2014/15

THE GUIDE TO

MAJOR TRUSTS VOLUME 2

ELEVENTH EDITION

Tom Traynor, Jude Doherty, Lucy Lernelius-Tonks,
Denise Lillya & Emma Weston

DIRECTORY OF SOCIAL CHANGE

Published by the Directory of Social Change (Registered Charity no. 800517 in England and Wales)
Head office: 24 Stephenson Way, London NW1 2DP
Northern office: Suite 103, 1 Old Hall Street, Liverpool L3 9HG
Tel: 08450 77 77 07

Visit www.dsc.org.uk to find out more about our books, subscription funding websites and training events. You can also sign up for e-newsletters so that you're always the first to hear about what's new.

The publisher welcomes suggestions and comments that will help to inform and improve future versions of this and all of our titles. Please give us your feedback by emailing publications@dsc.org.uk.

First published 1993
Second edition 1995
Third edition 1997
Fourth edition 1999
Fifth edition 2001
Sixth edition 2003
Seventh edition 2005
Eighth edition 2007
Ninth edition 2010
Tenth edition 2012
Eleventh edition 2014

ISBN 978 1 906294 86 1

British Library Cataloguing in Publication Data
A catalogue record for this book is available from the British Library

Cover and text design by Kate Bass
Typeset by Marlinzo Services, Frome
Printed and bound by Page Bros, Norwich

Contents

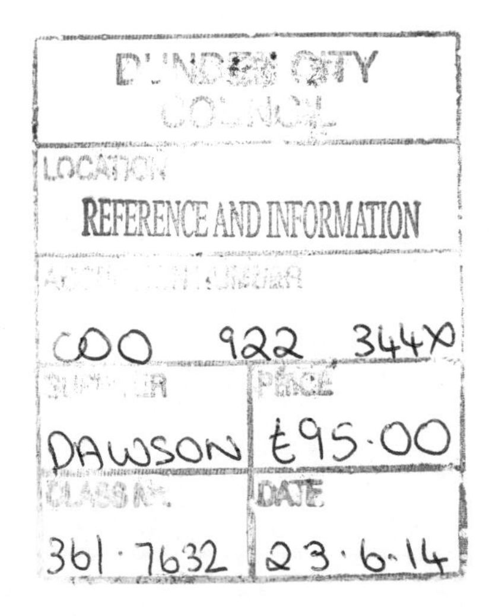

LOCATION
REFERENCE AND INFORMATION
C00 922 344X
DAWSON
£95.00
DATE
361.7632
23.6.14

Foreword

If there is anything akin to a Fundraiser's Bible then *The Guide to Major Trusts* is it, so I was delighted to be asked to write a foreword for the 2014/15 editions. I find it incredible that it is almost 30 years since the first edition was published in 1986. It is testament to these guides' enduring worth that they are still appearing in print version in this digital age.

Despite the economic downturn in recent years, the trust market is worth an estimated £2.8 billion per year and is a fundamental source of funding for charities both large and small. These DSC guides provide clear, concise summaries of each trust's policies and preferences, detailed information on how to apply and, in many ways most importantly, what a trust *won't* fund. They are essential resources for an organisation that is looking to develop its trust fundraising from scratch and one or both guides have a place on the desk of every trust fundraiser. They represent exceptional value for money in terms of the amount of funding on offer within it!

Research is the basis of good fundraising. Without insight into our donors and prospects we cannot forget those mutually beneficial donor journeys that deliver such an impact across our communities. Once we have some understanding of our donor motivations we can cultivate strong long-term partnerships and move away from a transactional approach that is less satisfying for both parties. These DSC guides help to broker these relationships and provide a key link between funder and grantee.

I hope those new to fundraising and more experienced practitioners alike benefit from and enjoy these new editions.

Lynda Thomas
Director of Fundraising, Macmillan Cancer Support

About the Directory of Social Change

The Directory of Social Change (DSC) has a vision of an independent voluntary sector at the heart of social change. The activities of independent charities, voluntary organisations and community groups are fundamental to achieve social change. We exist to help these organisations and the people who support them to achieve their goals.

We do this by:

- providing practical tools that organisations and activists need, including online and printed publications, training courses, and conferences on a huge range of topics;
- acting as a 'concerned citizen' in public policy debates, often on behalf of smaller charities, voluntary organisations and community groups;
- leading campaigns and stimulating debate on key policy issues that affect those groups;
- carrying out research and providing information to influence policymakers.

DSC is the leading provider of information and training for the voluntary sector and publishes an extensive range of guides and handbooks covering subjects such as fundraising, management, communication, finance and law. We have a range of subscription-based websites containing a wealth of information on funding from trusts, companies and government sources. We run more than 300 training courses each year, including bespoke in-house training provided at the client's location. DSC conferences, many of which run on an annual basis, include the Charity Management Conference, the Charity Accountants' Conference and the Charity Law Conference. DSC's major annual event is Charityfair, which provides low-cost training on a wide variety of subjects.

For details of all our activities, and to order publications and book courses, go to www.dsc.org.uk, call 08450 777707 or email publications@dsc.org.uk.

Introduction

Welcome to *The Guide to the Major Trusts Volume 2*. This edition contains more than 1,100 UK trusts, following on from the 400 largest detailed in Volume 1. The trusts in this book give £196.3 million a year collectively (trusts in Volume 1 gave a total of £2.8 billion).

The guide's main aim is to help people raise money from grant-making charities. We aim to provide as much information as we can to enable fundraisers to locate relevant grant-makers and produce suitable applications. There is also a secondary aim: to be a survey of the work of grant-making charities and to show where trust money is going and for what purposes.

For the 1,116 charities included in the guide, grants totalled £196.3 million with income standing at £398.6 million. Assets amounted to £4.36 billion in total (note that most of the financial information in this book was taken from 2011/12 accounts).

Comparing these figures to the previous edition shows that the value of grant-makers' assets has increased by £0.9 billion and income decreased by £26 million to £398 million. Despite this, total grants have remained the same at £196 million.

The continuing effects of the recession on charities

The recession of 2008/09, the change in government in 2010 plus the austerity measures that soon followed have had a dramatic effect on the sector (Alcock et al., 2012). During the period in which the research for this book is based, income has fallen while the total amount awarded in grants stayed the same as in the previous edition. This suggests that although grant-makers are struggling with less income, they understand the unfaltering need for grants, especially in harsh economic times.

Governmental cuts have been of particular interest to many third sector organisations that have either experienced funding cuts, or are anticipating cuts due to the government's austerity programme. A survey of more than 1,000 charity professionals hosted by *The Guardian*'s voluntary sector network in July 2013 showed that 'nearly one in 10 charities thinks it will not exist in 5 years'. However, 85% of respondents expect an increase in demand for their services (Bawden 2013).

A Centre for Local Economic Strategies research article entitled *Responsible Reform: Open Public Services for All* discusses the effects of the cuts on charities:

> Rather than having a positive impact upon voluntary and community sector group finances, big society for many is actually reducing and hindering access to funding, particularly through grants. The feeling was that cuts and the notion of big society were having an effect in a number of ways:
>
> - they were affecting some services directly: youth services, health and social care and advice services were seen to have been particularly affected;
> - with the main sources of future funding coming through contracts, local, well established groups were potentially threatened by competition from large voluntary and community sector organisations and from the private sector;
> - smaller voluntary and community sector organisations that supply niche and equalities group specific services, dependent both on volunteers and small grant funding to maintain their operations, were threatened by the loss of funding. *CLES 2012*

Take Newcastle City Council, for example, which had to make cuts of £43 million in 2011/12, followed by £30 million in 2012/13 and is considering cuts of a further £54 million in the following two years. When 53 third sector organisations working in the Newcastle area took part a survey in February 2012, 57% of respondents noted that they had to dip into reserves to keep afloat, whilst 59% had experienced cuts in statutory funding. A wide range of services were delivered by respondents; however, support for education and training, older people, disability, young people were most prevalent (Newcastle CVS 2013).

In June 2013 research based on 21 grant-making trusts by nfpSynergy on behalf of the Institute of Fundraising and the Office for Civil Society, discussed the impact of the recession on trusts. It showed that many grant-making trusts had received increasing numbers of applications to replace government funding whilst others had suffered a sufficient lull in applications. Grant-makers' responses to the recession and the subsequent austerity measures have been diverse and, at times, flexible and innovative in their approach to grant-making.

Grant-making trusts have adapted to the current economic climate by changing the forms that grants take and understanding the demands facing charities. Some more general and reactive grant-making trusts were willing to adjust their policies to fund charities that had faced

Top 25 trusts

	Guide to Major Trusts Volume 2 – 2012/13	Total grants		Guide to Major Trusts Volume 2 – 2014/15	Total grants
1	The Fuserna Foundation	£3.5 million	1 (-)	John Laing Charitable Trust	£1.8 million
2	The David and Elaine Potter Foundation	£3.2 million	2 (-)	J P Moulton Charitable Foundation	£1.7 million
3	The Exilarch's Foundation	£2.8 million	3 (25)	Lancashire Environmental Fund	£1.5 million
4	The M A Hawe Settlement	£1.8 million	4 (-)	The Porter Foundation	£1.5 million
5	The Marjorie and Arnold Ziff Charitable Foundation	£1.5 million	5 (-)	The Steinberg Family Charitable Trust	£1.5 million
6	The R D Crusaders Foundation	£1.4 million	6 (3)	The Exilarch's Foundation	£1.4 million
7	Bourneheights Limited	£1.2 million	7 (-)	Quercus Trust	£1.3 million
8	The Dinwoodie Settlement	£1.2 million	8 (-)	The Andrew Salvesen Charitable Trust	£1.3 million
9	The Ian Karten Charitable Trust	£1.1 million	9 (-)	LandAid Charitable Trust	£1.13 million
10	Country Houses Foundation	£1.1 million	10 (-)	Church Burgesses Trust	£1 million
11	Extonglen Limited	£1.1 million	11 (-)	The Alborada Trust	£1 million
12	The Lind Trust	£1 million	12 (-)	The Edith Winifred Hall Charitable Trust	£1 million
13	The Scotshill Trust	£1 million	13 (-)	The Linda and Gordon Bonnyman Charitable Trust	£1 million
14	Vyoel Moshe Charitable Trust	£1 million	14 (-)	Wychville Ltd	£1 million
15	The Langley Charitable Trust	£1 million	15 (-)	The Adrian Swire Charitable Trust	£997,000
16	The English Schools' Football Association	£984,000	16 (10)	Country Houses Foundation	£942,000
17	Truedene Co. Ltd	£960,000	17 (-)	The Clive Richards Charity	£942,000
18	The Charles Shorto Charitable Trust	£936,000	18 (-)	Heart Research UK	£939,000
19	Ambika Paul Foundation	£930,000	19 (-)	T and J Meyer Family Foundation Limited	£935,000
20	The Barbour Foundation	£925,000	20 (-)	The Ingram Trust	£909,000
21	The Talbot Village Trust	£884,000	21 (16)	The English Schools' Football Association	£853,000
22	Coutts Charitable Trust	£864,000	22 (-)	The Noon Foundation	£800,000
23	The Ireland Fund of Great Britain	£863,000	23 (17)	Truedene Co. Ltd	£788,000
24	The Queen Anne's Gate Foundation	£809,000	24 (-)	The Bransford Trust	£747,000
25	Lancashire Environmental Fund	£796,000	25 (-)	The J Isaacs Charitable Trust	£744,000
	Total	**£32.9 million**		**Total**	**£27.7 million**

* Figures in brackets show position in the previous edition

statutory funding cuts. Further research pointed out how grant-makers felt they could best assist charities:

> One grant-maker said they are trying to give out fewer but larger grants, hoping that their grants will have more impact. Another grant-maker has taken the opposite approach, giving less money to a larger number of charities.
>
> Similarly, some grant-making trusts said they try to minimise risk by having higher demands on charities' finances being in order; whereas others said they have become more flexible and understanding of charities having low reserves. One grant-making trust manages risk while being more flexible by paying out grants in smaller, quarterly instalments rather than annual payments. *nfpSynergy 2013*

Grant-making trusts have adapted in their own ways in order to deliver their objectives and they still remain an essential source of funding for many charities. Although grant-making trusts have shown flexibility and resilience, they still face challenges in maintaining grant levels in the midst of austerity.

What's new?

There are a number of trusts which are new to the series. There have also been trusts added that were in the previous edition of Volume 1 as they no longer give enough money to qualify for the top 400. Some trusts that were in the last edition of this guide have grown and now warrant entries in Volume 1. Others are newly established or newly discovered and include: The Linda and Gordon Bonnyman Charitable Trust, giving around £1 million in grants a year, and The Green Room Charitable Trust and Bag4Sport giving around £50,000.

DSC survey 2013

In our survey of 2013 we asked grant-makers whether they had received fewer, about the same or more applications than in their previous financial year. Out of 207 responses to this question, 130 trusts had received about the same number, 57 had received more applications and 20 had received fewer.

Of those that had received more applications, the majority stated that they had dealt with the increase by becoming proactive and not accepting unsolicited applications, narrowing the eligibility criteria, reducing the average amount given, making fewer awards and/or increasing administration hours. A recurring word was 'bin' and a recurring comment was that it had been necessary for trustees to be more selective.

The following comments, when asked 'What was your reaction to the increased demand?' show how grant-makers have endeavoured to deal (or not to deal) with the increase:

> Bin them!
>
> We can't begin to address it.

> We just send a card which says no funding available.
>
> Cannot meet increased demand, more applications denied.

And on a positive note:

> Happy to process.
>
> Increasing the number of hours spent processing applications.
>
> Proceeding normally.
>
> We now have a website.

Again, as in the last survey of 2011, another recurring comment was the amount of time it was felt was wasted by applicants in applying to grant-making charities that have stated clearly in both their own literature, and through publications such as this guide, that they do not consider unsolicited applications. Not only is this a waste of time for the applicant charity, it involves the grant-makers in unnecessary work. Our advice is that if trustees have stated that they will not consider applications they have not requested, then don't apply. If you consider that your project is so fitting to the grant-maker's criteria that they would actually welcome hearing about it, contact them and ask if they would be prepared to discuss the project briefly over the phone. However, be prepared for a swift 'No' and please don't call if the information we have provided or on the charity's website states that phone calls are not welcome.

Asked what common mistakes applicants made, the overwhelming response was that applications fell outside publicised guidelines or criteria and that applicants had not read these carefully (or at all). Many complained of cold-calling, mail-merged pro forma appeal letters, generic applications, applicants asking for far too much and individuals applying when the charity clearly only gives to organisations.

Here is a selection of comments taken from the survey about common mistakes:

> Letter too general, rabbits on about need instead of saying how specifically they will meet that need and how much each individual will be helped (in broad terms).
>
> Many seem not to have consulted any directories and do not know that we have a list of things we do not offer grants to.
>
> Not defining application. Too vague. Too large!
>
> Asking for unrealistically large grants.

Grant-making trusts are like all other charities: their resources are finite and often stretched. For this reason very few will spend time considering applications for projects which don't immediately appear to fall within their criteria, or where it is clear that the applicant has not read the published guidelines.

A number of respondents stated that applications often did not detail the need that would be met by the potential grant and how that need had been assessed. Some said that applications failed to provide a properly considered budget with validated costs, or details of how the work to be carried out would be planned, executed and monitored. In some cases trustees said they received too much information but none of it was tailored or relevant.

Indeed, many of the comments made were almost identical to the ones made in our earlier (2011) survey showing that, unfortunately, in many cases these issues have not been addressed.

Fundraisers need to dedicate time when applying for funding: time spent on initial research of the funder and its criteria is well spent and saves resources in the long run for both the applicant and the grant-making charity.

It has been particularly interesting to see over the course of the research for this guide a great number of grant-making charities which welcome and actively encourage dialogue with applicants in order to ensure as many as possible are successful, and also to help them to understand better the groups they set out to support.

However, whilst there are many that are open and accessible, there are still those that neglect their obligations. Some fail to be transparent or do not have application procedures that are clear to applicants, some still do not comply with the Charity Commission's guidelines on submitting accounts, or fail to include grants lists. Unfortunately, in some cases contact is actively discouraged. It is hoped that DSC's continuing Great Giving campaign will encourage more transparency in the future.

What trusts do we include?

Our criteria are as follows: trusts must have the potential to give at least £30,000 a year in grants and these grants should go to organisations in the UK. Many give far more than this: over 635 trusts have the potential to give £100,000 or more. There are actually 254 grant-making charities that have the potential to give £300,000 or more. These would appear to be large enough to be included in Volume 1. However, in a number of cases the income of the trust was lower than the total given in grants for the latest financial year – perhaps due to a substantial one-off donation from its capital – and therefore it is expected that the level of giving by such trusts will decrease in future. Other reasons are that the majority of its grants were distributed overseas or in a particular part of the UK, or its areas of work were too specific for Volume 1. For a full list of the grant-making charities in order of grant-total size see page xxi. Some have been included regardless of the fact that they gave less than £30,000, as they have the potential to increase this grant total in the future.

What is excluded?

Trusts which appear large enough to warrant inclusion in this guide may be excluded for the following reasons:

- Some or all of their money is given to individuals, meaning that £30,000 a year is not available for organisations. The following two guides provide information on trusts which support individuals: *The Guide to Grants for Individuals in Need* and *The Guide to Educational Grants*, both published by DSC. Alternatively our subscription website, www.grantsforindividuals.org.uk, contains the same information as these publications.
- Generally, they give exclusively to local causes in a restricted geographical area of England. There are many very large trusts which restrict their grant-making in

this way. So if giving is restricted to a single county or city (or smaller geographical area) it is generally excluded. In this way we hope that Volume 2 remains a national directory and therefore relevant to more people.
- They only, or predominantly, support international charities. Such grant-makers were previously included in this guide, but information on these can now be found in *The Directory of Grant Making Trusts.*
- They are company charities, established as a vehicle for a company's charitable giving. These are detailed in *The Guide to UK Company Giving* or at www.companygiving.org.uk.

DSC's subscription-based website www.trustfunding.org.uk contains details of over 4,500 trusts including those that give locally, UK-wide and internationally.

The layout of this book

The layout of the entries is similar to that established in the previous editions of Volumes 1 and 2, and is illustrated in 'A typical trust entry' on page xiii. Please also see page xii for other information on how to use this guide. We have rounded off the financial figures to allow for easier reading of the guide, which explains why in some places the totals do not add up exactly.

Indexes

The grant-makers are listed alphabetically in this guide. To help you locate the most relevant there are two indexes. They are a useful starting point.

- Subject index (see page 349). This can be useful for identifying those that have a particular preference for your cause. There are many which have general charitable purposes (either exclusively or as well as other specific criteria). However, we do not have a general category in the indexes. This is because it would include so many as to be useless. The subject index therefore should not be used as the definitive guide to finding the right grant-makers to apply to.
- Geographical index (see page 375). Although charities that limit their support to one particular area have been excluded, there are many which have some preference for one or more areas. These are listed in this index. Again, in a similar way to the subject index, care is needed. Many state their beneficial area as the UK, so are not included in this index.

It is important to note that the trusts which appear under a particular index may have other criteria which exclude your organisation. Always read the entry carefully so that you can be sure you fit in with all the trust's criteria. Do not just use the index as a mailing list.

How the guide was compiled

The following practical guidelines were followed to produce this guide:

- Concentrate on what the grant-maker does in practice rather than the wider objectives permitted by its formal governing document.
- Provide extensive information which will be of most use to readers; i.e. publish stated criteria and guidelines for applicants in full, where available.
- Include, where possible, details of a good sample of the beneficiary organisations which have received grants to give the reader an idea of what the grant-maker supports and the amounts it usually gives.
- Provide the most up-to-date information available at the time of the research.
- Include all which meet our criteria for inclusion.

Charities SORP Consultation 2013

What is the Charities SORP?

Statements of Recommended Practice, generally referred to as SORPs, provide recommendations for comprehensive accounting and reporting. In the charity world it is recommended that we follow the Charities SORP (currently Charities SORP 2005).

The Charities SORP provides a mechanism which enables charities to meet the legal requirement for their accounts; that is, to give a true and fair view of them. It also provides consistency in the sector's interpretation of accounting standards and details recommendations for annual reporting that are relevant to the charity sector and stakeholders' needs.

The Charities SORP 2005 was developed by the Charity Commission in conjunction with the Charities SORP Committee, an advisory committee made up of charity finance directors, charity auditors, academics, charity advisers and charity regulators. The committee is also structured to reflect the different charity jurisdictions of the UK. DSC's Chief Executive, Debra Allcock Tyler, is a SORP Committee member.

DSC's consultation response

In 2013, the Charity Commission and the Office of the Scottish Charity Regulator, now the joint SORP-making body for charities, developed a new draft of the SORP (the Exposure Draft), to reflect various changes in accounting standards since 2005, in partnership with the current Charities SORP Committee.

DSC has responded to the consultation because it affects the voluntary sector and its own beneficiaries, including many small and medium-sized charities. The requirements of the SORP can affect these organisations on a daily basis and for many reasons; for example, in keeping good records of monitoring and evaluation for projects to report annually on public benefit, or, in the case of grant-makers, to detail who their beneficiary organisations are, in the interests of transparency and in order to make applying for funds an easier task for applicants.

It was important for DSC and other charities to contribute to this consultation process in order to get the best outcome for those who have the often complex task of preparing annual reports and accounts, and also for those who will undoubtedly benefit from clarity, transparency and openness.

DSC's recommendations on the Exposure Draft

The consultation covered a range of often quite technical accounting questions to which DSC responded. In summary, our recommendations included the following:

1. **Grant-making charities – disclosure of grant awards**: DSC researches the activities of thousands of grant-making charities each year and we fully agree with the proposal in the Exposure Draft that grant-making charities should disclose the details of grants made in their accounts. It is our experience that too many charities fail to provide information about material grants. This is important information which allows fundraisers to target their applications more effectively to the most appropriate funder. Further, it is in the public interest and the interest of the grant-makers themselves to be transparent about where charitable funds are given and for what purposes.
2. **Disclosure of senior staff salaries:** DSC agrees with the proposal in the Exposure Draft that larger charities should be required to disclose the salary and job title of their highest paid employee. This is clearly a matter of public interest and charities should be transparent about how charitable funds are being spent for whatever reason, including on paid staff who act for the trustees to achieve the charity's aims and objectives.
3. **Removal of requirement to disclose *ex gratia* payments (part of Q23):** The Exposure Draft lists a number of things which are proposed to be removed from the SORP for the purposes of 'simplification' including *'only requiring the disclosure of ex gratia payments where regulatory consent for payment is required'*.
   We believe this is unclear and are concerned at its proposed removal. The SORP committee needs to further clarify why this has been removed. In line with the Charity Commission's booklet, CC7, it is our understanding that trustees must always seek authority from the Commission before making an *ex gratia* payment. If non-authorised payments are permitted we would see no benefit to removing the requirement to disclose these payments in the accounts. In fact, these are the very ones likely to go under the radar and therefore this proposal would not seem to aid or improve accountability or transparency. The SORP should make clear that disclosure of all payments made to trustees (*ex gratia* or otherwise) for whatever reason, is best practice.

In our submission, we also stated that:

> It is imperative that the Charity Commission continues to publish relevant guidance booklets to support the SORP, and that it updates its existing guidance to reflect the revised SORP as well (for example CC19: Charities and Reserves, which includes sections on small charities, and CC15b: Charity Reporting and Accounting: The Essentials).
>
> In our view the Exposure Draft does not make sufficiently clear how or whether this guidance will be provided in the future. DSC is concerned that this may not be prioritised by the Charity Commission as it deals with severe budget cuts.

The consultation document and other information on the SORP consultation process can be found at: www.charitysorp.org.

Failing to supply accounts

Charities are required to send their annual report and accounts to the Charity Commission and also to any member of the public who requests them in writing. Many charities recognise the importance of providing good, clear information about the work they do. However, there are some that wish to believe they are private bodies and ignore their statutory obligation to provide information to the public. Trustees are required to send these documents on request although they can make a 'reasonable charge' for this (i.e. the costs of photocopying and postage).

Accounts that are overdue at the Commission now have a red outline at the top of the page to show this, making it immediately apparent to the reader. When the overdue accounts are received the colour will revert to green. However, a record that a charity's accounts were late for a particular year will remain on the page for five years.

Accounts count

Research undertaken by DSC concluded that poor financial management could be prejudicing charities' funding bids. Our *Accounts Count* report found that 53% of funders will check whether a charity has filed their accounts on time with the Charity Commission (DSC 2013). If accounts have been submitted late, 17% of funders indicated that they would not take the application any further. Charity teams work towards the same goal and it's important that they work together. Make sure your fundraising effort is not being hampered because of accounts lingering on someone else's desk.

Failure to disclose grants

In SORP 2005, there is a clear emphasis on transparency. The report section is designed to help interested parties understand the work of charities and provide clarity and structure. It includes sections on charities':

- aims and objectives and the strategies and activities undertaken to achieve them;
- achievements and performance;
- plans for the future.

The SORP also provides guidance on how grants payable during the year should be analysed. This should be sufficient to give an understanding of how grant-making activity fits in with its particular charitable objectives. It also requires trusts to detail at least 50 grants (if these are of £1,000 or more). Of the trusts listed in this guide, more than 50 did not provide any details of the grants they made during the year. Where this is the case we have noted this in the 'information available' field.

Failing to provide a narrative report

All trusts should provide a narrative report describing their work. It is here that trustees should give an account of their activities during the year with some explanation and analysis of the grants they have made. Many trustee reports are extremely brief and give very little away about what has taken place over the year. However, following the introduction of the Charities Act 2006, a charity must now be able to demonstrate that, for each of its aims, there is a clear benefit for the public as a whole or a sufficient section of it. Charity trustees have a new duty to report on their charity's public benefit in their trustee annual reports and this necessitates those trustees who have been less than open in the past to give a more detailed account of the trust's activities.

Good trust reports

On a positive note, there are some trusts which provide excellent reports that go beyond the basic statement: 'The charity has carried out its objective this year by making grants to charitable institutions.' When they have been particularly interesting or informative for applicants, we have reproduced extracts in the entry.

Applying to trusts

There is a lot of competition for grants. Many trusts in this guide receive more applications than they can support. It is important to do the research: read the grant-maker's criteria carefully and target the right trusts. This can lead to a higher success rate and save you writing applications which are destined only for the bin. Applying to inappropriate trusts is bad practice and, as well as annoying trustees, can potentially cause problems for future applicants. Trustees tell us that around half the applications they receive are from organisations that work outside their stated areas of support.

Unsolicited applications

A number of grant-makers do not want to receive applications (and for this reason usually do not want to appear in the guide). There can be good reasons for this. For example, the trust may do its own research or support the same list of charities each year. There are some, however, which believe that they are 'private' trusts. No registered charity is a private body. We believe that the trustees should not resent applications but should be committed to finding those charities most eligible for assistance.

We include these trusts for two reasons. Firstly, some state 'no unsolicited applications' simply as a deterrent in an effort to reduce the number of applications they receive, but will still consider the applications they receive. The second reason relates to the secondary purpose of the guide: to act as a survey of grant-making trusts.

If you choose to write to one of these trusts, do so with caution. Only write to those where your organisation very clearly fits a trust's criteria. We would advise you to include a stamped, addressed envelope and to state that you do not expect a response unless you are eligible. If they do not reply, do not chase them.

DSC policy and campaigning

Over the years, DSC has campaigned on a number of fronts for better grant-making. We believe that funders have a responsibility that extends far beyond providing funding. The way funders operate and develop their programmes has a huge impact on the organisations, causes and beneficiaries which their funding supports, as well as on the wider voluntary sector. Transparency is a key principle for us: by providing information about funders in this book and other DSC publications we have sought to open up their practices to greater scrutiny. Clearer and more accessible information enables fundraisers to focus their efforts effectively, and encourages open review and discussions of good practice. Our Great Giving campaign has grown out of these long-established beliefs.

We have identified some specific campaigning areas that we wish to focus on as part of an overall campaign for better grant-making.

A clear picture of the funding environment

We think that to enable better planning and decision-making from funders and policymakers, more comprehensive information is needed about where money is going and what it supports. Many of the funders in this book are leading the way, although some fall short in terms of the level of detail they provide about their activities and effectiveness. We have recommended that the charity SORP requires funders to go further on this. (See more on this under 'DSC's recommendations on the Exposure Draft'.)

Accessible funding for campaigning

Financial support for campaigning is vital to the role organisations play in achieving social change. It was heartening to see the sector unite to fight the threat of the Lobbying Bill recently, proving that there is much to campaign about – even campaigning itself! Greater clarity from grant-making charities (and other funders) is needed so that campaigning organisations can find the support they need more easily.

An end to hidden small print

DSC is asking all funders to provide the terms and conditions which govern the use of the funds at the outset when people apply and to be open to negotiating terms when applicants request it.

No ineligible applications

We know that most funders receive applications that do not fall within their set guidelines. Clearer guidelines can help, but applicants also need to take more heed of funder guidelines and target their applications appropriately.

DSC has always believed that clear and open application and monitoring processes are essential for both funders and fundraisers to produce more effective applications and better eventual outcomes. The availability of such information has come a long way since the first edition of this guide and the internet continues to be invaluable in offering grant-makers an opportunity to open up. However, an important element of the funding process often remains hidden from wider scrutiny.

The detailed terms and conditions which set out what the applicant is required to do to obtain and retain the grant are too often unavailable until the point at which a formal offer of a grant is made. For an applicant, seeing these terms and conditions for the first time only when there is an offer of money on the table is not helpful. Even if negotiating the conditions is an option, the balance of power is still squarely with the funder. If the funder is not willing to negotiate, the applicant is faced with a difficult decision: should any conditions conflict with their organisation's values or the wider needs of their beneficiaries, they then face a dubious choice between accepting conditions which may threaten their independence, and turning down much needed funding.

We surveyed the largest charitable, corporate and government funders to find out more about the availability and accessibility of their terms and conditions, which culminated in a research report, *Critical Conditions* (DSC 2009). This research found that many trusts and foundations were demonstrating what we consider good practice – 72% of those that responded said they made their terms and conditions publicly available, and there were a number of good examples. However, nearly half of trusts that responded stated that their terms were non-negotiable, a stance we consider not in the best interests of funders or applicants. Overall these findings compared favourably to the central government funders that responded. By comparison these funders appeared to be less transparent and more averse to negotiating. They also tended to have more complicated and lengthy terms.

However, in late 2009, DSC asked similar questions of a much larger sample of trusts and foundations, and the results paint a different picture. In this research only half of respondents said their terms and conditions were publicly available, and a solid majority said they were non-negotiable. The rate of those which said their terms were not publicly available at all was three times greater than in the Critical Conditions survey. Some of the variation is accounted for by the fact that the larger sample contained a far greater number of smaller trusts and foundations that do not have any terms and conditions at all (49% of respondents to this survey said they had terms and conditions, compared with 86% in the *Critical Conditions* report). Nevertheless, this further research broadly suggests that there is room for improvement from trusts as regards the transparency of their funding terms and conditions.

Some may argue that providing more information at the beginning of the application process could make things more time consuming and costly, but DSC believes the benefits of greater transparency should take precedence. It is crucial that fundraisers have access to all the information they need to make an informed decision about whether to apply. It is also vital that such information is publicly available so that funders and others can make comparisons and share good practice. Further, in this age of digital communication, there is an ever-increasing expectation that all the relevant information, guidance and application forms will be available online. A link to a web page or a short document outlining the detailed terms and explaining their place in the application process is easy to provide and need not cost anything.

Clear instructions should be provided for the fundraiser about the importance of the terms and conditions, why they are necessary and what they mean, along with exhortations to read them thoroughly.

Again the onus is not entirely on the funder – fundraisers have a responsibility to inform themselves as fully as possible and to ask for relevant information if it isn't available or is not clearly presented by the funder. Reading and evaluating the criteria, guidance and detailed terms and conditions is part of making a well-targeted application which is more likely to be successful. More crucially it is about protecting the organisation's independence and building funding relationships that will work well for both parties. The fundraiser, therefore, has an important role to play in scrutinising the conditions of the funding arrangement at the outset, and communicating their views to other decision-makers in the organisation (see www.dsc.org.uk for more advice on terms and conditions for fundraisers).

DSC's Big Lottery Refund campaign

The National Lottery occupies a unique place in the grant-making world. Whilst the various distributors are statutory bodies which distribute what is, technically speaking, public money, their activities, aims and beneficiaries have much in common with charitable grant-making trusts.

DSC's campaign will therefore be of interest to fundraisers, fundraising charities, and anyone interested in the Big Lottery Fund in particular. The aim of the campaign is for the government to refund to the Big Lottery Fund £425 million of Lottery revenue which was diverted to help pay for the London 2012 Olympics. We argue that this decision, taken in 2007, was wrong in principle, as it should have been given out in grants to voluntary and community groups across the country, not to make up the budgetary shortfall for a one-off sporting event.

Both the previous and current government has committed to refund the Lottery using proceeds from selling Olympics assets after the Games. However, it is unfortunately not straightforward – asset sales are expected to take decades, which is not acceptable in our view. Learn more, sign up to support the campaign and stay updated with developments at www.biglotteryrefund.org.uk.

Finally . . .

The research for this book has been conducted as carefully as possible. Many thanks to those who have made this easier, especially the trusts themselves through their websites, their trust officers for providing additional information and the trustees and others who have helped us.

The availability of so much accessible, high-quality information from the Charity Commission website has been invaluable in the preparation of this guide. However, the cuts in the workforce there have resulted in fewer charities' accounts being available online; very often, although received at the Commission, a considerable time has elapsed before the accounts are published.

We are aware that some of the information in this guide may be incomplete or will become out of date. We are equally sure we will have missed some relevant charities. We apologise for these imperfections. If you come across any omissions or mistakes, or if you have any suggestions for future editions of this book, do let us know. We can be contacted at the Liverpool Office Research Department at the Directory of Social Change either by phone on 0151 708 0136 or by email: research@dsc.org.uk.

We hope this latest edition is as useful in its application as it has been interesting and inspiring in its preparation.

References

Alcock, Pete, Rob Macmillan, and Sarah Bulloch, (2012), *The Worst of Times?*, London, Third Sector Research Centre

Bawden, Anna (2013), 'Charities: we've got give years left, at best', *The Guardian*, www.theguardian.com/society/2013/jul/24/charities-voluntary-sector-five-years-existence , 24 July

Escadale, Warren, Matthew Jackson and Stuart Speeden, (2012), *Responsible Reform: Open Public Services for All*, Manchester, Centre for Local Economic Strategies

Newcastle CVS (2012), *Surviving or Thriving in Newcastle: Tracking the impact of spending cuts on Newcastle's third sector*, Newcastle Council for Voluntary Service

Lindstrom, Elin and Joe Saxton (2013), *Inside the mind of a grant-maker: Useful stuff on how grant-making works*, London, nfpSynergy

How to use this guide

The contents

The entries are in alphabetical order and describe the work of over 1,100 grant-making charities. The entries are preceded by a listing of the trusts in order of size and are followed by a subject index and geographical index. There is also an alphabetical index at the back of this guide.

Finding the trusts you need

There are three basic ways of using this guide.

1. You can simply read the entries through from A to Z (a rather time-consuming activity).
2. You can look through the trust ranking table which starts on page xxi and use the boxes provided to tick the trusts which might be relevant to you (starting with the biggest).
3. You can use the subject or geographical indexes starting on pages 349 and 375 respectively. Each has an introduction that explains how to use them.

If you use approaches (1) or (3), once you have chosen enough trusts to be getting on with, read each trust entry carefully before deciding to apply. Very often a trust's interest in your field will be limited and precise, and may demand an application specifically tailored to its requirements or often no application at all as they may not be currently accepting applications.

Sending off applications which show that the available information has not been read antagonises trusts and brings charities into disrepute within the grant-making sector. Carefully targeted applications, on the other hand, are usually welcomed by most trusts.

A typical trust entry

The Fictitious Trust

Welfare

£180,000 (2013)

Beneficial area

UK.

Correspondent: Ann Freeman, Appeals Secretary, The Old Barn, Main Street, New Town ZC48 2QQ

Trustees: Eva Appiah; Rita Khan; Lorraine Murphy.

CC Number: 123456

The trust supports welfare charities in general, with an emphasis on homelessness. The trustees will support both capital and revenue projects. 'Specific projects are preferred to general running costs.'

In 2013 the trust had assets of £2.3 million and an income of £187,000. Over 200 grants were given totalling £180,000. Grants ranged from £100 to £20,000, with about half given in New Town. Beneficiaries included: Homelessness UK (£18,000); Shelter (£15,000); Charity Workers Benevolent Society (£10,000); Children Without Families (£5,000); New Town CAB (£3,000); and Ex-Offenders UK (£1,000).

Smaller grants were given to a variety of local charities, local branches of national charities and a few UK welfare charities.

Exclusions

No grants to non-registered charities, individuals or religious organisations.

Applications

In writing to the correspondent. Trustees meet in March and September each year. Applications should be received by the end of January and the end of July respectively.

Applications should include a brief description of the project and audited accounts. Unsuccessful applicants will not be informed unless a stamped, addressed envelope is provided.

Percentage of awards given to new applicants: between 10% and 20%.

Common applicant mistakes

'They don't read our guidelines.'

Information gathered from:

Accounts; Charity Commission record; further information provided by the funder.

Name of the charity

Summary of main activities – what the trust will do in practice rather than what its trust deed allows it to do.

Grant total – total grants given for the most recent year available.

Geographical area of grantgiving – including where the trust can legally give and where it gives in practice.

Correspondent and contact details – including telephone and fax numbers, and email and website addresses, if available.

Trustees

Background/summary of activities – a quick indicator of the trust's policies to show whether it is worth reading the rest of the entry.

Financial information – noting the assets, ordinary income and grant total, and comment on unusual figures.

Typical grants range – indicates what a successful applicant can expect to receive.

Beneficiaries included – a list of typical beneficiaries which indicates where the main money is going. This is often the clearest indication of trust priorities. Where possible, we include the purpose of the grant. We also indicate whether the trust gives one-off or recurrent grants.

Exclusions – a list of any area, subjects or types of grant the trust will not consider.

Applications – this includes how to apply and when to submit an application.

Percentage of awards given to new applicants – the grant-maker's response to DSC's 2013 survey.

Common applicant mistakes – the grant-maker's response to DSC's 2013 survey.

Information gathered from – our researchers' sources of information.

Dates for your diary

X = the usual month of trustees' or grant allocation meetings, or the last month for the receipt of applications.

Please note that these dates are provisional, and that the fact of an application being received does not necessarily mean that it will be considered at the next meeting.

	Jan	*Feb*	*Mar*	*Apr*	*May*	*Jun*	*Jul*	*Aug*	*Sep*	*Oct*	*Nov*	*Dec*
The A B Charitable Trust	X			X			X			X		
The Adamson Trust			X			X			X			X
The Adnams Charity	X			X			X			X		
The Sylvia Aitken Charitable Trust			X						X			
The Ajahma Charitable Trust											X	
The Alabaster Trust			X			X			X			X
All Saints Educational Trust				X								
The Anchor Foundation				X							X	
The Animal Defence Trust							X					
The Appletree Trust				X								
Archbishop of Wales' Fund for Children			X					X				
The Ove Arup Foundation			X			X			X			X
The Ashworth Charitable Trust					X						X	
The Astor Foundation				X						X		
The Baker Charitable Trust	X			X			X			X		
William P Bancroft (No. 2) Charitable Trust and Jenepher Gillett Trust					X							
Lord Barnby's Foundation		X				X					X	
The Misses Barrie Charitable Trust				X				X				X
The Bestway Foundation			X									
Miss Jeanne Bisgood's Charitable Trust		X							X			
Sir Alec Black's Charity					X						X	
The Charlotte Bonham-Carter Charitable Trust	X						X					
The Oliver Borthwick Memorial Trust					X							

	Jan	*Feb*	*Mar*	*Apr*	*May*	*Jun*	*Jul*	*Aug*	*Sep*	*Oct*	*Nov*	*Dec*
The Bothwell Charitable Trust		X										
The Bransford Trust								X				X
The Harold and Alice Bridges Charity	X				X				X			
The British Dietetic Association General and Education Trust Fund					X						X	
Bill Brown 1998 Charitable Trust						X						X
Burdens Charitable Foundation			X			X			X			X
The Clara E Burgess Charity	X						X					
Henry T and Lucy B Cadbury Charitable Trust			X									
The Richard Carne Trust						X						
The Joseph and Annie Cattle Trust	X	X	X	X	X	X	X	X	X	X	X	X
The Wilfrid and Constance Cave Foundation					X					X		
The Chapman Charitable Trust			X						X			
Chrysalis Trust					X							X
Church Burgesses Trust	X			X			X			X		
The Marjorie Coote Animal Charity Trust										X		
The Cotton Trust	X						X					
Country Houses Foundation				X						X		
The Augustine Courtauld Trust					X							
Dudley and Geoffrey Cox Charitable Trust			X							X		
The Ronald Cruickshanks Foundation									X			
The Cumber Family Charitable Trust			X							X		
The Delves Charitable Trust	X		X			X			X			X
The Dickon Trust					X					X		
The DLM Charitable Trust		X					X				X	
Douglas Arter Foundation			X			X			X			X
The Dumbreck Charity				X	X							
Edinburgh Trust No. 2 Account				X								
Educational Foundation of Alderman John Norman					X	X						
The George Elias Charitable Trust	X	X	X	X	X	X	X	X	X	X	X	X
The Edith Maud Ellis 1985 Charitable Trust		X				X				X		
The Elmgrant Trust			X			X				X		
The Englefield Charitable Trust			X						X			
The Eventhall Family Charitable Trust	X	X	X	X	X	X	X	X	X	X	X	X
Elizabeth Ferguson Charitable Trust Fund	X						X					
Marc Fitch Fund				X					X			
The Fitton Trust				X				X				X
The Joyce Fletcher Charitable Trust										X	X	
The Forbes Charitable Foundation						X					X	
Ford Britain Trust						X					X	

	Jan	*Feb*	*Mar*	*Apr*	*May*	*Jun*	*Jul*	*Aug*	*Sep*	*Oct*	*Nov*	*Dec*
The Oliver Ford Charitable Trust										X		
The Gordon Fraser Charitable Trust	X			X			X			X		
The Joseph Strong Frazer Trust			X						X			
The Frognal Trust		X			X			X			X	
The Golsoncott Foundation		X			X			X			X	
Grand Charitable Trust of the Order of Women Freemasons							X					
The Grand Order of Water Rats' Charities Fund	X	X	X	X	X	X	X	X	X	X	X	X
The GRP Charitable Trust			X									
Hasluck Charitable Trust	X						X					
The Hawthorne Charitable Trust											X	
Help the Homeless	X			X			X			X		
The Christina Mary Hendrie Trust for Scottish and Canadian Charities			X	X						X	X	
The Charles Littlewood Hill Trust			X				X				X	
Hockerill Educational Foundation						X						
The Dorothy Holmes Charitable Trust	X		X									
The Holst Foundation			X			X			X			X
Mary Homfray Charitable Trust		X	X									
The Hope Trust						X						X
The Cuthbert Horn Trust												X
The Humanitarian Trust			X							X		
The Irish Youth Foundation (UK) Ltd (incorporating The Lawlor Foundation)		X										
The Ironmongers' Foundation	X		X					X		X		
The Ruth and Lionel Jacobson Trust (Second Fund) No. 2	X		X		X		X		X		X	
The John Jarrold Trust	X					X						
Rees Jeffreys Road Fund	X			X			X		X		X	
The Jenour Foundation			X									
The Jephcott Charitable Trust				X						X		
The Johnson Foundation	X	X	X	X	X	X	X	X	X	X	X	X
The Anton Jurgens Charitable Trust						X				X		
The Kelly Family Charitable Trust			X						X			
The Nancy Kenyon Charitable Trust												X
The Peter Kershaw Trust					X						X	
The David Laing Foundation			X			X				X		X
The Lambert Charitable Trust								X				
LWS Lancashire Environmental Fund Limited	X			X			X			X		
LandAid Charitable Trust			X									
Langdale Trust							X					
The R J Larg Family Charitable Trust		X						X				
Mrs F B Laurence Charitable Trust				X							X	

	Jan	*Feb*	*Mar*	*Apr*	*May*	*Jun*	*Jul*	*Aug*	*Sep*	*Oct*	*Nov*	*Dec*
The Kathleen Laurence Trust	X					X						
The Law Society Charity				X			X		X			X
The Edgar E Lawley Foundation	X											
The Leche Trust		X				X				X		
The Linmardon Trust		X			X			X			X	
The Loseley and Guildway Charitable Trust		X			X				X			
Michael Marks Charitable Trust	X						X					
The Marsh Christian Trust	X	X	X	X	X	X	X	X	X	X	X	X
The Charlotte Marshall Charitable Trust			X									
John Martin's Charity				X			X			X		X
Merchant Navy Welfare Board		X			X		X			X		
The Millfield House Foundation			X						X			
The Peter Minet Trust		X				X				X		
Monmouthshire County Council Welsh Church Act Fund			X			X			X			X
The Morgan Charitable Foundation				X						X		
S C and M E Morland's Charitable Trust			X									X
The Morris Charitable Trust	X	X	X	X	X	X	X	X	X	X	X	X
The Edwina Mountbatten Trust									X	X		
Mountbatten Festival of Music	X						X					
Murphy-Neumann Charity Company Limited											X	X
The Music Sales Charitable Trust			X			X			X			X
National Committee of the Women's World Day of Prayer for England and Wales and Northern Ireland											X	
The National Manuscripts Conservation Trust						X						X
The Norton Foundation							X					
The Oakdale Trust			X						X			
The Ogle Christian Trust					X						X	
The Oikonomia Trust		X										
The Ouseley Trust			X							X		
The Frank Parkinson Agricultural Trust				X								
Arthur James Paterson Charitable Trust			X						X			
The Constance Paterson Charitable Trust						X						X
Miss M E Swinton Paterson's Charitable Trust							X					
The David Pickford Charitable Foundation	X	X	X	X	X	X	X	X	X	X	X	X
The Bernard Piggott Charitable Trust					X						X	
The Austin and Hope Pilkington Trust						X					X	
The J S F Pollitzer Charitable Settlement				X							X	
The Porter Foundation			X				X				X	
The J E Posnansky Charitable Trust					X							

	Jan	*Feb*	*Mar*	*Apr*	*May*	*Jun*	*Jul*	*Aug*	*Sep*	*Oct*	*Nov*	*Dec*
The Puebla Charitable Trust							X					
The R V W Trust				X				X				X
The Radcliffe Trust						X						X
The Rainford Trust			X				X				X	
The John Rayner Charitable Trust	X											
REMEDI						X						X
The Clive Richards Charity	X	X	X	X	X	X	X	X	X	X	X	X
Rix-Thompson-Rothenberg Foundation						X						X
The Rowing Foundation		X			X			X			X	
The Jean Sainsbury Animal Welfare Trust			X				X				X	
The Saintbury Trust				X							X	
Sir Samuel Scott of Yews Trust				X						X		
The Linley Shaw Foundation		X	X									
The Sheldon Trust			X						X			
The Shipwrights' Company Charitable Fund		X				X					X	
The John Slater Foundation					X						X	
The SMB Charitable Trust			X			X			X			X
The N Smith Charitable Settlement					X							X
The South Square Trust			X			X					X	
The W F Southall Trust		X	X								X	
The Worshipful Company of Spectacle Makers' Charity				X								
The Jessie Spencer Trust			X			X			X			X
The Late St Patrick White Charitable Trust		X			X			X			X	
St Teilo's Trust		X			X				X			
The Stoller Charitable Trust			X			X			X			X
The W O Street Charitable Foundation	X			X			X			X		
Swan Mountain Trust		X				X				X		
The Adrian Swire Charitable Trust	X	X	X	X	X	X	X	X	X	X	X	X
The Tabeel Trust					X						X	
C B and H H Taylor 1984 Trust					X						X	
The Three Oaks Trust	X			X			X		X			
The Trefoil Trust		X					X					
The Ulverscroft Foundation			X			X			X			X
The Van Neste Foundation	X					X				X		
Mrs Maud Van Norden's Charitable Foundation					X							
The Scurrah Wainwright Charity		X				X				X		
The Thomas Wall Trust									X			
The F J Wallis Charitable Settlement			X						X			
Blyth Watson Charitable Trust						X						X
The Weavers' Company Benevolent Fund				X				X				X
The James Weir Foundation					X					X		

	Jan	*Feb*	*Mar*	*Apr*	*May*	*Jun*	*Jul*	*Aug*	*Sep*	*Oct*	*Nov*	*Dec*
The Barbara Welby Trust			X							X		
The Wessex Youth Trust					X						X	
Dame Violet Wills Charitable Trust			X						X			
Woodroffe Benton Foundation	X			X			X			X		X
The Woodward Charitable Trust	X						X					
Zephyr Charitable Trust							X					

The major trusts ranked by grant total

Trust	Grants	Main grant areas
☐ John Laing Charitable Trust	£1.8 million	Education, community regeneration, youth, homelessness and environment
☐ J P Moulton Charitable Foundation	£1.7 million	Medical, education, training and counselling
☐ LWS Lancashire Environmental Fund Limited	£1.5 million	Environment and community
☐ The Porter Foundation	£1.5 million	Jewish charities, environment, arts, general
☐ The Steinberg Family Charitable Trust	£1.5 million	Jewish, health
☐ The Exilarch's Foundation	£1.4 million	General, Jewish, education
☐ Quercus Trust	£1.3 million	Arts, general
☐ The Andrew Salvesen Charitable Trust	£1.3 million	General charitable purposes
☐ LandAid Charitable Trust	£1.13 million	Homelessness, relief of need, young people
☐ Church Burgesses Trust	£1 million	Ecclesiastical purposes, education, and other charitable purposes
☐ The Linda and Gordon Bonnyman Charitable Trust	£1 million	General charitable purposes
☐ The Edith Winifred Hall Charitable Trust	£1 million	General charitable purposes, with preference towards young people and social welfare
☐ Wychville Ltd	£1 million	Jewish, education, general
☐ The Alborada Trust	£1 million	Veterinary causes, social welfare
☐ The Adrian Swire Charitable Trust	£997,000	General charitable purposes
☐ The Clive Richards Charity	£942,000	Churches, schools, arts, disability and poverty
☐ Country Houses Foundation	£942,000	Preservation of buildings of historic or architectural significance
☐ Heart Research UK	£939,000	Medical research into the prevention, treatment and cure of heart disease and heart disease prevention through lifestyle choices
☐ T and J Meyer Family Foundation Limited	£935,000	Education, healthcare, environment
☐ The Ingram Trust	£909,000	General charitable purposes
☐ The English Schools' Football Association	£853,000	Association football
☐ The Noon Foundation	£800,000	General, education, relief of poverty, community relations, alleviation of racial discrimination
☐ Truedene Co. Ltd	£788,000	Jewish causes

Trust	Grant total	Purposes
☐ **The Bransford Trust**	**£747,000**	General charitable purposes
☐ **The J Isaacs Charitable Trust**	**£744,000**	General charitable purposes
☐ **The Swire Charitable Trust**	**£742,500**	General charitable purposes
☐ **Menuchar Ltd**	**£722,000**	Jewish causes
☐ **The Persula Foundation**	**£709,000**	Homeless, people with disabilities, human rights, animal welfare
☐ **The Kennel Club Charitable Trust**	**£703,000**	Dogs
☐ **The Catherine Cookson Charitable Trust**	**£695,000**	General charitable purposes
☐ **The Bestway Foundation**	**£681,000**	Education, welfare, medical
☐ **The Petplan Charitable Trust**	**£681,000**	Welfare of dogs, cats, horses and rabbits
☐ **The Ruth Berkowitz Charitable Trust**	**£677,000**	Jewish, medical research, youth, general charitable purposes
☐ **Vyoel Moshe Charitable Trust**	**£668,000**	Education, relief of poverty
☐ **Friends of Wiznitz Limited**	**£665,500**	Jewish education, relief of poverty, advancement of the Jewish religion
☐ **The Ulverscroft Foundation**	**£642,000**	People who are blind or partially sighted, ophthalmic research
☐ **The Robert McAlpine Foundation**	**£640,000**	Children, disability, older people, medical research, welfare
☐ **The Schapira Charitable Trust**	**£639,000**	Jewish, health, education
☐ **The Shears Foundation**	**£632,000**	Health, education, children, arts, culture, recreation, heritage, conservation, environment
☐ **Royal Masonic Trust for Girls and Boys**	**£617,000**	Children, young people
☐ **Lewis Family Charitable Trust**	**£612,000**	General, Jewish
☐ **The Horne Trust**	**£606,000**	Hospices
☐ **Marchig Animal Welfare Trust**	**£595,000**	Animal welfare
☐ **The Queen Anne's Gate Foundation**	**£590,000**	Educational, medical and rehabilitative charities and those that work with underprivileged areas of society
☐ **St Monica Trust**	**£584,000**	Older people, disability
☐ **Bay Charitable Trust**	**£583,000**	Jewish causes
☐ **Help the Hospices**	**£582,000**	Hospices
☐ **The Talbot Village Trust**	**£577,000**	General charitable purposes
☐ **The Desmond Foundation**	**£570,000**	General charitable purposes, especially for the relief of poverty and sickness amongst children
☐ **The Rothermere Foundation**	**£569,000**	Education, general
☐ **The John Beckwith Charitable Trust**	**£556,000**	Sport, youth, education, social welfare, medical research, arts
☐ **The Cayo Foundation**	**£555,500**	Medical research, crime, children and young people, performing arts, general
☐ **Newpier Charity Ltd**	**£540,000**	Jewish, general
☐ **The Ashley Family Foundation**	**£534,000**	Art and design, higher education, local projects in mid-rural Wales
☐ **The Robert Gavron Charitable Trust**	**£528,000**	Health and welfare, prisons and prison reform, arts and arts education, education and social policy and research
☐ **Extonglen Limited**	**£528,000**	Orthodox Jewish causes, education, the relief of poverty
☐ **Bourneheights Limited**	**£519,000**	Orthodox Jewish causes
☐ **The Barbara Ward Children's Foundation**	**£516,000**	Children
☐ **Trumros Limited**	**£513,500**	Jewish causes
☐ **The Barbour Foundation**	**£505,500**	Health, welfare, conservation/restoration, animal care, schools, churches, overseas aid
☐ **The Hospital Saturday Fund**	**£503,000**	Medical, health
☐ **Stevenson Family's Charitable Trust**	**£501,000**	Culture and arts, conservation and heritage, health, education, overseas aid and general charitable purposes

Trust	Grant total	Causes
☐ **The O'Sullivan Family Charitable Trust**	**£493,000**	Children and young people, care homes, genetic research
☐ **The Bishop Radford Trust**	**£495,000**	Church of England
☐ **Buckingham Trust**	**£493,000**	Christian purposes, relief of poverty and sickness and support for older people
☐ **Kollel and Co. Limited**	**£493,000**	Jewish, relief of poverty
☐ **J A Clark Charitable Trust**	**£487,000**	Health, education, peace, preservation of the earth, the arts
☐ **Seamen's Hospital Society**	**£478,000**	Seafarers and their dependants
☐ **Salo Bordon Charitable Trust**	**£477,500**	Jewish causes
☐ **Kirschel Foundation**	**£475,000**	Jewish, medical
☐ **The Stella and Alexander Margulies Charitable Trust**	**£470,000**	Jewish, general charitable purposes
☐ **The A B Charitable Trust**	**£468,500**	Human rights
☐ **The Union of Orthodox Hebrew Congregation**	**£468,000**	Jewish causes
☐ **TVML Foundation**	**£466,000**	General charitable purposes
☐ **The Horizon Foundation**	**£454,000**	General, education, women and children
☐ **The Ruzin Sadagora Trust**	**£454,000**	Jewish causes
☐ **The Ian Karten Charitable Trust**	**£454,000**	Technology centres for people with disabilities
☐ **The Merchants' House of Glasgow**	**£452,000**	General charitable purposes
☐ **The Connie and Albert Taylor Charitable Trust**	**£448,500**	Medical research, hospices, education and recreation, preservation
☐ **All Saints Educational Trust**	**£448,000**	Religious education, home economics
☐ **The Paul Bassham Charitable Trust**	**£444,000**	General charitable purposes
☐ **The Sackler Trust**	**£443,500**	Arts and culture, science, medical
☐ **Brian Mercer Charitable Trust**	**£437,000**	Welfare, medical particularly sight and liver, visual arts
☐ **The Francis Winham Foundation**	**£435,000**	Welfare of older people
☐ **The Lind Trust**	**£434,000**	Social action, youth, community and Christian service
☐ **The Rowlands Trust**	**£433,000**	General, but mainly medical research, social welfare, music and the arts and the environment
☐ **The Dinwoodie Settlement**	**£433,000**	Postgraduate medical education and research
☐ **The Dyers' Company Charitable Trust**	**£430,000**	General charitable purposes
☐ **The Esfandi Charitable Foundation**	**£416,000**	Jewish causes
☐ **The Odin Charitable Trust**	**£413,000**	General charitable purposes
☐ **Premierquote Ltd**	**£412,000**	Jewish, general
☐ **The George Elias Charitable Trust**	**£410,000**	Jewish, general
☐ **The W O Street Charitable Foundation**	**£407,500**	Education, people with disabilities, young people, health, social welfare
☐ **The Stoller Charitable Trust**	**£405,500**	Medical, children, general
☐ **The Truemark Trust**	**£404,000**	General charitable purposes
☐ **Lloyd's Charities Trust**	**£403,000**	General charitable purposes
☐ **E and E Kernkraut Charities Limited**	**£403,000**	General, education, Jewish
☐ **The Lolev Charitable Trust**	**£403,000**	Orthodox Jewish causes
☐ **The Derek Butler Trust**	**£402,000**	Medical research, health, music and music education
☐ **The Mactaggart Third Fund**	**£398,000**	General charitable purposes
☐ **Basil Samuel Charitable Trust**	**£398,000**	General charitable purposes
☐ **The Locker Foundation**	**£397,000**	Mainly Jewish charities
☐ **The Tanner Trust**	**£396,000**	General charitable purposes
☐ **The Ironmongers' Foundation**	**£392,000**	Youth, education, iron projects
☐ **The M J C Stone Charitable Trust**	**£390,000**	General charitable purposes
☐ **The Lauffer Family Charitable Foundation**	**£381,000**	Jewish, general
☐ **Cullum Family Trust**	**£381,000**	Social welfare, education and general charitable purposes
☐ **The George Cadbury Trust**	**£379,000**	General charitable purposes
☐ **Dromintee Trust**	**£376,000**	General charitable purposes

Trust	Grant total	Interests
☐ **The Whitaker Charitable Trust**	**£375,000**	Music, environment, countryside conservation
☐ **Ian Mactaggart Trust**	**£373,000**	Education and training, culture, welfare and disability
☐ **The Dezna Robins Jones Charitable Foundation**	**£371,000**	Medicine, education
☐ **The Park House Charitable Trust**	**£368,000**	Education, social welfare, ecclesiastical
☐ **The Park Charitable Trust**	**£367,000**	Jewish, patient care – cancer and heart conditions, hospitals
☐ **Millennium Stadium Charitable Trust**	**£367,000**	Sport, the arts, community, environment, youth
☐ **The M and C Trust**	**£362,000**	Jewish, social welfare
☐ **The Batchworth Trust**	**£362,000**	Medical, humanitarian aid, social welfare, general
☐ **The Reta Lila Howard Foundation**	**£360,000**	Children, arts, environment
☐ **The Essex Youth Trust**	**£360,000**	Youth, education of people under 25
☐ **The Englefield Charitable Trust**	**£358,500**	General charitable purposes with a preference for local charities in Berkshire
☐ **The Simon Heller Charitable Settlement**	**£358,000**	Medical research, science and educational research
☐ **The Booth Charities**	**£358,000**	Welfare, health, education
☐ **The Racing Foundation**	**£357,000**	Horseracing industry, welfare and education, equine research
☐ **The Johnson Foundation**	**£356,000**	Education, health, relief of poverty
☐ **The Ireland Fund of Great Britain**	**£354,000**	Welfare, community, education, peace and reconciliation, the arts
☐ **The Vandervell Foundation**	**£351,000**	General charitable purposes
☐ **The Joseph Strong Frazer Trust**	**£345,000**	General, with broad interests in the fields of social welfare, education, religion and wildlife
☐ **The Holden Charitable Trust**	**£345,000**	Jewish causes
☐ **The D G Charitable Settlement**	**£344,000**	General charitable purposes
☐ **The GRP Charitable Trust**	**£342,500**	Jewish, general
☐ **The Toy Trust**	**£340,500**	Children
☐ **Kupath Gemach Chaim Bechesed Viznitz Trust**	**£338,000**	Jewish causes
☐ **The Michael and Ilse Katz Foundation**	**£336,000**	Jewish, music, medical, general
☐ **The King/Cullimore Charitable Trust**	**£334,000**	General charitable purposes
☐ **EMI Music Sound Foundation**	**£334,000**	Music education
☐ **The Norman Family Charitable Trust**	**£330,000**	General charitable purposes
☐ **Sino-British Fellowship Trust**	**£329,000**	Education
☐ **The William Brake Charitable Trust**	**£324,000**	General charitable purposes
☐ **Beauland Ltd**	**£318,000**	Jewish causes
☐ **The Eleanor Rathbone Charitable Trust**	**£318,000**	Merseyside, women, deprivation, social exclusion and unpopular causes
☐ **St James' Trust Settlement**	**£317,500**	General charitable purposes
☐ **The Radcliffe Trust**	**£317,000**	Music, crafts, conservation
☐ **The Marr-Munning Trust**	**£316,000**	Overseas aid
☐ **The Mutual Trust Group**	**£315,000**	Jewish, education, poverty
☐ **The Jean Shanks Foundation**	**£315,000**	Medical research and education
☐ **The Rowland Family Foundation**	**£315,000**	Relief-in-need, education, religion, community
☐ **The Jean Sainsbury Animal Welfare Trust**	**£311,000**	Animal welfare
☐ **The Austin and Hope Pilkington Trust**	**£308,000**	Categories of funding repeated in a three-year rotation (see the entry for further information)
☐ **The De Laszlo Foundation**	**£305,000**	Arts, general
☐ **Stuart Hine Trust**	**£304,000**	Evangelical Christianity
☐ **The Lister Charitable Trust**	**£304,000**	Outdoor activities for disadvantaged young people
☐ **The Michael Heller Charitable Foundation**	**£304,000**	University and medical research projects, the arts
☐ **The Adint Charitable Trust**	**£302,500**	Health, social welfare
☐ **Solev Co. Ltd**	**£302,000**	Jewish charities
☐ **The Janet Nash Charitable Settlement**	**£301,000**	Medical, hardship, general
☐ **The Sir Peter O'Sullevan Charitable Trust**	**£300,000**	Animal welfare
☐ **The Costa Family Charitable Trust**	**£300,000**	Christian purposes

Trust	Grant total	Main areas
☐ **H and L Cantor Trust**	**£300,000**	Jewish, general
☐ **The Sylvia Aitken Charitable Trust**	**£300,000**	Medical research and welfare, general
☐ **The Annandale Charitable Trust**	**£299,000**	Major UK charities
☐ **Mrs Waterhouse Charitable Trust**	**£298,000**	Medical, health, welfare, environment, wildlife, churches, heritage
☐ **Golden Charitable Trust**	**£298,000**	Preservation, conservation, medical research
☐ **The Tufton Charitable Trust**	**£293,000**	Christian causes
☐ **The Ellerdale Trust**	**£291,000**	Children, families, disability and ill health
☐ **The John Coates Charitable Trust**	**£291,000**	Preference is given to education, arts and culture, children, environment and health
☐ **The Joseph and Annie Cattle Trust**	**£289,000**	General charitable purposes
☐ **The Sir Jack Lyons Charitable Trust**	**£285,000**	Jewish, arts, education
☐ **Briggs Animal Welfare Trust**	**£284,000**	Animal welfare
☐ **The Cecil Rosen Foundation**	**£283,000**	Welfare, especially older people, infirm, people who are mentally or physically disabled
☐ **The Nigel Vinson Charitable Trust**	**£282,000**	Economic/community development and employment, general
☐ **C B and H H Taylor 1984 Trust**	**£282,000**	General charitable purposes, Quaker
☐ **The M K Charitable Trust**	**£282,000**	Jewish orthodox charities
☐ **The David Lean Foundation**	**£280,000**	Film production, education and visual arts
☐ **The David Laing Foundation**	**£279,000**	Youth, disability, the arts, general
☐ **The Bagri Foundation**	**£278,000**	General charitable purposes
☐ **The Millfield House Foundation**	**£278,000**	Social disadvantage, social policy
☐ **The Huntingdon Foundation**	**£277,000**	Jewish education
☐ **Toras Chesed (London) Trust**	**£277,000**	Jewish, education
☐ **National Committee of the Women's World Day of Prayer for England and Wales and Northern Ireland**	**£277,000**	Promotion of the Christian faith
☐ **Viscount Amory's Charitable Trust**	**£277,000**	Welfare, older people, education, Christian churches
☐ **The Norwich Town Close Estate Charity**	**£276,000**	Education in and near Norwich
☐ **Webb Memorial Trust**	**£276,000**	Education, politics, social policy
☐ **The Mahavir Trust**	**£276,000**	General, medical, animal welfare, relief of poverty, overseas aid, religion
☐ **The Clara E Burgess Charity**	**£275,000**	Children and young people
☐ **Rokach Family Charitable Trust**	**£275,000**	Jewish, general
☐ **The Grimmitt Trust**	**£273,000**	General charitable purposes ranging from community causes to overseas aid
☐ **The Catholic Trust for England and Wales**	**£271,500**	Catholic causes
☐ **The Philips and Rubens Charitable Trust**	**£271,000**	General, Jewish
☐ **The Inman Charity**	**£271,000**	General, medical, social welfare, disability, older people, hospices
☐ **The Marcela Trust**	**£270,000**	Medical research, environment and animals
☐ **Dudley and Geoffrey Cox Charitable Trust**	**£267,000**	Education, medicine, welfare, youth
☐ **The Ellinson Foundation Ltd**	**£267,000**	Jewish, education
☐ **The Sigmund Sternberg Charitable Foundation**	**£267,000**	Jewish, inter-faith causes, general
☐ **R S Charitable Trust**	**£267,000**	Jewish, welfare
☐ **The Armourers' and Brasiers' Gauntlet Trust**	**£267,000**	Materials science, general charitable purposes
☐ **The Doughty Charity Trust**	**£267,000**	Orthodox Jewish, religious education, relief of poverty
☐ **The Norton Foundation**	**£267,000**	Young people in need under 25 years of age
☐ **The Alchemy Foundation**	**£264,000**	Health and welfare, famine relief overseas
☐ **The Weavers' Company Benevolent Fund**	**£264,000**	Helping disadvantaged young people, offenders and ex-offenders
☐ **The Roger and Sarah Bancroft Clark Charitable Trust**	**£264,000**	Quaker, general

Trust	Grant total	Purposes
☐ **Calleva Foundation**	**£263,000**	General charitable purposes
☐ **The Loftus Charitable Trust**	**£263,000**	Jewish causes
☐ **Roger Vere Foundation**	**£262,000**	General charitable purposes
☐ **The Ajahma Charitable Trust**	**£261,500**	Development, poverty, human rights, health, disability, social welfare
☐ **William Harding's Charity**	**£261,000**	Education and welfare
☐ **The Charlotte Heber-Percy Charitable Trust**	**£259,000**	General charitable purposes, including: animal welfare, the environment, health, overseas aid, education, and the arts
☐ **Friends of Boyan Trust**	**£258,000**	Orthodox Jewish
☐ **The Marjorie and Arnold Ziff Charitable Foundation**	**£256,000**	General, education, Jewish, arts, youth, older people, medicine
☐ **The Andrew Anderson Trust**	**£254,000**	Christian, social welfare
☐ **Burdens Charitable Foundation**	**£254,000**	General charitable purposes
☐ **Wychdale Ltd**	**£253,000**	Jewish causes
☐ **John Coldman Charitable Trust**	**£252,000**	General, Christian
☐ **Tudor Rose Ltd**	**£252,000**	Jewish causes
☐ **The Saints and Sinners Trust**	**£251,000**	General but in practice mainly welfare and medical
☐ **The Stafford Trust**	**£250,500**	Animal welfare, medical research, local community, relief in need
☐ **Elizabeth Ferguson Charitable Trust Fund**	**£250,500**	Children, medical research, health, hospices
☐ **Mazars Charitable Trust**	**£250,000**	General charitable purposes
☐ **The Schreiber Charitable Trust**	**£250,000**	Jewish with a preference for education, social welfare and medical
☐ **The Stewards' Charitable Trust**	**£250,000**	Rowing
☐ **Scott (Eredine) Charitable Trust**	**£250,000**	Service and ex-service charities, medical, welfare
☐ **The Coltstaple Trust**	**£250,000**	The relief of persons in need, poverty or distress in third world countries and the relief of persons who are homeless or in housing need in the UK or any other part of the world
☐ **Peter Barker-Mill Memorial Charity**	**£248,500**	General charitable purposes
☐ **The Lynn Foundation**	**£248,000**	General charitable purposes
☐ **The W F Southall Trust**	**£248,000**	Quaker, general
☐ **Clydpride Ltd**	**£247,000**	Relief of poverty, Jewish charities, general charitable purposes
☐ **The Suva Foundation Limited**	**£245,000**	General charitable purposes
☐ **The Second Joseph Aaron Littman Foundation**	**£245,000**	General charitable purposes, with a special preference for Jewish causes, as well as academic and medical research
☐ **The Sidney and Elizabeth Corob Charitable Trust**	**£245,000**	General, Jewish
☐ **The Chapman Charitable Trust**	**£245,000**	Welfare, general
☐ **The Barnwood House Trust**	**£244,500**	Disability and old age
☐ **The Woodward Charitable Trust**	**£243,000**	General charitable purposes
☐ **The R V W Trust**	**£243,000**	Music education and appreciation
☐ **The Sir Edward Lewis Foundation**	**£242,000**	General charitable purposes
☐ **The Martin Laing Foundation**	**£242,000**	General, environment and conservation, disadvantaged young people and the elderly and infirm
☐ **The Homelands Charitable Trust**	**£242,000**	The New Church, health, social welfare, children
☐ **The Doris Field Charitable Trust**	**£241,000**	General charitable purposes
☐ **The Schmidt-Bodner Charitable Trust**	**£241,000**	Jewish, general
☐ **George A Moore Foundation**	**£240,000**	General charitable purposes
☐ **Woodroffe Benton Foundation**	**£240,000**	General charitable purposes
☐ **The British Council for Prevention of Blindness**	**£240,000**	Prevention and treatment of blindness

Trust	Grant total	Purposes
☐ **The Millichope Foundation**	**£239,000**	General charitable purposes
☐ **The SMB Charitable Trust**	**£238,000**	Christian, general charitable purposes
☐ **The CBD Charitable Trust**	**£238,000**	General, children and young people
☐ **The Leche Trust**	**£238,000**	Preservation and conservation of art and architecture, education
☐ **The Lotus Foundation**	**£237,500**	Children and families, women, community, animal protection, addiction recovery, education
☐ **The John Oldacre Foundation**	**£237,000**	Research and education in agricultural sciences
☐ **Alan Edward Higgs Charity**	**£236,000**	Child welfare
☐ **The Hutton Foundation**	**£235,000**	Christian, general
☐ **The Monatrea Charitable Trust**	**£235,000**	General charitable purposes
☐ **The Platinum Trust**	**£235,000**	Children with special needs and adults with mental or physical disabilities
☐ **The Sir Victor Blank Charitable Settlement**	**£232,000**	Jewish organisations and general charitable purposes
☐ **The William Allen Young Charitable Trust**	**£231,500**	General, health, social welfare
☐ **The Sir John Eastwood Foundation**	**£230,500**	Social welfare, education, health
☐ **The Elizabeth Frankland Moore and Star Foundation**	**£230,000**	General in the UK
☐ **Annie Tranmer Charitable Trust**	**£229,000**	General charitable purposes, education
☐ **The Whitley Animal Protection Trust**	**£228,000**	Animal welfare, conservation
☐ **The Norwood and Newton Settlement**	**£228,000**	Christian causes
☐ **The Norda Trust**	**£227,500**	Prisoners, asylum seekers, disadvantaged communities
☐ **The Tay Charitable Trust**	**£225,000**	General charitable purposes
☐ **The Gershon Coren Charitable Foundation (also known as The Muriel and Gus Coren Charitable Foundation)**	**£225,000**	General charitable purposes, social welfare and Jewish causes
☐ **The Football Association National Sports Centre Trust**	**£225,000**	Play areas, community sports facilities
☐ **Mercury Phoenix Trust**	**£224,000**	AIDS/HIV
☐ **The Christina Mary Hendrie Trust for Scottish and Canadian Charities**	**£224,000**	Youth, people who are elderly, general
☐ **Ryklow Charitable Trust 1992 (also known as A B Williamson Charitable Trust)**	**£223,000**	Education, health, environment and welfare
☐ **Marbeh Torah Trust**	**£223,000**	Jewish education and religion, and the relief of poverty
☐ **The Cooks Charity**	**£222,000**	Catering, welfare
☐ **The David Tannen Charitable Trust**	**£222,000**	Jewish causes
☐ **The Persson Charitable Trust**	**£221,000**	Christian mission societies and agencies
☐ **The Sheldon Trust**	**£221,000**	General charitable purposes
☐ **The Alan Sugar Foundation**	**£220,000**	Jewish charities, general
☐ **The Bertie Black Foundation**	**£220,000**	Jewish, general
☐ **The Bowerman Charitable Trust**	**£218,000**	Church, the arts, medical, youth
☐ **The Anton Jurgens Charitable Trust**	**£218,000**	Welfare, general
☐ **Royal Artillery Charitable Fund**	**£217,000**	Service charities
☐ **Monmouthshire County Council Welsh Church Act Fund**	**£216,000**	General charitable purposes
☐ **Matliwala Family Charitable Trust**	**£216,000**	Islam, education, social welfare
☐ **Largsmount Ltd**	**£216,000**	Jewish charitable purposes
☐ **Educational Foundation of Alderman John Norman**	**£215,000**	Educational purposes
☐ **The Anson Charitable Trust**	**£215,000**	General charitable purposes
☐ **Grand Charitable Trust of the Order of Women Freemasons**	**£215,000**	General in the UK and overseas

☐ **The David Webster Charitable Trust**	**£214,000**	Ecological and broadly environmental projects
☐ **The Generations Foundation**	**£214,000**	Health, family support, environmental protection and conservation, sports, education and leadership, hospitals, hospices, overseas aid, children, people with disabilities
☐ **The Kyte Charitable Trust**	**£214,000**	Jewish causes, education, health
☐ **Songdale Ltd**	**£214,000**	Jewish, education
☐ **Newby Trust Limited**	**£214,000**	Welfare, poverty, education, medical
☐ **The Marsh Christian Trust**	**£213,000**	General charitable purposes, with a preference towards social welfare, environmental causes, health, education, arts, animal welfare, and overseas appeals
☐ **The Sandhu Charitable Foundation**	**£212,000**	General charitable purposes
☐ **The Grahame Charitable Foundation Limited**	**£212,000**	Jewish causes
☐ **The James Weir Foundation**	**£210,000**	General charitable purposes
☐ **Ner Foundation**	**£210,000**	Orthodox Jewish
☐ **John Martin's Charity**	**£210,000**	Religious activity, relief-in-need, education
☐ **The Sir Harry Pilkington Trust**	**£208,000**	General charitable purposes
☐ **The Harebell Centenary Fund**	**£208,000**	General, education, medical research, animal welfare
☐ **The Flow Foundation**	**£208,000**	Welfare, education, environment, medical
☐ **Merchant Navy Welfare Board**	**£207,000**	Seafarers, merchant navy, sailors, welfare, medical care
☐ **The Doris Pacey Charitable Foundation**	**£206,000**	Jewish, medical, educational and social
☐ **Closehelm Limited**	**£206,000**	Jewish, welfare, general
☐ **The Anchor Foundation**	**£205,000**	Christian causes
☐ **Old Possum's Practical Trust**	**£205,000**	General, arts
☐ **Sir Samuel Scott of Yews Trust**	**£205,000**	Medical research
☐ **The Van Neste Foundation**	**£205,000**	Welfare, Christian, developing world
☐ **The Thornton Foundation**	**£204,000**	General charitable purposes
☐ **Talteg Ltd**	**£203,000**	Jewish, welfare
☐ **The Stanley Foundation Ltd**	**£203,000**	Medical care and research, education, social welfare, culture
☐ **Rees Jeffreys Road Fund**	**£203,000**	Road and transport research and education
☐ **Woodlands Green Ltd**	**£202,000**	Jewish causes
☐ **The Russell Trust**	**£201,000**	General charitable purposes
☐ **Bear Mordechai Ltd**	**£201,000**	Jewish causes
☐ **The Panacea Society**	**£200,000**	Christian religion, relief of sickness
☐ **The Cyril Taylor Charitable Trust**	**£200,000**	Education
☐ **The D W T Cargill Fund**	**£200,000**	General charitable purposes
☐ **The Ratcliff Foundation**	**£200,000**	General charitable purposes
☐ **Keren Mitzvah Trust**	**£200,000**	General, Jewish
☐ **Stervon Ltd**	**£200,000**	Jewish causes
☐ **D D McPhail Charitable Settlement**	**£200,000**	Medical research, disability, older people
☐ **The Bridging Fund Charitable Trust**	**£200,000**	Social welfare, relief of poverty
☐ **The Hope Trust**	**£200,000**	Temperance, Reformed Protestant churches
☐ **Miss Jeanne Bisgood's Charitable Trust**	**£199,000**	Roman Catholic purposes, older people
☐ **The M A Hawe Settlement**	**£198,000**	General charitable purposes
☐ **The Edgar E Lawley Foundation**	**£197,000**	Older people, disability, children, community, hospices and medical
☐ **The Gale Family Charity Trust**	**£196,000**	General charitable purposes with preference to churches and church ministries, as well as community life
☐ **The William and Katherine Longman Trust**	**£259,000**	General charitable purposes
☐ **The Follett Trust**	**£195,000**	Welfare, education, arts
☐ **Localtrent Ltd**	**£194,000**	Jewish, education, religion
☐ **The Joron Charitable Trust**	**£193,000**	Jewish, education, medical research, general

☐ **The James Caan Foundation**	**£193,000**	Social welfare, education
☐ **The Three Oaks Trust**	**£193,000**	Welfare
☐ **Salters' Charitable Foundation**	**£192,000**	General, with project grants focused specifically on the environment, citizenship and community development and health
☐ **The Delves Charitable Trust**	**£191,000**	Environment, conservation, medical, general
☐ **The Clover Trust**	**£190,500**	Older people, young people, Catholicism, health, disability
☐ **Ranworth Trust**	**£190,000**	General charitable purposes
☐ **The Iliffe Family Charitable Trust**	**£190,000**	Medical, disability, heritage, education
☐ **The Scouloudi Foundation**	**£188,500**	General charitable purposes
☐ **G M Morrison Charitable Trust**	**£188,000**	General charitable purposes
☐ **Finnart House School Trust**	**£187,000**	Jewish children and young people in need of care and/or education
☐ **The Tisbury Telegraph Trust**	**£186,000**	Christian, overseas aid, general
☐ **The Bothwell Charitable Trust**	**£186,000**	Disability, health, older people, conservation
☐ **The Fulmer Charitable Trust**	**£184,000**	Developing world, general
☐ **The C A Redfern Charitable Foundation**	**£184,000**	General charitable purposes
☐ **The South Square Trust**	**£182,500**	General charitable purposes
☐ **Hockerill Educational Foundation**	**£182,000**	Education, especially Christian education
☐ **The G W Cadbury Charitable Trust**	**£182,000**	Family planning, conservation, general
☐ **MYA Charitable Trust**	**£182,000**	Jewish causes
☐ **The Craps Charitable Trust**	**£182,000**	Jewish, general charitable purposes
☐ **The Misses Barrie Charitable Trust**	**£182,000**	Medical, general
☐ **The Primrose Trust**	**£181,000**	General, animal welfare
☐ **Weatherley Charitable Trust**	**£180,000**	General charitable purposes
☐ **The Bulldog Trust Limited**	**£180,000**	General charitable purposes
☐ **Macdonald-Buchanan Charitable Trust**	**£180,000**	General charitable purposes
☐ **Gerald Micklem Charitable Trust**	**£180,000**	General, health
☐ **The Tinsley Foundation**	**£180,000**	Human rights, poverty and homelessness and health education in underdeveloped countries
☐ **The CH (1980) Charitable Trust**	**£180,000**	Jewish causes
☐ **The Forest Hill Charitable Trust**	**£179,000**	Mainly Christian causes and relief work
☐ **The Double 'O' Charity Ltd**	**£178,000**	General charitable purposes
☐ **The Hilda and Samuel Marks Foundation**	**£178,000**	Jewish, general
☐ **The Yapp Charitable Trust**	**£178,000**	Social welfare
☐ **The Earl Fitzwilliam Charitable Trust**	**£177,000**	General charitable purposes
☐ **The Lord Faringdon Charitable Trust**	**£177,000**	Medical, educational, heritage, social welfare, the arts and sciences, recreation and general charitable purposes
☐ **Marc Fitch Fund**	**£176,000**	Heritage, archaeology, history, heraldry, genealogy
☐ **Truemart Limited**	**£175,000**	General, Judaism, welfare
☐ **R H Southern Trust**	**£174,000**	education, relief of poverty, disability, preservation and conservation
☐ **The J & J Charitable Trust**	**£174,000**	General, Jewish
☐ **The Laurence Misener Charitable Trust**	**£174,000**	Jewish, general
☐ **The A M Fenton Trust**	**£173,000**	General charitable purposes
☐ **The Kathleen Laurence Trust**	**£172,500**	Heart disease, arthritis, mental disabilities, medical research, older people, children's charities
☐ **The Lillie Johnson Charitable Trust**	**£172,000**	Children, young people who are blind or deaf, medical
☐ **The Saintbury Trust**	**£172,000**	General charitable purposes
☐ **Bill Brown 1998 Charitable Trust**	**£172,000**	General, health, social welfare
☐ **Frederick Mulder Charitable Trust**	**£172,000**	International development, climate change, conflict prevention
☐ **Jusaca Charitable Trust**	**£172,000**	Jewish, arts, research, religion, housing

Trust	Grant total	Areas
☐ **Brian and Jill Moss Charitable Trust**	**£172,000**	Jewish, healthcare
☐ **Children's Liver Disease Foundation**	**£170,000**	Diseases of the liver and biliary system in children
☐ **The Irish Youth Foundation (UK) Ltd (incorporating The Lawlor Foundation)**	**£170,000**	Irish young people
☐ **The Green Hall Foundation**	**£170,000**	Social welfare, medicine, health, general charitable purposes
☐ **James Madison Trust**	**£170,000**	The study of federal government
☐ **The Bedfordshire and Hertfordshire Historic Churches Trust**	**£169,500**	Churches
☐ **The Arnold Lee Charitable Trust**	**£169,000**	Jewish, educational, health
☐ **Hinchley Charitable Trust**	**£167,000**	Mainly evangelical Christian
☐ **The Gretna Charitable Trust**	**£166,500**	General charitable purposes
☐ **The Boshier-Hinton Foundation**	**£165,000**	Children and adults with special educational or other needs
☐ **The National Manuscripts Conservation Trust**	**£165,000**	Conservation of manuscripts
☐ **The Barbers' Company General Charities**	**£165,000**	Medical education and relief in sickness
☐ **Lifeline 4 Kids**	**£164,000**	Equipment for children with disabilities
☐ **The Oakdale Trust**	**£164,000**	Social work, medical, general
☐ **The Ronald Cruickshanks Foundation**	**£164,000**	Welfare, education, medical, general
☐ **The Cotton Trust**	**£163,000**	Relief of suffering, elimination and control of disease, people who have disabilities and disadvantaged people
☐ **The Amalur Foundation Limited**	**£162,000**	General charitable purposes
☐ **Barchester Healthcare Foundation**	**£162,000**	Health and social care
☐ **Thackray Medical Research Trust**	**£161,500**	Research of medical procedures/products, medical supply trade
☐ **The Elise Pilkington Charitable Trust**	**£161,000**	Equine animals, older people
☐ **The Charles Littlewood Hill Trust**	**£161,000**	Health, disability, service, heritage, children (including schools), welfare
☐ **The Nani Huyu Charitable Trust**	**£161,000**	Welfare
☐ **The Mole Charitable Trust**	**£161,000**	Jewish causes, education and the relief of poverty
☐ **The Peltz Trust**	**£160,000**	Arts, education, health, Jewish, general
☐ **Schroder Charity Trust**	**£159,500**	General charitable purposes
☐ **Lord Barnby's Foundation**	**£158,000**	General charitable purposes
☐ **The Leslie Mary Carter Charitable Trust**	**£157,000**	Conservation/environment, welfare
☐ **Sue Hammerson Charitable Trust**	**£157,000**	General charitable purposes, with particular emphasis on medical research, relief in need, education
☐ **The Daniel Howard Trust**	**£157,000**	Jewish causes
☐ **The Susanna Peake Charitable Trust**	**£156,500**	General charitable purposes
☐ **The Ove Arup Foundation**	**£156,000**	Construction education and research
☐ **The Jephcott Charitable Trust**	**£156,000**	Development worldwide specifically in the areas of health, education, population control and environment
☐ **Mickleham Charitable Trust**	**£156,000**	Relief-in-need
☐ **The Kennedy Charitable Foundation**	**£156,000**	Roman Catholic ministries, general, especially in the west of Ireland
☐ **Mariapolis Limited**	**£155,000**	Christian ecumenism, young people and families
☐ **The Sir James Roll Charitable Trust**	**£155,000**	General charitable purposes
☐ **The Peter Kershaw Trust**	**£155,000**	Medical research, education, social welfare
☐ **The Shanley Charitable Trust**	**£155,000**	Relief of poverty
☐ **The Holst Foundation**	**£154,000**	Arts
☐ **The Leslie Smith Foundation**	**£152,500**	Children with illnesses, orphans and schools
☐ **The Bernard Kahn Charitable Trust**	**£152,000**	Jewish education, advancement of religion
☐ **The Ian Askew Charitable Trust**	**£151,000**	General charitable purposes
☐ **The Paget Charitable Trust**	**£151,000**	General charitable purposes

Trust	Grant total	Areas
☐ **The Peter Minet Trust**	**£151,000**	General, children/youth, health and people with disabilities, social welfare, culture and community
☐ **Premishlaner Charitable Trust**	**£151,000**	Jewish causes
☐ **The Huggard Charitable Trust**	**£150,000**	General charitable purposes
☐ **The Ronald Miller Foundation**	**£150,000**	General charitable purposes
☐ **The Inlight Trust**	**£150,000**	Religion, spiritual development
☐ **The Edwina Mountbatten Trust**	**£149,000**	Medical, general
☐ **The Alan Evans Memorial Trust**	**£149,000**	Preservation, conservation
☐ **Saint Sarkis Charity Trust**	**£148,000**	Armenian churches and welfare, offenders
☐ **Jack Livingstone Charitable Trust**	**£148,000**	Jewish, general
☐ **The Vivienne and Samuel Cohen Charitable Trust**	**£147,500**	Jewish, education, health, medical, culture, general charitable purposes
☐ **Sueberry Ltd**	**£147,500**	Jewish, welfare
☐ **The Henry C Hoare Charitable Trust**	**£147,000**	General charitable purposes
☐ **The Roger Raymond Charitable Trust**	**£147,000**	Older people, education, medical
☐ **The Artemis Charitable Trust**	**£147,000**	Psychotherapy, parent education, and related activities
☐ **The Farthing Trust**	**£146,000**	Christian, general
☐ **The Richard Carne Trust**	**£146,000**	Young people in the performing arts
☐ **The Beaverbrook Foundation**	**£145,000**	General charitable purposes
☐ **The AM Charitable Trust**	**£145,000**	Jewish, general
☐ **The John Jarrold Trust**	**£145,000**	Social welfare, arts, education, environment/conservation, medical research, churches
☐ **The Jewish Youth Fund**	**£144,000**	Jewish youth work
☐ **The N Smith Charitable Settlement**	**£143,500**	General including social work, medical research, education, environment/animals, arts and overseas aid
☐ **The Scott Bader Commonwealth Ltd**	**£143,000**	General, international
☐ **Coral Samuel Charitable Trust**	**£143,000**	General, with a preference for educational, cultural and socially supportive charities
☐ **The London Law Trust**	**£143,000**	Medical research
☐ **Rosalyn and Nicholas Springer Charitable Trust**	**£142,000**	Welfare, Jewish, education, general
☐ **The Dellal Foundation**	**£142,000**	Jewish causes
☐ **The Spear Charitable Trust**	**£141,500**	General, with some preference for animal welfare, the environment and health
☐ **The Company of Actuaries' Charitable Trust Fund**	**£141,000**	Actuaries, medical research, young and older people, disability
☐ **The Friends of Kent Churches**	**£141,000**	Churches
☐ **The Beryl Evetts and Robert Luff Animal Welfare Trust Limited**	**£140,000**	Animal welfare
☐ **The Gordon Fraser Charitable Trust**	**£140,000**	Children, young people, environment, arts
☐ **The Benham Charitable Settlement**	**£140,000**	General charitable purposes
☐ **The John Slater Foundation**	**£140,000**	Medical, animal welfare, general
☐ **The Archie Sherman Cardiff Foundation**	**£139,000**	Health, education, training, overseas aid, community and Jewish
☐ **The Mayfield Valley Arts Trust**	**£138,000**	Arts, especially chamber music
☐ **Christian Response to Eastern Europe**	**£137,000**	Christian, emergency relief
☐ **Thomas Betton's Charity for Pensions and Relief-in-Need**	**£136,000**	Education for children and young people, housing, disability, performing arts, family
☐ **The Wilfrid and Constance Cave Foundation**	**£135,000**	Conservation, animal welfare, health, social welfare, general
☐ **The Kelly Family Charitable Trust**	**£135,000**	Family support
☐ **Consolidated Charity of Burton upon Trent**	**£135,000**	General charitable purposes
☐ **Ford Britain Trust**	**£134,500**	Community service, education, environment, disability, schools, special needs education, youth
☐ **The GNC Trust**	**£134,000**	General charitable purposes
☐ **Michael Marks Charitable Trust**	**£133,000**	Culture, environment

Trust	Grant total	Areas
☐ **The Christopher Laing Foundation**	**£133,000**	Disabilities, social welfare, environment, culture, health and, children and youth
☐ **Blatchington Court Trust**	**£133,000**	Supporting vision-impaired people under the age of 30
☐ **The Marjorie Coote Animal Charity Trust**	**£133,000**	Wildlife and animal welfare
☐ **Henry Lumley Charitable Trust**	**£132,000**	General charitable purposes, with a preference towards medicine, education and the relief of poverty
☐ **The Arnold Burton 1998 Charitable Trust**	**£132,000**	Jewish, medical research, education, social welfare, heritage
☐ **Melodor Limited**	**£131,500**	Jewish, general
☐ **The Melanie White Foundation Limited**	**£131,000**	General charitable purposes
☐ **SEM Charitable Trust**	**£131,000**	General, with a preference for educational special needs and Jewish organisations
☐ **Peter Stormonth Darling Charitable Trust**	**£131,000**	Heritage, medical research, sport
☐ **Elshore Ltd**	**£131,000**	Jewish causes
☐ **The Ouseley Trust**	**£130,000**	Choral services of the Church of England, Church in Wales and Church of Ireland, choir schools
☐ **Philip and Judith Green Trust**	**£130,000**	Christian and missions
☐ **The Bay Tree Charitable Trust**	**£130,000**	Development work, general
☐ **The Hyde Charitable Trust**	**£130,000**	Disadvantaged children and young people
☐ **Miss A M Pilkington's Charitable Trust**	**£130,000**	General charitable purposes
☐ **The Fuserna Foundation General Charitable Trust**	**£130,000**	General charitable purposes, including education and training, the advancement of health, the relief of poverty, accommodation and housing, the arts, the environment, the armed forces, and human rights
☐ **Langdale Trust**	**£130,000**	General charitable purposes, young people, social welfare, health, Christian
☐ **Prison Service Charity Fund**	**£130,000**	General, medical
☐ **AF Trust Company**	**£130,000**	Higher education
☐ **The Estelle Trust**	**£130,000**	Overseas aid
☐ **The J E Joseph Charitable Fund**	**£129,000**	Jewish causes
☐ **Saint Luke's College Foundation**	**£129,000**	Research or studies in theology
☐ **The Homestead Charitable Trust**	**£128,000**	Medicine, health, welfare, animal welfare, Christianity and the arts
☐ **The Hawthorne Charitable Trust**	**£127,000**	General charitable purposes
☐ **Daisie Rich Trust**	**£127,000**	General charitable purposes
☐ **Minton Charitable Trust**	**£126,500**	Education
☐ **The Burden Trust**	**£126,000**	Christian, welfare, medical research, education, general
☐ **Disability Aid Fund (The Roger and Jean Jefcoate Trust)**	**£126,000**	Disability
☐ **The Thornton Trust**	**£126,000**	Evangelical Christianity, education, relief of sickness and poverty
☐ **The Ward Blenkinsop Trust**	**£126,000**	Medicine, social welfare, arts, education, general
☐ **The Cobalt Trust**	**£125,000**	General charitable purposes
☐ **The Hudson Foundation**	**£125,000**	Older people, general
☐ **Princess Anne's Charities**	**£124,000**	Children, medical, welfare, general
☐ **The Portrack Charitable Trust**	**£124,000**	General charitable purposes
☐ **The Patricia and Donald Shepherd Charitable Trust**	**£124,000**	General charitable purposes particularly those involving young people
☐ **The Edward and Dorothy Cadbury Trust**	**£124,000**	Health, education, arts
☐ **The Cyril Shack Trust**	**£124,000**	Jewish, general
☐ **The Idlewild Trust**	**£124,000**	Performing arts, culture, restoration and conservation, occasional arts education
☐ **The Cecil Pilkington Charitable Trust**	**£123,000**	Conservation, medical research, general

Trust	Grant total	Purposes
☐ **The Laduma Dhamecha Charitable Trust**	**£123,000**	General charitable purposes
☐ **The Morris Charitable Trust**	**£123,000**	Relief of need, education, community support and development
☐ **The Walter Guinness Charitable Trust**	**£122,600**	General charitable purposes
☐ **The Sue Thomson Foundation**	**£122,000**	Christ's Hospital School, education
☐ **Ambika Paul Foundation**	**£122,000**	Education, young people
☐ **The J E Posnansky Charitable Trust**	**£122,000**	Jewish charities, health, social welfare and humanitarian
☐ **The Ashworth Charitable Trust**	**£122,000**	Welfare
☐ **The Wessex Youth Trust**	**£122,000**	Youth, general
☐ **The Smith Charitable Trust**	**£121,000**	General charitable purposes
☐ **The DLA Piper Charitable Trust**	**£120,000**	General charitable purposes
☐ **R J M Charitable Trust**	**£120,000**	Jewish causes
☐ **The Viznitz Foundation**	**£120,000**	Jewish causes
☐ **The Astor Foundation**	**£120,000**	Medical research, general
☐ **The Forte Charitable Trust**	**£120,000**	Roman Catholic, Alzheimer's disease, senile dementia
☐ **The Colonel W H Whitbread Charitable Trust**	**£119,000**	Education, preservation of places of historic interest and natural beauty
☐ **The Kreditor Charitable Trust**	**£119,000**	Jewish, welfare, education
☐ **The Helen Roll Charitable Trust**	**£118,000**	General charitable purposes
☐ **The Rayne Trust**	**£118,000**	Jewish organisations, older and young people and people disadvantaged by poverty or socially isolation, understanding between cultures
☐ **Kinsurdy Charitable Trust**	**£117,000**	General charitable purposes
☐ **The Billmeir Charitable Trust**	**£117,000**	General, health and medical
☐ **Spears-Stutz Charitable Trust**	**£117,000**	Relief of poverty, general
☐ **The Harding Trust**	**£116,000**	Arts, education
☐ **The Jenour Foundation**	**£116,000**	General charitable purposes
☐ **The Gay and Keith Talbot Trust**	**£116,000**	Overseas aid, health, famine relief
☐ **Mountbatten Festival of Music**	**£115,500**	Royal Marines and Royal Navy charities
☐ **The Ogle Christian Trust**	**£115,000**	Evangelical Christianity
☐ **Moshal Charitable Trust**	**£115,000**	Jewish causes
☐ **Sellata Ltd**	**£115,000**	Jewish, welfare
☐ **The Geoffrey C Hughes Charitable Trust**	**£115,000**	Nature conservation, environment, performing arts
☐ **The Annie Schiff Charitable Trust**	**£115,000**	Orthodox Jewish education
☐ **Panahpur**	**£114,000**	Christian missionaries, general, social investment
☐ **Spar Charitable Fund**	**£114,000**	General, with a preference for children and young people
☐ **Rix-Thompson-Rothenberg Foundation**	**£114,000**	Learning disabilities
☐ **The Langley Charitable Trust**	**£113,000**	Christians, at risk groups, people who are disadvantaged by poverty, socially isolated or sick
☐ **The Casey Trust**	**£112,000**	Children and young people
☐ **Vision Charity**	**£112,000**	Children who are blind, partially sighted or dyslexic
☐ **Adenfirst Ltd**	**£112,000**	Jewish causes
☐ **The Law Society Charity**	**£112,000**	Law and justice, worldwide
☐ **The Scurrah Wainwright Charity**	**£112,000**	Social reform
☐ **The Kobler Trust**	**£111,000**	Arts, Jewish, general
☐ **Cardy Beaver Foundation**	**£111,000**	General charitable purposes
☐ **The Ampelos Trust**	**£111,000**	General charitable purposes
☐ **The Louis and Valerie Freedman Charitable Settlement**	**£111,000**	General charitable purposes
☐ **The DLM Charitable Trust**	**£111,000**	General charitable purposes
☐ **The Fidelio Charitable Trust**	**£111,000**	Arts, in particular the dramatic and operatic arts, music, speech and dance

Trust	Grant total	Areas
☐ **The Pyne Charitable Trust**	**£110,000**	Christian, health
☐ **The Scarfe Charitable Trust**	**£110,000**	Churches, arts, music, environment
☐ **The Puebla Charitable Trust**	**£110,000**	Community development work, relief of poverty
☐ **The Limbourne Trust**	**£108,000**	Environment, welfare, arts
☐ **Fordeve Limited**	**£108,000**	Orthodox Jewish causes
☐ **St Michael's and All Saints' Charities Relief Branch (The Church Houses Relief in Need Charity)**	**£107,000**	Health, welfare
☐ **Famos Foundation Trust**	**£107,000**	Jewish causes
☐ **The Leigh Trust**	**£106,500**	Addiction, children and youth, criminal justice, asylum seekers, racial equality and education
☐ **Maranatha Christian Trust**	**£106,000**	Christian, relief of poverty and education of young people
☐ **Balmain Charitable Trust**	**£106,000**	General charitable purposes
☐ **The Sir Jeremiah Colman Gift Trust**	**£106,000**	General charitable purposes
☐ **The Taurus Foundation**	**£106,000**	General charitable purposes
☐ **Ulting Overseas Trust**	**£106,000**	Theological training
☐ **Peter Storrs Trust**	**£105,000**	Education
☐ **The Breast Cancer Research Trust**	**£104,000**	Breast cancer research
☐ **The A H and E Boulton Trust**	**£104,000**	Evangelical Christianity
☐ **The River Trust**	**£103,000**	Christian causes
☐ **G M C Trust**	**£103,000**	General charitable purposes, organisations benefiting children, young adults and older people are largely supported
☐ **The Neville and Elaine Blond Charitable Trust**	**£103,000**	Jewish, general
☐ **The Sir John Ritblat Family Foundation**	**£130,000**	Jewish, general
☐ **The Albert Van Den Bergh Charitable Trust**	**£103,000**	Medical research, disability, community, general
☐ **The M J Samuel Charitable Trust**	**£102,000**	General, Jewish
☐ **Diana and Allan Morgenthau Charitable Trust**	**£102,000**	Jewish, general
☐ **The Sydney and Phyllis Goldberg Memorial Charitable Trust**	**£102,000**	Medical research, welfare, disability
☐ **Oizer Dalim Trust**	**£102,000**	Orthodox Jewish causes, social welfare, education
☐ **The Harold and Alice Bridges Charity**	**£101,000**	Capital projects in connection with rural and village life
☐ **The MSE Charity**	**£101,000**	Financial education, improving financial literacy
☐ **The Edith Lilian Harrison 2000 Foundation**	**£101,000**	General charitable purposes
☐ **The Samuel and Freda Parkinson Charitable Trust**	**£101,000**	General charitable purposes
☐ **G R Waters Charitable Trust 2000**	**£101,000**	General charitable purposes
☐ **Dixie Rose Findlay Charitable Trust**	**£101,000**	General charitable purposes with preference to children, seafarers, blindness and multiple sclerosis
☐ **Altamont Ltd**	**£101,000**	Jewish causes
☐ **The Worshipful Company of Spectacle Makers' Charity**	**£101,000**	Visual impairment, general
☐ **The R J Larg Family Charitable Trust**	**£100,000**	Education, health, medical research, arts particularly music
☐ **The Humanitarian Trust**	**£100,000**	Education, health, social welfare, Jewish
☐ **The Charlotte Bonham-Carter Charitable Trust**	**£100,000**	General charitable purposes
☐ **The Duke of Cornwall's Benevolent Fund**	**£100,000**	General charitable purposes
☐ **The Mickel Fund**	**£100,000**	General charitable purposes
☐ **The Paragon Trust**	**£100,000**	General charitable purposes
☐ **Wallace and Gromit's Children's Foundation**	**£100,000**	Improving the quality of life for sick children
☐ **Friends of Biala Limited**	**£100,000**	Jewish causes, education, relief of poverty
☐ **Lord and Lady Lurgan Trust**	**£100,000**	Medical charities, older people, children and the arts
☐ **The Violet and Milo Cripps Charitable Trust**	**£100,000**	Prison and human rights
☐ **The Rainford Trust**	**£100,000**	Social welfare, general

Trust	Grant total	Purposes
☐ **The International Bankers Charitable Trust (The Worshipful Company of International Bankers)**	**£100,000**	The recruitment and development of employees in the financial services
☐ **The J G Hogg Charitable Trust**	**£100,000**	Welfare, animal welfare, general
☐ **The Forbes Charitable Foundation**	**£99,500**	Adults with learning disabilities
☐ **Birthday House Trust**	**£99,500**	General charitable purposes
☐ **The Samuel Storey Family Charitable Trust**	**£99,500**	General charitable purposes
☐ **The Florence Turner Trust**	**£99,000**	General charitable purposes
☐ **The Worshipful Company of Chartered Accountants General Charitable Trust**	**£99,000**	General, education
☐ **The Harris Family Charitable Trust**	**£99,000**	Health, sickness
☐ **Child Growth Foundation**	**£99,000**	Institutions researching child/adult growth disorders, and people with such diseases
☐ **The Sutasoma Trust**	**£98,500**	Education, general
☐ **The W G Edwards Charitable Foundation**	**£98,500**	Projects benefiting older people
☐ **The Galanthus Trust**	**£98,000**	Medical, developing countries, environment, conservation
☐ **The Simon Whitbread Charitable Trust**	**£97,000**	General charitable purposes
☐ **The Raymond and Blanche Lawson Charitable Trust**	**£97,000**	General charitable purposes, with preference towards children, young adults, older people, people with disabilities and people within the armed forces
☐ **The Gibbs Charitable Trust**	**£97,000**	Methodism, international, arts
☐ **Daily Prayer Union Charitable Trust Limited**	**£96,500**	Evangelical Christianity
☐ **Garrick Charitable Trust**	**£96,500**	Theatre, music, literature, dance
☐ **The G D Charitable Trust**	**£96,000**	Animal welfare, the environment, disability, homelessness
☐ **The Kasner Charitable Trust**	**£96,000**	Jewish causes
☐ **The Equity Trust Fund**	**£96,000**	Theatre
☐ **The Lord Forte Foundation**	**£95,500**	Hospitality
☐ **The Merchant Taylors' Company Charities Fund**	**£95,000**	Education, training, church, medicine, general
☐ **The George and Esme Pollitzer Charitable Settlement**	**£95,000**	Jewish, general
☐ **Andrews Charitable Trust**	**£95,000**	Social welfare, Christian causes
☐ **The Normanby Charitable Trust**	**£94,000**	Arts, culture, heritage, social welfare
☐ **The Noel Buxton Trust**	**£94,000**	Child and family welfare, penal matters, Africa
☐ **The Lyndhurst Trust**	**£94,000**	Christianity
☐ **Jacqueline and Michael Gee Charitable Trust**	**£94,000**	Health, arts, education, Jewish causes
☐ **Minge's Gift and the Pooled Trusts**	**£94,000**	Medical, education, disadvantage, disability, footwear
☐ **The Harry Bottom Charitable Trust**	**£94,000**	Religion, education, medical
☐ **The Patrick & Helena Frost Foundation**	**£93,000**	General charitable purposes
☐ **The Magen Charitable Trust**	**£92,000**	Education, welfare, health with preference to Jewish causes
☐ **The Amelia Chadwick Trust**	**£92,000**	General charitable purposes
☐ **The Peter Samuel Charitable Trust**	**£92,000**	Health, welfare, conservation, Jewish care
☐ **The Westcroft Trust**	**£92,000**	International understanding, overseas aid, Quaker, Shropshire
☐ **The Mishcon Family Charitable Trust**	**£92,000**	Jewish, social welfare, medical, disability, children
☐ **P Leigh-Bramwell Trust 'E'**	**£92,000**	Methodist, general charitable purposes
☐ **The Lady Eileen Joseph Foundation**	**£92,000**	People who are disadvantaged by poverty or socially isolated and 'at-risk' groups Largely welfare, medical causes and general charitable purposes are supported
☐ **The Jessie Spencer Trust**	**£91,000**	General charitable purposes
☐ **The Lord Cozens-Hardy Trust**	**£91,000**	Medical/health, education, welfare, general
☐ **The Seedfield Trust**	**£90,000**	Christian, relief of poverty

Trust	Grant total	Purposes
☐ **The Argentarius Foundation**	**£90,000**	General charitable purposes
☐ **The Michael and Clara Freeman Charitable Trust**	**£90,000**	General charitable purposes
☐ **The Cleevely Family Charitable Trust**	**£90,000**	General, children and young people
☐ **The Trefoil Trust**	**£90,000**	Health, young people, disability, the arts, armed forces
☐ **The Strawberry Charitable Trust**	**£90,000**	Jewish, youth
☐ **The Leach Fourteenth Trust**	**£90,000**	Medical, disability, environment, conservation, general
☐ **The Gunter Charitable Trust**	**£89,500**	General charitable purposes including medical and wildlife causes in the UK
☐ **The Charles Skey Charitable Trust**	**£88,000**	General charitable purposes
☐ **The C S Kaufman Charitable Trust**	**£88,000**	Judaism
☐ **The Cheruby Trust**	**£88,000**	Welfare, education, general, overseas aid
☐ **Leslie Sell Charitable Trust**	**£87,500**	Scout and guide groups
☐ **Mrs F B Laurence Charitable Trust**	**£87,500**	Social welfare, animal welfare, medical, disability, environment
☐ **The Marjorie and Geoffrey Jones Charitable Trust**	**£87,000**	General charitable purposes
☐ **Andor Charitable Trust**	**£87,000**	Health, arts, Jewish, general
☐ **The Thriplow Charitable Trust**	**£87,000**	Higher and further education and research
☐ **Sir Clive Bourne Family Trust**	**£87,000**	Jewish causes
☐ **The Anna Rosa Forster Charitable Trust**	**£87,000**	Medical research, animal welfare, famine relief
☐ **The Willie and Mabel Morris Charitable Trust**	**£87,000**	Medical, general
☐ **The Wyseliot Charitable Trust**	**£87,000**	Medical, welfare, arts
☐ **The P and C Hickinbotham Charitable Trust**	**£87,000**	Social welfare
☐ **R G Hills Charitable Trust**	**£86,500**	Health, poverty, education, general
☐ **The David Pearlman Charitable Foundation**	**£86,000**	Jewish, general
☐ **The Shipwrights' Company Charitable Fund**	**£86,000**	Maritime or waterborne connected charities
☐ **The Owen Family Trust**	**£85,000**	Christian, general
☐ **The Mason Porter Charitable Trust**	**£85,000**	Christian, health
☐ **David Solomons Charitable Trust**	**£85,000**	Learning difficulties
☐ **The Linden Charitable Trust**	**£85,000**	Medical, healthcare, the arts
☐ **C and F Charitable Trust**	**£85,000**	Orthodox Jewish charities
☐ **Philip Smith's Charitable Trust**	**£85,000**	Welfare, older people, children, environment, armed forces
☐ **The British Dietetic Association General and Education Trust Fund**	**£84,000**	Dietary and nutritional issues
☐ **The H and M Charitable Trust**	**£84,000**	Education, relief of poverty and other charitable purposes with a particular focus on seafaring
☐ **Liberum Foundation**	**£84,000**	General charitable purposes with a focus on disadvantaged young people
☐ **The Stanley Smith UK Horticultural Trust**	**£84,000**	Horticulture
☐ **REMEDI**	**£84,000**	Medical research
☐ **The Millward Charitable Trust**	**£84,000**	Social welfare, performing arts, medical research and animal welfare
☐ **The Children's Research Fund**	**£83,000**	Child health research
☐ **Edinburgh Trust No. 2 Account**	**£83,000**	Education, armed services, scientific expeditions
☐ **Samuel William Farmer Trust**	**£83,000**	Education, health, social welfare
☐ **Rita and David Slowe Charitable Trust**	**£83,000**	General charitable purposes
☐ **The J R S S T Charitable Trust**	**£82,000**	Democracy and social justice
☐ **The Tory Family Foundation**	**£82,000**	Education, Christian, medical
☐ **The Mizpah Trust**	**£82,000**	General charitable purposes
☐ **The Ardwick Trust**	**£82,000**	Jewish, welfare, general
☐ **The Barnsbury Charitable Trust**	**£81,000**	General charitable purposes
☐ **Yankov Charitable Trust**	**£81,000**	Jewish causes

Trust	Grant total	Areas
☐ **Douglas Arter Foundation**	**£81,000**	People with mental or physical disabilities
☐ **The Eleni Nakou Foundation**	**£80,000**	Education, international understanding
☐ **The Marjory Boddy Charitable Trust**	**£80,000**	General charitable purposes
☐ **The Andy Stewart Charitable Foundation**	**£80,000**	General charitable purposes
☐ **The BACTA Charitable Trust**	**£80,000**	General charitable purposes
☐ **The Thomas Sivewright Catto Charitable Settlement**	**£80,000**	General charitable purposes
☐ **The Altajir Trust**	**£79,500**	Islam, education, science and research
☐ **The Joseph and Lena Randall Charitable Trust**	**£79,000**	General charitable purposes
☐ **The Lili Tapper Charitable Foundation**	**£79,000**	Jewish causes
☐ **The Ruth and Stuart Lipton Charitable Trust**	**£79,000**	Jewish charities and general charitable purposes
☐ **The Seneca Trust**	**£79,000**	Social welfare, education, children and young people
☐ **The Animal Defence Trust**	**£78,000**	Animal welfare and conservation
☐ **The Rock Foundation**	**£78,000**	Christian ministries and charities
☐ **The Moss Charitable Trust**	**£78,000**	Christian, education, poverty, health
☐ **The Elaine and Angus Lloyd Charitable Trust**	**£78,000**	General charitable purposes
☐ **Garthgwynion Charities**	**£78,000**	Medical research, community projects, general
☐ **Greys Charitable Trust**	**£77,500**	General charitable purposes with preference towards church and historical building preservation, the arts
☐ **The Morel Charitable Trust**	**£77,000**	Arts and culture, race relations, inner-city projects UK and the developing world
☐ **C Richard Jackson Charitable Trust**	**£77,000**	General charitable purposes
☐ **Harbo Charities Limited**	**£77,000**	General charitable purposes and Jewish causes, education, relief in need, disability, ill health
☐ **Marmot Charitable Trust**	**£77,000**	General charitable purposes, 'green' organisations, conflict resolution
☐ **The Hugh and Ruby Sykes Charitable Trust**	**£77,000**	General, medical, education, employment
☐ **Dischma Charitable Trust**	**£77,000**	General, with a preference for Education, Arts and Culture, Conservation and Human and Animal Welfare
☐ **The Williams Charitable Trust**	**£77,000**	Education and training, the advancement of medicine and general charitable purposes
☐ **The Millfield Trust**	**£76,000**	Christian causes
☐ **The Gamma Trust**	**£76,000**	General, Christian, health, disability, arts, medical research
☐ **Ellador Ltd**	**£76,000**	Jewish organisations and individuals
☐ **The Tony Bramall Charitable Trust**	**£76,000**	Medical research, ill health, social welfare
☐ **Blyth Watson Charitable Trust**	**£76,000**	UK-based humanitarian organisations, hospices
☐ **The Bassil Shippam and Alsford Trust**	**£75,500**	Young and older people, health, education, learning disabilities, Christian
☐ **The Turtleton Charitable Trust**	**£75,000**	Arts, heritage, poverty, education
☐ **The Adamson Trust**	**£75,000**	Children under 18 with a physical or mental disability
☐ **The A M McGreevy No. 5 Charitable Settlement**	**£75,000**	General charitable purposes
☐ **The Treeside Trust**	**£75,000**	General charitable purposes
☐ **The Weinberg Foundation**	**£75,000**	General charitable purposes
☐ **B E Perl Charitable Trust**	**£75,000**	Jewish, general
☐ **T and S Trust Fund**	**£75,000**	Orthodox Jewish
☐ **The Oliver Morland Charitable Trust**	**£75,000**	Quakers, general
☐ **The Charlotte Marshall Charitable Trust**	**£75,000**	Roman Catholic, general
☐ **The Gaynor Cemlyn-Jones Trust**	**£75,000**	Welsh heritage, medical research, animal welfare, music and religion
☐ **The Modiano Charitable Trust**	**£74,000**	Arts, Jewish, general
☐ **The Dumbreck Charity**	**£74,000**	General charitable purposes

Trust	Grant total	Purposes
☐ **The Vernon N Ely Charitable Trust**	**£74,000**	General charitable purposes, with a preference to the London borough of Merton and sports charities
☐ **The Carr-Gregory Trust**	**£73,500**	Arts, social welfare, health, education
☐ **Armenian General Benevolent Union London Trust**	**£73,500**	Armenian education, culture and welfare
☐ **The David Pickford Charitable Foundation**	**£73,000**	Christian, general
☐ **The Salamander Charitable Trust**	**£73,000**	Christian, general charitable purposes
☐ **The Aurelius Charitable Trust**	**£73,000**	Conservation of culture and the humanities
☐ **The Chownes Foundation**	**£73,000**	Religion, relief-in-need, social problems
☐ **The Chipping Sodbury Town Lands Charity**	**£73,000**	Welfare, education, leisure, general charitable purposes
☐ **Ashburnham Thanksgiving Trust**	**£72,000**	Christian causes
☐ **Houblon-Norman/George Fund**	**£72,000**	Finance
☐ **The Spurrell Charitable Trust**	**£72,000**	General charitable purposes
☐ **The C L Loyd Charitable Trust**	**£72,000**	General charitable purposes
☐ **The Gilbert and Eileen Edgar Foundation**	**£72,000**	General charitable purposes with preference towards medical research, care and support, fine arts, education in the fine arts, religion, and recreation
☐ **The Witzenfeld Foundation**	**£72,000**	General charitable purposes, Jewish
☐ **The Jeremy and John Sacher Charitable Trust**	**£72,000**	General, including arts, culture and heritage, medical and disability, community and welfare, education, science and technology, children and youth, and religion
☐ **The Michael Harry Sacher Trust**	**£72,000**	General, with a preference for arts, education, animal welfare, Jewish, health and social welfare
☐ **Hasluck Charitable Trust**	**£72,000**	Health, welfare, disability, youth, overseas aid
☐ **The Benjamin Winegarten Charitable Trust**	**£72,000**	Jewish causes
☐ **Malbin Trust**	**£72,000**	Jewish causes, general charitable purposes, social welfare
☐ **Edith and Ferdinand Porjes Charitable Trust**	**£72,000**	Jewish, general
☐ **The Jill Franklin Trust**	**£71,500**	General charitable purposes with a preference towards welfare, prisons, church restoration and asylum
☐ **The B and P Glasser Charitable Trust**	**£71,500**	Health, disability, Jewish, welfare
☐ **The Chetwode Foundation**	**£71,000**	Education, churches, general
☐ **The Denise Cohen Charitable Trust**	**£71,000**	Health, welfare, arts, humanities, education, culture, Jewish
☐ **British Humane Association**	**£71,000**	Welfare
☐ **The R D Turner Charitable Trust**	**£70,500**	General charitable purposes
☐ **The Joyce Fletcher Charitable Trust**	**£70,500**	General charitable purposes with a preference towards children's welfare, music, disability
☐ **T F C Frost Charitable Trust**	**£70,500**	Research into the prevention of blindness
☐ **Wakeham Trust**	**£70,000**	Community development, education, community service by young people
☐ **Florence's Charitable Trust**	**£70,000**	Education, welfare, sick and inform, general charitable purposes
☐ **The Loke Wan Tho Memorial Foundation**	**£70,000**	Environment and conservation, general, medical causes, overseas aid
☐ **The Inverforth Charitable Trust**	**£70,000**	General charitable purposes
☐ **The Misselbrook Trust**	**£70,000**	General charitable purposes
☐ **Sumner Wilson Charitable Trust**	**£70,000**	General charitable purposes
☐ **Robyn Charitable Trust**	**£70,000**	General charitable purposes, particularly the support of young people
☐ **The Phillips Family Charitable Trust**	**£70,000**	Jewish charities, welfare, general
☐ **Harold and Daphne Cooper Charitable Trust**	**£70,000**	Medical, health, Jewish
☐ **Sir John Evelyn's Charity**	**£70,000**	Relief of poverty, as well as advance education and community development

☐ **The Blair Foundation**	**£70,000**	Wildlife, access to countryside, general
☐ **The Derek Hill Foundation**	**£69,000**	Arts and culture
☐ **The Felicity Wilde Charitable Trust**	**£69,000**	Children, medical research
☐ **The Association of Colleges Charitable Trust**	**£69,000**	Further education colleges
☐ **The Bernard Piggott Charitable Trust**	**£69,000**	General charitable purposes
☐ **Michael Davies Charitable Settlement**	**£69,000**	General charitable purposes
☐ **The Sir William Coxen Trust Fund**	**£69,000**	Orthopaedic hospitals or other hospitals or charities doing orthopaedic work
☐ **The Michael and Shirley Hunt Charitable Trust**	**£69,000**	Prisoners' families, animal welfare
☐ **The Hesed Trust**	**£68,000**	Christian causes
☐ **William Dean Countryside and Educational Trust**	**£68,000**	Education in natural history, ecology and conservation
☐ **The Norman Whiteley Trust**	**£68,000**	Evangelical Christianity, welfare, education
☐ **The B G S Cayzer Charitable Trust**	**£68,000**	General charitable purposes
☐ **The Francis Coales Charitable Foundation**	**£68,000**	Historical
☐ **The Diana Edgson Wright Charitable Trust**	**£67,500**	Animal conservation, social welfare, general
☐ **The Matt 6.3 Charitable Trust**	**£67,500**	Christian causes
☐ **The Tabeel Trust**	**£67,000**	Evangelical Christianity
☐ **The David and Ruth Behrend Fund**	**£67,000**	General charitable purposes
☐ **Vivdale Ltd**	**£67,000**	Jewish causes
☐ **The John Spedan Lewis Foundation**	**£67,000**	Natural sciences, particularly horticulture, environmental education, ornithology and conservation
☐ **The E L Rathbone Charitable Trust**	**£67,000**	Social work charities
☐ **The Gould Charitable Trust**	**£66,000**	Education and training, with preference towards Jewish organisations and causes
☐ **The Kreitman Foundation**	**£66,000**	Education, health and welfare
☐ **The Weinstein Foundation**	**£66,000**	Jewish, medical, welfare
☐ **The Seven Fifty Trust**	**£65,000**	Christian causes
☐ **P H Holt Foundation**	**£65,000**	General charitable purposes
☐ **The Searchlight Electric Charitable Trust**	**£65,000**	General charitable purposes
☐ **The Lionel Wigram Memorial Trust**	**£65,000**	General, particularly illness and disability
☐ **The Carpenter Charitable Trust**	**£65,000**	Humanitarian and Christian outreach
☐ **The Music Sales Charitable Trust**	**£64,000**	Children and youth, musical education, see below
☐ **P G and N J Boulton Trust**	**£64,000**	Christian causes
☐ **Limoges Charitable Trust**	**£64,000**	General, including health, heritage and community
☐ **The Friarsgate Trust**	**£64,000**	Health and welfare of young and older people
☐ **York Children's Trust**	**£64,000**	Young people under the age of 25
☐ **R S Brownless Charitable Trust**	**£63,000**	Disability, relief-in-need, ill health, accommodation and housing, education, job creation, voluntary work
☐ **The Pennycress Trust**	**£63,000**	General charitable purposes
☐ **Chrysalis Trust**	**£63,000**	General, education, social welfare
☐ **The Isaac and Freda Frankel Memorial Charitable Trust**	**£63,000**	Jewish, general
☐ **Highcroft Charitable Trust**	**£63,000**	Jewish, poverty
☐ **The Alfred And Peggy Harvey Charitable Trust**	**£63,000**	Medical, research, older people, children and young people with disabilities or disadvantages, visually and hearing impaired people
☐ **The G D Herbert Charitable Trust**	**£63,000**	Medicine, health, welfare, environmental resources
☐ **Mildred Duveen Charitable Trust**	**£62,000**	General charitable purposes
☐ **The Lawson Beckman Charitable Trust**	**£62,000**	Jewish, welfare, education, arts
☐ **The Ian Fleming Charitable Trust**	**£62,000**	Social welfare
☐ **The Simmons & Simmons Charitable Foundation**	**£62,000**	Social welfare, education
☐ **May Hearnshaw's Charity**	**£61,000**	General charitable purposes

Trust	Grant total	Purposes
☐ **The Richard Kirkman Charitable Trust**	**£61,000**	General charitable purposes
☐ **The Demigryphon Trust**	**£61,000**	Medical, education, children, general
☐ **The Cotton Industry War Memorial Trust**	**£61,000**	Textiles
☐ **The J M K Charitable Trust**	**£60,000**	Art and Music, religions and their relations with other faiths – Worldwide
☐ **The Monica Rabagliati Charitable Trust**	**£60,000**	Children, humanitarian, medical, general
☐ **The Oikonomia Trust**	**£60,000**	Christian causes
☐ **The Linley Shaw Foundation**	**£60,000**	Conservation
☐ **The Adnams Charity**	**£60,000**	General charitable purposes
☐ **The Dorothy Holmes Charitable Trust**	**£60,000**	General charitable purposes
☐ **The Epigoni Trust**	**£60,000**	General charitable purposes
☐ **Murphy-Neumann Charity Company Limited**	**£60,000**	Health, social welfare, medical research
☐ **Nesswall Ltd**	**£60,000**	Jewish causes
☐ **Tomchei Torah Charitable Trust**	**£60,000**	Jewish causes
☐ **The Acacia Charitable Trust**	**£60,000**	Jewish, education, general
☐ **Alan and Sheila Diamond Charitable Trust**	**£60,000**	Jewish, general
☐ **The Dunn Family Charitable Trust**	**£60,000**	Medical, general, conservation
☐ **The Morgan Charitable Foundation**	**£60,000**	Welfare, hospices, medical, Jewish, general
☐ **Criffel Charitable Trust**	**£59,500**	Christianity, welfare, health, overseas aid
☐ **J A R Charitable Trust**	**£59,500**	Roman Catholic, education, welfare
☐ **The Elephant Trust**	**£59,000**	Advancement of public education in all aspects of arts, development of artistic taste and knowledge, understanding and appreciation of the fine arts
☐ **The Alabaster Trust**	**£59,000**	Christian Church and related activities
☐ **The Gerald Fogel Charitable Trust**	**£59,000**	Jewish, general
☐ **Archbishop of Wales' Fund for Children**	**£58,000**	Children and their families
☐ **The Sydney Black Charitable Trust**	**£58,000**	Evangelical Christianity, social welfare, young people
☐ **The Dorus Trust**	**£58,000**	General charitable purposes
☐ **The Lambert Charitable Trust**	**£58,000**	Health, welfare, education, disability, Jewish causes
☐ **The Olga Charitable Trust**	**£58,000**	Health, welfare, youth organisations, children's welfare, carers' organisations
☐ **The Martin Smith Foundation**	**£57,000**	Art, music, sports and education
☐ **Clark Bradbury Charitable Trust**	**£57,000**	Environmental education and conservation, disability, disaster response
☐ **Dame Violet Wills Charitable Trust**	**£57,000**	Evangelical Christianity
☐ **The Barham Charitable Trust**	**£57,000**	General charitable purposes
☐ **The Sants Charitable Trust**	**£57,000**	General charitable purposes
☐ **The Lyons Charitable Trust**	**£57,000**	Health, animals, medical research, children
☐ **NJD Charitable Trust**	**£57,000**	Jewish causes
☐ **The Burry Charitable Trust**	**£57,000**	Medicine, health, disability and welfare
☐ **The Fitton Trust**	**£57,000**	Social welfare, medical
☐ **Rosanna Taylor's 1987 Charity Trust**	**£56,000**	General charitable purposes
☐ **The George Balint Charitable Trust**	**£56,000**	General, education, poverty relief and Jewish causes
☐ **The Rofeh Trust**	**£56,000**	General, religious activities
☐ **The Emerton-Christie Charity**	**£56,000**	Health, welfare, disability, arts
☐ **The Peter Morrison Charitable Foundation**	**£56,000**	Jewish, general
☐ **The Baker Charitable Trust**	**£56,000**	Mainly Jewish, older people, sickness and disability, medical research
☐ **The Golsoncott Foundation**	**£56,000**	Arts
☐ **The A S Charitable Trust**	**£55,500**	Christian, development, social concern
☐ **The Yardley Great Trust**	**£55,500**	General charitable purposes
☐ **The James Trust**	**£55,000**	Christianity
☐ **The Dennis Curry Charitable Trust**	**£55,000**	Conservation, general
☐ **The Loseley and Guildway Charitable Trust**	**£55,000**	General charitable purposes
☐ **The Barnett and Sylvia Shine No. 2 Charitable Trust**	**£55,000**	General charitable purposes

☐ **The Andrew Balint Charitable Trust** — **£55,000** General charitable causes, Jewish charities
☐ **The Ruth and Lionel Jacobson Trust (Second Fund) No. 2** — **£55,000** Jewish, medical, children, people with disabilities
☐ **The Oliver Ford Charitable Trust** — **£55,000** Mental disability, housing
☐ **The Christopher Cadbury Charitable Trust** — **£55,000** Nature conservation, general
☐ **The Catholic Charitable Trust** — **£54,000** Catholics
☐ **The Ebenezer Trust** — **£54,000** Evangelical Christianity, welfare

---

☐ **The Old Broad Street Charity Trust** — **£54,000** General charitable purposes
☐ **The Searle Charitable Trust** — **£54,000** Youth development with a nautical basis
☐ **Mageni Trust** — **£53,000** Arts
☐ **Col-Reno Ltd** — **£53,000** Jewish causes
☐ **The Stanley Kalms Foundation** — **£53,000** Jewish charities, general including arts, education and health
☐ **The Michael and Anna Wix Charitable Trust** — **£53,000** Jewish, general charitable purposes
☐ **The Ruth and Jack Lunzer Charitable Trust** — **£53,000** Jewish, children, young adults, education and the arts
☐ **The E C Sosnow Charitable Trust** — **£53,000** Mainly education and arts
☐ **The Boris Karloff Charitable Foundation** — **£53,000** Performing arts, cricket
☐ **The Baltic Charitable Fund** — **£53,000** Seafarers, fishermen, ex-service and service people

---

☐ **Nicholas and Judith Goodison's Charitable Settlement** — **£52,500** Arts, arts education
☐ **The Marina Kleinwort Charitable Trust** — **£52,000** Arts
☐ **The Whitecourt Charitable Trust** — **£52,000** Christian, general
☐ **The Williams Family Charitable Trust** — **£52,000** Jewish causes
☐ **The Rest Harrow Trust** — **£52,000** Jewish, general
☐ **Lindale Educational Foundation** — **£52,000** Roman Catholic, education
☐ **The Grand Order of Water Rats' Charities Fund** — **£51,500** General charitable purposes with a preference towards drama & theatre, overseas aid and medical & hospital equipment
☐ **The Almond Trust** — **£51,000** Christian, general charitable purposes
☐ **The Becker Family Charitable Trust** — **£51,000** General charitable purposes, orthodox Jewish causes
☐ **A J H Ashby Will Trust** — **£51,000** Wildlife, heritage, education and children

---

☐ **The Hare of Steep Charitable Trust** — **£50,500** General charitable purposes, in particular the advancement of social, cultural, medical, educational and religious projects
☐ **The Barbara Whatmore Charitable Trust** — **£50,000** Arts and music, relief of poverty
☐ **The Dorothy Hay-Bolton Charitable Trust** — **£50,000** Deaf, blind
☐ **The John and Freda Coleman Charitable Trust** — **£50,000** Disadvantaged young people
☐ **The Victor Adda Foundation** — **£50,000** Fan Museum, welfare
☐ **The Dickon Trust** — **£50,000** General charitable purposes
☐ **Laufer Charitable Trust** — **£50,000** General charitable purposes
☐ **The Matthews Wrightson Charity Trust** — **£50,000** General, smaller charities
☐ **The Chevras Ezras Nitzrochim Trust** — **£50,000** Jewish causes
☐ **The Crescent Trust** — **£50,000** Museums and the arts, ecology, health

---

☐ **The Edith Maud Ellis 1985 Charitable Trust** — **£50,000** Quaker work and witness, international peace and conflict resolution, interfaith and ecumenical understanding, community development work in the UK and overseas, work with asylum seekers and refugees including internally displaced people
☐ **The Edgar Milward Charity** — **£49,000** Christian, humanitarian
☐ **The Cumber Family Charitable Trust** — **£49,000** General, with preference being given to overseas projects, housing and welfare, children, youth and education, medical and disability and environment
☐ **The Solo Charitable Settlement** — **£49,000** Jewish, general
☐ **The Rhododendron Trust** — **£49,000** Overseas aid and development, social welfare and culture
☐ **eaga Charitable Trust** — **£48,500** Tackling fuel poverty

Trust	Grant total	Purposes
☐ **The Violet Mauray Charitable Trust**	**£48,000**	General charitable purposes, Jewish, medical
☐ **The Pharsalia Charitable Trust**	**£48,000**	General, relief of sickness
☐ **The Cuby Charitable Trust**	**£48,000**	Jewish causes
☐ **Philip Henman Trust**	**£46,000**	Overseas development
☐ **The Bartlett Taylor Charitable Trust**	**£47,500**	General charitable purposes
☐ **Alvor Charitable Trust**	**£47,000**	Christian, humanitarian, 'social change'
☐ **The Barleycorn Trust**	**£47,000**	Christian, relief of poverty, ill-health, older people, young people
☐ **Sir John and Lady Amory's Charitable Trust**	**£47,000**	General charitable purposes
☐ **The Sir Julian Hodge Charitable Trust**	**£47,000**	General charitable purposes
☐ **G S Plaut Charitable Trust Limited**	**£47,000**	General charitable purposes
☐ **The Sandy Dewhirst Charitable Trust**	**£47,000**	General charitable purposes, social welfare and community
☐ **The Moshulu Charitable Trust**	**£47,000**	Humanitarian', evangelical
☐ **The Emilienne Charitable Trust**	**£47,000**	Medical, education, addiction
☐ **The Heathcoat Trust**	**£47,000**	Welfare, local causes to Tiverton, Devon
☐ **The Augustine Courtauld Trust**	**£46,000**	General charitable purposes
☐ **Mary Homfray Charitable Trust**	**£46,000**	General charitable purposes
☐ **The Wilfrid Bruce Davis Charitable Trust**	**£46,000**	Health
☐ **Help the Homeless**	**£46,000**	Homelessness
☐ **The Adrienne and Leslie Sussman Charitable Trust**	**£46,000**	Jewish, general
☐ **Harry Bacon Foundation**	**£46,000**	Medical, animal welfare
☐ **The Frognal Trust**	**£46,000**	Older people, children, disability, blindness/ ophthalmological research, environmental heritage
☐ **The Balney Charitable Trust**	**£46,000**	Preservation, conservation, welfare, service charities
☐ **The Cleopatra Trust**	**£45,000**	General charitable purposes, health and disability
☐ **The Rayden Charitable Trust**	**£45,000**	Jewish causes
☐ **The Corona Charitable Trust**	**£45,000**	Jewish charitable causes, welfare, education, young people, the elderly
☐ **The Mountbatten Memorial Trust**	**£45,000**	Technological research in aid of disabilities
☐ **The David Brooke Charity**	**£45,000**	Youth, older people, medical
☐ **The Ann and David Marks Foundation**	**£44,500**	Jewish causes, health, education and welfare of communities, humanitarian aid
☐ **The Hamamelis Trust**	**£44,000**	Ecological conservation, medical research
☐ **The Charter 600 Charity**	**£44,000**	General charitable purposes
☐ **Zephyr Charitable Trust**	**£43,500**	Community, environment, social welfare
☐ **The E M MacAndrew Trust**	**£43,500**	Health, general
☐ **The Thistle Trust**	**£43,000**	Arts
☐ **Paul Lunn-Rockliffe Charitable Trust**	**£43,000**	Christianity, poverty, infirm people, youth
☐ **The Paul Balint Charitable Trust**	**£43,000**	General charitable purposes
☐ **The Eagle Charity Trust**	**£43,000**	General, international, welfare
☐ **MYR Charitable Trust**	**£43,000**	Jewish causes
☐ **The Gur Trust**	**£43,000**	Jewish causes
☐ **The P Y N and B Hyams Trust**	**£43,000**	Jewish, general
☐ **Swan Mountain Trust**	**£42,500**	Mental health, penal affairs
☐ **The Harbour Charitable Trust**	**£42,000**	General charitable purposes
☐ **The Huntly and Margery Sinclair Charitable Trust**	**£42,000**	General charitable purposes
☐ **Percy Hedley 1990 Charitable Trust**	**£42,000**	General charitable purposes
☐ **The Brendish Family Foundation**	**£42,000**	General, children, education, health care and access to food and water
☐ **Thomas Roberts Trust**	**£42,000**	Medical, disability, relief in need
☐ **William P Bancroft (No. 2) Charitable Trust and Jenepher Gillett Trust**	**£42,000**	Quaker causes

Trust	Grant total	Causes
☐ **The Robert Clutterbuck Charitable Trust**	**£42,000**	Service, sport and recreation, natural history, animal welfare and protection
☐ **John Bristow and Thomas Mason Trust**	**£41,500**	Education, relief in need, people with disabilities, community amenities
☐ **The André Christian Trust**	**£41,000**	Christian causes
☐ **The Nancy Kenyon Charitable Trust**	**£41,000**	General charitable purposes
☐ **The Oakmoor Charitable Trust**	**£41,000**	General charitable purposes
☐ **Mrs Maud Van Norden's Charitable Foundation**	**£41,000**	General charitable purposes
☐ **Mrs H R Greene Charitable Settlement**	**£41,000**	General, particularly at risk-groups, poverty, social isolation
☐ **Nazareth Trust Fund**	**£40,000**	Christian, in the UK and developing countries
☐ **Miss M E Swinton Paterson's Charitable Trust**	**£40,000**	Church of Scotland, young people, general
☐ **The Appletree Trust**	**£40,000**	Disability, sickness, poverty
☐ **St Teilo's Trust**	**£40,000**	Evangelistic work in the Church in Wales
☐ **The Fairway Trust**	**£40,000**	General charitable purposes
☐ **The Colin Montgomerie Charitable Foundation**	**£40,000**	General charitable purposes
☐ **The W L Pratt Charitable Trust**	**£40,000**	General charitable purposes
☐ **Edwin George Robinson Charitable Trust**	**£40,000**	Medical research
☐ **The Ericson Trust**	**£40,000**	Older people, community including the arts, offender rehabilitation and research, refugees, the environment, the developing world
☐ **The Tresillian Trust**	**£40,000**	Overseas aid, welfare
☐ **CLA Charitable Trust**	**£40,000**	People with disabilities or who are disadvantaged
☐ **The Thousandth Man – Richard Burns Charitable Trust**	**£39,500**	General charitable purposes directed towards the young, elderly and disabled
☐ **Panton Trust**	**£39,000**	Animal wildlife worldwide, environment UK
☐ **The Elmgrant Trust**	**£39,000**	General charitable purposes, education, arts, social sciences
☐ **Michael and Lesley Bennett Charitable Trust**	**£39,000**	Jewish causes
☐ **The Violet M Richards Charity**	**£39,000**	Older people, ill health, medical research and education
☐ **Elizabeth Cayzer Charitable Trust**	**£38,500**	Arts
☐ **The Montague Thompson Coon Charitable Trust**	**£38,000**	Children with muscular diseases, medical research, environment
☐ **The Alexis Trust**	**£38,000**	Christian causes
☐ **T B H Brunner's Charitable Settlement**	**£38,000**	Church of England, heritage, arts, general
☐ **Tegham Limited**	**£37,500**	Orthodox Jewish faith, welfare
☐ **D G Albright Charitable Trust**	**£37,000**	General charitable purposes
☐ **The R M Douglas Charitable Trust**	**£37,000**	General charitable purposes
☐ **The Linmardon Trust**	**£37,000**	General charitable purposes
☐ **The Maurice and Vivien Thompson Charitable Trust**	**£37,000**	General charitable purposes
☐ **The Shanti Charitable Trust**	**£37,000**	General, Christian, international development
☐ **Gilbert Edgar Trust**	**£37,000**	General, UK and overseas
☐ **Mejer and Gertrude Miriam Frydman Foundation**	**£37,000**	Jewish causes, general charitable purposes
☐ **Gamlen Charitable Trust**	**£37,000**	Legal education, the relief of poverty and the advancement of education through music and the arts
☐ **The Col W W Pilkington Will Trusts The General Charity Fund**	**£37,000**	Medical, arts, social welfare, international charities, drugs misuse, environment
☐ **Eva Reckitt Trust Fund**	**£37,000**	Welfare, relief-in-need, extension and development of education, victims of war
☐ **The John Feeney Charitable Trust**	**£36,500**	Arts, heritage and open spaces
☐ **The Charles Lloyd Foundation**	**£36,000**	Construction, repair and maintenance of Roman Catholic buildings, the advancement of Roman Catholic religion, and music

Trust	Grant total	Purposes
☐ **Cowley Charitable Foundation**	**£36,000**	General charitable purposes
☐ **A H and B C Whiteley Charitable Trust**	**£36,000**	General charitable purposes, particularly those causes based in Nottinghamshire
☐ **The Hinrichsen Foundation**	**£36,000**	Music
☐ **The Manny Cussins Foundation**	**£36,000**	Older people, children, health, Jewish, general
☐ **S C and M E Morland's Charitable Trust**	**£36,000**	Quaker, sickness, welfare, peace and development overseas
☐ **The Mirianog Trust**	**£35,000**	General charitable purposes
☐ **The John Rayner Charitable Trust**	**£35,000**	General charitable purposes
☐ **The Star Charitable Trust**	**£35,000**	General charitable purposes
☐ **The John Young Charitable Settlement**	**£35,000**	General charitable purposes
☐ **William Arthur Rudd Memorial Trust**	**£35,000**	General in the UK, and selected Spanish charities
☐ **The Hargrave Foundation**	**£35,000**	General, research, welfare
☐ **The Oliver Borthwick Memorial Trust**	**£35,000**	Homelessness
☐ **The ISA Charity**	**£35,000**	Arts, health and education
☐ **The Cazenove Charitable Trust**	**£34,500**	General charitable purposes
☐ **Gordon Cook Foundation**	**£34,000**	Education and training
☐ **CBRE Charitable Trust**	**£34,000**	General charitable purposes
☐ **The Barbara A Shuttleworth Memorial Trust**	**£34,000**	People with disabilities
☐ **The Lady Tangye Charitable Trust**	**£33,500**	Catholic, overseas aid, general
☐ **The Ormsby Charitable Trust**	**£33,000**	General charitable purposes
☐ **The John and Celia Bonham Christie Charitable Trust**	**£33,000**	General charitable purposes
☐ **The A and R Woolf Charitable Trust**	**£33,000**	General charitable purposes
☐ **The Red Rose Charitable Trust**	**£33,000**	General with particular reference to educational expenses for students and ill health
☐ **The Norman Joels Charitable Trust**	**£33,000**	Jewish causes, general
☐ **The A B Strom and R Strom Charitable Trust**	**£33,000**	Jewish, general
☐ **The Bintaub Charitable Trust**	**£33,000**	Jewish, medical and youth
☐ **The D C Moncrieff Charitable Trust**	**£33,000**	Social welfare, environment
☐ **The Gough Charitable Trust**	**£32,000**	General charitable purposes
☐ **Audrey Earle Charitable Trust**	**£32,000**	General, with some preference for animal welfare and conservation charities
☐ **The Carlton House Charitable Trust**	**£32,000**	Jewish, education/bursaries, general
☐ **The Simpson Education and Conservation Trust**	**£31,500**	Environmental conservation
☐ **The Late St Patrick White Charitable Trust**	**£31,500**	General charitable purposes
☐ **Bellasis Trust**	**£31,500**	General charitable purposes
☐ **The H P Charitable Trust**	**£31,500**	General charitable purposes, advancement of orthodox Judaism, poverty relief
☐ **The Sylvanus Charitable Trust**	**£31,000**	Animal welfare, Roman Catholics
☐ **The Barbara Welby Trust**	**£31,000**	General charitable purposes
☐ **Buckland Charitable Trust**	**£31,000**	General, health, international development and welfare
☐ **The Leslie Silver Charitable Trust**	**£31,000**	Jewish, general
☐ **The Metropolitan Drinking Fountain and Cattle Trough Association**	**£31,000**	Provision of pure drinking water for humans and animals
☐ **The Jim Marshall Charitable Trust**	**£30,500**	Children and young people, disabilities, local communities
☐ **The Max Reinhardt Charitable Trust**	**£30,000**	Deafness, fine arts promotion
☐ **The Dwek Family Charitable Trust**	**£30,000**	General charitable purposes
☐ **The Bernard Morris Charitable Trust**	**£30,000**	General charitable purposes
☐ **The Woodcock Charitable Trust**	**£30,000**	General, children
☐ **The Moette Charitable Trust**	**£30,000**	Jewish education and social welfare
☐ **The Mitchell Charitable Trust**	**£30,000**	Jewish, general
☐ **Arthur James Paterson Charitable Trust**	**£30,000**	Medical research, welfare of older people and children

Trust	Grant total	Purposes
☐ The Peter Beckwith Charitable Trust	**£30,000**	Medical, welfare, general charitable purposes
☐ The Forces Trust (Working Name)	**£30,000**	Military and Naval charities
☐ Henry T and Lucy B Cadbury Charitable Trust	**£30,000**	Quaker causes and institutions, health, homelessness, support groups, developing world
☐ The Dorcas Trust	**£29,000**	Christian, relief of poverty and advancement of education
☐ The Pat Allsop Charitable Trust	**£29,000**	Education, medical research, children, relief of poverty
☐ The Duncan Norman Trust Fund	**£29,000**	General charitable purposes
☐ Vale of Glamorgan – Welsh Church Fund	**£29,000**	General charitable purposes
☐ Miss V L Clore's 1967 Charitable Trust	**£29,000**	General, arts, social welfare, health, Jewish
☐ The Ripple Effect Foundation	**£29,000**	General, particularly disadvantaged young people, the environment and overseas development
☐ The Stephen R and Philippa H Southall Charitable Trust	**£28,500**	General charitable purposes
☐ R E Chadwick Charitable Trust	**£28,500**	General charitable purposes
☐ The Leonard Trust	**£28,000**	Christian, overseas aid, mental health
☐ Peter Cadbury Charitable Trust	**£28,000**	General, arts, conservation, cancer
☐ Garvan Limited	**£28,000**	Jewish causes
☐ The Torah Temimah Trust	**£28,000**	Orthodox Jewish
☐ Brian Abrams Charitable Trust	**£27,500**	Jewish causes
☐ Eric Abrams Charitable Trust	**£27,500**	Jewish causes
☐ The Astor of Hever Trust	**£27,500**	Youth, medical research, education, arts, conservation and sport
☐ The Nadezhda Charitable Trust	**£27,000**	Christian causes
☐ The Thomas Wall Trust	**£27,000**	Education, welfare
☐ The Birmingham Hospital Saturday Fund Medical Charity and Welfare Trust	**£27,000**	Medical
☐ The Pamela Champion Foundation	**£26,500**	General, disability
☐ The Calpe Trust	**£26,500**	Relief work
☐ The Roger Brooke Charitable Trust	**£26,000**	General charitable purposes
☐ The Hanley Trust (1987)	**£26,000**	General charitable purposes
☐ The RRAF Charitable Trust	**£26,000**	General, medical research, children who are disadvantaged, religious organisations, aid for the developing world and support for the elderly
☐ Sir Alec Black's Charity	**£26,000**	Relief in need
☐ The Rowing Foundation	**£26,000**	Water sports
☐ The Cuthbert Horn Trust	**£26,000**	General charitable purposes
☐ The Culra Charitable Trust	**£25,000**	General charitable purposes
☐ The Mushroom Fund	**£25,000**	General charitable purposes
☐ Lady Gibson's Charitable Trust	**£25,000**	General, arts, culture
☐ The Soli and Leah Kelaty Trust Fund	**£25,000**	General, education, overseas aid, religion
☐ The Jack Goldhill Charitable Trust	**£25,000**	Jewish, general
☐ The Nicholas Joels Charitable Trust	**£25,000**	Jewish, medical welfare, general
☐ The Emmanuel Kaye Foundation	**£25,000**	Medical research, welfare and Jewish organisations
☐ Sydney E Franklin Deceased's New Second Charity	**£25,000**	Relief of poverty, children, communities
☐ Evelyn May Trust	**£24,000**	Currently children, older people, medical, natural disaster relief
☐ Annette Duvollet Charitable Trust	**£24,000**	General charitable purpose, with preference towards young people
☐ The Green and Lilian F M Ainsworth and Family Benevolent Fund	**£24,000**	Youth, disability, health, medical research, disadvantage, older people, general
☐ The Oak Trust	**£23,000**	General charitable purposes
☐ West London Synagogue Charitable Fund	**£23,000**	Jewish, general

☐ **The Simpson Foundation**	**£23,000**	Roman Catholic purposes
☐ **The Late Sir Pierce Lacy Charity Trust**	**£23,000**	Roman Catholics, general
☐ **The Jack and Ada Beattie Foundation**	**£23,000**	Social welfare, injustice and inequality
☐ **The Beacon Trust**	**£22,000**	Christian causes
☐ **The Macfarlane Walker Trust**	**£22,000**	Education, the arts, social welfare, general
☐ **The John M Archer Charitable Trust**	**£22,000**	General charitable purposes
☐ **The Peggy Ramsay Foundation**	**£22,000**	Writers and writing for the stage
☐ **The Harold Joels Charitable Trust**	**£21,000**	Jewish causes
☐ **The Thames Wharf Charity**	**£20,500**	General charitable purposes
☐ **The Rock Solid Trust**	**£20,000**	Christian causes
☐ **The E H Smith Charitable Trust**	**£20,000**	General charitable purposes
☐ **The R H Scholes Charitable Trust**	**£20,000**	General, including children and young people who have disabilities or are disadvantaged, hospices, preservation and churches
☐ **The Richard and Christine Purchas Charitable Trust**	**£20,000**	Medical research, medical education and patient care
☐ **The Kathleen Trust**	**£20,000**	Music
☐ **The Kass Charitable Trust**	**£20,000**	Welfare, education, Jewish
☐ **The J S F Pollitzer Charitable Settlement**	**£19,000**	General charitable purposes
☐ **The Kitty and Daniel Nabarro Charitable Trust**	**£19,000**	Welfare, education, medicine, homeless, general
☐ **The Helen Isabella McMorran Charitable Foundation**	**£18,000**	General, Christian
☐ **The Dennis Alan Yardy Charitable Trust**	**£16,000**	General charitable purposes
☐ **The Constance Paterson Charitable Trust**	**£16,000**	Medical research, health, welfare of children, older people, service people
☐ **The Wilkinson Charitable Foundation**	**£16,000**	Scientific research
☐ **The Earl of Northampton's Charity**	**£16,000**	Welfare
☐ **Maurice Fry Charitable Trust**	**£14,500**	General charitable purposes
☐ **The Inland Waterways Association**	**£13,500**	Inland waterways
☐ **The Frank Parkinson Agricultural Trust**	**£13,000**	British agriculture
☐ **C J Cadbury Charitable Trust**	**£13,000**	Environment, conservation, music
☐ **Beatrice Hankey Foundation Limited**	**£12,000**	Christian causes
☐ **The Migraine Trust**	**£12,000**	Study of migraine
☐ **Haskel Family Foundation**	**£11,000**	Jewish, social-policy research, arts, education
☐ **The McKenna Charitable Trust**	**£10,250**	Education, health, disability, relief of poverty, the arts
☐ **The Carvill Trust**	**£10,000**	General charitable purposes
☐ **The Naggar Charitable Trust**	**£10,000**	Jewish, the arts, general
☐ **The TUUT Charitable Trust**	**£9,000**	General, particularly trade-union-favoured causes
☐ **The Hellenic Foundation**	**£8,000**	Greek education in the UK
☐ **Gableholt Limited**	**£8,000**	Jewish causes
☐ **The Geoffrey John Kaye Charitable Foundation**	**£6,300**	Jewish, general
☐ **Mandeville Trust**	**£6,000**	General charitable purposes, health and young people
☐ **The Boltons Trust**	**£6,000**	Social welfare, medicine, education
☐ **The Katzauer Charitable Settlement**	**£5,500**	Jewish causes
☐ **The Judith Trust**	**£5,000**	Mental health and learning disabilities with some preference for women and Jewish people
☐ **The F J Wallis Charitable Settlement**	**£4,500**	General charitable purposes
☐ **Rosa – the UK fund for women and girls**	**£3,800**	Women's organisations and projects supporting women
☐ **The Carron Charitable Settlement**	**£3,000**	Environment, education, medicine
☐ **The Avenue Charitable Trust**	**£3,000**	General charitable purposes

The A. B. Charitable Trust

Human rights

£468,500 (2012/13)

Beneficial area

Mainly UK.

Correspondent: Sara Harrity, Director, Monmouth House, 87–93 Westbourne Grove, London W2 4UL (tel: 020 7313 8070; fax: 020 7313 9607; email: mail@abcharitabletrust.org.uk; website: www.abcharitabletrust.org.uk)

Trustees: Claire Bonavero; Olivier Bonavero; Philippe Bonavero; Anne Bonavero; Yves Bonavero; Athol Harley; Alison Swan Parente; Peter Day.

CC Number: 1000147

The following information has been taken from the trust's website:

> The A B Charitable Trust (ABCT) is an independent, UK based grant-making organisation founded in 1990 that is concerned with promoting and defending human dignity.
>
> ABCT supports charities that defend human rights and promote respect for vulnerable individuals whatever their circumstances.
>
> The trust is particularly interested in charities that work with marginalised and excluded people in society, with a focus on:
> - Refugees and asylum seekers
> - Prisoners and penal reform
> - Human rights
>
> ABCT very occasionally undertakes special initiatives related to work in these fields.
>
> The A B Charitable Trust:
> - Seeks to support disenfranchised and forgotten groups
> - Builds mutually beneficial relationships with the people with whom it works
> - Aims to maximise opportunities inherent in its independent grant-making status
> - Is accessible and clear about priorities
> - Maintains high standards of administrative efficiency and cost-effectiveness
> - Is committed to learn from its grant making to inform future practice.

Grants are awarded to charities registered and working in the UK.

ABCT tends to support charities with annual income between £150k and £1.5 million which do not have substantial investments or surpluses.

Grants range in size, with most grants awarded being in the range £7,500 to £10,000. ABCT is happy to provide funding for core costs. Visit the trust's clear and helpful website for funding guidelines and deadlines.

In 2012/13 the trust had assets of £10,000 and an income of £430,000, mostly from Gift Aid and other contributions. From 368 applications received, grants to 56 organisations were made totalling £468,500. They were distributed as follows:

Refugees and asylum seekers	24	£198,500
Prisoners	14	£129,000
Human rights	7	£65,000
Abuse, addiction, mental health	7	£48,500
Older people and carers	4	£27,500

Beneficiaries across all categories included: Asylum Aid (£20,000); Detention Advice Service, Law Centres Network and Revolving Doors Agency (£15,000 each); Action on Elder Abuse, Circles UK, Prisoners' Education Trust and Prisoners of Conscience Appeal Fund (£10,000 each); UK Drugs Policy Commission (£6,000); and Finsbury Park Homeless Families Project, Music in Detention, Magic Me, Strong Roots and Zimbabwe Association (£5,000 each).

Exclusions

No grants are made to organisations principally concerned with:
- Animals
- Children
- Environment
- Formal education
- Individuals
- Medicine
- Religion
- Research

Capital appeals are not normally supported, nor are charities with large national or international links, or areas which should reasonably be funded by government.

Applications

Applications can be completed online at the trust's website.

As well as administrative and financial details, the online application form will ask for a two page summary of the organisation's work, including:
- Background
- Aims and objectives
- Activities
- Achievements

After filling in the online application form you will be sent a reference number. Send the director the following documents in hard copy quoting the reference number:
- The two page overview of the organisation's work
- A signed copy of the latest certified accounts/statements, with a reporting date that is no more than 12 months prior to the application deadline chosen (the trustees meet four times a year, in January, April, July and October – see the website for exact deadline dates)
- Up to two items of publicity material that illustrate the work of the organisation, such as annual reviews or leaflets

Information gathered from:

Accounts; Charity Commission record; funder's website.

Brian Abrams Charitable Trust

Jewish

£27,500 (2011/12)

Beneficial area

UK.

Correspondent: The Trustees, c/o Lyon Griffiths Ltd, Unit 17, Alvaston Business Park, Middlewich Road, Nantwich, Cheshire CW5 6PF (tel: 01270 624445)

Trustees: Betty Abrams; Brian Abrams; Eric Abrams; Gail Gabbie.

CC Number: 275941

The aims of the charity are to assist, by donation, registered charities established in the United Kingdom, for the advancement of education, welfare and relief of poverty, particularly amongst persons of the Jewish faith.

In 2011/12 this trust had an income of £37,000 and made 31 grants totalling £27,500.

Previous beneficiaries have included: Centre for Torah Education Trust, Friends of Ohr Akiva Institution, Halacha Lemoshe Trust, Hale Adult Hebrew Education Trust, the Heathlands Village, Manchester Jewish Federation, Rabbi Nachman of Breslov Charitable Foundation, Rainsough Charitable Trust, UK Friends of Magen David Adom and United Jewish Israel Appeal.

Exclusions

No grants to individuals.

Applications

The trust has stated that its funds are fully committed and applications are not invited.

Information gathered from:

Accounts; Charity Commission record.

Eric Abrams Charitable Trust

Jewish

£27,500 (2011/12)

Beneficial area

UK.

Correspondent: The Trustees, c/o Lyon Griffiths Ltd, Unit 17, Alvaston Business Park, Middlewich Road, Nantwich, Cheshire CW5 6PF (tel: 01270 624445)

Trustees: Brian Abrams; Eric Abrams; Marcia Anne Jacobs; Susan Melanie Abrams.

CC Number: 275939

The charity makes grants to registered charities established in the UK for the advancement of education, welfare and relief of poverty, particularly amongst persons of the Jewish faith.

In 2011/12 the trust had assets of £1 million and an income of £36,000. Grants to organisations totalled £27,500.

Previous beneficiaries have included: Friends of Ohr Akiva Institution, Centre for Torah Education Trust, Halacha Lemoshe Trust, Hale Adult Hebrew Education Trust, the Heathlands Village, Manchester Jewish Federation, Rabbi Nachman of Breslov Charitable Foundation, UK Friends of Magen David Adom and United Jewish Israel Appeal.

Exclusions

No grants to individuals.

Applications

The trustees do not invite appeals.

Information gathered from:

Accounts; Charity Commission record.

The Acacia Charitable Trust

Jewish, education, general

£60,000 (2011/12)

Beneficial area

UK and Israel.

Correspondent: The Secretary, c/o H. W. Fisher and Co., Acre House, 11–15 William Road, London NW1 3ER (tel: 020 7486 1884; email: acacia@dircon.co.uk)

Trustees: Kenneth Rubens; Angela Gillian Rubens; Simon Rubens; Paul Rubens.

CC Number: 274275

This trust supports charitable organisations with a range of causes.

In 2011/12 the trust had assets of £1.7 million and an income of £70,000. 27 grants to organisations totalled £60,000.

Grants were given in the following categories:

Arts and culture	£37,000
Overseas aid	£10,500
Community care and welfare	£9,500
Medical and disability	£1,800
General	£300
Education	£295

Previous beneficiaries included: The Jewish Museum (£41,000); Community Security Trust (£5,000); Norwood and Yad Vashem (£1,000 each); Royal National Theatre (£500); Nightingale House (£250); and Shelter, Jewish Council for Racial Equality and Riding for the Disabled (£100 each).

Exclusions

No grants to individuals.

Applications

In writing to the correspondent.

Information gathered from:

Accounts; Charity Commission record.

The Company of Actuaries' Charitable Trust Fund

Actuaries, medical research, young and older people, disability

£141,000 (2011/12)

Beneficial area

UK, with a preference for the City of London.

Correspondent: Patrick O'Keeffe, Honorary Almoner, Broomyhurst, Shobley, Ringwood, Hampshire BH24 3HT (tel: 01425 472810; email: almoner.cact@btinternet.com; website: www.companyofactuaries.co.uk/charitabletrust)

Trustees: Jeff Medlock; Michael Turner; Sally Bridgeland; Geraldine Kaye; Michael Pomery; Alan Smith.

CC Number: 280702

The following is taken from the trust's accounts:

> Objectives of the charity:
> 1 the relief of poverty of members of the profession of actuary
> 2 grants for the advancement of education of actuaries
> 3 grants for charitable research in the field of actuarial science and the award of bursaries
> 4 awards of educational exhibitions to persons intending to practice the profession of actuary
> 5 awards of prizes in connection with the examinations for actuaries
> 6 assisting the general education of persons in need who are preparing to be actuaries
> 7 assisting and benefiting persons who are endeavouring to qualify as actuaries
> 8 making donations to any registered charity

Information taken from the trust's website:

> The charitable giving policy of the trust is give priority in its donations to charities in which members of the livery or the wider actuarial profession are active, and the trustees actively encourage members to apply for support. However the trustees are prepared to consider applications from smaller charities where a contribution to a project can make a difference. All applications should be made to the Honorary Almoner using the form which can be downloaded from the website.
>
> Members of the actuarial profession or their dependents, and members of the Institute or Faculty suffering hardship may make an application for assistance to the trustees, who will give sympathetic consideration to any case of hardship brought to their notice.

The trustees have previously stated that they normally only donate to the following types of registered charities:

1 Those involved with supporting the elderly or disabled
2 Charities helping children and young people
3 Those involved in treating medical conditions or funding medical research
4 Other worthy charities, such as those working with the needy or disadvantaged

In 2011/12 the trust had assets of £350,000 and an income of £180,000. Grants were made to 61 organisations totalling £141,000. Awards were given ranging from £500 to £5,000, with one unusually large donation of £54,000 to the Royal Society. Grant funding was distributed as follows:

Donations made to charities	£55,000
Donations made to the Royal Society	£54,000
Awards made for educational purposes	£19,000
Master's donations	£10,000
Donations made from Master's events	£6,000

Beneficiaries included: Royal Society (£54,000); Children's Liver Disease Foundation (£5,000); Edmonton Sea Cadets (£4,000); Rainbow Trust (£3,500); Guildhall School of Music and Drama (£2,500); Fenland Association for Community Transport and Marine Society and Sea Cadets (£2,000 each); Just Different, Sailors' Families Society and Spadework (£1,000 each); and Carefree Kids, Gambia UpCountry and Traffic of the Stage (£500 each).

Exclusions

No grants for the propagation of religious or political beliefs, the maintenance of historic buildings or for conservation. The trustees do not usually support an organisation which has received a grant from the fund in the previous 24 months.

Applications

On a form which can be downloaded from the fund's website. Further information about the trust can be obtained from the correspondent.

Information gathered from:

Accounts; Charity Commission record; funder's website.

The Adamson Trust

Children under 18 with a physical or mental disability

Around £75,000 to organisations and individuals (2011/12)

Beneficial area

UK, but preference will be given to requests on behalf of Scottish children.

Correspondent: Edward Elworthy, Administrator, PO Box 26334, Crieff, Perthshire PH7 9AB (email: edward@elworthy.net)

Trustee: Information not available.

SC Number: SC016517

Officially this charity is the Robert and Agnes G Adamson's Fund, but its working title is the Adamson Trust. Grants are made to individuals and to organisations providing holidays for children under 18 with a physical or mental disability. Donations are usually one-off.

About £75,000 is given in grants each year.

Previous beneficiaries have included Barnardo's – Dundee Family Support Team, Children's Hospice Association Scotland, Lady Hoare Trust for Physically Disabled Children, Hopscotch Holidays, Over the Wall Gang Group, Peak Holidays, React, Scotland Yard Adventure Centre, Sense Scotland, Special Needs Adventure Play Ground and Scottish Spina Bifida Association.

Applications

In writing to the correspondent. A copy of the latest audited accounts should be included together with details of the organisation, the number of children who would benefit and the proposed holiday.

Percentage of awards given to new applicants: between 40% and 50%.

Common applicant mistakes

'Insufficient information.'

Information gathered from:

OSCR record; further information provided by the funder.

The Victor Adda Foundation

Fan Museum, welfare

Around £50,000 (2011/12)

Beneficial area

UK, but in practice Greenwich.

Correspondent: Kleinwort Benson Trustees Ltd, c/o Kleinwort Benson Trustees, 14 St George Street, London W1S 1FE (tel: 020 3207 7091)

Trustees: Helene Alexander; Susannah Alexander; Jeremy Hawes; Linda Estelle.

CC Number: 291456

Virtually since it was set up in 1984, the foundation has been a stalwart supporter of the Fan Museum in Greenwich and it continues with that support. Both the foundation and the museum share a majority of the same trustees; the foundation also owns the property in which the museum is sited and has granted it a 999-year lease.

In 2011/12 the trust had an income of £21,500 and a total expenditure of £62,000.

Previous beneficiaries have also included the Child Trust, Jewish Museum and St Christopher Hospice.

Applications

In writing to the correspondent. Only successful applications are notified of a decision.

Information gathered from:

Accounts; Charity Commission record.

Adenfirst Ltd

Jewish causes

£112,000 (2011)

Beneficial area

Worldwide.

Correspondent: Leonard Bondi, Trustee, c/o 479 Holloway Road, London N7 6LE (tel: 020 7272 2255)

Trustees: Mrs H. F. Bondi; Leonard Bondi; Mrs R. Cymerman; Sylvia Cymerman; Ian Heitner; Michael Cymerman; Sarah Heitner.

CC Number: 291647

The trust supports mostly Jewish organisations, with a preference for education and social welfare.

In 2011 the trust had assets of £1.5 million and made grants to 14 organisations totalling £112,000 which were broken down as follows:

Advancement of education	£54,000
Relief of poverty	£34,000
Advancement of religion	£20,000
Medical care	£4,500

There was no list of beneficiaries with the accounts but previously the following organisations have received awards: Beis Aaron Trust (£30,000); Ezer Vehatzolo and Kahal Chassidim Wiznitz (£20,000 each); and Beis Rochel D'Satmar, Lolev Charitable Trust and Mercaz Hatorah Belz Machnovke (£10,000 each).

Information was taken from the latest accounts available at the time of writing (October 2013).

Applications

In writing to the correspondent.

Information gathered from:

Accounts; Charity Commission record.

The Adint Charitable Trust

Health, social welfare

£302,500 (2012/13)

Beneficial area

Worldwide, in practice UK.

Correspondent: Douglas R. Oram, Trustee, Suite 42, 571 Finchley Road, London NW3 7BN (email: adintct@gmail.com)

Trustees: Anthony J. Edwards; Margaret Edwards; Douglas R. Oram; Brian Pate.

CC Number: 265290

This trust was established in 1972 by the settlor, Henry John Edwards. Most of the grants made are for £5,000 or £10,000 to a range of health and welfare charities, many concerned with children.

In 2012/13 the trust had assets of £6.8 million and an income of £250,500. Grants were made to 45 organisations totalling £302,500.

Beneficiaries included: Aldis Trust, BLISS, Dementia Relief Trust, KIDS, Meningitis Trust, Salvation Army and Springboard (£10,000 each); Acorn Children's Hospice, British Epilepsy Association, Cruse Bereavement Care, Help the Hospices, Listening Books, Prostate Cancer Charity, The Firefighters Charity and Thomas Coram Foundation (£5,000 each); Norwood Ravenswood (£1,000); and Noah's Ark Children's Hospice (£500).

Exclusions

Individuals are not supported.

Applications

In writing to the correspondent. Each applicant should make its own case in the way it considers best, but the application should include full details of the applicant charity. The trust states that it cannot enter into correspondence and unsuccessful applicants will not be notified.

Information gathered from:

Accounts; Charity Commission record.

The Adnams Charity

General

£60,000 (2011/12)

Beneficial area

Within a 25-mile radius of St Edmund's Church, Southwold.

Correspondent: Rebecca Abrahall, Charity Administrator, c/o The Street, Brockdish, Norfolk IP21 4JY (tel: 01502 727200; email: rebecca.abrahall@adnams.co.uk; website: www.adnams.co.uk/charity)

Trustees: Jonathan Adnams, Chair; Lizzy Cantwell; Guy Heald; Emma Hibbert; Melvyn Horn; Simon Loftus; Andy Wood; Alison Kibble; Ann Cross.

CC Number: 1000203

The Adnams Charity was founded in 1990 to mark the centenary of the Adnams company and is funded mainly by the annual donation from the profits of Adnams plc. It supports a wide variety of organisations within a 25 mile radius of Southwold, including those involved with health and social welfare, education, recreation, the arts, environment and conservation and historic buildings.

Applications from national charities which operate within a 25-mile area of Southwold may be considered if assurances can be given that the money will be used for a specific purpose within the area.

The charity prefers to make one-off grants for specific items which normally range from £100 to £2,500, the trustees expecting to see the result of its donations within twelve months.

In 2011/12 the charity held assets of £7,000 and had an income of £34,000. During the year 69 grants were made totalling £60,000.

Beneficiaries included: NWES World of Work and Peer Support (£2,500 each); Friends of John Turner House Day Centre, Prisoners' Education Trust, Suffolk Social Services and The Thirst Youth Cafe (£1,000 each); Alpington and Bergh Apton CE VA Primary School, Anglia Care Trust, Jubilee Opera, Mettingham Village Hall, New Cut Arts and Wacton Village Hall (£500 each); and Lowestoft Shopmobility (£400).

Exclusions

The charity does not normally make grants to religious organisations or private clubs unless they can demonstrate that the purpose of the grant is for something of clear public benefit, accessible to all. It does not provide raffle prizes or sponsorship of any kind. No grants are made to individuals. However, public bodies and charities may apply on behalf of individuals. Grants are not made in successive years.

Applications

Application forms are available on request to the charity administrator. Grants are considered at quarterly meetings, in January, April, July and October. Application deadlines usually fall in the previous month and are listed on the charity's website.

Information gathered from:

Accounts; Charity Commission record; funder's website.

AF Trust Company

Higher education

£130,000 (2011/12)

Beneficial area

England.

Correspondent: Paul Welch, Secretary, 34 Chapel Street, Thatcham, Reading, Berkshire RG18 4QL (tel: 01635 867222)

Trustees: Martin Wynne-Jones; Andrew Connolly; David Leah; Carol Wright.

CC Number: 1060319

Support is given for charitable purposes connected with the provision of higher education in England. The company currently provides property services and leasing facilities to educational establishments on an arm's length basis.

In 2011/12 the charity had assets of £451,000. The total income and expenditure for the year was £2.4 million. However, it is worth noting that this relates to the funds used to lease buildings from educational establishments and then enter into lease-back arrangements rather than describing the size of funds available. Grants were made totalling £130,000.

Beneficiaries were: Imperial College (£36,000); University of Nottingham, Samworthy Academy (£34,500); University of Reading (£33,500); University of Canterbury Christ Church (£17,000); and other institutions (£9,000).

Exclusions

No grants to individuals.

Applications

In writing to the correspondent. However, unsolicited applications are only accepted from higher education institutions within England.

Information gathered from:

Accounts; Charity Commission record.

The Green and Lilian F. M. Ainsworth and Family Benevolent Fund

Youth, disability, health, medical research, disadvantage, older people, general

£24,000 (2011/12)

Beneficial area

UK, with some preference for northwest England.

Correspondent: The Trust Section Manager, RBS Trust Services, Eden Building, Lakeside, Chester Business Park, Wrexham Road, Chester CH4 9QT (tel: 01244 625810)

Trustee: The Royal Bank of Scotland plc.

CC Number: 267577

The trust supports UK charities covering a wide range of interests mainly involving people of all ages who are disadvantaged by either health or other circumstances.

In 2011/12 the trust had assets of £850,000, an income of £22,500 and made 47 grants totalling £24,000.

Grants were all bar one for £500. Beneficiaries included: British Wireless for the Blind (£560); and Autism Initiatives UK, Bat Conservation Trust, Cross Roads Care, Donna Louise Children's Hospice, Ipswich Community Playbus, Kinship Care, Make A Wish, Martha Trust, Anthony Nolan Trust, Seashell Trust, Lee Smith Foundation, Wherever the Need and The Wildlife Trust (£500 each).

Exclusions

No grants to individuals or non-registered charities.

Applications

In writing to the trustees, there is no application form.

Information gathered from:

Accounts; Charity Commission record.

The Sylvia Aitken Charitable Trust

Medical research and welfare, general

About £300,000 (2011/12)

Beneficial area

UK, with a preference for Scotland.

Correspondent: The Administrator, Fergusons Chartered Accountants, 24 Woodside, Houston, Renfrewshire PA6 7DD (tel: 01505 610412)

Trustees: Mrs S. M. Aitken; Mrs M. Harkis; J. Ferguson.

SC Number: SC010556

Whilst this trust has a preference for medical projects, it has general charitable purposes, making small grants to a wide range of small local organisations throughout the UK, particularly those in Scotland. In 2011/12 the trust had an income of £98,000 and a total expenditure of £396,000.

Previous grant beneficiaries have included: Association for International Cancer Research, Barn Owl Trust, British Lung Foundation, British Stammering Association, the Roy Castle Lung Cancer Foundation, Disabled Living Foundation, Epilepsy Research Trust, Friends of the Lake District, Motor Neurone Disease Association, Network for Surviving Stalking, Royal Scots Dragoon Guards Museum Trust, Sense Scotland, Scottish Child Psychotherapy Trust, Tall Ships Youth Trust, Tenovus Scotland, Wood Green Animal Shelters and Young Minds.

Exclusions

No grants to individuals: the trust can only support UK registered charities.

Applications

In writing to the correspondent. Applicants should outline the charity's objectives and current projects for which funding may be required. The trustees meet at least twice a year, usually in March/April and September/October.

Information gathered from:

OSCR record.

The Ajahma Charitable Trust

Development, poverty, human rights, health, disability, social welfare

£261,500 (2011/12)

Beneficial area

Unrestricted.

Correspondent: Suzanne Hunt, Administrator, 275 Dover House Road, London SW15 5BP (tel: 020 8788 5388)

Trustees: Jennifer Sheridan; Elizabeth Simpson; James Sinclair Taylor; Carole Pound; Roger Paffard.

CC Number: 273823

This trust was established in 1977 for general charitable purposes. It aims to balance its donations between international and UK charities. Generally, established charities receive grants but new groups and those which may have difficulty finding funds from traditional sources are encouraged.

In 2011/12 the trust had assets of £2.8 million and an income of £85,000. During the year the Charity made 19 grant payments totalling £261,500 with an approximate balance of 74% (2011 – 70%) benefiting overseas work and 26% (2011 – 30%) benefiting work in the UK. A continuing substantial commitment to local Headway groups has been maintained, with Headway groups awards totalling £36,000 (7 grants).

Other beneficiaries included: CAMFED, Global Witness and Microloan Foundation (£50,000 each); Womankind Worldwide (£40,000); and Age Concern Ealing, Ashiana Network, Beat Bullying and Tower Hamlets Friends and Neighbours (£4,500 each).

Exclusions

Large organisations with a turnover above £4 million will not normally be considered, nor will applications with any sort of religious bias or those which support animal rights/welfare, arts, medical research, buildings, equipment, local groups or overseas projects where the charity income is less than £500,000 a year. Applications for grants or sponsorship for individuals will not be supported.

Applications

The trust has reviewed their grantmaking criteria and will now pro-actively seek and select organisations to which they wish to award grants. They will no longer consider unsolicited applications.

Information gathered from:

Accounts; Charity Commission record.

The Alabaster Trust

Christian Church and related activities

£59,000 (2011/12)

Beneficial area

UK and overseas.

Correspondent: John Caladine, Trust Administrator, Chantry House, 22 Upperton Road, Eastbourne, East Sussex BN21 1BF (tel: 01323 644579; email: john@caladine.co.uk)

Trustees: Jill Kendrick; Graham Kendrick; Abigail Sheldrake; Amy Waterman; Miriam Kendrick; Tamsin Kendrick.

CC Number: 1050568

This trust was set up to make grants to evangelical Christian organisations in the UK and abroad. In 2011/12 it had assets of £51,000 and an income of £66,500. Grants totalled £59,000. Further information was not available.

Exclusions

No grants to individuals.

Applications

In writing to the correspondent. The trustees meet to consider grants quarterly, usually in March, June, September and December.

Information gathered from:

Accounts; Charity Commission record.

The Alborada Trust

Veterinary causes, social welfare

£1 million (2012)

Beneficial area

Worldwide.

Correspondent: Jamie Matheson, Correspondent, Fladgate Fielder LLP, 16 Great Queen Street, London WC2 5DG (tel: 020 3036 7308; website: www.alboradatrust.com)

Trustees: Eva Rausing; David Way; Roland Lerner; James Nicholson.

CC Number: 1091660

This trust was established in October 2001 with an initial donation of £5 million being settled in April 2002. The trust is named after the racehorse Alborada.

Unsolicited applications are not requested as the trustees prefer to restrict the area of benefit to:

- Veterinary causes in the United Kingdom and Ireland with activities primarily devoted to the welfare of animals and/or in their associated research
- Projects throughout the world associated with the relief of poverty, human suffering, sickness or ill health

In 2012 the trust had assets of £13.2 million and an income of £120,500. Grants were made to nine organisations and totalled £1 million.

Beneficiaries included: Home of Horseracing Trust (£250,000); The Langford Trust for Animal Health and Welfare (£200,000); Alzheimer's Society (£139,000); Médecins Sans Frontières (£85,000); and Greatwood Charity (£14,000).

Applications

The 2012 annual report states that funds are fully committed. The trust does not accept unsolicited applications.

Information gathered from:

Accounts; Charity Commission record; funder's website.

D. G. Albright Charitable Trust

General

£37,000 (2011/12)

Beneficial area

UK, with a preference for Gloucestershire.

Correspondent: Richard Wood, Trustee, Old Church School, Hollow Street, Great Somerford, Chippenham, Wiltshire SN15 5JD (tel: 01249 720760)

Trustees: Hon. Dr Gilbert Greenall; Richard Wood.

CC Number: 277367

In 2011/12 the trust had assets of £1 million and an income of £45,000. Grants were made to 25 organisations totalling £37,000.

Grants included those to: Bromesberrow Church of England School (£6,500); Bromesberrow Parochial Church Council (£3,500); Independent Age (£2,500); Shelter – Gloucestershire Advice Service (£2,000); The Children's Society, Butterfly Conservation and Abbeyfield (Reading) Society (£1,000 each); and War Memorials Trust (£500).

Exclusions

No grants to individuals.

Applications

In writing to the correspondent.

Information gathered from:

Accounts; Charity Commission record.

The Alchemy Foundation

Health and welfare, famine relief overseas

£264,000 (2011/12)

Beneficial area

UK and overseas.

Correspondent: Richard Stilgoe, Trustee, Trevereux Manor, Limpsfield Chart, Oxted, Surrey RH8 0TL (tel: 01883 730600)

Trustees: Dr Jemima Stilgoe; Holly Stilgoe; Jack Stilgoe; Rufus Stilgoe; Richard Stilgoe; Alex Armitage; Andrew Murison; Annabel Stilgoe; Esther Rantzen; Joseph Stilgoe; Tony Elias.

CC Number: 292500

The charity was established, as The Starlight Foundation, by a charitable trust deed on 14 August 1985. The name was changed to The Alchemy Foundation on 2 June 1987.

The foundation's 2011/12 accounts state that its objects are, 'particularly focused on The Orpheus Centre, water projects in the developing world, disability (particularly mobility, access, helplines and communications), social welfare (inner city community projects, disaffected youth, family mediation, homelessness), personal reform, penal reform (work with prisoners, especially young prisoners, and their families), medical research and aid (especially in areas of blindness and disfigurement), individual enterprise (by helping Raleigh International and similar organisations to give opportunities to young people according to need) and respite for carers.'

In 2011/12 it had a total income of £352,000, of which £272,000 came from donations received and £80,000 was generated from assets, which totalled £2.4 million. There were 317 grants made totalling £264,000. Donations were broken down as follows:

Orpheus Centre	£104,000
Social welfare – inner city community projects	£59,000
Disability – mobility, helplines, access	£51,000
Respite for carers	£12,000
Individuals on behalf of registered charities	£11,000
Penal reform and work with prisoners and their families	£3,500
Medical research and blindness and disfigurement	£3,000
Other	£20,000
Disability – mobility, helplines, access	£0

A list of beneficiary organisations was not available.

Exclusions

The foundation does not fund organisations exclusive to one faith or political belief.

Applications

In writing to the correspondent.

Information gathered from:

Accounts; Charity Commission record.

The Alexis Trust

Christian causes

£38,000 (2011/12)

Beneficial area

UK and overseas.

Correspondent: Prof. Duncan Vere, Trustee, 14 Broadfield Way, Buckhurst Hill, Essex IG9 5AG

Trustees: Prof. Duncan Vere; Chris Harwood; Elisabeth Harwood; Vera Vere.

CC Number: 262861

Support is given to a variety of causes, principally Christian. In 2011/12 the trust had assets of £449,000 and an income of £37,000. Grants were made totalling £38,000.

The sum of £11,000 was distributed to various missionary societies with eight organisations receiving £1,000 or more, including: Barnabus Fund and Mission Aviation Fellowship (£2,000 each); UCCF (£1,200); and Epping Forest Youth for Christ and Tower Hamlets Mission (£1,000 each). A further 89 unlisted beneficiaries received a total of £22,000.

A further £5,000 was distributed to 53 short-term missionary projects.

Exclusions

No grants for building appeals, or to individuals for education.

Applications

In writing to the correspondent, although the trust states that most of the funds are regularly committed.

Information gathered from:

Accounts; Charity Commission record.

All Saints Educational Trust

Religious education, home economics

£260,000 to organisations (2011/12)

Beneficial area

UK and overseas.

Correspondent: The Clerk, Suite 8C, First Floor, VSC Charity Centre, Royal London House, 22–25 Finsbury Square, London EC2A 1DX (tel: 020 7248 8380; email: aset@aset.org.uk; website: www.aset.org.uk)

Trustees: Diane McCrea; Revd Canon Peter Hartley; Revd. Dr Keith Riglin; David J. Trillo; Dorothy Garland; Barbara E. Harvey; Dr Augur Pearce; Prof. Anthony R. Leeds; Ven. Stephan J. Welch; Stephanie Valentine; Joanna Moriarty; Frances M. Smith; Anna E. Cumbers; Michael C. Jacob; Stephen Brooker.

CC Number: 312934

The All Saints Educational Trust makes personal grant awards to teachers, intending teachers and students in Religious Studies, Home Economics and related areas. Corporate awards are made for imaginative new projects which will enhance the Church's contribution to higher and further education.

Its main purpose is to:

- Help increase the number of new teachers with Qualified Teacher Status
- Improve the skills and qualifications of experienced teachers

- Encourage research that can assist teachers in their work
- Support specifically the teaching of Religious Studies and Home Economics and related areas – such as the promotion of public health and nutrition, both at home and overseas

The trust offers both *Personal* and *Corporate* awards.

Corporate awards

The following description of the *Corporate Award* scheme has been taken from the trust's helpful website.

> The trust wishes to stimulate and support imaginative new projects that will enhance the Church's contribution to education, in accordance with our charitable scheme.
>
> The trustees are keen to identify and support pro-active projects that promote the development of education, particularly in the areas of Religious Education, Home Economics and related areas or subjects, and Multi-cultural/Inter-faith Education.
>
> Priority is given to projects in our core disciplines – especially pump-priming projects – whereby teachers are helped directly or indirectly.
>
> Projects most favoured are those that have the potential to result in lasting benefit, either through the intrinsic quality of the new ideas being put forward, or through the quantity of teachers and/or pupils who will share in the benefit.
>
> Larger corporate applications will be scrutinised carefully to ensure that they are sustainable and give value for money.
>
> Grants will not normally be made for a period in excess of five years.
>
> Our most distinctive and long-term Corporate Award is the All Saints Saxton Fellowship

In 2011/12 the trust had assets totalling £9 million which generated an income of £428,000. Grants totalled £448,000 and were distributed as follows:

Corporate awards (organisations)	£260,000
Scholarships and bursaries (individuals)	£187,000

Previous beneficiaries of corporate awards include: National Association of Teachers in Home Economics, Southwark Cathedral Education Centre, British Nutrition Foundation, Design and Technology Association, Sheffield Hallam University, Wulugu – Ghana, Scripture Union, Christian Education Movement and the Soil Association.

Exclusions

Note that the trust will not support:

- General or core funds of any organisation
- Public appeals
- School buildings, equipment or supplies (except library resources)
- The establishment of new departments in universities and colleges
- General bursary funds of other organisations

Applications

For applications from organisations (not individuals): applicants are invited to discuss their ideas informally with the clerk before making an application. In some cases, a 'link trustee' is appointed to assist the organisation in preparing the application and who will act in a liaison role with the trust. Completed applications are put before the awards committee in April/May, with final decisions made in June.

Application forms are available on the trust's website, either in interactive or printable form.

Information gathered from:

Accounts; Charity Commission record; funder's website.

The Pat Allsop Charitable Trust

Education, medical research, children, relief of poverty

£29,000 (2011/12)

Beneficial area

UK.

Correspondent: John Randel, Trustee, Lee Bolton Monier-Williams Solicitors, 1 The Sanctuary, London SW1P 3JT (tel: 020 7222 5381; email: jrandel@lbmw.com)

Trustees: John Randel; Patrick Kerr; Wayne Taylor; Neil MacKilligin.

CC Number: 1030950

A number of educational grants are made each year, e.g. towards research and organising educational events. The founder of the trust was a partner in Allsop and Co. Chartered Surveyors, Auctioneers and Property Managers, therefore the trust favours supporting those educational projects and charities which have connections with surveying and property management professions. The trustees have a policy of making a small number of major donations (over £2,500) and a larger number of smaller donations.

In 2011/12 it had assets of £908,000 and an income of £36,000. Grants were made to 20 organisations totalling £29,000.

Beneficiaries included: Jewish Care (£7,500); The Duke of Edinburgh's Award (£5,000); The Annington Trust (£3,000); Kids Company (£1,500); CORAM Children's Charity, Land Aid Charitable Trust and National Autistic Society (£500 each); and Maasai Heritage Foundation, Save the Children and Walk the Walk Worldwide (£250 each).

Exclusions

No grants to individuals.

Applications

The trust does not accept unsolicited applications.

Information gathered from:

Accounts; Charity Commission record.

The Almond Trust

Christian, general charitable purposes

£51,000 (2011/12)

Beneficial area

UK and worldwide.

Correspondent: Sir Jeremy Cooke, Trustee, 19 West Square, London SE11 4SN (tel: 020 7587 5167)

Trustees: Sir Jeremy Cooke; Jonathan Cooke; Lady Cooke.

CC Number: 328583

The trust's aims are the support of evangelistic Christian projects, Christian evangelism and the translation, reading, study and teaching of the Bible. Donations are often recurrent.

In 2011/12 the trust had assets of £356,500 and an income of £67,000, including £51,000 from donations. Grants totalled £50,000. The accounts listed 20 organisations with six having received grants in the previous year.

Beneficiaries included: Hertford House Trust (£10,000); The Attingham Trust (£8,500); Fairbridge London (£5,000); Donhead St Mary Parochial Church Council (£3,000); Impetus Trust, Courtauld Institute of Art and Shrewsbury School Foundation (£2,500 each); Mondo Challenge Foundation and Salisbury Hospice (£250 each); and Friends of Guy Marsh (£100).

Five payments totalling £8,800 were made to individuals.

Applications

In writing to the correspondent, but note that the trust states it rarely responds to uninvited applications.

Percentage of awards given to new applicants: less than 10%.

Information gathered from:

Accounts; Charity Commission record; further information provided by the funder.

The Altajir Trust

Islam, education, science and research

£79,500 to organisations (2012)

Beneficial area

UK and Arab or Islamic states.

Correspondent: The Trustees, 11 Elvaston Place, London SW7 5QG (tel: 020 7581 3522; fax: 020 7584 1977; email: awitrust@tiscali.co.uk; website: www.altajirtrust.org.uk)

Trustees: Prof. Alan Jones, Chair; Prof. Roger Williams; Dr Charles Tripp; Dr Noel Brehony.

CC Number: 284116

The Altajir Trust is a UK based charity supporting exhibitions, publications, educational activities and other programmes related to Islamic culture and Muslim – Christian relations. The trust provides scholarships for undergraduates and graduates, mainly from the Arab world, to undertake further studies at approved colleges of higher education within the United Kingdom. Funding may also be given towards the cost of conservation of Islamic artefacts and manuscripts in the United Kingdom, assisting conservation in Muslim countries, and to charitable and academic institutions assisting in rebuilding societies in the Islamic world after conflict.

In 2012 the trust had assets of £210,000 and an income of £567,000 mostly from donations. Direct charitable expenditure totalled £498,000 of which £79,500 was paid out in grants; £201,000 on student support and £68,000 on events and publications.

Grant beneficiaries were: University of York – Lectureship (£53,000); British Council – Chevening Scholarships (£19,000); St John of Jerusalem Eye Hospital (£14,000); Council for British Research in the Levant (£5,500); Chatham House – MENA programme (£5,000); and University of Sterling – Scholarships (£2,500).

Applications

On a form available from the trust's website. The trustees meet about four times a year. Applications can be submitted at any time but may have to await the next trustees' meeting for a decision. However, they will all be acknowledged when received and an indication of the time frame for a decision will be given.

Note: applications should be printed and signed before being sent to the trust.

Information gathered from:

Accounts; Charity Commission record; funder's website.

Altamont Ltd

Jewish causes

Around £101,000 (2011/12)

Beneficial area

Worldwide.

Correspondent: David Last, Trustee, 18 Green Walk, London NW4 2AJ (tel: 020 8457 8760)

Trustees: David Last; Henry Last; Mrs H. Kon; Mrs S. Adler; Gina Wiesenfeld.

CC Number: 273971

In 2011/12 the trust had an income of £16,000 and a total expenditure of £101,000. We have no further information regarding this charity.

Applications

In writing to the correspondent.

Information gathered from:

Accounts; Charity Commission record.

Alvor Charitable Trust

Christian, humanitarian, 'social change'

Around £47,000 (2011/12)

Beneficial area

UK, with a preference for Sussex, Norfolk and north east Scotland.

Correspondent: Ian Wilkins, Chair, Stone End, Fox Hill Close, Haywards Heath, West Sussex RH16 4RA (tel: 01444 473347)

Trustees: Clive Wills; Shaena Wills; Mark Atherton; Fiona Atherton; Ian Wilkins; Julie Wilkins.

CC Number: 1093890

Established in August 2002, this Christian and humanitarian charity predominately supports Christian social change projects in the UK and overseas. A proportion of its target funding goes to local projects around Sussex, Norfolk and north east Scotland where the trustees have personal interests. The trust tends to support smaller projects where the grant will meet a specific need. It typically makes a few larger donations each year and a number of smaller grants.

In 2011/12 the trust had no income. Total expenditure was £47,000. Despite the trust having no income for this accounting year, we have retained the entry as the charity remains on the Central Register of Charities and as far as we know, has not been dissolved.

Accounts were not available from the Charity Commission due to the low income but previous beneficiaries included: Kenward Trust (£50,000 in two grants); Salt Sussex Trading Ltd (£40,000 in four grants); Anne Marie School, Ghana (£35,000); Urban Saints (£33,000); Hymns Ancient and Modern (£30,000 in two grants); Care for the Family and Romance Academy (£25,000 each); Care, Hope UK, the Lighthouse Group, Message Trust, Mid-Sussex Citizen Advice Bureau, Saltmine Trust and World In Need (£20,000 each); Carey Films Ltd, Christians in Sport, Positive Parenting, Scripture Union, Trussell Trust and Youth For Christ (£15,000 each); Church Army, First Base Agency, Proclaim Trust and Release International (£10,000 each); Opera Brava (£8,000); Brighton FareShare, Furniture Now and N:Vision (£5,000 each); Caring 4 Life and Chestnut Tree House (£2,000 each); and Impact Initiatives (£500).

Exclusions

The trust does not look to support animal charities or medical charities outside of the geographic areas mentioned above.

Applications

In writing to the correspondent.

Information gathered from:

Accounts; Charity Commission record.

AM Charitable Trust

Jewish, general

£145,000 (2011/12)

Beneficial area

UK and overseas.

Correspondent: The Administrator, Kleinwort Benson Trustees Ltd, 14 St George Street, London W1S 1FE (tel: 020 3207 7091)

Trustee: Kleinwort Benson Trustees Ltd.

CC Number: 256283

This trust supports a range of causes, particularly Jewish organisations but also medical, welfare, arts and conservation charities. Certain charities are supported for more than one year, although no commitment is usually given to the recipient. Grants range between £100 and £15,000 each, but are mostly of £200 to £500.

In 2011/12 the trust had assets of £2 million and an income of £129,000. Grants were made to 47 organisations totalling £145,000.

Beneficiaries included: The Wallace Collection (£75,000); Youth Aliyah – Child Rescue and British ORT (£15,000 each); Friends of the Hebrew University of Jerusalem and Jerusalem Foundation (£10,000 each); Cancer Research Campaign (£3,000); and British Heart Foundation (£2,000); Blond McIndoe Research Foundation (£1,500); Royal Academy of Music (£1,000); Alzheimer's

Research Trust (£500); and Crimestoppers Trust (£200).

Exclusions

No grants to individuals.

Applications

> Donations are decided periodically by the trustee having regard to the wishes of the Settlor, and unsolicited appeals are considered as well as causes which have already been supported. Only successful applicants are notified of the trustee's decision. Certain charities are supported for more than one year, although no commitment is usually given to the recipients.

Information gathered from:

Accounts; Charity Commission record.

The Amalur Foundation Ltd

General

£162,000 (2011/12)

Beneficial area

Worldwide.

Correspondent: David Way, Trustee, Fladgate LLP, 16 Great Queen Street, London WC2B 5DG

Trustees: Claudia Garuti; David Way; Helen Mellor.

CC Number: 1090476

Registered in February 2002, in 2011/12 this charity had no income and a total expenditure of £162,000. Refer to the 'applications' section of this entry.

Previous beneficiaries include: Absolute Return for Kids (£110,000); St Patrick's Catholic Church (£50,000); Prostate Research Campaign UK (£10,000); Brain Tumour Research Campaign (£5,500); Breakthrough Breast Cancer (£3,000); and the Extra Care Charitable Trust (£2,000).

Applications

We were informed by the correspondent that the charity's income is diminishing and that it does not have a long-term future. While the trustees have funds available, they are pleased to consider applications. Applications should be made to the correspondent in writing.

Information gathered from:

Accounts; Charity Commission record.

Viscount Amory's Charitable Trust

Welfare, older people, education, Christian churches

£277,000 (2011/12)

Beneficial area

UK, primarily in Devon.

Correspondent: The Trust Secretary, The Island, Lowman Green, Tiverton, Devon EX16 4LA (tel: 01884 254899)

Trustees: Sir Ian Heathcoat Amory; Catherine Cavender.

CC Number: 204958

The trust's annual report 2011/12 states:

> The objectives of the trust are to donate the annual investment income to charitable institutions or other organisations primarily to benefit the inhabitants of the County of Devon; to assist young people, the poor and aged; and to advance education. The trustees invite or respond to applications from a wide variety of charities or groups promoting charitable causes. Their preference is to support smaller groups, mostly in the South West of England, which do not have access to sophisticated fundraising campaigns and on which a relatively small donation may have a significant effect.

In 2011/12 the trust had assets of £11.8 million and an income of £388,000. Grants were made to organisations totalling £277,000 and those over £5,000 were listed in the accounts.

Beneficiaries included: Rona Sailing Trust (£94,000); Blundells School (£25,500); Exeter Cathedral School (£16,500); Churches Housing Action Team (£6,500); Magdalen Court School (£5,500); and Calvert Trust Exmoor and Creative Cow (£5,000 each).

Exclusions

No grants to individuals from outside South West England.

Applications

In writing to the correspondent, giving general background information, total costs involved, amount raised so far and details of applications to other organisations.

Percentage of awards given to new applicants: between 20% and 30%.

Information gathered from:

Accounts; Charity Commission record; further information provided by the funder.

Sir John and Lady Amory's Charitable Trust

General

£47,000 to organisations (2011/12)

Beneficial area

UK, with a preference for Devon and the South West.

Correspondent: Lady Heathcoat Amory, Trustee, The Island, Lowman Green, Tiverton, Devon EX16 4LA (tel: 01884 254899)

Trustees: Sir Ian Heathcoat Amory; Lady Heathcoat Amory; William Heathcoat Amory.

CC Number: 203970

The trust was set up in 1961 with a bequest from Sir John and Lady Amory. It supports general charitable purposes and has a preference for funding smaller organisations in the south west of England that 'do not have access to sophisticated fundraising campaigns and on which a relatively small donation may have a significant effect'.

In 2011/12 the trust had assets of £1.9 million and an income of £306,000. Grants to charitable and other organisations totalled £47,000.

Only donations of £5,000 were listed in the accounts: National Trust (£8,500). A further £2,000 was given to individuals.

Applications

In writing to the correspondent.

Percentage of awards given to new applicants: between 30% and 40%.

Information gathered from:

Accounts; Charity Commission record; further information provided by the funder.

The Ampelos Trust

General

£111,000 (2011/12)

Beneficial area

UK.

Correspondent: Philip Hitchinson, Secretary, c/o Menzies LLP, Ashcombe House, 5 The Crescent, Leatherhead, Surrey KT22 8DY (tel: 01372 360130; email: leatherhead@menzies.co.uk)

Trustees: Baroness of Babergh Ruth Rendell; Ann Marie Witt; MMH. Trustees Ltd.

CC Number: 1048778

The trust was set up by Baroness Rendell of Babergh under a Trust Deed dated 12 June 1995, with the amount of

£5,000. The objects of the trust are to support charitable causes.

In 2011/12 the trust had assets of £464,000 and an income of £243,000. Grants were made to 15 organisations totalling £111,000.

Beneficiaries included: Handel House Trust and Shelter (£20,000 each); Little Hearts Matter (£15,000); National Clinical Group (£12,000); CLIC Sargent (£10,000); and Prostate Cancer Charity and Little Angels Theatre (£5,000 each).

Applications

The 2011/12 annual report states: 'Since the trustees anticipate being able to identify sufficient potential recipients to whom to distribute the income of the trust, the trustees do not wish to receive unsolicited applications for grants.'

Information gathered from:

Accounts; Charity Commission record.

The Anchor Foundation

Christian causes

£205,000 (2011/12)

Beneficial area

UK and occasionally overseas.

Correspondent: Catherine Middleton, Company Secretary, PO Box 21107, Alloa FK12 5WA (tel: 01159 500055; email: secretary@theanchorfoundation.org.uk; website: www.theanchorfoundation.org.uk)

Trustees: Revd Michael Mitton; Revd Robin Anker-Petersen; Nina Anker-Petersen.

CC Number: 1082485

The foundation was registered with the Charity Commission in September 2000, it supports Christian charities concerned with social inclusion, particularly through ministries of healing and the arts.

The grant range for a project is between £500 and £10,000. It is not the normal practice of the charity to support the same project for more than three years (projects which have had three years funding may apply again two years from the payment of the last grant). Applications for capital and revenue funding are considered. Only in very exceptional circumstances will grants be given for building work. Organisations with a number of projects operating are advised to choose a single project for their application.

In 2011/12 the foundation had assets of £5.8 million and an income of £306,000. Grants to over 42 organisations totalled £205,000.

Beneficiaries included: Al Massira, Oasis Cardiff and Fountain of Life (£7,500 each); Crisis Centre Ministries, Greenbelt, Hebrides Alpha Project and The Restorer Trust (£5,000 each); Tron Kirk (£4,000); and Coffee Craft, Derby City Church, Footprint Theatre, Genesis Trust, Living Well Trust, Streetlytes and Zephaniah Music (£3,000 each).

Exclusions

No grants to individuals.

Applications

An initial application form can be completed online at the foundation's website. Full guidelines for applicants are also available there. If the trustees decide they are interested in your application you will be contacted and asked to send further relevant information such as a project budget and your annual accounts. **Do not send these with your application form. Also note that applications should not be sent to the registered office in Nottingham.**

Applications are considered at twice yearly trustee meetings in April and November and need to be received by 31 January and 31 July each year. The foundation regrets that applications cannot be acknowledged.

Successful applicants will be notified as soon as possible after trustees' meetings – usually before the end of May or the end of November. Unsuccessful applicants may reapply after 12 months.

Percentage of awards given to new applicants: between 40% and 50%.

Information gathered from:

Accounts; Charity Commission record; further information provided by the funder; funder's website.

The Andrew Anderson Trust

Christian, social welfare

£254,000 (2011/12)

Beneficial area

UK and overseas.

Correspondent: Revd Andrew Robertson Anderson, Trustee, 1 Cote House Lane, Bristol BS9 3UW (tel: 01179 621588)

Trustees: Revd Andrew Robertson Anderson; Anne Alexander Anderson; Margaret Lillian Anderson.

CC Number: 212170

This trust is established for general charitable purposes. Most of its money appears to go to evangelical organisations and churches, but it also makes small grants to health, disability and social welfare charities.

In 2011/12 it had assets of £10.1 million and an income of £269,000. Grants totalled £254,000. No further information was available.

Previous beneficiaries have included: Aycliffe Evangelical Church, Christian Medical Fellowship, Concern Worldwide, Emmanuel Baptist Church – Sidmouth, Fellowship of Independent Evangelical Churches, Good Shepherd Mission, Kenward Trust, Latin Link, Proclamation Trust, Rehoboth Christian Centre – Blackpool, Scientific Exploration Society, St Ebbe's Parochial Church Council – Oxford, St Helen's Church – Bishopsgate, TNT Ministries, Trinity Baptist Church – Gloucester, Whitefield Christian Trust, Weald Trust and Worldshare.

Exclusions

Individuals should not apply for travel or education.

Applications

In writing to the correspondent.

Information gathered from:

Accounts; Charity Commission record.

Andor Charitable Trust

Health, arts, Jewish, general

£87,000 (2011/12)

Beneficial area

UK and overseas.

Correspondent: David Rothenberg, Trustee, c/o Blick Rothenberg Chartered Accountants, 16 Great Queen Street, Covent Garden, London WC2B 5AH (tel: 020 7486 0111)

Trustees: David Rothenberg; Nicholas Lederer; Dr Donald Dean; Jeanne Szego.

CC Number: 1083572

Registered with the Charity Commission in 2000, in 2011/12 the trust had assets of £3 million and an income of £76,000. Grants to 36 organisations totalled £87,000.

Beneficiaries included: The Chicken Shed Theatre Trust (£7,500 in two payments); Pavilion Opera Educational Trust and The Wiener Library Institute of Contemporary History (£5,000 each); The Prostate Cancer Charity (£4,000); The British Refugee Council (£2,500); London Mozart Players, Lupus UK and Riders for Health (£2,000 each); and Music in Hospitals and The Blond McIndoe Research Foundation (£1,000 each).

Applications

In writing to the correspondent.

Information gathered from:

Accounts; Charity Commission record.

The André Christian Trust

Christian

£41,000 (2012)

Beneficial area

UK.

Correspondent: Andrew K. Mowll, Trustee, 2 Clevedon Close, Exeter EX4 6HQ (tel: 01392 258681)

Trustees: Andrew K. Mowll; Stephen Daykin.

CC Number: 248466

The trust makes grants towards the advancement of Christianity, either through printing and distributing Bible scriptures or through evangelistic work. A number of charities are listed in the trust deed, and they are its principal beneficiaries. Grants appear to mainly be ongoing.

In 2012 the trust had assets of £1.19 million and an income of £51,000. Grants were made to 13 organisations totalling £41,000.

Beneficiaries in 2012 included: SIFT (£13,000); ECFT (£6,000); Care for the Family, Entheos Trust, Open Air Campaigners and Strangers' Rest Mission (£3,000 each); Choices Pregnancy Centre (£2,000); and Bible Society and Overseas Missionary Fellowship (£1,000 each).

Applications

In writing to the correspondent. However, the trust states that 'applications are discouraged since grants are principally made to those organisations which are listed in the trust deed'. Funds are therefore fully committed and unsolicited requests cannot be supported.

Information gathered from:

Accounts; Charity Commission record.

Andrews Charitable Trust

Social welfare, Christian causes

£95,000 (2012)

Beneficial area

UK and overseas.

Correspondent: Ms Sian Edwards, Director, The Clockhouse, Bath Hill, Keynsham, Bristol BS31 1HL (tel: 01179 461834; email: info@andrewscharitabletrust.org.uk; website: www.andrewscharitabletrust.org.uk)

Trustees: Andrew Radford, Chair; Michael Robson; David Saint; David Westgate; Nicholas Wright; Tony Jackson; Helen Battrick; Paul Heal; Alastair Page; Elisabeth Hughes; Chris Chapman.

CC Number: 243509

Established in 1965, the trust is funded by dividends from Andrews and Partners, a group of companies with activities including estate agents, letting agents, property management and financial services. The foundation describes its focus as: 'social innovation – tackling poverty and/or vulnerability, through support of new or emerging charities, social enterprises or Christian organisations'. In a May 2013 interview the trust's director Sian Edwards described their approach as venture philanthropy: 'We provide core funding for the start-up of the organisation. We are interested in finding real innovation and sustainable and replicable solutions. We look for inspirational founders that have a great idea.'

The following information is taken from the trust's comprehensive website:

> In all that we do, we seek to work with inspirational people who have **innovative, sustainable and replicable** solutions that meet human needs in the UK and internationally.
>
> In 2013/14 we will be prioritising ideas in the following fields, but not to the exclusion of great ideas in other areas:
>
> - Tackling the social barriers to educational achievement and improving the employment prospects of young people, especially girls
> - Care for the elderly
>
> We specialise in providing support for **young organisations** who have tested their innovative model, who know that they are offering something different and effective and who are looking for core funding and organisational development support to grow the enterprise as the vehicle for change.
>
> We support social entrepreneurs to set up charities and/or social enterprises as the vehicles for change. We are looking for entrepreneurs who have innovative ideas or new approaches that have the potential to make a real and positive difference to the lives of poor, vulnerable or excluded people.
>
> Typically we are looking for inspirational leaders who have the passion, skills and ambition to make a real impact. They will have tested their ideas, gathered some proof that they are addressing an identified need, and know how they will add to what is being done already. The approach will be sustainable with potential for diverse income streams.
>
> Whilst we operate from a Christian faith and values standpoint, we are keen to stress that we support work for and with all faiths and also those with none.
>
> Please note that we generally will not support innovations coming out of well-established or larger organisations. Ideally we are looking for organisations who have past the idea stage and can be typically described as looking for early revenue investment.
>
> *Funding Criteria*
>
> Please do not contact us unless your work fits the criteria advertised below.
>
> Core to our funding criteria are our two charitable objects which are:
>
> - The advancement of the Christian Religion including the declaration of Eternal Life, and
> - The relief of sickness, poverty and distress in any part of the world as an expression of Christian love
>
> *Applicants must have:*
>
> - An idea that has been tested and that is innovative, sustainable and replicable
> - An approach that has the potential to leave a mark on the world
> - Some evidence that the idea does make a significant difference and a commitment to embed performance and impact measurement
> - An approach which builds on the strengths of collaboration, networking and partnering
> - Strong and passionate leadership with some track record in (social) entrepreneurialism and at the early stages of setting up a new enterprise
> - Simple solutions to an identified need
> - A young organisation that is looking for early revenue investment and an engaged investor to support the growth of the enterprise
>
> *Trustee Preferences:*
>
> - Supporting a young organisation where it is 'the most effective way to make a sustainable and replicable difference'
> - Ideas that individual trustees feel passionate about
> - Ideas where the skills and experience of our trustees and director are most likely to add value
> - We work closely with the leadership of funded organisations. Applicants should be willing and open to this approach and will be able to recognize the need to invest time in the relationship to make this work on both sides
> - Willing to tolerate a degree of risk in the enterprise
> - Evidence of financial probity and a culture of financial discipline
> - Opportunities for leverage and co-funding
> - Building up a 'pipeline' of ideas to be incubated in advance of a funding commitment
>
> Please note that this is not an exhaustive list, and there is no guarantee that if you meet all these points then we will fund your venture. This is because we only have the capacity to take on a handful of funded partnerships at any one time. For each successful organisation we offer not just funding. We have a very engaged model of giving where the director and trustees can provide skills and experience to support funded organisations to achieve their goals. This will be discussed with organisations during the application process.

Characteristics of successful ventures

We have reviewed our funding and work relationships with organisations during the past years. Not all of the organisations we have worked with have been successful, for a range of reasons, and we have shared in this learning process.

We have identified some key characteristics which have significantly contributed to success. If you are thinking of applying to ACT then please do check these and consider them in regard to your idea, team and whether you think you and we might work well together.

You are:

- A champion to your cause, who is passionate and committed to addressing a social or faith issue or need
- Someone with a successful track record (though this does not have to be in the same field and young social entrepreneurs are not excluded)
- An entrepreneur, able to seize opportunities to make things happen and succeed
- Someone with a larger vision who may need help to make it a reality
- Someone who can recognise where extra support is needed and who is good at working with others to harness
- Able to communicate and network with a range of audiences
- From anywhere, any walk of life and any creed/culture/faith/gender

We are:

- Ready to offer our support to emerging and innovative work, often on causes that are not yet well understood or popular
- Prepared to take risks
- Wanting to work constructively with people/organisations wanting to promote the Christian Faith and/or who work to alleviate poverty
- Wanting to work constructively and add value to share the process of change which the implementation of grant funding leads to for new and step-change organisations
- Seeking to learn from our grant making so that we minimise risks and maximise the impact our limited funds and input can have and achieve with your help

In 2012 the trust had assets of £9 million, an income of £460,000 and gave grants totalling £95,000, broken down as follows:

Ending violence against women	£25,000
Support of carers	£50,000
Christian initiatives	£20,000

Beneficiaries listed on the website included: Carers Worldwide; Restored; Excellent Development; The Bristol Housing Partnership; Kainos Community; Advantage Africa; BasicNeeds; Digital Links; Catch Up; Credit Action and Opportunity International.

Exclusions

Do not apply if:

- You are an individual seeking support for educational expenses (academic or vocational)
- You are an individual undertaking charitable works in their own or another country on a project/'gap' year/work experience/exchange basis
- You are an organisation solely based outside of the UK
- You are seeking funding for ongoing work of any organisation
- Your project is a satellite aspect of an existing organisation
- You are looking to cover the costs of building, renovating or other capital works
- You offer something that is already done by other organisations
- You are not in a position to make your vision a reality
- You want funding for an event or project with a time limited span e.g. appeals
- You are not open to sharing learning, resources and materials with others working your field
- The work is NOT innovative, replicable and sustainable

Applications with any of the above characteristics will not be considered for funding and we urge you not to waste your time working on an application that will not be successful.

Applications

The trust provides the following information:

We don't have an application form or pack.

If you are in doubt about whether or not you 'fit' our criteria, then you can email us with a short introduction to your work and the initiative for which you were thinking of applying. We suggest this is done before writing a full application, if you are unsure of the suitability of your work to the interests of this trust.

Written applications can be in any format, but should aim to briefly answer the following questions in not more than three pages:

- What it is you want to do – explain the idea/work and its value. Are you looking to start a new initiative or is it a step change that you are looking to make?
- Why it should be done – present evidence of the need for it and why it is innovative/better than what is currently offered?
- Where do you want to work and how will this impact on the people/ communities you will work with?
- How many people are expected to benefit and who are they?
- How do you plan to deliver the change that you are seeking to make?
- How much will it cost and over what time frame are you looking for funding? (please include both the human and financial input you are looking for). As part of this please explain how you will sustain the work beyond the support requested
- Who are the key individuals that will lead the initiative? What experience do you, your organisation and its trustees/ board have which will give us confidence that you will be able to undertake the proposed work?

Information gathered from:

Accounts; Charity Commission record; funder's website.

The Animal Defence Trust

Animal welfare/protection

£78,000 (2011/12)

Beneficial area

UK.

Correspondent: Alan A. Meyer, Secretary, Horsey Lightly Fynn, Devon House, 12–15 Dartmouth Street, Queen Anne's Gate, London SW1H 9BL (tel: 020 7222 8844; email: ameyer@horseylightly.com; website: www.animaldefencetrust.org)

Trustees: Marion Saunders; Carole Bowles; Richard J. Vines; Jenny Wheadon.

CC Number: 263095

The trustees meet annually in July to consider applications from charities registered in the UK or Eire for capital projects for animal welfare or animal protection projects only.

In 2011/12 it had assets totalling £1.3 million and an income of £56,500. Grants were made to 42 organisations, including 27 that had been supported in the previous year, totalling £78,000.

Beneficiaries included: Brooke Hospital for Animals, Ferne Animal Sanctuary, Woodside Animal Welfare Trust and Worldwide Veterinary Service (£4,000 each); International Otter Survival Fund (£3,000); Greek Cat Welfare Society and Himalayan Animal Treatment Centre (£2,000 each); and Care4cats, Cat Register and Rescue, Fox Project, Greyhound Rescue, Rotherham Dog Rescue and Safe Haven for Donkeys in Holy Land (£1,000 each).

Exclusions

No grants to individuals.

Applications

On a form which, together with guidelines, can be downloaded from the trust's website.

Percentage of awards given to new applicants: between 20% and 30%.

Common applicant mistakes

'Not being a registered charity.'

Information gathered from:
Accounts; Charity Commission record; further information provided by the funder; funder's website.

The Annandale Charitable Trust

Major UK charities

£299,000 (2011/12)

Beneficial area
UK.

Correspondent: The Trust Manager, HSBC Trust Services, 10th Floor, Norwich House, Nelson Gate, Commercial Road, Southampton SO15 1GX (tel: 02380 722248)

Trustees: Carole Duggan; HSBC. Trust Company (UK) Ltd.

CC Number: 1049193

The trust supports a range of major UK charities. In 2011/12 it had assets of £10.7 million, an income of £259,500. Grants were made to 212 organisations totalling £299,000.

Beneficiaries included: Unicef East Africa Children's Appeal (£10,000); Age NI, Battersea Dogs and Cats Home, Dogs Trust, Just 42, Medequip4kids, Southampton Hospital Charity, The Horse Trust and Unicef Ivory Coast Emergency Appeal (£5,000 each); Breakthrough Breast Cancer, Cherished Memories, icandance, Marine Conservation Society and Talking with Hands (£3,000 each); and Unicef Libya Crisis Appeal (£2,000).

Applications
The trust has previously stated that it has an ongoing programme of funding for specific charities and all its funds are fully committed.

Information gathered from:
Accounts; Charity Commission record.

The Anson Charitable Trust

General

£215,000 (2011/12)

Beneficial area
UK.

Correspondent: George Anson, Trustee, The Lilies, High Street, Weedon, Aylesbury, Buckinghamshire HP22 4NS (tel: 01296 640331; email: ansonctrust@btinternet.com)

Trustees: George Anson; Kirsty Anson; Peter Nichols.

CC Number: 1111010

The trust was set up for general charitable purposes in 2005 and in 2011/12 it held assets of £646,000. During the year the trust had an income of £833,500 entirely from donations and gift aid, and made 280 grants totalling £215,000. Some organisations received more than one grant.

Beneficiaries included: The Pace Centre (£12,000); Royal Shakespeare Society and Tate Gallery (£10,000 each); Royal Opera House Foundation (£9,000); ABF The Soldiers' Charity and Weedon Methodist Church Trust (£6,000 each); Buckinghamshire Agricultural Association and Project Trust (£5,000 each); British Stammering Association, Listening Books and Queen Alexandra Hospital Home (£3,000 each); Prince's Regeneration Trust (£2,500); Braille Chess Association and Oundle School Foundation (£2,000 each); Anthony Nolan Trust and The Woodland Trust (£1,000 each); Water Aid (£600); and WNAA (£250).

Grants can also be made to individuals.

Applications
In writing to the correspondent.

Information gathered from:
Accounts; Charity Commission record.

The Appletree Trust

Disability, sickness, poverty

Around £40,000 (2011/12)

Beneficial area
UK and overseas, with a preference for Scotland and the north east Fife district.

Correspondent: The Royal Bank of Scotland plc, Administrator, The Royal Bank of Scotland plc, Trust and Estate Services, Eden Lakeside, Chester Business Park, Wrexham Road, Chester CH4 9QT

Trustee: The Royal Bank of Scotland plc.

SC Number: SC004851

This trust was established in the will of the late William Brown Moncour in 1982 to relieve disability, sickness and poverty. The settlor recommended that Action Research for the Crippled Child, British Heart Foundation and National Society for Cancer Relief should receive funding from his trust, particularly for their work in the north east Fife district.

In 2011/12 the trust had an income of £35,000 and a total expenditure of £54,000. No further information was available.

Previous grant beneficiaries have included: 1st St Andrews Boys' Brigade, Alzheimer's Scotland, Arthritis Care In Scotland, the Broomhouse Centre, Children's Hospice Association, Discovery Camps Trust, Home Start East Fife, Marie Curie Cancer Care, PDSA, Prince and Princess of Wales Hospice, RNID, the Salvation Army, Scottish Motor Neurone Disease Association and Scottish Spina Bifida Association.

Exclusions
No grants to individuals.

Applications
In writing to the correspondent. Trustees meet to consider grants in April.

Information gathered from:
OSCR record.

Archbishop of Wales' Fund for Children

Children and their families

£58,000 (2012)

Beneficial area
Wales.

Correspondent: Karen Phillips, Administrator, Church in Wales, 39 Cathedral Road, Cardiff CF11 9WH (tel: 02920 348234; email: awfc@churchinwales.org.uk)

Trustees: Revd J. Michael Williams, Chair; Cheryl Beach; Ruth Forrester; Caroline Owen; James Tovey.

CC Number: 1102236

This fund was established in 2004. Its purpose is to support children in need and their families and local communities, through the work of organisations in this order of priority:

- Those in the Dioceses of the Church in Wales
- Those associated with other Christian bodies which are members of Cytun (Churches Together in Wales)
- Other organisations working with children in Wales

In 2012 the trust had assets of £99,000 and an income of £32,500. Grants were made to 36 organisations and totalled £58,000 (including £7,500 liability to pay future grants). There was no list of beneficiaries contained within the accounts.

Previous beneficiaries have included: the Bridge Mentoring Plus Scheme; Cardiff People First; Family Awareness Drug and Support; MENFA; Pontllanfraith, Brecon, Aberdare and Merthyr Tydfil Contact Centres; and Valley Kids. A number of church-based projects were also supported.

Applications
Application forms are available from the correspondent. Telephone calls are welcome before application submitted.

Percentage of awards given to new applicants: between 40% and 50%.

Common applicant mistakes

'Do not include safeguarding policy or a third party letter of support.'

Information gathered from:

Accounts; Charity Commission record; further information provided by the funder.

The John M. Archer Charitable Trust

General

Around £22,000 (2011/12)

Beneficial area

UK and overseas.

Correspondent: Mrs E. Grant, Secretary, 10 Broughton Place Lane, Edinburgh EH1 3RS

SC Number: SC010583

The trust supports local, national and international organisations, in particular those concerned with:

- Prevention or relief of individuals in need
- Welfare of people who are sick, distressed or afflicted
- Alleviation of need
- Advancement of education
- Advancement of religious or missionary work
- Advancement of medical or scientific research and discovery
- Preservation of Scottish heritage and the advancement of associated cultural activities

In 2011/12 the trust had an income of £41,000 and a total expenditure of £25,000.

Previous beneficiaries have included Angkor Hospital For Children (Cambodia), the Canonmills Baptist Church, Castlebrae School Tutoring Programme, Erskine Stewarts Melville College – Arts Centre, Mercy Corps Scotland, the Bobby Moore Fund, Red Cross – Aberdeen Guest House and Royal Liverpool University Hospital – Macular Degeneration Research.

Applications

In writing to the correspondent.

Information gathered from:

OSCR record.

The Ardwick Trust

Jewish, welfare, general

£82,000 (2012/13)

Beneficial area

UK, Israel and the developing world.

Correspondent: Janet Bloch, Trustee, c/o Knox Cropper, 24 Petworth Road, Haslemere, Surrey GU27 2HR (tel: 01428 652788)

Trustees: Janet Bloch; Dominic Flynn; Judith Portrait.

CC Number: 266981

The trust supports Jewish welfare, along with a wide band of non-Jewish causes to include social welfare, health, education (especially special schools), older people, conservation and the environment, child welfare, disability and medical research. Although the largest grants made by the trust are to Jewish organisations, the majority of recipients are non-Jewish.

In 2012/13 it had assets of £1.1 million and an income of £88,500. Grants were made to 330 organisations totalling £82,000.

Ten organisations received grants of £1,000 or over: Nightingale Hammerson and Pinhas Rutenberg Educational Trust (£5,000 each); British Friends of the Hebrew University, Jewish Care and Technion UK (£3,000); World Jewish Relief (£1,500); and British ORT, Langdon Foundation, Norwood and UJIA (£1,000 each).

Remaining beneficiaries were all for £700, £500, £200 or £100 each. Beneficiaries included: Cancer Research UK, Cheltenham Ladies' College, Friends of Israel Educational Foundation, Great Ormond Street Hospital Charity, Jewish Deaf Association, North London Hospice, Pancreatic Cancer UK, Scope, Shelter, Shine, Springboard for Children, Stroke Association, Target Ovarian Cancer, Target Tuberculosis, Womankind Worldwide, World 4 Girls, WWF-UK, Y Care International YMCA England, Water Aid and Whizz-Kidz.

Exclusions

No grants to individuals.

Applications

In writing to the correspondent.

Percentage of awards given to new applicants: between 10% and 20%.

Common applicant mistakes

'They don't read the guidelines in the Directory or look at the type of organisations funded. Personal applications are particularly guilty concerning this.'

Information gathered from:

Accounts; Charity Commission record; further information provided by the funder.

The Argentarius Foundation

General

Around £90,000 (2011/12)

Beneficial area

UK.

Correspondent: Philip Goodman, Goodman and Co., 14 Basing Hill, London NW11 8TH (tel: 020 8458 0955; email: philip@goodmanandco.com)

Trustees: Emily Marbach; Judy Jackson; Anna Josse.

CC Number: 1079980

Set up by a trust deed in 2000, this foundation is established for general charitable purposes and gives grants to organisations. Income has steadily declined from around £50,000 in 2007/08 and last year income was recorded as nil.

In 2011/12 the foundation's income was £3,000 and there was a total expenditure of £95,000. Accounting documents had been received at the Commission but were not published. Unfortunately we have no information regarding the beneficiaries of the charity.

Applications

In writing to the correspondent.

Information gathered from:

Accounts; Charity Commission record.

Armenian General Benevolent Union London Trust

Armenian education, culture and welfare

Around £13,000 to organisations (2011)

Beneficial area

UK and overseas.

Correspondent: Dr Berge Azadian, Trustee, 51c Parkside, Wimbledon Common, London SW19 5NE

Trustees: Dr Berge Azadian; Berge Setrakian; Aris Atamian; Noushig Yakoubian Setrakian; Assadour Guzelian; Tro Manoukian; Arline Medazoumian; Armine Afrikian.

CC Number: 282070

The purpose of the trust is to advance education among Armenians, particularly those in the UK, and to promote the study of Armenian history, literature, language, culture and religion.

In 2011 it had assets of almost £3.7 million and an income of £143,000. Grants were made totalling £73,000 including £59,500 in 29 student loans and grants.

Grants categorised as 'Aid to Armenia, charitable and other grants' included those to: The Armenian Church Trust (£5,000) and the RP Musical for Remembrance Concert (£1,500). A further £4,000 was given under the grant category 'Education' to K Tahta Armenian Sunday School.

Exclusions

No support for projects of a commercial nature.

Applications

In writing to the correspondent. Applications are considered all year round.

Information gathered from:

Accounts; Charity Commission record.

The Armourers' and Brasiers' Gauntlet Trust

Materials science, general charitable purposes

£205,000 to organisations (2011/12)

Beneficial area

UK, with some preference for London.

Correspondent: Christopher Waite, Secretary, Armourers' Hall, 81 Coleman Street, London EC2R 5BJ (tel: 020 7374 4000; fax: 020 7606 7481; email: info@armourersandbrasiers.co.uk; website: www.armourersandbrasiers.co.uk)

Trustees: Prof. William Bonfield; Ven. C. J. H. Wagstaff; Jonathan Stopford Haw; David Chapman; Simon Archer; David Davies.

CC Number: 279204

The trust, which provides the charitable outlet for the Worshipful Company of Armourers and Brasiers, was set up in 1979. The following information is taken from the trust's website:

The objectives of the trust are:

- Support for education and research in materials science and technology and for basic science in schools
- Encouragement of the understanding and preservation of historic armour
- Encouragement of the armourers' trade in the armed services
- Encouragement of professional excellence in the training of young officers in the Royal Armoured Corps
- To consider appeals in the following overall categories: (i) community, social care and armed forces; (ii) children, youth and general education; medical and health; (iii) art, arms and armour; and (iv) Christian mission

Two-thirds of the charitable giving is directed to the first objective and is administered by the Company's Material Sciences Committee. The remaining one-third is applied by the trustees to the other objectives.

The trust is not a large charity, so the trustees prefer to make grants to smaller and less well known charitable organisations rather than to those with a high public profile. Over 100 such charities receive grants each year.

In 2011/12 the trust had assets of £6 million, an income of £397,000 and made grants totalling £346,000. Grants of £62,000 were made to 108 individuals and grants of over £205,000 were made to organisations.

Beneficiaries included: Royal Opera House and The Richard House Hospice (£2,000 each); Combat Stress, Just Different, Lumos Foundation, Medical Engineering Unit, Morning Star Trust, National Life Story Collection, and Spitalfields Festival Ltd (£1,000 each); and 4 Cancer Group, Cricklewood Homeless Concern, Hope UK, Local Employment Access Projects, My Voice London, Open Door Young People's Consultation Service, Siblings Together, Target Ovarian Cancer, The Eyeless Trust, The Migraine Trust, The National Tremor Foundation and Toucan Employment (£500 each).

Exclusions

In general grants are not made:

- To organisation or groups which are not registered charities
- In response to applications for the benefit of individuals
- To organisations or groups whose main object is to fund or support other charitable bodies
- Which are in direct relief of, or will lead to, a reduction of financial support from public funds
- To charities with a turnover in excess of £1\ million
- To charities which spend over 10% of their income on fundraising activities
- Towards general maintenance, repair or restoration of buildings, including ecclesiastical buildings, unless there is a connection with the Armourers and Brasiers' Company, or unless of outstanding importance to the national heritage
- To appeals for charitable sponsorship from individuals

Applications

In writing to the correspondent, with a copy of the latest annual report and audited accounts. Applications are considered quarterly. For full guidelines, visit the trust's website.

Information gathered from:

Accounts; Charity Commission record; funder's website.

The Artemis Charitable Trust

Psychotherapy, parent education, and related activities

£147,000 (2012)

Beneficial area

UK.

Correspondent: Richard Evans, Trustee, Brook House, Quay Meadow, Bosham, West Sussex PO18 8LY (tel: 01243 573475)

Trustees: Richard Evans; Dawn Bergin; David Evans; Mark Evans; Wendy Evans Menke.

CC Number: 291328

The trust was set up in 1985, its 2012 trustees' report states: 'The policy of the trust has continued to be the making of grants to aid the provision of counselling, psychotherapy, parenting, human relationship training and related activities.'

In 2012 it had assets of £1.5 million and an income of £50,000. Grants totalled £147,000. Beneficiaries were: Primary Care Psychological Services (£124,000); Chichester Festival Theatre (£17,000); The Expeditionary Trust (£5,000); Mental Health Informatics (£720); and Relate (£500).

Exclusions

Individuals or organisations which are not registered charities.

Applications

Applicants should be aware that most of the trust's funds are committed to a number of major ongoing projects and that spare funds available to meet new applications are very limited.

Information gathered from:

Accounts; Charity Commission record.

The Ove Arup Foundation

Construction – education and research

£156,000 (2011/12)

Beneficial area

Unrestricted.

Correspondent: Peter Klyhn, Ove Arup and Partners, Ove Arup and Partners, 13 Fitzroy Street, London W1T 4BQ (email: ovarfound@arup.com; website: www.theovearupfoundation.com)

Trustees: R. B. Haryott, Chair; A. Chan; F. Cousins; J. Kennedy; M. Shears;

D. Michael; R. T. M. Hill; C. Cole; R. Hough; P. Dilley.

CC Number: 328138

The trust was established in 1989 with the principal objective of supporting education in matters associated with the built environment, including construction-related academic research. The trustees are appointed by the board of the Ove Arup Partnership. It gives grants for research and projects, including start-up and feasibility costs.

In 2011/12 the foundation had assets of £2.8 million, an income of £197,000 and gave grants totalling £156,000.

Beneficiaries in 2011/12 were: The Royal Academy of Engineering (£50,000); The University of Edinburgh (£40,000); The London School of Economics (£35,000); The Industrial Trust (£13,500); Institution of Civil Engineers (£12,500); and The Royal Academy of Arts (£5,000).

Exclusions

No grants to individuals, including students.

Applications

On a form available to download from the foundation's website.

Information gathered from:

Accounts; Charity Commission record; funder's website.

The AS Charitable Trust

Christian, development, social concern

£55,500 (2009/10)

Beneficial area

UK and developing countries.

Correspondent: George Calvocoressi, Trustee, Bix Bottom Farm, Henley-on-Thames, Oxfordshire RG9 6BH

Trustees: Caroline Eady; George Calvocoressi; Simon Sampson.

CC Number: 242190

This trust makes grants in particular to projects which combine the advancement of the Christian religion, with Christian lay leadership, with third world development, with peacemaking and reconciliation or with other areas of social concern. In the accounts for 2008/09 the trustees made donations to charities known to them and whose aims they support.

Accounts for the year 2011/12 were overdue for submission at the Charity Commission and so not available at the time of writing.

In 2009/10 the trust had assets of £8.1 million and an income of £242,000. Grants to 13 organisations totalled £55,500.

Beneficiaries included: GRACE (£25,000 in two gifts); The De Laszlo Foundation (£10,000); Lambeth Partnership (£4,000 in two gifts); and The Message Trust and Vision 2025 (£1,000 each).

Exclusions

Grants to individuals or large charities are very rare. Such applications are discouraged.

Applications

In writing to the correspondent.

Information gathered from:

Accounts; Charity Commission record.

Ashburnham Thanksgiving Trust

Christian

£72,000 to organisations (2011/12)

Beneficial area

UK and worldwide.

Correspondent: The Charity Secretary, Brooke Oast, Jarvis Lane, Goudhurst, Cranbrook, Kent TN17 1LP (email: att@lookingforward.biz)

Trustees: E. R. Bickersteth; R. D. Bickersteth; Mrs R. F. Dowdy.

CC Number: 249109

The trust supports a wide range of Christian mission organisations and other Christian organisations which are known to the trustees, in the UK and worldwide. Individuals are also supported.
In 2011/12 the trust had assets of £5.6 million and an income of £174,000. Grants totalled £108,000, of which £72,000 was distributed in grants to 93 organisations. Further monies were distributed in restricted grants and grants to individuals.

Beneficiaries included: Genesis Arts Trust (£4,000); St Stephen's Society – Hong Kong (£3,800); Prison Fellowship (£2,900); Wycliffe Bible Translators (£2,800); Youth with a Mission and Interserve (£2,000 each); and Care Trust and Advantage Africa (£1,000 each).

The majority of beneficiaries received a small grant of £1,000 or less, including: Wonersh and Blackheath Parochial Church Council, Servants with Jesus, Movember, Lee Abbey Fellowship, Hebron Trust and Cherith Trust.

Exclusions

No grants for buildings.

Applications

Grants are typically made to organisations known to the trustees.

Information gathered from:

Accounts; Charity Commission record.

A. J. H. Ashby Will Trust

Wildlife, heritage, education and children

£51,000 (2011/12)

Beneficial area

UK, especially the Lea Valley area of Hertfordshire.

Correspondent: Sandra Hill, Trust Manager, HSBC Trust Company (UK) Ltd, Trust Services, Norwich House, Nelson Gate, Commercial Road, Southampton SO15 1GX (tel: 02380 722243)

Trustee: HSBC. Trust Company (UK) Ltd.

CC Number: 803291

The trust was established in 1990 to support wildlife throughout the UK, particularly birds, as well as heritage, education projects and young people specifically in the Lea Valley area of Hertfordshire.

In 2011/12 the trust held assets of £1.2 million had an income of £27,000. Grants were made to six organisations totalling £51,000.

Beneficiaries included: RSPB (£26,000 in four grants); Woodland Trust (£10,000); The Hertfordshire Groundwork Trust (£6,000); Wheelyboat Trust (£5,000); Harpenden Lions Club (£3,000); and Birchanger Wood Trust (£2,000).

Exclusions

No grants to individuals or students.

Applications

In writing to the correspondent.

Information gathered from:

Accounts; Charity Commission record.

The Ashley Family Foundation

Art and design, higher education, local projects in mid-rural Wales

£534,000 (2011/12)

Beneficial area

Mostly Wales, other areas considered.

Correspondent: Mia Duddridge, Correspondent, 6 Trull Farm Buildings, Trull, Tetbury, Gloucestershire GL8 8SQ (tel: 03030401005; email: info@ashleyfamilyfoundation.org.uk; website: www.ashleyfamilyfoundation.org.uk)

Trustees: Jane Ashley; Martyn C. Gowar; Emma Shuckburgh; Prof. Oriana

Baddeley; Prof. Sue Timney; Mike Hodgson; Jeremy McIlroy.

CC Number: 288099

In 1986, a year after the sad death of Laura Ashley, her family officially established The Laura Ashley Foundation. The change of name to The Ashley Family Foundation took place in 2011.

The foundation's ethos is primarily to strengthen rural communities, particularly those within Wales. Both in terms of the social and environmental aspects alongside giving back to the communities that helped the family develop the *Laura Ashley* company into an international success. Added to this are the promotion and support of traditional family values often retained within rural communities.

Developing the company in rural mid-Wales had a significant impact upon the local economy and the social well-being of its people with increased employment opportunity and the valued team spirit of the workforce. A commitment to maintaining these aspects remains within the activities of the foundation, with many grassroots voluntary groups benefiting from its funds.

The following information is taken from the foundation's helpful website:

> As a guide the foundation, for the past few years, has had a policy of giving half our funds to Welsh projects.
>
> *Grants Criteria*
>
> The foundation follows the ethos of the Ashley family and aims to support areas in which the family have a connection such as helping the communities of Mid Wales that supported the growth of the Laura Ashley business.
>
> The trustees wish to focus on the following priorities:
>
> - Support of charitable textiles projects, including small scale community textiles initiatives
> - Support for the arts
> - Support for projects which seek to strengthen rural communities in Wales, especially in Mid Wales
>
> Awards are mainly one-off and for a period of up to three years, subject to monitoring and review.

In 2011/12 the foundation had assets of £10.4 million and an income of over £204,000. According to the annual report, grants were made totalling £534,000 of which £230,000 was given towards arts projects and over £200,000 in educational grants. Over 50 organisations benefitted, many of them working on a grassroots level within the rural communities of Wales.

Beneficiaries included: Charleston Trust (£35,000); Royal College of Art (£18,000); London College of Communication and Music in Hospitals (£12,000 each); Phoenix Community Furniture, Quilt Association, Textprint and Wilderness Trust (£10,000 only); Bipolar UK (£5,000); Poems in the Waiting Room and Welsh National Sheepdog Trials (£3,000 each); A Voice for You (£2,000); Carno Bowling Club (£1,000); and Builth Wells Hand Bells, Volunteer Reading Help and Welsh Football Trust (£500 each).

Exclusions

The foundation does not generally fund individuals, business ventures, overseas projects, projects falling within the field of religion or retrospective work.

Applications

There is a two stage application process. Applications can be made throughout the year and are assessed in line with the guidelines available from the foundation's website. The final decision is made by the trustees during meetings held three times a year. The website states:

> Due to the economic downturn we are receiving an unprecedented increase in requests. We are therefore changing our long held policy of replying to all requests. If you have submitted a stage one proposal and have not heard within eight weeks please assume you have been unsuccessful.

Percentage of awards given to new applicants: between 20% and 30%.

Common applicant mistakes

'Not checking [our] website for criteria.'

Information gathered from:

Accounts; Charity Commission record; further information provided by the funder; funder's website.

The Ashworth Charitable Trust

Welfare

£117,000 to organisations

(2011/12)

Beneficial area

UK and worldwide, with some preference for certain specific needs in Honiton, Ottery St Mary, Sidmouth and Wonford Green surgery, Exeter.

Correspondent: Glenys Towner, Foot Anstey, Senate Court, Southernhay Gardens, Exeter EX1 1NT (tel: 01392 411221; fax: 01392 685220; email: ashworthtrust@btinternet.com; website: www.ashworthtrust.org)

Trustees: Shahin Saebnoori; Sharareh Rouhipour; Katherine Gray; Hoshmand Rouhipour; Kian Golestani; Wendi Cunningham Momen.

CC Number: 1045492

The trust was founded by Mrs C E Crabtree in 1995. The trust currently considers applications for and makes grants as appropriate to:

- Ironbridge Gorge Museum Trust
- People living in the areas covered by the medical practices and social services in Honiton, Ottery St Mary, Sidmouth and Wonford Green surgery, Exeter. Such grants are to be paid for particularly acute needs
- Humanitarian projects either to other charities or to individuals

The trust's website states that: 'for the most part, the trust looks to fund projects, not core funding.'

In 2011/12 the trust had assets of £4 million and an income of £136,000. Grants were made to 47 organisations totalling £122,000, of which £117,000 went to organisations.

Beneficiaries included: Ironbridge Gorge Museum Trust (£10,000); Appropriate Technology Asia, Excellent Development Ltd, Find Your Feet and Hospiscare Exeter (£5,000 each); Livingstone Tanzania Trust, Medical Assistance Sierra Leone and Wherever the Need (£3,000 each); Balloons, Exeter CAB, The Dignity Project and World Child Cancer (£2,000 each); and Accessible Coach Holidays, Devon Link-Up, Exeter Gateway Centre and Hope (£1,000 each).

A further £5,000 was given to 21 individuals from the Doctors' and Social Services Fund.

Note: these grant examples are not necessarily indicative of future giving.

Exclusions

No grants for:

- Research-based charities
- Individuals
- Non-UK registered charities
- Charities with a turnover of more than £1 million
- Charities with disproportionately large reserves, unless there is an exceptional reason. In such cases the trust requires an explanation
- Animal charities
- UK hospices – the trustees already contribute to one hospice of their choice
- 'heritage charities' such as National Trust or other organisations whose aim is the preservation of a building, museum, library and so on (with the exception of the Ironbridge Gorge Museum)
- The promotion of religious or political activities

Applications

In writing to the correspondent. There is no application form but applications should include:

- Registered charity number
- An email address
- A recent set of accounts
- A brief (not more than two pages) analysis of the main objectives of your

organisation and any particular project for which funding is required

Incomplete applications will not be considered. Do not send brochures, DVDs, books, annual reviews or any other bulky promotional material. If more information is needed, you will be contacted.

The trustees meet twice a year in May and November. Applications should be submitted by the middle of March or the middle of September respectively. Note that the trustees are unable to enter into any discussions regarding funding, successful or otherwise, as there are no funds designated for this purpose.

Information gathered from:

Accounts; Charity Commission record; funder's website.

The Ian Askew Charitable Trust

General

£151,000 (2011/12)

Beneficial area

UK, with a preference for Sussex.

Correspondent: The Trustees, c/o Baker Tilly, 18 Mount Ephraim Road, Tunbridge Wells, Kent TN1 1ED (tel: 01892 511944; email: bill.owen@bakertilly.co.uk)

Trustees: John Hecks; Cleone Pengelley; Richard Lewis; Rory Askew; James Rank.

CC Number: 264515

Grants are given to a wide variety of charitable bodies throughout the country with a preference for those connected with the county of Sussex. An educational sub-fund generally funds the maintenance and conservation of woodlands belonging to the trust which are used principally for educational purposes. There is also a conservation fund for the conservation and preservation of historic buildings.

In 2011/12 the trust had assets of £15.8 million and an income of £371,000. Grants to 215 charitable organisations totalled £129,000, excluding all support costs. Grants of £18,500 were also made from the Conservation fund and £4,200 from the Educational sub-fund.

The majority of grants to organisations were for £500 or less, with 15 for £1,000 or more. Beneficiaries of those grants included: Ditchling Museum, Friends of East Sussex Records Office and Ringmer Community College (£2,000 each); Commonwealth Housing Trust CPRE Sussex, Forces Support, The Georgian Group and The Victorian Society Appeal (£1,000 each).

Exclusions

None known.

Applications

In writing to the correspondent. Applications are considered every other month.

Information gathered from:

Accounts; Charity Commission record.

The Association of Colleges Charitable Trust

Further education colleges

£69,000 (2011/12)

Beneficial area

UK.

Correspondent: Alice Thiagaraj, Managing Trustee, 2–5 Stedham Place, London WC1A 1HU (tel: 020 7034 9917; email: alice_thiagaraj@aoc.co.uk; website: www.aoc.co.uk)

Trustees: Alice Thiagaraj; Peter Brophy; David Forrester; John Bingham; Martin Doel; Carole Stott; Wesley Streeting; Jane Samuels; Simon Francis; Shahida Aslam.

CC Number: 1040631

The Association of Colleges was created in 1996 as the single voice to promote the interests of further education colleges in England and Wales. It is responsible for administering two programmes, the largest of these is the Beacon Awards, which provide monetary grants to specific initiatives within further education colleges. The other programme that operates within the trust is the AoC Gold Awards.

Established in 1994, the Beacon Awards recognise and promote the interdependence of further education colleges and business, and, professional and voluntary sector organisations to their mutual advantage. Awards take the form of monetary grants of between £3,000 and £5,000 and are sponsored by various private and public sector organisations. The aim of the programme is to highlight the breadth and quality of education in colleges throughout the UK and increase understanding of colleges' contribution to UK educational skills policy and economic and social development.

The awards:

- Recognise imaginative and exemplary teaching and learning practice in colleges
- Draw attention to provision which encourages and supports learners to approach challenges positively and creatively
- Support learning and continuous improvement through the dissemination of Award-bearing practice
- Promote and celebrate the further education sector's commitment to pioneering approaches to equality and diversity

Applications may be for a programme, course, or project or for some other aspect of college provision – teaching, learning, guidance or support. To be eligible, initiatives should show evidence of imaginative yet sustainable teaching and learning practice or other relevant provision. It must also fulfil the following criteria:

- It must meet the specific requirements set out by the sponsors of the particular award (see relevant page in the Awards section of the Prospectus available from the association's website
- It must have regard to promoting equality and diversity in the delivery of the programme
- It must be subject to evaluation/ quality assurance to influence the continuing development of the initiative
- It must have been running for at least one academic session before the deadline for applications
- It must have features which actively promote exemplary teaching and learning
- It must be of benefit to one or more groups of students or trainees who will be identified and described in the application
- It must have wider relevance and applicability making it of value to other colleges as an example of good practice or innovation

Each award has separate criteria in the interests of the area of work of the sponsor. They range from broad educational development to the promotion of particular courses or subjects, covering most aspects of further education.

The other scheme operated by the trust is the AoC Gold Awards for Further Education Alumni, which reward former members of further education colleges who have since excelled in their chosen field or profession.

In 2011/12 the trust's assets stood at £148,000, with an income of £233,000. Charitable activities for the year amounted to £223,000, of which £69,000 was given in Beacon Awards – 14 were given in 2011/12.

Some of the awards and winners in 2011/12 included: Cardiff and Vale College (£5,000 for the Welsh Assembly Government – Overcoming Deprivation Award); West Cheshire College (£5,000 for the AoC – Inclusive Learning

Award); and Fareham College (£3,500 for the Jardine Lloyd Thompson – Health and Community Care Award).

Exclusions

Grants are not made to individuals.

Applications

The application process consists of submitting a standard application form and an anonymised description of the project (in no more than 3,000 words). Full details on the application process are available on the association's website.

Percentage of awards given to new applicants: between 40% and 50%.

Common applicant mistakes

'Colleges fail to address all of the criteria – particularly the one relating to equality and diversity. Some fail to follow the required format for submitting an application form.'

Information gathered from:

Accounts; Charity Commission record; further information provided by the funder; funder's website.

The Astor Foundation

Medical research, general

£120,000 (2011/12)

Beneficial area

UK.

Correspondent: Lisa Rothwell-Orr, Secretary, PO Box 3096, Marlborough, Wiltshire SN8 3WP (email: astor.foundation@gmail.com)

CC Number: 225708

The following extract is taken from the trust's 2011/12 accounts:

> The primary object of the foundation is medical research in its widest sense, favouring research on a broad front rather than in specialised fields. For guidance, this might include general medical equipment or equipment for use in research, or grants to cover travelling and subsistence expenses for doctors and students studying abroad.
>
> In general, the foundation gives preference to giving assistance with the launching and initial stages of new projects and filling in gaps or shortfalls.
>
> In addition to its medical connection, historically the foundation has also supported initiatives for children and youth groups, the disabled, the countryside, the arts, sport, carers groups and animal welfare.

In 2011/12 the foundation held assets of £3.4 million and had an income of £136,000. Grants were made to 67 organisations totalling £120,000.

The single biggest beneficiary was University College London Medical School (£16,000). Other beneficiaries included: University College London Hospitals Charitable Foundation (£5,000); Independence at Home (£4,500); Autistica (£3,000); Royal College of Music (£2,500); Meningitis Trust (£2,000); Royal Air Force Cadets and Penrith and District Red Squirrel Group (£1,500 each); and the Anaphylaxis Campaign and Parkinson's UK (£1,000 each).

Exclusions

No grants to individuals or towards salaries. Grants are given to registered charities only.

Applications

Applications should be in writing to the correspondent and must include accounts and an annual report if available.

The trustees meet twice yearly, usually in October and April. If the appeal arrives too late for one meeting it will automatically be carried over for consideration at the following meeting. An acknowledgement will be sent on receipt of an appeal. No further communication will be entered into unless the trustees raise any queries regarding the appeal, or unless the appeal is subsequently successful.

Percentage of awards given to new applicants: more than 50%.

Common applicant mistakes

'Ignoring advice regarding deadlines.'

Information gathered from:

Accounts; Charity Commission record.

The Astor of Hever Trust

Youth, medical research, education, arts, conservation and sport

£27,500 (2011/12)

Beneficial area

UK and worldwide, with a preference for Kent and the Grampian region of Scotland.

Correspondent: Gill Willis, Administrator, Frenchstreet House, Westerham, Kent TN16 1PW (tel: 01959 565070; email: astorofhevertrust@btinternet.com)

CC Number: 264134

The trust gives grants UK-wide and internationally. It states that there is a preference for Kent and the Grampian region of Scotland, although the preference for Kent is much stronger.

When Gavin Astor, second Baron Astor of Hever, founded the trust in 1955, its main areas of support were arts, medicine, religion, education, conservation, youth and sport. Reflecting the settlor's wishes, the trust makes grants to local youth organisations, medical research and educational programmes. Most beneficiaries are UK-wide charities or a local branch.

In 2011/12 the trust had assets of £1 million and an income of £34,000. Grants were made to 83 organisations totalling £27,500.

Beneficiaries included: Columbia Memorial Hospital, Combat Stress, Fields in Trust, Fifth Trust and Rochester Cathedral Trust (£1,000 each);Ambitious about Autism and Sound (£750 each); Buildings of Scotland Trust, Cage Green Autism Centre, Deafblind UK, Mercy Ships and National Memorial Arboretum (£500 each); Aberlour Child Care Trust, Books Abroad, Independence at Home and Street Pastors (£250 each); Chiddington Causeway Village Hall and Fund for Refugees in Slovenia (£100 each); and Tarland Agricultural Show (£50).

Exclusions

No grants to individuals.

Applications

In writing to the correspondent. Trustees meet twice each year. Unsuccessful applicants are not notified.

Information gathered from:

Accounts; Charity Commission record.

The Aurelius Charitable Trust

Conservation of culture and the humanities

£73,000 (2012/13)

Beneficial area

UK.

Correspondent: Philip Haynes, Trustee, Briarsmead, Old Road, Buckland, Betchworth, Surrey RH3 7DU (tel: 01737 842186; email: philip.haynes@tiscali.co.uk)

CC Number: 271333

During the settlor's lifetime, the income of the trust was distributed broadly to reflect his interests in the conservation of culture inherited from the past, and the dissemination of knowledge, particularly in the humanities field. Since the settlor's death in April 1994, the trustees have continued with this policy.

Donations are preferred to be for seed-corn or completion funding not otherwise available. They are usually one-off and range from £500 to £3,000.

In 2012/13 the trust had assets of over £2.3 million, which generated an income of £83,000. Donations were made to 28 organisations totalling £73,000 (one grant of £3,000 was committed, not paid).

Beneficiaries included: British School at Athens (£6,000); University of Westminster (£5,000); Bethel Chapel – Lye, Stourbridge (£4,000); British Exploring Society and Clophill Heritage Trust (£3,000 each); Lauderdale House Society and Society of Antiquaries of London (£2,000 each); Faversham Society (£1,000); and Christ Church Brockham Parochial Church Council (£500).

Exclusions

No grants to individuals.

Applications

In writing to the correspondent. Donations are generally made on the recommendation of the trust's board of advisors. Unsolicited applications will only be responded to if an sae is included. Trustees meet twice a year.

Information gathered from:

Accounts; Charity Commission record.

The Avenue Charitable Trust

General charitable purposes

Around £3,000 (2011/12)

Beneficial area

Worldwide.

Correspondent: Susan Simmons, Correspondent, Sayers Butterworth LLP, 3rd Floor, 12 Gough Square, London EC4A 3DW (tel: 020 7936 1910)

Trustees: Richard Astor; Bonny Astor; Alfred Astor; Geoffrey Todd.

CC Number: 264804

In 2011/12 the trust had an income of £1,500 and a total expenditure of over £3,000. We have no other information.

Previous beneficiaries included: Delta Trust (£225,000); Neuropsychoanalysis Fund (£65,000); David Astor Journalism Award Trust (£50,000); Adonis Mosat Project (£25,000); Living Landscape Project (£10,000); Adam von Trott Memorial Appeal (£5,000); Amnesty International, Cheek By Jowl and Koestler Trust (£1,000 each); and Prisoners Abroad (£500).

Applications

The trust has previously stated that all available income is now committed to existing beneficiaries.

Information gathered from:

Accounts; Charity Commission record.

Harry Bacon Foundation

Medical, animal welfare

£46,000 (2011/12)

Beneficial area

UK.

Correspondent: The Trust Manager, NatWest Bank plc, Trustee Department, 5th Floor, Trinity Quay 2, Avon Street, Bristol BS2 0PT (tel: 01179 403283)

Trustee: NatWest Bank plc.

CC Number: 1056500

In 2011/12 the trust had an income of £465,000 and made grants totalling £46,000.

The same charities are generally supported each year. Grants of £5,800 were given to the following eight charities: RNLI, Cancer Research UK, British Heart Foundation, PDSA, Parkinson's Disease Society, the Arthritis and Rheumatism Council for Research, The Donkey Sanctuary and World Horse Welfare.

Applications

In writing to the correspondent. The trustees meet regularly to consider applications.

Information gathered from:

Accounts; Charity Commission record.

The BACTA Charitable Trust

General charitable purposes

£80,000 (2011/12)

Beneficial area

UK.

Correspondent: Pru Kemball, Administration Assistant, 134–136 Buckingham Palace Road, London SW1W 9SA (tel: 020 7730 6444; email: pru@bacta.org.uk; website: www.bacta.org.uk)

Trustees: John Stergides; Mark Horwood; Jimmy Thomas; Stephen Hawkins; John Oversby-Powell; Anthony Boulton; Peter Weir; James Godden; Derek Petrie; Gabino Stergides; Michael Green; Neil Chinn.

CC Number: 328668

The trust only supports charities recommended by the British Amusement Catering Trade Association (BACTA) members.

In 2011/12 the trust had assets of £52,000 and an income of £36,000. Grants were made to seven organisations totalling £80,000. The main beneficiaries were Macmillan (£42,000); and Rays of Sunshine (£30,000). Other grants went to: Helen Rollason Cancer Charity (£3,000); Birmingham Children's Hospital (£3,000); Meningitis UK and The National Brain Appeal (£1,000 each); and Breast Cancer Campaign (£500).

The trust now works with a single charity partner for a three-year period, and up to early 2015 this will be Rays of Sunshine.

Exclusions

No grants for overseas charities or religious purposes.

Applications

BACTA have just entered into a three-year partnership with Rays of Sunshine Children's Charity, so unfortunately no other financial donations can be made at this time.

Information gathered from:

Accounts; Charity Commission record; funder's website.

The Scott Bader Commonwealth Ltd

General, international

£143,000 (2012)

Beneficial area

UK, Eire, Canada, France, South Africa, Croatia, Dubai, USA, Czech Republic, Sweden, Spain, China.

Correspondent: Sue Carter, Commonwealth Secretary, Scott Bader, Wollaston Hall, Wellingborough, Northamptonshire NN29 7RL (tel: 01933 666755; fax: 01933 666608; email: commonwealth_office@scottbader.com; website: www.scottbader.com)

Trustees: Andrew Radford; Syed Omar Hayat; Richard Stillwell; Julie Rogers; Anne Atkinson-Clark; Les Norwood; Jacquie Findlay; Barry Mansfield; Christian Caulier; Richard Hirst.

CC Number: 206391

This charity owns the share capital of Scott Bader Company Ltd and receives at least 1% of the Group's salary bill in donations each year. The charity fulfils its objectives by making grants to charitable organisations around the world whose purposes are to help young/disadvantaged people who suffer deprivation and discrimination or are poor, homeless, vulnerable children, women and minority communities and people affected by poverty, hunger and disease.

Funds are divided into two categories:

1. Central Fund.

- Large Project funding to the value of £25,000. Each year two large community-based environmental or educational projects that benefit young or disadvantaged people to the value of £25,000 each. These can be located anywhere in the world
- £10,000 was allocated in 2012 to a Small International Fund – to provide small grants of £500–£2,000 to support international projects that do not fit the local fund or large fund criteria
- £5,000 is made available for distribution to charities chosen by the Life President, Mr Godric Bader

2. Local Funds. Funds are made available to all the companies in the Scott Bader Group for them to submit applications to the trustees for charities they wish to support. Each company supports the work of charities associated with them or situated nearby. For example:

- Northamptonshire in the UK
- Co. Meath in Eire
- Amiens in France
- Falkenberg in Sweden
- Barcelona in Spain
- Liberec in the Czech Republic
- Zagreb in Croatia
- Dubai
- Durban in South Africa
- Ohio in the USA
- Shanghai in China
- Canada

In 2012 the charity had assets of £42 million and an income of £178,000 primarily in donations from the Scott Bader Company. Grants were made totalling £143,000. Of this grant total, £33,000 was given in the UK.

£13,000 of the UK grant total was given through the nomination scheme whereby staff of Scott Bader can nominate a charity of their choice to receive £120.

The remainder of the UK grant total was used to support local projects including: The Prince's Trust (£5,000); Nene Valley Care Trust (£3,500); Northampton Hope Centre (£3,000); Tall Ships Youth Trust (£2,000); and Mad Scientist (£1,000).

Exclusions

No support for charities concerned with the well-being of animals, individuals in need or organisations sending volunteers abroad. It does not respond to general appeals or support the larger well-established national charities. It does not provide grants for medical research. It does not make up deficits already incurred, or support the arts, museums, travel/adventure, sports clubs or the construction, renovation or maintenance of buildings.

Applications

Assessment criteria are available to download from the website. Application forms are available on request by post or email. Deadlines for the large project funding are available on the website. Applications for the Small International Fund are accepted all year round. Applications for local funds should be made to the local office.

Information gathered from:

Accounts; Charity Commission record; funder's website.

The Bagri Foundation

General charitable purposes

£278,000 to organisations and individuals (2011/12)

Beneficial area

Worldwide.

Correspondent: D. M. Beaumont, Correspondent, 80 Cannon Street, London EC4N 6EJ (tel: 020 7280 0000; email: enquiries@bagrifoundation.org; website: bagrifoundation.org)

CC Number: 1000219

The Bagri Foundation's principal activities relate to education, South Asian cultural heritage, and relief work primarily across the Indian subcontinent. The foundation's website states that:

> The foundation runs rich and diverse cultural programmes, particularly in the UK, and collaborates with other organisations to further its own charitable aims and objectives. The foundation's work is focused on a limited number of projects at any one time, and it does not accept unsolicited requests for financial assistance.

In 2011/12 it had assets of £14.5 million and an income of £12 million mainly from donations. Grants were made to organisations and individuals totalling £278,000. During the year the trustees agreed to donate £1 million over a period of five years between 2012 and 2016 to the London Business School for the advancement of education of the students at the school. The first £200,000 was made in this year.

No other information is given in its report and accounts.

Applications

All enquiries should be made by email.

Information gathered from:

Accounts; Charity Commission record; funder's website.

The Baker Charitable Trust

Mainly Jewish, older people, sickness and disability, medical research

£56,000 (2011/12)

Beneficial area

UK and overseas.

Correspondent: Dr Harvey Baker, Trustee, 16 Sheldon Avenue, Highgate, London N6 4JT (tel: 020 8340 5970)

CC Number: 273629

The trust makes grants to organisations that support people who are elderly, have a chronic sickness or disability and people who have had limited educational opportunity. The trust also supports medical research related to the above groups. There is a preference for Jewish organisations.

In 2011/12 it had assets of almost £1.2 million and an income of £58,000. Grants to 44 organisations totalled £56,000. A list of grants was not included in the accounts received at the Charity Commission.

Previous beneficiaries have included: British Council, Shaare Zedek Medical Centre, Chai Cancer Care, Community Security Trust, Disabled Living Foundation, Friends of Magen David Adom in Great Britain, Hillel Foundation, Institute of Jewish Policy Research, Jewish Care, Jewish Women's Aid, Marie Curie Cancer Care, National Society for Epilepsy, Norwood, United Jewish Israel Appeal, St John's Hospice, United Synagogue, Winged Fellowship and World Jewish Relief.

Exclusions

No grants to individuals or non-registered charities.

Applications

In writing to the correspondent. The trustees meet to consider applications in January, April, July and October.

Information gathered from:

Accounts; Charity Commission record.

The Andrew Balint Charitable Trust

General charitable causes, Jewish charities

£55,000 (2012/13)

Beneficial area

UK, Israel, Hungary.

Correspondent: Dr David Kramer, Correspondent, Carter Backer Winter, Enterprise House, 21 Buckle Street, London E1 8NN (tel: 020 7309 3800)

Trustees: Dr Gabriel Balint-Kurti; Angela Balint; Roy Balint-Kurti; Daniel Balint-Kurti.

CC Number: 273691

This trust gives to charitable organisations to assist with general causes in the UK and abroad. The accounts for 2012/13 state: 'The Andrew Balint Charitable Trust, The George Balint Charitable Trust, The Paul Charitable Trust and the Trust for Former Employees of Balint Companies are jointly administered. They have some trustees in common and are independent in other matters.'

In 2012/13 the trust held assets of £1.6 million and had an income of £47,000. Grants were made to 45 organisations and totalled £55,000.

Beneficiaries included: Nightingale House (£20,000); Hungarian Senior Citizens (£6,000); Former Employee Trust (£6,000); Jewish Care and United Jewish Israel Appeal £5,000 each); The Board of Deputies of British Jews (£500); and British Friends of Children's Town (£250).

Applications

In writing to the correspondent.

Information gathered from:

Accounts; Charity Commission record.

The Paul Balint Charitable Trust

General charitable purposes

Around £43,000 (2011/12)

Beneficial area

UK; Hungary; Israel.

Correspondent: Dr Andrew Balint, Trustee, 15 Portland Court, 101 Hendon Lane, London N3 3SH (tel: 020 8346 1266)

Trustees: Dr Andrew Balint; Dr Gabriel Balint-Kurti; Dr Marc Balint; Paul Balint.

CC Number: 273690

The trust was founded in 1977 and benefits organisations of general charitable purposes. It has helped a wide variety of organisations including those engaged in medical research, education, assisting the elderly and relieving poverty.

The Andrew Balint Charitable Trust, The George Balint Charitable Trust, The Paul Balint Charitable Trust and the Trust for Former Employees of Balint Companies are jointly administered. They have some trustees in common and are independent in other matters.

The trust makes grants to organisations operating in the UK, Israel and Hungary. In the year 2011/12 the trust had an income of £2,000 and a total expenditure of £44,000. No further information was available.

Applications

In writing to the correspondent.

Information gathered from:

Accounts; Charity Commission record.

The George Balint Charitable Trust

General, education, poverty relief and Jewish causes

Around £56,000 (2011/12)

Beneficial area

UK, Israel, Hungary.

Correspondent: David Kramer, Correspondent, Carter Backer Winter, Enterprise House, 21 Buckle Street, London E1 8NN (tel: 020 7309 3800)

Trustees: Dr Andrew Balint; George Rothschild; Dr Marc Balint.

CC Number: 267482

In 2011/12 the trust had an income of £21,000 and a total expenditure of £57,000. No further information was available.

In the past this trust has donated to general charitable organisations, this has included medical, educational and Jewish causes.

Previous beneficiaries include: United Jewish Israel Appeal (£15,000); Hungarian Senior Citizens (£10,200); Former Employees Trust (£8,500); Neviot Olam Institution and British Friends of Bar Ilan University (£2,000 each); Imperial College London (£1,000); Norwood: Children and Families First (£750); and Marie Curie Cancer Care (£200).

Previous accounts note:

> The George Balint Charitable Trust, the Paul Balint Charitable Trust and The Charitable Trust for Former Employees of Balint Companies operate from the same premises and are jointly administered. They have some trustees in common and are independent in all other matters.

Applications

In writing to the correspondent.

Information gathered from:

Accounts; Charity Commission record.

Balmain Charitable Trust

General

£106,000 (2011/12)

Beneficial area

UK.

Correspondent: Trust Administrator, c/o Rutter and Alhusen, 2 Longmead, Shaftesbury, Dorset SP7 8PL

Trustees: Andrew B. Tappin; Iain D. Balmain; Leonora D. Balmain; Charles A. G. Wells; Stewart Balmain; Penntrust Ltd.

CC Number: 1079972

Registered with the Charity Commission in March 2000, in 2011/12 the trust had assets of £2.6 million, an income of £117,000 and made 43 grants totalling £106,000.

Beneficiaries included: The Light Dragoons Regimental Charity (£10,000); British Red Cross Society and Oxfam (£8,000 each); Second Chance (£6,000); The Suzy Lamplugh Trust (£5,000); Wilderness Foundation UK, Unlock (National Association of Ex-Offenders); and RNLI (£2,000 each); The Wildfowl and Wetlands Trust (£1,500); and National Art Collections Fund, Cerebra and Age UK (£1,000 each).

Many of the beneficiaries are supported year after year.

Applications

In writing to the correspondent.

Information gathered from:

Accounts; Charity Commission record.

The Balney Charitable Trust

Preservation, conservation, welfare, service charities

£46,000 (2011/12)

Beneficial area

UK, with a preference for north Buckinghamshire and north Bedfordshire.

Correspondent: Helen Chapman, Correspondent, Hill Farm, North Crawley Road, Newport Pagnell, Buckinghamshire MK16 9HQ

Trustees: Ian Townsend; Robert Ruck-Keene; Ms J. Heaton.

CC Number: 288575

The objectives of the trust as stated in its accounts are as follows:

- The furtherance of any religious and charitable purposes in connection with the parishes of Chicheley, North Crawley and the SCAN Group i.e. Sherington, Astwood, Hardmead and churches with a Chester family connection
- The provision of housing for persons in need
- Agriculture, forestry and armed service charities
- Care of older people and the sick and people with disabilities from the Chicheley area
- Other charitable purposes

In 2011/12 the trust had assets of £804,000 and an income of £105,000. Charitable donations totalled £46,000.

The trust makes regular donations each year by standing order ranging from £25 to £1,000. A list of beneficiaries was not included in this year's accounts. However, previous beneficiaries included: Gurkha Welfare Trust (£1,000); St Lawrence Church – Chicheley (£500); Royal Agricultural Benevolent Institution (£350); Buckinghamshire Historic Churches Trust (£300); SSAFA (£250); Guards Museum Trust (£200); Country Landowners Association Charitable Trust (£100); and Friends of John Bunyan Museum – Bedford (£25).

Exclusions

Local community organisations and individuals outside north Buckinghamshire and north Bedfordshire.

Applications

In writing to the correspondent. Applications are acknowledged if an sae is enclosed, otherwise if the charity has not received a reply within six weeks the application has not been successful.

Information gathered from:

Accounts; Charity Commission record.

The Baltic Charitable Fund

Seafarers, fishermen, ex-service and service people

£53,000 (2011/12)

Beneficial area

UK, with a preference for the City of London.

Correspondent: The Company Secretary, The Baltic Exchange, 38 St Mary Axe, London EC3A 8BH (tel: 020 7623 5501)

Trustee: The Directors of the Baltic Exchange.

CC Number: 279194

The fund aims to support causes relating to the sea, including training for professionals and children, the City of London, Forces charities and for sponsorship for Baltic Exchange members. Support is given to registered charities only.

In 2011/12 the fund had assets of £2 million and an income of £83,000. Grants were made to 20 organisations totalling £53,000, including £11,000 given from the Bonno Krull Fund.

Beneficiaries included: London Nautical School (£30,000); Lord Mayor's Appeal (£7,500); Jubilee Sailing Trust (£5,000); Sailor's Society (£3,300); South Georgia Heritage Trust (£1,000); and Cancer Research and Sustrans (£300 each).

Exclusions

No support for advertising or charity dinners, and so on.

Applications

Unsolicited applications are not considered.

Information gathered from:

Accounts; Charity Commission record.

William P. Bancroft (No. 2) Charitable Trust and Jenepher Gillett Trust

Quaker causes

£42,000 (2011)

Beneficial area

UK and overseas.

Correspondent: Dr D. S. Gillett, Trustee, 13 Woodbury Park Road, Tunbridge Wells, Kent TN4 9NQ (tel: 01892 528150)

Trustees: Dr Godfrey Gillett; Martin B. Gillett; Dr D. S. Gillett; Jenepher Moseley; Dr Christopher Bancroft Wolff; Marion McNaughton.

CC Number: 288968

This trust is unusual as it consists of two separate trusts which are operated as one. For historical reasons there is a William P Bancroft Trust giving in the UK and a Jenepher Gillet Trust giving in Delaware, USA which shared a common settlor/joint-settlor; the two trusts are now being run jointly with the same trustees and joint finances.

It makes grants towards charitable purposes connected with the Religious Society of Friends, supporting Quaker conferences, colleges and Friends' homes for older people.

In 2011, the trust held assets of £735,000 and had an income of £43,000. Between the two trusts a total of £42,000 was given in grants to 29 organisations, with the William P Bancroft trust responsible for £24,500 of that total and the Jenepher Gillet Trust donating £17,500.

Beneficiaries included: Charney Manor Quake Course (£14,000); BYM (£5,000); Woodbrooke College (£2,000); Quaker Social Action (£2,500); Bootham School and Quaker Voluntary Action (£1,000 each); West Midland Quaker Peace Education, and Leaveners (£500 each).

This information was taken from the latest accounts available at the time of writing (November 2013).

Exclusions

No appeals unconnected with Quakers. No support for individual or student grant applications.

Applications

In writing to the correspondent. Trustees meet in May, applications must be received no later than April.

Information gathered from:

Accounts; Charity Commission record.

The Barbers' Company General Charities

Medical education and relief in sickness

£159,500 to organisations (2011/12)

Beneficial area

UK.

Correspondent: The Clerk, Barber-Surgeons' Hall, Monkwell Square, Wood Street, London EC2Y 5BL (tel: 020 7606 0741; email: clerk@barberscompany.org; website: barberscompany.org.uk)

Trustee: The Barbers' Company.

CC Number: 265579

The charities were registered in May 1973; grants are made to organisations and individuals. It no longer has direct contact with the hairdressing fraternity. However, a small amount is given each year to satisfy its historical links. Causes supported include those related to medical education and relief of the terminally ill.

In 2011/12 the charity had assets of £1.4 million and an income of £191,000. Grants totalled £165,000.

There were over 18 grants of £1,000 or more listed in the accounts. Beneficiaries included: Royal College of Surgeons (£40,000); Phyllis Tuckwell Hospice (£22,000); The Guildhall School Trust (£6,500); City of London School for Girls, Epsom College and Reeds School (£5,000 each); City of London Freemen's School (£4,000); and ABF- The Big Curry, Treloars and The Barbican Centre Trust (£1,000 each).

Applications

The trustees do not welcome unsolicited applications.

Information gathered from:

Accounts; Charity Commission record; funder's website.

The Barbour Foundation

Health, welfare, conservation/restoration, animal care, schools, churches, overseas aid

£505,500 (2011/12)

Beneficial area

England with a preference for Tyne and Wear, Northumberland and South Tyneside. Overseas aid.

Correspondent: Helen Tavroges, Trustee, J. Barbour and Sons Ltd, Simonside, South Shields, Tyne and Wear NE34 9PD (tel: 01914 554444; website: www.barbour.com)

CC Number: 328081

The objects of the charity are to support any charitable institution (grants are not made directly to individuals) the objects of which include:

- The relief of patients suffering from any form of illness or disease, the promotion of research in to the causes and treatment of such illnesses or disease and the provision of medical equipment for such patients
- The furtherance of education of children and young people who are in need of financial assistance by award of scholarship, exhibitions, bursaries or maintenance allowances tenable at any school, university or other educational establishment in England
- The protection and preservation for the benefit of the public in England, such features of cities, towns, villages and the countryside as are of special environmental, historical or architectural interest
- The relief of persons, whether resident in England or otherwise who are in conditions of need, hardship or distress as a result of local, national or international disaster, or by reason of their social and economic circumstances

In 2011/12 the foundation had assets of £9 million and an income of £445,000. Grants were made to 47 organisations totalling £510,000. Of this, almost £4,500 was in the form of goods supplied by J Barbour and Sons to the foundation.

Beneficiaries included: Newcastle School for Boys (£100,000); Hexham Abbey Project Appeal (£30,000); Princes Countryside Fund (£27,000); Marie Curie (£25,000); Duke of Edinburgh Award (£20,000); Barnardo's, British Red Cross and Calvert Trust (£5,000 each); East Africa Food Crisis, Revive Furniture Recycling and Sunnybank Centre (£3,000 each); Bubble Foundation, Contact (Morpeth Mental Health Group), Cedarwood Trust, Child Care Action Trust, Sailors' Families Society and YMCA (£2,000 each); and Arthritis Research UK, Bipolar Association, Brinkburn Music Festival and Target Ovarian Cancer (£1,000 each).

Exclusions

No support for:

- Requests from outside the geographical area
- Individual applications, unless backed by a particular charitable organisation
- Capital grants for building projects

Applications

Applications should be made in writing to the following address: PO Box 21, Guisborough, Cleveland TS14 8YH. The application should include full back-up information, a statement of accounts and the official charity number of the applicant.

A main grants meeting is held every three to four months to consider grants of £500 plus. Applications are processed and researched by the administrator and secretary and further information may be requested.

A small grants meeting is held monthly to consider grants up to £500.

The trust always receives more applications than it can support. Even if a project fits its policy priority areas, it may not be possible to make a grant.

Percentage of awards given to new applicants: less than 10%.

Common applicant mistakes

'Lack of information as requested in guidelines, usually financial.'

Information gathered from:

Accounts; Charity Commission record; further information provided by the funder; funder's website.

Barchester Healthcare Foundation

Health and social care

£59,000 to organisations (2012)

Beneficial area

England, Scotland and Wales.

Correspondent: Jon Hather, Correspondent, Suite 201, The Chambers, 2nd Floor, Design Centre East, Chelsea Harbour, London SW10 0XF (tel: 0800 328 3328; email: info@bhcfoundation.org.uk; website: www.bhcfoundation.org.uk)

CC Number: 1083272

The Barchester Healthcare Foundation was established in 2003 by Barchester Healthcare to reinvest into the communities it serves. It is a registered charity with independent trustees.

The trust's website states:

> We make grants available across England, Scotland and Wales to older people and other adults (18 plus) with a physical or mental disability whose health and/or social care needs cannot be met by the statutory public sector or by the individual. Our mission is to make a difference to the lives of older people and other adults with a physical or mental disability, supporting practical solutions that lead to increased personal independence, self-sufficiency and dignity.
>
> We are a unique charity that mostly helps individuals, but we also help small community groups and small local charities. We help people and groups based in England, Scotland and Wales.

In 2012 the foundation had an income of £167,000 and made grants totalling £162,000 of which £59,000 went to small charities/community groups and the remaining funds to individuals. 25 grants to organisations were over £1,000 and totalled £43,000 and 32 grants of under £1,000 went to organisations and totalled £16,000.

Beneficiary organisations were: Sefton Opera (£2,000); South Liverpool Voluntary Inclusion Programme (£1,500); and Barchester White Lodge, Canterbury Shopmobility, PHAB, Brandwood Community Centre, Galloping Grannies Community Riding Group, SERVE and Walsall Leisure Ramblers (£1,000 each).

Exclusions

Grants will not be made to community groups and small charities for:

- Core/running costs or salaries or financial support to general projects
- Indirect services such as help lines, newsletters, leaflets or research
- Major building projects or large capital projects
- Training of staff and volunteers

The trustees reserve the right to put a cap on grants to a single charity (including all of its branches) in any one year.

Applications

Application can be made via the foundation's website. A decision usually takes approximately ten weeks from the date of application.

All applications supported by Barchester Healthcare staff will be given priority.

Information gathered from:

Accounts; Charity Commission record; funder's website.

The Barham Charitable Trust

General

£57,000 (2012/13)

Beneficial area

UK.

Correspondent: The Trustees, Coutts and Co., 440 Strand, London WC2R 0QS (tel: 020 7663 6838)

Trustees: Dr John Barham; Dr Eugenia Metaxa-Barham; Coutts and Co.

CC Number: 1129728

The trust was established in 2009 for general charitable purposes.

In 2012/13 the trust had assets of £39,500 and an income of £54,500. Grants to eight organisations totalled £57,000 and ranged between £5,000 and £10,000.

Beneficiaries were: Medical Aid for Palestinians; The British Shalom Salaam Trust; War on Want; National Schizophrenia; Galilee Foundation; The Cambridge Foundation and IMET2000.

Applications

In writing to the correspondent.

Information gathered from:

Accounts; Charity Commission record.

Peter Barker-Mill Memorial Charity

General charitable purposes

Around £248,500 (2011/12)

Beneficial area

UK, with a preference for Hampshire, including Southampton.

Correspondent: Christopher Gwyn-Evans, Trustee, c/o Longdown Management Ltd, The Estate Office, Longdown, Marchwood, Southampton SO40 4UH (tel: 02380 292107; email: info@barkermillfoundation.com; website: www.barkermillfoundation.com)

Trustees: Christopher Gwyn-Evans; Tim Jobling; Richard Moyse.

CC Number: 1045479

The following information is taken from the charity's useful and informative website:

> The Barker-Mill Foundation was established in 1995 from funds provided by members of the Barker-Mill family in memory of their father and grandfather, Peter Barker-Mill.
>
> Previously known as the Peter Barker-Mill Memorial Charity, the Foundation mainly makes donations to local charities, schools, organisations and individuals needing support primarily in south west Hampshire.
>
> Whether you are a Scout group in search of funding for a new Scout hut or a charity looking to raise money for a particular project, the Barker-Mill Foundation may be able to help.
>
> Making single donations of up to £5,000, or sometimes more in special cases, the foundation has funded both large and small scale projects for numerous organisations and helped individuals in exceptional circumstances with much needed support.
>
> These donations include funding towards a new sensory room at local children's hospice, Naomi House, and financially supporting the renovation of Colbury Memorial Hall near Southampton. It has also granted funds to a local school girl, enabling her to fly to America for a life-changing operation.

In 2011/12 the trust had assets of over £3.6 million and an income of £140,000. Grants were made totalling £248,500. We do not have a breakdown of the amount given to organisations and the number of grants given to individuals.

Beneficiaries included: New Forest Ninth Centenary Trust and QK Southampton Football Club (£30,000 each); 4th New Forest Sea Scouts and Home-Start New Forest (£10,000 each); The Furzey Gardens Charitable Trust (£7,500); Redbridge Community School and Romsey Rugby Club (£5,000 each); Music at Beaulieu Trust and 10th Romsey Scout Group (£3,000 each); The Elizabeth Foundation and The Southern Spinal Injuries Trust (£2,000 each); New Forest CAB and Waterside Heritage (£1,000 each); and CLIC Sargent Cancer Care for Children (£350).

Applications

In writing to the correspondent.

Information gathered from:

Accounts; Charity Commission record; funder's website.

The Barleycorn Trust

Christian, relief of poverty, ill-health, older people, young people

£47,000 (2012)

Beneficial area

Worldwide.

Correspondent: Helen Hazelwood, Trustee, 32 Arundel Road, Sutton, Surrey SM2 6EU (email: partners@tudorjohn.co.uk)

Trustees: Helen Hazelwood; Sally Beckwith.

CC Number: 296386

This trust was formerly known as the Oasis Trust, however has since been renamed the Barleycorn Trust. According to the trustees' report for 2012: 'The object of the charity is the advancement of the Christian faith, furtherance of religious or secular education, the encouragement of missionary activity, relief of the poor and needy and help and comfort of the sick and aged.'

In 2012 its assets totalled £1.1 million, it had an income of over £39,000 and made grants totalling just over £47,000.

Beneficiaries include: Pathway (£15,000); Off the Fence (£10,000); Giving Insight (£6,000); Mustard Seed (£4,000); Romanian Aid Fund (£2,200); Hurn Zambia (£1,500); Yeldall Christian Centres, Sudbury Neighbourhood Centre, The Bridge and Kidz Club Leeds (£500 each).

Exclusions

No grants for building projects or gap year projects.

Applications

In writing to the correspondent, on no more than two sides of A4 including financial details of the proposed project.

Percentage of awards given to new applicants: between 10% and 20%.

Common applicant mistakes

'[Applications from] non-registered charities; [their] accounts do not indicate need for extra funding; building projects.'

Information gathered from:

Accounts; Charity Commission record; further information provided by the funder.

Lord Barnby's Foundation

General

£158,000 (2011/12)

Beneficial area

UK.

Correspondent: Jane Lethbridge, Secretary, PO Box 71, Plymstock, Plymouth PL8 2YP

CC Number: 251016

The foundation has established a permanent list of charities that it supports each year, with the remaining funds then distributed to other charities.

Its priority areas include the following:

- Heritage; the preservation of the environment; and the countryside and ancient buildings, particularly the 'great Anglican cathedrals'
- Charities benefiting people who are ex-service and service, Polish, disabled or refugees
- Welfare of horses and people who look after them
- Youth and other local organisations in Ashtead – Surrey, Blyth – Nottinghamshire and Bradford – Yorkshire

Many donations are also made to medical and disability charities.

In 2011/12 the trust had assets of £4.2 million, an income of £212,000 and made grants totalling £158,000.

'Permanent donations' totalled £3,000 and were given to Gurkha Welfare Trust (£2,000); and Ashtead Parochial Church Council and Blyth Parochial Church Council (£500 each).

Beneficiaries of discretionary donations included: Winston Churchill Memorial Trust (£8,000); The Joshua Project (£7,500); Canine Partners (£5,300); Christchurch Cathedral (£5,000); Cystic Fibrosis Trust and the Atlantic Salmon Trust (£2,000 each); Dame Vera Lynn Trust and Gloucester Cathedral (£1,000); RAF Wings Appeal, Leeds Templar and District Scouts and Plymouth Foyer (£500 each); and Anna Freud Centre (£200).

Exclusions

No grants to individuals.

Applications

Applications will only be considered if received in writing accompanied by a set of the latest accounts. Applicants do not need to send an sae. Appeals are considered three times a year, in February, June and November.

Percentage of awards given to new applicants: between 10% and 20%.

Information gathered from:

Accounts; Charity Commission record; further information provided by the funder.

The Barnsbury Charitable Trust

General

£81,000 (2011/12)

Beneficial area

UK, but no local charities outside Oxfordshire.

Correspondent: H. L. J. Brunner, Trustee, 26 Norham Road, Oxford OX2 6SF (tel: 01865 316431)

CC Number: 241383

In 2011/12 the trust had assets of £2.9 million and an income of £86,000. Grants were made to 46 organisations totalling £81,000.

Beneficiaries included: Oxford Chamber Music Festival (£10,000); National Trust (£8,000); Victoria History of Oxfordshire Trust (£7,500); Oxfordshire Family Mediation and Friends of Dorchester Abbey (£5,000 each); Age UK – Oxfordshire and Parochial Church Council of St John of Jerusalem, South Hackney (£2,500 each); St Margaret's War Memorial Appeal, Bookfeast and Disasters Emergency Committee (£1,000 each); and Music in Country Churches (£500).

Exclusions

No grants to individuals.

Applications

In writing to the correspondent.

Information gathered from:

Accounts; Charity Commission record.

The Barnwood House Trust

Disability and old age

£31,500 to organisations (2012)

Beneficial area

Gloucestershire.

Correspondent: Gail Rodway, Grants Manager, Ullenwood Manor Farm, Ullenwood, Cheltenham GL53 9QT (tel: 01452 614429; email: gail.rodway@barnwoodtrust.org; website: www.barnwoodtrust.org)

CC Number: 218401

General

Barnwood House Trust was established in its original form in 1792 and is now governed by a Charity Commission Scheme of 17 April 2000. It is one of Gloucestershire's largest charities providing assistance to people with disabilities, including those with mental disorders, who live in the county. Its current endowment arises principally from the sale of the land upon which Barnwood House Hospital stood until 1966.

Since the sale of the hospital the trust has developed as a provider of facilities and funding for people with disabilities. It offers grants to individuals and organisations and provides supported accommodation and day care, all of which is focused on improving opportunities and quality of life for individuals and subsequently their carers.

The trust has undergone a strategic review which means they will be phasing out services and have terminated the grants over £750 scheme. Instead the trust is running the community animation programme which aims to work in partnership with people living with disabilities and mental health problems, the voluntary and community and public sectors, and employers to strengthen capacity.

Grant Schemes

The following information is taken from the trust's website:

> On 3 May 2011 Barnwood Trust announced Unlocking Opportunities, its new ten-year investment plan which aims to transform opportunities for people with disabilities and mental health.
>
> Unlocking Opportunities will support the development of inclusive communities, where people with disabilities and mental health challenges can develop initiatives to help themselves, and each other. It will also promote the development of accessible housing and community spaces.

Currently, Barnwood Trust awards three types of grant:

- For constituted organisations
- Small Sparks – for people who want to come together in their community
- The Opportunities Award and the Wellbeing Fund – for individuals

Constituted organisations

Grants of less than £750 for organisations

Grants for holidays and play schemes are available to organisations with a demonstrable track record of providing holidays, trips or play schemes for Gloucestershire people with a disability. These grants are fast-tracked – and have a dedicated application form available from the website.

Small grants (under £750)
Awarded to organisations already known to the trust are unchanged. The application process for these grants will also remain the same – application form and instructions for applying, available from the website.

Grants for up to £750 for village halls
These grants, for the purpose of making adaptations for people with disabilities, are still available. These must meet the eligibility criteria agreed with Gloucestershire Rural Community Council. Apply to Barbara Pond at GRCC for details email bpond@grcc.org.uk or call 01452 528491.

Grants for organisations in excess of £750
The trust states:

> We no longer award open application grants for sums over £750. For the foreseeable future, the trust will be making funding available to communities across Gloucestershire on a proactive, not a reactive, basis. This means that the trust will be seeking to fund specific types of activity, not responding to requests from organisations.
>
> *The Small Sparks Fund*
> This fund has been created to help small groups of people throughout Gloucestershire to get together to do something they enjoy and make a difference to where they live.
>
> You might need gardening equipment to grow vegetables together, books or DVDs to get a club going, or wool and knitting needles for a group you are already a part of.
>
> You can apply for a grant of up to £250 if you can show us that:
> - At least one of you wanting to enjoy the activity has a disability or is an older person who would like to make more friends
> - There are at least four people involved in total
> - Everyone is prepared to contribute their time, energy and talents

For more information about Small Sparks download the checklist available from the website.

> **The Opportunities Award** gives people the chance to try something new that will enable them to move on to employment, volunteering or give them the ability to help others. It can also be used to fund training or equipment that will enhance their ability to pursue a current hobby.
>
> Some examples of what the Award could be used for include:
> - To fund a training course
> - Help towards the purchase of sporting equipment
> - Help towards equipment needed to further a hobby
> - Books, equipment or exam fees to support a training course
> - Specialist clothing for a work placement
>
> **The Wellbeing Fund** enables individuals to live independently – whether that means help with the purchase of domestic appliances, holidays, personal items, adaptations, disability-related equipment or other things that would otherwise be beyond their reach.
>
> Some previous examples include:
> - Equipment for use at home – such as riser/recliner chairs
> - Mobility aids and equipment – such as mobility deposits and pavement scooters
> - Domestic appliances – such as cookers, fridges and freezers
> - Household expenses – such as repairs, bedding and furniture
> - Sundry expenses – such as holidays and computers
>
> Grants typically range from £50 to £750.

Grantmaking in 2012

In 2012 the trust had assets of £72 million and an income of £2.4 million. Grants were made to organisations totalling just £31,500. (It is not clear whether this figure will increase, although as the trust has put a limit of £750 on grants, it may not again reach former levels of grant-giving.) A further £213,000 was awarded in grants to 745 individuals.

Previous beneficiary organisations included: Consortium of Mental Health Day Support Providers (£305,000); Crossroads Care – Cheltenham and Tewkesbury, Independence Trust and People and Places in Gloucestershire (£30,000 each); Whitefriars Sailing Club (£27,500); Stroke Association (£25,000); Forest of Dean Citizens Advice and Hop, Skip and Jump (Cotswold) (£18,000 each); Art Shape LTD, Barnwood Residents Association and Watershed Riding for the Disabled (£10,000 each).

Exclusions

Grants are not normally made in the following circumstances:
- To people or organisations outside Gloucestershire
- To people with problems relating to drugs or alcohol- unless they also have physical disabilities or a diagnosed mental illness
- To pay for funeral costs; medical equipment; private healthcare; counselling or psychotherapy; top-up nursing home fees; council tax; court fines; house purchase or rent; regular income supplements; needs of non-disabled dependents or carers

Grants will not be awarded retrospectively.

Applications

If you would like more information or to talk through your idea before applying, contact Gail Rodway, Grants Manager, on 01452 611292 or email gail.rodway@barnwoodtrust.org.

Information gathered from:

Accounts; Charity Commission record; funder's website.

The Misses Barrie Charitable Trust

Medical, general

£182,000 (2011/12)

Beneficial area

UK.

Correspondent: John A. Carter, Trustee, Raymond Carter and Co., 1b Haling Road, South Croydon CR2 6HS (tel: 020 8686 1686)

Trustees: John A. Carter; Robin Stuart Ogg; Rachel Fraser.

CC Number: 279459

This trust was established for general charitable purposes in 1979 by the late Sheila Coupar Barrie and the late Moira Morrison Barrie. The trustees support various small to medium-sized charities.

In 2011/12 the trust had assets of £5.6 million (there is a Designated Fund of £250,000 reserved for the possible future use of the Royal National Lifeboat Institution). An income of £213,000 was received and grants to 104 organisations totalled £182,000.

Beneficiaries included: Scottish Chamber Orchestra and University of Oxford Institute of Molecular Medicine (£10,000 each); East Neuk Festival (£5,000); Highlanders Museum (£3,000); Action for Blind people, Age Concern Dundee, Beating Bowel Cancer, Brighton and Hove Parents and Children Group, Croydon Voluntary Association for the Blind, Fairbridge, Hearts and Minds, I Can, Let's Face It, Lupus UK, Operation New World, Regain, Scottish Veterans' Residences, Sense, The Jennifer Trust, The Shakespeare Hospice and The Willow Trust (£2,000 each); React and Strongbones Children's Charitable Trust (£1,500 each); Addiscombe Boys and Girls Club, Ambitious About Autism, Baginton Village Hall, Braille Chess Association, CHICKS, Cued Speech, London Air Ambulance, Marine Conservation Society, Mid-Surrey Mencap, Parkinson's UK, RAFT, Raynaud's and Scleroderma Association, REHAB, RNLI, Seeing Ear, South Croydon Centre Trust, Steer Right and Wellbeing of Women (£1,000 each); and Over the Wall and The Encephalitis Society (£500 each).

Exclusions
No grants to individuals.

Applications
In writing to the correspondent accompanied, where appropriate, by up to date accounts or financial information. Trustees meet three times a year, in April, August and December.

The trustees regret that due to the large number of unsolicited applications for grants received each week they are not able to notify those which are unsuccessful.

Percentage of awards given to new applicants: between 10% and 20%.

Common applicant mistakes
'Incorrect trustees, name of charity or address.'

Information gathered from:
Accounts; Charity Commission record; further information provided by the funder.

The Bartlett Taylor Charitable Trust

General charitable purposes

£47,500 (2011/12)

Beneficial area
Preference for Oxfordshire.

Correspondent: Gareth Alty, Trustee, John Welch and Stammers, 24 Church Green, Witney, Oxfordshire OX28 4AT (tel: 01993 703941; email: galty@johnwelchandstammers.co.uk)

Trustees: Richard Bartlett; Gareth Alty; Katherine Bradley; Brenda Cook; James W. Dingle; Rosemary Warner; Ms S. Boyd.

CC Number: 285249

In 2011/12 the trust had assets of £1.8 million and an income of £177,000 which was unusually large due to the sale of land. Grants were made totalling £47,500. There were 106 grants awarded to organisations during the year which were covered in the following categories:

Local		
Community	26	£12,000
Medical	19	£8,500
Educational	6	£3,000
Other	2	£500
National		
Medical	27	£12,000
Educational	1	£250
Other	3	£1,000
International	5	£3,000
Individuals		
Relief	13	£6,000
Educational	4	£1,000

There was no list of beneficiaries available.

Applications
In writing to the correspondent. Trustees meet bi-monthly.

Information gathered from:
Accounts; Charity Commission record.

The Paul Bassham Charitable Trust

General

£444,000 (2011/12)

Beneficial area
UK, mainly Norwich and Norfolk.

Correspondent: Richard Lovett, Trustee, c/o Howes Percival, The Guildyard, 51 Colegate, Norwich NR3 1DD (tel: 01603 762103)

Trustees: Alexander Munro; Richard Lovett; Graham Tuttle; Patrick Harris.

CC Number: 266842

This trust was established in the early 1970s and has general charitable purposes. 'The trustees will seek to identify those projects where the greatest and widest benefit can be attained.'

In 2011/12 the trust had assets of £10.6 million, an income of £362,000 and made 187 grants totalling £444,000.

Beneficiaries included: Norfolk Community Foundation, Norwich Historic Churches and Norfolk Archaeological Trust (£10,000 each); Community Action Norwich (£7,000); MAP, Solo Housing and British Wireless for the Blind (£5,000 each); Norfolk County Council (Castle Museum) (£3,000); The Friends of Norfolk and Norwich University Hospital, RSPB, Norwich Cathedral and Norfolk Eating Disorder Association (£2,000 each); and Motor Neurone Disease Association, Costessey Baptist Church, Whizz-Kids and Bliss (£1,000 each).

Exclusions
Grant are not be made directly to individuals, nor to unregistered organisations.

Applications
Only in writing to the correspondent – no formal application forms issued. Telephone enquiries are not invited because of administrative costs. The trustees meet quarterly to consider general applications.

Percentage of awards given to new applicants: between 20% and 30%.

Common applicant mistakes
'Insufficient information to determine public benefit.'

Information gathered from:
Accounts; Charity Commission record; further information provided by the funder.

The Batchworth Trust

Medical, humanitarian aid, social welfare, general

£362,000 (2012/13)

Beneficial area
Worldwide.

Correspondent: Martin R. Neve, Administrative Executive, Haines Watts LLP, 3rd Floor, Consort House, Consort Way, Horley, Surrey RH6 7AF (tel: 01293 776411; email: mneve@hwca.com)

Trustee: Lockwell Trustees Ltd.

CC Number: 245061

The trust mainly supports nationally-recognised charities in a wide range of areas.

In 2011/12 it had assets of £12.3 million and an income of £394,000. Grants were made to 44 organisations totalling £362,000.

The trust has previously informed us that: 'The trustees have a policy of mainly distributing to nationally recognised charities but consider other charities where they felt a grant would be of significant benefit when matched with other funds to launch a new enterprise or initiative'.

During the year grants were mainly for medical research, youth charities and welfare both in the UK and overseas.

Beneficiaries included: The Francis Crick Institute (£30,000); Roger Feneley Project (£20,000); MOSS (£13,000); Blue Elephant Theatre, Copenhagen Youth Project, Crisis UK Re Oxford, International Red Cross – Syria, Oxfordshire Relate, Practical Action and The Archie Foundation (£10,000 each); Action Aid – Malawi (£5,000); Royal Highland Educational Trust (£3,000); and Dumfries and Galloway Arts Festival (£1,000).

Exclusions
No applications from individuals can be considered.

Applications
In writing to the correspondent. An sae should be included if a reply is required.

Information gathered from:
Accounts; Charity Commission record.

Bay Charitable Trust

Jewish

Around £583,000 (2012)

Beneficial area

UK and overseas.

Correspondent: Ian Kreditor, Trustee, Hermolis House, Abbeydale Road, Wembley, Middlesex HA0 1AY (tel: 020 8810 4321)

Trustees: Ian Kreditor; Michael Lisser.

CC Number: 1060537

Registered with the Charity Commission in February 2007, the objects of the charity are 'to give charity for the relief of poverty and the advancement of traditions of the Orthodox Jewish Religion and the study of Torah.'

In 2012 the trust had assets of £1 million and an income of nearly £1.2 million from donations. Grants totalled £583,000 and were payable to both individuals and organisations. There was no list of beneficiaries within the yearly accounts.

Applications

In writing to the correspondent.

Information gathered from:

Accounts; Charity Commission record.

The Bay Tree Charitable Trust

Development work, general

£130,000 (2012)

Beneficial area

UK and overseas.

Correspondent: The Trustees, PO Box 53983, London SW15 1VT

Trustees: Ian Benton; Emma Benton; Paul Benton.

CC Number: 1044091

This trust was established in 1994 for general charitable purposes. In 2012 it had assets of £3.5 million, an income of £122,000 and made 17 grants totalling £130,000.

Beneficiaries included: Age UK (£20,000); Combat Stress, Samaritans and Shelter (£10,000 each); and Bipolar UK, FareShare, Greenfingers and Support Dogs (£5,000 each).

Exclusions

No grants to individuals.

Applications

The 2012 accounts advise:

> All appeals should be by letter containing the following:
> - Aims and objectives of the charity
> - Nature of appeal
> - Total target if for a specific project
> - Contributions received against target
> - Registered charity number
> - Any other relevant factors
>
> Letters should be accompanied by a set of the charitable organisation's latest report and full accounts.

Information gathered from:

Accounts; Charity Commission record.

The Beacon Trust

Christian

£22,000 (2011/12)

Beneficial area

Mainly UK, but also some overseas (usually in the British Commonwealth) and Spain and Portugal.

Correspondent: Grahame Scofield, 3 Newhouse Business Centre, Old Crawley Road, Horsham, West Sussex RH12 4RU (tel: 01293 851715)

Trustees: Jillian Spink; Martin Spink; Joanna Benson.

CC Number: 230087

The trust's objects are 'to advance the Christian faith, relieve poverty and advance education'.

In 2011/12 the trust had assets of £2.5 million, an income of £52,000 and made grants totalling £22,000.

The emphasis of the trust's support is on Christian work overseas, particularly amongst students, although the trust does not support individuals. The trust has previously stated that it has a list of charities that it supports in most years. This leaves very little funds available for unsolicited applications.

Beneficiaries included: Latin Link (£5,000); Bible Society and Arocha (£4,000 each); Arbon Markland Project (£3,000); Alan Palister (£2,000); FEBA and Fegan's Homes (£1,500 each); L'Abri (£600); and David Cotton (£500).

Exclusions

Applications from individuals are not considered.

Applications

The trust does not respond to unsolicited applications.

Information gathered from:

Accounts; Charity Commission record.

Bear Mordechai Ltd

Jewish causes

£201,000 (2011/12)

Beneficial area

Worldwide.

Correspondent: Yechiel Benedikt, Trustee, 40 Fountayne Road, London N16 7DT

Trustees: Chaim Benedikt; Eliezer Benedikt; Yechiel Benedikt.

CC Number: 286806

Grants are made to Jewish organisations. The 2011/12 annual report states that the charity is established to advance religion in accordance with the Orthodox Jewish faith and other charitable purposes.

In 2011/12 this trust had assets of £1.5 million, an income of £188,000 and made grants totalling £201,000. There was no list of beneficiary organisations included in the accounts.

Previous beneficiaries have included: Agudat Yad Yemin Jerusalem, Almat, Chevras Mo'oz Ladol, Craven Walk Charities Trust, Havenpoint, Keren Tzedaka Vachesed, Lolev, UTA and Yetev Lev Yerusholaim.

Applications

In writing to the correspondent.

Information gathered from:

Accounts; Charity Commission record.

The Jack and Ada Beattie Foundation

Social welfare, injustice and inequality

£23,000 to individuals and organisations (2012/13)

Beneficial area

The Midlands and London.

Correspondent: Alexandra Taliadoros, Director, 203 Larna House, 116 Commercial Street, London E1 6NF (tel: 020 3287 8427; email: info@beattiefoundation.com; website: www.beattiefoundation.com)

Trustees: Trevor Beattie; Peter Beattie; Paul Beattie.

CC Number: 1142892

The foundation was established in July 2011 by Trevor Beattie, a marketing executive of the advertising company, Beattie McGuinness Bungay.

> I set up The Jack and Ada Beattie Foundation in honour and memory of my parents. It will adhere to their life-long held principles of fair play, care for the vulnerable and getting the job done. It will fight against inequality in all its forms

(when you come from a family of ten, you soon learn the importance of equality . . .) and it will probably bear the Beattie family trait of defiance in the face of adversity.

The following information is from the foundation's website:

Eligibility

- The Jack and Ada Beattie Foundation seeks to support those facing social injustice and inequality in the Midlands and London
- Our funding priorities are: Dignity; Freedom; and Sanctuary
- The foundation accepts applications from charitable organisations under these headings – please tailor your applications accordingly
- We are interested in funding credible projects with measured objectives and deliverable tangible outcomes
- The foundation holds an open grant programme for individuals facing social injustice and inequality

Guidelines for organisations

Proposal

- To apply, please send us a proposal
- For organisations, outline your project and anticipated achievements
- For individuals, give a summary of your situation

you can download guidelines for proposals from the website, along with our Data Protection policy

it would prove helpful if you detailed how your project is aligned to the foundation's objectives and values and how support from us can help your results

Application

- If your proposal is successful, we will invite you to submit an application
- You can download application forms for organisations and individuals to the right, along with our Data Protection policy
- Individual applicants must submit two references and identity documentation along with their application
- More information on this can be found within the Guidelines for Individual Applicants and our Data Protection policy

Evaluation

- All successful applicants are required to submit a project-end report illustrating the achievements as a direct result of the support provided by the Foundation
- Evaluative reports must be received before 12 weeks have passed from the project finish
- The Jack and Ada Beattie Foundation reserves the right to arrange a visit to the applicant/recipient of funding for monitoring and evaluation purposes
- Please note, recipients of support are asked to display the Jack and Ada Beattie Foundation's logo on all relevant material

The foundation also makes grants directly to individuals through its Fund for the Forgotten.

In 2012/13 the foundation had assets of £53,000, an income of £109,000 and made grants totalling £23,000. 'Charitable activities' were listed as £83,000 and this figure included administration and support costs such as salaries of £42,000.

Beneficiary organisations included: Contact the Elderly, Coventry Foodbank, Richard House Children's Hospice, Sense, SIFA Fireside, St Mungo's and Thrive.

Applications

Initial proposals should be emailed to the foundation. Eligible applicants will then be notified if the foundation is interested in receiving a full application, which is made using a form available on the foundation's website.

If your application is successful you will be required to monitor and evaluate the project and report back to the foundation. Details will be sent with the grant.

Application forms will only be accepted by email unless there are exceptional circumstances. Contact the foundation director if you have any queries.

The foundation endeavours to acknowledge each stage of the application process. Decisions will be reached within two months of each stage.

Percentage of awards given to new applicants: between 40% and 50%.

Common applicant mistakes

'Not relevant geographically. We receive applications from similar organisations to those we've just funded – we like diversity.'

Information gathered from:

Accounts; Charity Commission record; further information provided by the funder; funder's website.

Beauland Ltd

Jewish causes

£318,000 (2011/12)

Beneficial area

Worldwide, with some preference for the Manchester area.

Correspondent: Maurice Neumann, Trustee, 32 Stanley Road, Salford M7 4ES

Trustees: Fanny Neumann; Henry Neumann; Miriam Friedlander; Hannah Rosemann; Janet Bleier; Rebecca Delange; Maurice Neumann; Pinchas Neumann; E. Neumann; Esther Henry.

CC Number: 511374

The trust's objects are the advancement of the Jewish religion in accordance with the Orthodox Jewish faith and the relief of poverty. Most grants are made to educational institutions (including adult education) and institutions for the relief of poverty; although depending on the circumstances the trust may award a large donation to 'any particular cause that may arise in any year'.

In 2011/12 the trust had assets of £3.5 million and an income of £489,000. Grants totalled £318,000.

A list of beneficiaries was not available for 2011/12 but in previous years grants have included those to Asos Chesed, Cosmon Belz, Famos Charity Trust, Radford Education Trust, Sunderland Yeshiva and Yetev Lev.

Applications

In writing to the correspondent.

Information gathered from:

Accounts; Charity Commission record.

The Beaverbrook Foundation

General

£145,000 (2011/12)

Beneficial area

UK and Canada.

Correspondent: Ms Ford, Correspondent, Third Floor, 11/12 Dover Street, London W1S 4LJ (tel: 020 7042 9435; email: jane@beaverbrookfoundation.org; website: www.beaverbrookfoundation.org)

Trustees: Lord Beaverbrook; Lady Beaverbrook; Lady Aitken; Hon. Laura Levi; John Kidd; Hon. Maxwell Aitken.

CC Number: 310003

The objects of this foundation include:

- The erection or improvement of the fabric of any church building
- The purchase of books, papers, manuscripts or works of art
- Care of the aged or infirm in the UK

The Beaverbrook Foundation supports a variety of causes in the United Kingdom and Canada, including preserving heritage buildings and supporting charitable appeals. We have given three lifeboats to the British RNLI, and supported over 700 separate charitable bodies in the last fifty years. The Foundation has also been entrusted with various important collections of art, political cartoons and political papers, which we look after for future generations.

In 2011/12 the foundation had assets of £11.5 million and an income of £58,500. Grants to organisations totalled £145,000.

Grant beneficiaries include: Battle of Britain Memorial Trust (£80,000); RNLI (£12,000); Bright Ideas Trust (£10,000); Saints and Sinners Trust (£5,000); London Air Ambulance and Starlight

Children's Foundation (£2,000 each); and a number of other grants for under £2,000 each totalling £17,000.

Exclusions

Only registered charities are supported.

Applications

There is an online application form at the foundation's website.

Percentage of awards given to new applicants: between 40% and 50%.

Information gathered from:

Accounts; Charity Commission record; further information provided by the funder; funder's website.

The Becker Family Charitable Trust

General charitable purposes, Orthodox Jewish causes

£51,000 (2011/12)

Beneficial area

UK and overseas.

Correspondent: Allan Becker, Trustee, 33 Sinclair Grove, London NW11 9JH

Trustees: Allan Becker; Ruth Becker; Deanna Fried.

CC Number: 1047968

The trust makes grants for general charitable purposes, particularly to Orthodox Jewish organisations.

In 2011/12 the trust had assets of £329,000 and an income of £42,000, mainly from donations. Grants were made to organisations totalling £51,000.

Unfortunately a list of beneficiaries was not included with the accounts but previous beneficiaries have included: Keren Shabbas, Lolev CT, Menora Grammar School, Torah Temima and WST.

Applications

In writing to the correspondent. However, note that the trust has previously stated that its funds were fully committed.

Information gathered from:

Accounts; Charity Commission record.

The Peter Beckwith Charitable Trust

Medical, welfare, general charitable purposes

Around £30,000 (2011/12)

Beneficial area

UK.

Correspondent: Peter Beckwith, Trustee, Hill Place House, 55a High Street, Wimbledon Village, London SW19 5BA (tel: 020 8944 1288)

Trustees: Peter Beckwith; Clare Van Dam; Tamara Veroni.

CC Number: 802113

This trust was established in 1989. In 2011/12 it had an income of £21,000 and a total expenditure of £30,000.

Previous beneficiaries included: Wimbledon and Putney Common Conservators (£10,000); Richmond Theatre (£5,000); Imperial War Museum (£2,000); and BAAF, ORCHID and Starlight Children's Foundation (£1,000 each).

Applications

In writing to the correspondent.

Information gathered from:

Accounts; Charity Commission record.

The John Beckwith Charitable Trust

Sport, youth, education, social welfare, medical research, arts

£556,000 (2011/12)

Beneficial area

UK and overseas.

Correspondent: Ms Sally Holder, Administrator, 124 Sloane Street, London SW1X 9BW (tel: 020 7225 2250)

Trustees: Sir John Beckwith; Heather Beckwith; Christopher Meech.

CC Number: 800276

This trust is established for general charitable purposes with a preference for: sports programmes for young people; education; children's charities; medical research; the arts; and charities involved with overseas aid.

In 2011/12 it had assets of £1.2 million and an income of £322,000. There were 47 grants made totalling £556,000, broken down as follows:

Sport	£434,000	2
Social welfare	£56,000	34
Education	£46,000	4
Medical research	£20,000	7

The accounts listed 39 donations by far the largest was awarded to International Inspiration (£433,000). Other beneficiaries included: Wycombe Abbey School (£46,000); RNIB (£20,500); Great Ormond Street Children's Charity (£14,000); Rekindle (£5,000); Crisis (£2,000); New Ways (£1,500); and British Red Cross, Changing Faces, Dogs Trust, Parkinson's Disease Society, Shining Faces in India and Vision for Africa (£1,000 each).

Unlisted grants totalled £2,500.

Applications

In writing to the correspondent.

Information gathered from:

Accounts; Charity Commission record.

The Bedfordshire and Hertfordshire Historic Churches Trust

Churches

£169,500 (2011/12)

Beneficial area

Bedfordshire, Hertfordshire and that part of Barnet within the Diocese of St Albans.

Correspondent: Archie Russell, Grants Secretary, Wychbrook, 31 Ivel Gardens, Biggleswade, Bedfordshire SG18 0AN (tel: 01767 312966; email: grants@yahoo.co.uk; website: www.bedshertshct.org.uk)

Trustees: Stuart Russell; Aymeric Jenkins; Richard Genochio; Peter Griffiths; Jim May; Terry Warburton; Dr Christopher Green; P. Lepper; William Masterson.

CC Number: 1005697

The trust gives grants for the restoration, preservation, repair and maintenance of churches in Bedfordshire, Hertfordshire and that part of Barnet within the Diocese of St Albans. Annual income comes from member subscription and from the annual 'Bike 'n Hike' event. The trust also acts as a distributive agent for church grants made by the Wixamtree Trust and Waste Recycling Environmental Ltd (WREN).

In 2011/12 the trust had assets of £220,500 and an income of £206,000. There were 34 grants made totalling £169,500, which were in the range of £1,000 and £15,000.

Beneficiary Churches included: St Peter – Arlesey, St Lawrence – Ayot, St Mary – Haynes, St Catherine – Sacombe, All Saints – Sandon, All Saints – Shillington, St George – Toddington, St Mary – Westmill and St Michael and All Angels – Woolmer.

Exclusions

No grants to individuals.

Applications

Initial enquiries should be made to the grants secretary. Applications can only be made by members of the trust.

Information gathered from:

Accounts; Charity Commission record; funder's website.

The David and Ruth Behrend Fund

General charitable purposes

£67,000 (2011/12)

Beneficial area

UK, with a preference for Merseyside.

Correspondent: The Secretary, 151 Dale Street, Liverpool L2 2AH (tel: 01512 275177; website: www.merseytrusts.org.uk)

Trustee: Liverpool Charity and Voluntary Services.

CC Number: 261567

'The fund was established to make grants for charitable purposes. Grants are only made to charities known to the settlors and unsolicited applications are therefore not considered.' Set up in 1969, it appears to give exclusively in Merseyside.

In 2011/12 the fund had assets of £1.4 million and an income of £86,000. Grants totalled £67,000. There were 26 listed beneficiaries in receipt of grants of £1,000 or more.

Beneficiaries included: Merseyside Development Foundation (£6,000); Digital Production for Disabled People, Merseyside Somali Community Association, Porchfield Community Association, Top Spin Table Tennis Club, Tuebrook Community Centre Group and Wavertree Garden Suburb Institute (£2,000 each); and Bethlehem Community, British Red Cross, LGBT Choir Liverpool, Merseyside Holiday Service, Save the Children, Sheila Kay Fund, Support for Asylum Seekers and WAM Friendship Centre (£1,000 each).

Applications

This fund states that it does not respond to unsolicited applications. 'The charity only makes grants to charities already known to the settlors as this is a personal charitable trust.'

Common applicant mistakes

'Applying to a personal charitable trust.'

Information gathered from:

Accounts; Charity Commission record; funder's website.

Bellasis Trust

General charitable purposes

£31,500 (2011/12)

Beneficial area

UK.

Correspondent: Paul Wates, Trustee, Bellasis House, Headley Heath Approach, Mickleham, Dorking, Surrey RH5 6DH (tel: 01372 861058)

Trustees: Paul Wates; Annette Wates; Annabelle Elliott.

CC Number: 1085972

Established in March 2001, it is the 'intention of the trustees to support local charities including those for the disadvantaged persons'.

In 2011/12 the trust had assets of £936,000 and an income of £36,000. Grants were made to 25 different causes totalling £31,500.

There were 12 beneficiaries of £500 or more listed in the accounts. They included: Royal Horticultural Society and Wheelpower (£5,000 each); Institute of Economic Affairs (£4,000); Foundation for Social and Economic Thinking (£2,000); and Disability Sport and Walk the Walk (£1,000 each).

Applications

'The trustees research and consider applicants for grants.'

Information gathered from:

Accounts; Charity Commission record.

The Benham Charitable Settlement

General charitable purposes

£140,000 (2011/12)

Beneficial area

UK, with very strong emphasis on Northamptonshire.

Correspondent: The Secretary, Hurstbourne, Portnall Drive, Virginia Water, Surrey GU25 4NR

Trustees: Mrs M. M. Tittle; Lady Hutton; E. N. Langley; D. A. H. Tittle; Revd. J. A. Nickols.

CC Number: 239371

The charity was founded in 1964 by the late Cedric Benham and his wife Hilda, then resident in Northamptonshire, 'to benefit charities and other good causes and considerations'.

The object of the charity is the support of registered charities working in many different fields – including charities involved in medical research, disability, elderly people, children and young people, disadvantaged people, overseas aid, missions to seamen, the welfare of ex-servicemen, wildlife, the environment, and the arts. The trust also supports the Church of England, and the work of Christian mission throughout the world. Special emphasis is placed upon those churches and charitable organisations within the county of Northamptonshire [especially as far as new applicants are concerned].

In 2011/12 the charity had assets of £5.2 million and an income of £207,000. It made donations totalling £140,000 with the majority of grants ranging from £200 to £700.

Grants can be analysed as follows:

one-off cause (Northamptonshire Association of Youth Clubs)	1	£30,000
medical	35	£22,000
general	14	£15,000
persons with disabilities	31	£15,500
overseas aid and mission	12	£13,000
children, youth and schools	14	£11,500
elderly	16	£8,500
Christian mission	11	£12,000
church maintenance	13	£7,000
wildlife and conservation	9	£4,200
art and sport	3	£1,500
animal welfare	2	£800

Beneficiaries included: Northamptonshire Association of Youth Clubs (£30,000); William Wilberforce Trust (£6,000); Zimbabwe A National Emergency (£3,000); LifeCentre (£2,000); British Red Cross (£1,000); Anglo Peruvian Child Care Mission (£600); Action on Poverty, Tall Ships Youth Trust and Willen Hospice (£500 each); and Y Care International (£400).

Exclusions

No grants to individuals.

Applications

In recent years the trust has not been considering new applications.

Information gathered from:

Accounts; Charity Commission record.

Michael and Leslie Bennett Charitable Trust

Jewish

£39,000 (2011/12)

Beneficial area

UK.

Correspondent: Michael Bennett, Trustee, Bedegars Lea, Kenwood Close, London NW3 7JL (tel: 020 8458 4945)

Trustees: Michael Bennett; Lesley V. Bennett.

CC Number: 1047611

The trust supports a range of causes, but the largest donations are usually to Jewish organisations.

In 2011/12 the trust had assets of £291,000 and an income of £34,000. There were 30 grants made totalling £39,000.

Grants of £1,000 or more were made to eight organisations: World Jewish Relief (£10,000); Jewish Care (£8,500); Community Security Trust (£5,000); Chai Cancer Care and Norwood Ravenswood (£3,000 each); Magen David Adom and Nightingale Hammerson

(£2,500 each); and Anglo Israel Association (£1,400).

There were also 18 grants of less than £1,000, totalling £3,200.

Applications

In writing to the correspondent.

Information gathered from:

Accounts; Charity Commission record.

The Ruth Berkowitz Charitable Trust

Jewish, medical research, youth, general charitable purposes

£677,000 (2011/12)

Beneficial area

UK and overseas.

Correspondent: The Trustees, 39 Farm Avenue, London NW2 2BJ

Trustees: Philip Beckman; Brian Beckman.

CC Number: 1111673

Established for general charitable purposes, the trustees' current grantmaking policy is to make modest grants to numerous qualifying charities and some larger grants for specific projects. Grants are mostly made to Jewish organisations.

In 2011/12 the trust had assets of £3.8 million, an income of £104,000 and gave grants totalling £677,000, broken down as follows:

Children/youth/education	£321,000
Community and welfare	£253,000
Medical	£73,000
Small Grants Fund	£32,000

Beneficiaries included: Community Security Trust (£55,000); World Jewish Relief (£47,000); Bnai Nrith Hillel Foundation/Union of Jewish Students (£46,000); The Institute of Jewish Studies (£43,000); Magen David Adom UK (£35,000); Lord Ashdown Charitable Settlement (£32,000); Marie Curie cancer Care (£30,000); World ORT (£20,000); Nightingale House (£18,000); Jewish Women's Aid (£15,000); Simon Marks Jewish Primary School Trust (£10,000); British Friends of United Hatzalah Israel (£5,000); and One to One Children's Fund (£2,000).

Applications

The trustees stated in their annual report that as the trust is not reactive they will 'generally only make grants to charities that are known to them and will not normally respond to unsolicited requests for assistance. There is no application form.'

Information gathered from:

Accounts; Charity Commission record.

The Bestway Foundation

Education, welfare, medical

£497,000 to UK organisations (2011/12)

Beneficial area

UK and overseas.

Correspondent: M. Y. Sheikh, Trustee, Bestway Cash and Carry Ltd, Abbey Road, Park Royal, London NW10 7BW (tel: 020 8453 1234; email: zulfikaur.wajid-hasan@bestway.co.uk; website: www.bestwaygroup.co.uk/page/bestway-foundation)

Trustees: A. K. Bhatti; A. K. Chaudhary; M. Y. Sheikh; Z. M. Choudrey; M. A. Pervez.

CC Number: 297178

The objects of this foundation are the 'advancement of education by grants to schoolchildren and students who are of Indian, Pakistani, Bangladeshi or Sri Lankan origin; relief of sickness, and preservation and protection of health in the UK and overseas, especially in India, Pakistan, Bangladesh and Sri Lanka'. Grants are made to individuals, UK registered charities, non-registered charities and overseas charities. All trustees are directors and shareholders of Bestway (Holdings) Ltd, the parent company of Bestway Cash and Carry Ltd.

In 2011/12 this trust had assets of over £5.7 million, an income of £822,000 and made grants totalling £497,000 to 20 charities in the UK. £184,000 was awarded to foreign charities and individuals making a total of £681,000 in grants.

Grant beneficiaries included: Bestway Foundation Pakistan (£200,000); Imran Khan Cancer Appeal (£100,000); Crimestoppers (£34,000); Duke of Edinburgh Awards (£15,000); SOS Children's Villages (£5,000); British Pakistan Foundation (£4,000); The Priory School and John Ferneley College (£3,000 each); The Coexistence Trust and Silver Star Appeal (£2,000 each); and The Royal Commonwealth Society (£1,000).

Applications

In writing to the correspondent, enclosing an sae. Applications are considered in March/April. Telephone calls are not welcome.

Information gathered from:

Accounts; Charity Commission record; funder's website.

The Billmeir Charitable Trust

General, health and medical

£117,000 (2011/12)

Beneficial area

UK, with a preference for the Surrey area, specifically Elstead, Tilford, Farnham and Frensham.

Correspondent: Keith Lawrence, Secretary, Moore Stephens, 150 Aldersgate Street, London EC1A 4AB (tel: 020 7334 9191)

Trustees: Max Whitaker; Suzanne Marriott; Jason Whitaker.

CC Number: 208561

The trust states it supports a wide variety of causes. About a quarter of the grants are given to health and medical charities and about a third of the grants are given to local organisations in Surrey, especially the Farnham, Frensham, Elstead and Tilford areas.

In 2011/12 the trust had assets of £4.1 million, which generated an income of £191,000. Donations were made to 25 charities totalling £117,000, the majority of beneficiaries had received grants in previous years.

Beneficiaries included: Reed's School – Cobham (£10,000); Marlborough College (£8,000); Arundel Castle Cricket Foundation and Old Kiln Museum Trust (£7,000 each); RNIB and Woodlarks Campsite Trust (£5,000 each); Elstead Pavilion (£3,000); and Cancer Vaccine and Broomwood Hall School (£2,000 each).

Applications

The trust states that it does not request applications and they are very rarely successful.

Information gathered from:

Accounts; Charity Commission record.

The Bintaub Charitable Trust

Jewish, medical and youth

£33,000 (2011/12)

Beneficial area

Greater London, worldwide.

Correspondent: J. Wahnon, Secretary, Ki Tob Chartered Accountants, 125 Wolmer Gardens, Edgware HA8 8QF

Trustees: James Frohwein; Tonia Frohwein; Dahlia Rosenberg; Rabbi Eliot Stefansky.

CC Number: 1003915

This trust was set up in 1991 and provides grants to mainly London organisations, towards 'the advancement of education in and the religion of the Orthodox Jewish faith'. Grants are also given for other charitable causes, mainly towards medical and children's work.

In 2011/12 it had an income from donations of £38,000 and made grants totalling £33,000.

Beneficiaries included: Menorah Foundation School (£4,400); Yeshivah L'zeirnim (£3,000); Kupat Ha'ir (£2,600); Va'ad Harabbanim L'inyanei Tzedaka (£2,300); Jewish Teachers Training College (£2,000); and Midreshet Moriah (£1,600).

Applications

The trust has previously stated that new applications are not being accepted.

Information gathered from:

Accounts; Charity Commission record.

The Birmingham Hospital Saturday Fund Medical Charity and Welfare Trust

Medical

Around £27,000 (2012)

Beneficial area

UK, but mostly centred around the West Midlands and Birmingham area.

Correspondent: Philip Ashbourne, Correspondent, Gamgee House, 2 Darnley Road, Birmingham B16 8TE (tel: 01214 543601; email: charitabletrust@bhsf.co.uk)

CC Number: 502428

This trust supports the relief of sickness, with the trustees also having an interest in medical research. The trustees continue to give priority to charities that benefit those living in the West Midlands area with some interest in the south west for historical reasons. The trust no longer receives an income from the parent company and so the trustees are now working purely with reserves and the interest from them. This has resulted in a more critical look at projects at each meeting and donations are now generally less than £2,000. Projects that are appropriate and reflect well thought through projects with realistic cost breakdowns are given greater consideration.

In 2012 the trust had an income of just £550 and a total expenditure of £27,000. Income has been below £5,000 for the fourth year running (2008: £22,000) but expenditure has increased from last year (2011: £17,000). Full accounts were not required at the Charity Commission due to the low income this year and therefore further details on grants and beneficiaries were not available.

Previous beneficiaries included: Friends of Victoria School – Northfield (£3,800); NHS West Midlands (£3,400); Birmingham Centre for Arts Therapies and Starlight Children's Foundation (£2,500 each); Vascular Department, Selly Oak Hospital (£2,000); Dream Holidays, Isle of Wight (£1,900); the Mary Stevens Hospice, Stourbridge, West Midlands (£1,600); Institute of Ageing and Health, Birmingham (£1,500); Contact the Elderly, Birmingham (£1,200); Christian Lewis Trust – Cardiff (£1,100); Action Medical Research – Horsham, Children's Heart Foundation and REACT Surrey (£1,000); Katherine House – Stafford (£900); St Martin's Centre for Health and Healing (£750); Deep Impact Theatre Company and Birmingham Heart Care – Walsall (£500 each); and Acorns Children's Hospice – Birmingham (£315).

Exclusions

The trust will not generally fund: direct appeals from individuals or students; administration expenditure including salaries; bank loans/deficits/mortgages; items or services which should normally be publicly funded; large general appeals; vehicle operating costs; or motor vehicles for infrequent use and where subsidised vehicle share schemes are available to charitable organisations.

Applications

On a form available from the correspondent. The form requires basic information and should be submitted with financial details. Evidence should be provided that the project has been adequately considered through the provision of quotes or supporting documents, although the trust dislikes applications which provide too much general information or have long-winded descriptions of projects. Applicants should take great care to read the guidance notes on the application form. The trustees meet four times a year and deadlines are given when application forms are sent out.

Information gathered from:

Accounts; Charity Commission record.

Birthday House Trust

General

£50,000 to organisations (2011)

Beneficial area

England and Wales.

Correspondent: Laura Gosling, Trust Administrator, c/o Millbank Financial Services4th FloorSwan House17–19 Stratford PlaceLondonW1C 1BQ (tel: 020 7907 2100; email: charity@mfs.co.uk)

CC Number: 248028

Established in 1966, the main work of this trust is engaged with the running of a residential home for people who are elderly in Midhurst, West Sussex. In 2011 it had assets of £6.3 million and an income of £212,000. Grants to 12 organisations totalled £50,000. A further £50,000 was distributed to pensioners.

Beneficiaries were: Druk White Loftus School (£20,000); Climate Parliament and Merton Road Scouts (£10,000 each); Soil Association and The Ecology Trust (£2,500 each); Chichester Cathedral Trust (£2,000); Smile Support and Care (£1,000); Chichester Area Mind, Eastbourne Scout and Guide Hut Committee and Fire Services National Benevolent Fund (£500 each); and Murray Downland Trust (£50).

Exclusions

No applications will be considered from individuals or non-charitable organisations.

Applications

In writing to the correspondent, including an sae. No application forms are issued and there is no deadline. Only successful applicants are acknowledged.

Information gathered from:

Accounts for the latest year available at the time of writing; Charity Commission record.

Miss Jeanne Bisgood's Charitable Trust

Roman Catholic purposes, older people

£199,000 (2011/12)

Beneficial area

UK, overseas and locally in Bournemouth and Dorset, especially Poole.

Correspondent: Jeanne Bisgood, Trustee, 12 Waters Edge, Brudenell Road, Poole BH13 7NN (tel: 01202 708460)

CC Number: 208714

This trust has emerged following an amalgamation of the Bisgood Trust with Miss Jeanne Bisgood's Charitable Trust. Both trusts had the same objectives.

The General Fund has the following priorities:

1 Roman Catholic charities
2 Charities benefiting people in Poole, Bournemouth and the county of Dorset
3 National charities for the benefit of older people

No grants are made to local charities which do not fall under categories 1 or 2. Many health and welfare charities are supported as well as charities working in relief and development overseas.

In 2011/12 the trust had assets of £5.3 million, an income of £161,000 and made donations to charities totalling £199,000.

Previous beneficiaries from the general fund have included Apex Trust, ITDG, Horder Centre for Arthritis, Impact, St Barnabas' Society, St Francis Leprosy Guild, Sight Savers International and YMCA.

In considering appeals the trustees will give preference to charities whose fundraising and administrative costs are proportionately low.

The trust was given 12 paintings to be held as part of the trust funds. Most of the paintings were sold and the proceeds were placed in a sub-fund, the Bertram Fund, established in 1998, the income of which is purely for Roman Catholic causes. It is intended that it will primarily support major capital projects. Most grants are made anonymously from this fund.

Exclusions

Grants are not given to local charities which do not fit categories 1 or 2 listed in the general section. Individuals and non-registered charities are not supported.

Applications

In writing to the correspondent, quoting the UK registration number and registered title of the charity. A copy of the most recent accounts should also be enclosed. Applications should NOT be made directly to the Bertram Fund. Applications for capital projects 'should provide brief details of the main purposes, the total target and the current state of the appeal'. The trustees regret that they are unable to acknowledge appeals. The trustees normally meet in late February/early March and September.

The trust deed contains a proviso that 'the settlor as long as she is a trustee may make donations out of the income of the trust fund without consulting the other trustees'. The settlor (Jeanne Bisgood) has agreed that she will only do this in relation to donations of £100 or less.

Information gathered from:

Accounts; Charity Commission record.

The Sydney Black Charitable Trust

Evangelical Christianity, social welfare, young people

£58,000 (2011/12)

Correspondent: Jennifer Crabtree, Trustee, 30 Welford Place, London SW19 5AJ

Trustees: Jennifer Crabtree; Hilary Dickenson; Stephen Crabtree; Philip Crabtree.

CC Number: 219855

In 2001 The Edna Black Charitable Trust and The Cyril Black Charitable Trust were incorporated into this trust.

In 2011/12 the trust had assets totalling £3 million and an income of £71,000. Grants totalled £58,000. Unfortunately there was no list of grantees but a previous beneficiary was Endeavour, with an unusually large grant of £20,000. Grants are generally in the region of £125 and £250 each.

Applications

In writing to the correspondent.

Percentage of awards given to new applicants: less than 10%.

Information gathered from:

Accounts; Charity Commission record; further information provided by the funder.

The Bertie Black Foundation

Jewish, general

£220,000 (2011/12)

Beneficial area

UK, Israel.

Correspondent: Harry Black, Trustee, Abbots House, 13 Beaumont Gate, Shenley Hill, Radlett, Hertfordshire WD7 7AR (tel: 01923 850096; email: sonneborn@btconnect.com)

Trustees: Isabelle Seddon; Doris Black; Carolyn Black; Harry Black; Ivor Seddon.

CC Number: 245207

The trust tends to support organisations which are known to the trustees or where long-term commitments have been entered into. Grants can be given over a three-year period towards major projects.

Accounts and annual report for 2011/12 had been received at the Charity Commission but, in error, only the independent examiner's statement page was published online. Basic information is taken from the Commission's website.

In 2011/12 the foundation had an income of £103,000 and a total expenditure of £238,000.

Previous beneficiaries included: I Rescue (£50,000); Magen David Adom (£47,000 in three grants); Alyn Hospital (£49,000 in two grants); Emunah (£38,000); Laniardo Hospital and Shaare Zedek (£25,000 each); Friends of Israel Sports Centre for Disabled (£20,000); Child Resettlement Trust (£10,000 in four grants); Norwood (£7,600 in four grants); and Hope (£5,200 in four grants).

Applications

The trust states it 'supports causes known to the trustees' and that they 'do not respond to unsolicited requests'.

Information gathered from:

Accounts; Charity Commission record.

Sir Alec Black's Charity

Relief in need

£26,000 (2011/12)

Beneficial area

UK, with a preference for Grimsby.

Correspondent: Stewart Wilson, Trustee, Wilson Sharpe and Co., 27 Osborne Street, Grimsby, North East Lincolnshire DN31 1NU (email: sc@wilsonsharpe.co.uk)

Trustees: Stewart Wilson; Dr Diana F. Wilson; Michael Parker; Philip A. Mounfield; John N. Harrison.

CC Number: 220295

The primary purposes of the charity are:

- The purchase and distribution of bed linen and down pillows to charitable organisations caring for people who are sick or infirm
- The provision of pensions and grants to people employed by Sir Alec Black during his lifetime
- The benefit of sick, poor fishermen and dockworkers from the borough of Grimsby

In 2011/12 it had assets of £1.6 million and an unusually large income of £552,000 due mainly to the sale of investments. Grants totalled £26,500 and were distributed as follows:

Bed linen/pillows for charitable organisations	£14,500
Former employees	£11,000
Fishermen	£530

Applications

In writing to the correspondent. Trustees meet in May and November; applications need to be received in March or September.

Percentage of awards given to new applicants: less than 10%.

Information gathered from:
Accounts; Charity Commission record; further information provided by the funder.

Blackheart Foundation (UK) Ltd

General, health, education and sport

Beneficial area
UK.

Correspondent: Claire Heath, Trustee, c/o Tristan Capital Partners, Berkeley Square House, 8th Floor, Berkeley Square, London W1J 6DB (tel: 0204638900)

Trustees: Richard Lewis; Ilina Singh; Claire Heath.

CC Number: 1136813

The foundation was established in 2010 by Richard Lewis, chief executive of Tristan Capital Partners. Richard Lewis also serves on the board of several other charitable ventures, including the II Foundation, Teach First and Eastside Young Leaders Academy.

The objects of the foundation are to support individuals and organisations primarily in the areas health, education and sport.

In 2011/12 the foundation had an income of £120,000 and a total expenditure of £3,000. The 2012 annual report states: 'No grants were made in the year as donations were only received in April 2012.'

Applications
In writing to the correspondent.

Information gathered from:
Accounts; Charity Commission record.

The Blair Foundation

Wildlife, access to countryside, general

£70,000 (2011/12)

Beneficial area
UK, particularly southern England and Scotland; overseas.

Correspondent: The Trustees, Smith and Williamson, 1 Bishops Wharf, Walnut Tree Close, Guildford, Surrey GU1 4RA (tel: 01483 407100)

Trustees: Robert Thornton; Jennifer Thornton; Graham Healy; Alan Thornton.

CC Number: 801755

This foundation was originally established to create environmental conditions in which wildlife can prosper, as well as improving disability access to such areas. This work is focused on Scotland and southern England.

In 2011/12 the foundation had an income of £17,000 and a total expenditure of £78,000. Based upon expenditure in previous years grant expenditure probably totalled around £70,000.

Previous beneficiaries included: Ayrshire Wildlife Services (£12,000); King's School – Canterbury and Ayrshire Fiddler Orchestra (£10,000 each); Scottish National Trust (£7,000); Home Farm Trust (£5,000); CHAS (£2,000); Handicapped Children's Action Group and Penny Brohn Cancer Care (£1,500); Ro-Ro Sailing Project and Sustrans (£1,000 each).

Exclusions
Charities that have objectives which the trustees consider harmful to the environment are not supported.

Applications
In writing to the correspondent, for consideration at trustees' meetings held at least once a year. A receipt for donations is requested from all donees.

Information gathered from:
Accounts; Charity Commission record.

The Sir Victor Blank Charitable Settlement

Jewish organisations and general charitable purposes

£232,000 (2011/12)

Beneficial area
Worldwide.

Correspondent: Ronald Gulliver, Trustee, c/o Wilkins Kennedy, Bridge House, London Bridge, London SE1 9QR (tel: 020 7403 1877)

Trustees: Sir Maurice Blank; Lady Sylvia Blank; Ronald Gulliver.

CC Number: 1084187

Registered with the Charity Commission in December 2000, in 2011/12 this charity had assets of £2.1 million and an income of £43,000. Grants totalled £232,000.

There were 40 donations of £1,000 or more listed in the accounts. Beneficiaries included: United Jewish Israel Appeal (£31,000); Jewish Care (£30,000); Community Security Trust and Norwood Ravenswood (£15,000 each); Global Leadership Foundation and JLGB (£10,000 each); Jewish Deaf Association and Limmud (£5,000 each); University of Nottingham (£2,500); Ellenor Lions Hospice (£2,000); and Deafblind UK, Listening Books and Teenage Cancer Trust (£1,000 each).

Other grants of less than £1,000 each totalled over £11,000.

Applications
In writing to the correspondent.

Information gathered from:
Accounts; Charity Commission record.

Blatchington Court Trust

Supporting vision-impaired people under the age of 30

£46,000 to organisations (2011/12).

Beneficial area
UK, preference for Sussex.

Correspondent: The Executive Manager, Ridgeland House, 165 Dyke Road, Hove, East Sussex BN3 1TL (tel: 01273 727222; fax: 01273 722244; email: info@blatchingtoncourt.org.uk; website: www.blatchingtoncourt.org.uk)

Trustees: Richard Martin, Chair; Alison Acason; Daniel Ellman-Brown; Georgina James; Roger Jones; Stephen Pavey; Anna Hunter; Jonathan Wilson; Martin Reith Murdoch.

CC Number: 306350

This trust's initial income arose from the sale of the former Blatchington Court School for people who are partially sighted at Seaford. Its aim is the promotion of education and employment (including social and physical training) of blind and partially sighted persons under the age of 30 years. There is a preference for Sussex.

The Charity has two grantmaking programmes; financial assistance and capital grants:

(a) Sussex Programme
The primary and largest is the Sussex Programme, which provides services to individual clients including advocacy, counselling, education, training and assistance in finding employment and family support.

(b) Annual Awards Scheme
The second programme is for grants which cover all of the UK and through which the charity, usually in partnership with sister charities, will:

(i) Award grants for the provision of recreational and leisure facilities (or contributions towards such facilities), which enable vision impaired people to develop their physical, mental and moral capacities.

(ii) Make grants to any voluntary or charitable organisation approved by the trustees, the objects of which include the promotion of education, training and/or employment of vision impaired young people and their general well-being in pursuance of all the forgoing.

In 2011/12 the trust had assets of £10.9 million and an income mainly from investments of £496,000. Grants paid totalled £133,000, of which £46,000 went to organisations. The remaining £87,000 was given to individuals.

Applications

On a form available from the correspondent. Applications can be considered at any time. An application on behalf of a registered charity should include audited accounts and up-to-date information on the charity and its commitments.

Information gathered from:

Accounts; Charity Commission record; funder's website.

The Neville and Elaine Blond Charitable Trust

Jewish, general

£103,000 (2011/12)

Beneficial area

Worldwide.

Correspondent: The Trustees, c/o H. W. Fisher and Co., Chartered Accountants, Acre House, 11–15 William Road, London NW1 3ER (tel: 020 7388 7000)

Trustees: Dame Simone Prendergast; Peter Blond; Ann Susman; Simon Susman; Jennifer Skidmore.

CC Number: 206319

In 2011/12 the trust had assets of almost £1.2 million and an income of £43,000. Grants totalling £103,000 were made to 18 organisations in the following categories:

Education	£41,500
Overseas aid	£30,000
Community and welfare	£23,000
Arts and culture	£6,500
Health	£2,300
Total	£103,300

No list of grantees was available in this year's accounts. Previous beneficiaries included: Beth Shalom Holocaust Memorial Centre (£30,000); United Jewish Israel Appeal (£30,000); and British WIZO and Community Security Trust (£10,000 each); Holocaust Educational Trust (£5,000); Halle Orchestra (£4,000); Nordoff Robbins Music Therapy Centre (£2,000); Chicken Shed Theatre (£1,000); and Walk the Walk (£200).

Exclusions

Only registered charities are supported.

Applications

In writing to the correspondent. Applications should arrive by 31 January for consideration in late spring.

Information gathered from:

Accounts; Charity Commission record.

The Marjory Boddy Charitable Trust

General

£80,000 (2011/12)

Beneficial area

UK, with a preference for North West England.

Correspondent: Mrs Adele Bebbington-Plant, Administrator, c/o Cullimore Dutton Solicitors, 20 White Friars, Chester CH1 1XS (tel: 01244 356789; fax: 01244 312582; email: info@cullimoredutton.co.uk)

Trustees: Revd Canon Christopher Samuels; Edward Walton; Randal Hibbert; Richard Raymond.

CC Number: 1091356

The trust was established in 2002 for general charitable purposes.

In 2011/12 the trust had assets of £2.7 million and an income of £92,000. Grants were made totalling £80,000, although a list of beneficiaries was not included in the accounts.

Further research shows that the trust has supported organisations including the Brathay Trust, Motability, Nightingale House Hospice – Wrexham, Chance to Shine, the Christie Charitable Fund and Chester Mystery Plays.

Applications

In writing to the correspondent.

Information gathered from:

Accounts; Charity Commission record.

The Boltons Trust

Social welfare, medicine, education

£6,000 (2011/12)

Beneficial area

Unrestricted.

Correspondent: Mrs Mai Brown, Blick Rothenberg, 12 York Gare, Regent's Park, London NW1 4QS (tel: 020 7544 8862)

Trustees: C. Albuquerque; R. M. Baldock; S. D. Albuquerque.

CC Number: 257951

The main aims of the trust are:

- The pursuit of understanding and the reduction of innocent suffering
- Support for education, research and welfare projects

In 2011/12 the trust had assets of £1.2 million, an income of £46,000 and a total expenditure of £28,000, the majority of which went towards investment and accountancy fees. Two grants were made in the year totalling £6,000 (£55,000 in 2010/11): Heifer International (£5,000); and Movember Europe (£1,000).

Applications

In writing to the correspondent. The trustees meet on a regular basis to consider applications.

Information gathered from:

Accounts; Charity Commission record.

The John and Celia Bonham Christie Charitable Trust

General charitable purposes

£33,000 (2011/12)

Beneficial area

UK, with some preference for the former county of Avon.

Correspondent: Rosemary Ker, Trustee, PO Box 9081, Taynton, Gloucester GL19 3WX

Trustees: Richard Bonham Christie; Robert Bonham Christie; Rosemary Ker.

CC Number: 326296

In 2011/12 the trust had an income of £47,000 and a total expenditure of £33,000. Accounts had been received at the Commission but had not been published online.

Previous beneficiaries have included: BIBIC, Butterwick Hospice, Cancer Research Campaign, Derby TOC, Digestive Disorder Foundation, Dorothy House, Elizabeth Finn Trust, Foundation for the Study of Infant Cot Deaths, Frome Festival, Home Start South Wiltshire, Inspire Foundation, Kings Medical Trust, Royal Society for the Blind Winsley, Sea Cadet Association, St John Ambulance and Ten of Us.

Exclusions

No grants to individuals.

Applications

In writing to the correspondent. Only a small number of new applications are supported each year.

Information gathered from:

Accounts; Charity Commission record.

The Charlotte Bonham-Carter Charitable Trust

General

Around £100,000 (2011/12)

Beneficial area

UK, with some preference for Hampshire.

Correspondent: Jenny Cannon, Administrator, Chelwood, Rectory Road, East Carleton, Norwich NR14 8HT (tel: 01508 571230)

Trustees: Sir Matthew Farrer; David Bonham-Carter; Eliza Bonham-Carter; Georgina Nayler.

CC Number: 292839

The trust is principally concerned with supporting charitable bodies and purposes which were of particular concern to Lady Bonham-Carter during her lifetime or are within the county of Hampshire. 'The trustees continue to support a core number of charities to whom they have made grants in the past as well as reviewing all applications received and making grants to new charities within their grant-giving criteria.'

In 2011/12 the trust had an income of £124,000 and a total expenditure of £103,000. Although the trust's annual report and accounts had been received at the Commission, they were not published online. Grants generally range from £500 to £10,000.

Previous beneficiaries included: National Trust (£10,000); Florence Nightingale Museum (£5,000); City and London Guilds Bursary Fund (£4,000); British Museum – Friends of the Ancient Near East (£3,500); British Institute for the Study of Iraq (£3,000); Chelsea Physic Garden (£2,000); British Schools Exploring Society, Enterprise Education Trust and Firefly International (£1,000 each); Fields in Trust, National Council for the Conservation of Plants and Gardens and Sir Joseph Banks Archive Project (£500 each).

Exclusions

No grants to individuals or non-registered charities.

Applications

In writing to the correspondent. The application should include details of the funds required, funds raised so far and the timescale involved. The trust states that: 'unsolicited general applications are unlikely to be successful and only increase the cost of administration'. There are no application forms. Trustees meet in January and July; applications need to be received by May or November.

Percentage of awards given to new applicants: between 20% and 30%.

Information gathered from:

Accounts; Charity Commission record; further information provided by the funder.

The Linda and Gordon Bonnyman Charitable Trust

General charitable purposes

Around £1 million (2011/12)

Beneficial area

Unrestricted.

Correspondent: Linda Bonnyman, Trustee, Ely Grange, Bells Yew Green Road, Frant, Tunbridge Wells, East Sussex TN3 9DY

Trustees: James Gordon Bonnyman; Linda Bonnyman; James Wallace Taylor Bonnyman.

CC Number: 1123441

This trust was established in 2008 for general charitable purposes. Accounts were received at the Charity Commission but not published online due to the charity's low income.

In 2011/12 the charity had an income of £8,000 and a total charitable expenditure of £1 million. No further information was available.

Applications

In writing to the correspondent.

Information gathered from:

Accounts; Charity Commission record.

The Booth Charities

Welfare, health, education

£358,000 (2012/13)

Beneficial area

Salford.

Correspondent: Jonathan Aldersley, Clerk to the Trustees, Butcher and Barlow, 34 Railway Road, Leigh, Greater Manchester WN7 4AU (tel: 01942 674144; email: enquiries@butcher-barlow.co.uk)

Trustees: William Whittle, Chair; David Tully; Philip Webb; Richard Kershaw; Edward Wilson Hunt; Roger Weston; Michael Prior; John Willis; Alan Dewhurst; Richard Fildes; Jonathan Shelmerdine.

CC Number: 221800

The Booth Charities are two charities supporting disadvantaged people in Salford. Together they provide a wide range of support including pension payments to individuals and grants to local charities and facilities. A large number of grants go to organisations which have a direct connection with the charities and a substantial number of these institutions bear the Booth name.

Humphrey Booth the Elder's Charity is for the benefit of the inhabitants of Salford and is established 'for the relief of the aged, impotent or poor' with a preference for people over sixty years of age; the relief of distress and sickness; the provision and support of facilities for recreation and other leisure time occupation; the provision and support of educational facilities; and any other charitable purpose.

Humphrey Booth the Grandson's Charity is established for the income to be applied in or towards the repair and maintenance of the Church of Sacred Trinity, Salford, and in augmenting the stipend of the rector of the Church. The remaining income is then applied in furtherance of the same objects as apply to the Humphrey Booth the Elder Charity.

In 2012/13 the trust had assets of £31.7 million. Income stood at £964,000. Grants were made to 55 organisations during the year totalling £358,000. Support costs were relatively high at £176,000. Grants were categorised as follows:

Relief of distress and sickness	£91,000
Education	£90,000
Leisure and recreation	£57,000
Other	£44,000
Relief of aged, impotent and poor	£38,000
Sacred Trinity Church	£38,000

Beneficiaries included: RECLAIM Project (£30,000); Macmillan Cancer Support (£20,000); Wood Street Mission (£10,000); Eccles Community Hall Organisation (£8,000); Together Trust and Salford Mayoral Appeal (£5,000 each); Live Music Now (£3,000); PDSA and Start in Salford (£1,500); and Manchester University Guild of Change Ringers (£100).

Applications

In writing to the correspondent.

Information gathered from:

Accounts; Charity Commission record.

Salo Bordon Charitable Trust

Jewish causes

£477,500 (2011/12)

Beneficial area

UK and worldwide.

Correspondent: Marcel Bordon, Trustee, 39 Gresham Gardens, London NW11 8PA

Trustees: Marcel Bordon; Salo Bordon; Lilly Bordon.

CC Number: 266439

This trust makes grants mainly to Jewish organisations, for social welfare and religious education.

In 2011/12 it had assets amounting to £7.6 million and an income of £594,000. Grants totalled £477,500. A list of grant beneficiaries was not included in the accounts.

Previous beneficiaries include: Agudas Israel Housing Association Ltd, Baer Hatorah, Beth Jacob Grammar School, Brisk Yeshivas, Golders Green Beth Hamedrash Congregation Jaffa Institute, Jewish Learning Exchange, London Academy of Jewish Studies, Society of Friends of Torah and WST Charity.

Applications

In writing to the correspondent.

Information gathered from:

Accounts; Charity Commission record.

The Oliver Borthwick Memorial Trust

Homelessness

£35,000 (2011/12)

Beneficial area

UK.

Correspondent: Anthony Blake, Correspondent, c/o Donor Grants Department, Charities Aid Foundation, Kings Hill, West Malling, Kent ME19 4TA (tel: 01732 520107; email: tblake@charaplus.co.uk)

Trustees: Michael Bretherton; David Scott; The Earl Bathurst; James MacDonald; John Toth; Andrew Impey; Virginia Buckley; Sebastian Cresswell-Turner.

CC Number: 256206

The intention of the trust is to provide shelter and help the homeless. The trustees welcome applications from small but viable charities where they are able to make a significant contribution to the practical work of the charity, especially in disadvantaged inner-city areas.

In 2011/12 it had assets of £1 million which generated an income of £54,500. Grants totalling £35,000 were made to nine organisations.

Beneficiaries included: Christian Action and Response in Society, Clock Tower Sanctuary – Brighton, Notting Hill Churches – Homeless Concern and Vine Drop-In Centre; (£5,000 each); and Slough Homeless Our Concern and Winchester Churches Night Shelter (£3,000 each).

Exclusions

No grants to individuals, including people working temporarily overseas for a charity where the request is for living expenses, together with applications relating to health, disability and those from non-registered charitable organisations.

Applications

Letters should be set out on a maximum of two sides of A4, giving full details of the project with costs, who the project will serve and the anticipated outcome of the project. Meetings take place once a year in May. Applications should be received no later than April.

Information gathered from:

Accounts; Charity Commission record.

The Boshier-Hinton Foundation

Children and adults with special educational or other needs

£165,000 (2011/12)

Beneficial area

England and Wales.

Correspondent: Dr Peter Boshier, Trustee, Yeomans, Aythorpe Roding, Great Dunmow, Essex CM6 1PD (tel: 01245 231032; email: boshierhinton@yahoo.co.uk; website: www.boshierhintonfoundation.org.uk)

Trustees: Thea Boshier, Chair; Dr Peter Boshier; Colin Flint; Janet Beale.

CC Number: 1108886

Set up in 2005, the foundation's main area of interest is children and adults with special educational or other needs and their families. The website states:

> the founding trustees are experienced in working and caring for children and adults with special needs and their families. It is also their experience that funding for projects to promote the welfare of individuals and groups of individuals continues to be difficult to obtain as grants have become more restricted and limited in recent years. The purpose of this Charity is to identify areas of need and make appropriate grants, where possible.

In 2011/12 the foundation had assets of £962,000, an income of £239,000 and made 92 grants totalling £165,000.

Beneficiaries included: Paralympics GB (£20,000); Starlight Children's Foundation (£5,000); Disability Partnership (£2,500); Afasic, Asperger East Anglia, Asthma UK, Barnardo's, Communications for Blind People, Hearing Dogs for Deaf People, Treehouse Trust and Us in a Bus (£2,000 each); Green Light Trust, Just Different and Wheelyboat Trust (£1,000 each); Movement Foundation (£750); and Tyneside Challenge (£500).

Exclusions

No repeat grants are made within two years.

Applications

The application form can be downloaded from the website. The foundation welcomes informal email enquiries prior to the submission of a formal application.

Percentage of awards given to new applicants: between 10% and 20%.

Common applicant mistakes

'Not reading our guidelines. Those re-applying know that we use an application form, but others do not request a copy.'

Information gathered from:

Accounts; Charity Commission record; further information provided by the funder; funder's website.

The Bothwell Charitable Trust

Disability, health, older people, conservation

£186,000 (2011/12)

Beneficial area

England, particularly the South East.

Correspondent: Paul Leonard James, Trustee, 25 Ellenbridge Way, South Croydon CR2 0EW (tel: 020 8657 6884)

Trustees: Paul L. James; Crispian M. P. Howard; Theresa McGregor.

CC Number: 299056

The trust makes grants towards health, people with disabilities, conservation, children's and older people's causes.

In 2011/12 the trust had assets of £4.3 million with an income of £206,000. Grants were made to organisations totalling £186,000 in the following amounts:

People with disabilities/social work	£68,000
Medical research	£57,000
Hospices	£31,000
Children's causes	£27,000
Countryside projects	£3,000

Previously grants were for either £2,000 or £1,000 and beneficiaries included: Arthritis Research UK, Blackthorn Trust, British Heart Foundation, ECHO International Health Services Ltd, Friends of the Elderly, Invalid Children's Aid Nationwide, Leukaemia Research Fund (£2,000 each); and Brain Research Trust, British Trust for Conservation Volunteers, Childlink Adoption Society, Multiple Sclerosis Society and Riding for the Disabled Association (£1,000 each).

Exclusions

No grants for animal charities, overseas causes, individuals, or charities not registered with the Charity Commission.

Applications

In writing to the correspondent. Distributions are usually made in February or March each year.

Information gathered from:

Accounts; Charity Commission record.

The Harry Bottom Charitable Trust

Religion, education, medical

£94,000 (2011/12)

Beneficial area

UK, with a preference for Yorkshire and Derbyshire.

Correspondent: John Hinsley, c/o Westons, Chartered Accountants, Queen's Buildings, 55 Queen Street, Sheffield S1 2DX (tel: 01142 738341)

Trustees: Revd. James Kilner; Prof. Terence Lilley; Prof. Andrew Rawlinson.

CC Number: 204675

The trust states that support is divided roughly equally between religion, education and medical causes. Within these categories grants are given to:

- Religion – small local appeals and cathedral appeals
- Education – universities and schools
- Medical – equipment for hospitals and charities concerned with disability

In 2011/12 the trust had assets of £5.3 million and an income of £226,000. Grants were made totalling £94,000 and were broken down as follows:

Educational and other activities	£41,000
Religious activities	£37,000
Medical activities	£16,000

Beneficiaries included: Yorkshire Baptist Association (£35,000); St Luke's Hospice (£5,000); and Cherry Tree Children's Home and Sheffield Mencap (£3,000 each).

Exclusions

No grants to individuals.

Applications

In writing to the correspondent at any time enclosing your most recent set of annual accounts.

Percentage of awards given to new applicants: between 10% and 20%.

Common applicant mistakes

'They don't submit accounts/financial information; they don't check Charity Commission website to check eligibility criteria (numerous applicants from outside the supported area).'

Information gathered from:

Accounts; Charity Commission record; further information provided by the funder.

P. G. and N. J. Boulton Trust

Christian causes

£64,000 (2011/12)

Beneficial area

Worldwide.

Correspondent: Andrew L. Perry, Trustee, PO Box 72, Wirral CH28 9AE (website: www.boultontrust.org.uk)

Trustees: Andrew L. Perry; Shirley Perry; Peter H. Stafford; Margaret Jardine-Smith.

CC Number: 272525

The trust describes its general funding policy on its website as follows:

1. **Main Commitment –** Our giving is largely restricted to organisations and activities that are of special interest to the trustees and this is largely concentrated in the area of Christian missionary work
2. **Other Areas –** The trust has from time to time made donations in the following areas:
   - Disaster and poverty relief
   - Medical research and healthcare
   - Disability relief and care of elderly

In 2011/12 it had assets of £3.4 million, an income of £129,000 and made grants totalling £64,000.

Grants of £1,000 or more were made to twelve organisations and were listed in the accounts. Beneficiaries were: Vision for China (£23,000); New Life Centre (£10,000); Shalom Christian Trust (£6,000); Longcroft Christian Trust (£5,000); Children Alone (£4,500); Just Care (£4,000); International Mission Project (£2,250); Barnabas Fund (£2,000); and Christian Institute, Creation Research Trust and Shepherd's Purse Trust (£1,500 each). Other donations totalled (£2,000).

Other donations of £1,000 or less totalled £5,000.

Exclusions

No grants for:

- Individuals
- Environment and conservation
- Culture and heritage
- Sport and leisure
- Animal welfare
- Church building repairs

Applications

Note the following statement from the trust's website:

> We are currently undergoing a long-term review of our policies and this means that in practice, we are currently only making donations to organisations to whom we have an existing commitment. This unfortunately means that any new requests for funding at the present time will almost certainly be unsuccessful.

Information gathered from:

Accounts; Charity Commission record; funder's website.

The A. H and E. Boulton Trust

Evangelical Christian

£104,000 (2011/12)

Beneficial area

Worldwide, with some preference for Merseyside.

Correspondent: Brian McGain, Correspondent, c/o Moore Stephens LLP, 110–114 Duke Street, Liverpool L1 5AG (tel: 01517 031080)

Trustees: Dr Frank Gopsill; Jennifer Gopsill; Michael Gopsill; Peter Gopsill.

CC Number: 225328

The trust mainly supports the erection and maintenance of buildings to be used for preaching the Christian gospel and for relieving the sick or needy. The trustees can also support other Christian institutions, especially missions in the UK and developing world.

In 2011/12 the trust had assets of £2.8 million and an income of £76,000. Grants totalled £104,000.

Beneficiaries were: Boulton's Cottage Homes Trust (£45,000); Holy Trinity Church (£21,000); Pioneer People Wirral (£15,000); Peel Beech Mission (£10,500); Bethesda Church (£10,000). Sundry small grants to individual ministers totalled £2,000.

Applications

In writing to the correspondent. The trust tends to support a set list of charities and applications are very unlikely to be successful.

Information gathered from:

Accounts; Charity Commission record.

Sir Clive Bourne Family Trust

Jewish causes

£87,000 (2012/13)

Beneficial area

UK.

Correspondent: Janet Bater, Correspondent, Gardiner House, 6B Hemnall Street, Epping, Essex CM16 4LW (tel: 01992 560500)

Trustees: Lady Joy Bourne; Katie Cohen; Lucy Furman; Claire Lefton; Merryl Flitterman.

CC Number: 290620

The trustees favour Jewish causes. A number of health and medical charities (particularly relating to cancer) have also benefited.

In 2012/13 the trust's assets totalled £4.1 million and it had an income of £83,000. Grants were made to 23 organisations totalling £87,000.

Beneficiaries included: Prostate Action (£13,500); Jewish Care (£12,500); Norwood Ravenswood (£8,000); WIZO UK (£6,000); One Family UK (£5,000); Magen David Adom and Community Security Trust (£2,000 each); World Jewish Relief (£1,000); and Jewish Museum and Zionist Federation (£500 each).

Applications

In writing to the correspondent.

Information gathered from:

Accounts; Charity Commission record.

Bourneheights Ltd

Orthodox Jewish causes

£519,000 (2011/12)

Beneficial area

UK.

Correspondent: Schloime Rand, Trustee, Flat 10, Palm Court, Queen Elizabeth's Walk, London N16 5XA (tel: 020 8809 7398)

Trustees: Chaskel Rand; Esther Rand; Erno Berger; Yechiel Chersky; Schloime Rand.

CC Number: 298359

Registered with the Charity Commission in February 1998, in 2011/12 this charity had assets of £6.2 million and an income of £1.2 million. Grants were made totalling £519,000. There was no list of grant beneficiaries included in the annual report and accounts.

Previous beneficiaries include: Moreshet Hatorah, Mercaz Torah Vahesed Ltd, BFOT, Belz Synagogue, Telz Academy Trust, Gevurath Ari Academy, UTA, Toreth Emeth, Olam Chesed Yiboneh, Before Trust, Heaven Point, Yeshivas Avas Torah and Lubavitch Mechina.

Applications

In writing to the correspondent.

Information gathered from:

Accounts; Charity Commission record.

The Bowerman Charitable Trust

Church, the arts, medical, youth

£218,000 (2011/12)

Beneficial area

UK, with a preference for West Sussex.

Correspondent: D. W. Bowerman, Trustee, Champs Hill, Coldwatham, Pulborough, West Sussex RH20 1LY (tel: 01798 831205)

Trustees: D. W. Bowerman; C. M. Bowerman; J. M. Taylor; K. E. Bowerman; A. M. Downham; J. M. Capper; M. Follis.

CC Number: 289446

The trust maintains a music room, art gallery, conference centre and campsite as well as making charitable donations. Grants tend to be made at the trustees' discretion in Sussex and London. In 2011/12 the trust had assets of £10.8 million and an income of £168,000. Grants were made to organisations totalling £218,000 and were broken down as follows:

Church activities	£124,000
The arts	£63,000
Medical charities	£24,000
Youth work	£3,000
Other	£3,000

Grants may also be given for the rehabilitation of offenders, relief of poverty, distress or disadvantage.

The largest grants went to St Paul's Hammersmith (£100,000); St Margaret's Trust (£12,000); British Youth Opera (£10,000); and Royal Academy of Music (£8,000).

Applications

In writing to the correspondent. The trustees have previously stated that they are bombarded with applications and unsolicited applications will not be considered.

Information gathered from:

Accounts; Charity Commission record.

The William Brake Charitable Trust

General

£324,000 (2011/12)

Beneficial area

UK, with a preference for Kent.

Correspondent: The Trustees, c/o Gill Turner and Tucker, Colman House, King Street, Maidstone, Kent ME14 1JE (tel: 01622 759051)

Trustees: Philip R. Wilson; Deborah J. Isaac; Penelope A. Lang; Michael Trigg.

CC Number: 1023244

The charity invites applications from the William Brake family for funding of worthy charitable causes each year, with a particular emphasis on local charities where the family know the charity's representative.

In 2011/12 the trust had assets of £9.4 million and an income of £95,000. The trust made 77 grants totalling £324,000. No list of beneficiaries was available.

Previous beneficiaries included: Whitely Fund for Nature; the Royal Masonic Benevolent Institution; NSPCC; the Duke of Edinburgh's Award; the Ecology Trust; Wooden Spoon Society; Aurora Tsunami Orphanage; Mike Collingwood Memorial Fund; League of Remembrance; Friends of St Peter's Hospital Chertsey; Canterbury Cathedral Development; Cancer Research UK; Elimination of Leukaemia Fund; Maidstone Mencap Charitable Trust; RNLI; Alzheimer's Society; Breast Cancer Care; Courtyard – Petersfield; Dorothy Grinstead Memorial Fund; Macmillan and Portland College.

Applications

The 2011/12 accounts note that, 'the charity invites applications from the William Brake family for funding of worthy registered charities each year, with a particular emphasis on local charities where the family know the charity's representative.'

Information gathered from:

Accounts; Charity Commission record.

The Tony Bramall Charitable Trust

Medical research, ill health, social welfare

£76,000 (2012/13)

Beneficial area

UK, with some preference for Yorkshire.

Correspondent: The Trustees, 12 Cardale Court, Beckwith Head Road, Harrogate, North Yorkshire HG3 1RY (tel: 01423 535300; email: alison.lockwood@bramallproperties.co.uk)

Trustees: Tony Bramall; Karen Bramall Odgen; Melanie Foody; Geoffrey Tate; Anna Bramall.

CC Number: 1001522

'The charity was established in 1988 by Mr D C A Bramall with an initial sum of £600,000. The charity is focused on assisting people less able to finance their medical/health needs, particularly children and particularly those causes based in the northern part of the country.

In 2012/13 the trust had assets of £4.4 million, an income of £157,000 and made 33 grants totalling £76,000.

Beneficiaries included: Tree of Hope (£10,000); BEN, Help Harry Help Others, St Luke's and Saint Gemma's Hospice (£5,000 each); Children Heart Surgery Fund (£3,000); Helen's Trust and Well-being of Women (£2,500 each); Toy Libraries Association (£500); and Caring Hands Skydive (£250).

Applications

In writing to the correspondent.

Percentage of awards given to new applicants: between 10% and 20%.

Common applicant mistakes

'Causes of charities do not fit with the objectives of our trust.'

Information gathered from:

Accounts; Charity Commission record; further information provided by the funder.

The Bransford Trust

General

£747,000 (2011/12)

Beneficial area

Preference for the West Midlands.

Correspondent: Julia Kirkham, Administrator, Bransford Facilities Management, 6 Edgar Street, Worcester WR1 2LR (tel: 0870 066 2446; email: julia@bransford-facilities.co.uk)

CC Number: 1106554

Established in 2004 for general charitable purposes (in consultation with the settlor), the trust primarily supports the arts and music and the education of young people in Worcestershire who are from disadvantaged backgrounds.

In 2011/12 the trust had assets of £12.6 million and an income of £5 million. Grants were made to over 16 organisations totalling almost £747,000.

Beneficiaries included: University of Worcester (£200,000); the Leys School (£150,000); St Richard Hospice (£110,000); Sing (UK) (£37,000); Acorns Children's Trust (£35,000); Worcester Porcelain Museum (£20,000); English Symphony, Vitalise Trust and Worcester Live (£10,000 each); Noah's Ark Trust (£7,500); and County Air Ambulance (£6,000).

Applications

In writing to the correspondent.

Information gathered from:

Accounts; Charity Commission record.

The Breast Cancer Research Trust

Breast cancer research

£104,000 (2011/12)

Beneficial area

UK.

Correspondent: Mrs Rosemary Sutcliffe, Executive Administrator, PO BOX 861, Bognor Regis PO21 9HW (tel: 01243–583143; email: bcrtrust@bt.internet.com; website: www.breastcancerresearchtrust.org.uk)

CC Number: 272214

'The Breast Cancer Research Trust is a charity dedicated to funding clinical and laboratory project research, undertaken in recognised cancer centres or research institutions in the UK, directly aimed at improving the prevention, early diagnosis and treatment of breast cancer.' Limited grants are available up to a term of three years. Grants reviewed annually.

In 2011/12 the trust had assets of £527,000 and an income of £105,000. Grants were made to more than four institutions totalling £104,000.

Beneficiaries included: Southampton University (£50,000); Southampton General Hospital (20,000); University of Leeds (£19,000); and CBC Research (£10,000). Other grants totalled £5,000.

Exclusions

No grants to students.

Applications

Application forms available only from the trust's website. The trust has stated that they are not open for new applications until 2015.

Percentage of awards given to new applicants: between 30% and 40%.

Information gathered from:

Accounts; Charity Commission record; further information provided by the funder; funder's website.

The Brendish Family Foundation

General, children, education, health care and access to food and water

Around £42,000 (2011/12)

Beneficial area

UK and overseas, with a preference for India.

Correspondent: Graham Chambers, Trustee, Dixon Wilson Chartered Accountants, 22 Chancery Lane, London WC2A 1LS (tel: 020 7680 8100)

CC Number: 1079065

The trust was established in 2000 for general charitable purposes. The trustees stated in their 2009/10 accounts that in the future they would like to support projects including those that involve children, education, health care and access to food and water.

In 2011/12 the foundation had an income of £24,000 and a total expenditure of £42,000. Accounts had been received at the Charity Commission but not published due to the charity's low income.

Beneficiaries in previous years have included: Brendish Foundation (£30,000); Child in Need Institute – India (£10,000); the Children with Special Needs Foundation (£5,000); the Busoga Trust (£3,000); Marie Curie Cancer Care (£2,500); Digital Himalayan Project – Cambridge University (£1,500); and Haiti Earthquake Appeal (£1,000).

Applications

In writing to the correspondent.

Information gathered from:

Accounts; Charity Commission record.

The Harold and Alice Bridges Charity

Capital projects in connection with rural and village life

£101,000 (2011/12)

Beneficial area

South Cumbria and North Lancashire (as far south as Preston).

Correspondent: Richard N. Hardy, Trustee, Linder Myers, 21–23 Park Street, Lytham FY8 5LU (tel: 0844 984 6001; email: richard.hardy@lindermyers.co.uk; website: www.haroldandalicebridgescharity.co.uk)

Trustees: Richard N. Hardy; Irene Greenwood.

CC Number: 236654

'The trustees normally make grants to local causes in the Lancashire and South Cumbria area with special preference to the River Ribble area and northwards, the Blackburn area, and the South Lakes area. Generally, grants are made to benefit the young and the elderly, are mainly towards capital projects in connection with rural and village life especially where there is associated voluntary effort.'

In 2011/12 the charity had assets of £3 million and an income of £560,000. Grants to 59 organisations totalled £101,000. There was no list of grant beneficiaries provided with the accounts.

Previous beneficiaries included: Stainton Institute and Rosemere Cancer Foundation – Preston (£5,000 each); St John's Churchyard – Tunstall (£4,000); Emmanuel Parish Church – Southport (£2,500); British Wireless for the Blind Fund (£2,000); Rainbow Trust Children's Charity (£1,000); and Dolly Mops and Springfield Bowling Club – High Bentham (£500 each).

Exclusions

No grants to individuals.

Applications

Refer to the charity's website for full guidelines and application form. The trustees meet three times a year to discuss and approve grant applications and review finances. Cheques are sent out to those successful applicants within days of each meeting.

Information gathered from:

Accounts; Charity Commission record; funder's website.

The Bridging Fund Charitable Trust

Social welfare, relief of poverty

About £200,000 (2012)

Beneficial area

UK.

Correspondent: Debbie Cockrill, Trustee, PO Box 3106, Lancing, West Sussex BN15 5BL (tel: 01903 750008; email: info@bridgingfund.org)

Trustees: Debbie Cockrill; David Reeds; Mike Richardson; Rosemary Mackay; Gordon Hayes.

CC Number: 1119171

The trust was established in 2007 with a legacy of £1.3 million received from the estate of the late Frank E Newman. The objects of the trust are to make grants to organisations working with individuals in financial hardship to help them 'get back on their feet'. Grants are typically made to charities working with people in crisis, and the money has previously been used for purposes such as 'clearing utility debts, rent arrears, the purchase of essential household items and buying disability equipment – but in all cases the individual had no other means of assistance'.

In 2012 the trust had an income of £21,000 and a total expenditure of £211,000. Grants totalled about £200,000. No further information was available.

Exclusions

No grants for running costs or directly to individuals.

Applications

In writing to the correspondent.

Information gathered from:

Accounts; Charity Commission record.

Briggs Animal Welfare Trust

Animal welfare

Around £284,000 (2011/12)

Beneficial area

UK and overseas.

Correspondent: Louise Hartnett, Trustee, Little Champions Farm, Maplehurst Road, West Grinstead, Horsham, West Sussex RH13 6RN

Trustees: Louise Hartnett; Adrian Schouten.

CC Number: 276459

This trust derives most of its income from shares in the company Eurotherm International plc. Although the original objects of the trust were general, but with particular support for animal welfare, the trust's policy is to support only animal welfare causes. There are five named beneficiaries in the trust deed: RSPCA, Reystede Animal Sanctuary Ringmer, Brooke Hospital for Animals Cairo, Care of British Columbia House and the Society for the Protection of Animals in North Africa.

The income of the trust has been declining year on year recently, from a high of £37,000 in 2007/08 to £600 in 2011/12. However, expenditure seems to have been unaffected, reaching a high of £284,000 in 2011/12. No further information was available.

Applications

In writing to the correspondent.

Information gathered from:

Accounts; Charity Commission record.

John Bristow and Thomas Mason Trust

Education, relief in need, people with disabilities, community amenities

£41,500 (2012)

Beneficial area

Parish of Charlwood (as the boundaries stood in 1926).

Correspondent: Miss M. Singleton, Secretary, 3 Grayrigg Road, Maidenbower, Crawley RH10 7AB (tel: 01293 883950; email: trust.secretary@jbtmt.org.uk; website: www.jbtmt.org.uk)

Trustees: Martin James; Revd Bill Campen; Feargal Hogan; Alison Martin; Howard Pearson; Julie King; Carole Jordan; Richard Parker.

CC Number: 1075971

The trust's objectives are:

- The promotion of education in the area of benefit
- The relief of inhabitants who are in need, hardship or distress, or who are sick, convalescent, have disabilities or are infirm
- The provision and support of facilities for recreation and other leisure time occupation of the inhabitants or any sufficient sector of them
- The provision and support of other charitable purposes for the benefit of the inhabitants

In 2012 the trust had assets of £2.4 million and an income of £65,000. Grants amounted to £41,500.

Grants approved were: St Nicholas Parochial Church Council £3,500); Parish Venture Week (£3,000); Hello Hookwood (£2,500); 8th Horley (Charlwood) Scouts (£1,000); Charlwood Evening Women's Institute (£850); and Charlwood Day Centre (£350).

Exclusions

Any application that will not benefit the residents of the Parish of Charlwood (as the boundaries stood in 1926) will not be considered.

Applications

Applications should be made on a form available from the correspondent upon written request, and should include an estimate of the total cost of the project, with three quotations where applicable.

Information gathered from:

Accounts; Charity Commission record; funder's website.

The British Council for Prevention of Blindness

Prevention and treatment of blindness

£240,000 (2011/12)

Beneficial area

Worldwide.

Correspondent: Stephen Silverton, Correspondent, 4 Bloomsbury Square, London WC1A 2RP (tel: 020 7404 7114; email: info@bcpb.org; website: www.bcpb.org)

Trustees: Stephen Brooker; Arvind Chandna; Prof. James Morgan; Prof. Paul Foster; Dr Jeffrey Jay; Dr Clare O'Neill.

CC Number: 270941

The following information is taken from the council's website:

> *Fellowships and Research Grants*
>
> There is a great need for trained eyecare personnel in the developing world. That is why one of the key Vision 2020 objectives is to build up the eyecare resources in developing countries by providing specialist training, from community level to policy planning at national and regional levels.
>
> The BCPB has two Fellowship Programmes.
>
> **Boulter Fellowships** provide trained personnel at MSC level.
>
> **Prevention of Blindness Fellowships** provide both key research outcomes and top level personnel trained to Doctoral level.
>
> To achieve these aims, an Advisory Panel of leading experts in global blindness has been set up.
>
> Two types of Fellowship are offered. Barrie Jones Fellowships are awarded to UK based Fellows who carry out research in a developing country. Sir John Wilson Fellowships are awarded to students from developing countries who come to the UK to carry out research.
>
> Applicants for Fellowships should download, read and complete the Fellowship Guidelines and Fellowship Application Form.
>
> BCPB also funds **Research grants** worth up to £60,000 in total over one, two or three years. Research grants are available to clinicians, scientists or epidemiologists: a) for 'pump-priming' to develop their research ideas and generate pilot data to facilitate a future application for a substantial grant; or b) to provide funding for a non-clinical PhD or DrPH studentship.
>
> Research Grant Projects further the goals of 'VISION 2020: The Right to Sight' – the elimination of avoidable blindness – and benefit low income countries. Grants are awarded to UK research/training institutions.
>
> Applicants for Pump-Priming Grants should download, read and complete the Research Grant Guidelines and the Pump-Priming Grants Application Form.
>
> Applicants for Studentships should download, read and complete the Research Grant Guidelines and the Non-clinical PhD Studentship Application Form.
>
> From April 2014 BCPB will also fund **Research Mentorship Awards**. These will build research links between hospitals and universities in developing countries and UK universities or NHS Trusts, with the goal of building research capacity. Successful projects will further the goals of 'VISION 2020: The Right to Sight', the elimination of avoidable blindness in low-income countries. Grants between £5,000 and £15,000 will be awarded to enable applicants from developing countries with a colleague or mentor in the UK to work together to develop a research project. For applicants who do not have a contact in the UK, BCPB is building a database of specialist 'BCPB mentors' who work in a variety of fields of ophthalmic and vision science.

Guidelines and application forms are available from the website.

In 2011/12 the organisation had assets of £352,000 and an income of £193,000. Grants awarded in the year totalled £240,000. Beneficiaries included: International Centre for Eye Health, London School of Hygiene and Tropical Medicine (£60,000); Southampton University (£59,000); and Aberdeen University (£45,000).

Exclusions

This trust does not deal with the individual welfare of blind people in the UK.

Applications

Applications can be made throughout the year.

Information gathered from:

Accounts; Charity Commission record; funder's website.

The British Dietetic Association General and Education Trust Fund

Dietary and nutritional issues

£84,000 (2011/12)

Beneficial area

UK.

Correspondent: The Secretary to the Trustees, 5th Floor, Charles House, 148–149 Great Charles Street, Queensway, Birmingham B3 3HT (tel: 01212 008080; email: info@bda.uk.com; website: www.bda.uk.com)

Trustees: P. Brindley; W. T. Seddon; M. Mackintosh; H. Davidson; S. Acreman.

CC Number: 282553

The British Dietetic Association General and Education Trust exists 'to advance education and other purposes related to the science of dietetics'. The trust can make grants to individuals and to recognised associations or groups of people engaged in dietetic research and associated activities. Grants can be made for core as well as project costs and if necessary for help with salaries.

In 2011/12 it had assets of £1.4 million and an income of £47,000. Six research grants were made totalling £79,000. A number of awards were also made to dietetic practitioners totalling £5,000.

The website advises that previous successful projects have included:

- Funding for a study trip to the USA to evaluate diabetes management
- A research project to evaluate the impact of clinical placements on professional training
- 'start up' funding for a post to monitor developments in clinical effectiveness for dietitians

Funding bids have been rejected in the past on the grounds that the methodology has not been rigorous enough; there is no clear benefit to dietetic practice or increase in the knowledge base in the profession; or the project is too local and the funding sought should be available elsewhere, e.g. from the NHS.

Exclusions

No grants for buildings; postgraduate qualifications or to support dietetic students in training.

Applications

Application forms can be downloaded from the trust's website. Trustees meet twice a year, usually in May and November and applications should be received at least six weeks prior to the meeting. Urgent requests may be considered between meetings.

Information gathered from:

Accounts; Charity Commission record; funder's website.

British Humane Association

Welfare

£71,000 (2012)

Beneficial area

UK.

Correspondent: Henry Grant, Company Secretary, The Cottage, New Road, Cutnall Green, Droitwich WR9 0PQ (tel: 01299 851588)

Trustees: Dr John Breen; David Eldridge; Benedict Campbell-Johnston; Rachel Campbell-Johnston; Duncan Cantlay; Philip Gee; John Huntington-Whiteley; Anthony Chignell; Michael Nemko.

CC Number: 207120

The charity's 2012 trustees' report states:

> The primary aim of the company, which is a registered charity, is the promotion of benevolence for the good of humanity and the community, through grant making. The directors of the Association have decided, that in order to increase the amount available for grant distribution to beneficiaries, they will transfer funds to other charitable organisations, which have in place systems for identifying and assisting deserving cases in need. By so doing, they will not duplicate selection processes and the resultant costs. It is the intention that any one or more of the directors will examine requests for assistance received and submit a proposal to the board to award a one-off, set period or continuing grant to anybody, which has applied for assistance.
>
> Three classes of charities have been designated to receive support in accordance with our Articles of Association these are:
>
> - Charities directly involved in the relief of inhumane activities
> - Charities distributing grants to individuals
> - Charities providing relief of poverty, sickness or benefit to the community

In 2012 the charity had an income of £129,000 and assets of £3.9 million. Grants were made to 11 organisations totalling £71,000.

Beneficiaries included: St John Wales (£20,000); St John of Jerusalem Eye Hospital (£12,000); Karabuni Trust and GARAS (£6,000 each); Close House Hereford (£5,000); and Ardent Hare and MERU (£2,000 each).

Applications

Applications not considered – see 'General' section.

Information gathered from:

Accounts; Charity Commission record.

The Roger Brooke Charitable Trust

General

£26,000 (2011/12)

Beneficial area

UK, with a preference for Hampshire.

Correspondent: The Trustees, Withers LLP, 16 Old Bailey, London EC4M 7EG (tel: 020 7597 6123)

Trustees: Nancy Brooke; Stephen Brooke.

CC Number: 1071250

Established in 1998, this trust has general charitable purposes, including medical research, support for carers and social action.

In 2011/12 the trust had an income of £6,000 and a total expenditure of £26,000. Accounts had been received at the Charity Commission but were not published online due to the charity's low income. No other financial information was available.

Previous beneficiary: The Southampton University Development Fund (£100,000).

Exclusions

In general, individuals are not supported.

Applications

The trustees advised us as follows: 'We are suspending grants for the foreseeable future due to the decreased value of the underlying assets of the trust.'

Information gathered from:

Accounts; Charity Commission record.

The David Brooke Charity

Youth, older people, medical

£45,000 (2011/12)

Beneficial area

UK.

Correspondent: David Rusman, Trustee, Cook Sutton, Tay Court, Blounts Court Road, Sonning Common, Oxfordshire RG4 9RS (tel: 01491 573411)

Trustees: David Rusman; Peter Hutt; Nigel Brooke.

CC Number: 283658

The charity supports youth causes, favouring disadvantaged young people, particularly through causes providing self-help programmes and outdoor-activity training. Grants are also given to medical organisations and organisations supporting older people.

In 2011/12 the charity had assets of £2 million and an income of £114,000. The 2011/12 trustee report states that there has been a significant reduction in income this year. Voluntary income in recent years was comprised of donations from J. M. Brooke and these ceased with her death in 2010. Grants in this year were given to 27 organisations totalling £45,000, which were broken down into the following two categories:

Children and young people	£12,000
Other institutions	£33,000

Beneficiaries included: Great Ormond Street Hospital (£3,000); Arthritis Research Campaign and ASTO (£2,500 each); British Stammering Association and YMCA (£2,000 each); and Independence at Home, Kennet and Avon Canal Trust and the Mission to Seafarers (£1,000 each).

Applications

The correspondent stated that the trust's annual income is not for general distribution as it is committed to a limited number of charities on a long-term basis.

Information gathered from:

Accounts; Charity Commission record.

Bill Brown 1989 Charitable Trust

General, health, social welfare

£172,000 (2011/12)

Beneficial area

UK, preference for South England.

Correspondent: The Trustees, BM BOX 4567, London WC1N 3XX (website: www.billbrowncharity.org)

Trustees: G. S. Brown; A. J. Barnett.

CC Number: 801756

This trust was founded in 1989 by Percy William Ernest Brown, a civil engineer and businessman who also served in the RAF during the second world war. There is a preference for charities in the south of England and trustees are particularly interested in the following areas:

- Research into blindness
- General medical research
- Deaf and blind people
- Elderly
- People with disabilities
- General welfare
- Hospices

In 2011/12 the trust had assets of £10 million and an income of £364,000. Grants to 18 organisations totalled £172,000. Grants are often recurrent.

Beneficiaries included: Charities Aid Foundation Trust (£65,000 in two grants); Macmillan Cancer Support and Salvation Army (£13,000 each); Scout

Council – Greater London Middlesex West County, Contact the Elderly and Alzheimer's Society (£6,500 each); and Richmond Borough Association for Mental Health (£3,250).

Exclusions

No grants to individuals. No grants for animal welfare; small/local charitable causes; wildlife or environmental charities; building maintenance; regional branches of national charitable organisations or religious charities.

Applications

In writing containing the following:

- Aims and objectives of the charity
- Nature of appeal
- Total target if for a specific project
- Contributions received against target
- Registered charity number
- Any other relevant factors

Appeals should be accompanied by a set of the organisation's latest report and full accounts. Trustees meet to consider applications in mid-June and December; applications should be received by the end of May and October to be considered at the respective meeting. Only successful applicants will be notified.

Information gathered from:

Accounts; Charity Commission record; funder's website.

R. S. Brownless Charitable Trust

Disability, relief-in-need, ill health, accommodation and housing, education, job creation, voluntary work

£63,000 (2011/12)

Beneficial area

Mainly UK and occasionally overseas.

Correspondent: Philippa Nicolai, Trustee, Hennerton Holt, Hennerton, Wargrave, Reading RG10 8PD (tel: 01189 404029)

Trustees: Frances Plummer; Philippa Nicolai.

CC Number: 1000320

The trust makes grants to causes that benefit people who have disabilities, are disadvantaged or seriously ill. Charities working in the fields of accommodation and housing, education, job creation and voluntary work are also supported. Grants are usually one-off, ranging between £100 and £2,000.

In 2011/12 the trust had assets of £1.2 million and an income of £61,000. Grants were made totalling £63,000.

Previous beneficiaries have included: Alzheimer's Society, Camp Mohawk, Casa Allianza UK, Crisis, Foundation for Study of Infant Deaths, Prader-Willi Foundation, St Andrew's Hall, UNICEF, Wargrave Parochial Church Council and Witham on the Hill Parochial Church Council.

Exclusions

Grants are rarely given to individuals for educational projects or to education or conservation causes or overseas aid.

Applications

In writing to the correspondent. The trustees meet twice a year, but in special circumstances will meet at other times. The trust is unable to acknowledge all requests.

Information gathered from:

Accounts; Charity Commission record.

The T. B H. Brunner Charitable Settlement

Church of England, heritage, arts, general

£38,000 (2011/12)

Beneficial area

UK with some preference for Oxfordshire.

Correspondent: Timothy Brunner, Trustee, Flat 4, 2 Inverness Gardens, London W8 4RN (tel: 020 7727 6277)

Trustees: Timothy Brunner; Helen Brunner; Dr Imogen Brunner.

CC Number: 260604

The trust offered the following guidance on its grantmaking policy in the latest accounts: 'The trustees seek to make donations to other charities and voluntary bodies for the benefit of Church of England preservation projects and other charities dealing with historical preservation, both local to Oxfordshire and nationally. The trustees may also seek to make donations to other charities, voluntary bodies and individuals relating to the arts, music and also for general charitable purposes.'

In 2011/12 this trust had assets of £1.7 million and an income of £51,000. There were 48 grants made during the year totalling £38,000.

Beneficiaries included: Rotherfield Greys Parochial Church Council (£7,000); Institute of Economic Affairs (£2,500); Care International, King Edward Hospital, the London Library and Opera Holland Park (£1,000 each); the Children's Society and the Pearl Harris Trust (£500 each); and Friends of Dorchester Abbey (£250).

Applications

In writing to the correspondent.

Information gathered from:

Accounts; Charity Commission record.

Buckingham Trust

Christian purposes, relief of poverty and sickness and support for older people

£487,000 to organisations

(2011/12)

Beneficial area

UK and worldwide.

Correspondent: The Trustees, Foot Davson, 17 Church Road, Tunbridge Wells, Kent TN1 1LG (tel: 01892 774774)

Trustees: Richard Foot; Tina Clay.

CC Number: 237350

The trust's objects are the advancement of religion and other charitable purposes.

In 2011/12 the trust held assets of £619,000 and had an income of £244,000, mostly from voluntary donations. Grants were made totalling £487,000, broken down as follows:

Charities	£386,000
Churches	£101,000

Beneficiaries included: Tear Fund (£38,000); Barnabas Fund (£37,000); OMF International (£33,000); Church Mission Society (£32,000); All Saints – Crowborough (£30,000); Battle Methodist Church (£29,000); Cure International (£7,400); World in Need (£6,000); Christchurch Claypath Durham (£3,000); Giddeons (£1,400); and The Manor Preparatory School (£1,200).

A small amount (£5,900) was also distributed to individuals.

Applications

Unsolicited applicants are not considered. As an agency charity, the trustees allow the donors to choose which registered charities or churches their funds are given to.

Information gathered from:

Accounts; Charity Commission record.

Buckland Charitable Trust

General, health, international development and welfare

£31,000 (2011/12)

Beneficial area

UK and overseas.

Correspondent: The Trustees, c/o Smith and WIlliamson Ltd, 1 Bishops Wharf,

Walnut Tree Close, Guildford, Surrey GU1 4RA (tel: 01483 407100)

Trustees: Paul Bannister; Ali Afsari; Anna Bannister.

CC Number: 273679

In 2011/12 the trust held assets of £1.6 million, had an income of £34,000 and made grants to 33 organisations totalling £31,000. During the year the majority of support was given to health related activities.

Beneficiaries included: Macmillan (£3,000); Médecins Sans Frontières, Eden Valley Hospice and Cancer Research (£2,000 each); East Cumbria Family Support and Scope (£1,000 each); Camphill Village Trust, Kids in Action and RNLI (£500 each); and The Smile Train (£200).

Applications

In writing to the correspondent.

Information gathered from:

Accounts; Charity Commission record.

The Bulldog Trust Ltd

General charitable purposes

£180,000 to organisations (2011/12)

Beneficial area

Worldwide, with a preference for the South of England.

Correspondent: Mary Gunn, Correspondent, 2 Temple Place, London WC2R 3BD (tel: 0207246044; email: info@bulldogtrust.org; website: www.bulldogtrust.org)

Trustees: Martin Riley; Brian Smouha; Charles Hoare; Hamish McPherson; Kim Hoare; Alex Williams.

CC Number: 1123081

The following information is taken from the trust's website:

> Operating since 1983, the Bulldog Trust has donated more than £4m to a range of charities. The trust aims to support charity in ways which ensure that smaller donations provide maximum benefit.
>
> ***The Golden Bottle Trust and the Bulldog Trust Funding Initiative***
>
> In 2012, the trust launched its first collaborative funding initiative with The Golden Bottle Trust. The initiative has been hailed by Philanthropy UK as a 'revolutionary criteria-free grant-making scheme' and aims to provide small to medium sized charitable organisations with the chance to access funding of between £1,000 and £30,000 without a complicated and time consuming application process.
>
> The funding year runs from 1 April – 31 March and in 2012/13, £250,000 was available for distribution. In 2013/14 a total of £300,000 was offered over three rounds.

For full application guidelines and forms visit the trust's website.

In 2011/12 the trust had assets of £9.9 million and an income of £595,000. Grants were made to 76 organisations and totalled £180,000.

Beneficiaries included: University of Winchester (£22,500); Public Catalogue Foundation (£16,500); English Heritage Foundation, Park and Gardens Data Service and Special Boat Service Association (£10,000 each).

Exclusions

No grants are given to individuals or to unsolicited applications.

Applications

The trust regrets that unsolicited applications cannot be accepted.

Information gathered from:

Accounts; Charity Commission record; funder's website.

The Burden Trust

Christian, welfare, medical research, education, general

£126,000 (2011/12)

Beneficial area

UK and overseas.

Correspondent: Patrick O'Conor, Secretary, 51 Downs Park West, Westbury Park, Bristol BS6 7QL (tel: 01179 628611; email: p.oconor@netgates.co.uk; website: www.burdentrustbristol.co.uk)

Trustees: A. C. Miles, Chair; Dr Joanna Bacon; R. E. J. Bernays; Dr M. G. Barker; Prof. A. Halestrap.

CC Number: 235859

The trust operates in accordance with various trust deeds dating back to 1913. These deeds provide for grants for medical research, hospitals, retirement homes, schools and training institutions, homes and care for the young and people in need. The trust operates with an adherence to the tenets and principles of the Church of England.

Grants are generally for around £5,000 and the trust prefers to 'build a relationship with the organisation concerned and always look to see how best a project that is funded can be effectively sustained for the future'.

In 2011/12 the trust had assets of £3.8 million and an income of £85,000. There were 20 grants totalling £126,000 which were made under the following categories:

Schools and training institutions	5	£55,000
Support of the marginalised	12	£48,000
Organisations for care and training of young people	3	£23,000
Total	20	£126,000

Beneficiaries included: Langham Research Scholarships (£18,000); Oxford Centre for Mission Studies (£16,000); Easton Families Project (£17,500); Crisis Centre Ministries and Trinity College Bristol (£10,000 each); Changing Tunes (£7,800); Barton Camp and Wheels Project (£4,000); Urban Saints (£3,000); The Seed Project and Frontier Youth Trust (£2,500); Avon Riding Camp (£2,000); and BCAN (£1,000).

Exclusions

No grants to individuals.

Applications

Via the online form available on the trust's website by 31 March each year in preparation for the trustee meeting in June. Once an online application is submitted the trustees will make further contact before the June meeting if they want a full application.

Information gathered from:

Accounts; Charity Commission record; funder's website.

Burdens Charitable Foundation

General charitable purposes

£254,000 (2010/11)

Beneficial area

UK, but mostly overseas, with special interest in Sub-Saharan Africa.

Correspondent: Arthur James Burden, Trustee, St George's House, 215–219 Chester Road, Manchester M15 4JE (tel: 01618 324901)

Trustees: Arthur James Burden; Godfrey Wilfred Burden; Hilary Margaret Perkins; Sally Anne Schofield; Anthony David Burden; Professor Burden.

CC Number: 273535

'There are no formal restrictions on the charitable activities that can be supported, but the trustees' main activities currently embrace the prevention and relief of acute poverty, substantially through the medium of education and healthcare and most especially in countries such as those of sub-Saharan Africa.'

Accounts for 2010/11 are the latest available at the time of writing.

In 2010/11 the foundation had assets of £20.8 million, an income of £587,000 and made 39 grants totalling £254,000 a significant number of which went overseas.

Beneficiaries of grants of £3,000 or more included: Build-it (£49,000); The Message Trust (£20,000); REAP (£11,000); Kings World Trust India and Wuluga (£10,000 each); and Zagalona Workshop (£3,000).

Exclusions

Causes which rarely or never benefit include animal welfare (except in less developed countries), the arts and museums, political activities, most medical research, preservation etc. of historic buildings and monuments, individual educational grants and sport, except sport for people with disabilities. No grants are made to individuals.

Applications

In writing to the correspondent, accompanied by recent, audited accounts and statutory reports, coupled with at least an outline business plan where relevant. Trustees usually meet in March, June, September and December.

Information gathered from:

Accounts; Charity Commission record.

The Clara E. Burgess Charity

Children and young people

£275,000 (2011/12)

Beneficial area

UK and worldwide.

Correspondent: The Trust Section Manager, RBS Trust Services, Eden, Lakeside, Chester Business Park, Wrexham Road, Chester CH4 9QT (tel: 01244 625810)

Trustee: The Royal Bank of Scotland plc.

CC Number: 1072546

Registered in 1998, this trust makes grants to registered charities where children are the principal beneficiaries of the work. Grants are towards 'the provision of facilities and assistance to enhance the education, health and physical well-being of children particularly (but not exclusively) those under the age of ten years who have lost one or both parents'. Within these boundaries grants can be made to the following causes: education/training, overseas projects, disability, social welfare, hospitals/hospices, medical/ health and medical research.

In 2011/12 the trust had assets of £10.4 million and an income of £282,000. Grants were made to 57 organisations totalling £275,000. Most grants were for £5,000 or less.

Beneficiaries included: Operation Orphan, Positive Action on Cancer and Rucksack (£10,000 each); Smile Train (£7,500); Autism Initiatives (£5,500); Douglas Bader Foundation, Play Train, Richard House and Sign Post (£5,000 each); Nelson's Journey and Toybox (£3,000 each); Dove Service and Royal Horticultural Society (£2,000 each); and Human Farleigh Hospice (£500).

Exclusions

No grants to non-registered charities.

Applications

In writing to the correspondent. Applications are considered in January and July.

Information gathered from:

Accounts; Charity Commission record.

The Burry Charitable Trust

Medicine, health, disability and welfare

£57,000 (2011/12)

Beneficial area

UK, with a preference for Highcliffe and the surrounding and further areas.

Correspondent: Robert J. Burry, Trustee, 261 Lymington Road, Highcliffe, Christchurch, Dorset BH23 5EE (tel: 01425 277661)

Trustees: Robert Burry; Adrian Osman; Judith Knight; James Lapage.

CC Number: 281045

In 2011/12 the trust had assets of £930,000 and an income of £81,000. Grants were made to 22 mainly local organisations totalling £57,000.

Beneficiaries included: Oakhaven Hospital Trust (£15,000); Canine Partners and Salvation Army (£5,000 each); British Red Cross and Isle of Wight Air Ambulance (£2,500 each); St John Ambulance (£2,000); Wessex Autistic Society, Christchurch Music Centre and Parkinson's Disease Society (£1,500 each); Myeloma UK, New Milton Guides and 3rd Ringwood Scout Group £1,000 each); and Sway Welfare Aid Group (£250).

Exclusions

No grants to individuals or students.

Applications

This trust states that it does not respond to unsolicited applications.

Information gathered from:

Accounts; Charity Commission record.

The Arnold Burton 1998 Charitable Trust

Jewish, medical research, education, social welfare, heritage

£132,000 (2011/12)

Beneficial area

Worldwide.

Correspondent: The Trust Managers, c/o Trustee Management Ltd, 19 Cookridge Street, Leeds LS2 3AG (tel: 01132 436466)

Trustees: Arnold Burton; Mark Burton; Jeremy Burton; Nicholas Burton.

CC Number: 1074633

Established in 1998, this trust gives special consideration to appeals from Jewish charities and projects related to medical research, education, social welfare and heritage. No grants are made to individuals. In 2011/12 it had assets of £5.3 million, an income of £140,000 and 238 grants were made totalling £132,000. Donations were broken down as follows:

Jewish/Israel	43	£42,000
Health	59	£35,500
Social welfare	82	£31,000
Third world	23	£9,000
Education	15	£7,000
Arts and amenities	16	£7,000

Beneficiaries included: Hillel Foundation B'nai Brith (£10,000); JNF Charitable Trust and Lubavitch Foundation (£5,000 each); Berkshire School, Clothing Solutions, NSPCC, Pain Relief Foundation and Paperworks (£1,000 each); Apex Challenge, Macular Disease Society and Sign Health (£500 each); Scope (£250); and Cued Speech Association (£30).

Applications

In writing to the trust managers. Unsuccessful appeals will not necessarily be acknowledged.

Information gathered from:

Accounts; Charity Commission record.

Consolidated Charity of Burton upon Trent

General

£57,000 to organisations (2012)

Beneficial area

The former county borough of Burton upon Trent and the parishes of Branston, Stretton and Outwoods.

Correspondent: T. J. Bramall, Clerk to the Trustees, Talbot and Co., 148 High Street, Burton upon Trent, Staffordshire DE14 1JY (tel: 01283 564716; email:

clerk@consolidatedcharityburton.org.uk; website: www.consolidatedcharityburton.org.uk)

Trustees: Valerie Burton; Gwendoline Foster; Patricia Phyllis Hill; Beryl Toon; John Peach; Marie Lorain Nash; Peter Davies; Margaret Heather; Dennis Fletcher; Patricia Ackroyd; Gerald Hamilton; Elizabeth Staples; Ben Robinson; David Clegg Leese; Revd Robert Styles; Leonard Milner; George Faragher; Geoffrey Brown.

CC Number: 239072

This large local trust supports individuals and organisations within the area of benefit. In 2012 the trust had assets of £11.1 million and an income of £426,000. Grants to organisations totalled £57,000 and a further £77,000 was given to individuals for relief-in-need purposes and educational purposes. The trust also operates almshouse accommodation.

Numerous organisations receive funding from the charity including churches, other registered charities, and voluntary groups within the area of benefit. Grants are made for capital and revenue cost, but not salaries.

Beneficiaries included: Burton and District Operatic Society (£8,700); Winshill Parish Youth Council and St Peter's Church Stapenhill PC (£5,000 each); ESBC Sports Development and Pulse for Music Staffordshire (£3,000 each); Able Too Forum (£2,000); Burton and District Arts Council (£1,000); Waterside Youth Project (£900); and Harvey Girls (£500).

Exclusions

No grants for salaries.

Applications

On a form which can be downloaded from the trust's website. Applications for grants from organisations are considered by the main committee which meets three times a year. Meeting dates and deadlines are available published along with the application form and guidelines.

Percentage of awards given to new applicants: between 10% and 20%.

Common applicant mistakes

'Incomplete application forms.'

Information gathered from:

Accounts; Charity Commission record; further information provided by the funder; funder's website.

The Derek Butler Trust

Medical research, health, music and music education

£344,000 to organisations

(2011/12)

Beneficial area

Worldwide, in practice UK.

Correspondent: James McLean, Trustee, c/o Underwood Solicitors LLP, 40 Welbeck Street, London W1G 8LN (tel: 020 7526 6000; email: info@thederekbutlertrust.org.uk; website: www.thederekbutlertrust.org.uk)

Trustees: James McLean; Donald F. Freeman; Revd Michael Fuller; Hilary A. E. Guest.

CC Number: 1081995

The trust was established in 2000 for general charitable purposes, with an interest in medical research, health, music and music education. The following information is taken from the 2011/12 annual report:

> The charity has established its current grant making policy to achieve in particular its objects for the public benefit to:
>
> (a) promote cancer research (including into oesophageal cancers) and to improve the lives of sufferers from such cancers and related conditions through a grant to establish a specialist nursing post.
>
> (b) promote music education by grants to organisations which promote musical education for young musicians, including grants by way of bursary to music colleges, generally for post-graduate education.
>
> The charity carries out these objects by (following the numbering above):
>
> (a) Funding pure research (by meeting the direct costs of research posts of specific research projects carried out by other charitable organisations, such as CORE). Making grants to hospices in the London area for specific and general purposes.
>
> (b) Making grants, principally by post-graduate music scholarships to four London Music Colleges through the Derek Butler London Scholarship, which provides an annual scholarship to the participants (nominated by their respective colleges). In addition, the trustees support other charitable organisations for young musicians, such as the National Opera Studio, the National Youth Orchestra and British Youth Opera.

In 2011/12 the trust had assets of £12 million and an income of £343,000. Grants were made during the year totalling £402,000, which included £58,000 in awards through the Derek Butler London Prize.

There were 21 grants made to organisations, with beneficiaries including: Awards for Young Musicians (£100,000); The Digestive Disorders Foundation (£68,500); St Luke's Hospice Plymouth (£45,000); The International Organ Festival Society (£18,000); Kensington and Chelsea Cruse (£20,000); Anglican Centre in Rome and Seventy4 Foundation (£15,000 each); Akamba Aid Fund Charity (£2,000); Royal College of Music (£1,500); and St Martin-in-the-Fields (£1,000).

Applications

In writing to the correspondent. 'The trustees continue to seek new charities to which they can make suitable donations.'

Information gathered from:

Accounts; Charity Commission record; funder's website.

The Noel Buxton Trust

Child and family welfare, penal matters, Africa

£94,000 (2012)

Beneficial area

UK, eastern and southern Africa.

Correspondent: The Trustees, PO Box 520, Fleet, Hampshire GU51 9GX (website: www.noelbuxtontrust.org.uk)

Trustees: Simon Buxton; Jon Snow; Jo Tunnard; John Littlewood; Brendan Gormley; Emma Compton-Burnett; Katie Aston; Katie Buxton.

CC Number: 220881

The following information is taken from the trust's helpful website:

> When Lord Noel-Buxton set up the Trust in 1919, he intended to foster a 'worldwide view of human welfare and a belief that it can be affected by human action'. The trustees today remain committed to this broad aim, and fulfil it by supporting voluntary and community based organisations in Great Britain and in some of the most vulnerable parts of Africa.
>
> The trust has a long-standing concern for the welfare of both families and prisoners, and its work in Britain continues to focus on these areas. In Africa, the trustees seek to support community-led organisations working to build local sustainable livelihoods. In all three areas, the Trustees have an interest in funding work which, although pressing, does not easily attract funding from other sources.
>
> Each area of funding has specific guidelines and exclusions. Please read them carefully if you wish to make an appeal. An appeal is more likely to be successful when the applicant shows how the work fits within our guidelines.

In 2012 the trust had assets of £2.3 million and an income of £112,000. Donations were made totalling £94,000. The trustees considered 132 appropriate new appeals and made 22 new grants. In addition, trustees renewed 16 grants to existing beneficiaries. The 38 grants comprised 11 for Africa, 7 to support vulnerable families and 20 for work with prisoners. Trustees were able to support 17% of the new appeals they received.

Beneficiaries included: Family Rights Group, Fatherhood and Vida (£5,000 each); Exeter Ethiopia Link, Microloan Foundation and Renewable World (£4,000 each); International Childcare Trust (£3,500); African Children's Fund and Find Your Feet (£3,000 each); Fair Shares, Forest of Mercia and Prison Fellowship (£2,000 each); The Forgiveness Project and Women Acting in Today's Society (£1,500 each); Daylight, Mentoring Plus and Prison Advice and Care Trust (£1,000 each); and Cumbria Reducing Offending Partnership Trust (£500).

Exclusions

In addition to the specific exclusions of each programme, grants are not made for: academic research; advice centres; animal charities including those running sanctuaries, rescue or adoption services; the arts for their own sake; buildings; conferences; counselling for individuals; expeditions, exchanges, holidays, study tours, visits; housing and homelessness; human rights; HIV/AIDS programmes; grants are not made to INDIVIDUALS for any purpose; Northern Ireland; organisations set up primarily to treat medical conditions, physical disabilities or mental health issues; playgrounds; prizes; race relations; contribution to a specific salaried post; schools, including school infrastructure and teaching equipment; vehicles; victims of crime (except those affected by domestic violence and victims involved with restorative justice projects); videos and IT.

Applications

Visit the trust's website for guidance on how to apply to each programme.

Information gathered from:

Accounts; Charity Commission record; funder's website.

C. and F. Charitable Trust

Orthodox Jewish charities

£85,000 (2011/12)

Beneficial area

UK and overseas.

Correspondent: The Trustees, 50 Keswick Street, Gateshead, Tyne and Wear NE8 1TQ

Trustees: Fradel Kaufman; Simon Kaufman.

CC Number: 274529

The trust income derives mainly from investment properties and other investments. Grants are made to Orthodox Jewish charities.

In 2011/12 the trust had assets of £1.2 million, an income of £176,000 and made grants totalling £85,000.

Previous beneficiaries have included Community Council of Gateshead, Ezras Nitrochim, Gur Trust, Kollel Shaarei Shlomo, SOFT and Yetev Lev Jerusalem Trust.

Exclusions

Registered charities only.

Applications

In writing to the correspondent.

Information gathered from:

Accounts; Charity Commission record.

The James Caan Foundation

Social welfare, education

£193,000 (2011/12)

Beneficial area

UK and Pakistan.

Correspondent: Hanah Caan, Trustee, Hamilton Bradshaw, 60 Grosvenor Street, London W1K 3HZ (tel: 020 7399 6700; email: hanah@thejcf.co.uk; website: www.thejcf.co.uk)

Trustees: James Caan; Deepak Jalan; Hanah Caan.

CC Number: 1136617

Registered with the Charity Commission in 2010, this is the charitable foundation of James Caan, entrepreneur. The objects of the foundation are broadly social welfare and education in the UK and Caan's native Pakistan.

The foundation is currently focused on the 'Build a Village Project' – constructing villages in Pakistan to help those who were affected by the 2010 floods. A full description of the project and details on the other individuals and organisations involved can be found on the foundation's website.

In 2011/12 the foundation had assets of £350,000 and an income of £142,000. Grants were approved to 24 organisations totalling £193,000.

International Aid	9	£152,000
Other	10	£30,000
Education	5	£10,500

Previously, Caan, either personally or through the foundation, has supported organisations in the UK and Pakistan including: Prince's Trust; NSPCC; Care Foundation; BBC Children in Need; Big Issue; Comic Relief; Sport Relief; vInspired; Marie Curie Cancer Care; Mosaic; and the British Asian Trust.

Applications

In writing to the correspondent.

Information gathered from:

Accounts; Charity Commission record; funder's website.

Peter Cadbury Charitable Trust

General, arts, conservation, cancer

£28,000 (2011/12)

Beneficial area

UK and overseas.

Correspondent: Derek Larder, Trustee, KS Carmichael Accountants, PO Box 4UD, London W1A 4UD (tel: 020 7258 1577; email: dlarder@kscarmichael.com)

Trustees: Derek Larder; Peter Cadbury; Sally Cadbury.

CC Number: 327174

The trust makes grants to registered charities for general charitable purposes, with a preference for the arts, conservation and cancer-related causes. Grants range from between £25 and £3,500.

In 2011/12 the trust had assets of £540,000 and an income of £31,000. There were 15 grants made totalling £28,000. Many beneficiaries are supported on a regular basis.

Beneficiaries included: The Royal Ballet School (£3,000 in two grants); Tate Gallery (£2,000); Garsington Opera, Trinity Hospice and The Wallace Collection (£1,500 each); The Reliance Trust (£1,300); and Natural History Museum (£1,000).

Applications

The trust does not usually respond to unsolicited applications.

Percentage of awards given to new applicants: less than 10%.

Information gathered from:

Accounts; Charity Commission record; further information provided by the funder.

Henry T. and Lucy B. Cadbury Charitable Trust

Quaker causes and institutions, health, homelessness, support groups, developing world

Around £30,000 (2012)

Beneficial area

Mainly UK, but also the Third World.

Correspondent: The Secretary, c/o B. C. M, Box 2024, London WC1N 3XX

Trustees: Candia Carolan; Ruth Charity; Bevis Gillett; Elizabeth Rawlins; Tamsin Yates; Dr Emma Hambly.

CC Number: 280314

In 2012 the trust had an income of £22,500 and a total expenditure of over £31,000.

Grant recipients are usually those that are personally chosen by one of the trustees. Previously beneficiaries included: Quaker United Nations Office (£5,000); Battle Against Tranquillizers, British Pugwash Trust, the People's Kitchen and Slower Speeds Trust (£2,000 each); Action for ME, Money for Madagascar and Tools for Self Reliance (£1,500 each); and Calcutta Rescue Fund, Quaker Opportunity Playgroup and Youth Education Service Midnapore (£1,000 each).

Exclusions

No grants to non-registered charities.

Applications

The trust's income is committed each year and so unsolicited applications are not normally accepted. The trustees meet in March to consider applications.

Information gathered from:

Accounts; Charity Commission record.

C. J. Cadbury Charitable Trust

Environment, conservation, music

£13,000 (2011/12)

Beneficial area

UK.

Correspondent: Deborah Ashbourne, Martineau LLP, No. 1 Colmore Square, Birmingham B4 6AA (tel: 0870 763 2000; fax: 0870 763 2001)

Trustees: Hugh Carslake; Joy Cadbury; Thomas Cadbury; Lucy Cadbury.

CC Number: 270609

In 2011/12 the trust had assets of £700,000 and an income of £36,000. There were 15 grants awarded totalling £13,000.

Only those beneficiaries in receipt of £1,000 or more in grants were listed in the accounts. They were: Island Conservation Society UK (£8,000); and Devon Wildlife Trust (£1,000).

Applications

The trust does not generally support unsolicited applications.

Information gathered from:

Accounts; Charity Commission record.

The G. W. Cadbury Charitable Trust

Family planning, conservation, general

£182,000 (2011/12)

Beneficial area

Worldwide.

Correspondent: The Trust Administrator, PFK (UK) LLP, GW Cadbury Charitable Trust, New Guild House, 45 Great Charles Street, Queensway, Birmingham B3 2LX

Trustees: Jennifer Boal; Jessica Woodroffe; Peter Boal; Lyndall Boal; Nick Woodroffe; Caroline Woodroffe.

CC Number: 231861

This trust established in 1955 is for general charitable purposes.

In 2011/12 the trust had assets of £5.7 million and an income of £245,000. There were 73 grants made totalling £182,000, given in the following geographical areas:

UK	£81,000
USA	£96,000
Africa	£5,000

Beneficiaries included: Colston's Primary School (£35,000); Pacific Northwest Ballet – USA (£30,000); Gender and Development Network (£10,000); British Pregnancy Advisory Service (£6,000); Compassion in Dying (£5,000); Brook (£4,000); Birmingham Royal Ballet (£2,000); and Swaledale Friends (£1,000).

Other smaller grants of less than £999 were made to 34 organisations and totalled £6,000.

Exclusions

No grants to individuals or non-registered charities, or for scholarships.

Applications

In writing to the correspondent.

Information gathered from:

Accounts; Charity Commission record.

The Christopher Cadbury Charitable Trust

Nature conservation, general

£55,000 (2011/12)

Beneficial area

UK, with a preference for the Midlands.

Correspondent: The Trust Administrator, PKF (UK) LLP, New Guild House, 45 Great Charles Street, Queensway, Birmingham B3 2LX (tel: 01212 122222)

Trustees: Roger Cadbury; Tim Peet; Dr James Cadbury; Tina Benfield; Virginia Reekie; Peter Cadbury.

CC Number: 231859

In 2011/12 the trust had assets of £1.8 million, which generated an income of £87,000. Grants totalled £55,000.

The majority of beneficiaries were supported in previous years; grants included those made to: Fircroft College and Island Conservation Society UK (£10,500 each); Playthings Past Museum Trust (£7,500); Devon Wildlife Trust (£6,000); Bower Trust, R. V. J. Cadbury Charitable Trust, Norfolk Wildlife Trust, R. A. and V. B. Reekie Charitable Trust and Sarnia Charitable Trust (£2,000 each); Survival International (£1,000); and Avoncroft Arts Society and Selly Oak Nursery School (£500 each).

Exclusions

No support for individuals.

Applications

Unsolicited applications are unlikely to be successful.

Information gathered from:

Accounts; Charity Commission record.

The Edward and Dorothy Cadbury Trust

Health, education, arts

£124,000 (2011/12)

Beneficial area

Preference for the West Midlands area.

Correspondent: Susan Anderson, Company Secretary/Trust Manager, Rokesley, University of Birmingham Selly Oak, Bristol Road, Selly Oak, Birmingham B29 6QF (tel: 01214 721838; email: e-dcadburytrust@btconnect.com; website: www.e-dcadburytrust.org.uk)

Trustees: Dr Cathleen Elliott; Philippa Ward; Susan Anfilogoff; Julia Gillett; Julie Cadbury.

CC Number: 1107327

This trust was registered in December 2004, and is the recipient of funds transferred from the now defunct Edward and Dorothy Cadbury Trust (1928), registered charity number 221441. The objects of the new trust remain the same, i.e. general charitable purposes in the West Midlands, with areas of work funded including music and the arts, children's charities, disadvantaged groups and support for the voluntary sector. The normal range of grants is between £500 and £2,500, with occasional larger grants made.

In 2011/12 this trust had assets of £5.5 million, which generated an income of £172,000. Grants were made to 110 organisations totalling £124,000, which were distributed under the following categories:

Category	No.	Amount
Compassionate support	39	£38,000
Arts and culture	17	£28,000
Community projects and integration	25	£20,500
Education and training	19	£18,500
Conservation and the environment	6	£12,500
Research	4	£7,000

Beneficiaries included: Birmingham Royal Ballet (£15,000); Acorns Children's Hospice, Quaker Memorial Service Trust and RSPB (£5,000 each); Bromsgrove Festival (£4,000); Birmingham Settlement, Camphill Village Trust, Motability and RNIB (£1,000 each); Foundation for Conductive Education and SENSE (£750 each); Association for Rehabilitation of Communication and Oral Skills, British Wireless for the Blind Forum, Contact a Family, Orchestra of the Swan, Send a Cow and Worcestershire Wildlife Trust (£500 each).

Exclusions

No grants to individuals.

Applications

The following is taken from the trust's helpful website:

> An application for funding may be made at any time and should be submitted in writing to the trust manager either by post or email. Trustees request that the letter of application should provide a clear and concise description of the project for which the funding is required as well as the outcomes and benefits that it is intended to achieve. They also require an outline budget and explanation of how the project is to be funded initially and in the future together with the latest annual report and accounts for the charity.
>
> Applications for funding are generally considered within a three month timescale. Please note that applications which fall outside the trust's stated areas of interest may not be considered or acknowledged.

The trust's 2011/12 annual report states:

> As a matter of good practice, trustees undertake a programme of visits to organisations where a grant of high value has been made or the activity is of particular interest to the trust in terms of future development. This has proved helpful in building up positive relationships with grantees and providing networking opportunities.

Information gathered from:

Accounts; Charity Commission record; funder's website.

The George Cadbury Trust

General

£379,000 (2011/12)

Beneficial area

Preference for the West Midlands, Hampshire and Gloucestershire.

Correspondent: Sarah Moss, PKF Accountants, New Guild House, 45 Great Charles Street, Queensway, Birmingham B3 2LX (tel: 01216 093282)

Trustees: Anne L. K. Cadbury; Sir Adrian Cadbury; Mark Cadbury; Roger V. J. Cadbury; A. Jane Cadbury.

CC Number: 1040999

The trust was set up in 1924 and maintains a strong financial interest in the Cadbury company.

In 2011/12 the trust had assets of £10.4 million, an income of £412,000 and made grants totalling £379,000.

Beneficiaries included: Birmingham Royal Ballet (£33,000); Dean and Chapters Gloucester Cathedral (£20,000); Cheltenham College Charity Fund (£15,000); ForceSelect Foundation (£12,000); Gloucestershire Community Foundation and Green Oasis Appeal (£10,000 each); Peter H. G. Cadbury Trust (£6,000); Fircroft College, Soil Association and Sydney Children's Hospital Foundation (£5,000 each); Hackwood Festival (£4,000); Friends of Bournville Carillon Ltd (£3,600); Help for Heroes (£3,000); Second Chance (£2,000); and St Luke's Hospice, Hillside Animal Sanctuary and Gosford Forest Guide House Co. Armagh (£1,000 each).

Exclusions

No support for individuals for projects, courses of study, expeditions or sporting tours. No support for overseas appeals.

Applications

In writing to the correspondent to be considered quarterly. Note that very few new applications are supported due to ongoing and alternative commitments.

Information gathered from:

Accounts; Charity Commission record.

Calleva Foundation

General charitable purposes

£263,000 (2011)

Beneficial area

UK and worldwide.

Correspondent: The Trustees, PO Box 22554, London W8 5GN (email: contactcalleva@btopenworld.com)

Trustees: Caroline Butt; Stephen Butt.

CC Number: 1078808

Registered with the Charity Commission in January 2000, this foundation can give in the UK and worldwide for general charitable purposes.

In 2011 the trust had assets of £168,000, an income of £395,000, and paid out £263,000 in grants which were categorised as follows:

Education	£155,000
Social services	£42,000
Overseas/international relief	£29,500
Children's holidays	£15,000
Environment	£11,000
Medical research	£10,000

No further information on beneficiaries was available.

Applications

This trust does not accept unsolicited applications.

Percentage of awards given to new applicants: less than 10%.

Common applicant mistakes

'Too much information; requests [for funding] too frequent.'

Information gathered from:

Accounts; Charity Commission record; further information provided by the funder.

The Calpe Trust

Relief work

£26,500 (2011/12)

Beneficial area

Worldwide.

Correspondent: Reggie Norton, Trustee, The Hideaway, Sandy Lane, Hatford Down, Faringdon, Oxfordshire SN7 8JH (tel: 01367 870665; email: reggienorton@talktalk.net)

Trustees: Reggie Norton; Beatrice Norton; Edward Perks.

CC Number: 1004193

The trust makes grants towards registered charities benefiting people in need including refugees, homeless people, people who are socially disadvantaged, victims of war, victims of disasters and so on.

In 2011/12 the trust had assets of £1 million and an income of £32,000. It made 10 grants totalling £26,500.

Beneficiaries included: Ecumenical Project for International Cooperation (£8,000); New Israel Fund and Salt of the Earth (£5,000 each); Womankind for Nepal (£1,000); and Peace Trails through London (£500).

Exclusions

No grants towards animal welfare or to individuals.

Applications

In writing to the correspondent. Applicants must contact the trust before making an application.

Percentage of awards given to new applicants: less than 10%.

Information gathered from:

Accounts; Charity Commission record; further information provided by the funder.

H. and L. Cantor Trust

Jewish, general

Around £300,000 (2011/12)

Beneficial area

UK, with some preference for Sheffield.

Correspondent: Lilly Cantor, Trustee, 3 Ivy Park Court, 35 Ivy Park Road, Sheffield S10 3LA (tel: 01142 306354)

Trustees: Lily Cantor; Nicholas Jeffrey.

CC Number: 220300

The principal objective of the trust is to provide benefit for charities, particularly Jewish charities.

In 2011/12 the trust had an income of just £465 and an unusually high expenditure of £315,000 (£48,000 in 2010/11). No further information was available.

Previous beneficiaries include: Delamere Forest School Ltd, Sheffield Jewish Congregation and Centre, Sheffield Jewish Welfare Organisation, I Rescue, Jewish Childs Day, Sense, Share Zadek UK, Brain Research Trust, PDSA – Sheffield and World Cancer Research.

Applications

Unsolicited applications are not considered.

Information gathered from:

Accounts; Charity Commission record.

Cardy Beaver Foundation

General

£111,000 (2012/13)

Beneficial area

UK with preference for Berkshire.

Correspondent: John James, Trustee, Clifton House, 17 Reading Road, Pangbourne, Berkshire RG8 7LU (tel: 01189 614260)

Trustees: John James; Mary Cardy; Sandra Rice.

CC Number: 265763

Registered with the Charity Commission in May 1973, in 2012/13 the foundation had assets of £2.4 million and an income of £159,000. Grants totalled £111,000. Unfortunately, no list of grant recipients was included with the annual report. Grants tend to be for amounts of around £5,000 or less.

Previous beneficiaries have included: Cancer Research UK, Watermill Theatre Appeal, Wallingford Museum, NSPCC, Berkshire Blind Society, Adventure Dolphin, St Peter's Parochial Church Council, Church House Trust, RNLI and Asthma Relief, Julia's House, Elizabeth Foundation, Com Exchange – Newbury and Pangbourne Fete.

Exclusions

Registered charities only.

Applications

In writing to the correspondent.

Information gathered from:

Accounts; Charity Commission record.

The D. W T. Cargill Fund

General

Around £200,000 (2011/12)

Beneficial area

UK, with a preference for the West of Scotland.

Correspondent: Norman A. Fyfe, Trustee, Miller Beckett and Jackson Solicitors, 190 St Vincent Street, Glasgow G2 5SP

Trustees: A. C. Fyfe; W. G. Peacock; N. A. Fyfe; Mirren Elizabeth Graham.

SC Number: SC012703

This fund has the same address and trustees as two other trusts, W A Cargill Charitable Trust and W A Cargill Fund, although they all operate independently.

It supports 'any hospitals, institutions, societies or others whose work in the opinion of the trustees is likely to be beneficial to the community'.

In 2011/12 the fund had an income of £285,500. Grants have previously totalled around £200,000 a year.

Previous beneficiaries have included City of Glasgow Society of Social Service, Colquhoun Bequest Fund for Incurables, Crathie Opportunity Holidays, Glasgow and West of Scotland Society for the Blind, Glasgow City Mission, Greenock Medical Aid Society, North Glasgow Community Forum, Scottish Maritime Museum – Irvine, Scottish Episcopal Church, Scottish Motor Neurone Disease Association, Lead Scotland and Three Towns Blind Bowling/Social Club.

Exclusions

No grants are made to individuals.

Applications

In writing to the correspondent, supported by up-to-date accounts. Trustees meet quarterly.

Information gathered from:

OSCR record.

The Carlton House Charitable Trust

Jewish, education/bursaries, general

£32,000 (2011/12)

Beneficial area

UK and overseas.

Correspondent: Stewart Cohen, Trustee, Craven House, 121 Kingsway, London WC2B 6PA (tel: 020 7242 5283)

Trustees: Stewart Cohen; Pearl Cohen; Fiona Stein.

CC Number: 296791

The charity's main aim is to provide support to other charities in the UK and overseas. The charity supports a limited number of graduate and postgraduate students- in particular those in engineering, the physical sciences, drama and stage management.

In 2011/12 the trust had assets of £1.2 million and an income of £173,000. Grants were made to 147 organisations totalling £32,000.

Beneficiaries of the 23 grants of £100 or more included: Western Marble Arch Synagogue (£3,000); Community Security Trust and Bnai Brith Hillel Foundation, National Trust (£2,000 each); Royal Academy of Music and Board of Deputies Charitable Foundation (£1,000 each); Beit Halechem and London Philharmonic Orchestra (£500); Nightingale House and Ovarian Cancer Action (£250 each); and

Bnai Brith First Lodge of England (£170).

124 donations were made for £100 or less totalling £5,000.

Applications

In writing to the correspondent.

Information gathered from:

Accounts; Charity Commission record.

The Richard Carne Trust

Young people in the performing arts

£146,000 to organisations and individuals (2012)

Beneficial area

UK.

Correspondent: Christopher Gilbert, Administrator, Kleinwort Benson Trustees Ltd, 14 St George Street, London W1S 1FE (tel: 020 3207 7356)

Trustees: Kleinwort Benson Trustees Ltd; Philip Edward Carne; Marjorie Christine Carne.

CC Number: 1115903

Set up in 2006, 'the objects of the charity are to assist young people in the performing arts, and will be largely focused towards individuals in institutions dedicated to music and theatre. In addition, the trust may also wish to help fringe theatrical groups or musical groups in the early stages of their careers'.

In 2012 the trust had assets of £978,000 and an income of £219,000. Grants were made to 27 organisations totalling £146,000.

Beneficiaries included: Royal College of Music (£30,000); Trinity Laban Conservatoire of Dance and Music (£16,000); Royal Welsh College of Music and Drama (£15,000); Classical Opera Company and Theatre 503 (£5,000 each); Red Handed Theatre Company (£3,000); and British Isles Music Festival (£2,000).

The trust's annual report states: 'The trustees current policy is to annually distribute the trust's income to certain selected charities, although no commitment is given to the recipients.'

Applications

The trust's annual report gives the following information about the application process:

> The trustees' current policy is to consider all written appeals received, but only successful applications are notified of the trustees' decision. The trustees review the selected charities, and consider new appeals received at their annual trustee meeting, normally held in June.

Information gathered from:

Accounts; Charity Commission record.

The Carpenter Charitable Trust

Humanitarian and Christian outreach

Around £65,000 (2011/12)

Beneficial area

UK and overseas.

Correspondent: Michael Carpenter, Trustee, 1 Codicote Road, Welwyn, Hertfordshire AL6 9LY (tel: 01438 718439)

Trustees: Michael Carpenter; Gabriel Carpenter.

CC Number: 280692

'The charity is established on wide grant giving terms. The trustees continue to pursue their 'preferred' list approach – a list of charities with which the trustees have developed a good relationship over the years.'

In 2011/12 the trust had an income of £14,000 and a total expenditure of £65,000. A full list of beneficiaries for the year was unavailable.

Previous grants have included: Mission Aviation Fellowship Europe (£7,500); ORBIS Charitable Trust (£6,000); Andrew Christian Trust, Barnabas Fund, Help in Suffering UK; Relationships Foundation (£5,000 each); DEC Bangladesh (£2,500); Brooke Hospital for Animals, Crisis UK, Merlin and Salvation Army (£1,000 each); Blue Cross, Fight for Sight, Mercy Ships, Prison Fellowship, RSPB, Send a Cow and Tibet Relief (£500 each); and Cats Protection League (£250).

Exclusions

'The trustees do not consider applications for church repairs (other than in respect of Kimpton Church) nor applications from individuals nor any applications received from abroad unless clearly 'sponsored' by an established charity based in England and Wales.'

Applications

In writing to the correspondent including sufficient details to enable a decision to be made. However, as about half the donations made are repeat grants, the amount available for unsolicited applications remains small.

Percentage of awards given to new applicants: less than 10%.

Common applicant mistakes

'Not eligible; assume we make much larger grants than we have ever done; show lack of vision.'

Information gathered from:

Accounts; Charity Commission record; further information provided by the funder.

The Carr-Gregory Trust

Arts, social welfare, health, education

£66,500 to organisations (2012)

Beneficial area

UK.

Correspondent: Russ Carr, Trustee, 56 Pembroke Road, Clifton, Bristol BS8 3DT

Trustees: Russ Carr; Heather Wheelhouse; Linda Carr; Hannah Nicholls.

CC Number: 1085580

Grants are mainly made to charities operating in London or the Bristol area. Priority is given to the performing arts and health and social needs.

In 2012 the trust had assets of £432,000 and an income of £61,000. Grants were made to 42 organisations and totalled £66,500. One grant of £7,000 was awarded to an individual.

Awards were broken down as follows:

Arts/culture	£32,000
Social needs	£14,000
Health	£13,000
Education	£4,500

Grant beneficiaries included: the Royal National Theatre (£25,000); The Royal Academy of Music (£7,500); Quartet Charitable Foundation (£2,500); Alzheimer's Society, Diana Award and Penny Brohn Cancer Care (£2,000 each); Beating Bowel Cancer and Shakespeare at the Tobacco Factory (£1,000 each); and Centrepoint and St Mungo's (£500 each).

Applications

Applications should be made in writing to the correspondent and should not exceed two A4 pages.

Information gathered from:

Accounts; Charity Commission record.

The Carron Charitable Settlement

Environment, education, medicine

Around £3,000 (2011/12)

Beneficial area

UK and overseas.

Correspondent: Amanda Dorman, Correspondent, c/o Rothman Panthall and Co., 10 Romsey Road, Eastleigh, Hampshire SO50 9AL (tel: 02380 614555)

Trustees: Peter Fowler; David Morgan.

CC Number: 289164

The trust was created for charitable purposes in connection with wildlife, education, medicine, the countryside and the printing and publishing trade. Ongoing support is given to the St Bride's Church – Fleet Street.

Income for this charity has been steadily declining, however, it is still on the Central Register of Charities and while it remains on the register will be included here in case it should come to life again. In 2011/12 there was no income received by the charity and there was a total expenditure of £3,000.

Previous beneficiaries included: St Bride's Church Appeal (£20,000); INTBAU (£10,000); Academy of Aviation and Space Medicine (£3,000); and Curwen Print Study Centre (£1,500).

Exclusions

No grants to individuals.

Applications

The trust does not invite applications from the general public.

Information gathered from:

Accounts; Charity Commission record.

The Leslie Mary Carter Charitable Trust

Conservation/environment, welfare

£157,000 (2012)

Beneficial area

UK, with a preference for Norfolk, Suffolk and North Essex.

Correspondent: Sam Wilson, Trustee, c/o Birketts, 24–26 Museum Street, Ipswich IP1 1HZ (tel: 01473 232300)

Trustees: Sam Wilson; Leslie Carter; Martyn Carr.

CC Number: 284782

The trust has a preference for welfare organisations and conservation/environment causes, with an emphasis on local projects including those in Suffolk, Norfolk and North Essex. Grants generally range from £500 to £5,000 but larger grants are sometimes considered.

In 2012 the trust had assets of £3 million, an income of £116,000 and made grants totalling £157,000.

Beneficiaries included: Animal Health Trust (£50,000); Action Medical Research, Essex Wildlife Trust, RNIB, St Nicholas Hospice Care and The Long Shop Project Trust (£5,000 each); National Search and Rescue Dog Association and Shelter (£3,000 each); Excelsior Trust and Suffolk Accident Rescue Service (£2,000 each); and RSPB and Suffolk Preservation Society (£1,000 each).

The trustees prefer well thought-out applications for larger gifts, than many applications for smaller grants.

Exclusions

No grants to individuals.

Applications

In writing to the correspondent. Telephone calls are not welcome. There is no need to enclose an sae unless applicants wish to have materials returned.

Applications made outside the preferred areas for grant giving will be considered, but acknowledgements may not always be sent.

Percentage of awards given to new applicants: less than 10%.

Common applicant mistakes

'Repeat applications where grants never previously made.'

Information gathered from:

Accounts; Charity Commission record; further information provided by the funder.

The Carvill Trust

General

£10,000 (2011/12)

Beneficial area

UK.

Correspondent: R. J. MacGregor, Trustee, 5th Floor, Minories House, 2–5 Minories, London EC3N 1BJ (tel: 020 7780 6900)

Trustees: R. K. Carvill; R. J. MacGregor.

CC Number: 1036420

The trust was established for general charitable purposes in 1994. The income of the trust has dropped considerably in recent years from a high of £121,000 in 2008 to £1,400 in 2012. Expenditure has fluctuated, averaging £52,000 a year in the same period. In 2011/12 expenditure was £12,000. No further information was available.

Previous beneficiaries included: Irish Youth Foundation (£14,000); and Academy Ocean Reef and War Child (£10,000 each).

Applications

In writing to the correspondent, although the trust states that it only supports beneficiaries known to or connected with the trustees. Unsolicited applications from individuals will not be supported.

Information gathered from:

Accounts; Charity Commission record.

The Casey Trust

Children and young people

£112,000 (2011/12)

Beneficial area

UK and developing countries.

Correspondent: Kenneth Howard, Trustee, 27 Arkwright Road, London NW3 6BJ (tel: 020 7435 9601; website: www.caseytrust.org)

Trustees: Kenneth Howard; Edwin Green; Leonard Krikler.

CC Number: 1055726

This trust was established to help children and young people in the UK and developing countries by supporting new projects, in a variety of countries.

In 2011/12 the trust had assets of £2.8 million, an income of £194,000 and made grants totalling £112,000.

Beneficiaries included: WMF (World Monuments Fund) (£12,500); Norwood (£10,000); Youth Aliyah (£7,000); Save the Children (£5,000); Princess Royal Trust Carers and Hope (£3,000 each); Kisharon and Barnstondale Centre (£2,000 each); Trinity Hospice (£1,500); Lothians Autistic Society and Dame Vera Lynn Trust (£1,000 each); and Yes Outdoors (£900).

Exclusions

Grants are not given to 'individual applicants requesting funds to continue studies or travel'.

Applications

The trust's accounts note: 'Not being a reactive trust, it is regretted that the trustees will be unable to respond to the majority of requests for assistance. In order to both reduce costs and administration the trustees will respond mainly to those charitable institutions known to them.' There is no application form. Trustees meet four times a year.

The trustees will only notify unsuccessful applicants if an sae is enclosed.

Percentage of awards given to new applicants: between 30% and 40%.

Common applicant mistakes

'Apart from the obvious ones like not reading online or elsewhere what the trust objectives are, many give either too little or too much information, not stating what they are specifically asking for. Many don't enclose saes and demand to know why they haven't been contacted. Many re-apply after being successful, with no reference to earlier grants.'

Information gathered from:

Accounts; Charity Commission record; further information provided by the funder; funder's website.

The Catholic Charitable Trust

Catholic

£54,000 (2012)

Beneficial area

America and Europe.

Correspondent: Wilfrid Miles, Trustee, c/o Hunters, 9 New Square, London WC2A 3QN (tel: 020 7412 0050)

Trustees: John C. Vernor-Miles; W. E. Vernor-Miles; D. P. Orr.

CC Number: 215553

The trust supports traditional Catholic organisations in America and Europe.

In 2012 it had assets of £1.9 million, which generated an income of £71,000. Grants were made to 14 organisations totalling £54,000.

Beneficiaries included: Society of Saint Pius X – England (£16,000); White Fathers (£5,000); Little Sisters of the Poor (£4,000); California Friends of the Society of St Pius X and Holy Cross Parish Fulham (£2,000 each); and Carmelite Monastery Carmel California (£1,000).

Exclusions

Grants are not made to individuals.

Applications

Applications can only be accepted from registered charities and should be in writing to the correspondent. The trust does not normally support a charity unless it is known to the trustees. In order to save administration costs replies are not sent to unsuccessful applicants. For the most part funds are fully committed.

Information gathered from:

Accounts; Charity Commission record.

The Catholic Trust for England and Wales

Catholic causes

£271,500 (2012)

Beneficial area

England and Wales.

Correspondent: Revd Marcus Stock, Secretary, 39 Eccleston Square, London SW1V 1BX (tel: 020 7901 4810; email: secretariat@cbcew.org.uk; website: www.catholicchurch.org.uk)

Trustees: Rt Revd Malcolm McMahon; Ben Andradi; Richard King; Revd John Nelson; Michael Prior; Dr Elizabeth Walmsley; William Moyes; Nigel Newton.

CC Number: 1097482

The fund was established in 1968 and is concerned with 'the advancement of the Roman Catholic religion in England and Wales'. In order to fulfil its charitable aims and objectives, the activities of CaTEW are determined by the requirements of the Bishops' Conference of England and Wales.

The 2010 accounts give this background detail:

> The Catholic Bishops' Conference of England and Wales is a permanent body within the organisation of the Catholic Church that brings together the Bishops of England and Wales. As a Conference the Bishops 'jointly exercise certain pastoral functions for the Christian faithful . . . in order to promote the greater good which the Church offers to humanity, especially through forms and programs of the apostolate fittingly adapted to the circumstances of time and place' (cf. Code of Canon Law can 447).
>
> The departments of CaTEW identify the present broad areas of activity for the Bishops in supporting the Dioceses of England and Wales and witnessing to the Gospel in the contemporary world: Catholic Education and Formation, Christian Life and Worship, Christian Responsibility and Citizenship, Dialogue and Unity, Evangelisation and Catechesis and International Affairs.
>
> Each committee is concerned with a different area of work of the Church. Grants are only given to organisations which benefit England and Wales as a whole, rather than local projects.

In 2012 the trust had assets of £12 million and an income of £4 million. Grants totalled £271,500.

Beneficiaries included: CARITAS Social Action Network (£119,500); Catholic Voices (£60,000); Churches Legislation Advisory Service (£18,000); National Board of Catholic Women (£10,000); International Eucharistic Congress (£8,000); Diocese of Menevia (£3,500); and MACSAS (£2,000).

Exclusions

No grants to individuals, local projects or projects not immediately advancing the Roman Catholic religion in England and Wales.

Applications

In writing to the correspondent. The trust has stated previously that it does not respond to unsolicited applications.

Information gathered from:

Accounts; Charity Commission record; funder's website.

The Joseph and Annie Cattle Trust

General

£265,000 to organisations (2011/12)

Beneficial area

Worldwide, with a preference for Hull and East Yorkshire.

Correspondent: Roger Waudby, Administrator, PO Box 23, Hull HU12 OWF (tel: 01964 671742; fax: 01964 671742; website: www.jacattletrust.co.uk)

Trustees: Paul Edwards; Michael Gyte; Christopher Munday; S. C. Jowers.

CC Number: 262011

The object of the charity is to provide for general charitable purposes by making grants, principally to applicants in the Hull area. Older people and people who have disabilities or who are underprivileged are assisted wherever possible, and there is a particular emphasis on giving aid to children with dyslexia.

In 2011/12 the trust had assets of £7.3 million and an income of £365,000. Grants totalled £289,000 which includes £24,000 awarded to individuals. The grants (of £1,000 or more) to organisations were broken down into three main categories as follows:

Purpose	No. of grants over £1,000
Local societies and activities	38
National societies	32
Churches and missions	8

Beneficiaries included: Sobriety Project (£15,000); Dyslexia Action (£14,000); Anlaby Park Methodist Church and Prince's Trust (£5,000 each); Hull and East Riding Institution for the Blind (£3,000); Bath Institute of Medical Engineering and Ocean Youth Trust (£2,000 each); and Age UK East Riding, Longhill Primary School and Prison Fellowship (£1,000 each).

Exclusions

The trust **only** works with charitable bodies or statutory authorities and does not provide grants directly to individuals.

Applications

The following information is taken from the trust's website:

> There are two main types of application that we are looking to support:
>
> Firstly, there are applications by charitable or statutory bodies on behalf of individuals or families. The application form available through this web page must be completed by the charitable organisation/statutory body concerned and not the individual/family. Supporting papers should be attached where necessary.
> Secondly, there are applications for projects and work with the groups of people who are outlined in our key objective above. Please submit full details to the [correspondent] including the following:
>
> - The charitable organisation including contact details and the latest financial statements
> - Projects/work successfully completed to date that support the current application. Please outline work already carried out in the Hull & East Riding area. Because we will request that our grants are used exclusively in the Hull & East Riding area please identify how your organisation will guarantee this is achieved
> - The project/work together with detailed costings and supporting information (e.g. estimates/planning permission etc.)
> - Identify other grants received or currently being considered by other bodies
> - How the grant is to be spent. In considering applications the trustees may require further information so please remember it is in your interests to give as much detail as possible
>
> Application forms should be printed, **completed in handwriting** and sent to the correspondent by post or fax.

Information gathered from:

Accounts; Charity Commission record; funder's website.

The Thomas Sivewright Catto Charitable Settlement

General charitable purposes

£80,000 (2011/12)

Beneficial area

Unrestricted (for UK-based registered charities).

Correspondent: The Secretary to the Trustees, PO Box 47408, London N21 1YW

Trustees: Lord Catto; Olivia Marchant; Zoe Richmond-Watson.

CC Number: 279549

This trust has general charitable purposes, making a large number of smaller grants to a wide range of organisations and a few larger grants of up to £20,000. Despite the large number of grants made, there appears to be no strong preference for any causes or geographical areas.

In 2011/12 the trust had assets of £7.2 million, an income of £74,000 and made donations of £80,000. There was no list of beneficiaries contained within the accounts.

Previous beneficiaries included: Royal College of Music (£14,000); Royal Scottish Academy of Music and Drama (£12,000); Bowel Cancer Research and King VII's Hospital for Officers (£10,000 each); Haddo House Choral and Operatic Society and World YWCA (£5,000 each); Aviation for Paraplegics and Tetraplegics Trust (£2,000); NACRO (£1,500); Alzheimer's Research Trust, Elizabeth Finn Care, Concern Worldwide, the Fostering Network, Outward Bound Trust, Refugee Council, St Mungo's, Shelter and Charlie Waller Memorial Trust (£1,000 each); Crisis, Disabled Living Foundation, Matthew Trust, REACT and Royal London Society for the Blind (£750 each); and Clubs for Young People, Motability, Nepal Leprosy Trust, Prisoners' Advice Service, Queen Elizabeth's Foundation, Sportability and VSO (£500 each).

Exclusions

The trust does not support non-registered charities, expeditions, travel bursaries and so on, or unsolicited applications from churches of any denomination. Grants are unlikely to be considered in the areas of community care, playschemes and drug abuse, or for local branches of national organisations.

Applications

In writing to the correspondent, including an sae.

Information gathered from:

Accounts; Charity Commission record.

The Wilfrid and Constance Cave Foundation

Conservation, animal welfare, health, social welfare, general

£135,000 (2011/12)

Beneficial area

UK, with preference for Berkshire, Cornwall, Devon, Dorset, Hampshire, Oxfordshire, Somerset, Warwickshire and Wiltshire.

Correspondent: The Secretary, New Lodge Farm, Drift Road, Winkfield, Windsor SL4 4QQ (email: tcf@eamo.co.uk)

Trustees: Toni Jones; Jacqueline Archer; Mark Pickin; Nicola Thompson; Glyn Howells; Francois Jones; Janet Pickin; Melanie Waterworth; Roy Walker; William Howells.

CC Number: 241900

The trust supports local and UK-wide organisations and has general charitable purposes.

In 2011/12 it had assets of £4.1 million which generated an income of £248,000. Grants were made to 39 organisations totalling £135,000, with Oxford Museum of Children's Literature receiving the largest grant of £40,000.

Other beneficiaries included: Royal Academy of Music (£10,000); Farmers' Club Pinnacle Award (£7,000); East Berkshire Women's Aid and Moorland Mousie Trust (£5,000 each); Twitchen Parish Hall (£3,000); Two Moors Festival (£2,000); and Himalayan Children and Shooting Star Children's Hospice (£1,000 each).

Exclusions

No grants to individuals.

Applications

In writing to the correspondent a month before the trustees' meetings held twice each year, in May and October.

Percentage of awards given to new applicants: between 20% and 30%.

Common applicant mistakes

'Too much paperwork.'

Information gathered from:

Accounts; Charity Commission record; further information provided by the funder.

The Cayo Foundation

Medical research, crime, children and young people, performing arts, general

£555,500 (2011/12)

Beneficial area

UK.

Correspondent: Angela E. McCarville, Trustee, 7 Cowley Street, London SW1P 3NB (tel: 020 7248 6700)

Trustees: Angela E. McCarville; Stewart A. Harris.

CC Number: 1080607

The foundation supports the fight against crime, medical research and training, performing arts and children's charities.

In 2011/12 it had assets of £1.7 million an income of £751,000. Grants were made to 39 organisations totalling £555,500.

Previous beneficiaries included: NSPCC (£125,000); the Disability Foundation, PACT and the Royal Opera House (£25,000 each); the Princes Foundation (£20,000); Wessex Youth Trust (£10,000); Christian Blind Mission (£6,000); Wellbeing of Women (£3,000); Institute for Policy Research and Royal Humane Society (£2,500 each); and Sue Ryder Care – St John's Hospice (£1,000).

Applications

In writing to the correspondent.

Information gathered from:

Accounts; Charity Commission record.

Elizabeth Cayzer Charitable Trust

Arts

£38,500 (2011/12)

Beneficial area

UK.

Correspondent: The Hon. Elizabeth Gilmour, Trustee, The Cayzer Trust Company Ltd, Cayzer House, 30 Buckingham Gate, London SW1E 6NN (tel: 020 7802 8080)

Trustees: The Hon. Elizabeth Gilmour; Diana Lloyd; Dominic Gibbs.

CC Number: 1059265

This charity was established by The Honourable Elizabeth Gilmour, who has made significant donations to the charity since 1996. In formulating policy the trustees have taken into account the wishes of the settlor, which are that the assets of the charity should be used in supporting and promoting the work of museums, galleries and the architectural heritage of the British Isles.

The trustees in their report of 2011/12 state that they expect the level of grants in 2012/13 to increase significantly, as the income from recent increased portfolio holdings also increases.

In 2011/12 the trust had assets of £3.4 million, an income of £822,000 and made grants totalling £38,500, broken down as follows: education (£10,000); and conferences and exhibitions (£28,500). All grants in the year were made to art galleries and museums which are registered charities except for one to the Ashmolean Museum of Art and Archeology at the University of Oxford. A list of beneficiaries was not contained within the accounts.

Previous beneficiaries have included Elias Ashmole Trust; Dulwich Picture Gallery; the National Gallery and Sir John Soane's Museum.

Applications

Note the following statement taken from the charity's 2011/12 accounts:

> The trustees identify the projects and organisations they wish to support and so do not consider grants to people or organisations who apply speculatively. The trust also has a policy of not responding to any correspondence unless it relates to grants it has agreed to make or to the general management of the trust.

Information gathered from:

Accounts; Charity Commission record.

The B. G S. Cayzer Charitable Trust

General

£68,000 (2011/12)

Beneficial area

UK.

Correspondent: Mrs Sonia Barry, Trust Administrator, The Cayzer Trust Company Ltd, Cayzer House, 30 Buckingham Gate, London SW1E 6NN (tel: 020 7802 8439)

Trustees: Mr P. R. Davies; Mrs M. Buckley; Mrs A. M. Hunter; Mrs R. N. Leslie.

CC Number: 286063

In 2011/12 the trust had assets of £2.8 million, an income of £101,000 and made grants totalling £68,000, broken down as follows:

Education and training	£24,000
Medical	£17,000
Heritage and conservation	£11,500
General	£7,500
Relief of poverty	£4,500
Religion	£2,300
Arts and culture	£1,000

Limited information on beneficiaries was available although grants to the Feathers Association (£3,000), The Patricia Baines Trust (£2,500) and the Westerkirk Parish Trust (£300) were published in the accounts. Previous beneficiaries have included: Friends of the National Maritime Museum, Hike for Hope, Marie Curie Cancer Care, RAFT, St Paul's Cathedral Foundation, Scottish Countryside Alliance Education Trust and Worshipful Company of Shipwrights Charitable Fund.

Exclusions

No grants to organisations outside the UK.

Applications

The trust tends to support only people/projects known to the Cayzer family or the trustees. Unsolicited appeals will not be supported.

Information gathered from:

Accounts; Charity Commission record.

The Cazenove Charitable Trust

General

£34,500 (2012)

Beneficial area

UK.

Correspondent: Edward Harley, Trustee, Cazenove, 12 Moorgate, London EC2R 6DA (tel: 020 3479 0102)

Trustees: David Mayhew; Edward M. Harley; Michael Wentworth-Stanley; Michael Power.

CC Number: 1086899

Established in 1969, this trust primarily supports the charitable activities sponsored by current and ex Cazenove employees.

In 2012 the trust had assets of nearly £2.4 million and an income of £70,000. Grants totalled £34,500.

Beneficiaries included: Starlight Children's Foundation (£9,000); Disability Snowsport, NCC Foundation and Wheelpower (£2,500); Essex Community Foundation (£2,000); and Mayor of Havering Appeal (£1,000).

£15,000 worth of grants were made in sums of less than £1,000.

Applications

This trust does not respond to unsolicited applications.

Information gathered from:

Accounts; Charity Commission record.

The CBD Charitable Trust

General, children and young people

£238,000 (2011/12)

Beneficial area

Worldwide.

Correspondent: Coutts and Co., Trustee Dept, Coutts and Co., 440 Strand, London WC2R 0QS (tel: 020 7663 6825)

Trustees: Coutts and Co.; Ingrid Scott.

CC Number: 1136702

The trust was established in 2010 for general charitable purposes and is connected to CBD Interfaith Ministries. The trust has a preference for organisations working with children and young people.

In 2011/12 the trust had assets of £41,000 and an income of £149,000. The trustees awarded £238,000 in 71 grants ranging in value from £60 – £16,000 to a range of charities.

Beneficiaries included: Earthway, Hope Community Village, Martlets Hospice, Self Help Africa, Unity Church New York.

Applications

In writing to the correspondent.

Information gathered from:

Accounts; Charity Commission record.

CBRE Charitable Trust (formerly CB Richard Ellis Charitable Trust)

General

£34,000 (2011/12)

Beneficial area

Unrestricted.

Correspondent: Mr A. C. Naftis, Secretary to the Trustees, St Martin's Court, 10 Paternoster Row, London EC4M 7HP (tel: 020 7182 3452)

Trustees: Matthew D. Black; Nicholas E. Compton; Guy Gregory; Lena Ubhi; David Hitchcock; Miles Skinner.

CC Number: 299026

The aim of the trust is primarily to respond to clients of CBRE Ltd requests for support and to provide sponsorship to staff who are personally involved in fundraising activities. The trust will also consider applications from any other party with whom C B Richard Ellis has a significant relationship.

In 2011/12 the trust had assets of £106,000 and an income of £78,000, mostly received as funding from CBRE Ltd. There were 94 grants made totalling £34,000.

Beneficiaries included: Cancer Research UK (£2,500); Breast Cancer Campaign (£2,000); UNICEF (£1,200); ME Research UK (£1,000); Age UK (£750); Sparks (£500); Deafblind, London Legal Support Trust, Footprints and Different Strokes (£250 each); and Meningitis Research Foundation (£200).

Exclusions

Recognised charitable causes only. No grants to third parties, such as fundraising organisations or publication companies producing charity awareness materials.

Applications

In writing to the correspondent. The trust stated that in recent years they have received as many as two hundred unsolicited requests for support that do not meet with the above donations criteria. Given the size of the trust, a response to such requests is not always possible.

Information gathered from:

Accounts; Charity Commission record.

The Gaynor Cemlyn-Jones Trust

Welsh heritage, medical research, animal welfare, music and religion

£75,000 (2011/12)

Beneficial area

North Wales and Anglesey.

Correspondent: Philip G. Brown, Trustee, Park Cottage, Gannock Park, Deganwy, Conwy LL31 9PZ (tel: 01492 596360; email: philip.brown@brewin.co.uk)

Trustees: Philip G. Brown; Janet Lea; Eryl G. Jones; Colin Wickens.

CC Number: 1039164

This trust was registered in 1994, and has a welcome preference for making grants to small local projects in North Wales and Anglesey. Its objects, listed in the annual report, are:

- Conservation and protection of general public amenities, historic or public interests in Wales
- Medical research
- Protection and welfare of animals and birds
- Study and promotion of music
- Activities and requirements of religious and educational bodies

In 2011/12 the trust had assets of £1 million and an exceptional income of £377,000, largely due to the sale of investments. Grants were made totalling £75,000.

The beneficiaries were: Bangor University SEACAMs Project (£50,000); the Scholarship Fund (£15,000); Music in Hospitals (£4,000); Beaumaris Band (£3,000); and Llandudno Youth Music Theatre (£2,800).

Exclusions

No grants to individuals or non-charitable organisations.

Applications

In writing to the correspondent.

Information gathered from:

Accounts; Charity Commission record.

The CH (1980) Charitable Trust

Jewish

£180,000 (2011/12)

Beneficial area

UK and Israel.

Correspondent: The Administrator, Kleinwort Benson Trustees Ltd, 14 St George Street, London W1S 1FE (tel: 020 3207 7000)

Trustee: Kleinwort Benson Trustees Ltd.

CC Number: 279481

Established in 1980, in 2011/12 the trust had assets of £1.4 million and an income of £40,000. Twelve grants totalled £180,000.

Grants went to: Oxford Centre for Hebrew and Jewish Studies (£100,000); Jewish Care (£20,000); World Jewish Relief (£15,000); Anglo Israel Foundation (£12,000); British Friends of Israel Free Loan Association (£4,000); and West London Synagogue Charitable Fund (£3,000).

Applications

In writing to the correspondent.

Information gathered from:

Accounts; Charity Commission record.

R. E. Chadwick Charitable Trust

General charitable purposes

£28,500 (2011/12)

Beneficial area

UK.

Correspondent: Peter Chadwick, Trustee, Hathenshaw Farm, Hathenshaw Lane, Denton, Ilkley, West Yorkshire LS29 0HR (tel: 01132 446100)

Trustees: Peter Chadwick; Esme Knowles; Paul Knowles; Ann Chadwick.

CC Number: 1104805

Set up in 2004, in 2011/12 the trust had assets of £867,000 and an income of £35,000. Grants totalling £28,500 were made to 49 organisations.

Beneficiaries included: Action Aid, British Refugee Council, Henshaws College, Leeds Community Foundation and Unicef (£1,000 each); Age UK, British Heart Foundation, Claro Enterprises, Martin House Children's Hospice, Save the Children Fund and Sightsavers International (£500 each); and Donna's Dream House (£200).

Exclusions

No grants for individuals.

Applications

In writing to the correspondent.

Percentage of awards given to new applicants: between 10% and 20%.

Common applicant mistakes

'We do not support individuals.'

Information gathered from:

Accounts; Charity Commission record; further information provided by the funder.

The Amelia Chadwick Trust

General charitable purposes

£92,000 (2011/12)

Beneficial area

UK, especially Merseyside.

Correspondent: The Trustees, c/o Liverpool Charity and Voluntary Services, 151 Dale Street, Liverpool L2 2AH (tel: 01512 275177)

Trustees: Liverpool Charity and Voluntary Services; Ruth Behrend; Caroline Dawson; Christopher Bibby.

CC Number: 213795

The trust supports a wide range of charities, especially welfare causes. Although grants are given throughout the UK, there is a strong preference for Merseyside.

In 2011/12 the trust had assets of £3.6 million, an income of £145,000 and made 34 grants totalling £92,000.

Beneficiaries included: Merseyside Development Foundation (£25,000); Liverpool PSS (£11,500); European Play-Work Association (£9,000); Merseyside Holiday Service (£3,000); Centrepoint, Farms for City Children, Kensington Housing Trust, Kid's Cookery School and Sue Ryder Home (£2,000 each); Sheila Kay Fund (£1,500); Age Concern – Liverpool and Shrewsbury House (£1,000 each); British Red Cross (£750); Fortune Centre (£500); and St Helens and District Women's Aid (£100).

Exclusions

No grants to individuals.

Applications

All donations are made through Liverpool Charity and Voluntary Services. Grants are only made to charities known to the trustees, and unsolicited applications are not considered.

Information gathered from:

Accounts; Charity Commission record.

The Pamela Champion Foundation

General, disability

£26,500 (2012)

Beneficial area

UK, with a preference for Kent.

Correspondent: Elizabeth Bell, Trustee, Wiltons, Newnham Lane, Eastling, Faversham, Kent ME13 0AS (tel: 01795 890233)

Trustees: Caroline Winser; Elizabeth Bell; Peter Williams.

CC Number: 268819

In 2012 the trust had assets of over £748,000 and an income of over £47,000. There were 24 grants made totalling £26,500.

Beneficiaries included: Heart of Kent Hospice, Kent Community Foundation and Macmillan (£2,000 each); Afghanistan Trust and Carers UK (£1,000 each); Beacon Church, Cancer Research UK, Odyssey Project and Phyllis Tuckwell Hospice (£500 each).

Exclusions

No grants to non-registered charities.

Applications

In writing to the correspondent.

Information gathered from:

Accounts; Charity Commission record.

The Chapman Charitable Trust

Welfare, general

£245,000 (2011/12)

Beneficial area

UK, with preference for North Wales, London and South East England.

Correspondent: Roger S. Chapman, Trustee, Crouch Chapman, 62 Wilson Street, London EC2A 2BU (tel: 020 7782 0007; email: cct@rpgcrouchchapman.co.uk; website: www.chapmancharitabletrust.org.uk)

Trustees: Roger Chapman; Richard Chapman; Bruce Chapman; Guy Chapman; Bryony Chapman.

CC Number: 232791

Established in 1963 with general charitable purposes, the trust mainly supports culture and recreation, education and research, health, social services, environment and heritage causes.

In 2011/12 the trust has assets of £6.5 million and an income of £249,000. 134 grants were made totalling £245,000.

Beneficiaries included: Pesticide Action Network UK (£20,000); Action for Children, Aldeburgh Music and Methodist Homes for the Aged (£12,000 each); A Rocha UK and TreeHouse Trust (£6,000 each); and Yateley Industries for the Disabled, Global Rescue Services, Mind, The National Police Community Trust and Working Families (£2,000 each).

In addition, there were 91 grants of £1,000 each made to organisations.

Exclusions

No grants to or for the benefit of individuals, local branches of national charities, animal welfare, sports tours, research expeditions or sponsored adventure holidays.

Applications

In writing at any time. The trustees advise that 'it is helpful if the application begins with a short paragraph giving a short summary of the project requiring support'. The trustees currently meet to consider grants twice a year at the end of September and March. They receive a large number of applications and regret that they cannot acknowledge receipt of them. The absence of any communication for six months would mean that an application must have been unsuccessful.

Percentage of awards given to new applicants: between 10% and 20%.

Common applicant mistakes

'The wrong geographical area; amount of grant [requested] outside our guidelines.'

Information gathered from:

Accounts; Charity Commission record; further information provided by the funder; funder's website.

The Charter 600 Charity

General

£44,000 (2011/12)

Beneficial area

UK.

Correspondent: Mr M. McGregor, The Clerk, Mercers' Hall, Ironmongers Lane, London EC2V 8HE (website: www.mercers.co.uk)

Trustee: The Mercers Company.

CC Number: 1051146

The Charter 600 charity was established to commemorate the 600th anniversaries of the Grant of the Mercers' Company's first Charter in 1394 and of the first Mastership of Sir Richard Whittington in 1395. Established in 1994, it operates under a trust deed dated October 1995.

The annual report for 2011/12 states that:

The trustee's aims are to support a range of organisations with the common theme of delivering charitable services and facilities to those in need and to local communities. The Charity has achieved these aims during the period by supporting community-based, grass-roots organisations with particular emphasis on education, social and medical welfare support for young people and communities.

In 2011/12 the charity has assets of £920,000 and an income of £136,500. Grants totalling £44,000 were made to 45 organisations during the year and were distributed for the following purposes:

Welfare – youth and community	£18,250
Welfare – social and medical	£14,500
Church	£5,500
Education	£3,750
Performing arts	£1,000
Heritage – wildlife	£1,000

Beneficiaries included: Claire House Children's Hospice, Howbury Friends and Meadow Orchard Project (£1,500 each); Emma's Bubble Trust, Headway, Musical Moving and West Lavington Youth Club (£1,000 each); Addis Yimer, Samuel Lithgow Youth Centre and Student Volunteers Abroad (£500 each); and Federation of London Youth Clubs, Friends of Workholt Park and Salmon Youth Centre in Bermondsey (£250 each).

Exclusions

Applications for charitable grants will only be accepted when put forward by a member of the Mercers' Company.

Applications

The charity does not consider unsolicited applications.

Information gathered from:

Accounts; Charity Commission record; funder's website.

The Worshipful Company of Chartered Accountants General Charitable Trust (also known as CALC)

General, education

£99,000 (2011/12)

Beneficial area

UK.

Correspondent: Peter Lusty, Clerk, Hampton City Services, Hampton House, High Street, East Grinstead, West Sussex RH19 3AW (tel: 01342 319038; email: peterlusty@btconnect.com)

Trustees: Richard Dyson; Richard Green; Adam Vere Broke; Nigel Turnbull; Richard Battersby; Peter Wyman; Andrew Popham.

CC Number: 327681

In general, the trust supports causes advancing education and/or benefiting disadvantaged people. It has a tendency to focus on a particular theme each year, as well as making grants to other causes and organisations of particular relevance to members of the company.

In 2011/12 the trust had assets of £1.2 million, an income of £119,000 and made grants totalling £99,000.

£36,000 was distributed between 30 Primary Schools to promote numeracy and literacy.

Major beneficiaries included: The Master's Project (£30,000); Institute of Chartered Accountants – bursary (£18,000); MANGO and St Paul's Cathedral Foundation (£5,000 each); and The Lord Mayor's Appeal 2012 (£2,500).

Applications

Applications must be sponsored by a liveryman of the company.

Information gathered from:

Accounts; Charity Commission record.

The Cheruby Trust

Welfare, education, general, overseas aid

£88,000 (2011/12)

Beneficial area

UK and worldwide.

Correspondent: Mrs S. Wechsler, Trustee, 62 Grosvenor Street, London W1K 3JF (tel: 020 7499 4301)

Trustees: A. L. Corob; L. E. Corob; T. Corob; C. J. Cook: S. A. Wechsler.

CC Number: 327069

The trust's charitable objectives are the relief of poverty, the advancement of education and such other charitable purposes as the trustees see fit. In 2011/12 the trust had assets of £42,000 and an income of £115,000, mostly from donations. There were 33 grants made totalling £88,000.

Grants went to: World Jewish Relief (£6,000); Alzheimer's Society and Save the Children (£5,000 each); Family Action (£3,500); APT Enterprise Development and Indian Rural Health Trust (£3,000 each); Breadline Africa and National Autistic Society (£2,000 each); Cruse Bereavement Care (£1,000); and London Wildlife Trust (£100).

Applications

In writing to the correspondent.

Information gathered from:

Accounts; Charity Commission record.

The Chetwode Foundation

Education, churches, general

£71,000 (2011/12)

Beneficial area

UK, with a preference for Nottinghamshire, Leicestershire and Derby.

Correspondent: Grants Administrator, Samworth Brothers (Holdings) Ltd, Chetwode House, 1 Samworth Way, Leicester Road, Melton Mowbray LE13 1GA (tel: 01664 414500; email: info@thechetwodefoundation.co.uk; website: www.thechetwodefoundation.co.uk)

Trustees: J. G. Ellis; R. N. J. S. Price.

CC Number: 265950

This foundation has general charitable purposes, with preference for 'the most disadvantaged, under-privileged young people in the [Nottinghamshire] area, giving them opportunities to fulfil their potential, and benefit the wider community.'

Current priorities, taken from the trust's website, include:

- Support for disenfranchised young people
- Support for those affected by the current economic climate
- Projects that train the trainer to build the confidence, life skills and employment skills of young people
- Projects working with prisoners and ex-offenders to improve their life skills and reduce re-offending
- Projects which help children/young people realise their potential through education, sport and art
- Projects which encourage and give opportunities to young people with learning and/or physical disabilities
- Other projects which will benefit the community as a whole will also be considered

The trustees seek projects which can demonstrate short-term, quantifiable and sustainable benefit. The outcomes must offer long-term benefits for the beneficiaries and be based in the Nottinghamshire/East Midlands area. The website also notes that 'consideration will also be shown where a project of particular interest to the trustees is being carried out outside the locality (but within the UK) which could be put into practice for the benefit of our local community.'

In 2011/12 the foundation had assets of £1.6 million and an income of £77,000. Grants totalling £71,000 were made to over 20 organisations.

Beneficiaries included: The Vineyard Arches Trust and Hope for the Homeless

(£15,000 each); The Canaan Trust (£6,200); The Rotary Club of Nottingham Trust Fund (£5,000); Tythby and Cropwell Butler Parochial Church Council (£3,000); Radcliffe on Trent Advice Centre (£1,300); and The Prostate Cancer Charity, Remar Association and Derby Toc H Children's Camp (£1,000 each).

Exclusions

No grants to individuals, national charities or organisations outside the UK.

Applications

On an application form available to download from the website or by contacting the trust via email or post. The application form is basic, with the majority of detail to be included in a written statement outlining the project on no more than two sides of A4. Consult the application guidelines for an idea of what the trustees want to see. Applications can be submitted at any time and the trust aims to acknowledge all relevant applications within four weeks. If you are unsuccessful at the initial assessment you will be informed within eight weeks of receipt of your application.

Multiple grants over successive years will only be considered in exceptional circumstances.

Information gathered from:

Accounts; Charity Commission record; funder's website.

Child Growth Foundation

Institutions researching child/adult growth disorders, and people with such diseases

£99,000 (2011/12)

Beneficial area

UK.

Correspondent: Tam Fry, Trustee, 2 Mayfield Avenue, Chiswick W4 1PY (tel: 020 8995 0257; email: tamfry@childgrowthfoundation.org; website: www.childgrowthfoundation.org)

Trustees: Tam Fry; Nick Child; Russell Chaplin; Rachel Pidcock; Linda Washington; Mark Coyle; Sue Davies; Nikos Tzvadis; Kevin Kirk; Simon Lane.

CC Number: 274325

Among the objects of this foundation are to promote and fund research into the causes and cure of growth disorders in children within the area of benefit and to publish the results of such research. The foundation makes grants to major medical establishments in the UK to fund research projects into growth disorders and related areas.

The conditions covered by the foundation are:

- Turner syndrome
- Russell silver syndrome/intrauterine growth retardation
- Bone dysplasia
- Sotos syndrome
- Premature sexual maturity
- Growth/multiple pituitary hormone deficiency

In 2011/12 the accounts for the charity show that the trust had assets of £437,000 and an income of £189,000. Grants were made totalling £99,000.

Beneficiaries included: Bradford Hospitals NHS Trust (£47,000); University of Birmingham (£20,000); Institute of Child Health (£5,000); and King's College Hospital (£2,000).

Applications

In writing to the correspondent.

Information gathered from:

Accounts; Charity Commission record; funder's website.

Children's Liver Disease Foundation

Diseases of the liver and biliary system in children

£170,000 (2011/12)

Beneficial area

UK.

Correspondent: Alison Taylor, Correspondent, 36 Great Charles Street, Queensway, Birmingham B3 3JY (tel: 01212 123839; fax: 01212 124300; email: info@childliverdisease.org; website: www.childliverdisease.org)

Trustees: Thomas Ross; David Tildesley; Mairi Everard; Kellie Charge; Nicholas Budd; Georgina Sugden.

CC Number: 1067331

The Children's Liver Disease Foundation (CLDF) is a national registered charity founded in 1980. Its mission is to advance knowledge of childhood liver disease through:

- Funding pioneering medical research
- Providing effective education
- Giving a professional and caring support service to families and young people with liver disease

CLDF supports a wide range of projects, including clinical and laboratory-based research, and social research which looks at topics such as how to improve quality of life. Further details on the research priorities for specific years are available to download from the website.

The foundation has a major grants programme which awards project grants for a maximum three years. The small grants programme distributes £20,000 per annum in grants of up to £5,000. PhD fellowship funding is also offered on an ad hoc basis.

In 2011/12 the foundation had assets of £488,000, an income of £649,000 and a total expenditure of £789,000. 'Research grants and expenditure' totalled £170,000.

Beneficiaries included: King's College Hospital; University of Birmingham; University College Medical School.

Exclusions

The charity does not accept applications from organisations whose work is not associated with paediatric liver disease. No grants to individuals, whether medical professionals or patients. No grants for travel or personal education. No grants for general appeals.

Applications

Applicants are strongly advised to visit the foundation's website where further information and application forms are available.

Information gathered from:

Accounts; Charity Commission record; funder's website.

The Children's Research Fund

Child health research

£83,000 (2011/12)

Beneficial area

UK.

Correspondent: The Trustees, 6 Scarthill Property, New Lane, Aughton, Ormskirk L39 4UD (tel: 01695 420928; email: children'sresearchfund@btinternet.com; website: www.children'sresearchfund.org.uk)

Trustees: Hugh Greenwood; Gerald Inkin; Hugo Greenwood; Elizabeth Theobald; David Lloyd.

CC Number: 226128

The fund supports research into children's diseases, child health and prevention of illness in children, carried out at institutes and university departments of child health. The policy is to award grants, usually over several years, to centres of research. It will also support any charitable project associated with the well-being of children.

In 2011/12 it had assets of £1.4 million, an income of £53,000 and made research grants totalling £83,000.

Beneficiaries included: the British Association of Paediatric Surgeons and The Peninsula Foundation (£30,000 each); Dubai – War Damaged Children (£9,600); The Not Forgotten Association

(£3,000); Alder Hey Children's Hospital (£2,100); and Coming Home (£2,000).

Exclusions

No grants for capital projects.

Applications

Applicants from child health research units and university departments are invited to send in an initial outline of their proposal; if it is eligible they will then be sent an application form. Applications are considered in March and November.

Information gathered from:

Accounts; Charity Commission record; funder's website.

The Chipping Sodbury Town Lands Charity

Welfare, education, leisure, general charitable purposes

£49,000 to organisations (2012)

Beneficial area

The parishes of Chipping Sodbury and Old Sodbury.

Correspondent: Nicola Gideon, Clerk, Town Hall, 57–59 Broad Street, Chipping Sodbury, Bristol, South Gloucestershire BS37 6AD (tel: 01454 852223; email: nicola.gideon@chippingsodburytownhall.co.uk)

Trustees: Paul Tily; David Shipp; Bill Ainsley; Michelle Cook; Wendy Whittle; Colin Hatfield; Jim Elsworth; Bryan Seymour; Paul Robins.

CC Number: 236364

The charity gives grants for relief-in-need and educational purposes, and also other purposes within Sodbury, including the provision of leisure facilities.

In 2012 the charity had assets of £8.2 million, an income of £357,000 and made grants totalling £73,000 of which £49,000 was given to organisations.

Beneficiaries included: Chipping Sodbury Endowed School (£20,000); Sodbury Town Council Playscheme (£4,000 each); Old Sodbury School (£3,000); St John the Baptist Nativity Celebration (£1,000).

Applications

In writing to the correspondent. The trustees meet on the third week of each month except August. Retrospective applications are not considered.

Information gathered from:

Accounts; Charity Commission record.

The Chownes Foundation

Religion, relief-in-need, social problems

£45,000 to organisations (2011/12)

Beneficial area

UK, priority is given to charities based in Sussex, particularly in mid-Sussex.

Correspondent: Sylvia Spencer, Secretary, The Courtyard, Beeding Court, Shoreham Road, Steyning, West Sussex BN44 3TN (tel: 01903 816699; email: chownes@russellnew.com)

Trustees: Mrs U. Hazeel; The Rt Revd S. Ortiger; M. Woolley.

CC Number: 327451

The foundation's objects are 'the advancement of religion, the advancement of education among the young, the amelioration of social problems, the relief of poverty amongst the elderly and the former employees of Sound Diffusion plc who lost their pensions when the company went into receivership and the furtherance of any other lawful charitable purpose.' Priority is given to charities based in Sussex, particularly in mid-Sussex, being the former home of the founder. Preference will be given to projects where a donation by the foundation may have some meaningful impact on an identified need rather than simply being absorbed into a larger funding requirement. Applications from smaller charities whose aims mirror those of the founder, Paul Stonor, will be favoured.

In 2011/12 the foundation had assets of £1.6 million, which generated an income of £31,000. Grants were made totalling £73,000 which included £27,000 in grants to individuals and £45,000 in grants to organisations, which was distributed as follows:

Social problems	£33,000
Religion	£3,500
Other	£9,200

Beneficiaries included: Age Unlimited (£10,000 in two grants); Worth Abbey (£3,500); CamFed and FareShare Brighton and Hove (£3,000 each); Amnesty International (£2,500); and the Howard League for Penal Reform and Mencap (£1,000 each).

Applications

In writing to the correspondent.

Information gathered from:

Accounts; Charity Commission record.

Christian Response to Eastern Europe

Christian, emergency relief

£49,500 to organisations (2012)

Beneficial area

Eastern Europe (in practice Romania and Moldova).

Correspondent: David Northcote-Passmore, Trustee, Cherith, 130 Honiton Road, Exeter EX1 3EW (tel: 01392 367692; email: davidnpass@aol.com; website: www.cr2ee.org.uk)

Trustees: David Northcote Passmore; Timothy Mason; Hugh Scudder.

CC Number: 1062623

'The objects of the charity are to provide relief to disadvantaged and vulnerable people living in Eastern Europe. Help is given by supporting families, churches and medical organisations through financial gifts, taking humanitarian aid and medical supplies, and setting up projects to provide long-term benefits and independence.'

In 2012 the trust had assets of £41,000 and an income of £143,000. Grants were made totalling £137,000 mainly to assist people in Romania and Moldova.

Grants were made to 92 individuals and families totalling £87,500. 56 grants were made to organisations and totalled £49,500.

Beneficiaries included: Gura Biculu Centre (£20,000); Gura Bicului VW Transporter (£8,000); Soup Kitchen (£4,000); Orhei Church and Soup Kitchen (£3,000); and Children's Parties (£500).

Applications

No grants to unsolicited applications.

The charity has informed us that: 'As the funds we are given are raised for specific projects that we support in Moldova, we are unable to donate to charities that are not directly linked with us. We are linked with one specific charity in Moldova.'

Information gathered from:

Accounts; Charity Commission record; funder's website.

Chrysalis Trust

General, education, social welfare

£63,000 (2011/12)

Beneficial area

North East of England, UK national organisations providing benefit across the UK, overseas.

Correspondent: Sarah Evans, Trustee, Piper Close House, Aydon Road, Corbridge, Northumberland NE45 5PW (email: info@chrysalis-trust.co.uk; website: www.chrysalis-trust.co.uk)

Trustees: Mark Price Evans; Sarah Evans; Andrew Playle; Alba Lewis.

CC Number: 1133525

The trust was registered in 2010 for general charitable purposes, with a particular interest in education, social welfare and disability. The trust considers funding unpopular causes and projects that may find it difficult to attract funding elsewhere. Funding is divided between North East England, the rest of the UK and overseas. The following further information is taken from the trust's website:

> All grants are made at the discretion of the trustees without discrimination on any grounds. Amongst other things, the trustees will consider the following criteria:
> - The ability of the applicant to demonstrate that they already provide or will provide public benefit
> - The impact the grant will make with regard to relieving hardship, distress or sickness and/or promoting social welfare
> - The number of people the grant will benefit and for how long
> - How any shortfall in funding for the project will be raised
> - The time scale for the project

In 2011/12 the trust had an income of £1.4 million and made grants totalling £63,000.

Beneficiaries included: Cry in the Dark (£20,000); Greggs Foundation (£10,000); Huntington's Association (£4,000); Wamba Community Trust (£2,000); and Sunshine Fund (£1,000).

Exclusions

Grants are not made for:

- Research – academic or medical
- Holidays or outings
- Arts or entertainment activities
- Animal welfare
- General appeals

Applications

The trust provides the following helpful information on its website:

> *Application Checklist*
>
> There is no application form. Please outline your project on no more than 4 A4 sides using the following checklist:
>
> 1. What is the name of your organisation and what is your charitable registration number if you have one?
> 2. What does your organisation do?
> 3. Who are you helping, how many and how?
> 4. How many staff and volunteers do you have?
> 5. Which statutory and voluntary organisations do you have links with, if any?
> 6. How much money do you need? [e.g., a contribution of £X towards a total budget of £Y]. Where will the balance of the funds required come from?
> 7. What do you need the money for?
> 8. When do you need the money?
> 9. Have you applied to other sources? If so, give details and outcomes
> 10. Who is your key contact regarding this application and what are their contact details (including telephone, email and mailing address)?
>
> Please attach:
>
> - A 250 word summary of your proposal
> - The contact details of 2 organisations or individuals able to provide a reference on your behalf
> - A copy of your latest audited annual report and accounts or a copy of your most recent bank statement if you do not have accounts
> - A budget for the project for which the application is made
> - Please do not attach any unnecessary documentation
>
> Applications should then be submitted preferably by email; if necessary, applications may be sent by post.
>
> *What will happen next?*
>
> - You will receive an acknowledgement that your application has been received
> - Applications are considered by the Trustees twice a year – usually in June and December, however, applications for amounts less than £1,001 may be considered sooner
> - We may contact you by telephone or email to discuss your application or to arrange a visit
> - We aim to let applicants know whether or not their application has been successful within 2 weeks of the trustees meeting at which the application is being considered
>
> *What are the terms and conditions of a grant?*
>
> - Successful applicants will be asked to sign a simple grant agreement setting out their obligations in relation to the grant
> - Grants must be used for the purposes outlined in the application. If the project is unable to go ahead as planned we are happy to consider variations as to how the money is to be spent, however, the money must not be used for any other purposes without our agreement. It must be returned if the project does not go ahead
> - Recipients of a grant will be required to provide a report on the funded project to the trustees within 6 months of receiving the grant

Percentage of awards given to new applicants: between 40% and 50%.

Common applicant mistakes

'Do not meet published criteria or send general appeals rather than applications.'

Information gathered from:

Accounts; Charity Commission record; further information provided by the funder; funder's website.

Church Burgesses Trust

Ecclesiastical purposes, education, and other charitable purposes

£1 million (2012)

Beneficial area

Sheffield.

Correspondent: Godfrey J. Smallman, Law Clerk, Sheffield Church Burgesses Trust, 3rd Floor, Fountain Precinct, Balm Green, Sheffield S1 2JA (tel: 01142 675594; fax: 01142 763176; email: godfrey.smallman@wrigleys.co.uk; website: www.sheffieldchurchburgesses.org.uk)

Trustees: D. F. Booker; Revd S. A. P. Hunter; Nicholas J. A. Hutton; Julie Banham; Peter W. Lee; J. F. W. Peters; Prof. G. D. Sims; Ian G. Walker; Mike R. Woffenden; D. Stanley; B. R. Hickman; Mrs S. Bain.

CC Number: 221284

The trust's website gives an account of the origin of the trust:

> The charity now known as the Church Burgesses Trust has served Sheffield quietly and unobtrusively, for over 450 years. Edward VI had seized for his own use land and property belonging to the town. Protest was made but to no avail. When Queen Mary Tudor succeeded Edward, a petition was presented asking for the return of the lands. This she granted on 8 June 1554 in a royal charter which gave the land and property in trust to a new corporate body: The Twelve Capital Burgesses and Commonalty of the Town and Parish of Sheffield in the County of York.

The trust's income is divided 71.5% for ecclesiastical purposes, which includes Cathedral maintenance and the building and adaptation of churches and halls and the furthering of ministry in the four Sheffield Anglican deaneries; 10.7% for general charitable purposes in the city; and, the remaining 17.8% for educational purposes administered by a separate charity, the Church Burgesses Educational Foundation.

The website states:

> The trust seeks to respond positively to the needs of a large modern city through its support for: the parishes carved out of the ancient Parish of Sheffield; the work of Sheffield Cathedral; organisations working for the needy and the deprived, the elderly, the marginalised and for the revitalisation of inner city communities; the Church Burgesses Educational Foundation (schools, educational organisations and individuals).

The General Charitable Purposes Committee welcomes applications for funds from a wide range of charities and groups whose activities are carried out within the city of Sheffield to the benefit of local inhabitants, with particular emphasis upon:-

- The relief for those who are aged, ailing, disabled, poor or otherwise disadvantaged
- The relief of distress and sickness
- The provision and support of facilities for recreation and other leisure time occupation
- The provision and support of educational facilities

The trust is not able to make grants to individuals under this heading. Individuals under 25 can apply to the Church Burgesses Educational Foundation for specific educational help. Visit the trust's website for further details.

In 2012 the trust had an income of £2.2 million and held assets of £39 million. Grants were made totalling £1 million, distributed as follows:

Ecclesiastical grants to institutions	£560,000
Cathedral expenditure	£341,000
General grants to organisations	£176,500
Ecclesiastical grants to clergy	£12,000

Beneficiaries included: St Luke's Hospice (£35,000); University of Sheffield Chaplaincy (£16,000); Attercliffe Deanery (£12,500); Families Action Support – Sheffield (£7,000); Macmillan Cancer Relief and Whirlow Grange Ltd (£5,000 each); Share Psychotherapy (£4,000); Shine (£2,500); Action for Children, Action for Stannington, FareShare South Yorkshire, Grenoside Community Association, Sheffield Mencap and Gateway and Trinity Day Care Trust (£2,000 each); and Whizz-Kidz (£1,500).

Applications

In writing to the correspondent. The trustees meet in January, April, July and October and at other times during the year through its various committees. The day to day administration of the trust (work in connection with its assets, liaison with outside bodies such as the Diocese of Sheffield, the administration of its grant programmes and the processing and handling of applications prior to their consideration by relevant committees) is delegated to the Law Clerk. Completed application forms and all supporting papers need to be received by the Law Clerk before the beginning of the second week of December, March, June and September.

The trust invites applications from Anglican parishes, from individuals involved in Christian work of a wide variety of types and from charities both national and local, involved in general charitable work within the trust's geographical area of remit.

Further information, guidelines for applying and application forms are available on the trust's website.

Percentage of awards given to new applicants: between 20% and 30%.

Common applicant mistakes

'Ignoring the geographical restriction.'

Information gathered from:

Accounts; Charity Commission record; further information provided by the funder; funder's website.

CLA Charitable Trust

People with disabilities or who are disadvantaged

£40,000 (2011/12)

Beneficial area

England and Wales only.

Correspondent: Peter Geldart, Director, Hopbine Farm, Main Street, Ossington, Newark NG23 6LJ (tel: 01636 823835; website: www.cla.org.uk)

Trustees: Sir Henry Aubrey-Fletcher; Gordon Lee Steere; Anthony Duckworth-Chad; Hugh Duberly; Neil Mainwaring.

CC Number: 280264

The trust was founded in 1980 by CLA members. Its objects are threefold:

- To encourage education about the countryside for those who are disabled or disadvantaged, particularly youngsters from urban areas
- To provide facilities for those with disabilities to have access to recreation in the countryside
- To promote education in agriculture, forestry, horticulture and conservation for those who are disabled or disadvantaged

It prefers to support smaller projects where a grant from the trust can make a 'real contribution to the success of the project'. It gives grants for specific projects or items rather than for ongoing running costs.

In 2011/12 it had assets of £313,000 and an income of £59,000. Grants totalled £40,000.

There were 10 grants of £1,000 or more listed in the accounts. Beneficiaries included: Farms for City Children (£10,000); Harper Adams College (£6,000); East Kent Sports Club and Wirral Swallows and Amazons (£2,000 each); British Red Squirrel (£1,500); and Calvert Trust (£1,100).

Other grants of less than £1,000 each totalled £12,000.

Exclusions

No grants to individuals.

Applications

In writing to the correspondent. Trustees meet four times a year.

Information gathered from:

Accounts; Charity Commission record; funder's website.

Clark Bradbury Charitable Trust

Environmental education and conservation, disability, disaster response

£57,000 (2012/13)

Beneficial area

UK and overseas with a preference for Cambridgeshire.

Correspondent: Dr Mike Clark, Trustee, 124 Richmond Road, Cambridge CB4 3PT (tel: 01223 740237; email: contact@cbct.org.uk)

Trustees: Dr Mike Clark; Dr Jane Bradbury; Prof. Elizabeth Morris; Robin Hodgkinson.

CC Number: 1129841

Established in 2009, this is the charitable trust of Dr Mike Clark and Dr Jane Bradbury, directors of Clark Bradbury Ltd, a consultancy to the biotechnology and biopharmaceutical industries. The trust was established with an initial donation of £5,000 from Dr Clarke, and receives subsequent donations from Clark Bradbury Ltd.

The objects of the trust, as set out in its annual report, are:

- To provide support to charities involved in environmental conservation and in educating the public about the environment
- To provide support to charities helping people with disabilities to experience the outdoors
- To respond to specific world crises

In 2012/13 the trust had an income of £60,000 from donations. There were 20 grants made totalling £57,000.

The beneficiaries included: Jubilee Sailing Trust (£3,000); Disability Snowsport UK (£2,500); Nancy Oldfield Trust (£2,000); Tall Ships Youth Trust (£1,500); and Garden Science Trust (£1,200).

Applications

In writing to the correspondent, via email. The trust checks applicants' Charity Commission records.

Information gathered from:

Accounts; Charity Commission record.

J. A. Clark Charitable Trust

Health, education, peace, preservation of the earth, the arts

£487,000 (2012)

Beneficial area

UK, with a preference for South West England.

Correspondent: Jackie Morgan, Secretary, PO Box 1704, Glastonbury, Somerset BA16 0YB

Trustee: William Pym.

CC Number: 1010520

In 2012 the trust had assets of £16.6 million and an income of £650,000. Grants made totalled £487,000.

Beneficiaries included: Eucalyptus Charitable Foundation (£99,000); SHIN (£55,000); Khwendo Kor-Pakistan (£50,000);Conflicts Forum and Innercity Scholarship (£20,000 each); Oval House (£18,000); Ground Work (£13,000); Combatants for Peace (£9,000); Peacock Gym (£7,500); and Hamlin Fistula (£5,000).

Applications

This trust does not respond to unsolicited applications.

Information gathered from:

Accounts; Charity Commission record.

The Roger and Sarah Bancroft Clark Charitable Trust

Quaker, general

£264,000 (2012)

Beneficial area

UK and overseas, with preference for Somerset.

Correspondent: Lynette Cooper, Correspondent, 40 High Street, Somerset BA16 0EQ (email: lynette.cooper@clarks.com)

Trustees: Mary Lovell; Alice Clark; Martin Lovell; Caroline Gould; Roger Goldby; Robert Robertson.

CC Number: 211513

The Roger and Sarah Bancroft Clark Charitable Trust was set up by a trust deed in 1960. The trust's accounts for 2012 state that:

> The income of the trust is to be distributed solely for charitable purposes to charitable institutions or individuals. Grants are made for general charitable purposes. In the past grants have been made to Religious Society of Friends and associated bodies, charities connected with Somerset and education.

In 2012 the trust had an income of £252,000 and assets of £5.8 million. 310 grants were made totalling £264,000 consisting of 131 grants to organisations, which totalled £213,000 and 184 grants to individuals, which totalled £57,000.

Beneficiaries included: Hindhayes School (£40,000); Street Quaker Meeting House (£15,000); Britain Yearly Meeting (£14,000); Oxfam (£10,000); Barts and London School of Medicine and Dentistry and the Society for the Protection of Ancient Buildings (£5,000 each); Arthritis Research UK (£4,000); Retreat Grants Fund and Royal Academy of Music (£2,000 each); Alfred Hillett Trust (£1,900); Amnesty International and Alzheimer's Society (£1,000 each); Age UK and Womankind Worldwide (£500 each); African Initiatives (£300); Ziyraet Tepe Archaeological Trust (£250); and Penicuik and District YMCA (£200).

Exclusions

Students.

Applications

In writing to the correspondent.

Information gathered from:

Accounts; Charity Commission record.

The Cleevely Family Charitable Trust

General, children and young people

£90,000 (2011/12)

Beneficial area

Worldwide.

Correspondent: Coutts and Co., Coutts and Co., Trustee Dept, 440 Strand, London WC2R 0QS (tel: 020 7753 1000)

Trustees: Dr David Cleevely; Rosalind Cleevely; Olivia Florence.

CC Number: 1137902

Established in 2010 for general charitable purposes, this is the charitable trust of Dr David Cleevely and his family. Dr Cleevely is the founding director of the Centre for Science and Policy at the University of Cambridge and he has had a distinguished career in communications technology.

As Dr Cleevely and his wife Rosalind are patrons of The Prince's Trust, it is likely that the trust has a preference for organisations working with children and young people. There may also be a preference for education and the Cambridge area.

In 2011/12 the trust had assets of £530,000 and an income of £7,000. Grants were made to three charities totalling £90,000.

Beneficiaries were: Cambridge Science Centre; Teenage Cancer Trust and The Prince's Trust. The individual amounts given were not listed in the trustees' annual report and accounts.

Applications

Applications for grants must be in writing to the correspondent. The trustees meet regularly. Recipients of grants are required to provide copies of receipts for expenditure and the grant may be subject to an ongoing monitoring programme – further instalments of grants only released subject to timescales being reached.

Information gathered from:

Accounts; Charity Commission record.

The Cleopatra Trust

General charitable purposes, health and disability

£45,000 (2012)

Beneficial area

Mainly UK.

Correspondent: Charles Peacock, Trustee, Charities Aid Foundation, 25 Kings Hill Avenue, Kings Hill, West Malling ME19 4TA (tel: 01732 520028)

Trustees: Bettine Bond; Charles Peacock; Dr Clare Peacock.

CC Number: 1004551

The trust has common trustees with two other trusts, the Dorus Trust and the Epigoni Trust (see separate entries), with which it also shares the same aims and polices. All three trusts are administered by Charities Aid Foundation. The trust has general charitable purposes, with preference towards health and disability.

In 2012 it had assets of almost £3.2 million, which generated an income of £32,000. Grants were made totalling £45,000. 11 grants were made to organisations in 2012.

Beneficiaries included: Environmental Vision, Maggie Keswick Jencks Cancer Caring Centres Trust and PSP Association (£10,000 each); Relate Brighton (£3,500); and St Barnabas Hospice, Southern Spinal Injuries Unit and Casa Alianza Charitable Co. (£1,000 each).

Exclusions

Organisations only.

Applications

In writing to the correspondent.

Information gathered from:

Accounts; Charity Commission record.

Miss V. L. Clore's 1967 Charitable Trust

General, arts, social welfare, health, Jewish

Around £29,000 (2011/12)

Beneficial area

UK.

Correspondent: Sally Bacon, Executive Director, The Clore Foundation, Unit 3, Chelsea Manor Studios, Flood Street, London SW3 5SR (tel: 020 7351 6061; email: info@cloreduffield.org.uk; website: www.cloreduffield.org.uk)

Trustees: Dame Vivien Duffield; Caroline Deletra; David Digby Harrel.

CC Number: 253660

The trust was formed under a trust deed in 1967 and was established for general charitable purposes, but broadly speaking is concerned with the performing arts, education, social welfare, health and disability. Grants usually range from £500 to £5,000. It is administered alongside the much larger Clore Duffield Foundation.

In 2011/12 the trust had assets of £1.2 million, an income of £40,000 and made grants totalling almost £29,000. A breakdown of grants payable was provided:

Arts, heritage and education	£23,000
Health and social care	£6,000
Jewish support	£0

Beneficiaries included: Bloomsbury Art Fair, Chickenshed Theatre and Blond McIndoe Foundation (£5,000 each); and European Union Youth Orchestra and Lady Joseph Trust (£1,000 each).

An anonymous grant of £10,000 was made to an organisation within the arts, heritage and education sector.

Exclusions

No grants are given to individuals.

Applications

In writing to the correspondent on one to two sides of A4, enclosing an sae.

Information gathered from:

Accounts; Charity Commission record; funder's website.

Closehelm Ltd

Jewish, welfare, general

£206,000 (2011/12)

Beneficial area

UK and Israel.

Correspondent: Mr A. Van Praagh, Trustee, 30 Armitage Road, London NW11 8RD (tel: 020 8201 8688)

Trustees: A. Van Praagh; Hanna Grosberg; Henrietta Van Praagh.

CC Number: 291296

Closehelm Ltd was established in 1983 with its principal activity being to support poor people in financial need. According to the Charity Commission's website at the time of writing (October 2013), the trust also looks to support the advancement of religion in accordance with the Orthodox Jewish faith and other charitable purposes.

In 2011/12 the trust had assets of £3.5 million and an income of £349,000. Grants were made during the year totalling £206,000. The trustees' report for 2011/12 states that grants are made to individuals in financial need. These grants typically cover the housing costs of individuals on low incomes. Grants totalling £73,000 were given to individuals and £134,000 to organisations.

Support was also given to nine organisations. These included: Zaks (£111,200); the Mutual Trust (£5,000); Beenstock Home (£1,700); Yeshivat and Kol Torah (£1,000); Hayomi Trust (£800); Friends of Mir (£500); and Friends of Karlin Stolin (£200).

Applications

In writing to the correspondent.

Information gathered from:

Accounts; Charity Commission record.

The Clover Trust

Older people, young people, Catholicism, health, disability

£190,500 (2012)

Beneficial area

UK, and occasionally overseas, with a slight preference for West Dorset.

Correspondent: George Wright, Correspondent, DTE Herbert Pepper, Park House, 26 North End Road, London NW11 7PT (tel: 020 8458 4384)

Trustees: Sara Woodhouse; Nicholas Haydon; Benedict Woodhouse; Charlotte Morrison.

CC Number: 213578

The Clover Trust was established in 1961. According to the Charity Commission's website, the trust supports organisations concerned with the advancement of health, disability, relief of poverty, overseas aid, amateur sport, young people, older people and Catholic activities.

In 2012, the trust had assets of £4.3 million and an income of £209,000. Grants were made to 33 organisations totalling £190,500.

Beneficiaries included: Friends of Children in Romania (£35,000); Action Medical Research, CAFOD, Childhood First and Downside Fisher Youth Club (£8,000 each); West London Action, JOLT and 999 Club (£6,500 each); Orchard Vale Trust, Brainwave and Bridport Stroke Club (£4,000 each); and Disability Snowsport UK, The Car Care Support Group and W4B Wavelength (£2,000 each).

Applications

In writing to the correspondent. Replies are not given to unsuccessful applicants.

Information gathered from:

Accounts; Charity Commission record.

The Robert Clutterbuck Charitable Trust

Service, sport and recreation, natural history, animal welfare and protection

£42,000 (2011/12)

Beneficial area

UK, with preference for Cheshire and Hertfordshire.

Correspondent: George Wolfe, Secretary, 28 Brookfields, Calver, Hope Valley, Derbyshire S32 3XB (tel: 01433 631308; email: secretary@clutterbucktrust.org.uk; website: www.clutterbucktrust.org.uk)

Trustees: Roger Pincham; Ian Pearson; Lucy Pitman.

CC Number: 1010559

Major Clutterbuck donated £1 million at the time of the trust's inception in 1992. Major Clutterbuck died in April 2012 leaving a further £500,000 to the trust in his will.

The trust prefers to make grants towards buying specific items rather than running costs to assist:

- Personnel within the armed forces and ex-servicemen and women
- Sport and recreational facilities for young people benefiting Cheshire and Hertfordshire
- The welfare, protection and preservation of domestic animal life benefiting Cheshire and Hertfordshire
- Natural history and wildlife
- Other charities associated with the counties of Cheshire and Hertfordshire
- Charities which have particular appeal to the founder, Major Robert Clutterbuck

According to the trust's website, 'the trustees do not consider applications for payments to individuals and do not generally pay grants below £1,000 or over £3,000'.

In 2011/12 the trust had assets totalling just over £1.2 million, an income of £40,000 and made 45 grants totalled £42,000.

Beneficiaries included: Wood Green Animal Charity (£2,800); Churches Housing Trust, 9 Lives Furniture and North West Air Ambulance (£2,000 each); Leonard Cheshire Disability and Cheshire MS Support (£1,500 each); Wheathampstead Cricket Club, National Deaf Children's Society, MedEquip4Kids and Barnstonedale Centre (£1,000 each); Buxton Sea Cadets, Walton Lea Project and Seal and Bird Rescue (£750 each); Penrith Red Squirrel Group, PDSA, Evergreen and Harpenden Lions Club (£500 each); and Honeypot (£400).

Exclusions

No grants to individuals.

Applications

In writing to the correspondent. There are no application forms. Applicants should write to the secretary giving details of what they propose to do with any grant made and of their current financial position. The deadlines for the rounds of applications are 30 June and 31 December in each year. The trustees generally meet in March and September. The trustees will not normally consider appeals from charities within two years of a previous grant being approved.

Percentage of awards given to new applicants: between 30% and 40%.

Common applicant mistakes

'Not knowing our guidelines.'

Information gathered from:

Accounts; Charity Commission record; further information provided by the funder; funder's website.

Clydpride Ltd

Relief of poverty, Jewish charities, general charitable purposes

£247,000 (2012)

Correspondent: L. Faust, Trustee, c/o Rayner Essex Accountants, Tavistock House South, Tavistock Square, London WC1H 9LG (tel: 020 8731 7744)

Trustees: L. Faust; M. H. Linton; Aron Faust.

CC Number: 295393

The objects of this trust are to advance religion in accordance with the Jewish Orthodox faith, the relief of poverty and general charitable purposes. The main focus is to support the 'renaissance of religious study and to alleviate the plight of poor scholars'.

In 2012 the trust had assets of £19.6 million and an income of £4.8 million. Grants were made totalling £247,000; this comprised: £106,000 to educational institutions to support the advancement of religion through education; £99,500 for the relief of poverty; £31,000 which was donated to institutions that benefit the Jewish community in ways such as through medical facilities; and £9,700 was given to individuals. According to the 2012 annual report, 'the decrease in grants made arose as a result of the decreased funds available which in turn were as a result of the payments due to the vendor of the Newcom Ltd Group acquired last year'.

No list of beneficiaries was available but previously has included: Achiezer; Achisomoch Aid Company; Beis Chinuch Lebonos; Beis Soroh Scheneirer Seminary; Bnei Brak Hospital; Comet Charities Ltd; EM Shasha Foundation; Friends of Mir; Gevurath Ari Torah Academy Trust; Mosdos Tchernobil; Notzar Chesed; Seed; Society of Friends of Torah; and Telz Talmudical Academy Trust.

Applications

The trust states that unsolicited applications are not considered.

Information gathered from:

Accounts; Charity Commission record.

The Francis Coales Charitable Foundation

Historical

£68,000 (2012)

Beneficial area

UK, with a preference for Bedfordshire, Buckinghamshire, Hertfordshire and Northamptonshire.

Correspondent: Trevor Parker, Correspondent, The Bays, Hillcote, Bleadon Hill, Weston-super-Mare, Somerset BS24 9JS (tel: 01934 814009; email: fccf45@hotmail.com; website: franciscoales.co.uk)

Trustees: Martin Stuchfield; Guy Harding; Revd Brian Wilcox; Ian Barnett; Matthew Saunders.

CC Number: 270718

In 1885 Francis Coales and his son, Walter John Coales, acquired a corn merchant's business in Newport Pagnell, Buckinghamshire. Over the years similar businesses were acquired, but after a major fire it was decided to close down the business. From the winding-up was established The Francis Coales Charitable Trust in 1975.

The objectives of the foundation, taken from the website, are:

> To provide grants for the structural repair of buildings (built before 1875) which are open to the public. Preference is given to churches in the counties of Bedfordshire, Buckinghamshire, Hertfordshire and Northamptonshire. There is no territorial restriction in respect of the conservation of monuments and monumental brasses. Grants are occasionally made towards publication of architectural and archaeological books and papers; towards the purchase of documents and items for record offices and museums; for archaeological research and related causes.

In 2012 the foundation had assets of £3.6 million and an income of £123,000. 44 grants were made totalling £68,000.

Beneficiaries included: Paulerspury – Northants, Upton – Bucks and Ivinghoe – Beds (£2,500 each); Wingrave – Bucks and Hockliffe – Beds (£2,000 each); Alpheton – Suffolk and Cransley – Northants (£1,000 each); Tibenham – Norfolk and Laindon – Essex (£750 each); Harlaxton Series (£500); and Church Monuments Soc. (£250).

Exclusions

In respect of buildings, assistance is only given towards fabric repairs, but not to 'domestic' items such as heating, lighting, wiring, installation of facilities etc.

Applications

On a form which can be downloaded from the foundation's website. Trustees normally meet three times a year to consider grants. The foundation's website offers the following guidance:

> In respect of a building or contents, include a copy of the relevant portion only of the architect's (or conservator's) specification showing the actual work proposed. Photographs illustrating this are a necessity, and only in exceptional circumstances will an application be considered without supporting photographs here.
>
> It is of help if six copies of any supporting documentation are submitted in order that each trustee may have a copy in advance of the meeting.

Percentage of awards given to new applicants: between 10% and 20%.

Common applicant mistakes

'Do not read requirement as set out in our brochure.'

Information gathered from:

Accounts; Charity Commission record; further information provided by the funder; funder's website.

The John Coates Charitable Trust

Preference is given to education, arts and culture, children, environment and health

£291,000 (2011/12)

Beneficial area

UK, mainly southern England.

Correspondent: Rebecca Lawes, Trustee, 3 Grange Road, Cambridge CB3 9AS

Trustees: Gillian McGregor; Rebecca Lawes; Phyllida Youngman; Catharine Kesley; Claire Cartledge.

CC Number: 262057

According to the Charity Commission's website at the time of writing (September 2013), the trust supports the following:

- Education and training
- Health
- The relief of poverty
- Arts, culture and heritage
- Science
- The environment and conservation

Grants are made to large UK-wide charities, or small charities of personal or local interest to the trustees.

In 2011/12 the trust had assets of £10 million and an income of £381,000. Grants to 76 organisations totalled £291,000.

Beneficiaries included: National Trust (£10,000); Action for Addiction, Campaign to Protect Rural England, Age UK and National Ankylosing Spondylitis Association- NASS (£5,000 each); British Association for Adoption and Fostering and the National Literacy Trust (£4,000 each); Amberley Museum and Heritage Centre, Calibre Audio Library and Fine Cell Work (£3,000 each); Breast Cancer Haven, Hampshire and Wight Trust for Maritime Archaeology and Kidscape (£2,000 each); and the Barn Owl Trust and Lifelites (£1,000 each).

Exclusions

Grants are given to individuals only in exceptional circumstances.

Applications

In writing to the correspondent. Small local charities are visited by the trust before grants are committed.

It is the trust's policy to request a post-grant report detailing how a donation has been spent for any single donation over £15,000.

Information gathered from:

Accounts; Charity Commission record.

The Cobalt Trust

General

Around £125,000 (2011/12)

Beneficial area

UK and overseas.

Correspondent: Stephen Dawson, Trustee, 17 New Row, London WC2N 4LA

Trustees: Stephen Dawson; Brigitte Dawson.

CC Number: 1096342

This trust was set up in 2002 with general charitable purposes. The trustees do not respond to unsolicited applications.

The trust's 2009/10 report states:

> Criteria for grants are reviewed on a regular basis. The latest review has led to focusing a substantial proportion of the amounts donated on a small number of larger and regular donations. These are generally to organisations well known to the trustees or where the trustees have undertaken a thorough review before deciding to donate. The trustees have a preference in their strategic donations for smaller organisations where they feel their contribution will have a greater impact.

Accounts were not available for the 2011/12 due to the trust's low income. The trust had an income of £16,000 and a total expenditure of £135,000. Based on past performance, grants probably totalled around £125,000.

Previous beneficiaries included: Impetus Trust (£169,000); EVPA (£26,000); Streets Ltd (£14,000); Enable Ethiopia and Tree Aid (£12,000 each); Rose Trees Trust and Money for Madagascar (£10,000 each); Beat – Eating Disorders Association (£5,000); Wherever the Need (£1,000); Red Squirrel Survival Trust (£500); Wessex MS Therapy Centre (£100); and Bath RSPB (£50). Many of the beneficiaries were supported on a recurrent basis.

Applications

The trustees do not respond to unsolicited applications.

Information gathered from:

Charity Commission record.

The Denise Cohen Charitable Trust

Health, welfare, arts, humanities, education, culture, Jewish

£71,000 (2011/12)

Beneficial area

UK.

Correspondent: Martin Paisner, Trustee, Berwin Leighton and Paisner, Adelaide House, London Bridge, London EC4R 9HA (tel: 020 3400 1000)

Trustees: Denise Cohen; Martin Paisner; Sara Cohen.

CC Number: 276439

Registered with the Charity Commission in 1978, the trust has general charitable purposes, with a preference for work in the following areas: health, welfare, arts, humanities, education, culture, and Jewish organisations. In 2011/12 the trust had assets of £1.4 million and an income of £58,000. Grants were made to 96 charities totalling £71,000.

Grants included those made to: Chai Cancer Charity (£7,000); Nightingale (£6,000); Jewish Women's Aid (£3,500); Community Security Trust (£3,000); Lewis W. Hammerson Memorial Home (£2,500); Ben Uri Gallery (£2,000); British Friends of Herzog Hospitality and Royal British Legion (£1,000 each); The Shalom Foundation (£750); Jewish Child's Day and Royal Star and Garter Home (£500 each); Youth Aliyah-Child Rescue (£250); and Institute for Jewish Policy Research (£100).

Applications

In writing to the correspondent incorporating full details of the charity for which funding is requested. No acknowledgements will be sent out to unsuccessful applicants.

Information gathered from:

Accounts; Charity Commission record.

The Vivienne and Samuel Cohen Charitable Trust

Jewish, education, health, medical, culture, general charitable purposes

£147,500 (2011/12)

Beneficial area

UK and Israel.

Correspondent: Dr Vivienne Cohen, Trustee, Clayton Start and Co., 5th Floor, Charles House, 108–110 Finchley Road, London NW3 5JJ (tel: 020 7431 4200)

Trustees: Jonathan Lauffer; Gershon Cohen; Michael Ben-Gershon; Dr Vivienne Cohen; Gideon Lauffer.

CC Number: 255496

The majority of the trust's support is to Jewish organisations. In 2011/12 the trust had assets of almost £3 million and an income of £131,000. Grants totalled £147,500.

There were 278 grants made in the year which were broken down into the following categories:

Education	50	£67,000
Medical care and welfare	73	£37,500
Care and welfare	69	£23,000
Cultural and recreation	64	£13,500
Religious activities and communal	22	£6,500

Beneficiaries included: the Spiro Ark, Ariel, Yeshivat Har Hamor and Mishkan David (£7,000 each); Nidrash Shmuel and Friends of Tiferet Shlomo (£6,500 each); Friends of S H Hospital and World Jewish Relief (£5,000 each); Glazer Institute of Jewish Studies (£4,000); East London NHS Foundation Trust (£3,500); Friends of the Israel Opera, University Jewish Chaplaincy Board and Society for the Protection of Nature in Israel (£2,000 each); Israel Free Loan Association, Friends of Jerusalem College of Technology and National Osteoporosis Society (£1,000 each); and Home for Aged Jews and Bridge Lane Beth Hamedrash (£500 each).

Exclusions

No grants to individuals.

Applications

In writing only, to the correspondent.

Information gathered from:

Accounts; Charity Commission record.

John Coldman Charitable Trust

General, Christian

£252,000 (2011/12)

Beneficial area

UK, with a preference for Edenbridge in Kent.

Correspondent: Charles Warner, Trustee, Warners Solicitors, Bank House, Bank Street, Tonbridge, Kent TN9 1BL (tel: 01732 770660; fax: 01732 362452; email: charles.warner@warners-solicitors.co.uk)

Trustees: John Coldman; Graham Coldman; Charles Warner.

CC Number: 1050110

The trust gives grants to community and Christian groups in Edenbridge, Kent and UK organisations whose work benefits that community such as children's and medical charities and schools.

In 2011/12 the trust had assets of £1.3 million and an income of £25,000. Grants were made to 20 organisations totalling £252,000.

Beneficiaries included: Hever Primary School (£50,000); St Luke's Parochial Church Council (£30,000); Oasis International (£27,000); Prince's Trust and Tonbridge School Foundation (£20,000 each); Citizens Advice, Edenbridge and Westerham Branch (£15,000); St Mary's Church, Chiddingstone (£9,000); Domestic Abuse Volunteer Support Service (£5,000); Prostrate Cancer Charity (£2,500); Age UK Sevenoaks and Tonbridge (£1,300); and CARE International (£250).

During the year an additional £35,000 went towards the running of the Holcot Residential Centre, which operates as a hostel, holiday centre and community centre for the use of young people and others.

Applications

In writing to the correspondent.

Information gathered from:

Accounts; Charity Commission record.

The John and Freda Coleman Charitable Trust

Disadvantaged young people

£50,000 (2011/12)

Beneficial area

Hampshire and Surrey and surrounding areas.

Correspondent: Jeanette Bird, Trustee, 3 Gasden Drive, Witley, Godalming, Surrey GU8 5QQ (tel: 01428 681333; email: questrum.holdings@gmail.com)

Trustees: Paul Coleman; Jeanette Bird; Brian Coleman.

CC Number: 278223

The trust aims to provide: 'an alternative to an essentially academic education, to encourage and further the aspirations of young people with talents to develop manual skills and relevant technical knowledge to fit them for satisfying careers and useful employment. The aim is to develop the self-confidence of individuals to succeed within established organisations or on their own account and to impress upon them the importance of service to the community, honesty, good manners and self-discipline.'

In 2011/12 the trust had assets of £834,000, an income of £37,000 and made 11 grants totalling £50,000.

Beneficiaries included: Surrey Care Trust (£11,000); Surrey SATRO (£10,000); Transform (£8,000); Guildford YMCA (£5,500); Second Chance (£3,000); the Yvonne Arnaud Theatre Youth Drama Training (£2,500); Step by Step (£1,500); and Leonard Cheshire (£500).

Exclusions

No grants are made to students.

Applications

In writing to the correspondent. Telephone calls are not welcome.

Percentage of awards given to new applicants: between 20% and 30%.

Common applicant mistakes

'They haven't read the criteria – we only give to Surrey and Hampshire area and [grants have] to help young, disadvantaged adults/children.'

Information gathered from:

Accounts; Charity Commission record; further information provided by the funder.

The Sir Jeremiah Colman Gift Trust

General

£106,000 (2011/12)

Beneficial area

UK, with a preference for Hampshire, especially Basingstoke.

Correspondent: Mrs V. R. Persson, Secretary to the Trustees, Malshanger, Basingstoke, Hampshire RG23 7EY (tel: 01256 780252)

Trustees: Michael Colman; Judith Colman; Oliver Colman; Cynthia Colman; Jeremiah Colman; Sue Colman.

CC Number: 229553

The trust makes grants for general charitable purposes with special regard to:

- Advancement of education and literary scientific knowledge
- Moral and social improvement of people
- Maintenance of churches of the Church of England and gifts and offerings to the churches
- Financial assistance to past and present employees/members of Sir Jeremiah Colman at Gatton Park, J. and J. Colman Ltd or other clubs and institutions associated with Sir Jeremiah Colman

In 2011/12 the trust had assets of £4.8 million and an income of £145,000. Grants were made totalling £106,000, comprised of £57,000 in 'annual donations' and £49,000 in 'special donations'.

Beneficiaries included: The Bucke Collins Charitable Trust (£5,000); The Nehemiah Project (£3,000); The Art Fund (£2,000); Basingstoke and North Hants Medical Trust, Royal Horticultural Society and Oakley Parochial Church Council (£1,500 each); and Hackney Academy, National Trust, The Hunting Office, Royal Alexandra and Albert School, Spinal Injuries Association, Wessex Counselling Service,

St Michael's Hospice and Youth for Christ (£1,000 each).

Exclusions

Grants are not made to individuals requiring support for personal education, or to individual families for welfare purposes.

Applications

The trust states that unsolicited applications are unwelcome.

Percentage of awards given to new applicants: less than 10%.

Common applicant mistakes

'They haven't read the fact that unsolicited applications are unwelcome.'

Information gathered from:

Accounts; Charity Commission record; further information provided by the funder.

Col-Reno Ltd

Jewish

£53,000 (2011/12)

Beneficial area

UK, USA and Israel.

Correspondent: The Trustees, 10 Hampshire Court, 9 Brent Street, London NW4 2EW (tel: 020 8202 7013)

Trustees: Martin Stern; Alan Stern; Keith Davis; Rhona Davis; Chaim Stern; Libbie Goldstein.

CC Number: 274896

The trust supports Jewish organisations in the UK and Israel.

In 2011/12 it had assets of £1.1 million and an income of £111,000. Grants to 29 organisations totalled £53,000.

Beneficiaries included: Society of Friends of the Torah (£17,000); Chabad of Hendon and Lubavitch of Liverpool (£8,500 each); Hasmonean High School (£2,000); Friends of Small Communities (£1,600); Yad Eliezer Trust (£1,250); Zionist Federation (£1,150); Ohel Torah Trust (£800); and Jerusalem College for Girls (£400).

Applications

In writing to the correspondent.

Information gathered from:

Accounts; Charity Commission record.

The Coltstaple Trust

The relief of persons in need, poverty or distress in third world countries and the relief of persons who are homeless or in housing need in the UK or any other part of the world

£250,000 (2011/12)

Beneficial area

Worldwide.

Correspondent: Lord Oakeshott of Seagrove Bay, Trustee, Pollen House, 10–12 Cork Street, London W1S 3NP (tel: 020 7439 4400)

Trustees: Lord Oakeshott of Seagrove Bay; Lord Stoneham of Droxford; Elaine Colville; Dr Philippa Oakeshott.

CC Number: 1085500

According to the trustees' report for 2011/12, the trust was set up in 2001 with the following objects: 'The relief of persons in need, poverty or distress in third world countries and the relief of persons who are homeless or in housing need in the UK or any other part of the world.'

In 2011/12, the trust had assets of £4.5 million, an income of £218,000 and made grants totalling £250,000.

Five grants were made and these were awarded to: Oxfam (£140,000); St Mungo's and Opportunity International (£40,000 each); Sport for Life (£20,000); and The Connection at St Martin's (£10,000).

Applications

Unfortunately the trust's funds are fully committed. The trustees intend to continue providing grants in a similar way to the recent past while retaining flexibility as to the timing and scale of grants.

Information gathered from:

Accounts; Charity Commission record.

Gordon Cook Foundation

Education and training

£34,000 (2011/12)

Beneficial area

UK.

Correspondent: Sharon Hauxwell, Foundation Secretary, 15 Golden Square, Aberdeen AB10 1WF (tel: 01224 571010; email: gordoncook@btconnect.com; website: www.gordoncook.org)

Trustees: Anne Harper; David Adams; Gavin Ross; Dr D. Sutherland; James Anderson.

SC Number: SC017455

The Gordon Cook Foundation was established in 1974 with the aim to promote and develop values education. According to the trustees' report for 2011/12, 'values education includes social and moral education, health education and projects likely to promote character development, citizenship and ethical behaviour'. Values education aims to extend character development into school, work and everyday life. Projects are particularly aimed at young people.

The overall objects of the trust are to:

- Sponsor and deliver educational projects designed to promote character development and good citizenship
- Promote social and moral education: complementary to religious education
- Provide support, advice and information to teachers and others relating to personal development of the child
- Disseminate the results of related research and development
- Promote citizenship in its widest terms including moral education, aesthetic appreciation, youth activities, co-operation between the home and the school
- Promote health education
- Receive and manage funds from other appropriate sources

In 2011/12 the foundation had assets of £9.4 million and an income of £312,000. Grants totalling £34,000 were made during the year. Grants usually range from around £3,000 to £30,000.

The foundation collaborates with a wide range of other institutions involved in values education including: Comino Foundation, Association of Directors of Education in Scotland, Royal Highland Education Trust and Education Scotland. Sponsored projects involve both the formal education sector and other informal groups.

Beneficiaries included: Tan Dance (£15,000); Five Nations (£9,000); and Royal Highland Education Trust and Association of Directors Education in Scotland (£5,000 each).

Exclusions

Individuals are unlikely to be funded.

Applications

Applications not accepted unless recommended through a trustee. The foundation has stated (November 2013) the following:

> The Gordon Cook Foundation operates a proactive policy in making grants to other bodies which means that the foundation itself identifies areas of work in values education which would benefit from further work and development and does not normally invite or respond to unsolicited applications for grant aid.

Percentage of awards given to new applicants: less than 10%.

Common applicant mistakes

'We do not invite or respond to unsolicited applications for grant aid. All of the grants we provide are through areas of work that are identified by the trustees themselves.'

Information gathered from:

Accounts; OSCR record; further information provided by the funder; funder's website.

The Cooks Charity

Catering, welfare

£222,000 (2011/12)

Beneficial area

UK, especially City of London.

Correspondent: Peter Wilkinson, 18 Solent Drive, Warsash, Southampton SO31 9HB (email: clerk@cookslivery.org.uk)

Trustees: Hugh Thornton; George Rees; Bev Puxley; Oliver Goodinge.

CC Number: 297913

The Cooks Charity was established in 1987 by the Worshipful Company of Cooks of London. According to the 2011/12 accounts: 'The fundamental objects of the charity are the advancement of education and the general welfare of persons who are in any way associated with the catering trade and the support of any charitable purposes connected with the City of London.'

In 2011/12 the trust had an income of £178,000 and assets of £4.4 million. Grants were made to 15 organisations totalling £222,000, which were broken down as follows:

Advancement of education	9	£184,000
Purposes connected with the City of London	4	£32,000
General welfare	3	£6,000

Beneficiaries included: Academy of Culinary Arts (£65,000); Springboard and FareShare (£25,000 each); Treloar Trust, Jamie Oliver Foundation and Bridge Project (£15,000 each); City University (£10,500); and Christ's Hospital (£5,000).

Exclusions

No individuals.

Applications

In writing to the correspondent. Applications are considered in spring and autumn.

Information gathered from:

Accounts; Charity Commission record.

The Catherine Cookson Charitable Trust

General

£695,000 (2011/12)

Beneficial area

UK, with some preference for the North East of England.

Correspondent: Peter Magnay, Trustee, Thomas Magnay and Co., 13 Regent Terrace, Gateshead, Tyne and Wear NE8 1LU (tel: 01914 887459)

Trustees: David S. S. Hawkins; Peter Magnay; Hugo F. Marshall; Daniel E. Sallows; Jack E. Ravenscroft.

CC Number: 272895

This trust was registered with the Charity Commission in February 1977. In 2011/12 the trust had assets of £24 million and an income of just over £929,000 derived from investments and royalties from many of the literary works of Dame Catherine Cookson. Grants were made during the year totalling £695,000 and were broken down as follows:

Arts and culture	£255,000	23
Education and training	£137,000	9
Disability	£118,000	23
Medical	£111,000	20
Religious activity	£37,000	21
Other	£21,000	43
Children and young people	£14,000	40
Animal welfare	£1,000	1

The majority of grants were between £100 and £500 with a notable number of larger grants spread across all categories. Larger grants were made to: The British Library (£250,000); RNIB and Cancer Research (£100,000 each); Newcastle Dioceses Education Board (£50,000); Newcastle Royal Grammar School (£35,000); Clore Leadership Programme (£30,000); South West Tyneside Methodist Church (£25,000); Bedes World (£20,000); and Cystic Fibrosis (£10,000).

Smaller grants were made to: Willow Burn Hospice (£1,000); Moorview Percy Hedley School, Lupus UK, 23rd South Shields Scout Group, Tall Ships Youth Trust, St Marys Church – Horden and The Wheelyboat Trust (£500 each); Listening Books (£300); and Whizz-Kidz, Sedgefield Players and Family Action (£250 each).

Applications

In writing to the correspondent.

Information gathered from:

Accounts; Charity Commission record.

Harold and Daphne Cooper Charitable Trust

Medical, health, Jewish

£70,000 (2011/12)

Beneficial area

UK.

Correspondent: Alison Burton, Trust Administrator, c/o Portrait Solicitors, 21 Whitefriars Street, London EC4Y 8JJ (tel: 020 7092 6984)

Trustees: Judith Portrait; Timothy Roter; Abigail Roter; Dominic Roter.

CC Number: 206772

The trust was established in 1962 with general charitable purposes, although in practice support is focused on medical research, health and Jewish charities. Most grants are small and one-off but ongoing support may be considered.

In 2011/12 the trust had assets of £2.8 million and an income of £94,000. Three grants were made totalling £70,000.

The beneficiaries were: Jewish Care (£45,000); Action Against Cancer (£20,000); and Macmillan Cancer Support (£5,000).

Exclusions

No grants to individuals.

Applications

In writing to the correspondent; applications are not acknowledged.

Information gathered from:

Accounts; Charity Commission record.

The Marjorie Coote Animal Charity Trust

Wildlife and animal welfare

£133,000 (2011/12)

Beneficial area

Worldwide.

Correspondent: Mrs Jill P. Holah, Trustee, End Cottage, Terrington, York YO60 6PU (email: info@mcacharity.org.uk)

Trustees: Sir Hugh Neill; Jill P. Holah; Lady Neill; Mrs S. E. Browne; Mrs N. C. Baguley.

CC Number: 208493

The trust was established in 1954 for the benefit of five named charities and any other charitable organisation which has as its main purpose the care and protection of horses, dogs or other animals or birds.

The trustees concentrate on research into animal health problems and on the protection of the species, and apply a small proportion of the income to general animal welfare, including sanctuaries. The trustees give ongoing support, subject to annual review, and also one-off grants to organisations requiring funds for specific projects.

In 2011/12 it had assets of £3.3 million and an income of £106,000. Grants paid totalled £133,000.

Regular Grants (£72,000 in 18 grants)
Beneficiaries included: Animal Health Trust (£20,000); Pet Aid Hospital Sheffield (£8,000); RSPCA Sheffield (£5,000); Friends of Conservation and Brooke Hospital for Animals (£3,000 each); Wildfowl and Wetlands Trust and Devon Wildlife Trust (£2,000 each); and Sheffield Wildlife Trust (£1,000).

One-off grants (£61,000 in 19 grants)
PSDA (New Sheffield Centre (£50,000); The David Shepherd Wildlife Foundation, Save the Rhino International and Elephant Family (£1,000 each); Cat Abuse Treatment Society, Nowzad Dogs Charity and South West Equine Protection (£500); and World Society for the Protection of Animals (£250).

Exclusions
No grants to individuals.

Applications
In writing to the correspondent. Applications should reach the correspondent during September for consideration in October/November. Appeals received at other times of the year are deferred until the following Autumn unless they require consideration for an urgent 'one-off' grant for a specific project.

Information gathered from:
Accounts; Charity Commission record.

The Gershon Coren Charitable Foundation (also known as The Muriel and Gus Coren Charitable Foundation)

General charitable purposes, social welfare and Jewish causes

£225,000 (2011/12)

Beneficial area
UK and the developing world.

Correspondent: Muriel Cohen, Trustee, 5 Golders Park Close, London NW11 7QR

Trustees: Walter Stanton; Anthony Coren; Muriel Coren.

CC Number: 257615

The trust supports charitable organisations, particularly Jewish organisations. In 2011/12 the trust had assets that totalled £2.6 million and it had an income of £233,000. Grants were made to 55 organisations and totalled £225,000.

Beneficiaries included: Gategi Village Self-Help Group (£75,000); Friends of the United Institute of Arad (£30,000); Laniado UK (£9,000); Aish UK (£7,000); Jewish Care, Hobrifa and Spiro Ark (£5,000 each); Manchester Balfour Trust and UKLFI (£3,000 each); Jewish Renaissance and Kisharon (£2,000 each); Prostate Cancer Research Fund and Macmillan Cancer Support (£1,000 each); and Royal British Legion, Crisis and CPRE (£500 each).

Applications
In writing to the correspondent.

Information gathered from:
Accounts; Charity Commission record.

The Duke of Cornwall's Benevolent Fund

General

£100,000 (2011/12)

Beneficial area
UK, with a number of grants made in the Cornwall area.

Correspondent: Robert Mitchell, 10 Buckingham Gate, London SW1E 6LA (tel: 020 7834 7346)

Trustees: Bertie Ross; The Hon. James Leigh-Pemberton.

CC Number: 269183

According to the trustees' report for 2011/12:

> The fund receives donations from the Duke of Cornwall (Prince Charles) based on amounts received by the Duke as Bona Vacantia (the casual profits of estates of deceased intestates dying domiciled in Cornwall without kin) after allowing for costs and ex-gratia payments made by the Duke in relation to claims on any estate.

The Duke of Cornwall's Benevolent Fund was established in 1975. Its main objectives are as follows:

- The relief of persons in need of assistance because of sickness, poverty or age
- The provision of alms-houses, homes of rest, hospitals and convalescent homes
- The advancement of education
- The advancement of the arts
- The advancement of religion
- The preservation for the benefit of the public of lands and buildings.

In 2011/12 the fund had assets of £3.3 million and an income of £541,000. Grants were made totalling £100,000. Of the 151 grants made during the year, there were 37 grants of £1,000 or more listed in the accounts.

Beneficiaries included: Business in the Community (£20,000); Strata Florida and Gordonstown School (£5,000 each); St Mary's Pilot Gig and Dorchester Festival (£2,000 each); and Phoenix Stroke Appeal, Friends of the Countryside, Soil Association and Echo Cornwall (£1,000 each).

Exclusions
No grants to individuals.

Applications
In writing to the correspondent.

Information gathered from:
Accounts; Charity Commission record.

The Sidney and Elizabeth Corob Charitable Trust

General, Jewish

£245,000 (2011/12)

Beneficial area
UK.

Correspondent: The Trustees, c/o Corob Holdings, 62 Grosvenor Street, London W1K 3JF (tel: 020 7499 4301)

Trustees: A. L. Corob; E. Corob; C. J. Cook; J. V. Hajnal; S. A. Wechsler; S. Wiseman.

CC Number: 266606

The trust has general charitable purposes, supporting a range of causes including education, arts, welfare and Jewish charities.

In 2011/12 the trust had assets of £364,000 and an income of £535,000, mainly from donations. Grants totalled £245,000.

Beneficiaries included: Oxford Centre for Hebrew and Jewish Studies (£50,000); University College London (£40,000); British Friends of Feuerstein and London Jewish Cultural Centre (£10,000 each); The Council of Christians and Jews and Ohel Torah Beth David (£5,000 each); JNF – Jewish Botanical Gardens (£3,000); Ben-Gurion University Foundation and Community Security Trust (£2,500 each); and Israel Educational Foundation, Royal National Theatre and World Jewish Relief (£2,000 each).

Exclusions
No grants to individuals or non-registered charities.

Applications
In writing to the correspondent. The trustees meet at regular intervals.

Information gathered from:

Accounts; Charity Commission record.

The Corona Charitable Trust

Jewish charitable causes, welfare, education, young people, the elderly

£50,000 (2011/12)

Beneficial area

UK and overseas.

Correspondent: The Trustees, 16 Mayfield Gardens, Hendon, London NW4 2QA

Trustees: Abraham Levy; Alison Levy; Ben Levy.

CC Number: 1064320

In 2011/12 the trust had an income of £21,000 and an expenditure of £50,000. The income of the foundation has been declining over the past few years. No further information was available.

Previous beneficiaries have included: Menorah Foundation School, the ZSV Trust, Ahavas Shalom Charity Fund, WST Charity Ltd, and Edgware Jewish Primary School.

Applications

In writing to the correspondent.

Percentage of awards given to new applicants: between 10% and 20%.

Information gathered from:

Accounts; Charity Commission record; further information provided by the funder.

The Costa Family Charitable Trust (formerly the Morgan Williams Charitable Trust)

Christian purposes

Around £300,000 (2011/12)

Beneficial area

UK.

Correspondent: Kenneth Costa, Trustee, 43 Chelsea Square, London SW3 6LH (tel: 07785 467441)

Trustees: Kenneth Costa; Ann Costa.

CC Number: 221604

This charity was established in 1959 for general charitable purposes and supports organisations that focus on Christian activities.

The accounts for the year 2011/12 had been received by the Commission but were not published online. In that accounting year, the trust had an income of £361,000. We have estimated that grants totalled around £300,000.

Previous beneficiaries included: Alpha International (£250,000); VSO (£12,000); Pentecost Festival (£10,000); the Chase Trust and the Philo Trust (£5,000 each); British Museum (£2,000); and the Wallace Collection (£1,000).

Applications

The trust states that only charities personally connected with the trustees are supported and absolutely no applications are either solicited or acknowledged.

Information gathered from:

Accounts; Charity Commission record.

The Cotton Industry War Memorial Trust

Textiles

£61,000 (2012)

Beneficial area

UK.

Correspondent: Hilda Ball, Secretary, 42 Boot Lane, Heaton, Bolton BL1 5SS (tel: 01204 491810)

Trustees: Peter Booth; Christopher Trotter; Prof. Albert Lockett; Keith Lloyd; Keith Garbett; Peter Reid; Philip Roberts; John Reed.

CC Number: 242721

According to the Charity Commission's website at the time of writing (October 2013), the trust makes grants to all aspects of aid and assistance to employees, former employees and students of the textile industry. The trust also makes pension payments to former employees of the textile industry and to the Cotton Industry Convalescence Home. Major support has also been given to other causes, including those related to young people and people with disabilities.

In 2012 it had assets of £6 million and an income of £305,000. Grants totalled £61,000. One grant of £500 was made to an individual.

Beneficiaries included: Children's Adventure Farm Trust (£30,000); Samuel Crompton Fellowship Award (£12,000); the Society of Dyers and Colourists (£10,000); Participation Works (£6,600); Bradford Textile Society (£1,500); and Salford Children Holiday Camp (£130).

Applications

In writing to the correspondent. The trustees meet at least four times a year to consider requests for funds and grants.

Information gathered from:

Accounts; Charity Commission record.

The Cotton Trust

Relief of suffering, elimination and control of disease, people who have disabilities and disadvantaged people

£163,000 (2011/12)

Beneficial area

UK and overseas.

Correspondent: Joanne Congdon, Trustee, PO Box 6895, Earl Shilton, Leicester LE9 8ZE (tel: 01455 440917)

Trustees: Joanne Congdon; Erica Cotton; Tenney Cotton.

CC Number: 1094776

The Cotton Trust was established in 1956. According to the trustees' report for 2011/12:

> The object of the trust is to give grants to UK registered charities working to relieve suffering, eliminate and control disease, and to those that work with people with disabilities and disadvantaged people of all ages. Originally helping only a small number of charities working in the area of Hinckley in Leicestershire, the trust now supports a large number of UK registered charities, a significant number of which are operating internationally.

Grants are primarily awarded for capital costs or for items of specialist equipment and occasionally for running costs where predicted budgets and costs are provided.

In 2011/12 the trust had assets of £5.9 million, an income of £158,000 and made grants totalling £163,000.

A total of 78 organisations were supported. Of these awards, 57.5% of the total amount distributed was awarded to projects operating overseas, primarily in Africa, Asia and South America with £35,000 of this granted for emergency and disaster appeals. The remaining £69,000 was awarded to charities operating within the UK.

Donations were broken down as follows:

Overseas aid	20	£55,500
Community and welfare-specialist schools	21	£49,800
Medical and disability	20	£23,900
Education (non-UK)	9	£22,200
Relief of poverty	7	£11,600
General	1	£10

Beneficiaries included: Leicester Charity Link (£30,500); Merlin (£25,000); Camfed (£15,000); Earl Shilton Social Institute, British Red Cross, Save The Children and Concern Worldwide (£5,000 each); Cecily's Fund and the Queen Alexandra Hospital Home (£2,000 each); Computer Aid International, Health Poverty Action and

Resolve International (£1,000 each); Special Toys Educational Postal Service, Strongbones Children's Charitable Trust and Inter Care (£500 each); Orcadia Creative Learning Centre (£250); and the Leysian Mission (£10).

Exclusions

Grants are only given to UK-registered charities that have been registered for at least one year. The charity has stated that it does not support 'overly political or religious organisations and those that appear exclusive on grounds of religion, gender, race, etc.'

Applications

In writing to the correspondent. According to the trustees' report for 2011/12, trustees reach decisions on applications by taking into account the following:

- How effective the grant is expected to be towards fulfilling a charity's stated objective
- The size of the grant requested in relation to the stated overall project and/or capital costs
- The financial standing of the charity as presented in its latest report and accounts with respect to: the extent of the applicant's exclusively charitable expenditure in relation to its annual income; the extent of expenditure on fundraising and management as a proportion of the charity's annual income; the level of a charity's free and restricted reserves against its annual spending on charitable activities.

Percentage of awards given to new applicants: between 20% and 30%.

Common applicant mistakes

'Non specific applicants; lack of accounts; excessive financial expectations; professional fundraisers' professional speak (patronising blarney).'

Information gathered from:

Accounts; Charity Commission record; further information provided by the funder.

Country Houses Foundation

Preservation of buildings of historic or architectural significance

£942,000 (2011/12)

Beneficial area

England.

Correspondent: David Price, Company Secretary, The Manor, Sheephouse Farm, Uley Road, Dursley, Gloucestershire GL11 5AD (tel: 0845 402 4102; fax: 0845 402 4103; email: david@countryhousesfoundation.org.uk; website: www.countryhousesfoundation.org.uk)

Trustees: Christopher Taylor, Chair; Oliver Pearcey; Nicholas Barber; Michael Clifton; Norman Hudson; Sir John Parsons; Mary King.

CC Number: 1111049

The CHF was born out of the Country Houses Association, an Industrial and Provident Society which was formed in 1955 by Admiral Greathed for the purposes of preserving historic buildings for the benefit of the nation. During its lifetime, the Association acquired nine large country houses and restored and preserved these until their sale in 2003 and 2004. During their ownership by the Association, all the houses were converted into retirement apartments, with the rental income helping to pay for extensive renovations and repairs. The houses were open to members of the Association and also members of the public.

Following a restructuring of the Association in 2004, all the properties were sold which resulted in a substantial surplus. The majority of these funds have been donated to the Country Houses Foundation to ensure that the work of preserving historic buildings continues. It is the intention of the CHF Trustees that these funds will be used to award substantial grants to the most deserving of qualifying projects.

The main aims of the foundation are to advance for the public benefit, the preservation of buildings of historic or architectural significance together with their gardens and grounds, and/or to protect and augment the amenities and furnishings of such buildings, gardens and grounds. Beneficiaries can include registered charities, building preservation trusts and private owners.

The following extract is taken from the foundation's 2011/12 accounts:

'Since the launch of the grants scheme in February 2006, the number of applications for funding has steadily increased. At the end of the financial year [2011/12] the foundation had supported 75 projects with grant offers totalling over £4.5 million.'

In 2011/12 the foundation had assets of £12 million and an income of £397,000. Grants totalled £942,000. Beneficiaries included: Hadlow Tower (£75,000); Godolphin House (£70,000); Wolfeton (£56,000); Duncombe Park, Llanthony Secunda and Wellbrook (£50,000 each); Astley Castle (£42,000); Eastnor Castle (£40,000); Compton Verney (£25,000); Cockle Park Tower and Harrowden Hall (£20,000 each); Faringdon Folly (£11,000); Sinai Park (£10,000); New Hall Farm (£6,000); and Heritage Alliance (£2,000).

Exclusions

The following extract is taken from the foundation's website:

As a general rule we do not offer grants for the following:

- Buildings and structures which have been the subject of recent purchase and where the cost of works for which grant is sought should have been recognized in the purchase price paid.
- Projects which do not principally involve the repair or conservation of a historic building or structure.
- Churches and chapels unless now or previously linked to a country house or estate.
- Alterations and improvements, and repairs to non historic fabric or services.
- Routine maintenance and minor repairs.
- General running costs.
- Demolition unless agreed as part of a repair and conservation programme.
- Rent, loan or mortgage payments.
- Conservation of furniture, fittings and equipment except where they are themselves of historic or architectural significance, have a historic relationship with the site, are relevant to the project, and can be secured long-term from sale or disposal.
- Work carried out before a grant offer has been made in writing and accepted.

Applications

Refer to the foundation's very helpful website for full information on how to make an application. *Pre-Application Forms* can be completed online, or in a hard copy and returned by post. The foundation tries to respond within 28 days of receipt. If a project fits the criteria then a unique reference number will be issued which must be quoted on the *Full Application Form.*

Applications can be made at any time.

Information gathered from:

Accounts; Charity Commission record; funder's website.

The Augustine Courtauld Trust

General

£46,000 (2011/12)

Beneficial area

UK, with a preference for Essex.

Correspondent: Bruce Ballard, Clerk, Birkett Long Solicitors, Essex House, 42 Crouch Street, Colchester, Essex CO3 3HH (tel: 01206 217300; fax: 01206 572393; email: julienc@summershall.com; website: www.augustinecourtauldtrust.org)

Trustees: Revd. A. C. Courtauld, Chair; Lord John P. Petre; Julien Courtauld; Derek Fordham; Sir Anthony Denison-

Smith; Thomas J. R. Courtauld; Bruce R. Ballard.

CC Number: 226217

This trust was founded in 1956 by Augustine Courtauld, an Arctic explorer who was proud of his Essex roots. His charitable purpose was simple: 'my idea is to make available something that will do some good.' Among the main areas of work supported before his death in 1959 were young people, people with disabilities, the countryside, certain churches, Arctic exploration and the RNLI. The current guidelines are to support organisations that are:

- Working within the historical boundaries of the county of Essex
- Involved in expeditions to the Arctic and Antarctic regions
- Known to one of the trustees

Within Essex, the preference is to support disadvantaged young people, conservation projects and certain charities that the founder specifically wanted to help. Grants for projects and core costs and can be for multiple years, but only if the charity applies for a grant in consecutive years.

In 2011/12 the trust had assets of £1.2 million and an income of £54,000. There were 33 grants made to organisations totalling £46,000.

The largest grants went to: Gino Watkins Memorial Trust (£9,000) and Cirdan Sailing Trust and Essex Boys and Girls Clubs (£5,000 each). Other beneficiaries included: Stubbers Adventure Centre (£2,500); Rural Community Council of Essex (£2,350); Marie Curie Cancer Care (£2,000); Stanley Hall Opera and The Peaceful Place Ltd (£1,000 each); Country Holidays for Inner City Kids (£800); and SOS Domestic Abuse Projects, Crossroads Care Essex and St Andrew's Church – Great Yeldham (£500 each).

Exclusions

No grants to individuals. No grants to individual churches for fabric repairs or maintenance.

Applications

Applications must be submitted via the online form on the trust's website. Written applications will not be accepted. Trustees meet in the spring to consider applications; precise deadlines and trustee meeting dates are published on the trust's website.

Information gathered from:

Accounts; Charity Commission record; funder's website.

Cowley Charitable Foundation

General

£36,000 (2011/12)

Beneficial area

Worldwide, with some preference for south Buckinghamshire and the Aylesbury area.

Correspondent: The Secretary, 140 Trustee Co. Ltd, 2nd Floor, 17 Grosvenor Gardens, London SW1W 0BD (tel: 020 7834 9797)

Trustees: 140 Trustee Co. Ltd; Harriet M. M. Cullen.

CC Number: 270682

The charity was established in 1973 with general charitable purposes.

In 2011/12 the trust had assets of £915,000 and an income of £36,000. Grants to 33 organisations totalled £36,000.

Beneficiaries included: Tau Zero Foundation (£5,000); MAST (£4,000); Underwater Archaeology Research Centre – University of Nottingham (£3,500); Age UK (£2,200); Children with Cancer UK and John Soane Museum (£1,000 each); and Camphill Village Trust, Save the Children and Shelter (£500 each).

Exclusions

No grants to non-registered charities. No grants to individuals or for causes supposed to be serviced by public funds or with a scope considered to be too narrow.

Applications

The trust states that unsolicited applications are not invited, and that the trustees carry out their own research into charities.

Information gathered from:

Accounts; Charity Commission record.

Dudley and Geoffrey Cox Charitable Trust

Education, medicine, welfare, youth

£267,000 (2011/12)

Beneficial area

UK.

Correspondent: Matthew Dear, Charities Officer, c/o Merchant Taylors' Company, 30 Threadneedle Street, London EC2R 8JB (tel: 020 7450 4440; email: mdear@merchant-taylors.co.uk)

Trustees: Ian Ferres; Bill Underwood; Ted Drake; John Sharpe; John Wosner; Michael Boyle.

CC Number: 277761

According to the trustees' report for 2011/12, 'the trustees endeavour to make the best use of the monies available from the funds of the trust. In particular donations are made to projects they believe to be inadequately supported.'

The trustees support registered charities in geographical areas that they know well.

In the past grants have fallen into three main categories:

- Education: grants to schools, colleges and universities
- Medical: grants to hospitals and associated institutions and to medical research
- Youth and welfare: primarily to include former Haymills' staff and support for training schemes to assist in the education, welfare and training of young people

In 2011/12 it had assets of £6.6 million and an income of £222,000. Grants totalled £267,000 and were broken down as follows:

Youth and welfare	£157,500
Medical	£75,000
Education	£34,500

Beneficiaries included: Merchant Taylor's School- Geoffrey Cox scholarships (£32,500); and British Red Cross, RAFT, Royal College of Physicians, Independent Age and Workaid (£5,000 each).

Exclusions

No personal applications will be considered unless endorsed by a university, college or other appropriate authority.

Applications

In writing to the correspondent. Trustees meet at least twice a year.

Information gathered from:

Accounts; Charity Commission record.

The Sir William Coxen Trust Fund

Orthopaedic hospitals or other hospitals or charities doing orthopaedic work

£69,000 (2011/12)

Beneficial area

England.

Correspondent: Caroline Webb, Correspondent, The Town Clerk's Office, City of London, PO Box 270, Guildhall, London EC2P 2EJ (tel: 020 7332 1416; website: www.cityoflondon.gov.uk/about-the-city/what-we-do/Pages/trusts-charities-awards)

Trustees: John Stuttard; Neil Redcliffe; Michael Savory; Michael Bear; John Garbutt; Andrew Parmley.

CC Number: 206936

This trust was established following a bequest from the late Sir William Coxen in 1940. Expenditure is mainly applied for the support of orthopaedic hospitals or other hospitals or charities doing orthopaedic work.

In 2011/12 the trust had assets of £2 million and an income of £104,000. Grants were made to 19 organisations totalling £69,000.

Beneficiaries included: Fire Fighters Charity (£4,500); Child Care Action Trust (£4,100); British School of Osteopathy (£4,000); and Action Medical Research Council, Association for Spina Bifida and Hydrocephalus, Conductive Education, Motability, Royal Manchester Children's Hospital, Strongbones and Therapy Centre (£3,500 each).

Exclusions

No grants to individuals or non-charitable institutions.

Applications

In writing to the correspondent, guidelines are available from the correspondent.

Information gathered from:

Accounts; Charity Commission record; funder's website.

The Lord Cozens-Hardy Trust

Medical/health, education, welfare, general

£91,000 (2011/12)

Beneficial area

Merseyside and Norfolk.

Correspondent: The Trustees, PO Box 28, Holt, Norfolk NR25 7WH

Trustees: J. E. V. Phelps; Mrs L. F. Phelps; J. Ripman.

CC Number: 264237

The trustees' policy is to assist as many UK registered charities as possible but with particular interest in supporting medicine, health, education and welfare causes in Norfolk and Merseyside.

In 2011/12 the trust had assets of £2.7 million and an income of £104,000. Grants totalled £91,000 and were broken down as follows:

Community	£44,000
Medical	£34,000
Children, youth and education	£12,000
Other	£2,000

Beneficiaries included: Cancer Research UK (£11,000); Waveney Stardust (£10,000); Action for Children – Warrington, Help and Woodlands Hospice Charitable Trust (£5,000 each); St John Ambulance (£3,000); and Norfolk and Norwich Association for the Blind, World Association of Girl Guides and Girl Scouts and Liverpool School of Tropical Medicine (£1,000 each).

Exclusions

No grants to individuals.

Applications

In writing to the correspondent. Applications are reviewed quarterly.

Percentage of awards given to new applicants: less than 10%.

Common applicant mistakes

'We only give grants to registered charities in Norfolk and Merseyside.'

Information gathered from:

Accounts; Charity Commission record; further information provided by the funder.

The Craignish Trust

Education, the arts, heritage, culture, science and environmental protection and improvement

Around £120,000

Beneficial area

UK, with a preference for Scotland.

Correspondent: The Trustees, c/o Geoghegan and Co., 6 St Colme Street, Edinburgh EH3 6AD

Trustees: Ms M. Matheson; J. Roberts; Ms C. Younger.

SC Number: SC016882

This trust was established in 1961 by the late Sir William McEwan Younger; its funding criteria are summarised as follows:

- No grants to large national charities
- There is a Scottish bias, but not exclusively
- Arts, particularly where innovative and/or involved in the community
- Education
- Environment
- Organisations/projects of particular interest to a trustee

It aims to advance education, the arts, heritage, culture, science and environmental protection and improvement.

In 2012/13 the trust had an income of £134,000.

Previous beneficiaries have included Art in Healthcare, Boilerhouse Theatre Company Ltd, Butterfly Conservation – Scotland, Cairndow Arts Promotions, Centre for Alternative Technology, Edinburgh International Book Festival, Edinburgh Royal Choral Union, Friends of the Earth Scotland, Human Rights Watch Charitable Trust and Soil Association Scotland.

Exclusions

Running costs are not normally supported.

Applications

There is no formal application form; applicants should write to the correspondent. Details of the project should be included together with a copy of the most recent audited accounts.

Information gathered from:

OSCR record.

The Craps Charitable Trust

Jewish, general charitable purposes

£182,000 (2011/12)

Beneficial area

UK, Israel.

Correspondent: The Trustees, Grant Thornton, Chartered Accountants, 202 Silbury Boulevard, Milton Keynes MK9 1LW

Trustees: Caroline Dent; Jonathan Dent; Louisa Dent.

CC Number: 271492

This trust mostly supports Jewish charities, although medical and other organisations are also supported.

In 2011/12 it had assets of £3.8 million, which generated an income of £177,000. Grants were made to 30 organisations totalling £182,000.

Beneficiaries included: British Technion Society (£25,000); Jewish Care (£20,000); WIZO.UK and Nightingale- Home for Aged Jews (£16,000 each); Jerusalem Foundation and Friends of the Hebrew University (£14,000 each); CBF World Jewish Relief (£5,000); Ravenswood Foundation, British Friends of Herzog Hospital and British Friends of Haifa University (£4,000 each); the United Jewish Israel Appeal and Medical Foundation for Care of Victims of Torture (£3,000 each); and Shelter and National Theatre (£1,000 each).

Applications

In writing to the correspondent.

Information gathered from:

Accounts; Charity Commission record.

The Crescent Trust

Museums and the arts, ecology, health

£50,000 (2011/12)

Beneficial area

UK.

Correspondent: Christine Akehurst, 9 Queripel House, 1 Duke of York Square, London SW3 4LY (tel: 020 7730 5420)

Trustees: John Tham; Richard Lascelles.

CC Number: 327644

The trust concentrates on arts, heritage and ecology.

In 2011/12 the trust had assets of £356,500 and an income of £67,000, the majority of which came from donations. Grants were made to 20 organisations totalling £50,000.

Beneficiaries included: Hertford House Trust and University of Oxford (£10,000 each); the Attingham Trust (£8,500); Fairbridge London (£5,000); Courtauld Institute of Art, Impetus Trust and Sea the Future (£2,500 each); Countryside Alliance (£500); Galapagos Conservation Trust and Save the Children (£250 each); and Mondo Challenge Fund (£125).

Applications

This trust states that it does not respond to unsolicited applications.

Information gathered from:

Accounts; Charity Commission record.

Criffel Charitable Trust

Christianity, welfare, health, overseas aid

£59,500 (2011/12)

Beneficial area

UK and overseas.

Correspondent: Mr and Mrs Lees, Trustees, Ravenswood Lodge, 1a Wentworth Road, Sutton Coldfield B74 2SG (tel: 01213 081575)

Trustees: Jim Lees; Joy Harvey; Juliet Lees.

CC Number: 1040680

The Criffel Charitable Trust was established in 1991. According to the trustees' report for 2011/12 'the principal objects of the charity continued to be the relief of the poor and needy, the advancement of Christianity, and the relief of sickness'.

In 2011/12 it had assets of £907,000 and an income of £47,000. Grants totalled £59,500 and were broken down as follows:

Advancement of Christianity	£24,000
Relief of poor and needy	£21,000
Relief of sickness	£13,500
Miscellaneous	£1,500

The only beneficiary of a grant over £2,000 was Four Oaks Methodist Church (£3,000).

Exclusions

Individuals.

Applications

The trust states that 'unsolicited applications are declined on each of two applications and shredded on a third application'.

Common applicant mistakes

'Applying at all when no funds are available.'

Information gathered from:

Accounts; Charity Commission record; further information provided by the funder.

The Violet and Milo Cripps Charitable Trust

Prison and human rights

£115,000 (2011/12)

Beneficial area

UK.

Correspondent: The Trustees, Wedlake Bell, 52 Bedford Row, London WC1R 4LR

Trustees: Richard Linenthal; Anthony Newhouse; Jennifer Beattie.

CC Number: 289404

The trust supports large prison and human rights organisations. In 2011/12 the trust had an income of £3,000 and an expenditure of £115,000. No further information was available.

Previous beneficiaries have included: Lancaster University, the Prison Advice and Care Trust, Dorothy House Hospice Care, Frank Langford Charitable Trust and Trinity Hospice.

Applications

The trust states that unsolicited applications will not receive a response.

Information gathered from:

Accounts; Charity Commission record.

The Ronald Cruickshanks Foundation

Welfare, education, medical, general

£164,000 (2011/12)

Beneficial area

UK, with some preference for Folkestone, Faversham and the surrounding area.

Correspondent: I. F. Cloke, Trustee, 34 Cheriton Gardens, Folkestone, Kent CT20 2AX (tel: 01303 251742)

Trustees: I. F. Cloke, Chair; J. S. Schilder; Mrs S. E. Cloke.

CC Number: 296075

The settlor of this charity died in 1995 leaving his shareholding in Howe Properties Ltd to the foundation, under the terms of his will. The foundation's objects are to provide general charitable and educational assistance as the trustees deem suitable with the knowledge of the wishes given to them by the settlor in his lifetime. The assistance is to include those in poverty and need in Folkestone and Faversham and their surrounding areas.

In 2011/12 the foundation had assets of £1.8 million and an income of £257,000. Grants to 147 organisations totalled £164,000.

Beneficiaries included: The Pilgrims Hospice (The Hospice on the Hill) (£9,000); The Pilgrims Hospice (Canterbury) and Demelza House Children's Hospice (£8,500); Parish Church of St Mary and St Eanswythe – Fabric Fund (£6,000); Kent Air Ambulance (£5,500); Operation Sunshine (£4,000); Jesuit Missions (3,500); Marie Curie Cancer Centre (£2,000); Disasters Emergency Committee – East African drought/ starvation crisis, St Stephens Church, Lympne, The Fire Fighters Charity and PDSA (£1,000 each); Kent Autistic Trust, Action for Kids and Volunteer Reading Help (£500 each); and The Folkestone Pipes and Drums and Shelter (£250 each).

Applications

In writing to the correspondent.

Information gathered from:

Accounts; Charity Commission record.

The Cuby Charitable Trust

Jewish

£48,000 (2011/12)

Beneficial area

UK, overseas.

Correspondent: Sidney Cuby, Trustee, 16 Mowbray Road, Edgware HA8 8JQ (tel: 020 7563 6868)

Trustees: C. Cuby; Sidney Cuby; Jonathan Cuby; Raquel Talmor.

CC Number: 328585

The Cuby Charitable Trust was established in 1990. According to the trustees' report for 2011/12, the main objectives are 'to provide charitable assistance in any part of the world and in particular for the advancement of Orthodox Jewish religious education'.

In 2011/12 the trust had assets of £350,000 and an income of £75,000, mainly from donations. Grants totalled £48,000. No list of grants was provided with the accounts to indicate the size or number of beneficiaries during the year.

Applications

In writing to the correspondent.

Information gathered from:

Accounts; Charity Commission record.

Cullum Family Trust

Social welfare, education and general charitable purposes

£381,000 (2011/12)

Beneficial area

UK.

Correspondent: Peter Cullum, Trustee, Wealden Hall, Parkfield, Sevenoaks TN15 0HX

Trustees: Ann Cullum; Claire Cullum; Peter Cullum; Simon Cullum.

CC Number: 1117056

The trust was established in 2006 by the entrepreneur, Peter Cullum. According to the trustees' report for 2011/12, the trust's aim is to focus on the support of children related issues of deprivation, impairment and education, as well as to provide for the protection and prevention of cruelty to animals and financial support to selected community foundations.

In 2011/12 the foundation had assets of £21 million and an income of £660,000. Grants were made totalling £381,000.

Beneficiaries included: City University (£337,000); the Sussex Community Foundation (£25,000); and Kids Company (£10,000).

Applications

In writing to the correspondent.

Information gathered from:

Accounts; Charity Commission record.

The Culra Charitable Trust

General

£25,000 (2011/12)

Beneficial area

UK.

Correspondent: Mary Kitto, Correspondent, Victoria House, 1–3 College Hill, London Ec4R 2RA (tel: 020 7489 8076)

Trustees: Charles Cook; Guy Needham; George Francis; Henry Byam-Cook.

CC Number: 274612

This trust has general charitable purposes, giving grants to a wide variety of active charitable organisations throughout the UK. In 2011/12 the trust had an income of £23,000 and spent £25,000.

No more information was available.

Exclusions

Grants are not given to non-registered charities or individuals. The trust does not tend to support large national charities.

Applications

The trust tends to support organisations known to the trustees, rather than responding to unsolicited applications. The trustees meet twice a year.

Percentage of awards given to new applicants: between 40% and 50%.

Common applicant mistakes

'Culra does not tend to support large national charities.'

Information gathered from:

Accounts; Charity Commission record; further information provided by the funder.

The Cumber Family Charitable Trust

General, with preference being given to overseas projects, housing and welfare, children, youth and education, medical and disability and environment

£49,000 (2011/12)

Beneficial area

Worldwide, with a preference for the developing world and Berkshire and Oxfordshire.

Correspondent: Ms Mary Tearney, Secretary, Manor Farm, Mill Road, Marcham, Abingdon OX13 6NZ (tel: 01865 391327; email: mary.tearney@hotmail.co.uk; website: www.cumberfamilycharitabletrust.org.uk)

Trustees: William Cumber; Mary Tearney; Alec Davey; Margaret Freeman; Marian Cumber; Julia Mearns.

CC Number: 291009

The Cumber Family Charitable Trust was established in 1985 by a Berkshire farming family and the current trustees are still family members. Current interest for grants includes farming and the countryside. Agricultural and conservation work is supported locally-in Oxfordshire and Berkshire, nationally and in the third world. The trustees prefer to support charities working through the UK but will fund small-scale agricultural projects in the third world. Educational needs are supported, especially for projects which involve disadvantaged children and medical appeals, especially cancer research.

The trust favours the following causes:

- Overseas
- Housing and welfare
- Children
- Youth and education
- Medical and disability
- Environment

Christian work in all of these fields is favoured.

In 2011/12 the trust had assets of £766,000 and an income of £38,000. Grants ranging from £200 to £8,000 were made to 41 organisations totalling £49,000.

Beneficiaries included: Thames Valley and Chiltern Ambulance (£8,000); Helen and Douglas House (£4,000); Shelter, Nuffield Orthopaedic Centre and Bradfield Primary Project (£2,000 each); Marcham Village Shop (£1,500); Vale and Downland Museum, Riders for Health and Mission Aviation Fellowship-MAF (£1,000 each); Tools for Self Reliance and Rushmoor Healthy Living (£500 each); and Rakome School Education Day (£200).

Exclusions

Individuals are not usually supported. Individuals with local connections and who are personally known to the trustees are occasionally supported.

Applications

Applications must be sent in paper format and not via email. There is no formal application; however the trust has provided guidelines which can be found on its website. Applications must be sent to the secretary. Trustees meet twice a year to consider applications, usually in March and October. Applications need to be made at least a month before the meeting date. First time applicant must provide a copy of the latest annual report and accounts.

Percentage of awards given to new applicants: between 20% and 30%.

Common applicant mistakes

'We receive a lot of applications from individuals and clearly state that we only support individuals who are known to a trustee personally. Also local projects not in our local area are not eligible.'

Information gathered from:

Accounts; Charity Commission record; further information provided by the funder; funder's website.

The Dennis Curry Charitable Trust

Conservation, general

£55,000 (2011/12)

Beneficial area

UK.

Correspondent: Nigel Armstrong, Secretary to the Trust, Alliotts, Imperial House, 15 Kingsway, London WC2B 6UN (tel: 020 7240 9971; email: denniscurryscharity@alliotts.com)

Trustees: Michael Curry; Anabel Sylvia Curry; Margaret Curry-Jones; Patricia Rosemary Edmund.

CC Number: 263952

The trust has general charitable objects with a special interest in the environment and education; occasional support is given to churches and cathedrals. In 2011/12 it had an income of £74,000, distributing £55,000 to ten organisations. Assets stood at £3.1 million.

Beneficiaries were: University of Oxford – Dept. of Zoology, Wildlife Conservation Research Unit (£15,000); The British Museum Friends, The Frozen Ark Project and Friends of Little Chalfont Library (£10,000 each); Galapagos Conservation Trust (£5,000); University of Glasgow Trinidad Expedition (£3,000); Project Trust (£1,000); and Medicines Sans Frontieres and The Open Spaces Society (£500 each).

Applications

In writing to the correspondent.

Information gathered from:

Accounts; Charity Commission record.

The Manny Cussins Foundation

Older people, children, health, Jewish, general

£36,000 (2011/12)

Beneficial area

Mainly UK, with some emphasis on Yorkshire.

Correspondent: The Trustees, Rotherhill, Lower Street, Fittleworth, Pullborough RH20 1EJ

Trustees: A. Reuben; A. Cussins; A. J. Cussins; B. Cussins; A. Zucker.

CC Number: 219661

The settlor, the late Manny Cussins, was a businessman who made his fortune in the furniture retail trade. He had close ties to Leeds United serving as the club chair for a period in the 1970s and 1980s.

The foundation's objects are as follows:

- To support the welfare and care of the elderly
- Welfare and care of children at risk
- Health care in the Yorkshire region and abroad
- Charities in Yorkshire and the former county of Humberside
- Charitable need amongst Jewish communities in the UK and abroad
- General charitable purposes

The 2011/12 accounts note: 'The trustees... aim to support charitable causes that are local to the Leeds area and have some Jewish and medical content in a way that will perpetuate the name and work of the settlor, the late Manny Cussins.' There is a preference for supporting projects rather than giving towards general funds. In 2011/12 the foundation had assets of £746,000, an income of £56,000 and made grants totalling £36,000. The accounts did not include a list of beneficiaries.

Previous beneficiaries have included Angels International, Christie Hospital – Children Against Cancer, Forgiveness Project, Hadassah Lodge, Leeds International Piano Competition, Leeds Jewish Education Authority, Leeds Jewish Welfare Board (where a family project is named after the settlor), Lifeline for the Old Jerusalem, Martin House Hospice, United Jewish Israel Appeal, Wheatfields Hospice and Women's International Zionist Organisation.

Exclusions

No grants to individuals.

Applications

The correspondent states that applications are not sought as the trustees carry out their own research.

Information gathered from:

Accounts; Charity Commission record.

D. C. R. Allen Charitable Trust

General charitable purposes

£117,000 (2012/13)

Beneficial area

England and Wales.

Correspondent: Julie Frusher, Trustee, Estate Office, Edgcote House, Edgcote, Banbury, Oxfordshire OX17 1AG

Trustees: Julie Frusher; Martin Allen; Colin Allen.

CC Number: 277293

This trust was established in 1979 and has general charitable purposes.

In 2012/13 the trust had assets of £336,000 and an income of £299,000. Grants totalled £117,000. A list of beneficiaries was unavailable.

Exclusions

No individuals.

Applications

In writing to the correspondent.

Information gathered from:

Accounts; Charity Commission record.

The D. G. Charitable Settlement

General

£344,000 (2011/12)

Beneficial area

UK.

Correspondent: Joanna Nelson, Secretary, PO Box 62, Heathfield, East Sussex TN21 8ZF (tel: 01435 867604; email: joanna.nelson@btconnect.com)

Trustees: David Gilmour; Patrick Grafton-Green; Polly Samson.

CC Number: 1040778

This charity makes regular donations to a fixed list of organisations and does not consider unsolicited applications. In 2011/12 the charity had assets of £1 million and an income of £3,500. Grants were made to 24 organisations and totalled £344,000.

Beneficiaries included: Oxfam (£100,000); Crisis (£40,000); Great Ormond Street Hospital and Shelter (£25,000 each); Cancer Research UK, Environmental Investigation Agency Charitable Trust, Friends of the Earth and Reprieve UK (£10,000 each); Defend the Right to Protest, Media Standards Trust – Hacked Off and University of

St Andrews (£5,000 each); and Terrence Higgins Trust (£2,000).

Applications

This trust does not consider unsolicited applications.

Information gathered from:

Accounts; Charity Commission record.

Daily Prayer Union Charitable Trust Ltd

Evangelical Christianity

£29,500 to organisations (2011/12)

Beneficial area

UK.

Correspondent: Clare Palmer, Secretary, 12 Weymouth Street, London W1W 5BY

Trustees: Revd David Jackman; Revd Timothy Sterry; Anne Tompson; Elizabeth Bridger; Fiona Ashton; Dr Joanna Sudell; Giles Rawlinson; Revd Raymond Porter; Carolyn Ash.

CC Number: 284857

The purpose of the trust is to make grants for the advancement of the Christian religion. Levels of fixed grants are set each year for training, children's education and missionaries.

In 20011/12 the trust had assets of £41,500 and an income of £33,000. Grants totalled £96,500, of which £29,500 went to organisations and £67,000 to 50 individuals.

Beneficiaries included: Monkton Combe School (£7,000); Jesus Lane Trust (£3,000); London City Mission and People International (£2,000 each); Interserve (£1,500); and AIM International (£1,000).

Applications

The trustees meet regularly to review applications for new grants and grants which are due for renewal.

Information gathered from:

Accounts; Charity Commission record.

Oizer Dalim Trust

Orthodox Jewish causes, social welfare, education

£102,000 (2011/12)

Beneficial area

UK and overseas.

Correspondent: Mordechai Cik, Trustee, 68 Osbaldeston Road, London N16 7DR

Trustees: Mordechai Cik; Maurice Freund; Moshe Cohen.

CC Number: 1045296

According to the trustees' report for 2011/12, 'the trust was established to help alleviate poverty amongst members of the Orthodox Jewish faith both in the UK and overseas. It assists also in the furtherance of Orthodox Jewish education throughout the world.'

In 2011/12 the trust had an income of £94,000, entirely from donations. Assets stood at £16,000. Grants were made for 'poverty alleviation' totalling £102,000. A list of grant beneficiaries was not available.

Applications

In writing to the correspondent.

Information gathered from:

Accounts; Charity Commission record.

Michael Davies Charitable Settlement

General charitable purposes

£69,000 to organisations (2011/12)

Beneficial area

UK.

Correspondent: Kenneth Hawkins, Trustee, Lee Associates, 5 Southampton Place, London WC1A 2DA (tel: 020 7025 4600)

Trustees: Michael Davies; Kenneth Hawkins.

CC Number: 1000574

This charity was established in 1990 for general charitable purposes.

In 2011/12 it had assets of £799,000 and an income of £118,000. Grants were made totalling £69,000.

Beneficiaries were: Marie Curie Cancer Care and The Sorrell Foundation (£20,000 each); Docklands Scout Project and RNLI (£10,000 each); University of Westminster Prize and Scholarship Fund (£3,000); Cycle to Cannes (£2,000); Macmillan Cancer Support (£1,250); Royal Parks Foundation and Super Strings Club (£1,000 each); and NSPCC (£500).

Applications

In writing to the correspondent.

Information gathered from:

Accounts; Charity Commission record.

The Wilfrid Bruce Davis Charitable Trust

Health

£46,000 (2011/12)

Beneficial area

UK, but mainly Cornwall; India.

Correspondent: W. B. Davis, Trustee, La Feock Grange, Feock, Truro, Cornwall TR3 6RG (tel: 01872 862795)

Trustees: W. B. Davis; Mrs D. F. Davis; Mrs D. S. Dickens; Mrs C. A. S. Pierce.

CC Number: 265421

The trust was set up in 1967, the objects being 'such charities as the settlor in his lifetime and the trustees after his death shall determine'. The trust presently concentrates on 'improving the quality of life for those who are physically disadvantaged and their carers'. The geographical area covered is almost exclusively Cornwall, however the main thrust of the trust's activities is now focused on India.

The trust is fully committed to its current beneficiaries.

In 2011/12 the trust had assets of £157,000 and an income of £59,000. Grants to 19 organisations totalled £46,000.

Beneficiaries included: Pallium India (£20,000); Merlin Project and Guwahati Pain Clinic (£5,000 each); Cornwall Community Foundation (£2,000); and Precious Lives Appeal and Jubilee Sailing Trust (£1,000 each).

Exclusions

No applications from individuals are considered.

Applications

Unsolicited applications are generally not supported.

Information gathered from:

Accounts; Charity Commission record.

The De Laszlo Foundation

The arts, general

£305,000 (2011/12)

Beneficial area

UK and worldwide.

Correspondent: Christabel Wood, 5 Albany Courtyard, London W1J 0HF (tel: 020 7437 1982)

Trustees: Damon de Laszlo; Lucy Birkbeck; Robert de Laszlo; William de Laszlo.

CC Number: 327383

Registered with the Charity Commission in March 1987, the foundation has the following objects:

1. The advancement and promotion of education and interest in the visual arts with special reference to encouraging knowledge of the works of contemporary painters, in particular those of the late Philip de Laszlo
2. To encourage research into the restoration of works of art and their preservation and the location of suitable venues for them

3 To acquire and maintain a collection of the works of art of the late Philip de Laszlo and of appropriate works of art of the same or any other period
4 To advance education and research generally in the areas of arts, science, economics and medicine
5 To encourage the study, reproduction and cataloguing of works of art and the publication of books and literature in connection therewith
6 To promote the founding of scholarships and prizes related to the above

We understand that it has increasingly been the policy of the trustees to make a small number of targeted large grants. In 2011/12 the foundation had assets of £1.87 million and an income of £444,000. Grants totalled £305,000.

Grants were broken down into the following categories:

Archive Trust	£130,000
Arts	£42,000
Education	£36,500
Scholarship and grants	£28,500
Other charities	£28,000
Medicine	£26,500
Science	£15,000

Previous beneficiaries included: the De Laszlo Archive Trust (£188,000); Gordonstoun School Arts Centre (£20,000); Durham University and Royal Marsden (£10,000 each); Foundation for Liver Research (£8,000); Southampton University (£5,000); Federation of British Artists (£3,000); AGORA (£2,500); National Youth Orchestra (£1,500); Tate Foundation (£1,000); Cardboard Citizens (£500); and Chelsea Open Air Nursery School (£250).

Applications

No grants to unsolicited applications.

Percentage of awards given to new applicants: less than 10%.

Common applicant mistakes

'Not to enclose an sae.'

Information gathered from:

Accounts; Charity Commission record; further information provided by the funder.

William Dean Countryside and Educational Trust

Education in natural history, ecology and conservation

£68,000 (2012)

Beneficial area

Principally Cheshire; also Derbyshire, Lancashire, Staffordshire and the Wirral.

Correspondent: Brenda Bell, Correspondent, St Mary's Cottage, School Lane, Astbury, Congleton CW12 4RG (tel: 01260 290194; email: bellstmarys@hotmail.com)

Trustees: John Ward; David Daniel; William Crawford; Margaret Williamson; David Crawford.

CC Number: 1044567

The trust was established in 1994 in accordance with the will of William Dean. According to the trustees' report for 2011/12, the objects of the trust are to 'promote the advancement of education for the public benefit relating to natural history, ecology and conservation of the natural environment'.

In 2012 it had assets of £1.3 million, an income of £64,000 and made grants totalling almost £68,000. There were 65 organisations in receipt of grants.

Beneficiaries included: Cheshire Wildlife Trust (£15,000); St Mary's Church Astbury Conservation (£8,000); Congleton Projects Garden Festival (£3,000); Lower Moss Wood Animal Hospital (£2,000); Riverside Concern, Friends of Sandbach Park and Staffordshire Wildlife Trust (£1,000 each); Centre for Alternative Technology and Garden Organic Schools Program (£700 each); Derbyshire Wildlife Trust, Autism Initiatives UK and National Lobster Hatchery (£500 each); and Songbird Survival (£100).

Exclusions

The trust stated that education is not funded, unless directly associated with one of the eligible categories.

Applications

In writing to the correspondent. The Trustees meet four times each year in March, June, September and December when applications for grants are considered.

Information gathered from:

Accounts; Charity Commission record.

The Dellal Foundation

Around £142,000 (2011/12)

Beneficial area

UK.

Correspondent: S. Hosier, 25 Harley Street, London W1G 9BR (tel: 020 7299 1400)

Trustees: Edward Azouz; Guy Dellal.

CC Number: 265506

The foundation gives 'a significant proportion of the grants towards charities whose aim is the welfare and benefit of Jewish people'.

In 2011/12 it had an income of £1,000 and a total expenditure of £142,000. Unfortunately further information was not available.

Exclusions

No grants to individuals.

Applications

In writing to the correspondent.

Information gathered from:

Accounts; Charity Commission record.

The Delves Charitable Trust

Environment, conservation, medical, general

£191,000 (2011/12)

Beneficial area

UK and overseas.

Correspondent: The Trust Administrator, Luminary Finance LLP, PO Box 135, Longfield, Kent DA3 8WF (tel: 01732 822114)

Trustees: Elizabeth Breeze; John Breeze; George Breeze; Charles Breeze; William Breeze; Mark Breeze; Catharine Mackey.

CC Number: 231860

The trustees only release grants to UK registered charities (this can of course include charities that undertake work overseas).

In 2011/12 the trust had assets of £6.7 million, which generated an income of £236,000. The annual report states that 'subscriptions' were paid to 21 organisations totalling £134,000 and 'donations' were made to 16 charities totalling £57,000.

The largest grants went to: Action Medical Research (£20,500); SEQUAL Trust (£18,000); British Heart Foundation (£16,000); Macmillan Cancer Support (£15,500); Alzheimer's Society (£15,000); Medecins Sans Frontieres (£10,500; and Parkinson's UK (£10,000).

Other beneficiaries of subscriptions and donations included: CRISIS and DEC East Africa – crisis appeal (£5,000 each); William Morris Craft Fellowship Trust and Tree of Life for Animals (£4,000 each); Ghana Education Project and Motivation (£3,000 each); and Big Issue Foundation (£1,500).

Exclusions

The trust does not give sponsorships or personal educational grants.

Applications

In writing to the correspondent. The trust provides the following information:

Concisely explain the objective, activities, intended public benefit and anticipated achievements. Enclosures such as detailed accounts and brochures should not be sent at the initial application stage and are indeed discouraged on environmental grounds. Applications are accepted on a rolling basis and reviewed by the trustees quarterly, whose decision is final. No response is made to unsuccessful unsolicited applications.

Information gathered from:

Accounts; Charity Commission record.

The Demigryphon Trust

Medical, education, children, general

£61,000 (2011/12)

Beneficial area

UK, with a preference for Scotland.

Correspondent: Laura Gosling, c/o Millbank Financial Services, 4th Floor, Swan House, 17–19 Stratford Place, London W1C 1BQ (tel: 020 7907 2100; email: charity@mfs.co.uk)

Trustee: The Cowdray Trust Ltd.

CC Number: 275821

This trust was established in February 1978 for general charitable purposes. In 2011/12 it had assets of £2.5 million and an income of £52,000. Grants to organisations totalled £13,000 with a further £48,000 being paid to pensioners.

Beneficiary organisations included: Game and Wildlife Conservation Trust (£5,000); Leeds University – Cowdray Legacy Exhibition (£2,000); Friends of St Mary's Petworth (£1,000); The Silver Circle and Tillington Parochial Church Council (£500 each); and The Amber Foundation, Breakthrough Breast Cancer and Help for Heroes (£250 each).

Exclusions

No grants to individuals; only registered charities are supported.

Applications

No grants to unsolicited applications.

Information gathered from:

Accounts; Charity Commission record.

The Desmond Foundation (formerly known as the RD Crusaders Foundation)

General charitable purposes, especially for the relief of poverty and sickness amongst children

£570,000 (2012)

Beneficial area

Worldwide.

Correspondent: Allison Racher, Correspondent, The Northern and Shell Building, Number 10 Lower Thames Street, London EC3R 6EN (tel: 020 8612 7760; email: allison.racher@express.co.uk)

Trustees: Richard Desmond; Northern and Shell Services Ltd; Northern and Shell Media Group Ltd.

CC Number: 1014352

The RD Crusaders Foundation was renamed the Desmond Foundation in 2013. According to the trustees' report for 2012, the foundation gives grants for general charitable purposes, especially for the relief of poverty and sickness amongst children.

In 2012 the foundation had assets of £90,000 and an income of £618,000. There were 70 grants made totalling £570,000.

Beneficiaries include: Norwood (£157,000); World Jewish Relief (£61,500); Dalaid and Fight for Sight (£50,000 each); IC Trust (£19,500); Well Being of Women (£15,000); Forward Thinking, University of Nottingham and Community Security Trust (£10,000 each); Creative Access, the Disability Foundation and Caron Keating Foundation (£5,000 each); Tsu'Chu Biz Foundation and Richard House Trust (£2,000 each); and the Holocaust Centre and St Bride's Church (£1,000 each).

Applications

In writing to the correspondent. All grant requests are considered and awards made are based on the merits of each proposal.

Information gathered from:

Accounts; Charity Commission record.

The Sandy Dewhirst Charitable Trust

General charitable purposes-social welfare and community

£47,000 (2012)

Beneficial area

UK, with a strong preference for East and North Yorkshire.

Correspondent: Louise Cliffe, Correspondent, Addleshaw Goddard, 100 Barbirolli Square, Manchester M2 3AB (tel: 01619 346373)

Trustees: Paul Howell; Timothy Dewhirst.

CC Number: 279161

The trust was established in 1979, firstly for the welfare of people connected through employment with I J Dewhirst Holdings Ltd or the settlor of the trust and secondly for general charitable purposes, with a strong preference for East and North Yorkshire. The charity makes donations to local and national organisations.

In 2012 the trust held assets of £1.6 million and had an income of £62,000. The trustees made grants totalling £47,000 and of this almost £20,000 was given to local organisations and £17,000 to national organisations.

23 grants to organisations included: Sargent Cancer Care for Children (£10,000); Help for Heroes (£5,000); Salivation Army, the Army Benevolent Fund and Yorkshire Air Ambulance (£3,000 each); Action Medical Research (£2,000); Driffield Town Cricket and Recreation Club (£1,500); and St Catherine's Hospice, Hull Sea Cadets and All Saints Church – Nafferton (£500 each).

Applications

The trust does not accept unsolicited applications.

Information gathered from:

Accounts; Charity Commission record.

The Laduma Dhamecha Charitable Trust

General

£123,000 (2011/12)

Beneficial area

UK and overseas.

Correspondent: Pradip Dhamecha, Trustee, 2 Hathaway Close, Stanmore, Middlesex HA7 3NR (tel: 020 8903 8181)

Trustees: K. R. Dhamecha; S. R. Dhamecha; P. K. Dhamecha.

CC Number: 328678

The trust was founded by the Dhamecha family who founded and operate the Dhamecha cash and carry group based in Greater London. The trust supports a wide range of organisations in the UK and overseas. The aims of the trust are listed in the annual report as being:

- To provide relief of sickness by the provision of medical equipment and the establishing or improvement of facilities at hospitals
- To provide for the advancement of education and/or an educational establishment in rural areas to make children self-sufficient in the long term
- Other general charitable purposes

In 2011/12 the trust had assets of almost £1.6 million and an income of £367,000 including £300,000 from Dhamecha Foods Ltd. Grants totalled £123,000. No information was available on the size or number of beneficiaries during this year.

Applications

In writing to the correspondent.

Information gathered from:

Accounts; Charity Commission record.

Alan and Sheila Diamond Charitable Trust

Jewish, general

£60,000 (2011/12)

Beneficial area

UK.

Correspondent: The Trustees, Mazars LLP, 8 New Fields, 2 Stinsford Road, Nuffield, Poole, Dorset BH17 0NF (tel: 01202 680777)

Trustees: Alan Diamond, Chair; Sheila Diamond; Jonathan Kropman; Kate Goldberg.

CC Number: 274312

About two-thirds of the trust's grantmaking is to Jewish organisations. The trust supports the same organisations each year which are listed in its trust deed, and cannot consider other applications.

In 2011/12 the trust had assets of £1.5 million and an income of £70,000. Grants totalled £60,000.

Beneficiaries included: British School of Osteopathy (£10,000); Norwood (£8,000); Youth Aliyah Child Rescue (£7,800); Anglo Israel Association (£6,000); The Royal Navy and Royal Marines (£5,000); Community Security Trust (£4,000); and Sidney Sussex College (£2,000).

Exclusions

No grants to individuals.

Applications

The trust states that it will not consider unsolicited applications or engage in preliminary telephone calls. There are no regular trustees' meetings. The trustees frequently decide how the funds should be allocated. The trustees have their own guidelines, which are not published.

Information gathered from:

Accounts; Charity Commission record.

The Dickon Trust

General

£50,000 (2011/12)

Beneficial area

North East England and Scotland.

Correspondent: Helen Tavroges, Dickinson Dees, St Anne's Wharf, 112 Quayside, Newcastle NE99 1SB (tel: 01912 799698; website: www.dickontrust.org.uk)

Trustees: Diana Linda Barrett; Maj.-General Robin Brims; Richard Younger Barrett; M. L. Robson; A. Copeman.

CC Number: 327202

The trust has general charitable purposes giving grants to local groups in North East England (from the Tees in the south to Cumbria in the west) and Scotland. The trustees in particular favour charities that are beneficial to children and young people.

In 2011/12 the trust had assets of £1.3 million and an income of £55,000. Grants to 48 organisations totalled £50,000.

All grants but two were for £1,000 each. Beneficiaries included: B.U.G.S. and Kids' Company (£2,000 each); and Age Concern Gateshead, Bobath Scotland, Butterwick House Children's Hospice, Esh Winning Residents Group, Fairbridge Tyne and Wear, Heel and Toe, Mental Health Matters, Partners in Advocacy, Pathfinder Guide Dogs, Samaritans of Kirkcaldy and District, Spinal Injuries Association, Tweed Valley Mountain Rescue Team (£1,000 each).

Exclusions

No support for individuals, unregistered charities or churches.

Applications

Applications can be made online at the trust's website. The trustees meet twice a year in summer and winter to consider appeals. Any applications received by the end of October will be considered at the winter meeting and any applications made after that time, up to the end of May, will be considered at the summer meeting.

Information gathered from:

Accounts; Charity Commission record; funder's website.

The Dinwoodie Settlement

Postgraduate medical education and research

£433,000 (2011/12)

Beneficial area

UK.

Correspondent: The Clerk to the Trustees, c/o Thomas Eggar, The Corn Exchange, Baffins Lane, Chichester, West Sussex PO19 1GE

Trustees: William A. Fairbairn; John Black; Christian Webster; Rodney B. N. Fisher; John A. Gibson.

CC Number: 255495

The trustees outlined their grant policy in their 2011/12 accounts:

> The trustees endeavour to be pro-active in pursuing the objectives of the charity. There is a sub-group which evaluates grant applications. Site visits prior to commitment are made by one or more trustees with follow up visits as appropriate. Grant making policy is reviewed in light of changes and developments in the delivery and widening of postgraduate education.
>
> The trustees find themselves unable to look favourably on appeals of a general nature, especially when they come from organisations acting as intermediaries and even though postgraduate medical research may be involved.

Postgraduate Medical Centres (PMC's): Support is almost invariably of a participatory nature with other funding sources. Projects typically fall into two categories, small and large, divided by a £500,000 total spend threshold.

Smaller PMC Projects: The trustees normally limit their contributions to £40,000 – £200,000, and the charity's participation rarely exceeds 50% of the total cost.

In 2011/12 the trust had assets of £4.2 million and an income of £278,000. Grants were made to totalling £433,000. Beneficiaries included: Blackpool Victoria Hospital (£133,000); Pembury Hospital, Tunbridge Wells (£121,000); Royal Wolverhampton Hospital (£100,000); N W Kent Postgraduate Medical Association (£50,000); Imperial College London (£15,000); and Royal Free Hospital, Hampstead (£12,500).

Exclusions

Anything falling outside the main areas of work referred to above. The trustees do not expect to fund consumable or equipment costs or relieve the NHS of its financial responsibilities.

Applications

The trustees state they are proactive rather than reactive in their grant-giving. Negotiating for new PMCs and monitoring their construction invariably takes a number of years.

Information gathered from:

Accounts; Charity Commission record.

Disability Aid Fund (The Roger and Jean Jefcoate Trust)

Disability

£126,000 to organisations

(2011/12)

Beneficial area

UK.

Correspondent: Roger Jefcoate, Trustee, 2 Copse Gate, Winslow, Buckingham MK18 3HX (tel: 01296 715466)

Trustees: Vivien Dinning, Chair; Roger Jefcoate; Valerie Henchoz; Rosemary McCloskey; Carol Wemyss.

CC Number: 1096211

The following statement was taken from the trust's 2011/12 accounts and explains its grantmaking strategy:

> We support a few carefully selected local, regional and small national healthcare and disability charities for older people in Buckinghamshire and Milton Keynes and adjacent counties, especially charities which promote health and wellbeing through information, advice and practical help like developing or providing special needs technology. We look for charities showing strong support from service users and volunteers and only modest expenditure on fundraising and administration.

The trust is particularly interested in charities for people with 'hidden disabilities' like dementia, deafness and poor mental health as well as charities for carers.

In 2011/12 the trust had assets of £3.3 million, an income of £163,000 and made grants totalling £126,000.

Beneficiaries included: Pace – Aylesbury – refurbishment of local centre and Canine Partners – Midhurst – towards a Midlands training centre (£25,000 each); L'Arche Community – Bognor – appeal for Jericho Community House (£15,000); Friends of Bedford House – Pinner – wheelchair vehicle (£10,000); SHARE Community – Wadsworth – general needs (£5,000); and Carers Milton Keynes – new communications system (£3,600).

Applications

Information provided by the trust:

> If you think that your charity might fit our remit please telephone Roger Jefcoate on 01296 715466 weekdays before 7pm to discuss your proposal. You may then be invited to submit a written application summarising your request on just one side of paper, with minimal supporting information like a single sheet general leaflet or a magazine article; do not send your annual review, we would ask for that if we need it. We would normally only consider a further request after two years, and then only by invitation.

Percentage of awards given to new applicants: between 20% and 30%.

Common applicant mistakes

'Not reading carefully our criteria in your [DSC's] guides and on the Charity Commission website with our list of grants.'

Information gathered from:

Accounts; Charity Commission record; further information provided by the funder.

Dischma Charitable Trust

General, with a preference for Education, Arts and Culture, Conservation and Human and Animal Welfare

£77,000 (2012)

Beneficial area

Worldwide, with a strong preference for London and the south east of England.

Correspondent: Linda Cousins, Secretary, Rathbone Trust Company Ltd, 4th Floor, 1 Curzon Street, London W1J 5FB (tel: 020 7399 0820; email: linda.cousins@rathbones.com)

Trustees: Simon Robertson; Edward Robertson; Lorna Robertson Timmis; Virginia Robertson; Selina Robertson; Arabella Brooke.

CC Number: 1077501

The Dischma Charitable Trust was established in 1999. The trustees have recently reviewed their grant-giving policy and decided to support principally, but not exclusively, projects concerned with education, arts and culture, conservation and human and animal welfare.

In 2012 the trust had assets of £4.9 million and income of £113,000. Grants were made to 52 organisations totalling £77,000 and were broken down as follows:

General	£19,000
Children and youth welfare	£17,000
Wildlife and conservation	£14,500
General medical, mental health and disabled	£12,000
The relief of poverty	£8,000
Education	£5,000
Elderly welfare	£2,000

Beneficiaries included: Trinity Hospice (£5,000); International Animal Rescue (£4,300); Guide Dogs (£3,400); Epic Arts (£3,000); Fields in Trust, Forces Support, Camden Arts Centre, Contact the Elderly and West London Churches Homeless Concern (£2,000 each); the Gorilla Organisation and Theatre for a Change (£1,000 each); and Tall Ships Youth Trust (£500).

Exclusions

The trust does not support charities that carry out medical research.

Applications

The trustees meet half-yearly to review applications for funding. Only successful applicants are notified of the trustees' decision. Certain charities are supported annually, although no commitment is given.

Information gathered from:

Accounts; Charity Commission record.

The DLM Charitable Trust

General charitable purposes

£111,000 (2011/12)

Beneficial area

UK, especially the Oxford area.

Correspondent: Jeffrey Alan Cloke, Trustee, c/o Cloke and Co., 475 Salisbury House, London Wall, London EC2M 5QQ (tel: 020 7638 8992)

Trustees: Jeffrey Alan Cloke; Dr Eric Anthony de la Mare; Jennifer Elizabeth Pyper; Philippa Sawyer.

CC Number: 328520

The trust was established in 1990, after R. D. A. de la Mare left 25% of the residue of his estate for charitable purposes. It supports charities that were supported by the settlor and local Oxford organisations 'where normal fundraising methods may not be successful.' In 2011/12 the trust had assets of £5.2 million and an income of £136,000. Grants were given to 20 organisations totalling £111,000.

Beneficiaries included: Ley Community (£20,000); See Saw (£15,000); Stillbirth and Neonatal Death Charity and Wildlife Conservation Research Unit (£10,000 each); Brainwave and Home Farm Trust (£5,000 each); Action for Blind People and Cecily's Fund (£3,000 each); and

OXRAD and Prison Phoenix Trust (£2,000 each).

Exclusions

No grants to individuals.

Applications

In writing to the correspondent. Trustees meet in February, July and November to consider applications.

Percentage of awards given to new applicants: between 30% and 40%.

Information gathered from:

Accounts; Charity Commission record; further information provided by the funder.

The Dorcas Trust

Christian, relief of poverty and advancement of education

£29,000 (2011/12)

Beneficial area

UK.

Correspondent: I. Taylor, c/o Rathbone Trust Co. Ltd, Port of Liverpool Building, Pier Head, Liverpool L3 1NW (tel: 01512 366666)

Trustees: James Cecil Lionel Broad; Jan Broad; Peter Butler.

CC Number: 275494

The trustees make grants for the advancement of the Christian religion, the relief of poverty and the advancement of education. They will also consider making loans to organisations and individuals. In 2011/12 the trust had assets of over £1.5 million and an income of £41,000. Grants were made totalling £29,000.

Beneficiaries included: Navigators (£16,000); British Youth for Christ (£3,000); Tear Fund (£2,500); Chippenham Cricket Club and Coach House Riding for the Disabled (£1,000 each); New Hope Ministries (£750); Salvation Army (£500); New Market Day Centre (£100); and Movember (£50).

Applications

In writing to the correspondent, although the trustees have stated that applications cannot be considered as funds are already committed.

Information gathered from:

Accounts; Charity Commission record.

The Dorus Trust

General charitable purposes

£58,000 (2012)

Beneficial area

Mainly UK but sometimes overseas.

Correspondent: Charles Peacock, Trustee, c/o Charities Aid Foundation, 25 Kings Hill Avenue, Kings Hill, West Malling ME19 4TA (tel: 01732 520028)

Trustees: Bettine Bond; Charles Peacock; Sarah Peacock.

CC Number: 328724

The Dorus Trust was established in 1990. The trust has common trustees with two other trusts, the Cleopatra Trust and the Epigoni Trust (see separate entries) with which it also shares the same aims and polices. All three trusts are administered by Charities Aid Foundation. Generally the trusts support different organisations each year.

In 2012 the trust had assets of £3 million, which generated an income of £32,000. Grants were made to ten organisations totalling £58,000.

Beneficiaries included: St Raphael's Hospice (£8,000); Practical Action and Home-Start Merton (£7,000 each); Volunteer Centre Merton and Switchback (£5,000 each); and St Catherine's – Oxford (£3,000).

Exclusions

No grants to individuals.

Applications

This trust no longer accepts applications.

Information gathered from:

Accounts; Charity Commission record.

The Double 'O' Charity Ltd

General

£175,000 (2011/12)

Beneficial area

UK and overseas.

Correspondent: The Trustees, c/o 4 Friars Lane, Richmond, Surrey TW9 1NL (tel: 020 8940 8171)

Trustees: Peter Townshend; Karen Townshend.

CC Number: 271681

The primary objective of the trust is to make grants towards the relief of poverty, preservation of health and the advancement of education. The trust considers all requests for aid.

In 2011/12 the trust held assets of £34,000 and had an income of £179,000. Grants to 13 organisations totalled £175,000, with an additional £2,750 awarded to individuals.

Beneficiaries included: Spirit of Recovery (£38,000); Refuge (£30,000); NAPAC (£27,000); Promise Clinic and Richmond Bridge Friendship Club (£25,000 each); Livewire Youth Music Project (£10,000); The Wroxham Trust (£1,000); and The William Donkin Memorial Fund (£200).

Applications

In writing to the correspondent.

Information gathered from:

Accounts; Charity Commission record.

The Doughty Charity Trust

Orthodox Jewish, religious education, relief of poverty

£267,000 (2012)

Beneficial area

England, Israel.

Correspondent: Gerald Halibard, Trustee, 22 Ravenscroft Avenue, London NW11 0RY (tel: 020 8209 0500)

Trustees: Gerald Halibard; M. Halibard.

CC Number: 274977

According to its 2012 accounts, the Doughty Charity Trust was established 'to promote the relief of poverty and the advancement of religion and religious education'.

This trust appears to confine its giving to Orthodox Jewish causes.

In 2012 the trust had an income of £325,000 and made grants totalling £267,000. Its assets stood at £115,000. Various donations of £5,000 and under amounted to £89,500.

Beneficiaries included: FKHS (£24,000); Ezras Nitrochim (£17,500); Kerren Shabbos (£13,500); Torah Vodaas and Torah Emes (£10,000 each); Zichron Menachem (£8,500); and Mir and Yad Elizer (£6,000 each).

Applications

In writing to the correspondent. The trustees are experiencing increasing demands upon the charities resources. They have decided to not add to the list of present donees.

Information gathered from:

Accounts; Charity Commission record.

Douglas Arter Foundation

People with mental or physical disabilities

£81,000 (2012)

Beneficial area

UK, with preference for Bristol, Somerset and Gloucestershire.

Correspondent: Peter Broderick, Trustee, 16 Westway, Nailsea, Bristol BS48 2NA (tel: 01275 851051; email: gntbristol@aol.com)

Trustees: Geoffrey Arter; John Gurney; Peter Broderick; John Hudd.

CC Number: 201794

According to the trustees' report for 2012:

> The trustees' policy is to make grants principally for the benefit of the mentally and physically disabled of all ages within the UK, mainly through registered charities whose activities are for the benefit of the disabled. The trustees make awards where they are considered to be most effective, taking into account the feasibility of projects concerned, financial situation of the organisations, funding already available, numbers of people benefiting and voluntary and self help aspects.

In 2012 the trust had assets of £2.6 million and an income of £106,000. Grants totalling £81,000 were made to 126 organisations, ranging from £250 to £10,000. 98 grants were for amounts between £250 and £500, and 27 grants of £1,000. Grants were broken down geographically as follows:

	No. of grants	Amount
National	82	£53,500
Local	44	£27,500

Beneficiaries included: SCOPE (£10,000); Amber Trust, Macmillan Cancer Support – Somerset, Marches Family Network, British Wireless for the Blind Fund and Music Alive (£1,000 each); Penny Brohn Cancer Care – Bristol, North Devon Voluntary Services, Where Next Association and Weston Hospicecare – Weston-super-Mare (£500 each); and Prostate Cancer Support Group, Rainbow Centre – Bristol and Merseyside Thursday Club (£250 each).

Exclusions

Support is not given: for overseas projects; general community projects*; individuals; general education projects*; religious and ethnic projects*; projects for unemployment and related training schemes*; projects on behalf of offenders and ex-offenders; projects concerned with the abuse of drugs and/or alcohol; wildlife and conservation schemes*; and general restoration and preservation of buildings, purely for historical and/or architectural reasons. (* If these projects are mainly or wholly for the benefit of people who have disabilities then they may be considered.)

Ongoing support is not given, and grants are not usually given for running costs, salaries, research and items requiring major funding. Loans are not given.

Applications

The trust does not have an official application form. Appeals should be made in writing to the secretary. Telephone calls are not welcome. The trust asks that the following is carefully considered before submitting an application:

Appeals must:

- Be from registered charities
- Include a copy of the latest audited accounts available (for newly registered charities a copy of provisional accounts showing estimated income and expenditure for the current financial year)
- Show that the project is 'both feasible and viable' and, if relevant, give the starting date of the project and the anticipated date of completion
- Include the estimated cost of the project, together with the appeal's target-figure and details of what funds have already been raised and any fundraising schemes for the project

The trustees state that 'where applicable, due consideration will be given to evidence of voluntary and self-help (both in practical and fundraising terms) and to the number of people expected to benefit from the project'. They also comment that their decision is final and 'no reason for a decision, whether favourable or otherwise, need be given' and that 'the award and acceptance of a grant will not involve the trustees in any other commitment'.

Appeals are dealt with on an ongoing basis, but the trustees meet formally four times per year usually in March, June, September and December.

Information gathered from:

Accounts; Charity Commission record.

The R. M. Douglas Charitable Trust

General

£37,000 to organisations (2011/12)

Beneficial area

UK with a preference for Staffordshire.

Correspondent: Juliet Lees, Trustee, c/o Geens, 68 Liverpool Road, Stoke-on-Trent ST4 1BG (tel: 01782 847952)

Trustees: Juliet Lees, Jonathan Douglas; Murray Lees.

CC Number: 248775

The trust was set up for the relief of poverty (including provision of pensions) especially for present and past employees (and their families) of Robert M Douglas (Contractors) Ltd, and for general charitable purposes especially in the parish of St Mary, Dunstall. In practice grants are only given to organisations previously supported by the trust. Grants range from £200 to £5,000, although only a few are for over £500.

In 2011/12 the trust had assets of £944,000 and an income of £40,000. Grants to organisations totalled £37,000. Grants were also given to individuals connected with the company, totalling £6,700.

Previous beneficiaries included: Bible Explorer for Christian outreach, British Red Cross for general purposes, Burton Graduate Medical College to equip a new lecture theatre, Four Oaks Methodist Church for its centenary appeal, Lichfield Diocesan Urban Fund for Christian mission, St Giles Hospice – Lichfield for development, SAT-7 Trust for Christian outreach and John Taylor High School – Barton in Needwood for a performing arts block.

Applications

The trust has previously stated that its funds were fully committed.

Information gathered from:

Accounts; Charity Commission record.

The Drayson Foundation

Relief of sickness, education

£0 (2011/12)

Beneficial area

UK.

Correspondent: Clare Maurice, Trustee, 201 Bishopsgate, London EC2M 3AB (tel: 020 7456 8610; email: clare.maurice@MTGLLP.com)

Trustees: Clare Maurice; Lord Paul Drayson; Lady Elspeth Drayson.

CC Number: 1076700

Set up in 1999, the main objects of the foundation are the relief of sickness, with particular emphasis on children and the advancement of education by the provision of scholarships, exhibitions, grants and allowances at any education or training establishment. The trustees continue to review educational projects with a particular bias towards science.

In 2011/12 it had assets of almost £3.8 million and an income of £88,000. No grants were made this year.

Applications

In writing to the correspondent.

Information gathered from:

Accounts; Charity Commission record.

Dromintee Trust

General

£376,000 (2011/12)

Beneficial area

UK and developing countries.

Correspondent: Hugh Murphy, Trustee, The Manor House, Main Street, Thurnby, Leicester LE7 9PN (tel: 01162 415100)

Trustees: Hugh Murphy; Margaret Murphy; Mary Murphy; Patrick Hugh Murphy; Robert Smith; Paul Tiernan; Joseph Murphy.

CC Number: 1053956

Established in March 1996, this trust gives for people in need by reason of age, illness, disability or socio-economic circumstances; for charitable purposes connected with children's welfare; the advancement of health and education; research into rare diseases and disorders, in particular metabolic disorders; and for general charitable purposes. Grants are made locally, nationally and in developing countries.

In 2011/12 the trust had assets of £1.2 million and an income of £312,000. Grants were made to 16 organisations totalling £376,000.

As in previous years the largest beneficiary was Great Ormond Street Hospital Charity (£250,000).

Other beneficiaries were: CAFOD – Assumption Sisters of Nairobi (£35,000); Consolata Fathers – Ikonda Hospital (£25,000); Intercare (£20,000); Let the Children Live and Belinda Stanford Memorial Fund (£5,000 each); African Mission (£3,000); and UCL – two professors' trip to Namibia (£1,500).

Applications

In writing to the correspondent.

Information gathered from:

Accounts; Charity Commission record.

The Dumbreck Charity

General

£74,000 (2011/12)

Beneficial area

Worldwide, especially the West Midlands.

Correspondent: Mrs P. M. Spragg, c/o PS Accounting, 41 Sycamore Drive, Hollywood, Birmingham B47 5QX

Trustees: Chris Hordern; Hugh Carslake; Jane Uloth; Judith Melling.

CC Number: 273070

The trust focuses on animal welfare and conservation, children's welfare, care of the elderly, people with disabilities and medicine and health. A small number of new grants are awarded each year to charities in Worcestershire, Warwickshire and West Midlands. Grants can be one-off and recurring.

In 2011/12 the trust had assets of £3.6 million, an income of £134,000 and gave grants totalling £74,000, broken down as follows:

Category	Regular grants	One-off grants	Total
Medical	3	10	£16,500
Care of the elderly and disabled	6	7	£14,500
Children's welfare	2	9	£7,000
Animal welfare/ conservation	3	3	£7,500
Miscellaneous	2	26	£28,000

Beneficiaries included: DEC East Africa Crisis Appeal and CHARMS – Birmingham Children's Hospital (£5,000 each); Shipston Home Nursing (£3,000); Brooke Hospital for Animals Cairo and Macular Disease Support Group Leamington (£2,000 each); Army Benevolent Fund, Taste for Adventure, Greatwood – Horse Power Programme, Hunt Staff Benefit Society and Friends of Pershore Abbey (£1,000 each); and Academy Chamber Orchestra, Kenwood Eagles FC, Mobility Trust and Teenage Cancer Trust (£500 each).

Exclusions

No grants to individuals.

Applications

In writing to the correspondent. The trustees meet annually in April/May. Unsuccessful applicants will not be notified. In general, priority is given to applications from the Midlands counties.

Percentage of awards given to new applicants: between 40% and 50%.

Common applicant mistakes

'Out of area applications.'

Information gathered from:

Accounts; Charity Commission record; further information provided by the funder.

The Dunn Family Charitable Trust

Medical, general, conservation

£60,000 (2011/12)

Beneficial area

UK, with a strong preference for Nottinghamshire.

Correspondent: Mrs Jacky Chester, Rushcliffe Estates Ltd, Tudor House, 13–15 Rectory Road, West Bridgford, Nottingham NG2 6BE (tel: 01159 455300; email: jrc@rushcliffe.co.uk)

Trustees: Graham R. Dunn; Jacky R. Dunn; Lisa J. Dunn; Nigel A. Dunn; Peter M. Dunn; Richard M. Dunn.

CC Number: 297389

This trust supports health, multiple sclerosis research, conservation, ecology and general community and voluntary organisations.

In 2011/12 the trust had assets of £1.8 million, an income of £69,000 and gave 28 grants to organisations totalling £60,000.

Beneficiaries included: The Oakes Trust (Sheffield) (£4,500); Nottingham Multiple Sclerosis Therapy Centre Ltd (£4,000); Treetops Hospice (£3,500); Support Dogs (£3,000); Nottinghamshire Historic Churches Trust (£2,500); Seafarers UK and West Bridgford Shopmobility (£2,000 each); Age UK and Rainbow Children's Hospice (£1,500 each); RNLI (Wells-next-the-Sea) and Nottinghamshire Wildlife Trust (£1,000 each); and Dolly Parton Imagination Library (£500).

Exclusions

No grants to individuals or unsolicited applications.

Applications

In writing to the correspondent.

Information gathered from:

Accounts; Charity Commission record.

Mildred Duveen Charitable Trust

General

£62,000 (2011/12)

Beneficial area

Worldwide.

Correspondent: Peter Holgate, Trustee, Devonshire House, 60 Goswell Road, London EC1M 7AD (tel: 020 7566 4000)

Trustees: Peter Holgate; Adrian Houstoun; Peter Loose; John Shelford.

CC Number: 1059355

Registered with the Charity Commission in November 1996, in 1999/2000 this trust received a substantial income of £1.3 million.

In 2011/12 the trust had assets of £1.1 million and an income of £27,000. Grants to 37 organisations totalled £62,000.

Beneficiaries included: Missing People (£10,000); Almedia Theatre and Masterclass Trust (£5,000 each); Charlie Waller Memorial Trust (£3,300); Whittington Babies (£2,500); Three Wings Trust, St John's College and Hearing Dogs for Deaf People (£2,000 each); Combat Stress, Lingfield and District RDA, Old Meeting URC

Bedworth and The Firefighters Charity (£1,000 each); Centrepoint (£750); and ACT (Prostrate Cancer Charity), Cruse Bereavement Care, Shooting Start and The Rainbow Centre for Children (£500 each).

Applications

In writing to the correspondent.

Information gathered from:

Accounts; Charity Commission record.

The Annette Duvollet Charitable Trust

General charitable purpose, with preference towards young people

£24,000 (2011/12)

Beneficial area

UK.

Correspondent: Peter Clarke, Trustee, 18 Nassau Road, London SW13 9QE (tel: 020 8748 5401; email: peteaclarke@yahoo.com)

Trustees: Peter Clarke; Richard Shuttleworth; Caroline Dawes.

CC Number: 326505

Registered with the Charity Commission in 1984, this trust gives grants to charities whose work supports young people aged 14 to 25. In 2011/12 the trust had assets of £677,000 and an income of £29,000. Grants were given to ten organisations totalling £24,000.

Beneficiaries include: DePaul Trust and Pathway Workshop (£5,000); NMC Charity (£3,000); Island Trust Ltd, Support Line and Tiverton Market Centre (£2,000 each); Sense (£1,500); and Sayers Croft Environmental Educational Trust (£1,000).

Applications

In writing to the correspondent.

Information gathered from:

Accounts; Charity Commission record.

The Dwek Family Charitable Trust

General

About £30,000 (2011/12)

Beneficial area

UK, with a preference for the Greater Manchester area.

Correspondent: Joseph Claude Dwek, Trustee, Suite One, Courthill House, 66 Water Lane, Wilmslow, Cheshire SK9 5AP (tel: 01625 549081)

Trustees: Anthony Jack Leon; Jonathan Victor Dwek; Joseph Claude Dwek.

CC Number: 1001456

In 2011/12 the trust had an income of £23,000 and an expenditure of £35,000. No further information was available.

Previous major beneficiaries have included: Manchester International Festival; The Wilbraham Road Manchester Trust and The Royal Society.

Applications

In writing to the correspondent.

Percentage of awards given to new applicants: less than 10%.

Information gathered from:

Accounts; Charity Commission record; further information provided by the funder.

The Dyers' Company Charitable Trust

General charitable purposes

£430,000 (2011/12)

Beneficial area

UK.

Correspondent: The Clerk of the Dyers, Dyer's Hall, Dowgate Hill, London EC4R 2ST (tel: 020 7236 7197; website: www.dyerscompany.co.uk)

Trustee: The Dyers Company.

CC Number: 289547

According to the trustees' report for 2011/12, the trust was established in 1984 and 'makes a large number of grants to registered charities in support of general charitable purposes'. The trust gives to both one-off and long standing projects. The trust distributes only to UK registered charities which are local/small. The trust does not consider applications unless they are supported/sponsored by one of their liverymen.

In 2011/12 the trust had assets of £10 million and an income of £877,000. Grants to organisations totalled £430,000, which were in the following categories:

Education and the young	32	£108,000
Craft	14	£65,500
Health and welfare	35	£41,500
Arts	15	£20,500
Services	8	£13,500
The Church	9	£7,000
Local community/city/inner London	7	£7,000

Beneficiaries included: Boutcher C. of E. Primary School and Archbishop Tenison's School (£25,000 each); Society of Dyers and Colourists (£20,000); University of Manchester (£17,000); Cirdan Sailing Trust (£4,000); HANDS (£3,000); Combat Stress (£2,500); Orchid Cancer Appeal and National Memorial Arboretum (£2,000 each); Oakhaven Hospice and River Thames Boat Project (£1,000 each); Fashion and Textile Children's Trust and Fairbridge West (£500 each); and Association of Weavers (£200).

Exclusions

No grants to individuals or international charities.

Applications

The company's website provides information regarding applications and is as follows:

> Please note that the company does not accept unsolicited applications as a matter of policy unless supported/endorsed by a member of the company. Nevertheless, the charitable activities of our company continue to be as flexible as we can manage to accommodate requests for funds.

Information gathered from:

Accounts; Charity Commission record; funder's website.

eaga Charitable Trust

Tackling fuel poverty

£48,500 (2011/12)

Beneficial area

UK and European Union.

Correspondent: Dr Naomi Brown, Trust Manager, PO Box 225, Kendal LA9 9DR (tel: 01539 736477; email: eagact@aol.com; website: www.eagacharitabletrust.org)

Trustees: William Baker; Anne Toms; Prof. Dave Gordon; Elizabeth Gore; Virginia Graham; Pedro Guertler; Jack Harrison.

CC Number: 1088361

The trust currently provides grants to fund research and other projects within the following programme:

Understanding and combating fuel poverty – Ensuring energy services are fair and accessible for all groups in society

Grant applications should consist of one or more of the following elements:

- Rigorous academic or policy-related research
- Robustly evaluated action projects that can offer new models for use on a wider scale and
- Wider promotion of good practice (for example through toolkits and workshops)

The main focus of support is to promote a better understanding of fuel poverty and more effective means of tackling it. This includes understanding the causes of fuel poverty, how to prevent it and which groups are most likely to suffer fuel poverty. It also includes how best to target assistance to those in fuel poverty or at risk of it. Essential to this is improving energy efficiency and comfort in homes.

The following information is taken from the guidelines available on the trust's website:

> Although we cannot support physical energy efficiency measures, we do support evaluation and promotion of targeted energy efficiency strategies.
>
> Groups of consumers in fuel poverty are likely to suffer other, related forms of financial and social deprivation and exclusion. These groups may thus be the targets of multiple policies and programmes to combat poverty. This may lead to confusion. By understanding better the links and interactions between these policies and programmes, and how they impact on different groups, there are opportunities to increase effectiveness and efficiency of delivery and take-up. We are therefore keen to support work that promotes a better understanding of the links between fuel poverty and other financial and social exclusion agendas at the national, devolved and local levels.
>
> We welcome well-presented, rigorous applications for financial support for work that is relevant to the themes of our programme, as outlined above. In addition, during 2013 we are prioritising for funding grant applications which address any one or more of the following linked subject areas: fuel poverty and disability; fuel poverty and young children; the links between fuel poverty and migrant communities; real and perceived barriers to the take-up of assistance; fuel poverty and the climate change agenda; and fuel poverty definition and target.

The trust does not have minimum or maximum grant levels but it does encourage the co-funding of projects where appropriate. Grants usually run from one to three years. The trust will accept the inclusion of reasonable overhead costs within a project budget (in addition to the project's direct costs) providing the applicant can explain what the overhead costs include, how the full costs have been analysed and how the allocation was calculated.

Local projects

The trust gives priority to funding proposals that have the potential to inform or influence national perceptions and policies and have a wide geographic focus. A project that operates at a local level will only be considered for a grant if it: clearly demonstrates innovation; identifies the policy relevance of the project; has wide applicability; and has well-developed evaluation and dissemination plans.

In 2011/12 the trust had assets of £765,000, an income of £83,000 and grants awarded in the year totalled £48,500. Beneficiaries include: Association for the Conservation of Energy (ACE); Centre for Consumers and Essential Services, University of Leicester; Centre for Sustainable Energy; Department of Social Policy and Social Work, University of York; and Joanne Wade and Impetus Consulting Ltd.

Exclusions

No grants for: general fundraising appeals; projects that comprise solely of capital works; retrospective funding; energy advice provision materials; maintenance of websites; or local energy efficiency/warm homes initiatives. No grants to individuals.

Applications

Application forms and detailed guidance on the application process are available on the trust's website. Potential applicants are encouraged to contact the trust's manager, Naomi Brown at an early stage to discuss whether their ideas are likely to fall within the trust's areas of interest.

Percentage of awards given to new applicants: between 20% and 30%.

Common applicant mistakes

'Not answering questions specifically; insufficient detail with project budget and finances; insufficient development of methodological approach.'

Information gathered from:

Accounts; Charity Commission record; further information provided by the funder; funder's website.

The Eagle Charity Trust

General, international, welfare

£43,000 (2012)

Beneficial area

UK, in particular Manchester, and overseas.

Correspondent: The Trustees, c/o Nairne Son and Green, 477 Chester Road, Cornbrook, Manchester M16 9HF (tel: 01618 721701)

Trustees: Laura Gifford; Daphne Gifford; Elizabeth Williams; Sarah Nowakowski; Robert Gifford.

CC Number: 802134

The trust stated it supports a wide variety of charities, including UK and international charities and local charities in Manchester. There is a preference for those concerned with medicine and welfare. Grants are made on a one-off basis, with no commitment to providing ongoing funding.

In 2012 the trust had assets of £1 million and an income of £44,000. There were 26 grants made totalling £43,000. The trustees opted not to publicise a list of beneficiaries. The majority of grants were for either £500 or £1,000.

Previous beneficiaries include: Oxfam – Darfur and Chad (£2,500); Médecins Sans Frontières, UNICEF and Shelter (£2,000 each); British Red Cross – Bangladesh and Macmillan Cancer Support (£1,500 each); Amnesty International, Sight Savers International and Samaritans (£1,000 each); and Turning Point, Claire House and WaterAid (£500 each).

Applications

Unsolicited applications are not invited.

Information gathered from:

Accounts; Charity Commission record.

Audrey Earle Charitable Trust

General, with some preference for animal welfare and conservation charities

£32,000 (2011/12)

Beneficial area

UK.

Correspondent: Paul Sheils, Trustee, 24–25 Bloomsbury Square, London WC1A 2PJ (tel: 020 7359 4135; email: psheils@mail.com)

Trustees: Paul A. Sheils; Roger J. Weetch; Richard H. Fleetwood Fuller.

CC Number: 290028

In 2011/12 this trust had assets of just under £5 million and an income of £80,000. Grants totalled £32,000. A list of beneficiaries was not available, however, many beneficiaries are supported year after year.

Previous beneficiaries have included: Wells Hospital and Hospice Trust (£7,000); Animal Health Trust, British Red Cross Society, Royal British Legion, People's Dispensary for Sick Animals – PDSA, Age Concern England, Redwings Horse Sanctuary, Salvation Army and Oxfam (£4,000 each); Burnham Market and Norton Village Hall (£3,000); Burnham Overy Parochial Church Council (£1,000); and Farming and Wildlife Advisory Group (£500).

Applications

In writing to the correspondent.

Information gathered from:

Accounts; Charity Commission record.

The Sir John Eastwood Foundation

Social welfare, education, health

£230,500 (2011/12)

Beneficial area

UK, but mainly Nottinghamshire in practice.

Correspondent: David Marriott, Trustee, PO Box 9803, Mansfield NG18 9FT (fax: 01623 847955)

Trustees: Diana Cottingham; Constance Mudford; Gordon Raymond; Valerie Hardingham; David Marriott.

CC Number: 235389

The charity was originally established by Sir John Eastwood in 1964. According to the trustees' report for 2011/12:

> The objects of the charity are to support other registered charities and priority is given to local charities benefiting Nottinghamshire, although appeals are considered from organisations which operate further afield. Particular emphasis is given to charities which help the disabled, the elderly and children with special needs.
>
> The charity supports a number of registered charities on a regular basis by making grants each year to those particular charities. The prime target of the trustees each year is to ensure the continuance of these regular grants. Once these have been ensured, the trustees consider special projects and then other individual applications.

In 2011/12 the trust had assets of £7.6 million and an income of £416,000. The foundation's income has reduced significantly following the cessation of trading of Adam Eastwood and Sons Ltd, a company which is wholly owned by the foundation and from where income was derived. Grants were made during the year totalling £230,000. Most grants were for less than £3,000, with some organisations receiving more than one grant during the year.

The larger beneficiaries, listed in the accounts, were: Nottingham Hospice (£24,000); Newark and Nottinghamshire Agricultural Society, the Oaklands and Sherwood Forest Hospital Voluntary Services (£10,000 each); Nottingham University (£9,000); Macmillan Cancer Support, Disability Living Centre and Southwell Minster (£5,000 each); and British Wireless for the Blind (£3,000).

Exclusions

No grants to individuals.

Applications

In writing to the correspondent.

Information gathered from:

Accounts; Charity Commission record.

The Ebenezer Trust

Evangelical Christianity, welfare

£54,000 (2011/12)

Beneficial area

UK and overseas.

Correspondent: Nigel Davey, Trustee, Longwood Lodge, Whites Hill, Stock, Ingatestone CM4 9QB (tel: 01277 829893)

Trustees: Nigel Davey; Ruth Davey.

CC Number: 272574

The trust gives grants to evangelical Christian charities. In 2011/12 the trust had assets of £716,000 and an income of £77,000. Grants were made to 41 organisations totalling £54,000.

Beneficiaries included: Christ Church-Stock (£5,000); Barnabas Fund and TEAR Fund (£4,000 each); Stepping Stones Trust (£3,000); Gideons International (£2,500); Alpha Partners (£2,000); Brentwood Christian Schools Worker Trust (£1,500); Wheels for the World and Christians Against Poverty (£1,000 each); Spurgeon's Child Care and Scripture Union (£500 each); London Institute of Contemporary Christianity and Sierra Leone Mission (£250 each); and Arsenal Charitable Trust (£50).

Exclusions

No grants to individuals.

Applications

The trust states that they 'are most unlikely to consider unsolicited requests for grants.'

Percentage of awards given to new applicants: less than 10%.

Common applicant mistakes

'Applying when they know that unsolicited applications are not being sought.'

Information gathered from:

Accounts; Charity Commission record; further information provided by the funder.

The Gilbert and Eileen Edgar Foundation

General charitable purposes with preference towards medical research, care and support, fine arts, education in the fine arts, religion, and recreation

£72,000 (2012/13)

Beneficial area

UK (and a few international appeals).

Correspondent: Adam Gentilli, Trustee, Greville Mount, Milcote, Stratford upon Avon, Warwickshire CV37 8AB (tel: 01491 848500; email: info@jamescowper.co.uk)

Trustees: Simon Gentilli; Adam Gentilli.

CC Number: 241736

The Gilbert and Eileen Edgar Foundation was created by a deed in 1965. According the trustees' report for 2012/13, the foundation has widely drawn objects and its objectives are as follows:

- Medical research – the promotion of medical and surgical science in all forms
- Care and support – helping people who are young, old and in need
- Fine arts – raising the artistic taste of the public in music, drama, opera, painting, sculpture and the fine arts
- Education in the fine arts – the promotion of education in the fine arts
- Religion – the promotion of religion
- Recreation – the provision of facilities for recreation or other leisure time activities

According to the trustees' report for 2012/13:

> The foundation has continued to make substantial grants for scholarships in the arts and donations to charities which raise the artistic taste of the public. It has also made a one-off grant towards building facilities for use by a charity providing education to young people in the art of silversmithing. The foundation has also made donations to charities providing support overseas by the provisions of tools and skills to enable people in Africa to earn a sustainable livelihood, and by providing educational books. It has also continued to donate to a charity which gives sight to cataract-blind people.

In 2012/13 the trust had assets of £1.8 million and an income of £83,000. Grants were made to 87 organisations totalling £72,000.

Beneficiaries included: Royal College of Music (£9,000); Royal Academy of Arts (£6,000); Royal Academy of Dramatic Art (£5,000); English National Ballet (£2,000); Worshipful Company of

Clockmakers, Gurkha Welfare Trust, Coram Life Education and Atlantic Salmon Trust (£1,000 each); Action for Elder Abuse, Child Brain Injury Trust and National Eye Research Centre (£500 each); and Hambledon Surgery Medical Fund (£250).

Exclusions

Grants for education in the fine arts are made by way of scholarships awarded by academies.

Applications

In writing to the correspondent. There are no application forms.

Information gathered from:

Accounts; Charity Commission record.

Gilbert Edgar Trust

General, UK and overseas

£37,000 (2011/12)

Beneficial area

Predominantly UK, limited overseas.

Correspondent: Simon Gentilli, Trustee, Barnwell House, Skirmett Road, Fingest, Oxon RG9 6TH

Trustees: Simon Gentilli; Adam Gentilli; Dr Richard Solomons.

CC Number: 213630

Registered with the Charity Commission in 1955, this trust supports organisations concerned with the welfare of people in the UK and overseas.

In 2011/12 the trust had assets of £900,000 and an income of £42,000. Charitable activities in the accounts are given as £5,200, however, this is because £31,500 of the previous year's grants were withdrawn or not taken up. Grants payable for the year came to £37,000 payable in 51 grants, which were broken down as follows:

Children	7	£5,000
Deaf/blind	2	£1,000
Disabled	9	£4,500
Drug abuse	4	£2,000
Homeless	5	£7,000
Hospice	3	£1,500
Medical	3	£2,000
Overseas	5	£5,000
Research	5	£3,000
Social	6	£4,000
Youth	3	£1,500
Other	1	£100

Beneficiaries included: British Red Cross, Samaritans, Shelter and Simon Community (£1,500 each); Echo, Impact Foundation, Macmillan Cancer Support, Nottinghill Foundation and Prostate Cancer Charity (£1,000 each); Broadreach House, East Anglia's Children's Hospices, Pain Relief Foundation, Prisoners Abroad, Re-Solv, Saint John's Ambulance and Spinal Injuries Foundation, (£500 each); and Worshipful Company of Clockmakers (£100).

Exclusions

No grants to individuals or non-registered charities.

Applications

In writing to the correspondent, with a copy of a brochure/flyer describing your work.

Information gathered from:

Accounts; Charity Commission record.

Edinburgh Trust No. 2 Account

Education, armed services, scientific expeditions

£83,000 (2011/12)

Beneficial area

UK and worldwide.

Correspondent: The Secretary, The Duke of Edinburgh's Household, Buckingham Palace, London SW1A 1AA (tel: 020 7024 4107)

Trustees: Charles Woodhouse; Sir Brian McGrath; Brigadier Archie Miller-Bakewell.

CC Number: 227897

According to the trustees' report for 2011/12:

> The trust supports general charitable purposes, however each year a proportion of the income is applied for the promotion and advancement of education and of the efficiency of the armed services of the crown. Income is applied by making grants and awarding prizes of scholarships and bursaries for successful achievements in the field of education and by awarding prizes and trophies for competitions and activities which increase the efficiency of the armed forces of the crown.
>
> The trust aims to make grants to the public benefit in the following areas: general charitable purposes, development of educational expedition research projects and support to the armed services of the crown.

In 2011/12 the trust had assets of £2.4 million and an income of £97,000. Grants were made to 82 organisations totalling £83,000 and were distributed into the following categories:

General	£52,000
Armed Services	£26,000
Education	£4,000

Beneficiaries included: Edwina Mountbatten Trust (£2,800); the Federation of London Youth Clubs, Royal Marines General Fund and the Game and Wildlife Conservancy Trust (£2,000 each); Burma Star Association, the Cutty Sark Trust and British Trust for Conservation Volunteers (£1,500 each); and the Countryside Foundation for Education and Royal Air Force Benevolent Fund (£1,000 each).

Exclusions

No grants to individuals; only scientific expeditions are considered with the backing of a major society. No grants to non-registered charities.

Applications

In writing to the correspondent.

Information gathered from:

Accounts; Charity Commission record.

Educational Foundation of Alderman John Norman

Educational purposes

£49,000 to organisations (2011/12)

Beneficial area

Norwich and Old Catton.

Correspondent: N. F. Saffell, Clerk, The Atrium, St George's Street, Norwich NR3 1AB (tel: 01603 629871)

Trustees: Revd Jonathan Boston; Roger Sandall; Dr Julia Leach; Revd Canon Martin Smith; Derek Armes; Tracey Hughes; Stephen Slack; Christopher Brown; Francis Whymark; James Hawkins; Roy Hughes.

CC Number: 313105

The original aims of the foundation were laid out in the will of the late Alderman John Norman who died in 1724. According to the Charity Commission, the income of the foundation is to be applied in one or more of the following ways, namely to assist:

- The education of children and young people descended from Alderman John Norman
- The education of children and young people resident in the parish of Old Catton
- Educational organisations within the parish of Old Catton, the city of Norwich and its immediate suburbs

In 2011/12 the foundation held assets of £6.3 million and had an income of £225,000. Grants to 448 descendants and 4 Old Catton residents totalled £166,000. A further £49,000 was given to 22 organisations.

Beneficiaries included: 1st Norwich Sea Scouts (£7,000); the Matthew Project and How Hill Trust (£5,000 each); East Norwich Youth Project, Norfolk Eating Disorders Association and Norfolk Archaeological Trust – St Benet's Abbey (£3,000 each); West Norwich Partnership and Your Future (£2,000 each); Norwich Cycle Speedway and Eaton Vale Scouts and Guides Activity Centre (£1,000 each); and Sewell Toy Library (£500).

Exclusions

No applications from outside Norwich and Old Catton will be considered.

Applications

In writing to the correspondent. Grants to organisations are considered at the trustees' meeting in May/June. All applications should be made through the clerk.

Information gathered from:

Accounts; Charity Commission record.

The W. G. Edwards Charitable Foundation

Projects benefiting older people

£98,500 (2012/13)

Beneficial area

UK.

Correspondent: Janet Brown, Clerk, 123A Station Road East, Oxted, Surrey RH8 0QE (tel: 01883 714412; email: janetbrown@wgedwardscharitablefoundation.org.uk; website: www.wgedwardscharitablefoundation.org.uk)

Trustees: Gillian Shepherd Coates; Wendy Savage; Yewande Savage; William Mackie.

CC Number: 293312

The W G Edwards Charitable Foundation is constituted under a trust deed of 1985 following the death of William George Edwards.

According to the trustees' report for 2012/13, the trustees have adopted the following grantmaking policy as a result of the wishes of the late Mr Edwards:

> To assist with the provision of care for older people through existing charities, principally with capital projects but also other innovative schemes for on-going care.
>
> The aims of the foundation are:
>
> - To support as many projects as possible, even if this means smaller individual grants
> - To donate to refurbishment/building projects nearing completion rather than those in the planning stage
> - To support all kinds of groups of older people
> - To sponsor individual named items of expenditure rather than donate into a pool/unrestricted fund
> - To ensure that any funding is properly spent on those specific items sponsored.

In 2012/13 the foundation had an income of £126,000 and assets of £3 million. A total of 147 applications were received, of which 46 were successful. Grants totalled £98,000. Types of donations as listed in the accounts were broken down as follows:

Furniture/equipment	£42,500
Refurbishment	£25,500
Recreational activity	£22,500
New building	£4,000
Outreach/care projects	£1,500
IT for older people	£1,500
Research	£900

Beneficiaries included: Family Support Clacton and Garvald Glenesk (£5,000 each); Aspire Living Ltd and Age UK Lewisham and Southwark (£4,000 each); West Herts Against Crime (£3,500); Independent Age (£3,000); NBFA Assisting the Elderly and Newent Association for the Disabled (£2,000 each); Vine Community Trust and Alive Activities Ltd (£1,000 each); and AM Arts Ltd (£500).

Exclusions

No grants to individuals.

Applications

The trust's website states that applications should be in writing to the correspondent, including: confirmation of charitable status (charity number on letterhead will suffice); brief details of the project; budget statement for the project; current fundraising achievements and proposals for future fundraising; items of expenditure within project costing approx. £1,000 to £5,000 – trustees currently prefer to give towards a named item rather than into a pool building fund; copy of latest accounts if available.

There are no forms or deadlines for applications. If your project fulfils the foundation's policy criteria, your details will be passed on to the trustees for consideration at their next meeting.

According to the trustees' report for 2012/13, 'beneficiaries must be established registered charities that assist with the care of old people – the trustees consider than an older person is generally assumed to be over 60 years of age, but they will also look at projects for over 50s'.

Percentage of awards given to new applicants: more than 50%.

Common applicant mistakes

'They ask for revenue funding; their projects are not for the benefit of older people.'

Information gathered from:

Accounts; Charity Commission record; further information provided by the funder; funder's website.

The Elephant Trust

Advancement of public education in all aspects of arts, development of artistic taste and knowledge, understanding and appreciation of the fine arts

£26,000 to organisations (2011/12)

Beneficial area

England and Wales.

Correspondent: Ruth Rattenbury, Bridge House, 4 Borough High Street, London SE1 9QR (tel: 020 7403 1877; email: ruth@elephanttrust.org.uk; website: www.elephanttrust.org.uk)

Trustees: Prof. Dawn Ades; Antony Forwood; Rob Tufnell; Benjamin Cook; Jeremy Deller; Elizabeth Carey-Thomas; Melissa Gronlund; Elizabeth Price; Antony Penrose.

CC Number: 269615

As the trust's website states, 'the Elephant Trust was created in 1975 by Roland Penrose and Lee Miller with a view to develop and improve the knowledge, understanding and appreciation of the fine arts in the United Kingdom'. The trust makes grants to individual artists, arts organisations and publications concerned with the visual arts. It aims to extend the frontiers of creative endeavour, to promote the unconventional and the imaginative and, to make it possible for artists and arts organisations to realise and complete specific projects.

In 2011/12 the trust had assets of £2.8 million and an income of £1.3 million. Grants were given totalling £59,000 with £33,000 distributed to 20 individuals and £26,000 distributed to 17 organisations.

Beneficiaries included: Transmission Gallery, University of Dundee, Artists Collective Gallery, Cubbits Artist Ltd, Chisenhale Gallery, Barts and the London Charity, North Devon Theatres Trust, Electra and Redmond Entwistle (£2,000 each); Sierra Metro Ltd and Salisbury Artists Centre (£1,500 each); and the Pavillion, Spike Island Artspace, Lido Projects and RGAP (£1,000 each).

The trust also administers both the George Melhuish Bequest and the Shelagh Wakely Bequest, which have similar objectives.

Exclusions

The following categories are not supported:

- Arts festivals
- Group exhibitions
- Charities organising community projects

- Students
- Educational or other studies
- Residencies or research
- Symposia or conferences
- Publications or catalogues
- Projects taking place outside the UK

Applications

Only postal applications are accepted. Applications should include:

- Synopsis of the project
- Budget
- Brief CV
- Visual material

The trust's website states that 'priority is given to artists and small organisations and galleries who should submit well argued, imaginative proposals for making or producing new work or exhibitions'.

If not contacted within six months, the trust states that you should assume that your application has been unsuccessful.

Further information available on the website or upon request.

Common applicant mistakes

'Do not read guidelines on website or read and ignore them.'

Information gathered from:

Accounts; Charity Commission record; further information provided by the funder; funder's website.

The George Elias Charitable Trust

Jewish, general

£410,000 (2011/12)

Beneficial area

Some preference for Manchester.

Correspondent: Stephen Elias, Trustee, Shaws Fabrics Ltd, 1 Ashley Road, Altrincham, Cheshire WA14 2DT (tel: 01619 287171; email: textiles@kshaw.com)

Trustees: Ernest Elias; Stephen Elias.

CC Number: 273993

The trust was established in 1977 by the late Mr George Elias. The trust states that it gives grants to charities supporting educational needs and the fight against poverty as well as organisations promoting the Jewish faith. Support is given to UK organisations as well as overseas.

In 2011/12 the trust had assets of £729,000 and an income of £257,000. Grants totalled £410,000. A list of beneficiaries was not provided.

Previous beneficiaries included: UK Friends of Nadar Deiah (£50,000); Ahavat Shalom (£45,000); UJIA (£30,000); Hale and District Hebrew Congregation (£24,000); JEM (£5,000); South Manchester Mikva Trust (£4,000); British Friends of Rinat Aharon (£2,500); Moracha LTD (£1,000); Chai Lifeline Cancer Trust (£300); and Friends of the Sick (£100).

Applications

In writing to the correspondent. Trustees meet monthly.

Information gathered from:

Accounts; Charity Commission record.

Ellador Ltd

Jewish organisations and individuals

£76,000 (2011/12)

Beneficial area

UK and overseas.

Correspondent: Mrs Helen Schreiber, Trustee, 20 Ashtead Road, London E5 9BH (tel: 020 7242 3580)

Trustees: Joel Schreiber; Helen Schreiber; Rivka Schreiber; Mr J. Schreiber; Mr Y. Schreiber; Mrs S. Reisner; Mrs C. Hamburger; Mrs R. Benedikt.

CC Number: 283202

The charity supports organisations benefiting Jewish people and also Jewish individuals, mainly for educational and religious purposes. In 2011/12 it had assets of £524,000 and an income of £67,000. Grants totalled £76,000, however a list of beneficiaries was not included in the accounts.

Applications

In writing to the correspondent.

Information gathered from:

Accounts; Charity Commission record.

The Ellerdale Trust

Children, families, disability and ill health

£291,000 (2011/12)

Beneficial area

Norfolk.

Correspondent: Mary Adlard, Director of Grantmaking, The Parlour, The High Street, Ketteringham, Wymondham, Norfolk NR18 9RU (tel: 01603 813340; email: mary.adlard@btconnect.com)

Trustees: Alistair Macfarlane; P. C. Kurthausen; S. P. Moores.

CC Number: 1073376

This trust was established to relieve poverty, distress or suffering in any part of the world particularly children who are disadvantaged or in need. In practice, the majority of funding is given to local and national organisations for projects based in Norfolk.

In 2011/12 the trust had assets of £4.3 million, and an income of £1.4 million. Grants were made to 43 organisations totalling £291,000.

Beneficiaries included: The Atrium Project (£35,000); Action for Kids (£30,000); Rainbow Centre (£20,000); The Nancy Oldfield Trust (£16,000); Mind (£15,000); Break and Autism Anglia (£10,000 each); British Blind Sport (£8,000); Africa Equipment for Schools and BLISS (£6,000 each); Inspire and Musical Keys (£5,000 each); Nelson's Journey and NORCAS (£4,000 each); Home Start Norwich (£3,000); Norwich MIND (£2,000); and Whatever the Need (£1,500).

Applications

In writing to the correspondent.

Percentage of awards given to new applicants: less than 10%.

Common applicant mistakes

'Not realising that we primarily fund community projects for children, only in the county of Norfolk.'

Information gathered from:

Accounts; Charity Commission record; further information provided by the funder.

The Ellinson Foundation Ltd

Jewish, education

£267,000 (2011/12)

Beneficial area

Worldwide.

Correspondent: The Trustees, Robson Laidler and Co., Fernwood House, Fernwood Road, Jesmond, Newcastle upon Tyne NE2 1TJ (tel: 01912 818191)

Trustees: A. Ellinson; A. Z. Ellinson; U. Ellinson.

CC Number: 252018

The foundation supports hospitals, education and homelessness in the UK and overseas, usually with a Jewish-teaching aspect. The trust regularly supports organisations such as boarding schools for boys and girls teaching the Torah.

In 2011/12 the trust had assets of £3.5 million, an income of £310,000 and gave grants totalling £267,000.

Beneficiaries included: Kesser Yeshua Refua – Israel (£150,000); Friends of Yeshivas Brisk (£35,000); Three Pillars (£20,000); Mifaley Tzedoka Vochesed (£13,000); Yad Eliezer (Jerusalem) (£12,000); Kollel Ohel Torah (Jerusalem) (£9,000); Tomchei Yotzei Anglia

(£5,000); British Friends of Rinat Aharon (£4,000); Vaani Sfolosi Kitat Tzanz (£3,000); The Bridge Lane Beth Hamedrash (£2,000); Kollel America (£1,500); and Darcey Miriam (Jerusalem) (£1,000).

Donations of less than £1,000 totalled £6,200.

Exclusions

No grants to individuals.

Applications

In writing to the correspondent. However, the trust generally supports the same organisations each year and unsolicited applications are not welcome.

Information gathered from:

Accounts; Charity Commission record.

The Edith Maud Ellis 1985 Charitable Trust

Quaker work and witness, international peace and conflict resolution, interfaith and ecumenical understanding, community development work in the UK and overseas, work with asylum seekers and refugees including internally displaced people

£50,000 (2011/12)

Beneficial area

UK and overseas.

Correspondent: Jacqueline Baily, Virtuosity Executive Support, 6 Westgate, Thirsk, North Yorkshire YO7 1QS (tel: 01845 574882; email: jackie@virtuosity-uk.com; website: www.theedithmellischaritabletrust.org)

Trustees: Michael Phipps; Jane Dawson; Elizabeth Cave; Nicholas Sims.

CC Number: 292835

Edith M Ellis was a passionate Quaker and worked tirelessly for international peace and reconciliation. The Edith Ellis Charitable Trust was established by her for general charitable purposes. The trust aims to give small grants to a broad range of Quaker and other UK registered charities, or non-governmental organisations.

Grants tend to be either: one-off; time limited in support; or, are given in the form of seed money for start-up projects. Usually small grants of up to £3,000 (in exceptional circumstances larger grants may be given) or interest free loans of up to £5,000 repayable over five years. Grants are usually made in the following categories:

- Quaker work and witness
- International peace and conflict resolution
- Interfaith and ecumenical understanding
- Community development work in the UK and overseas
- Work with asylum seekers and refugees, including internally displaced people

In 2011/12 the trust had assets of £227,000 and an income of £410,000. Grants were made to 50 organisations totalling £50,000.

Beneficiaries included: Barmoor 1982 Trust Appeal and Quaker Council for European Affairs (£3,000 each); Association of Visitors to Immigration Detainees and Glenthorne Bursary Fund (£2,000 each); UNHCR (£1,500); Off the Fence, Jubilee Debt Campaign and Pathway Project (£1,000 each); Build Africa and Afrinspire (£750 each); and Fairtrade Foundation (£500).

Exclusions

In general the trust does not support the following:

- Core funding for organisations
- Individuals
- Infrastructure organisations
- Conferences or seminars
- On-going work
- General appeals
- Educational bursaries
- Humanitarian relief appeals
- Medical research and services

Applications

According to the trust's website:

> Applications should be received by the end of January, May and September, in order to be considered at one of the trustee meetings. It is sensible to get applications in well ahead of these dates. Late applicants will be considered in the next funding round. Successful applicants will be informed as soon as possible of the trustees' decisions. If you have not heard within one calendar month of the relevant closing date you should assume you have been unsuccessful. Successful applicants will be encouraged to contribute to our website in a variety of ways and may be approached to showcase the work of the trust.

Information gathered from:

Accounts; Charity Commission record; funder's website.

The Elmgrant Trust

General charitable purposes, education, arts, social sciences

£39,000 to organisations (2011/12)

Beneficial area

South West of England (Cornwall, Devon, Somerset, Dorset, Wiltshire and Gloucestershire).

Correspondent: Amanda Horning, Secretary, The Elmhirst Centre, Dartington Hall, Totnes, Devon TQ9 6EL (tel: 01803 863160; email: info@elmgrant.org.uk; website: www.elmgrant.org.uk)

Trustees: Marian Ash, Chair; Sophie Young; Paul Elmhirst; David Young; Mark Sharman.

CC Number: 313398

This trust has general charitable purposes, but in particular aims to encourage local life through education, the arts and social sciences. Although there is a preference for South West England, grants to organisations are awarded throughout the UK. Individuals in the South West are also supported. Grants are typically for £150 to £1,500.

In 2011/12 the trust had assets of £1.9 million and an income of £60,000. Grants were given totalling £44,000, with £4,800 given in 11 grants to individuals, and £39,000 given in 72 grants to organisations. Grants were distributed under the following categories:

Social sciences and scientific	£17,000
Arts and arts research	£10,000
Education and educational research	£11,000
Pensions and compassionate	£2,500

A list of beneficiaries was not included in the accounts. Previous beneficiaries have included: Dartington International Summer School; Kinergy; Prison Phoenix Trust; Centre for the Spoken Word; Dawlish Gardens Trust; the Towersey Foundation; and the Daisy Garland and Guild of St Lawrence.

Exclusions

The following are not supported:

- Postgraduate study or related expenses
- Second and subsequent degrees
- Overseas student grants
- Expeditions, travel and study projects overseas
- Training in counselling courses
- Large-scale national organisations
- Organisations which have received a grant in the last two years

Applications

In writing to the correspondent, giving full financial details and dates, and where possible, a letter of support or acceptance onto a course. Applications from organisations should include the previous year's accounts. Initial telephone calls are welcome if advice is needed.

Trustee meetings are three times a year on the last Saturday in February, June and October and the deadlines are one month before the meetings. All applications are acknowledged and applicants will be informed if they are shortlisted for presentation at the trustee meeting.

Information gathered from:

Accounts; Charity Commission record; funder's website.

Elshore Ltd

Jewish

£131,000 (2011/12)

Beneficial area

Worldwide.

Correspondent: Hersz M. Lerner, Trustee, c/o Michael Pasha and Co., 220 The Vale, Golders Green, London NW11 8SR (tel: 020 8209 9880)

Trustees: Hersz M. Lerner; Susan Yanofsky; Ahuva Ann Lerner.

CC Number: 287469

This trust appears to make grants solely to Jewish organisations. In 2011/12 the trust held assets of £78,000 and it had an income of £100,000, mainly from donations. Grants were made totalling £131,000. A grants list was not included with the accounts for this year.

Further information has been unavailable since 1994/95, when grants to 40 beneficiaries totalled £178,000. Beneficiaries included: Eminor Educational Centre (£26,000); Cosmon Belz (£20,000); Gur Trust and Marbe Torah Trust (£10,000 each). Most other grants were less than £1,000, although some were for up to £8,000.

Applications

In writing to the correspondent.

Information gathered from:

Accounts; Charity Commission record.

The Vernon N. Ely Charitable Trust

General charitable purposes, with a preference to the London borough of Merton and sports charities

£74,000 (2011/12)

Beneficial area

Worldwide, with a preference for London borough of Merton.

Correspondent: Derek Howorth, Trustee, Grosvenor Gardens House, 35–37 Grosvenor Gardens, London SW1W 0BY (tel: 020 7828 3156; email: dph@helmores.co.uk)

Trustees: Derek Howorth; John Moyle; Richard Main.

CC Number: 230033

The trust was established in 1962 by Mr Vernon Ely. The trust prefers to make donations of a reasonable size to a limited number of charities. The majority of these donations are made to charities based in the London borough of Merton. Other donations have been made to sports charities.

In 2011/12 the trust had assets of almost £1.7 million and an income of £64,000. Grants totalled £74,000. There was no list of beneficiaries with the accounts.

Previous beneficiaries included: Age Concern, Cardiac Risk in the Young, Samaritans, London Sports Forum for Disabled People, Christchurch URC, Polka Children's Theatre and Community Housing Therapy (£4,000 each); British Tennis Foundation (£1,750); and West Barnes Singers and Sobell Hospice (£500 each).

Exclusions

No grants to individuals.

Applications

In writing to the correspondent.

Information gathered from:

Accounts; Charity Commission record.

The Emerton-Christie Charity

Health, welfare, disability, arts

£56,000 (2011/12)

Beneficial area

UK.

Correspondent: The Trustees, c/o Cartmell Shepherd, Viaduct House, Victoria Viaduct, Carlisle CA3 8EZ (tel: 01228 516666; email: joanna.jeeves@cartmells.co.uk)

Trustees: Norman Walker; William Niekirk; Claire Mera-Nelson; Sally Walker.

CC Number: 262837

The Emerton Charitable Settlement was established in 1971 by Maud Emerton, with additional funds subsequently added by Vera Bishop Emerton. In April 1996, it became the Emerton-Christie Charity following a merger with another trust, The Mrs C M S Christie Will Trust.

In 2011/12 it had assets totalling £2.4 million and an income of £70,000. Grants totalled £56,000.

Beneficiaries included: Trinity Laban Conservatoire of Music and Dance (£4,600); Action Medical Research, Centre for Sustainable Health, Disability North, Médecins Sans Frontières, Music in Detention, The Calvert Trust, The Life Centre and Trinity Hospice (£3,000 each); Papworth Trust (£2,400); Whizz-Kidz (£1,000); and BBACT (£500).

Exclusions

Generally no grants to: individuals; religious organisations; restoration or extension of buildings; start-up costs; animal welfare and research; cultural heritage; or environmental projects.

Applications

In writing to the correspondent. A demonstration of need based on budgetary principles is required and applications will not be acknowledged unless accompanied by an sae. Trustees normally meet once a year in the autumn to select charities to benefit.

Information gathered from:

Accounts; Charity Commission record.

EMI Music Sound Foundation

Music education

£334,000 to organisations (2011/12)

Beneficial area

UK and Ireland.

Correspondent: Janie Orr, Chief Executive, Beaumont House, Avonmore Road, Kensington Village, London W14 8TS (tel: 020 7550 7898; fax: 020 7550 7809; email: enquiries@musicsoundfoundation.com; website: www.emimusicsoundfoundation.com)

Trustees: David Hughes; Charles Ashcroft; Jim Beach; John Deacon; Paul Gambaccini; Jo Hibbit; Leslie Hill; Max Hole; Richard Lyttleton; Rupert Perry; Tony Wadsworth; Christine Walter.

CC Number: 1104027

According to the foundation's website, 'EMI Music Sound Foundation is an independent music education charity, established in 1997 to celebrate the centenary of EMI Records and to improve young peoples' access to music education in the UK & Ireland.'

The trustees' report for 2011/12 states that:

> The aim of the charity is to support music education in all its forms, and more particularly:
> - The education of the public, and in particular young people, in all aspects of music
> - The provision of grants to enable persons in need to buy instruments and music tuition which they would otherwise be unable to afford

Funds are distributed as bursaries for music students in eight colleges and individual grants generally not exceeding £2,000. These are given in the following areas:

> - Funding music education in schools (primary, secondary and tertiary), for the purchase of instruments/equipment
> - Purchasing musical instruments/ equipment for students in full time education
> - Funding music teachers to advance training and attend relevant courses.

Every year EMI Music Sound Foundation awards bursaries to students at eight music colleges in the UK and Ireland. These bursaries are distributed at each college's discretion, based on criteria provided by the foundation.

In 2011/12 the foundation had assets totalling £7.1 million and an income of £298,000. Grants totalled £501,000 of which £167,000 was awarded to individuals and £334,000 to organisations.

Grant beneficiaries include: Royal Welsh College of Music and Drama (£10,000); and Royal Conservatoire of Scotland, National Children's Orchestra and Brighton Institute of Modern Music (£5,000 each).

Exclusions

The foundation does not support:

- Applications from applicants based outside the United Kingdom and Ireland
- Non-school based community groups
- Applications for tuition fees and living expenses other than as described under the bursary awards section on the foundation's website
- Applications over £2,000
- Independent music teachers
- Payment of staffing costs to cover the teaching of the national curriculum or peripatetic teaching costs
- Retrospective grants

Applications

On a form which can be downloaded from the foundation's website. Guidance notes are also available regarding applications.

Information gathered from:

Accounts; Charity Commission record; funder's website.

The Emilienne Charitable Trust

Medical, education, addiction

£47,000 (2011/12)

Beneficial area

Hampshire.

Correspondent: M. Howson-Green, Trustee, Ashton House, 12 The Central Precinct, Chandler's Ford, Eastleigh, Hampshire SC53 2GB (tel: 02380 274555)

Trustees: M. Howson-Green; B. M. Baxendale; Mrs M. A. Howson-Green; David Hoare.

CC Number: 327849

Set up in 1988, the trustees are particularly interested in support for charities involved in the treatment of addiction and in promoting education.

In 2011/12 the trust had assets of £575,000 and an income of £31,000. Grants were given to 54 organisations totalling £47,000.

Beneficiaries of grants over £1,000 each were: Streetscene (£7,300); SCRATCH (£5,000); Wessex Medical Trust (£2,000); and Myositis Support Group (£1,500).

A further 50 grants of less than £1,000 were made totalling £31,000.

Applications

In writing to the correspondent.

Information gathered from:

Accounts; Charity Commission record.

The Englefield Charitable Trust

General charitable purposes with a preference for local charities in Berkshire

£358,500 (2011/12)

Beneficial area

Worldwide. In practice, UK with a special interest in Berkshire.

Correspondent: Alexander Reid, Secretary, The Quantocks, North Street, Theale, Reading RG7 5EX (tel: 01189 323582; email: charity@englefield.co.uk)

Trustees: Catherine Haig; James Shelley; Lady Elizabeth Benyon; Richard Benyon; Sir William Benyon; Zoe Benyon; Melissa Owston; Richard Bampfylde.

CC Number: 258123

The trust was established in 1968 for general charitable purposes by the settlor Sir William Benyon. The trustees consider each application on its own merit and give preference to local causes in Berkshire.

In 2011/12 the trust had assets of £13.6 million and an income of £448,000. During the year the trustees approved donations of almost £358,000. 122 donations were made, varying in size from £200 to £100,000. Approximately 700 applications were received during the year.

Beneficiaries included: Ufton Court Educational Trust (£100,000); Englefield Parochial Church Council (£36,500); Thames Valley Chiltern Air Ambulance (£5,500); Trooper Potts VC Memorial Trust and Watermill Theatre (£5,000 each); Thrive and Corn Exchange Newbury (£3,000 each); 14–21 Time to Talk, Children's Trust and Church Housing Trust (£2,000 each); Christians Against Poverty, Andover Mind and British Horseracing Education (£1,000 each); Aldermaston Parish Hall (£500); and Volunteer Centre West Berks (£350).

Exclusions

Individual applications for study or travel are not considered.

Applications

In writing to the correspondent enclosing the latest accounts, stating the charity's registered number and the purpose for which the money is to be used. Applications are considered in March and September. Only applications going before the trustees will be acknowledged.

Information gathered from:

Accounts; Charity Commission record.

The English Schools' Football Association

Association football

£853,000 (2012)

Beneficial area

England.

Correspondent: John Read, Chief Executive, 4 Parker Court, Staffordshire Technology Park, Stafford ST18 0WP (tel: 01785 785970; email: office@efsa.co.uk; website: www.esfa.co.uk)

Trustees: Philip Harding; Nigel Brown; Michael Coyne.

CC Number: 306003

Support is given for the mental, moral and physical development and improvement of schoolchildren and students through playing association football. Assistance is also given to teachers' charities and 'other such charitable purposes'.

In 2012 the association had an income of £1.4 million and a total expenditure of £1 million. Grants totalled £853,000 and were broken down as follows:

National competitions	£224,000
FA growth and retention	£212,000
Management and administration	£144,000
International matches	£142,000
Festivals of football	£58,000
Council and AGM	£46,500
Coaching courses	£25,000
Fundraising and publicity	£2,500

Exclusions

Grants are restricted to membership and teacher charities.

Applications

In writing to the correspondent. Check the association's website for up-to-date information on future deadlines.

Information gathered from:

Accounts; Charity Commission record; funder's website.

The Epigoni Trust

General charitable purposes

£60,000 (2012)

Beneficial area

UK.

Correspondent: Charles Peacock, Trustee, c/o Charities Aid Foundation, 25 Kings Hill Avenue, Kings Hill, West Malling ME19 4TA (tel: 01732 520028)

Trustees: Bettine Bond; Charles Peacock; Andrew Bond.

CC Number: 328700

The trust has common trustees with two other trusts, the Cleopatra Trust and the Dorus Trust (see separate entries) with which it also shares the same aims and policies. All three trusts are administered by Charities Aid Foundation. Generally the trusts support different organisations.

In 2012 the trust had an income of £32,000 and assets of £3.2 million. It made 6 grants totalling £60,000.

Beneficiaries included: Pallant House Gallery (£20,000); Chichester Festival Theatre and Mondo Challenge Foundation (£10,000 each); and St Richard of Chichester Christian Care Association (£5,000).

Exclusions

No grants to individuals.

Applications

This trust no longer accepts applications.

Information gathered from:

Accounts; Charity Commission record.

The Equity Trust Fund

Theatre

£96,000 (2011/12)

Beneficial area

UK.

Correspondent: Kaethe Cherney, Secretary, Plouviez House, 19–20 Hatton Place, London EC1N 8RU (tel: 020 7831 1926; fax: 020 7242 7995; email: kaethe@equitycharitabletrust.org.uk; website: www.equitycharitabletrust.org.uk)

Trustee: The Trustees.

CC Number: 328103

The charity is a benevolent fund for professional performers and stage managers and their dependents. It offers help with welfare rights, gives free debt counselling and information and can offer financial assistance to those in genuine need. It also has an education fund to help members of the profession with further training provided they have at least ten years' professional adult experience. It also makes grants and loans to professional theatres or theatre companies.

In 2011/12 the trust had assets of £8.7 million and an income of £394,000. Grants to seven organisations totalled £96,000, broken down into:

Theatrical grants	3	£51,000
Education grants	1	£40,000
John Fernald Award	3	£5,000

Beneficiaries were: Interact Reading Services (£45,000); Dancers' Career Development (£40,000); Birmingham Repertory Theatre, Chickenshed Theatre and Tricycle Theatre (£3,000 each); Soho Theatre (£1,000); and Stone Crabs Theatre (£950).

A further £173,000 was given in 121 grants to individuals for welfare and education.

Exclusions

No grants to non-professional performers, drama students, non-professional theatre companies, multi-arts venues, community projects or projects with no connection to the professional theatre.

Applications

In the first instance call the office to ascertain if the application is relevant. Failing that, submit a brief letter outlining the application. A trustee meeting takes place about every six to eight weeks, ring for precise dates. Applications are required at least two weeks beforehand.

Information gathered from:

Accounts; Charity Commission record; funder's website.

The Ericson Trust

Older people, community including the arts, offender rehabilitation and research, refugees, the environment, the developing world

Around £40,000 (2011/12)

Beneficial area

UK, developing countries, Eastern and Central Europe.

Correspondent: Ms Claudia Cotton, Flat 2, 53 Carleton Road, London N7 0ET (email: claudia.cotton@googlemail.com)

Trustees: R. C. Cotton; V. J. Barrow; A. M. C. Cotton.

CC Number: 219762

Exclusions

No grants to individuals or to non-registered charities. Applications from the following areas are generally not considered unless closely connected with one of the above: children's and young people's clubs, centres and so on; schools; charities dealing with illness or disability (except psychiatric); or religious institutions, except in their social projects.

Applications

Unsolicited applications cannot be considered as the trust has no funds available. The correspondent stated:

> We are increasingly worried by the waste of applicants' resources when they send expensive brochures at a time when we are unable to consider any new appeals and have, indeed, reduced some of our long standing grants due to the bad economic situation. It is particularly sad when we receive requests from small charities in Africa and Asia.

Percentage of awards given to new applicants: less than 10%.

Common applicant mistakes

'Many seem not to have consulted any directories and do not know that we have a list of things we do not offer grants to at present; however, most new applications can be considered 'mistakes' as our funds are too limited for most new applicants.'

Information gathered from:

Accounts; Charity Commission record; further information provided by the funder.

The Esfandi Charitable Foundation

Jewish causes

£416,000 (2011/12)

Beneficial area

UK and overseas.

Correspondent: Joseph Esfandi, Trustee, 36 Park Street, London W1K 2JE (tel: 020 7629 6666)

Trustees: Joseph Esfandi; Denise Esfandi.

CC Number: 1103095

Set up in 2004, in 2011/12 the foundation had an income of £462,000, assets of £140,000 and made grants totalling £416,000.

Beneficiaries included: Schlomo High School (£250,000); British Friends of Migdal Or (£60,000); Jewish Care and Jewish Community Secondary School Trust (£12,500); Naima Jewish Preparatory School (£8,000); Royal National Theatre and Chief Rabbinate Trust (£5,000 each); British Friends of Gesher (£2,000); Western Marble Arch Synagogue (£1,500); and Norwood (£750).

Applications

In writing to the correspondent.

Information gathered from:

Accounts; Charity Commission record.

The Essex Youth Trust

Youth, education of people under 25

£360,000 (2011/12)

Beneficial area

Essex.

Correspondent: J. P. Douglas-Hughes, Clerk, Gepp and Sons, 58 New London Road, Chelmsford, Essex CM2 0PA (tel: 01245 493939; fax: 01245 493940; email: douglas-hughesj@gepp.co.uk)

Trustees: Richard Wenley; Julien Courtauld; Michael Dyer; Revd Duncan Green; William David Robson; Lady Julia Denison-Smith; Claire Cottrell; Michael Biegel; Julie Rogers.

CC Number: 225768

The Essex Youth Trust comprises four charities administered under a scheme dated 24 February 1993. The four charities are Essex Home School for Boys, The Charity of George Stacey Gibson, The Charity of George Cleveley and The Charity of Adelia Joyce Snelgrove.

The trust's objectives are the advancement of education for people under the age of 25 who are in need of assistance. Preference is given to those who are in need owing to 'being temporarily or permanently deprived of normal parental care or who are otherwise disadvantaged'.

'The trustees favour organisations which develop young people's physical, mental and spiritual capacities through active participation in sports and indoor and outdoor activities. As a result they are particularly supportive of youth clubs and other organisations which provide facilities for young people to take active part in an assortment of activities as well as single activity organisations.'

In 2011/12 the trust had assets of £7.2 million, an income of £427,000 and gave grants totalling £360,000.

Beneficiaries included: Summer Action Programme (£45,000); Cirdan Sailing Trust (£50,000 in two grants); Essex Boys and Girls Club (£28,000 in two grants); The College of St Mark (£10,000); Chain Reaction Theatre Company (£8,000); Maldon Essex Mind (£7,000); Barking and Dagenham Training Centre (£5,000); Market Field School (£3,000); Dream Holidays (£1,500); and Harp Acorn Project (£400).

Exclusions

No grants to individuals.

Applications

On a form available from the correspondent. The trustees meet on a quarterly basis.

Information gathered from:

Accounts; Charity Commission record.

The Estelle Trust

Overseas aid

£130,000 (2011/12)

Beneficial area

Not defined, but in practice Zambia.

Correspondent: Caroline Harvey, Fisher Phillips, 170 Finchley Road, London NW3 6BP (tel: 020 7483 6100)

Trustees: Nigel Farrow; G. R. Ornstein; D. Wise; Rachel Lynch; Katherine Farrow; Imogen Abed; Sarah Davies.

CC Number: 1101299

Registered in December 2003, the trust focuses on funding community and educational projects in Zambia but also makes smaller grants for general charitable purposes in the UK.

In 2011/12 the trust had assets of £1.3 million and an income of £103,000. Grants totalled £130,000.

Beneficiaries included: Project Luangwa and University of Bradford (£15,000 each); Nagwaza (£13,000); Microloan Foundation (£10,000); Arulussa School Development (£9,000); Queens College Cambridge (£7,000); Baynards Zambia Trust (£6,300); Zambia Orphans of AIDS (£6,600); International Rescue Committee (£5,000); Suntech Solar Pump (£4,500); Twavwane Home Based Care (£3,400); Kachele Village (£2,800); St Catherine's Hospice (£1,000); ABF The Soldiers Charity and Prostrate Action (£500 each); and Assist Sheffield (£200).

Applications

In writing to the correspondent.

Information gathered from:

Accounts; Charity Commission record.

The Alan Evans Memorial Trust

Preservation, conservation

£149,000 (2011/12)

Beneficial area

UK.

Correspondent: The Trustees, Lemon and Co., 34 Regent Circus, Swindon SN1 1PY (tel: 0800 135 7917; email: aevans@lemon-co.co.uk)

Trustees: David Halfhead; Deirdre Moss.

CC Number: 326263

The trust's Summary Information Return states that the objectives of the trust are:

> To promote the permanent preservation for the benefit of the nation of land and tenements (including buildings) of beauty or historic interest and with regards to land the preservation (so far as practicable) with their natural aspect features and animal and plant life.

In 2011/12 the trust had assets of £456,000 and an income of £33,000. Grants ranged from £400 to £1,500 and were given to 123 organisations totalling £149,000. A list of beneficiaries was not available.

Previous beneficiaries include: English Hedgerow Trust, Landmark Trust, Zoological Society of London, St Wilfrid's Church – Leeds, Thatcham Charity, Cathedral Church of the Holy Spirit – Guildford, Peterborough Cathedral Development and Preservation Trust, Wells Cathedral – Somerset, Lincoln Cathedral and, the Church of Our Lord, St Mary and St Germaine – Selby Abbey.

Exclusions

Grants are given to registered charities only. General appeals will not be acknowledged.

Applications

There is no formal application form, but appeals should be made in writing to the correspondent, stating why the funds are required, what funds have been promised from other sources (for example, English Heritage) and the amount outstanding. The trust has also stated previously that it would be helpful when making applications to provide a photograph of the project. The trustees normally meet four times a year, although in urgent cases decisions can be made between meetings. The trustees may wish to see the work undertaken out of the proceeds of the grant. Grant recipients might be asked to provide copies of receipts for expenditure.

Information gathered from:

Accounts; Charity Commission record.

Sir John Evelyn's Charity

Relief of poverty, advancing education and community development

£70,000 to organisations (2012)

Beneficial area

Ancient parishes of St Nicholas Deptford and St Luke Deptford.

Correspondent: Colette Saunders, Clerk's Office, Armada Court Hall, 21 Macmillan Street, Deptford, London SE8 3EZ (tel: 020 8694 8953)

Trustees: Kay Ingledew; Bridget Perry; Revd Jack Lucas; Janet Miller; Maureen O'Mara; Margaret Mythen; Revd Louise Cordington-Marshall.

CC Number: 225707

Originally registered in 1876, the charity received a small boost to its endowment with the amalgamation of 19 small charities under a Charity Commission scheme of 1992. It operates within the ancient parishes of St Nicholas and St Luke in Deptford. The charity has continued its support of community projects, as well as grants and through this has directly benefited residents' lives and wellbeing.

According to the trustees' report for 2012, the charity has the following objectives:

- Prevention and relief of poverty
- Advancement of education
- Advancement of citizenship and community development
- Relief of those in need by reason of youth, age, ill health, disability, financial hardship or other disadvantage

In 2012 the trust had assets of £2.5 million and an income of over £75,000. Grants were made to individuals (£1,100) and six organisations and totalled just under £70,000.

Beneficiaries were: Armada Community Project (£48,000); Hughes Field and Henrietta Young People's Project (£10,000); Partworks (£9,000); Creekside Forum (£3,000); Evelyn 190 Centre (£500); and St Nicholas and St Luke's (£400).

Exclusions

Exclusively for the area specified.

Applications

In writing to the correspondent.

Information gathered from:

Accounts; Charity Commission record.

The Eventhall Family Charitable Trust

General charitable purposes

£253,000 (2012/13)

Beneficial area

UK with a preference for the north west of England.

Correspondent: The Trustees, PO Box 490, Altrincham WA14 22T

Trustees: Julia Eventhall; David Eventhall.

CC Number: 803178

The Eventhall Family Charitable Trust was established in 1986.

In 2012/13 the trust had assets of £3.5 million, an income of £99,000 and made grants totalling £253,000.

Previous beneficiaries have included: Aish Hatorah, ChildLine, Clitheroe Wolves Football Club, Community Security Trust, Greibach Memorial, Guide Dogs for the Blind, Heathlands Village, International Wildlife Coalition, JJCT, MB Foundation Charity, Only Foals and Horses Sanctuary, Red Nose Day, RNLI, Sale Ladies Society, Shelter and South Manchester Synagogue.

Applications

In writing to the correspondent. Note, however, previous research highlighted that the trust stated it only has a very limited amount of funds available.

Information gathered from:

Accounts; Charity Commission record.

The Beryl Evetts and Robert Luff Animal Welfare Trust Ltd

Animal welfare

£140,000 (2011/12)

Beneficial area

UK.

Correspondent: Richard Price, Trustee, Waters Edge, Ferry Lane, Moulsford, Wallingford, Oxfordshire OX10 9JF (email: rpjprice@gmail.com)

Trustees: Jean Tomlinson; Sir Robert Johnson; Brian Nicholson; Revd Matthew Tomlinson; Richard Price; Melanie Lydiate Condon; Lady Ruth Bodey.

CC Number: 283944

The principal objective of the trust is the funding of veterinary research and the care and welfare of animals.

In 2011/12 the trust had assets of £4.1 million, which generated an income of £259,000. Grants were made to 11 organisations totalling £140,000.

Beneficiaries included: Animal Health Trust (£65,000); Royal Veterinary College (£60,000); Blue Cross (£8,000); Brooke Hospitals for Animals, St Tiggy Winkles and Kent Wildlife Trust (£1,000 each); and the Cats Protection League and the National Fox Welfare Society (£500 each).

Applications

Applications from organisations that the trust has never previously funded are considered, however the trust has stated that it is very unlikely that grants of any higher than £5,000 are likely to be considered. Grants are made annually and administered in June. Applications should be submitted by 31 March and should be longer than three A4 pages.

Information gathered from:

Accounts; Charity Commission record.

The Exilarch's Foundation

General, Jewish, education

£1.4 million (2012)

Beneficial area

Mainly UK, occasionally overseas.

Correspondent: Dr Naim Dangoor, Trustee, 4 Carlos Place, Mayfair, London W1K 3AW

Trustees: David Dangoor; Elie Dangoor; Robert Dangoor; Michael Dangoor; Dr Naim Dangoor.

CC Number: 275919

The trust has the following objectives:

- The advancement of education and the Jewish religion in Iraq
- Educational projects and scholarships
- Universal monotheism

In 2012 the foundation had assets of £60.4 million, £10 million of which is specifically designated towards the plans for Iraq. Income totalled £6 million and grants were made to the value of £1.4 million, broken down as follows:

Education	£1.2 million
Social welfare	£206,000

Beneficiaries included: Open University (£1 million); Gateshead Talmudical College and Memorah Grammar School Charitable Trust (£50,000 each); Spanish and Portuguese Jews' Congregation (£34,000); Jewish Chronicle (£21,000); Sephardi Voices and Council of Christians and Jews (£15,000 each); Jewish Association for Business Ethics (£10,000); Westminster Academy (£5,000); and Weizmann UK (£3,000).

Applications

In writing to the correspondent.

Information gathered from:

Accounts; Charity Commission record.

Extonglen Ltd

Orthodox Jewish causes, education, the relief of poverty

£528,000 (2011)

Beneficial area

UK.

Correspondent: Mrs C. Levine, Trustee, New Burlington House, 1075 Finchley Road, London NW11 0PU (tel: 020 8731 0777; email: ml@rowdeal.com)

Trustees: Meir Levine; Mrs C. Levine; Isaac Katzenberg.

CC Number: 286230

Registered with the Charity Commission in January 1983, this trust accepts applications from representatives of Orthodox Jewish charities. The trust has a particular focus on education and the relief of poverty.

The latest accounts available were for 2011, the 2012 accounts being overdue at the Commission. The trust had assets of £13 million and an income of £805,000. Grants totalled £528,000. Investment management costs were £286,000 and governance costs were £24,000. The trustees annual report for 2011 states that the charitable donations have been detailed in a separate publication 'Extonglen Ltd – Schedule of Charitable Donations', copies of which are available from the trustees 'on payment of the appropriate fee'.

No further information concerning grants was available but previous beneficiaries have included: Kol Halashon Education Programme (£470,000); Ahavas Chesed (£95,000); Pikuach Nefesh (£50,000); Kupath Gemach Chaim Bechesed Viznitz Trust (£40,000); British Friends of Nishmat Yisrael (£12,000); and Children's Town Charity (£3,600).

Applications

In writing to the correspondent.

Information gathered from:

Accounts; Charity Commission record.

The Fairway Trust

General

£40,000 (2011/12)

Beneficial area

UK and worldwide.

Correspondent: Mrs J. Gudrun Grimstone, Trustee, The Gate House, Coombe Wood Road, Kingston upon Thames, Surrey KT2 7JY

Trustees: Janet Gudrun Grimstone; Kirsten Suenson-Taylor.

CC Number: 272227

The trust's accounts state it will continue support for charities engaged in the fields of education, religion and social welfare.

In 2011/12 the trust had assets of £50,000 and an income almost entirely from donations of £42,000. Grants were made totalling £40,000.

Beneficiaries included: Family Education Trust (£20,000); Textile Conservation (£6,000); Clubs for Young People Northern Ireland and Welsh National Opera (£2,000); CIVITA's, Fan Museum, Lucy Cavendish and Prayer Book Society (£1,000 each); Grantchester Parochial Church Council (£750); and 4th Ormskirk Guides (£200).

Exclusions

No grants to medical charities.

Applications

The trustees have an established list of charities which they support on a regular basis. Unsolicited applications are not therefore considered.

Information gathered from:

Accounts; Charity Commission record.

Famos Foundation Trust

Jewish causes

£107,000 (2011/12)

Beneficial area

UK and overseas.

Correspondent: Rabbi S. M. Kupetz, Trustee, 4 Hanover Gardens, Salford, Greater Manchester M7 4FQ (tel: 01617 405735)

Trustees: Rabbi S. M. Kupetz; Fay Kupetz; Isaac Kupetz; Joseph Kupetz.

CC Number: 271211

The trust mainly supports a wide range of Jewish organisations, including those concerned with education and the relief of poverty. Organisations and individuals are supported both in the UK and abroad. Many grants are recurrent and are of up to £5,000 each.

In 2011/12 the trust had assets of £1.6 million and an income of £327,000. Grants totalled £107,000, broken down into the following categories:

Relief of poverty	£50,000
Education	£30,000
Places of Worship	£17,500
Medical	£9,500

Applications

In writing to the correspondent, at any time. The trust does not accept telephone enquiries.

Information gathered from:

Accounts; Charity Commission record.

The Lord Faringdon Charitable Trust

Medical, educational, heritage, social welfare, the arts and sciences, recreation and general charitable purposes

£177,000 (2011/12)

Beneficial area

UK.

Correspondent: Mrs S. L. Lander, Secretary to the Trustees, The Estate Office, Buscot Park, Faringdon SN7 8BU (tel: 01367 240786; email: estbuscot@aol.com)

Trustees: A. Forbes; The Hon J. Henderson; S. Maitland Robinson; Bernard Cazenove.

CC Number: 1084690

This trust was formed in 2000 by the amalgamation of the Lord Faringdon First and Second trusts. The trust supports well run national and local institutions (Oxfordshire) which set out to make life more tolerable and fuller for those in difficult circumstances.

According to the trustees' report for 2011/12, it specifically supports:

- Educational objectives
- Hospitals and the provision of medical treatment for the sick
- Purchase of antiques and artistic objects for museums and collections that have public access
- Care and assistance of people who are elderly or infirm
- Development and assistance of arts and sciences, physical recreation and drama
- Research into matters of public interest
- Relief of poverty
- Support of matters of public interest
- Maintaining and improving the Faringdon Collection

In 2011/12 it had assets of £6.8 million and an income of £171,000. Grants to 64 organisations totalled £177,000.

Beneficiaries included: Faringdon Collection (£30,000); Buscot Centenary and Millennium Fund (£20,000); the National Trust and the Gordon Palmer Memorial Trust (£10,000 each); the Royal Horticultural Society, Royal Opera House and Royal Choral Society (£5,000 each); Root and Branch and Taunton and Somerset Spinal Unity (£2,000 each); Salvation Army, the Woodland Trust and Prospect Hospice (£1,000 each); and Living Memorial Historical Association, Historical Chapels Trust and Red Squirrel Survival Trust (£500 each).

Exclusions

No grants to individuals, just to registered charities.

Applications

In writing to the correspondent. According to the trustees' report for 2011/12:

> Grant applications are accepted from registered charities and other recognised bodies. All grant applications are required to provide information on the specific purpose and expected beneficiaries of the grants. This information helps the charity assess how its programme of discretionary grantmaking achieves a spread of benefit.

Information gathered from:

Accounts; Charity Commission record.

Samuel William Farmer's Trust

Education, health, social welfare

£81,500 to organisations (2012)

Beneficial area

Mainly Wiltshire.

Correspondent: Melanie Linden-Fermor, Administrator, 71 High Street, Market Lavington, Devizes SN10 4AG (tel: 01380 813299)

Trustees: Bruce Waight; Jennifer Liddiard; Peter Fox-Andrews; Charles Brockis; Jean Simpson.

CC Number: 258459

According to the trustees' report for 2012, the trust was set up for 'the benefit of poor persons who through ill health or old age are unable to earn their own livelihood, for educational purposes and for the benefit of hospitals, nursing and convalescent homes or similar objectives'. The trustees aim to acknowledge the original objectives; however will apply a modern interpretation where necessary. Both individuals and organisations, sometimes with a preference towards Wiltshire, are supported.

In 2012 the trust had assets of £2.2 million and an income of £85,000. 34 'special' grants for this year totalled £71,500 and annual grants totalled £10,000. The sum of £1,200 went to individuals. Grants totalled £83,000.

Beneficiaries included: Field in Trust (£10,000); the Crown Centre (£6,000); Sevington Victorian School Appeal (£4,000); SWIFT Medics and Hop, Skip and Jump – Wiltshire (£3,000 each); Wiltshire Blind Association, Epilepsy Society and Wiltshire Scout Council (£2,000 each); and Wiltshire Air Ambulance Appeal, Bath Institute of Medical Engineering and Swindon Therapy Centre for Multiple Sclerosis (£1,000 each).

Applications

In writing to the correspondent. Trustees meet half-yearly. Trustees bring suggestions and applications for grants to their half yearly meetings. Grants must be formally approved before they are made. There must be at least three trustees present at a meeting for decisions to be made.

Percentage of awards given to new applicants: between 30% and 40%.

Information gathered from:

Accounts; Charity Commission record; further information provided by the funder.

The Farthing Trust

Christian, general

£146,000 to organisations and individuals (2011/12)

Beneficial area

UK and overseas.

Correspondent: Heber Martin, PO Box 277, Cambridge CB7 9DE

Trustees: C. H. Martin; Mrs E. Martin; Mrs J. Martin; Mrs A. White.

CC Number: 268066

This trust was established to meet charitable causes in any area of the world. It has wide charitable objectives but the main focus is on the advancement of religion, education, health and human rights and the reconciliation and promotion of religious and racial harmony, equality and diversity.

In 2011/12 the trust had assets of £2.9 million and an income of £118,000. Grants were made totalling £146,000, and were broken down as follows:

UK Churches	£44,000
UK Christian causes	£39,000
Christ's servants	£25,000
Education – UK and overseas	£14,500
Overseas Christian causes	£12,000
Local grants	£7,000
Individuals in need – UK and overseas	£2,500
Overseas general charities	£1,000
UK general charities	£750

Applications

Applications and enquiries should be made in writing to the correspondent. Applicants, and any others requesting information, will only receive a response if an sae is enclosed. Most beneficiaries are known to the trustees personally or through their acquaintances, although applications from other organisations are considered.

Information gathered from:

Accounts; Charity Commission record.

The John Feeney Charitable Bequest

Arts, heritage and open spaces

£36,500 (2012)

Beneficial area

Birmingham.

Correspondent: Amanda Cadman, Secretary, 55 Wychall Lane, Birmingham B38 8TB (tel: 01216 243865; email: secretary@feeneytrust.org.uk; website: www.feeneytrust.org.uk)

Trustees: John Smith; Hugh Carslake; James Lloyd; Michael Darby; Charles King-Farlow; Geoffrey Oakley; Merryn Ford Lloyd; Anouk Perinpanayagam; William Southall; Sally Luton; Lucy Reid.

CC Number: 214486

The trust was set up in 1907 when John Feeney directed that one tenth of his residue estate be invested and the income used for the benefit of public charities in the city of Birmingham, for the promotion and cultivation of art in the city and for the acquisition and maintenance of parks, recreation grounds or open spaces in or near the city.

In 2012 the charity had assets of almost £1.6 million and an income of £82,000. There were 18 grants made to organisations totalling £36,500, which are broken down as follows:

Arts	£24,000
Open spaces	£5,500
Commissions	£5,000
Heritage	£2,000

Beneficiaries included: Birmingham Bach Choir, the City of Birmingham Museums and Art Gallery Development Trust and MSC Birmingham (£5,000 each); Performances Birmingham Ltd (£3,000); Warley Woods Community Trust Ltd, Castle Bromwich Hall Gardens Trust and Royal Birmingham Society of Artists (£2,000 each); Orchestra of the Swan and Ackers Adventure (£1,500 each); Birmingham Pen Trade Heritage Association, Black Country Living Museum Trust and Stage 2 Youth Theatre Company (£1,000 each); and Moby Duck Theatre Company (£500).

Exclusions

Applications will not be accepted: from, or on behalf of, individuals; which do not directly benefit the Birmingham area or Birmingham charitable organisations; which could be considered as political or denominational.

Applications

Priority will be given to applications from charitable organisations operating in the fields of the arts, music, heritage and open spaces. Trustees will seek to give grants to organisations where they feel that the grants, whatever size, will have a significant impact. Applications will only normally be considered from registered charities.

Application forms are available from the trust's website. When the form is completed post or email it with a supporting letter and other documents to the correspondent.

Information gathered from:

Accounts; Charity Commission record; funder's website.

The A. M. Fenton Trust

General

£173,000 (2012)

Beneficial area

UK, preference for North Yorkshire, and overseas.

Correspondent: James Fenton, Trustee, 14 Beech Grove, Harrogate HG2 0EX (tel: 01423 504442)

Trustees: James Fenton; C. Fenton.

CC Number: 270353

The trust was created by Alexander Miller Fenton in 1975. After his death in 1977, the residue of his estate was transferred to the trust which is established for general charitable purposes. Although the trust has general charitable purposes, preference is given to health, disability support and medical charitable organisations, as well as those that work with young people.

In 2012 the trust had assets of £4.3 million, an income of £143,000, and made grants totalling £173,000. Grants were made to over 65 organisations.

Beneficiaries included: Yorkshire County Cricket Club Charitable Youth Trust (£20,000); Hipperholme Grammar School (£10,000); the Tweed Foundation and Dewsbury League of Friendship (£8,000 each); Horticap, Arthritis Research Council and Police Treatment Centres (£4,000 each); Marie Curie Cancer Care and Epilepsy Research UK (£3,000 each); Every Child and Institute of Medical Engineering (£2,000 each); Crimestoppers Trust, Abandoned Animals Charity and Ability Beyond Disability (£1,000 each); Macmillan Centre Fund and Girl Guides Brighouse (£500 each); and Checkheaton Boxing Academy (£200).

Exclusions

The trust is unlikely to support local appeals, unless they are close to where the trust is based.

Applications

In writing to the correspondent.

Information gathered from:

Accounts; Charity Commission record.

Elizabeth Ferguson Charitable Trust Fund

Children, medical research, health, hospices

£250,500 to organisations and individuals (2011/12)

Beneficial area

UK, with some interest in Scotland.

Correspondent: The Trustees, c/o 27 Peregrine Crescent, Droylsden, Manchester M43 7TA

Trustees: Sir Alex Ferguson; Cathy Ferguson; Huw Roberts; Ted Way; Les Dalgarno; Paul Hardman; Jason Ferguson.

SC Number: SC026240

This trust was created by Sir Alex Ferguson in 1998 in memory of his mother. It supports a range of children's and medical charities. Grants range from £250 to £10,000 and can be recurrent. Various high-profile events have contributed to the trust's income in recent years. Grants are distributed in the areas where the income is raised.

In 2011/12 the trust had an income of £821,000. Grants totalled £250,500.

Charities supported by the founder in his home town of Govan will continue to be supported through the trust. Recent beneficiaries have included the Govan Initiative and Harmony Row Boys' Club.

Exclusions

Non-registered charities are not supported. The trust does not make grants overseas.

Applications

An application form and guidelines should be requested in writing from the correspondent. The committee meets to consider grants at the end of January and July. Applications should be received by December and June respectively.

Information gathered from:

Accounts; OSCR record.

The Fidelio Charitable Trust

The arts, in particular the dramatic and operatic arts, music, speech and dance

£111,000 to institutions (2011/12)

Beneficial area

UK.

Correspondent: A. Wingate, 2nd Floor, 20–22 Stukeley Street, London WC2B 5LR (email: fidelio@act.eu.com; website: www.fideliocharitabletrust.org.uk)

Trustees: Jennifer Wingate; Tony Wingate; John Sotheby Boas.

CC Number: 1112508

The Fidelio Charitable Trust was established in 2008 in support of the arts in the United Kingdom. According to the trustees' report for 2011/12, the trust's objectives are:

> The advancement of education of the public in the arts and in particular in the dramatic and operatic arts, music,

> speech, drama and dance. The charity aims to support individual performers and artists who have been recommended by educational institutions and others in a similar capacity.

In 2011/12 the trust had assets of almost £1.2 million and an income of £19,500. Grants were made to institutions totalling £111,000.

Beneficiaries included: IMS Prussia Cove (£10,000); Central School of Speech and Drama and Handel House Trust (£5,000 each); RADA (£4,000); Tête à Tête Opera, Southbank Sinfonia and Oxford Lieder (£3,500 each); Dartington Hall Trust and Academy Concert Society (£2,000 each); Spitalfields Music (£1,000); and Birmingham Chamber Orchestra (£750).

Exclusions

Applications from individuals or groups seeking support for themselves will not be accepted.

Applications

Application forms are available from the trust's website, with full details on how to apply. The following information was taken from the trust's website:

> institutions, colleges, arts festivals and other arts organisations in the United Kingdom, may seek financial support for individuals or groups of exceptional ability, whom they have been responsible for selecting, to enable them:
> - To receive special tuition or coaching (e.g. in the case of musicians to attend master classes)
> - To participate in external competitions
> - To be supported for a specially arranged performance
> - To receive support for a special publication, musical composition or work of art

Information gathered from:

Accounts; Charity Commission record; funder's website.

The Doris Field Charitable Trust

General

£241,000 (2011/12)

Beneficial area

UK, with a preference for Oxfordshire.

Correspondent: Helen Fanyinka, c/o Morgan Cole, Buxton Court, 3 West Way, Oxford OX2 0SZ (tel: 01865 262183)

Trustees: John Cole; N. Harper; Wilhelmina Church.

CC Number: 328687

The Doris Field Charitable Trust was established in 1990. One-off and recurrent grants are given to large UK organisations and small local projects for a wide variety of causes. The trust states that it favours local causes in Oxfordshire. In 2011/12 the trust had assets of £7.9 million and an income of £353,000. Grants were made totalling £241,000 to 168 organisations. No grants were made to individuals.

Beneficiaries included: Meningitis UK (£40,000); Cancer Research UK (£30,000); Greenpower (£15,000); Medical and Life Sciences Research Fund (£9,000); Vale and Downland Museum, Oxfordshire Historical Churches and Royal British Legion (£5,000 each); the Pegasus School Trust (£3,000); Pathway Workshop (£2,000); Whizz-Kidz, Wesley Memorial Methodist Church- Oxford and Oxford PHAB Club (£1,000 each); and Blackbirds Leys Adventure Playgroup, the Movement Foundation and the Parasol Project (£500 each).

Exclusions

It is unlikely that grants would be made for salaries, training or higher education costs.

Applications

According to the trustees' report for 2011/12, 'the trustees receive applications from diverse sources. Each applicant is required, except in exceptional cases, to complete a standard application form and to submit information in support of that application.' Applications are considered three times a year or as and when necessary.

Information gathered from:

Accounts; Charity Commission record.

Dixie Rose Findlay Charitable Trust

General charitable purposes with preference to children, seafarers, blindness and multiple sclerosis

£101,000 (2012/13)

Beneficial area

UK.

Correspondent: S. Hill, Trust Manager, HSBC Trust Company UK Ltd, Trust Services, 10th Floor, Norwich House, Nelson Gate, Southampton SO15 1GX (tel: 02380 722243)

Trustee: HSBC. Trust Company (UK) Ltd.

CC Number: 251661

The trust was established through the trust deed of the late Dixie Rose Findlay in 1967. The trust is concerned with children, seafarers, blindness, multiple sclerosis and similar conditions.

In 2012/13 it had assets of almost £4.5 million, an income of £99,000 and made grants to 48 organisations totalling £101,000.

Beneficiaries included: St John's Wood Church (£6,000); St John's Wood Adventure Playground and Hampshire and Isle of Wight Air Ambulance (£5,000 each); Kent, Surrey and Sussex Air Ambulance Trust (£4,000); Brighton and Hove Parents and Children's Group and Shooting Star CHASE (£3,000 each); Multiple Sclerosis Trust, Pathfinder Guide Dog Programme and Reading Association for the Blind (£2,000 each); and the Legacy Rainbow House and Surrey Association for Visual Impairment (£1,500 each).

Applications

In writing to the correspondent.

Information gathered from:

Accounts; Charity Commission record.

Finnart House School Trust

Jewish children and young people in need of care and/or education

£187,000 (2011/12)

Beneficial area

Worldwide.

Correspondent: Jamie Wood, Correspondent, Radius Works, Back Lane, London NW3 1HL (tel: 07804 854905; email: info@finnart.org; website: www.finnart.org)

Trustees: Dame Hilary Blume; Robert Cohen; Linda Paterson; Sue Leifer; Gideon Lyons; Gil Cohen; Mervyn Kaye; Anthony Yadgaroff.

CC Number: 220917

The trust supports the relief of children and young people (aged under 21) of the Jewish faith. Bursaries and scholarships are given to Jewish secondary school pupils and university entrants who are capable of achieving, but would probably not do so because of family and economic pressures. Grants to schools are also made to help Jewish pupils with small grants to enable them to pay fares, buy clothes and books and go on school trips. The trust may also support work concerned with people who are disaffected, disadvantaged socially and economically through illness or neglect or in need of care and education.

In 2011/12 the trust had assets of £4.5 million, which generated an income of £153,000. Grants totalled £187,000.

The majority of grant expenditure financed the Finnart Scholarship to individual students (£171,000). Grants were made to two schools: JFS School

(£10,000); and King Solomon High School (£6,000).

Applications

Note the following statement taken from the trust's website:

> If you are a charity (working for Jewish children in need) seeking support, please understand that the major part of Finnart's income goes to fund the Finnart Scholars. If you wish to apply, though realising the chances of success are slim, please check by telephone, email or letter before doing so. If you are a school seeking a hardship fund, please remember that our trust deed restricts our grant giving to Jewish children in need. We may also require evidence of the eligibility of any pupil. We will require a report on how any funds have been dispersed.

Percentage of awards given to new applicants: between 30% and 40%.

Common applicant mistakes

'Don't read the criteria. Ours is a very restricted trust: i.e. [ineligible applicants are] over 21 years of age, not Jewish, not poor, not from UK, they want to study abroad.'

Information gathered from:

Accounts; Charity Commission record; further information provided by the funder; funder's website.

Marc Fitch Fund

Heritage, archaeology, history, heraldry, genealogy

£176,000 to organisations and individuals (2011/12)

Beneficial area

UK.

Correspondent: Christopher Catling, Director, 19 The Avenue, Cirencester, Gloucestershire GL7 1EJ (tel: 01608 811944; email: admin@marcfitchfund.org.uk; website: www.marcfitchfund.org.uk)

Trustees: David White; Lindsay Allason-Jones; Andrew Howard Murison; Dr Helen Forde; Prof. John Blair; Prof. David Hey; Dr Michael Hall; David Palliser; Bernard Nurse; Christiana Payne.

CC Number: 313303

The trust makes grants to organisations and individuals for publication and research in archaeology, historical geography, history of art and architecture, heraldry, genealogy, use and preservation of archives, conservation of artefacts and other antiquarian, archaeological and historical studies. The primary focus of the fund is the local and regional history of the British Isles.

Grants range from relatively minor amounts to more substantial special project grants which may be paid over more than one year. In many cases, the awards enable work to be undertaken, or the results published either in print or online form, which would not otherwise be achieved.

In 2011/12 the trust had assets of £5.2 million and an income of £194,000. Grants to 58 organisations totalled £176,000, including £18,000 which was given in research grants to individuals.

Beneficiaries included: College of Arms and Newcastle University (£25,000 each); Public Catalogue Foundation and Sulgrave Archaeology Group (£10,000 each); Christ Church Oxford (£6,000); North Wales Dendro Project and University of Reading (£5,000 each); University of York (£4,000); London Metropolitan University (£3,000); Royal Cornwall Museum (£2,500); Moothill and Abbey Survey Scone and Romney Society (£2,000 each); Hebden Bridge Society (£1,500); Manchester University Press and Norfolk Heraldry Society (£1,000 each); and Boydell and Brewer (£500).

Exclusions

No grants are given towards foreign travel or for research outside the British Isles (unless the circumstances are exceptional); building works; mounting exhibitions; or general appeals. No awards are made in connection with vocational or higher education courses or to people reading for higher degrees.

Applications

In writing to the correspondent, providing a brief outline of the project. The Council of Management meets twice a year, in spring and autumn, to consider applications. The deadlines for receipt of completed applications and references are 1 March and 1 August. The fund requests that any application enquiries be made well in advance of these deadlines as the application process is likely to take at least a few weeks to complete.

Percentage of awards given to new applicants: between 40% and 50%.

Common applicant mistakes

'Not reading the award criteria, or assuming that their case is exceptional.'

Information gathered from:

Accounts; Charity Commission record; further information provided by the funder; funder's website.

The Fitton Trust

Social welfare, medical

£57,000 (2011/12)

Beneficial area

UK.

Correspondent: Mrs Rosalind Gordon-Cumming, The Secretary, PO Box 661, West Broyle, Chichester PO19 9JS

Trustees: Dr R. P. A. Rivers; D. V. Brand; R. Brand; K. J. Lumsden; E. M. Lumsden; L. P. L. Rivers.

CC Number: 208758

The trust was established in 1928 for general charitable purposes.

In 2011/12 the trust had assets of £1.5 million, an income of £92,000 and made grants of £57,000,

The majority of grants were for between £150 and £350; no charities received grants of more than £1,000. A list of grant beneficiaries was not included in the accounts. Previous grant beneficiaries have included King's Medical Research Trust.

Exclusions

No grants to individuals.

Applications

In writing to correspondent. The secretary scrutinises and collates applications in preparation for the trustee meetings. The trustees meet three times each year, usually in April, August and December and they consider all applications.

Information gathered from:

Accounts; Charity Commission record.

The Earl Fitzwilliam Charitable Trust

General

£177,000 (2011/12)

Beneficial area

UK, with a preference for areas with historical family connections, chiefly in Cambridgeshire, Northamptonshire and Yorkshire.

Correspondent: R. W. Dalgleish, Secretary to the Trustees, Estate Office, Milton Park, Peterborough PE6 7AH (tel: 01733 267740)

Trustees: Sir Philip Naylor-Leyland; Lady Isabella Naylor-Leyland.

CC Number: 269388

The trust tends to favour charities that benefit rural communities, especially those with a connection to Cambridgeshire, Peterborough, South Yorkshire and Malton in North Yorkshire where the Fitzwilliam family have held their landed estates for many centuries. It was established in 1975 by the Rt Hon. Earl Fitzwilliam and has since had various capital sums and property gifted to it. Grants tend to be one-off and are usually for £5,000 or less.

In 2011/12 the trust had assets of £13 million and an income of £198,000. Grants were made to 87 organisations totalling £177,000.

Beneficiaries included: Malton Amenity CIFC (£60,000); Peterborough Cathedral Development and Preservation Trust (£25,000); Eton College (New Foundation) (£5,000); I CAN – Million Lost Voices Appeal (£2,500); Break, Hunt Servants Fund, Peterborough Streets and St Margaret's Church – Fletton (£2,000 each); Warwickshire and Northamptonshire Air Ambulance, Safe Haven Children's Trust, National Autistic Society and Mepal Outdoor Centre (£1,000 each); Sheffield Academy of Young Leaders and Support Dogs (£500 each); and Wednesday Phab Club and Movember (£250 each).

Exclusions

No grants to individuals.

Applications

In writing to the correspondent. 'Trustees take decisions on applications for charitable grants in consultation with the secretary at meetings throughout the year.'

Information gathered from:

Accounts; Charity Commission record.

The Ian Fleming Charitable Trust

Social welfare

£20,000 to organisations (2011/12)

Beneficial area

UK.

Correspondent: Archibald Fleming, Trustee, Fairfax House, 15 Fulwood Place, London WC1V 6AY (tel: 020 7969 5500; email: dmcgowan@haysmacintyre.com)

Trustees: Archibald Fleming; A. Isaacs; Gordon Wyllie.

CC Number: 263327

The Ian Fleming Charitable Trust supports national charities who support the relief and welfare of men, women and children who for any reason are disabled or otherwise in need of help, care and attention; and for charities who actively engage in the promotion, financing and encouragement of research into human diseases, particularly their prevention and cure. The trust also supports music awards under a scheme administered by the Musicians Benevolent Fund.

In 2011/12 it had assets of £1 million, which generated an income of £109,000. Grants were made totalling just over £62,000, of which £20,000 was given in 18 grants to organisations and £42,000 was awarded to the Musicians Benevolent Fund Awards.

Beneficiaries included: Music in Hospitals, National Blind Children's Society and Edinburgh Young Carers (£1,500 each); and Action Medical Research Child Cataracts Appeal, Army Benevolent Fund, Brain Research Trust, Gurkha Welfare Fund and Mental Health Foundation (£1,000 each).

Exclusions

No grants to individuals except under the music education award scheme. No grants to purely local charities.

Applications

In writing to the correspondent.

Information gathered from:

Accounts; Charity Commission record.

The Joyce Fletcher Charitable Trust

General charitable purposes with a preference towards children's welfare, music, disability

£70,500 (2011/12)

Beneficial area

England, almost entirely south west.

Correspondent: Robert Fletcher, Trustee, 68 Circus Mews, Bath BA1 2PW (tel: 01225 314355; website: www.joycefletchercharitabletrust.co.uk)

Trustees: Robert Fletcher; Stephen Fletcher; Susan Sharp; William Reddihough Fletcher.

CC Number: 297901

The trust was established in 1987 by William Fletcher as a way of directing some of the family's wealth to good causes. The trust supports institutions and organisations that are registered charities, specialising in music in a social or therapeutic context, music and special needs, and children and young people's welfare. Other organisations which are supported outside these areas are usually known to the trustees and/or are in the south west. Grants usually range between £500 and £5,000, occasionally more is given. A good proportion are repeat grants although there are always some new ones. In recent years, there has been an increasing emphasis on grants to arts bodies which work with children and are usually based in the south west.

In 2011/12 the trust had assets of £2.1 million, an income of £56,000 and made grants totalling £70,500. Of the 36 organisations receiving support, 25 were based in the south west, ten were national charities, and one was based in another UK region. Grants were broken down as follows:

Music and arts education	48%	£33,500
Music in a social/therapeutic context	40%	£28,000
Children and young people	4%	£3,000
Organisations outside the immediate objectives	8%	£6,000

Beneficiaries included: Welsh National Opera (£5,000); Wiltshire Music Centre, RUH Arts Fund and Bath Festivals (£4,000 each); Drake Music, English Touring Opera and Iford Arts (£3,000 each); Bath Area Play Project, International Guitar Festival and National Star College- Cheltenham (£2,000 each); and Beckford Tower Trust, Wessex Foundation and Friends of Music at Wells Cathedral School (£1,000 each).

Exclusions

Grants to individuals and students are exceptionally rare. No support for areas which are the responsibility of the local authority. No support is given to purely professional music/arts promotions. No support for purely medical research charities.

Applications

In writing to the correspondent before 1 November each year. Applications are considered in the months of October and November. There are no application forms. Letters should include the purpose for the grant, an indication of the history and viability of the organisation and a summary of accounts. Preliminary telephone calls are accepted. Applications via email will not be acknowledged.

Percentage of awards given to new applicants: between 10% and 20%.

Common applicant mistakes

'Outside our preferred geographical area or outside our stated objectives.'

Information gathered from:

Accounts; Charity Commission record; further information provided by the funder; funder's website.

Florence's Charitable Trust

Education, welfare, sick and inform, general charitable purposes

£70,000 to organisations (2011/12)

Beneficial area

UK, with preference to Lancashire.

Correspondent: Brian Terry, Secretary, E. Suttons and Sons Ltd, PO Box 2, Bacup OL13 0DT (tel: 01706 874961)

Trustees: Christopher Harrison; Gordon Dewhirst Low; Bob Uttley; Michael Kelly; Simon Holding; Angela Jepson.

CC Number: 265754

The trust was formed, amongst other things, to:

- Establish, maintain and support places of education and to give scholarships and other awards to encourage proficiency in education
- Establish, maintain and support places providing relief for sickness and infirmity, and for the aged
- Relieve poverty of any person employed or formerly employed in the shoe trade
- Provide general charitable public benefits

In 2011/12 the trust had assets of £962,000 and an income of £54,000. Grants totalled £70,000 and were broken down as follows:

General charitable public benefits	34	£39,000
Educational support	29	£22,000
Relief for sickness and infirmity	6	£9,000

A list of grant beneficiaries was not included in the latest accounts.

Previous beneficiaries have included: Pioneer Community Club; Bacup Family Centre; Whitworth Water Ski; Rossendale Search and Rescue; Rossendale United Junior Football Club; North West Air Ambulance; British Heart Foundation; Rochdale Special Needs; Macmillan Cancer Support; Children with AIDS; SENSE; Tenovus; All Black Netball Fund; Sport Relief and Heart of Lancashire appeal. A number of local primary schools and playgroups also benefitted.

Applications

In writing only to the correspondent (no telephone calls please).

Information gathered from:

Accounts; Charity Commission record.

The Flow Foundation

Welfare, education, environment, medical

£208,000 (2011/12)

Beneficial area

UK.

Correspondent: Nita Sowerbutts, Trustee, 22 Old Bond Street, London W1S 4PY (tel: 020 7499 9099)

Trustees: Nathalie Shashou; Nita Sowerbutts; Harold Woolf; Josiane Woolf.

CC Number: 328274

In 2011/12 this foundation had assets of £981,000 and an income of £305,000, including a donation of £294,000 from the Woolf family. 15 grants totalling £208,000 were made and this year were focused on: arts and culture; health and medical issues; and education.

By far the largest grant was made to Imperial College (£143,000). Other beneficiaries included: Westminster School (£15,000); Norwood Ravenswood and The Tate Foundation (£10,000 each); British ORT and Sight Savers (£5,000 each); Families of the Fallen and The British Friends of Haifa University (£2,500 each); and Leuka (£1,000).

Applications

In writing to the correspondent on one sheet of paper only.

Information gathered from:

Accounts; Charity Commission record.

The Gerald Fogel Charitable Trust

Jewish, general

£59,000 (2011/12)

Beneficial area

UK.

Correspondent: David Truman, Accountant, Morley and Scott, Lynton House, 7–12 Tavistock Square, London WC1H 9LT

Trustees: David Fogel; Joseph Fogel; Steven Fogel; Benita Fogel.

CC Number: 1004451

The trust stated in its annual report that its policy is 'to make a wide spread of grants', however mainly Jewish charities are supported in practice.

In 2011/12 the trust had assets of £884,000, an income of £71,000 and made grants totalling £59,000.

Beneficiaries included: Chai Cancer Care (£18,000); World Jewish Relief (£5,500); Norwood (£4,500); Community Security Trust (£2,500); Youth Aliya (£2,300); United Jewish Israel Appeal (£2,000); Royal National Theatre (£1,300); and Crohn's and Colitis in Childhood – 3C's, Ben-Gurion University Foundation, Magen David Adom and Royal Academy of the Arts (£1,000 each).

Small grants below £1,000 each totalled £5,200.

Exclusions

No grants to individuals or non-registered charities.

Applications

In writing to the correspondent.

Information gathered from:

Accounts; Charity Commission record.

The Follett Trust

Welfare, education, arts

£195,000 (2011/12)

Beneficial area

UK and overseas.

Correspondent: Brian Mitchell, Trustee, Po Box 4, Knebworth, Herts SG3 6UT (tel: 01438 222908)

Trustees: Brian Mitchell; Ken Follett; Barbara Follett.

CC Number: 328638

The trust's policy is to: give financial assistance to organisations in the field of education and individual students in higher education including theatre; support organisations concerned with disability and health; support trusts involved with writers and publishing; and respond to world crisis appeals for help.

In 2011/12 the trust had funds of £46,000 and an income of £162,000. Grants to over 38 organisations totalled £195,000.

Grants of £1,000 or more included those to: George Orwell Memorial Trust (£26,000); Impilo Place of Safety (£20,000); Canon Collins Education Trust (£18,000); Stevenage Citizens Advice (£15,000); UCL Development Fund (£13,000); Rosenhof Ahrensburg (£12,000); APEC and Battersea Arts Centre (£5,000 each); and English Pen, Education for Choice, Piggy Bank Kids, Scope and Turn the Boats Tide (£1,000 each).

Grants of less than £1,000 totalled £8,500.

Applications

The trust states, 'A high proportion of donees come to the attention of the trustees through personal knowledge and contact rather than by written application. Where the trustees find it impossible to make a donation they rarely respond to the applicant unless a stamped addressed envelope is provided'.

Information gathered from:

Accounts; Charity Commission record.

The Football Association National Sports Centre Trust

Play areas, community sports facilities

£225,000 (2012)

Beneficial area

UK.

Correspondent: Richard McDermott, Secretary to the Trustees, Wembley National Stadium Ltd, PO Box 1966, London SW1P 9EQ (tel: 0844 980 8200 ext. 6575; email: richard.mcdermott@thefa.com)

Trustees: Brian Adshead; Raymond Berridge; Barry Bright; Geoff Thompson; Mervyn Leggett.

CC Number: 265132

The trust supports the provision, maintenance and improvement of facilities for use in recreational and leisure activities. Grants are made to county football associations, football clubs and other sports associations.

In 2012 the trust had assets of £4.5 million and an income of £26,500. Grants totalled £225,000.

Exclusions

No grants to individuals.

Applications

In writing to the correspondent.

Information gathered from:

Accounts; Charity Commission record.

The Forbes Charitable Foundation

Adults with learning disabilities

£99,500 (2011/12)

Beneficial area

UK.

Correspondent: John Shepherd, PO Box 6256, Nuneaton CV11 9HT (tel: 01455 292881; email: info@theforbescharitablefoundation.org; website: www.theforbescharitablefoundation.org)

Trustees: John Waite; C. Packham; Nicolas Townsend; Ian Johnson; John Williamson; Robert Bunting.

CC Number: 326476

According to the trust's website, 'the Forbes Charitable Foundation's objective is to provide benefits for people with learning disabilities'.

It prefers to support capital rather than revenue projects. The foundation prefers to make grants to small and medium sized organisations where its support will make a real impact. The foundation also prefers to support capital expenditure and certain types of revenue expenditure, such as holidays for the disabled and the costs of training towards employment.

In 2011/12 it had assets of £4.6 million and an income of £1.4 million, which mostly came from a substantial legacy donation. Grants to organisations totalled £99,000.

Beneficiaries included: Cottage and Rural Enterprises Ltd (£31,500); Acre Housing, Bridge Priory Trust and Down's Syndrome Association (£5,000 each); Sussex Association for Spina Bifida and Hydrocephalus and Calvert Trust (£3,000 each); Camden Society, the Fircroft Trust and the Norman Laud Association (£2,000 each); and Scottish Autism (£1,700).

Exclusions

Support is only given to charitable organisations whose work primarily benefits people with learning disabilities.

Applications

On the foundation's application form. Applications should be received close to but no later than the last day of February, June or October. A copy of the latest accounts should be provided along with the application form. Application forms can be obtained from the foundation's website or in writing to the correspondent. Successful applicants will be expected to justify the expenditure of the grant given.

Percentage of awards given to new applicants: 78%.

Common applicant mistakes

'This charity only provides funding to applicants who primarily provide a service to people with learning disabilities – some applicants do not meet this remit.'

Information gathered from:

Accounts; Charity Commission record; further information provided by the funder; funder's website.

The Forces Trust

Military and Naval charities

£30,000 (2011/12)

Beneficial area

UK.

Correspondent: Richard Nugee, Drews Mill, Potterne Road, Devizes, Wiltshire SN10 5LH (email: j.d@gilbert-allen.co.uk)

Trustees: Richard Nugee; Andrew Niekirk; William Niekirk; Brooke Vansittart Bowater.

CC Number: 211529

The trust can only support military and naval charities or institutions. The trustees prefer to support service charities that assist people rather than support buildings or property.

In 2011/12 the trust had assets of £1.1 million, an income of £41,000 and gave grants totalling £30,000.

The beneficiaries were: Sir Oswald Stoll Foundation (£20,000); League of Remembrance and Vitalise (£4,000 each); and Queen Alexandra Hospital Home (£2,000).

Exclusions

No grants to any non-naval or military charities, individuals, scholarships or education generally.

Applications

In writing to the correspondent at any time, preferably on one side of A4.

Percentage of awards given to new applicants: less than 10%.

Common applicant mistakes

'Not being relevant.'

Information gathered from:

Accounts; Charity Commission record; further information provided by the funder.

Ford Britain Trust

Community service, education, environment, disability, schools, special needs education, youth

£123,000 (2012/13)

Beneficial area

Local to the areas in close proximity to Ford Motor Company Ltd's locations in the UK. These are Essex (including East London), Bridgend, Southampton and Daventry.

Correspondent: Gary Smith, 68 Blackheath, Colchester CO2 0AD (tel: 01268 404831; email: fbtrust@ford.com; website: www.ford.co.uk/fbtrust)

Trustees: Michael Callaghan; David Russell; Michael Brophy; Dr June-Alison Sealy; Mitra Janes; Wendy James; Stephen Evison.

CC Number: 269410

The Ford Britain Trust serves the communities in which Ford Motor Company Ltd and its employees are located. The trust provides grants mainly to registered charities and schools that are in support of youth development; schools and education, with particular emphasis on special educational needs; disabilities; and community related services.

The trust particularly encourages applications from Ford employees, but is open to all, provided that applicants meet the selection criteria.

Grants are typically one-off, provided for specific capital projects or parts of a project, and fall into two categories:

- Small grants – for amounts up to £250, available four times a year
- Large grants – for amounts over £250 and usually up to £3,000, available twice a year

Applications for new Ford vehicles are considered when two-thirds of the purchase price is available from other sources. These grants are not usually more than £2,000, but registered charities may be able to arrange a reduction from the recommended retail price. Grants are not available for second-hand vehicles.

In 2012/13 the trust had assets of £322,000 and an income of £187,000. Grants totalled £123,000, broken down as follows:

Schools/education	57	£57,500
Youth	46	£28,000
Community service	74	£25,500
Disability	24	£11,000
Special needs education	1	£1,500

The five largest grants went to: St Joseph's Primary School (£3,400); Llanharan Primary School and Sick Children's Trust (£3,000 each); Leigh Beck Infant School (£2,800); and DACT (£2,600).

Grants of £2,000 each or less totalled £101,500.

Exclusions

Grant applications are not considered if they support the following purposes or activities: major building works; sponsorship or advertising; research; overseas projects; travel; religious projects; political projects; purchase of second hand vehicles; third party fundraising initiatives (exceptions may be made for fundraising initiatives by Ford Motor Company Ltd employees and retirees).

National charities are assisted rarely and then only when the purpose of their application has specific benefit to communities located in close proximity to Ford locations.

Applications for core funding and major building projects are rarely considered.

Grants cannot be provided to individuals.

Applications

On a form available from the correspondent or to download from the trust's website. Applications for large grants should include a copy of the organisation's most recent report and accounts.

Small grant applications are considered in March, June, September and November and should be submitted by the 1st of each month. Applications for large grants are considered in March and September.

Information gathered from:

Accounts; Charity Commission record; funder's website.

The Oliver Ford Charitable Trust

Mental disability, housing

£55,000 to organisations (2011/12)

Beneficial area

UK.

Correspondent: Matthew Pintus, 20 Cursitor Street, London EC4A 1LT (tel: 020 7831 9222)

Trustees: Lady Wakeham; Martin Levy.

CC Number: 1026551

The objects of the trust are to educate the public and advance knowledge of the history and techniques of interior decoration, the designs of fabric and other decorative materials and landscape gardening, including Oliver Ford's own work. Income and capital not used for these purposes is used for the Anthroposophical Society of Great Britain, Camphill Village Trust, Norwood or any other charity providing housing, educational or training facilities for children, young persons or adults who have learning disabilities or learning difficulties.

In 2011/12 the trust had assets of £2.4 million and an income of £102,000. Grants to 22 organisations and three students totalled £83,000. Grants were given to students at the Furniture and History Society (£4,000); the Royal Horticultural Society (£5,000); and the Victoria and Albert Museum (£19,000).

Beneficiaries included: Livability (£10,000); Camphill Devon (£7,000); Autism Sussex Ltd and Enham (£5,000 each); National Star College and Papworth Trust (£4,000 each).

Applications

In writing to the correspondent. Trustees meet in March and October.

Information gathered from:

Accounts; Charity Commission record.

Fordeve Ltd

Orthodox Jewish causes

£108,000 (2011/12)

Beneficial area

UK.

Correspondent: Jeremy Kon, Trustee, Hallswelle House, 1 Hallswelle Road, London NW11 0DH (tel: 020 8209 1535)

Trustees: Helen Kon; Jeremy Kon.

CC Number: 1011612

The main objective of the trust is to advance religion in accordance with the Orthodox Jewish faith.

In 2011/12 it had assets of £582,000, an income of £107,000 and gave grants totalling £108,000. No further information about the beneficiaries or the grants they received was available from this year's accounts.

Previous beneficiaries include: the Gertner Charitable Trust; Lubavitch Foundation; the Yom Tov Assistance Fund; the Society of Friends of the Torah; Lolev Charitable Trust; Beth Jacob Grammar School for Girls.

Applications

In writing to the correspondent.

Information gathered from:

Accounts; Charity Commission record.

The Forest Hill Charitable Trust

Mainly Christian causes and relief work

£179,000 (2011/12)

Beneficial area

UK and overseas.

Correspondent: Dr Francis Horace Pile, Trustee, 104 Summercourt Way, Brixham, Devon TQ5 0RB (tel: 01803 852857; email: horacepile@tiscali.co.uk)

Trustees: Dr Horace Francis Pile; Ronald Stanley Pile; Marianne Sylvia Tapper; Michael Thomas; Patricia Jean Pile.

CC Number: 1050862

This trust gives grants mainly to Christian causes and for relief work (80%), although support is given to agencies helping people who are disabled, in need or sick.

In 2011/12 the trust had assets of £3.2 million and an income of £180,000.

Grants were made to approximately 140 charities totalling £179,000 and in the following categories:

Christianity	£82,000
Health and respite care	£51,500
Social	£19,500
Foreign relief	£15,000
Education	£11,000

In the main, grants average £1,000 – £2,000 however, there were two exceptional grants: LiNX (£21,000); and Great Parks Chapel (£10,000).

Other beneficiaries included: Marilyn Baker Trust, Caring for Life, Christian Blind Mission, Concern Worldwide, Emmaus, Interserve, Mercy Ships, ROPE and World Emergency Relief (£2,000 each); Christians Against Poverty, Compass Braille, DELTA, Gate Christian Fellowship, Harvest Trust, Prison Fellowship and Time for Families (£1,000 each); and Evangelical Housing Association and Farm Crisis Network (£500 each).

Applications

The trustees have previously stated that their aim was to maintain regular and consistent support to the charities they are currently supporting. New requests for funding are therefore very unlikely to succeed and unsolicited applications are rarely considered.

Information gathered from:

Accounts; Charity Commission record.

The Anna Rosa Forster Charitable Trust

Medical research, animal welfare, famine relief

£87,000 (2011/12)

Beneficial area

Worldwide.

Correspondent: R. W. Napier, Trustee, c/o R. W. Napier Solicitors, Floor E, Milburn House, Dean Street, Newcastle upon Tyne NE1 1LF (tel: 01912 301819; email: rogerw.napier@gmail.com)

Trustees: R. W. Napier; A. W. Morgan.

CC Number: 1090028

Registered with the Charity Commission in January 2002, in 2011/12 the trust had assets of £2 million and an income of £89,000. Grants were made totalling £87,000, distributed into the following categories:

Medical research	£29,000
Animal welfare	£29,000
Famine relief	£29,000
Memorial maintenance	£540

A list of grants was not available but previously has included: Alzheimer's Research Trust, Cancer Research UK, British Red Cross, Farm Africa, Cats Protection League, CARE International UK, Motor Neurone Disease Association, the Donkey Sanctuary, PDSA, RSPCA, International Spinal Research Trust and the World Medical Fund.

Applications

In writing to the correspondent.

Information gathered from:

Accounts; Charity Commission record.

The Forte Charitable Trust

Roman Catholic, Alzheimer's disease, senile dementia

Around £43,000 (2012/13)

Beneficial area

UK and overseas.

Correspondent: Judy Lewendon, Correspondent, Rocco Forte Hotels Ltd, 70 Jermyn Street, London SW1Y 6NY (email: jlewendon@roccofortehotels.com)

Trustees: Sir Rocco Forte; George Proctor; The Hon Olga Polizzi de Sorrentino; Lowndes Trustees Ltd.

CC Number: 326038

The trust has narrowed its areas of work down to those in relation to the Roman Catholic faith, Alzheimer's disease and senile dementia.

In 2012/13 the trust had an income of £1,500 and a total expenditure of £45,000. We have estimated the grant total to be around £40,000.

Applications

In writing to the correspondent.

Information gathered from:

Charity Commission record.

The Lord Forte Foundation

Hospitality

£95,500 (2011/12)

Beneficial area

UK.

Correspondent: Judy Lewendon, Administrator, Rocco Forte Hotels Ltd, 70 Jermyn Street, London SW1Y 6NY (tel: 020 7235 6244; email: jlewendon@roccofortehotels.com)

Trustees: Sir Rocco Forte; Lord Janner of Braunstone; George Proctor; The Hon Olga Polizzi di Sorrentino; Nick Scade; Andrew McKenzie.

CC Number: 298100

According to the annual report for 2011/12, the trust was set up in 1987 'to encourage excellence within the fields of hospitality, encompassing the hotel, catering, travel and tourism industries within the UK and overseas'. It does this by giving grants directly to educational establishments which provide training courses or carry out research projects in these fields.

In 2011/12 it had assets of £2.1 million, which generated an income of £65,000. Grants were made totalling £95,000 to 11 educational institutions providing training courses in the hospitality industry.

Beneficiaries included: British Institute of Innkeeping (£25,500); WCI General Charity Fund (£20,000); Thames Valley University (£11,000); Springboard Charitable Trust and University of Bedfordshire (£7,000 each); Westminster Kingsway College and Jamie Oliver Foundation (£5,000 each); and Cornwall College (£500).

Exclusions

Grants are given to those organisations which fulfil the objectives of the foundation.

Applications

In writing to the correspondent.

Information gathered from:

Accounts; Charity Commission record.

The Isaac and Freda Frankel Memorial Charitable Trust

Jewish, general

£63,000 (2011/12).

Beneficial area

UK and overseas, particularly Israel.

Correspondent: M. D. Frankel, Trustee, 33 Welbeck Street, London W1G 8LX (tel: 020 7872 0023)

Trustees: M. D. Frankel; Geraldine Frankel; J. Steinhaus; J. Silkin.

CC Number: 1003732

The Isaac and Freda Frankel Memorial Charitable Trust was established in July 1991 by members of the Frankel family to support mainly Jewish causes.

In 2011/12 the trust had assets of £409,000 and an income of £45,000. Grants totalled £63,000. A list of beneficiaries was not included with the accounts filed at the Charity Commission.

Exclusions

No grants to individuals or students, for expeditions or scholarships.

Applications

In writing to the correspondent.

Information gathered from: Accounts; Charity Commission record.

The Elizabeth Frankland Moore and Star Foundation

General in the UK

£230,000 (2011/12)

Beneficial area

UK.

Correspondent: Marianne Neuhoff, Neuhoff and Co., 11 Towcester Road, Whittlebury, Towcester NN12 8XU (tel: 01327 858171)

Trustees: R. A. Griffiths; Anne Ely; Dr David Spalton; Janine Cameron.

CC Number: 257711

The Elizabeth Frankland Moor and Star Foundation was established in 1968. The foundation aims to give grants to a range of charitable organisations and individuals.

In 2011/12 the trust had an income of £263,000, assets of £9.4 million and made grants to 33 organisations totalling £230,000.

Beneficiaries included: Iceni Project and Kids Company (£20,000 each); Alzheimer's Society (£17,500); Salvation Army (£16,000); Erskine (£15,000); the Not Forgotten Association, Centre Point and Age Scotland (£10,000 each); Eyes for East Africa (£8,500); Prisoners Abroad and Queen Alexandra Hospital Home (£5,000 each); Gardening Leave and RNLI (£1,000 each); and Warminster Food Bank (£500).

Applications

In writing to the correspondent. Trustees meet twice a year.

Information gathered from:

Accounts; Charity Commission record.

Sydney E. Franklin Deceased's New Second Charity

Relief of poverty, children, communities

Around £25,000 (2011/12)

Beneficial area

Worldwide. Priority is given to developing world projects.

Correspondent: Dr Rodney Franklin, Trustee, 39 Westleigh Avenue, London SW15 6RQ

Trustees: Dr Rodney Franklin; Natasha Franklin; Roxanne Smee; Julia Edwards.

CC Number: 272047

The trust supports small charities with low income (under £300,000), which are involved in the relief of poverty and disability and the protection of endangered species. Priority is given to children in the developing world, education and communities working towards self-sufficiency.

In 2011/12 the trust had an income of £24,000 and a total expenditure of £29,000. No further information was available.

Previous beneficiaries have included: Kerala Federation for the Blind, Water for Kids, Narwhal/Niaff, United Charities Fund, Ashram International, Books Abroad, Children of the Andes, Kaloko Trust, Microloan Foundation, Tools for Self Reliance, Tree Aid, Window for Peace UK, Forest Peoples Project, African Initiatives, Lake Malawi Projects, World Medical Fund and Gwalior Children's Hospital.

Exclusions

Individuals.

Applications

Written applications only. Must include most recent audited accounts.

Percentage of awards given to new applicants: between 20% and 30%.

Common applicant mistakes

'We only give to small charities with turnover under £300,000. Most 'mistakes' are due to applications from larger charities.'

Information gathered from:

Accounts; Charity Commission record; further information provided by the funder.

The Jill Franklin Trust

General charitable purposes with a preference towards welfare, prisons, church restoration and asylum

£71,500 (2011/12)

Beneficial area

UK.

Correspondent: Norman Franklin, Trustee, Flat 5, 17–19 Elsworthy Road, London NW3 3DS (tel: 020 7722 4543; email: jft@jill-franklin-trust.org.uk; website: www.jill-franklin-trust.org.uk)

Trustees: Sally Franklin; Norman Franklin; Andrew Franklin; Dr Samuel Franklin; Thomas Franklin.

CC Number: 1000175

The Jill Franklin Trust was established in 1988. Apart from special grants selected by the trustees, the six areas the trustees have concentrated their giving on are:

- Self-help groups etc. for people with a mental illness or learning difficulties
- Holidays for carers to provide respite for their caree – mainly provided as a block grant to the Princess Royal Trust for Carers
- Organisations helping and supporting asylum seekers and refugees coming to the UK
- Restoration of churches of architectural importance
- Grants to prisoners for education and training – mainly as a block grant to the Prisoners Education Trust
- Camden Bereavement Service, with which Jill Franklin was closely associated

In 2011/12 the trust had assets of almost £1.5 million, an income of £70,000 and made grants totalling £72,000, broken down as follows.

Bereavement	1	£12,000
Church restoration	20	£25,000
Education	2	£14,000
Holidays for carers	7	£10,000
Mental health and learning difficulties	20	£10,000
Other	3	£500
Overseas	1	£2,500
Refugees	19	£9,500

Beneficiaries included: Prisoners Education Trust and CCIWBS (£12,000 each); Princess Royal Trust for Carers (£7,000); Pevsner Books Trust (£4,000); Camara (£2,500); and Devon and Cornwall Refugee Support Council, Hackney Migrant Centre and Respite Association (£1,000 each).

Exclusions

Grants are not given to:

- Appeals for building work
- Endowment funds
- Branches of a national organisations, and to the centre itself (unless it is a specific grant, probably for training in the branches)
- Replace the duties of government, local authorities or the NHS
- Encourage the 'contract culture', particularly where authorities are not funding the contract adequately
- Religious organisations set up for welfare, education etc. of whatever religion, unless the service is open to and used by people from all denominations
- Overseas projects
- Heritage schemes
- Animal charities
- Students, nor to any individuals nor for overseas travel
- Medical research

Applications

In writing to the correspondent, enclosing a copy of the latest annual report and accounts and a budget for the project. Organisations based outside the UK should provide the name, address and telephone number of a correspondent or referee in the UK.

According to the annual report for 2011/12, 'the trustees tend to look more favourably on an appeal which is simply and economically prepared: glossy, 'prestige' and mail sorted brochures do not impress the trustees'.

Unsolicited enquiries are not usually acknowledged.

Information gathered from:

Accounts; Charity Commission record; funder's website.

The Gordon Fraser Charitable Trust

Children, young people, environment, arts

£140,000 (2012/13)

Beneficial area

UK, with a preference for Scotland.

Correspondent: Claire Armstrong, Administrator, Gaidrew Farmhouse, Drymen, Glasgow G63 0DN

Trustees: M. A. Moss; W. F. T. Anderson; Sarah Moss; Susannah Rae; Alexander Moss; Alison Priestley.

CC Number: 260869

The trustees are particularly interested in supporting children/young people in need, the environment (including the built environment) and visual arts (including performance arts). Most grants are given within these categories. Applications from or for Scotland will receive favourable consideration, but not to the exclusion of applications from England, Wales or Northern Ireland.

In 2012/13 the trust had assets of £3.2 million and an income of £167,000. Grants were made to 92 organisations totalling £140,000.

The trustees rarely make donations to the same charity more than once in the same year and a donation rarely exceeds £20,000 or is less than £100 although there are no minimum or maximum amounts for donations.

Beneficiaries included: the National Galleries of Scotland (£13,500); Hunterian Art Gallery (£10,000); Artlink Central (£6,000); London Children's Flower Society and Royal Scottish National Orchestra (£4,000 each); British Red Cross and the Edinburgh International Festival Society (£2,000 each); Fly Cup Catering Ltd, the Glasgow School of Art and John Muir Trust (£1,000 each); Christians Against Poverty and East End Kids and Co. (£500 each); and the Council for Music in Hospitals (£300).

Exclusions

No grants are made to organisations which are not recognised charities, or to individuals.

Applications

In writing to the correspondent. Applications are considered in January, April, July and October.

Percentage of awards given to new applicants: between 10% and 20%.

Common applicant mistakes

'Applying as individuals or unregistered charities; applying for sums far beyond the trust's means.'

Information gathered from:

Accounts; Charity Commission record; further information provided by the funder.

The Joseph Strong Frazer Trust

General, with broad interests in the fields of social welfare, education, religion and wildlife

£345,000 (2011/12)

Beneficial area

Unrestricted, in practice, England and Wales only.

Correspondent: The Trustees, Joseph Miller and Co., Floor A, Milburn House, Dean Street, Newcastle upon Tyne NE1 1LE (tel: 01912 328065; fax: 01912 221554; email: uf@joseph-miller.co.uk)

Trustees: Sir William A. Reardon Smith, Chair; David A. Cook; R. M. H. Read; William N. H. Reardon Smith; William I. Waites.

CC Number: 235311

Established in 1939, the trust has general charitable purposes and gives to a wide range of causes, with broad interests in the fields of medical and other research, social welfare, people with disabilities, children, hospitals, education, maritime, youth, religion and wildlife. Recipients are based throughout England and Wales.

In 2011/12 the trust had assets of £12 million and an income of £446,000. There were 275 grants made totalling £345,000, categorised in the accounts as follows:

Medical and other research	62	£84,000
Other trusts and funds	37	£40,000
Caring organisations	28	£33,000
Children	25	£32,500
Deaf and blind	17	£28,000
Hospitals and home	21	£25,000
Youth	22	£21,500
Disability	14	£19,000
Leisure activities, animals and wildlife	13	£15,500
Maritime	13	£14,500
Armed forces	7	£9,000
Older people	4	£7,000
Religious bodies	5	£7,000
Mental Health	4	£4,500
Schools and colleges	3	£4,500

Grants of £2,000 were paid to 67 organisations including: Addaction, Archway Project, British Retinitis Pigmentosa Society, Counsel and Care for the Elderly, Iris Fund, Leonard Cheshire Wales and West, Royal School for the Blind Liverpool and Welsh National Opera. There were a further 208 grants to organisations of less than £2,000 which were not detailed in the accounts.

Exclusions

No grants to individuals.

Applications

In writing to the correspondent. Trustees meet twice a year, usually in March and September. Application forms are not necessary. It is helpful if applicants are concise in their appeal letters, which must include an sae if acknowledgement is required.

Information gathered from:

Accounts; Charity Commission record.

The Louis and Valerie Freedman Charitable Settlement

General

£111,000 (2011/12)

Beneficial area

UK, especially Burnham.

Correspondent: Francis Hughes, Trustee, c/o Bridge House, 11 Creek Road, East Molesey, Surrey KT8 9BE (tel: 020 8941 4455)

Trustees: Francis Hughes; Michael Ferrier.

CC Number: 271067

According to the trustees' report for 2011/12, the trust was initially established by a gift from Louis Freedman in 1976 followed by gifts to the charity from various companies that Louis Freedman assisted during his professional life and legacies to the charity after his death and the death of his wife Valerie Freedman.

The trust supports medical research as well as health and sickness charities and youth education. Local charities in the area of Burnham in Buckinghamshire are supported.

In 2011/12 it had assets of £3.9 million, an income of £143,000 and made grants totalling £111,000.

Beneficiaries were: Burnham Health Promotion Trust (£50,000); Second

Chance Children's Society (£15,000); Prostate Cancer Research UK and Cheam School Educational Trust (£10,000 each); and Disability Challenges, Rekindle and SSAFA Forces Help (£5,000 each).

Exclusions

No grants to individuals. Only registered charities are considered for support.

Applications

There is no application form. The following information was obtained from the trustees' report 2011/12:

> The trustees meet periodically (and are also in regular contact) to consider what grants they will make and to review any feedback they have received relating to past donations. The trustees receive many applications for assistance but are normally minded to help those with a link to the Freedman family.

Information gathered from:

Accounts; Charity Commission record.

The Michael and Clara Freeman Charitable Trust

General

£90,000 (2011/12)

Beneficial area

UK and overseas.

Correspondent: Michael Freeman, Trustee, 9 Connaught Square, London W2 2HG

Trustees: Michael Freeman; Clara Freeman; Laura Freeman; Edward Freeman.

CC Number: 1125083

The trust was established in 2008 for general charitable purposes with an initial donation of almost £2 million from the settlors, Michael Freeman, co-founder of Argent Property Developers and his wife Clara, a former executive on the board of Marks and Spencer and currently on the University of the Arts London board of governors.

In 2011/12 the trust had no income and spent £92,000. It is likely grants totalled around £90,000.

Previous accounts have noted that a gift of £450,000 had been pledged to Balliol College, Oxford, and it is possible that some of the funds were donated here in the year. Other previous beneficiaries included: Help for Heroes (£23,000); Chipping Norton Theatre (£5,000); Combat Stress and the British Legion (£2,500); Kids Company and St Giles' Trust (£2,000 each); and Mary's Meals (£1,000).

Applications

In writing to the correspondent.

Information gathered from:

Accounts; Charity Commission record.

The Friarsgate Trust

Health and welfare of young and older people

£64,000 (2011/12)

Beneficial area

UK, with a strong preference for West Sussex, especially Chichester.

Correspondent: Miss Amanda King-Jones, Thomas Eggar LLP, The Corn Exchange, Baffins Lane, Chichester PO19 1GE (tel: 01243 786111)

Trustees: A. C. Colenutt; Mrs V. Higgins; Mr N. M. Proctor.

CC Number: 220762

The objectives of the trust are:

- To provide funds for the academic and general education of orphans and children (whether infant or adult) whose parents are in poor or reduced circumstances
- To promote the mental, moral, physical, technical and social education of children, young persons and adults
- To provide, equip and maintain for the purposes referred to above camping grounds, holiday camps, playing fields, club rooms or other accommodation and facilities
- To provide for the relief and care of impotent persons including in that expression all persons suffering either temporarily or permanently from disease or disability of any kind affecting their body or mind
- To provide for the relief of persons over the age of sixty years by the provision of maintenance, food, clothing and housing
- To promote and support or aid any charitable institutions, purposes or projects in any way connected with the objects aforesaid or calculated to further such objects or any of them

In 2011/12 the trust had assets of £2.1 million and an income of £87,000. There were 44 grants made during the year totalling £64,000, split into two categories: education (£36,000); and care and welfare (£28,000).

Beneficiaries included: Chichester District Scouts (£10,000); St Wilfrid's Hospice (£3,200); The Douglas Bader Foundation, Chichester Community Transport and Contact 88 (£2,000 each); The Sussex Snowdrop Trust, Fields in Trust, Shelter, Jubilee Sailing Care and Elizabeth Finn Care (£1,000 each); and Brighton and Hove Unwaged Christmas Appeal (£500).

Exclusions

Local organisations outside Sussex are unlikely to be supported.

Applications

In writing to the correspondent. Applicants are welcome to telephone first to check they fit the trust's criteria.

Information gathered from:

Accounts; Charity Commission record.

Friends of Biala Ltd

Jewish causes, education, relief of poverty

Around £100,000 (2011/12)

Beneficial area

UK and overseas.

Correspondent: The Trustees, Rosenthal and Co., 106 High West Street, Gateshead, Tyne and Wear NE8 1NA (tel: 01914 772814)

Trustees: B. Rabinowitz; T. Weinberg.

CC Number: 271377

The trust supports religious education in accordance with the Orthodox Jewish faith and registered welfare charities.

In 2011/12 the trust had an income of £11,000 and a total expenditure of £106,000. No further information was available.

Previous beneficiaries include: Friends of Biala Israel, Aguda Hadadit, Yeshiva Beis Ephraim, Gemach Ezra Hadadit and Freebee Foundation Ltd.

Applications

In writing to the correspondent.

Information gathered from:

Accounts; Charity Commission record.

Friends of Boyan Trust

Orthodox Jewish

£258,000 (2012)

Beneficial area

Worldwide.

Correspondent: Jacob Getter, Trustee, 23 Durley Road, London N16 5JW (tel: 020 8809 6051)

Trustees: Jacob Getter; Mordechai Freund; Nathan Kuflik.

CC Number: 1114498

Set up in 2006, 'the charity was formed for the advancement of the Orthodox Jewish faith, Orthodox Jewish religious education, and the relief of poverty in the Orthodox Jewish community'.

In 2012 the trust had assets of £78,000 and an income of £325,000. Grants were made totalling £258,000.

A list of beneficiaries was not available with the accounts. Previous beneficiaries included: Gomlei Chesed of Chasidei Boyan (£84,000); Mosdot Tiferet Yisroel Boyan (£31,000); Kimcha De'Pischa Boyan (£21,000); Kimcha De'Pischa Beitar Ilit (£13,000); Chevras Mo'oz Ladol (£12,000); Kolel Avrechim Boyan, Betar Ilit (£6,000); Ezer Mikoidesh Foundation (£2,000); Beis Rizhin Trust (£1,500); and Yad Vochessed (£1,000).

Applications

In writing to the correspondent.

Information gathered from:

Accounts; Charity Commission record.

The Friends of Kent Churches

Churches

£141,000 (2012)

Beneficial area

County of Kent.

Correspondent: Jane Bird, Parsonage Farm House, Hampstead Lane, Yalding, Maidstone ME18 6HG (tel: 01622 815569; website: www.friendsofkentchurches.co.uk)

Trustees: Charles Banks; Charles Oliver; Paul Smallwood; Angela Parish; Leslie Smith; Richard Latham; Jane Boucher; Mary Gibbins; Jane Bird.

CC Number: 207021

According to the trustees' report for 2012, the objective of the Friends of Kent Churches 'is to promote the preservation of churches in use of architectural merit or historical interest in the county of Kent (pre-April 1965 boundaries) and to help maintain in good order their fabric and fixtures of special importance'.

A large amount of the trust's income is raised by an annual sponsored bike ride where half of the money raised is returned to the church of the riders' choice and the other half is allocated by the trust to the churches that have applied for a grant.

The following is taken from the trustees' report for 2012: 'the Friends paid out £181,200 in grants to churches in 2012 on completion of work carried out. During the year 27 successful applications were made for help and grants offered amounting to £141,700, payable on completion of works.'

In 2012 the trust had assets of £666,500 and an income of £237,000. 27 grants were paid out totalling £141,000.

Beneficiaries included: St Mary – Westwell (£15,000); St Mary the Virgin – Chiddingstone and St Nicholas – Wade (£10,000 each); St Augustine – Ramsgate and St Mary of Charity – Faversham (£8,000 each); St Martin of Tours – Ashurst and St Eanswythe – Folkestone (£5,000 each); St John the Baptist – Meopham (£3,000); St Mary the Virgin – Stone in Oxney, St Mary the Virgin – West Malling and St Mary the Virgin – Westerham (£1,000 each); and St John the Baptist – Bredgar (£500).

Exclusions

No grants for reordering, new extensions, toilets and kitchens; heating, redecorating and rewiring; bells, clocks and organs.

Applications

In writing to the correspondent. Grants are offered twice a year at meetings in January and July. Applications should be sent to the secretary by 1 May or 1 November. There are no formal architectural or financial requirements, however proposals must be sensible.

Applications can also be made for the National Churches Trust Partnership grants, which are available for structural repair projects with a total cost of up to £50,000. Forms and guidance notes can be downloaded from the trust's website.

Grants are also distributed on behalf of WREN (Waste Recycling Environmental Ltd) for the maintenance, repair and restoration of places of religious worship. More information can be found on the trust's website.

Information gathered from:

Accounts; Charity Commission record; funder's website.

Friends of Wiznitz Ltd

Jewish education, relief of poverty, advancement of the Jewish religion

£665,500 (2011/12)

Beneficial area

UK and overseas.

Correspondent: E. Gottesfeld, Correspondent, 8 Jessam Avenue, London E5 9DU

Trustees: Heinrich Feldman; Shulom Feldman; Ralph Bergman.

CC Number: 255685

The trust's objectives are the advancement of religion, religious education and the relief of poverty with special regards to Wiznitz institutions. The trust grants the free use of its buildings, for educational purposes, to other Wiznitz charities in order to fulfil the aforementioned objectives.

This trust is mainly concerned with supporting major educational projects being carried out by Orthodox Jewish institutions.

In 2011/12 the trust had assets of almost £1.5 million and an income of £1.1 million. Grants were made totalling £665,000 and distributed as follows:

Relief of poverty	£287,000
Religious education	£257,000
Advancement of religion	£108,000
Individuals (relief of poverty)	£13,000
Support	£700

There was a limited list of beneficiaries included; however those that were given the largest grants are as follows: Igud Mosdos Wiznitz (£250,000); Zidkat Zadik (£191,500); Lehachzikom Velchachyosom (£56,000); and Ahavat Israel Synagogue (£26,000).

Exclusions

Exclusively Jewish causes.

Applications

In writing to the correspondent.

Information gathered from:

Accounts; Charity Commission record.

The Frognal Trust

Older people, children, disability, blindness/ophthalmological research, environmental heritage

£46,000 (2011/12)

Beneficial area

UK.

Correspondent: Susan Hickley, Correspondent, Wilson Solicitors LLP, Alexandra House, St Johns Street, Salisbury SP1 2SB (tel: 01722 427536)

Trustees: Philippa Blake-Roberts; Jennifer Helen Fraser; Peter Fraser.

CC Number: 244444

The trust supports smaller charities rather than national organisations or local branches of large national charities. In 2011/12 it had assets of £2.1 million, which generated an income of £84,000. Grants were made to organisations totalling £46,000, which were broken down as follows:

Disability and blindness	£11,000
Children and young people	£10,500
Medical research	£10,000
Older people	£7,500
Environmental heritage	£7,000

Unfortunately a grants list was not available in this year's accounts.

Previous beneficiaries have included: Action Medical Research, Aireborough Voluntary Services to the Elderly, Canniesburn Research Trust, Elderly Accommodation Counsel and Leeds

Society for Deaf and Blind People, Friends of the Elderly, Gloucestershire Disabled Afloat Riverboat Trust, National Rheumatoid Arthritis Society, Royal Liverpool and Broad Green University Hospitals, Samantha Dickson Research Trust, Stubbers Adventure Centre, Wireless for the Bedridden Society and Yorkshire Dales Millennium Project.

Applications

In writing to the correspondent. Applications should be received by February, May, August and November, for consideration at the trustees' meeting the following month.

Information gathered from:

Accounts; Charity Commission record.

T. F. C. Frost Charitable Trust

Research into the prevention of blindness

£70,500 (2011/12).

Beneficial area

UK and overseas.

Correspondent: John Holmes, 10 Torrington Road, Claygate, Esher, Surrey KT10 0SA (tel: 01372 465378; email: holmes_and_co@hotmail.com)

Trustees: Michael Miller; Thomas Frost; Prof. John Marshall; Dr Elizabeth Graham.

CC Number: 256590

According to the 2011/12 accounts, the objectives of the trust are 'to foster research into the prevention of blindness by supporting programmes submitted by senior trainees and by enhancing their horizons by underwriting the costs of educational or research periods of training at home or abroad at recognised centres'.

In 2011/12 it had assets of £2.6 million and an income of £83,000. Grants totalled £71,000.

There were two beneficiaries in which funding was distributed between three individuals. These beneficiaries were: University of Southampton (£45,500); and William Beaumont Hospital-Michigan, USA (£25,000).

Exclusions

There are no available resources for the relief of blind people or people suffering from diseases of the eye.

Applications

In writing to the correspondent. Trustees meet twice a year.

Information gathered from:

Accounts; Charity Commission record.

The Patrick and Helena Frost Foundation

General charitable purposes

£93,000 (2011/12)

Beneficial area

UK.

Correspondent: Allan Twitchett, Administrator, c/o Trowers and Hamlins LLP, 3 Bunhill Row, London EC1Y 8YZ (tel: 020 7423 8276; email: atwitchett@trowers.com)

Trustees: Luke Valner; Dominic Tayler; Neil Hendriksen.

CC Number: 1005505

The foundation makes general welfare grants to organisations and grants to help small charities that rely on a considerable amount of self-help and voluntary effort.

In 2011/12 the foundation had assets of £5 million and an income of £39,000. Grants were paid to 31 organisations totalling £93,000.

Beneficiaries included: Jubilee Sailing Trust (£7,500); Action for Blind People and Humberside Police Authority (£5,000 each); Practical Action, Tree Aid and Yeldall Christian Centres (£2,500 each); and Bowel and Cancer Research and the Gurkha Welfare Trust (£1,000 each).

Exclusions

No grants to individuals.

Applications

In writing to the correspondent, accompanied by the last set of audited accounts. The trustees regret that due to the large number of applications they receive, they are unable to notify unsuccessful applicants.

Percentage of awards given to new applicants: between 10% and 20%.

Information gathered from:

Accounts; Charity Commission record; further information provided by the funder.

Maurice Fry Charitable Trust

General charitable purposes

£14,500 (2011/12)

Beneficial area

UK and overseas.

Correspondent: Leaf Fry, Trustee, 98 Savernake Road, London NW3 2JR

Trustees: Leaf Fry; Lisa Weaks; Felicity Cooklin; Sam Cooklin-Smith.

CC Number: 327934

The Maurice Fry Charitable Trust was created by a declaration of trust in 1988 with funds derived from a similar trust created by the late Maurice Fry in 1958. The trust was established for general charitable purposes.

In 2011/12 the trust had assets of £1.25 million and an income of £37,000. Grants to 14 organisations totalled £14,500.

Beneficiaries included: Southbank Centre, British Red Cross, NSPCC and the Maypole Project (£2,000 each); Marie Curie Centre and Special Olympics GB (£1,000 each); and Fairtrade Foundation (£500).

Exclusions

No grants to individuals.

Applications

The trustees meet twice a year to consider applications from a wide range of sources. It states that it does not respond to unsolicited applications.

Percentage of awards given to new applicants: less than 10%.

Information gathered from:

Accounts; Charity Commission record; further information provided by the funder.

Mejer and Gertrude Miriam Frydman Foundation

Jewish causes, general charitable purposes

£37,000 (2011/12)

Beneficial area

UK and overseas.

Correspondent: David Frydman, Trustee, Westbury, 145–157 St John Street, London EC1V 4PY (tel: 020 7253 7272)

Trustees: Keith Graham; David Frydman; Gerald Frydman; Louis Frydman.

CC Number: 262806

The Mejer and Gertrude Miriam Frydman Foundation was established by a trust deed in 1971. It has general charitable purposes with a preference towards Jewish causes.

In 2011/12 the foundation had assets of £82,500 and an income of £42,000. Grants were made totalling £37,000.

Beneficiaries included: North West London Jewish Day School (£4,000); Friends of Yeshiva OHR Elchanan (£3,000); Chai Cancer Care and Friends of Eretz Hemdah (£2,500 each); Kesser Torah (£2,000); Achisomoch Aid Co. (£1,000); and Talia Trust for Children (£500).

Exclusions

No grants to individuals for scholarships or any other purpose.

Applications

In writing to the correspondent.

Information gathered from:

Accounts; Charity Commission record.

The Fulmer Charitable Trust

Developing world, general

£184,000 (2011/12)

Beneficial area

Worldwide, especially the developing world and Wiltshire.

Correspondent: The Trustees, Estate Office, Street Farm, Compton Bassett, Calne, Wiltshire SN11 8SW (tel: 01249 760410)

Trustees: J. S. Reis; Mrs S. Reis; Mrs C. Mytum.

CC Number: 1070428

Most of the support is given in the developing world, although UK charities are also supported, especially those working in Wiltshire.

In 2011/12 the trust had assets of £7.8 million, an income of £284,000 and gave grants totalling £184,000.

Beneficiaries included: The Sequal Trust (£7,000); Save the Children (£4,500); Send a Cow (£4,000); The Leys Youth Programme (£3,000); Micro Loan Foundation (£2,750); Stars Appeal (£2,500); Christian Aid (£2,000); Ashram International, Brooke Hospital for Animals and Cerebral Palsy Africa (£1,000); Aid for the Aged in Distress, Joshua Foundation, Samaritans (£750); Release International and Wiltshire Wildlife Trust (£500 each); and Help Counselling Services (£250).

Exclusions

No support for gap year requests.

Applications

In writing to the correspondent. Very few unsolicited applications are accepted.

Information gathered from:

Accounts; Charity Commission record.

The Fuserna Foundation General Charitable Trust

General charitable purposes, including education and training, the advancement of health, the relief of poverty, accommodation and housing, the arts, the environment, the armed forces, and human rights

£130,000 (2012)

Beneficial area

UK and overseas.

Correspondent: Louise Creasey, Trustee, 6th Floor, 6 Chesterfield Gardens, London W1J 5BQ (tel: 020 7409 3900; email: info@fusernafoundation.org; website: www.fusernafoundation.org)

Trustees: Patrick Maxwell; Ariadne Getty; Louise Creasey.

CC Number: 1107895

The Fuserna General Charitable Trust was established in November 2004. The trust has a US branch which aims to work in tandem with the Fuserna General Charitable Trust in order to achieve its charitable objectives.

Fuserna's core focus, as stated on the trust's website, is to:

- Revitalize existing charities and individual charitable projects that are failing in their objectives due to financial constraints and/or a lack of exposure and publicity. This includes vital projects that have difficulty raising funds, without much in the way of cash reserves, statutory funding or good contacts and patrons to assist them
- Fund projects that alleviate poverty and financial hardship; relieve sickness and poor health; and also support certain 'unpopular' causes. The emphasis is on self-help and community values and assisting individuals and communities in making changes

Fuserna aims to partner with charitable organisations that:

- Enable individuals to reach their full potential despite their social, economic, physiological, and environmental limitations
- Provide opportunities and experiences for individuals that they may not otherwise have access to
- Assist, promote, and encourage sustainable projects that create long-term benefits for disadvantaged local communities and individuals that are intent on improving their environment
- Assist in the treatment and care of individuals suffering from mental or physical illness or those in need of rehabilitation as a result of such illness

In 2012 the foundation had an income of £2.5 million, assets of £2.8 million and made 16 grants totalling £130,000 (2009: £3.5 million).

Grants are usually of between £5,000 and £15,000 each. They can be broken down as follows:

Arts	2	£20,000
Community	1	£5,000
Children/young people	4	£23,000
Disabilities/medical	6	£49,000
Education	1	£2,500
Mental health	2	£23,000

Beneficiaries included: Tandem Befriending Project (£20,000); Immediate Theatre and Lakelands Day Care (£15,000 each); the Child Brain Injury Trust (£12,000); Tiverton Market Centre (£10,000); Tuberous Sclerosis Association (£7,000); My Voice London and West Sussex Association for the Blind (£5,000 each); and Support Line and Bag Books (£2,500 each).

Exclusions

The trust will not normally consider making a grant to any charity that has an income over £3 million.

Applications

Trustees may approach certain charities and ask them to submit a funding request based on Fuserna's interest in their projects.

The trust's website states the following:

> All applications must have a clear sense of objective, how to achieve that objective, and have a very good chance of making a real difference in the field it which it operates. Applications should be submitted in writing and include:
>
> - A full outline of the project for which funding is needed
> - The cost of the project
> - The community affected
> - The benefits and impact of the project intended
> - Other sources of funding secured in relation to the project
> - A full outline of the charity itself, its history, financial position and forecast, as well as its overall strategy
>
> In addition, financial statements, management accounts, tax returns, and any cash-flow statements should also accompany the application.
>
> Applications are reviewed on a quarterly basis throughout the calendar year. Certain applications are shortlisted for the trustees and board members. Following an initial review of the shortlist, those applications approved will go through a further stage of assessment before the trustees and board members make a final determination of the successful applications for that quarter and the amount of any grant awarded.
>
> If a grant application is successful, the Fuserna team requires regular updates as to the progress of the project funded and the charity itself. This will also benefit the project by giving the charity a way to track its own impact.

Information gathered from:
Accounts; Charity Commission record; funder's website.

The G. D. Charitable Trust

Animal welfare, the environment, disability, homelessness

£96,000 (2012)

Beneficial area
Worldwide.

Correspondent: Jonathan Brinsden, Correspondent, Bircham Dyson Bell, 50 Broadway, London SW1H 0BL (tel: 020 7227 7000)

Trustees: George Duffield; Alexander Fitzgibbons; Natasha Duffield.

CC Number: 1096101

Registered in February 2003, the trust aims to support the following charitable areas:
- The relief of animal suffering
- The preservation of the environment
- The promotion of equal opportunities for people who are disabled
- The relief of people who are homeless

In 2012 the trust had assets of £3.5 million, an income of £93,000 and grants to eight organisations were made totalling £96,000.

Beneficiaries were: Blue Marine Foundation (£50,000); Whitley Fund for Nature (£25,000); Save the Children UK (£17,000); SWHP, Naomi House and BDFA (£1,000 each); Hart Wildlife Hospital (£500); and Sarah Greene Breakthrough Tribute Fund (£200).

Exclusions
No grants to individuals.

Applications
In writing to the correspondent.

Information gathered from:
Accounts; Charity Commission record.

G. M. C. Trust

General charitable purposes, organisations benefiting children, young adults and older people are largely supported

£103,000 (2011/12)

Beneficial area
UK, predominantly West Midlands.

Correspondent: Rodney Pitts, Secretary, Flat 4 Fairways, 1240 Warwick Road, Knowle, Solihull B93 9LL (tel: 01564 779971)

Trustees: Bes Cadbury; Sir Adrian Cadbury; M. J. Cadbury; C. E. Fowler-Wright.

CC Number: 288418

According to the trustees' report for 2011/12, 'the object of the charity is to promote and assist charitable work by direct grants. The charity awards grants to other charitable institutions in varying amounts of £200 and £20,000; preferring an area of benefit in the West Midlands.'

In 2011/12 the trust had assets of £2.7 million and an income of £138,000. Grants to 19 organisations totalled £103,000.

Beneficiaries included: Ellern Mede School and UN Women UK (£20,000 each); the Salvation Army and ZANE-Zimbabwe A National Emergency (£10,000 each); King's College-Cambridge, Listening Books and London and North Western Railway Society (£5,000 each); King's Lynn Arts Centre Trust (£2,000); Royal Birmingham Society of Artists (£1,500); Institute of Economic Affairs and Oundle Music Trust (£1,000 each); the Society of King's Economists (£500); and Arden School (£200).

Exclusions
No grants to individuals, or to local or regional appeals outside the West Midlands.

Applications
In writing to the correspondent. The trust largely supports projects which come to the attention of its trustees through their special interests and knowledge. General applications for grants are not encouraged.

Percentage of awards given to new applicants: between 10% and 20%.

Information gathered from:
Accounts; Charity Commission record; further information provided by the funder.

Gableholt Ltd

Jewish causes

£8,000 (2011/12)

Beneficial area
Worldwide.

Correspondent: Etelka Noe, Trustee, 115 Craven Park Road, London N15 6BL (tel: 020 8802 4782)

Trustees: Philip Noe; Etelka Noe; Salomon Noe; Aron Bude.

CC Number: 276250

Set up as a limited company in 1978, the trust gives most of its funds to Jewish institutions, particularly those working in accordance with the Orthodox Jewish faith. The trust gives to many educational institutions, as well as other charitable institutions both in the UK and overseas.

In 2011/12 the trust held assets of £22 million and an income of £831,000. Grants to organisations and individuals totalled just over £8,000.

Unfortunately no information on grants was included with the trust's accounts that were on file at the Charity Commission. In previous years beneficiaries have included: Afula Society; Child Resettlement; Friends of Harim Establishment; Friends of the Sick; Gur Trust; Mengrah Grammar School; Rachel Charitable Trust and Torah Venchased Le'Ezra Vasad.

Applications
In the past this trust has stated that 'in the governors' view, true charitable giving should always be coupled with virtual anonymity' and for this reason they are most reluctant to be a party to any publicity. Along with suggesting that the listed beneficiaries might also want to remain unidentified, they also state that the nature of the giving (to Orthodox Jewish organisations) means the information is unlikely to be of much interest to anyone else. Potential applicants would be strongly advised to take note of these comments.

Information gathered from:
Accounts; Charity Commission record.

The Galanthus Trust

Medical, developing countries, environment, conservation

Around £98,000 (2011/12)

Beneficial area
UK and overseas.

Correspondent: Juliet Rogers, Trustee, Pile Oak Lodge, Donhead St Andrew, Shaftesbury, Dorset SP7 9EH (tel: 0747829138; email: galanthustrust@yahoo.co.uk)

Trustees: S. F. Rogers; Mrs J. M. Rogers.

CC Number: 1103538

This trust was registered with the Charity Commission in April 2004. 'Our aim is to help finance a variety of smaller local projects and good causes, in addition to supporting the work of existing organisations, both in the UK and abroad.

There are several areas of particular interest to the trustees:
- Medical and healthcare needs including research, and patient support (for example, stroke, MS, heart disease and cancer). This might also include help for disability access, support groups or individuals with special needs resulting from illness or injury

- Projects in the third world: health, education, water supplies and sustainable development. Here the intention is to fund ongoing projects being managed by charitable organisations in the developing world
- Environmental and wildlife concerns, including the restoration and maintenance of the UK's natural habitats, such as local woodlands and chalk downland. The trust will also give grants for the creation of new footpaths, particularly those facilitating access for disabled people
- Conservation and preservation projects of historic and cultural value (for example, the National Trust's work at Tyntesfield).

In 2011/12 the trust had an income of £4,500 and a total expenditure of £98,000. Previously grants had been distributed between three categories: medical and healthcare, projects in the third world and environment and welfare.

Applications

In writing to the correspondent. 'All requests for grants are considered carefully by the trustees. The trustees decide whether to donate and the amount to donate.'

Percentage of awards given to new applicants: less than 10%.

Common applicant mistakes

'Not being aware of criterion, e.g. we do not support educational projects but they apply.'

Information gathered from:

Accounts; Charity Commission record; further information provided by the funder.

The Gale Family Charity Trust

General charitable purposes with preference to churches and church ministries, as well as community life

£196,000 (2011/12)

Beneficial area

UK, mainly Bedfordshire.

Correspondent: Alistair Law, Administrator, Northwood House, 138 Bromham Road, Bedford MK40 2QW (tel: 01234 354508; fax: 01234 349588; email: alistair.law@garnerassociates.co.uk)

Trustees: Anthony Ormerod; Gary Payne; John Tyley; Doreen Watson; Warwick Browning; Russell Beard; David Fletcher; Gerry Garner.

CC Number: 289212

The trust was founded in 1984 by Horace and Marjorie Gale. The trust's main aim is to apply funds to charitable causes both locally and nationally. Funds are also donated to churches to further their work. According to the trustees' report for 2011/12, the trust gives support in three areas:

- For churches and church ministries, with emphasis on Bunyan Meeting Free Church in Bedford and the ministries of the Baptist Union in England and Wales
- Donations to charities and organisations active in the community life of Bedford and Bedfordshire
- Donations to UK charities and organisations active in community life

In 2011/12 the trust had assets of £5.4 million and an income of £117,000. Grants were made totalling £196,000.

There were 58 grants made to organisations, which included payments to: Bedford Day Care Centre (£20,000); Bedford Modern School (£10,000); Cecil Higgins Arts Gallery, St John's Hospice – Moggerhanger and Bedford Concern for the Homeless and Rootless – Prebend Street Day Centre (£5,000 each); Bedford Guild House and Bedford and District Cerebral Palsy Society (£3,000 each); Soundabout and Douglas Bader Foundation (£2,000 each); Action for Sick Children, Dream Holidays and Marie Curie Cancer Care (£1,000 each); and War Memorials Trust (£500).

A further 20 grants were made to churches, including those made to: Bunyan Meeting Free Church (£17,000); St Paul's Church – Bedford (£14,000); Central Baptist Association (£10,000); Bunyan Trustees (£5,000); Breachwood Green Baptist Church, Elstow Bunyan Christian Fellowship and LCET (£2,000 each); and St Peter's Church – Bedford, Cockayne Baptist Church and St Owen's Church – Bromham (£1,000 each).

Exclusions

Grants are rarely given to individuals.

Applications

In writing to the correspondent.

Percentage of awards given to new applicants: between 30% and 40%.

Common applicant mistakes

'Not in the correct geographical area.'

Information gathered from:

Accounts; Charity Commission record; further information provided by the funder.

Gamlen Charitable Trust

Legal education, the relief of poverty and the advancement of education through music and the arts

£37,000 (2012/13)

Beneficial area

UK.

Correspondent: Julian Chadwick, Trustee, c/o Thomas Eggar LLP, Newbury House, 20 Kings Road West, Newbury, Berkshire RG14 5XR (tel: 01635 571000)

Trustees: Julian Chadwick; Rodney Stubblefield; Paul Eaton.

CC Number: 327977

The Gamlen Charitable Trust was established in 1988 by Miss Catherine Gamlen. According to the trustees' report for 2012/13, the objectives of the trust are as follows:

- Advancement and promotion of legal education and in particular to provide for the financial assistance of law students and trainee solicitors whether in further education or training. This object includes the creation of scholarships, bursaries and prizes for law students and trainee solicitors
- To carry out such charitable purposes for the relief of poverty or the advancement of education as the trustees from time to time decide, in particular promotion of education through music and arts.

During 2012/13, the trust had assets of £1.7 million, and an income of £47,000. Grants to four organisations totalled £37,000.

Beneficiaries were: Christ Church – Law Fellowship (£30,000); Newbury Spring Festival and Grange Park Opera (£3,000 each); and Orpheus Foundation (£1,000).

Exclusions

In accordance with charitable objectives, we can surmise that the trust funds exclusively to law students and trainee solicitors, as well as to organisations that aim to relieve poverty and advance education through music and the arts.

Applications

The trust does not accept unsolicited applications.

Information gathered from:

Accounts; Charity Commission record.

The Gamma Trust

General charitable purposes- Christian, health, disability, arts, medical research

About £76,000 (2011/12)

Beneficial area

UK, with preference to Scotland.

Correspondent: Fiona Tedford, Trust Team Leader, c/o Mazars CYB Services Ltd, 90 St Vincent Street, Glasgow G2 5UB (tel: 01412 254953; email: glasgowtrustteam@mazars.co.uk)

Trustee: Clydesdale Bank plc.

SC Number: SC004330

The trust's objects, as stated in the trustees' report for 2011/12, are as follows:

- To support Christian churches of any denomination, including Christian missionary organisations
- To support organisations that alleviate suffering arising from childbirth; mental and physical disability; and alcohol or drug addiction
- To aid individuals through further education with grants and bursaries
- To donate to organisations that study, preserve or publically display Scottish architecture, art, history, customs, buildings or monuments
- To support organisations which promote disaster relief and help refugees
- To support scientific and medical research
- To especially promote assistance to Scottish organisations and individuals

In 2011/12 the trust had assets of £1.5 million, an income of £86,000 and made grants totalling £76,000 to 40 organisations.

Previous beneficiaries have included British Red Cross, British Heart Foundation, Cancer Research Campaign and Erskine Hospital.

Applications

In writing to the correspondent for consideration quarterly.

Information gathered from:

Accounts; OSCR record.

Garrick Charitable Trust

Theatre, music, literature, dance

£96,000 (2011/12)

Beneficial area

UK.

Correspondent: Fiona Murray, Trust Administrator, Garrick Club, 15 Garrick Street, London WC2E 9AY (tel: 020 7395 4136; email: michaelkb@garrickclub.co.uk; website: www.garrickclub.co.uk)

Trustees: David Sigall; Sir Stephen Waley-Cohen; Roger Braban; Stephen Aris; Ion Trewin.

CC Number: 1071279

The Garrick Charitable Trust aims to encourage theatre, music, literature and dance. According to the trust's website at the time of writing (October 2013):

> Named after the great actor-manager David Garrick, the Garrick Club in London has an outstanding theatrical and artistic background. It was founded in 1831 and occupies a building in Garrick Street on the edge of Covent Garden, in the heart of London's theatreland. The trust is independent of the club. We focus on helping professional organisations in need of financial support. We have a particular interest in helping actors, directors, writers, musicians, composers and choreographers in the early stages of their careers.

Grants are usually for amounts of £2,500, only in exceptional circumstances will they exceed £10,000.

In 2011/12 the trust had assets of £4.9 million, which generated an income of £168,000. Grants were made to 33 organisations totalling £96,000 and were broken down as follows:

Music	50%	£48,000
Theatre	27%	£26,500
Literature	15%	£14,000
Dance	8%	£7,500

Beneficiaries included: Alternative Theatre Company, Africa 95, Birmingham Royal Ballet and Buxton Festival (£5,000 each); Ledbury Petry Festival (£4,000); Arches Theatre, Charleston Trust, Darlington International Summer School and Northern Ballet (£2,500 each); and Brockley Jack Theatre (£1,000).

Exclusions

Drama training or academic studies amateur productions projects outside the UK.

Applications

Initial applications are reviewed by the trustees who decide whether or not to send an application form. Trustees meet quarterly.

The trust's website states:

> First, please write us a short letter – preferably one, but not more than two, pages, perhaps with a publicity flyer.
>
> In your letter please tell us: about your organisation and the project you want us to support how much money you are asking for how your organisation will benefit from a grant what will happen if you do not receive a grant. Occasionally we are able to make an immediate grant, but normally we will then send you a form asking for more detailed information about your request and your organisation.
>
> The form also asks you for your most recent accounts and income, including earnings and support in kind. You may wish to include CVs of the people involved in the project, reviews of previous productions or publicity flyers.

Percentage of awards given to new applicants: 50%.

Common applicant mistakes

'Not checking our objectives.'

Information gathered from:

Accounts; Charity Commission record; further information provided by the funder; funder's website.

Garthgwynion Charities

Medical research, community projects, general

£78,000 (2011/12)

Beneficial area

Primarily the parishes of Isygarreg and Uwchygarreg at Machynlleth, Powys.

Correspondent: Mrs June Baker, 13 Osborne Close, Feltham, Hounslow, London TW13 6SR (tel: 020 8890 0469)

Trustees: Eleanor R. Lambert; David Owen; Edward Owen.

CC Number: 229334

The trust supports organisations benefiting people with various diseases and medical conditions. Support is also given to at risk groups, and people who are disadvantaged by poverty or socially isolated.

In 2011/12 the charities had assets of £1.4 million and an income of £56,000. Grants were made to 12 organisations totalling £78,000, with beneficiaries including Machynlleth Tabernacle Trust, Harrow School, Powys Eisteddfod, the Tannery Appeal and Gonville and Caius College, Cambridge.

Applications

In writing to the correspondent.

Information gathered from:

Accounts; Charity Commission record.

Garvan Ltd

Jewish

£28,000 (2011/12)

Beneficial area

UK.

Correspondent: The Trustees, Flat 9, Windsor Court, Golders Green Road, London NW11 9PP

Trustees: Ahron Ebert; Lilly Ebert.

CC Number: 286110

The objectives of this charity are the advancement of religion in accordance with the Orthodox Jewish faith and the relief of poverty.

In 2011/12 the trust had assets of £1.5 million and an income of £183,000. It gave grants totalling £28,000. No further information was available.

Applications

In writing to the correspondent.

Information gathered from:

Accounts; Charity Commission record.

The Robert Gavron Charitable Trust

Health and welfare, prisons and prison reform, arts and arts education, education and social policy and research

£528,000 (2011/12)

Beneficial area

Mainly UK.

Correspondent: Ms Yvette Dear, Secretary, 44 Eagle Street, London WC1R 4FS (tel: 020 7400 4300)

Trustees: Sarah Gavron; Charles Corman; Lord Robert Gavron; Jessica Gavron; Lady Katharine Gavron.

CC Number: 268535

According to the trustees' report for 2011/12, the trust continued to support a wide range of charitable causes. The principal fields of interest continue to be the arts, education, social policy and research and charities for the disabled. The trust concentrated on the following areas:

- Health and welfare
- Human rights, legal and prison reform
- Arts and arts education
- Sports and education
- Social policy and research
- Community projects

> In many cases the trustees prefer to make grants to organisations whose work they personally know and admire. This does not, however, mean that charities unknown to the trustees personally do not receive grants. One freelance adviser visits and reports on new applicants to the trust and his reports are taken into account by the trustees when they make their decisions. This leads to a number of grants to new organisations during each financial year. These include small charities working in areas which cannot easily raise funds and which are without the resources themselves for professional fund raising. Small charities supported during the year include those working in prisons and with ex-offenders, and those working with adults and children with disabilities. The trust has also continued to help previously funded small charities which come into these categories.

In 2011/12 the trust had assets of £8 million and an income of £708,000. Grants were made totalling £528,000.

Major beneficiaries during the year were: Arab Israel Children's Tennis Charity (£59,500); High Pay Unit and Tricycle Theatre (£50,000 each); Action on Addiction (£30,000); Reprieve (£29,000); House of Illustration (£17,000); Redlands Primary School (£12,500); National Film and TV School (£10,000); Charleston Trust and Mudchute Association (£5,000 each); and Arts for All (£3,000).

Smaller grants of less than £3,000 totalled £65,000.

Exclusions

The trust does not give donations to individuals.

Applications

The trustees' report for 2011/12 states the following:

> At present the trust is fully committed to its existing areas of interest. Furthermore, the trustees are unlikely to be able to consider further applications for funding in the current financial climate (written in November 2012).

Information gathered from:

Accounts; Charity Commission record.

Jacqueline and Michael Gee Charitable Trust

Health, arts, education, Jewish causes

£94,000 (2011/12)

Beneficial area

UK and overseas.

Correspondent: Michael Gee, Trustee, Flat 27 Berkeley House, 15 Hay Hill, London W1J 8NS (tel: 020 7493 1904)

Trustees: Michael Gee; Jacqueline Gee.

CC Number: 1062566

The Jacqueline and Michael Gee Charitable Trust was established in 1997. According to the trustees' report for 2011/12, 'the trust makes charitable contributions for wide charitable purposes at the discretion of the trustees almost exclusively to benefit health, education and training, arts and culture, overseas aid and general charitable purposes'.

In 2011/12 the trust had assets of £119,000 and an income of £156,000 made up mostly from donations. Grants were made to 49 organisations totalling £94,000 and were distributed as follows:

General donations and overseas aid	9	£29,000
Arts and culture	16	£29,000
Medical, health and sickness	13	£19,000
Education and training	11	£17,000

Beneficiaries included: Yad Vashem – UK Foundation (£10,000); United Synagogue (£6,800); Youth Aliyah – Child Rescue, SJP Charity Trust Ltd, Philharmonia Chorus and Nightingale Hammerson (£5,000 each); Child Resettlement Trust Fund and Garsington Opera Ltd (£3,300 each); Israel Philharmonic Orchestra Foundation, Jewish Child's Day and Kisharon (£2,000 each); Lifelites and the Churchill Centre (£1,000 each); Royal Brompton and Harefield Hospital Charitable Fund and Weizmann Institute Foundation (£500 each); and West London Synagogue Charitable Fund and Musicworks (£200 each).

Applications

In writing to the correspondent.

Information gathered from:

Accounts; Charity Commission record.

Sir Robert Geffery's Almshouse Trust

Education for children and young people, housing, disability, performing arts, family

£136,000 (2011/12)

Beneficial area

UK.

Correspondent: The Charities Administrator, Ironmongers' Hall, Barbican, London EC2Y 8AA (tel: 020 7776 2311; email: helen@ironhall.co.uk; website: www.ironhall.co.uk)

Trustee: The Worshipful Company of Ironmongers.

CC Number: 219153

The trust's website states:

> Sir Robert Geffery was twice Master of the Company and was Lord Mayor of London in 1685. Born in the village of Landrake in Cornwall, he died in London in 1704 having made his fortune in overseas trade. He left a substantial endowment for almshouses which were

built in Shoreditch, east London. These were sold in 1910 to London County Council and now house the Geffrey Museum. The Company then built new almshouses at Mottingham in Kent, which in turn were sold, in 1972, to the Greater London Council.

Today the Trust owns two almshouses in Hampshire, one at Hook built in 1976 and enlarged in 1987 and one at Basingstoke which was opened in 1984. These provide sheltered housing for 125 retired people of limited means. There are resident Wardens at both Homes, with the overall management carried out from Ironmongers' Hall.

Grants are made by the Trust for relief in need, focusing on educational projects for children and young people in disadvantaged areas. A bursary is given to support a student at the City of London School for Girls.

In 2011/12 the almshouse trust had assets of £12 million and an income of £933,000. Grants totalling £136,000 were made to 18 organisations.

Beneficiaries included: MakeBelieve Arts (£21,000); Lyric Hammersmith (£17,000); The Art Room (£14,000); St Vincent's Family Project (£10,000); Royal Academy of Arts (£7,000); North East Theatre Trust (£5,500); and the London Federation of OCA's (£250).

Exclusions

Applications for grants to individuals are accepted only from registered social workers or other agencies, not directly from individuals.

Applications

In writing to the correspondent.

Information gathered from:

Accounts; Charity Commission record; funder's website.

The Generations Foundation

Health, family support, environmental protection and conservation, sports, education and leadership, hospitals, hospices, overseas aid, children, people with disabilities

Around £214,000 (2011/12)

Beneficial area

UK, Merton and overseas.

Correspondent: Rohini Finch, Trustee, 36 Marryat Road, Wimbledon, London SW19 5BD (tel: 020 8946 7760; email: rfinch@rfinch.plus.com; website: www.generationsct.co.uk)

Trustees: Robert Finch, Stephen Finch; Rohini Finch.

CC Number: 1110565

The trust's website provides a useful overview of its activities:

> Generations Charitable Trust was set up in July 2005 by the Finch Family. The trust is funded by the family and aims to provide a better quality of life for children who need it the most; those who are disabled, disadvantaged, or struggle with ill health. The trust supports local causes in the Borough of Merton where the family is resident and also works abroad in developing countries. The trust also supports projects for environmental protection and conservation; the central aim being to leave a gift for future generations.

In 2011/12 the foundation had assets of £228,000 and an income of £437,500. Grants totalled £214,000.

Awards ranging from £5,000 to £31,000 were made to 17 organisations, including: Right to Dream (£16,000); Whizz-Kidz (£13,000); Billy Riordan Memorial Trust, Home Start Merton IT4CH and Mothers to Mothers UK (£10,000 each); Save the Children (£6,000); and Cherished Memories, FoCT and Rosemary Foundation (£5,000 each).

Further grants of less than £5,000 were made totalling £30,000.

Applications

In writing to the correspondent.

Percentage of awards given to new applicants: between 40% and 50%.

Common applicant mistakes

'Cold calling/posting.'

Information gathered from:

Accounts; Charity Commission record; further information provided by the funder; funder's website.

The Gibbs Charitable Trust

Methodism, international, arts

£97,000 (2011/12)

Beneficial area

UK with a preference for the south of England and worldwide.

Correspondent: Dr James M. Gibbs, Trustee, 8 Victoria Square, Clifton, Bristol BS8 4ET (email: jamesgibbs@btinternet.com; website: www.gibbstrust.org.uk)

Trustees: John N. Gibbs, Chair; James Gibbs; Andrew Gibbs; Celia Gibbs; Elizabeth Gibbs; Jessica Gibbs; John E. Gibbs; Juliet Gibbs; Patience Gibbs; Rebecca Gibbs; William Gibbs; James D. Gibbs.

CC Number: 207997

The trust supports Methodist churches and organisations, other Christian causes (especially those of an ecumenical nature) and creative arts, education and social and international causes. It has a slight preference for projects which can be easily visited by the trustees and it also occasionally supports overseas applications.

In 2011/12 the trust had assets of £2 million and an income of £88,000. Grants totalled £97,000, which were broken down as follows:

International	23	£42,500
Social, educational and medical need	13	£18,000
Arts, drama and music	13	£15,000
Other Methodist initiatives	8	£9,500
Other Christian initiatives	8	£7,000
Methodist churches, circuits and districts	8	£4,500

Beneficiaries included: Christian Aid and Langley House Trust (£5,000 each); Nixon Memorial Hospital, Sierra Leone, Oxfam, Practical Action and St Paul's Carnival (£3,000 each); Africa Now, Canon Collins Trust, Hope and Homes for Children, Pentecost Festival 2012 and Welsh National Opera (£2,000 each); Brecon and District Contact Association, Fairbridge, Magnet Resources, Splice Productions and Sound Affairs (£1,000 each); and Daylight Christian Prison Trust, Lees Methodist Church and Llangynidr Village Hall (£500 each).

Exclusions

A large number of requests are received by the trust from churches undertaking improvement, refurbishment and development projects, but only a few of these can be helped. In general, Methodist churches are selected, sometimes those the trustees have particular knowledge of.

No unsolicited applications from individuals and no animal charities.

Applications

The trust has no application forms, although an application cover sheet is available on the trust's website along with a policy and guidelines page. Requests should be made in writing to the correspondent. The trustees meet three times a year, after Christmas, near Easter and late summer. Unsuccessful applicants are not normally notified. The trustees do not encourage telephone enquiries or speculative applications. They also state that they are not impressed by applicants that send a huge amount of paperwork. They suggest a maximum of four sides of A4 including a summary of the budget.

Information gathered from:

Accounts; Charity Commission record; funder's website.

Lady Gibson's Charitable Trust

General, arts, culture

About £25,000 (2011/12)

Beneficial area

Overseas and the UK, with a preference for East Sussex, Kent, Surrey and West Sussex.

Correspondent: Laura Gosling, Administrator, c/o Millbank Financial Services, 4th Floor, Swan House, 17–19 Stratford Place, London W1C 1BQ (tel: 020 7907 2100; email: charity@mfs.co.uk)

Trustee: The Cowdray Trust Ltd.

CC Number: 261442

The trust makes grants to a range of organisations including a number that are arts and culture related. Priority is given to grants for one year or less; grants for up to two years are considered. Grants range from £20 up to around £10,000, but the majority tend to be below £1,000.

In 2011/12 the trust had an income of £21,500 and an expenditure of £25,000.

Previous beneficiaries included: Withyham Parochial Church Council (£11,000); Royal National Theatre (£1,500); Royal Academy Trust (£1,300); Blond McIndoe Centre (£1,000); Bowles (£500); Chichester Cathedral Restoration and Development Trust (£350); Combat Stress (£250); London Philharmonic Orchestra (£120); Southbank Centre (£45); and Friends of Friendless Churches (£20).

Exclusions

No grants to individuals or non-registered charities.

Applications

In writing to the correspondent. Acknowledgements will only be sent if a grant is being made.

Information gathered from:

Accounts; Charity Commission record.

The B. and P. Glasser Charitable Trust

Health, disability, Jewish, welfare

£71,500 (2011/12)

Beneficial area

UK and worldwide.

Correspondent: Julia Strike, Correspondent, Chantrey Vellacott DFK, Russell Square House, 10–12 Russell Square, London WC1B 5LF (tel: 020 7623 9490)

Trustees: James Cullingham; Michael Glasser; John Glasser.

CC Number: 326571

This trust makes grants mainly to health and disability-related charities and Jewish charities, but also for general social-welfare purposes.

In 2011/12 the trust had assets of £2.2 million and an income of £87,000. Grants to 30 organisations totalled £71,500.

Grant beneficiaries included: Practical Action (£8,000); Jewish Care (£6,000); Royal National Institute for the Blind and Sight Savers International (£5,000 each); Ian Rennie Hospice at Home (£2,500); Camphill Village Trust and Jewish Deaf Association (£2,000 each); Help the Aged and Jewish Blind and Disabled (£1,500 each); Action Aid UK, British Red Cross and Fair Trials International (£1,000 each); and Gurkha Welfare Trust and The Samaritans – Chiltern branch (£500 each).

Exclusions

No grants to individuals or students.

Applications

In writing to the correspondent. To keep administrative costs to a minimum the trust is unable to reply to unsuccessful applicants.

Information gathered from:

Accounts; Charity Commission record.

The GNC Trust

General charitable purposes

£134,000 (2012)

Beneficial area

UK, with preferences for Birmingham and Cornwall.

Correspondent: Mrs Paddy Spragg, Correspondent, 41 Sycamore Drive, Hollywood, Birmingham B47 5QX (tel: 07976 848390)

Trustees: G. Cadbury; Jayne Cadbury; P. Richmond-Watson; I. Williamson.

CC Number: 211533

Support is given to general worthy causes as the trustees see fit.

In 2012 the trust had assets of £939,000 and an income of £38,000 and made 77 grants totalling £134,000. Grants were broken down as follows:

Disability	£1,000
Education	£55,000
Medicine	£18,000
The Arts	£50,000

Beneficiaries included: Downing College-Everitt Butterfield Foundation (£50,000); Birmingham Royal Ballet (£44,000); St John of Jerusalem Eye Hospital (£10,000); National Youth Ballet and University of Birmingham (£5,000 each); and Elmhurst School for Dance and Alzheimer's Research Trust (£1,000 each).

61 grants for under £900 totalling £10,000 were also made.

Applications

In writing to the correspondent at any time. There are no application forms and applications are not acknowledged.

Information gathered from:

Accounts; Charity Commission record.

The Sydney and Phyllis Goldberg Memorial Charitable Trust

Medical research, welfare, disability

£102,000 (2011/12)

Beneficial area

UK.

Correspondent: Michael Church, Trustee, Coulthards Mackenzie, 17 Park Street, Camberley, Surrey GU15 3PQ (tel: 01276 65470)

Trustees: Christopher Pexton; Howard Vowles; Michael Church.

CC Number: 291835

According to the trustees' report for 2011/12, 'the objects of the trust are to perpetuate the memory of Sydney Goldberg and his wife Phyllis by using the funds available to it for charitable purposes'. The trust particularly focuses on charitable causes that deal with medical research, welfare and disability.

The income for the trust comes from its investments which are mainly held in Syona Investments Ltd. Phyllis Goldberg initially bequeathed her shareholding in Syona Investments Ltd to the trust and since then the trust has bought the balance of the shares.

In 2011/12 the trust had assets of £3.3 million with an income of £107,000 with grants totalling £102,000.

Beneficiaries included: Children with Special Needs Foundation, Life Centre, Heart 2 Heart and the British Stammering Association (£12,000 each); and the Isaac Goldberg Charity Trust (£6,000).

Applications

In writing to the correspondent. Telephone requests are not appreciated. Applicants are advised to apply towards the end of the calendar year.

According to the trustees' report for 2011/12:

> The trust has established its grant making policy to achieve its objects for the public benefit by inviting applications from

existing and previous donee charities and charitable causes favoured by Sydney and Phyllis Goldberg and by advertising the objectives in the *Directory of Grant Making Trusts*.

The Charity requests a copy of the final reports on all research for which grants are made.

Information gathered from:

Accounts; Charity Commission record.

Golden Charitable Trust

Preservation, conservation, medical research

£298,000 (2012/13)

Beneficial area

UK with a preference for West Sussex.

Correspondent: Lewis Golden, Correspondent, Little Leith Gate, Angel Street, Petworth GU28 0BG (tel: 01798 342434)

Trustees: Sara Solnick; Jeremy Solnick.

CC Number: 263916

The Golden Charitable Trust was established in 1972 by Jacqueline Golden. The trust has general charitable purposes.

The trust appears to have a preference in its grantmaking for organisations in West Sussex in the field of the preservation and conservation of historic articles and materials; church restoration and medical research charities.

In 2012/13 the trust had an income of £35,000 and assets of £864,000. Grants totalling £298,000 were made to 20 organisations.

Beneficiaries included: The London Library (£250,000); the Friends of St Mary's Petworth (£22,000); Westminster Synagogue (£7,000); Friends of Pallant House Gallery and the Langdon Foundation (£2,000 each); the Royal Star and Garter Homes and the Royal School of Needlework (£1,000 each); the Wordsworth Trust, Petworth Film House and the Dermatitis and Allied Diseases Research Trust (£500 each); the National Trust and the Parachute Regimental Association (£100 each); and St Wilfred's Hospice (£50).

Applications

In writing to the correspondent.

Information gathered from:

Accounts; Charity Commission record.

The Jack Goldhill Charitable Trust

Jewish, general

£25,000 (2011)

Beneficial area

UK.

Correspondent: Michael Louis Goldhill, Trustee, 85 Kensington Heights, Campden Hill Road, London W8 7BD (tel: 020 7727 4326)

Trustees: Grete Goldhill; Michael Louis Goldhill; Anthony Frederick Abrahams.

CC Number: 267018

In 2011 the trust had assets of £967,000 and an income of £100,000. Grants were made totalling £147,000, however no details of beneficiaries were provided in the trust's accounts. These were the latest accounts available at the time of writing (November 2013).

Previous beneficiaries have included: CST, City and Guilds of London School of Art, Jack Goldhill Award Fund, JNF Charitable Trust, Jewish Care, Joint Jewish Charitable Trust, Nightingale House, Royal Academy of Arts, Royal London Hospital, Tate Gallery, Tricycle Theatre Co., West London Synagogue and Atlantic College.

Exclusions

No support for individuals or new applications.

Applications

The trustees have a restricted list of charities to which they are committed and no unsolicited applications can be considered.

Information gathered from:

Accounts; Charity Commission record.

The Golsoncott Foundation

The arts

£56,000 (2011/12)

Beneficial area

UK.

Correspondent: Hal Curtlandt Bishop, Administrator, 53 St Leonard's Rd, Exeter EX2 4LS (tel: 01392 252855; email: golsoncott@btinternet.com; website: www.golsoncott.org.uk)

Trustees: Josephine Lively, Chair; Penelope Lively; Stephen Wick; Dr Harriet Harvey Wood.

CC Number: 1070885

The trust states its objects as follows: 'to promote, maintain, improve and advance the education of the public in the arts generally and in particular the fine arts and music. The fostering of the practice and appreciation of the arts, especially amongst young people and new audiences, is a further specific objective.

'Grants vary according to context and are not subject to an inflexible limit, but they are unlikely to exceed £5,000 and are normally given on a non-recurrent basis.'

In 2011/12 the foundation had assets of £1.8 million and an income of £69,000. Grants to 54 organisations totalled £56,000 and ranged between £100 and £4,500.

Beneficiaries included: Somerset Museums (£4,500); Rodhuish Parochial Church Council (£4,000); National Children's Orchestra (£3,000); Marian Concert and Poetry Book Society (£2,000 each); National Theatre and Shakespeare Schools (£1,000 each); Oxford Lieder (£750); Arts in Hanworth, Forestage Theatre and Live Music Now (£500 each); and Public Catalogue Foundation (£140).

Exclusions

No grants to individuals.

Applications

The trustees meet quarterly to consider applications, in February, May, August and November. Applications, made by hard copy with an email contact address, should be sent to the correspondent by the end of the month preceding the month of the trustees' meeting. They should include the following:

- A clear and concise statement of the project, whether the award sought will be for the whole project or a component part. Is the applicant organisation of charitable status?
- Evidence that there is a clear benefit to the public, i.e. does the project conform with the declared object of the trust
- The amount requested should be specified, or a band indicated. Is this the only source of funding being sought? All other sources of funding should be indicated, including those that have refused funding
- If the grant requested is part of the match-funding required by the Heritage Lottery Foundation (HLF) following an award, state the amount of that award and the percentage of match-funding required by the HLF and the completion date
- Wherever possible an annual report and accounts should accompany the application, as may other supporting information deemed relevant

Second or further applications will not be considered until a minimum of 12 months has elapsed since determination of the previous application, whether successful or not.

Percentage of awards given to new applicants: between 30% and 40%.

Common applicant mistakes

'Not reading or following the guidelines; unrealistic aspirations.'

Information gathered from:

Accounts; Charity Commission record; further information provided by the funder; funder's website.

Golubovich Foundation

Arts

£0 (2011/12)

Beneficial area

UK.

Correspondent: Tim Lewin, c/o MVL Business Services, 15a High Street, Battle, East Sussex TN33 0AE (tel: 01424 830723; email: tim.lewin@btinternet.com)

Trustees: Alexei Golubovich; Olga Mirimskaya; Andrey Lisyanski; Arkadiy Golubovich.

CC Number: 1113965

Set up in 2006, the foundation seeks to foster relationships between Russia and the UK in the area of performing arts. This is done mainly through encouraging established UK arts centres to identify and develop the talents of young Russian nationals.

In 2011/12 the foundation had assets of £8,300 and an income of £28,000. There were no payments to beneficiary organisations but £28,000 was spent on governance costs.

Although there were no grants awarded this year, (2011/12), the trustees are actively fundraising and funds could be available again in future years.

Previous beneficiaries have included: Trinity College of Music London (£75,000); and University of the Arts London (£65,000).

Applications

In writing to the correspondent.

Information gathered from:

Accounts; Charity Commission record.

Nicholas and Judith Goodison's Charitable Settlement

Arts, arts education

£52,500 (2012/13)

Beneficial area

UK.

Correspondent: Sir Nicholas Goodison, Trustee, PO Box 2512, London W1A 5ZP

Trustees: Sir Nicholas Goodison; Judith Goodison; Katharine Goodison.

CC Number: 1004124

The trust supports registered charities in the field of the arts and arts education. Grants are often given to institutions in instalments over several years towards capital projects.

In 2012/13 the trust had assets of £1.4 million and an income of £61,000. Grants were made to 28 organisations totalling £53,000. Management and administration expenses for the year were very low at just £900.

Beneficiaries included: Victoria and Albert Museum (£10,000); Courtauld Institute (£6,000); English National Opera, Academy of Ancient Music and Handel House (£2,500 each); Crafts Council (£1,500); Attingham Trust and Public Catalogue Foundation (£1,000 each); Royal Society of Arts and Chippendale Society (£500 each); and Venice in Peril (£200).

Exclusions

No grants to individuals.

Applications

The trust states that it cannot respond to unsolicited applications.

Percentage of awards given to new applicants: between 10% and 20%.

Information gathered from:

Accounts; Charity Commission record; further information provided by the funder.

The Gough Charitable Trust

General charitable purposes

Around £32,000 (2011/12)

Beneficial area

UK.

Correspondent: The Trustees, Lloyds Private Banking Ltd, Trust Centre, The Clock House, 22–26 Ock Street, Abingdon Oxon OX14 5SW (tel: 01235 232712)

Trustee: Lloyds TSB. Private Banking.

CC Number: 262355

Income is paid to various charities as advised by the Right Honourable Sir Shane Hugh Maryon Fifth Viscount Gough. In 2011/12 the trust had an income of £34,000 and assets of £34,000. Grants totalled £32,000. A list of beneficiaries was included but grant amounts were not provided. 13 organisations were provided with grants.

Beneficiaries included: Herbert Old Wellington; the Lifeboat Service Memorial Book Trust; Royal Ballet School Trust; Trinity Hospice; and Irish Guards Lieutenant Colonels Fund.

Applications

In writing to the correspondent.

Information gathered from:

Accounts; Charity Commission record.

The Gould Charitable Trust

Education and training, with preference towards Jewish organisations and causes

£66,000 (2011/12)

Beneficial area

Worldwide.

Correspondent: S. Gould, Trustee, Cervantes, Pinner Hill, Pinner HA5 3XU (tel: 020 8868 2700)

Trustees: Jean Gould; Simon Gould; Sidney Gould; Lawrence Gould; Matthew Gould.

CC Number: 1035453

The trust was established in 1993 between Sidney Gould, Lawrence Gould, Simon Gould and Matthew Gould. According to the trustees' report for 2011/12, 'the objects of the trust are to provide general education and training through charitable or voluntary bodies'.

In 2011/12 the trust had assets of £921,000 and an income of £25,000. Grants were made totalling £66,000.

Beneficiaries included: Kibbutz Eshbal (£20,000); UJIA (£18,000); One to One (£7,000); World Jewish Relief (£3,000); NSPCC and Dignity in Dying (£1,000 each); Youth at Risk and Notting Hill Housing (£200 each); Watford New Hope Trust and Latitude Global Volunteers (£100 each); and Orchestra of Age Enlightenment and National Osteoporosis (£50 each).

Exclusions

No support for non-registered charities. No grants to individuals.

Applications

In writing to the correspondent.

Information gathered from:

Accounts; Charity Commission record.

The Grahame Charitable Foundation Ltd

Jewish

£212,000 (2012)

Beneficial area

UK and worldwide.

Correspondent: Miki Shaw, Secretary, 5 Spencer Walk, Hampstead High Street, London NW3 1QZ (tel: 020 7794 5281)

Trustees: Alan Grahame; J. M. Greenwood.

CC Number: 1102332

The charity's objects and its principal activities are that of the advancement of education, religion and the relief of poverty anywhere in the world. The trustees support mainly Jewish causes.

In 2012 the foundation had assets of £1 million and an income of £230,000. Grants were made to nine organisations totalling £212,000. Beneficiaries included: Avraham Bezalel Foundation and Jerusalem College of Technology (£25,000 each); Emunah – The Child Resettlement Fund (£20,000); Beis Rizhin Trust and Yad Rachel (£10,000 each); and Beit Haknesset Caesarea (£7,500).

Exclusions

No grants to individuals.

Applications

The trustees allocate funds on a long-term basis and therefore have none available for other applicants.

Information gathered from:

Accounts; Charity Commission record.

Grand Charitable Trust of the Order of Women Freemasons

General in the UK and overseas

£215,000 to non-masonic organisations (2011/12)

Beneficial area

UK and overseas.

Correspondent: The Trustees, 27 Pembridge Gardens, London W2 4EF (tel: 020 7229 2368; website: www.owf.org.uk)

Trustees: Zuzanka Penn; Jean Masters; Sylvia Major; Ms H. Maldrett; Dr Iris Boggia-Black; Beryl Daniels.

CC Number: 1059151

The charity's objectives are the general charitable purposes which the trustees shall in their absolute discretion think fit to support or establish throughout England and Wales. These include:

- Medical – assistance in getting operations or treatment carried out privately to relieve pain or suffering where there is a long wait for NHS treatment
- Relief of poverty – assistance with costly utility bills where hardship has occurred
- Accommodation – help given especially where floods or serious fires have occurred
- Children, elderly and disabled – donations mainly to hospitals, hospital appeals and help with mobility appliances
- Grants to individuals/organisations – sponsorship always considered and special appeals
- Other charities and voluntary bodies – donations given when applications are made. The amount is at the trustees' discretion

In 2011/12 the trust had assets of £702,000, an income of £234,000 and made grants totalling £268,000. During the year the trust has gifted £215,000 to outside charities including a grant of £150,000 to Breast Cancer Campaign Tissue Bank Appeal.

Specific gifts from members have also enabled the trust to make donations to the Adelaide Litten Charitable Trust which was set up to assist with the running of two properties and also to give general assistance to Order members. These donations totalled £53,000.

Applications

In writing to the correspondent. Applications should be submitted by the end of July each year for consideration by the trustees.

Information gathered from:

Accounts; Charity Commission record; funder's website.

The Grand Order of Water Rats' Charities Fund

General charitable purposes with a preference towards drama and theatre, overseas aid and medical and hospital equipment

£51,500 (2012)

Beneficial area

Worldwide.

Correspondent: Mike Martin, Correspondent, 328 Gray's Inn Road, London WC1X 8BZ (tel: 020 7278 3248; email: charities@gowr.net; website: www.gowr.net)

Trustees: Wyn Calvin; Roy Hudd; Kaplan Kaye; Keith Simmons; Chas McDevitt.

CC Number: 292201

The trust was established in 1985. The objects of the charity are as follows:

- To relieve or assist in the relief of poor or necessitous members of the Grand Order of Water Rats and their widows and also such persons engaged or formerly engaged as theatrical entertainers and their dependents
- To support or aid any other charitable organisation connected with or calculated to benefit theatrical entertainers and their dependents
- To relieve or assist in the relief of distress, poverty or famine in any part of the world
- To relieve or assist in the relief of sickness amongst individuals in particular, by the provision of equipment in hospitals and to outpatients
- To promote other charitable purposes in particular, by making donations to national fundraising appeals

In 2012, the trust had an income of £105,000 and assets of £1.7 million. Charitable activities amounted to £51,000.

Previous grants included those made to Actors Church Union, British Legion Wales, Bud Flanagan Leukaemia Fund, Cause for Hope, Northwick Park Hospital and Queen Elizabeth Hospital for Children.

Exclusions

No grants to students. No grants to cover debts.

Applications

In writing to the correspondent.

According to the trustees' report for 2012:

> The trustees require written requests for assistance. Grants, both one-off and regular, can be made to members of the theatrical profession and their dependents. To qualify, a professional must have been a performer for a minimum of seven years in the theatrical profession. The trustees do not make grants for student's fees or for education. Nor do they make grants to cover debts incurred by credit card usage, bank loans or overdrafts or for local or national taxes. From time to time the trustees may also grant a one-off payment to organisations or individuals who the trustees feel are in need of assistance.

Information gathered from:

Accounts; Charity Commission record; funder's website.

The Green Hall Foundation (formerly known as the Constance Green Foundation)

Social welfare, medicine, health, general charitable purposes

£170,000 (2011/12)

Beneficial area

Mainly England, with some preference for West Yorkshire; overseas.

Correspondent: S. Hall, Correspondent, Centenary House, La Grande Route De St, Pierre, St Peter, Jersey JE3 7AY (tel: 01534 487757; email: greenhallfoundation@fcmtrust.com)

Trustees: Michael Collinson; Margaret Hall; Sue Collinson; Nigel Hall; Peter Morgan.

CC Number: 270775

The foundation makes grants mainly in the fields of social welfare and medicine. There is a special emphasis on the needs of young people and people who are mentally or physically disabled. Preference is given to making grants to assist in funding special projects being undertaken by charities rather than grants to supplement funds used for general purposes.

In 2011/12 the foundation had assets of £7.7 million and an income of £338,000. Grants were made to 69 organisations totalling £170,000. A further breakdown of grants by category and expenditure can be seen as follow:

Medical and social care	34%	£57,000
Disabled and aged	22%	£38,000
Homeless	6%	£10,500
Children and young persons	29%	£50,000
Church and community projects	9%	£14,500

Beneficiaries included: Marie Curie Cancer Care (£10,000); St Martin-in-the-Fields (£7,500); Blond McIndoe Research Foundation, Brathay Trust and Disability Action Yorkshire (£5,000 each); Kidz Club Coventry, Commonwealth Society for the Blind and Cerebra (£2,000 each); and Human Relief, Living Water Satisfies and Malaika Kids UK (£1,000 each).

Exclusions

Organisations only.

Applications

At any time in writing to the correspondent (no special form of application required). Applications should include clear details of the need the intended project is designed to meet, plus an outline budget.

According to the trustees' report for 2011/12:

> Applications for grants should be submitted to the administrator. A grant application form was implemented in the year financial year 2011/12 and all applicants should complete the prescribed application form with clear details of the need the intended project is designed to meet plus an outline budget.

Percentage of awards given to new applicants: between 20% and 30%.

Common applicant mistakes

'Not being submitted on the official application form. Not being succinct enough in explaining reason for application.'

Information gathered from:

Accounts; Charity Commission record; further information provided by the funder.

Philip and Judith Green Trust

Christian and missions

£130,000 to organisations (2011/12)

Beneficial area

UK and Africa.

Correspondent: Philip Green, Trustee, Marchfield, Flowers Hill, Pangbourne, Berkshire RG8 7BD (tel: 01189 845935)

Trustees: Philip Green; Judith Green.

CC Number: 1109933

Registered with the Charity Commission in 2005, the charity's objects are:

> To advance the education and support the development of pupils in underprivileged communities both overseas and in the UK and to advance the Christian faith for the benefit of the public by supporting missionaries and to include the upkeep and provision of places of worship both overseas and in the UK.

In 2011/12 the trust had assets of £131,000 and an income of £74,000. Grants were made totalling £130,000. A further £15,200 was given in grants to missionaries.

Beneficiaries included: Hope Through Action (£51,000); Sentebale (£20,000); Queen Mary's School (£10,000); Greyfriars Church (£8,400); Bible Society (£7,300); Five Talents (£6,200); Rinell Carey Holmquist (£5,300); Alpha International (£5,000); Stewardship Services (£1,700); and Greyfriars Mission (£1,200).

Applications

In writing to the correspondent.

Information gathered from:

Accounts; Charity Commission record.

Mrs H. R. Greene Charitable Settlement

General, particularly at risk-groups, poverty, social isolation

£41,000 (2011/12)

Beneficial area

UK, with a preference for Norfolk and Wistanstow in Shropshire.

Correspondent: N. G. Sparrow, Trust Administrator, Birketts LLP, Kingfisher House, 1 Gilders Way, Norwich, Norfolk NR3 1UB (tel: 01603 232300)

Trustees: Revd J. B. Boston; C. N. E. Boston; J. R. Boston.

CC Number: 1050812

The founder of this trust lived in Wistanstow in Shropshire and the principal trustee was for many years based in Norwich. Both these factors influence the grantmaking of the trust, with several grants given in both the parish of Wistanstow and in the Norfolk area. The trust has an additional preference for supporting organisations helping at-risk groups and people who are disadvantaged by poverty or socially isolated.

In 2011/12 the trust had assets of £2.2 million, an income of £77,000 and made grants totalling £41,000 which included £4,700 in Christmas gifts. This is the only information available for this year.

Previous beneficiaries included: St Michael's Hospital Bartestree, Norfolk and Norwich Clergymen's Widows' and Children's Charity, Brittle Bone Society, Children's Food Fund, Macmillan Cancer Relief, Muscular Dystrophy Group, Orbis, Beeston Church Organ, Friends of Norwich Cathedral, Horsford and St Faith's Scout Group and Litcham Parochial Church Council.

Applications

The trust states that it does not respond to unsolicited applications.

Information gathered from:

Accounts; Charity Commission record.

The Gretna Charitable Trust

General

£166,500 (2011/12)

Beneficial area

UK, with a preference for Hertfordshire and London.

Correspondent: Richard Walduck, Trustee, Imperial London Hotels Ltd, Russell Square, London WC1B 5BB

Trustees: Richard Walduck; Susan Walduck; Alexander Walduck; Colin Bowles.

CC Number: 1020533

This trust gives grants to a wide range of voluntary organisations in the UK, with a preference for Hertfordshire and London.

In 2011/12 the trust had assets of £1.5 million and an income of £99,000. Grants totalling £166,500 were made to 50 organisations, and ranged from £250–£7,500.

There was an unusually large grant of £110,000 made to St Alban's Cathedral – Saints Statues. Other beneficiaries included: Prince William Jubilee Playing Fields (£7,500); St John's Church – Notting Hill (£5,000); Basketmakers' Company (£3,000); Brunel University (£2,000); Age UK (£1,500); British Australia Society, Garden House Hospice, Hertfordshire Scouts and Rosalind Runcie Memorial Fund (£1,000 each); and All Hallows by the Tower, Mensah Recovery Support Agency, St Olave's Church and The Mill Museum (£500 each).

Exclusions

The trust will not provide support to fund salaries or administration costs.

Applications

This trust does not encourage applications.

Information gathered from:

Accounts; Charity Commission record.

The Greys Charitable Trust

General charitable purposes with preference towards church and historical building preservation, the arts

£77,500 (2011/12)

Beneficial area

UK and locally in Oxfordshire.

Correspondent: The Trustees, The Greys Charitable Trust, Flat 4, 2 Inverness Gardens, London W8 4RN (tel: 020 7727 6277)

Trustees: Jacob Brunner; Timothy Brunner.

CC Number: 1103717

Registered in May 2004, this charity's trust fund consists solely of shares in the Brunner Investment Trust plc and cash.

The trust seeks to make donations for the benefit of Church of England preservation projects and other charities dealing with historical preservation, both local to Oxfordshire and nationally, and may also seek to make donations to the arts.

In 2011/12 it had assets of £980,000 and income of £26,000. Grants were made totalling £77,500. 23 grants were made to organisations.

Beneficiaries included: the National Trust- two grants (£12,000); Trinity College- Oxford (£10,000); Indo-Myanmar Conservation (£6,000); Sophie Elwes Trust and George Orwell Memorial Trust (£5,000 each); OHCT and the University Church of St Mary-Oxford (£2,000 each); and Ditchling Museum and British Red Cross (£1,000 each).

Applications

In writing to the correspondent, the trustees usually meet twice a year.

Information gathered from:

Accounts; Charity Commission record.

The Grimmitt Trust

General charitable purposes ranging from community causes to overseas aid

£273,000 (2012/13)

Beneficial area

Worldwide, locally Birmingham and the surrounding areas.

Correspondent: Vanessa Welch, Correspondent, 151B All Saints Road, Kings Heath, Birmingham B14 6AT (tel: 01212 512951; email: admin@grimmitt-trust.org.uk)

Trustees: Patrick Welch; Sue Day; Leon Murray; David Owen; Tim Welch; Jenny Dickins; Sarah Wilkey; Phil Smith.

CC Number: 801975

The Grimmitt Trust was established under a trust deed in 1986. According to the trustees' report for 2012/13:

> The objects of the trust are the encouraging and strengthening of local communities, together with an awareness of national and international responsibilities particularly those within the active interest and geographical areas of the trustees and the Kite Connexion group employees.

In 2012/13 the trust had assets of £7.6 million and an income of £312,000. There were 235 grants made in the year totalling £273,000, broken down as follows:

Community	92	£106,000
Cultural and educational	44	£57,000
Children and youth	59	£57,500
Overseas	3	£20,500
Medical and health	23	£21,000
Elderly	14	£10,500

Support was given to projects where local government funding was withdrawn.

Beneficiaries included: King Edwards School Birmingham Trust, Methodist Relief and Development Fund and the Ackers (£10,000 each); Aston University and the Ironbridge Gorge Museum (£5,000 each); Allens Croft Project, Dream Makers and the Royal Institution (£3,000 each); and Action Centres UK, Prince's Trust and Wellington Methodist Church Centre (£2,500 each).

Smaller grants of less than £2,500 were made to 208 organisations, totalling £158,500.

Exclusions

The trust welcomes applications from charities, charitable organisations and individuals.

Applications

Potential applicants should contact the secretary who will advise on the best way to design a grant request and to ensure that all the necessary information is included. The trustees meet three times a year to consider applications.

Applicants must demonstrate that their project and the grant received is used in line with the trust's objectives.

Information gathered from:

Accounts; Charity Commission record.

The GRP Charitable Trust

Jewish, general

£342,500 (2011/12)

Beneficial area

UK.

Correspondent: The Secretary, 14 St George Street, London W1S 1FE (tel: 020 3207 7000)

Trustee: Kleinwort Benson Trustees Ltd.

CC Number: 255733

The GRP of the title stands for the settlor, George Richard Pinto, a London banker who set up the trust in 1968. Most of the grants are given to Jewish organisations.

In 2011/12 the trust had assets of £5.2 million and an income of £229,000.

A total of £342,500 was given in 30 grants.

Beneficiaries included: Oxford Centre for Hebrew and Jewish Studies (£102,000); The Wallace Collection (£75,000); Jerusalem Foundation (£31,000); Traditional Alternatives Foundation (£25,000); Magen David Adom – UK and United Jewish Israel Appeal (£10,000 each); Anglo Jewish Association and Trinity College (£5,000 each); Thames Diamond Jubilee (£3,000); Alexandra Wylie Tower Foundation, Royal British Legion and Simon Marks Jewish Primary School Trust (£1,000 each); Chicken Shed Theatre Company (£500); Spotlight Appeal (£200); and King Edward VII Hospital Sister Agnes (£100).

Exclusions

No grants to individuals.

Applications

In writing to the correspondent. Trustees meet annually in March.

Information gathered from:

Accounts; Charity Commission record.

The Walter Guinness Charitable Trust

General

£122,600 (2011/12)

Beneficial area

UK with a preference for Wiltshire and overseas.

Correspondent: The Secretary, Biddesden House, Andover, Hampshire SP11 9DN

Trustees: Hon. F. B. Guinness; Hon. Mrs R. Mulji; Hon. Catriona Guinness.

CC Number: 205375

The trust was established in 1961 by Bryan Walter, the second Lord Moyne, in memory of his father, the first Lord Moyne. Most grants are given to a number of charities which the trust has been consistently supporting for many years.

In 2011/12 the trust had assets of £6.8 million and an income of £141,000. Grants were made to the total value of £122,600. There were 71 grants of £1,000 or more made to 71 organisations totalling £100,000. Further grants of less than £1,000 were made to organisations totalling £22,600.

Beneficiaries included: DEC Disaster Emergencies Committee (£5,000;) Nursing Cancer Patients (£3,000); Arts Together (£2,500) Inspire Foundation, Prospect Hospice, SCOPE, Shelter, Wiltshire South Girl Guides (£2,000 each); Samaritans (£1,500); Barnardo's, Break Combat Stress and National Deaf Children's Society (£1,000 each).

Exclusions

No grants to individuals.

Applications

In writing to the correspondent. Replies are only sent when there is a positive decision. Initial telephone calls are not possible. There are no application forms, guidelines or deadlines. No sae is required.

Information gathered from:

Accounts; Charity Commission record.

The Gunter Charitable Trust

General charitable purposes including medical and wildlife causes in the UK

£89,500 (2011/12)

Beneficial area

UK and occasionally overseas.

Correspondent: The Trustees, c/o Forsters LLP, 31 Hill Street, London W1J 5LS (tel: 020 7863 8333)

Trustees: James de Cardonnel Findlay; Geoffrey Worrall.

CC Number: 268346

The trust gives grants to a wide range of local and UK organisations, including countryside, medical and wildlife causes. In 2011/12 the trust had assets of £2.1 million and an income of £111,000. There were 63 grants made totalling £89,000.

Beneficiaries included: The Medical Foundation for the Care of Victims of Torture (£6,500); Practical Action (£6,000); Humanitarian Aid Relief Trust (£5,000); Entelechy Arts Ltd (£4,500); St Mary's Church – Fordingbridge, Friends of Dr Pearay Lal Hospital and Liverpool School of Tropical Medicine (£1,000 each); and Guideposts Trust Ltd and Scottish Wildlife Trust (£400 each).

Exclusions

No support for unsolicited applications.

Applications

Applications are considered by the trustees twice a year. No unsolicited applications are accepted.

Information gathered from:

Accounts; Charity Commission record.

The Gur Trust

Jewish causes

£43,000 (2011/12)

Beneficial area

Worldwide.

Correspondent: Sheldon Morgenstern, Correspondent, 206 High Road, London N15 4NP (tel: 020 8801 6038)

Trustees: Sheldon Morgenstern; David Cymerman; Shaye Traube.

CC Number: 283423

The objectives of the Gur Trust are to assist in the provision of Orthodox Jewish education.

In 2011/12 the trust had assets of £1.4 million and an income of £46,000. Grants were made totalling £43,000; however a list of beneficiaries was not available in this year's accounts.

Previous beneficiaries have included Beis Yaacov Casidic Seminary, Beth Yaacov Town, Bnei Emes Institutions, Central Charity Fund, Gur Talmudical College, Kollel Arad, Yeshiva Lezeirim, Pri Gidulim, Maala and Mifal Gevura Shecehessed.

Applications

In writing to the correspondent. The trust has previously stated that: 'Funds are raised by the trustees. All calls for help are carefully considered and help is given according to circumstances and funds then available.'

Information gathered from:

Accounts; Charity Commission record.

The H. and M. Charitable Trust

Education, relief of poverty and other charitable purposes with a particular focus on seafaring

£84,000 (2011/12)

Beneficial area

UK, with some preference for Kent.

Correspondent: David Harris, Trustee, Lilac Cottage, Highwood Hill, London NW7 4HD (tel: 020 8906 3767; email: david@brooksgreen.com)

Trustees: David Harris; Pamela Lister; John Lister.

CC Number: 272391

According to the trustees' report for 2011/12, the object of the charity is the advancement of education, the relief of poverty and other charitable purposes. A particular focus is given towards seafaring.

In 2011/12 the trust had assets of £2.6 million and an income of £54,000. Grants totalled £84,000.

Previous beneficiaries included: Arethusa Venture Centre, Fairbridge – Kent, Guide Dogs for the Blind, Hand in Gillingham, Jubilee Sailing Trust, Kent Air Ambulance, North London Hospice, RSPCA, Royal Engineers Association, Royal National Lifeboat Association and Royal Star and Garter Home.

The trust has previously stated that 'resources are committed on a regular annual basis to organisations that have come to rely upon us for their funding'.

Applications

The trustees said they do not wish their trust to be included in this guide since it leads to disappointment for applicants. Unsolicited applications will not be successful.

Information gathered from:

Accounts; Charity Commission record.

The H. P. Charitable Trust

General charitable purposes, advancement of Orthodox Judaism, poverty relief

£31,500 (2011/12)

Beneficial area

UK and overseas.

Correspondent: Aron Piller, Trustee, 26 Lingwood Road, London E5 9BN (tel: 020 8806 2432)

Trustees: Arthur Zonszajn; Aron Piller; Hannah Piller.

CC Number: 278006

The H P Charitable Trust was created by Hannah Piller in 1979 and makes grants to Orthodox Jewish charities.

According to the trustees' report for 2011/12:

> The charity was formed for general charitable purposes, in particular the advancement of religion in accordance with the Orthodox Jewish faith, the relief of poverty, and other charitable purposes.
>
> The trustees seek to direct grants towards the relief of poverty among Orthodox Jewish communities and the advancement of the Orthodox Jewish religion by way of grants to educational and community institutions, both in the UK and abroad. The trustees mainly entertain applications by recommendation from workers known to them in the above areas.

In 2011/12 its assets stood at £1.8 million and it had an income of £205,000. Grants totalled £31,000, an increase from the previous year's figure (£5,600). There was no explanation for this in the trust's accounts, except the following quote: 'during the year the charity continued to receive investment income, and the trustees have been able to resume their grant-making activities'.

Previous beneficiaries included: Craven Walk Charities, Emuno Educational Centre Ltd, Gur Trust, Ponivez, Yad Eliezer, Yeshuas Caim Synagogue and Yetev Lev.

Applications

In writing to the correspondent.

Information gathered from:

Accounts; Charity Commission record.

The Edith Winifred Hall Charitable Trust

General charitable purposes, with preference towards young people and social welfare

£1 million (2011/12)

Beneficial area

UK, with a preference for Northamptonshire.

Correspondent: David Endicott, Trustee, Spratt Endicott, 52–54 South Bar Street, Banbury OX16 9AB (tel: 01295 204000)

Trustees: David Endicott; David Reynolds; Lucie Burgess-Lumsden; Pamela Reynolds.

CC Number: 1057032

This trust has stated that it wants its funds to make a difference. Documentation provided was limited to four pages from the annual accounts for 2011/12 detailing charitable expenditure.

In 2011/12 grants were made to 16 organisations totalling £1 million.

Beneficiaries included: Youthscape (£450,000); Reachout Plus (£225,000); Northamptonshire Association of Youth Clubs (£150,000); Beds Garden Carers (£80,000); Northampton Community Foundation and St Mary's – Titchmarsh (£20,000 each); Rothwell Parochial Church (£7,000); and Sue Ryder Thorpe Hall Hospital and St Peter's Centre (£1,000 each).

Applications

In writing to the correspondent.

Information gathered from:

Accounts; Charity Commission record.

The Hamamelis Trust

Ecological conservation, medical research

£44,000 (2011/12)

Beneficial area

UK, but with a special interest in the Godalming and Surrey areas.

Correspondent: Mrs L. Dadswell, Trustee, c/o Penningtons Solicitors LLP, Highfield, Brighton Road, Godalming, Surrey GU7 1NS (tel: 01483 791800)

Trustees: Mrs L. Dadswell; Dr A. F. M. Stone; Mrs Mirouze.

CC Number: 280938

The trust was set up in 1980 by John Ashley Slocock and enhanced on his death in 1986. The main areas of work are medical research and ecological conservation. Grants are occasionally made to other projects. Preference is given to projects in the Godalming and Surrey areas.

In 2011/12 the trust had assets of £3.3 million and an income of £117,000. Grants totalling £44,000 were given to 15 organisations.

Beneficiaries included: The Sussex Community Foundation – Slindon Forge Fund (£10,000); Fight for Sight (£3,000); Gwent Wildlife Trust, Surrey Care Trust, The John Muir Trust, Wildlife Aid, The Gatton Trust, Stroke Association, Juvenile Diabetes Research Foundation and The National Trust – Speckled Wood Project (£2,500 each); Deafness Research and Autistica (£2,000 each); and Godalming Museum Trust (£1,600).

Exclusions

Projects outside the UK are not considered. No grants to individuals.

Applications

In writing to the correspondent. All applicants are asked to include a short summary of the application including costings, along with any published material and references. Unsuccessful appeals will not be acknowledged. Dr Adam Stone, one of the trustees, who is medically qualified, assesses medical applications.

Information gathered from:

Accounts; Charity Commission record.

Sue Hammerson Charitable Trust

General charitable purposes, with particular emphasis on medical research, relief in need, education

£157,000 (2011/12)

Beneficial area

UK, with a preference for London.

Correspondent: Trust Administrator, c/o H. W. Fisher and Company, Acre House, 11–15 William Road, London NW1 3ER (tel: 020 7388 7000)

Trustees: Sir Gavin Lightman; David Hammerson; Patricia Beecham; Peter Hammerson; Anthony Bernstein; Anthony Thompson; Rory Hammerson.

CC Number: 235196

The trust was established in 1957. The trust gives particular consideration to the advancement of medical learning and research and to the relief of sickness and poverty, with first consideration being given to the needs of the Lewis W. Hammerson Memorial Home. A wide range of health care, educational and religious causes are also funded.

In 2011/12 it had assets of £8 million and an income of £180,000. Grants were made to three organisations totalling £157,000.

The largest beneficiary by far was Lewis W Hammerson Memorial Home, which received a grant of £150,000. Other beneficiaries included: Painter-Stainers Fine Art Fund (£5,200); and Army Benevolent Fund (£2,000).

Exclusions

No grants to individuals.

Applications

In writing to the correspondent.

Information gathered from:

Accounts; Charity Commission record.

Beatrice Hankey Foundation Ltd

Christian

£12,000 (2012)

Beneficial area

UK and overseas.

Correspondent: Melanie Churchill, Secretary, 11 Staverton Road, Peterborough PE4 6LY (tel: 01733 571794)

Trustees: Hilary Walker; Angela Stewart; Revd David Faulks; Revd David Savill; Canon David Haokip; Christine Legge; Wendyanne Hill; Selina Ormond; Daphne Sampson; Margaret Faulks; Crispin Wedell; David Walker.

CC Number: 211093

The Beatrice Hankey Foundation Ltd was established in 1962. According to the trustees' report for 2012, the charity's principal activities are as follows:

- To continue the work of Beatrice and Eva Hankey in connection with the fellowship knows as 'the knighthood' and for 'blue pilgrims' to work for the advancement of the Christian religion in co-operation with the Christian churches at home and in the international field
- To train and send forth persons to act as Christian leaders, teachers and missionaries in deprived areas or where the churches need the services of men and women of the Christian vocation

In 2012 the foundation had assets of £1 million and an income of £49,000. Grants were made to organisations totalling £12,000.

Beneficiaries included: Bangladesh Knighthood Fellowship (£4,000); Friends of Burma, Mathieson Music Trust and Hope on the Horizon (£1,000 each); and Christian Response to Eastern Europe and Christian Solidarity Worldwide (£500 each).

Exclusions

No grants for buildings or equipment.

Applications

Unsolicited applications cannot be considered.

Information gathered from:

Accounts; Charity Commission record.

The Hanley Trust (1987)

General charitable purposes

£26,000 (2011/12)

Beneficial area

UK.

Correspondent: Hon. Sarah Price, Trustee, 21 Buckingham Gate, London SW1E 6LS

Trustees: Hon. Sarah Price; William Swan; Hon. Samuel Butler.

CC Number: 299209

The trust supports general charitable purposes and makes grants to charitable foundations.

In 2011/12 the trust had assets of £1 million and an income of £35,000. Grants were made to 72 organisations totalling £26,000 and ranged between £50 and £2,500.

Beneficiaries included: Butler Trust and Irene Taylor Trust (£2,500 each); Canine Partners and Shelter (£1,000 each); Helen Arkell Dyslexia Centre, Amnesty International and Prader Willi Syndrome (£500 each); Prison Phoenix Trust, Parentline Plus and Corby Voluntary and Community Services (£250 each); Leicestershire and Rutland Headway, Homestart – Leicester and Youth Brass 2000 (£100 each); and Duke of Cornwall Spinal Appeal- Cornwall (£50).

Exclusions

Grants are not made to individuals or to non-registered charities.

Applications

In writing to the correspondent.

Information gathered from:

Accounts; Charity Commission record.

Harbo Charities Ltd

General charitable purposes and Jewish causes, education, relief in need, disability, ill health

£77,000 (2011/12)

Beneficial area

Worldwide.

Correspondent: Harry Stern, Trustee, 13 Fairholt Road, London N16 5EW

Trustees: Harold Gluck; Harry Stern; Barbara Stern.

CC Number: 282262

The trust supports Orthodox Jewish, religious and educational charities both in the UK and abroad. The trust supports charities that provide the following:

- Financial support to the poor
- Provision of basic necessities to the poor
- Relief of sickness and disabilities
- Jewish education and places of worship for the Jewish community

In 2011/12 the trust had assets of £744,000, an income of £93,000 and made grants totalling £77,000. There was no list of grants available in the 2011/12 accounts.

Previous beneficiaries have included: Beis Chinuch Lebonos Girls School, Beth Rochel d'Satmar, Bobov Trust, Chevras Maoz Ladol, Craven Walk Charitable Trust, Edgware Yeshiva Trust, Keren Yesomim, Kollel Shomrei HaChomoth, Tevini Ltd, Tomchei Shabbos, Yad Eliezer, Yesode Ha Torah School and Yeshiva Chachmay Tsorpha.

Applications

In writing to the correspondent.

Information gathered from:

Accounts; Charity Commission record.

The Harbour Charitable Trust

General

£42,000 (2011/12)

Beneficial area

UK.

Correspondent: Mr Aldina, Correspondent, Barbican House, 26–34 Old Street, London EC1V 9QQ

Trustees: Barbara Brenda Green; Elaine Knobil; Zena Sandra Blackman; Tamar Eisenstat.

CC Number: 234268

The trust makes grants for the benefit of childcare, education and healthcare and to various other charitable organisations. In 2011/12 it had assets of £4.2 million and an income of £192,000. Grants were made totalling £42,000 and were categorised as follows:

Joint Jewish Charitable Trust	£31,000
Childcare	£6,000
Aged care	£3,000
Other donations	£1,000
Healthcare	£500

No further information was available on the charities supported.

Exclusions

Grants are given to registered charities only.

Applications

In writing to the correspondent.

Information gathered from:

Accounts; Charity Commission record.

The Harding Trust

Arts, education

£116,000 (2011/12)

Beneficial area

Mainly, but not exclusively, Staffordshire and surrounding areas.

Correspondent: Peter O'Rourke, Correspondent, Horton House, Exchange Flags, Liverpool L2 3YL (tel: 01516 003000; email: peter.orourke@brabnerscs.com)

Trustees: Geoffrey Snow; Geoffrey Wall; John Fowell; Michael Lloyd.

CC Number: 328182

The trust was established in 1989 and according to the trustees' report for 2011/12:

> Aims to promote, improve, develop and maintain public education in and appreciation of the art and science of music, mainly but not exclusively in Staffordshire and surrounding areas, inter alia, by sponsoring or by otherwise supporting public concerts, recitals and performances by amateur and professional organisations.

In 2011/12 the trust had assets of £3.7 million and an income of £143,000. Grants were made to 26 organisations totalling £116,000.

Beneficiaries included: Stoke on Trent Festival (£32,000); Harding Trust Piano Recitals (£18,000); Malvern Theatres Trust (£10,000); European Union Chamber Orchestra and Royal Philharmonic Orchestra (£6,000 each); Clonter Farm Music Trust (£3,500); Help for Heroes and English Haydn Festival (£2,000 each); British Red Cross Society, Midlands Air Ambulance and Codsall Arts Festival (£1,000 each); Tettenhall Operatic Society (£750); and Uttoxeter Choral Society and English Music Festival (£500 each).

Applications

In writing to the correspondent. The trustees meet annually in spring/early summer. Accounts are needed for recurrent applications.

Information gathered from:

Accounts; Charity Commission record.

William Harding's Charity

Education and welfare

£261,000 (2012)

Beneficial area

Aylesbury.

Correspondent: John Leggett, Correspondent, 14 Bourbon Street, Aylesbury, Buckinghamshire HP20 2RS (tel: 01296 318501; email: doudjag@pandclip.co.uk)

Trustees: Les Sheldon; Anne Brooker; Freda Roberts; Bernard Griffin; Penni Thorne; Roger Evans; William Chapple; Lennard Wakelam; Susan Hewitt.

CC Number: 310619

Under a scheme of 1978, Harding's Eleemosynary Charity and Harding's Educational Charity (both set up in the eighteenth century) merged to become William Harding's Charity. Its objects, limited to the town of Aylesbury, include the provision of alms-houses and other benefits for older people; the provision of special benefits of any kind not normally provided by the local authority for any maintained school or any college of education or other institution of further education in or substantially serving the town of Aylesbury; awarding maintenance allowances tenable at any school, university or college of further education; relief in need and provision of general benefit in Aylesbury.

The trust owns 35 properties in Aylesbury itself, land in or adjacent to Aylesbury and is a member of the National Association of Alms-houses.

In 2012 the charity had assets of £23.7 million, an income of £834,000 and made grants totalling £261,000.

Grants to organisations totalled £220,000 and were broken down into the following categories:

Schools and other educational establishments	£102,000
General benefits/relief in need	£100,500
Travel for clubs/societies/groups	£46,500
Youth groups	£12,000
Equipment and tools for young people	£500

A further £143,500 was awarded to 185 individuals.

Beneficiaries included: Aylesbury Project Community Interest Company (£15,000); QPAC (£12,000); Aylesbury Youth Action (£10,000); Youth Concern Aylesbury (£7,000); IQRA (£5,000); Monday Contact Club and SPACE (£4,000 each); and Buckingham St Youth Club and 14th Vale of Aylesbury Sea Scout (£2,500 each).

Exclusions

All persons and organisations not based in Aylesbury Town.

Applications

In writing to the correspondent. Trustees meet on a regular basis to consider and determine applications for charitable assistance.

Percentage of awards given to new applicants: between 10% and 20%.

Common applicant mistakes

'They fail to read guidance notes properly – this results in insufficient information and so delays the outcome of the applications.'

Information gathered from:

Accounts; Charity Commission record; further information provided by the funder.

The Hare of Steep Charitable Trust

General charitable purposes, in particular the advancement of social, cultural, medical, educational and religious projects

£50,500 (2011/12)

Beneficial area

UK, with preference for the south of England, especially Petersfield and East Hampshire.

Correspondent: Mrs S. M. Fowler, Hon. Secretary, 56 Heath Road, Petersfield GU31 4EJ (tel: 01730 267953)

Trustees: S. M. Fowler; P. L. F. Baillon; J. R. F. Fowler; S. E. R. Johnson-Hill; Stephanie Grenfell.

CC Number: 297308

The Hare of Steep Charitable Trust was established in 1987. According to the trustees' report for 2011/12:

> The principal objects of the charity are to contribute towards any charitable purpose for the benefit of the community and in particular the advancement of social, cultural, medical, educational and religious projects. It intends to operate without discrimination in relation to ethnicity, disability, sex, age, religion or belief.

The trust supports small local charities and local branches of national charities where contributions have most impact.

In 2011/12 the trust had assets of £115,000 and an income of £48,000. Grants were made to 33 organisations totalling £50,000. The trust made no donations greater than 5% of the total distributed.

Unfortunately an exact breakdown of the grant beneficiaries was not provided by the trust. Previous grants have been made to Alzheimer's Disease Society, Arthritis and Rheumatism Council – Petersfield, British Heart Foundation, Rainbow House Trust and SSAFA.

Applications

The trust has previously stated that 'the trustees already support as many charities as they could wish. Unsolicited requests are not acknowledged.'

Information gathered from:

Accounts; Charity Commission record.

The Harebell Centenary Fund

General, education, medical research, animal welfare

£208,000 (2012)

Beneficial area

UK.

Correspondent: Penelope Chapman, Trustee, 50 Broadway, Westminster, London SW1H 0BL (tel: 020 7227 7000; email: pennychapman@bdb-law.co.uk)

Trustees: Michael Goodbody; Penelope Chapman; Angela Fossick.

CC Number: 1003552

The Harebell Centenary Fund was established in 1991. According to the trustees' report for 2012, the objectives of the trust are to:

> Further the advancement of the education of the general public particularly in matters of providing funding to young persons to further their education, the promotion of neurological and neurosurgical research and the relief of sickness and suffering amongst animals.

The current policy of the trustees is to concentrate on making donations to charities that do not receive widespread public support and to keep administrative expenses to a minimum. For this reason the trustees have decided to make donations only to registered charities and not to individuals.

In 2012 it had assets of £5.7 million, which generated an income of £182,000. Grants totalling £208,000 were made to 37 organisations, many of which were hospices. Governance costs were £15,000.

Beneficiaries included: PACE (£10,000); Partially Sighted Society, Meningitis Trust and Penumbra (£7,000 each); St Helena Hospice and Nordoff-Robbins Music School (£5,000 each); and the Blue Cross (£2,000).

Exclusions

No grants are made to individuals.

Applications

In writing to the correspondent. The trust meets every six months to consider applications. Unsolicited applications are not requested, as the trustees prefer to make donations to charities whose work they have come across through their own research.

Percentage of awards given to new applicants: between 10% and 20%.

Common applicant mistakes

'We still get a number of applications from individuals despite saying we do not give to individuals.'

Information gathered from:

Accounts; Charity Commission record; further information provided by the funder.

The Hargrave Foundation

General, research, welfare

£35,000 (2011/12)

Beneficial area

Worldwide.

Correspondent: Stephen Hargrave, Trustee, 47 Lambs Conduit Street, London WC1N 3NG

Trustees: Stephen Hargrave; Dominic Moseley; Adam Parkin.

CC Number: 1106524

The trust was established in 2004 with general charitable purposes, with preference towards welfare and medical research.

In 2011/12 it had assets of £2.8 million, an income of £108,000 and made grants to organisations totalling £35,000. This figure was significantly lower than previous years of grantmaking (2009/10: £129,000).

A list of beneficiaries was not provided, however previous beneficiaries have included: Institute of Healing of Memories; Reform Research Trust; British Liver Trust; Prostate Cancer Charity; Writers and Scholars Educational Trust; and English Pen.

Applications

In writing to the correspondent.

Information gathered from:

Accounts; Charity Commission record.

The Harris Family Charitable Trust

Health, sickness

£99,000 (2011/12)

Beneficial area

UK.

Correspondent: Ronnie Harris, Trustee, 64 New Cavendish Street, London W1G 8TB (tel: 020 7467 6300)

Trustees: Ronnie Harris; Loretta Harris; Charlotte Harris; Sophie Harris; Toby Harris.

CC Number: 1064394

Set up in 1997, the trust makes grants to organisations dealing with health issues and the alleviation of sickness.

In 2011/12 it had an income of £408,000 and assets of £1.3 million. Donations totalling £99,000 were made to organisations, however a list of beneficiaries was not provided.

Applications

According to the trustees' report for 2011/12, 'the charity invites applications for funding of projects through various sources. The applications are reviewed by the trustees that they are in accordance with the charity's objectives.'

Information gathered from:

Accounts; Charity Commission record.

The Edith Lilian Harrison 2000 Foundation

General

£101,000 (2011/12)

Beneficial area

UK.

Correspondent: Geoffrey Peyer, Trustee, TWM Solicitors LLP, 40 West Street, Reigate RH2 9BT (tel: 01737 221212; email: reigate.reception@twmsolicitors.com)

Trustees: Geoffrey Peyer; Clive Andrews; Paul Bradley.

CC Number: 1085651

The foundation was established in 2000 for general charitable purposes, although grantmaking activities only commenced in 2008/09 after receiving £3.5 million from the estate of the late Edith Lilian Harrison.

The foundation's accounts give this insight into its funding strategy:

> In terms of identifying grant recipients, the trustees have followed the general directions set out in a Letter of Wishes signed by Mrs Harrison on 5th September 2000.

In 2011/12 the foundation had assets of £2.7 million and an income of £78,000. Grants were made to 12 organisations totalling £101,000.

Beneficiaries included: Salisbury Hospice, PDSA and Macmillan Cancer Support (£20,000 each); Transport for All, Centre for Alternative Technology and Cobalt Heart Mind and Body Scanner Appeal (£5,000 each); and Rotary Club of Salisbury (£1,000).

Applications

In writing to the correspondent. The trustees meet every six months. At each regular meeting, applications for grants are considered and duly dealt with.

Information gathered from:

Accounts; Charity Commission record.

The Alfred And Peggy Harvey Charitable Trust

Medical, research, older people, children and young people with disabilities or disadvantages, visually and hearing impaired people

£63,000 (2011/12)

Beneficial area

UK, with a strong preference for Kent, Surrey and South East London.

Correspondent: Colin Russell, Trustee, c/o Manches LLP, Aldwych House, 81 Aldwych, London WC2B 4RP (tel: 020 7404 4433)

Trustees: Kevin Custis; Colin Russell; John Duncan.

CC Number: 1095855

The trust has four main objects:

- The advancement and funding of medical and surgical studies and research
- The care of the elderly and the provision of accommodation for the elderly
- The care of and provision of financial support for disabled children and young people and for children and young people suffering from the lack of stable family upbringing or other social or educational disadvantages
- The care of blind and deaf people

The trust will only consider applications from charities in Kent, Surrey and South East London.

In 2011/12 the trust had assets of £424,000 and an income of £70,000. Grants totalled £63,000.

A list of beneficiaries was not provided, however previous beneficiaries included: Macular Disease Society; Country Holidays For Inner City Kids; Lighthouse Educational Scheme; E-Learning Foundation; Hope UK; Children's Country Holiday Fund; Kidscape; Happy Days; Action for Kids; Child Victims of Crime.

Exclusions

Charitable organisations in Kent, Surrey and south east London only.

Applications

In writing to the correspondent.

Information gathered from:

Accounts; Charity Commission record.

The Haskel Family Foundation

Jewish, social-policy research, arts, education

£11,000 (2012)

Beneficial area

UK.

Correspondent: Lord Simon Haskel, 12 Rosemont Road, Richmond upon Thames, Surrey TW10 6QL (tel: 020 8948 7711)

Trustees: Alan Davis; Susan Haskel; Lady Haskel; Lord Haskel.

CC Number: 1039969

The charity funds projects concerned with social-policy research, Jewish communal life, arts and education.

In 2012 the foundation had assets of £620,000 and an income of £31,000. Grants totalled £11,000.

Beneficiaries were: UCL Development (£5,000); Liberal Judaism and the Rosetree Trust (£5,000 each); Blythe Valley Chamber Music (£2,500); Kisharon (£2,000); and Institute for Jewish Policy Research (£1,500).

Applications

This trust states that it does not respond to unsolicited applications.

Information gathered from:

Accounts; Charity Commission record.

Hasluck Charitable Trust

Health, welfare, disability, youth, overseas aid

£72,000 (2011/12)

Beneficial area

UK.

Correspondent: John Billing, Trustee, Rathbone Trust Company Ltd, 4th Floor, 1 Curzon Street, London W1J 5FB (tel: 020 7399 0447; email: john.billing@rathbones.com)

Trustees: Matthew James Wakefield; John Billing.

CC Number: 1115323

The Hasluck Charitable Trust was established in 2006. Half of the income received is allocated to eight charities (Barnardo's, Mrs R. H. Hotblacks Michelham Priory Endowment Fund, International Fund for Animal Welfare, Macmillan Cancer Relief, the Riding for the Disabled Association, RNLI, RSPB and Scope), which are of particular interest to the settlor. The remaining monies are distributed to such charitable bodies as the trustees decide.

In 2011/12 the trust had assets of £1.2 million and an income of £96,000. Grants totalled £72,000.

The sum of £35,000 was given to the trust's eight primary beneficiaries. There were a further 34 grants made in the range of £500 to £2,500.

Beneficiaries included: Alzheimer's Society (£2,500); Riders and World Vision – Somalia Appeal (£1,500 each); Living Hope, Family Care, Just Different, Ipswich Community Playbus and Seafarers UK (£1,000 each); and the Message and Leukaemia and Lymphoma Research (£500 each).

Exclusions

No grants are made to individuals.

Applications

In writing to the correspondent. Grants are generally distributed in January and July, although consideration is given to appeals received at other times of the year.

Percentage of awards given to new applicants: between 40% and 50%.

Information gathered from:

Accounts; Charity Commission record; further information provided by the funder.

The M. A. Hawe Settlement

General

£198,000 to organisations (2011/12)

Beneficial area

Lancashire with a preference for the Fylde coastal area.

Correspondent: M. A. Hawe, Trustee, 94 Park View Road, Lytham St Annes, Lancashire FY8 4JF (tel: 01253 796888)

Trustees: M. A. Hawe; Mrs G. Hawe; M. G. Hawe.

CC Number: 327827

In April 1993 the trustees purchased a property with the intention that it should be converted in order to provide suitable accommodation on a short stay basis for young homeless people. A company, The Kensington House Trust Ltd, operating under the name The Kensington Foundation (Charity commission no. 1044235) was established for the purpose of operating the accommodation. The hostel was closed in 2008/09.

The trust states that:

> The settlement is committed to the support of the Kensington Foundation to which 96% of the grants (by value) made in this year have gone. The Kensington Foundation intends to focus its efforts into developing the Daisy Chain Project at Norcross farm as their main activity.

In 2011/12 the trust had assets of £3 million and an income of £65,000. Grants were given to organisations totalling £198,000. Grants to individuals totalled £2,500.

The main beneficiary was Kensington House Trust Ltd (£191,000). Other beneficiaries included: Youth Service Events and Young Persons' Visits to Lourdes (£1,000 each); Holy Cross Church and Soup Kitchen (£840); and Fylde Mayor's Charity and Fr Dunstan Cooper (£500 each).

Applications

In writing to the correspondent.

Information gathered from:

Accounts; Charity Commission record.

The Hawthorne Charitable Trust

General

£127,000 (2011/12)

Beneficial area

UK, especially Hereford and Worcester.

Correspondent: Mrs Evaline Sarbout, c/o Baker Tilly, 25 Farringdon Street, London EC4A 4AB (tel: 020 3201 8298)

Trustees: Alexandra Berington; Roger Jackson Clark; Thomas Berington; Richard White.

CC Number: 233921

The trust supports a wide range of organisations, particularly health and welfare causes but also charities concerned with animal welfare, disability, heritage and young people.

In 2011/12 it had assets of £7.2 million, which generated an income of £178,000. Grants were made to 65 organisations totalling £127,000. Donations were broken down into the following categories:

Medical	21	£47,000
Other	23	£41,000
Environment, conservation& heritage	9	£18,000
People with disabilities	7	£12,000
Animal welfare	4	£7,000
Relief of poverty	1	£2,000

Beneficiaries included: St Laurence – Winchenford (£5,250); Malvern Festival Theatre Trust Ltd, Canine Partners for Independence, Combat Stress and Elizabeth Finn Trust (£2,500 each); Motor Neurone Disease Association and The Passage (£2,000 each); National Art Collections Fund and Birmingham Hippodrome (£1,000 each); and Asthma Relief (£500).

A number of the above beneficiaries have been supported in previous years.

Exclusions

Grants are given to registered charities only. No grants to individuals.

Applications

In writing to the correspondent, including up-to-date accounts. Applications should be received by October for consideration in November.

Information gathered from:

Accounts; Charity Commission record.

The Dorothy Hay-Bolton Charitable Trust

Deaf, blind

Around £50,000

Beneficial area

UK, with a preference for the South East of England and overseas.

Correspondent: The Trustees, Reeves and Co. LLP, 24 Chiswell Street, London EC1Y 4YX (tel: 020 7382 1820; email: brian.carter@reeves.co.uk)

Trustees: Brian Carter; Stephen Gallico.

CC Number: 1010438

The trust makes grants towards charities working with people who are deaf or blind, particularly children, young people and elderly people. In 2011/12 the trust had an income of £23,000 and a total expenditure of £57,000. Further information was not available.

Previous beneficiaries have included: Hearing Dogs for the Deaf, Action for Blind People, Sussex Lantern, Telephones for the Blind, Eyeless Trust, British Blind Sport, Esther Benjamin's Trust, East Sussex Association for the Blind, the Seeing Ear and East Kent Cycling Club.

Exclusions

The trust states that it does not generally give to individuals.

Applications

In writing to the correspondent.

Information gathered from:

Accounts; Charity Commission record.

May Hearnshaw's Charity

General

£61,000 (2011/12)

Beneficial area

UK, particularly South Yorkshire, North Nottinghamshire, Derbyshire, East Lancashire and Cheshire areas.

Correspondent: Michael Ferreday, Trustee, Barber Harrison and Platt, 2 Rutland Park, Sheffield S10 2PD

Trustees: Marjorie West; Michael Ferreday; Richard Law; William Munro.

CC Number: 1008638

This trust was established by the will of the late May Hearnshaw who died in 1988. It was her wish that the trust be used for the promotion of education, advancement of religion and relief of poverty and sickness. Support is mostly given to children's organisations within these themes. Grants are made to UK-wide charities or local charities working in the South Yorkshire, North Nottinghamshire, Derbyshire, East Lancashire and Cheshire areas.

In 2011/12 the trust had assets of £1.9 million and an income of £77,000. Grants were made to 23 organisations totalling £61,000. Governance costs were £10,000.

Beneficiaries were: St Luke's Capital Appeal (£25,000); Air Ambulance and St Cuthbert's Church (£5,000 each); Brains Trust (£3,000); Amy's Trust and Cherry Tree (£2,000 each); Christians Against Poverty and Strongbones Children's Charitable Trust (£1,000 each); and Barnsley Asperger's Parent Group and The Stroke Association (£500 each).

Information gathered from:

Accounts; Charity Commission record.

Heart Research UK

Medical research into the prevention, treatment and cure of heart disease and heart disease prevention through lifestyle choices

£939,000 (2012)

Beneficial area

UK.

Correspondent: M. Clark, Heart Research UK, Suite 12D, Joseph's Well, Leeds LS3 1AB (tel: 01132 347474; email: mail@heartresearch.org.uk; website: www.heartresearch.org.uk)

Trustees: Keith Loudon; Richard Hemsley; Christine Mortimer; Dr David Dickinson; Heather Stewart; Joan Villiers; Kevin Watterson; Anthony Knight; Antony Oxley; Paul Rogerson; Dr Catherine Dickinson; Anthony Kilner; Paul Smith; Richard Brown; Jean Hill; Peter Braidley.

CC Number: 1044821

Heart Research UK (formerly the National Heart Research Fund) was founded in 1967 by a working heart surgeon. The stated function of the Charity is the promotion of medical research into heart disease and related disorders and into the prevention treatment and cures of such complaints and the dissemination of any useful results. The provision of practical help and rehabilitation for those with, or vulnerable to, heart disease or any related complaint.

The objects are fulfilled by funding medical research projects at centres throughout the UK, all projects undertaken being allocated and controlled in line with the guiding principles of the Association of Medical Research Charities (AMRC). In addition, an ongoing programme is undertaken to raise awareness of the issue of heart disease and related illnesses, coupled with the promotion of healthier lifestyles through Healthy Heart community grants and initiatives in schools and workplaces. The charity has also forged partnerships with organisations and companies to promote heart health and highlight particular conditions and issues.

Grants Programmes

Translational Research

Translational research bridges the gap between scientific research and patient care, bringing about clinical benefits in the most efficient way. This may advance current practice or enable innovative discoveries to be efficiently transferred into practical tools to prevent, diagnose and treat human disease. [The maximum award is £150,000].

Novel and Emerging Technologies

This unique grant gives researchers the opportunity to apply for funding to develop a novel and emerging technology. Proposals can involve an innovative novel and emerging technology or a new application of an existing technology. A maximum of £200,000 is available each year. The grant selection process is rigorous and the scheme is competitive with a typical success rate in previous years of 1 in 8.

HRUK Healthy Heart Grants

Heart Research UK Healthy Heart Grants of up to £10,000 are available for new, original and innovative projects that actively promote Heart Health and help to prevent, or reduce, the risk of heart disease in specific groups or communities.

HRUK and Subway Healthy Heart Grants

These grants have the same criteria as the HRUK Healthy Heart grants. The grants are awarded to not-for-profit organisations, from small voluntary or grass-root development groups right through to the charitable arms of sporting organisations

Grantmaking in 2012

In 2012 the foundation had assets of £2.9 million and an income of £1.8 million. Grants totalled £939,000 consisting of £755,000 in medical research grants and £184,000 in Healthy Heart grants.

Beneficiaries of medical research grants included: University College London and Great Ormond Street Hospital for Children (£186,000); University of Nottingham (£145,000); William Harvey Research Institute, Queen Mary University of London (£112,000); Kings College London (£75,000); and Oxford Spires Four Pillars Hotel (£19,000).

Beneficiaries of Healthy Heart grants included: The Fresh – Sportsmen Study (£10,000); Heart Smart (£8,000); Northern Star's Healthy Hearts (£5,700); Run for a Healthy Heart (£4,700); and YMCA Fitness Challenge – Love Your Heart (£2,300).

Exclusions

Government and local authority funded institutions are not eligible.

Applications

Application forms, full guidelines and grant terms and conditions for each programme can be requested by telephone or downloaded from the website.

For **Translational Research** grants the deadline is 1 February each year with applications being accepted from the beginning of January.

For **Novel and Emerging Technologies** grants outline applications are accepted from 1 March until 1 April each year and the deadline for full applications is 1 July each year.

For **Healthy Heart** grants there are two rounds each year, one in May and one in November.

Subway Healthy Heart grants are available in specific regions at certain times of the year; check the website for these details.

Information gathered from:

Accounts; Charity Commission record; funder's website.

The Heathcoat Trust

Welfare, causes local to Tiverton, Devon

£47,000 to organisation (2011/12)

Beneficial area

Mainly Tiverton, Devon.

Correspondent: Lowman Manufacturing Co. Ltd, Secretary, The Island, Lowman Green, Tiverton EX16 4LA (tel: 01884 254899; website: www.heathcoat.co.uk)

Trustees: Sir Ian Heathcoat Amory; Lady Amory; WF. Heathcoat Amory.

CC Number: 203367

The trust was established in 1945. Its objectives as stated in the 2006 accounts are 'for the relief of financial hardship, for education and training, for building or making grants to health institutions, and in certain circumstances for making contributions to any charity but mostly in Tiverton in Devon and its neighbourhood, or in places where the firms John Heathcoat and Company Ltd and Lowman Manufacturing Company Ltd and their subsidiaries carry on business. In so far as the income cannot be applied towards the objects specified in the trust deed, it may be applied for any charitable purpose.'

Over 100 grants a year, mostly under £1,000 each, are made to organisations and nearly all to local causes around the Tiverton area. Other grants are made to individuals, employees and pensioners of the Heathcoat group of companies. Educational grants are given to children of those employees or pensioners and also to local students attending schools and colleges in Tiverton, or beyond if courses are not available locally.

In 2011/12 the trust had assets of £1.9 million and an income of £306,000. Grants to organisations totalled £47,000. A further £2,000 was given in grants to individuals.

Applications

In writing to the correspondent. There are application forms for certain education grants.

Information gathered from:

Accounts; Charity Commission record; funder's website.

The Charlotte Heber-Percy Charitable Trust

General charitable purposes, including: animal welfare, the environment, health, overseas aid, education, and the arts

£259,000 (2011/12)

Beneficial area

Worldwide.

Correspondent: The Administrator, Rathbone Trust Company Ltd, 4th Floor, 1 Curzon Street, London W1J 5FB (tel: 020 7399 0820)

Trustees: Joanna Prest; Charlotte Heber-Percy.

CC Number: 284387

Set up by a deed created in 1981. In 2011/12 the trust had assets of £6 million, which generated an income of £253,000. Grants were made to 51 organisations totalling £259,000, which were distributed in the following categories:

Animal welfare and the local environment	£51,000
Medical, cancer and hospices	£30,000
International charities	£28,000
Local organisations	£19,000
Education and children	£39,000
General charitable organisations	£64,000
The arts and museums	£28,000

Beneficiaries included: Countryside Foundation (£34,000); ABF The Soldier's Charity (£20,000); Royal Shakespeare Company, Rugby Football Foundation and Ronald McDonald House (£10,000 each); Dumfries and Galloway Action (£8,000); Katherine House Hospice and Lawrence's Roundabout Well Appeal (£5,000 each); Remount (£3,000); St Andrew's Church – Naunton and War Memorial Trust (£2,000 each); and St John's Ambulance and the Children's Trust (£1,000 each).

Exclusions

No grants to individuals.

Applications

The trustees meet on an ad hoc basis to consider applications.

Information gathered from:

Accounts; Charity Commission record.

Percy Hedley 1990 Charitable Trust

General charitable purposes

£42,000 (2011/12)

Beneficial area

UK with a preference for Northumberland and Tyne and Wear.

Correspondent: John Armstrong, Trustee, 10 Castleton Close, Newcastle upon Tyne NE2 2HF (tel: 01912 815953)

Trustees: John Armstrong; Bill Meikle; Fiona Ruffman.

CC Number: 1000033

In 2011/12 the trust had assets of £1.4 million and an income of £46,000. Grants were made to 59 organisations totalling £42,000. Many beneficiaries are supported on a regular basis.

Beneficiaries included: Percy Hedley Foundation (£5,000); Newcastle Royal Grammar School Bursary Fund and Central Newcastle High School GDST Bursary Fund (£3,000 each); St Oswald's Hospice, Anaphylaxis Campaign and Samaritans – Newcastle (£1,000 each); and Howick Church, Landmark Trust, Stroke Association, Combat Stress, Northumberland Wildlife Trust and The Grassland Trust (£500 each).

Applications

In writing to the correspondent. Trustees meet twice a year. 'We are happy to receive succinct applications. A financial statement can be welcome, but full annual report accounts are too much.'

Percentage of awards given to new applicants: 14%.

Common applicant mistakes

'None.'

Information gathered from:

Accounts; Charity Commission record; further information provided by the funder.

The Hellenic Foundation

Greek education in the UK

Around £8,000 (2012)

Beneficial area

UK.

Correspondent: The Secretary, 150 Aldersgate Street, London EC1A 4AB (tel: 020 7251 5100)

Trustees: Stamos J. Fafalios; Nicos H. Sideris; Constantinos I. Caroussis; Mary Bromley; George J. D. Lemos; Louisa Williamson; Joanna Caroussis; Nikki Chandris; Pantelis Michelakis.

CC Number: 326301

The foundation was set up in 1982 to 'advance and propagate education and learning in Great Britain in the cultural tradition and heritage of Greece and particularly in the subjects involving education, research, music and dance, books and library facilities and university symposia'.

In 2012 the trust had an income of £22,000 and a total expenditure of £8,000. We have no information regarding beneficiaries.

Previous beneficiaries: Royal Academy Byzantine exhibition (£15,000); Theatro Technis (£1,000); and Aghia Shophia School (£200).

Exclusions

The foundation is unable to offer scholarships or grants to cover tuition fees and living expenses.

Applications

In writing to the correspondent.

Information gathered from:

Accounts; Charity Commission record.

The Michael Heller Charitable Foundation

University and medical research projects, the arts

£304,000 (2011/12)

Beneficial area

Worldwide.

Correspondent: Michael Heller, Trustee, 24 Bruton Place, London W1J 6NE (tel: 020 7415 5000)

Trustees: Morven Heller; Michael Heller; W. S. Trustee Company Ltd.

CC Number: 327832

This trust was established in 1988, and funds specific projects relating to medical research, science and educational research. This usually involves making large grants to universities for research purposes, particularly medical research.

In 2011/12 the trust had assets of £3.8 million and an income of £240,000. Grants totalled £203,000, broken down as follows:

Education	£94,000
Humanitarian	£65,000
Research	£44,000

A list of beneficiaries was not provided in the trust's accounts.

Exclusions

No support for individuals.

Applications

In writing to the correspondent.

Information gathered from:

Accounts; Charity Commission record.

The Simon Heller Charitable Settlement

Medical research, science and educational research

£358,000 (2011/12)

Beneficial area

Worldwide.

Correspondent: The Trustees, 24 Bruton Place, London W1J 6NE (tel: 020 7415 5000)

Trustees: Michael Heller; Morven Heller; W. S. Trustee Company Ltd.

CC Number: 265405

This trust was established in 1972, and funds specific projects relating to medical research, science and educational research. This usually involves making large grants to universities for research purposes, particularly medical research. In practice, there appears to be some preference for Jewish organisations.

In 2011/12 the trust had assets of £7.2 million and an income of £385,000. Grants were made totalling £358,000. Broken down as follows: humanitarian (£184,000); education (£93,000); and research (£61,000). The accounts state that:

> The trustees consider that as this is a private charitable trust to which no public funds have been contributed, the disclosure requirements relating to grants in excess of £1,000 do not apply as the inclusion of such information would, in certain circumstances, be likely to prejudice the furtherance of the purposes of the charitable trust or recipient.

Previous beneficiaries include: Institute for Jewish Policy Research (£35,000); Jewish Care (£30,000), Aish Hatora (£15,000 in two grants), Spiro Institute (£13,000), Scopus (£12,000 in two grants); and Chief Rabbinate Charitable Trust (£10,000).

Exclusions

No grants to individuals.

Applications

In writing to the correspondent.

Information gathered from:

Accounts; Charity Commission record.

Help the Homeless

Homelessness

£46,000 (2011/12)

Beneficial area

UK.

Correspondent: Terry Kenny, Secretary, 6th Floor, 248 Tottenham Court Road, London W1T 7QZ (email: hth@help-the-homeless.org.uk; website: www.help-the-homeless.org.uk)

Trustees: F. J. Bergin; T. S. Cookson; T. Rogers; P. Fullerton; J. Rose; S. Holmes.

CC Number: 271988

The trust makes grants to smaller or new voluntary organisations (with a turnover of less than £1 million a year), who are registered charities, for capital costs directly relating to projects that assist individuals in their return to mainstream society, rather than simply offer shelter or other forms of sustenance. Grants to larger charities are considered if the project is suitably innovative and it is only possible for a large organisation to develop it. Grants do not normally exceed £3,000.

In 2011/12 the trust had assets of £1.2 million, an income of £75,000 and gave grants totalling £46,000.

Beneficiaries included: Bradford City Centre Project, West London Day Centre, Homeless in Action, Say Women and Youth Shelter (£3,000 each); Room at the Inn (£2,800); Furniture Plus, Ross-shire Women's Aid and St George's Hub (£2,000 each); Urban Outreach and South Birmingham Young Homeless Project (£1,500 each); and The Nehemiah Project (£400).

Exclusions

Charities with substantial funds are not supported. No grants to individuals.

Applications

Application forms can be downloaded from the trust's website. The quarterly deadlines for applications each year are: 31 March, 30 June, 30 September and 31 December.

Percentage of awards given to new applicants: between 40% and 50%.

Common applicant mistakes

'They do not properly review our website.'

Information gathered from:

Accounts; Charity Commission record; further information provided by the funder; funder's website.

Help the Hospices

Hospices

£582,000 to organisations (2011/12)

Beneficial area

UK and overseas.

Correspondent: Grants Team, 34–44 Britannia Street, London WC1X 9JG (tel: 020 7520 8200; fax: 020 7278 1021; email: info@helpthehospices.org.uk; website: www.helpthehospices.org.uk)

Trustees: Lee Barker; Peter Holliday; Andrew Ryde; Michael Howard; Bay Green; Paul Dyer; Patrick Beasley; Ros Taylor; Susan Newman; Christine Miles; Rosalind Scott.

CC Number: 1014851

The objects of the charity are:

- To facilitate and promote the relief, care and treatment of the sick, especially of the dying, and the support and care of their families and carers and of the bereaved
- To facilitate and promote the charitable activities of independent hospices
- To provide or facilitate education and training for professionals and volunteers engaged in palliative care
- To increase awareness among the general public of the values, principles and practice of hospice and palliative care

These objectives are met by providing education and training as well as funding hospices and palliative care units through a number of grant schemes. See the charity's website for up-to-date details of open and forthcoming programmes.

In 2011/12 the charity had assets of £6.8 million, an income of £5.7 million and made grants to organisations totalling £582,000. A further £1 million was given in grants to individuals for education, training and professional development.

Beneficiaries included: St Luke's Hospice (£78,000); St Giles Hospice (£51,000); St Catherine's Hospice (£49,000); Rowcroft – Torbay and S Devon Hospice (£30,000); Farleigh Hospice (£7,000); Children's Hospice Association Scotland (£5,000); Richard House Children's Hospice (£2,000).

Applications

The trust's website provides guidelines for each programme and clear information on application procedures and deadlines. Depending on the programme, application forms can be downloaded or completed through the online application system.

Information gathered from:

Accounts; Charity Commission record; funder's website.

The Christina Mary Hendrie Trust for Scottish and Canadian Charities

Youth, people who are elderly, general

£224,000 (2011/12)

Beneficial area

Scotland and Canada.

Correspondent: Alan Sharp, Secretary, 1 Rutland Court, Edinburgh EH3 8EY (tel: 01312 707700; website: www.christinamaryhendrietrust.com)

Trustees: Charles Cox; John Scott-Moncrieff; Caroline Irwin; Anthony Cox; Mary-Rose Grieve; Susie Hendrie; Andrew Desson; Caron Hughes.

SC Number: SC014514

The trust was established in 1975 following the death in Scotland of Christina Mary Hendrie. According to the trust's website:

> Although the trust's charitable purposes are broadly stated, our focus is specifically on assisting other charities operating in Scotland and Canada, specialising in work related to the young and the old. Within these criteria we have a particular but not exclusive or predominant interest in hospices and veterans of the armed forces.

In 2011/12 the trust's assets stood at £6 million with an income of £103,000. Grants totalled £224,000.

Beneficiaries included: Camphill Blair Drummond (£20,000); PKAVS, Portage Program and ACCORD Hospice Paisley (£10,000 each); Freeing the Human Spirit and Wester Hailes Youth Society (£9,000 each); Down's Syndrome Scotland and Fernandez Earle Scholarship Foundation (£5,000 each); and Highland Skate Park (£2,000).

Exclusions

Grants are not given to individuals.

Applications

Application forms can be accessed via the trust's website. Applications forms must be sent to the trust by post. The trustees meet twice yearly in March and October. To be considered for the meeting in March, applications must be made no later than 15 February and 15 September for the October meeting. Applications are acknowledged via email.

Information gathered from:

Accounts; OSCR record; funder's website.

Philip Henman Trust

Overseas development

£46,000 to organisations (2011/12)

Beneficial area

Worldwide.

Correspondent: Joseph Charles Clark, Trustee, 16 Pembury Road, Tonbridge TN9 2HX (tel: 01732 362227; email: info@pht.org.uk; website: www.pht.org.uk)

Trustees: Joseph Charles Clark; David James Clark; Jason Colin Duffey.

CC Number: 1054707

The Philip Henman Trust offers grants to major UK development organisations based overseas requiring partnership funding for projects lasting between three and five years. These grants are split into annual payments (normally between £3,000 and £5,000 per annum) with a maximum total of £25,000. Once the grant has been approved the organisation will be guaranteed an annual grant for the duration of the project, as long as receipts and reports are sent back to the trust. Once a grant has been given, the organisation cannot apply for a further grant in respect of the same project.

The trust only has resources to guarantee an average of two new long-term grants a year, and therefore it is important to be sure any project fits the criteria before applying. Successful applications are normally those that prove the following:

- The project is being run professionally by an established major UK registered charity (normally defined as having an income of over £100,000 per annum)
- The project is concerned with long-term overseas development
- The project will start and finish within five years – no funding is given for ongoing concerns
- The funding from the trust is important to the project (normally the grant should account for between 20% and 80% of the total project budget)
- The project will provide a lasting beneficial impact to the people or environment it seeks to help
- The project is being partly funded by other sources – voluntary work and central office administration costs can be counted as other source funding

In 2011/12 the trust had assets of £1.8 million and an income of £60,000. Grants were awarded to 15 organisations and totalled £48,000. They were broken down as follows:

Overseas aid	£40,000
Medical and community work	£5,000
Individuals	£2,000
Other	£850

Unfortunately, a list of beneficiaries was not included in the accounts.

Applications

Applications are only considered once a year – the deadline is always 10 September. Applications are no longer accepted by post. Use the online form (available on the 'Applications' page) to submit a request for funding.

Percentage of awards given to new applicants: between 10% and 20%.

Common applicant mistakes

'Sending by post; looking for one-off grants.'

Information gathered from:

Accounts; Charity Commission record; further information provided by the funder; funder's website.

The G. D. Herbert Charitable Trust

Medicine, health, welfare, environmental resources

£63,000 (2011/12)

Beneficial area

UK.

Correspondent: Mr M. J. Byrne, Trustee, Veale Wasbrough Vizards, Barnards Inn, 86 Fetter Lane, London EC4A 1AD (tel: 020 7405 1234)

Trustees: M. E. Beaumont; J. M. Cuxson.

CC Number: 295998

The trust makes grants in the areas of medicine, health, welfare and environmental resources. It mainly gives regular grants to a set list of charities, with a few one-off grants given each year in the fields of health and welfare.

In 2011/12 this trust had assets of £1.8 million, which generated an income of £46,000. There were 25 'regular donations' made totalling £63,000.

All beneficiaries except two (Ogbourne St George Parochial Church Council and Wiltshire Wildlife Trust (£600 each)) received grants totalling £2,700, they included: The National Trust, The Abbeyfield Society, Canterbury Oast Trust, Campaign to Protect Rural England, Friends of the Elderly, Marie

Curie Cancer Care, NSPCC, Catch 22, Disability Rights UK, St Christopher Hospice and The Woodland Trust.

Applications

In writing to the correspondent. No applications are invited other than from those charities currently supported by the trust.

Information gathered from:

Accounts; Charity Commission record.

Hesed Trust

Christian causes

£68,000 (2010/11)

Beneficial area

UK and overseas.

Correspondent: Glyn Rawlings, Trustee, 14 Chiltern Avenue, Cosby, Leicestershire LE9 1UF (tel: 01162 862990; email: glynrawlings@btopenworld.com)

Trustees: Ronald Eagle; Glyn Rawlings; Charles Smith.

CC Number: 1000489

The trust's objectives are:

- The advancement of the Christian faith
- The relief of persons who are in conditions of need, hardship or distress or who are aged or sick
- The provision of instruction the Christian faith at any educational establishment
- The provision of facilities for recreation for persons in need of, for the benefit of the public at large with the object of improving the conditions of life for such persons

The accounts for 2011/12 were overdue at the Commission being 319 days late at the time of writing. In 2010/11 the trust had assets of £74,500 and an income £180,000. Grants were made to more than six charitable organisations and totalled £68,000.

Beneficiaries were: Ministries without Borders (£42,000); All Nations Church (£24,000); Blackpool Church and City Church Coventry (£10,000 each); and Covenant Life Church Leicester (£750).

Exclusions

No support for expeditions and individual requests.

Applications

In writing to the correspondent.

Information gathered from:

Accounts; Charity Commission record.

The P. and C. Hickinbotham Charitable Trust

Social welfare

£87,000 (2011/12)

Beneficial area

UK, with a preference for Leicestershire and Rutland.

Correspondent: Roger Hickinbotham, Trustee, 9 Windmill Way, Lyddington, Oakham, Leicestershire LE15 9LY (tel: 01572 821236; email: roger@hickinbothamtrust.org.uk; website: www.hickinbothamtrust.org.uk)

Trustees: Catherine Hickinbotham; Roger Hickinbotham; Rachel Hickinbotham; Anna Steiger; Charlotte Hickinbotham; Frances Hickinbotham.

CC Number: 216432

Grants are generally not recurrent and are largely to social welfare organisations, with some churches and Quaker meetings also receiving support. Grants are mainly between £1,000 – £2,000, with some smaller grants made to a variety of registered charities. The trust gives occasional, one-off larger grants usually between £5,000 and £20,000.

In 2011/12 the trust had assets of £3.5 million and an income of £65,000. Grants totalled £87,000.

Beneficiaries included: DeMontfort University – Women in Technology Programme (£9,000); Community Foundation for Northern Ireland and Lyddington Village Hall Trust (£5,000 each); Altnaveigh House (£3,500); Mullaghdun Community Association (£2,000); Belgrave Playhouse (£1,500) LOROS, RNLI, Pen Green Centre and Staffordshire Area Quaker Meeting (£1,000 each).

Exclusions

No grants to individuals applying for bursary-type assistance or to large UK charities.

Applications

In writing to the correspondent, giving a brief outline of the purpose of the grant. Replies will not be sent to unsuccessful applicants. Successful applicants are usually contacted within six weeks.

Common applicant mistakes

'Don't match our criteria'

Information gathered from:

Accounts; Charity Commission record; further information provided by the funder; funder's website.

Alan Edward Higgs Charity

Child welfare

£236,000 (2010/11)

Beneficial area

Within 25 miles of the centre of Coventry only.

Correspondent: Peter Knatchbull-Hugessen, Clerk, Ricoh Arena Ltd, Phoenix Way, Coventry CV6 6GE (tel: 02476 221311; email: clerk@higgscharity.org.uk)

Trustees: Peter J. Davis; Marilyn F. Knatchbull-Hugessen; Andrew Young.

CC Number: 509367

Grants are made to benefit 'wholly or mainly the inhabitants of the area within 25 miles of the centre of Coventry'. The main activity supported is 'the promotion of child welfare, and particularly the welfare of underprivileged children'. It is the aim of the trustees to reach as wide a selection of the community as possible within the geographical limitations. They are happy to receive applications for grants from local bodies or associations and from national organisations that can show that any grant from the charity would be used to benefit people resident within the geographical area. The increasing range and diversity of donations continue to be welcomed.

At the time of writing, the accounts for the year 2011/12 were almost a year overdue at the Charity Commission and so we have used the information provided in the most recent published, those for 2010/11. In that accounting year the charity had assets of £19 million, an income of £477,000 and grants were made to 50 organisations totalling £236,000.

There was no list of beneficiaries contained within the accounts but previous grant beneficiaries included: Coventry Institute of Creative Enterprise (£40,000); The Living Environment Trust (£28,000); Belgrade Theatre (£20,000); Family Holiday Association (£10,000); Shakespeare Hospice Appeal (£5,000); Guideposts Trust (£3,000); and the RSPB (£1,000).

Exclusions

No grants for individuals or the funding of services usually provided by statutory services, medical research, travel outside the UK or evangelical or worship activities.

Applications

In writing to the clerk to the trustees, along with:

- A copy of the latest audited accounts
- Charity number (if registered)

- A detailed description of the local activities for the benefit of which the grant would be applied
- The specific purpose for which the grant is sought
- A copy of the organisation's policy that ensures the protection of young or vulnerable people and a clear description of how it is implemented and monitored

Information gathered from:

Accounts; Charity Commission record.

Highcroft Charitable Trust

Jewish, poverty

Around £63,000 (2011/12)

Beneficial area

UK and overseas.

Correspondent: Rabbi R. Fischer, Trustee, 15 Highcroft Gardens, London NW11 0LY

Trustees: Rabbi Richard Fischer; Sarah Fischer.

CC Number: 272684

The trust supports the advancement and study of the Jewish faith and the Torah, and also the relief of poverty and advancement of education among people of the Jewish faith. Grants have previously ranged between £150 and £5,000.

The income of the trust varies, averaging around £64,000 between 2008 and 2012. In 2011/12 the trust had an income of £17,000 and a total expenditure of £69,000. Grants totalled around £63,000.

Unfortunately, a list of beneficiaries was not available, however previous beneficiaries have included: Friends of Beer Miriam, Institute For Higher Rabbinic Studies and Kollel Ohr Yechiel (£5,000 each); Kollel Chibas Yerushalayim (£4,200); Craven Walk Charity Trust (£2,500); London Friends of Kamenitzer (£2,000); Hachzakas Torah Vachesed Charity (£1,900); Amutat Shaarei Harama, Beis Yaacov High School and Tashbar Manchester (£1,000 each); Belt Haknesset Kehilat Yaacov (£700); and British Friends of College Technology and Delamere Forest School (£100 each).

Applications

In writing to the correspondent.

Information gathered from:

Accounts; Charity Commission record.

The Derek Hill Foundation

Arts/culture

£66,000 to organisations (2011/12)

Beneficial area

UK.

Correspondent: The Trustees, Rathbone Trust Company Ltd4th Floor1 Curzon StreetLondonW1J 5FB (tel: 020 7399 0000)

Trustees: Rathbone Trust Company Ltd; Earl of Gowrie; Lord Armstrong of Ilminster; Josephine Batterham; Ian Paterson.

CC Number: 801590

This foundation was set up in 1989, by the writer and artist Derek Hill. Following his death in 1990, a specific legacy was left to the foundation including properties, furniture and pieces of art. In 2011/12 it had assets of £1.4 million and an income of £27,000. Grants totalled £69,000, of which £66,000 went to organisations.

Beneficiaries included: the British School at Rome (£12,000); Arvon Foundation (£7,500); The George Orwell Memorial Trust and Thelma Holt (£5,000 each); Llanfyllin Festival Association (£3,000); Welsh National Opera (£2,500); Bulgarian Orphans Fund (£1,500); Yale University Press and Friary Guildford Brass Band (£1,000 each).

In addition, grants were made to six individuals amounting to £2,900.

Applications

In writing to the correspondent.

Information gathered from:

Accounts; Charity Commission record.

The Charles Littlewood Hill Trust

Health, disability, service, heritage, children (including schools), welfare

£161,000 (2012)

Beneficial area

UK, with a preference for Nottinghamshire and Norfolk.

Correspondent: John Thompson, c/o Shakespeares, Park House, Friar Lane, Nottingham NG1 6DN (tel: 01476 552429; fax: 01159 480234)

Trustees: Charles Barratt; Tim Farr; Nigel Savory; John Pears.

CC Number: 286350

The trust supports schools, disability, health, service and children's organisations. It gives UK-wide, although particular preference is given to applications from Norfolk and Nottinghamshire.

In 2012 the trust had assets of £4.1 million and an income of £204,000. Grants were made to over 62 organisations totalling £161,000. Beneficiaries included: Norfolk Community Foundation (£15,000); Royal Norfolk Agricultural Association (£12,500); The Norfolk Churches Trust (£7,500); St John Waterwing (£6,000); Churches Conservation Trust and Nottinghamshire Wildlife Trust (£5,000 each); Dragon Hall and Family Care (£2,000 each); and Ovarian Cancer Action and Victim Support – Norfolk (£1,000 each).

Other grants totalled £17,500.

Exclusions

Applications from individuals are not considered. Grants are seldom made for repairs of parish churches outside Nottinghamshire.

Applications

In writing to the correspondent, including the latest set of audited accounts, at least one month before trustees' meetings in March, July and November. Unsuccessful applicants will not be notified.

Percentage of awards given to new applicants: between 10% and 20%.

Common applicant mistakes

'They ignore the geographic preferences of the trustees noted on the Charity Commission website. They do not include a copy of their latest audited accounts.'

Information gathered from:

Accounts; Charity Commission record; further information provided by the funder.

R. G. Hills Charitable Trust

Health, poverty, education, general

£86,500 (2011/12)

Beneficial area

UK and overseas.

Correspondent: Harvey Barrett, Trustee, Furley Page, 39 St Margaret's Street, Canterbury, Kent CT1 2TX (tel: 01227 763939)

Trustees: David Pentin; Harvey Barrett.

CC Number: 1008914

This trust was dormant until Mrs E M Hill's death in March 1996, when she left three-quarters of the residue of her estate to the trust. The balance was received in June 1999. The trust supports local and national registered charities mainly, but not exclusively, in the fields of health, poverty and education.

In 2011/12 it held assets of £3 million and had an income of £105,000. The trust made grants to 39 organisations totalling £86,500.

Beneficiaries included: Canterbury Festival Foundation (£10,000); Odyssey Project Ltd (£3,500); Swinfen Charitable Trust and Wildwood Trust (£3,000 each); Porchlight and Project Mala (£2,500 each); African Mission, Asthma Relief, Dyslexia Institute, Fynvola Foundation and The Grasslands Trust (£2,000 each); Tall Ships Trust (£1,750); Action Against Hunger and Hope Romania (£1,500 each); and The B 17 Charitable Trust (£1,000).

Applications

In writing to the correspondent.

Information gathered from:

Accounts; Charity Commission record.

Hinchley Charitable Trust

Mainly evangelical Christian

£167,000 (2011/12)

Beneficial area

UK and overseas.

Correspondent: Mrs Emma Northcott, Secretary, 10 Coplow Terrace, Coplow Street, Birmingham B16 0DQ (tel: 01214 556632)

Trustees: Prof. Brian Stanley, Chair; John Levick; Mark Hobbs; Roger Northcott.

CC Number: 1108412

The trust gives grants in the following categories in the UK:

- Training of Christian leaders
- Holistic mission and evangelism
- Christian youth organisations
- Christian organisations in local communities
- Christian influence in the public sphere

And in the following categories in the rest of the world:

- Leadership training for the South
- Community development work with strong with a strong local partnership
- Evangelism – consistent with sustainability and training

It is particularly keen to support smaller charities where a grant can make a significant difference to their work.

In 2011/12 the trust had assets of £2.8 million and an income of £163,000. Grants to 19 organisations totalled £167,000.

During the year beneficiaries included: Langham Partnership (£13,000); Christchurch Canterbury University, ACK Masabit Mission, Faith2Share, Spurgeons College (£10,000 each); Elim Church – Huddersfield (£8,000); and Urban Saints (£7,500).

Applications

The trustees adopt a proactive approach to grantmaking meaning unsolicited applications are rarely supported.

Information gathered from:

Accounts; Charity Commission record.

Stuart Hine Trust

Evangelical Christianity

£304,000 (2011/12)

Beneficial area

UK and overseas.

Correspondent: Raymond Bodkin, Trustee, 'Cherith', 23 Derwent Close, Hailsham, East Sussex BN27 3DA (tel: 01323 843948)

Trustees: Raymond Bodkin; Amelia Gardner; Roland Dumford-Slater; Jonathan Birdwood Juby; Leonard Chipping.

CC Number: 326941

This trust receives the royalties produced by the hymn 'How Great Thou Art'. It gives grants to evangelical Christian organisations, churches and missionary societies. The majority of grants go to Wycliffe Bible Translators and organisations supported by Stuart Hine during his lifetime.

In 2011/12 the trust had assets of £371,000, an income of £223,000 and gave grants totalling £304,000.

The only grant beneficiary listed in the accounts was Wycliff Bible Translators, which received a donation of £159,000. Grants to other organisations totalled £145,000.

Applications

The trust states that 'unsolicited requests for funds will not be considered'. Funds are basically distributed in accordance with the wishes of the settlor.

Common applicant mistakes

'They are not aware that we are restricted by a wish as to whom we can make grants.'

Information gathered from:

Accounts; Charity Commission record; further information provided by the funder; funder's website.

The Hinrichsen Foundation

Music

£29,000 to organisations (2012)

Beneficial area

UK.

Correspondent: The Administrator, 2–6 Baches Street, London N1 6DN (email: hinrichsen.foundation@editionpeters.com; website: www.hinrichsenfoundation.org.uk)

Trustees: Professor Jonathan Cross; Keith Potter; Dr Linda Hirst; Professor Stephen Walsh; Patric Standford; Paul Strang; Sue Lubbock; Tim Berg; Tabby Estell; Eleanor Gussman.

CC Number: 272389

The following information is taken from the foundation's website:

> The Hinrichsen Foundation is a charity devoted to the promotion of music.
>
> It was founded in 1976 by Carla Eddy Hinrichsen to ensure the continuation of the tradition established by the Hinrichsen family as the proprietors of 'Edition Peters' the music publishers, established more than 200 years ago in the German city of Leipzig.
>
> At the trustees meeting at the beginning of January 2012 the foundation considered its financial position and prospects, which the foundation believe to be positive. We are currently evaluating the role that the foundation may play within the contemporary music environment, particularly against the current economic backdrop, and assessing where its support may be most effective. We are now accepting applications, albeit at a modest level: further announcements will be posted on the website.
>
> During the 32 years since the foundation was set up, 1330 grants have been awarded, totalling £1.4 million. (This amounts to approximately £45,000 per year with an average grant of £1,000).
>
> Throughout this time the majority of awards have been made to subsidise the public performance of works by living composers – these have included performances in standard concert halls, churches, railway stations and other conventional spaces. Awards have also been made to fund scholarships and bursaries at academic institutions and some festivals. In the early years a number of musicological projects were funded, assisting with the publications of a number of books, music scores and three recordings. While grants towards recordings are no longer made, the publication of the results of research continues to be an important though minor part of our funding programme.
>
> In 1994 the first Hinrichsen Composition Bursary was awarded: to date six awards have been made totalling £70,000, the

first three direct to composers and the other three in association with institutions.

In 2012 the foundation's statement of financial activities declared assets of £1.2 million and an income of £522,000. Grants payable totalled £36,000 representing £29,000 to 20 organisations and £7,000 to individuals.

Beneficiaries included: ENO (£2,500); Birmingham Contemporary Music Group, Dartington International Summer Festival and Sound Festival (£2,000 each); Wednesdays at the Forge and York Late Music (£1,500 each); and Clod Ensemble and Trio Scordatura (£1,000 each).

Exclusions

The foundation does not:

- Fund the commissioning of new works
- Make donations towards the costs of making recordings, either by private or commercial companies
- As a general rule, finance degree courses. The aim is to encourage composition and research, but not to finance the acquisition of basic skills in these subjects
- Consider applications for assistance in purchasing musical instruments or equipment including the electronic or computer variety
- Make grants retrospectively

Applications

On a form which can be downloaded from the foundation's website, where full information on how to apply, including a useful FAQ section, is also available. Trustees meet quarterly.

Information gathered from:

Accounts; Charity Commission record; funder's website.

The Henry C. Hoare Charitable Trust

General

£147,000 (2011/12)

Beneficial area

UK.

Correspondent: Trust Administrator, C. Hoare and Co., 37 Fleet Street, London EC4P 4DQ (tel: 020 7353 4522)

Trustees: Henry C. Hoare; Hoare Trustees.

CC Number: 1088669

This trust was established in 2001 with general charitable purposes. One-off and annual donations are made.

In 2011/12 the trust held assets of £3.8 million and had an income of £198,000. Grants were made totalling £147,000.

Donations were broken down as follows:

Health	£42,000
Environmental protection and improvement	£36,000
Citizenship and Community Development	£23,000
Youth, age, ill health, disability and financial hardship	£22,000
Education	£15,000
Animal welfare	£3,600
Religion	£2,200
Arts	£2,200
Crime	£1,000
Public policy	£250

The accounts listed donations of £5,000 or more. These included: Beckley Foundation (£10,500); Transform Drug Policy Foundation, Prospect Burma, Future Trees Trust and Autism Research (£10,000 each); Worldwide Volunteers, Tree Aid, The March Foundation, Leaping Frogs Kindergarten, League of Friends of Westminster Hospital, Ataxia UK and Burma Campaign UK (£5,000 each).

Applications

In writing to the correspondent.

Information gathered from:

Accounts; Charity Commission record.

Hockerill Educational Foundation

Education, especially Christian education

£182,000 to organisations (2011/12)

Beneficial area

UK, with a preference for the dioceses of Chelmsford and St Albans.

Correspondent: Derek J. Humphrey, Secretary, 3 The Swallows, Harlow, Essex CM17 0AR (tel: 01279 420855; email: info@hockerillfoundation.org.uk; website: www.hockerillfoundation.org.uk)

Trustees: Mrs H. Potter; Jonathan Reynolds; Venerable Elwin Cockett; Lesley Barlow; Colin Graham Bird; Harry Marsh; Revd Paul Bayes; Bishop of Colchester; Janet Scott; Jonathan Longstaff; Revd Dr Alan Smith; Revd Stephen Cottrell.

CC Number: 311018

The foundation was set up in 1978 following the closure of Hockerill College, which was established in 1852 to train women teachers who 'would go to schools in the service of humanity'. When the Secretary of State for Education and Science decided in 1976 to wind down Hockerill College, the proceeds of the sale of its assets were given to this foundation to use for the purposes for which the college was created.

The foundation makes grants in the field of education in three main areas:

- individual grants to support the education and training of teachers
- Research, development and support grants to organisations in the field of religious education
- Grants to develop the church's educational work in the dioceses of Chelmsford and St Albans

The trustees will normally consider applications from corporate bodies or institutions associated with education on Christian principles. There is a religious dimension to all education, but the trustees expect any activity, course, project or research supported to be of real benefit to religious education and/or the church's educational work. They will give priority to imaginative new projects which will enhance the Church of England's contribution to higher and further education and/or promote aspects of religious education in schools.

Grants are renewable for up to three years, or occasionally a maximum of five years, subject to the trustees being satisfied on an annual basis that the grant has been used satisfactorily. Grants are always made for specific programmes or projects. Grants for the funding of research or the appointment of staff may be paid by instalments and are subject to funds being available. The trustees will monitor research or the progress of a project as appropriate, and expects regular progress reports. It may also ask for a line of credit in the final report of a research project.

In 2011/12 the foundation had assets of £5.3 million and an income of £274,000. Grants totalling £233,000 were paid during the year and were distributed as follows:

Diocese of St Albans	£75,000
Diocese of Chelmsford	£75,000
Other corporate grants	£32,000
Individuals	£51,000

Exclusions

Grants are not given for general appeals for funds, 'bricks and mortar' building projects or purposes that are the clear responsibility of another body.

Applications

On a form available to download from the foundation's website. Applications should include some official documentation, such as the most recent annual report and accounts, which clearly show the status, objects and ideals of the organisation and its financial position, and an sae. They should be submitted by 31 March each year. Grants are usually awarded between July and September.

Percentage of awards given to new applicants: between 40% and 50%.

Common applicant mistakes
'Do not read the guidance notes for making applications.'

Information gathered from:
Accounts; Charity Commission record; further information provided by the funder; funder's website.

The Sir Julian Hodge Charitable Trust

General

£47,000 (2011/12)

Beneficial area
UK.

Correspondent: Margaret Cason, Trustee and Secretary, 31 Windsor Place, Cardiff CF10 3UR (tel: 02920 787674)

Trustees: Jonathan Hodge; Joyce Harrison; Derrek Jones; Margaret Cason; Eric Hammonds.

CC Number: 234848

The trust was established by a gift from Sir Julian Hodge and in 2006 received a further substantial bequest under the terms of his will.

The principal objective of the trust is to allocate trust income for charitable purposes, with special regard to the following areas:

- The encouragement of medical and surgical studies and research and in particular the study and research in connection with the causes, diagnosis, treatment and cure of cancer, poliomyelitis, tuberculosis and diseases affecting children
- The general advancement of medical and surgical science
- The advancement of education
- The advancement of religion
- The relief of aged and disabled persons in needy circumstances

In 2011/12 the trust had assets of £1.4 million and an income of £59,000. Grants were made totalling £47,000 and were broken down as follows:

Medical	£17,000
Other	£23,250
Education	£6,000
Religion	£1,000

Beneficiaries included: The Conservation Foundation and Strongbones Children's Charitable Trust (£2,000 each); Sense, Douglas Macmillan Hospice and The Firefighters Charity (£1,500 each); National Search and Rescue Dog Association, All Saints Church, Ammanford, Disabled Travel Service, Watford and Three Rivers Furniture Recycling, YHA (England and Wales) Ltd and North Wales Deaf Association (£1,000 each); and Northampton Volunteering Centre (£750).

Exclusions
No grants to individuals or companies.

Applications
In writing to the correspondent. The trust invites applications for grants from charitable organisations. Organisations should submit a summary of their proposals to the trustees in a specific format. Applications for grants are considered by the trustees against its objectives.

Information gathered from:
Accounts; Charity Commission record.

The J. G. Hogg Charitable Trust

Welfare, animal welfare, general

Around £100,000 (2011/12)

Beneficial area
UK.

Correspondent: C. M. Jones, Trustees' Accountant, Chantrey Vellacott DFK, Russell Square House, 10 -12 Russell Square, London WC1B 5LF (tel: 020 7509 9000; email: cjones@cvdfk.com)

Trustees: Sarah Jane Houldsworth; Joanna Wynfreda Turvey.

CC Number: 299042

The trust states that it has no set policy on the type of charity supported, but would give favourable consideration to those based primarily in the UK that support the relief of human and animal suffering.

In 2011/12 the trust had an income of £15,000 and total expenditure of £100,000. We have no information regarding beneficiary organisations but previously the trust made awards to: Kids Company and Oxfam (£15,000 each); Medicinema and Teddy Bear Air Care (£10,000 each); and Addiction Recovery Foundation (£7,000).

Exclusions
No grants to individuals. Registered charities only are supported.

Applications
In writing to the correspondent. To keep administration costs to a minimum, the trust is unable to reply to unsuccessful applicants.

Information gathered from:
Accounts; Charity Commission record.

The Holden Charitable Trust

Jewish causes

£377,000 (2011/12)

Beneficial area
UK, with a preference for the Manchester area.

Correspondent: The Clerk, c/o Lopian Gross Barnett and Co., Cardinal House, 20 St Mary Parsonage, Manchester M3 2LG (tel: 01618 328721)

Trustees: David Lopian; Marian Lopian; Michael Lopian.

CC Number: 264185

The Holden Charitable Trust exists to receive and distribute charitable donations to worthy causes primarily within the Jewish community.

In 2011/12 the trust had assets of £687,000 and an income of £302,000. Grants amounted to £377,000.

There was no list of beneficiary organisations contained within the annual accounts, however previous beneficiaries have included: Broom Foundation (£59,000); Ohel Bnei Yaakob (£50,000); Ohr Yerushalayim Synagogue (£33,000); Friends of Beis Eliyahu Trust (£24,000); the FED (£7,500); and King David's School (£5,000).

Applications
In writing to the correspondent.

Information gathered from:
Accounts; Charity Commission record.

The Dorothy Holmes Charitable Trust

General

Around £60,000 (2011/12)

Beneficial area
UK, with a preference for Dorset.

Correspondent: Michael Kennedy, Smallfield Cody and Co., 5 Harley Place, Harley Street, London W1G 8QD (tel: 020 7631 4574)

Trustees: Margaret Cody; Dr Susan Roberts; James Roberts.

CC Number: 237213

The trust's policy is to make a substantial number of relatively small donations to groups working in many charitable fields – including those involved in medical research, disability, older people, children and young people, churches, the disadvantaged, the environment and the arts. The trust can give throughout the UK but has a preference for Dorset, especially Poole. In practice nearly all grants are given to either national charities or those based in Dorset. In 2011/12 the trust had an income of £25,000 and an expenditure of £65,000. Further information was not available.

Previous beneficiaries included: Wallingford School (£6,000); Children in Touch, Crisis and Christmas and RNLI (£5,000 each); Hyman Cen Foundation (£4,000); Army Benevolent Fund (£3,000); Action on Elder Abuse and Clic Sargent Cancer Fund (£2,000 each); National Autistic Society and Raleigh International (£1,000 each); and Royal Free Hospital Retirement Fellowship (£300).

Exclusions

Only applications from registered charities will be considered.

Applications

In writing to the correspondent, preferably in January to March each year.

Information gathered from:

Accounts; Charity Commission record.

The Holst Foundation

Arts

£154,000 (2011/12)

Beneficial area

UK.

Correspondent: The Grants Administrator, 43 Alderbrook Road, London SW12 8AD (tel: 020 8673 4215 (answerphone only); email: holst@dpmail.co.uk; website: www.holstfoundation.org)

Trustees: Andrew Clements; Prof. Arnold Whittall; Peter Carter; Bayan Northcott; Noel Periton; Julian Anderson.

CC Number: 283668

The trust has two objects: firstly, to promote public appreciation of the musical works of Gustav and Imogen Holst; and secondly, to encourage the study and practice of the arts.

In practice the trust tends to be proactive. Funds are available for the composition and performance of new music. The trust has historical links with Aldeburgh in Suffolk and is a major funder of new music at the annual Aldeburgh Festival. It also promotes the recording of new music by means of funding to the recording label NMC, which the foundation also provided the funds to set up. The 2011/12 accounts note:

> With the expiry of the majority of the copyrights in Holst's music at the end of 2004, the Foundation has adopted a policy of distributing funds from capital as well as income, with a view to maintaining its existing grants policy for at least a further ten years. The main aim of the Foundation over this period will be to safeguard the future of the recording label NMC (itself a charitable company). This will mean that other grants will be gradually reduced.

In 2011/12 it had assets of £1.1 million and an income of £76,000. Grants totalled £154,000.

As in previous years the largest donation of £120,000 went to NMC Recordings. Other beneficiaries included: New Music House (£3,800); Holst Birthplace Trust, London Sinfonietta and Birmingham Contemp Music Group (£3,000 each); Aldeburgh Music (£2,500); and Mornington Trust and Tête à Tête Productions (£1,000).

A further 22 unlisted grants of less than £1,000 each totalled £11,300.

Exclusions

No support for

- The recordings or works of Holst that are already well supported
- Capital projects
- Individuals for educational purposes, research, travel, purchase of instruments, equipment or publications
- The commissioning of new works, although help is sometimes available for the copying and rehearsal costs of works receiving first performances
- Festivals (other than Aldeburgh) or orchestras or other large organisations

Applications

In writing to the correspondent. Trustees meet four times a year. There is no application form. Six copies of the application should be sent. Applications should contain full financial details and be as concise as possible. If you are applying to other funders you should also make note of this in your application form. Funding is not given retrospectively.

Percentage of awards given to new applicants: less than 10%.

Common applicant mistakes

'Not reading our guidelines.'

Information gathered from:

Accounts; Charity Commission record; further information provided by the funder; funder's website.

P. H. Holt Foundation

General

£65,000 (2011/12)

Beneficial area

UK, with a preference for Merseyside.

Correspondent: Anne Edwards, Trust Administrator, LCVS, 151 Dale Street, Liverpool L2 2AH (tel: 01512 372663; email: administrator@phholtfoundation.org.uk; website: www.phholtfoundation.org.uk)

Trustees: Neil Kemsley, Chair; Tilly Boyce; Martin Cooke; Paige Earlam; Nikki Eastwood; Anthony Hannay; Ken Ravenscroft; Elspeth Christie.

CC Number: 1113708

The foundation makes a large number of mostly small grants mostly in Merseyside. It is a welcome and exceptional example of Liverpool shipping money staying in and around the city. The foundation concentrates its giving on projects in Merseyside but also recognises that some parts of Cheshire West and Chester, Halton and West Lancashire are linked to Merseyside and so also considers these as within its beneficial area. The trust also offers support and professional advice to charities in the area. The 'Holt Tradition' grant programme has been discontinued since 2011.

> *Current priorities*
>
> We are currently particularly interested in some themes which cross boundaries: for example, in the links between community development and economic activity, in educational initiatives in a wide sense, in using the arts to serve the community, in breaking down barriers between social and cultural groupings, in health education, and in community participation in the care of the natural and built environment.
>
> Nearly all our grants are for specific projects not general running costs. Exceptionally, we may assist with routine costs of organisations which are having major financial difficulties if we think their work has special value.

Grants are rarely given for core, staffing or capital costs. A full discussion of the trust's priorities and criteria is available on the website.

Grantmaking

In 2011/12 the foundation had assets of £13.9 million and an income of £754,000. 41 grants were made during the year, 37 of which went to applicants who were previously supported. Staffing costs were proportionately high at £69,000. Grants committed during the year totalled £75,000 (although only £65,000 was paid in the year) and were categorised as follows:

Grants by category 2011/12

	Merseyside
Community development and participation	£33,000
Visual and performing arts	£15,600
Education	£14,900
Social welfare	£7,300
Natural environment	£2,800
Heritage and built environment	£1,100
Total committed in year	**£75,000**

Grants totalled £75,000 although a budget of £160,000 was available. The 2011/12 accounts offer the following:

> The principal generic reason for our comparatively low grant expenditure was that, as indicated in previous years, the vast majority of the applications which we currently receive are for worthy but routine causes seeking help to cover day-to-day expenditure, more and more often including staff costs. We remain conscious of our comparatively small size as a grant maker and also continue to think that the cuts in public expenditure and the general downturn in the economy both mean that Merseyside's charitable sector might still not have reached the time when it will be most in need of grants from foundations such as ours.

A full list of grants was not included in the accounts, however, previous beneficiaries included: Speke Baptist Church (£10,000); Lodestar Theatre Company (£6,000); Collective Encounters and Liverpool Arts Interface Ltd (£5,000 each); Plaza Community Cinema (£4,400); Garston and District Community Council (£3,000); Hurricane Film Foundation (£2,500); Creative Ideas in Action and Merseyside Refugee and Asylum Seekers Pre and Post Natal Support Group (£2,000 each); Steps to Freedom (£1,500); Kensington Remembers (£1,000); and China Pearl, Rotunda Community College and Elim Christian Centre (£500 each).

Exclusions

No grants for:

- Individuals
- Sectarian causes
- Appeals for help with minibuses, holidays and animal welfare work
- Organisations based outside of Merseyside

The trust tends to dislike appeals from intermediary bodies and will only support national charities working on Merseyside when the activity is important for the area and there are good reasons why it is not being carried out by a local organisation.

Applications

From the website:

> There is currently no application form. What we want is a short letter about your project, backed up as appropriate by a budget, your annual report and accounts, and indications of who else is supporting the work or willing to recommend it. Explain how much you hope we will give and why you need that amount. Remember that, with limited resources, we prefer to make fairly small grants but also want them to be significant in their impact; when we make larger grants, it is normally after a series of meetings and discussions.
>
> We can only judge how your project fits those priorities if your application includes the answers to five specific questions:
>
> - What are you trying to do?
> - How does it fit in with the rest of your work?
> - How does it fit in with what other organisations are doing?
> - If we make a grant, how will you and we know whether what you do with it is worthwhile and successful?
> - Why do you need PH Holt Foundation, rather than anyone else, to support this piece of work?
>
> It helps if you give us a telephone contact so we can follow up any queries. We accept applications throughout the year and try to take decisions about them within three months. Inevitably, we receive far more applications than we can help. Contacting individual trustees about applications is not a good idea! However, we welcome enquiries even at the early stage when you are considering an application.

Information gathered from:

Accounts; Charity Commission record; funder's website.

The Homelands Charitable Trust

The New Church, health, social welfare, children

£242,000 (2011/12)

Beneficial area

UK.

Correspondent: Nigel Armstrong, Trustee, c/o Alliotts, 4th Floor, Imperial House, 15 Kingsway, London WC2B 6UN (tel: 020 7240 9971)

CC Number: 214322

This trust was established in 1962, the settlors were four members of the Curry family and the original endowment was in the form of shares in the Curry company.

In 2011/12 it had assets of £6.8 million and a total income of £260,000. Grants were made totalling £242,000. No list of beneficiary organisations was available. The trustees state in their 2011/12 annual report that they intend to continue supporting registered charities with a bias towards: General Conference of the New Church; medical research; care and protection of children; and hospices, including those for children.

Previous beneficiaries included: General Conference of the New Church (£68,000); Broadfield Memorial Fund (£15,000); New Church College (£11,000); Bournemouth Society (£10,000); Jubilee Sailing Trust, Manic Depression Fellowship and National Children's Homes (£2,400 each); and the Attic Charity – Youth Project, Bikeability, Eyeless Trust and Pestalozzi (£1,600 each).

Applications

In writing to the correspondent.

Information gathered from:

Accounts; Charity Commission record.

The Homestead Charitable Trust

Medicine, health, welfare, animal welfare, Christianity and the arts

£128,000 to organisations (2011/12)

Beneficial area

UK.

Correspondent: Lady Nina Bracewell-Smith, Trustee, Flat 7, Clarence Gate Gardens, Glentworth Street, London NW1 6AY

CC Number: 293979

This trust makes grants towards medical, health and welfare, animal welfare, Christianity and the arts.

In 2011/12 it had assets of £5.1 million, which generated an income of £88,000. Grants given to individuals and institutions totalled £131,000.

Beneficiaries included: Ahkshaya Patra Foundation (£21,000); British Heart Foundation (£15,000); Missionaries of Charity – Calcutta, water.org and Angel Covers (£6,200 each); Nottingham Trent University, National Osteoporosis Society and County History Trust (£5,000 each); Fight Against Blindness (£3,500); Prostate Cancer Charity and Kingswold Trust for Children (£2,000 each); Finsbury Park Community Hub (£1,500); Down's Heart Group and South East Dog Rescue (£1,000 each); and YMCA (£250).

Applications

In writing to the correspondent.

Information gathered from:

Accounts; Charity Commission record.

The Mary Homfray Charitable Trust

General

£46,000 (2011/12)

Beneficial area

UK, with a preference for Wales.

Correspondent: Angela Homfray, Trustee, 5 Callaghan Square, Cardiff CF10 5BT (tel: 02920 264391)

Trustees: Angela Homfray; Simon Gibson; Josephine Homfray.

CC Number: 273564

The trust supports a wide range of organisations. Support is mainly given in Wales, although some national charities are also supported.

In 2011/12 the trust had assets of £1.4 million and an income of £160,000. Grants were made to 25 organisations totalling £46,000 and were mostly recurrent.

Beneficiaries included: Age Concern, Teenage Cancer Trust and Welsh Sinfonia (£3,000 each); Barnardo's, National Botanic Garden of Wales, Prince's Trust Cymru, St David's Foundation, Wales Millennium Centre and Wildfowl and Wetland Trust (£2,000 each); Y Bont, St Dunstan's, RSPB, Maes-y-Dyfan, Alzheimer's Society and Ashgrove School (£1,000 each).

Applications

In writing to the correspondent. Applications should be made towards the end of the year, for consideration at the trustees' meeting in February or March each year.

Information gathered from:

Accounts; Charity Commission record.

The Hope Trust

Temperance, Reformed Protestant churches

About £200,000 (2012)

Beneficial area

Worldwide, with a preference for Scotland.

Correspondent: The Secretary, Drummond Miller, 31–32 Moray Place, Edinburgh EH3 6BZ (tel: 01312 265151; email: reception@drummond-miller.co.uk)

SC Number: SC000987

The trust was established to promote the ideals of temperance in the areas of drink and drugs, and Protestant church reform through education and the distribution of literature. PhD students of theology studying at Scottish universities are also supported.

In 2012 its income was £215,000. Grants totalled around £200,000.

Previous beneficiaries have included Church of Scotland Priority Areas Fund, World Alliance of Reformed Churches, National Bible Society for Scotland, Feed the Minds and Waldensian Mission Aid.

Exclusions

No grants to gap year students, scholarship schemes or to any individuals, with the sole exception of PhD students of theology studying at Scottish universities. No grants for the refurbishment of property.

Applications

In writing to the correspondent. The trustees meet to consider applications in June and December each year. Applications should be submitted by mid-May or mid-November each year.

Percentage of awards given to new applicants: less than 10%.

Information gathered from:

OSCR record; further information provided by the funder.

The Horizon Foundation

General, education, women and children

£454,000 (2012/13)

Beneficial area

Worldwide.

Correspondent: Trust Administrator, c/o Coutts and Co., 440 The Strand, London WC2R 0QS (tel: 020 7663 6814)

Trustees: Kirkland Caroline Smulders; Patrick Lance Smulders; Coutts and Co.

CC Number: 1118455

Established in 2007, the objects of the foundation are:

- To promote and advance the education of women and children
- The relief of financial hardship, either generally or individually, of women and children by making grants of money for providing or paying for items services or facilities
- General charitable purposes

In 2012/13 the foundation had both an income and total expenditure of £458,000. Grants were made to 17 organisations totalling £454,000.

Beneficiaries include: Future Hope UK and Rugby School (£65,600 each); UWC Atlantic College and The National Boarding Bursary Foundation (£50,000 each); Eton College (£48,000); The Hotchkiss School (£22,000); University College London (£18,500); School for Oriental and African Studies (£14,000); Medical Aid for Palestinians (£8,000); and Friends of Ubunto Education Fund (£5,000).

Applications

In writing to the correspondent.

Information gathered from:

Accounts; Charity Commission record.

The Cuthbert Horn Trust

£26,000 (2012)

Beneficial area

Worldwide.

Correspondent: Laurie Wilson, Trust Manager, Capita Trust Company Ltd, 4th Floor, 40 Dukes Place, London EC3A 7NH (tel: 020 3367 8209; email: lwilson@capitafiduciary.co.uk)

Trustees: Alan Flint; Prosper Marr-Johnson; Rory Johnston; Capita Trust Co. Ltd.

CC Number: 291465

Registered with the Charity Commission in 1985, this trust makes grants for general charitable purposes. In 2012 the trust had assets of over £1.3 million and a total income of £231,000. Grants were made to 11 organisations totalling £26,000.

Beneficiaries included: BISYOC and The Island Trust (£3,000 each); and Charleston Trust, Norfolk Wherry Trust, Population Matters, Pesticide Action Network UK and Progressive Farming Trust (£2,000 each).

Exclusions

No grants are made to individuals.

Applications

Unsolicited applications are discouraged. For the time being the trustees have decided to rely on their own research, usually giving to organisations that have an income of less than £100,000.

Information gathered from:

Accounts; Charity Commission record.

The Horne Trust

Hospices

£606,000 (2011/12)

Beneficial area

UK and the developing world.

Correspondent: J. T. Horne, Trustee, Kingsdown, Warmlake Road, Chart Sutton, Maidstone, Kent ME17 3RP (tel: 01622 842638; email: contact@horne-trust.org.uk)

Trustees: Jeff Horne; Jon Horne; Emma Horne.

CC Number: 1010625

The vast majority of support is given to hospices, particularly children's hospices. Grants can also be given to medical support charities and organisations helping to develop self-reliant technology in Africa and the developing world. The 2011/12 accounts note:

> The trustees have determined to continue the policy of concentrating on annual maintenance grants to our regularly supported charities, whilst expanding in the area of hospice funding. We also intend to keep options open for emergency grants and researching future grant strategies.

In 2011/12 it had assets of £6.4 million and an income of £788,000. Grants to 110 organisations totalled £606,000.

Beneficiaries included: World Medical Fund (£20,000); St Andrew's Hospice – Grimsby, Practical Action (IDTG) and Demelza House Children's Hospice (£10,000 each); Ardgowan Hospice – Greenock (£7,500); Acorns Children's Hospice – Worcester, Alzheimer's Society, Donna Louise Children's Hospice – Stoke, Humberstone Hydrotherapy Pool, Julia's House Children's Hospice – Dorset (£5,000 each); Soundabout (£2,500); and Whitby Dog Rescue and Winfield Trust (£1,000 each).

Applications

Normally in writing to the correspondent, although the trust has stated that currently unsolicited applications cannot be supported.

Information gathered from:

Accounts; Charity Commission record.

The Hospital Saturday Fund

Medical, health

£478,000 to organisations (2012)

Beneficial area

UK, the Republic of Ireland, the Channel Islands and the Isle of Man.

Correspondent: Paul Jackson, Chief Executive, 24 Upper Ground, London SE1 9PD (tel: 020 7202 1381; email: charity@hsf.eu.com)

Trustees: John Greenwood; Jane Laidlaw Dalton; Michael Boyle; John Randel; David Thomas; Christopher Bottomley; Pauline Lee.

CC Number: 1123381

The Hospital Saturday Fund is a healthcare cash plan organisation, which was founded in 1873. In 1987 it established a charitable trust to support a wide range of hospitals, hospices and medical charities for care and research, as well as welfare organisations providing similar services. The trustees continue to provide support to smaller, lesser-known charities connected with diseases and disabilities about which there is little public awareness. Individuals can also be supported by the trust, usually for special equipment to relieve their condition or in cases where their health has contributed to their financial hardship, although sponsorship can be given to people studying for a medically-related career.

> *What is funded?*
>
> The Hospital Saturday Fund will consider giving grants towards medical capital projects, medical care or research and in support of medical training. The Hospital Saturday Fund will also consider grants for running costs.

In 2012 the fund had an income of £27 million. This was mostly from trading turnover from the charity's subsidiary company HSF health plan Ltd. Grants were made to 413 organisations totalling £478,000 and to individual medical students totalling £25,000. Grants to organisations were broken down as follows:

Other medical charities	£357,000
Hospices	£60,000
Hospitals	£31,000
Sponsorship	£30,000

The majority of grants were for £1,000. Eight higher grants ranging between £1,400 and £10,000 were awarded to charities where a specific need was deemed by the Committee to warrant a larger award.

> The committee endeavours to ensure that not only is there a wide geographical spread in the grantmaking but that, within the charities supported, many different types of illness, disability, care, research and age groups are represented. Grants are made to both local and national institutions.

A full list of grants was not available with the accounts; however, some beneficiaries are listed: Rainbow Living, St Joseph's Hospice – Hackney, DeafHear, Maggie's Cancer Caring Centre, Yeovil Hospital, the National Osteoporosis Society, Hope House Children's Hospices, Happy Days Charity, Trinity College Dublin, Cardiff University, Clatterbridge Cancer Centre and Meningitis UK. Further details of recent grants are available on the fund's website.

Exclusions

Organisations should be registered with the Charity Commission, OSCR, Charity Commission for Northern Ireland, Isle of Man General Registry, HM Revenue and Customs, the Revenue Commissioners in Ireland or the appropriate regulatory body in the Channel Islands.

Applications

Applications by letter to the Chief Executive detailing the scope of the request with supporting documentation, the amount requested and a copy of the latest annual report. The letter should clearly state the reason for your application (specific project or running costs); your charity registration number or details of registration with one of the other named bodies and the correct wording for a cheque should your application be successful.

Information gathered from:

Accounts; Charity Commission record.

Houblon-Norman/ George Fund

Finance

£72,000 (2011/12)

Beneficial area

UK.

Correspondent: Miss Emma-Jayne Coker, Secretary, Bank of England, Threadneedle Street, London EC2R 8AH (tel: 020 7601 3778; email: ma-hngfund@bankofengland.co.uk; website: www.bankofengland.co.uk/research/houblonnorman)

Trustees: Andrew Haldane; Charles Bean; David Prentis.

CC Number: 213168

The trust supports research into the interaction and function of financial and business institutions, the economic conditions affecting them, and the dissemination of knowledge thereof. Fellowships are tenable at the Bank of England. The research work to be undertaken is intended to be full-time work, and teaching or other paid work must not be undertaken during the tenure of the fellowship, without the specific consent of the trustees. In considering applications the trustees will pay particular regard to the relevance of the research to current problems in economics and finance.

In 2011/12 the trust had assets of £2 million, an income of £164,300, and made one fellowship grant totalling £72,000.

Applications

Application forms and guidance notes are available on the website, to be returned by email or post to the secretary. Any queries about the form or an application should also be directed to the secretary.

Information gathered from:

Accounts; Charity Commission record; funder's website.

The Reta Lila Howard Foundation

Children, arts, environment

£360,000 (2011/12)

Beneficial area

UK and Republic of Ireland.

Correspondent: The Company Secretary, Jamestown Investments, 4 Felstead Gardens, Ferry Street, London E14 3BS (tel: 020 7537 1118; email: jamestown@btinternet.com)

Trustees: Pilar Bauta; Charles Burnett; Garfield Mitchell; Alannah Weston; Galvin Weston; Melissa Murdoch; Tamara Lila Rebanks.

CC Number: 1041634

The founder of this trust had an interest in children's charities and the trust's grantmaking focus is 'to support a few innovative projects that benefit children up to the age of 16 within the British Isles'. Funds are directed to selected projects, 'to support the education of young people or to ameliorate their physical and emotional environment'. In practice the trust also supports arts and environmental organisations. Donations are given over a finite period, with the aim that the project can be self-supporting when funding has ended.

In 2011/12 the trust had assets of £14 million and an income of £47,000. Grants were made totalling £360,000.

Previous beneficiaries included: Countryside Education Trust (£70,000); Barnardo's (£68,500); Civitas (£60,000); The Tree Council (£53,000); Farms for City Children (£40,000); Children's Hospice Association Scotland (£35,000); Teach First (£30,000); New Forest Museum and Library (£20,000); The Bridge End Community Centre (£15,000); and Bibles for Children (£10,000).

Exclusions

Grants are not given to individuals, organisations which are not registered charities, or towards operating expenses, budget deficits, (sole) capital projects, annual charitable appeals, general endowment funds, fundraising drives or events, conferences, or student aid.

Applications

The trust states that it does not accept unsolicited applications, since the trustees seek out and support projects they are interested in.

Information gathered from:

Accounts; Charity Commission record.

The Daniel Howard Trust

Jewish causes

£157,000 (2011/12)

Beneficial area

UK and Israel.

Correspondent: Sarah Hunt, 22 Arlington Street, London SW1A 1RD

Trustees: Dame Shirley Porter; Linda Streit; Steven Porter; Brian Padgett; Andrew Peggie.

CC Number: 267173

The trust mostly supports Jewish or Israeli organisations, in particular those promoting education, culture, the environment and welfare. There is ongoing support for the Daniel Amichai Education Centre and the Israel Philharmonic Orchestra.

In 2011/12 the trust held assets of £5.2 million and had an income of £40,000. Grants totalled £157,000 and were broken down as follows:

Education	£74,000
Culture	£63,000
Environment	£11,200
Welfare	£9,300

Beneficiaries included: Friends of Daniel for Rowing Association (£40,000); V&A (£30,000); Tel Aviv Foundation (for Daniel Centre) (£22,000); Council for a Beautiful Israel (£10,000); Ringling Museum of Art (£9,600); Israel Philharmonic (£6,400); The Wharton Fund (£6,100); Israeli Opera Friends Association (£2,500); and Habitat for Humanity (£1,200).

Exclusions

Grants are only made to registered charities. No grants to individuals.

Applications

In writing to the correspondent.

Information gathered from:

Accounts; Charity Commission record.

The Hudson Foundation

Older people, general

£125,000 (2011/12)

Beneficial area

UK, with a preference for the Wisbech area.

Correspondent: David W. Ball, Trustee, 1–3 York Row, Wisbech, Cambridgeshire PE13 1EA (tel: 01945 461456)

Trustees: Hayward A. Godfrey; David W. Ball; Stephen G. Layton.

CC Number: 280332

The object of the foundation is the relief of infirm and/or older people, in particular the establishment and maintenance of residential accommodation for relief of infirm and/or older people and to make donations to other charitable purposes with a preference for the Wisbech area. The accounts state that 'whilst the trustees do make contributions to revenue expenditure of charitable organisations, they prefer to assist in the funding of capital projects for the advancement of the community of Wisbech and district'.

In 2011/12 the foundation had assets of £2 million and an income of £870,000. Grants to 12 organisations totalled £125,000.

Beneficiaries were: Wisbech Grammar School (£42,000); National Trust (£25,000); Wisbech Swimming Club (£9,100); Fenland Association Community Transport (£7,900); WisARD (£7,500); Wisbech Angles Theatre (£6,000); and Listening Books (£2,000).

Applications

In writing to the correspondent. Trustees meet quarterly.

Information gathered from:

Accounts; Charity Commission record.

The Huggard Charitable Trust

General

Around £150,000 (2011/12)

Beneficial area

UK, with a preference for South Wales.

Correspondent: Stephen Thomas, Trustee, 25 Harvey Crescent, Aberavon, Port Talbot SA12 6DF (tel: 01639 681539)

Trustees: Anne Helme; Stephen Thomas; Anne Chiplen.

CC Number: 327501

In 2011/12 the trust had an income of £16,000 and a total expenditure of £156,000.

Previous beneficiaries included: Amelia Methodist Trust, Vale of Glamorgan, Bro Morgannwg NHS Trust, CURE Fund – Cardiff, Laparoscopy Laser Fund – UHW, SWS Cymru and Whitton Rosser Trust – Vale of Glamorgan.

Applications

The trustees are not inviting applications for funds, they support a list of charities provided by their founder.

Information gathered from:

Accounts; Charity Commission record.

The Geoffrey C. Hughes Charitable Trust

Nature conservation, environment, performing arts

£115,000 (2011/12)

Beneficial area

UK.

Correspondent: Paul Solon, Trustee, c/o Mills and Reeve, Francis House, 112 Hills Road, Cambridge CB2 1PH (tel: 01223 222290)

Trustees: John Young; Paul Solon; William Bailey.

CC Number: 1010079

This trust is essentially interested in two areas: nature conservation/environment and performing arts, particularly ballet or opera with a bias towards modern work.

In 2011/12 the trust had an income of £6,800 and total expenditure of £117,000. Expenditure fluctuates and has averaged around £57,000 over the last five years.

Exclusions

No grants to individuals.

Applications

In writing to the correspondent.

Information gathered from:

Accounts; Charity Commission record.

The Humanitarian Trust

Education, health, social welfare, Jewish

Around £100,000

Beneficial area

Worldwide, mainly Israel.

Correspondent: Miss J. Myers, Secretary, c/o Prism the Gift Fund, 20 Gloucester Place, London W1U 8HA (tel: 020 7486 7760)

Trustees: Jacques Gunsbourg; Pierre Halban; Anthony Lerman; Emanuelle Gunsbourg-Kasavi.

CC Number: 208575

The trust was founded in 1946. In the early years donations were made overwhelmingly to educational causes in Israel. Nowadays the trust is giving to a wider range of causes, still mainly Jewish, but some smaller grants are given to non-Jewish organisations. Most grants are for between £1,000 and £5,000.

'The trustees consider grant applications from organisations and individuals in the UK and abroad, especially in the fields of education, health, social welfare, civil society, Jewish communal life and general charitable purposes.'

In 2011/12 the trust held assets of £4.3 million and had an income of £137,000. Grants totalled £93,000 and were broken down as follows:

Academic and education	£56,000
Social service	£25,000
Medical and charitable	£12,000

Beneficiaries included: Friends of Hebrew University of Jerusalem (£25,000 in two equal awards for scholarships); New Israel Fund (£6,000); Etz Hayyim Synagogue (£5,000); Jerusalem Foundation and Friendship Village (£4,000 each); Share Zedek UK (£3,000); Anne Frank Trust UK (£2,500); Nightingale House and Leo Baeck College (£2,000 each); Glasgow Jewish Educational Forum, Jewish Music Institute and Diabetes UK (£1,000 each); and Tommy's The Baby Charity, Oxford University Jewish Society and University of Warwick (£500 each).

Applications

In writing to the correspondent, including annual report and accounts, projected budgets and future plans. Applications are considered at trustees' meetings in March and October. Less than 10% of grants are given to new applicants.

Percentage of awards given to new applicants: less than 10%.

Information gathered from:

Accounts; Charity Commission record; further information provided by the funder.

The Michael and Shirley Hunt Charitable Trust

Prisoners' families, animal welfare

£69,000 to organisations and individuals (2011/12)

Beneficial area

UK and overseas.

Correspondent: Mrs Debra Jenkins, Trustee, Ansty House, Henfield Road, Small Dole, West Sussex BN5 9XH (tel: 01903 817116; fax: 01903 879995)

Trustees: Chester Hunt; Deborah Jenkins; Kathy Mayberry; Shirley Hunt; Wanda Baker.

CC Number: 1063418

The trust makes grants for the benefit of prisoners' families, animals which are unwanted, sick or ill-treated and general charitable purposes. The trustees prefer to award grants for emergency operational funding rather than capital projects or overhead expenses.

In 2011/12 the trust had assets of £5.8 million and an income of £206,000. Grants were made totalling £69,000, broken down as follows:

Prisoners and their families	8	£22,000
Animal welfare	18	£20,000
Miscellaneous	5	£15,500

Grants to 71 individuals (under the prisoners category) totalled £12,000.

Beneficiaries included: St Barnabas Hospice (£6,000); Storybook Dads, DEC East Africa Crisis and Time for Families (£5,000 each); Miracles to Believe in (£2,500); Church Housing Trust (£2,000); and Rocking Horse, Alberts Horse Sanctuary and Dog Action Welfare Group (£1,000 each).

Exclusions

No grants for capital projects, support costs, fines, bail, legal costs, rent deposits and so on.

Applications

In writing to the correspondent. The trustees meet to consider applications 'as and when necessary, and at least annually'.

Information gathered from:

Accounts; Charity Commission record.

The Huntingdon Foundation

Jewish education

£277,000 (2011/12)

Beneficial area

Mainly Jewish communities in the UK. There is some grant giving in the US.

Correspondent: Benjamin Perl, 8 Goodyers Gardens, London NW4 2HD (tel: 020 8202 2282)

Trustees: Benjamin Perl; Dr Shoshana Perl; R. Jeidel; Jonathan Perl; Naomi Sorotzkin; Joseph Perl.

CC Number: 286504

The foundation was established in 1960 for general charitable purposes. It defines its principal activity as 'the establishment and continued support of Jewish schools'. The foundation also supports other educational organisations, charities and Orthodox Jewish higher education establishments in the U.S.

In 2011/12 the trust had assets of £11 million and an income of £652,000. Grants were made totalling £277,000.

Beneficiaries included: Yavneh College, Beis Yaccov Primary School, Bnos Beis Yaakov Primary School Ltd, Menorah High School, Moreshet Hatorah and Simon Marks Jewish Primary School.

'In addition the trustees have supported numerous institutions for the relief of poverty and other Jewish educational institutions and have been and continue to be instrumental in the development of Yavneh College, Borehamwood.'

The accounts do not list the amounts given to individual recipient organisations.

Exclusions

No grants to individuals.

Applications

In writing to the correspondent. The trustees meet several times a year.

Information gathered from:

Accounts; Charity Commission record.

The Hutton Foundation

Christian, general

£235,000 (2012)

Beneficial area

UK and overseas.

Correspondent: Jackie Hart, Secretary and Treasurer, Hutton Collins Partners LLP, 50 Pall Mall, London SW1Y 5JH (tel: 020 7004 7000; fax: 020 7004 7001; email: jackie.hart@huttoncollins.com; website: www.huttoncollins.com/about-us/hutton-collins-foundation)

Trustees: Graham Hutton; Amanda Hutton; Richard Hutton; James Hutton; Helen Hutton.

CC Number: 1106521

The foundation was established in 2004 by Graham Hutton of private equity firm Hutton Collins, and his family. The objects of the foundation are stated as general charitable purposes, although the main, major donations listed in the accounts are usually to Christian organisations. The firm's website lists Build Africa, Sheffield Institute for Motor Neurone Disease, Club Itaca and Macmillan as among other beneficiaries.

In 2012 the foundation had assets of £1.7 million and an income of £97,000. Grants were made totalling £253,000.

International Theological College (£64,000) and Emmanuel College (£7,200) both received grants in previous years. The only other named beneficiary was the Cardinal Hume Centre (£35,000). Other donations totalled £147,000.

Applications

Unsolicited applications are not supported. Those interested in learning more about the foundation are encouraged to contact the secretary.

Information gathered from:

Accounts; Charity Commission record; funder's website.

The Nani Huyu Charitable Trust

Welfare

£161,000 (2011/12)

Beneficial area

UK, particularly but not exclusively within 50 miles of Bristol.

Correspondent: The Trustees, Rusling House, Butcombe, Bristol BS40 7XQ (tel: 01275 474433; email: maureensimonwhitmore@btinternet.com)

Trustees: Ben Whitmore; Charles Thatcher; Maureen Whitmore; Susan Webb.

CC Number: 1082868

The trust was registered with the Charity commission in October 2000. Its aims are to assist people who are underprivileged, disadvantaged or ill, young people in matters of health, accommodation and training and those requiring assistance or medical care at the end of their lives, principally within Bristol and its surroundings.

In 2011/12 the trust had assets of £4.1 million and an income of £161,000. Grants were made to 23 organisations totalling £161,000.

Beneficiaries included: Womankind and Rainbow (£13,000 each); Southside Family Project (£12,000); Jessie May Trust (£11,000); Young Bristol and Fairshare South West (£10,000 each); Fairbridge West and Bristol Drugs Project (£8,000 each); Grounds 4 Change (£7,000); Kingergy (£6,000); Blenheim Scouts (£4,000); and Bristol Children's Help Society (£3,000).

Applications

In writing to the correspondent.

Information gathered from:

Accounts; Charity Commission record.

The P. Y N. and B. Hyams Trust

Jewish, general

£43,000 (2011/12)

Beneficial area

Worldwide.

Correspondent: N. Shah, Trustee, Lubbock Fine, Russell Bedford House, City Forum, 250 City Road, London EC1V 2QQ (tel: 020 7490 7766)

Trustees: Mrs M. Hyams; D. Levy; N. Shah.

CC Number: 268129

In 2011/12 the trust had assets of £1.1 million and an income of £84,000. Grants to organisations totalled £43,000. No list of grants was included with the accounts.

In previous years, grants have been mostly given to Jewish organisations, although other causes are also funded.

Applications

In writing to the correspondent, but note, the trust states that funds are fully committed and unsolicited applications are not welcomed.

Information gathered from:

Accounts; Charity Commission record.

The Hyde Charitable Trust – Youth Plus

Disadvantaged children and young people

£130,000 to organisations and individuals (2011/12)

Beneficial area

The areas in which the Hyde Group operates (currently London, Kent, Surrey, Sussex and Hampshire).

Correspondent: The Trustees, Hyde Charitable Trust, 30 Park Street, London SE1 9EQ (tel: 020 3207 2762; email: hydeplus@hyde-housing.co.uk; website: www.hyde-housing.co.uk/about-us/hyde-plus)

Trustees: Geron Walker; Kishwer Falkner; Jonathan Prichard; Julie Hollyman; Jacqueline Puddifoot; Ronald Brookes; Andrew Moncrieff; Sharon Darcy; Christopher Carlisle.

CC Number: 289888

Hyde Charitable Trust is a charitable company established in 1984. It 'works to help improve the condition and quality of life of people from the poorest communities.'

The trust is part of the Hyde Group and is managed by Hyde Plus, the Social and Economic Investment department of The Hyde Group. It provides grants to organisations providing services to residents of Hyde Housing Association and other Hyde Group members. The trust also provides bursaries directly to residents to improve life opportunities.

Current grant programmes focus on young people, financial and digital inclusion, employment and enterprise, and community development. The grant allocation was £300,000 for 2013/14.

In 2011/12 the trust had assets of £2.9 million, an income of £431,000 and made grants totalling £130,000 to organisations and individuals through the following programmes:

Young Pride Awards (£34,000); Family Support/Parenting (£26,000); Flexible

Pot (£16,000); Navi Learning Fund and Activities Communities (£13,000 each); Jobs Plus (£11,000); Older People and Green Living (£9,000); Digital Inclusion (£7,000); and Youth Plus Pilot (£6,000).

Exclusions

No funding for:

- Unsolicited applications
- Projects outside of the area where Hyde is working. No areas outside the South East of England
- Sporting, social or fundraising events
- Medical research, hospices, residential homes for the elderly
- Any other projects which the trustees deem to fall outside the trust's main criteria

Applications

The trust has informed us that:

> Because the funding available is limited – and targeted at Hyde residents – the Trust does not encourage unsolicited applications.

Information gathered from:

Accounts; Charity Commission record; funder's website.

The Idlewild Trust

Performing arts, culture, restoration and conservation, occasional arts education

£124,000 (2012)

Beneficial area

UK.

Correspondent: Mrs Angela Hurst, Administrator, 1a Taylors Yard, 67 Alderbrook Street, London SW12 8AD (tel: 020 8772 3155; email: info@idlewildtrust.org.uk; website: www.idlewildtrust.org.uk)

Trustees: Jonathan Ouvry; Tony Ford; Dr Tessa Murdoch; Helen McCabe; John Gittens; Tessa Mayhew.

CC Number: 268124

The trust was founded in 1974 by Peter Brissault Minet, who had previously set up the Peter Minet Trust. Its policy is to support charities concerned with the encouragement of performing and fine arts and preservation for the benefit of the public of lands, buildings and other objects of beauty or historic interest. Occasionally support is given to bodies for educational bursaries in these fields or for conservation of the natural environment. The trust prefers to support UK-charities and it is unlikely to support a project of local interest only. Applications for up to £5,000 are considered.

Criteria (taken from the trust's website):

> **Education:** the trust funds education projects and initiatives within the fine arts (performing arts and visual arts) whose primary objective is to nurture and develop talent, working with those aged 16 or over. Occasionally, excellent projects for younger students will be considered. The projects must be professionally run and should demonstrate best practice in their field.
>
> The trust does not fund projects aimed at pre-school or primary school aged children.
>
> **Museums and galleries:** the trust funds exhibitions, projects and capital works within museums, galleries and other venues concerned with the visual arts and crafts. The trust will need to be satisfied that the work is of a high standard and will attract visitors from outside its immediate community, if not nationally. Priority is gen to projects of a national interest with a national or regional audience.
>
> **Performing arts:** the trust funds projects, events and performances within the performing arts including music, dance, poetry, drama and film. The trust will need to be satisfied that the work is of a high standard and will attract an audience from outside its immediate community, if not nationally. Priority is generally given to projects of national interest with a national or regional audience.
>
> **Preservation and conservation:** the trust funds the conservation or restoration for the benefit of the public of lands, buildings and other objects of beauty or historical interest in the UK. However the trust does not fund new work within a restoration project such as new heating systems, annexes or facilities.

In 2012 the trust had assets of £4.7 million, an income of £178,000 and made grants totalling £124,000.

Grants were categorised in the trust's annual report as follows:

Preservation and Restoration	25	£58,000
Performing Arts	14	£35,000
Education	9	£24,000
Museums, Galleries and Fine Art	4	£7,000

Beneficiaries included: National Youth Choirs of Great Britain (£4,000); National Theatre (£3,600); Lake District Summer Music (£3,500); Birmingham Royal Ballet, Buxton Festival, Holdgate Church and Oxford University Museum of Natural History (£3,000 each); The National Trust, The Friends of St Bridget's – Skenfirth, The Friends of Portaferry Presbyterian Church and Classical Opera (£2,500); Handel House Museum, Barbican Art Gallery and Northamptonshire Music and Performing Arts Trust (£2,000 each); and Vale of Glamorgan Festival and Abbot's Hospital (£1,000 each).

Exclusions

- Work which has been completed
- Individuals
- New work within churches, such as heating systems, annexes, facilities
- Community-based projects or festivals largely involving and attracting people in the immediate area
- Education work unless it is within the fine arts (performing or visual arts)
- Education work with pre-school or primary school aged children
- Endowment or deficit funding
- Nationwide appeals by large charities
- Appeals where all or most of the recipients live outside the UK
- Appeals whose sole or main purpose is to make grants from funds collected
- Projects based in the channel islands or Isle of Man

Applications

The trust now uses an online application process via its website. Potential applicants are welcome to telephone the trust to discuss their application and check eligibility; however, opening times are limited so check the website before calling. Trustees meet twice a year usually in May and November – exact dates and deadlines are published on the website. The trust will check your Charity Commission record if your charity's annual returns and accounts are up-to-date.

The trust will let you know the outcome of your application within a fortnight of the trustees' meeting. Grants will not be awarded to any one charity more frequently than every two years. Unsuccessful applicants can re-apply immediately.

Information gathered from:

Accounts; Charity Commission record; funder's website.

The Iliffe Family Charitable Trust

Medical, disability, heritage, education

£190,000 (2011/12)

Beneficial area

UK and Worldwide.

Correspondent: Secretary to the Trustees, Barn Close, Yattendon, Berkshire RG18 0UX (tel: 01635 203929)

Trustees: Lord Iliffe; Edward Iliffe; Catherine Fleming.

CC Number: 273437

The trust gives grants towards groups concerned with medical causes, disability, heritage and education. The bulk of the grants made are to charities already known to the trustees, to which funds are committed from year to year. Other donations are made for a wide range of charitable purposes in which the trust has a special interest.

In 2011/12 the trust had assets of £1.4 million and an income of £96,000.

Grants totalled £190,000 and were broken down as follows:

Heritage	£50,000
Welfare	£46,000
Education	£42,000
Medical	£29,000
Conservation	£15,000
Religious	£8,300

Beneficiaries included: Royal Shakespeare Company and Mary Rose Trust (£20,000 each); Berkshire Community Foundation (£16,000); Arthur Rank Centre (£12,000); Coventry University, Godiva Awakes Trust and Prostate Cancer Research (£10,000 each); Game and Wildlife Conservation Trust (£2,500); Army Benevolent Fund and Welsh Guards Afghanistan Appeal (£2,000 each); University of Cambridge Vet School Trust (£1,400); National Rheumatoid Arthritis Society, Marine Society and Sea Cadets and Farm Africa (£1,000); National Trust Newbury (£500); and Hampshire and Isle of Wight Wildlife Trust (£100).

Exclusions

No grants to individuals and rarely to non-registered charities.

Applications

In writing to the correspondent. Only successful applications will be acknowledged. Grants are considered at ad hoc meetings of the trustees, held throughout the year.

Information gathered from:

Accounts; Charity Commission record.

The Ingram Trust

General

£909,000 (2011/12)

Beneficial area

UK and overseas, with a local preference for Surrey.

Correspondent: Joan Major, Administrator, Ground Floor, 22 Chancery Lane, London WC2A 1LS (email: theingramtrust@nqpllp.com)

Trustees: Christopher Ingram; Clare Maurice; Janet Ingram.

CC Number: 1040194

The trust's policies are as follows:

- It selects a limited number of charities which it commits itself to support for three to five years
- It prefers to support specific projects which can include identifiable costs for special services provided by the charity or equipment that is required
- Beneficiaries will generally be major national and international charities together with some local ones in the county of Surrey
- The majority of grants will be made for periods of three to four years at a time in order to better assess grant applications and monitor progress
- The only overseas aid charities which are considered are those dedicated to encouraging self-help and providing more permanent solutions to problems
- No animal charities are considered except those concerned with wildlife conservation

The accounts also note that:

> The trustees continue to focus on making larger grants to few charities with the aim of having larger grants to few charities with the aim of having a greater impact within the areas chose for support. Although the number of charities will reduce, the trustees will be able to assess more effectively the way in which funds are being deployed and monitor the recipients and the impact of the funding more comprehensively.

In 2011/12 the trust had assets of £10.6 million, an income of £147,000 and made grants to 29 organisations totalling £909,000. Many beneficiaries are supported on a regular basis.

Beneficiaries included: WWF – UK (£242,000); Shelter (£75,000); NSPCC (£65,000); ActionAid (£52,000); the National Theatre (£50,000); Queen Elizabeth Foundation for Disabled People (£35,000); Almeida Theatre Company Ltd and the Prince's Trust (£30,000 each); Alzheimer's Society (£22,000); Countryside Learning (£20,000); Rainbow Trust Children's Charity and St Giles Trust (£15,000 each); Pimlico Opera and SouthEast Cancer Help Centre Ltd (£12,000 each); The Woodland Trust and The Princess Alice Hospice (£10,000 each); and Age UK – Surrey (£2,000).

Exclusions

No grants to non-registered charities or to individuals.

Applications

In writing to the correspondent, although the trust states that it receives far more worthy applications than it is able to support.

Information gathered from:

Accounts; Charity Commission record.

The Inland Waterways Association

Inland waterways

£13,500 (2012)

Beneficial area

UK and Ireland.

Correspondent: Helen Elliott-Adams, Correspondent, Island House, Moor Road, Chesham HP5 1WA (tel: 01494 783453; email: iwa@waterways.org.uk; website: www.waterways.org.uk)

Trustees: Vaughan Welch; Les Etheridge; Alan Platt; Paul Roper; Raymond Carter; Peter Scott; Ivor Caplan; James Shead; Paul Strudwick; Gordon Harrower; Clive Henderson; Gillian Smith; Roger Holmes; Grenville Messham.

CC Number: 212342

The trust supports organisations promoting the restoration of inland waterways (i.e. canal and river navigations).

The trust's objectives are to advocate the conservation and maintenance of British inland waterways; promote the fullest use of the inland waterways; educate the public and other bodies about inland waterways; promote and commission research regarding inland waterways.

In 2012 the trust had assets of £1.7 million and an income of £1.3 million, most of which was derived from membership subscriptions, legacies, donations and related funds such as Gift Aid. Charitable expenditure during the year totalled £663,000 of which a large amount (£479,000) was designated to 'campaign and restoration costs'. Grants were made totalling £13,500 during the year.

Projects are awarded mainly for the following:

- Professional services
- Administration
- Construction
- Land purchase
- Research on matters affecting waterway restoration
- Education

Four grants were awarded to the following organisations during the year: Pocklington Canal Amenity Society and Shrewsbury and Newport Canals Trust (£5,000 each); Lichfield and Hatherton Canals Restoration Trust (£2,500); and Wilts and Berks Canals Trust (£1,000).

Exclusions

No grants to individuals. No retrospective grants for projects where expenditure has already been incurred or committed.

Applications

In writing to the correspondent. Applications should comply with the guidelines for applicants, also available from the correspondent. Application forms can be downloaded from the IWA website.

Applications are considered by the IWA's Restoration Committee. The committee will prioritise work involving practical restoration.

Each applicant should provide a full description of the proposal. The guidelines state that proposals should include the following:

- Location plans
- Proposed programme of activities
- Information on land ownership and consents
- Timescales
- Totals costs of the project
- How value for money will be achieved
- Maintenance after construction

Applications for up to £2,000 are assessed under a simplified procedure – each application should demonstrate that the grant would be used to initiate or sustain a restoration scheme or significantly benefit a specific small project.

Applications for over £2,000 should demonstrate that the grant would be applied to one of the types of projects (1–6). Applicants should also demonstrate the extent to which the project satisfies one or more of the following conditions:

- The grant would unlock (lever) a grant several times larger from another body
- The grant would not replace grants available from other sources
- The project does not qualify for grants from major funding sources
- The grant would enable a key project to be undertaken which would have a significant effect on the prospect of advancing the restoration and gaining funds from other sources for further restoration projects
- The result of the project would have a major influence over the progress of a number of other restoration projects
- The Inland Waterways Association Restoration Committee would have a major influence in the management of the project, including monitoring of expenditure

Percentage of awards given to new applicants: less than 10%.

Common applicant mistakes

'Don't read all the application and guidelines fully, thus wrong or ineligible applications are made.'

Information gathered from:

Accounts; Charity Commission record; further information provided by the funder; funder's website.

The Inlight Trust

Religion, spiritual development

£150,000 (2012/13)

Beneficial area

UK.

Correspondent: Clare Pegden, Correspondent, PO Box 2, Liss, Hampshire GU33 6YP (tel: 01730 894120)

CC Number: 236782

The trust makes grants for the advancement of religion only. It states that its funding priorities are: 'To make donations on an undenominational basis to charities providing valuable contributions to spiritual development and charities concerned with spiritual healing and spiritual growth through religious retreats.'

Grants are usually one-off for a specific project or part of a project. Bursary schemes may also be supported. Core funding and/or salaries are rarely considered.

In 2012/13 it had an income of £298,000 and a total expenditure of £289,047. We have estimated the grants total to be around £150,000.

Previous beneficiaries included: Drukpa UK (£10,000); St Albans Cathedral Music Trust (£5,000): Christians in Care (£3,000); and Acorn Christian Healing Foundation (£2,000).

Exclusions

Grants are made to registered charities only. Applications from individuals, including students, are ineligible. No grants are made in response to general appeals from large national organisations. Grants are seldom available for church buildings.

Applications

In writing to the correspondent including details of the need the intended project is designed to meet plus an outline budget and the most recent available annual accounts of the charity. Only applications from eligible bodies are acknowledged. Applications must be accompanied by a copy of your trust deed or of your entry in the Charity Commission register. They are considered four times a year. Only successful applicants are informed.

Information gathered from:

Accounts; Charity Commission record.

The Inman Charity

General, medical, social welfare, disability, older people, hospices

£271,000 (2012)

Beneficial area

UK.

Correspondent: The Trustees, BM Box 2831, London WC1N 3XX (website: www.inmancharity.org)

CC Number: 261366

'The directors operate a grant giving policy, providing funds for such charitable object or institution as the directors think fit. In addition to supporting a wide range of charitable organisations, the charity makes a regular payment (currently £20,000 per annum) to the Victor Inman Bursary Fund at Uppingham School of which the settlor had been a lifelong supporter.' The directors aim to make grants totalling approximately £275,000 per year. Areas supported are:

- Medical research
- Care of the elderly
- General welfare
- Hospices
- Deaf and blind
- Care of the physically and mentally disabled
- Armed forces

In 2012 the trust held assets of £4.8 million generating an income of £172,000. Grants to 69 organisations totalled £271,000.

Beneficiaries included: Help the Hospices (£10,000); Wellbeing of Women, Parkinson's UK, Multiple Sclerosis Society, Juvenile Diabetes Research Foundation, Vitalise, Royal British Legion, Changing Faces and St Mark's Hospital Foundation (£5,000 each); Back to Work for the over 40's, The Pavement, Thrift Urban Housing and Farleigh Hospice (£3,500); Hearing Dogs for Deaf People, St Cuthbert's Hospice, Support for Living and Remap (£3,000 each); Cornwall Blind Association, The Royal Star and Garter Homes and Swinfen Telemedicine (£2,000 each); and Communication for Blind and Disabled People (£1,500).

Exclusions

No grants to:

- Individuals
- Young children and infants
- Maintenance of local buildings (e.g. churches and village halls)
- Animal welfare
- Wildlife and environmental conservation
- Religious charities

Applications

In writing to the correspondent accompanied by the charity's latest report and full accounts. Applications should contain the following: aims and objectives of the charity; nature of the appeal; total target if for a specific project; contributions received against target; registered charity number; any other relevant factors.

Directors' meetings are held in April and October; applications should be received by the end of February and August to be considered at the respective meetings. Only successful applicants will be contacted.

Information gathered from:

Accounts; Charity Commission record; funder's website.

The International Bankers Charitable Trust (The Worshipful Company of International Bankers)

The recruitment and development of employees in the financial services

£100,000 (2011/12)

Beneficial area

UK with preference for inner London.

Correspondent: Tim Woods, Clerk, 3rd Floor, 12 Austin Friars, London EC2N 2HE (tel: 020 7374 0212; email: clerk@internationalbankers.co.uk; website: www.internationalbankers.co.uk)

Trustee: The Worshipful Company of International Bankers.

CC Number: 1087630

'As a representative of the major commercial activity in the city, banking and financial services, the company combines the traditions of the City Livery Companies with a modern outlook on the financial services sector. With more than 600 members, drawn from over 250 companies and institutions and with almost 50 nationalities represented, the company has a truly international character.'

Set up in 2001, 'The company will seek to promote recruitment and development of employees in the financial services industry with particular emphasis on those younger people in the immediate area of the city who would not normally be able to aspire to a city job.' Grants are made to registered charities only.

The company may support:

1 Specific projects where a donation from the company would cover either a significant proportion of the cost or an identified element of it
2 Long-term funding of scholarships and/or bursaries

In 2011/12 the trust had assets of £899,000 and an income of £142,000, mostly from members of the Worshipful Company of International Bankers. Grants were made totalling £100,000.

Beneficiaries included: the Brokerage Citylink (£30,000); City Experience (£11,000); Lord George Memorial Scholarship – Dulwich College (£7,500); Brokerage Citylink Essay Competition, Mansion House Scholarship Scheme and the City of London School for Girls (£5,000 each); University Academic Prizes (£3,000); Mudchute Park and Farm (£1,500); and Debt Doctors Foundation, Blind in Business, Into University and ENO Opera Squad Proposal (£1,000 each).

Exclusions

The following areas are excluded from company grants:

- Large projects towards which any contribution from the company would have limited impact
- General appeals or circulars
- Replacement of statutory funds
- Salaries
- Counselling
- Course fees for professionals
- Medical research
- Fundraising events and sponsorship

Applications

On a form with can be downloaded from the trust's website. Previous grant recipients must allow two years from the date the original grant was awarded to reapply.

Information gathered from:

Accounts; Charity Commission record; funder's website.

The Inverforth Charitable Trust

General

£70,000 (2012)

Beneficial area

UK.

Correspondent: Mrs Clarinda Kane, Secretary and Treasurer, 58A Flood Street, London SW3 5TE

Trustees: Elizabeth Lady Inverforth; Dr Andrew Weir; Mrs J. Kane.

CC Number: 274132

Established in 1977 the trust exists to support general charitable causes. It has given widely in the past by supporting organisations concerned with health, the arts, youth and education, churches and heritage. The trust supports UK and international charities.

In 2012 the trust had assets of £4.1 million, which generated an income of £39,000. Grants to 12 organisations totalled £70,000. No list of beneficiaries was included, however, grants were categorised under music, physical and mental health, hospices, youth and education and sundry including international.

Previous beneficiaries have included: Help for Heroes (£5,000); Herriot Hospice Homecare and CHASE Hospice Care for Children (£2,000 each); the ART Fund, British Lung Foundation, Voluntary Services Overseas and National Youth Orchestra of Great Britain (£1,500 each); National Playbus Association, Kidscape, Contact the Elderly and Farms for City Children (£1,000 each); and Book Aid International, Bowel Cancer UK and the Gurkha Welfare Trust (£500 each).

Applications

In writing to the trustees.

Information gathered from:

Accounts; Charity Commission record.

The Ireland Fund of Great Britain

Welfare, community, education, peace and reconciliation, the arts

£354,000 (2012)

Beneficial area

Ireland and Great Britain.

Correspondent: Sheila Bailey, 2nd Floor, Wigglesworth House, 69 Southwark Bridge Road, London SE1 9HH (tel: 020 7940 9850; fax: 020 7378 8376; email: shenderson@irlfunds.org; website: www.irelandfund.org)

Trustees: Sheila Bailey; Seamus McGarry; Peter Kiernan; John Rowan; Ruth McCarthy; Ivan Fallon; Michael Casey; Ruari Conneely; Zach Webb; Eileen Kelliher; Rory Godson.

CC Number: 327889

Founded in 1976 by Sir Anthony O'Reilly and a number of key American businessmen, The Worldwide Ireland Funds is an international charitable organisation operating in 12 countries and has raised over $430 million.

In 1988 the Ireland Fund of Great Britain (IFGB) was established: 'to distribute funding to community groups, voluntary organisations, charities and establishments who seek to promote Irish arts and culture and develop relationships between our communities; advancement of education; [and] promote Irish culture to the friends of Ireland.'

In 2012 the fund had assets of £680,000, an income of £630,000 mainly from donations and memberships. Grants totalled £354,000 and were broken down as follows:

Community development and relief of poverty	£231,000
Education	£84,000
Sharing and developing Irish arts and culture	£39,000

In 2012 beneficiaries included: The Irish Women Survivors Support Network (£45,000); St John's Ward – Crumlin (£25,000); Justice for Magdalenes (£14,000); Southwark Irish Pensioners (£10,000); Federation of Irish Societies (£6,100); Irish in Birmingham (£6,000); Irish Heritage Foundation Scotland (£4,200); Coventry Irish Society (£3,500); and St John Bosco Youth Club (£2,000).

Eligibility

IFGB supports projects in the following categories:

- Projects which help marginalised people in society, such as homeless people
- Vulnerable and/or older Irish people who do not, cannot or who are reluctant to access existing services
- Projects that tackle loneliness and isolation, such as lunch clubs
- Projects that support survivors of institutional abuse
- Social, cultural or educational activities for vulnerable and/or elderly Irish people
- Projects that help young people

Exclusions

No grants for: organisations based outside of England, Scotland or Wales; general appeals – assistance must be sought for clearly specified purposes; individuals; tuition or student fees; medical costs; purchase of buildings or land; construction or refurbishment projects; events; debt; retrospective costs or salary costs.

Applications

On an application form available to download from the website. Applicants must attach a copy of their audited accounts. Only one application per organisation per year. Staff or donors may visit your organisation.

Information gathered from:

Accounts; Charity Commission record; funder's website.

The Irish Youth Foundation (UK) Ltd (incorporating The Lawlor Foundation)

Irish young people

£170,000 (2012)

Beneficial area

UK.

Correspondent: Linda Tanner, The Irish Cultural Centre, 26–28 Hammersmith Grove, London W6 7HA (tel: 020 8748 9640; fax: 020 8748 7386; email: info@iyf.org.uk; website: www.iyf.org.uk)

CC Number: 328265

Irish Youth Foundation (UK) Ltd merged with the Lawlor Foundation (effective from 30 June 2005). The work of the Lawlor Foundation, towards the advancement of education in Northern Ireland, continues with support for Irish students and educational organisations.

The foundation supports organisations anywhere in the UK working with young Irish people aged up to 25 who are socially, educationally or culturally disadvantaged.

A wide range of projects are supported which include: training/counselling; drug rehabilitation; advice/advocacy; youth work; family support; homelessness; educational, cultural and social activities; cross-community initiatives; travellers and disability.

Organisations based in Northern Ireland may apply for grants of up to £5,000. Grants for organisations in England, Scotland and Wales fall into two categories:

- Small grants up to £2,500
- Standard grants of between £2,500 and £12,000

A wide variety of projects are supported, including: training/counselling; drug rehabilitation; advice/advocacy; youth work; family support; homelessness; educational, cultural and social activities; cross-community initiatives; travellers; and disability.

The Irish Youth Foundation (UK) and the Irish Youth Foundation (Ireland) have established a joint fund to provide support for community and voluntary groups in Northern Ireland. Grants for organisations in Northern Ireland are up to £5,000.

In 2012 the foundation had assets of £2.4 million and an income of £343,000. Grants totalled £170,000.

Great Britain beneficiaries included: New Horizon Youth Centre – London, Solace Women's Aid – London and Irish Community Care Merseyside (£9,500 each); Tyneside Irish Cultural Society, Luton Irish Forum, Liverpool Irish Festival Society, Irish Traveller Movement in Britain and Tricycle Theatre Company – London (£2,000 each); Manchester Irish Education Group (£1,500); Reading Community Radio (£1,000); and Irish Arts Foundation – Leeds (£500).

Previous beneficiaries in Northern Ireland included: The National Deaf Children's Society, Northern Ireland (£4,500); Artillery Youth Centre – Belfast (£4,000); Drake Music Project – Newry (£3,500); Down Community Arts – Downpatrick (£3,000); Headliners – Derry (£2,500); and Our Lady Queen of Peace Youth Club – Belfast (£1,000).

Exclusions

The foundation generally does not support: projects for people over 25; general appeals; large/national charities; academic research; alleviating deficits already incurred; individuals; capital bids; overseas travel; or multiple applications from a single organisation.

Applications

Applications are assessed on an annual basis and application forms are only available during the annual round either on the website or by request. The application period is short as forms are only available during December with grant awards being made the following May. Unsolicited applications at other times of the year are not accepted.

Applications are assessed on the following requirements: need; continuity; track record/evaluation; disadvantaged young people; innovativeness; funding sources; and budgetary control. Faxed or emailed applications are not considered. Unsolicited applications outside the annual round of grant applications will not be considered or acknowledged.

Information gathered from:

Accounts; Charity Commission record; funder's website.

The Ironmongers' Foundation

Youth, education, iron projects

£392,000 (2012/13)

Beneficial area

UK with some preference for inner London.

Correspondent: Helen Sant, Charities Administrator, Ironmongers' Hall, Barbican, London EC2Y 8AA (tel: 020 7776 2311; fax: 020 7600 3519; email: helen@ironhall.co.uk; website: www.ironhall.co.uk)

CC Number: 219153–10

The Ironmonger's Foundation and its assets are, for administrative and organisational purposes, bound up with five other charitable funds administered by the Ironmongers' Company. They are registered under the name 'Sir Robert Geffery's Almshouse Trust'. The assets, income and expenditure listed below are therefore not entirely linked to the work listed below.

Youth/Education

The Ironmongers' Company wishes to support projects that provide opportunities for disadvantaged children and young people to fulfil their potential [in the UK].

Grants will be made for projects in the UK that meet all of the following criteria:

1 Children and young people up to the age of 25 who are disadvantaged
2 Consist of educational activities that develop learning, motivation and skills
3 Have clear aims and objectives to be met within a planned timescale

The average grant is around £4,000 but they range from a few hundred pounds up to £10,000. The trustees will consider making grants over more than one year to longer term projects, subject to a satisfactory evaluation of progress at the end of each year. The company's support should make a recognisable difference; therefore preference will be given to requests which cover a significant element of the cost and to those from smaller organisations.

The Company is particularly interested in enabling primary age children to develop a strong foundation for the future. Projects could, for example, support special educational needs, address behavioural problems or promote citizenship, parenting or life skills. Preference will be given to projects piloting new approaches where the outcomes will be disseminated to a wider audience.

From the accounts:

Relationships with four partner charities were continued during the year. The Art Room, Lyric Hammersmith and MakeBelieve Arts all use arts to enable children and young people to develop basic skills such as literacy. The fourth, St Vincent's Family Project, provides support to parents of young children in challenging circumstances.

Iron

The Ironmongers' Company, as part of its charitable activities, works to promote the craft of ironwork. Support is given primarily for the conservation of historic ironwork or the creation of new decorative iron or steel work.

The Company does not make grants for other restoration projects.

Grants are made for charitable purposes and not for the benefit of private individuals. Applications are accepted from registered charities, churches and schools for projects in the UK only.

The Company prefers to fund entire projects, or specific elements of a project. The majority of grants awarded are under £5,000. Grants are paid on completion of the project and must be claimed within eighteen months of the date awarded.

In 2012/13 the foundation had assets of £23.5 million, an income of £1.3 million and made grants to organisations totalling £392,000.

Beneficiaries included: Lyric Hammersmith (£17,000); MakeBelieve Arts (£16,000); St Paul's Cathedral School (£12,500); St Vincent's Family Project (£10,000); Museum of London (£8,600); The Comedy Trust (£4,700); University of Sheffield (£4,500); University of Manchester and University of Cambridge (£4,000 each); REAL (£3,400); Liverpool Lighthouse, Froglife Trust and Leaders in Community (£2,500 each); Sheriff's and Recorder Fund (£2,000); City of London and North East Sector Army Cadet Force (£1,000); and City of London Police Widows and Orphans Fund (£200).

Exclusions

No grants towards:

- Large projects towards which any contribution from the Company would have limited impact
- General appeals or circulars
- Replacement of statutory funds
- General running costs (a reasonable proportion of overheads will be accepted as part of project costs)
- Counselling and therapy
- Course fees for professionals
- Medical research
- Fundraising events and sponsorship
- Retrospective appeals and projects starting before the date of the relevant Committee meeting
- Building work
- Holidays

Applications

Youth/Education projects

The Company's 'Grant Application Summary Sheet' must be completed and returned including a description of the project, of no more than three A4 pages. Summary sheets can be downloaded from the fund's website.

A description of the project on no more than three A4 pages, typed on one side of each sheet, should be provided. Use the following headings:

- Aims and objectives of the organisation
- How the need for the work has been identified
- Why the project is the best way to address this need
- The anticipated outcomes and the methods by which the success of the project will be evaluated
- A full breakdown of the costs involved, explaining how the figures have been calculated

If your most recent audited accounts are not available on the Charity Commission website enclose a copy. There is no need to send additional material.

The Appeals Committee meets twice a year in March and October. The deadlines for receipt of applications are 31 December and 31 July respectively.

Note that applications are not accepted by email.

Grants must be spent within twelve months from the date of the award.

Iron projects

The Company's Iron Committee meets annually in May to review grants for Iron Projects and the deadline for receipt of applications is 31 March. Applicants should write to the Charities Manager at the address below with details of the project, including:

- A description of the property, the ironwork, its relevance and the work required
- Conservation plan/craftsman's drawings/photographs as applicable
- A full breakdown of the costs involved, indicating specific elements of the project for which a grant could be made and itemising VAT separately. Please state whether VAT will be reclaimed
- The amount of money already raised for the project and any applications made or pending to other potential funders
- The proposed dates for starting and finishing the work
- Plans for ongoing preventative maintenance of the ironwork
- Public access arrangements and visitor numbers where appropriate

The company expects any conservation of historic ironwork to follow the National Heritage Ironwork Group's Conservation Principles (see: www.nhig.org.uk). Your application should confirm that your project will meet these standards.

Information gathered from:

Accounts; Charity Commission record; funder's website.

The ISA Charity

The arts, health and education

£35,000 (2011/12)

Beneficial area

UK.

Correspondent: Richard Paice, Trustee, 2 The Mansion, Northwick Park, Blockley, Moreton-in-Marsh Gl56 9RJ (tel: 01386 700121; website: www.isacharity.org)

Trustees: Monique Paice; Adriana Kent; Richard Paice.

CC Number: 326882

Founded in 1985 by Richard Paice, the ISA Charity supports causes related to the arts, health and education in the broadest sense. This can include both UK and overseas initiatives. The following information is taken from the charity's website:

Travel Award

This travel award has grown and now runs in a number of schools and university across the U.K. from Edinburgh to

Sussex. Every year 12–15 students are awarded funding and support to embark on their travels.

Personal Development Award at Goldsmith's University
This new award aims to give a design student/s the encouragement and direction to realise a project of their dreams. Past winners have included a design collective of six students starting up their own studio and working on a variety of different projects, (including a large event at the London Design Festival 2006) and a student running a charity that recycles used bicycles and sends them to Africa. The award is still in its infancy and we are looking forward to working with many more exciting winners.

Open Book, Goldsmiths University
This exciting initiative encourages and provides the opportunity for ex-offenders, addicts and those with mental health problems to enter higher education. Joe Baden, an ex-offender who founded the programme, believes strongly that people will not re-offend or re-abuse if they are taught self-worth and have pride in what they achieve. Our involvement with this excellent scheme has just begun and we are supporting people within the Open Book community who have learning difficulties, such as dyslexia. We are currently working with a member of the community who has decided to embark on a Remedial Teaching course, specialising in dyslexia. Once she has trained she will become an invaluable resource for the Open Book community.

Mentoring Programme, Oxford Brookes
For the past ten years we have run a successful programme at the university that offers candidates a one-to-one mentoring experience, to help them focus on and realise their professional ambitions.

In 2011/12 the charity had assets of almost £1.7 million and an income of £59,000. Grants totalled £35,000.

Unfortunately a list of the beneficiaries was not available.

Applications

The following is taken from the charity's website from which can be downloaded an application form:

How to Apply
When applying for the award please bear in mind that we would like either a written report outlining your experience once you return (minimum of 500 words with lots of images) or a blog whilst you are travelling (with at least four entries of 250 words and plenty of pictures). We also encourage winners to share their experience with their school or University when they return and inspire new candidates to apply.

Information gathered from:

Accounts; Charity Commission record; funder's website.

The J. Isaacs Charitable Trust

General

Around £744,000 (2011/12)

Beneficial area

England and Wales.

Correspondent: The Trustees, JRJ Group, 61 Conduit Street, London W1S 2GB (tel: 020 7220 2305)

Trustees: Jeremy Isaacs: Joanne Isaacs; Helen Eastick.

CC Number: 1059865

Registered with the Charity Commission in 1996, the trust states that it:

> Strives to support causes connected to the following:
> - Children
> - Respite for parents/children
> - Cancer
> - Sponsorship for causes supported by Lehman employees
> - London-based organisations

In 2011/12 it had an income of £16,000 and a total expenditure of £744,500. Due to the low income, accounts were not published on the Commission's website.

Previous beneficiaries included: Jewish Care (£200,000); the Jewish Museum London (£100,000); Community Security Trust (£75,000); Greenhouse Schools Project (£25,000); Policy Exchange Ltd (£15,000); UCLH Fund (£7,500); UK Jewish Film (£5,000); and Royal National Theatre (£1,000).

Applications

In writing to the correspondent.

Information gathered from:

Accounts; Charity Commission record.

The Ithaca Trust

General, education, social welfare

Beneficial area

Greater London.

Correspondent: James Midgley, Trustee, MacIntyre Hudson, New Bridge Street House, 30–34 New Bridge Street, London EC4V 6BJ (tel: 020 7429 4100; email: james.midgley@mhllp.co.uk)

Trustees: James Midgley; Ralph Fiennes; Julian Wadham.

CC Number: 1145502

Registered in January 2012, this is the charitable trust of the actor, Ralph Fiennes. The objects of the trust are general charitable purposes, education and social welfare. No further information was available. Unfortunately at the time of writing (December 2013) the trust's first accounts were overdue with the Charity Commission.

Applications

In writing to the correspondent.

Information gathered from:

Accounts; Charity Commission record.

The J. and J. Charitable Trust

General, Jewish

£174,000 (2011/12)

Beneficial area

UK.

Correspondent: Leon Angel, Administrator, Hazlems Fenton LLP, Palladium House, 1–4 Argyll Street, London W1F 7LD (tel: 020 7437 7666; fax: 020 7734 0644; email: leonangel@hazlemsfenton.com)

Trustees: Jahnene Green; Jonathan Green.

CC Number: 1065660

The trust was established in 1997 for general charitable purposes. Jonathan Green is a former Goldman Sachs trader and co-founder of London hedge fund GLG.

In 2011/12 the trust had an income of £62,500, all of which came from donations from Jonathan Green. Grants were made during the year totalling £174,000.

The main beneficiary during the year was the Harefield Academy (£145,000), of which Mr Green is listed as a sponsor. The other beneficiaries were: Great Ormond Street Hospital (£7,000); Western Marble Arch Synagogue (£6,200); Myeloma UK and London Business School (£5,000 each); Kisharon (£2,000); British Technion Society (£1,500); The Presidents' Club and the National Society for Epilepsy (£1,000 each); and Jewish Care (£140).

Applications

In writing to the correspondent.

Information gathered from:

Accounts; Charity Commission record.

J. A. R. Charitable Trust

Roman Catholic, education, welfare

£59,500 (2011/12)

Beneficial area

Worldwide.

Correspondent: Philip R. Noble, Trustee, Hunters, 9 New Square, London WC2A 3QN (tel: 020 7412 0050)

Trustees: Philip R. Noble; Revd William Young; Revd Paschal Ryan.

CC Number: 248418

The trust makes grants towards: Roman Catholic missionaries, churches, schools and other causes; education for people under 30; and food and clothing for people over 55 who are in need. In practice, the trust gives regular grants to support mainly Roman Catholic organisations.

In 2011/12 the trust had assets of £2.4 million and an income of £78,000. Grants were made to 28 organisations totalling £59,500.

Beneficiaries included: Oxford Oratory and the Passage (£4,000 each); Catholic Children's Society – Brentwood, Liverpool Archdiocesan Youth Pilgrimage, St Joseph's Hospice and the Venerable English College Rome (£3,000 each); Friends of Tumaini, Little Sisters of the Poor and St Anthony's Church (£2,000 each); and Marriage Care, Tongabezi Trust School and Walsingham Parish (£1,000 each).

Exclusions

The trust does not normally support a charity unless it is known to the trustees and it does not support individuals.

Applications

In writing to the correspondent. Note that the trust's funds are fully committed to regular beneficiaries and it states that there is very little, if any, for unsolicited appeals. In order to save administration costs replies are not sent to unsuccessful applicants.

Information gathered from:

Accounts; Charity Commission record.

The J. M. K. Charitable Trust

Art and Music, religions and their relations with other faiths – Worldwide

£60,000 (2011/12)

Beneficial area

Worldwide.

Correspondent: The Trustees, c/o Saffery Champness, Lion House, 72–75 Red Lion Street, London WC1R 4GB (tel: 020 7841 4000)

Trustees: Jill Karaviotis; Joseph Karaviotis.

CC Number: 274576

This trust supports registered charities, with a current preference for those concerned with the appreciation of art and music. 'We also assist religious organisations to help relations with other faiths.'

In 2011/12 the trust had assets of £2 million and an income of £70,000. Grants to 18 organisations totalled £60,000.

Beneficiaries include: Royal Academy of Music – Scholarship (£17,000); English Touring Opera (£13,000); Royal Opera House (£5,400); Les Azuriales Opera Trust (£4,000); Friends of the Salzburg Festival (£3,400); Central British Fund for World Jewish Relief (£1,400); London Jewish Cultural Centre and English National Opera (£1,000 each); British Friends of Haifa University (£200); and Opera Holland Park (£100).

Applications

Unsolicited applications will not be considered.

Information gathered from:

Accounts; Charity Commission record.

The JRSST Charitable Trust

Democracy and social justice

£82,000 (2012)

Beneficial area

UK.

Correspondent: Tina Walker, The Garden House, Water End, York YO30 6WQ (tel: 01904 625744; email: info@jrrt.org.uk; website: www.jrrt.org.uk)

Trustees: Christine Day; Dr Christopher Greenfield; Amanda Cormack; Peadar Cremin; Baroness Sal Brinton; Andrew Neal; Alison Goldsworthy.

CC Number: 247498

The trust was originally endowed by the non-charitable Joseph Rowntree Reform Trust Ltd. It will consider and sometimes instigate charitable projects which relate specifically to the work of The Joseph Rowntree Reform Trust Ltd in supporting the development of an increasingly democratic and socially-just society in Great Britain. The trust does not have a defined grants programme.

In 2012 the trust had assets of £2.8 million and an income of over £105,500. 21 grants were paid to organisations totalling £82,000.

Beneficiaries of grants approved during the year included: Reuters Institute for the Study of Journalism (£20,000); Rowntree Society (£15,000); Democratic Audit (£9,000); Education for Choice (£5,000); Bureau of Investigative Journalism (£4,000); and Institute of Race Relations (£2,000).

Exclusions

No student grants are funded. Non-charitable, political and campaigning activities only.

Applications

The trustees meet quarterly. They do not invite applications.

Initial assessments should be submitted to the Grants and Projects Adviser via email. The email should include an outline (up to a side of A4 which includes the amount required) of the proposal.

There is no standard application form; however an application should include the following:

- Application registration form (available from the trust's website)
- Proposal (up to four pages long)
- Full project budget
- Most recent accounts
- CV (if applying as an individual)

Applications for small grants of up to £5,000 are considered at any time. The deadline for grants over £5,000 is four to five weeks before the trustees' meeting. All applications should be received before 12 noon on the deadline day.

Information gathered from:

Accounts; Charity Commission record; funder's website.

C. Richard Jackson Charitable Trust

General charitable purposes

£77,000 (2011/12)

Beneficial area

England and Wales.

Correspondent: Charles Richard Jackson, Trustee, Loftus Hill, Ferrensby, Knaresborough, North Yorkshire HG5 9JT (tel: 01904 694000; fax: 01904 694090)

Trustees: Charles Richard Jackson; Jeremy P. Jackson; Lucy Crack.

CC Number: 1073442

The trust was established for general charitable purposes in 1998 by Charles Richard Jackson, who was awarded an MBE in 2002 for 'services in the community of West and North Yorkshire'. Mr Jackson is a director of United Health, a company providing care homes and supported living accommodation.

In 2011/12 the trust had an income of £71,000, all of which came from donations. Grants were made to 62 organisations totalling £77,000. Most grants were for less than £500.

The largest grants were made to: The Prince's Trust (£43,000); Teenage Cancer Trust and St Peter's Church (£5,000 each); The Variety Club Children's Charity and Macmillan Cancer Support (£3,500 each); Kohima Educational Trust (£3,000); Leeds Teaching Hospitals

Charitable Foundation and Prince of Wales Hospice (£2,500 each); and Two Ridings Community Fund (£2,000).

Applications

In writing to the correspondent.

Information gathered from:

Accounts; Charity Commission record.

The Ruth and Lionel Jacobson Trust (Second Fund) No. 2

Jewish, medical, children, people with disabilities

£55,000 (2011/12)

Beneficial area

UK, with a preference for North East England.

Correspondent: Malcolm Jacobson, Trustee, 14 The Grainger Suite, Dobson House, The Regent Centre, Newcastle upon Tyne NE3 3PF

Trustees: Anne Jacobson; Malcolm Jacobson.

CC Number: 326665

The trust supports UK charities and organisations based in the north east of England. The trust states that it supports the advancement of Jewish religious education and healthcare charities. Charities outside the north east of England are supported whenever possible.

In 2011/12 the trust had assets of £1.3 million, an income of £168,000 and made grants to six organisations totalling £55,000. Beneficiaries were: Newcastle University (£20,000); Calvert Trust (£15,000); United Jewish Israel Appeal (£12,500); WIZO UK (£6,000); Anne Frank Trust (£1,500); and NE Jewish Community Services (£200).

Exclusions

No grants for individuals. Only registered charities will be supported.

Applications

In writing to the correspondent. Enclose an sae. Applications are considered every other month.

Information gathered from:

Accounts; Charity Commission record.

The James Trust

Christianity

£55,000 (2011/12)

Beneficial area

UK and overseas.

Correspondent: R. J. Todd, Trustee, 27 Radway Road, Upper Shirley, Southampton, Hampshire SO15 7PL (tel: 02380 788249)

Trustees: Richard Todd; George Blue.

CC Number: 800774

Principally, the trust has a preference for supporting Christian organisations. It operates primarily as a channel for the giving of a small group of donors. Grants are primarily to churches and Christian organisations involved in overseas development and work with young people.

In 2011/12 the trust had assets of £77,000, an income of £47,000 and gave grants totalling £55,000, broken down as follows:

Organisations working overseas	£18,000
Churches and church organisations	£14,000
Organisations working in the UK	£13,000
Development and relief work	£10,000

During the year donations were made to the local churches of the donors and to a wide range of Christian organisations. The main beneficiaries were Above Bar Church, Church Mission Society, Food for the Hungry, Highfield Church and Wycliffe Translators.

Unfortunately a full grants list was not provided in this year's set of accounts, however previous beneficiaries have included: Archbishops Council; UCCF; Crusaders; Christian Aid; Bible Society; and Cancer Research.

Exclusions

No grants to individuals not personally known to the trustees.

Applications

In writing to the correspondent. Unsolicited applications are not acknowledged. Phone calls are welcome before an application is submitted.

Percentage of awards given to new applicants: less than 10%.

Common applicant mistakes

'Not telephoning first; explaining activities rather than benefits.'

Information gathered from:

Accounts; Charity Commission record; further information provided by the funder.

The John Jarrold Trust

Social welfare, arts, education, environment/conservation, medical research, churches

£145,000 (2011/12)

Beneficial area

Norfolk.

Correspondent: Caroline Jarrold, Trustee, Jarrold and Sons Ltd, St James Works, 12–20 Whitefriars, Norwich NR3 1SH (tel: 01603 677360; email: caroline.jarrold@jarrold.com; website: www.jarrold.com)

Trustees: Caroline Jarrold; Juliet Jarrold; Richard Jarrold; Waltraud Jarrold; Joan Jarrold; Peter Jarrold; Antony Jarrold; Charles Jarrold.

CC Number: 242029

The trust supports a wide range of organisations, see the table below, and in particular those supporting education and research in all or any of the natural sciences. It prefers to support specific projects, rather than contribute to general funding. In practice, most of the funds are given in Norfolk.

In 2011/12 the trust had assets of over £2.4 million and an income of £99,000. Grants made to 145 organisations totalled £145,000, and were broken down as follows:

Social and Welfare	£54,500
Education	£43,500
Arts	£19,000
Developing countries	£8,000
Churches and historic buildings	£7,000
Health and Medical	£5,500
Environment	£4,000
Jarrold Staff Charity Challenge	£4,000

Beneficiaries included: UEA Jubilee Appeal (£30,000); Hamlet Centre and YMCA Norfolk (£7,500 each); Thorpe St Andrew School (£5,000); Norfolk and Norwich Festival and Theatre Royal Norwich (£3,000 each); Community Action Norwich, East Anglia Art Fund, Emmaus, Smallpiece Trust and Woodland Trust (£2,000 each); Big C, Childhood First, CLIC Sargent, Criminon UK, Hebron Trust, Leeway Norwich Women's Aid, Mercy Ships, Self Help Africa, Sightsavers, The Hamlet Centre and SNCLS (£1,000 each); Feed the Minds, Friends of the Elderly, Halvergate Parish Council, Leonard Cheshire Disability, Magdalene Group and Theatre Royal Norwich (£500 each); Garveston Parish Council, Geographical Association and Norfolk Titanic Association (£100 each); and Magdalen Gates Primary School (£50).

Exclusions

Educational purposes that should be supported by the state will not be helped by the trust. Local groups outside Norfolk are very unlikely to be supported unless there is a personal connection to the trust. Individual educational programmes and gap year projects are not supported.

Applications

Trustees meet in January and June each year and applications should be made in writing by the end of November and April respectively. Grants of up to £250 can be made between meetings.

Percentage of awards given to new applicants: between 10% and 20%.

Common applicant mistakes

'Not reading the criteria; long letters.'

Information gathered from:

Accounts; Charity Commission record; further information provided by the funder; funder's website.

Rees Jeffreys Road Fund

Road and transport research and education

£203,000 to organisations and individuals (2012)

Beneficial area

UK.

Correspondent: Brian Smith, Fund Secretary, Merriewood, Horsell Park, Woking, Surrey GU21 4LW (tel: 01483 750758; email: briansmith@reesjeffreys.org; website: www.reesjeffreys.co.uk)

CC Number: 217771

The late William Rees Jeffreys established the trust in 1950, shortly after he wrote 'The King's Highway'. He campaigned extensively for the improvement of better roads and transport and was described by Lloyd George as 'the greatest authority on roads in the United Kingdom and one of the greatest in the world', due to his unrivalled expertise in this field. He was the first Secretary of the Road Board, the precursor of the Department of Transport.

The trust's objectives are:

- To contribute to the cost of lectures, studies and scholarship calculated to foster the improvement of design and layout of public highways and adjoining lands
- To promote schemes for the provision of roadside parks and open spaces
- To encourage the improvement of existing and provision of additional public highways, bridges, tunnels, footpaths, verges, and cycleways to secure the maximum of safety and beauty
- To do any other matter or thing which may conduce to the carrying out of the forgoing object and thereby carry out the wishes and continue the life work of the founder

The trust will support projects and pump priming for longer-term ventures for up to a maximum of five years. Operational or administrative staff costs are rarely supported. In almost all cases applicants are expected to provide or arrange match funding.

In 2012 the fund held assets of £6.8 million and had an income of £17,000. Grants totalled £203,000 and were broken down as follows:

Educational bursaries and support	£99,000
Research and other projects	£94,000
Roadside improvements (Wildlife Trusts) grants	£11,000

As in previous years the trust continued its longstanding support of the Wildlife Trusts, with four grants totalling £11,000. Education grants were made to eight postgraduate transport students as well as to the Arkwright Trust and Headstart. The 2012 accounts also note that the trustees:

> Have continued as a high priority to seek to extend the number of research grant recipients particularly where projects have the potential to influence UK transport policy. It was pleasing to note therefore that research expenditure totalled £104,000 in 2012 compared with £46,000 in 2011. The Motorway Archive Trust, PACTS, CIHT and the Independent Transport Commission (ITC) were among the recipients in 2012, and the wide range of topics covered included Transport in the Urban Environment, Paying for Road Use, Cycling Safety, Verge Maintenance and Older Driver Safety.

The chair notes in his 2012 report that they were keen on seeing more research projects around 'mobility, economics and environmental aspects of transport policy and practice'. And in general 'there remained a shortage of good quality research applications'. He also emphasised that applicants should 'give a clear indication of the potential application of the results of their work and how these would be disseminated'.

Exclusions

Grants are not given to environmental projects not related to highways, individual works for cycle tracks or works of only local application. Also, operational and administrative staff costs are rarely considered.

Applications

Applications should be made in writing to the fund secretary and include the following details:

- The purpose for which funding is sought – outlining the objects, relevance and the proposed methodology of the project including the names of the principal participants
- The expected costs by category, along with the project timetable
- Evidence of the willingness of other parties (where the project requires their contribution or participation) to get involved
- Appropriate evidence of the applicant's in-depth knowledge of the subject of the application and their familiarity with previous work in the field

Applications should not be more than three A4 pages. All necessary supporting material and a digital version of the application should also be submitted.

The trustees meet five times a year, usually in January, April, July, September and November (see the fund's website for specific dates). The deadline for submission of applications or other agenda items is normally a fortnight before the meeting. Informal contact prior to submitting a formal application is welcomed.

Information gathered from:

Accounts; Charity Commission record; funder's website.

The Jenour Foundation

General charitable purposes

£116,000 (2011/12)

Beneficial area

UK, with a special interest in Wales.

Correspondent: Cecilia St Clair, Correspondent, Deloitte PCS Ltd, 5 Callaghan Square, Cardiff CF10 5BT (tel: 02920 264391)

CC Number: 256637

This foundation has general charitable purposes, with a preference for Welsh causes. The trustees will award donations to capital projects and also towards ordinary charitable purposes.

In 2011/12 the foundation had assets of £3.1 million, an income of £118,000 and made 33 grants totalling £116,000.

Beneficiaries included: Army Benevolent Fund (£9,000); Atlantic College and Cancer Research Wales (£8,000 each); British Heart Foundation and Welsh National Opera (£7,000 each); Macmillan Cancer Care Fund (£6,000); St Arvan's Church- Chepstow, St Woolos Cathedral and British Red Cross (£5,000 each); Wales Millennium Centre, Llandovery College and British Scoliosis Research Foundation (£3,000 each); Parish of Llanishen (£1,000); and Society for Welfare of Horses and Ponies and Bridge VIS (£500 each).

Exclusions

Registered charities only.

Applications

Applications should be in writing and reach the correspondent by February for the trustees' meeting in March.

Information gathered from:

Accounts; Charity Commission record.

The Jephcott Charitable Trust

Development worldwide specifically in the areas of health, education, population control and environment

£156,000 (2011/12)

Beneficial area

Worldwide.

Correspondent: Dr Felicity Gibling, Secretary to the Trustees, The Threshing Barn, Ford, Kingsbridge, Devon TQ7 2LN (website: www.jephcottcharitabletrust.org.uk)

CC Number: 240915

The following information is taken from the trust's website:

The trust's funding priorities are:

- *Population control* – The trust is prepared to consider support for schemes, particularly educational ones, which help to control excessive growth in population
- *The natural environment* – The trust has supported a number of projects involved in conserving the natural environment. It does not support projects involving animal welfare or heritage sites or buildings
- *Education* – Projects will be considered benefiting people of all ages and backgrounds. They may be able to provide formal education, to teach vocational skills to enhance the possibility of employment, to enhance computer skills, health awareness, distance learning
- *Health* – A wide range of healthcare projects are supported. Projects which require long-term funding are not normally considered. The trust prefers to make one-off donations to get many projects started, rather than support fewer projects over a long period

The trust prefers to support projects which are pump-priming – helping to get an organisation up and running, or make a significant step forward. 'We like to make grants which will make a difference, preference will be given to charities or projects which are having difficulty getting started, or raising funds from other sources. This often means that the trust is funding capital projects, e.g. for equipment or materials, rather than running costs. Grants are made to charities in all parts of the world.

Grants are made in the range of £2,000 to £10,000, and in exceptional cases only, up to £20,000. For further information visit the trust's helpful website.

In 2011/12 the trust had assets of £5.4 million, an income of £212,000 and made 18 grants totalling £156,000, which were distributed as follows:

Health	£91,000
Educational	£39,500
Environment relief	£20,000
Music	£5,000

Beneficiaries included: Possibilities (£20,000); Catherine Bullen Trust (£15,000) Lessons for Life and Zisize (£10,000 each); Lotus Flower Trust (£8,000); Flora and Fauna International and Kagando (£5,000 each); Potosi (£4,000); and African Village Support (£2,000).

Exclusions

The trust does not support:

- Organisations whose administrative expenses form more than 15% of their annual income
- Individuals
- Animal welfare
- Heritage

Projects which require long-term funding are not normally considered.

Applications

Full and detailed guidelines and application forms can be downloaded from the trust's website. Trustees meet twice a year (in April and October) and must have detailed financial information about each project before they will make a decision. Only applications from eligible bodies are acknowledged, when further information about the project may be requested. Monitoring of grant expenditure is a requirement of all successful grants and donations from the trust.

Information gathered from:

Accounts; Charity Commission record; funder's website.

The Jewish Youth Fund

Jewish youth work

£144,000 (2011/12)

Beneficial area

UK.

Correspondent: Julia Samuel, Secretary, Haskell House, 152 West End Lane, London NW6 1SD (tel: 020 7443 5169; email: info@jyf.org.uk)

CC Number: 251902

The fund's objectives are to promote and protect religious, moral, educational, physical and social interests of young members of the Jewish community in the UK.

In 2011/12 the trust had assets of £3.4 million and an income of £101,000. Grants totalling £144,000 went to ten organisations. The grants ranged in size from £1,000 to £104,000.

Beneficiaries were: London Jewish Cultural Centre (£104,000); JLGB (£10,000); Step by Step (£8,000); Camp Simcha (£5,000); Friends of B'nei Akiva (£4,000); FZY, Noam, Habonim Dror and Kisharon (£3,000 each); and The BBYO Charitable Trust (£1,000).

Exclusions

Grants are not made in response to general appeals. Formal education is not supported.

Applications

On an application form available from the correspondent, enclosing a copy of the latest accounts and an annual report.

Information gathered from:

Accounts; Charity Commission record.

The Nicholas Joels Charitable Trust

Jewish, medical welfare, general

Around £25,000 (2011/12)

Beneficial area

UK and overseas.

Correspondent: Nicholas Joels, Trustee, 20 Copse Wood Way, Northwood HA6 2UF (tel: 01923 841376)

CC Number: 278409

The trust makes grants to registered charities only, and from the list of beneficiaries it appears to support Jewish causes and medical and welfare charities.

In 2011/12 it had an income of £19,000 and a total expenditure of £25,500. No information was available regarding beneficiary organisations.

Previous beneficiaries included: World Jewish Relief (£9,000); Norwood (£5,300); Emunah (£4,300); United Jewish Israel Appeal (£3,800); Jewish Care (£2,000); Zionist Federation (£1,000); United Synagogue (£900); I Rescue (£750); Chinese Disaster Fund (£500); Jewish Women's Aid (£200); and Friends of the Tate Gallery (£100).

Applications

In writing to the correspondent.

Information gathered from:

Accounts; Charity Commission record.

The Harold Joels Charitable Trust

Jewish

£21,000 (2011/12)

Beneficial area

UK and overseas.

Correspondent: Harold Joels, Trustee, 11a Arkwright Road, London NW3 6AA (email: hjoles7@aol.com)

Trustees: Harold Joels; Mr N. Joels; Valerie Joels; Prof. Norman Joels.

CC Number: 206326

The trust makes grants to Jewish organisations in the UK and US.

In 2011/12 the trust had assets of £595,000, an income of £28,000 and a total expenditure of £23,000. Grants totalled £21,000, with £4,600 awarded to 23 British organisations and £16,400 awarded to 32 American organisations.

Beneficiaries in the UK include: United Synagogue (£1,600); and Chai Cancer Care, Norwood, Samaritans, Shaare Zedek UK, St John Ambulance and Tricycle Theatre Company Ltd (all grants under £500).

Applications

In writing to the correspondent.

Information gathered from:

Accounts; Charity Commission record.

The Norman Joels Charitable Trust

Jewish causes, general

£33,000 (2011/12)

Beneficial area

UK, Israel and the Middle East.

Correspondent: The Trustees, Grunberg and Co. Ltd, 10 - 14 Accommodation Road, London NW11 8EP (tel: 020 8458 0083)

Trustees: Jessica Joels; Norman Joels; Harold Joels; Myriam Joels.

CC Number: 206325

In 2011/12 the trust had assets of £1.2 million and an income of £36,000. Grants were made totalling £33,000. A grants breakdown was not included in the accounts.

Previous beneficiaries have included: Friends of Magen David Action in Great Britain, Jewish Aid Committee, Jewish Care, Joint Jewish Charitable Trust, New London Synagogue, Norwood Ravenswood, The Spiro Institute and World Jewish Relief.

Applications

In writing to the correspondent.

Information gathered from:

Accounts; Charity Commission record.

The Lillie Johnson Charitable Trust

Children, young people who are blind or deaf, medical

£172,000 (2011/12)

Beneficial area

UK, with a preference for the West Midlands.

Correspondent: John Desmond, Trustee, Heathcote House, 39 Rodbourne Road, Harborne, Birmingham B17 0PN (tel: 01214 721279)

Trustees: Victor Lyttle; Peter Adams; John Desmond; Verena Adams.

CC Number: 326761

In 2011/12 the trust had assets of £5.3 million and an income of £204,000. Grants to 152 organisations were made totalling £172,000.

Donations under £1,000 were made to 109 organisations. Beneficiaries of grants of £1,000 or more included: LEC – Worcester (£40,000); Family Care Trust and Marie Curie Cancer Care (£10,000 each); British Tinnitus Association and Samaritans Solihull (£5,000 each); Birmingham and Midland Operatic Society – Youth (£4,500); and Blind Veterans UK, Cambridge Performing Arts, Pan Asia Community Housing, Sense, Sunfield Home and Warwickshire Junior Tennis Foundation (£1,000 each).

Exclusions

No support for individuals.

Applications

Applications are only considered from charities which are traditionally supported by the trust. The trust stated that it is inundated with applications it cannot support and feels obliged to respond to all of these.

Information gathered from:

Accounts; Charity Commission record.

The Johnson Foundation

Education, health, relief of poverty

£356,000 (2012/13)

Beneficial area

Merseyside.

Correspondent: Peter Johnson, Trustee, c/o Park Group plc, 1 Valley Road, Birkenhead, Wirral CH41 7ED (tel: 01516 531700)

Trustees: Christopher Johnson; Peter Johnson.

CC Number: 518660

The foundation's main aim is to support charitable activities in the City of Liverpool. The objects for which the foundation is established are:

- To promote any charitable purposes for the benefit of the City of Liverpool or the immediate neighbourhood at the discretion of Liverpool City Council
- To promote any charitable purposes and in particular the advancement of education, the preservation and protection of health and relief of poverty and sickness

In 2012/13 the foundation had assets of £3.8 million and an income of £127,000. Grants totalling £356,000 were awarded to 75 organisations.

Beneficiaries included: Liverpool and Merseyside Theatre Trust (£200,000); Liverpool Heart and Chest Hospital (£50,000); Birkenhead School (£25,000); Age UK Wirral (£19,000); Old Parkonians Youth Development and Sara's Hope Foundation Children's Hospice (£10,000 each); Wirral St John's Hospice (£5,000); Christians Against Poverty and the Prince's Trust (£2,500 each); and the Snowdrop Appeal, Birkenhead Gang Show and Shining Faces in India (£1,000 each).

Exclusions

Grants are not normally given to individuals.

Applications

In writing to the correspondent. The trustees meet monthly.

Information gathered from:

Accounts; Charity Commission record.

The Dezna Robins Jones Charitable Foundation

Medicine, education

£371,000 (2012/13)

Beneficial area

Preference for south Wales.

Correspondent: Bernard Jones, Trustee, Greenacres, Laleston, Bridgend CF32 0HN (tel: 01656 768584)

Trustees: Bernard Jones; Louise Boobyer; Alexia Cooke.

CC Number: 1104252

The trustees' report for 2012/13 states that 'the objectives are to support primarily local medical and educational (both sporting and arts) causes.'

The trust supports the University Hospital of Wales Cardiff, as well as a range of other local medical and educational charitable causes with benefit the local south Wales community.

In 2012/13 the trust had assets of £2.3 million, an income of nearly £4,000. It made grants of just over £371,000.

Beneficiaries included: University Hospital Wales (£88,000); Neil Boobyer Rugby Solutions Ltd (£56,000); Performance Arts Education (£54,000); Tredegar Band and St John's School Porthcawl (£50,000 each); Cory Band (£42,000); St David's Hospice and Save the Children Fund (£5,000 each); Maggie's Cancer Care Centre (£2,000); and Cancer Information and Support Services (£1,000).

Applications

In writing to the correspondent. Trustees meet at least twice a year.

Information gathered from:

Accounts; Charity Commission record.

The Marjorie and Geoffrey Jones Charitable Trust

General

£87,000 (2011/12)

Beneficial area

UK, preference south west of England.

Correspondent: Sophia Honey, Correspondent, Carlton House, 30 The Terrace, Torquay, Devon TQ1 1BN (tel: 01803 213251; email: sophia.honey@wollenmichelmore.co.uk)

Trustees: Nigel Wollen; William Coplestone Boughey; Philip Kay; Katrina Vollentine.

CC Number: 1051031

The trust was set up under the terms of the will of Rose Marjorie Jones, who died in 1995, leaving the gross of her estate amounting to £2.2 million for grantmaking purposes. In her will she donated amounts of £15,000 and £10,000 to charities based in Devon, such as the Donkey Sanctuary – Sidmouth, Paignton Zoological and Botanical Gardens Ltd, the Rowcroft Hospital – Torquay, the Torbay Hospital League of Friends and RNIB – Torquay. Other organisations named in the will were UK-wide, such as RNLI, RSPCA and NSPCC – although grants were probably given to local branches.

In 2011/12 the trust had assets of £1.4 million and an income of £23,000. Grants were made to 43 organisations totalling £87,000.

Beneficiaries included: Torquay Child Contact Centre (£5,000); Children and Families in Grief (£4,000); British Wireless for the Blind Fund, Devon Wildlife Trust and Parkinson's UK (£3,000 each); Epilepsy Society (£2,500); Changing Faces and The Sailors' Families Society (£2,000 each); and 66 Route Youth Trust, Double Elephant Print Workshop and Home-Start Torbay (£1,000 each).

Applications

In writing to the correspondent. The trustees meet four times a year to consider applications.

Information gathered from:

Accounts; Charity Commission record.

The Joron Charitable Trust

Jewish, education, medical research, general

£193,000 (2011/12)

Beneficial area

UK.

Correspondent: Bruce D. G. Jarvis, Chair, 115 Wembley Commercial Centre, East Lane, North Wembley, Middlesex HA9 7UR (tel: 020 8908 4655)

Trustees: Bruce D. G. Jarvis; Sandra C. Jarvis; Joseph R. Jarvis.

CC Number: 1062547

The trust's policy is to make grants to registered charities in the fields of education, medical research and other charities who can demonstrate that the grants will be used effectively.

In 2011/12 the trust had assets of £220,000 and an income of £347,500, largely in donations from Ravensale Ltd. Grants to six organisations totalled £193,000.

The beneficiaries were: The Wilderness Foundation (£112,000 for the protection of wilderness areas); Hammersmith Hospital Imperial Healthcare Charity (£63,000 to fund the oncology department for prostate cancer research); St John's Hospice (£10,000); Keeping Kids Company (£5,000); the Wellchild Trust (£2,500); and Breast Cancer Care (£1,000).

Applications

In writing to the correspondent. 'There is no formal grants application procedure. The trustees retain the services of a charitable grants advisor and take account of the advice when deciding on grants.'

Information gathered from:

Accounts; Charity Commission record.

The J. E. Joseph Charitable Fund

Jewish

£129,000 (2011/12)

Beneficial area

London, Manchester, Israel, India and Hong Kong.

Correspondent: Roger J. Leon, Secretary, 10 Compass Close, Edgware, Middlesex HA8 8HU (tel: 020 8958 0126)

Trustees: E. Mocatta, Chair; P. Sheldon; J. H. Corre; S. Horesh; A. Simon; R. Shemtob; S. Kendal.

CC Number: 209058

The trust was established for the benefit of Jewish communities for any purposes, mainly in the fields of education, disability and the relief of poverty. The accounts note a preference for assisting Jews of Sephardic origin and their institutions, in accordance with the wishes of the settlor. In 2011/12 it had assets of £4.2 million, an income of £131,000 and made grants totalling £120,000. The trust has recently developed a preference for funding smaller, local organisations in both the UK and abroad.

Grants included those made to: The Future Generation Fund (£11,000); Sir Jacob Sassoon Charity Trust (£8,500); Old Yosef Hai Yeshiva and Edinburgh House Elderly Home (£6,000 each); University Jewish Chaplaincy Board (£5,000); Ezra U'Marpeh (£4,000); Alyn Paediatric and Adolescence Rehabilitation Centre (£3,500); and British Ort Foundation, ICLEP and Spanish and Portuguese Synagogue Hebrew Classes (£3,000 each).

Exclusions

No grants to individuals. No support for capital projects.

Applications

In writing to the correspondent, including a copy of the latest accounts. The trustees respond to all applications which are first vetted by the secretary. The accounts have noted that, 'as in previous years the trust received far more applications that it can support from its limited funds. However, the trust does try, if possible, to respond favourably to one or two new applications per year'.

Information gathered from:

Accounts; Charity Commission record.

The Lady Eileen Joseph Foundation

People who are disadvantaged by poverty or socially isolated and 'at-risk' groups. Largely welfare, medical causes and general charitable purposes are supported

Around £92,000 (2012/13)

Beneficial area

UK.

Correspondent: Thurlstan W. Simpson, Trustee, Colbrans Farm, Cow Lane, Laughton, Lewes BN8 6BZ

Trustees: Judith M. Sawdy; Thurlstan W. Simpson; Gael Lynn Simpson.

CC Number: 327549

The trust was registered in 1987. It supports people who are disadvantaged by poverty or who are socially isolated. Medical causes are also supported.

In 2012/13 the foundation had an income of £10,000 and a total expenditure of £95,000. Grants totalled about £92,000.

Previous beneficiaries include: Second Chance (£7,500); Coldstream Guards Association (£6,500); Alzheimer's Research Trust and Friends of the Home Physiotherapy Service (£5,000 each); Havens Hospices (£4,500); Ellenor Foundation and Queen Alexandra Hospital (£3,000 each); Independent Age and Wellbeing of Women (£2,000 each); and Cystic Fibrosis Trust, Foundation for the Prevention of Blindness and Action for Kids (£1,000 each).

Applications

The trust states that unsolicited requests will not be considered.

Information gathered from:

Accounts; Charity Commission record.

The Judith Trust

Mental health and learning disabilities with some preference for women and Jewish people

£5,000 (2011/12)

Beneficial area

UK.

Correspondent: Dr Annette Lawson, Trustee, 5 Carriage House, 88–90 Randolph Avenue, London W9 1BG (tel: 020 7266 1073; email: judith.trust@lineone.net; website: www.judithtrust.org.uk)

Trustees: Dr Annette Lawson; Peter Lawrence; Dr George Lawson; Charlotte Collins; Dr Geraldine Holt; Dr Colin Samson.

CC Number: 1063012

Established in 1997, the Judith Trust focuses its work on the problems faced by people who have both a learning disability and mental ill-health.

The following information is taken from the trust's website:

> Named for Judith Lawrence, sister of the current Chair, and current Honorary Treasurer, the Judith Trust ensures its work closely follows the nature of Judith's own problems, her background and personal characteristics. The trust supports multi-disciplinary, preventative and innovative approaches and pays particular attention to the needs of women and Jewish people.
>
> The Judith Trust:
> - Commissions and carries out research and supports innovative projects
> - Forms strategic alliances with government departments, voluntary organisations and academic institutions
> - Brings together groups of professionals and others, including service users, for specific purposes
> - Campaigns on behalf of and with people with learning disabilities and mental health needs
> - Promotes examples of good practice and the sharing of knowledge in its publications, seminars and conferences
> - Takes a gendered perspective in all its work

In 2011/12 the trust had an income of £30,000. Expenditure on charitable activities was £68,000. Grants payable was listed as £5,000. A list of grants was not available.

Exclusions

No grants to individuals.

Applications

In writing to the correspondent; however, note that most grants are made through experts and advisors. The trust does not accept unsolicited applications for funding, but is pleased to hear from organisations who wish the trust to be aware of their work.

Information gathered from:

Accounts; Charity Commission record; funder's website.

The Anton Jurgens Charitable Trust

Welfare, general

£218,000 (2011/12)

Beneficial area

UK with a preference for the south east of England.

Correspondent: Maria E. Edge-Jurgens, Trustee, Saffrey Champness, Lion House, 72–75 Red Lion Street, London WC1R 4GB (tel: 020 7841 4000)

Trustees: Eric M. C. Deckers; Steven R. D. Jurgens; Frans A. W. Jurgens; F. A. W. Jurgens; Maria E. Edge-Jurgens; Frans C. M. Tilman.

CC Number: 259885

This trust has general charitable purposes, although welfare and children's groups feature prominently in the grants, as do organisations based in the south east of England. The trust states its main aim is 'alleviating suffering by making grants to charitable organisations that try to help those who are vulnerable in our society.'

In 2011/12 the trust had assets of £6.3 million and an income of £263,000. Grants to over 80 organisations were made totalling £218,000.

Beneficiaries included: Spinal Injuries Association (£20,000); Motor Neurone Disease Association (£10,000); Bristol Children's Help Society (£7,500); Autism Anglia and Fairbridge (£5,000 each); Suffolk Artlink, St Francis Hospice and Jennifer Trust for Spinal Muscular Atrophy (£3,000 each); Peterborough Streets and Cerebral Palsy Sport (£2,000 each); and Cross Roads Care (£1,000).

Applications

In writing to the correspondent. The trustees meet twice a year in June and October. The trustees do not enter into correspondence concerning grant applications beyond notifying successful applicants.

Information gathered from:

Accounts; Charity Commission record.

Jusaca Charitable Trust

Jewish, arts, research, religion, housing

£172,000 (2011/12)

Beneficial area

UK, Israel and worldwide.

Correspondent: Sara Emanuel, Trustee, 17 Ashburnham Grove, London SE10 8UH

Trustees: Ralph Neville Emanuel; Sara Jane Emanuel; Carolyn Leonora Emanuel; Maurice Seymour Emanuel; Diana Clare Franklin; Donald Franklin; Rachel Paul.

CC Number: 1012966

The following statement from the trust's 2011/12 annual accounts outlines its grant policy:

> The trust aims to give grants to alleviate poverty, promote health and education, to support the arts, research, religious

> activities and the provision of decent housing. The objective is to distribute at least 50% of donations to Jewish charities (in the UK, overseas and Israel), of the remainder about 40% to be donated to charities operating in the UK and about 60% outside the UK.

The majority of grants are given to the same organisations each year in order to provide a long-term stream of funding.

In 2011/12 the trust had assets of over £1.3 million and an income of £125,000. Grants to 84 organisations totalled £172,000, of which 32 exceeded £1,000. No further information was available.

Applications

Grants are made at the discretion of the trustees. Unsolicited applications are not encouraged.

Information gathered from:

Accounts; Charity Commission record.

The Bernard Kahn Charitable Trust

Jewish education, advancement of religion

£152,000 (2011/12)

Beneficial area

UK and Israel.

Correspondent: Yaacov Zvi Kahn, Trustee, 24 Elmcroft Avenue, London NW11 0RR

CC Number: 249130

The trustees' report for 2011/12 states that 'the objects of the trust are the relief and the advancement of education and religion in the Jewish community'.

In 2011/12 the trust had assets of £1.4 million and an income of £52,000. Grants were made to 18 organisations totalling £152,000.

Beneficiaries included: Marbeh Torah Trust and Achlsomoch Aid Company Ltd (£23,000 each); Orthodox Council of Jerusalem Ltd and Friends of Be'er Miriam (£20,000 each); Tashbar and Mishkovas Yaacov (£10,000 each); the Menorah Primary School (£5,000); the Rowans Hospice (£3,000); NW London Communal Mikvah Ltd and Menorah High School (£1,000 each); Shori Torah (£400); and CRI (£100).

Exclusions

Jewish causes only.

Applications

In writing to the correspondent.

Information gathered from:

Accounts; Charity Commission record.

The Stanley Kalms Foundation

Jewish charities, general including arts, education and health

£53,000 (2011/12)

Beneficial area

UK and overseas.

Correspondent: Mrs Jane Hunt-Cooke, 84 Brook Street, London W1K 5EH (tel: 020 7499 3494)

CC Number: 328368

Established in 1989 by Lord Stanley Kalms, the president of DSG International plc (formerly Dixons Stores Group plc), this charity states its objectives as the encouragement of Jewish education in the UK and Israel. Other activities include support for the arts and media and other programmes, both secular and religious.

In 2011/12 the foundation held assets of £248,000 and had an income of £100,000. Grants were made to 28 organisations totalling £53,000. Grants of £5,000 were made to Churchillian Centre UK, Dixons City Academy, Lifelites, Oxford Centre for Hebrew and Jewish Studies and Taxpayers Alliance. Grants under £5,000 were not listed individually.

Applications

In writing to the correspondent, but note that most of the trust's funds are committed to projects supported for a number of years.

Information gathered from:

Accounts; Charity Commission record.

The Boris Karloff Charitable Foundation

Performing arts, cricket

£53,000 (2011/12)

Beneficial area

Worldwide.

Correspondent: Andrew Studd, Correspondent, Russell Cooke Solicitors, 2 Putney Hill, London SW15 6AB (tel: 020 8789 9111; fax: 020 8780 1194)

CC Number: 326898

This foundation was set up in 1985, by Evelyn Pratt (Karloff), wife of the famous horror actor, Boris Karloff (whose real name was William Henry Pratt). When Evelyn Pratt died in June 1993, she bequeathed over £1.4 million to the assets of the foundation. Grants are made with particular reference to the performing arts and cricket.

In 2011/12 the foundation had assets of £2.1 million and an income of £60,000. Grants to eight organisations were made totalling £53,000.

Beneficiaries were: Young Vic (£13,000); Surrey County Cricket (£10,000); Soho Theatre (£7,000); LAMDA, RADA, Royal Theatrical Fund and Shakespeare's Globe Trust (£5,000 each); and National Media Museum (£4,000).

Exclusions

No grants for individuals or charities with large resources.

Applications

In writing to the correspondent.

Percentage of awards given to new applicants: between 40% and 50%.

Common applicant mistakes

'Not reading our criteria. We do not make grants to individuals, nor do we give grants to any bodies unless it relates to performing arts or cricket.'

Information gathered from:

Accounts; Charity Commission record; further information provided by the funder.

The Ian Karten Charitable Trust

Technology centres for people with disabilities

£454,000 to organisations (2011/12)

Beneficial area

UK and Israel, with some local interest in Surrey and London.

Correspondent: Timothy Simon, Trustee, The Mill House, PO Box 386, Lymington SO41 1BD (tel: 01590 681345; fax: 01483 222420; email: kartentrust@aol.com; website: www.karten-network.org.uk)

CC Number: 281721

The trust states its objects in its 2011/12 accounts:

> The objects of the trust are to carry out legally charitable purposes for the relief of poverty, the advancement of education or religion or otherwise for the benefit of the community and the trustees shall pay particular regard to the UK, the state of Israel and for persons of the Jewish faith wherever they may be.

'The trust currently concentrates on

- 'Improving the quality of life and independence of people with severe physical, sensory, cognitive disability or mental health problems by providing Centres for Computer-aided Training, Education and Communication (CTEC Centres). These are typically established by and located in colleges of further education or (mainly residential) host charities concerned with rehabilitation and education, especially vocational, of people with one or more of the above mentioned disabilities
- 'the support of higher education by funding studentships for postgraduate studies and research at selected universities in the UK'

'The trust also has a separate modest budget from which it makes small donations to other selected registered charities, mostly local to the trust (London or Surrey).'

In 2011/12 it had assets of £6.6 million and an income of £214,000. Grants paid to organisations totalled £454,000, broken down as follows and shown with examples of beneficiaries:

CTEC Centres – 20 grants totalling £345,000

Scope – Beaumont College (£86,000); Cedar Foundation – Northern Ireland (£26,000); Bridge College – Manchester and Linkage Colleges (£25,000 each); Percy Hedley (£22,000); Jewish Care – Redbridge (£12,000); and White Lodge – Chertsey (£5,800). The trustees have resolved to not open any new centres other than in very exceptional circumstances and instead intend to fund existing centres.

Large grants – 11 grants totalling £44,000

Southampton (£37,000); Jewish Care (£1,500) Commonwealth Jewish Trust and World Jewish Relief (£1,000 each); Spiro Ark (£500); and Community Security Trust (£300).

Further funding was given for scholarships to eight institutions, including Haifa University and Southampton University, totalling £62,000; an individual scholarship of £6,800; and, the sum of £2,900 was also given in small grants.

Applications

The trust currently only considers grants to charities supported in the past. Grants are no longer being made for new CTEC centres. The trustees meet at least twice a year to review grants.

Information gathered from:

Accounts; Charity Commission record; funder's website.

The Kasner Charitable Trust

Jewish

£96,000 (2011/12

Beneficial area

UK and Israel.

Correspondent: Josef Kasner, Trustee, 1a Gresham Gardens, London NW11 8NX (tel: 020 8455 7830)

Trustees: Baruch Erlich; Josef Kasner; Elfreda Erlich.

CC Number: 267510

The objects of the trust are for general charitable purposes and in practice grants are given to Jewish organisations. They are subject to the approval of Josef Kasner during his lifetime and thereafter at the discretion of the trustees.

In 2011/12 the trust had assets of £844,000, an income of £146,000 and made grants to around 400 organisations totalling £96,000. The majority of grants are below £500.

Beneficiaries included: British Committee for Israel and U.J.I.A. (£10,000 each); Gevurath Ari Academy Trust (£5,000); Gateshead Talmudical College (£1,600); and British Friends of Nishmas Yisroel, British Friends of Shalom, British Friends of the Hebrew University, Friends of Michas, Friends of Seret Vishnitz, Chashei Dovid, Jewish Genetic Disorder Ltd, Neve Yerushalayim and Union of Orthodox Hebrew (£100 each).

Applications

In writing to the correspondent. The trust gives grants to most of the organisations that apply. Certain organisations are investigated personally by the trustees and may receive larger grants.

Information gathered from:

Accounts; Charity Commission record.

The Kass Charitable Trust

Welfare, education, Jewish

Around £20,000

Beneficial area

UK.

Correspondent: D. E. Kass, Trustee, 37 Sherwood Road, London NW4 1AE (email: dkass@vintange.co.uk)

Trustees: David Elliot Kass; Shulamith Malkah Sandler.

CC Number: 1006296

The trust now focuses on 'poverty and education for disadvantaged children'.

In 2011/12 the trust had an income of £26,000 and a total expenditure of £30,000. The income tends to come from donations. In the past some of the expenditure has been used to help individuals. Grants are typically small (less than £500).

Applications

In writing to the correspondent.

Percentage of awards given to new applicants: less than 10%.

Common applicant mistakes

'Not checking what we provide grants for!!'

Information gathered from:

Accounts; Charity Commission record; further information provided by the funder.

The Kathleen Trust

Music

£20,000 (2011/12)

Beneficial area

UK, with a preference for London.

Correspondent: E. R. H. Perks, Trustee, Currey and Co., 21 Buckingham Gate, London SW1E 6LS (tel: 020 7828 4091)

Trustees: E. R. H. Perks; Sir O. C. A. Scott; Lady P. A. Scott; Mrs C. N. Withington.

CC Number: 1064516

Established in 1997, it is the policy of the trustees to 'assist young and impecunious musicians'.

In 2011/12 the trust had an income of £28,000 and total expenditure of £91,000. One grant was made to the Oxford Chamber Music Festival (£20,000) with £66,000 paid in grants to individuals.

Applications

In writing to the correspondent.

Information gathered from:

Accounts; Charity Commission record.

The Michael and Ilse Katz Foundation

Jewish, music, medical, general

About £336,000 (2011/12)

Beneficial area

Worldwide.

Correspondent: Osman Azis, Trustee, Counting House, Trelill, Bodmin PL30 3HZ (tel: 01208 851814)

Trustees: Norris Gilbert; Osman Azis.

CC Number: 263726

Established in 1971, this foundation supports many Jewish organisations, although musical and medical charities also received funds. The trustees' report for 2011/12 states that 'applications are considered in relation to the prevention and relief of suffering and those in need. Applications from organisations focusing on medical and age support are given particular consideration.'

In 2011/12 it had assets of £2.1 million and an income of £2 million. Grants to organisations totalled £336,000, of which £9,500 was allocated in grants not exceeding £1,000 each.

Beneficiaries included: Jewish Hospice Care (£252,000); Jewish Care (£17,500); Fight for Sight (£15,000); the Worshipful Company of Butchers (£10,000); Bournemouth Orchestral Society (£8,000); Community Security Trust and Norwood Children and Families First (£7,000 each); Hannah Levy House Trust (£2,000); and Council of Christians and Jews, Variety Club of Jersey and Starlight Children's Foundation (£1,000 each).

Applications

In writing to the correspondent.

Information gathered from:

Accounts; Charity Commission record.

The Katzauer Charitable Settlement

Jewish

About £5,500 (2011/12)

Beneficial area

UK, but mainly Israel.

Correspondent: Walter Lian, Trustee, c/o Citroen Wells and Partners, Devonshire House, 1 Devonshire Street, London W1W 5DR (tel: 020 7304 2000; email: walter.lian@citroenwells.co.uk)

Trustees: Gordon Smith; Elisabeth Moller; Mark Bailey; Walter Lian.

CC Number: 275110

In 2011/12 the trust had an income of £3,000 and a total expenditure of £6,000.

Previous beneficiaries included: Chabad Ra'anana (£26,000); Moriah Community and Meir Hospital (£10,000); Nahalat Yehiel (£6,000); Mercaz Hatorah (£4,000); Rabbi K Gross (£3,800); Kollel Ralanana (£3,200); Friends of Lubavitch (£2,900); Beit Hatavshil (£1,000);.

Applications

In writing to the correspondent.

Information gathered from:

Accounts; Charity Commission record.

The C. S. Kaufman Charitable Trust

Judaism

£88,000 (2011/12)

Beneficial area

UK.

Correspondent: The Trustees, 162 Whitehall Road, Gateshead, Tyne and Wear NE8 1TP

Trustees: I. I. Kaufman; Mrs L. L. Kaufman; J. J. Kaufman; S. Kaufman.

CC Number: 253194

In 2011/12 the trust had assets of £877,000 and an income of £92,000. There were 31 grants made totalling £88,000.

Grants ranged from £50 to £25,000 and included those made to: The New Rachmistrivke Synagogue Trust (£25,000); Mercaz Torah Belz Machnovke (£15,000); Ezer Mikoldesh Foundation and Chevras Machzikei Mesivta (£10,000 each); Jewish Teachers' Training College (£9,000 in three grants); Tat Family Relief Fund (£6,000); and Matana (£1,500).

Applications

In writing to the correspondent.

Information gathered from:

Accounts; Charity Commission record.

The Geoffrey John Kaye Charitable Foundation

Jewish, general

£6,300 to organisations (2011/12)

Beneficial area

UK and overseas.

Correspondent: Robert Shaw, Chartered Account, Macilvin Moore Reveres, 7 St John's Road, Harrow, Middlesex HA1 2EY (tel: 020 8863 1234; email: charity@mmrca.co.uk)

Trustees: G. J. Kaye; Mrs S. Rose; J. Pears.

CC Number: 262547

In 2011/12 the foundation had assets of £1 million and an income of £54,000.

There were three grants made totalling £18,000, two of which appear to have been paid to individuals. One grant of £6,300 was made to Animal Shelter A.C.

Applications

In writing to the correspondent, but note that the foundation has previously stated that funds were fully committed.

Information gathered from:

Accounts; Charity Commission record.

The Emmanuel Kaye Foundation

Medical research, welfare and Jewish organisations

Around £25,000 (2011/12)

Beneficial area

UK and overseas.

Correspondent: The Secretary to the Trustees, Oakleigh House, High Street, Hartley Wintney, Hampshire RG27 8PE (tel: 01252 843773)

Trustees: David Kaye; John Forster; Michael Cutler.

CC Number: 280281

The foundation supports organisations benefiting medical professionals, research workers, scientists, Jewish people, at risk groups, people who are disadvantaged by poverty and socially isolated people.

In 2011/12 it had an income of £24,000 and total expenditure of £25,000.

Previous beneficiaries included: St James Conservation Trust (£6,000); Imperial College London and Nightingale (£5,000 each); Royal Academy of Arts and St Michael's Hospice – North Hampshire (£2,500 each); Jewish Care, the Holocaust Education Trust, Shaare Zedek UK, Community Links Trust, Laniado UK and UK Friends of Magen David Adom (£2,000 each); and Caius (£1,500).

Exclusions

Only registered charities are supported.

Applications

In writing to the correspondent.

Information gathered from:

Accounts; Charity Commission record.

The Caron Keating Foundation

Supports small but significant cancer charities

£0 (2011/12)

Beneficial area

UK.

Correspondent: Mary Clifford Day, PO Box 122, Sevenoaks, Kent TN13 1UM (email: info@caronkeating.org; website: www.caronkeating.org)

Trustees: Michael Keating; Gloria Hunniford.

CC Number: 1106160

Registered with the Charity Commission in October 2004, this foundation is a fundraising charity that aims to target and financially assist 'small but significant cancer charities and support groups'.

The foundation's overall aim is to help small cancer charities in their work with professional carers, complimentary healing practitioners as well as groups that provide support and advice to cancer patients and the people closest to them who are affected by the disease.

> It will also financially help a number of cancer charities with their ongoing quest for prevention, early detection and hopefully ultimate cure.

In 2011/12 the trust had assets of £1.1 million and an income of £200,000. No grants were made during the year due to illness in the trustee's family. Shortly after the year end over £250,000 was paid out in grants, which will appear in the next accounts.

Previous beneficiaries have included: Action Cancer Belfast; The Lavender Touch; The Rosemary Foundation; Sarah Lee Trust; Variety Club; and the Rainbow Centre.

Exclusions

No grants to individuals.

Applications

In writing to the correspondent.

Information gathered from:

Accounts; Charity Commission record; funder's website.

The Soli and Leah Kelaty Trust Fund

General, education, overseas aid, religion

Around £25,000 (2011/12)

Beneficial area

Not defined.

Correspondent: Frederick Kelaty, Trustee, Block O, OCC Building, 105 Eade Road, London N4 1TJ (tel: 020 8800 2000; email: freddy.kelaty@asiatic.co.uk)

CC Number: 1077620

Registered with the Charity Commission in September 1999, grants can be made to organisations and individuals.

In 2011/12 the trust had both an income and total expenditure of around £25,000. No list of grant beneficiaries was available.

Applications

In writing to the correspondent.

Information gathered from:

Accounts; Charity Commission record.

The Kelly Family Charitable Trust

Family support

£135,000 (2011/12)

Beneficial area

UK.

Correspondent: Stuart Armstrong, Administrator, 8 Mansfield Place, Edinburgh EH3 6NB (tel: 01313 154879; email: s.armstrong@kfct.org; website: www.kfct.org.uk)

CC Number: 1102440

Established in 2004, the trust supports organisation that encourage family welfare and cohesion. The following information is taken from the trust's website:

> The trust has decided to prioritise its funding in favour of charities whose activities involve all or most family members in initiatives that support and encourage the family to work as a cohesive unit in tackling problems that face one or more of its members. The overall objective is to reinforce the potential benefit and support that family members as a unit can give to each other.
>
> Applications are also welcomed from sports and health-related charities whose activities comply with the above criteria.
>
> The trust will consider both capital and revenue grants. The trust is happy to support requests for core funding as well as project-based grants, and actively encourages applications from relatively new organisations to help them become established.

Grants are generally for £1,000 to £10,000. In the 2011/12 annual report the trust outlined the criteria that they consider when evaluating applications:

- The financial situation and sustainability of the charity
- The size of the charity
- The reach of the charity
- The number of people being helped
- The number of salaried staff as compared to the number of volunteers
- Whether other charities are offering the same service

In 2011/12 the trust had assets of £2.6 million and an income of £132,000. Grants totalling £135,000 were made to 23 organisations.

Beneficiaries included: Homestart Teesside; Quaker Social Action; Westminster Befriending; Winchester Young Carers; Relate North East; Parent to Parent Dundee; Survive; Guy's Gift; Moira Anderson Foundation; Homestart Perth; Relationship Scotland (Orkneys); Families Talking and Meningitis Trust.

Exclusions

The following will not be considered:

- Non-registered charities
- Grants directly to individuals
- National charities (only regional projects will be considered)
- General appeals
- Organisations with specific religious or political agendas

Applications

Applications should be made using the application form, which can be downloaded from the trust's website. Applications should be sent by email, and should be supported by annual accounts where available.

Grants are awarded twice a year to charities and are usually for amounts between £1,000 and £5,000, but the trustees will consider requests for higher amounts.

Applications must be submitted by 1 March and 1 September to be considered at the subsequent meeting. The trustees will ask for more detail for those applications that pass the initial screening and may visit the projects they wish to support.

Percentage of awards given to new applicants: between 40% and 50%.

Common applicant mistakes

'Stretching their perception of what we will support.'

Information gathered from:

Accounts; Charity Commission record; further information provided by the funder; funder's website.

The Kennedy Charitable Foundation

Roman Catholic ministries, general, especially in the west of Ireland

£156,000 (2011/12)

Beneficial area

Unrestricted, but mainly Ireland with a preference for County Mayo and County Sligo.

Correspondent: The Trustees, 12th Floor, Bank House, Charlotte Street, Manchester M1 4ET (tel: 01612 368191; fax: 01612 364814; email: kcf@pye158.freeserve.co.uk)

CC Number: 1052001

Established in 1995, the foundation is funded by donations. Grants are predominantly made to organisations connected with the Roman Catholic faith, mainly in Ireland.

In 2011/12 the foundation had assets of £187,000, an income of £98,000 and made 44 grants totalling £156,000.

Beneficiaries included: Newman Institute (£27,000); Knock Shrine (£18,000); Catholic Truth Society and Cornerstone (£10,000 each); Ballintubber Abbey Trust (£8,000); Little Sisters of the Poor, Elizabeth Hardie Ferguson Charitable Trust and Rainbow Family Trust (£5,000 each); Lancaster Roman Catholic Diocese Trustees (£3,000); Hearts and Minds Challenge, Irish Community Care, St Ann's Hospice, St Vincent de Paul Society, Wythenshawe and Society of African Missions (£2,000 each); Diocese of Salford, Francis House and Restoration Ministries (£1,000 each); Diocese of Shrewsbury (£500); and The Urology Foundation (£200).

Applications

The foundation says that 'unsolicited applications are not accepted'.

Information gathered from:

Accounts; Charity Commission record.

The Kennel Club Charitable Trust

Dogs

£703,000 (2012).

Beneficial area

UK.

Correspondent: Richard Fairlamb, Administrator, 1–5 Clarges Street, Piccadilly, London W1J 8AB (tel: 020 7518 6874; fax: 020 7518 1014; email: dholford@the-kennel-club.org.uk; website: www.thekennelclub.org.uk/charitabletrust)

Trustees: Michael Townsend; Bill King; Steven Dean; Michael Herrtage; John Spurling; Jennifer Fairhall.

CC Number: 327802

The trust describes its objects as 'science, welfare and support'. It supports the furthering of research into canine diseases and hereditary disorders of dogs and also organisations concerned with the welfare of dogs in need and those which aim to improve the quality of life of humans by promoting dogs as practical or therapeutic aids. The trust gives both ongoing and one-off grants. The following information is taken from the charity's website:

> ***Grantmaking policy***
>
> We provide grants for welfare, rescue and support organisations. The trust provides funds for three purposes, in accordance with its trust deed:
>
> - To promote the advancement of education and science by furthering research into canine diseases and hereditary disorders of dogs
> - To promote the quality of life of human beings by promoting dogs as therapeutic and practical aids to humans
> - To promote the relief of suffering of dogs which are in need of care and attention
>
> ***How to apply for a grant***
>
> You should state clearly the specific details of the costs for which you are requesting funding, and for what purpose and over what period the funding is required.
>
> The trustees meet four times a year and will wish to see your organisation's latest audited and signed report and accounts and (if applicable) the registered number of your charity.
>
> Generally, pure building costs or requests from organisations whose concern is not predominantly with the dog (e.g. general animal sanctuaries) do not receive favourable attention from the trustees. Similarly, grants are rarely made to individuals and not to organisations having a political reason.
>
> Grants which are payable over a number of years will be subject to a satisfactory annual review and report of progress.
>
> Please send information to: Mr Richard Fairlamb (email), The Kennel Club, 1-5 Clarges Street, London W1J 8AB. Tel: 020 7518 6874, fax: 020 7518 1014.

In 2012 the trust had assets of almost £2.5 million and an income of nearly £728,000. Grants were made totalling £703,000. These were divided into 'scientific and research project support' – 10 grants amounting to £383,000, and 48 'other grants' totalling £320,000.

Beneficiaries included: Animal Health Trust (£250,000); Hearing Dogs for Deaf People (£30,000); Support Dogs (£24,000); Mayhew Animal Rescue Home and Stokenchurch Dog Rescue (£10,000 each); Pets as Therapy (£7,000); BAARK (£6,000); Bristol Dog Action Welfare Group (£3,000); and Bulldog Rescue and Rehoming Trust and Supporters of Stray and Abandoned Dogs (£2,000 each).

Exclusions

The trust does not give grants directly to individuals; veterinary nurses can apply to the British Veterinary Nursing Association where bursaries are available. The trustees tend not to favour funding the costs of building work.

Applications

In writing to the administrator, including latest accounts. State clearly details of the costs for which you are requesting funding, and for what purpose and over what period the funding is required. The trustees meet three or four times a year.

Information gathered from:

Accounts; Charity Commission record; funder's website.

The Nancy Kenyon Charitable Trust

General

£34,000 to organisations (2011/12)

Beneficial area

UK.

Correspondent: Alison Smith, c/o Brook Financial Management Ltd, Meads Barn, Ashwell Business Park, Ilminster, Somerset TA19 9DX (tel: 01460 259852)

Trustees: Lucy Phipps; Maureen Kenyon; Christopher Kenyon; Sally Kenyon; Peter Kenyon; Kieron Kenyon.

CC Number: 265359

The trust makes grants primarily for people and causes known to the trustees.

In 2011/12 the trust had assets of £1.5 million and an income of £47,000. Grants were made to 19 organisations totalling £34,000, while individuals received a total of £7,000.

Beneficiaries include: Nancy Oldfield Trust (£10,500); St Nicholas Church, Ashchurch (£3,500); One More Child (£3,000); The Good Shepherd Project and The Starfish Cafe, Cambodia (£2,000 each); Cheltenham Youth for Christ and the Starfish Cafe – Cambodia (£2,000 each); Church Mission Society (£1,500); African Workshop, Epic Arts and Earls Court Community Project (£1,000 each); and Cheltenham Youth for Christ and The Family Haven (£500 each).

Applications

In writing to the correspondent at any time. Applications for causes not known to the trustees are considered annually in December.

Information gathered from:

Accounts; Charity Commission record.

E. and E. Kernkraut Charities Ltd

General, education, Jewish

£403,000 (2011/12)

Beneficial area

UK.

Correspondent: Eli Kernkraut, Trustee, Eli Kernkraut, The Knoll, Fountayne Road, London N16 7EA (tel: 020 8806 7947)

Trustees: Eli Kernkraut; Esther Kernkraut; Joseph Kernkraut; Jacob Kernkraut.

CC Number: 275636

The trust states that it makes grants for educational, Jewish and other charitable purposes. Unfortunately the trust did not include a list of beneficiaries with their annual accounts.

In 2011/12 the trust had assets of £6.2 million and an income of £897,000. Grants were made totalling £403,000.

Applications

In writing to the correspondent.

Information gathered from:

Accounts; Charity Commission record.

The Peter Kershaw Trust

Medical research, education, social welfare

£155,000 (2011/12)

Beneficial area

Manchester and the surrounding district only.

Correspondent: Bryan Peak, Correspondent, 22 Ashworth Park, Knutsford, Cheshire WA16 9DE (tel: 01565 651086; email: pkershawtrust@btinternet.com; website: www.peterkershawtrust.org)

Trustees: David Tully; Margaret Rushbrooke; Richard Kershaw; Rosemary Adams; Tim Page.

CC Number: 268934

The principal activities of the trust are to provide grants for social welfare and to provide school bursaries in the Greater Manchester and North Cheshire area; to provide grants for medical research; and to make an annual award in memory of Peter Kershaw, of £50,000 spread over three years and specifically targeted at innovative youth work.

There are three types of grants available from the trust: ordinary grants, medical research grants and school bursaries. According to the trust's website:

> Ordinary grants are made for a wide variety of purposes under the general heading of 'social welfare.
>
> A limited amount of grants are made available to medical research establishments, especially for anything connected with cancer research. Generally, a maximum of three years' costs will be supported. Grants will not normally be made which represent a small element of a large appeal.

Also, 'bursaries are available to assist parents with children at secondary school who encounter financial problems after the child has started'.

Another award is provided annually called the Peter Kershaw Memorial Bursary: 'The bursary is intended to fund the costs of a youth leader, though other forms of youth work will be considered.' Charitable organisations located in Greater Manchester are invited to apply.

In 2011/12 the trust had assets of £6.4 million and an income of £195,000. 31 grants were made totalling £155,000 and were broken down as follows:

Social welfare institutions	£68,000
Memorial bursary	£47,500
School bursaries	£39,500

Beneficiaries included: N-Gage (£25,000); South Chadderton Methodist Church (£15,000); Factory Youth Zone (£12,500); Bolton School (£6,000); Broughton House, Manchester Grammar School and Commitment in Communities (£5,000 each); Cornerstone Day Centre, Depaul UK and Disability Snowsport UK (£2,000 each); Ace Centre North (£1,500); and ECHG Sash Project and ECHG Stopover (£500 each).

Exclusions

No grants to individuals or for building projects.

Applications

In writing to the correspondent, however the trust is always oversubscribed. The trustees normally meet twice a year in May and November to consider recommendations for grant aid which will be disbursed in June and December respectively.

The trustees' report for 2011/12 states that

> applications for social welfare grants and medical research are received by the secretary in writing. These must give an outline of the organisation and the project for which financial assistance is being sought, together with budgetary forecasts and a copy of the latest financial accounts. Applications for school bursaries are usually made by the relevant educational establishment on behalf of the pupil. These must give the background to the family circumstances of the pupil together with a financial statement and a justification for why the trust should continue to support the pupil.

Percentage of awards given to new applicants: between 20% and 30%.

Common applicant mistakes

'Do not read the criteria, e.g. capital building work, geographic requirement, registered charity.'

Information gathered from:

Accounts; Charity Commission record; further information provided by the funder; funder's website.

The King/Cullimore Charitable Trust

General

£334,000 (2011/12)

Beneficial area

UK.

Correspondent: Peter Cullimore, Trustee, 52 Ledborough Lane, Beaconsfield, Buckinghamshire HP9 2DF (tel: 01494 678811)

Trustees: Christopher King; Peter Cullimore; Alastair McKechnie; Christopher Gardner.

CC Number: 1074928

This trust has general charitable purposes and was registered with the Charity Commission on 30 March 1999.

In 2011/12 the trust had assets of £6.3 million and an income of £716,000. Donations totalled £334,000.

Beneficiaries included: Splash (£150,000); Jubilee Sailing Trust and Scannappeal (£25,000 each); Countryside Foundation for Education (£20,000); Sussex Snowdrop Trust (£15,000); Woodland Trust, Alzheimer's Research UK and London Youth (£10,000 each); Leukaemia and Lymphoma Research (£7,500); Music in Hospitals (£5,000); and Chiltern MS Centre and St Agnes Pre-School (£2,000 each).

Applications

In writing to the correspondent.

Percentage of awards given to new applicants: between 20% and 30%.

Information gathered from:

Accounts; Charity Commission record; further information provided by the funder.

Kinsurdy Charitable Trust

General charitable purposes

£117,000 (2011/12)

Beneficial area

UK.

Correspondent: James Mann, Trustee, c/o Cheviot Asset Management Ltd, 90 Long Acre, London WC2E 9RA (tel: 020 7438 5600; email: dominic.goumal@cheviot.co.uk)

Trustees: James Mann; Ian Brasington.

CC Number: 1076085

Registered in June 1999, in 2011/12 this trust had assets of £3.7 million and an income of £690,000. Grants to 16 organisations totalled £117,000

All beneficiaries were awarded with the same grant amount of £7,300. Beneficiaries included: the National Trust, the Samaritans, Age UK, Multiple Sclerosis Society, West Berks Community Hospital League of Friends, Macmillan Cancer Support and the Children's Trust.

Applications

The trustees do not respond to unsolicited requests.

Information gathered from:

Accounts; Charity Commission record.

The Richard Kirkman Charitable Trust

General charitable purposes

£61,000 to organisations and individuals (2011/12)

Beneficial area

UK, with a preference for Hampshire.

Correspondent: Michael Howson-Green, Trustee, Ashton House, 12 The Central Precinct, Winchester Road, Chandlers Ford, Eastleigh, Hampshire SO53 2GB (tel: 02380 274555)

Trustees: Michael Howson-Green; Frances Kirkman; Brian Baxendale; David Hoare; M. Howson-Green.

CC Number: 327972

This trust supports a range of causes with a preference for Hampshire, especially Southampton.

In 2011/12 the trust had assets of £1.5 million and an income of £52,000. Grants of over £1,000 were given to ten organisations and grants of less than £1,000 were given to 63 organisations and individuals, altogether totalling £61,000.

Beneficiaries of more than £1,000 were: British Limbless Ex-Servicemen Association and Rose Road (£4,000 each); Southampton Society for the Blind (£2,500); and Diabetes UK, Mayor of Southampton's Charity Fund, Southampton Churches Rent Deposit Scheme, Southampton Rotary Club Trust Fund, Southampton Young Carers Project and Stroke Association (£2,000 each).

Grants of less than £1,000 to individuals and organisations totalled £37,000.

Applications

The trust carries out its own research for beneficiaries and does not respond to applications by post or telephone.

Information gathered from:

Accounts; Charity Commission record.

Kirschel Foundation

Jewish, medical

£475,000 (2011/12)

Beneficial area

UK.

Correspondent: Stephen Pinshaw, Trustee, 26 Soho Square, London W1D 4NU (tel: 020 7437 4372)

Trustees: Laurence Grant Kirschel; Ian Lipman; Stephen Pinshaw.

CC Number: 1067672

This trust states its aims and objectives are 'to provide benefits to underprivileged persons, who may be either disabled or lacking resources' and 'the promotion of internal spirituality and harmony which leads to positive thought and action'. In practice this includes mostly Jewish organisations.

In 2011/12 the foundation had assets of £305,000 and an income of £400,000, mainly from donations. Grants were made totalling £475,000.

There were 70 grants of £1,000 or more listed in the accounts. Beneficiaries included: Hampstead Village Shul (£74,000); Aharat Shalom Charity Fund (£73,000); Rays of Sunshine (£41,000); Jewish Learning Exchange (£33,000); Gateshead Academy for Torah Studies (£20,000); Jewish Care (£13,000); The Israel Film Festival London (£9,300); Great Ormond Street Hospital and TUT (£5,000); Diabetes UK (£3,000); Immanuel College (£2,500); Keren Hayeled (£2,000); and ETC Youth, Jewish Deaf Association and Beis Yehudis Moscow (£1,000 each).

Grants of less than £1,000 totalled £13,600.

Applications

In writing to the correspondent.

Information gathered from:

Accounts; Charity Commission record.

The Marina Kleinwort Charitable Trust

Arts

£52,000 (2011/12)

Beneficial area

UK.

Correspondent: Nicholas Kerr-Sheppard, Secretary, c/o Kleinwort Benson Trustees Ltd, 14 St George Street, London W1S 1FE (tel: 020 3207 7337; email: elizabeth.fettes-neame@kleinwortbenson.com)

Trustees: Marina Kleinwort, Chair; David Robinson; Tessa Bremner.

CC Number: 1081825

In 2011/12 this trust had assets of £1.3 million and an income of £50,000. Grants totalling £52,000 were made to nine organisations.

Beneficiaries were: Rambert Dance Company (£25,000); LAMDA (£5,000); The Art Room and The Old Vic Theatre Trust (£4,000 each); Notting Hill Churches (£3,500); Endymion Ensemble (£3,000); Almeida Theatre (£2,700); Opera Brava (£2,500); and Polka Theatre (£2,000).

Exclusions

No grants to individuals.

Applications

The trustees' current policy is to consider written appeals from charities working in the field of the arts, but only successful applications are notified of the trustees' decision. The trustees do not normally respond favourably to appeals from individuals, nor to those unconnected with the arts. The charity requests a copy of the most recent report and financial statements from applicants.

Information gathered from:

Accounts; Charity Commission record.

The Kobler Trust

Arts, Jewish, general

£111,000 (2011/12)

Beneficial area

UK.

Correspondent: The Trustees, c/o Lewis Silkin LLP, 10 Clifford's Inn Passage, London EC4A 1BL (tel: 020 7074 8000; email: info@lewissilkin.com)

Trustees: A. Xuereb; A. H. Stone; Ms J. L. Evans; J. W. Israelsohn.

CC Number: 275237

The Kobler Charitable Trust was established in 1963 by the settlor, Fred Kobler, for charitable purposes in the UK. In 2011/12 the trust had assets of £2.7 million and an income of £90,000 from investments. Grants totalling £111,000 were given to 68 organisations.

Beneficiaries included: Tricycle Theatre (£15,000); Pavilion Opera Educational Trust (£12,000); Arkwright Scholarship (£8,000 in two grants); Jewish Museum London (£5,000); Disability Law Service (£3,000); Place2Be, St Mungo's and Jewish Blind and Disabled (£1,000 each); and Merseyside Thursday Club (£500).

Exclusions

Grants are only given to individuals in exceptional circumstances.

Applications

Applications should be in writing and incorporate full details of the charity for which funding is requested. Trustees meet two to three times a year. Acknowledgements are not generally sent out to unsuccessful applicants.

Information gathered from:

Accounts; Charity Commission record.

Kollel and Co. Limited

Jewish, relief of poverty

£493,000 (2012/13)

Beneficial area

Worldwide.

Correspondent: S. Low, Trustee, 7 Overlea Road, London E5 9BG (tel: 020 8806 1570)

Trustees: S. Low; J. Lipschitz; Z. Rothschild.

CC Number: 1077180

Set up in 1999, the objects of this charity are the:

1 Advancement of education and religion in accordance with the doctrines of the Jewish religion
2 Relief of poverty
3 General charitable purposes

In 2012/13 it had assets of £1.9 million and an income of £856,000. Grants totalled £493,000 and were given under the following headings:

Synagogues	£125,000
General	£120,000
Education	£115,000
Relief of poverty	£65,000
Religious institutions	£33,000
Talmudical colleges	£20,500
Publication of religious books	£7,000
Orphanage	£1,500
Integrated school	£1,000
Needy	£1,000
Community organisation	£500

Only the largest grants were listed in the accounts. They were: Congregation Beth Hamadrash Vyoel Moshe D'Satmar (£120,000); Ezer V'hatzolah (£85,000); Hadras Kodesh Trust (£34,000); Shaarei Chesed – London (£33,500); Inspirations (£28,500); and Chochmas Shloime Chasidi Talmud Torah Jerusalem (£25,000).

Applications

Grants are made upon application by the charity concerned. Grants are made in amounts thought appropriate by the directors/trustees.

Information gathered from:

Accounts; Charity Commission record.

The Kreditor Charitable Trust

Jewish, welfare, education

£119,000 (2011/12)

Beneficial area

UK, with preferences for London and North East England.

Correspondent: Paul Kreditor, Trustee, Hallswelle House, 1 Hallswelle Road, London NW11 0DH (tel: 020 8209 1535; email: admin@gerald-kreditor.co.uk)

Trustees: Paul Kreditor; Merle Kreditor; Sharon Kreditor.

CC Number: 292649

This trust was established in 1985 for general charitable purposes, including the relief of poverty and the advancement of the Jewish religion.

In 2011/12 the trust had assets of £1,700 and an income of £84,000. Grants totalled £119,000.

In previous years, grants have been mostly for less than £100 and have been given mainly to Jewish organisations working in education and social and medical welfare. Beneficiaries have been scattered across London and the north-east of England. The vast majority of grants were for less than £100.

Recipients have included Academy for Rabbinical Research, British Friends of Israel War Disabled, Fordeve Ltd, Jerusalem Ladies' Society, Jewish Care, Jewish Marriage Council Kosher Meals on Wheels, London Academy of Jewish Studies, NW London Talmudical College and Ravenswood. Non-Jewish organisations supported included British Diabetic Association, RNID and UNICEF UK.

A reduction in grants received in recent years may lead to a decline in charitable causes that the charity may be able to support in the future.

Applications

In writing to the correspondent.

Information gathered from:

Accounts; Charity Commission record.

The Kreitman Foundation

Education, health and welfare

£66,000 (2011/12)

Beneficial area

UK.

Correspondent: The Trustees, Citroen Wells, Devonshire House, 1 Devonshire Street, London W1W 5DR

Trustees: Jill Luck-Hille; Peter Luck-Hille; Gareth Morgan.

CC Number: 269046

This trust was established in 1975 as the Jill Kreitman Charitable Trust which changed its name to the Luck-Hille Foundation and in 2009 changed its name again to The Kreitman Foundation. The foundation generally supports projects in the fields of education, health and welfare. It makes grants to registered charities or those which are exempt from charitable registration.

In 2011/12 the trust held assets of £4.6 million and had a total income of £183,000. Three grants totalling £66,000 were made. These were: Middlesex University (£56,000); and University of Bristol and Isha Institute of Inner Sciences (£5,000 each).

Exclusions

No grants to individuals.

Applications

To the correspondent in writing. The trustees seem to have a list of regular beneficiaries and it may be unlikely that any new applications will be successful.

Information gathered from:

Accounts; Charity Commission record.

Kupath Gemach Chaim Bechesed Viznitz Trust

Jewish causes

£123,000 to organisations (2011/12)

Beneficial area

UK and Israel.

Correspondent: Saul Weiss, Trustee, 171 Kyverdale Road, London N16 6PS (tel: 020 8442 9604)

Trustees: Israel Kahan; Saul Weiss; Alexander Pifko.

CC Number: 1110323

The charity was established by Deed of Trust dated 18 May 2005.

The objects of the charity are:

- The relief of the poor, sick, feeble and frail throughout the world and in particular but not exclusively amongst members of the Jewish faith
- The advancement of the Orthodox Jewish faith
- The advancement of the Orthodox Jewish religious education

In 2011/12 the trust had assets of £20,000, an income of £318,000 from donations and made grants to organisations totalling £123,000, which were broken down as follows:

advancement of religion	£67,000
education	£39,000
relief of poverty	£10,000
medical	£7,000

Organisations to benefit included: Keren Habinyan (£50,000); Kollel Imrei Boruch (£13,000); Talmud Torah Viznitz (£8,000); and Mercaz Refuah (£7,000).

During the year, a further £215,000 was granted to individuals.

Applications

In writing to the correspondent.

Information gathered from:

Accounts; Charity Commission record.

The Kyte Charitable Trust

Jewish causes, education, health

£214,000 (2011/12)

Beneficial area

UK.

Correspondent: Carly McKenzie, Correspondent, Business Design Centre, 52 Upper Street, London N1 0QH (tel: 020 7704 7791)

Trustees: David Kyte; Tracey Kyte; James Kyte; Ilana Kyte.

CC Number: 1035886

The trust supports general charitable purposes; however the list of beneficiaries indicates that the trust has a preference towards Jewish causes and educational and medical charitable organisations.

In 2011/12 the trust had assets of £70,000 and an income of £250,000 from covenants and Gift Aid received. Grants were made to 19 organisations totalling £214,000, and were broken down into the following categories:

Community support	£125,000
Sports	£32,000
Healthcare	£10,000
International aid	£9,500
Educational support	£2,500
Arts, culture and heritage	£2,000

Beneficiaries included: United Jewish Israel Fund (£27,500); Jewish Care (£26,000); Jewish Community Secondary School (£20,000); Chai Cancer Care and Norwood Ravenswood (£16,000 each); One Family UK and United Kingdom Jewish Film Festival (£5,000 each); and Rays of Sunshine, Wizo and Union of Jewish Students (£1,000 each).

Applications

In writing to the correspondent.

Information gathered from:

Accounts; Charity Commission record.

The Late Sir Pierce Lacy Charity Trust

Roman Catholics, general

£23,000 (2011/12)

Beneficial area

UK and overseas.

Correspondent: Aviva Insurance Ltd, Capita Trust Company, 4th Floor, 40 Dukes Place, London EC3A 7NH (tel: 020 3367 8142)

Trustee: Aviva Insurance Ltd.

CC Number: 1013505

In 2011/12 the trust has an income of £27,000 and made grants totalling £23,000 although a list of beneficiaries was not available. Grants are only made to Roman Catholic and associated institutions. Newly established and UK organisations are supported, benefiting children, young adults, older people, Roman Catholics, at- risk groups, carers, people who have disabilities and people disadvantaged by poverty.

Recurrent small grants of £1,000 or less are made, and grants can be for buildings, capital, core costs, project, research and start-up costs. Funding for more than three years may be considered.

Previous beneficiaries have included : Crusade of Rescue (£1,400); St Francis' Children's Society (£900); Poor Mission Fund and St Cuthbert's Mayne RC School – special donation (£800 each); Society of St Vincent De Paul (£700); Poor Mission Fund (£600); Catholic Children's Society (£550); and St Francis' Leprosy Guild (£500).

Exclusions

The trust only supports the Roman Catholic Church or associated institutions.

Applications

In writing to the correspondent, at any time.

Information gathered from:

Accounts; Charity Commission record.

John Laing Charitable Trust

Education, community regeneration, youth, homelessness, environment

£1.2 million to organisations

(2012)

Beneficial area

UK.

Correspondent: Jenny Impey, Correspondent, 33 Bunns Lane, Mill Hill, London NW7 2DX (tel: 020 7901 4216; email: jenny.impey@laing.com; website: www.laing.com)

Trustees: Christopher Laing; Sir Martin Laing; Lynette Krige; Christopher Waples; Daniel Partridge.

CC Number: 236852

The following information is taken from the company's website:

> The trust exists to enable John Laing plc and its subsidiaries to make charitable donations and provide welfare support to existing and former employees. The work of the Trust is split into four distinct areas including:
>
> - Welfare
> - Charitable donations
> - Staff applications and
> - Named funds
>
> The scope of the trust is widespread. The trust deed sets out that the trust should apply its assets for 'such charitable purposes for relief of poverty, incapacity or sickness; or the advancement of education, religion or such other charitable purposes.
>
> In addition, the trustees 'shall have special regard to the relief of poverty of employees or their dependents by the provision of gratuities or allowances... and in particular for those employees of their dependents who are in special need of financial assistance on account of any illness, old age or from other causes.
>
> The John Laing Charitable Trust has always tried to match its areas of donations to sectors allied to the Company's business.
>
> More recently, the trust has concentrated its support on charities which support the following main themes:
>
> 1. education
> 2. community regeneration
> 3. disadvantaged young people
> 4. homelessness with a particular emphasis on day centres
> 5. environment
>
> The John Laing Charitable Trust takes a pro-active role in seeking charities that fit the criteria.
>
> Donations range from £250 to £25,000 with up to 12 charities receiving more than £10,000. Usually, charities receive one-off donations, but a small number are

supported for an agreed period, often up to three years.

In addition, the trust will match the fundraising efforts of the staff of John Laing plc with predetermined limits.

In 2012 the trust had assets of £52.7 million, an income of £1.9 million and 'distributed and accrued' grants totalling £1.8 million of which £1.2 million went to organisations. Grants to individuals totalled £585,000. The trustees' report for 2012 states:

The total of approved and accrued donations made to charitable organisations in 2012 amounted to £1,236,000 (£952,000: 2011). During the year an additional offer was made to National Communities Resource Centre of £24, 000 which has been accrued. In addition, the trustees decided to make a donation to Bury Lake Young Mariners of £500,000 which has also been accrued.

Beneficiaries included: Bury Lake Young Mariners (£500,000); Young Enterprise London (£30,000); Homeless Link, Hertfordshire Groundwork and TCV (£25,000 each); Fairshare and National Literacy Trust (£20,000 each); Place 2 Be (£15,000); Envision and Outreach (£10,000 each); Darton College, Safe and Sound Derby and Westminster Befriend a Family (£5,000 each); 999 Club and Hounslow Seniors Trust (£2,500 each).

Exclusions

No grants to individuals (other than to Laing employees and/or their dependents).

Applications

In writing to the correspondent. Telephone enquiries are welcome to avoid abortive work. The trust does not have an application form and applicants are asked to keep the initial request as brief as possible. There is no deadline for receipt of applications. All applications are dealt with on a rolling basis. The trust says that all applications are acknowledged.

Information gathered from:

Accounts; Charity Commission record; funder's website.

The Martin Laing Foundation

General, environment and conservation, disadvantaged young people and the elderly and infirm

£242,000 (2012/13)

Beneficial area

UK and worldwide, particularly Malta.

Correspondent: Elizabeth Harley, Correspondent, 33 Bunns Lane, London NW7 2DX (tel: 020 8238 8890; website: www.laingfamilytrusts.org.uk)

Trustees: Edward Laing; Sir Martin Laing; Lady Laing; Nicholas Gregory; Colin Fletcher; Alexandra Gregory; Graham Sillett.

CC Number: 278461

This foundation is established for general charitable purposes and operates through its grantmaking programme. Through this programme, the trustees support charitable projects in areas identified as being of particular interest to them. These areas include environmental and conservation work, projects benefiting disadvantaged young people or the elderly/infirm, and Norfolk-based activities. A small number of grants are made to overseas projects, particularly in Malta; in such cases the trustees will have a thorough working knowledge of the organisations involved.

A small number of larger grants are made, including one to the Charities Aid Foundation (CAF) which is then disbursed in smaller grants to a large number of organisations. The foundation is administered alongside the Beatrice Laing Trust, Kirby Laing Foundation and Maurice and Hilda Laing Charitable Trust.

In 2012/13 the foundation had assets of £6.4 million and an income of £191,000. Governance and support costs totalled £23,000, while the investment manager's charges totalled £13,000. Grants were made totalling £242,000 of which £65,000 was distributed through CAF.

Grants made directly by the foundation were broken down as follows:

Overseas development	6	£38,000
Social welfare	11	£33,000
Health and medicine	10	£19,500
Religion	4	£16,000
Child and youth	6	£11,500
Cultural and environmental	5	£8,500

Beneficiaries included: WWF (£35,000); East Anglian Air Ambulance, Student's Education Trust and Macmillan Cancer Support (£10,000 each); John Laing Charitable Trust (£7,500); the Pushkin Trust and Friends of the Castle of Mey (£5,000 each); Norfolk Community Foundation (£4,000); Hands Around The World and Coming Home (£2,000 each); the Nancy Oldfield Trust and Cure Parkinson's Trust (£1,000 each); Spinal Injuries Association (£500); and Choppin's Charity (£250).

Exclusions

The trust's website states that the following cannot be funded:

- General appeals or circulars
- Campaigning or lobbying activities
- Umbrella, second tier or grant-making organisations
- Professional associations or projects for the training of professionals
- Feasibility studies and social research
- Individual sponsorship requirements
- Grants to individuals for educational, medical or travel purposes including gap year projects and overseas exchange programmes
- Summer activities for children/young people or after-school clubs
- State maintained or independent schools other than those for pupils with special educational needs
- Uniformed groups such as scouts and guides
- Costs of staging one-off events, festivals or conferences
- Animal welfare
- Core running costs of hospices, counselling projects and other local organisations
- Church restoration or repair (including organs and bells)

Applications

The trustees meet three times a year to consider grants.

The trust's website states that 'the Laing Family Trusts are administered and co-ordinated centrally. An application to one is therefore considered as an application to all'. Applications should be made by letter, accompanied by a concise proposal of three to four pages. Information regarding details of the project for which funding is needed, such as project activities and budget breakdown, plus a copy of the charity's most recent annual report and accounts should be included.

A list of other supporting documents e.g. annual review, business plan, drawings for capital building projects etc. can also be included.

For more information visit the trust's website.

Information gathered from:

Accounts; Charity Commission record; funder's website.

The David Laing Foundation

Youth, disability, the arts, general

£279,000 (2012/13)

Beneficial area

Worldwide with a preference for the East Midlands and the south of England.

Correspondent: David Laing, Trustee, The Manor House, Grafton Underwood, Kettering NN14 3AA (email: david@david-laing.co.uk)

Trustees: David Laing; Stuart Lewis; Frances Laing; Francis Barlow.

CC Number: 278462

The foundation has general charitable purposes with an emphasis on youth, disability and the arts. Previous information has shown the foundation to make large grants to a wide and varied number of organisations as well as donating smaller grants through Charities Aid Foundation. The trust gives to community foundations to ensure that local needs are met.

In 2012/13 the foundation had assets of £4.2 million and an income of £110,000. Grants totalled £279,000, which were broken down into the following categories:

General charitable purposes	£173,000
Disability/disadvantaged/health/ sickness/medical	£38,000
Child and youth	£24,000
Arts and culture	£15,000
Religion	£13,000
Social welfare/sports/recreation	£9,000
Overseas aid	£8,000

Grants for over £5,000 were awarded to: Nottinghamshire Community Foundation (£122,000); Hertfordshire Community Foundation and Reach Out Plus (£20,000 each); Wooden Spoon (£16,500); Peterborough Cathedral (£12,000); and Marie Curie Cancer (£11,800).

Applications

In writing to the correspondent.

Information gathered from:

Accounts; Charity Commission record.

The Christopher Laing Foundation

Disabilities, social welfare, environment, culture, health and, children and youth

£133,000 (2011/12)

Beneficial area

UK.

Correspondent: Vince Cheshire, Administrator, c/o TMF Management UK Ltd, 400 Capability Green, Luton LU1 3AE (tel: 01582 439200)

CC Number: 278460

The foundation has general charitable purposes and had until recently held a preference for organisations in Hertfordshire, but now they are focusing on organisations supporting adults with disabilities.

In 2011/12 the trust had assets of £6.6 million, which generated an income of £239,000. Grants totalled £133,000, which were distributed under the following categories:

Child and youth	£43,000
Cultural and environmental	£40,000
Charities Aid Foundation	£30,000
Social welfare	£17,000
Health and medicine	£3,000

Beneficiaries included: Charities Aid Foundation and Fields in Trust (£30,000 each); The Lord's Taverners (£25,000); The Duke of Edinburgh's Award, The John Clements Sports and Community Centre and Hertfordshire Groundwork Trust (£10,000 each); Action on Addiction and Youth Create (£5,000 each); Wooden Spoon (£2,000); and Stroke Association (£1,000).

Exclusions

Donations are only made to registered charities.

Applications

In writing to the correspondent. The accounts note: 'an enormous and increasing number of requests for donations are received and unfortunately only a small proportion of these requests can be fulfilled'.

Information gathered from:

Accounts; Charity Commission record.

The Lambert Charitable Trust

Health, welfare, education, disability, Jewish causes

£58,000 (2011/12)

Beneficial area

UK and Israel.

Correspondent: George Georghiou, Correspondent, Mercer and Hole, 72 London Road, St Albans, Hertfordshire AL1 1NS (tel: 01727 869141)

CC Number: 257803

The trust supports Jewish and Israeli causes, and organisations for people with disabilities, the elderly, medical, welfare and education.

In 2011/12 the trust had assets of £3 million and an income of £90,000. Grants totalled £58,000 and investment management and governance costs totalled £34,500.

Beneficiaries included: Jewish Care (£15,000); Action on Addiction (£4,000); Medical Engineering Resource Unit and Ro-Ro Sailing Project (£3,000 each); Action Medical Research, Anne Frank Trust, Meningitis Research Foundation, New Horizon Youth Centre and Quaker Social Action (£2,000 each); Jewish Association for the Mentally Ill and Kids' Cookery School (£1,000 each); and Ponevez Yeshivah Israel (£250).

Applications

In writing to the correspondent.

Information gathered from:

Accounts; Charity Commission record.

LWS Lancashire Environmental Fund Ltd

Environment and community

£1.5 million (2012)

Beneficial area

Lancashire.

Correspondent: Andy Rowett, Correspondent, The Barn, Berkeley Drive, Bamber Bridge, Preston PR5 6BY (tel: 01772 317247; fax: 01772 628849; email: general@lancsenvfund.org.uk; website: www.lancsenvfund.org.uk)

CC Number: 1074983

This fund was established in June 1998 from a partnership of four organisations: SITA (Lancashire) Ltd, Lancashire County Council, the Wildlife Trust for Lancashire, Manchester and North Merseyside and Community Futures.

The fund enables community groups and organisations throughout the country to take advantage of the funding opportunities offered by landfill tax credits. It achieves this by supporting organisations and projects based within Lancashire, or nationwide research or development with a relevance to Lancashire, which are managed by an Enrolled Environmental Body, as recognised by Entrust.

The trustees' report for 2012 states: 'LWT is established to promote the conservation of nature for the purpose of study and research and to educate the public in the understanding and appreciation of nature, the awareness of its value and the need for conservation.'

In 2012 the fund had assets of £2.1 million and an income of £1.1 million. Grants were awarded to 65 organisations and totalled £1.5 million. Grants were broken down as follows:

Community facility improvements	32	£797,000
General environmental improvements	20	£532,000
Parks, gardens and open spaces	4	£140,000
Play areas and recreational facilities	5	£96,000
Habitat creation and management	4	£89,000

Beneficiaries included: Thornton Methodist Church, Haslingden St Mary's Community Centre and Lytham Hall (£40,000 each); RSPB- Leighton Moss and Clitheroe United Reformed Church (£30,000 each); Leyland Baptist Community Hall (£25,000); Grimsargh Village Hall (£20,000); Lostock Hall (£15,000); Wycoller Ruparian Habitat Restoration Project (£11,500); the Meadow Skate Area (£10,000); Oakhill Park (£7,000); and Clivigier Village Hall (£5,000).

Exclusions

Funding is not given for the following:

- Core cost of an organisation
- Retrospective funding
- Projects in school grounds
- Allotment or food growing projects
- Car parks and public conveniences
- Recycling projects
- Projects within the unitary authority districts of Blackpool and Blackburn

All projects must satisfy at least one objective of the Landfill Communities Fund. For more information about the scheme contact Entrust, the regulatory body, by visiting their website at or telephoning 01619 720074.

Applications

Detailed and helpful guidance notes and application forms for each funding strand are available from the correspondent or may be downloaded from the fund's website. Institutional applications are invited to submit a summary of their proposals in a specified format. The applications are reviewed against specific criteria.

The board meets quarterly in January, April, July and October.

Staff are willing to have informal discussions before an application is made. Potential applicants are strongly advised to visit the website and view the guidelines before contacting the trust.

Information gathered from:

Accounts; Charity Commission record; funder's website.

LandAid Charitable Trust

Homelessness, relief of need, young people

£1.13 million (2012/13)

Beneficial area

Worldwide.

Correspondent: Joanna Averley, Chief Executive, St Albans House, 5th Floor, 57–59 Haymarket, London SW1Y 4QX (tel: 020 3102 7190; email: enquiries@landaid.org; website: www.landaid.org)

Trustees: Robin Broadhurst; Robert Bould; Michael Slade; Suzanne Avery; Elizabeth Peace; David Taylor; Lynette Lackey; Timothy Roberts; Robert Noel; Jeremy Newsum; Alistair Elliott; Jenny Buck; David Erwin.

CC Number: 295157

The principal activity of LandAid, as stated in the trustees' report for 2012/13, is as follows:

> LandAid works to improve the lives of children and young people in the UK who experience disadvantages due to their economic or social circumstances. As a charitable foundation supported by the property industry, LandAid finds ways to apply the generosity and expertise of the industry to this cause.

The objects of the charity are to:

- Relieve poverty and sickness in the UK and worldwide
- Advance education in hunger and disaster-stricken countries around the world
- Advance all other purposes that are charitable

LandAid focuses on capital grants to support the improvement and extension of buildings plus the refurbishment or building of facilities.

In 2012/13 the trust had assets of £450,000 and an income of almost £1.4 million, mainly from donations. Grants totalled £1.13 million and were given to 21 organisations.

Beneficiaries included: Roots and Shoots and St Basils (£150,000 each); FRE Flyers (£85,000); Llamau (£75,000); Fuse Youth Cafe Glasgow and Jericho Foundation (£50,000 each); Goodwin Development Trust and St Edmunds Society (£35,000 each); East Cleveland Youth Housing Trust and Grimsby and Cleethorpes Area Doorstep (£25,000 each); Burley Lodge Centre (£10,000); and Motiv8 South Ltd (£9,500).

As well as its grants programme, the trust has been providing pro bono work to organisations by imparting technical and professional advice relating to property issues. 16 projects were involved in 2012/13.

LandAid has also partnered with Centrepoint since 2009 through its Foundations for Life (FFL) programme. Both organisations work together to provide fully resourced learning facilities in Centrepoint hostels where homeless young people are given the opportunity to learn independent living skills.

Exclusions

No grants to individuals.

Applications

Organisations should apply online through the trust's website. Supporting documentation, including a copy of the latest annual report and financial statements, is required.

Written applications for grant support are required to ensure that they fall within the stated criteria; projects are then shortlisted and reviewed by the grants committee.

Organisations receiving grant support are required to report on the progress of the project being funded and to provide evidence of the impact of the grant.

Percentage of awards given to new applicants: 66%.

Common applicant mistakes

'They are a charity focused on health issues and our criteria is not health issues but primarily social and economic disadvantage. They apply for support for over 25 year olds which is outside our age range criteria.'

Information gathered from:

Accounts; Charity Commission record; further information provided by the funder; funder's website.

Langdale Trust

General charitable purposes, young people, social welfare, health, Christian

£130,000 (2011/12)

Beneficial area

Worldwide, with some preference towards Birmingham.

Correspondent: Ruth Barron, Correspondent, c/o DWF LLP, 1 Scott Place, 2 Hardman Street, Manchester M3 3AA (tel: 01618 380487)

Trustees: Timothy Wilson; Theresa Wilson; Jethro Elvin.

CC Number: 215317

The trust was established in 1960 by the late Antony Langdale Wilson. There is a preference for local charities in the Birmingham area and those in the fields of social welfare and health, especially with a Christian context.

In 2011/12 the trust had assets of almost £3.7 million, which generated an income of £135,000. Grants were made to 42 organisations totalling £130,000.

Beneficiaries included: Girlguiding (£10,000); Shelter Cymru and Save the Children Fund (£6,000 each); Macmillan Cancer Relief and Make a Wish Foundation (£5,000 each); Buttle UK (£4,000); National Foundation for Conductive Education, Deafblind UK, Birmingham Settlement and Birmingham Federation of Clubs for Young People (£3,000 each); and Survival International, Help the Aged, Quaker Social Action and Off the Rail Contemporary (£1,000 each).

Exclusions

No grants to individuals.

Applications

In writing to the correspondent.

Information gathered from:
Accounts; Charity Commission record.

The Langley Charitable Trust

Christians, at risk groups, people who are disadvantaged by poverty, socially isolated or sick

£113,000 (2012)

Beneficial area
UK and worldwide, with a preference for the West Midlands.

Correspondent: John Gilmour, Trustee, Wheatmoor Farm, 301 Tamworth Road, Sutton Coldfield B75 6JP (tel: 01213 080165)

Trustees: John Gilmour; Sylvia Gilmour.

CC Number: 280104

The trustees' report for 2012 states that 'the principal activity of the trust is to advance the gospel of Jesus Christ and Christianity and the general welfare of humanity in its creation, nurturing and development of Christian outreach in varied dimensions'. It makes grants in the UK and worldwide but appears to have a slight preference for the West Midlands.

In 2012 the trust had an income of £101,000 and assets of almost £3.9 million. Grants were made totalling just over £113,000 to seven organisations.

Beneficiaries were: Northamptonshire Association of Youth Clubs (£50,000); Coton Green Church and United Christian Broadcasters (£25,000 each); Youth for Christ (£10,000); Sutton Coldfield Vineyard (£2,000); the Gap (£1,000); and Two Rivers School (£400).

No grants to individuals were made during the year.

Applications
The trustees' report for 2012 states that 'trustees only reply where they require other information. No telephone calls or correspondence will be entered into concerning any proposed or declined applications.'

Information gathered from:
Accounts; Charity Commission record.

The R. J. Larg Family Charitable Trust

Education, health, medical research, arts – particularly music

Around £100,000

Beneficial area
UK but generally Scotland, particularly Tayside.

Correspondent: The Trustees, Whitehall House, Yeaman Shore, Dundee DD1 4BJ

Trustees: R. Gibson; D. Brand; S. Stewart.

SC Number: SC004946

In 2013, the trust has an annual income of £141,000. Grants, which total about £100,000 each year, range between £250 and £6,000 and are given to a variety of organisations. Expenditure totalled £130,000.

These include organisations concerned with cancer research and other medical charities, youth organisations, university students' associations and amateur musical groups. No further recent information was available.

Previous beneficiaries include High School – Dundee, Whitehall Theatre Trust, Macmillan Cancer Relief – Dundee and Sense Scotland Children's Hospice.

Exclusions
Grants are not available for individuals.

Applications
In writing to the correspondent. Trustees meet to consider grants in February and August.

Information gathered from:
OSCR record.

Largsmount Ltd

Jewish charitable purposes

£216,000 (2012)

Beneficial area
UK and overseas.

Correspondent: Simon Kaufman, Trustee, 50 Keswick Street, Gateshead NE8 1TQ (tel: 01914 900140)

Trustees: ZM. Kaufman; Simon Kaufman; Naomi Kaufman.

CC Number: 280509

Registered in 1980, the trust states that its aims are to advance religion in accordance with the Orthodox Jewish faith, promote education and relieve poverty. The charity gives to religious educational and other institutions in the UK and abroad. The trustees' report for 2012 states that 'the charity accepts application for grants from representatives of Orthodox Jewish charities in England and abroad. The trustees consider all requests which they receive and make donations based on the level of funds available.'

In 2012 the trust had an income of £673,000 and assets of £4.25 million. Grants made during the year totalled £216,000.

Details of beneficiaries during the year were not available, although previously the M Y A Charitable Trust, a connected charity, has been the largest beneficiary every year.

Exclusions
Gives mainly to Jewish charitable organisations.

Applications
In writing to the correspondent.

Information gathered from:
Accounts; Charity Commission record.

Laufer Charitable Trust

General charitable purposes

£50,000 (2012/13)

Beneficial area
UK.

Correspondent: Rowland Aarons, Trustee, 342 Regents Park Road, London N3 2LJ (tel: 020 8343 1660)

Trustees: Stanley Laufer; Della Laufer; Simon Goulden; Rowland Aarons; Mark Hoffman.

CC Number: 275375

The trust makes grants mainly to Jewish organisations and has a list of charities which it has a long-term commitment to and supports annually or twice a year. It rarely adds new charities to the list.

In 2012/13 the trust had assets of £925,000 and an income of £66,000. Grants were made totalling £50,000.

Unfortunately, we have no information regarding the beneficiaries.

Exclusions
No grants to individuals, as grants are only made to registered charities.

Applications
New beneficiaries are only considered by the trust in exceptional circumstances, as the trustees seek to maintain support for an existing group of charities. In view of this it is suggested that no applications be made.

Information gathered from:
Accounts; Charity Commission record.

The Lauffer Family Charitable Foundation

Jewish, general

£381,000 (2011/12)

Beneficial area

Commonwealth countries, Israel and USA.

Correspondent: Jonathan Simon Lauffer, Trustee, Clayton Stark and Co., 5th Floor, Charles House, 108–110 Finchley Road, London NW3 5JJ (tel: 020 7431 4200; email: jonathanlauffer13@gmail.com)

Trustees: Jonathan Lauffer; Robin Lauffer; Gideon Lauffer.

CC Number: 251115

The trust has general charitable purposes, supporting Jewish causes in the UK, Commonwealth, Israel and USA.

In 2011/12 the trust had assets of £5.4 million, an income of £35,000 and made 251 grants to organisations totalling £381,000.

Grants were broken down as follows:

Education	60	£129,000
Recreation and culture	42	£89,000
Welfare and care of children and families	92	£88,000
Medical Healthcare	30	£50,000
Religious Activities	22	£23,000
Environment	5	£600

Beneficiaries of over £1,000 included: Lyttleton Playing Fields Redevelopment (£35,000); Jewish Learning Exchange (£22,000); British Friends of Sarah Herzog Memorial Hospital (£20,000); Friends of Tifereth Shlomo (£17,000); Chicken Shed Theatre Trust and Teenage Cancer Trust (£8,300 each); British Friends of Ariel (£7,000); Bridge Lane Beth Hamidrash (£5,200); Lincoln College Development Fund (£3,500); and Jewish Women's Aid, The Royal Ballet School and Nightingale (Home for Aged Jews) (£1,000 each).

Exclusions

No support for individuals.

Applications

In writing to the correspondent; applications are considered once a year.

Information gathered from:

Accounts; Charity Commission record.

Mrs F. B. Laurence Charitable Trust

Social welfare, animal welfare, medical, disability, environment

£87,500 (2011/12)

Beneficial area

UK and overseas.

Correspondent: The Trustees, BM Box 2082, London WC1N 3XX

Trustees: Caroline Fry; Camilla Carr; Elizabeth Lyle.

CC Number: 296548

The trust produces guidelines which state:

> The stated object of the charity in its deed of trust is to provide for the benefit of the Royal National Lifeboat Institution, King George's Fund for Sailors (now known as Seafarers UK), Stock Exchange Benevolent Fund, Royal Air Force Benevolent Fund and such other charitable object or institution as the trustees in their absolute discretion think fit.
>
> The trustees' preference is to make grants for the care and improvements of conditions experienced by disadvantaged members of society both within the United Kingdom and overseas for whom the United Kingdom owes a duty of care.
>
> The trustees are willing to support small organisations and those that by the nature of their work, find it difficult to attract funding.

In 2011/12 the trust had assets of over £2.3 million and a total income of £80,000. Grants were made totalling £87,500.

Beneficiaries included: DEC East Africa Crisis Appeal and the Cambridge Foundation (£5,000 each); Halow Project (£4,000); Multiple Sclerosis Trust (£3,500); Shooting Star Chase and Wiltshire Air Ambulance (£2,000 each); Winston's Wish and Brooke Hospital for Animals (£1,500 each); and Fernhurst Recreation (£1,300).

Exclusions

No support for individuals. The following applications are unlikely to be considered:

- Appeals for endowment or sponsorship
- Overseas projects, unless overseen by the charity's own fieldworkers
- Maintenance of buildings or landscape
- Provision of work or materials that are the responsibility of the state
- Where administration expenses, in all their guises, are considered by the trustees to be excessive
- Where the fundraising costs in the preceding year have not resulted in an increase in the succeeding years' donations in excess of these costs

Applications

In writing to the correspondent, including the latest annual report and accounts, as filed with the Charity Commission. Applications should be no more than two sides of A4 and should include the following information:

- Who you are
- What you do
- What distinguishes your work from others in your field
- Where applicable describe the project that the money you are asking for is going towards and include a business plan/budget
- What funds have already been raised and how
- How much are you seeking from us
- How do you intend to measure the potential benefits of your project or work as a whole?

Only registered charities will be considered.

Information gathered from:

Accounts; Charity Commission record.

The Kathleen Laurence Trust

Heart disease, arthritis, mental disabilities, medical research, older people, children's charities

£172,500 (2011/12)

Beneficial area

UK.

Correspondent: Trust Manager, Coutts and Co., Trustee Department, 440 Strand, London WC2R 0QS (tel: 020 7663 6825)

Trustee: Coutts and Co.

CC Number: 296461

Donations are given to a wide range of organisations, particularly favouring smaller groups and those raising funds for specific requirements, such as for the caring and support of people with mental disabilities, arthritic and rheumatoid research, cancer research, research into respiratory and cardiac illnesses, and children's charities.

In 2011/12 the trust had assets of £787,000 and an income of £1 million, most of which came from the sale of assets. Grants were made to 68 organisations totalling £172,500.

Beneficiaries included: Arthritis Research UK; Cancer Research UK; British Heart Foundation; Society for Horticultural Therapy; Greenwich Toys and Leisure Library Association; Fair Play for Children; I CAN – Children's

Communication Charity; Aylsham Care Trust; QED – UK; Contact the Elderly; Dr Bell's Family Centre; Home Start – Stroud and Dursley; Calvert Trust; Birmingham Settlement; Disability Challengers; and Step by Step – Autistic School.

Exclusions

No donations are made for running costs, management expenses or to individuals.

Applications

In writing to the correspondent. Trustees meet in January and June.

Information gathered from:

Accounts; Charity Commission record.

The Law Society Charity

Law and justice, worldwide

£112,000 (2011/12)

Beneficial area

Worldwide.

Correspondent: Andrew Dobson, Company Secretary, 110–113 Chancery Lane, London WC2A 1PL (tel: 020 7316 5597; email: lawsocietycharity@lawsociety.org.uk; website: www.lawsociety.org.uk)

CC Number: 268736

As the charity of the Law Society of England and Wales, this trust is concerned with causes connected to the legal profession, particularly in advancing legal education and access to legal knowledge as well as the promotion of human rights. Organisations protecting people's legal rights and lawyers' welfare are also supported, as are law-related projects from charities without an identifiable legal connection. The charity also seeks to champion and support projects which can be supported by local law societies and groups as well as with the charitable arms of firms of solicitors. The charity is also interested in international work which promotes human rights and the development of law, such as pro bono assistance for people facing capital punishment or the promotion of legal education.

Grants

Grants are up to a maximum of £15,000 and the charity warns that 'we may regard your asking for a very large amount as an indication that the project and your hopes for funding it, are unrealistic, and reject it on that basis'.

Criteria

The following are taken into account (taken from the Law Society website):

- The degree of need you have demonstrated, and how crucial a grant from the charity is for your organisation (taking into account, for example, the size of your organisation, whether you have an established fundraising operation, and the amount of income generated)
- How many people are likely to be helped through the project
- Whether other charities or public bodies are active in the same field as the organisation or help through similar projects
- Whether funding will also be required from other sources and the likelihood of this being obtained
- Whether the project would particularly promote the needs of excluded, under-represented or disadvantaged groups and minorities
- Whether the organisation has a good track record in running the kind of project concerned and is able to do so (and manage its other operations) cost-effectively
- Whether the project is of too localised or limited a nature – we aim to help projects covering as wide an area and as many people as possible
- Whether the overriding requirement of 'public benefit' has been met

In 2011/12 the trust held assets of £727,000 and had an income of £275,000 and a total expenditure of £141,000. Grants totalled £112,000.

Beneficiaries included: Liverpool Mombasa Access to Justice Project and Personal Support Unit (£15,000 each); City of Westminster and Holborn Law Society – Caravana Colombia (£12,500); Just Fair – Economic, Social and Cultural Rights UK (£10,000); Advocates for International Development (£8,000); Fair Trials International (£7,500); UK Lesbian and Gay Immigration Group and Detention Advice Service (£5,000 each); and University of Cape Town (£3,500).

Applications

On an application form available from the society's website. Applications are considered at quarterly trustees' meetings, usually held in April, July, September and December with precise dates available on the website. Applications should be received four weeks before the date of the meeting. Feedback on unsuccessful applications may be available on request.

Information gathered from:

Accounts; Charity Commission record; funder's website.

The Edgar E. Lawley Foundation

Older people, disability, children, community, hospices and medical

£197,000 (2011/12)

Beneficial area

UK, with a preference for the West Midlands.

Correspondent: F. S. Jackson, Trustee, P.O. Box 456, Esher KT10 1DP (tel: 01372 805760; email: frankjackson1945@yahoo.com; website: www.edgarelawleyfoundation.org.uk)

CC Number: 201589

The foundation currently funds six broad areas: elderly people, hospices, children and young people, community, disabilities and medical and medical research. Grants are given throughout the UK but there is some preference for smaller charities in the West Midlands.

In 2011/12 the foundation had assets of £4 million and an income of £188,000. Grants were made to 131 organisations and totalled £197,000. The website notes that grants are typically in the region of £1,500.

Beneficiaries were listed in the accounts, but without any indication of the size of grant received. They included: Rugby Mountaineering Club, Samaritans, Toynbee Hall, Woking and Sam Beare Hospices, SSAFA Forces Help, Dogs for the Disabled, Inspire Foundation, Newman University College – Birmingham, Cockermouth Mountain Rescue Team and Babies in Prison.

Exclusions

No grants to individuals.

Applications

Applications should be made in writing to the correspondent by 31 October. Applicants should outline the reasons for the grant request and the amount of grant being sought. Any supporting information that adds to the strength of the application should be included.

The trustees make grant decisions in January. The foundation regrets that it is not possible, unless a stamped addressed envelope has been provided, to communicate with unsuccessful applicants and the fact that a grant has not been received by the end of January indicates that it has not been possible to fund it. The trustees advise that around one in seven applications is successful.

Percentage of awards given to new applicants: between 40% and 50%.

Common applicant mistakes

'Failure to understand that we only assist registered charities and similar organisations.'

Information gathered from:

Accounts; Charity Commission record; further information provided by the funder; funder's website.

The Lawson Beckman Charitable Trust

Jewish, welfare, education, arts

£62,000 (2011/12)

Beneficial area

UK and overseas.

Correspondent: Melvin Lawson, Trustee, A. Beckman plc, PO Box 1ED, London W1A 1ED (tel: 020 7637 8412)

Trustees: Melvin Lawson; Lynton Stock; Francis Katz.

CC Number: 261378

The trust gives grants for the 'relief of poverty, support of the arts and general charitable purposes.' Grants are allocated two years in advance.

In 2011/12 the trust had assets of £2.5 million and an income of £65,000. A total of £62,000 was distributed in 17 grants broken down as follows:

General charitable purposes	£9,000
Education/training	£5,000
Medical/health/sickness	£115,000
Relief of poverty	£3,000
Religious activities	£1,000

Beneficiaries included: Jewish Care (£21,000); Norwood Ravenswood (£11,000); World Jewish Relief (£5,000); United Jewish Israel Appeal (£3,000); Dalaid Ltd and the Prince's Teaching Institute (£2,000 each); and the Anne Frank Trust (£1,000).

Exclusions

No grants to individuals.

Applications

In writing to the correspondent.

Information gathered from:

Accounts; Charity Commission record.

The Raymond and Blanche Lawson Charitable Trust

General charitable purposes, with preference towards children, young adults, older people, people with disabilities and people within the armed forces

£97,000 (2011/12)

Beneficial area

UK, with an interest in West Kent and East Sussex.

Correspondent: The Trustees, 28 Barden Road, Tonbridge, Kent TN9 1TX (tel: 01732 352183; email: philip.thomas@worrinlawson.co.uk)

Trustees: Philip Thomas; Sarah Hill.

CC Number: 281269

The Raymond and Blanche Lawson Charitable Trust was established in 1980. The trust has a preference for local organisations and generally supports charities within the following categories:

- Local voluntary organisations
- Preservation of buildings
- Local hospices
- Care in the community
- Assistance for people who are disabled
- Armed forces and benevolent funds

In 2011/12 the trust had assets of £1.6 million, an income of £140,000 and made grants to 99 organisations totalling £97,000. Grants ranged from £500–£5,000.

The two largest grants during the year were for £5,000 and were awarded to the following charities: Royal British Legion and the Royal London Society for the Blind.

Smaller grants included: Crisis, Royal Marsden and Kent Air Ambulance (£2,500 each); Scots Project Trust, Cancer Research UK, Young Lives Foundation and the Heart of Kent Hospice (£2,000 each); Worldwide Volunteering (£1,500); British Lung Foundation, Canine Partners, Fire Fighters Charity and Age Concern (£1,000 each); and the National Autistic Society, the Dame Vera Lynn Trust and Action for Deafness (£500 each).

Exclusions

No support for individuals.

Applications

In writing to the correspondent.

Information gathered from:

Accounts; Charity Commission record.

The Leach Fourteenth Trust

Medical, disability, environment, conservation, general

Around £90,000 (2011/12)

Beneficial area

UK, with some preference for south west England and overseas only via a UK charity.

Correspondent: Guy Ward, Trustee, Bathurst House, 86 Micklegate, York YO1 6LQ (tel: 01904 628551; email: info@barronyork.co.uk)

Trustees: Roger Murray-Leach; Judith Murray-Nash; Guy Ward; John Henderson; Tamsin Murray-Leach; Grant Nash; Richard Moore.

CC Number: 204844

Although the trust's objectives are general, the trustees tend towards medical and disability organisations. The trust also has a preference for conservation (ecological) organisations. In practice there is a preference for South West England and the Home Counties.

A few charities receive regular donations. The trustees prefer to give single grants for specific projects rather than towards general funding and also favour small organisations or projects.

In 2011/12 the trust had an income of £115,000 and a total expenditure of £126,000. Although the accounts for this financial year had been received at the Commission, they had not been published online. We estimate the total grant giving to be around £90,000.

Previous beneficiaries included: Merlin (£10,000); the Country Trust (£4,500); Hope and Homes for Children (£3,000); Orbis, Deafblind UK and International Otter Survival Fund (£2,000 each); Roy Kinnear Trust and Salvation Army (£1,500 each); and Armed Forced Fund, Dogs for the Disabled and Isles of Scilly Museum (£1,000 each).

Exclusions

Only registered charities based in the UK are supported.

Applications

In writing to the correspondent.

Information gathered from:

Accounts; Charity Commission record.

The David Lean Foundation

Film production, education and visual arts

£280,000 to organisations (2012)

Beneficial area

UK.

Correspondent: The Trustees, The Bradshaws, Oaken, Codsall, Stoke On Trent WV8 2HU (tel: 01902 754024; email: aareeves@davidleanfoundation.com; website: www.davidleanfoundation.org)

Trustees: Anthony Reeves; Stefan Breitenstein.

CC Number: 1067074

The foundation was registered in 1997 and was given rights to the royalties of four of the major films directed by the late Sir David Lean. This provides the foundation's principal, current and future source of income.

The foundation's objects are to promote public interest in the visual arts by stimulating original and creative work in the field of film production. The foundation awards grants to other charitable institutions whose aims include those similar to the British Film Institute, British Academy of Film and Television Arts and Royal Academy of Arts and to the National Film and Television School.

In 2012 the foundation had assets of £979,000 and an income of £950,000. Grants totalled £280,000.

The beneficiaries were: National Film and Television School (£88,000); Royal Academy of Arts (£75,000); British Film Institute (£65,000); British Academy of Film and Television (£31,000); and Film Club UK (£13,000).

Applications

Scholarship grants for students attending the National Film and Television School, Royal Holloway or Leighton Park School, are normally only awarded on the recommendation of the course provider with the trustees.

Other applications for grants that would meet the aims of the foundation are invited in writing, enclosing full details of the project and including financial information and two references.

Progress reports should be provided when required.

Information gathered from:

Accounts; Charity Commission record; funder's website.

The Leche Trust

Preservation and conservation of art and architecture, education

£215,000 to organisations (2011/12)

Beneficial area

UK.

Correspondent: Louisa Lawson, Correspondent, 84 Cicada Road, London SW18 2NZ (tel: 020 8870 6233; email: info@lechetrust.org; website: www.lechetrust.org)

Trustees: Martin Williams; Dr Ian Bristow; Simon Wethered; Lady Greenstock; Ariane Bankes; Caroline Laing; Thomas Howard.

CC Number: 225659

The trust was founded and endowed by the late Mr Angus Acworth in 1950. It supports the following categories:

- 'the promotion of amity and good relations between Britain and third world countries by financing visits to such countries by teachers or other appropriate persons, or providing financial assistance to students from overseas especially those in financial hardship during the last six months of their postgraduate doctorate study in the UK or those engaged in activities consistent with the charitable objects of the trust
- 'assistance to academic, educational or other organisations concerned with music, drama, dance and the arts
- 'the preservation of buildings and their contents and the repair and conservation of church furniture (including such items as monuments, but excluding structural repairs to the church fabric); preference is to be given to buildings and objects of the Georgian period
- 'assistance to conservation in all its aspects, including in particular museums and encouraging good practice in the art of conservation by supporting investigative and diagnostic reports
- 'the support of charitable bodies or organisations associated with the preservation of the nation's countryside, towns, villages and historic landscapes.

In 2011/12 the trust had assets of almost £5.9 million and an income of £231,000. Grants paid totalled £238,000.

Historic buildings – 16 grants totalling £42,000. These included: the Illam Cross Trust and Chawton House Library (£5,000 each); Sneath's Mill Trust and Compton Verney (£3,000 each); Sir William Turner's Hospital and the International Trust for Croatian Monuments (£2,000 each); and William Morris Society and Pakenham Water Mill (£1,000 each).

Churches – 13 grants totalling £42,000. These included: St Mary's Bow Church – London, St George's Church – Somerset and St Giles Church – Wrexham (£5,000 each); St Peter's Church – Devon and St Mary's Church – Berkshire (£4,000 each); St Mary the Virgin Church – Kent (£2,500); St Botolph Church – Norfolk (£1,000); and All Saints Church – Northamptonshire and Sheffield Cemetery Trust – Yorkshire (£500 each).

Institutions and museums – 21 grants totalling £67,000. These included: Furniture History Society (£20,000); Warwickshire Museum Service (£8,000); City and Guilds of London Art School (£5,000); Holbourne Museum and Oxford Conservation Consortium (£2,000 each); Frome Museum and Haslemere Education Museum (£1,000 each); and the Library of Innerpeffray – Scotland (£400).

Arts – 33 grants totalling £65,000. These included: Leeds College of Music (£5,000); London Shobana Jeyasingh Dance Company and NI Opera (£3,000 each); Young Musicians Symphony Orchestra and Classical Opera (£2,000 each); Théâtre Sans Frontières, Sound Festival and Barefaced Theatre Company (£1,000 each); and English Folk Dance and Song Society (£600).

Education (individuals) – 2 grants of £3,500.

Overseas students – 13 grants totalling £19,000. This enables the publication of their theses to make them available to other members of the academic community.

Exclusions

No grants are made for: religious bodies; overseas missions; schools and school buildings; social welfare; animals; medicine; expeditions; or British students other than music students.

Applications

In writing to the correspondent. Trustees meet three times a year, in February, June and October; applications need to be received the month before. Applications must be submitted via letter along with relevant supporting documents and budgets. Unsuccessful applicants will be notified within two weeks.

Funding for overseas students is on a rolling programme and students can apply at any time. Applications can only be made by students in the final six months of a PhD course and if they are under 35 years of age. Application forms and guidance notes can be obtained from the secretary.

Percentage of awards given to new applicants: between 20% and 30%.

Information gathered from:

Accounts; Charity Commission record; further information provided by the funder; funder's website.

The Arnold Lee Charitable Trust

Jewish, educational, health

£169,000 (2012/13)

Beneficial area

UK.

Correspondent: Hazlems Fenton LLP, Correspondent, Hazlems Fenton LLP, Palladium House, 1–4 Argyll Street, London W1F 7LD (tel: 020 7437 7666)

Trustees: Edward Lee; Alan Lee.

CC Number: 264437

The policy of the trustees is to distribute income to established charities of high repute for any charitable purpose or object. The trust supports a large number of Jewish organisations.

In 2012/13 the trust had assets of nearly £2 million and an income of £466,000. Grants were made totalling £169,000. The annual report states that grants were made to charities of high repute but there was no list of beneficiaries.

Jewish community support	£155,000
Education	£12,500
Healthcare	£1,300

The largest beneficiaries for the year were: Project Seed (£15,000); Aleph Society (£13,000); Policy Exchange Ltd (£7,500); Mesila UK (£6,500); JRoots (£5,000); and the Institute of Jewish Studies (£2,000).

Exclusions

Grants are rarely made to individuals.

Applications

In writing to the correspondent.

Information gathered from:

Accounts; Charity Commission record.

The Leigh Trust

Addiction, children and youth, criminal justice, asylum seekers, racial equality and education

£106,500 (2011/12)

Beneficial area

UK and overseas.

Correspondent: The Trustees, Begbies Chettle Agar, Epworth House, 25 City Road, London EC1Y 1AR (tel: 020 7628 5801; fax: 020 7628 0390)

Trustees: Hon. David Bernstein; Caroline Moorehead.

CC Number: 275372

The Leigh Trust was registered in 1978. Its current policy is to distribute investment revenue and a proportion of capital gains. The trust makes grants to a variety of registered charities concerned with:

- Drug and alcohol rehabilitation
- Criminal justice
- Asylum seekers and refugees
- Racial equality
- Education

'The policy of the trustees is to support those organisations which they believe to be in greatest need. The trustees can respond favourably to very few applicants.'

In 2011/12 the trust had assets of £2.9 million and an income of over £85,000. Gants totalling £106,500 were categorised by the trust as follows:

Drug and alcoholic addiction	20	£44,000
Criminal justice/young offenders/youth at risk	15	£43,000
Asylum seekers and refugees	8	£16,500
Other	1	£3,000

Beneficiaries included: The Amber Foundation (£6,000); Action on Addiction, Outside Edge Theatre Company and Shelter (£5,000 each); Music in Detention (£3,000); Bedfordshire Refugee and Asylum Support, Mentoring Plus and One North East London (£2,000 each); and Good News Family Care, Solace and The Trust Women's Project (1,500 each).

Exclusions

The trust does not make grants to individuals.

Applications

Organisations applying for grants must provide their most recent audited accounts, a registered charity number, a cash flow statement for the next 12 months, and a stamped addressed envelope.

Applicants should state clearly on one side of A4 what their charity does and what they are requesting funding for. They should provide a detailed budget and show other sources of funding for the project.

Information gathered from:

Accounts; Charity Commission record.

P Leigh-Bramwell Trust 'E'

Methodist, general charitable purposes

£92,000 (2012/13)

Beneficial area

UK, with a preference for Bolton.

Correspondent: Mrs L. Cooper, Secretary, Suite 2E, Atria, Spa Road, Bolton BL1 4AG (tel: 01204 364656)

Trustees: Helen Leigh-Bramwell; Jennifer Leigh Mitchell; Brian Leigh-Bramwell.

CC Number: 267333

The trustees' annual report for 2012/13 states that the objects of the charity are the 'advancement of the Christian religion, education, the RNLI and any other legal charitable institutions by the provision of funds'.

In 2012/13 the trust had assets of over £2.2 million, an income of £90,000 and made grants totalling £92,000. Distributions were made to both regular beneficiaries together with six additional charitable organisations. There was no list of beneficiary organisations.

Previous beneficiaries include: King's College School (£30,000). Other large beneficiaries included: Leigh-Bramwell Fund (£23,000); The Methodist Church – Bolton (£11,000); Rivington Parish Church (£7,500); The Unicorn School (£7,000); and The Methodist Church – Delph Hill and The Methodist Church – Breightmet (£3,400 each); Barnabus, Bolton Choral Union, Bolton Deaf Society, ChildLine North West, NCH Bypass, West London Mission and YWCA (£500 each).

Exclusions

No grants to individuals.

Applications

In writing to the correspondent; however, note that previous research suggests that there is only a small amount of funds available for unsolicited applications and therefore success is unlikely.

Information gathered from:

Accounts; Charity Commission record.

The Leonard Trust

Christian, overseas aid, mental health

£28,000 (2012)

Beneficial area

Overseas and UK, with a preference for Winchester.

Correspondent: Tessa E. Feilden, Correspondent, 18 Edgar Road, Winchester, Hampshire SO23 9TW (tel: 01962 854800)

Trustees: Dominic Gold; Christopher Smiley.

CC Number: 1031723

This trust makes grants to registered charities ranging from small local (Hampshire) groups to large nationals. According to its actives listed at the Charity Commission website, historically the trustees have tended to concentrate on Christian based charities, mental health and overseas aid (often in response to specific disaster relief). Grants generally range between £500 and £5,000 each.

In 2012 the trust had assets of £191,000 an income of £29,000 and made grants to 14 organisations totalling just under £28,000.

Grant recipients included: Care for the Family, Christian Aid and Christian Missionary Society (£3,000 each); Intercare, Scripture Union and Tower Hamlets Mission (£2,000 each); and VIVA Together for Children (£1,000).

Exclusions

No grants to individuals. Medical research or building projects are no longer supported.

Applications

Unsolicited applications cannot be considered.

Percentage of awards given to new applicants: less than 10%.

Common applicant mistakes

'Far too much information, including accounts; requesting money for something way outside the remit of the trust.'

Information gathered from:

Accounts; Charity Commission record; further information provided by the funder.

Lewis Family Charitable Trust

General, Jewish

£612,000 (2011/12)

Beneficial area

UK and Israel.

Correspondent: The Secretary, Chelsea House, West Gate, Ealing, London W5 1DR (tel: 020 8991 4601)

Trustees: Julian Lewis; Deborah Lewis; Benjamin Lewis; Simon Lewis.

CC Number: 259892

The trust's annual report stated that 'The trust was initially established to give expression to the charitable intentions of members of the families of David, Bernard, Geoffrey and Godfrey Lewis and certain companies which they control. The legally permitted objectives are very wide and cover virtually every generally accepted charitable object, in practice the causes to which the trustees have devoted the bulk of their resources in recent years have been:

- General charitable funding
- Medical research
- Educational funding
- Child care.'

Jewish charities are prominent throughout the categories of giving.

In 2011/12 the trust had assets of £8 million and an income of £1.6 million. Grants were made to over 48 organisations totalling £612,000 and broken down as follows:

General charitable funding	£156,000
Medical research	£135,000
Educational funding	£119,000
Child care	£65,000
Support for the elderly	£53,000
Medical – general support	£43,000
Jewish religious support	£25,000
Poverty relief	£15,000

While the majority of beneficiaries had a Jewish connection, support was also given to a number of non-Jewish organisations.

Beneficiaries included: Israel Centre for Social and Economic Progress (£66,000); University of Nottingham (£53,000); United Jewish Israel Appeal (£50,000); Bowel Disease Research Foundation (£40,000); Weizmann Institute (£25,000); Reform Judaism and Norwood (£20,000 each); Centre for Media Research, FRODO and The Common Security Trust (£10,000 each); Council for a Beautiful Israel, Jewish Marriage Council and NSPCC (£5,000 each); and Ajex Museum, Jewish Museum and Lupus UK (£1,000 each).

Exclusions

No grants to individuals.

Applications

In writing to the correspondent.

Information gathered from:

Accounts; Charity Commission record.

The Sir Edward Lewis Foundation

General charitable purposes

£242,000 (2011/12)

Beneficial area

UK and overseas, with a preference for Surrey.

Correspondent: Darren Wing, Administrator, Rawlinson and Hunter, The Lower Mill, Kingston Road, Ewell, Surrey KT17 2AE (tel: 020 7842 2000)

Trustees: Richard Lewis; Mark Harris; Christine Lewis; Sarah Dorin.

CC Number: 264475

The trust was established in 1972 by Sir Edward Roberts Lewis. The trust has revised its policy and now plans to make one substantial donation every two or three years to an appropriate cause as well as smaller donations on an annual basis. Therefore it will not distribute all its income every year. The trustees prefer to support charities known personally to them and those favoured by the settlor.

In 2011/12 the foundation had assets of £7.8 million, an income of £256,000 and made 114 grants to organisations totalling £242,000.

Beneficiaries included: The Arnold Foundation for Rugby School (£60,000); Arthritis Research UK (£15,000); FareShare (£10,000); The Children's Trust Tadworth, Ex-Services Mental Welfare Society (Combat Stress), Gurkha Welfare Trust and St Bartholomew's Church, Leigh (£5,000 each); Rugby Clubs (£4,000); Opthalmic Aid to Eastern Europe (£3,000); Musicians Benevolent Fund (£2,500); The Airey Neave Trust, St Catherine's Hospice and Wildlife Aid (£2,000); WaterAid (£1,000); and Elizabeth Finn Care (£500).

Exclusions

Grants are only given to charities, projects or people known to the trustees. No grants are given to individuals.

Applications

In writing to the correspondent. The trustees meet every six months.

Percentage of awards given to new applicants: less than 10%.

Information gathered from:

Accounts; Charity Commission record; further information provided by the funder.

The John Spedan Lewis Foundation

Natural sciences, particularly horticulture, environmental education, ornithology and conservation

£67,000 (2012/13)

Beneficial area

UK.

Correspondent: Ms Bridget Chamberlain, Secretary, Partnership House, Carlisle Place, London SW1P 1BX (tel: 020 7592 6121; email: bridget_chamberlain@johnlewis.co.uk)

Trustees: Charlie Mayfield; David Jones; Dr Vaughan Southgate; Dr John David; Gerrard Keogh-Peters.

CC Number: 240473

The trust makes grants in the areas of horticulture, environmental education, ornithology and conservation, and to associated educational and research projects. Donations are mainly one-off.

In 2012/13 it had assets of £2.6 million and an income of £88,000. Grants were made to 19 organisations and one individual totalling £67,000.

The beneficiaries included: Clyde River Foundation (£6,000); Highland Biological Recording Group, Natural History Museum and Yorkshire Wildlife Trust (£5,000 each); Kent Wildlife Trust and The Manchester Museum (£4,000 each); and Snowdon Trust and Birding for All (£1,000 each).

Exclusions

Local branches of national organisations, or for salaries, medical research, welfare projects, building works or overseas expeditions.

Applications

In writing to the correspondent with latest report and accounts and a budget for the proposed project.

Information gathered from:

Accounts; Charity Commission record.

Liberum Foundation

General charitable purposes with a focus on disadvantaged young people

£84,000 (2012)

Beneficial area

Not defined, in practice UK.

Correspondent: Justine Rumens, Secretary to the Foundation, Ropemaker Place, Level 12, 25 Ropemaker Street, London EC2Y 9LY (tel: 020 3100 2000; email: info@liberumfoundation.com; website: www.liberumcapital.com/LiberumFoundation)

Trustees: Carolyn Doherty; Simon Stilwell; Antony Scawthorn; Dean Butterfield; Timothy Mayo.

CC Number: 1137475

This charity was set up in March 2010 for general charitable purposes. The area of benefit is not defined but in practice is mainly national and the focus is on disadvantaged young people. It is funded by donations from Liberum Capital Ltd and fundraising activities by employees. Grants will be given to individuals and organisations and includes those for education; training and employment; the prevention or relief of poverty; sport/recreation and community development. The foundation's website states:

> We hold two big fundraising events each year. In addition we encourage individual employees to organise and/or participate in smaller ad-hoc events during the year on behalf of the foundation.
>
> We support 3 anchor charities for specific projects per year using approx 65% of the funds held within the foundation. Our first three anchor charities are School Home Support, St Giles Trust and Tiny Tickers. We intend to build a partnership with these charities and take an active and participative role within the projects to monitor the progress of them and assist in adding value where possible. The remaining 35% of donations will be made to smaller causes. We anticipate limiting these to other registered charities for the first year. These donations will be made upon receipt of proposals from staff and we expect a level of participation and commitment from those who are proposing the donations.

In 2012 the foundation held assets of £116,000 and had an income of £139,000. Grants were made (as stated above) to three charities totalling £84,000.

Beneficiaries were: St Giles Trust (£30,000); Tiny Tickers (£29,000); and School Home Support (£24,000).

Exclusions

Adult health; hospitals; animals; older people; the armed services; housing; heritage; environment; and religion.

Applications

In writing to the Secretary.

Information gathered from:

Accounts; Charity Commission record; funder's website.

Lifeline 4 Kids

Equipment for children with disabilities

£164,000 (2012)

Beneficial area

Worldwide.

Correspondent: Roger Adelman, Trustee, 215 West End Lane, West Hampstead, London NW6 1XJ (tel: 020 7794 1661; fax: 020 7794 1161; email: rda@lifeline4kids.org; website: www.lifeline4kids.org)

Trustees: Jeffrey Bonn; Paul Maurice; Beverley Emden; Roberta Harris; Roger Adelman; Irving Millman.

CC Number: 200050

This charity supports children who are disabled up to 18 years old. The following description is taken from its website:

> We are a UK National children's charity established in 1961. Originally known as the Handicapped Children's Aid Committee, in 2000 our working name changed to Lifeline 4 Kids. Our members work on an entirely voluntary basis and we have no paid staff.
>
> We were formed for one purpose- to provide essential equipment to help improve the quality of life for children with disabilities and special needs irrespective of race or creed.

The trust provides equipment to individual children, schools, children's hospices, respite care homes, support centres and hospital neonatal units. No appeal is too large to consider for the trust.

In 2012 the charity had assets of £394,000, an income of £25,000 and gave £164,000 in response to appeals. Details of the successful applicants were not included with the accounts.

Note that the trust does not give financial support, but purchases equipment directly for and on behalf of the beneficiary.

Assistance given in 2006 included that to: Central Middlesex Hospital, towards equipment for its outdoor play area (£5,000); the Living Paintings Trust, funding the production of 20 copies of a new Living Picture Book (£2,500); the New Jumbulance Travel Trust, providing two portable instant resuscitation packs (£2,400); Vision Aid, providing a specialised flat screen video magnifier (£2,000); and the Lothian Autistic Society, for equipment for its various play schemes (£1,500).

Exclusions

Building projects, research grants and salaries will not be funded. According to the trust's website, the trust does not fund the following:

- Building or garden works
- Carpets/floor covering
- Ovens/cookers
- Refrigerators (unless for medical needs)
- Clothing
- Shoes (unless specialist)
- Transport costs
- Tuition/school lessons or fees
- Driving lessons
- Holidays.

Applications

Applications for help indicating specific requirements and brief factual information must initially be made in writing, addressed to the correspondent, or by email (appeals@lifeline4kids.org).

The charity states on its website that:

> Each request will be acknowledged and provided it meets our criteria, an application form will be sent by post or email. The form contains comprehensive questions relating to the child/children's medical condition and requires backup information from health professionals together with a financial statement of the applicant/organisation.
>
> After we have received the completed application form, if appropriate, the appeal will be investigated personally by one of our members.
>
> The majority of appeals are discussed and decided upon at our monthly meetings. If approved, a maximum sum is allocated and we take full responsibility for the purchase and safe delivery of the approved item.

Initial telephone calls from applicants are not welcome.

Information gathered from:

Accounts; Charity Commission record; funder's website.

The Limbourne Trust

Environment, welfare, arts

£108,000 (2012/13)

Beneficial area

UK and overseas.

Correspondent: Elisabeth Thistlethwayte, Trustee, Downs Farm, Homersfield, Harleston IP20 0NS

CC Number: 1113796

The trust was established in 2006 with wide charitable objects. According to the trustees' report for 2012/13, the trust looks to:

> Benefit communities throughout the world, and in particular the advancement of education, the protection of health, and the relief of poverty, distress and sickness.
>
> The charity will also seek to challenge all forms of oppression and inequality, and will prioritise funding for groups who assist people who are unable to take a full role in society due to economic, political and social disadvantage.
>
> The charity will seek to achieve these objectives by providing grant funding for other charities working in the following fields:
>
> - Research into renewable energy sources
> - Development of organic farming methods
> - Development of environmentally sustainable projects
> - Overcoming adverse effects of climate change
> - Community projects to assist those at disadvantage
> - Protection and conservation of the environment
> - Promote the public education in and appreciation of literature, music and drama
> - Other charitable purposes as the trustees from time to time may decide

In 2012/13 the trust had assets of £2.7 million and an income of £105,000. Grants totalled nearly £108,000 and were made to 17 organisations.

Beneficiaries included: The Reader Organisation (£12,500); Farms for City Children and Jubilee Sailing Trust (£10,000 each); Seachange Arts and CHICKS (£9,000 each); Voluntary Action Maidstone (£7,500); English Pen, Hope and Homes for Children and Vauxhall City Farm (£5,000 each); and Eden Community Outdoors- ECO (£2,000).

Applications

The trustees' report for 2012/13 states that 'the trustees will seek to identify those projects where the greatest and widest benefit can be attained, and usually will only consider written applications and, where necessary, make further enquiries'.

Information gathered from:

Accounts; Charity Commission record.

Limoges Charitable Trust

General, including health, heritage and community

£64,000 (2011/12)

Beneficial area

UK, with a preference for Birmingham.

Correspondent: Judy Ann Dyke, Trustee, c/o Tyndallwoods Solicitors, 29 Woodbourne Road, Edgbaston, Birmingham B17 8BY (tel: 01216 932222; fax: 01216 930844)

CC Number: 1016178

The trust has general charitable purposes, although there are preferences for animal, health, heritage and community organisations. Many of the beneficiaries are based in Birmingham.

In 2011/12 the trust had assets of £701,000 and an income of £27,000. Grants to 59 organisations totalled £64,000 and were distributed as follows:

Heritage and community	£32,000
Health and welfare	£17,000
Education	£6,900
Youth	£3,5000
Animals	£2,800
Other	£1,500
Nautical	£1,000

Beneficiaries included: Edward's Trust and Moseley Community Development Trust (£10,000 each); Portsmouth Cathedral (£4,000); Birmingham Civic Society and Birmingham St Mary's Hospice (£2,000 each); University of Birmingham (£1,700); and St Ildemas Church (£1,600).

Applications

In writing to the correspondent. Trustees usually meet four times a year to consider applications.

Information gathered from:

Accounts; Charity Commission record.

The Lind Trust

Social action, youth, community and Christian service

£434,000 to organisations and individuals (2011/12).

Beneficial area

UK.

Correspondent: Gavin Croft Wilcox, Trustee, Drayton Hall, Hall Lane, Norwich, Norfolk NR8 6DP (tel: 01603 262626; email: john.savery@dacrepropertyholdings.com)

CC Number: 803174

This trust makes grants to individuals and organisations and also lets its properties to charities at a peppercorn rent. It owns various properties and land in Norwich and is primarily focused on Christian causes and youth work.

In 2011/12 the trust had assets of £20 million, an income of £652,000 and made 'monetary gifts and donations' of £434,000.

Beneficiaries included: The Open Youth Trust (£185,000); and other charities not listed. The trustees have made a £5,000 commitment to the Matthew Project.

Applications

In writing to the correspondent at any time. However, the trust commits most of its funds in advance, giving the remainder to eligible applicants as received.

Percentage of awards given to new applicants: less than 10%.

Common applicant mistakes

'Not related to young people or the Christian faith, and/or not based in Norfolk.'

Information gathered from:

Accounts; Charity Commission record; further information provided by the funder.

Lindale Educational Foundation

Roman Catholic, education

£52,000 (2011/12)

Beneficial area

UK and overseas.

Correspondent: Jack Valero, Correspondent, 6 Orme Court, London W2 4RL (tel: 020 7243 9417)

Trustees: Dawliffe Hall Educational Foundation; Greygarth Association; Netherhall Educational Association.

CC Number: 282758

The foundation supports the Roman Catholic religion and the advancement of education. Its aims are to:

- Train priests
- Establish, extend, improve and maintain churches, chapels, oratories and other places of worship
- Establish, extend, improve and maintain university halls and halls of residence for students of all nationalities
- Arrange and conduct courses, camps, study centres, meetings, conferences and seminars
- Provide financial support for education or research by individuals or groups of students
- Provide financial support for other individuals or institutions which meet the trust's criteria, including the corporate trustees

In 2011/12 the foundation had assets of £5,000 and an income of £33,000. Grants were made totalling £52,000. A total of eleven grants were made to organisations.

Beneficiaries were: Thornycroft Hall (five grants totalling £29,000); Netherhall Educational Association Centre for Retreats and Study (four grants totalling £16,500); and Hazelwood House (two grants totalling £6,500).

Exclusions

No grants to individuals.

Applications

In writing to the correspondent, but note that most funds are already committed.

Information gathered from:

Accounts; Charity Commission record.

The Linden Charitable Trust

Medical, healthcare, the arts

£85,000 (2011/12)

Beneficial area

UK, with a preference for West Yorkshire.

Correspondent: Baker Tilly Tax and Accounting Ltd, 2 Whitehall Quay, Leeds, West Yorkshire LS1 4HG

Trustees: Margaret Heaton Pearson; Gerald Holbrook; John Swales; Robert Swales.

CC Number: 326788

Currently, the trust's policy is to benefit charities specialising in cancer relief and research, those particularly involved with hospices, those involved in arts and also a wider range of charities based in and around Leeds, West Yorkshire.

The trustees agreed (in 2009/10) to make a regular donation to Leeds international Pianoforte Competition of £10,000 per year.

In 2011/12 the trust had assets of £2.5 million and an income of £66,000. Grants were made totalling £85,000. 51 grants were made to organisations. Grants were made totalling £85,500

Beneficiaries included: Leeds International and Pianoforte Competition (£10,000); Macmillan Cancer Care (£5,000); Yorkshire Air Ambulance, Henshaws for the Blind and Leeds Lieder (£3,000 each); David Wood Yellow Bird and Caring for Life (£2,000 each); Yorkshire Eye Research, the Sick Children's Trust and West Yorkshire Playhouse (£1,000 each); and Yorkshire Dales Millennium and Phillip Harvey Horse and Do (£500 each).

Exclusions

No grants to individuals.

Applications

In writing to the correspondent.

Information gathered from:

Accounts; Charity Commission record.

The Linmardon Trust

General

£37,000 (2011/12)

Beneficial area

UK, with a preference for the Nottingham area.

Correspondent: Lee Topp, Trust Manager, HSBC Trust Company (UK) Ltd, Norwich House, Nelson Gate, Commercial Road, Southampton SO15 1GX (tel: 02380 722240)

Trustee: HSBC. Trust Company (UK) Ltd.

CC Number: 275307

The trust supports charities in the UK with a preference for those in the Nottingham area. The trustees prefer to support a greater number of small donations to various charities throughout the year.

In 2011/12, it held assets of £1.2 million and had an income of £361,000. Grants totalling £37,000 were made to 24 organisations. The trust has a preference for awarding a larger number of small grants.

Beneficiaries included: Animal Health Trust, Bath Cats and Dogs Home, Great North Air Ambulance and Sheltered Work Opportunities Project (£2,000 each); The Nottingham Historic Churches Trust and Age UK Andover and District (£1,250 each); and Demand, Friends of St Francis Special School and Newport Cottage Care Centre (£1,000 each).

Exclusions

Grants are made to registered charities only. No support to individuals.

Applications

In writing to the correspondent. The trustees meet quarterly, generally in February, May, August and November.

Information gathered from:

Accounts; Charity Commission record.

The Ruth and Stuart Lipton Charitable Trust

Jewish charities and general charitable purposes

£79,000 (2011/12)

Beneficial area

UK and overseas.

Correspondent: Neil Benson, Trustee, c/o Lewis Golden and Co., 40 Queen Ann Street, London W1G 9EL (tel: 020 7580 7313)

Trustees: Sir Stuart Lipton; Lady Lipton; Neil Benson.

CC Number: 266741

The trust was founded by property/art mogul Stuart Lipton and his wife in 1973.

In 2011/12 the trust had assets of £593,000 and an income of £72,000. Grants to 23 organisations totalled £79,000. There is no minimum limit for any grant and all grants must be approved unanimously by the trustees.

Beneficiaries include: Community Security Trust (£28,000); United Jewish Israel Appeal (£12,500); The Royal Opera House Foundation (£8,000); Western Marble Arch Synagogue (£4,000); Barbican Centre (£3,000); Chai Cancer Care (£2,500); National Portrait Gallery and Haileybury Youth Trust (£1,000 each); Royal Ballet School (£500); Oxfam (£200); and Motor Neurone Disease Association and Jewish Women's Aid (£100 each).

Exclusions

No grants to individuals.

Applications

In writing to the correspondent.

Information gathered from:

Accounts; Charity Commission record.

The Lister Charitable Trust

Outdoor activities for disadvantaged young people

£304,000 (2011/12)

Beneficial area

UK and overseas.

Correspondent: Nicholas Yellowlees, Correspondent, 44 Welbeck Street, London W1G 8DY (tel: 020 7486 0800; email: info@apperleylimited.co.uk)

Trustees: Noel Lister; David Collingwood; Paul Lister; Penny Horne; Sylvia Lister.

CC Number: 288730

The trust's annual report and accounts for 2011/12 included the following statement:

> The trust formerly had strong links to the UK Sailing Academy but this is now primarily supported by the Whirlwind Charitable Trust having been seeded with £4m capital sum by the trust in June 2007. This has enabled the Lister Charity to have greater impact in other areas of charitable support as demonstrated by the list of donations made during the year.

In 2011/12 the trust had assets of £7.7 million, an income of £216,000, and made 10 grants totalling £304,000.

Beneficiaries included: The European Nature Trust (£191,000); the Stroke Association (£40,000); Nyaka School (£19,000); Sponsored Arts for Education and Home Start Ashford (£10,000 each); Oxford Transplant Foundation (£5,000); and Embercombe (£3,000).

Exclusions

Applications from individuals, including students, are ineligible. No grants are made in response to general appeals from large UK organisations or to smaller bodies working in areas outside its criteria.

Applications

In writing to the correspondent. Applications should include clear details of the need the intended project is designed to meet, plus an outline budget. Only applications from eligible bodies are acknowledged, when further information may be requested.

Information gathered from:

Accounts; Charity Commission record.

The Second Joseph Aaron Littman Foundation

General charitable purposes, with a special preference for Jewish causes, as well as academic and medical research

£245,000 (2011/12)

Beneficial area

UK.

Correspondent: Robert Littman, Trustee, Manor Farm, Mill Lane, Charlton Mackrell, Somerton, Somerset TA11 7BQ

Trustees: Robert Littman; Glenn Hurstfield; C. Littman.

CC Number: 201892

The trust states in its annual report for 2011/12 that its objects are to relieve poverty anywhere in the world and to advance knowledge anywhere in the world. This trust has general charitable purposes with special preference for Jewish causes, as well as academic and medical research.

In 2011/12 it had assets of £5.6 million and an income of £295,000. Grants were made to totalling £245,000.

The main beneficiary, as in previous years, was Littman Library of Jewish Civilisation which received £208,000. There were ten further donations listed in the accounts.

The main beneficiary, as in previous years, was Littman Library of Jewish Civilisation which received £192,000. Other beneficiaries included: Hadassah UK, University Jewish Chaplaincy and Coronary Flow Trust (£5,000 each); Leo Baeck College UK (£2,500); University College London and Great Ormond Street Hospital (£2,000 each); Holocaust Educational Trust (£1,500); and Fight for Sight (£1,000).

Donations of less than £1,000 totalled £12,000.

Exclusions

Applications from individuals are not considered.

Applications

In writing to the correspondent.

Information gathered from:

Accounts; Charity Commission record.

Jack Livingstone Charitable Trust

Jewish, general

£148,000 (2011/12)

Beneficial area

UK and worldwide, with a preference for Manchester.

Correspondent: Janice Livingstone, Trustee, Westholme, The Springs, Bowdon, Altrincham, Cheshire WA14 3JH (tel: 01619 283232)

Trustees: Janice Livingstone; Terence Livingstone; Brian White.

CC Number: 263473

This trust gives grants to organisations for general purposes, with a preference for Jewish charities.

In 2011/12 the trust had assets of £1.9 million, an income of £52,000 and gave grants totalling £148,000.

Beneficiaries included: LCCC Foundation (£105,000); Federation of Jewish Services (£8,000); Community Security Trust and Manchester Jewish Community Care (£5,000 each); Langdon FDN Patrons (£3,000); J Roots Ltd (£2,500); British Friends of Darche Noam (£1,600); South Manchester Synagogue (£1,500); Southport New Synagogue, Project Seed, Stockdales, UK Toremet and Brookvale (£1,000 each).

Grants of less than £1,000 totalled £11,000.

Applications

The trust does not respond to unsolicited applications.

Information gathered from:

Accounts; Charity Commission record.

The Elaine and Angus Lloyd Charitable Trust

General

£78,000 (2011/12)

Beneficial area

UK, with a preference for Surrey, Kent and the South of England.

Correspondent: Ross Badger, 3rd Floor, North Side, Dukes Court, 32 Duke Street, St James's, London SW1Y 6DF (tel: 020 7930 7797)

Trustees: Angus Lloyd; John Gordon; James Lloyd; Philippa Satchwell-Smith; Virginia Best; Christopher Lloyd; Michael Craig-Cooper; Richard Lloyd.

CC Number: 237250

In 1992, the Elaine Lloyd Charitable Trust and the Mr Angus Lloyd Charitable Settlement were amalgamated and are now known as the Elaine and Angus Lloyd Charitable Trust. Many grants are recurrent, some may be paid quarterly. Grants are mainly to UK charities and local organisations in the Surrey and Kent area and elsewhere in the South of England. Grants are given in practice to those charities known to one or more of the trustees. Donations are made to:

- Any charitable institution whether incorporated or not
- Any individual recipients to assist them in meeting education expenses either for themselves or their children
- Any individual recipients whose circumstances are such they come within the legal conception of poverty

In 2011/12 the trust had assets of £2.5 million, an income of £88,000 and gave grants totalling £78,000.

Beneficiaries included: Positive Initiative Trust (£7,500); EHAS (£3,800); Diabetes UK, Monday to Wednesday club, Rhema Partnership Anitoch, Rhema New Bible College and Skillaway (£2,000 each); East Kent Hospice Project and Martha Trust (£1,500 each); Croce Rossa Italiana Menaggio, Hever School, National Youth Orchestra of Great Britain, RNLI and The Afghan Connection (£1,000 each).

Grants of less than £1,000 totalled £27,000.

Applications

In writing to the correspondent. The trustees meet regularly to consider grants.

Information gathered from:

Accounts; Charity Commission record.

The Charles Lloyd Foundation

Construction, repair and maintenance of Roman Catholic buildings, the advancement of Roman Catholic religion, and music

£36,000 (2012/13)

Beneficial area

Roman Catholic Dioceses of Menevia and Wrexham.

Correspondent: Vincent Ryan, Trustee, 8–10 Grosvenor Road, Wrexham LL11 1BU (tel: 01978 291000; email: susanelder@allingtonhughes.co.uk)

Trustees: Richard Thorn; Patrick Walters; Vincent Ryan; Steven Davies.

CC Number: 235225

The foundation supports the construction, repair or maintenance of Roman Catholic churches, houses, convents and monasteries, the advancement of Roman Catholic charities in the beneficial area and the promotion and advancement of music, either religious or secular, for public appreciation in or towards national Catholic charities operating in the area of benefit. It prefers to give one-off donations for specific projects.

In 2012/13 it had assets of £1.4 million, which generated an income of £46,000. Grants were made to three organisations totalling £36,000; which went to: Flint Catholic Church (£16,000); and Hawarden Catholic Church and Barmouth Catholic Church (£10,000 each).

Applications

In writing to the correspondent. Four copies of the income and expenditure pages of the latest financial return; plans and estimates of the project; plus what finances the parish can contribute must be provided once details of the project are known.

Information gathered from:

Accounts; Charity Commission record.

Lloyd's Charities Trust

General charitable purposes

£403,000 (2012)

Beneficial area

UK, with particular interest in East London.

Correspondent: Suzanna Nagle, Correspondent, 1 Lime Street, London EC3M 7HA (tel: 020 7327 6075; email: communityaffairs@lloyds.com; website: www.lloyds.com/lct)

Trustees: John Spencer; David Gittings; Lawrence Holder; Iain Wilson; Charles Hamond; Rupert Atkin; Graham Clarke; Chris Harman; Neil Smith; Vicky Mirfin.

CC Number: 207232

The charity was set up in 1953, and is the charitable arm of Lloyd's insurance market in London. There are three separate funds that are used to administer grants. Through these, the trust looks to support London-based charities in the fields of education, employability, enterprise, and sport. It also seeks to support emergency appeals.

According to the trust's website at the time of writing (October 2013), the trust focuses on three main areas of giving and these are as follows:

- Making a great city greater: at home in London, we give to tackle disadvantage and foster opportunity
- Responding to disasters and emergencies: around the world, we give to relieve suffering and rebuild lives
- Preparing for the future: we give to equip individuals and communities with the resources and skills they need to meet the challenges of a rapidly changing world

In 2012 the trust had assets of £2.5 million and an income of £469,000. Grants were made in the form of donations and bursaries totalling £403,000.

Beneficiaries included: the Prince's Trust (£75,000); and Bromley By Bow Centre (£50,000).

Exclusions

The trust's website states:

> Lloyd's Charities Trust will not fund the following:
>
> - Organisations that are not registered charities or non-UK registered charities (except at the occasional discretion of trustees)
> - Political parties or lobbying organisations
> - Local charities outside London, unless there is significant involvement from a person currently working in the Lloyd's market, in which case the application must come from that individual (see: www.lloyds.com)
> - Mainstream schools, PTAs and educational establishments unless there is significant involvement from a person currently working in the Lloyd's market, in which case the application must come from that individual (see: www.lloyds.com)
> - Grant-making bodies to make grants on our behalf
> - Animal welfare causes, zoos, animal rescue
> - The promotion of religion or other beliefs
> - Individuals, including student grants, bursaries, medical costs or financial assistance
> - Sponsorship of events or individuals including taking tables at gala dinners

- Advertising including in brochures for charitable events
- Costs associated with expeditions
- Retrospective funding for work that has already taken place

Lloyd's Charities Trust will typically not fund the following:

- Military causes
- Arts, culture or heritage charities
- Outward bound courses and adventure experiences
- Conferences, cultural festivals, exhibitions and events
- Churches, cathedrals and other historic buildings

Applications

Lloyd's Charities Trust makes ad hoc donations, however the majority of funds are committed to supporting the partnership charities the trust works with. The trust has previously stated that as funds are committed over a three-year period 'we are unable to respond positively to the numerous appeals we receive'.

Information gathered from:

Accounts; Charity Commission record; funder's website.

Localtrent Ltd

Jewish, education, religion

£194,000 (2011/12)

Beneficial area

UK, with some preference for Manchester.

Correspondent: A. Kahan, Administrator, Lopian Gross Barnett and Co., 6th Floor, Cardinal House, 20 St Mary's Parsonage, Manchester M3 2LG (tel: 01618 328721)

Trustees: Hyman Weiss; Mina Weiss; Philip Weiss; Zisel Weiss; Bernardin Weiss; Yocheved Weiss.

CC Number: 326329

The trust was established in 1983 for the distribution of funds to religious, educational and similar charities for the advancement of the Jewish religion.

In 2011/12 the trust had assets of £749,000 and an income of £214,000. Grants totalling £194,000 were described in the trust's accounts as being made to:

> A number of institutions which carry out activities such as providing Orthodox Jewish education and other activities which advance Jewish religion in accordance with the Orthodox Jewish faith (e.g. Yetev Lev: grant £41,300, Dushinsky Trust: grant £20,000 and Kesser Torah School: grant £7,305).

Applications

In writing to the correspondent.

Information gathered from:

Accounts; Charity Commission record.

The Locker Foundation

Mainly Jewish charities

£397,000 (2011/12)

Beneficial area

UK and overseas.

Correspondent: Irving Carter, Trustee, 9 Neville Drive, London N2 0QS (tel: 020 8455 9280)

Trustees: I. Carter; M. Carter; Mrs S. Segal.

CC Number: 264180

The trust mainly supports Jewish organisations. Its objects are for general charitable purposes with a preference for the welfare of the sick and those with disabilities and the teaching of the Jewish religion.

In 2011/12 it had assets of £4.5 million and an income of £540,000. It made 35 grants totalling £397,000.

Beneficiaries included: Magen David Adom (£65,000); Kahal Chassidim Babov (£64,000); British Friends of Israel War Disabled (£30,000); Chai Cancer Care (£25,000); Jewish Blind and Disabled (£20,000); Youth Aliyah (£17,000); Shaare Zedak Hospital (£15,000); Norwood Children and Families First (£12,000); The Shalom Foundation and World Jewish Relief (£10,000); Jewish Museum (£5,000); Jewish Lads and Girls Brigade (£2,500); North London Hospice (£1,000); and Zionist Foundation (£250).

Applications

In writing to the correspondent.

Information gathered from:

Accounts; Charity Commission record.

The Loftus Charitable Trust

Jewish

£263,000 (2011/12)

Beneficial area

UK and overseas.

Correspondent: Anthony Loftus, Trustee, Asher House, Blackburn Road, London NW6 1AW (tel: 020 7604 5900; email: post@rhodesandrhodes.com)

Trustees: R. I. Loftus; A. L. Loftus; A. D. Loftus.

CC Number: 297664

The trust was established in 1987 by Richard Ian Loftus. Its objects are the:

- Advancement of the Jewish religion
- Advancement of Jewish education and the education of Jewish people
- Relief of the Jewish poor

In 2011/12 the trust had an income of £244,000 and made grants totalling £263,000. These were categorised as follows: relief of poverty and ill-health (£118,000); religious organisations (£54,000); and education (£91,000).

The largest grants were to: Jewish Care (£30,000); Zichron Moshe Educational and Education Trust (£25,000); United Synagogue (£22,000); and Kirsharon and Norwood (£20,000 each).

Smaller grants included those to: Community Security Trust (£15,000); Tikva Children's Home (£10,000); Nightingale and Lubavitch Foundation (£5,000 each); Magen David Adom UK (£3,000); and Project SEED (£2,500).

Applications

The trustees prefer to invite applications rather than considering unsolicited applications.

Information gathered from:

Accounts; Charity Commission record.

The Lolev Charitable Trust

Orthodox Jewish causes

£403,000 to organisations (2011)

Beneficial area

Worldwide.

Correspondent: Abraham Tager, Trustee, 14a Gilda Crescent, London N16 6JP

Trustees: Abraham Tager; Eve Tager; Michael Tager.

CC Number: 326249

The objects of the charity are the relief of the sick and needy and the support of Orthodox Jewish education.

The latest accounts available at the time of writing (December 2013) were for 2011. In this year the trust had an income of £3.7 million and assets of £6,000. The trust gave £3.7 million in grants of which £403,000 was given to organisations and £3.3 million was given to individuals.

Grants to organisations were broken down as follows:

Religious education	£219,000
Poor and needy	£108,000
Medical	£43,000
Schools (including repairs)	£36,000

Applications

In writing to the correspondent. Applications by individuals must be accompanied by a letter of recommendation by the applicant's minister or other known religious leader.

Information gathered from:

Accounts; Charity Commission record.

The London Law Trust

Medical research

£143,000 (2011/12)

Beneficial area

UK.

Correspondent: Graham Olgilvie, Correspondent, Hunters, 9 New Square, Lincoln's Inn, London WC2A 3QN (tel: 020 7412 0050; email: londonlawtrust@hunters-solicitors.co.uk; website: www.thelondonlawtrust.org)

Trustees: Prof. Anthony Mellows; Roger Pellant; Sir Michael Hobbs; Sir Ian Gainsford.

CC Number: 1115266

The London Law Trust's website states at the time of writing (October 2013) the following:

> The London Law Trust has entered into arrangements for funding medical research and leadership development programmes which are being run in conjunction with other institutions. As for the foreseeable future the trust will be applying all of its available funds on these programmes, it regrets that it is no longer able to accept any new applications for grants.

During the year 2011/12, the trustees have continued with the recently introduced the London Law Trust Medal, in association with King's College London. The fellowship is awarded for research in medicine or dentistry which is designed to impact on patient care. Candidates are selected on merit by a panel constituted by the college and including up to two trustees of the London Law Trust. Two Medals may be awarded in any year.

In 2011/12 the trust had assets of £3.9 million and an income of £143,000. Grants were made to organisations totalling £111,000. The beneficiaries were not listed in the accounts.

Previous beneficiaries have included: BRIC, British Lung Foundation, Deans and Canons of Windsor, Great Ormond Street and St George's Hospital Medical School (£5,000 each); Envision (£3,000); Activenture and Swan Syndrome (£2,500 each); and Circomedia (£1,000).

Exclusions

Applications from individuals, including students, are ineligible.

Applications

In writing to the correspondent, however funds are currently fully committed.

Information gathered from:

Accounts; Charity Commission record; funder's website.

The William and Katherine Longman Trust

General

£259,000 (2011/12)

Beneficial area

UK.

Correspondent: Mrs G. Feeney, Charles Russell LLP, 5 Fleet Place, London EC4M 7RD (tel: 020 7203 5196)

Trustees: Paul Harriman; A. C. O. Bell.

CC Number: 800785

The trust supports a wide range of organisations with grants ranging from £1,000 to £30,000 each, mostly at the lower end of the scale.

In 2011/12 it had assets of £3.2 million, which generated an income of £68,000. Grants were made totalling £259,000. Management and administration charges were relatively high at £32,000.

Past beneficiaries of grants of £10,000 or more included: Vanessa Grant Trust (£30,000); Chelsea Festival and World Child Cancer Fund (£20,000 each); Care (£12,000); and Hope Education Trust and RADA (£10,000 each).

Other beneficiaries included: Action for ME (£5,000); The Children's Society (£4,500); Age Concern – Kensington and Chelsea (£3,500); RSPCA – Harmsworth Hospital (£3,000); St Mungo's (£2,500); and Prisoners Abroad (£1,000).

Exclusions

Grants are only made to registered charities.

Applications

The trustees believe in taking a proactive approach in deciding which charities to support and it is their policy not to respond to unsolicited appeals.

Information gathered from:

Accounts; Charity Commission record.

The Loseley and Guildway Charitable Trust

General

£55,000 (2011/12)

Beneficial area

International and UK, with an interest in Guildford.

Correspondent: Miss Helen O'Dwyer, Secretary, The Estate Offices, Loseley Park, Guildford, Surrey GU3 1HS (tel: 01483 405114; fax: 01483 302036; email: charities@loseleypark.co.uk; website: www.loseley-park.com/charities)

Trustees: Maj. James More-Molyneux, Chair; Susan More-Molyneux; Michael More-Molyneux; Alexander More-Molyneux; Glye Hodson.

CC Number: 267178

The trust was founded in 1973, when 'the More-Molyneux family injected private capital and transferred five of their own properties to the trust'. The rent of these properties provides about half the trust's present income. Two of these properties have now been sold in order to finance the purchase of land on which CHASE Children's Hospice has now been built.

The trust's accounts state that: 'The objects of the charity are widely drawn to include making grants to charitable associations, trusts, societies and corporations whether they are local, national or international. The major part of the available funds tend to be distributed locally to charitable institutions which the trustees consider to be particularly worthy of support'. In effect this means that major grants tend to be given to charities with which various members of the More-Molyneux family and trustees are associated.

In 2011/12 the trust had an income of £61,000 and a total expenditure of £78,000. Grants were made grants totalling about £55,000.

Previous beneficiaries include: CHASE and Disability Challengers (£5,000 each); Brooke Hospital, Cherry Trees, Crisis, Gurkha Welfare Trust, National Society for Epilepsy, Phyllis Tuckwell Hospice, RNLI and Wells for India (£1,000 each).

Exclusions

No grants to non-registered charities.

Applications

In writing to the correspondent. The trustees meet in February, May and September to consider applications. However, due to commitments, new applications for any causes are unlikely to be successful.

Information gathered from:

Accounts; Charity Commission record; funder's website.

The Lotus Foundation

Children and families, women, community, animal protection, addiction recovery, education

£237,500 (2012)

Beneficial area

UK, especially London and Surrey; occasionally overseas.

Correspondent: Barbara Starkey, Trustee, c/o Startling Music Ltd, 90 Jermyn Street, London SW1Y 6JD

(tel: 020 7930 5133; website: www.lotusfoundation.com)

Trustees: Barbara Starkey; Richard Starkey; Emma Turner.

CC Number: 1070111

The trust was established in 1998 and aims to make grants to other established and newly-formed charities. The trust states that:

> The objectives of the Lotus Foundation are to fund, support, participate in and promote charitable projects aimed at advancing social welfare in diverse areas including, but not limited to: substance abuse, cerebral palsy, brain tumours, cancer, battered women and their children, homelessness and animals in need.

In 2012 the trust had an income of £208,500 and holds assets of £87,000. They made grants totalling £237,500 which were broken down as follows:

Substance abuse/domestic violence	5	£91,500
Medical	5	£53,000
Children/youth	11	£45,000
Community	2	£30,000
Animals	3	£16,000
Education	1	£2,000

Beneficiaries included: RAPT (£31,500); British Red Cross and ACLIM and Addaction (£25,000 each); Whizz-Kidz and Macmillan Cancer Relief (£10,000 each); Fine Cell Workers (£7,000); Scope and Variety the Children's Charity (£5,000 each); and Alone in London and Happy Days (£1,000 each).

Applications

In writing to the correspondent giving a brief outline of the work, amount required and project/programme to benefit. The trustees prefer applications which are simple and economically prepared rather than glossy 'prestige' and mail sorted brochures.

Note: In order to reduce administration costs and concentrate its efforts on the charitable work at hand, unsolicited requests will no longer be acknowledged by the foundation.

Information gathered from:

Accounts; Charity Commission record; funder's website.

The C. L. Loyd Charitable Trust

General charitable purposes

£72,000 (2011/12)

Beneficial area

UK, with a preference for local causes.

Correspondent: Thomas Loyd, Trustee, The Lockinge Estate Office, Ardington, Wantage OX12 8PP (tel: 01235 833200)

Trustees: Christopher Loyd; Thomas Loyd; Alexandra Loyd.

CC Number: 265076

The trust supports any UK charities and local charities, especially those involved in welfare, animals, churches, medical and disability, children, youth and education.

In 2011/12 the trust had assets of £2.3 million, which generated an income of £85,000. Grants were made to organisations totalling £72,000.

Grants of £1,000 or more went to eleven organisations which included: County Buildings Protection Trust (£31,000); Wantage Vale and Downland Museum (£10,000); Coldstream Guards (£5,000); Iran Liberty Association (£3,000); Christian Aid, Mango Tree and Pond Conservation (£1,000 each).

Other grants of less than £1,000 amounted to £10,000.

Exclusions

No support for individuals or medical research.

Applications

In writing to the correspondent. Grants are made several times each month.

Information gathered from:

Accounts; Charity Commission record.

Henry Lumley Charitable Trust

General charitable purposes, with a preference towards medicine, education and the relief of poverty

£132,000 (2012)

Beneficial area

UK and overseas.

Correspondent: Peter Lumley, Trustee, c/o Lutine Leisure Ltd, Windlesham Golf Club, Bagshot, Surrey GU19 5HY (tel: 01276 472273)

Trustees: Peter Lumley; Henry Lumley; James Porter; Robert Lumley.

CC Number: 1079480

Registered in February 2000, the trust's objective is to further charitable purposes in any part of the world.

In 2012 the trust had assets of £3.3 million and an income of £87,000. Grants totalling £132,000 were made to 38 organisations. Although established as a general charitable trust, grants usually cover three main areas, namely, medical, educational and relief of poverty and hardship. Grants were broken down as follows:

Medical	33	£120,500
Educational	1	£2,500
Relief of poverty and hardship	1	£2,500
Other	3	£6,000

Beneficiaries included: Royal College of Surgeons (£15,000); Royal Australasian College of Surgeons (£10,000); Stroke Association and Cancer Research UK (£5,000 each); Action on Addiction, Bowel Disease Research Foundation and Meningitis Research Fund (£4,000 each); Juvenile Diabetes Research Foundation, Outward Bound Trust and Royal Star and Garter Home for Disabled Ex-Service Men and Women (£2,500 each); and Royal School of Needlework and Wings for Life Spinal Cord Research (£1,000 each).

Applications

In writing to the correspondent.

Information gathered from:

Accounts; Charity Commission record.

Paul Lunn-Rockliffe Charitable Trust

Christianity, poverty, infirm people, youth

£43,000 (2011/12)

Beneficial area

UK and developing world.

Correspondent: James Lunn-Rockliffe, Trustee, 6A Barnes Close, Winchester, Hampshire SO23 9QX (email: plrcharitabletrust@gmail.com)

Trustees: Jacqueline Lunn-Rockliffe; James Lunn-Rockliffe; Bryan Boult.

CC Number: 264119

The 2011/12 annual report states that:

> The object of the charity is to make grants to any charity or for any charitable purpose, at the trustees discretion, but preferably to those recipients likely to further Christianity, support the relief of poverty and assist the aged and infirm.
>
> The charity has supported 70 separate charities during the year . . . [and] maintains a database of details and financial data for the charities supported. The latest financial information for recipient charities is reviewed and their achievements assessed, prior to donating further funds.
>
> The trustees have a policy of restricting the total number of recipient charities in order to ensure that each receives a more significant donation and has a preference for smaller and locally based charities, or those known to the trustees or members of their families.
>
> The trustees allocate a proportion of the funds for donation to be applied to charities not previously supported and for special one-off causes.

In 2011/12 the trust had assets of £1.4 million and an income of £205,000. Grants totalled £43,000 and were distributed as follows:

Third world	£12,400
Disabled	£4,800
Youth	£4,100
Needy, drug addicts, homeless and unemployed	£4,000
Mission	£3,600
Prisoners	£3,000
Family	£2,800
Children	£2,500
Radio/mission	£1,800
Education and students	£1,600
Others	£1,500
Aged	£1,000

Beneficiaries included: Christians Against Poverty (£1,000); Community of Holy Fire (Zimbabwe children) and Parish of St George Hanworth (£600 each); Action for Elder Abuse, Children Country Holiday Fund, Consequences, Forgiveness, Koestler Awards, Parkinson Disease Society, Shepherds Down School, Street Pastors, Under Tree Schools and Way to Life (£500 each); and Gateway Club (£300).

Exclusions

The trustees will not fund individuals; for example, student's expenses and travel grants. Repair and maintenance of historic buildings are excluded.

Applications

In writing to the correspondent. The trust will generally only reply to written correspondence if an sae has been included.

Information gathered from:

Accounts; Charity Commission record.

The Ruth and Jack Lunzer Charitable Trust

Jewish, children, young adults, education and the arts

£53,000 (2011/12)

Beneficial area

UK.

Correspondent: Martin Paisner, Trustee, c/o Berwin Leighton Paisner, Adelaide House, London Bridge, London EC4R 9HA (tel: 020 7760 1000)

Trustees: J. V. Lunzer; M. D. Paisner.

CC Number: 276201

The trust says it makes grants to organisations benefiting children, young adults and students; primarily educational establishments. In practice many such beneficiaries are Jewish organisations.

In 2011/12 the trust had assets of £513,000 and an income of £56,000. Grants to 39 organisations were made totalling £53,000.

Beneficiaries included: Yesodey Hatorah Schools (£8,500); Kahal Chassidim Boboy and Lubavich Foundation (£6,000); Chai Cancer Care and Trenhill Ltd (£3,000 each); British Friends of Ohel Sarah and Weizmann UK (£1,000 each); British Friends of Ezer Mizion and The Committee for the Rescue of Immigrant Children in Israel £500 each); Institute for Higher Rabbinical Studies (£250); and Chesdei Ephraim Ltd (£100).

Applications

In writing to the correspondent. Unsuccessful applicants are not acknowledged.

Information gathered from:

Accounts; Charity Commission record.

Lord and Lady Lurgan Trust

Medical charities, older people, children and the arts

£107,000 (2012)

Beneficial area

England, Northern Ireland and South Africa.

Correspondent: Andrew Stebbings, Trustee, 45 Cadogan Gardens, London SW3 2AQ (tel: 020 7591 3333; fax: 020 7591 3300; email: charitymanager@pglaw.co.uk; website: www.lurgantrust.org)

Trustees: Andrew Stebbings; Simon Ladd; Diana Graves; Brendan Beder.

CC Number: 297046

The trust's website states the following:

> In the UK the grants are focused on:
> - Music education
> - Education with an emphasis on the arts
> - The elderly
> - Medical research
> - Medical relief including hospice support
> - Disability with a bias towards deafness
>
> In Northern Ireland and South Africa grants are awarded rather by the trustees' perception of need, although they may reflect the general categories listed above.
>
> Grants are made at regular intervals during the year and the total level of grants annually is approximately £100,000. Grants are generally made as single payments of between £1,000 and £5,000.

In 2012 the trust had an income of £22,000 and an expenditure of £107,000. Accounts were not available from the Charity Commission's website.

Previous beneficiaries have included: Royal College of Music, English National Opera, Queen's University – Belfast, Greater Shankhill Business Forum, Deafblind UK, Help the Aged, Macmillan Cancer Relief, Oesophageal Patients Association, St Joseph's Hospice and Water Aid.

Exclusions

No grants to individuals or for expeditions. No support for organisations in Scotland.

Applications

Complete the downloadable application form which is available on the trust's website. Also read the grant policy there before completing the form. Trustees meet three or four times a year. There is no deadline for applications. All successful applications will be required to provide a written report within six months of receiving the grant.

Information gathered from:

Accounts; Charity Commission record; funder's website.

The Lyndhurst Trust

Christianity

£56,000 to organisations in the UK (2012)

Beneficial area

UK and overseas, with preferences for North East England and the developing world.

Correspondent: The Secretary, PO Box 615, North Shields NE29 1AP

Trustees: Revd Dr Robert Ward; Jane Hinton; Ben Hinton; Sally Tan.

CC Number: 235252

The trust's accounts stated:

> The trustees have continued to support opportunities to promote and advance the spreading of the Christian religion in any part of the world. The policy has been continued of supporting regularly charities that are promoting the awareness of the Christian gospel, in those areas of the World where people are prevented from hearing it through normal channels of communication. Agencies operating in difficult circumstances are given special consideration.
>
> The trustees have continued their policy of making funds available to the disadvantaged in the United Kingdom. In addition, the trustees give special consideration to charities involved in supporting members of the persecuted church around the world. Churches in the North East of England have been given increased support due to the particular needs of the communities where they are operating.

According to the trustees' report for 2012, the trust's objects are as follows:

- The maintenance or support of any body or institution having exclusively charitable objects connected to the propagation of the gospel or the promotion of the Christian religion

- The distribution of Bibles and other Christian religious works
- The establishment, maintenance or support of Christian missions whether in the United Kingdom or abroad
- The provision of clergy or the augmentation of the stipends of the clergy of any Christian denomination
- The provision or maintenance of churches or chapels of any Christian denomination or of buildings ancillary to and used in connection with such churches or chapels.

In 2012 the trust had an income of £42,000 and grants totalled £94,000, of which £56,000 went to organisations within the UK. Assets stood at £1.3 million. Grants were broken down as follows:

North East England	19	£42,000
Third World countries	8	£32,500
United Kingdom	6	£13,500
Rest of the World	3	£5,500

Grants in the UK and North East of England included: Sowing Seeds (£12,000); Junction 42 (£5,000); Lydia's House, St Luke's Church and Friends International (£3,000 each); Ichthus Christian Fellowship, Newcastle Chaplaincy and St Barnabas Church (£2,000 each); Eden North East and Healing on the Streets (£1,000 each); and Action Foundation, Blue Sky Trust and Trinity Church – Gosforth (£500 each).

Exclusions

No support for individuals or buildings.

Applications

In writing to the correspondent.

Information gathered from:

Accounts; Charity Commission record.

The Lynn Foundation

General

£248,000 (2011/12)

Beneficial area

UK and overseas.

Correspondent: Guy Parsons, Trustee, 17 Lewes Road, Haywards Heath RH17 7SP (tel: 01444 454773)

Trustees: Guy Parsons; Ian Fair; John Emmott; Philip Parsons; John Sykes.

CC Number: 326944

The trust has previously stated that it supports a very wide range of organisations, including those in the areas of music, the arts, Masonic charities, people with disabilities, older people and children.

In 2011/12 the trust had assets of £4.9 million, an income of £277,000 and made grants totalling £248,000. Grants were made to 429 organisations and totalled £248,000. Details of individual beneficiary organisations were not available, although the total was broken down as follows:

Disabled children	139	£70,000
Disabled adults	140	£70,000
Arts	9	£28,000
Music	27	£22,000
Youth sponsorship	36	£21,000
Medical research	39	£18,000
Hospices	35	£18,000
Sundry	4	£2,000

Applications

In writing to the correspondent.

Percentage of awards given to new applicants: between 20% and 30%.

Information gathered from:

Accounts; Charity Commission record; further information provided by the funder.

The Lyons Charitable Trust

Health, animals, medical research, children

£57,000 (2011/12)

Beneficial area

UK.

Correspondent: Michael Scott Gibbon, Trustee, 74 Broad Walk, London N21 3BX (tel: 020 8882 1336)

Trustees: M. Scott Gibbon; J. Scott Gibbon; G. Read; Robin Worby.

CC Number: 1045650

The trust in particular makes grants in the fields of health, medical research, animals and children in need. Historically, the same 11 charities are supported each year.

In 2011/12 it had assets of £1.6 million and an income of £66,000. Eight grants were made totalling £57,000 and all beneficiaries had previously been supported. They were: Helen House (£12,000); Streetsmart (£10,000); The Royal Marsden Hospital, Macmillan and St Thomas Hospital (£8,000 each); CLIC (£5,000); and Children with Aids and Cambridge Curwen Print Study Centre (£3,000).

Applications

The trustees have decided that the most effective method of applying the charity's resources is to make distributions to known charitable organisations.

Information gathered from:

Accounts; Charity Commission record.

The Sir Jack Lyons Charitable Trust

Jewish, arts, education

£285,000 (2011/12)

Beneficial area

UK and Israel.

Correspondent: Paul Mitchell, Gresham House, 5–7 St Pauls Street, Leeds LS1 2JG (tel: 01332 976789)

Trustees: Lady Roslyn Marion Lyons; M. J. Friedman; D. S. Lyons; Miss A. R. J. Maude-Roxby; P. D. Mitchell; Belinda Lyons-Newman.

CC Number: 212148

This trust shows a particular interest in Jewish charities and also a consistent interest in the arts, particularly music. In 2011/12 it had assets of £2.9 million and an income of £117,000. Grants were made to seven organisations totalling £285,000.

Beneficiaries included: Federation CJA (£130,000 in four grants); UJIA (£86,000 in two grants); Jerusalem Foundation (£40,000); Beit Halohem Geneva (£11,000); Yezreel Valley College (£10,000); and Jewish Institute of Music (£7,500).

Exclusions

No grants to individuals.

Applications

In writing to the correspondent. In the past the trust has stated: 'In the light of increased pressure for funds, unsolicited appeals are less welcome and would waste much time and money for applicants who were looking for funds which were not available.'

Information gathered from:

Accounts; Charity Commission record.

The M. and C. Trust

Jewish, social welfare

£362,000 (2011/12)

Beneficial area

UK.

Correspondent: Helen McKie, Correspondent, c/o Mercer and Hole Trustees Ltd, Gloucester House, 72 London Road, St Albans, Herts AL1 1NS (tel: 01727 869141)

Trustees: Rachel Lebus; Kate Bernstein; Elizabeth Marks.

CC Number: 265391

The trust's primary charitable objects are Jewish causes and social welfare.

In 2011/12 the trust had assets of £4.2 million and an income of £172,000.

24 grants totalling almost £362,000 were made.

The four largest grants went to Jerusalem Foundation (£120,000); and Jewish Care, One Voice Europe and OXPIP (£20,000 each).

Other beneficiaries included: World Jewish Relief and Connect-Communication Disability Network (£10,000 each); Helen and Douglas House, Princes Royal Trust for Carers and Refugee Resources (£7,000 each); Community Security Trust and Deafblind UK (£5,000 each); and Changing Faces and Chicken Shed Theatre Company (£3,000 each).

Exclusions

No grants to individuals.

Applications

In writing to the correspondent.

Information gathered from:

Accounts; Charity Commission record.

The M. K. Charitable Trust

Orthodox Jewish charities

£282,000 (2011/12)

Beneficial area

Unrestricted, in practice mainly UK.

Correspondent: Simon Kaufman, Trustee, 50 Keswick Street, Gateshead NE8 1TQ (tel: 01914 900140)

CC Number: 260439

This trust was established in 1966 for general charitable purposes and applies its income for the provision and distribution of grants and donations to Orthodox Jewish Charities.

In 2011/12 it had assets of £7.9 million and an income of £985,000. Grants were made totalling £282,000.

Unfortunately, no further information was available regarding the trust's grantmaking activities.

Applications

In writing to the correspondent. The trust accepts applications for grants from representatives of Orthodox Jewish charities, which are reviewed by the trustees on a regular basis.

Information gathered from:

Accounts; Charity Commission record.

The E. M. MacAndrew Trust

Health, general

£43,500 (2011/12)

Beneficial area

UK.

Correspondent: James Thornton, Administrator, J. P. Thornton and Co., The Old Dairy, Adstockfields, Adstock, Buckingham MK18 2JE (tel: 01296 714886; fax: 01296 714711)

CC Number: 290736

The trust is mainly interested in health charities and those supporting people with disabilities. In 2011/12 it had assets of £988,000 and an income of £47,000. Grants totalling £43,500 were made to 29 organisations.

Beneficiaries included: MacIntyre (£3,000); Bucks Community Foundation, Calibre Audio Library, The Pepper Foundation, Puzzle Pre School and Willen Hospice (£2,000 each); and Action Medical Research, Addington Fund, Cancer Research UK, Restore and Scannappeal (£1,000 each).

Information gathered from:

Accounts; Charity Commission record.

The Macdonald-Buchanan Charitable Trust

General charitable purposes

£180,000 (2012)

Beneficial area

UK, with a slight preference for Northamptonshire.

Correspondent: Linda Cousins, Rathbone Trust Company Ltd, 4th Floor, 1 Curzon Street, London W1J 5FB (tel: 020 7399 0820; email: linda.cousins@rathbone.com)

CC Number: 209994

The Hon. Catherine Macdonald-Buchanan set up this trust in 1952 for general charitable purposes.

In 2012 the trust had assets of £3.2 million and an income of £146,000. Grants were made to 145 organisations and totalled £180,000. The majority of these were £1,000 or less.

Overall, grants by category of the recipient charity were broken down as follows:

General welfare	£118,000
Medical and research	£22,200
Disability	£8,500
Armed forces	£7,600
Animal welfare	£6,900
Youth welfare	£5,900
Older people	£5,300
Hospices	£3,800
Religion	£3,300

Beneficiaries included: Carrijo and Orrin (£30,000 each); Racing Welfare (£29,000); AMB Charity Trust (£15,000); Royal National Lifeboat Institution (£1,300); the Gurkha Welfare Trust, the Holy Sepulchre Northampton Restoration Trust and Victim Support (£650 each); the Royal Mencap Society, the Scots Guards Association and St John's Hospice (£500 each); the National Association of Almshouses (£400); the Wordsworth Trust and International Fund for Animal Welfare (£200 each); and the James Mackaness Family Charitable Trust and Warning Zone (£50 each).

Exclusions

No grants to individuals.

Applications

In writing to the correspondent, for consideration once a year.

Information gathered from:

Accounts; Charity Commission record.

The Macfarlane Walker Trust

Education, the arts, social welfare, general

£22,000 to organisations (2011/12)

Beneficial area

UK, with priority for Gloucestershire.

Correspondent: Sophie Walker, Correspondent, 4 Shooters Hill Road, London SE3 7BD (tel: 020 8858 4701; email: sophiewalker@mac.com)

CC Number: 227890

The trustees' report for 2011/12 states:

> The Macfarlane Walker Trust was founded in 1963 by James Macfarlane of Cheltenham for general charitable purposes and in particular for provision of facilities for recreation and social welfare in Gloucestershire; the relief of poverty and hardship among employees and former employees of Walker Crosweller & Co. Ltd; the provision of educational facilities particularly in scientific research; and the encouragement of music, drama and the fine arts.

In 2011/12 the trust had assets of £661,000, an income of £27,000 and made grants totalling £22,000. 19 grants were made to organisations.

Beneficiaries included: Gloucestershire Society (£2,000); Wellchild and Cotswold Volunteers (£1,500 each); Music Alive, Under The Edge and Root and Branch (£1,000 each); Guideposts (£600); and New Brewery Arts (£500).

Exclusions

No grants for tuition fees; gap year trips; large charities; animal charities; foreign charities; or major building projects.

Applications

In writing to the correspondent.

Percentage of awards given to new applicants: between 10% and 20%.

Common applicant mistakes

'Not a problem.'

Information gathered from:

Accounts; Charity Commission record; further information provided by the funder.

The Mactaggart Third Fund

General charitable purposes

£398,000 (2011/12)

Beneficial area

UK and abroad.

Correspondent: The Trustees, 2 Babmaes Street, London SW1Y 6HD (website: www.mactaggartthirdfund.org)

SC Number: SC014285

The following information is taken from the charity's website:

> The Mactaggart Third Fund is a grant-making charity, established in 1968 by Deed of Trust granted by Western Heritable Investment Company Ltd. The objectives of the trust are to distribute funds by way of charitable donations to suitable charities in the United Kingdom and abroad. The trustees have decided to take a proactive approach to their grant-making. Their present policy is to make grants to those charities whose aims they support and who they believe have demonstrated excellence in their achievements. The trust aims to make grants of circa £250,000 each year and since its inauguration it has made grants of over £6m to a range of charitable organisations. Please note the fund does not accept unsolicited applications.

In 2011/12 it had an income of £11.9 million and expenditure was £1.2 million of which £398,000 was awarded in grants. There was no information available on beneficiary organisations for this accounting year.

Previous beneficiaries included: University of Miami (£50,000); Robin Hood Trust (£13,000); Bahamas National Trust (£11,000); Amazon Conservation Team (£8,000); Mactaggart Community Cybercafé (£7,000); Terrence Higgins Trust (£5,000); Hearing Dogs for Deaf People (£4,000); Harris Manchester College (£2,000); Greatwood (£1,000); and Diabetes UK (£100).

Applications

The fund's website states:

> The trustees are solely responsible for the choice of charitable organisations to be supported. Trustees are proactive in seeking out charities to support and all projects are chosen on the initiative of the trustees. Unsolicited applications are not supported.

Information gathered from:

Accounts; OSCR record; funder's website.

Ian Mactaggart Trust

Education and training, culture, welfare and disability

£373,000 (2011/12)

Beneficial area

UK, with a preference for Scotland.

Correspondent: The Trustees, 2 Babmaes Street, London SW1Y 6HD (website: www.ianmactaggarttrust.org)

SC Number: SC012502

The Ian Mactaggart Trust is a grantmaking charity, established in 1984. The objectives of the trust are to distribute funds by way of charitable donations to suitable charities in the United Kingdom and abroad. The trustees have decided to take a proactive approach to their grantmaking. Their present policy is to make grants to those charities whose aims they support and who they believe have demonstrated excellence in their achievements.

In 2011/12 the trust had an unusually high income of £8.7 million recorded on the OSCR's website, (it is normally around £500,000). This was approximately what was declared as assets in the previous accounts. Grants to organisations were made totalling £373,000.

Previous beneficiaries included: Slough Immigration Aid Unit (£31,000); Robin Hood Foundation (£22,000); Alzheimer's Society (£21,000); Oxfordshire Community Foundation (£20,000); Eagle Hill Foundation (£13,000); Game and Wildlife Conservation Trust (£10,000); Rights of Women (£5,000); Millbrook Early Childhood Education Centre (£3,000); Medical Foundation for the Victims of Torture (£2,500); Breakthrough Breast Cancer (£2,000); Dragon School Trust Ltd (£1,000); and Ashmolean Museum (£750).

Applications

The trustees are committed to seeking out charitable organisations that they wish to support and therefore they do not respond to unsolicited applications.

Information gathered from:

Accounts; OSCR record; funder's website.

James Madison Trust

The study of federal government

Around £170,000 (2011/12)

Beneficial area

UK.

Correspondent: David Grace, Correspondent, 68 Furnham Road, Chard TA20 1AP (tel: 01460 67368)

CC Number: 1084835

'The objects of the charity are to support and promote studies of federal government whether within or among states and of related subjects, including the processes that may lead towards the establishment of such government, and to support or promote education and dissemination of knowledge of these subjects. These objects govern all decisions of trustees without the need for further specific annual objectives.'

In 2011/12 the trust had an income of £9,000 and a total expenditure of £185,000. No further information was available.

Previous beneficiary organisations have included: University of Kent, Federal Trust, University of Edinburgh, Unlock Democracy, University of Middlesex, London Metropolitan University, and University of Cardiff.

The trust has also usefully broken down grant totals according to project, as well as by recipient organisations. Previous projects funded by grants have included: Comparative Devolution, Centre for Federal Studies, Federal Trust Projects, Additional Constitutionalism, Autonomy Website, Regions of England, European Foreign and Security Policy, Welsh Papers, Climate Change Research and Book of Federal Studies 06.

Applications
In writing to the correspondent.

Information gathered from:
Accounts; Charity Commission record.

The Magen Charitable Trust

Education, welfare, health with preference to Jewish causes

£92,000 (2011/12)

Beneficial area
UK.

Correspondent: The Trustees, New Riverside, 439 Lower Broughton, Salford M7 2FX (tel: 01617 922626)

Trustees: Jacob Halpern; Rosa Halpern.

CC Number: 326535

The trust's objects are for the relief of poverty; supporting educational establishments; and supporting religious education.

In 2011/12 the trust had assets of £1.45 million and an income of £136,000. Grants were made totalling £92,000. There was no list of grant recipients included in the accounts.

Previous beneficiaries have included Manchester Yeshiva Kollel, Talmud Educational Trust, Bnos Yisroel School and Mesifta Tiferes Yisroel.

Applications
In writing to the correspondent.

Information gathered from:
Accounts; Charity Commission record.

Mageni Trust

Arts

£53,000 (2011/12)

Beneficial area
UK.

Correspondent: Garfield Collins, Trustee, 5 Hyde Vale, Greenwich SE10 8QQ (tel: 020 8469 2683; email: garfcollins@gmail.com)

Trustees: Garfield Collins; Gillian Collins; Alex Collins.

CC Number: 1070732

In 2011/12 the trust had assets of £1.1 million, an income of £27,000 and made grants to the total of £53,000.

Beneficiaries included: Charities Aid Foundation (£10,000); British Red Cross, Esther Benjamins Trust and LPO Thomas Beecham Group (£5,000 each); National Theatre (£2,500); Foundation for Young Musicians (£2,000); Medicine Sans Frontier and RNLI (£1,000 each); Primavera (£600); and Care International (£500).

Applications
In writing to the correspondent.

Percentage of awards given to new applicants: between 10% and 20%.

Common applicant mistakes
'Assuming that this small fund has unlimited resources.'

Information gathered from:
Accounts; Charity Commission record; further information provided by the funder.

The Mahavir Trust (also known as the K. S. Mehta Charitable Trust)

General, medical, animal welfare, relief of poverty, overseas aid, religion

£276,000 (2011/12)

Beneficial area
UK.

Correspondent: Jay Mehta, Trustee, 19 Hillersdon Avenue, Edgware, Middlesex HA8 7SG (tel: 020 8958 4883; email: mahavirtrust@googlemail.com)

Trustees: Jay Mehta; Nemish Mehta; Pravinchandra Mehta; Pushpa Mehta; Kumar Mehta; Sheena Mehta Sabharwal; Sangita Mehta.

CC Number: 298551

Established in 1987, this trust operates with a Jain philosophy.

In 2011/12 the trust had assets of £334,000 and an income of £274,000 mainly from donations and gifts. Grants totalled £276,000 and were broken down as follows:

Land and property donated	£147,000
Promoting Jain religion	£103,000
Medical services	£10,000
Promote vegetarianism and humane behaviour towards animals	£5,300
Rehabilitation of children with disabilities	£5,300
Advancement of education	£4,300
Disaster relief	£500
Community welfare and interfaith	£500
Poverty relief	£100

Beneficiaries included: Shantiniketan Ltd (£147,000); Mahavir Foundation Ltd UK (£61,000); Shivanand Mission Virpur India (£3,400); Samast Mahajan Mumbai India (£3,300); and Jain Vishwa Bharti UK (£1,200).

Applications
In writing to the correspondent.

Information gathered from:
Accounts; Charity Commission record.

Malbin Trust

Jewish causes, general charitable purposes, social welfare

£72,000 (2010/11)

Beneficial area
Worldwide.

Correspondent: Benjamin Leitner, Trustee, 8 Cheltenham Crescent, Salford M7 4FP (tel: 01617 927343)

Trustees: Benjamin Leitner; Benjamin Leitner; Jehuda Waldman; Margaret Leitner.

CC Number: 1045174

The latest accounts available for this trust were from 2010/11. In this year the trust held assets of £436,000 and had an income of £65,000. Grants totalled £72,000 and the trust also has investments to provide long-term support for orphaned children. Donations are also given to support families following childbirth.

A list of beneficiaries was not included with the accounts.

Applications
In writing to the correspondent.

Information gathered from:
Accounts; Charity Commission record.

The Mandeville Trust

General charitable purposes, health and young people

Around £8,000 (2011/12)

Beneficial area
UK.

Correspondent: Robert Mandeville, Trustee, The Hockett, Hockett Lane, Cookham, Maidenhead SL6 9UF (tel: 01628 484272)

Trustees: Robert Mandeville; Pauline Mandeville; Dr Justin Mandeville; Peter Murcott.

CC Number: 1041880

In 2011/12 the trust had an income of £10,000 and a total expenditure of £8,000. Due to the trust's low income no further information was available.

Previous beneficiaries have included: University College London and Imperial College for research purposes; and the Berkshire Community Foundation.

Applications
In writing to the correspondent.

Information gathered from:
Accounts; Charity Commission record.

Maranatha Christian Trust

Christian, relief of poverty and education of young people

£106,000 (2011/12)

Beneficial area

UK and overseas.

Correspondent: The Secretary, 208 Cooden Drive, Bexhill-On-Sea TN39 3AH

Trustees: Alan Bell; Lyndon Bowring; Viscount Crispin Brentford.

CC Number: 265323

The trust was established in 1972. According to the trustees' report for 2011/12, the objects of the charity are to aid 'the promotion of education among young persons and the relief of poverty, particularly among those professing the Christian religion or working to promote such religion'.

In 2011/12 the trust had assets of £957,000 and an income of £27,000. Grants were made totalling £106,000.

Beneficiaries included: CARE (£5,000); Cafe Africa Trust (£3,000); Concordis International (£2,500); and Ashburnham Christian Trust and Stewards Trust (£2,000 each).

Applications

In writing to the correspondent.

Information gathered from:

Accounts; Charity Commission record.

Marbeh Torah Trust

Jewish education and religion, and the relief of poverty

£223,000 (2012)

Beneficial area

UK and Israel.

Correspondent: Moishe Elzas, Trustee, 116 Castlewood Road, London N15 6BE

Trustees: Jacob Elzas; Moishe Elzas; Simone Elzas.

CC Number: 292491

The trust's objects are to further and support Orthodox Jewish education and religion, as well as the relief of poverty. The trust primarily supports Jewish educational establishments. The trust aims to continue to provide funds for Jewish educational establishments.

In 2012 the trust had an income of £228,000, assets of £2,500 and made grants totalling £223,000.

Beneficiaries included: Yeshiva Marbeh Torah (£124,000); Chazon Avraham Yitzchak (£34,000); Tashbar (£19,000); Yad Gershon (£17,000); Mishkenos Yaakov (£8,000); Torah Bezalel (£6,000); Beis Dovid (£1,000); and British Friends of Igud Hokollim (£300).

Exclusions

Mainly Jewish causes.

Applications

In writing to the correspondent.

Information gathered from:

Accounts; Charity Commission record.

The Marcela Trust

Medical research, environment and animals

£270,000 (2011/12)

Beneficial area

UK.

Correspondent: Josephine Paxton, OMC Investments Ltd, 2nd Floor, 14 Buckingham Street, London WC2N 6DF (tel: 020 7925 8095)

Trustees: Brian Groves; Dawn Rose; Dr Martin Lenz; Mark Spragg.

CC Number: 1127514

The trust was established in 2009 for general charitable purposes. All of the trust's income comes from OMC Investments Ltd – two of the trustees, Dawn Rose and Brian Groves, are also directors of OMC. Donations may be made to the trust by the company for restricted purposes, i.e. to then be awarded to specific organisations.

In 2011/12 the trust had assets of £65.8 million and an income of over £5.8 million. Grants were made totalling £270,000 to two organisations. They were: Fauna and Flora International (£170,000); and Consensus Action on Salt and Health (£100,000).

Applications

In writing to the correspondent, although potential applicants should be aware that grant recipients may be pre-determined by the directors of OMC Investments Ltd.

Information gathered from:

Accounts; Charity Commission record.

Marchig Animal Welfare Trust

Animal welfare

£595,000 (2012)

Beneficial area

Worldwide.

Correspondent: Alastair Keatinge, Trustee, Caledonian Exchange, 10A Canning Street, Edinburgh EH3 8HE (tel: 01316 565746; email: info@marchigtrust.org; website: www.marchigtrust.org)

Trustees: Colin Moor; Les Ward; Dr Jerzy Mlotkiewicz; Alastair Keatinge; Janice McLoughlin.

CC Number: 802133

The Marchig Animal Welfare Trust was established in 1989 by the late Madam Jeanne Marchig of Geneva for nature and animals and in memory of her husband, the painter Giannino Marchig.

The trustees' report for 2012 states that the objects of the charity are:

> To encourage initiatives designed to improve animal welfare, promote alternative methods to the use of animals in experiments and their practical implications and encourage practical work in alleviating suffering, preventing cruelty and improving conditions for animals.

Projects supported by the trust have included mobile spay/neuter clinics, alternatives to the use of animals in research, poster campaigns, anti-poaching programmes, establishment of veterinary hospitals, clinics and animal sanctuaries. There are no restrictions on the geographical area of work, types of grants or potential applicants, but all applications must be related to animal welfare and be of direct benefit to animals.

The trust's website states the following:

> All applications meeting the following criteria will be considered by the trust:
>
> - Those encouraging initiatives designed to improve animal welfare
> - Those promoting alternative methods to animal experimentation and their practical implementation
> - Those promoting and encouraging practical work in alleviating suffering and preventing cruelty to animals
>
> As well as giving grants, the trust also makes Jeanne Marchig Awards. These awards, which take the form of a financial donation in support of the winner's animal welfare work, are given in either of the following two categories: (a) the development of an alternative method to the use of animals in experimental procedures and the practical implementation of such an alternative resulting in a significant reduction in the number of animals used in experimental procedures; (b) practical work in the field of animal welfare resulting in significant improvements for animals either nationally or internationally.

In 2012 the trust had assets of £18.2 million, an income of £1 million and made grants totalling £595,000.

UK beneficiaries included: Freshfield Animal Rescue Centre; Prevent Unwanted Pets; Farm Animal and Bird Sanctuary Trust; Rain Rescue; Society for Abandoned Animals; and Save Our Strays.

Non-UK beneficiaries included: Gozo SPCA – Malta; Aegean Wildlife Hospital – Greece; Kleinmond Animal Welfare Society – South Africa; Dog and Cat Rescue Samui – Thailand; Free the Bears – Australia; Chats de Quercy – France; Animal House – Jamaica; and McKee Project – Costa Rica.

Exclusions

The trust will reject any application failing to meet its criteria. Additionally, applications relating to educational studies or other courses, expeditions, payment of salaries, support of conferences and meetings, or activities that are not totally animal welfare related, will also be rejected.

Applications

On an application form available from the correspondent or via the website. Entries should be submitted by email or via post. Full support documentation must be submitted with the form. Applications are accepted throughout the year.

Information gathered from:

Accounts; Charity Commission record; funder's website.

The Stella and Alexander Margulies Charitable Trust

Jewish, general charitable purposes

£470,000 (2011/12)

Beneficial area

UK.

Correspondent: Leslie Michaels, Trustee, 34 Dover Street, London W1S 4NG

Trustees: Martin Paisner; Sir Stuart Lipton; Alexander Sorkin; Marcus Margulies; Leslie Michaels.

CC Number: 220441

Established in 1962, the trust has general charitable purposes, with a preference for Jewish organisations. The trustees search out appropriate projects to fulfil the objectives of the trust and grants are made at their discretion. A significant project with The Jerusalem Foundation has now commenced and is expected to be completed in June 2011.

In 2011/12 it had assets of £7.5 million and an income of £151,000. Grants were made to 20 organisations totalling £470,000. The largest grants were awarded to Shaare Zedek (£236,000); and Jerusalem Foundation – Har Herzl (£187,000).

Beneficiaries included: Royal Opera House Foundation and Alma Hebrew College (£25,000 each); Chief Rabbinate Trust and B'nai B'rith Hillel Foundation (£5,000 each); Nightingale House (£2,000); Jewish Literary Trust and Jewish Association of Business Ethics (£1,000 each); Beaconsfield Talking Papers and Cancer Research UK (£500 each); and Lolev Charitable Trust (£200).

Exclusions

Mainly Jewish causes.

Applications

In writing to the correspondent.

Information gathered from:

Accounts; Charity Commission record.

Mariapolis Ltd

Christian ecumenism, young people and families

£155,000 (2011/12)

Beneficial area

UK and overseas.

Correspondent: Rumold Van Geffen, Correspondent, 57 Twyford Avenue, London W3 9PZ (tel: 020 8992 7666; email: rumold1949@gmail.com)

Trustees: Barry Redmond; Manfred Kochinky.

CC Number: 257912

According to the trust's Summary Information Return for 2011/12, the charity's principal aims are the following:

- Relief of poverty, sickness and old age
- Advancement of education
- Promotion of higher standards of moral life in the individual, the family and the community
- Advancement of religion.

The trust promotes the international Focolare Movement in the UK, and grantmaking is only one area of its work. It works towards a united world and its activities focus on peace and cooperation. It has a related interest in ecumenism and also in overseas development. Activities include organising conferences and courses, and publishing books and magazines.

There was little financial information available, however the trust did state that it provided £155,000 in grants to support the network of communities in which it works.

Previous beneficiaries have included: Pia Associazione Maschile Opera di Maria; family welfare grants; Anglican Priests Training Fund; and Focolare Trust.

Applications

In writing to the correspondent.

Information gathered from:

Accounts; Charity Commission record.

The Michael Marks Charitable Trust

Culture, environment

£133,000 (2011/12)

Beneficial area

UK and overseas.

Correspondent: Lady Marina Marks, 5 Elm Tree Road, London NW8 9JY (tel: 020 7286 4633)

Trustees: Lady Marina Marks; Prof. Sir Christopher White; Noel Annesley.

CC Number: 248136

The trust supports the arts (including galleries and museums), and environmental groups, with grants generally ranging from £1,000 to £25,000, although larger grants have been given.

In 2011/12 it had assets of £5.8 million and an income of £178,000. Grants were given to 17 organisations totalling £133,000.

Beneficiaries included: British Library (£19,000); The Burlington Magazine (£15,000); The Bach Choir, Suffolk Wildlife Trust and Woodland Trust (£10,000 each); Canterbury Cathedral (£9,000); St Pancras Community Trust (£7,700); London Zoological Society (£6,000); Oxford Philomusica Trust (£5,000); National Library of Scotland (£4,300); Benaki Museum and Harvard Centre of Hellenic Studies (£3,000); Campaign for the Protection of Rural England (£2,000); and Greek Archaeological Committee (UK) (£500).

Exclusions

Grants are given to registered charities only. No grants to individuals or profit organisations.

Applications

In writing to the correspondent. Applications should include audited accounts, information on other bodies approached and details of funding obtained. The trustees meet twice a year, usually in January and July, to consider applications. Requests will not receive a response unless they have been successful.

Information gathered from:

Accounts; Charity Commission record.

The Ann and David Marks Foundation

Jewish causes, health, education and welfare of communities, humanitarian aid

£44,500 (2012)

Beneficial area

Worldwide.

Correspondent: David Marks, Trustee, Mutley Properties Ltd, Mutley House, 1 Ambassador Place, Stockport Road, Altrincham WA15 8DB (tel: 01619 413183; email: davidmarks@mutleyproperties.co.uk)

Trustees: A. Marks; A. Marks; G. Marks; David Marks; Marcelle Palmer.

CC Number: 326303

The trust mainly supports Jewish charities, especially in the Manchester area. The Charity Commission website states at the time of writing (October 2013) that the trust's objectives are 'to promote and support health, education and welfare of communities. It also supports humanitarian aid when required.'

It has a number of regular commitments and prefers to distribute to charities known to the trustees.

In 2012 the foundation had assets of £574,000 and an income of £29,000. Grants totalled £44,500. Unfortunately a list of grants was unavailable, although the trustees' report for 2012 states that the following organisation was a beneficiary: Finchley Jewish Primary Trust – Morasha (£20,000).

Applications

Previous research suggested that the trust's funds are mostly committed and unsolicited applications are not welcome.

Information gathered from:

Accounts; Charity Commission record.

The Hilda and Samuel Marks Foundation

Jewish, general

£178,000 (2011/12)

Beneficial area

UK and Israel.

Correspondent: David Marks, Trustee, 1 Ambassador Place, Stockport Road, Altrincham, Cheshire WA15 8DB (tel: 01619 413183; email: davidmarks@mutleyproperties.co.uk)

Trustees: David Marks; Samuel Marks; Hilda Marks; Rochelle Selby.

CC Number: 245208

The foundation mainly gives support to UK charities and to charities based in Israel. The 2011/12 annual report states that: 'The object of the foundation is to provide relief and assistance to poor and needy persons; for the advancement of education, religion or for other purposes beneficial to the community.'

Furthermore: 'As stated in previous years, the foundation has supported a number of organisations on a long-term basis.'

In 2011/12 the foundation had assets of £3.1 million and an income of £111,000. Grants totalling £178,000 were made during the year.

A list of beneficiaries was unavailable, however grants were broken down as follows:

Community/education	£64,000	35.9%
Health	£58,000	32.5%
Welfare	£56,000	31.6%

Exclusions

No grants to individuals.

Applications

The trust primarily supports projects known to the trustees and its funds are fully committed. Therefore unsolicited applications are not being sought.

Information gathered from:

Accounts; Charity Commission record.

Marmot Charitable Trust

General charitable purposes, 'green' organisations, conflict resolution

£77,000 (2011/12)

Beneficial area

Worldwide.

Correspondent: Bevis Gillett, Trustee, c/o BM Marmot, London WC1N 3XX

Trustees: Bevis Gillett; Jonathan Gillett; Jeanni Barlow.

CC Number: 1106619

The trust was registered with the Charity Commission in November 2004. The trust makes grants for general charitable purposes. The trustees' report for 2011/12 states that:

> In practice, a policy reflecting the interests of the settlors has been implemented along with the interests of the late David Gillett, who left a major legacy to the trust. There is a concentration on 'green' organisations that support changes that will pave the way for a sustainable future. In addition, there is an interest in supporting peace and security organisations; in particular those that are working on nuclear disarmament and non-proliferation.

In 2011/12 the trust had assets of £2.8 million and an income of £102,000. Grants totalling £77,000 were made to 23 organisations.

Beneficiaries included: Unit for Research into Changing Institutions (£15,000); Organic Research Centre (£7,000); Centre for Alternative Technology- Zero Carbon Britain Appeal (£5,000); Earth Resources Research- Nuclear Research for Parliamentarians and War on Want-Stamp Out Poverty (£4,000 each); Margaret Hayman Charitable Trust and Missionary Society of St Columban (£2,000 each); Christian Peace Education Fund and Quaker Service Memorial Trust (£500 each).

Applications

The trust has informed us directly that they do not accept unsolicited applications.

Common applicant mistakes

'Assuming that because our name appears in various directories and on the Charity Commission website that we would consider an application for funding.'

Information gathered from:

Accounts; Charity Commission record; further information provided by the funder.

The Marr-Munning Trust

Overseas aid

£316,000 (2011/12)

Beneficial area

Indian Subcontinent, South-East Asia and Sub-Saharan Africa.

Correspondent: James Fitzpatrick, Executive Director, 9 Madeley Road, Ealing, London W5 2LA (tel: 020 8998 7747; fax: 020 8998 9593; email: info@marrmunningtrust.org.uk; website: www.marrmunningtrust.org.uk)

Trustees: Glen Barnham; Marianne Elliott; Guy Perfect; Pierre Thomas; Martin Sarbicki; Dr Geetha Oommen.

CC Number: 261786

The trust was founded in 1970 by the late Frank Harcourt-Munning. An extract from the trust's 2011/12 accounts encapsulate its purposes:

> To support charities giving overseas aid ... for the relief of poverty suffering and distress particularly among the inhabitants of territories which are economically underprivileged through want of development or of support of the necessities of life or of those commodities and facilities which enhance human existence enriched by education and free from the threat of poverty, disease, under nourishment or starvation.

Policies and Priorities

We wish to make a real difference to the lives of people in some of the poorest communities in the world and believe that the most long-lasting solutions are likely to be those rooted in the communities themselves. To make every penny count we prioritise applications from registered, independent non-governmental organisations with an annual income of no more than £1 million.

The trust does this by:

- Supporting organisations working in the Indian Subcontinent, South-East Asia or Sub-Saharan Africa
- Supporting projects which focus on children's education – with a preference for primary and pre-primary education
- Skills training for adults which will directly increase their ability to earn a living for themselves and their families. Under this category the trust stresses that they will not fund capital projects (such as irrigation or sanitation) which do not improve the livelihood skills of local people

Applicants can have their headquarters in any country provided the funds which they are applying for are for use in a country in the specified areas.

Types of grants

- Project costs – full or part-funding of projects. In part-funding cases you must be able to show how the rest of the costs will be met
- Capital costs and revenue costs – you must explain how you will sustain the running and maintenance costs after the grant has been spent
- Grants are generally made over 2-year periods or longer in exceptional cases

The trustees have continued to support a number of projects on an ongoing basis as well as funding new applicants and making one-off grants.

In 2011/12 the trust had assets of £12.4 million and an income of £651,000. Grants totalling £316,000 were made to organisations working overseas and were broken down as follows:

Educational support	£165,000
Self-sustaining projects	£56,000
Food and shelter	£53,000
Healthcare projects	£24,000
Natural disaster response	£17,000
Wateraid and wells	£1,000

Major beneficiaries were: Marr-Munning Ashram (£23,000); Gram Niyojan Kendra (£18,000); and Friends of Ibba Girls' School (£15,000).

Recipients of smaller grants included: Woodford Foundation (£10,000); The Joe Homan Charity (£8,800); Kasilsi Porridge Project (£6,000); Children in Crisis (£4,000); World Wide Cancer (£3,000); Seeds for Africa (£2,000); and Ebenezer Woman Welfare Sangam (£1,900).

Exclusions

No grants to individuals or for work taking place outside the defined beneficial area (Indian Subcontinent, South-East Asia and Sub-Saharan Africa). No retrospective funding.

Applications

The trust has an application form available on its website. Completed forms should be emailed to the trust. The trust no longer accepts applications not made on their application form.

Applicants must submit the following supporting documentation:

- A copy of the organisation's most recent audited accounts
- A copy of the governing document
- If an NGO or charitable organisation based outside the UK, a copy of your registration certificate

Applicants may also, if they wish, supply further information which they think may help the trustees make their decision, for example, a recent annual report, business plan, project plan, newsletter or newspaper report about your project. If you supply an email address the trust will acknowledge receipt of your application and the outcome. Do not send CDs or memory sticks. Applications are typically reviewed twice yearly and precise dates will be published on the trust's website. No feedback for unsuccessful applicants.

More detailed application guidelines, including common reasons why applications are unsuccessful, are available from the website.

Information gathered from:

Accounts; Charity Commission record; funder's website.

The Marsh Christian Trust

General charitable purposes, with a preference towards social welfare, environmental causes, health, education, arts, animal welfare, and overseas appeals

£213,000 (2011/12)

Beneficial area

UK.

Correspondent: Brian Marsh, Trustee, 36 Broadway, London SW1H 0BH (tel: 020 7233 3112; website: www.marshchristiantrust.org)

Trustees: Brian Marsh; Natalie Marsh; L. Ryan; Antonia Marsh; Camilla Kenyon; Charles Micklewright.

CC Number: 284470

According to the trust's website:

> The Marsh Christian Trust was founded by Brian Marsh in 1981 based on the Christian principles of reaching out, caring for the natural world and helping those in need. These principles continue to remain a core part of the charity's ethos and it provides support on this basis which is distinctly inclusive of all organisations, including those of other faiths or no faith.

Its main areas are as follows: social welfare; environmental causes; health care and medical research; education and training; arts and heritage; animal welfare; and overseas appeals.

In 2011/12 the trust had assets of £7 million and an income of £619,000. Grants and awards were made to 263 organisations and totalled £213,000. Grants/awards were broken down as follows:

Social and welfare	£99,000
Literature, arts and heritage	£65,000
Environmental causes and animal welfare	£41,000
Education and training	£7,000
Healthcare and medical research	£1,200

Beneficiaries included: English Speaking Union of the Commonwealth (£6,500); Butterfly Conservation (£2,500); Refugee Council (£2,000); Bible Reading Fellowship and Ataxia UK (£1,000 each); Born Free Foundation and Seven Stories (£800 each); Clean Rivers Trust and the Fircroft Trust (£700 each); Barnabus, Barnardo's, Church Mission Society and Children's Country Holidays Fund (£500 each); Disability Challengers and Mother's Union (£400 each); the Holly Lodge Centre and the Queen Alexandra Hospital Home (£300 each); Amnesty International, Housing Justice and Marie Curie Cancer Care (£250 each); Zoological Society of London (£100); English Heritage (£80); National Army Museum (£50); and NADFAS (£10).

Exclusions

The trust's website states that:

- No grants are made to individuals or towards individual sponsorship proposals
- No funding is provided for building work or individual restoration projects
- No funding is provided to individual churches, as the Trustees consider it is the responsibility of congregations and the church to maintain these
- No funding is provided for individual hospices or hospitals, as the Trustees consider it is the responsibility of the local and national community to maintain these

Applications

In writing to the correspondent. Applications should be one or two sides of A4 plus a copy of the most recent set of accounts. Applications can be made at any point throughout the year.

Percentage of awards given to new applicants: less than 10%.

Common applicant mistakes

'Do not research the type of funding we provide.'

Information gathered from:

Accounts; Charity Commission record; further information provided by the funder; funder's website.

The Jim Marshall Charitable Trust

Children and young people, disabilities, local communities

£30,500 (2012)

Beneficial area

Milton Keynes.

Correspondent: The Trustees, Simpson Wreford and Co., Wellesley House, Duke of Wellington Avenue, London SE18 6SS (tel: 020 8317 6460)

Trustees: Jonathon Ellery; Kenneth Saunders; Richard Willis; David Cole.

CC Number: 328118

Established in 1989 by the founder of Marshall Amplification plc, this trust supports organisations concerned with children, young people, families and people who are sick or have disabilities and the local community generally. Grants are also made directly to individuals.

In 2012 the trust had an income of £3 million and had assets of £3.1 million. Grants totalling £30,500 were made to organisations. A total of £4,500 was made in grants of £1,000 or less.

Beneficiaries included: MK Lions Basketball Club (£10,000); Willen Hospice (£5,000); and Action 4 Youth and MK Victors Boxing Club (£3,000 each).

Applications

In writing to the correspondent at any time. Applications will only be considered for those charitable organisations benefiting communities in and around Milton Keynes.

Information gathered from:

Accounts; Charity Commission record.

The Charlotte Marshall Charitable Trust

Roman Catholic, general

£75,000 (2011/12)

Beneficial area

UK.

Correspondent: The Trustees, Sidney Little Road, Churchfields Industrial Estate, St Leonards on Sea, East Sussex TN38 9PU (tel: 01424 856655)

Trustees: Elizabeth Cosgrave; Joseph Cosgrave; Kevin Page; John Russell; Rachel Cosgrave.

CC Number: 211941

The trust has general charitable purposes in the UK, mainly supporting educational, religious and other charitable purposes for Roman Catholics.

In 2011/12 the trust had assets of £520,000 and an income of £77,000. During the year, grants were made to organisations and totalled £75,000. Of this, over £50,000 went towards Roman Catholic activities in the UK. Grants were further broken down as follows:

Disability and illness	21	£18,500
Needy and underprivileged	12	£17,000
Education	5	£16,000
Other	7	£10,000
Parents and children/young people	3	£7,500
Homelessness	3	£6,000
Abuse addiction, refugee and torture	1	£1,250

Beneficiaries included: Sacred Heart Primary School (£5,000); Society of St Vincent de Paul (£3,500); Catholic Trust for England and Wales and Kent Association for the Blind (£2,000 each); African Swahili Community Project in the UK and The Clock Tower Sanctuary (£1,500 each); 4Sight, Demelza House Children's Hospice, Pett Level Rescue Boat Association and St John Ambulance Sussex (£1,000 each); and Pestalozzi and St Wilfrid's Hospice (£500 each).

Exclusions

No grants are given to individuals.

Information gathered from:

Accounts; Charity Commission record.

John Martin's Charity

Religious activity, relief-in-need, education

£210,000 to schools and organisations (2012/13)

Beneficial area

Evesham and 'certain surrounding villages' only.

Correspondent: John Daniels, Clerk, 16 Queen's Road, Evesham, Worcestershire WR11 4JN (tel: 01386 765440; email: enquiries@johnmartins.org.uk; website: www.johnmartins.org.uk)

Trustees: Nigel Lamb; John Smith; Richard Emson; Cyril Scorse; Revd Andrew Spurr; Diana Raphael; Josephine Sandalls; Joyce Turner; Julie Westlake; John Wilson; Revd Mark Binney; Catherine Evans; Gabrielle Falkiner.

CC Number: 527473

The charity was created following the death of John Martin of Hampton, Worcestershire in 1714. His property was left for the benefit of local residents, and over the years some of this property has been sold to generate income to enable the charity to carry out its objectives in accordance with his wishes. It was formally registered with the Charity Commission in 1981.

The overall aim of the charity is to benefit the residents of the town and neighbourhood of Evesham, Worcestershire. It does this through the implementation of four specific aims:

- Religious support – to assist the Vicars and Parochial Church Councils within the town of Evesham
- Relief in need – to assist individuals and organisations within the town of Evesham who are in conditions of need, hardship and distress
- Promotion of education – to promote education to persons who are or have a parent residing within the town of Evesham and to provide benefits to schools within Evesham
- Health – the trustees have wide ranging authority within the scheme to provide such charitable purposes as they see fit, for either assisting beneficiaries within the town of Evesham or within the immediate neighbourhood. The trustees currently utilise this authority to support people with chronic health problems and other related health issues

In 2012/13 the charity had assets of £20.5 million and an income of £749,000. Grants were made to 25 organisations (including schools) totalling £210,000, broken down as follows:

Religious support	3	£69,000
Relief in need	8	£67,000
Promotion of education	13	£54,000
Health	1	£20,000

Beneficiaries included: St Andrews Parochial Church Council Hampton (£31,000); Heart of England Mencap and St Richard's Hospice (£20,000 each); St Peter's Parochial Church Council Bengeworth and All Saints Parochial Church Council Evesham (£19,000 each); South Worcestershire Citizens Advice (£12,000); Evesham and District Mental Health (£10,000); Evesham Shop Mobility (£6,500); Acquired Aphasia Trust (£5,000); Evesham Methodist Church (£3,000); Life Education Centre (£1,500); and Youth Music Festival (£500).

Grants were also made to individuals across all four categories totalling £428,000.

Exclusions

No grants for the payment of rates or taxes, or otherwise to replace statutory benefits.

Applications

Grant applications are considered from organisations in, or supporting, the town of Evesham where the requested support is considered to fit within the governing schemes of the charity. Details of the application procedure for individuals are also contained on the trust's website.

There is no limit on the amount of grants that an organisation can apply for but trustees cannot commit to renewals. Requests are considered for both capital items and general expenditure, including project costs. Organisations which show self-help or those which give valid reasons why alternative sources of finance are not available will be given preference.

Forms are available from the correspondent or via the website. Applicants are asked to provide the following with their application: the latest set of annual accounts; latest bank statement showing the current balance and name of the organisation; any relevant literature about the organisation e.g. a leaflet or flyer.

The annual closing dates for applications are as follows: 1 June, 1 September, 20 November and 1 March.

Information gathered from:

Accounts; Charity Commission record; funder's website.

The Mason Porter Charitable Trust

Christian, health

£85,000 (2011/12)

Beneficial area

UK.

Correspondent: The Secretary, Liverpool Charity and Voluntary Services, 151 Dale Street, Liverpool L2 2AH (tel: 01512 275177)

Trustees: Sue Newton, Chair; Mark Blundell; Dil Daly; Adeyinka Olushonde; Charles Feeny; William Fulton; Prof. Phillip Love; Andrew Lovelady; Christine Reeves; Hilary Russell; Heather Akehurst; Perminder Bal.

CC Number: 255545

The trust supports mainly Christian causes in the UK, including those which provide relief or missionary work overseas.

In 2011/12 the trust had assets of £1.7 million, an income of £91,000 and gave grants totalling £85,000.

Grants of £1,000 and over were made to: St Luke's Methodist Church Hoylake (£23,000); Abernethy Trust Ltd (£10,500); Cliff College (£10,000); St John's Hospice in Wirral (£7,000); Proclaim Trust, ECG Trust and Just Care (£5,000 each); and Sisters of Jesus Way; One Rock International; Messengers and Crusade for World Revival (£1,000 each).

Applications

The trust states that it only makes grants to charities known to the settlor and unsolicited applications are not considered.

Information gathered from:

Accounts; Charity Commission record.

Matliwala Family Charitable Trust

Islam, education, social welfare

£216,000 (2012/13)

Beneficial area

UK and overseas, especially Bharuch – India.

Correspondent: Ayub Bux, Trustee, 9 Brookview, Fulwood, Preston PR2 8FG (tel: 01772 706501)

Trustees: Ayub Bux; Yousuf Bux; Abdul Patel; Usman Salya; Fatima Ismail.

CC Number: 1012756

The trust's areas of giving are:

- The advancement of education for pupils at Matliwala School of Bharuch in Gujerat – India, including assisting with the provision of equipment and facilities
- The advancement of the Islamic religion
- The relief of sickness and poverty
- The advancement of education

In 2012/13 the trust had assets of £4.4 million and an income of £426,000. Grants totalled £216,000, the vast majority of which was given to various projects in Bharuch, Gujarat – India. The grants were broken down as follows:

Matliwala Relief Trust	£145,000
Religion (UK)	£51,000
Education (overseas)	£19,000
Relief of poverty (overseas)	£500
Education (UK)	£150

No grants were given to individuals. Unfortunately, there was no list of beneficiaries.

Applications

In writing to the correspondent.

Information gathered from:

Accounts; Charity Commission record.

The Matt 6.3 Charitable Trust

Christian causes

£67,500 (2012/13) to organisations and individuals

Beneficial area

UK.

Correspondent: Ian Harding Davey, Secretary, Progress House, Progress Park, Cupola Way, Off Normanby Road, Scunthorpe DN15 9YJ (tel: 01724 863666)

Trustees: Doris Dibdin; Christine Barnett.

CC Number: 1069985

According to the trustees' report for 2012/13:

> The objective of the MATT 6.3 Charitable Trust is to advance and promote the Christian faith among all ages, and achieve this objective by making grants and donations to evangelical societies and others. The trust has established a number of long-term relationships with organisations and individuals who share its vision to promote the Christian faith.

The trust has also stated that because it is a small family charity with limited funds that is already supporting two long-term projects, it only occasionally supports fresh applicants.

In 2012/13 the trust had assets of £4.3 million and an income of £345,000. Grants totalling £67,500 were made,

£2,400 of which was given to individuals. The only organisational grant made was awarded to Christian Centre (Humberside) Ltd (£65,000).

Applications

The trustees' report states the following: 'due to the fact that the charity's income is largely unpredictable, the trustees have adopted a policy of maximising the reserves in order to provide ongoing funding in future years for the organisations they wish to support.'

Percentage of awards given to new applicants: less than 10%.

Information gathered from:

Accounts; Charity Commission record; further information provided by the funder.

The Violet Mauray Charitable Trust

General charitable purposes, Jewish, medical

£48,000 (2012/13)

Beneficial area

UK.

Correspondent: John Stephany, Trustee, 9 Bentinck Street, London W1U 2EL (tel: 020 7935 0982)

Trustees: Robert Stephany; John Stephany; Alison Karlin.

CC Number: 1001716

The Violet Mauray Charitable Trust was set up in 1990. The trust supports general charitable causes, with preference for medical charities and Jewish organisations.

In 2012/13 the trust had assets of £2 million and an income of £52,000. Grants totalled £48,000 and were made to 28 organisations.

Beneficiaries included: Wikimedia UK (£5,000); Action on Hearing Loss, Aquabox and Straight Talking (£3,000 each); Merlin, Jewish Marriage Council and Jewish Deaf Association (£2,000 each); Bletchley Park Trust and British Institute for Brain-Injured Children (£1,000 each); and British Shalom-Salaam Trust (£750).

Exclusions

No grants to individuals.

Applications

In writing to the correspondent. Grants are made on an ad hoc basis. Grants are made to assist the funding of projects of other charities.

Information gathered from:

Accounts; Charity Commission record.

Evelyn May Trust

Currently children, older people, medical, natural disaster relief

£24,000 (2012)

Beneficial area

Worldwide.

Correspondent: Ms Kim Gray, Trustee, 70 St George's Square, London SW1V 3RD (tel: 020 7821 8211)

Trustees: Jill McDermid; Kim Gray; Lisa Webb.

CC Number: 261038

According to the trustees' report for 2012:

> The Evelyn May Trust was established by a trust deed dated 20 January 1970, having been settled by Evelyn May Riddach during her lifetime and was the residuary beneficiary of her estate. The purpose of the charity is to provide grants to causes of interest to the settlor namely the advancement of education; relief of poverty and sickness; supporting conservation and heritage; relief of the aged and disabled; supporting social welfare and the Christian religion.

In 2012 the trust had assets of £763,000, an income of £30,000 and made grants to ten organisations totalling £24,000.

Beneficiaries included: MACS (£3,800); Edward's Trust (£3,000); the Rainbow Centre for Children and Children's Heart Foundation (£2,000 each); and Independent Parental Special Education Advice (£1,000).

Exclusions

No grants to individuals, including students, or to general appeals or animal welfare charities.

Applications

In writing to the correspondent.

Information gathered from:

Accounts; Charity Commission record.

The Mayfield Valley Arts Trust

Arts, especially chamber music

£138,000 (2012/13)

Beneficial area

Unrestricted, but with a special interest in Sheffield and South Yorkshire.

Correspondent: James Thornton, Trustee, 12 Abbots Way, Abbotswood, Ballasalla, Isle of Man IM9 3EQ (email: jamesthornton@manx.net)

Trustees: David Brown; David Whelton; John Rider; Anthony Thornton; Priscilla Thornton; James Thornton.

CC Number: 327665

Established in 1987, the objects of the trust are as follows:

- To support those organisations which are committed to helping young artists of recognised potential, by offering them a platform/audience, which otherwise they would have difficulty in achieving
- To support those organisations who specialise in educational music, including special needs schools

In 2012/13 the trust had assets of nearly £2.3 million and an income of £126,000. Grants totalling £138,000 were made to six organisations.

The beneficiaries were: Wigmore Hall (£45,000); York Early Music Foundation and Live Music Now (£30,000 each); Music in the Round (£18,000); Prussia Cove (£10,000); and MIR Piano Donation (£5,000).

Exclusions

The trust has stated that 'it will not be involved in the education of individual students nor will it provide grants to individual students; it will not be involved in the provision of musical instruments for individuals, schools or organisations'.

Applications

The trust states that no unsolicited applications are considered. The trust has also stated that 'it considers its financial support on a three year cycle. The next review being summer 2016. If a charity/organisation meets our criteria it should submit a summary request at that time.'

Information gathered from:

Accounts; Charity Commission record.

Mazars Charitable Trust

General charitable purposes

Around £250,000 (2011/12)

Beneficial area

UK, overseas.

Correspondent: Bryan Rogers, Trust Administrator, 1 Cranleigh Gardens, South Croydon CR2 9LD (tel: 020 8657 3053)

Trustees: Phil Verity; Alan Edwards; David Evans; Bob Neate.

CC Number: 1150459

The charity known as Mazars Charitable Trust, (Charity Commission no. 287735), established in 1983 for the advancement of the Christian faith and general charitable purposes, was a conduit for most of the charitable giving of Mazars, chartered accountants. It was removed from the Central Register of Charities in April 2013 as it had ceased to exist.

A new charity (no. 1150459) established for general charitable purposes was registered in January 2013 and has the same name, a majority of the same trustees and the same correspondent address. Neither trust had accounts available at the time of writing (December 2013). Unfortunately, it is not possible to provide details of the new trust apart from those given here; however, we have retained the entry for updating in the future when accounts are published. We have estimated the grant total based on previous years.

The former charity's grants policy was as follows:

> The trustees operate through the management committee who meet annually to consider nominations for national (major) grants. Some funds are allocated to ten regional 'pots' whose appointed representatives approve smaller grant nominations from within their own region.
>
> Nominations for national grants must be known to and be sponsored by team members of Mazars LLP and comply with stated criteria. Applicants known to team members of Mazars LLP can obtain a copy of the stated criteria upon request to the trust administrator. National and regional criteria are regularly reviewed but, in general, the trustees consider that the national grant-making policy should avoid core funding. Most national grants are therefore made towards one-off projects covering a defined period. Successful national nominations cannot normally be repeated within three years.

Previous beneficiaries included: UK Youth (£25,000); Chickenshed Theatre and Parkinson's Disease Society of the United Kingdom (£15,000 each); The Johari Foundation (£12,000); Hope HIV and The Waterside Charitable Trust (£10,000 each); Emmanuel Global Network (UK) Ltd, Hope for Konya and Redbridge Breast Funds (£5,000 each); and Sense and The National Deafblind and Rubella Association (£2,250 each).

Exclusions

Refer to the 'General information' section.

Applications

See 'General information' for further details. Unsolicited appeals are usually rejected.

Information gathered from:

Accounts; Charity Commission record.

The Robert McAlpine Foundation

Children, disability, older people, medical research, welfare

£640,000 (2011/12)

Beneficial area

UK.

Correspondent: Brian Arter, Correspondent, Eaton Court, Maylands Avenue, Hemel Hempstead, Hertfordshire HP2 7TR (tel: 01442 233444; email: b.arter@sir-robert-mcalpine.com)

Trustees: Adrian McAlpine; Cullum McAlpine; The Hon David McAlpine; Kenneth McAlpine.

CC Number: 226646

In 2011/12 the trust had assets of almost £13.7 million and had an income of £813,000. Grants paid during the year totalled £640,000. There were 45 grants paid during the year.

Beneficiaries included: Ewing Foundation (£100,000); Royal Marsden NHS Trust (£50,000); Prostate UK (£46,000); National Eye Research Centre (£31,000); the Towers School and 6th Form Centre (£25,000); Community Self Build Agency, Merchants Academy Withywood and Downside Fisher Youth Club (£20,000 each); Age Concern (£15,000); DENS Action Against Homelessness, St Johns Youth Centre and James Hopkins Trust (£10,000 each); and Grateful Society, National Benevolent Fund for the Aged and the Golden Oldies (£5,000 each).

Exclusions

The trust does not like to fund overheads. No grants to individuals.

Applications

In writing to the correspondent at any time. Considered annually, normally in November.

Information gathered from:

Accounts; Charity Commission record.

The A. M. McGreevy No. 5 Charitable Settlement

General

£75,000 (2011/12)

Beneficial area

UK, with a preference for the Bristol and Bath area.

Correspondent: Karen Ganson, Trust Administrator, KPMG, 100 Temple Street, Bristol BS1 6AG (tel: 01179 054000)

Trustees: Avon Executor and Trustee Co. Ltd; Anthony McGreevy; Elise McGreevy-Harris; Katrina Paterson.

CC Number: 280666

The trust was established in 1979 by Anthony M McGreevy. In previous years there has been a preference for charities based in the former county of Avon.

Grants have been in the range of £500 to £40,000.

In 2011/12 the trust had assets of £2.2 million, an income of £36,000 and gave 3 grants totalling £75,000.

The beneficiaries were: NSPCC, UCL Development Fund and Christchurch Oxford (£25,000 each).

Exclusions

No support for individuals.

Applications

In writing to the correspondent.

Information gathered from:

Accounts; Charity Commission record.

The McKenna Charitable Trust

Education, health, disability, relief of poverty, the arts

£10,250 to organisations (2011/12)

Beneficial area

England and Wales.

Correspondent: John Boyton, Trustee, Ingenious Media plc, 15 Golden Square, London W1F 9JG (tel: 020 7319 4000)

Trustees: Howard Jones; John Boyton; Margaret McKenna; Patrick McKenna.

CC Number: 1050672

The McKenna Charitable Trust was established in 1995. According to the trustees' report for 2011/12, the principal aims and objectives of the trust are:

- To assist with the education, medical welfare and relief of suffering of individuals with disabilities
- To provide funds for education as a means of relieving poverty

- To make grants to other charities whose aims include the relief of suffering children
- To make grants for any other charitable purpose which the trustees consider should be supported

In 2011/12 the trust had assets of £311,000 and an income of £272,000. Grants were made to three beneficiaries and totalled just over £10,200. The beneficiaries were: Clic Sargent and Miracles (£5,000 each); and St Paul's Church (£250).

Applications
The 2011/12 trustees' report states that 'the trustees will consider applications for grants from individuals and charitable bodies on their merits but will place particular emphasis on the educational needs and the provision of support for disabled people'.

Information gathered from:
Accounts; Charity Commission record.

The Helen Isabella McMorran Charitable Foundation

General, Christian

£18,000 (2011/12)

Beneficial area
UK and overseas.

Correspondent: NatWest Trust Services, NatWest Trust Services, 5th Floor, Trinity Quay 2, Avon Street, Bristol BS2 0PT (tel: 0551 657 7371)

Trustee: NatWest Trust Services.

CC Number: 266338

The trust makes one-off grants towards older people's welfare, Christian education, churches, the arts, residential facilities and services, social and moral welfare, cultural and religious teaching, special needs education, health, medical and religious studies, conservation, animal welfare, bird sanctuaries and heritage.

In 2011/12 the foundation had an income of £28,000 and made 11 grants of £1,625 to the following organisations: Cambridge Preservation Society, The Samaritans, National Churches Trust, Save the Children Fund, St John Ambulance, Salvation Army, National Art Collection Fund, DIBS Charitable Trust, Edinburgh Festival Appeal, Royal Commonwealth Society for the Blind and Cambridge House.

Exclusions
No grants to individuals.

Applications
In writing to the correspondent. Brief guidelines are available. The closing date for applications is February each year.

Information gathered from:
Accounts; Charity Commission record.

D. D. McPhail Charitable Settlement

Medical research, disability, older people

£200,000 (2011/12)

Beneficial area
UK.

Correspondent: Sheila Watson, Administrator, PO Box 285, Pinner, Middlesex HA5 3FB

Trustees: Julia Noble; Patricia Cruddas; Catherine Charles-Jones; Christopher Yates; Tariq Kazi; Michael Craig; Mary Meeks.

CC Number: 267588

The D. D. McPhail Charitable Settlement was established in 1973. The trustees' report for 2011/12 states that the charity's objectives are:

- The furtherance of medical research
- The care of the disabled, particularly disabled children
- The care of the aged and infirm

In 2011/12 the trust had assets of £8.5 million and an income of £390,000. Grants were made to 17 organisations totalling £200,000. Governance costs for grant distribution totalled £19,000 (nearly 10% of the total grants distributed).

Beneficiaries included: Pulmonary Hypertension Clinical Trials (£128,000); CHAMPS (£35,000); Dove Cottage Day Hospice and Vocal Eyes (£5,000 each); Diabetes UK, the Cure Parkinson's Trust and BLISS (£2,000 each); and RASCALS (£1,000).

Applications
In writing to the correspondent. The charity's accounts for 2011/12 state that:

> To date, the trust has supported small and medium sized charities to make an investment and/or step change in their activities by making a relatively large grant award over a period of 2 to 3 years. Trustees identify potential projects for assessment by the executive director. The trust makes no commitment to respond to unsolicited applications. There have also been on-going smaller grants to causes supported by the founder and trustees.

Information gathered from:
Accounts; Charity Commission record.

Melodor Ltd

Jewish, general

£131,500 (2011/12)

Beneficial area
UK and overseas.

Correspondent: Bernardin Weiss, Correspondent, 10 Cubley Road, Salford M7 4GN (tel: 01617 206188)

Trustees: Hyman Weiss; Philip Weiss; Zisel Weiss; Pinchas Neumann; Yocheved Weiss; Eli Neumann; Esther Henry; Henry Neumann; Janet Bleier; Maurice Neumann; Miriam Friedlander; Rebecca Delange; Rivka Ollech; Rivka Rabinowitz; Pesha Kohn; Yehoshua Weiss.

CC Number: 260972

The trust supports Orthodox Jewish institutions in the areas of education, relief of poverty and the advancement of religion in accordance with the Orthodox Jewish faith.

In 2011/12 it had assets of £571,000 and an income of £87,500. Grants to organisations totalled £131,500. A list of grants was not available. However, the trust did state that all charitable donations were to 'religious, educational and medical institutions, as well as institutions to help relieve poverty in accordance with the objects of the charity'.

Previously, beneficiaries of the largest grants were the Centre for Torah Education Trust, Beis Rochel and Chasdei Yoel.

Other beneficiaries include: Beth Hamedrash Hachodosh, Yeshivas Ohel Shimon, Beis Minchas Yitzhok, Talmud Torah Education Trust, Dushinsky Trust, Kollel Chelkas Yakov, Yetev Lev, Delman Charitable Trust, Ovois Ubonim and Friends of Viznitz.

Applications
The trust's accounts for 2011/12 state:

> The governors receive many applications for grants, mainly by mail, but also verbally. Each application is considered against the criteria established by the charity. Although the charity does not advertise, it is well known within its community and there are many requests received for grants. Feedback received is used to monitor the quality of grants.

Information gathered from:
Accounts; Charity Commission record.

Meningitis Trust

Meningitis in the UK

£0 to organisations (2011/12)

Beneficial area
UK.

Correspondent: Financial Grants Officer, Link House, Britton Gardens, Kingswood, Bristol BS15 1TF (tel: 01179 476320; fax: 01179 600427; email: catherine@meningitisuk.org; website: www.meningitisuk.org)

Trustees: Gill Noble; Richard Greenhalgh; Alastair Irvine; Mitchell Wolfe; Stephen Gazard; Michelle Harvey-Jones; Anna Freeman; Richard Gillett.

CC Number: 803016

The trust is an international charity with a strong community focus, which aims to fight meningitis through the provision of support, education and awareness and research.

In 2011/12 the trust had assets of £1.6 million and an income of £3.2 million. No research grants were made during the year, previously grants have fluctuated from £2,000 to £150,000. There were grants to individuals made totalling £294,000.

Applications
On a form available from the website along with guidelines, to be submitted by mid-August. See the website for exact deadlines. Decisions are announced in late December.

Information gathered from:
Accounts; Charity Commission record; funder's website.

Menuchar Ltd

Jewish

£722,000 (2011/12)

Beneficial area
UK.

Correspondent: The Trustees, c/o Barry Flack and Co., Knight House, 27–31 East Barnet Road, Barnet EN4 8RN (tel: 020 8275 5186)

Trustees: Norman Bude; Gail Bude.

CC Number: 262782

The main objects of the trust are the advancement of religion in accordance with the Orthodox Jewish faith and the relief of people in need.

In 2011/12 the trust had assets of £154,000 and an income of £738,000, mostly from donations. Grants totalled £722,000.

A list of beneficiaries was not included in the accounts however they stated that most grants went to religious organisations.

Exclusions
No grants to non-registered charities or to individuals.

Applications
In writing to the correspondent.

Information gathered from:
Accounts; Charity Commission record.

Brian Mercer Charitable Trust

Welfare, medical particularly sight and liver, visual arts

£437,000 (2011/12)

Beneficial area
UK and overseas.

Correspondent: Alan Rowntree, Trustee, c/o Beever and Struthers, Central Buildings, Richmond Terrace, Blackburn BB1 7AP (tel: 01254 686600; fax: 01254 682483; email: info@brianmercercharitabletrust.org; website: www.brianmercercharitabletrust.org)

Trustees: Christine Clancy; Kenneth Merrill; Alan Rowntree; Roger Duckworth; Mary Clitheroe.

CC Number: 1076925

The trust awards grants in the following main areas:

- Eyesight – in particular research into and assistance for age related macular degeneration
- Liver – research into and support for people who are affected by liver cancer
- Art – supporting the development of young artists in the north west of the UK

Grants are also made more generally in the fields of youth, disability and medicine, in Blackburn and the North West.

In 2011/12 the trust had assets of £22 million, an income of £511,000 and gave grants totalling £437,000.

Beneficiaries included: British Liver Trust (£82,000); British Council for the Prevention of Blindness (£59,000); Blackburn Youth Zone (£25,000); Sculpture Residency in Pietrasanta (£21,000); Marie Curie Cancer Care, The Living Paintings Trust and Micro Loan Foundation (£10,000 each); NADFAS North West Area (£9,000); East\(£9,000); Talking Newspapers and Magazines (£3,000); Baines School and Our Lady Catholic College (£2,500 each).

Applications
Via email at least four weeks before trustee meetings. Dates of upcoming trustee meetings can be found on the trust's website; they are generally twice yearly.

Information gathered from:
Accounts; Charity Commission record; funder's website.

Merchant Navy Welfare Board

Seafarers, merchant navy, sailors, welfare, medical care

£207,000 (2012)

Beneficial area
UK.

Correspondent: David Parsons, Chief Executive, 8 Cumberland Place, Southampton SO15 2BH (tel: 02380 337799; email: enquiries@mnwb.org.uk; website: www.mnwb.org)

Trustees: Anthony Dickinson; Barry Bryant; Timothy Springett; Michael Jess; Stephen Todd; Edward McFadyen; Graham Lane; Robert Jones; Ian Ballantyne; Revd Kenneth Peters; Deanne Thomas; Andrew Cassels; Mark Carden; David Colclough.

CC Number: 212799

The board is an umbrella charity for the maritime charity sector. It makes grants to over 40 constituent charities towards capital and start-up costs. Its aim is to promote and support the welfare of merchant seafarers and their dependents.

Grants of up to £5,000 for small projects are considered throughout the year. The board will normally allocate a maximum of £50,000 each year in grants in this category. Grants in excess of £5,000 will normally be decided towards the end of each calendar year and applications should be submitted no later than 1 September. In the case of larger projects the trustees may consider partnership funding with other charities.

In 2012 the trust had assets totalling £12.5 million and an income of £622,000. Grants totalled £207,000.

Beneficiaries include: Maritime Charities Funding Group (£50,000); Nautilus Welfare Fund (£41,000); Mission to Seafarers (£33,000); Royal National Mission to Deep Sea Fishermen (£20,000); Royal Alfred Seafarers' Society – Belvedere Care Home, Surrey (£19,000); Sir Gabriel Woods Mariners Horne, Greenock, Scotland (£12,500); Queen Victoria Seamen's Rest, London (£6,000); Invergordon Seafarers' Centre (£800); and Merchant Navy Medal Fund (£100).

Exclusions

No retrospective funding.

Applications

On an application form available to download from the website. Applicants seeking amounts over £5,000 should submit their latest annual report and accounts. Those applying for amounts over £25,000 should also supply a five-year business plan. Applications may be submitted by email. Applicants should call the office to let the board know that an application has been sent. The trust is open to enquiries regarding the application process. Trustees meet to consider applications in February, May, July and October.

Applications should contain the following information:

- A demonstration of need which highlights the direct benefit to seafarers
- A summary of the organisations reserves policy, stating whether the policy is to reduce, maintain or increase reserves and why that policy is appropriate
- Whether or not the organisation is able to reclaim VAT

Capital grants will only be paid on proof of expenditure or the submission of a valid invoice.

Information gathered from:

Accounts; Charity Commission record; funder's website.

The Merchant Taylors' Company Charities Fund

Education, training, church, medicine, general

£95,000 (2012)

Beneficial area

UK, especially inner London.

Correspondent: Nick Harris, Chief Executive Officer, Merchant Taylor's Hall, 30 Threadneedle Street, London EC2R 8JB (tel: 020 7450 4440; fax: 020 7588 2776; email: charities@merchant-taylors.co.uk; website: www.merchanttaylors.co.uk)

Trustees: Hugh Stubbs; Duncan Macdonald Eggar; Peter Magill; Rupert Bull.

CC Number: 1069124

Grants are considered for the arts, social care and community development, disability, the elderly, poverty, medical studies and research, addiction, homelessness, children, and education, with priority for special needs. Grants are focused on London but may exceptionally be made for national work especially where it benefits members or ex-members of the forces or has some connection to tailoring or clothing. The majority of grants are for between £5,000 and £15,000.

Grants are generally made for projects and can be made for up to three years. Potential applicants must be able to demonstrate that they have also applied for funding elsewhere.

In 2010 the trust had assets of £698,000 and an income of £293,000, mostly from donations. Grants were made totalling £95,000 and were broken down as follows:

Livery and Freeman fund	£79,000
Church and Clergy	£8,000
Education Awards	£6,900
Church and Clergy	£1,000
Miscellaneous	£300

Beneficiaries included: Veterans Aid (£14,000); UNLOCK and Cricket for Change (£10,000 each); Westside School (£9,000); Guildhall School of Music and Drama (£6,000); Addaction (£5,000); St John's Church, Hackney (£3,000); Tailors' Benevolent Institute (£1,500); Master Tailors' Benevolent Association (£1,000); Merchant Taylors' School, Crosby and St Paul's Cathedral Choir School (£500 each); and Brandram Road Community Association (£300).

The Merchant Taylors' Company also administers the Charities for the Infirm (214266) and the Charities for the Poor (214267).

Exclusions

No grants for:

- bricks and mortar, although they will consider contributing to the fitting out or refurbishment of new or existing buildings
- Medical research, although the Company provides administrative services to a third-party trust with a small reactive capacity in this area, to which such applications may be referred
- Funds for 'on-granting' to third-party charities or individuals
- Generalised appeals
- Very large charities, except occasionally in support of localised work in the trustees' geographical area of interest
- Revenue funding

Applications

Awards are restricted at present to charities nominated by the Livery Committee. Applications may only be made with the support of a member of the Merchant Taylors' Company or by invitation.

Information gathered from:

Accounts; Charity Commission record; funder's website.

The Merchants' House of Glasgow

General

£452,000 (2012)

Beneficial area

Glasgow and the west of Scotland.

Correspondent: The Directors, 7 West George Street, Glasgow G2 1BA (tel: 01412 218272; fax: 01412 262275; email: theoffice@merchantshouse.org.uk; website: www.merchantshouse.org.uk)

Trustee: The Directors.

SC Number: SC008900

The charity's main activities included paying 'pensions to pensioners, who may or may not have membership qualifications, and to provide assistance in the form of grants to charitable institutions within and around Glasgow'. It will normally consider applications from the following:

- Organisations providing care and assistance to people with disabilities, older people, people who are terminally ill and people who have been socially deprived
- Organisations providing for the care, advancement and rehabilitation of youth
- Universities, colleges of further education and schools
- Organisations connected with the arts, including music, theatre and the visual arts

- Institutions that are connected with and represented by the Merchants' House

In 2012 the charity had an income of £928,000 and spent £452,000 on 'grants and donations'.

Previous grant recipients have included: Erskine Hospital, the National Youth Orchestra of Scotland, Scottish Motor Neurone Disease, the Castle Howard Trust, Delta, the National Burns Memorial Homes, Quarriers Village and Shelter.

Exclusions

The trust will not, unless in exceptional circumstances, make grants to:

- Individuals
- Churches other than Glasgow Cathedral
- Organisations that have received support in the two years preceding an application

Applications

In writing to the correspondent at any time, supported by copy of accounts and information about the organisation's principal activities.

Information gathered from:

Accounts; OSCR record; funder's website.

Mercury Phoenix Trust

AIDS, HIV

£224,000 (2011/12)

Beneficial area

Worldwide.

Correspondent: Peter Chant, Administrator, 22 Cottage Offices, Latimer Park, Latimer, Chesham, Buckinghamshire HP5 1TU (tel: 01494 766799; email: mercuryphoenixtrust@ idrec.com; website: www. mercuryphoenixtrust.com)

CC Number: 1013768

The trust was set up in memory of Freddie Mercury by the remaining members of the rock group, Queen, and their manager. It makes grants to 'help relieve the poverty, sickness and distress of people with AIDS and HIV and to stimulate awareness and education in connection with the disease throughout the world'.

The trust's website states:

> Since 1992 the Mercury Phoenix Trust has been responsible for donating more than $15 million in the fight against AIDS making over 750 grants to charities worldwide. Applications for grants have come in from many countries around the world and collaboration has been realised with groups as far removed as the World Health Organisation to grass-root organisations run partly by voluntary workers in Uganda, Kenya, South Africa, Zambia, Nepal and India. The trust has adapted its policy to concentrate on HIV/ AIDS education and awareness in the developing world

In 2011/12 the trust had assets of £1.4 million and an income of £539,000. Grants totalled £224,000, of which 49 were listed in the accounts.

Beneficiaries included: Help Age International – Thailand (£10,500); UNICEF, Azafady – Madagascar and AIDS Care Education and Training UK – Democratic Republic of Congo (£10,000 each); Teaching Aids at Low Cost – Mozambique (£7,500); Joint Efforts for Youth Uganda, Concern Worldwide – Zimbabwe and Build Africa UK – Kenya (£5,000 each); Karunya Social Services Society – India (£3,000); Rural Development Welfare Society – India (£2,000); and Terrence Higgins Trust (£1,600).

Exclusions

No funding for individuals or travel costs.

Applications

Application forms are available on request from funding@mercuryphoenixtrust.com. In addition to a completed application form, the trust requires the following documents:

- A budget
- Registration certificate
- Audited accounts for the last financial year
- Constitution or memorandum and articles of association
- Annual report
- Equal opportunities policy

Information gathered from:

Accounts; Charity Commission record; funder's website.

The Metropolitan Drinking Fountain and Cattle Trough Association

Provision of pure drinking water for humans and animals

£31,000 (2012)

Beneficial area

UK, mainly London, and overseas.

Correspondent: R. P. Baber, Secretary, Oaklands, 5 Queenborough Gardens, Chislehurst, Kent BR7 6NP (tel: 020 8467 1261; email: ralph.baber@tesco.net; website: www.drinkingfountains.org)

CC Number: 207743

The objectives of the association are to promote the provision of drinking water for people and animals in the United Kingdom and overseas, and the preservation of the association's archive materials, artefacts, drinking fountains, cattle troughs and other installations.

In principle about one third of the net income is allocated to overseas projects. Grants are for £50 to £3,000. In practise the foundation tends to give grants for restoration works to public fountains installed by the foundation over the years, grants for school fountains and grants for overseas projects.

For schools the association typically gifts a Novus drinking fountain to a school on the condition that the school pays £25 to join the association. Generally one fountain is donated per 100 children. The school is responsible for the installation and the maintenance of the fountain.

In 2012 the trust had assets of £618,000, an income of £31,000 and gave grants totalling £31,000.

Beneficiaries included: Restoration of Horse Troughs (£10,000); Busogu Trust, Excellent Development, Appropriate Technology and Village Water (£2,000 each); Teso (£1,400); Friends of Mayow Park (£900); Newport Parish Council (£750); Friends of Hope (£740); and Schools for Kenya (£600).

Grants paid to schools not exceeding £1,000 each totalled £9,000. During the year 21 fountains were donated to schools throughout the UK.

Exclusions

Registered charities only.

Applications

There are separate application forms depending on whether an application is being made for a schools fountain; a UK project; an overseas project or a restoration work. These forms are all available on the website. In addition the trustees require the following information:

- A copy of the most recent audited accounts
- How has the cost of the project been ascertained, such as by a qualified surveyor
- How many people/animals is it estimated would use the fountain/ trough in a day
- Will the charity supervise the project, if not who would
- Where is it anticipated the remainder of the funds to complete the project will come from

Percentage of awards given to new applicants: less than 10%.

Common applicant mistakes

'Unregistered charities [applying].'

Information gathered from:

Accounts; Charity Commission record; further information provided by the funder; funder's website.

T. and J. Meyer Family Foundation Ltd

Education, healthcare, environment

£935,000 (2012)

Beneficial area

UK and overseas.

Correspondent: T. H. Meyer, 3 Kendrick Mews, London SW7 3HG (email: info@tjmff.org)

Trustees: A. C. Meyer; J. D. Meyer; Q. H. Meyer; I. T. Meyer; M. M. Meyer.

CC Number: 1087507

Set up in 2001, this foundation focuses primarily on education, healthcare and the environment. The criteria for charities are:

- Organisations which alleviate the suffering of humanity through health, education and environment
- Organisations with extremely high correlation between what is gifted and what the beneficiary receives
- Organisations which struggle to raise funds either because either they are new, their size or their access to funds is constrained
- Organisations which promote long-term effective sustainable solutions

In 2012 the trust had assets of £25 million, an income of £594,000 and gave grants totalling £935,000, broken down in the accounts into the categories shown in the table below.

Beneficiaries included: Partners in Health (£200,000); Royal Marsden Cancer Trust (£198,000); Sisters SHJ&Mary (£129,000); Hope and Homes for Children (£63,000); Angkor Children's Hospital (£50,000); Pepo La Tumaini (£35,000); Nyaya Health and Heifer International (£25,000 each); Friends of the Citizens Foundation (£17,000); Healthprom and Rwanda Works (£16,000 each); Qespina (£11,000); Project Muso (£10,000); Riders for Health (£7,900); and Toniic (£4,200).

Applications

No grants to unsolicited applications. Trustees meet four times a year.

Information gathered from:

Accounts; Charity Commission record.

T. AND J. MEYER FAMILY FOUNDATION LTD

Education	Asia, South America, Southern Africa and Global	£209,000
Healthcare	Asia, Southern, Western and Eastern Africa	£435,000
Private	Central Eastern and Western Europe	£287,000
Membership	Global	£4,200

The Mickel Fund

General

Around £100,000 each year

Beneficial area

UK, with a preference for Scotland.

Correspondent: Lindsay McColl, 1 Atlantic Quay, 1 Robertson Avenue, Glasgow G2 8JB (tel: 01412 427528; email: admin@mickelfund.org.uk; website: www.mickelfund.org.uk)

Trustees: Mairi Mickel; Bruce Mickel; Findlay Mickel; Alan Hartley; Oliver Bassi.

SC Number: SC003266

The following information on the charity and its activities is taken from its website:

> The charity was founded on 14th May 1970 by Deed of Trust and is funded currently by investments. The charity was originally set up to assist hardship cases within Mactaggart & Mickel Ltd, with the original start up funding being provided by Douglas Mickel and later upon his death substantially added to by his wife Marjorie. During the past 10 years [2002–2012] we have gifted £730,000 to a number of charities. Over the years the criteria for granting donations has been redefined and currently we donate approximately £100,000 annually.
>
> The trustees of the Mickel Fund would like to support a broad range of charities and individuals working in different fields. The trustees would prefer to fund direct service delivery to people in Scotland in need of this support.
>
> This enables the trustees to donate to a wide range of charitable activities which take place in, or have a direct impact on Scotland. To achieve an effective distribution of funds the Mickel Fund has recently reviewed their funding strategy.
>
> The types of funding available fall into three categories:
>
> *Major Donations*
> The Mickel Fund prefers to support organisations where our contributions 'make a difference'. Major Donations will be considered for one large-scale local project at a time, for example the donation of £5,000 – £10,000 on a one-off basis.
>
> *Capital towards Major Building Projects*
> As trustees we've made a decision on how we can best contribute towards capital building projects given the limited nature of our financial resource but the wider scope of building experience amongst the trustees. As an alternative to writing a relatively modest cheque towards the capital cost of a building project we will offer our free 'value engineering' service at an early stage in the project. This would allow us to engage with charities before they have considered design and set costs in order to add value at the earliest possible stage in technical and construction support; this idea is still very much embryonic.
>
> *Annual Donations*
> For those charities looking towards annual contributions funding, The Mickel Fund will donate £500 – £2,000 per year to the chosen national charity, with the view of being updated and reassessed annually. The annual contributions funding can be donated to both long-term supported charities and/or newly assessed charities.
>
> Due to the high volume of applications we are only able to make donations to one charity per category annually.
>
> *Hardship Donations*
> This type of funding will only apply to people who are socially disadvantaged e.g. through health, education, location, poverty etc and who live in Scotland. If you do not live in Scotland please do not apply.

In 2011/12 the fund had an income of £367,000 and a total expenditure of £145,000.

Beneficiaries include: Barnardo's; Macmillan Cancer Support; Guide Dogs for the Blind; Glasgow Association for Mental Health; Royal National Lifeboat Institution; FUSE Youth Cafe; The Royal Zoological Society of Scotland; and Erskine Hospital.

Exclusions

The charity will not make grants:

- For events such as conferences, seminars and exhibitions
- To fee charging residential home, nurseries and care facilities
- For fundraising events
- To individuals – other than through the hardship fund
- As loans or for the repayments of loans – other than through the hardship fund
- For religious promotion
- For the replacement of statutory funds
- To schools other than pre-school and after-school clubs and activities promoting parental and community involvement

Applications

On an application form available from the charity's website, which should be email to the charity upon completion. A check-list of requirements and eligibility criteria is also available on the charity's website.

The following information is provided by the charity:

> The Mickel Fund aims to be a flexible and helpful funder that builds relationships with the organisations we fund. We have a small team who work hard to provide the support required by charities that wish to make applications. We recognise that charities are often dealing with complex issues and we try to provide as much advice and support as we can in addition to donations. We are always happy to answer telephone and email enquiries and to give pre-application support as appropriate. We sometimes meet with potential applicants but only once we have received an application.
>
> Our aim is to fund effective people and organisations that can make a difference. We are an independent grant-maker and we are willing to take risks and support new ideas; however, we will also fund ongoing work, which can show it makes a difference. Donations can take the form of core funding including salaries and general running costs, project grants or capital grants for building or equipment.

Information gathered from:

Accounts; OSCR record; funder's website.

Mickleham Charitable Trust

Relief-in-need

£156,000 (2011/12)

Beneficial area

UK, with a preference for Norfolk.

Correspondent: Philip Norton, Trustee, c/o Hansells, 13–14 The Close, Norwich NR1 4DS (tel: 01603 615731; email: philipnorton@hansells.co.uk)

Trustees: Philip Norton; Revd Sheila Nunney; Anne Richardson.

CC Number: 1048337

Set up in 1995, the trust's main object is to provide relief for the abused and disadvantaged, particularly young people, and the blind.

In 2011/12 the trust had assets of £3.2 million, an income of £124,000 and made grants totalling £156,000, mostly to organisations that had been supported in the previous year. The grants were split across the objectives of the charity with £127,000 made in support of charities providing assistance to the abused and disadvantaged and £29,000 in support of the blind or partially sighted.

Beneficiaries included: YMCA Norfolk and Norfolk and Norwich Association for the Blind (£20,000 each); Motability for Norfolk (£7,500); Barnardo's and Connects and Co. (£5,000 each); Foundation for Conductive Education and Mercy Ships (£2,000 each); and British Wireless for the Blind, Moorfields Eye Hospital, The Benjamin Foundation, Prisoners of Conscience Appeal Fund, Norwich Door to Door, East Norwich Youth Project and Canine Partners (£1,000 each).

Applications

In writing to the correspondent.

Information gathered from:

Accounts; Charity Commission record.

Gerald Micklem Charitable Trust

General, health

£180,000 (2012)

Beneficial area

UK and East Hampshire.

Correspondent: Mrs S. J. Shone, Trustee, Bolinge Hill Farm, Buriton, Petersfield, Hampshire GU31 4NN (tel: 01730 264207; email: mail@geraldmicklemct.org.uk; website: www.geraldmicklemct.org.uk)

Trustees: Susan J. Shone; Joanna L. Scott-Dalgleish; Helen Ratcliffe.

CC Number: 802583

The trust was established in November 1989 with a bequest left in the will of Gerald Micklem. The trust states that the charities:

> It is most interested in are UK charities working on a national basis in the following areas: disability; deafness and blindness; medical conditions affecting both adults and children; medical research, but not in substitution of NHS spending; people with learning disabilities; children and young people, especially the disadvantaged; environment and wildlife.

On occasion, the trust will make grants to charities working in East Hampshire outside the above fields. It does not make grants to local charities operating elsewhere in the UK. Donations are generally for between £3,000 and £4,000.

In 2012 the trust had assets of £1.1 million, an income of £220,000 and made grants totalling £180,000.

Beneficiaries included: Self Unlimited (£60,000); Cecily's Fund (£6,000); Whizz-Kidz and The Rowans Hospice (£5,000 each); British Schools Exploring Society, CLIC Sargent, Foundation for Paediatric Osteopathy and Target Ovarian Cancer (£4,000 each); I CAN and Kinlochbervie High School (£3,000 each); and Halow Project (£2,000).

Exclusions

The trust does not make grants to individuals, does not enter into sponsorship arrangements with individuals and does not make grants to organisations that are not UK-registered charities.

> The areas of charitable activity that fall outside the trust's current funding priorities are: drug/alcohol abuse and counselling; museums, galleries and heritage; performing arts and cultural organisations; churches; and overseas aid.

Applications

Applications may be made to the correspondent by letter – not by email. Enquiries prior to any application may be made by email.

> There is no application form. Applications may be made at any time, but preferably not in December, and should be accompanied by the latest report & accounts of the applicant organisation.
>
> Applicants should note that, at their main meeting early in the calendar year, the trustees consider applications received up to 31 December each year, but do not carry them forward. Having regard for the time of year when this meeting takes place, it makes sense for applications to be made as late as possible in the calendar year so that the information they contain is most up to date when the trustees meet.
>
> **Note:** The trustees receive a very substantial number of appeals each year. It is not their practice to acknowledge appeals, and they prefer not to enter into correspondence with applicants other than those to whom grants are being made or from whom further information is required. Only successful applicants are notified of the outcome of their application.

Information gathered from:

Accounts; Charity Commission record; funder's website.

The Migraine Trust

Study of migraine

£12,000 in research fellowships (2012/13)

Beneficial area

UK and overseas.

Correspondent: Adam Speller, 2nd Floor, 52–53 Russell Square, London WC1B 4HP (tel: 020 7631 6970; fax: 020 7436 2886; email: info@migrainetrust.org; website: www.migrainetrust.org)

Trustees: P. J. Goadsby; Jennifer Mills; Mark Wetherall; Brendan Davies; Ian Watmore; Suzanne Marriot; Fayyaz Ahmed; David Cubitt; Denis O'Connor.

CC Number: 1081300

Amongst other objects in relation to the study of migraine, the trust provides research grants, fellowships and studentships (studentships are applied for by host institution only). The trust also provides information and advice to sufferers and health professionals as well as advocacy and awareness raising.

Funds are provided for research into migraine at recognised institutions, such as hospitals and universities. The Migraine Trust website provides the following information:

- **Training Fellowships:** Fellowships are usually awarded for three years, to give clinicians and scientists protected time to undertake research. All candidates are either clinical or non-clinical with a strong interest in clinical or basic science research related to migraine or other primary headaches
- **Studentships:** Studentships are usually awarded for three years and candidates must apply with a named supervisor at a recognised university
- **Project grants:** We also provide project grants to enable scientists to examine a particular research question or small group of related questions. They are usually up to a maximum of three years

In 2012/13 the trust had assets of £388,000, an income of £583,000 and had 'research fellowship costs' of £12,000.

Organisations previously supported that are detailed on the trust's website included the University of California.

Applications

Contact the trust to discuss an application.

Information gathered from:

Accounts; Charity Commission record; funder's website.

Millennium Stadium Charitable Trust

Sport, the arts, community, environment, youth

£367,000 (2011/12)

Beneficial area

Wales.

Correspondent: Sarah Fox, Suite 1 4, Bessemer Road, Cardiff CF11 8BA (tel: 02920 022143; email: info@millenniumstadiumtrust.org.uk; website: www.millenniumstadiumtrust.co.uk)

CC Number: 1086596

The trust was established by an agreement between the Millennium Commission and the Millennium Stadium plc. Its income is generated through a levy on every ticket purchased for public events at the stadium.

Aims

Through its grant funding the trust aims to improve the quality of life of people who live and work in Wales. In particular the trust aims to promote education, history, language and culture, particularly for those who face disadvantage or discrimination.

Wales is a country rich in culture, history, language and sporting successes. In today's era of globalisation people often forget what is in their locality. As a result the trust is keen to help young people learn more about their country via exchange programmes and has made provision to support youth exchange programmes which fall in to any of the funding categories of the trust.

Guidelines

The trust has chosen to make grants in the following four categories:

Sport

Sport embraces much more than traditional team games and competition. Sport can mean physical activity or the improvement of physical fitness and mental well-being, and can assist in the formation of social relationships and individual and team confidence.

The trust is particularly interested in supporting projects that improve the quality of life of people and communities facing disadvantage.

Funding Priorities

The trust strives to make a difference to sporting organisations throughout Wales and appreciates that sport relies heavily on volunteers.

The trust is keen to support volunteer-based projects, particularly from ethnic minorities and people with disabilities. In addition, the trust recognises the difference that coaching can make to the development of a sport and is keen to fund equipment and coaching costs if the need has been clearly identified.

The arts

The trust is keen to support arts projects that are creative, unique and work with the disadvantaged or deprived individuals and groups throughout Wales. In particular, the trust wishes to develop and improve the knowledge and practice of the arts and to increase opportunities for people to see and participate in the arts throughout Wales.

Funding Priorities

The trust aims to give more people the opportunity to enjoy the diversity of performing and visual arts in Wales. The trust particularly favours proposals which expand and improve arts provision in parts of the country less well served than others and will give priority to organisations which strive to work together to share experiences, practices and ideas.

The environment

The environment of Wales varies dramatically between north, south, east and west of the country. From the mountains of the north to the valleys of the south, the trust welcomes applications relating to environmental groups from both rural and urban areas in Wales.

Funding Priorities

The trust encourages applications relating to recycling, developing green spaces, the development and promotion of green practices and the promotion of public transport schemes. Projects that improve the quality of Wales' environment, protect and create a vibrant countryside, and develop and promote sustainable land-use planning will be a priority for support.

The trust aims to fund programmes that protect and enhance Wales' natural heritage and promote its sustainable use and enjoyment in a way which contributes to local economic prosperity and social inclusion.

The community

The trust is keen to target local communities suffering from greatest disadvantage in Wales.

Funding Priorities

The trust will give priority to organisations that are looking to tackle social, personal, economic or cultural barriers within their own communities. In particular projects that lead to greater independence and give people more control over their lives will be given priority. The trust welcomes applications that give people a voice to express their needs and hopes.

The trust is keen help disabled people to challenge barriers and to be active and visible in their local communities.

Youth Exchange Programmes

The trust will give priority to projects [in the above categories] that foster greater understanding and friendship among the young people of Wales through exchange programmes. Organisations may wish to consider applying for costs towards travel and accommodation to visit another similar group in Wales. Examples of projects such as this may include one football club in Wales travelling to visit another football club to undertake a sporting and social weekend. In particular the trust is keen to support youth programmes that bring together 11 to 25 year olds through sporting or cultural exchanges. Exchange projects should demonstrate long-term benefits for the groups and communities involved and must be between groups based within Wales. These benefits will be as a result of new experiences that are educative, participative, empowering and expressive. The trust recognises that such exchanges can lead to a better appreciation of the different cultural, linguistic and social characteristics that make up the communities of Wales.

The trust supports:

- Not-for-profit organisations
- Properly constituted voluntary organisations
- Charitable organisations
- Voluntary groups working with local authorities (applicant cannot be the local authority)
- Applications from groups of any age (not just youth projects)

Priority is given to organisations serving groups and communities suffering from the greatest disadvantage.

The trust issues funding according to the size of geographical area that an organisation has a remit to cover:

- National organisations (covering the whole of Wales) – up to £12,500
- Regional organisations (covering a region or local authority area) – up to £7,500
- Local organisations (covering a local community or town) – up to £2,500

Full guidelines are provided on the trust's website.

Grantmaking in 2011/12

During the year the trust had assets of £152,000 and an income of £342,000. Grants to organisations totalled £367,000.

Recent beneficiaries listed on the website included: Cardiff Foodbank; South Gwent Children's Foundation; The Bridge to Cross Charitable Trust; Rhyl Yacht Club; and Take Part Community Group.

Exclusions

The trust does not support:

- Projects outside of Wales
- Day-to-day running costs
- Projects that seek to redistribute grant funds for the benefit of third party organisations
- Payments of debts/overdrafts
- Retrospective requests
- Requests from individuals
- Payment to profit making organisations
- Applications made solely in the name of a local authority

Note: In addition to the above, successful applicants may not-reapply to the trust until a three year period from the date of grant offer has elapsed. The grant offer letter will advise applicants of the date when they will be eligible to re-apply.

Applications

The trust holds three rounds a year; one for each type of application – national, regional and local. Deadline dates can be found on the trust's website, along with full guidelines and application forms.

Information gathered from:

Accounts; Charity Commission record; funder's website.

The Ronald Miller Foundation

General

About £150,000 (2011/12)

Beneficial area

UK, with a preference for Scotland, especially Glasgow.

Correspondent: The Secretary, Maclay Murray and Spens, 151 St Vincent Street, Glasgow G2 5NJ

Trustees: C. Fleming-Brown; G. R. G. Graham; J. Simpson; G. F. R. Fleming-Brown.

SC Number: SC008798

The foundation supports a wide range of charitable activities, primarily in Scotland, but also in other parts of the UK. Arts, social welfare, education, environment and health have all been supported. Grants generally range from £500 to £2,000, with the majority of them recurrent.

In 2011/12 the foundation had an income of £181,000. Grants are made totalling around £150,000 each year. No further information was available.

Exclusions

No grants to individuals.

Applications

In writing to the correspondent.

Information gathered from:

OSCR record.

The Millfield House Foundation

Social disadvantage, social policy

£278,000 (2011/12)

Beneficial area

North east England particularly Tyne and Wear.

Correspondent: Fiona Ellis, Trusts Manager, Brunswick House, Whaelton, Morpeth, Northumberland NE61 3UZ (tel: 07500 057825; email: fiona.ellis@mhfdn.org.uk; website: www.mhfdn.org.uk)

Trustees: Grigor McClelland; Stephen McClelland; Sheila Spencer; Robert Williamson; Toby Lowe; Jane Streather; Rhiannon Bearne; Peter Deans; Betty Weallans; John Williamson; Andrew Curry.

CC Number: 271180

Millfield House Foundation (MHF) helps to tackle poverty, disadvantage and exclusion and to promote social change in the North East of England, particularly Tyne and Wear. The current priority is to promote social change by funding projects that inform discussion and influence public policy and attitudes, with the aim of diminishing social deprivation and empowering communities.

The foundation stated in 2010:

> It is not MHF's role, nor does it have the resources, to protect those parts of the VCS which may be facing substantial cuts and MHF cannot provide a safety net for organisations at risk of failing or closing. But the trustees are committed to continuing to support policy functions, and particularly the 'voices' of vulnerable groups in North East communities, especially if they are disproportionately affected by public expenditure cuts, reduction in services and the withdrawal or loss of grant aid to the VCS.

Grants Policy

The foundation funds in three ways:

- We invite a limited number of policy-focused organisations to become our strategic partners
- We are developing the capacity and policy skills of the North East voluntary sector through placements we are setting up with accomplished policy-focused organisations
- Through our open grants programme we support applications from the field

The strategic partners are currently IPPR North and VONNE. The placement scheme is supporting two people a year.

They offer the following guidelines for applicants on their website:

- We expect you to be able to describe the change you want to achieve, your part in the process and who else is helping or working in the area. You may refer to our 'mosaic of change' to help you do so, or you may have other ways of articulating your role in change
- We do not expect you to manage serious change alone, but we do look for signs that show you can be effective, so you need to show us how you understand the wider context
- We do not require grant recipients to attribute particular outcomes to our funding, but we do want you to say how you will track progress and measure results appropriate to your particular intervention and its timescale. We are as interested in unexpected and undesired outcomes, and what can be learned from them, as we are in goals being met as planned
- MHF will support national as well as local bodies, provided that the work being funded is in the North East of England. Proposals for very local work may occasionally be considered so long as it makes sense as part of the mosaic of change and you have made sufficient connections to others who can ensure your findings or ideas reach those who can make the changes sought

As a charity, the foundation must confine its grants to purposes accepted in law as charitable. However, official guidance makes it clear that charities may include a variety of political and campaigning activities to further their purposes.

In 2011/12 the foundation had assets of £5.3 million, an income of £169,000 and gave grants totalling £278,000.

Beneficiaries listed on the website included: Regional Refugees Forum North East (£161,000 over three years); Mental Health North East (£70,000); Voluntary Organisations North East (£60,000 over two years); IPPR North and Regional Youth Work Unit North East (£35,000 each); Northumbria University (£31,000); Centrepoint (£22,000); Age UK North Tyneside (£20,000); Cyrenians (£17,000); and Blyth Valley Citizens Advice (£6,000).

Exclusions

The foundation 'will not fund straightforward service provision, or mainline university research, or the wide range of other projects that are eligible for support elsewhere'.

Applications

Applications can only be made using the trust's application form available on its website. The following documents should be attached with the form:

- A copy of the most recent annual report and accounts or a reference to the Charity Commission website if they are available on there
- The governing document
- A job description for and requests for funding towards a salaried post

The trustees meet twice a year, in May and November and the deadlines for the trustees' meetings are end March or end September. If the trustees are interested the trust manager may request further information and/or a meeting.

For further information potential applicants are strongly advised to visit the trust's website.

Percentage of awards given to new applicants: between 20% and 30%.

Common applicant mistakes

'They are ineligible; disguising service as policy.'

Information gathered from:

Accounts; Charity Commission record; further information provided by the funder; funder's website.

The Millfield Trust

Christian

£76,000 to organisations (2011/12)

Beneficial area

UK and worldwide.

Correspondent: D. Bunce, Trustee, Millfield House, Bell Lane, Liddington, Swindon, Wiltshire SN4 0HE (tel: 01793 790181)

Trustees: Andrew Bunce; David Bunce; Philip Bunce; Stephen Bunce; Rita Winifred Bunce.

CC Number: 262406

The trust was setup to provide grants to Christian organisations, and has supported a number of missionary societies for the last 50 years. Grants are given solely to organisations known to the trustees and new applications are not considered.

In 2011/12 the trust had assets of £168,000 and an income of £98,000, mostly from donations. Grants to organisations totalled £76,000 with a further £2,000 being given to 'individual evangelists and missionaries' and £80 to pensioners and widows.

Beneficiaries of over £1,000 included: Gospel Mission to South America (£14,000); Gideons International (£13,000); Ashbury Evangelical Free Church (£6,000); Mission to Europe (£3,000); Overseas Council for Theological Education and Mission (£2,500); Revival and Armonia (UK) Trust (£2,000 each); Scripture Union (£1,800); and Abacus Trust and Send a Cow (£1,100 each).

Grants of less than £1,000 totalled £25,000.

Applications

No replies to unsolicited applications.

Information gathered from:

Accounts; Charity Commission record.

The Millichope Foundation

General

£239,000 (2011/12)

Beneficial area

UK, especially the West Midlands and Shropshire.

Correspondent: Mrs S. A. Bury, Trustee, The Old Rectory, Tugford, Craven Arms, Shropshire SY7 9HS (tel: 01584 841234; email: sarah@millichope.com)

Trustees: Bridget Marshall; Sarah Bury; Lindsay Bury; Frank Bury; H. M. Horne.

CC Number: 282357

The foundation makes donations in the UK to arts, culture, conservation and heritage. Grants are made specifically within Shropshire for general charitable purposes. Worldwide conservation projects and disaster funds are also occasionally supported.

In 2011/12 the foundation had assets of £6.1 million, an income of £510,000 and gave grants totalling £239,000.

Beneficiaries included: Fauna and Flora International (£20,000); Shropshire Historic Churches Trust (£10,000); Manali School/Hospital (£5,000); Community of the Holy Fire (£2,500); Macmillan Cancer Support and Welsh National Opera (£2,000 each); Age Concern Ludlow, Shropshire Victim Support and Relate Shropshire (£1,000 each); Isle of Jura Music Festival (£500); and Frank Haines Memorial Trust (£200).

Exclusions

No grants to individuals or non-registered charities.

Applications

In writing to the correspondent. Trustees meet several times a year to consider grants.

Information gathered from:

Accounts; Charity Commission record.

The Millward Charitable Trust

Social welfare, performing arts, medical research and animal welfare

£84,000 (2009/10)

Beneficial area

UK and overseas.

Correspondent: John Hulse, Trustee, c/o Burgis and Bullock, 2 Chapel Court, Holly Walk, Leamington Spa, Warwickshire CV32 4YS (tel: 01926 451000)

Trustees: Maurice Millward; Sheila Millward; John Hulse.

CC Number: 328564

The trust has general charitable purposes and supports a variety of causes including social welfare, performing arts, medical research and animal welfare.

The trust has had consistently overdue accounts at the Charity Commission. The last financial information available was for 2009/10, when the trust had assets of £2 million, and income of £68,000 and gave grants totalling £84,000.

Performing arts	8	£61,500
Social welfare	19	£16,500
Animal welfare	5	£3,500
Medical research	6	£2,600

Institutional grants greater than £1,000 each included: Birds Eye View (£36,000 in three grants); Music in the Round (£6,400); City of Birmingham Symphony Orchestra (£10,000 in two grants); CORD Sudan Appeal and Leamington Music RSPCA (£5,000 each); and Barnardo's, Christian Relief, Howard League for Penal Reform and RSPCA (1,000 each).

Applications

In writing to the correspondent.

Information gathered from:

Accounts; Charity Commission record.

The Edgar Milward Charity

Christian, humanitarian

£49,000 (2012/13)

Beneficial area

UK and overseas, with an interest in Reading.

Correspondent: A. S. Fogwill, Corresponding Secretary, 53 Brook Drive, Corsham, Wiltshire SN13 9AX (tel: 01832 270055)

CC Number: 281018

The object of the charity is to distribute all of its income as it arises in the following manner:

- One-half for the furtherance of the Christian religion within the UK and throughout the world
- Two-fifths for general charitable purposes
- One-tenth for educational purposes within a 15-mile radius of the Civic Centre in Reading

Within this, the trust's grantmaking policy is to support a limited number of causes known to the trustees, particularly those supported by the settlor.

In 2012/13 the trust had assets of £1.3 million and an income of £52,000. Grants were made totalling £49,000, which were distributed under the categories displayed in the box below.

Beneficiaries included: Connect4Life (£5,000); Bransgore Community Church and Global Outreach (£2,000 each); Africa Inland Mission (£1,500); and Christian Legal Centre, Greyfriars Missionary Trust, Open Doors and REAP (£1,000 each).

Exclusions

New applications will not be supported.

Applications

Unsolicited applications are not normally considered.

Information gathered from:

Accounts; Charity Commission record.

The Peter Minet Trust

General, children/youth, health and people with disabilities, social welfare, culture and community

£151,000 (2011/12)

Beneficial area

Mainly south east London boroughs, particularly Lambeth and Southwark.

Correspondent: Rachel Oglethorpe, 1a Taylors Yard, 67 Alderbrook Road, London SW12 8AD (tel: 020 8772 3155; email: info@peterminet.org.uk; website: www.peterminet.org.uk)

CC Number: 259963

In the mid-sixties, the Minet family sold much of their property to local councils. Part of the proceeds were used by Peter Brissault Minet to set up the trust in 1969.

The trust aims to improve the quality of life for people living in the inner city boroughs of South East London, especially Lambeth and Southwark. It does this by making grants to UK registered charities in the following areas: community; cultural; health and disability and youth.

The Peter Minet Trust is interested in new ventures as well as established projects. It awards main grants of up to £5,000 and runs a small grants programme (£500 and under) for one-off events and smaller projects such as Christmas parties, summer play schemes and trips.

In 2011/12 the trust had assets of £4.7 million, an income of £203,000 and made 67 grants totalling £151,000. Grants were distributed in the following categories:

Children and youth	£49,000	19
Community projects	£46,000	18
Health and people with disabilities	£36,000	11
General and cultural	£14,000	6
Small grants	£6,200	13

Beneficiaries included: Alzheimer's Society, FareShare and Latin American Disabled People's Project (£5,000 each); Slade Gardens Community Play Association and Raw Material (£4,250 each); Cardboard Citizens (£4,000); Somali Mental Health and Advocacy Project (£3,300); Futures Theatre Company, London Philharmonic Orchestra and Springfield Community Flat (£3,000 each); Stockwell Partnership (£2,500); The Guild of Psychotherapists and Bermondsey Artists' Group (£2,000); Dog Kennel Hill Adventure Playground (£1,500); Kings College London (£1,000); and Little Starz Children's Services and Sickle Cell and Young Stroke Survivors (£500 each).

Exclusions

The trust does not make grants for:

- Individuals
- National appeals by large charities
- Appeals outside the inner boroughs of South East London
- Appeals whose sole purpose is to make grants from collected funds
- Research.

Applications

Using the online application process on the trust's website.

Main grants are awarded in February, June and October. Applications should be submitted approximately two months beforehand. See the application guidelines for exact dates. Applications for small grants can be made at any time and a decision will be communicated within four weeks.

The office is open Monday and Tuesday 9.00–15.00 and Wednesday 10.00–14.00.

Information gathered from:

Accounts; Charity Commission record; funder's website.

THE EDGAR MILWARD CHARITY

	Christianity (no. of grants)	Trustees' discretion	Educational	Total
Over £1,000	£8,000 (6)	£13,000 (8)	£1,000 (1)	£22,000 (15)
Under £1,000	£15,000 (34)	£9,900 (23)	£2,500 (5)	£28,000 (62)
Total	£23,000 (40)	£23,000 (31)	£3,500 (6)	£49,000 (77)

Minge's Gift and the Pooled Trusts

Medical, education, disadvantage, disability, footwear

£94,000 to organisations (2011/12)

Beneficial area

UK, with some preference for the City of London.

Correspondent: John Miller, Company Clerk, The Worshipful Company of Cordwainers, Clothworkers Hall, Dunster Court, Mincing Lane, London EC3R 7AH (tel: 020 7929 1121; fax: 020 7929 1124; email: office@cordwainers.org; website: www.cordwainers.org)

Trustees: Charles Fairweather; Lance Bridgman Shaw; Glenn Bridgman Shaw.

CC Number: 266073

Minge's Gift – The trust was established for general charitable purposes as directed by the Master and Wardens of the Worshipful Company of Cordwainers. The income of Minge's Gift is generally allocated for the support of educational and medical establishments with which the company has developed long-term relationships, ex-service organisations, charities connected with the footwear, fabric and leather trades and towards assistance for disabled and/or disadvantaged youth.

In 2011/12 the trust had assets of £1.4 million and an income of £142,000 (excluding the pooled trusts). Grants were made to 43 organisations totalling £93,000.

Beneficiaries included: University of Northampton (£17,000); Urswick School Hackney, Library Books (£13,000); Royal London Society for the Blind (Dorton House) (£8,000); Capel Manor College (2 Bursaries) (£6,000); University of the Arts, London (£5,300), Footwear Friends (£4,500); University College London (£4,000); Guildhall School of Music and Drama (£2,100); British Footwear Development Trust (£2,000); Lord Mayor's Fund (£1,500); Leather Conservation Centre (£1,000); St Dunstan-in-the-West Church (£700); St Mary Magdalene Enfield (£500); and Museum of London (£100).

Pooled Trusts – Also included in the accounts for Minge's Gift, were details of the giving of the Common Investment Fund (Pooled Trusts).This combines a number of small trusts which are administered by the Worshipful Company of Cordwainers for the benefit of scholars, the blind, deaf, clergy widows, spinsters of the Church of England, ex-servicemen and their widows and those who served in the merchant services. It also provides for the upkeep of the Company's almshouses in Shorne, Kent. A total of £11,600 was given to individuals and £1,000 to organisations in 2011/12.

Exclusions

Grants to individuals are only given through the Pooled Trusts.

Applications

In writing to the correspondent.

Information gathered from:

Accounts; Charity Commission record; funder's website.

Minton Charitable Trust

Education

£126,500 (2011/12)

Beneficial area

UK.

Correspondent: Sir Anthony Armitage Greener, Trustee, Flat 26 Hamilton House, Vicarage Gate, London W8 4HL

Trustees: Sir Anthony Armitage Greener; Richard Edmunds; Lady Audrey Greener.

CC Number: 1112106

Set up in 2005, the trust's objects are, 'the advancement and promotion of the education of the public through the provision of, or assisting with, the provision of facilities, support, education, advice and financial assistance to individuals and organisations'.

In 2011/12 the trust had assets of £607,000 and an income of £212,000, mostly from donations. Grants totalled £126,500.

The main beneficiary was St Giles Trust (£125,000), with £500 distributed to other organisations and £1,000 awarded to individuals.

Applications

In writing to the correspondent.

Information gathered from:

Accounts; Charity Commission record.

The Mirianog Trust

General

£35,000 (2011/12)

Beneficial area

UK.

Correspondent: Canon W. E. L. Broad, Trustee, Moorcote, Thornley, Tow Law, Bishop Auckland DL13 4NU (tel: 01388 731350)

Trustees: Canon William Broad, Chair; Daphne Broad; Elizabeth Jeary.

CC Number: 1091397

Set up in 2002 with general charitable purposes, currently the trustees give preference to:

- Relief of poverty
- Overseas aid and famine relief
- Accommodation and housing
- Environment, conservation and heritage

In 2011/12 the trust had assets of £637,000, an income of £29,000 and made grants to 15 organisations totalling £35,000.

Beneficiaries included: Justice First (£6,100); Medical Aid for Palestine and Freedom of Torture (£3,000); Shelter, Children with Aids, RIDERS and Bwindi Hospice (£2,000); Key (£1,500); and Temwa (£1,000).

Applications

In writing to the correspondent. The trustees meet twice each year.

Percentage of awards given to new applicants: between 30% and 40%.

Common applicant mistakes

'Not sending proper receipts.'

Information gathered from:

Accounts; Charity Commission record; further information provided by the funder.

The Laurence Misener Charitable Trust

Jewish, general

£174,000 (2011/12)

Beneficial area

UK.

Correspondent: David Lyons, Correspondent, c/o Leonard Jones and Co., 1 Printing Yard House, London E2 7PR (tel: 020 7739 8790)

Trustees: Jillian Legane; Capt. George Frederick Swaine.

CC Number: 283460

The trust was established for general charitable purposes by a Deed of Settlement in June 1981. When allocating grants the trustees have in mind charities that would have been approved of by the settlor.

In 2011/12 the trust had assets of £2.4 million and an income of £96,000. Grants were made totalling £174,000.

The largest grants were to: Jewish Association for the Physically Handicapped, Jewish Care and Nightingale House (£15,000 each); and Cancer Research UK (£14,000).

Other grants included: Seafarers UK (£10,000); Jews' Temporary Shelter (£8,000); and Blond McIndoe Centre, Cassel Hospital Families Centre Appeal, Elimination of Leukaemia Fund, Great

Ormond Street Children's Hospital Fund, Sussex Stroke and Circulation Fund, Royal Marsden Hospital and World Jewish Relief (£7,000 each).

Applications
In writing to the correspondent.

Information gathered from:
Accounts; Charity Commission record.

The Mishcon Family Charitable Trust

Jewish, social welfare, medical, disability, children

£92,000 (2011/12)

Beneficial area
UK.

Correspondent: The Trustees, Summit House, 12 Red Lion Square, London WC1R 4QD

Trustees: P. A. Mishcon; R. O. Mishcon; Mrs J. Landau.

CC Number: 213165

The trust supports mainly Jewish charities, but also gives grants to general social welfare and medical/disability causes, especially children's charities.

In 2011/12 the trust had assets of £1.8 million, and an income of £61,000. Grants were made to 97 organisations totalling £92,000.

As in previous years the largest grant went to the United Jewish Israel Appeal (£34,000). Smaller grants included: University College London (£16,500); One to One Children's Fund (£6,500); Ambitious about Autism (£1,800); Centre for Jewish Life (£1,500); Marie Curie Cancer Care (£1,300); Royal Free Charity and Barts and the London Charity (£1,000 each); WWF (£250); and The Cardiomyopathy Association (£100).

Applications
In writing to the correspondent.

Information gathered from:
Accounts; Charity Commission record.

The Misselbrook Trust

General

£70,000 (2011/12)

Beneficial area
UK with a preference for the Wessex area.

Correspondent: Michael Howson-Green, Trustee, Ashton House, 12 The Central Precinct, Winchester Road, Eastleigh, Hampshire SO53 2GB (tel: 02380 274555)

Trustees: Michael Howson-Green; Brian M. Baxendale; David A. Hoare; Mrs M. A. Howson-Green.

CC Number: 327928

The trust was established in 1988 for general charitable purposes in the UK. In 2011/12 assets stood at £1 million and the trust received an income of £53,000. Grants were made totalling £70,000 and those over £1,000 were listed in the accounts.

Beneficiaries included: Enham Trust (£2,000); and Aidis Trust, Marwell Preservation Trust and St Dunstan's (£1,000 each).

Other grants of £1,000 or less were made to 26 organisations and totalled £65,000.

Applications
In writing to the correspondent.

Information gathered from:
Accounts; Charity Commission record.

The Mitchell Charitable Trust

Jewish, general

£30,000 (2011/12)

Beneficial area
UK, with a preference for London and overseas.

Correspondent: Ashley Mitchell, Trustee, 28 Heath Drive, London NW3 7SB (tel: 020 7794 5668)

Trustees: Ashley Mitchell; Elizabeth Mitchell; Antonia Mitchell; Keren Mitchell.

CC Number: 290273

The trust was established in 1984. It has general charitable purposes but in practice appears to have a strong preference for welfare charities, Jewish organisations and health charities.

In 2011/12 the trust had assets of £1.1 million and an income of £40,000. There were 18 grants made during the year totalling £30,000, broken down as follows:

Community and welfare	£25,000
Medical and disability	£3,000
Arts and culture	£1,000
Education	£1,000

There was no list of beneficiaries available in the 2011/12 accounts. Previous beneficiaries included: Hammersmith Clinical Research (£37,000); Ovarian Cancer Care (£34,500); and Prostate Cancer Research Foundation (£25,000). Smaller grants have included: London School of Economics and Political Science (£6,000); Community Security Trust and Norwood (£5,000 each); National Council for Epilepsy (£500); and Kidney for Kids (£30).

Exclusions
No grants to individuals or for non-Jewish religious appeals. Applicants from small charities outside London are unlikely to be considered.

Applications
In writing to the correspondent. Applications must include financial information. The trust does not reply to any applications unless they choose to support them. Trustees do not meet on a regular basis, thus applicants may not be advised of a grant for a considerable period.

Percentage of awards given to new applicants: between 20% and 30%.

Common applicant mistakes
'They don't bother to research the types of charities we support.'

Information gathered from:
Accounts; Charity Commission record; further information provided by the funder.

Keren Mitzvah Trust

General, Jewish

£200,000 (2012)

Beneficial area
UK.

Correspondent: Mrs Naomi Crowther, 1 Manchester Square, London W1U 3AB

Trustees: Manny Weiss; Alan McCormack; Neil Bradley.

CC Number: 1041948

In 2012 the trust had assets of £55,000 and an income of £212,000, almost entirely from donations. Grants totalled £200,000 and were broken down into the following categories:

Religious advancement	£99,000
Education	£61,000
Poverty relief	£21,000
Other	£15,000
Health	£3,300

Beneficiaries included: Friends of Yeshivas Mir (£31,000); CML (£16,000); Cosmon Beiz Ltd and Woodstock Sinclair Trust (£11,000 each); Edgware Jewish Primary School and KKL Charity (£10,000 each); Yesamach Levav Foundation (£7,000); NRST (£6,300); and European Beis Din and Centre for Advanced Rabbinics (£5,000).

Applications
The trust stated that the trustees support their own personal charities.

Information gathered from:
Accounts; Charity Commission record.

The Mizpah Trust

General

£82,000 to organisations (2011/12)

Beneficial area

UK and overseas.

Correspondent: A. C. O. Bell, Trustee, Foresters House, Humbly Grove, South Warnborough, Hook, Hampshire RG29 1RY

Trustees: Alan Bell; Julia Bell.

CC Number: 287231

The trust is proactive and makes grants to a wide range of organisations in the UK and, to a lesser extent, overseas for the relief of poverty, aid and famine relief and Christianity.

In 2011/12 the trust had assets of £45,000 and an income of £83,000, mostly from donations. There were 7 grants made totalling £82,000, with a further £500 given to individuals.

Beneficiaries during the year were: The Vanessa Grant Trust (£60,000); CARE (£5,000); Micah Trust (£4,000); and The Stewards Trust, The Wilberforce Trust and The Saville Foundation (£1,000 each).

Applications

No unsolicited applications.

Information gathered from:

Accounts; Charity Commission record.

The Modiano Charitable Trust

Arts, Jewish, general

£74,000 (2011/12)

Beneficial area

UK and overseas.

Correspondent: Michael Modiano, Trustee, Broad Street House, 55 Old Broad Street, London EC2M 1RX (tel: 020 7012 0000)

Trustees: Barbara Modiano; Laurence Modiano; Michael Modiano.

CC Number: 328372

In 2011/12 the trust had assets of £167,000, an income of £140,000 and made grants totalling £74,000. The trust supports the arts, Jewish charities and those which relieve poverty, both in the UK and overseas.

No list of grants was available but previous beneficiaries have included: Philharmonic Orchestra (£20,000); the Weiznam Institute Foundation (£10,000); DEC Haiti Appeal, St Paul's School and UJIA (£5,000 each); World Jewish Relief (£4,000); Life Action Trust (£3,500); CCJ and The Holocaust Educational Trust (£2,500 each); YMCA and the Reform Research Trust (1,000 each); and British Forces Association, Jewish Assoc. for the Mentally Ill (JAMI); and The St John of Jerusalem Eye Hospital (£100 each).

Applications

In writing to the correspondent.

Information gathered from:

Accounts; Charity Commission record.

The Moette Charitable Trust

Jewish education and social welfare

£30,000 (2011/12)

Beneficial area

UK and overseas.

Correspondent: Simon Lopian, Trustee, 1 Holden Road, Salford M7 4NL (tel: 01618 328721)

Trustees: Jonathan Brodie; Simon Lopian; Pearl Lopian.

CC Number: 1068886

The principal activity of the trust is to make grants for the support of 'the poor and needy as well as other charitable institutions'.

In 2011/12 the trust had assets of £423,000 and an income of £101,500. Grants made in accordance with the trust's objectives totalled £30,000. A list of beneficiaries was unavailable.

Previous beneficiaries have included: Finchley Road Synagogue (£15,000); King David Schools (Manchester) and Manchester Charitable Trust (£2,500); The Purim Fund (£2,000); Yad Voezer and Yeshivas Lev Aryeh (£1,000 each); Hakalo and London School of Jewish Studies (£500); Manchester Jewish Federation (£400); and Manchester Seminary for Girls (£50).

Applications

In writing to the correspondent.

Information gathered from:

Accounts; Charity Commission record.

The Mole Charitable Trust

Education, relief of poverty

£161,000 (2011/12)

Beneficial area

UK, with a preference for Manchester.

Correspondent: Martin Gross, Trustee, 2 Okeover Road, Salford M7 4JX (tel: 01618 328721; email: martin.gross@lopiangb.co.uk)

Trustees: Leah Pearl Gross; Martin Gross.

CC Number: 281452

The objects of the charity are to make donations and loans to educational institutions and charitable organisations, and for the relief of poverty.

In 2011/12 the trust had assets of almost £2.4 million and an income of £157,000. Grants totalling £161,000 were broken down as follows:

- Education (£98,000)
- Religious institutions and charitable organisations (£63,000)

A list of beneficiaries for the year was unavailable.

Grants have previously included those to: Three Pillars Charity (£60,000); Manchester Jewish Grammar School (£26,000); Chasdei Yoel Charitable Trust and United Talmudical Associates Ltd (£20,000 each); Binoh of Manchester (£6,000); Beis Ruchel Girls School (£3,000); Manchester Jewish Federation (£2,500); and Our Kids (£1,000).

Information gathered from:

Accounts; Charity Commission record.

The Monatrea Charitable Trust

General

£235,000 (2011/12)

Beneficial area

UK.

Correspondent: Coutts and Co., Coutts and Co., 440 Strand, London WC2R 0QS (tel: 020 7663 6838)

Trustees: Patrick Vernon; Mary Vernon; Coutts and Co.

CC Number: 1131897

The trust was established in 2009 with an endowment of £503,500 for general charitable purposes. It is the charitable trust of Stephen Vernon, chair of Green Property Ltd.

In 2011/12 the trust had assets of £212,000 and an income of £216,000. There were 16 grants of between £2,000 and £27,000 made totalling £235,000.

The beneficiaries during the year were: Children Welfare Home, Samata Samaj, Dr Ambrosoli Memorial Health Care Centre, Prisoners' Advice Service, Family Action, Roses Charitable Trust, Samata Hospital, South Central Youth and Africa Conservation.

Applications

In writing to the correspondent.

Information gathered from:

Accounts; Charity Commission record.

The D. C. Moncrieff Charitable Trust

Social welfare, environment

£33,000 (2011/12)

Beneficial area

UK and worldwide, with a preference for Norfolk and Suffolk.

Correspondent: R. E. James, Trustee, 8 Quinnell Way, Lowestoft, Suffolk NR32 4WL

Trustees: M. I. Willis; R. E. James; M. F. Dunne.

CC Number: 203919

The trust was established in 1961. It supports a number of large UK organisations but tends to concentrate on charities local to the Norfolk and Suffolk areas.

In 2011/12 the trust had assets of £2.1 million and an income of £44,000. Grants were made to organisations totalling £33,000. A list of beneficiaries for the year was unavailable.

Previous grants have included those to: All Hallows Hospital, East Anglia's Children's Hospices, the Society for Lincolnshire History and Archaeology, Hemley Church Parochial Church Council, Lowestoft Girl Guides Association and The Scouts Association, BREAK, Strongbones Children's Charitable Trust and East Anglian Air Ambulance Association.

Exclusions

No grants for individuals.

Applications

In writing to the correspondent. The trust has previously stated that demand for funds exceeded available resources; therefore no further requests are currently invited.

Information gathered from:

Accounts; Charity Commission record.

Monmouthshire County Council Welsh Church Act Fund

General

£216,000 to organisations (2011/12)

Beneficial area

Blaenau Gwent, Caerphilly, Monmouthshire, Torfaen and Newport.

Correspondent: Joy Robson, Head of Finance, Monmouthshire County Council, Innovation House, PO Box 106, Magor, Caldicot NP26 9AN (tel: 01633 644657; fax: 01633 644260)

Trustee: Monmouthshire County Council.

CC Number: 507094

An annual budget set by the local authority for grant payments is split between the administrative areas of Blaenau Gwent, Caerphilly, Monmouthshire, Torfaen and Newport on a population basis. A committee set up by the authority approves grant applications on a quarterly basis. The trust supports individuals or organisations that are known to the trustees. It has supported a wide variety of causes including education, people who are blind, sick or in need, older people, medical and social research, recreation, culture and the arts, historic buildings, churches and burial grounds, emergencies and disaster appeals.

In 2011/12 assets stood at £4.7 million. The trust had an unusually low income of £84,000 (£70,000 in 2010/12 and £280,000 in 2008/09), which it attributed to underperforming financial markets. Grants to organisations during the year totalled £216,000 broken down as: purposes beneficial to the community (£115,000); the advancement of religion (£100,500); and the advancement of education (£1,200).

A list of beneficiary organisations was not available but previous beneficiaries include: Parish Church Llandogo, Parish Church Llangybi, Bridges Community Centre, St David's Foundation Hospice Care and North Wales Society for the Blind.

Applications

On a form available from the correspondent, this must be signed by a county councillor. They are considered in March, June, September and December.

Information gathered from:

Accounts; Charity Commission record.

The Montague Thompson Coon Charitable Trust

Children with muscular diseases, medical research, environment

£38,000 (2011/12)

Beneficial area

UK.

Correspondent: Philippa Blake-Roberts, Trustee, Old Rectory, Church Lane, Colton, Norwich NR9 5DE (tel: 07766 072592)

Trustees: Peter Clarke, Chair; John Lister; Philippa Blake-Roberts.

CC Number: 294096

This trust was registered with the Charity Commission in 1986. The trust's objects are: 'to relieve sickness in children with muscular dystrophy and/or other muscular diseases, to carry out and provide for research into infant diseases and to advance the education of the public in the study of ecology and wildlife'.

In 2011/12 the trust had assets of £1.2 million and an income of £55,000. There were 10 grants made in the year totalling £38,000.

Beneficiaries included: Livability (£10,000); The Wildfowl and Wetlands Trust (£7,500); Muscular Dystrophy Campaign (£6,000); Keech Hospice Care (£5,000); Farms for City Children (£4,000); and CP Sport (£1,000).

Exclusions

No grants to individuals.

Applications

In writing to the correspondent.

Information gathered from:

Accounts; Charity Commission record.

The Colin Montgomerie Charitable Foundation

General

Around £40,000 (2011)

Beneficial area

UK.

Correspondent: Miss Donna Cooksley, Trustee, c/o Catella, Chiswick Gate, 3rd Floor, 598–608 Chiswick High Road, London W4 5RT

Trustees: Colin Montgomerie; Guy Kinnings; Jonathan Dudman; Donna Cooksley.

CC Number: 1072388

Set up in November 1998, the foundation aims to support the relief of poverty, the advancement of education and religion, and any other charitable purposes as decided by the trustees.

At the time of writing, accounts for 2011 were a year overdue at the Charity Commission. In 2011 the trust had an income of £88,000 and an expenditure of £75,000. Previously grants have totalled around £40,000 annually. Further information was not available.

Previous beneficiaries have included: British Lung Foundation, Cancer Vaccine Institute, NSPCC for the Full Stop Campaign, and University of Glasgow MRI Scanner Fund.

Applications

In writing to the correspondent.

Information gathered from:

Accounts; Charity Commission record.

George A. Moore Foundation

General

£240,000 (2011/12)

Beneficial area

Principally Yorkshire and the Isle of Man.

Correspondent: Mrs James, Chief Administrator, The Stables, Bilton Hall, Bilton-in-Ainsty, York YO26 7NP (tel: 01423 359446; email: info@gamf.org.uk; website: www.gamf.org.uk)

Trustees: George Moore; Elizabeth Moore; Jonathan Moore; Paul Turner.

CC Number: 262107

The trustees of the foundation select causes and projects from applications received during the year, as well as using independent research to identify specific objectives where they wish to direct assistance. Education, health, the forces, community and sports have all been supported.

In 2011/12 the trust had assets of £5.7 million and an income of £281,000. There were 75 grants of up to £50,000 made totalling £240,000.

Beneficiaries included: National Institute for Cardiovascular Outcomes Research (£50,000); Boston Charitable Foundation (£44,000); Marrick Priory (£25,000); North Yorkshire Waste Action Group (£10,000); 49th Eastfield Scout Group (£5,000); Blood Pressure Association, Disability Action Yorkshire, Living Paintings Trust and Northallerton and District Voluntary Service (£1,000 each); Time Together (£500); and Sulby Horticultural Show (£250).

Exclusions

No assistance will be given to individuals, courses of study, expeditions, overseas travel, holidays, or for purposes outside the UK. Local appeals for UK charities will only be considered if in the area of interest. Because of present long-term commitments, the foundation is not prepared to consider appeals for religious property or institutions.

Applications

In writing to the correspondent. No guidelines or application forms are issued. The trustees meet approximately four times a year, on variable dates, and an appropriate response is sent out after the relevant meeting. For large grants of over £5,000, the trust will normally hold a meeting with the applicant to determine how the money will be spent.

Percentage of awards given to new applicants: between 20% and 30%.

Common applicant mistakes

'We are a traditional grantmaking charity and find that applicants can be too "familiar" in their initial approach, often using Christian names which is not always appropriate, especially if the trustees are elderly and prefer a more formal address. Also database incorrectly set up when the applicant puts "Dear Mrs A L James", rather than the correct "Dear Mrs James".'

Information gathered from:

Accounts; Charity Commission record; further information provided by the funder; funder's website.

The Nigel Moores Family Charitable Trust

Arts

£0

Beneficial area

UK, but mostly Liverpool and Wales.

Correspondent: P. Kurthausen, Accountant and Trustee, c/o Macfarlane and Co., 2nd Floor, Cunard Building, Water Street, Liverpool L3 1DS (tel: 01512 366161; email: mail@bwm.co.uk)

Trustees: J. C. S. Moores; Portia Kennaway; Paul Kurthausen.

CC Number: 1002366

The trustees have determined that their principal objective should be the raising of the artistic taste of the public, whether in relation to music, drama, opera, painting, sculpture or otherwise in connection with the fine arts, the promotion of education in the fine arts and academic education, the promotion of the environment, the provision of facilities for recreation or other leisure time occupation and the advancement of religion.

This foundation primarily funded the A Foundation in Liverpool, which is now defunct. The foundation had little assets and has had very low income and expenditure since 2010. Accounts for 2011/12 were also very overdue at the Charity Commission. The trust did not respond to our request for clarification; however, it may be inactive.

In 2010/11 the foundation had an income of £60 and an expenditure of £2,500. Previous beneficiaries have included: The A Foundation (£525,000); London Library (£20,000); Mostyn Gallery (£10,000); University of York (£6,750); Art School Palestine (£1,000); and Matts Gallery (£500).

Applications

In writing to the correspondent.

Information gathered from:

Accounts; Charity Commission record.

The Morel Charitable Trust

Arts/culture, race relations, inner-city projects. UK and the developing world

£77,000 (2011/12)

Beneficial area

UK and the developing world.

Correspondent: Simon Gibbs, Trustee, 34 Durand Gardens, London SW9 0PP (tel: 020 7582 6901)

Trustees: James Gibbs; William Gibbs; Benjamin Gibbs; Simon Gibbs; Thomas Gibbs; Dr Emily Parry; Abigail Keane.

CC Number: 268943

The trust supports: the arts, particularly drama; organisations working for improved race relations; inner-city projects and developing-world projects. Also supported are: culture and recreation; health; conservation and environment; education and training; and social care and development. Projects supported are usually connected with places that the trustees have lived and worked, including the cities of Bristol, Leeds, Brecon and London and the countries of Ghana, Zambia, Malawi and the Solomon Islands.

In 2011/12 the trust had assets of £1.2 million and an income of £55,000. 42 grants were made totalling £77,000 and were broken down as follows:

Social and development	£53,000
Health	£7,000
Drama and the arts	£7,000
Humanitarian and welfare	£4,000
International	£3,500
Other	£3,000

Beneficiaries included: Oxfam (£15,000); Christian Aid – Kailahun (£5,000); Motor Neurone Disease (£3,000); Collective Artistes, Computer Aid International, Health Poverty Action, Kaloko Trust, KidzClub Leeds (£2,000 each); African Initiatives and Afrika Eye Bristol (£1,500 each); and Brecon Arts Trust, ACET, Medical Aid Palestine and Renewable World (£1,000 each).

Exclusions

No grants to individuals.

Applications

In writing to the correspondent. The trustees normally meet three times a year to consider applications.

Information gathered from:

Accounts; Charity Commission record.

The Morgan Charitable Foundation

Welfare, hospices, medical, Jewish, general

£60,000 (2012)

Beneficial area

UK.

Correspondent: The Trustees, PO Box 57749, London Nw11 1FD (tel: 07968 827709)

CC Number: 283128

The Morgan Charitable Foundation (previously known as The Erich Markus Charitable Foundation) was established in 1979 when, following Erich Markus's death, half of his residual estate was left to the trust.

In 2012 the foundation had an income of £107,000 and an expenditure of £99,000. No further financial information was available. Previously, grants have been made totalling around £60,000.

Previous beneficiaries included: Magen David Adom, World Jewish Relief, Chai Cancer Care, In Kind Direct Charity, Jewish Care, Jewish Blind and Disabled, Afrikids, Aleh Charitable Foundation, Institute for Philanthropy, London Pro Arte Choir, Marie Curie Cancer Care, Ohel Sarah, Pears Foundation, and Royal National Lifeboat Institution.

Exclusions

No grants to individuals.

Applications

In writing to the correspondent. Applications will only be considered if accompanied by a copy of the charitable organisation's latest report and accounts. Trustees meet twice a year, usually in April and October. No telephone enquiries please.

Information gathered from:

Accounts; Charity Commission record.

Diana and Allan Morgenthau Charitable Trust

Jewish, general

£102,000 (2011/12)

Beneficial area

Worldwide.

Correspondent: Allan Morgenthau, Trustee, Flat 27, Berkeley House, 15 Hay Hill, London W1J 8NS (tel: 020 7493 1904)

CC Number: 1062180

Registered with the Charity Commission in April 1997, grants are made to a range of Jewish, medical, education and arts organisations.

In 2011/12 the trust had assets of £34,000 and an income of £131,000, almost all of which was a donation from The Archie Sherman Charitable Trust. Grant totalled £102,000 and were broken down as follows:

General donations and overseas aid	£83,000
Medical, health and sickness	£8,000
Arts and culture	£5,400
Education and training	£5,600

Beneficiaries included: Belsize Square Synagogue (£30,000); The Central British Fund for World Jewish Relief (£18,000); The British Friends of the Jaffa Institute (£10,000); Marie Curie Cancer Care (£5,000); Holocaust Educational Trust (£4,000); Tricycle Theatre Company (£1,700); Lifelites (£1,500); The Royal Marsden Hospital (£250); and The Royal Free Hampstead Charities (£150).

A further £16,000 was given in grants to individuals.

Applications

In writing to the correspondent.

Information gathered from:

Accounts; Charity Commission record.

The Oliver Morland Charitable Trust

Quakers, general

Around £75,000 (2011/12)

Beneficial area

UK.

Correspondent: J. M. Rutter, Trustee, Thomas House, Stour Row, Shaftesbury, Dorset SP7 0QW (tel: 01747 853524)

CC Number: 1076213

The trustees state that the majority of funds are given to Quaker projects or Quaker-related projects, which are usually chosen through the personal knowledge of the trustees.

In 2011/12 the trust had an income of £20,000 and a total expenditure of £87,000. The Commission did not publish the most recent accounts as the trust's income fell below the £25,000 threshold. Based on previous performance it is likely that grants totalled around £75,000 once investment and accounting costs are taken into account.

Previous beneficiaries have included: Quaker Peace and Service (£32,500); Quaker Home Service – children and young people (£16,000); Refugee Council (£2,000); Leap Confronting Conflict, Living Again, Medical Aid for Palestine and Sightsavers International (£1,000 each); Come to God (£850); and Brooke Animal Hospital (£300).

Exclusions

No grants to individuals.

Applications

'Most of our grants are for continuing support of existing beneficiaries (approx 90%) so there is little left for responding to new appeals. We receive unsolicited applications at the rate of six or seven each week, 99% are not even considered.'

Information gathered from:

Accounts; Charity Commission record.

S. C. and M. E. Morland's Charitable Trust

Quaker, sickness, welfare, peace and development overseas

£36,000 (2011/12)

Beneficial area

UK.

Correspondent: Victoria Morland, Trustee, 14 Fairmont Terrace, Sherborne DT9 3JS

CC Number: 201645

The trust states in its annual report and accounts that it 'gives to Quaker, local and national charities which have a strong social bias, and also to some UK-based international charities'. Also, that it supports those charities concerned with the relief of poverty and ill health, and those promoting peace and development overseas.

The trust generally makes grants to charities it has supported on a long-term basis, but each year this list is reviewed and new charities may be added.

In 2011/12 the trust had assets of £904,000 and an income of £41,000. There were 94 grants to organisations made totalling £36,000.

There was one grant of £8,000 made to Britain Yearly Meeting. Other grants totalling £28,000 were for less than £1,000 therefore were not listed in the accounts.

Exclusions

The trust does not usually give to animal welfare, individuals or medical research.

Applications

In writing to the correspondent. The trustees meet two times a year to make grants, in March and December. Applications should be submitted in the month before each meeting.

Information gathered from:

Accounts; Charity Commission record.

The Morris Charitable Trust

Relief of need, education, community support and development

£123,000 (2011/12)

Beneficial area

UK, with a preference for Islington; and overseas.

Correspondent: Jack A. Morris, Trustee, c/o Management Office, Business Design Centre, 52 Upper Street, London N1 0QH (tel: 020 7359 3535; fax: 020 7226 0590; email: info@morrischaritabletrust.com; website: www.morrischaritabletrust.com)

Trustees: Jack A. Morris; Paul B. Morris; Alan R. Stenning; Gerald Morris; Dominic Jones.

CC Number: 802290

The Morris Charitable Trust was established in 1989 to provide support for charitable causes. It was founded by the Morris Family, whose principal business – The Business Design Centre Group Ltd – is based in Islington, London. The group contributes a proportion of its annual profits to facilitate the trust's charitable activities.

The trust has general charitable purposes, placing particular emphasis on alleviating social hardship and deprivation, supporting national, international and local charities. There is a preference for supporting causes within the borough of Islington.

In 2011/12 the trust had assets of £185,000 and an income of £125,000 mainly from donations received from the above mentioned company. Grants totalling £123,000 were made to 62 organisations, the majority of which (23) received a grant of less than £500 each. 21 organisations received a grant of between £501 and £1,000, while 16 received grants of between £1,001 and £5,000 and just two received grants of over £5,001. No further information was available.

No list of beneficiaries was available with this year's accounts but previous beneficiaries include: Age Concern – Islington (an unusually large grant of £25,000); The Bridge School – Islington; (£5,000); and Islington Senior Citizens Fund (£1,000).

Exclusions

No grants for individuals. No repeat donations are made within 12 months.

Information gathered from:

Accounts; Charity Commission record; funder's website.

The Willie and Mabel Morris Charitable Trust

Medical, general

£87,000 (2011/12)

Beneficial area

UK.

Correspondent: Angela Tether, 41 Field Lane, Letchworth Garden City, Hertfordshire SG6 3LD (tel: 01462 480583)

Trustees: Michael Macfadyen; Alan Bryant; Peter Tether; Andrew Tether; Angela Tether; Suzanne Marriott; Verity Tether.

CC Number: 280554

The trust was established in 1980 by Mr and Mrs Morris. It was constituted for general charitable purposes and specifically to relieve physical ill-health, particularly lupus, cancer, heart trouble, cerebral palsy, arthritis and rheumatism. Grants are usually only given to registered charities.

In 2011/12 the trust had assets of £3.6 million and an income of £130,000. Grants were made totalling £87,000. A further £58,000 was spent on governance and administration.

Beneficiaries included: St Thomas Lupus Trust (£10,000); UCLH Epilepsy (£7,500); London Centre for Children with Cerebral Palsy (£5,000); St Mary's Church (£4,400); The Prostrate Cancer Charity (£2,500); Gainsborough House Society (£550); Historic Royal Palaces (£500); British Heart Foundation (£350); English National Ballet (£200); and Dementia UK (£100).

Exclusions

No grants for individuals or non-registered charities.

Applications

The trustees 'formulate an independent grants policy at regular meetings so that funds are already committed'.

Information gathered from:

Accounts; Charity Commission record.

The Bernard Morris Charitable Trust

General

About £35,000 (2011/12)

Beneficial area

UK.

Correspondent: Simon Ryde, Trustee, 5 Wolvercote Green, Oxford OX2 8BD (tel: 01865 516593)

Trustees: Simon Ryde; Judith Silver; Simon Fineman; Jessica Ryde; Anne Pelton.

CC Number: 266532

In 2011/12 the trust had an income of £23,000 and a total expenditure of £38,000. Accounts were submitted but not available to view at the Charity Commission due to a low income. Interestingly the trust has spent three times as much as it has received in income across the past five years.

Previous grant recipients included: Oxford Synagogue (£16,000); Dragon School Trust (£12,000); One Voice (£2,500), OCJHS – Oxford Centre for Jewish and Hebrew Studies (£2,000), Soundabout (£1,000), the Story Museum (£500); and Centrepoint Homeless (£200).

Applications

In writing to the correspondent.

Information gathered from:

Accounts; Charity Commission record.

The Peter Morrison Charitable Foundation

Jewish, general

£56,000 (2011/12)

Beneficial area

UK.

Correspondent: J. Payne, Begbies Chettle Agar, Chartered Accountants, Epworth House, 25 City Road, London EC1Y 1AR (tel: 020 7628 5801)

Trustees: M. Morrison; I. R. Morrison; Louise Greenhill; Jane Morrison.

CC Number: 277202

In the trust's annual report it states that 'The trustees are concerned to make donations to charitable institutions which in the opinion of the trustees are most in need and which provide a beneficial service to the needy.'

In 2011/12 the trust had assets of £888,000 and an income of £27,000. Grants were made totalling £56,000.

Beneficiaries included: Hawk Conservancy Trust Ltd (£10,000); RNLI (£4,300); Grange Park Opera (£3,400);

Maccabi GB (£2,000); Alzheimer's Society (£1,000); Cystic Fibrosis Trust (£900); Jewish Care (£500); Langalanga Scholarship Fund (£200); and Friends of the Sick (£50).

Applications

In writing to the correspondent.

Information gathered from:

Accounts; Charity Commission record.

G. M. Morrison Charitable Trust

General

£188,000 (2011/12)

Beneficial area

UK.

Correspondent: Anthony Cornick, Trustee, c/o Currey and Co., 21 Buckingham Gate, London SW1E 6LS (tel: 020 7802 2700)

Trustees: N. W. Smith; Elizabeth Morrison; Anthony Cornick; Jane Hunt.

CC Number: 261380

Grants are mostly given to a wide variety of activities in the social welfare, medical and education/training fields. The trust maintains a list of beneficiaries that it has regularly supported.

In 2011/12 the trust had assets of £9.8 million and an income of £344,000. There were 234 grants made to organisations totalling £188,000, broken down as follows:

Medical and health	£78,000
Social welfare	£58,000
Others	£34,000
Education and training	£17,000

Beneficiaries included: Save the Children (£3,000); British Red Cross Society – Pakistan Floods Appeal, Royal Society of Arts Endowment Fund (£2,000 each); University of Cambridge (£1,200); Enterprise Education Trust, Psychiatry Research Trust, St Luke's Hospital for the Clergy and YMCA England (£1,050 each); Refugee Council Day Centre (£1,000); Crossroads Care and St Mungo's Association (£850 each); British Lung Foundation and Family Action (£750 each); Missionaries of Africa (£700); Musicians Benevolent Fund (£650); and Liverpool School of Tropical Medicine and Salmon Youth Centre (£600 each).

Exclusions

No support for individuals, charities not registered in the UK, retrospective applications, schemes or activities which are generally regarded as the responsibility of statutory authorities, short-term projects or one-off capital grants (except for emergency appeals).

Applications

The trust's annual report states:

> Beneficiaries of grants are normally selected on the basis of the personal knowledge and recommendation of a trustee. The trust's grant making policy is however to support the recipient of grants on a long-term recurring basis. The scope of its giving is determined only by the extent of its resources, and is not otherwise restricted. The trustees have decided that for the present, new applications for grants will only be considered in the most exceptional circumstances, any spare income will be allocated to increasing the grants made to charities currently receiving support. In the future this policy will of course be subject to periodic review. Applicants understanding this policy who nevertheless wish to apply for a grant should write to the [correspondent].

Monitoring is undertaken by assessment of annual reports and accounts which are required from all beneficiaries, and by occasional trustee visits.

Information gathered from:

Accounts; Charity Commission record.

Moshal Charitable Trust

Jewish

£115,000 (2011/12)

Beneficial area

UK.

Correspondent: The Trustees, c/o Sefton Yodaiken and Co., Fairways House, George Street, Prestwich, Manchester M25 9WS (tel: 01617 739411)

CC Number: 284448

This trust is established for general charitable purposes and benefits mainly Jewish causes. In 2011/12 it had assets of £370,000 and an income of £160,000 mainly from donations. Grants during the year totalled £115,000 but a list of beneficiaries was not included in the accounts.

Applications

In writing to the correspondent.

Information gathered from:

Accounts; Charity Commission record.

Vyoel Moshe Charitable Trust

Education, relief of poverty

£668,000 (2010/11)

Beneficial area

UK and overseas.

Correspondent: Mr Berish Berger, Secretary, 2–4 Chardmore Road, London N16 6HX

Trustees: Jacob Frankel; Berish Berger; S. Seidenfeld.

CC Number: 327054

Accounts for this trust are consistently filed more than a year overdue at the Charity Commission. The most recent financial information available at the time of writing was for 2010/11. During this year, the trust had assets of £34,000 and an income of £622,000. Grants were made totalling £668,000, most of which went to overseas organisations. A list of beneficiaries was not included.

Applications

In writing to the correspondent.

Information gathered from:

Accounts; Charity Commission record.

The Moshulu Charitable Trust

'Humanitarian', evangelical

£47,000 (2011/12)

Beneficial area

UK.

Correspondent: H. J. Fulls, Trustee, Devonshire Road, Heathpark, Honiton, Devon EX14 1SD (tel: 01404 540770)

Trustees: H. J. Fulls; D. M. Fulls; G. N. Fulls; S. M. Fulls; G. F. Symons.

CC Number: 1071479

Set up in September 1998, in 2011/12 the trust had an income of £0 and an expenditure of £47,000. No more financial information was available, previously the trust has received all its income from donations and nearly all of the expenditure has been on grants.

Previous beneficiaries included: SWYM (£15,900); Christ Church (£11,700); Tear Fund (£5,400); Partnership UK (£3,000); Care for the Family (£2,400); and Seaway Trust (£1,600).

Applications

In writing to the correspondent.

Information gathered from:

Accounts; Charity Commission record.

Brian and Jill Moss Charitable Trust

Jewish, healthcare

£172,000 (2011/12)

Beneficial area

Worldwide.

Correspondent: The Trustees, c/o Deloitte, 5 Callaghan Square, Cardiff CF10 5BT (tel: 02920 264391)

Trustees: Brian Moss; Jill Moss; David Moss; Sarah Levy.

CC Number: 1084664

Established in 2000, this trust makes grants for capital projects and towards 'ordinary charity expenditure'. In 2011/12 assets stood at £3.2 million, income was £124,000 and grants were made totalling £172,000.

No list of beneficiaries was available for this accounting year but previous beneficiaries include: United Jewish Israel Appeal (£43,000); Magen David Adom UK (£31,000); Jewish Care (£16,000); World Jewish Relief (£15,000); Norwood (£13,000); Chai Cancer Care (£12,000); United Synagogue-Tribe (£11,000); Cancer Bacup (£6,300); WIZO UK (£6,000);National Jewish Chaplaincy Board (£5,500); Prostate Cancer Charitable Trust (£5,000); Jewish Association for the Mentally Ill (£3,500); Myeloma UK (£3,000); Holocaust Centre and Israel Folk Dance Institute (£500 each); and Jewish Museum and Operation Wheelchairs (£250 each).

Exclusions

Donations are made to registered charities only.

Applications

In writing to the correspondent. 'Appeals are considered as they are received and the trustees will make donations throughout the year.'

Information gathered from:

Accounts; Charity Commission record.

The Moss Charitable Trust

Christian, education, poverty, health

£78,000 to organisations (2011/12)

Beneficial area

Worldwide, with an interest in Dorset, Hampshire and Sussex.

Correspondent: P. D. Malpas, 7 Church Road, Parkstone, Poole, Dorset BH14 8UF (tel: 01202 730002)

Trustees: J. H. Simmons; A. F. Simmons; D. S. Olby.

CC Number: 258031

The objects of the trust are to benefit the community in the county borough of Bournemouth and the counties of Hampshire, Dorset and Sussex, and also the advancement of religion in the UK and overseas, the advancement of education and the relief of poverty, disease and sickness.

The trust achieves this by providing facilities for contributors to give under Gift Aid or direct giving and redistributes them according to their recommendations. The trustees also make smaller grants from the general income of the trust.

In 2011/12 the trust had assets of £146,000 and an income of £199,000. Grants were given totalling £83,000, broken down as follows:

UK institutions	£63,000
Overseas institutions	£15,000
UK individuals	£2,600
Overseas individuals	£2,000

Beneficiaries receiving grants of £1,000 or more included: Palawan Partners (£12,000); Christ Church Westbourne (£6,400); Tamil Church (£4,400); Chichester Counselling Service (£3,500); Echo Worldwide (£2,400); Slindon Parochial Church Council (£2,100); Barnabas Fund (£1,900); Care Trust (£1,700); Crosslinks (£1,400); Napam (£1,300); Youth Action for Holistic development (£1,200); European Christian Mission (£1,100); and Trinity Methodist Church (£1,000).

Applications

No funds are available by direct application. Because of the way in which this trust operates it is not open to external applications for grants.

Information gathered from:

Accounts; Charity Commission record.

J. P. Moulton Charitable Foundation

Medical, education, training and counselling

£1.7 million (2012)

Beneficial area

UK.

Correspondent: Jon Moulton, Trustee, c/o Better Capital LLP, 39–41 Charing Cross Road, London WC2H 0AR (tel: 020 7440 0860)

Trustees: Jon Moulton; Spencer Moulton; Sara Everett.

CC Number: 1109891

Registered in 2005, this is the foundation of venture capitalist, Jon Moulton. The foundation provides:

> Charitable donations for community service projects of any kind and to further the aims of the community by promoting education, training, counselling for disadvantaged persons of any age; to provide donations to hospitals, hospices, medical and care projects of any kind and to generally promote the relief of suffering.

In 2012 the foundation had assets of £2 million and an income of £72,000. Grants were made totalling just over £1.7 million. All grants made during the year were for medical research projects.

The beneficiaries were: University of Manchester (£491,000); University College London (£396,500); University of Bristol (£300,000); London School of Tropical Medicine (£189,000); Imperial College London (£142,000); University of Cambridge (£65,000); King's College Hospital (£46,000); Brain Tumour Charity (£32,500); Myasthenia Gravis Association (£30,000); King's College London (£13,000); Liverpool Women's NHS Foundation Trust (£11,000); and University of Leicester (£10,000).

Applications

In writing to the correspondent.

Information gathered from:

Accounts; Charity Commission record.

The Edwina Mountbatten and Leonora Children's Foundation

Medical, general

£149,000 (2011/12)

Beneficial area

UK and overseas.

Correspondent: John Moss, Secretary, Estate Office, Broadlands, Romsey, Hampshire SO51 9ZE (tel: 01794 529750)

Trustees: Countess Mountbatten of Burma, Chair; Hon. Alexandra Knatchbull; Lord Brabourne; Peter H. T. Mimpriss; Dame Mary Fagan; Lady Brabourne; Myrddin Rees; Sir Evelyn De Rothschild.

CC Number: 228166

The Edwina Mountbatten Trust was established in 1960 to honour the causes Edwina, Countess Mountbatten of Burma was involved with during her lifetime. Each year support is given to St John Ambulance (of which she was superintendent-in-chief) for work in the UK and its Commonwealth, and Save the Children (of which she was president) for the relief of children who are sick, distressed or otherwise in need. Nursing organisations are also supported, as she was the patron or vice-president of a number of nursing organisations. Grants, even to the core beneficiaries, are only given towards specific projects rather than core costs.

Charity Commission approval was received to merge the trust with The Leonora Children's Cancer Fund and to adopt a working title of The Edwina Mountbatten and Leonora Children's Foundation. The merger took place on 1 January 2010, and the assets of The Leonora Children's Cancer Fund were transferred to the Edwina Mountbatten Trust.

In 2012 the trust had assets of £5 million and an income of £153,000. Grants to 14 organisations totalled £149,000.

Beneficiaries included: St John Jerusalem Eye Hospital, Brecknock Hospice and Rainbow Trust (£30,000 each); Save the Children (£25,000); Cancer Research UK (£10,000); Home Start Eastleigh (£5,000); Riders for Health and Malaria No More (£3,000 each); Ashram International and Hope 4 the World (£2,000 each); and Queens Nursing Institute (£1,000).

Exclusions

No grants for research or to individual nurses working in the UK for further professional training.

Applications

Details of how to apply for grants can be obtained from the Trust Secretary. The trustees meet once a year, generally in September/October.

Information gathered from:

Accounts; Charity Commission record.

Mountbatten Festival of Music

Royal Marines and Royal Navy charities

£115,500 (2011/12)

Beneficial area

UK.

Correspondent: Lt Col Ian Grant, Corps Secretary, The Corps Secretariat, Building 32, HMS Excellent, Whale Island, Portsmouth PO2 8ER (tel: 02392 547201; email: royalmarines.charities@charity.vfree.com; website: www.royalmarinesregimental.co.uk)

Trustees: Commandant General Royal Marines; Director of Royal Marines; Naval Personnel Team (RM) Team Leader.

CC Number: 1016088

The trust was set up in 1993 and is administered by the Royal Marines. It raises funds from band concerts, festivals of music and beating retreat. The main beneficiaries are service charities connected with the Royal Marines and Royal Navy. The only other beneficiaries are those hospitals or rehabilitation centres and so on, which have recently directly aided a Royal Marine in some way and Malcolm Sergeant Cancer Care. One-off and recurrent grants are made.

In 2011/12 the charity had an income of £495,000 and made grants to 15 organisations totalling £115,500.

Beneficiaries included: Royal Marines Charitable Trust Fund (£53,500); CLIC Sargent (15,000); RN Benevolent Trust, Royal Marines Museum and Royal Navy and Royal Marines Children's Fund (£10,000 each); Combat Stress (£4,000); Blind Veterans UK (£3,000); BLESMA (£2,000); and Erskine Hospital and Women's Royal Naval Service Benevolent Trust (£1,000 each).

Exclusions

Charities or organisations unknown to the trustees.

Applications

Unsolicited applications are not considered as the trust's income is dependent upon the running and success of various musical events. Any money raised is then disbursed to a set of regular beneficiaries.

Information gathered from:

Accounts; Charity Commission record; funder's website.

The Mountbatten Memorial Trust

Technological research in aid of disabilities

£45,000 (2012)

Beneficial area

Mainly UK, but some overseas.

Correspondent: John Moss, Secretary, The Estate Office, Broadlands, Romsey, Hampshire SO51 9ZE (tel: 01794 529750)

Trustees: Countess Mountbatten of Burma; Lady Pamela Hicks; Ben Moorhead; Ashley Hicks; Hon. Michael John Knatchbull; Hon. Philip Knatchbull; William Fox and Kelly Knatchbull.

CC Number: 278691

The trust was set up in 1979 to honour the ideals of the Admiral of the Fleet, the Earl Mountbatten of Burma. It supports charities and causes 'working to further the humanitarian purposes with which he was associated in his latter years'. The trust mainly focuses on making grants towards the development of technical aids for people with disabilities. Another focus has been to support the United World Colleges movement, which has the aim of providing a broad education to students from around the world and community projects are also an interest of the trust.

Following the merger with the Mountbatten Community Trust in January 2008, grants are now also made to aid the young and disadvantage in various communities throughout Britain. Grants are usually made to UK based charities, although their work can be worldwide, on a one year basis although three to four year projects have been supported in the past.

In 2011/12 the trust had assets of £549,000 and an income of £37,000. Grants were made totalling £45,000, with £40,000 given for educational projects and £4,600 for 'technological and other grants'.

The beneficiaries during the year were: Atlantic College (£40,000); Canine Partners (£1,600); and British Wireless for the Blind, The Elizabeth Foundation and Sign Health (£1,000 each).

Exclusions

No grants are made towards the purchase of technology to assist people with disabilities.

Applications

In writing to the correspondent, at any time. Further details of how to apply can be obtained from the Secretary.

Information gathered from:

Accounts; Charity Commission record.

Mrs Waterhouse Charitable Trust (formerly known as the Houghton Dunn Charitable Trust)

Medical, health, welfare, environment, wildlife, churches, heritage

£298,000 (2012/13)

Beneficial area

UK, with an interest in North West England.

Correspondent: Mark Dunn, Carlton Place, 28–32 Greenwood Street, Altrincham WA14 1RZ

Trustees: Alistair Houghton Dunn; Richard Houghton Dunn.

CC Number: 261685

According to the trustees' report for 2012/13:

> The trust makes donations to bodies embracing a wide range of charities; the

> main fields supported being medical and health, welfare in the community, environment and wildlife, and church and heritage with special reference to charities in, or with branches in the North West of England.

In 2012/13 the trust had assets of £7.2 million and an income of £302,000. Grants were made to 29 organisations totalling £298,000. Grants were broken down as follows:

Welfare in the community – children and youth	11	103,000
Medical and health – general	7	81,000
Welfare in the community – general	4	44,000
Medical and health – children	3	35,000
Medical and health – research	2	20,000
Environment and wildlife	2	15,000

Previous beneficiaries have included: AMEND, Arthritis Research Campaign, Cancer BACUP, Cancer Research UK, Christie Hospital NHS Trust, East Lancashire Hospice Fund, Lancashire Wildlife Trust, Marie Curie Cancer Care, Macmillan Cancer Relief, National Eczema Society, National Trust Lake District Appeal and National Youth Orchestra.

Exclusions

No grants to individuals.

Applications

In writing to the correspondent.

Information gathered from:

Accounts; Charity Commission record.

The MSE Charity

Financial education, improving financial literacy

£101,000 (2011/12)

Beneficial area

UK.

Correspondent: Anthony Jeffrey, Administrator, PO Box 240, Gatley, Cheadle SK8 4XT (tel: 01618 349221; email: stuart@msecharity.com; website: www.msecharity.com)

Trustees: Tony Tesciuba; John Hewison, Chair; Katie Birkett; Vanessa Bissessur; Teej Dew.

CC Number: 1121320

This trust was founded in 2007 by the popular television and radio personality and founder of the Money Saving Expert website, Martin Lewis.

According to the trust's website:

> The MSE Charity addresses the UK's massive problem of financial illiteracy by funding relevant guidance and education for individuals and groups.
>
> The MSE Charity will support eligible individuals and groups who want to help eradicate this illiteracy through self-development or innovative projects.

The trust sets out a number of helpful criteria for groups or applicants seeking to establish innovative projects:

- Projects must assist people to improve their quality of life through knowledge and understanding of how to manage and take control of their own financial situation
- Groups will need to demonstrate that they have researched and assessed the need for the project
- Groups must demonstrate that the project will make a significant difference to the beneficiaries so the OUTPUTS must be achievable, measurable, deliverable within budget and within a time frame and be sustainable
- Groups will also need to show that the project will also provide outcomes that will benefit their wider communities
- Groups should demonstrate that they have the skills, ability and experience to deliver the project
- The trust will consider full project cost recovery, but costs must only relate to the project itself and not the organisation's core funding
- Projects must demonstrate value for money
- Projects should seek to provide long-term solutions rather than short one-off events
- For existing projects with a proven success record, consideration will only be given to those that can demonstrate that funding will be used to extend the project beyond its existing boundaries in terms of the scope of project, number of beneficiaries and/or time frame

Applicants must be a 'constituted group', meaning they must have a bank accounts and a set of rules which make it accountable. Grants are generally for around £5,000 or less.

In 2011/12 the trust had assets of £270,000 and an income of £230,000, mostly from donations. Grants were made totalling £101,000, consisting of £87,000 for 'projects' and £14,000 to fund training courses.

No list of beneficiaries was included in the accounts however the website lists all the beneficiaries the trust has supported since its inception.

Beneficiaries in 2013 included: North Liverpool CAB, Whitlawburn Community Resource Centre, Wintercomfort for the Homeless, Building Bridges, Jubilee Family Centre, Financial Inclusion Derbyshire, Durham Christian Partnership, East Ayrshire Carers centre, Solihull Action through Advocacy, Institute of Money Advisers, The Elfrida Society Parents Project and Mancunian Way.

Exclusions

No funding for career development, vocational courses, undergraduate or postgraduate courses. No applications directly from persons under 18 years of age, such applicants will need a parent or guardian to apply on their behalf.

Applications

Applications must be made via the online application form. The trust is open to applications for a month three times a year, usually January, May and September check the website for upcoming deadlines. It will close to applications either after a month or when 40 completed applications have been received, whichever is the earlier.

After a provisional eligibility check the application will be given to the Grant Approval Panel, which meets three times a year. Only one application will be accepted from an organisation within a two year period.

If you have a project you consider to be special, and which does not appear to fit into the other criteria, then write directly to the Operations Manager (stuart@msecharity.com), who will bring it to the attention of the trustees.

Information gathered from:

Accounts; Charity Commission record; funder's website.

Frederick Mulder Charitable Trust (formerly the Prairie Trust)

International development, climate change, conflict prevention

£172,000 (2011/12)

Beneficial area

Worldwide.

Correspondent: Dr Frederick Mulder, 83 Belsize Park Gardens, London NW3 4NJ (tel: 020 7722 2105; email: info@frederickmulder.com)

Trustees: Dr Frederick Mulder; Hannah Mulder; Robin Bowman; Rhodes Pinto.

CC Number: 296019

The trust does not consider unsolicited applications and instead develops its own programme to support a small number of organisations working on issues of third world development, climate change and conflict prevention, particularly to support policy and advocacy work in these areas. The trustees are also interested in supporting innovative and entrepreneurial approaches to traditional problems and organisations encouraging the development of philanthropy.

Many grants are now made through the Funding Network, to projects which have presented at both the London and non-London events, and the trust also helps to support the Network's operating costs. The trust states that this trend is likely to continue and possibly increase in future years.

In 2011/12 the trust had assets of £1.6 million and an income of £155,000. Grants to organisations totalled £172,000.

Beneficiaries included: The Funding Network (for various projects, TFN London and other TFN groups plus operational costs) (£79,000); 10:10 (carbon emissions) (£35,000); and Novim Group (climate change) (£30,000).

Exclusions

No grants to individuals or for expeditions.

Applications

The trust states: 'As we are a proactive trust with limited funds and administrative help, we are unable to consider unsolicited applications.'

Percentage of awards given to new applicants: between 20% and 30%.

Information gathered from:

Accounts; Charity Commission record; further information provided by the funder.

Murphy-Neumann Charity Company Ltd

Health, social welfare, medical research

£60,000 (2011/12)

Beneficial area

UK.

Correspondent: Mark Lockett, Trustee, Hayling Cottage, Upper Street, Stratford-St-Mary, Colchester, Essex CO7 6JW (tel: 01206 323685; email: mncc@keme.co.uk)

Trustees: Mark J. Lockett; Paula Christopher; Marcus Richman.

CC Number: 229555

The trust has three main objects:

- To support projects aimed at helping those in society who suffer economic or social disadvantages or hardship arising from disability and/or social exclusion
- To assist those working to alleviate chronic illness and disabling disease
- To help fund research into medical conditions (particularly among the very young and the elderly) for which there is not yet a cure

In 2011/12 the trust had assets of £1.5 million and an income of £67,000. Grants totalled £60,000. The trust provided the following analysis of its grantmaking in the latest accounts:

> Of the sixty one charities to which donations were made around twenty fell into the core category with whom Murphy Neumann has had an on-going, long-term relationship. In most cases these are relatively high profile organisations serving a large and well attested client base. Murphy Neumann made donations to around some fifteen charities primarily concerned with ameliorating the conditions of those who suffer specific economic or social disadvantage or hardship, approximately twenty charities most active in the investigation and alleviation of disabling and potentially terminal diseases and the remainder, charities mostly fairly small and community based, providing a mix of services to a clientele broadly drawn from among those who fall within the charity's overall catchment.
>
> The trustees do not have a fixed policy with regard to the number of charities that can be supported. Each year a decision is taken on how much money is available for distribution without putting Murphy Neumann at risk. The trustees are mindful that donations should not be so small that they make little or no impact on the needs of the recipient. Not only could such donations hinder rather than help recipients but they would diminish the funds available to other charities with a perceived greater claim. With these considerations in mind the trustees have reached the conclusion that for the time being grants should be fixed at a maximum of £2,500 and a minimum of £500. The majority of grants fall within the range £750 -£2,000.
>
> [...] It is difficult to measure the impact of (relatively) small grants on large organisations. In a number of cases grants are made to general funds rather than to support specific initiatives. In the case of smaller charities grants are invariably made towards named and known projects. This might include the purchase of specialist equipment, sponsoring programmes or activities or funding long-term research into disabling diseases. In recent years charities have been obliged to comply with new legislation and in many cases this has entailed the provision of new facilities and the adaptation of old buildings to meet current needs. In several such cases the trustees have been able to support projects essential to the well-being or even survival of relatively large organisations. In one or two cases top-up grants have been made to small charities, particularly those with outreach programmes, where funding is essential to maintain their role in the community.

Beneficiaries during the year included: Evening Argus Christmas Appeal and Contact the Elderly (£2,000 each); Acorn Villages and Autistica (£1,500 each); Hospice in the Weald and Action on Elder Abuse (£1,250 each); Vitalise, Chicks Camping Holidays, Housing the Homeless Central Fund, The Prostrate Cancer Charity, Dream Makers, Daisy's Eye Cancer Fund and Tourettes Action (£1,000 each); Lowe Syndrome Trust (£750); and Youth Talk (£500).

Exclusions

No grants to individuals, or non-registered charities.

Applications

In writing to the correspondent, in a letter outlining the purpose of the required charitable donation. Telephone calls are not welcome. There are no application forms, guidelines or deadlines. No sae required. Grants are usually given in November and December. Printed grant criteria is available on request.

Percentage of awards given to new applicants: less than 10%.

Common applicant mistakes

'Our grantmaking criteria are clearly specified in the annual/financial report available via Companies House and the Charity Commission. We also have printed criteria which may be had on application. A small minority of applications fall outside our criteria but it is evident that most applicants have searched the relevant register before applying.'

Information gathered from:

Accounts; Charity Commission record; further information provided by the funder.

The Mushroom Fund

General charitable purposes

£25,000 (2011/12)

Beneficial area

UK and overseas, with a preference for St Helens.

Correspondent: The Trustees, Liverpool Charity and Voluntary Services, 151 Dale Street, Liverpool L2 2AH (tel: 01512 275177; email: enquiries@charitycheques.org.uk)

Trustees: Rosalind Christian; Guy Pilkington; James Pilkington; Harriet Christian; Liverpool Charity and Voluntary Services.

CC Number: 259954

The trust has general charitable purposes, only supporting causes known to the trustees.

In 2011/12 the trust had assets of £987,000 and an income of £35,000. Grants were made totalling £25,000 of which 11 were listed in the accounts.

Beneficiaries receiving grants of £1,000 or more each included: Save the Family (£5,000); Liverpool CVS (£2,000); and Age UK (mid-Mersey), Halton and St Helens Voluntary Community Action, SENSE, Samaritans and Walesby Village Hall (£1,000 each).

Exclusions

No grants to individuals or to organisations that are not registered charities.

Applications

The trust does not consider or respond to unsolicited applications.

Percentage of awards given to new applicants: less than 10%.

Common applicant mistakes

'Applying to a personal charitable trust.'

Information gathered from:

Accounts; Charity Commission record; further information provided by the funder.

The Music Sales Charitable Trust

Children and youth, musical education, see below

£64,000 (2011)

Beneficial area

UK, but mostly Bury St Edmunds and London.

Correspondent: Neville Wignall, Clerk, Music Sales Ltd, Dettingen Way, Bury St Edmunds, Suffolk IP33 3YB (tel: 01284 702600; email: neville.wignall@musicsales.co.uk)

Trustees: Robert Wise; Mr T. Wise; Ian Morgan; Christopher Butler; David Rockberger; Mildred Wise; Mr A. E. Latham; Mr M. Wise; Jane Richardson.

CC Number: 1014942

The trust was established in 1992 by the company Music Sales Ltd. It supports registered charities benefiting children and young adults, musicians, people who are disabled and people disadvantaged by poverty', particularly those resident in London and Bury St Edmunds. The trust is also interested in helping to promote music and musical education, again with a particular interest in children attending schools in London and Bury St Edmunds.

In 2011 the trust had assets of £30,000 and an income of £75,000, from donations. There were 76 grants made totalling £64,000, broken down as follows:

Medical, health, sickness	37	£23,000
Arts and culture	15	£21,000
Education/training	12	£7,300
Religion	2	£5,500
Disability	3	£2,300
General	4	£2,200
Overseas aid/famine relief	3	£2,100

Beneficiaries included: Bury St Edmunds Borough Council (£6,500); Westminster Synagogue and Bury St Edmunds Bach Society (£5,000 each); Royal College of Music (£2,500); St Nicholas Hospice Care (£2,300); The Salmon Trust – Thurston Festival and Action Medical Research for Children for Life (£1,500 each); and Save a Child – India, Fulfil the Wish, Great Ormond Street Hospital Children's Charity, Paralympics 2012 and Young People Taking Action (£1,000 each).

Exclusions

No grants to individuals.

Applications

In writing to the correspondent. The trustees meet quarterly, generally in March, June, September and December.

Information gathered from:

Accounts; Charity Commission record.

The Mutual Trust Group

Jewish, education, poverty

£315,000 (2012)

Beneficial area

UK.

Correspondent: Rabbi Benzion Weitz, Trustee, 12 Dunstan Road, London NW11 8AA (tel: 020 8458 7549)

Trustees: Rabbi Benzion Weitz; Michael Weitz; Adrian Weisz.

CC Number: 1039300

In 2012 the trust had assets of £153,000, an income of £304,000 and made grants totalling £315,000.

Beneficiaries included: Yeshivat Kesser Hatalmud (£217,000); Yeshivat Shar Hashamayim (£89,000); and 'other' (£1,000).

Applications

In writing to the correspondent.

Information gathered from:

Accounts; Charity Commission record.

MYA Charitable Trust

Jewish

£182,000 to organisations (2011/12)

Beneficial area

Worldwide.

Correspondent: Myer Rothfeld, Trustee, Medcar House, 149a Stamford Hill, London N16 5LL (tel: 020 8800 3582)

Trustees: Myer Rothfeld; Eve Rothfeld; Hannah Schraiber; Joseph Pfeffer.

CC Number: 299642

Grants are given for the advancement of Orthodox Judaism including religious education and the relief of poverty and distress.

In 2011/12 the trust had assets of £980,000 and an income of £201,000. Grants to organisations were made totalling £182,000. A further £6,500 was given in grants to individuals.

A list of beneficiaries was not included in the accounts. Previous beneficiaries have included: ZSV Trust, KZF, Beis Rochel, Keren Zedoko Vochesed, London Friends of Kamenitzer Yeshiva, Maos Yesomim Charitable Trust, Bikkur Cholim De Satmar, Keren Mitzva Trust and Wlodowa Charity Rehabilitation Trust.

Applications

In writing to the correspondent.

Information gathered from:

Accounts; Charity Commission record.

MYR Charitable Trust

Jewish

£43,000 (2011/12)

Beneficial area

In practice, Israel, USA and England.

Correspondent: Z. M. Kaufman, Trustee, 50 Keswick Street, Gateshead, Tyne and Wear NE8 1TQ

Trustees: Z. M. Kaufman; S. Kaufman; A. A. Zonszajn; J. Kaufman.

CC Number: 1104406

In 2012 the trust had assets of £1.1 million, an income of £94,000 and gave grants totalling £43,000.

A list of beneficiaries was not included in the accounts. Previous beneficiaries included: Cong Beth Joseph, HP Charitable Trust, UTA, Gateshead Jewish Boarding School, Keren Eretz Yisorel, SCT Sunderland and GJLC.

Applications

In writing to the correspondent. The trustees consider all requests which they receive and make donations based on the level of funds available.

Information gathered from:

Accounts; Charity Commission record.

The Kitty and Daniel Nabarro Charitable Trust

Welfare, education, medicine, homeless, general

Around £19,000 (2011/12)

Beneficial area

UK.

Correspondent: Daniel Nabarro, Trustee, 24 Totteridge Common,

London N20 8NE (email: admin.nabarro.charity@gmail.com)

Trustees: Daniel Nabarro; Katherine Nabarro; Allan Watson.

CC Number: 1002786

The trust makes grants towards the relief of poverty, advancement of medicine and advancement of education, with some preference for work with homeless people. This trust will consider funding: information technology and computers; support and self-help groups; nature reserves; environmental issues; IT training; literacy; training for work; vocational training; and crime prevention schemes.

In 2011/12 the trust had an income of £21,000 and total expenses of £19,000. As the income was below £25,000 accounts were not displayed on the Commission's website. Previous beneficiaries include: Cambridge Foundation Discovery Fund (£5,000); and OCD Action (£2,000).

Exclusions

No grants to individuals.

Applications

The trustees allocate grants on an annual basis to an existing list of charities. The trustees do not envisage grants to charities which are not already on the list. This trust states that it does not respond to unsolicited applications.

Information gathered from:

Accounts; Charity Commission record.

The Nadezhda Charitable Trust

Christian

£27,000 (2011/12)

Beneficial area

UK and worldwide, particularly Zimbabwe.

Correspondent: Mrs Jill Kingston, Trustee, c/o Ballard Dale Syree Watson LLP, Oakmore Court, Kingswood Road, Hampton Lovett, Droitwich Spa WR9 0QH

Trustees: William M. Kingston; Jill M. Kingston; Anthony R. Collins; Ian Conolly.

CC Number: 1007295

The trust makes grants to projects for the advancement of Christianity in the UK and overseas, especially Zimbabwe.

In 2011/12 the trust had assets of £33,000 and an income of £28,000, all from donations. Grants were made totalling £27,000.

Beneficiaries included: Mind the Gap Africa (£5,700); Family Impact (£2,400); All Saints Kemble (£2,000); Impact Giving (£1,200); and World Horizons (£1,000).

Exclusions

No grants to individuals.

Applications

From the trust's annual report: 'The Trust has continued to operate on the basis of not supporting projects from unsolicited contacts.'

Information gathered from:

Accounts; Charity Commission record.

The Naggar Charitable Trust

Jewish, the arts, general

Around £10,000 (2011/12)

Beneficial area

UK and overseas.

Correspondent: G. Naggar, Trustee, 61 Avenue Road, London NW8 6HR (tel: 020 7034 1919)

Trustees: Guy Naggar; Hon. Marion Naggar; Marc Zilkha.

CC Number: 265409

The trust mainly supports Jewish organisations and a few medical charities and arts organisations.

The trust has had an irregular income in recent years ranging from £527,000 in 2007/08 to £0 in 2011/12. Total expenditure has also fallen from a high of £424,000 to just £13,000 in 2011/12.

Previous beneficiaries included: British Friends of the Art Museums of Israel (£15,000); Western Marble Arch Synagogue (£11,000); CST (£8,500); The Contemporary Arts Society and The Royal Parks Foundation (£5,000 each); Jewish Care and One Family UK (£2,500 each); Royal Academy of Arts (£1,000); and St John's Wood Society (£15).

Applications

In writing to the correspondent.

Information gathered from:

Accounts; Charity Commission record.

The Eleni Nakou Foundation

Education, international understanding

Around £80,000 (2011/12)

Beneficial area

Worldwide, mostly Continental Europe.

Correspondent: Chris Gilbert, Secretary, Kleinwort Benson Trustees Ltd, 14 St George Street, London W1S 1FE (tel: 020 3207 7000; email: chris.gilbert@kbpb.co.uk)

Trustee: Kleinwort Benson Trustees Ltd.

CC Number: 803753

The main aim of the trust is to advance the education of the people of Europe in each other's culture.

In 2011/12 the foundation had an income of just £600 and an expenditure of £88,000. No further details were available.

Previous beneficiaries have included: Danish Institute at Athens (£45,000); Hellenic Foundation (£17,500); Eleni Nakou Scholarship Athens (£9,000); Scandinavian Society for Modern Greek Studies (£1,000).

Applications

In writing to the correspondent. Applications are considered periodically. However, the trustees' state: 'It is unusual to respond favourably to unsolicited appeals'.

Information gathered from:

Accounts; Charity Commission record.

The Janet Nash Charitable Settlement

Medical, hardship, general

£301,000 to organisations and individuals (2011/12)

Beneficial area

UK.

Correspondent: Ronald Gulliver, Trustee, Ron Gulliver, The Old Chapel, New Mill Lane, Eversley, Hampshire RG27 0RA (tel: 01189 733194)

Trustees: Ronald Gulliver; Mark Stephen Jacobs; Charlotte Emma Westall.

CC Number: 326880

Established in March 1985, this charity supports medical research and education, particularly in the area of pathology. Grants are made to fund medical students who wish to have an extra research year at medical school and also to other research projects the trustees consider worthwhile.

In 2011/12 the charity had assets of £85,000 and an income of £304,000. Grants totalled £301,000 of which £26,500 went to organisations.

Beneficiary organisations were: Get-a-Head Charitable Trust (£15,000); Sense (£5,000); Dyslexia Institute (£4,000); County Air Ambulance Trust (£1,500); and Birmingham Children's Hospital (£1,000).

Applications

Absolutely no response to unsolicited applications. The trustees have stated:

'The charity does not, repeat not, ever consider any applications for benefit from the public'. Furthermore, that: 'Our existing charitable commitments more than use up our potential funds and were found personally by the trustees themselves, never as a result of applications from third parties'.

Information gathered from:

Accounts; Charity Commission record.

National Committee of the Women's World Day of Prayer for England and Wales and Northern Ireland (formerly known as Women's World Day of Prayer)

Promotion of the Christian faith

£277,000 (2012)

Beneficial area

UK and worldwide.

Correspondent: Mary Judd, Administrator, Commercial Road, Tunbridge Wells TN1 2RR (tel: 01892 541411; email: office@wwdp-natcomm.org; website: www.wwdp-natcomm.org)

CC Number: 233242

The trust's website states:

> Women's World Day of Prayer is a global, ecumenical movement of informed prayer and prayerful action, organised and led by Christian women who call the faithful together on the first Friday in March each year to observe a common day of prayer and who, in many countries, have a continuing relationship in prayer and service.

According to the trustees' report for 2012, 'the main object of the charity is to unite Christians in prayer.' The object of the charity is achieved by fulfilling the following:

- Holding services on the first Friday in March in each year
- Fostering local interdenominational prayer groups and other activities bringing women together in closer fellowship, understanding and action throughout the year
- Distribution of Christian literature
- Supporting women throughout the world with informed prayer and prayerful action
- Assisting projects, financially or otherwise, run by Christian charities throughout the world

> After meeting overhead expenses and maintaining reserves as stated, the National Committee allocates surplus income to assist projects run by Christian charities throughout the world.

In 2012 the trust had assets of £444,000 and an income of £552,000. Grants were made to 48 organisations totalling £277,000.

Beneficiaries included: Foundation for Relief and Reconciliation in the Middle East (£30,000); Friends of Ebenezer Child Care (£20,000); Bible Society and Feed the Minds (£15,000 each); United Society for Christian Literature and Wycliffe UK Ltd (£10,000 each); Hope Christian Trust (£8,000); Bible Reading Fellowship, International Bible Reading Association and People International (£3,000 each); Mission India (£2,000); Wales Sunday Schools Council (£1,600); Welsh Council on Alcohol and Drugs (£500); and Christian Aid and Cafod (£300 each).

Exclusions

No grants to individuals.

Applications

In writing to the correspondent.

Percentage of awards given to new applicants: between 40% and 50%.

Common applicant mistakes

'They ignore our basic criteria, i.e. our constitution requirements, wasting both their time and ours.'

Information gathered from:

Accounts; Charity Commission record; further information provided by the funder; funder's website.

The National Manuscripts Conservation Trust

Conservation of manuscripts

£165,000 (2011/12)

Beneficial area

UK.

Correspondent: Mrs Nell Hoare, Secretary, PO Box 4291, Reading, Berkshire RG8 9JA (tel: 020 8392 5218; email: info@nmct.org.uk; website: www.nmct.co.uk)

CC Number: 802796

The object of the trust is to advance the education of the public by making grants towards the cost of conserving manuscripts and archives which are of historic or educational value. Funding is given:

- To record offices and libraries in the United Kingdom offering public access and not directly funded by the government including local authorities universities and specialised record repositories
- To owners of manuscripts and archives resident in the United Kingdom which are conditionally exempt from capital taxation or which are owned by a charitable trust subject to assurances regarding adequate public access to such manuscripts
- Towards the cost of repair, binding and conservation including reprography of manuscripts which in the opinion of the Trustees are of historic or educational value and towards the cost of first stage listing but not for capital cost or equipment

Grants are awarded in June and December, for up to 90% of the cost of conservation of manuscripts held by any record office, library or by an owner of manuscript material that is exempt from capital taxation or owned by a charitable trust.

In 2012 the trust had assets of £2 million and an income of £175,000. Grants totalled £165,000.

Beneficiaries included: Dr Williams' Library (£22,000); Cambridge Fitzwilliam Museum and Church of England Record Centre (£15,000 each); University of Southampton (£15,500); Bangor University Archive (£12,000); Essex Record Office (£9,500); Glamorgan Archive Aberystwyth University Archive (£4,400); Cornwall Record Office (£3,300); Anglesey Archives (£1,800); and Ceredigion Archives (£1,400).

Exclusions

The following are not eligible: public records within the meaning of the Public Records Act; official archives of the institution or authority applying except in the case of some older records; loan collections unless exempt from capital taxation or owned by a charitable trust; and photographic, audio-visual or printed materials.

Applications

On a form available to download from the website, along with guidance notes. Applicants must submit six copies of the application form including six copies of a detailed description of the project. The applicant should also submit one copy of their most recent annual reports and accounts and details of its constitution.

The deadlines are usually 1 April and 1 October, check the website for the deadlines and full details of how to apply.

> In deciding whether an application should be awarded a grant, the Trustees take into account the significance of the manuscript or archive, the suitability of the storage conditions, the applicant's commitment to continuing good preservation practice, and the requirement for the public to have

reasonable access to it. Written reports on each application are given to the trustees by specialist staff from the National Archives working on a pro bono basis, but there is no other contribution by volunteers.

Information gathered from:

Accounts; Charity Commission record; funder's website.

Nazareth Trust Fund

Christian, in the UK and developing countries

£40,000 (2011/12)

Beneficial area

UK and developing countries.

Correspondent: Dr Robert W. G. Hunt, Trustee, Barrowpoint, 18 Millennium Close, Salisbury, Wiltshire SP2 8TB (tel: 01722 349322)

CC Number: 210503

The trust funds churches, Christian missionaries, Christian youth work and overseas aid. Grants are only made to people or causes known personally to the trustees.

In 2011/12 the trust had assets of £37,000 and an income of £38,000, mostly from gift aid. Grants to organisations totalled £40,000, with a further £1,800 being given in grants to individuals.

Beneficiaries included: Hamham Free Church (£8,000); IREF (£5,500 in two grants); Durham Rd Baptist Church (£2,000 in two grants); Crusaders (£1,000); London School of Theology (£300); Christian Viewpoint for Men (£250); and Jubilee Centre and Scripture Union (£100 each).

Exclusions

No support for individuals not known to the trustees.

Applications

'We only give to people we know personally. Unsolicited applications are unsuccessful.'

Percentage of awards given to new applicants: less than 10%.

Common applicant mistakes

'Applying when they are not know to us personally.'

Information gathered from:

Accounts; Charity Commission record; further information provided by the funder.

Ner Foundation

Orthodox Jewish

£210,000 (2011/12)

Beneficial area

UK and Israel.

Correspondent: A. Henry, Trustee, 309 Bury New Road, Salford, Manchester M7 2YN

CC Number: 1104866

Set up in July 2004 as a company limited by guarantee:

> The objects of the charity are the relief of poverty amongst the elderly or persons in need, hardship or distress in the Jewish Community; the advancement of the Orthodox Jewish Religion and the advancement of education according to the tenets of the Orthodox Jewish Faith.

In 2011/12 the foundation had assets of £392,000 and an income of £190,000. A list of beneficiaries was not included in the accounts but grants totalling £210,000 were broken down as follows:

Relief of poverty	£81,000
Schools	£45,000
Community projects	£40,000
Yeshivos and seminaries	£17,000
Advancement of religion	£6,800
Grants under £1,000 each	£15,000.

Applications

In writing to the correspondent.

Information gathered from:

Accounts; Charity Commission record.

Nesswall Ltd

Jewish

£60,000 (2011/12)

Beneficial area

UK.

Correspondent: Mrs R. Teitelbaum, Secretary, 28 Overlea Road, London E5 9BG (tel: 020 8806 2965)

CC Number: 283600

In 2011/12 the trust had assets of £569,000 and an income of £61,000. Grants and donations totalled £60,000. A list of grants was not available. Previous beneficiaries have included: Friends of Horim Establishments, Torah Vochesed L'Ezra Vesaad and Emunah Education Centre.

Applications

In writing to the correspondent, at any time.

Information gathered from:

Accounts; Charity Commission record.

Newby Trust Ltd

Welfare, poverty, education, medical

£214,000 to organisations and individuals (2011/12)

Beneficial area

UK.

Correspondent: Wendy Gillam, Secretary, Hill Farm, Froxfield, Petersfield, Hampshire GU32 1BQ (tel: 01730 827557; email: info@newby-trust.org.uk; website: www.newby-trust.org.uk)

CC Number: 227151

The aims of the trust are to promote medical welfare, training and education and the relief of poverty. The following is taken from the trust's annual report:

> The company works nationally, in particular to promote medical welfare, education, training and research, and the relief of poverty. The company does not generally provide funding for non UK activities or education, but takes steps to ensure the grants disbursed are spread as widely as possible to those in need within the United Kingdom.
>
> *Medical Welfare*
>
> To help alleviate physical and mental suffering within the United Kingdom, the company provides:
>
> - Small grants to individuals towards essential equipment, such as mobility aids, specialist chairs and beds
> - Larger grants on occasions, to registered charities for medical research, equipment, building improvements, etc. These are often related to the company's annual special category, as noted below
>
> *Education, Training and Research*
>
> The company promotes education by providing grants to:
>
> - United Kingdom educational establishments in the form of bursaries and scholarships for postgraduate and post-doctoral research students, a condition of the grant being that its disbursement is based on merit and need
> - Registered charities and educational establishments for educational, cultural, sporting, or other projects. These are often associated with the annual special category
>
> *Relief of Poverty*
>
> Recognising that there is widespread poverty and privation within the United Kingdom, some of which manifests itself

as crime, violence, bullying, or domestic intimidation, the company makes:

- Small grants to individuals for home comforts, clothing, school uniforms, footwear, white goods, flooring etc
- Larger grants to registered charities for community projects, refurbishment of community halls and buildings, the alleviation of homelessness, etc, again often related to the company's annual special category

Annual Special Category

Under the general headings above, the directors have a policy of selecting one category for special support each year:

- In 2011/12 it was assisting disabled people with education, qualifications and independent living
- In 2012/13 it was mental health

In 2011/12 the trust had assets of £15 million and an income of £382,000. Grants were made totalling £214,000. The success rate excluding individual grants was less than 10%. Grants were broken down as follows:

Special category	13	£107,000
Relief of poverty	360	£68,000
Education, training and research	6	£23,000 (£12,000 to individuals)
Medical welfare	3	£16,000

Beneficiaries included: The Bridge Foundation, Snowden Award Scheme, Spinal Injuries Association, Treloar School and College and U Can Do I.T. (£10,000 each); Greenhouse (White City Youth Theatre); Medical Foundation for the Care of Victims of Torture, Birmingham Royal Ballet and Royal School of Needlework (£5,000 each); Action for Children (£2,100); The Textile Conservation Centre Foundation and Canine Partners (£2,000); and Eaves Housing for Women (£1,000).

Applications

The application procedure differs between each category as follows:

Annual special category: unsolicited applications will not be considered.

Education, training and research: since 2008 the trust has supported education at the postgraduate or postdoctoral level only by allocating funds to selected universities or institutions in the United Kingdom. These are City University, London, the London School of Economics and Political Science, the University of Edinburgh and the University of Manchester. Grants are awarded at the discretion of these universities subject to guidelines related to the purposes of the trust.

Medical welfare and *Relief of poverty:* Social Services, NHS Trusts, Citizens Advice or similar organisations may apply **only online** on behalf of individuals in need using the pre-application screening form on the trust's website.

Responsibility for smaller individual grants is delegated to the Secretary. Main grants are decided at meetings in March and November.

Information gathered from:

Accounts; Charity Commission record; funder's website.

Newpier Charity Ltd

Jewish, general

£540,000 (2011/12)

Beneficial area

UK.

Correspondent: Charles Margulies, Trustee, 186 Lordship Road, London N16 5ES (tel: 020 8802 4449)

Trustees: Charles Margulies; Helen Knopfler; Rachel Margulies.

CC Number: 293686

The main objectives of the charity are the advancement of the Orthodox Jewish faith and the relief of poverty.

In 2011/12 it had assets of £3 million and an income of £1 million. Grants totalling £540,000 were made during the year. Unfortunately, no list of grantees was included with the accounts at the Charity Commission.

Previous beneficiaries include: BML Benityashvut, Friends of Biala, Gateshead Yeshiva, KID, Mesdos Wiznitz and SOFT for redistribution to other charities.

Applications

In writing to the correspondent.

Information gathered from:

Accounts; Charity Commission record.

The Chevras Ezras Nitzrochim Trust

Jewish

£50,000 to organisations (2012)

Beneficial area

UK, with a preference for London.

Correspondent: Hertz Kahan, Trustee, 53 Heathland Road, London N16 5PQ (tel: 020 8800 5187)

Trustees: Kurt Stern; Hertz Kahan; Moshe Rottenberg.

CC Number: 275352

'The objects of the charity are the relief of the poor, needy and sick and the advancement of Jewish religious education.' There is a preference for Greater London, but help is also given further afield. The majority of grants are made to individuals.

In 2012 the trust had assets of £13,000 and an income of £263,000. Grants to organisations totalled £50,000, broken down as follows:

Poor and needy	£37,000
Education	£6,100
Religion	£6,300

A further £199,000 was given in grants to individuals.

There was no detailed list of beneficiary organisations but the trustees' report states that the following organisations benefited: Yesamach Levav Trust (£7,200); and Notzar Chesed (£7,100). Previous beneficiaries included Mesifta, Kupas Tzedoko Vochesed, Beis Chinuch Lenonos, Hachzokas Torah Vochesed Trust, Ezras Hakohol Trust, Woodstock Sinclair Trust, Side by Side, Yeshivas Panim Meiros, Yeahuas Chaim Synagogue, TYY Trust, Square Yeshiva and Stanislow.

Applications

In writing to the correspondent.

Information gathered from:

Accounts; Charity Commission record.

NJD Charitable Trust

Jewish

£57,000 (2011/12)

Beneficial area

UK and Israel.

Correspondent: Alan Dawson, Trust Administrator, Crowe Clark Whitehill, St Bride's House, 10 Salisbury Square, London EC4Y 8EH (tel: 020 7842 7306; email: info@igpinvest.com)

Trustees: Nathalie Dwek; Jean Glaskie; Jacob Wolf; Alexander Dwek.

CC Number: 1109146

Set up in 2005, the objects of this trust are:

- The relief of poverty and hardship of members of the Jewish faith
- The advancement of Jewish religion through Jewish education

In 2011/12 the trust had assets of £186,000, an income of £100,000 and made grants totalling £57,000.

Beneficiaries included: Jewish Care (£15,000); UJIA (£10,000); Jewish Leadership Council (£7,500); Community Security Trust (£6,600); and Holocaust Educational Trust (£5,000).

Grants of less than £2,000 totalled (£13,000).

Applications

In writing to the correspondent.

Information gathered from:

Accounts; Charity Commission record.

The Noon Foundation

General, education, relief of poverty, community relations, alleviation of racial discrimination

Around £800,000 (2012)

Beneficial area

UK.

Correspondent: The Trustees, 25 Queen Anne's Gate, St James's Park, London SW1H 9BU (tel: 020 7654 1600; email: grants@noongroup.co.uk)

Trustees: Lord Noon; Akbar Shirazi; Zeenat Harnal; A. M. Jepson; A. D. Robinson; Zarmin N. Sekhon.

CC Number: 1053654

The trust was set up in 1996 by Sir Gulam Noon, the founder of Noon Products. Grants are generally given for education, sickness, community relations and the arts. The trust has previously stated that it will continue to make substantial capital grants where this furthers its purposes over the longer term.

In 2012 the foundation had an income of £10,000 and an expenditure of £812,000.

Previous beneficiaries included: Marie Curie Cancer Care, Birkbeck University of London, Breast Cancer Care, Macmillan Cancer Support, Co-existence Trust, Horizon Medical, Garsington Opera, London School of Economics, Oxfam, Muslim Aid and Wellbeing.

Applications

All applications and queries should be made by email.

Information gathered from:

Accounts; Charity Commission record.

The Norda Trust

Prisoners, asylum seekers, disadvantaged communities

£227,500 (2012)

Correspondent: Martin Ward, Administrator, The Shieling, St Agnes, Cornwall TR5 0SS (tel: 01871 553822; email: enquiries@thenordatrust.org.uk; website: www.thenordatrust.org.uk)

CC Number: 296418

The trustees allocate funds principally in support of those working for the rehabilitation of prisoners both before and after release and support for the partners and families of prisoners. A special interest is taken in charities and organisations that support immigration detainees and the welfare of young offenders.

As funds permit, the trust can also support small local charities whose primary aim should be to improve the quality of life for the most severely disadvantaged communities or individuals.

The majority of awards are made on a one-off basis, with very few commitments made over two or more years.

The trustees have a particular interest in helping to support new initiatives where there is a high level of volunteer involvement.

When funds allow, applications will be considered from charities and organisations that, by the nature of the work they undertake, do not attract popular support.

In 2012 the trust's assets stood at £2.7 million. It had an income of £72,000 and made grants totalling £227,500. Grants were made in three categories as follows:

General	£128,500 (3 grants)
Asylum seekers and refugees	£60,000 (14 grants)
Prisoners and their families	£39,000 (12 grants)

Beneficiaries included: Workhubs Network CIC (£125,000); Samaritans Listening Scheme (£8,000); Detention Action, Dover Detainee Visitors Group and Asylum Welcome (£5,000 each); HOPE, Not Shut Up and TRAIN (£3,000 each) and Personal Support Unit (£1,000).

Exclusions

The following areas are not funded by the trust:

- Medical causes
- Animal causes
- Individuals
- School fees
- Proselytising

Applications

Via letter or email, outlining the appeal. All applicants should leave at least a year before re-applying. Up to date financial information is required from all applicants. The trust will then make contact to request any further information they need.

Information gathered from:

Accounts; Charity Commission record; funder's website.

The Norman Family Charitable Trust

General

£330,000 (2012/13)

Beneficial area

Primarily Cornwall, Devon and Somerset.

Correspondent: R. J. Dawe, Chair of the Trustees, 14 Fore Street, Budleigh Salterton, Devon EX9 6NG (tel: 01395 446699; email: info@nfct.org; website: www.nfct.org)

Trustees: R. J. Dawe, Chair; Mrs M. H. Evans; M. B. Saunders; Mrs M. J. Webb; Mrs C. E. Houghton; Mrs S. Gillingham.

CC Number: 277616

The trust gives grants to registered charities in Devon, Cornwall and Somerset. Most grants are made for specific projects. The trust is keen to receive applications from smaller charities in the South West. The recent focus has been on charities that assist homeless people, and training young people for employment or otherwise better enabling them in their life and their search for employment.

In 2012/13 the trust had assets of £8.4 million and an income of £387,000. Grants were made totalling £330,000 and broken down by category (including support costs) as follows:

Medical (inc. research)	91,000
Community projects	44,000
Children's welfare	43,000
Physical disabilities, visual and auditory	38,000
Sport and leisure	28,000
Youth	26,000
Homelessness and social welfare	25,000
Animals, environment and conservation	24,000
Forces, ex-forces, emergency services	14,000
Senior welfare	13,000
Mental health and learning disabilities	8,300
Crime prevention, rehabilitation, addiction	2,800
Miscellaneous	1,400

Beneficiaries included: University of Exeter – Peninsular Foundation (£25,000); Children's Hospice South West and Exmouth Community Transport (£10,000 each); West of England School for Children with Little or No Sight, Topsham Rugby and Football Club, Hospicare Exeter, Shilhay Community and East Budleigh Community Shop (£5,000 each); Exmouth Community College (£4,900); Knowle Village Hall (£4,000); Fire Fighters Charity (£3,000); and Kingfisher Award Scheme (£2,500).

Exclusions

No grants to individuals. No funding for religious buildings or to assist any organisations using animals for live experimental purposes or generally to fund overseas work.

Applications

Applications can be made using the online form, or by downloading the form, completing it and sending via post. Trustees meet in March, June, September and December to consider grants over £5,000. A subcommittee meets every six to eight weeks to deal with applications for less than £5,000. Meeting dates can be found on the website and applications should be submitted at least two weeks in advance.

Percentage of awards given to new applicants: between 10% and 20%.

Information gathered from:

Accounts; Charity Commission record; further information provided by the funder; funder's website.

The Duncan Norman Trust Fund

General

£29,000 (2011/12)

Beneficial area

UK, with a preference for Merseyside.

Correspondent: Liverpool Charity and Voluntary Services, Liverpool Charity and Voluntary Services, 151 Dale Street, Liverpool L2 2AH (tel: 01512 275177; email: enquiries@charitycheques.org.uk; website: www.merseytrusts.org.uk)

Trustees: Mr R. K. Asser; Caroline Chapman; Ms V. S. Hilton; Caroline Elizabeth Lazar; William Stothart; Clare Louise Venner.

CC Number: 250434

The trust has general charitable purposes, but particularly supports organisations in the Merseyside area. In 2011/12 the trust had assets of £826,000 and an income of £32,000. Grants were made totalling £29,000.

Grants of £1,000 or more were made to: Hertford College, Oxford (£2,000); DEC – East Africa Crisis Appeal and LCVS – Thrive at Five Project (£1,000 each). Grants of less than £1,000 each totalled £25,000.

Exclusions

No grants to individuals.

Applications

The trust states that it only makes grants to charities known to the settlor and unsolicited applications are not considered.

Information gathered from:

Accounts; Charity Commission record; funder's website.

The Normanby Charitable Trust

Arts, culture, heritage, social welfare

£94,000 (2011/12)

Beneficial area

UK, with a special interest in North Yorkshire and north east England.

Correspondent: The Trustees, 52 Tite Street, London Sw3 4JA

Trustees: The Marquis of Normanby; The Dowager Marchioness of Normanby; Lady Lepel Kornicki; Lady Evelyn Buchan; Lady Peronel Phipps de Cruz; Lady Henrietta Burridge.

CC Number: 252102

'The trustees have decided that only exceptionally will they help individuals in the future, and that they will confine their assistance for the moment, to mainly North Yorkshire and the North East of England.'

'In accordance with the objectives under the trust deed the trustees do exceptionally make grants outside the preferred area and this has happened during the current year in respect of the grant paid to The Moyne Institute.'

The trust concentrates its support on general charitable purposes, however previous research has suggested a preference for supporting arts culture, heritage, social welfare and disability. The trust has occasionally considered giving grants for the preservation of religious and secular buildings of historical or architectural interest.

In 2011/12 the trust had assets of £9.7 million, an income of £288,000 and gave grants totalling £94,000 to 40 organisations.

Beneficiaries included: Ley Hall Zealholme (£10,000); Mickleby Village Hall (£7,500); ZANE (£7,000); Yorkshire Air Ambulance, Scarborough and District CAB and the Captain Cook School Room Museum (£5,000 each); Education Centre for Children with Down Syndrome and North Yorkshire Moors Chamber Music Festival (£3,000 each); The Prince's Trust (£2,500); St Hilda's Playgroup (£2,000); Red Squirrel Survival Trust (£1,000); and Braille Chess Association (£500).

Exclusions

No grants to individuals, or to non-UK charities.

Applications

In writing to the correspondent. Trustees meet two or three times a year to award grants, although there are no regular dates. Note, only successful applications will be acknowledged.

Information gathered from:

Accounts; Charity Commission record.

The Earl of Northampton's Charity

Welfare

£16,000 (2011/12)

Beneficial area

England, with a preference for London and the South East.

Correspondent: M. McGregor, Clerk to the Mercers' Company, Mercers' Hall Offices, Mercers' Hall, Ironmonger Lane, London EC2V 8HE (tel: 020 7726 4991; fax: 020 7600 1158; email: info@mercers.co.uk; website: www.mercers.co.uk)

Trustee: The Mercers' Company.

CC Number: 210291

Shortly before his death in 1614, Henry Howard, Earl of Northampton, founded a 'hospital' or almshouse for poor men at Greenwich, known as Trinity Hospital, and although he was not a member of the Mercers' Company he entrusted the management to the Company's care.

In 2011/12 the trust had assets of £23 million and income of £1.2 million, most of which was spent on the upkeep of almshouses.

Grants totalled £16,000 and were made to four organisations: Jubilee Trust Almshouses (£2,000); Trinity Hospital Castle Rising (£10,000); Trinity Hospital Clun (£4,000); and St Michael's Church Framlingham (£250).

Applications

Note: The trust is currently not accepting any applications. It is under the trusteeship of the Mercers' Company and one application to the Company is an application to all of its trusts including the Mercers' Charitable Foundation and the Charity of Sir Richard Whittington.

Information gathered from:

Accounts; Charity Commission record; funder's website.

The Norton Foundation

Young people in need under 25 years of age (currently restricted to the areas of Birmingham, Coventry and the County of Warwick)

£267,000 to organisations

(2011/12)

Beneficial area

UK, with a preference for Birmingham, Coventry and the County of Warwick.

Correspondent: Mr Richard C. Perkins, Correspondent, PO Box 10282, Redditch, Worcestershire B97 9ZA (tel: 01527 544446; email: correspondent@nortonfoundation.org; website: www.nortonfoundation.org)

CC Number: 702638

The trust was created in 1990. Its objects are to help children and young people under 25 who are in need of care or rehabilitation or aid of any kind, particularly as a result of deprivation, maltreatment or neglect or who are at risk of becoming involved with anti-social behaviour or offending.

Grants of up to £5,000 (usually £500–£2,500) are available for vocational development, entry to employment, establishing a home, provision of equipment and personal development.

Once every five years the trust intends making a donation of £100,000 to a capital project and a designated fund has been created for this purpose.

Grants of up to £500 are also available for individuals.

In 2011/12 the charity had assets of £4.1 million, an income of £128,000 and gave £267,000 in grants to organisations, broken down as follows:

Capital grants for building projects	2	£200,000
Education and training	48	£60,000
Holidays	3	£3,800
Medical	5	£3,400

Note the total grants figure for this financial year is inflated as the five yearly capital grant was given during the year, plus another one-off capital grant of £100,000. Grantmaking to organisations generally totals around £60–70,000. A further £34,000 was given in grants to individuals.

Beneficiaries of the £100,000 capital grant given every five years were: Alcester Town Council and free@last.

Other beneficiaries included: Construction Youth Trust (£5,000); Coventry City Mission (£3,250); Volunteer Reading Help Birmingham Branch, The Jericho Foundation, Life Space Trust and Pan-Asia Community Housing (£2,000 each); Envision and Brathay Trust (£5,000); Tall Ships Youth Trust (£1,200); and The Salvation Army, Cruse Bereavement Care and Bedworth Heath Youth Project (£1,000 each).

Exclusions

No grants for the payment of debts that have already been incurred. Grants are not made for further education (except in very exceptional circumstances).

Applications

On a form, available with guidance notes from the trust's website. Applications from organisations are normally processed by the trustees at their quarterly meetings.

The trust expects that it will make the next capital donation of £100,000 in summer 2015. Applications for this are being accepted from Monday 3 November 2014, when the application form and process for this award will become available on the trust's website.

Percentage of awards given to new applicants: between 10% and 20%.

Common applicant mistakes

'Failure to recognise our advertised criteria and guidance available on our website.'

Information gathered from:

Accounts; Charity Commission record; further information provided by the funder; funder's website.

The Norwich Town Close Estate Charity

Education in and near Norwich

£276,000 to organisations

(2011/12)

Beneficial area

Within a 20-mile radius of the Guildhall of the city of Norwich.

Correspondent: David Walker, Clerk, Mr David Walker, 1 Woolgate Court, St Benedict's Street, Norwich NR2 4AP (tel: 01603 621023; email: david.walker@norwichcharitabletrusts.org.uk)

Trustees: David Fullman; John Rushmer; Michael Quinton; Brenda Ferris; Geoffrey Loades; Philip Blanchflower; Anthony Hansell; Nigel Back; Richard Gurney; Jeanette Southgate; Robert Self; Pamela Scutter; Brenda Arthur; Heather Tyrrell; Michael Quinton; John Symonds.

CC Number: 235678

The charity has the following objects:

- To provide 'relief in need' and pensions to Freemen or their widows or daughters where required
- The promotion of education of those in need of financial assistance who are Freemen or the sons or daughters of Freemen
- To make grants for educational purposes to bodies whose beneficiaries reside within the 20-mile radius of the Norwich Guildhall

The trust has close links with Norwich Consolidated Charities and Anguish's Educational Foundation. They share their administration processes and collaborate on grantmaking. Grants to individuals are prioritised, particularly for pensions and education.

In 2011/12 the charity had assets of £19.6 million and an income of £722,000. Grants to organisations totalled £276,000. Grants to individuals were also made, totalling £165,000.

Beneficiaries of organisational grants included: Norfolk Record Office (£34,000); Cultural Communities Consortium (£30,000); Whittingham Boathouses Foundation (£25,000); Morley C of E VA Primary School and Hamlet Centre Trust (£20,000 each); CAST (Centre for the Advancement of Science and Technology), Community Action Norwich and Stalham Brass Band (£10,000 each); Hethersett High School and Science College (£6,700); Norwich City (FC) Community Sports Foundation (£6,000); Asperger East Anglia, The Wherry Yacht Charter Charitable Trust and Mancroft Advice project (£5,000 each); Norfolk SEN Network (£3,000); Hub Community Project (£2,500); and The Chermond Trust (£760).

Exclusions

No grants to: individuals who are not Freemen (or dependents of Freemen) of the city of Norwich; charities more than 20 miles from Norwich; or charities which are not educational. Revenue funding for educational charities is not generally given.

Applications

After a preliminary enquiry, in writing to the clerk.

When submitting an application the following points should be borne in mind:

- Brevity is a virtue. If too much written material is submitted there is a risk that it may not all be assimilated
- The trustees like to have details of any other financial support secured
- An indication should be given of the amount that is being sought and also how that figure is arrived at
- The trustees will not reimburse expenditure already incurred
- Nor, generally speaking will the trustees pay running costs, e.g. salaries

Percentage of awards given to new applicants: between 10% and 20%.

Common applicant mistakes

'Individuals who write to us think that anyone can apply to Norwich Town Close Estate charity, but in fact the only individuals who can apply are Freeman, their sons and daughters. That is Freeman of Norwich. Other charities who apply to us do not have the same criteria, but the [applicant] charity has to be within 20 miles of Norwich Guildhall.'

Information gathered from:

Accounts; Charity Commission record; further information provided by the funder.

The Norwood and Newton Settlement

Christian

£228,000 (2011/12).

Beneficial area

England and Wales.

Correspondent: David M. Holland, Trustee, 126 Beauly Way, Romford, Essex RM1 4XL (tel: 01708 723670)

Trustees: P. Clarke; D. M. Holland; Stella Holland; R. Lynch; Susan Newsom.

CC Number: 234964

The trust supports Methodist and other mainline Free Churches and some other smaller UK charities in which the founders had a particular interest. As a general rule, grants of £1,000 to £20,000 are given for capital building projects which aim to improve the worship, outreach and mission of the church.

Where churches are concerned, the trustees take particular note of the contribution and promised contributions towards the project by members of the church in question.

In 2011/12 the charity had assets of £7.3 million and an income of £333,000. There were 33 grants made totalling £228,000. Grants were made to 37, mainly Methodist, organisations and totalled £308,000.

Beneficiaries included: New Malden Baptist Church (£320,000); Lichfield Methodist Church, Staffordshire (£15,000); Shirrell Heath Methodist Church, Hampshire (£10,000); The Crown Centre, Plymouth; Sea Mills Community Initiative, Bristol; Christ Church Methodist Church, Addiscombe, Croydon; Trinity Methodist Church, Skipton and Tissington Methodist Chapel, Derby (£5,000 each); Horton Heath Methodist Church, Wimborne (£3,000); and YMCA England Memorial at the National Aborelum (£1,000).

Exclusions

Projects will not be considered where an application for National Lottery funding has been made or is contemplated. No grants to individuals, rarely to large UK charities and not for staff/running costs, equipment, repairs or general maintenance.

Applications

In writing to the correspondent. In normal circumstances, within seven days an applicant will be sent either a refusal or an application form. Applications are then considered at the quarterly trustee meetings. The trust states:

> At all times applicants are kept informed of the Trustees' time scale.

Information gathered from:

Accounts; Charity Commission record.

The Sir Peter O'Sullevan Charitable Trust

Animal welfare

£300,000 (2011/12)

Beneficial area

Worldwide.

Correspondent: Nigel Payne, Trustee, The Old School, Bolventor, Launceston, Cornwall PL15 7TS (tel: 07768 025265; email: nigel@earthsummit.demon.co.uk; website: www.thevoiceofracing.com)

Trustees: Christopher Spence; Sir Peter O'Sullevan; Nigel Payne; Geoffrey Hughes; Michael Dillon; John McManus; Michael Keer-Dineen.

CC Number: 1078889

Established in 2000 by Peter O'Sullevan, a horse racing commentator, in order to improve the welfare of retired, injured or ill-treated animals. The trust supports six horse/animal welfare charities: Blue Cross, Brooke Hospital for Animals, Compassion in World Farming, World Horse (formerly International League for the Protection of Horses), the Racing Welfare Charities and the Thoroughbred Rehabilitation Centre.

In 2011/12 the trust had assets of £106,000 and an income of £433,000. Each beneficiary charity detailed above received £50,000, altogether totalling £300,000.

Applications

In writing to the correspondent although applications are very unlikely to be successful as the trust supports the same six charities every year.

Information gathered from:

Accounts; Charity Commission record; funder's website.

The Oak Trust

General

£23,000 (2011/12)

Beneficial area

UK with a preference for East Anglia.

Correspondent: Bruce Ballard, Clerk to the Trustees, Birkett Long, Number One, Legg Street, Chelmsford, Essex CM1 1JS (tel: 01206 217300; email: julienc@summershall.com; website: www.oaktrust.org.uk)

Trustees: Revd A. C. C. Courtauld; J. Courtauld; Dr Elizabeth Courtauld; Miss C. M. Hart; Dr Christopher.

CC Number: 231456

The trust has a preference for supporting those charities that it has a special interest in, knowledge of or association with and with a turnover of below £1 million. Consideration is specifically given for disadvantage, personal development through adventure, the environment, medicine and life changing benefits. Grants are for £250–£4,000.

In 2011/12 the trust had assets of £667,000 and an income of £28,000. Grants were made to 29 organisations totalling £23,000.

Beneficiaries included: The Cirdan Sailing Trust (£3,000); Christian Aid (£2,000); Save the Children Fund, Voice and School Home Support (£1,000 each); Dhaka Ahsania Mission and Tower Hamlets Mission (£750 each); and Essex Youthbuild, Practical Action, MS Society, Tools for Self Reliance and FareShare (£500 each).

Exclusions

No support to individuals.

Applications

Applications must be submitted via the online form on the trust's website.

Details of the next submission date are included on the application form. Applicants will receive an acknowledgement of their application and notification of the outcome within ten days of the Review Meeting by email.

Information gathered from:

Accounts; Charity Commission record; funder's website.

The Oakdale Trust

Social work, medical, general

£164,000 (2011/12)

Beneficial area

UK, especially Wales, and overseas.

Correspondent: Rupert Cadbury, Correspondent and Trustee, Tansor House, Tansor, Oundle, Peterborough PE8 5HS (tel: 01832 226386; email: oakdale@tanh.co.uk; website: www.oakdaletrust.org.uk)

CC Number: 218827

The trust's main areas of interest include:

- Welsh-based social and community projects
- Medical – support groups operating in Wales and UK-based research projects
- UK-based charities working in the third world
- Environmental conservation in the UK and overseas
- Penal reform

Some support is also given to the arts, particularly where there is a Welsh connection. The average grant is approximately £900.

In 2011/12 the trust had assets of £8.8 million, an income of £304,000 and gave grants totalling £164,000.

Beneficiaries included: The Brandon Centre (£7,000); F.P.W.P Hibiscus (£5,000); Quaker Service Memorial Trust (£4,000); Cambridge Female Education Trust (£2,000); Play Montgomeryshire, Action for Prisoners Families and International Refugee Trust (£1,000 each); The Brecon Cathedral Choir Appeal, Roy Castle Lung Cancer Foundation and the Benefits Advice Shop (£750 each); Rethink, Disabled Workers Co-operative and Valleys Healing and Life (£500 each); and Hearing Dogs for Deaf People, The National Lobster Hatchery and Freeplay Network (£250 each).

Exclusions

No grants to individuals, holiday schemes, sport activities or expeditions.

Applications

An online application form is available on the trust's website. The trust gives the following guidelines:

> Applications can be submitted online or sent in by post if preferred. An official application form is available for download although applicants are free to submit requests in any format so long as applications are clear and concise, covering – aims and achievements, plans and needs supported by a budget for the project in question. Applicants applying for a grant in excess of £1,000 are asked to submit a recent set of audited accounts **only** if not already available on the Charity Commission web site. Please give a web address where supporting information is available on-line. In order to minimise the waste of time and material, large organisations in particular are asked to submit one application only per trustees' meeting and to avoid sending in duplicate applications.
>
> The trustees meet twice a year in April and October to consider applications and to award grants. No grants are awarded between meetings. The deadline for applications for the April meeting is the 1 March and for the October meeting the 1 September.
>
> The trust is administered by the trustees at no cost and in view of the numerous requests received unsuccessful applicants are not normally notified and similarly applications are not acknowledged even when accompanied by a stamped addressed envelope.

Percentage of awards given to new applicants: between 20% and 30%.

Common applicant mistakes

'Failing to take account of conditions and criteria set out in our guidelines.'

Information gathered from:

Accounts; Charity Commission record; further information provided by the funder; funder's website.

The Oakmoor Charitable Trust

General

£41,000 (2011/12)

Beneficial area

UK.

Correspondent: The Administrator, Rathbone Trust Company Ltd, Rathbone Trust Company Ltd, 4th Floor, 1 Curzon Street, London W1J 5FB (tel: 020 7399 0807)

CC Number: 258516

Established in 1969 the trust receives regular donations from the settlor, Peter Andreae.

In 2011/12 the trust had assets of £1.5 million and an income of £31,000. Grants were made to 23 organisations totalling £41,000, broken down into the following categories:

Local charities and hospices	£9,800
The arts and museums	£3,300
Religious organisations	£1,500
Youth and education	£1,000
Other national and international charities	£25,000

Beneficiaries included: Marine Society and Sea Cadets (£15,000); Byways (£5,000); National Gallery Trust (£2,500); Newnham College Cambridge, Smile Support and Care and The Soldiers Charity (£1,000 each); Winchester Festival, RNLI, Hertford House Trust and Friends of St Cross Winchester (£500 each); Grange Park Opera (£300); and Irish Guards Appeal (£200).

Exclusions

No grants to individuals.

Applications

The trust states that it does not respond to unsolicited applications.

Information gathered from:

Accounts; Charity Commission record.

The Odin Charitable Trust

General

£413,000 (2011/12)

Beneficial area

UK.

Correspondent: Mrs S. G. P. Scotford, Trustee, PO Box 1898, Bradford-on-Avon, Wiltshire BA15 1YS (email: kelly.donna@virgin.net)

CC Number: 1027521

Although the objects of the charity are wide, the trust has a preference for making grants towards: furthering the arts; providing care for people who are disabled and disadvantaged; supporting hospices, the homeless, prisoners' families, refugees, gypsies and 'tribal groups'; and furthering research into false memories and dyslexia.

The trustees are more likely to support small organisations and those that by the nature of their work, find it difficult to attract funding. Grants range from one-off donations to three year awards. Grants range from £1,000 to £5,000.

In 2011/12 the trust had assets of £5 million, an income of £402,000 and made grants totalling £413,000.

The largest grant went to BFMS (£47,000). Other beneficiaries included: Helen Arkell Dyslexia Centre and Julian House (£5,000 each); Bath Recital Arts Centre (£3,500); St Peter's Hospice; Music Alive and Asylum Aid (£3,000); Roma Support Group, Castle Gate Family Trust and Music in Prisons (£2,500 each); and UCanDoIT, City Gate Community Project and Young and Free (£2,000 each).

Exclusions

Applications from individuals are not considered.

Applications

All appeals should be by letter containing the following:

- Aims and objectives of the charity
- Nature of appeal
- Total target if for a specific project
- Contributions received against target
- Registered Charity Number
- Any other relevant factors.

Letters should be accompanied by a set of the charitable organisation's latest report and full accounts and should be addressed to the correspondent. Trustees meet twice a year to approve grants.

Information gathered from:

Accounts; Charity Commission record.

The Ogle Christian Trust

Evangelical Christianity

£115,000 (2011)

Beneficial area

Worldwide.

Correspondent: Mrs F. J. Putley, Trustee, 43 Woolstone Road, Forest Hill, London SE23 2TR (tel: 020 8699 1036)

Trustees: Mrs F. J. Putley; R. J. Goodenough; S. Proctor; Mrs L. M. Quanrud; Dr D. Harley.

CC Number: 1061458

The trust mainly directs funds to new initiatives in evangelism worldwide, support of missionary enterprises, publication of scriptures and Christian literature, pastor training and famine and other relief work.

In 2011 the trust had assets of £2.3 million and an income of £129,000. There were 56 grants made totalling £115,000, broken down as follows:

Regularly supported organisations	£54,000
Occasionally supported organisations	£59,000
Regularly supported individuals	£2,000

By far the largest grant, as in previous years, went to Operation Mobilisation (£22,000). Other beneficiaries included: CCSM (£8,000); OMF International UK (£6,000); RedCliffe College (£4,000); ELAM Ministries and South Asian Concern (£3,000 each); Dehra Dun and France Mission Trust (£2,000 each); INNOVISTA (£1,500); and Release International (£1,000).

Exclusions

Applications from individuals are discouraged; those granted require accreditation by a sponsoring organisation. Grants are rarely made for building projects. Funding will not be offered in response to general appeals from large national organisations.

Applications

In writing to the correspondent, accompanied by documentary support and an sae. Trustees meet in May and November, but applications can be made at any time.

Percentage of awards given to new applicants: between 10% and 20%.

Common applicant mistakes

'Lack of personal details/references.'

Information gathered from:

Accounts; Charity Commission record; further information provided by the funder.

The Oikonomia Trust

Christian

£66,000 (2011/12)

Beneficial area

UK and overseas.

Correspondent: Colin Mountain, Trustee, 98 White Lee Road, Batley, West Yorkshire WF17 8AF (tel: 01924 502616; email: colin.mountain@gmail.com)

Trustees: Douglas Metcalfe; Richard Metcalfe; Stephen Metcalfe; Colin Mountain; Revd Robert Owens.

CC Number: 273481

The trust supports evangelical work, famine and other relief through Christian agencies. The trust is not looking for new outlets as it states those it has knowledge of are sufficient to absorb its available funds.

In 2011/12 the trust had an income of £0 and a total expenditure of £69,000. There has been an income of £0 for the past two years. No beneficiary information was available.

Previous beneficiaries have included: Barnabus Trust (£5,500); Slavic Gospel Association (£5,000); Bethel Church (£4,000); Asia Link, Association of Evangelists and Caring for Life (£3,000 each); Japan Mission (£2,500); Starbeck Mission (£2,000); People International (£1,000); and Carey Outreach Ministries (£500).

Exclusions

No grants made in response to general appeals from large national organisations.

Applications

In writing to the correspondent, although the trust has stated that most grants are made to the same organisations each year and as such new applications are unlikely to be successful. If an applicant desires an answer, an sae should be enclosed. Applications should arrive in January.

Information gathered from:

Accounts; Charity Commission record.

The Old Broad Street Charity Trust

General

£54,000 to organisations (2011/12)

Beneficial area

UK and overseas.

Correspondent: Simon Jennings, Secretary to the Trustees, Rawlinson and Hunter, Eighth Floor, 6 New Street Square, London EC4A 3AQ (tel: 020 7842 2000; email: obsct@rawlinson-hunter.com)

Trustees: Simon Jennings; Eric Frank; Christopher J. Sheridan; Clare Gough.

CC Number: 231382

The objects of the trust are general, although most of the funds are given towards the arts. It was the wish of Louis Franck, the founder, that part of the income should be used to fund scholarships, preferably for UK citizens to reach the highest levels of executive management in banking and financial institutions. The trust makes provision for this each year by setting aside an annual amount and funding scholarships for people serving in a bank or financial institution in the UK to spend time in any seat of learning (principally INSEAD) to attain the highest level of executive management.

In 2011/12 the trust had assets of £1.5 million and an income of £29,000. Grants to organisations totalled £54,000, with a further £48,000 being given in scholarships to individuals.

The organisations that received grants not in relation to scholarships were: Foundation Henri Cartier-Bresson (£43,000); Hospital of St Cross and Almshouse of Noble Property (£10,000); Whitechapel Gallery (£1,000); and Serpentine Gallery (£500).

Exclusions

The trustees only support organisations of which they personally have some knowledge.

Applications

In writing to the correspondent. The annual report states that 'general appeals for funding are sent in to the registered office by post or email. They are collated and distributed to the trustees for consideration on an annual basis.'

Percentage of awards given to new applicants: between 40% and 50%.

Information gathered from:

Accounts; Charity Commission record; further information provided by the funder.

Old Possum's Practical Trust

General, arts

£205,000 (2011/12)

Beneficial area

UK.

Correspondent: The Trustees, PO Box 5701, Milton Keynes MK9 2WZ (email: generalenquiry@old-possums-practical-trust.org.uk; website: www.old-possums-practical-trust.org.uk)

CC Number: 328558

This trust was established by Valerie Eliot in 1990, 25 years after her husband T S Eliot's death. The following information on its aims and objectives is taken from the trust's website:

> The trust's mission is to manage the funds at its disposal to support literary, artistic, musical and theatrical projects and organisations.
>
> Priority is given to requests that display enterprise in artistic endeavour and demonstrate high sustainability and contextual impact. Particular interest is taken in those projects that will have an impact on future literary work.
>
> Special contributions made by the trust to other related types of organisation reflect both the personal history of Old Possum's Practical Trust and the wishes of the trustees. Support is more likely for those projects which best reflect the literary reputation and name of T. S. Eliot and the special interests of his wife.

In 2011/12 the trust had assets of £6.2 million and an income of £214,000. Grants were made totalling £205,000, broken down as follows:

Arts and historical conservation	£118,000
Educational support	£71,000
Support for the disabled and disadvantaged	£16,000

Beneficiaries included: High Tide (£80,000); First Story (£45,000); Story Vault (£25,000); Chickenshed Theatre Company (£10,000); Arete (£5,000); English Stage Co. (£3,800); Gersington Opera (£1,000); Big Heart Bike Ride and Southampton Amateur Boxing Club (£500 each); and Fitzroy (£300).

Exclusions

The trust does not support the following:

- Activities or projects already completed
- Capital building projects
- Personal training and education e.g. tuition or living costs for college or university
- Projects outside the UK
- Medical care or resources
- Feasibility studies
- National charities having substantial amounts of potential funding likely from other sources

Applications

Applications can only be made online through the trust's website. The trustees meet regularly to consider applications but state in the latest accounts that: 'the emphasis will be on continued support of those institutions and individuals who have received support in the past. Unfortunately we have to disappoint the great majority of applicants who nevertheless continue to send appeal letters. The trustees do not welcome telephone calls or emails from applicants soliciting funds.'

To keep administration costs to a minimum the trust does not give reasons for unsuccessful applications or allow applicants to appeal a decision.

Information gathered from:

Accounts; Charity Commission record; funder's website.

The John Oldacre Foundation

Research and education in agricultural sciences

£237,000 (2011/12)

Beneficial area

UK.

Correspondent: Stephen J. Charnock, Trustee, Bohicket, 35 Broadwater Close, Burwood park, Walton on Thames, Surrey KT12 5DD

CC Number: 284960

Grants are made to universities and agricultural colleges towards the advancement and promotion, for public benefit, of research and education in agricultural sciences and the publication of useful results.

In 2011/12 the foundation had assets of £7.8 million, an income of £195,000 and gave 11 grants totalling £237,000.

Beneficiaries included: University of Bristol (£58,000); Royal Agricultural College (2 grants totalling £40,000); Nuffield Farming Trust and University of Exeter (£20,000 each); Reading University and Wolverhampton University (£19,000 each); NIAB (£15,000); and Game and Wildlife Conservation Trust (£12,000).

Exclusions

No grants towards tuition fees.

Applications

In writing to the correspondent stating how the funds would be used and what would be achieved.

Information gathered from:

Accounts; Charity Commission record.

The Olga Charitable Trust

Health, welfare, youth organisations, children's welfare, carers' organisations

£58,000 (2011/12)

Beneficial area

UK and overseas.

Correspondent: Adam Broke, Accountant, International Press Centre, 76 Shoe Lane, London EC4A 3JB (tel: 020 7353 1597)

CC Number: 277925

The trust supports health, welfare and youth organisations, children's welfare and carers' organisations. All must be known to the trustees.

In 2011/12 the trust had assets of £934,000 and an income of £49,000. Grants totalling £58,000 were made to 35 organisations.

Beneficiaries included: Holy Trinity Church, St Andrews (£10,000); Sightsavers (£6,000); Imperial College Healthcare Charity (£5,000); Crisis and The Cystic Fibrosis Trust (£2,000 each); Brain Tumour Campaign, British Red Cross, Cancer Research UK, RNLI, Save the Children, The Ruth Winston Centre and ZAWT (£1,000 each); and The Great North Air Ambulance Pride of Cumbria (£500).

Applications

In writing to the correspondent, although the trust states that its funds are fully committed and applications made cannot be acknowledged.

Information gathered from:

Accounts; Charity Commission record.

The Ormsby Charitable Trust

General

£33,000 (2011/12)

Beneficial area

UK, London and the South East.

Correspondent: Mrs K. McCrossan, Trustee, The Red House, The Street, Aldermaston, Reading RG7 4LN (tel: 01189 710343)

Trustees: Rosemary Ormsby David; Angela Ormsby Chiswell; Katrina Ormsby McCrossan.

CC Number: 1000599

The Ormsby Charitable Trust was established in 1990 and has general charitable purposes.

In 2011/12, the trust had an income of £44,000, assets of £1.7 million and made grants totalling £33,000.

Beneficiaries included: Newbury Community Resource Centre (£3,500); Honeypot House (£3,000); In Kind and Crisis (£2,000 each); St Michaels Hospice (North Hampshire) (£1,900); Marie Curie and Action 4 Blind (£1,500 each); REACT, Move Europe and NSPCC (£1,000 each); and Wheely Boat, Teenage Cancer and The Living Paintings Trust (£500 each).

Exclusions

No grants to individuals, animals or religious causes.

Applications

In writing to the correspondent. Grants are made to organisations known to the trustees.

Information gathered from:

Accounts; annual report; Charity Commission record.

The O'Sullivan Family Charitable Trust

Children and young people, care homes, genetic research

£493,000 (2011/12)

Beneficial area

Unrestricted, UK in practice.

Correspondent: Diana O'Sullivan, Trustee, 36 Edge Street, London W8 7PN

Trustees: Diana O'Sullivan; Finian O'Sullivan; Emily O'Sullivan; Sophie O'Sullivan; Tessa O'Sullivan.

CC Number: 1123757

The trust was established in 2008 with a £5 million donation from Finian O'Sullivan, founder of Burren Energy, who reportedly made £67 million from the sale of the company in 2007.

The trustees state their aims for the trust are to:

> Provide advancement of health or relief for those in need because of ill health, disability, financial hardship or other disadvantage; particularly by the provision of respite care for children and young adults affected by sever long-term disability and the promotion of genetic research into the causes of such disability and the dissemination of the useful results of such research.

The main focus of the trust in the long term is to support a large scale capital project which will provide respite care for severely disabled children, although applications from other organisations whose work fits in with the trustees' interests will also be considered.

In 2011/12 the trust had assets of £5.2 million and an income of £168,000. Grants were made totalling £498,000, most of which went in one grant of £325,000 to Smile Support and Care.

Other beneficiaries included: Galway University Foundation (£32,000); University of Southampton (£30,000); The Rose Road Foundation (£20,000); The Duke of Edinburgh International Award (£15,000); The Cheshire Residential Homes Trust (£10,000); The Honey Pot Children's Charity (£7,000); Canine Partners (£5,000); Bal Ashram (£3,000); On Course Foundation (£2,500); Debra (£2,000); and Romsey Good Neighbours (£1,000).

Applications

In writing to the correspondent.

Information gathered from:

Accounts; Charity Commission record.

The Ouseley Trust

Choral services of the Church of England, Church in Wales and Church of Ireland, choir schools

£130,000 (2012)

Beneficial area

England, Wales and Ireland.

Correspondent: Martin Williams, Clerk, PO Box 281, Stamford, Lincolnshire PE9 9BU (tel: 01780 752266; email: ouseleytrust@btinternet.com; website: www.ouseleytrust.org.uk)

Trustees: Dr Christopher Robinson, Chair; Revd Canon Mark Boyling; Dr Stephen Darlington; Gillian Perkins; Canon Martin Pickering; Adam Ridley; Dr John Rutter; Canon Richard White; Timothy Byram-Wigfield; Paul Mason; Adrian Barlow.

CC Number: 527519

The trust administers funds made available from trusts of the former St Michael's College, Tenbury. Its object is 'projects which promote and maintain to a high standard the choral services of the Church of England, the Church in Wales and the Church of Ireland', including grants for: courses of instruction; endowment grants; choir school fees; and the purchase of music.

In 2012 the trust had assets of £3.8 million and an income of £153,000. Grants were authorised to 34 organisations totalling £130,000.

Grants *authorised* in the year were broken down as follows:

Endowments	10	65,000
Fees	12	55,000
Music	4	4,500
Other	1	5,500

Grants will be awarded only where there is a clear indication that an already acceptable standard of choral service will be raised. Under certain circumstances grants may be awarded for organ tuition. Each application will be considered on its merits, keeping in mind the specific terms of the trust deed. Unique, imaginative ventures will receive careful consideration.

The trust does not normally award further grants to successful applicants within a two-year period. The trustees' policy is to continue making grants to cathedrals, choral foundations and parish churches throughout England, Wales and Ireland.

Authorised grants for the year 2012 included: Blackburn Cathedral, Chester Cathedral and Sheffield Cathedral (£10,000 each); Dean Close School (£8,000); Salisbury Cathedral (£7,000); St Mary the Virgin – Bury (£4,000); King's College School – Cambridge (£3,000); and Hereford Sixth Form College and St James the Great – Derby (£1,000 each).

Exclusions

Under normal circumstances, grants will not be awarded for building projects, the making of recordings, the purchase of furniture or liturgical objects, the repair of organs, the purchase of pianos or other instruments, the design or acquisition of robes, or tours and visits.

Applications

Applicants are strongly advised to refer to the trust's guidelines and FAQ section of its website before drafting an application. Applications must be submitted by an institution on a form available from the correspondent. Closing dates for applications are 31 January for the March meeting and 30 June for the October meeting.

Percentage of awards given to new applicants: between 20% and 30%.

Common applicant mistakes
'Failure to read the guidelines which are posted on our website.'

Information gathered from:
Accounts; Charity Commission record; further information provided by the funder; funder's website.

The Owen Family Trust

Christian, general

£85,000 (2012/13)

Beneficial area
UK, with a preference for West Midlands.

Correspondent: David Owen, Trustee, c/o Rubery Owen Holdings Ltd, PO Box 10, Wednesbury WS10 8JD (tel: 01215 263131)

Trustees: Grace Jenkins; David Owen.

CC Number: 251975

Grants are given to independent and church schools, Christian youth centres, churches, community organisations, arts, conservation and medical charities. Support is given throughout the UK, with a preference for the West Midlands.

In 2012/13 the trust had assets of £1.1 million and an income of £45,000. Grants totalled £85,000.

The largest grants were made to: Oundle School Foundation (£15,000); and Black Country Museum Development Trust, Lichfield Cathedral, The Feast and Frontier Youth Trust (£5,000 each).

Beneficiaries included: Black Country Living Museum and Lichfield Cathedral (£5,000 each); Birmingham Federation of Clubs for Young People and NAYC Action Centre UK (£3,000 each); Sutton Coldfield YMCA (£2,500); Birmingham Royal Ballet (£2,000); Little Aston Village Hall (£1,500); and Chaplaincy Plus, St Giles Hospice, Elmhurst School for Dance and Shakespeare Birthplace Trust (£1,00 each).

Exclusions
The trust states 'No grants to individuals unless part of a charitable organisation'.

Applications
In writing to the correspondent including annual report, budget for project and general information regarding the application. Organisations need to be a registered charity; however an 'umbrella' body which would hold funds would be acceptable. Only a small number of grants can be given each year and unsuccessful applications are not acknowledged unless an sae is enclosed. The trustees meet quarterly.

Percentage of awards given to new applicants: between 10% and 20%.

Common applicant mistakes
'We do not respond to individuals but we still get requests.'

Information gathered from:
Accounts; Charity Commission record; further information provided by the funder.

The Doris Pacey Charitable Foundation

Jewish, medical, educational and social

£206,000 (2010/11)

Beneficial area
UK and Israel.

Correspondent: J. D. Cohen, Trustee, 30 Old Burlington Street, London W1S 3NL (tel: 020 7468 2600)

Trustees: J. D. Cohen; R. Locke; L. Powell.

CC Number: 1101724

In 2010/11 the foundation had assets of £5.9 million, an income of £104,000 and gave grants totalling £206,000.

Grants were made to: OR Movement and Jewish Chaplaincy (£50,000 each); UJIA – Jewish Curriculum (£40,000); UJIA – Hemed Project (£25,000); ALEF (£11,000); Heart Cells Foundation (£10,000); Surrey Opera (£9,300); and Courtauld Institute of Art and Nightingale (£5,000 each).

Applications
Unsolicited applications are not considered.

Information gathered from:
Accounts; Charity Commission record.

The Paget Charitable Trust

General

£151,000 (2011/12)

Beneficial area
Worldwide, with an interest in Loughborough.

Correspondent: Joanna Herbert-Stepney, Trustee, Old Village Stores, Dippenhall Street, Crondall, Farnham, Surrey GU10 5NZ (tel: 01252 850253)

Trustees: Joanna Herbert-Stepney; Meg Williams.

CC Number: 327402

The trust (full name: The Joanna Herbert-Stepney Charitable Settlement) supports UK and local charities for general charitable purposes. Priorities include international aid and development, children who are disadvantaged, older people, animal welfare and environmental projects. The trust states that there is a preference for the 'unglamorous' and 'projects where a little money goes a long way'. In many cases ongoing support is given to organisations.

In 2011/12 the trust had assets of £8.1 million and an income of £197,000. During the year 128 grants were made to organisations totalling £151,000 (2009/10: £225,000). Investment management costs were relatively high at £62,000 to produce an investment income of £191,000.

Beneficiaries included: Oxfam (£4,000); Farms for City Children (£3,000); ActionAid, Childhood First, Freedom from Torture and Children's Family Trust (£2,000 each); Vitalise (£1,500); Wells for India, Tree Aid, Toynbee Hall, St Nicholas Hospice, Splash, Refugee Council, Quaker Social Action, Deafblind UK and Concern Worldwide (£1,000 each); and Dhaka Ahsania Mission, Feed the Children, Cambodia's Dump Children, Asthma UK, Afghan Action and Jubilee Action (£500 each).

Exclusions
The trust states that 'sheer need is paramount, in practice, nothing else is considered'. Grants are only given to registered UK charities. Overseas projects can only be funded via UK charities; no money can be sent directly overseas. The trust does not support individuals (including students), projects for people with mental disabilities, medical research or AIDS/HIV projects.

Applications
In writing to the correspondent; there is no application form. The trustees meet in spring and autumn. The trust regrets that it cannot respond to all applications.

Percentage of awards given to new applicants: less than 10%.

Common applicant mistakes
'Using jargon, trying to sound correct. I'd like them to tell me what they do, in their own words, in plain simple English.'

Information gathered from:
Accounts; Charity Commission record; further information provided by the funder.

The Panacea Society

Christian religion, relief of sickness

£200,000 to unconnected organisations (2012)

Beneficial area

UK, with a strong preference for Bedford and its immediate region.

Correspondent: David McLynn, Executive Officer, 14 Albany Road, Bedford MK40 3PH (tel: 01234 359737; email: admin@panacea-society.org; website: www.panacea-society.org)

CC Number: 227530

The charity is a Christian society. It was originally set up as a religious community, which thrived in Bedford between the First and Second World Wars. Over the years members of the Society have donated money and property to the charity to further the life of the community and its religious aims. The society ceased to exist as a religious organisation in 2012 and consequently changed its name from The Panacea Society to The Panacea Charitable Trust.

The Panacea Museum in Bedford tells the story of the Panacea Society, in its original setting. The trust is also the custodian of a large amount of material relating to the Society which it is currently in the process of conserving, cataloguing and digitising in order to make the collection more available for academic research. Catalogues of these archives are available to researchers on application to the trust.

In addition to the above the charity makes grants and donations to deserving causes. The trustees expect to be able to continue applying a proportion of the income towards the work of recognised local health and social care related organisations, insofar as available funding permits, provided applications fall within the designated criteria.

Grants

Education grants

Funding is given in three ways:

- Through supporting research projects at various UK universities
- By providing individual scholarship funding to doctoral scholars
- By sponsoring or supporting academic conferences

Grants in this area are mainly for the field of historical theology, in particular: Prophecy; the Book of Revelation; The Second Coming of Christ; Jewish Apocalyptic literature and Christian Theology and Millennialism and Christian millenarian movements.

Poverty, sickness and social related grants

The charity does not provide direct funding in this area. It now channels this through the Bedfordshire and Luton Community Foundation working in partnership with Community and Voluntary Service Bedfordshire. Details of how to apply for funding can be obtained from these organisations.

The trust states that grants will be made for charitable purposes to UK-based organisations only. Priority will be given to funding requests that promote the religious aims of the society, benefit large numbers of people and are made on behalf of organisations rather than individuals.

In 2012 the trust had assets of £25 million and an income of £773,000. Grants were made totalling £501,000, broken down as follows:

Bedford project	£302,000
Universities research and conference grants	£150,000
Health/social	£50,000

Beneficiaries included: Bedford Project – Charity's properties, chapel and gardens, archives and library (£302,000); Bedford Hospitals Charity, Cambridge University and Goldsmiths College (£75,000 each); Kings College London (£54,000); Bedfordshire and Luton Community Foundation (£50,000); Gray Research Scholarship (£21,000); and Buntan Meeting Broomhall (£2,400).

Exclusions

The society will not consider funding:

- Political parties or political lobbying
- Pressure groups
- Commercial ventures
- Non-charitable activities
- Replacement of statutory funding

Applications

The trust has previously stated that it receives many applications that they are unable or unwilling to support. Read the grant criteria carefully before submitting an application. Unsolicited applications are not responded to.

Any organisation considering applying for funding support should make a formal application in writing to the correspondent. The application should set out the purpose for which the funding is required, and explain how it falls within the funding criteria and complies with their requirements. Full information on the work of the applicant body together with details of how the proposed funding will be applied should be given.

The correspondent will acknowledge receipt of an application, and indicate if the application falls within their parameters. At this point the society may call for additional information, or indicate that it is unable to consider the application further. Most applications fail because they fall outside the criteria, however the society does not provide additional reasons why it is unable to support a particular application.

When all relevant information has been received the application will be discussed at the next meeting of the society's trustees together with other valid applications. The trustees may at that meeting refuse or defer any application or request further information without giving reasons. Applicants will be advised in writing of the trustees' decision.

For full details visit the society's website.

Information gathered from:

Accounts; Charity Commission record; funder's website.

Panahpur

Christian missionaries, general, social investment

£114,000 to organisations (2011/12)

Beneficial area

UK, overseas in particular India.

Correspondent: James Perry, Trustee, 84 High Street, Tonbridge, Kent TN9 1AP

CC Number: 1130367

This trust was formed in 2009 from the assets of the previous Panahpur Charitable Trust. It supports Christian missionary organisations operating both in the UK and overseas. It will also continue the trend of forming long-term partnerships with a small number of suitable organisations and individuals. The fund operates three 'investment portfolios':

- Impact – Programme related and mixed purpose investments managed by an intermediary
- Hope – Programme related investments managed in-house
- Venture – Mixed-purpose investments managed in-house

The charity is not a traditional grantmaker rather it champions and support social and impact investment with a Christian ethos. There are three investment themes for the future:

- Democratising resources
- Future of welfare in the developed world
- Future of welfare in emerging economies

In 2011/12 the trust had assets of £5 million, an income of £144,000 and gave grants totalling £150,000 including £36,000 to individuals.

Beneficiaries included: Mission Now Cambodia (£51,000); Youth for Christ International (£35,000); ResPublica (£12,000); InterHealth (£9,400); Trans World Radio (£8,600); Romance Academy (£6,000); Molly's Network (£5,000); Cinnamon Network (£4,000); Ambassadors in Sport (£2,100); and Serving in Mission (£1,500); and Door of Hope (£1,300).

Applications

The trustees do their own research and do not respond to unsolicited applications.

Information gathered from:

Accounts; Charity Commission record.

The Panton Trust

Animal wildlife worldwide, environment UK

£39,000 (2011/12)

Beneficial area

UK and overseas.

Correspondent: Laurence Slavin, Trustee, Ramsay House, 18 Vera Avenue, Grange Park, London N12 1RA (tel: 020 8370 7700)

Trustees: L. M. Slavin; R. Craig.

CC Number: 292910

The trust's annual report states:

> The objects of the Charity are … concerned with any animal or animals or with wildlife in any part of the world, or with the environment of the UK or any part thereof, for the benefit of the public.
>
> The trustees consider applications from a wide variety of sources and favour smaller charities which do not have the same capacity for large-scale fundraising as major charities in this field.

In 2011/12 the trust had assets of £187,000, an income of £60,000 and made grants totalling £39,000.

Beneficiaries included: St Tiggywinkles Wildlife Hospital (£4,000); PDSA (£3,000); Sunshine Club, Flora and Fauna International and William Ellis School (£2,000 each); and Dogs Trust, Gorilla Organisation, Wroxton Parish Council, Moor Bear Rescue and Barn Owl Trust (£1,000 each).

Applications

In writing to the correspondent.

Information gathered from:

Accounts; Charity Commission record.

The Paragon Trust

General

£82,000 (2010/11)

Beneficial area

UK and overseas.

Correspondent: Stuart Goodbody, c/o Thomson Snell and Passmore Solicitors, 3 Lonsdale Gardens, Tunbridge Wells, Kent TN1 1NX (tel: 01892 510000)

Trustees: The Lord Wrenbury; Revd Canon R. Coppin; Ms L. J. Whistler; P. Cunningham; Dr Fiona Cornish; Patricia Russell.

CC Number: 278348

In 2010/11 the trust had assets of £1.7 million, an income of £83,000 and gave grants totalling £82,000.

Beneficiaries included: Compassion in World Farming 'YouTube Video Project' (£8,000); British Red Cross (£3,000); Zane Zimbabwe (£2,500); Canterbury Cathedral and Médecins Sans Frontières (£2,000 each); Dallington Parochial Church Council Spire Restoration Fund (£1,500); Send a Cow, Army Benevolent Fund, Prison Reform Trust and The Art Fund (£1,000 each); and Women's Holiday Fund, Hospice in the Weald and Changing Faces (£500 each).

Applications

The trust states that it does not respond to unsolicited applications; all beneficiaries 'are known personally to the trustees and no attention is paid to appeal literature, which is discarded on receipt. Fundraisers are therefore urged to save resources by not sending literature.'

Information gathered from:

Accounts; Charity Commission record.

The Park Charitable Trust

Jewish, patient care – cancer and heart conditions, hospitals

£367,000 (2011/12)

Beneficial area

UK.

Correspondent: E. Pine, Trustee, 69 Singleton Road, Salford M7 4LX

Trustees: D. Hammelburger; Mrs M. Hammelburger; E. Pine.

CC Number: 1095541

> The objects of the charity are the advancement of the Jewish Faith; the advancement of Jewish education; the relief of poverty amongst the Jewish community; the relief of patients suffering from cancer and heart conditions; giving financial support to hospitals and furthering such other charitable purposes as the trustees may from time to time determine in support of their charitable activities.

In 2011/12 the trust had assets of £1.6 million and an income of £847,000. Grants totalled £367,000, broken down as follows:

Relief of poverty	£234,000
Grants paid under £1,000	£42,000
Community projects	£39,000
Yeshivot and seminaries	£29,000
Schools	£22,000

A list of beneficiaries was not included in the accounts.

Applications

In writing to the correspondent.

Information gathered from:

Accounts; Charity Commission record.

The Park House Charitable Trust

Education, social welfare, ecclesiastical

£368,000 (2012)

Beneficial area

UK and overseas, with a preference for the Midlands, particularly Coventry and Warwickshire.

Correspondent: Paul Varney, Dafferns LLP, One Eastwood, Harry Weston Road, Binley Business Park, Coventry CV3 2UB (tel: 02476 221046)

Trustees: N. P. Bailey; Mrs M. Bailey; P. Bailey.

CC Number: 1077677

The trust was established in September 1999. In 2012 it had assets of £1.4 million, an income of £301,000 and made 30 grants totalling £368,000, categorised as follows:

Social welfare	£320,000
Ecclesiastical	£21,000
Medical	£20,000
Education	£7,000

Beneficiaries included: Scottish International Relief and St Joseph and the Helpers Charity (£100,000 each); Aid to the Church in Need, Columban Fathers, CAFOD and St John of Jerusalem Eye Hospital (£10,000 each); Smile Train, Y Care International and The Passage (£5,000 each); Community of Holy Fire (£4,000); and Bibles for Children (£3,000).

Exclusions

No grants to individuals.

Applications

In writing to the correspondent. The trust has stated that it does not expect to have surplus funds available to meet the majority of applications.

Information gathered from:
Accounts; Charity Commission record.

The Frank Parkinson Agricultural Trust

British agriculture

£13,000 (2012)

Beneficial area
UK.

Correspondent: Miss Janet Smith, Secretary to the Trustees, 11 Alder Drive, Pudsey LS28 8RD (tel: 01132 578613; email: janetpudsey@live.co.uk)

Trustees: C. Bourchier; Prof. Paul Webster; D. Gardner; Prof. David Leaver; Alastair Morrison.

CC Number: 209407

The trust's principal object is the improvement and welfare of British agriculture. Its aims are:

- The improvement and welfare of British agriculture
- The undertaking of agricultural research or the provision of grants for such means
- The establishment of scholarships, bursaries and exhibitions at any university, college or other technical institution in any branch of the agricultural industry
- The granting of financial assistance to young people of ability who are in need of assistance and are working in the agricultural industry to improve their education and experience by working, training or otherwise
- The encouragement and assistance of the social and cultural welfare of people working in the agricultural industry
- The making of grants to any charity or organisation which is carrying on any work in connection with the provision of any such benefits as aforesaid

The trust fulfils these objects primarily by making grants to educational or research institutions.

In 2012 the trust had assets of £1.2 million, an income of £60,000 and made grants to four organisations totalling £13,000.

The beneficiaries were: St George's House and Yorkshire and Harrogate Beekeepers' Association (£5,000 each); John Innes Centre (£2,400); and AgriFood Charities Partnership (£250).

Exclusions
Grants are given to corporate bodies and the trust is not able to assist with financial help to any individuals undertaking postgraduate studies or degree courses.

Applications
In writing to the correspondent. The trustees meet annually in April and applicants are expected to make an oral presentation. Further details of the whole application process can be found in the useful 'Guidelines for Grant Applications' which is available from the trust. Note, however: 'The chair has the authority to approve small grants between annual meetings, but these are only for minor sums and minor projects.'

Information gathered from:
Accounts; Charity Commission record.

The Samuel and Freda Parkinson Charitable Trust

General

£101,000 (2011/12)

Beneficial area
UK.

Correspondent: Trust Administrator, Regent House, 25 Crescent Road, Windermere, Cumbria LA23 1BJ (tel: 01539 446585)

Trustees: John Crompton; Judith Todd; Michael Fletcher.

CC Number: 327749

This trust was established in 1987 with?100. The fund stayed at this level until 1994/95 when?2.1 million worth of assets were placed in the trust on the death of the settlor. It supports the same eight beneficiaries each year, although for varying amounts.

In 2011/12 the trust had assets of?3 million, an income of?105,000 and gave grants totalling?101,000.

Grant beneficiaries were: Salvation Army (?26,000); The Leonard Cheshire Foundation (?25,000); Church Army and RNLI (?15,000); and RSPCA, Animal Concern, Animal Rescue Cumbria and Animal Welfare (?5,000 each).

Applications
The founder of this charity restricted the list of potential beneficiaries to named charities of his choice and accordingly the trustees do not have discretion to include further beneficiaries, although they do have complete discretion within the stated beneficiary list.

Information gathered from:
Accounts; Charity Commission record.

Arthur James Paterson Charitable Trust

Medical research, welfare of older people and children

£30,000 each (2011/12)

Beneficial area
UK.

Correspondent: Anita Carter, Trust Administrator, Royal Bank of Canada Trust Corporation Ltd, Riverbank House, 2 Swan Lane, London EC4R 3BF (tel: 020 7653 4756; email: anita.carter@rbc.com)

Trustee: Royal Bank of Canada Trust Corporation Ltd.

CC Number: 278569

In 2011/12 the trust had assets of £1.7 million and an income of £45,000. Grants to seven organisations totalled £30,000.

The beneficiaries were: Glenalmond College and Worcester College (£6,200 each); Shine and Eureka (£4,000 each); Woodlands Hospice and Home Start Bristol (£3,900 each); and British Eye Research and British Forces (£1,100 each).

Applications
There are no application forms. Send your application with a covering letter and include the latest set of report and accounts. Deadlines are February and August.

Information gathered from:
Accounts; Charity Commission record.

The Constance Paterson Charitable Trust

Medical research, health, welfare of children, older people, service people

£16,000 (2012/13)

Beneficial area
UK.

Correspondent: Ms Anita Carter, Administrator, Royal Bank of Canada Trust Corporation Ltd, Riverbank House, 2 swan lane, London EC4R 3BF (tel: 020 7653 4756; email: anita.carter@rbc.com)

Trustee: Royal Bank of Canada Trust Corporation Ltd.

CC Number: 249556

The trust makes grants in support of medical research, healthcare, welfare of elderly people and children (including accommodation and housing) and service people's welfare.

In 2012/13 the trust had assets of £1.2 million, an income of £31,000 and gave grants totalling £16,000.

The beneficiaries were: Ambitious About Autism, Golden Oldies, Joe Glover Trust, Thames Hospice Care and The Speech Language and Hearing Centre (£2,000 each); and It's your Choice, Forest Bus Ltd, The Eyeless Trust and Extend Exercise Trading Ltd (£1,500 each).

Exclusions

No grants to individuals.

Applications

In writing to the correspondent, including covering letter and the latest set of annual report and accounts. The trust does not have an application form. Deadlines for applications are June and December.

Information gathered from:

Accounts; Charity Commission record.

Miss M. E Swinton Paterson's Charitable Trust

Church of Scotland, young people, general

Around £40,000

Beneficial area

Scotland.

Correspondent: The Trustees, Lindsays Solicitors, Calendonian Exchange, 19a Canning Street, Edinburgh EH3 8HE

SC Number: SC004835

The trust was set up by the will of Miss M E Swinton Paterson who died in October 1989. The objectives of the trust are the support of charities in Scotland, specifically including schemes of the Church of Scotland.

In 2012/13 the trust had an income of £50,000 and an expenditure of £42,000. Grants are usually made totalling around £40,000.

Previous beneficiaries include: L'Arche Edinburgh Community, Livingstone Baptist Church, Lloyd Morris Congregational Church, Haddington West Parish Church, Acorn Christian Centre, Stranraer YMCA, Care for the Family, Boys' and Girls' Clubs of Scotland, Fresh Start, Friends of the Elms, Iona Community, Edinburgh Young Carers' Project, Epilepsy Scotland, Stoneykirk Parish Church, Scotland Yard Adventure Centre, Atholl Centre, Scottish Crusaders, Disablement Income Group Scotland and Artlink.

Exclusions

No grants to individuals or students.

Applications

In writing to the correspondent. Trustees meet once a year in July to consider grants.

Information gathered from:

OSCR record.

Ambika Paul Foundation

Education, young people

£122,000 (2011/12)

Beneficial area

Mainly UK and India.

Correspondent: Lord Paul of Marylebone, Trustee, Caparo House, 103 Baker Street, London W1U 6LN (tel: 020 7486 1417; email: georgina.mason@caparo.com)

Trustees: Lord Paul of Marylebone; Lady Aruna Paul; Hon. Angad Paul; Hon. Anjli Paul; Hon. Ambar Paul; Hon. Akash Paul.

CC Number: 276127

The foundation supports large organisations, registered charities, colleges and universities benefiting children, young adults and students mostly in the UK and India. Main areas of interest are to do with young people and education. Grants usually range from £100 to £3,000.

In 2011/12 the foundation had assets of £7.5 million and an income of £576,000. Grants to nine organisations totalled £122,000 and were broken down as follows:

Educational projects	£87,000
Social projects	£29,000
Medical trust funds	£5,000

The beneficiaries were: Loreto College, India (£76,000); Zoological Society of London (£15,000); Shri Venkateswara (£11,000); Indian Orthopaedic Society (£10,000); Lamu Dispensary (£5,000); Anglican Communion Ministries (£2,600); Bharatiya Vidya Bhawan (£1,500); and Sindi Nari Sabha and CST (protecting Jewish Community) (£500 each).

Exclusions

Applications from individuals, including students, are mainly ineligible. Funding for scholarships is made directly to colleges/universities, not to individuals. No expeditions.

Applications

In writing to the trustees at the correspondence address. Acknowledgements are sent if an sae is enclosed. However, the trust has no paid employees and the enormous number of requests it receives creates administrative difficulties.

Information gathered from:

Accounts; Charity Commission record.

The Susanna Peake Charitable Trust

General

£156,500 (2011/12)

Beneficial area

UK, with a preference for the South West of England, particularly Gloucestershire.

Correspondent: The Administrator, Rathbone Trust Company Ltd4th Floor1 Curzon StreetLondonW1J 5FB (tel: 020 7399 0811)

Trustees: Susanna Peake; David Peake.

CC Number: 283462

This is one of the Kleinwort family trusts. It was set up by Susanna Peake in 1981 for general charitable purposes and has a preference for charities based in the Gloucestershire area. In addition, non-local appeals when received are accumulated and considered by the trustees annually.

In 2011/12 the trust had assets of £5.5 million and an income of £154,000. Grants were made to 57 organisations totalling £156,500 and were broken down as follows:

Local charities	£44,000
General and animal charities	£33,500
Medical, cancer and hospices	£28,000
Education and children	£24,500
International and overseas	£16,500
Elderly people	£10,000

Beneficiaries included: Longborough School (£10,000); Speech, Language and Hearing Centre (£6,000); Gloucester County Council for the Blind and Rutland Houses School Parents (£5,000 each); Charity Search and Cotswold Care Hospice (£4,000 each); Friends of St Lawrence Church and Training for Life (£3,000 each); PDSA and WaterAid (£2,000 each); Victim Support (£1,000); and Kidscape (£100).

Exclusions

No grants to individuals.

Applications

In writing to the correspondent. 'The trustees meet on an ad hoc basis to review applications for funding, and a full review is undertaken annually when the financial statements are available. Only successful applications are notified of the trustees' decision.'

Information gathered from:

Accounts; Charity Commission record.

The David Pearlman Charitable Foundation

Jewish, general

£86,000 (2011/12)

Beneficial area

UK.

Correspondent: Mr D. Goldberger, Trustee, New Burlington House, 1075 Finchley Road, London NW11 0PU (tel: 020 8731 0777)

Trustees: D. A. Pearlman; M. R. Goldberger; S. Appleman; J. Hager.

CC Number: 287009

Set up in 1983, in 2011/12 the foundation had assets of £2.5 million and an income of £178,000. Grants were made totalling £86,000. The accounts did not contain a list of beneficiaries.

Previous beneficiaries have included: British Friends of Igud Hakolelim B'Yerushalayim (£60,000); Lolev Charitable Trust (£30,000); Jewish Care (£16,000); Chevras Mo'oz Ladol (£15,000); Norwood (£12,000); the Duke of Edinburgh Trust (£7,000); Community Security Trust (£6,000); London Academy of Jewish Studies (£1,500); Jewish Music Institute and United Jewish Israel Appeal (£1,000).

Applications

In writing to the correspondent.

Information gathered from:

Accounts; Charity Commission record.

The Peltz Trust

Arts, education, health, Jewish, general

£160,000 (2011/12)

Beneficial area

UK and Israel.

Correspondent: Martin Paisner, Trustee, Berwin Leighton Paisner, Adelaide House, London Bridge, London EC4R 9HA (tel: 020 3400 2356)

Trustees: Martin Paisner; Daniel Peltz; Hon. Elizabeth Wolfson Peltz.

CC Number: 1002302

In 2011/12 the trust had assets of £640,000 and an income of £1 million. Grants were made to 26 organisations totalling £160,000, broken down into the following categories:

Education and training	8	£90,000
Economic and community development	7	£33,500
Religious activities	3	£17,000
Medical, health and sickness	5	£10,500
Arts and culture	3	£9,500

Beneficiaries included: Birkbeck College (£50,000); British Technion Society (£21,000); Central Synagogue General Charities Fund (£13,000); Norwood Ravencourt (£10,000); City of London School, UK Friends of Magen David Adom, One Family and United Jewish Israel Appeal (£5,000 each); Nightingale House (£2,500); AISH Hatorah UK Ltd (£1,500); Willow Foundation (£1,000); and Mousetrap Theatre Projects (£500).

Applications

In writing to the correspondent. The trustees meet at irregular intervals during the year to consider appeals from appropriate organisations.

Information gathered from:

Accounts; Charity Commission record.

The Pennycress Trust

General charitable purposes

£63,000 (2011/12)

Beneficial area

UK and worldwide, with a preference for Cheshire and Norfolk.

Correspondent: Mrs Doreen Howells, Secretary to the Trustees, Flat D, 15 Millman Street, London WC1N 3EP (tel: 020 7404 0145)

Trustees: Lady Aline Cholmondeley; Lady Rose Cholmondeley. Anthony J. M. Baker; C. G. Cholmondeley; Sybil Sassoon.

CC Number: 261536

The trust's policy is to make donations to smaller charities and especially those based in Cheshire and Norfolk, with some donations to UK and international organisations. Grants are generally for £100 to £500, occasionally larger.

In 2011/12 the trust had assets of £2.2 million and an income of £79,000. Grants were made to 209 organisations totalling £63,000. A list of beneficiaries was not included with the latest accounts.

Previous beneficiaries have included All Saints' Church – Beeston Regis, Brain Research Trust, Brighton and Hove Parents' and Children's Group, British Red Cross, Crusaid, Depaul Trust, Elimination of Leukaemia Fund, Eyeless Trust, Genesis Appeal, Help the Aged, Matthew Project, RUKBA, St Peter's – Eaton Square Appeal, Salvation Army, Tibet Relief Fund, West Suffolk Headway, Women's Link and Youth Federation.

Lady Aline and Charles Cholmondeley are also trustees of Aaron David Sassoon (Charity Commission no. 210731; and Anthony Baker is also a trustee of Aaron David Sassoon and Beeston Regis Church Field (Charity Commission no. 241840).

Exclusions

No support for individuals.

Applications

In writing to the correspondent. 'No telephone applications please.' Trustees meet regularly. They do not have an application form as a simple letter will be sufficient.

Percentage of awards given to new applicants: between 10% and 20%.

Common applicant mistakes

'Asking for a specific amount and sending too many enclosures.'

Information gathered from:

Accounts; Charity Commission record; further information provided by the funder.

B. E. Perl Charitable Trust

Jewish, general

£75,000 (2011/12)

Beneficial area

UK.

Correspondent: Benjamin Perl, Trustee, Foframe House, 35–37 Brent Street, Hendon, London NW4 2EF

Trustees: Benjamin Perl; Dr Shoshanna Perl; Jonathan Perl; Joseph Perl; Naomi Sorotzkin; Rachel Jeidal.

CC Number: 282847

The trust's main focus is the advancement of education in and the religion of the Orthodox Jewish faith. Grants are made to Jewish schools, other educational organisations and other charities.

In 2011/12 the trust had assets of £15.5 million and an income of over £1.8 million. Grants totalled £75,000.

Major beneficiaries were: Hasmonean High School, JNF, Society of Friends of the Torah and Yavenh College. No details of grant amounts were available.

Plans for future periods

Note the following statement taken from the 2011/12 annual report and accounts:

> The trustees have considered and approved plans for the establishment of a major educational project in the UK. It is anticipated that the cost of this project will be in the order of £5 million and it is the intentions of the trustees to accumulate this amount over the next ten years. During the period an amount of £500,000 (2011–£500,000) was transferred to the Educational Reserve in order to fund this project. The Educational Reserve for this purpose stands at £3 million as at the balance sheet date.

Applications

In writing to the correspondent.

Information gathered from:

Accounts; Charity Commission record.

The Persson Charitable Trust (formerly Highmoore Hall Charitable Trust)

Christian mission societies and agencies

£221,000 (2011/12)

Beneficial area

UK and overseas.

Correspondent: Paul Persson, Trustee, Long Meadow, Dark Lane, Chearsley, Aylesbury, Buckinghamshire HP18 0DA (tel: 01844 201955; email: paulpersson@xalt.co.uk)

Trustees: Paul Persson; Andrew Persson; John Persson; Ann Persson.

CC Number: 289027

The trust makes grants for the prevention and relief of poverty, the advancement of religion, health and humanitarian aid both nationally and internationally. In practice grants are given to Christian relief and mission societies.

In 2011/12 the trust had assets of £615,000 and an income of £254,000. Grants were made totalling £221,000, broken down as follows in the trust accounts:

Home missions	£130,000
Overseas missions and relief	£91,000

Beneficiaries included: Bible Reading Fellowship (£111,000); Tearfund – Christian Relief (£55,000); All Nations Christian College (£12,000); and Christian Solidarity Worldwide (£10,000).

Other grants totalled £33,000.

Exclusions

No grants to non-registered charities.

Applications

The trust states that it does not respond to unsolicited applications. Telephone calls are not welcome.

Information gathered from:

Accounts; Charity Commission record.

The Persula Foundation

Homeless, people with disabilities, human rights, animal welfare

£709,000 (2011/12)

Beneficial area

Predominantly UK; overseas grants are given, but this is rare.

Correspondent: Fiona Brown, Chief Executive, Gallery Court, Hankey Place, London SE1 4BB (tel: 020 7551 5343; fax: 020 7357 8685; email: fiona@persula.org)

Trustees: J. Richer; D. Robinson; Mrs R. Richer; Mrs H. Oppenheim; Robert Rosenthal; Jonathan Levy.

CC Number: 1044174

The trust works in collaboration with organisations to support projects that are innovative and original in the UK and worldwide.

The foundation has core charity interests which they call Generic Research Projects (GRPs) and from this base, they decide on the charity and amount they donate.

- Animal welfare
- Disabilities (blind and visually impaired, deaf and hard of hearing, learning disabilities, mental health, physical disabilities)
- Human welfare (bullying, children and young people, homeless, welfare)
- Human rights

> Our projects continued to run successfully in 2011/2012. The 'Storytelling Tour' gave over 100 free sessions of storytelling and music to the visually impaired, the elderly, and disabled children & adults and throughout the UK. The 'On The Right Track Project' provides free touch-screen computerised kiosks giving information to homeless people and young runaways in London and 'Tapesense' is our mail-order service offering subsidised blank media and popular hi fi accessories to Blind and Visually Impaired people throughout the UK.

In 2011/12 the foundation had assets of £40,000 and an income of £807,000. Grants totalled £709,000. The principal source of funding was donated by Richer Sounds plc of which Julian Richer is the founder. The following table gives a breakdown of the purposes for which the grants were made:

Human welfare	£454,000
Animal welfare	£132,000
Human rights	£30,000
People with disabilities	£58,000
Tapesense	£22,000
Storytelling	£13,000

One of the largest listed went to Tapesense (£22,000). This project was set up a few years ago by the foundation and offers subsidised equipment and accessories to blind and visually impaired people. The other beneficiaries listed in the accounts were: Impact Youth Project Work (£45,000); WSPA Humane Slaughter (£35,000); Amnesty International UK (£25,000); and Parent Circle Families Forum (£20,000)

Previous beneficiaries have included Action for ME, African Children's Educational Trust, the Aids Trust, the Backup Trust, The Helen Bamber Foundation, Bullying Online, Disability Challengers, Dogs Trust, Emmaus, Humane Slaughter Association, Interact Worldwide, Kidscape, League Against Cruel Sports, The Mango Tree, the MicroLoan Foundation, National Deaf Children's Society, Practical Action, Prisoners Abroad, Prison Reform Trust, Respect for Animals, RNIB, RNID, St Mungo's, SOS Children, Stonewall, VIVA! and WSPA.

Exclusions

No grants to individuals, including sponsorship, for core costs, buildings/building work or to statutory bodies.

Applications

In writing to the correspondent. Trustees meet every two months. The foundation states:

> We consider applications which fit our broad criteria, but they must also fulfill the following:
>
> 1. They must come from a registered charity or other appropriate organisation
> 2. The project should be an original idea, and not duplicating an existing service or suchlike
> 3. The project should be or have the potential to be of national application, rather than local to one area
> 4. We will not consider applications from charities that have substantial financial reserves (3 to 6 months running costs), and ask to see an annual report from any charity making an application
> 5. Any charity with whom we work must be prepared to co-operate in a professional manner, for example, meet deadlines, return calls, perform mutually agreed work, in short, to behave 'commercially'
> 6. The project, in most cases, must fall within the remit of one or more GRPs
> 7. They must provide value for money
>
> This list is by no means exhaustive, nor is it final. We will attempt to consider every application but, in general, the above should apply.

Information gathered from:

Accounts; Charity Commission record.

The Petplan Charitable Trust

Welfare of dogs, cats, horses and rabbits

£681,000 (2012)

Beneficial area

UK.

Correspondent: Catherine Bourg, Administrator, Great West House GW2, Great West Road, Brentford, Middlesex TW8 9EG (tel: 020 8580 8013; fax: 020 8580 8186; email: catherine.bourg@allianz.co.uk; website: www.petplantrust.org)

Trustees: David Simpson, Chair; Clarissa Baldwin; Patsy Bloom; John Bower; Ted Chandler; Neil Brettell.

CC Number: 1032907

The trust was established in 1994 by a pet insurance company by adding an optional £1.50 a year to the premiums paid by its members. 'The trust provides grants towards the welfare of dogs, cats, horses and rabbits by funding clinical veterinary investigation, education and welfare projects.'

Funding is given in three areas:

Scientific grants

- Full grants for in depth research for up to three years
- Pump priming grants of up to £10,000

Clinical research that will potentially help vets in practice to treat and care for animals. Only work which involves the study of companion animals will be funded. The trust strictly will not fund anything that involves even the slightest invasive treatment. Full terms and conditions are on the website.

Welfare grants

- One major welfare grants of up to £20,000 towards an innovative project
- Up to £40,000 to be distributed in general grants of between £5,000 and £7,500
- Up to £40,000 to be distributed for general grants of up to £5,000
- Up to 3 grants to assist with vehicle purchase

General grants can include items such as neutering, kennelling and veterinary costs but not for general overheads. Projects involving pet therapy have also been supported.

Capital grants

Usually given to veterinary schools to support rebuilding and modernising facilities.

In 2012 the trust had assets of £382,000, an income of £683,000 and gave grants totalling £681,000, broken down as follows:

Scientific grants	£399,000
Welfare and educational grants	£182,000
Pedigree adoption scheme grants	£100,000

Beneficiaries included: Royal Veterinary College (£133,000); University of Cambridge (£86,000); Ashbourne and District Animal Welfare Society (£20,000); Rain Rescue (£12,000); University of Edinburgh, Gable farm Dogs and Cats Home (£10,000 each); Animal Health Trust (£9,400); Wood Green Animal Shelter (£7,500); Oldies Club (£5,000); Labrador Rescue England (£2,000); Camp Nibble (£1,500); Joseph Clark School (£500); and English Springer Spaniel Welfare (£100).

Exclusions

No grants to individuals or non-registered charities. The trust does not support or condone invasive procedures, vivisection or experimentation of any kind.

Applications

Closing dates for scientific and welfare applications vary so check the trust's website first. Grant guidelines and application forms can also be downloaded from the trust's website.

Information gathered from:

Accounts; Charity Commission record; funder's website.

The Pharsalia Charitable Trust

General, relief of sickness

£48,000 (2011/12)

Beneficial area

Unrestricted, with a particular interest in Oxford.

Correspondent: Trudy Sainsbury, Trustee, The Ham, Ickleton Road, Wantage, Oxfordshire OX12 9JA (tel: 01235 426524)

Trustees: Nigel Stirling Blackwell; Christina Blackwell; Trudy Sainsbury.

CC Number: 1120402

Established in 2007, the trust gives grants for general charitable purposes, with particular emphasis on the relief of sickness. It is the charitable trust of Nigel Stirling Blackwell of Blackwell's books and publishing – the name of the trust derives from a Roman epic poem by Lucan.

In 2011/12 the trust had assets of £2.2 million, an income of £73,000 and gave grants totalling £48,000.

The major beneficiary during the year was Oxford Radcliffe Hospital Charitable Funds, which received £25,000.

Other grant beneficiaries included: The Vale House Appeal (£15,000); The Haig Housing Trust and Oxford Radcliffe Hospital Charitable Funds (£5,000 each); Bromsgrove Day Centre (£1,700); DEC East Africa Appeal, Helen and Douglas House, Motability, Sobell House Hospice and the Salvation Army (£1,000 each); Glacier Trust and Royal British Legion (£500 each); and Alzheimer's Research UK (£250).

Applications

In writing to the correspondent.

Information gathered from:

Accounts; Charity Commission record.

The Phillips and Rubens Charitable Trust

General, Jewish

£271,000 (2011/12)

Beneficial area

UK.

Correspondent: M. L. Phillips, Trustee, 67–69 George Street, London W1U 8LT

Trustees: Michael L. Philips; Ruth Philips; Martin D. Paisner; Paul Philips; Gary Philips; Carolyn Mishon.

CC Number: 260378

The trust supports a wide range of causes, including medical research, education, disability, old age, poverty, sheltered accommodation and the arts. In practice, almost all the grants are made to Jewish/Israeli organisations.

In 2011/12 the trust had assets of £8.7 million and an income of £305,000. Grants totalled £271,000.

Beneficiaries included: The Phillips Family Charitable Trust (£80,000); United Jewish Israel Appeal (£42,000); Charities Aid Foundation (£25,000); Jewish Community Secondary School (£20,000); Simon Wiesenthal Centre (£16,000); Holocaust Educational Trust and Jewish Care (£7,500 each); The Churchill Centre United Kingdom, The Community Security Trust and British ORT (£5,000 each); and Nightingale House and UK Friends of the Association for the Wellbeing of Israel's Soldiers (£2,500 each).

Grants of less than £2,500 each totalled £17,000.

Exclusions

No grants are made to individuals.

Applications

In writing to the correspondent at any time, although the trust has stated that the majority of grants are to beneficiaries they already support.

Percentage of awards given to new applicants: less than 10%.

Information gathered from:

Accounts; Charity Commission record; further information provided by the funder.

The Phillips Family Charitable Trust

Jewish charities, welfare, general

£70,000 (2012/13)

Beneficial area

UK.

Correspondent: Paul S. Phillips, Trustee, 67–69 George Street, London W1U 8LT (tel: 020 7487 5757)

Trustees: Michael L. Phillips; Ruth Phillips; Martin D. Paisner; Paul S. Phillips; Gary M. Phillips.

CC Number: 279120

This trust stated that it makes grants to Jewish organisations and to a range of other organisations, including elderly, children and refugee charities and educational establishments.

In 2012/13 the trust had assets of £25,000 and an income of £80,000. The income each year comes from a grant from the related Phillips and Rubens Charitable Trust. Grants totalled £70,000.

Beneficiaries included: London School of Jewish Studies (£6,000); Community Security Trust and United Synagogue (£5,000 each); Jewish Leadership Council (£4,500); Jewish Learning Exchange (£4,000); Norwood Ravenswood (£3,200); London Jewish Cultural Centre (£3,000); Tree of Life, Council of Christians and Jews, Interface Parent Carer Forum and Beth Shalom Ltd (£1,000 each); and Chabad Lubavitch UK.

Exclusions

No grants to individuals.

Applications

In writing to the correspondent. Note, the trust informed us that there is not much scope for new beneficiaries.

Percentage of awards given to new applicants: less than 10%.

Common applicant mistakes

'No common mistakes.'

Information gathered from:

Accounts; Charity Commission record; further information provided by the funder.

The David Pickford Charitable Foundation

Christian, general

£73,000 (2011/12)

Beneficial area

UK (with a preference for Kent and London) and overseas.

Correspondent: E. J. Pettersen, Trustee, Benover House, Rectory Lane, Saltwood, Hythe, Kent CT21 4QA (tel: 01303 268322)

Trustees: C. J. Pickford; E. J. Pettersen;.

CC Number: 243437

The general policy is to make gifts to Christian organisations especially those helping youth, and with special needs in the UK and overseas.

In 2011/12 the foundation had assets of £1.1 million, an income of £39,000 and gave 37 grants totalling £73,000. A list of beneficiaries was not included in the accounts.

Previous beneficiaries included: CARE; Chaucer Trust; Oasis Trust; Brighter Future and Pastor Training international; Toybox; Alpha International, Flow Romania and Mersham Parish Church; Compassion; Samaritans and Lionhart.

Exclusions

No grants to individuals. No building projects.

Applications

In writing to the correspondent. The deadline for applications is November. Applications will not be acknowledged. The correspondent states: 'It is our general policy only to give to charities to whom we are personally known.' Unsolicited applications are rarely funded. Those falling outside the criteria mentioned above will be ignored.

Percentage of awards given to new applicants: between 10% and 20%.

Common applicant mistakes

'The grants are not for activities that our charity will sponsor – they must be linked to Christian activities.'

Information gathered from:

Accounts; Charity Commission record; further information provided by the funder.

The Bernard Piggott Charitable Trust

General

£69,000 (2011/12)

Beneficial area

North Wales and Birmingham.

Correspondent: Jenny Whitworth, Administrator, Jenny Whitworth, 4 Streetsbrook Road, Shirley, Solihull, West Midlands B90 3PL (tel: 01217 441695)

Trustees: Mark Painter; Derek Lea; Nigel Lea; Richard Easton; Venerable Paul Davies.

CC Number: 260347

This trust provides one-off grants for Church of England, Church of Wales, educational, medical, drama and youth organisations in Birmingham and North Wales only. It is the trustees' policy to allocate approximately one-third of income to charitable organisations operating within North Wales and two-thirds to the Birmingham area.

In 2011/12 the trust had assets of £1.4 million, an income of £105,000 and made grants totalling £69,000. Grants ranged from £500 to £2,000.

Beneficiaries included: The Joseph Foote Trust and Wales Air Ambulance (£2,000 each); InterAct Reading Service and Llandysilio Church Parochial Church Council (£1,500 each); Christian Mountain Centre Pensarn Harbour, Inclusion 4U, Birmingham Clubs for Young People, Combat Stress, Relate, Elmhurst, Motor Neurone Disease Association and Birmingham Children's Hospital (£1,000 each); Northfield Festival of Music and Speech (£750); and BUDS (Better Understanding of Dementia in Sandwell) (£500).

Exclusions

No grants to individuals.

Applications

The trustees meet in May/June and November. Applications should be in writing to the secretary including annual accounts and details of the specific project including running costs and so on. General policy is not to consider any further grant to the same organisation within the next two years. 'Trustees meet every six months to consider recommended applications. Those successful are sent the approved grant as soon as possible.'

Percentage of awards given to new applicants: between 20% and 30%.

Common applicant mistakes

'Re-applying too soon or being outside the areas specified by the original [deed], or applications made by individuals.'

Information gathered from:
Accounts; Charity Commission record; further information provided by the funder.

The Elise Pilkington Charitable Trust

Equine animals, older people

£161,000 (2011/12)

Beneficial area
UK.

Correspondent: Kenton Lawton, Trust Administrator, Ridgecot, Lewes Road, Horsted Keynes, Haywards Heath, West Sussex RH17 7DY (tel: 01825 790304; website: elisepilkingtontrust.org.uk)

Trustees: Caroline Doulton, Chair; Tara Economakis; Revd Rob Merchant; Helen Timpany.

CC Number: 278332

The trust's objects are:

- To prevent cruelty to equine animals, to relieve suffering and distress amongst such equine animals and to care for and protect such equines in need of care and protection
- To provide social services for the relief of the aged

Grantmaking is split with approximately two thirds to equine charities and the remaining third to charities for older people. The trust supports small specific projects of a capital nature and occasionally larger charities, but over a period of three years. Grants are not usually given towards running costs.

In 2011/12 the trust had assets of £2.8 million. It had an income of £90,000 and made 28 grants totalling £161,000.

To prevent cruelty to equine animals	8	£90,000
To provide help for the aged	20	£72,000

A list of beneficiaries was not available.

Applications
In writing to the correspondent including:

- 5 copies of your full application letter along with 5 copies of your latest consolidated statement of financial activity and balance sheet (we don't need 5 full sets of the accounts)
- Detail in your application what percentage of your income is actually used for charitable purposes
- In the case of equine application, please outline the number of equines your charity currently has in the centre, the number taken in during the last twelve months and the number rehomed during the same period

The deadlines are 28 March for consideration in May and 30 September for consideration in October.

Successful applicants must wait three years before reapplying.

Percentage of awards given to new applicants: between 20% and 30%.

Common applicant mistakes
'Applications not benefiting the elderly or equine.'

Information gathered from:
Accounts; Charity Commission record; further information provided by the funder; funder's website.

The Cecil Pilkington Charitable Trust

Conservation, medical research, general

£123,000 (2010/11)

Beneficial area
UK, particularly Sunningwell in Oxfordshire and St Helens.

Correspondent: Anthony Bayliss, Duncan Sheard Glass, Castle Chambers, 43 Castle Street, Liverpool L2 9TL

Trustees: Arnold Pilkington; Mark Feeny; Vanessa Pilkington; Heloise Pilkington.

CC Number: 249997

This trust supports conservation and medical research causes across the UK, supporting both national and local organisations. It also has general charitable purposes in Sunningwell in Oxfordshire and St Helens.

The latest accounts available were for 2010/11. During the year the trust had assets of £7.8 million, an income of £272,000 and gave 12 grants totalling £123,000.

Beneficiaries included: Psychiatry Research Trust (£50,000); Prostrate Cancer Research Centre (£33,000); Peninsular Medical School Foundation (£24,000); Allergy UK, Epilepsy Research, Oxford Preservation Trust and Beating Bowel Cancer (£2,000 each); and British Horse Loggers Charitable Trust and Gordon Russell Trust (£1,000 each).

Exclusions
No grants to individuals or non-registered charities.

Applications
The trust does not respond to unsolicited appeals.

Information gathered from:
Accounts; Charity Commission record.

The Austin and Hope Pilkington Trust

Categories of funding repeated in a three-year rotation (see the entry for further information)

£308,000 (2012)

Beneficial area
Unrestricted, but see exclusions field.

Correspondent: Karen Frank, Administrator, PO Box 124, Stroud, Gloucestershire GL6 7YB (email: admin@austin-hope-pilkington.org.uk; website: www.austin-hope-pilkington.org.uk)

Trustees: Jennifer Jones; Deborah Nelson; Penny Shankar.

CC Number: 255274

The trustees welcome applications for projects within the following areas for the next three years. These categories are then repeated on a three-year rotation.

- 2011 – music and the arts; overseas (*the last year grants will be made to overseas projects*)
- 2012 – community; medical
- 2013 – children and youth
- 2014 – music and the arts; elderly

Registered charities only. National projects are preferred to those with a local remit. Grants are usually between £1,000 and £3,000. The majority of grants made were for £1,000 because the trustees decided to make a large number of small grants in order to make the trust's resources as effective as possible given the exceptional demand on the charity. Exceptionally, grants of up to £10,000 are made, but these are usually for medical research projects. Grants are usually awarded for one year only.

In 2012 the trust had assets of £9.5 million and an income of £328,000. Grants were made totalling £308,000.

Beneficiaries included: Cancer Research UK (£10,000); Genesis Breast Cancer Prevention (£5,000); CLIC Sargent, Shelter, Tommy's and Westminster Befriend a Family (£3,000 each); and Emmaus, Kirby Trust, April Centre, Big Issue, Cardiff bond Board, Housing for Woman, Lesbian and Gay Foundation, Sign Health and Spadework (£1,000 each).

Exclusions
Grants only to registered charities. No grants to individuals, including individuals embarking on a trip overseas with an umbrella organisation. Overseas projects are no longer supported. National organisations are more likely to be supported than purely local organisations. Charities working in the following areas are not supported:

religion (including repair of Church fabric); animals (welfare and conservation); scouts, guides, cubs, brownies; village halls; individual hospices (national organisations can apply); capital appeals; schools; and minibuses.

Applications

Applicants are strongly advised to visit the trust's website as projects supported and eligibility criteria change from year to year. Grants are made twice a year, with deadlines for applications being 1 June and 1 November.

Applications should be made in writing to the correspondent – do not use signed for or courier. To apply for a grant, submit *only* the following:

- A letter summarising the application, including acknowledgement of any previous grants awarded from the trust
- A maximum of two sides of A4 (including photographs) summarising the project
- A detailed budget for the project
- A maximum of two sides of A4 (including photographs) summarising the charity's general activities
- The most recent accounts and annual report

'Do not send CDs, DVDs, or any other additional information. If we require further details, we will contact the charity directly. Charities are therefore advised to send in applications with sufficient time before the June or November deadlines to allow for such enquiries.'

With the increased level of applications, the trust has stated that all successful applicants will in future be listed on their website on the 'recent awards' after each trustee meeting. All applicants will still be contacted by letter in due course. Early applications are strongly encouraged.

Information gathered from:

Accounts; Charity Commission record; funder's website.

The Sir Harry Pilkington Trust

General charitable purposes

£208,000 (2011/12)

Beneficial area

UK, in practice Merseyside.

Correspondent: The Trustees, Liverpool Charity And Voluntary Services, 151 Dale Street, Liverpool L2 2AH (tel: 01512 275177)

Trustee: Liverpool Charity and Voluntary Services.

CC Number: 206740

The trust operates in Merseyside and St Helens and has general charitable objects, with a preference for arts and culture, youth work and health and general social welfare.

In 2011/12 the trust had assets of £5 million and an income of £190,000. Grants were made totalling £208,000.

Beneficiaries included: Liverpool Charity and Voluntary Services (£160,000); Fazakerley Community Federation (£2,600); Croxteth and Gilmoss Community Council and Belle Vale Adventure Playground (£2,000 each); Woodchurch Amateur Boxing Club, West Derby Tuition and Choices Lifelong Learning (£1,500 each); and East 14 Film and Theatre Productions, Liverpool Homeless Football Club, Somali Welfare Development Trust and Woodlands Christian Revival Centre (£1,000 each).

Applications

In writing to the correspondent. The trust welcomes an initial phone call to discuss the proposal.

Information gathered from:

Accounts; Charity Commission record.

The Col W. W. Pilkington Will Trusts – The General Charity Fund

Medical, arts, social welfare, international charities, drugs misuse, environment

£37,000 (2011/12)

Beneficial area

Mainly UK, with a preference for Merseyside.

Correspondent: Sarah Nicklin, Administrator, Rathbones, Port of Liverpool Building, Pier Head, Liverpool L3 1NW (tel: 01512 366666)

Trustees: Arnold Pilkington; Jennifer Jones; Neil Pilkington Jones.

CC Number: 234710

The trust gives grants to registered charities only, with a preference for the Merseyside area and the arts.

In 2011/12 the trust had assets of £1.8 million and an income of £63,000. Grants to 37 organisations totalled £37,000, distributed as follows:

Medical	9	£9,000
Welfare	7	£7,200
Environment	6	£6,000
Arts	8	£5,500
International	5	£5,500
Drugs	2	£2,000

Beneficiaries included: Everyman Theatre Liverpool, Anti-Slavery and Prisoners' Education Trust (£1,500 each); Hope UK, Lupus UK, Tourettes Action, Bug Life, Tree Aid and Minority Rights Group International (£1,000 each); and North End Writers and Hope Centre St Helens (£700).

Exclusions

No support for non-registered charities, building projects, animal charities or individuals.

Applications

In writing to the correspondent, outlining clear statement of need and including recent accounts.

Percentage of awards given to new applicants: between 10% and 20%.

Information gathered from:

Accounts; Charity Commission record; further information provided by the funder.

Miss A. M. Pilkington's Charitable Trust

General

Around £130,000 (2012/13)

Beneficial area

UK, with a preference for Scotland.

Correspondent: The Clerk, Carters Chartered Accountants, Pentland House, Saltire Centre, Glenrothes, Fife KY6 2AH

SC Number: SC000282

The trust supports a wide variety of causes in the UK, with few causes excluded (see exclusions). In practice there is a preference for Scotland – probably half the grants are given in Scotland. There is a preference for giving recurring grants, which normally range from £500 to £1,500.

In 2012/13 the trust had an income of £130,000 and an expenditure of £143,000.

Exclusions

Grants are not given to overseas projects or political appeals.

Applications

The trustees state that, regrettably, they are unable to make grants to new applicants since they already have 'more than enough causes to support'.

Information gathered from:

OSCR record.

The DLA Piper Charitable Trust

General

£120,000 (2011/12)

Beneficial area

UK.

Correspondent: G. J. Smallman, Secretary, Wrigleys Solicitors LLP, Fountain Precinct, Balm Green, Sheffield S1 1RZ (email: godfrey.smallman@wrigleys.co.uk)

Trustees: N. G. Knowles; P. Rooney; S. Mahon.

CC Number: 327280

In 2011/12 this trust had an income of £75,000 derived from donations from DLA Piper and made 50 grants totalling £120,000.

The trust seems to be moving towards aligning its giving with the charitable endeavours of DLA Piper staff through matched funding and encouraging applications from staff on behalf of charities.

Beneficiaries included: British Red Cross – Japan Tsunami Appeal (£30,000); Room to Read (£21,000); British Red Cross – Queensland Floods and Marie Curie Big Build (£15,000 each); The Prince's Trust (£5,000); Cancer Research (£3,300 in 5 grants); and Weston Park Hospital Cancer Charity (£1,300).

Exclusions

No grants to individuals.

Applications

In writing to the correspondent, for consideration every three months. Applications from members, partners and employees of DLA Piper for grants in support of charities are encouraged.

Percentage of awards given to new applicants: between 40% and 50%.

Common applicant mistakes

'Asking for unrealistically large grants.'

Information gathered from:

Accounts; Charity Commission record; further information provided by the funder.

The Platinum Trust

£235,000 (2011/12)

Beneficial area

UK.

Correspondent: The Secretary, Sedley Richard Laurence Voulters, 89 New Bond Street, London W1S 1DA (tel: 020 7079 8814)

Trustees: Georgios K. Panayiotou; Stephen Marks; Christopher Organ.

CC Number: 328570

This trust gives grants in the UK for the relief of children with special needs and adults with mental or physical disabilities 'requiring special attention'. The trust was established by Georgios Panayiotou, AKA the singer George Michael.

In 2011/12 the trust had an income of £330,000 and assets stood at £272,000. Grants to 17 organisations totalled £235,000.

Beneficiaries included: United Kingdom Disabled People's Council (£32,500); Centre for Studies on Inclusive Education and Disability, Pregnancy and Parenthood International (£30,000 each); Parents for Inclusion (£27,000); Alliance for Inclusive Education and Independent Panel for Special Education Advice (£20,000 each); Crescent Support Group and Vassal Centre Trust (£15,000 each); Disabled Parents Network (£10,000); Worldwide Volunteering (£5,000); and Earthworks and The Cambridge Foundation (£2,500).

Exclusions

No grants for services run by statutory or public bodies, or from mental-health organisations. No grants for: medical research/treatment or equipment; mobility aids/wheelchairs; community transport/disabled transport schemes; holidays/exchanges/holiday playschemes; special-needs playgroups; toy and leisure libraries; special Olympic and Paralympics groups; sports and recreation clubs for people with disabilities; residential care/sheltered housing/respite care; carers; conservation schemes/city farms/horticultural therapy; sheltered or supported employment/ community business/social firms; purchase/construction/repair of buildings; and conductive education/ other special educational programmes.

Applications

The trust does not accept unsolicited applications; all future grants will be allocated by the trustees to groups they have already made links with.

Information gathered from:

Accounts; Charity Commission record.

G. S. Plaut Charitable Trust Ltd

General charitable purposes

£47,000 (2012/13)

Beneficial area

Predominantly UK.

Correspondent: Dr Richard Speirs, Secretary, 39 Bay Road, Wormit, Newport-on-Tay, Fife DD6 8LW

Trustees: A. D. Wrapson; T. A. Warburg; W. E. Murfett; B. A. Sprinz; R. E. Liebeschuetz; Dr J. D. Hall.

CC Number: 261469

This trust appears to make grants across the whole spectrum of the voluntary sector.

In 2012/13 the trust had assets of £1.5 million, an income of £61,000 and awarded 23 grants totalling £47,000.

Beneficiaries included: Veterans Aid and Anglo Jewish Association and British Eye Research Foundation (£4,500 each); Victoria County History of Essex Appeal (£4,000); British Retinitis Pigmentosa Society (£3,500); Chilterns Multiple Sclerosis Centre and Médecins Sans Frontières (£2,500 each); Southend Toy Library, Magen David Adorn UK, Home Farm Trust and Cancer Research UK (£2,000 each); Action For Kids, Ben-Gurion University Foundation, Council of Christians and Jews, Tall Ships Youth Trust and Sight Savers International (£1,000 each); and Home-Start Dundee (£250).

Exclusions

No grants to individuals or for repeat applications.

Applications

In writing to the correspondent. Applications are reviewed twice a year. Only successful applications are acknowledged.

Percentage of awards given to new applicants: between 10% and 20%.

Common applicant mistakes

'Enclosing excessive documentation or lack of information with appeal. Sending an appeal to trust's registered address rather than preferred correspondence one; using incorrect recipient and/or destination address details, presumably due to 'cut and paste' or automated letter generation methods.'

Information gathered from:

Accounts; Charity Commission record; further information provided by the funder.

The George and Esme Pollitzer Charitable Settlement

Jewish, general

£95,000 (2011/12)

Beneficial area

UK.

Correspondent: Miss L. E. Parrock, Saffery Champness, Beaufort House, 2 Beaufort Road, Clifton, Bristol BS8 2AE (tel: 01179 151617)

Trustee: Jeremy Barnes.

CC Number: 212631

This trust has general charitable purposes with no exclusions. Most funds are given to Jewish causes.

In 2011/12 the settlement's assets stood at £2.9 million. It had an income of £122,000 and made grants to 31organisations totalling £95,000. All grants bar two were for £2,000 each.

Beneficiaries included: Jewish Museum (£10,000); Royal Hospital for Neuro-disability (£5,000); and Big Issue, Coram, I Can, Macmillan Cancer Support, Marie Curie Cancer Care, Médecins Sans Frontières, The National Brain Appeal, Samaritans, SBS Association and Target Ovarian Cancer (£2,000 each).

Applications

In writing to the correspondent.

Information gathered from:

Accounts; Charity Commission record.

The J. S F. Pollitzer Charitable Settlement

General

£19,000 (2011/12)

Beneficial area

UK and overseas.

Correspondent: Mr J. R. Webb, Mary Street House, Mary Street, Taunton, Somerset TA1 3NW (tel: 01823 286096)

Trustees: Mr R. F. C. Pollitzer, Chair; Mrs E. Pettit; Mrs S. C. O'Farrell.

CC Number: 210680

The trust supports a range of UK and local charities.

In 2011/12 the trust had assets of £733,000 and an income of £52,000. There were 19 grants of £1,000 to organisations totalling £19,000, broken down into the following categories:

Health	£5,000
Cultural	£4,000
Disabled	£4,000
Children and youth	£2,000
Conservation and environment	£2,000
Education, science and technology	£1,000
Social and community welfare	£1,000

Beneficiaries included: Happy House; Home Start Richmond; Renewable World; Clean Rivers Trust; Merlin Theatre; Jackdaws Music Education Trust; Manchester Camerata; Orchard Vale Trust; Tourettes Action; Autism Plus; The Hope Centre; Noah's Ark Appeal; Dorset and Somerset Air Ambulance; National Osteoporosis Society; Brain Research UK; Relatives and Residents Association (£1,000 each).

Exclusions

No grants to individuals or students, i.e. those without charitable status.

Applications

In writing to the correspondent. Grants are distributed twice a year, usually around April/May and November/ December.

Information gathered from:

Accounts; Charity Commission record.

Edith and Ferdinand Porjes Charitable Trust

Jewish, general

£72,000 (2011/12)

Beneficial area

UK and overseas.

Correspondent: M. D. Paisner, Trustee, Adelaide House, London Bridge, London EC4R 9HA (tel: 020 7760 1000)

Trustees: M. D. Paisner; A. S. Rosenfelder; H. Stanton.

CC Number: 274012

Although the trust has general charitable purposes, the trust is inclined to support applications from the Jewish community in the UK and overseas. The trustees have set aside a fund, referred to as the 'British Friends of the Art Museums of Israel Endowment fund' with the specific aim of supporting the British Friends of the Art Museums of Israel.

In 2011/12 the trust had assets of £1.5 million, an income of £56,000 and gave six grants totalling £72,000.

The beneficiaries were: The London School of Jewish Studies (£30,000); Jewish Book Council (£17,000); Yesodey Hatorah Grammar School (£10,000); International Institute for Jewish Genealogy (£7,900); Shaare Zedek (£5,000); and British Friends of OHEL Sarah (£2,500).

Applications

In writing to the correspondent.

Information gathered from:

Accounts; Charity Commission record.

The Porter Foundation

Jewish charities, environment, arts, general

£1.5 million (2011/12)

Beneficial area

Israel and the UK.

Correspondent: Paul Williams, Executive Director, Silex Administration S.A., 22 Arlington Street, London SW1A 1RD (tel: 0204991957; email: theporterfoundation@btinternet.com)

Trustees: Albert Castle; Dame Shirley Porter; Steven Porter; Sir Walter Bodmer; John Porter; Linda Streit.

CC Number: 261194

Summary

The foundation supports 'projects in the fields of education, the environment, culture and health and welfare, which encourage excellence, efficiency and innovation and enhance the quality of people's lives'.

During recent years it has cut back on the number of beneficiaries supported and is making fewer, larger grants, mainly to the connected Porter School of Environmental Studies at Tel Aviv University, or the university itself, and to other causes in Israel. This has led to a temporary reduction in UK-based activity. A limited number of community awards continue to be given, although usually to organisations already known to the foundation. These are focused on access to the arts.

In 2012 the foundation set up the Porter Foundation Switzerland with a donation of £40,000 to support projects similar to the Verbier Festival which they have supported for many years.

General

The foundation was set up in 1970 by Sir Leslie Porter and Dame Shirley Porter, a former leader of Westminster City Council.

In 2011/12 the foundation has assets of £39 million and an income of £923,000. Grants were made totalling £1.5 million.

New grant commitments comprised of: Tel Aviv University Trust – Porter School of Environmental Studies (£1.1 million); Friends of Daniel for Rowing Association (£183,000); and Jewish Deaf Association (£12,000).

Other grant beneficiaries included: Porter Foundation Switzerland (£40,000); New Israel Fund and The Israel Opera Trust (£25,000); English National Opera (£15,000); British Friends of the Council for a Beautiful Israel (£13,000); The Royal Parks Foundation (£10,000); British Friends of the Verbier Festival and Academy (£7,000); The Royal National Theatre (£2,500); and Mencap, Sadler Wells Trust Ltd, Kisharon and Whitechapel Gallery (£1,000 each).

Exclusions

The foundation makes grants only to registered charitable organisations or to organisations with charitable objects that are exempt from the requirement for charitable registration.

Grants will not be made to:

- General appeals such as direct mail circulars
- Charities which redistribute funds to other charities
- Third-party organisations raising money on behalf of other charities
- Cover general running costs

No grants are made to individuals.

Applications

An initial letter summarising your application, together with basic costings and background details on your organisation, such as the annual report and accounts, should be sent to the director. Speculative approaches containing expensive publicity material are not encouraged.

If your proposal falls within the foundation's current funding criteria you may be contacted for further information, including perhaps a visit from the foundation staff. There is no need to fill out an application form.

Applications fulfilling the criteria will be considered by the trustees, who meet three times a year, usually in March, July and November. You will hear shortly after the meeting whether your application has been successful. Unfortunately, it is not possible to acknowledge all unsolicited applications (unless a stamped, addressed envelope is enclosed). If you do not hear from the foundation, you can assume that your application has been unsuccessful. Due to limits on funds available, some excellent projects may have to be refused a grant. In such a case the trustees may invite the applicant to re-apply in a future financial year, without giving a commitment to fund.

Information gathered from:

Accounts; Charity Commission record.

The Portrack Charitable Trust

General

£124,000 (2011/12)

Beneficial area

Some preference for Scotland.

Correspondent: George Holmes, Butterfield Bank, 99 Gresham Street, London EC2V 7NG (tel: 020 7776 6700)

Trustees: Charles Jencks; Keith Galloway; John Jencks.

CC Number: 266120

In 2011/12 the trust had assets of £4.7 million, an income of £104,000 and gave grants totalling £124,000. Most grants were for £1,000 or £2,000.

Beneficiaries included: Maggie's Cancer Centres (£45,000 in three grants); Payment to Medical Aid for Palestinians (£6,000 in two grants); Dumfries and Galloway Endowment Fund (£5,000); Victoria and Albert Museum (£3,000); Human Rights Watch Charitable Trust, Who Care Trust, Dumfries and Galloway Mental Health and Musicians Benevolent Fund (£2,000 each); and Lifelites, British Eye Research Foundation, Princess Royal Trust for Carers, Just for Kids Law and St John's Hospice (£1,000 each).

Exclusions

Grants are not given to individuals.

Applications

In writing to the correspondent.

Information gathered from:

Accounts; Charity Commission record.

The J. E. Posnansky Charitable Trust

Jewish charities, health, social welfare and humanitarian

£122,000 (2011/12)

Beneficial area

UK and overseas.

Correspondent: Mr N. S. Posnansky, Trustee, Sobell Rhodes, Monument House, 215 Marsh Road, Pinner, Middlesex, London HA5 5NE (tel: 020 8429 8800; fax: 020 7435 1516)

Trustees: Mrs G. Raffles; A. Posnansky; P. A. Mishcon; Mrs E. J. Feather; N. S. Posnansky.

CC Number: 210416

The trust was created in 1958 for general charitable purposes in the UK and elsewhere and grant giving now concentrates on the areas of Jewish, health, education, social welfare and humanitarian causes. The trust incorporates the A V Posnansky Charitable Trust.

In 2011/12 the trust had assets of £3.6 million, an income of £109,000 and made grants totalling £122,000.

Beneficiaries included: UJIA and Magen David Adom UK (£20,000 each); Wizo. UK (£15,000); Friends of Alyn (£13,000); Jewish Care (£7,500); British Technion Society and World Jewish Relief (£5,000 each); Sight Savers International and Water Aid (£2,500 each); British Limbless Ex-Servicemen, Hazion Yeshaya and Terrance Higgins Trust (£1,000 each); Amnesty International, Jewish Childs Day and The Council for Christians and Jews (£500); and The Sue Ryder Foundation (£250).

Exclusions

No grants to individuals.

Information gathered from:

Accounts; Charity Commission record.

The W. L. Pratt Charitable Trust

General

£40,000 (2011/12)

Beneficial area

UK, particularly York, and overseas.

Correspondent: Christopher Goodway, Trustee, Grays, Duncombe Place, York YO1 7DY (tel: 01904 634771; email: christophergoodway@grayssolicitors.co.uk)

Trustees: John Pratt; Christopher Tetley; Christopher Goodway.

CC Number: 256907

The trust divides its grant-giving between overseas charities, local charities in the York area and UK national charities. UK and overseas grants are restricted to well-known registered charities.

Support is given:

- In the UK: to support religious and social objectives with a priority for York and district, including health and community services
- Overseas: to help the developing world by assisting in food production and relief of famine and disease

In 2011/12 the trust's assets stood at over £1.6 million. It had an income of £49,000 and made 48 grants totalling almost £40,000, broken down into the following categories:

Local charities	20	£18,000
One-off donations	5	£11,000
UK National charities	15	£5,000
Overseas	8	£5,000

Beneficiaries included: York Minister Development Campaign (£5,000); York Diocesan Board of Finance (£3,750); Christian Aid, York Cancer Relief and York Samaritans (£1,000 each); British Humanitarian Aid Ltd, British Red Cross, Guide Dogs for the Blind, Oxfam, RNLI, and St John Ambulance (£500 each); and Action Research, Age UK, Marie Curie Memorial Foundation and Wellbeing/Birthright (£250 each).

Exclusions

No grants to individuals. No grants for buildings or for upkeep and preservation of places of worship.

Applications

In writing to the correspondent. Applications will not be acknowledged unless an sae is supplied. Telephone applications are not accepted.

Percentage of awards given to new applicants: less than 10%.

Information gathered from:
Accounts; Charity Commission record; further information provided by the funder.

Premierquote Ltd

Jewish, general

£412,000 (2011/12)

Beneficial area
Worldwide.

Correspondent: D. Last, Trustee, 18 Green Walk, London NW4 2AJ (tel: 020 7247 8376)

Trustees: D. Last; Mrs L. Last; H. Last; M. Weisenfeld.

CC Number: 801957

The trust was established in 1985 for the benefit of Jewish organisations, the relief of poverty and general purposes. In 2011/12 the trust had assets of £6 million, an income of £846,000 and gave grants totalling £412,000. Grants for over £1,000 each totalled £345,000 and those for under £1,000 each, £67,000.

A full list of beneficiaries for the year was not included with the accounts, however, previous beneficiaries have included: Achisomoch, Belz Yeshiva Trust, Beth Jacob Grammar School for Girls Ltd, British Friends of Shuvu, Friends of Ohel Moshe, Friends of Senet Wiznitz, Friends of the United Institutions of Arad, Kehal Chasidel Bobov, Meadowgold Ltd, Menorah Primary School, North West London Communal Mikvah and Torah Vedaas Primary School.

Applications
In writing to the correspondent.

Information gathered from:
Accounts; Charity Commission record.

Premishlaner Charitable Trust

Jewish

£151,000 (2011/12)

Beneficial area
UK and worldwide.

Correspondent: C. M. Margulies, Trustee, 186 Lordship Road, London N16 5ES (tel: 020 8802 4449)

Trustees: C. Freudenberger; C. M. Margulies.

CC Number: 1046945

This trust was founded in 1995; its principal objects are:

- To advance Orthodox Jewish education
- To advance the religion of the Jewish faith in accordance with the Orthodox practice
- The relief of poverty

In 2011/12 the trust had assets of £388,000, an income of £181,000 and gave grants totalling £151,000.

Beneficiaries included: Chochmas Shlomo Chasidi (£23,000); Chen Vochessed Vrachamim and Beis Rochel (£13,000 each); Emunoh Educational Centre (£10,000); U.T.A. (£9,500); Yeshiva Gedola Sevenoaks (£7,500); J. and R. Charitable Trust (£6,500); and Vaad Horabonim, Binyan Torah Charity and Tevini (£5,000 each).

Other donations under £5,000 each totalled £35,000.

Applications
In writing to the correspondent.

Information gathered from:
Accounts; Charity Commission record.

The Primrose Trust

General, animal welfare

£181,000 (2011/12)

Beneficial area
UK.

Correspondent: Steven Allan, 5 Callaghan Square, Cardiff CF10 5BT (tel: 02920 264394)

Trustees: M. G. Clark; Susan Boyes-Korkis.

CC Number: 800049

The trust was established in 1986 with general charitable purposes. In 2011/12 it had assets of £3.5 million, an income of £137,000 and gave grants totalling £181,000.

The grant recipients were: Animal Health Trust (£85,000); St Mary's School Calne (£30,000); British Hen Welfare Trust (£21,000); Langford Trust and World Veterinary Service (£20,000 each); and Swan Advocacy Network (£5,000).

Exclusions
Grants are given to registered charities only.

Applications
In writing to the correspondent, including a copy of the most recent accounts. The trust does not wish to receive telephone calls.

Information gathered from:
Accounts; Charity Commission record.

Princess Anne's Charities

Children, medical, welfare, general

£124,000 (2011/12)

Beneficial area
UK.

Correspondent: Capt. N. Wright, Farrer and Co. LLP, 66 Lincoln's Inn Fields, London WC2A 3LH

Trustees: Hon. M. T. Bridges; Sir T. J. H. Laurence; B. Hammond.

CC Number: 277814

This trust has general charitable purposes, with a preference for registered charities in which the Princess Royal has a particular interest.

In 2011/12 the trust had assets of £5 million, an income of £150,000 and made 33 grants totalling £124,000.

Social welfare	12	£43,000
Medical	9	£26,000
Children and youth	3	£25,000
Armed forces	6	£24,000
Environment and wildlife	3	£6,500

Previous beneficiaries have included: Butler Trust, the Canal Museum Trust Cranfield Trust, Dogs Trust, Dorothy House Foundation, Durrell Wildlife Conservation Trust, the Evelina Children's Hospital Appeal, Farms for City Children, Farrer and Co. Charitable Trust, Fire Services National Benevolent Fund, the Home Farm Trust, Intensive Care Society, and International League for the Protection of Horses.

Exclusions
No grants to individuals.

Applications
The Trustees receive numerous grant application letters throughout the year which are considered by the Trustees at their meeting. They discuss the merits of the applications against the criteria for support referred to above, having taken account of the funds available to them.

Information gathered from:
Accounts; Charity Commission record.

Prison Service Charity Fund

General, medical

£130,000 (2011/12)

Beneficial area

UK.

Correspondent: Neville Joseph, The Lodge, 8 Derby Road, Garstang, Preston PR3 1EU (tel: 01995 604997; email: bob@pscf.co.uk; website: www.prisonservicecharityfund.co.uk)

Trustees: A. N. Joseph, Chair; P. Ashes; J. Goldsworthy; P. McFall; C. F. Smith; K. Wingfield; J. White; Bob Howard.

CC Number: 801678

The fund gives grants for general charitable purposes, particularly medical. The fund's website states:

> The fund will cover those appeals which are to assist those in need of medical treatment/equipment.
>
> If fund raising involves raising monies for a Trust Hospital, the PSCF will only give a donation to specifically nominated units, or direct to suppliers of the required equipment as opposed to monies being donated directly into the Trust's account.
>
> It is the fund's policy not to donate more than has been raised by the applicant, and then only to a ceiling of £5,000.

In 2012 the fund had assets of £699,000, an income of £166,000 and gave grants to 66 organisations totalling £130,000, the majority of which were for £1,000 or less.

Grant beneficiaries included: Leeds Prison Charity Fund (£2,000); The Twins Appeal and the David Cross Appeal (£1,600 each); Five Charity Appeal, The Alfie Gough Trust and Steps to America Appeal (£1,000 each); Help for Heroes (£750); Chadsgrove Special School (£670); Claire House Children's Hospice and Prostrate Cancer Charity (£600 each); Neurofibromatosis Association; Woodlands Hospice (£500); MS Society (£300); and Lymphoma and Leukaemia Association (£220).

Applications

The trust does not accept outside applications – the applicant must be a member of prison service staff.

Information gathered from:

Accounts; Charity Commission record; funder's website.

The Puebla Charitable Trust

Community development work, relief of poverty

£110.000 (2011/12)

Beneficial area

Worldwide.

Correspondent: The Clerk, Ensors, Cardinal House, 46 St Nicholas Street, Ipswich IP1 1TT (tel: 01473 220022)

Trustees: J. Phipps; M. A. Strutt.

CC Number: 290055

The trust has stated that: 'At present, the council limits its support to charities which assist the poorest sections of the population and community development work – either of these may be in urban or rural areas, both in the UK and overseas.'

Grants are normally in the region of £5,000 to £20,000, with support given over a number of years where possible. Most of the trust's income is therefore already committed, and the trust rarely supports new organisations.

In 2011/12 the trust had assets of £2.4 million, an income of £98,000 and gave six grants totalling £110,000.

The beneficiaries were: Shelter, South West London Law Centres, Child Poverty Action Group and Family Action (£20,000 each); and Action on Disability and Development and Mines Advisory Group (£15,000 each).

Exclusions

No grants for capital projects, religious institutions, research or institutions for people who are disabled. Individuals are not supported and no scholarships are given.

Applications

In writing to the correspondent. The trustees meet in July. The trust is unable to acknowledge applications.

Information gathered from:

Accounts; Charity Commission record.

The Richard and Christine Purchas Charitable Trust

Medical research, medical education and patient care

About £20,000 (2011/12)

Beneficial area

UK.

Correspondent: Daniel Auerbach, Trustee, 46 Hyde Park Gardens Mews, London W2 2NX (tel: 020 7580 2448)

Trustees: Daniel Auerbach; Pauline Auerbach; Dr Douglas Rossdale; Robert Auerbach.

CC Number: 1083126

Applications

In writing to the correspondent.

Information gathered from:

Accounts; Charity Commission record.

The Pyne Charitable Trust

Christian, health

£110,000 (2011/12)

Beneficial area

UK and overseas, particularly Malawi, Moldova, Slovakia and Ukraine.

Correspondent: Pauline Brennan, Secretary, 26 Tredegar Square, London E3 5AG (tel: 020 8980 4853)

Trustees: Michael Brennan; Pauline Brennan; Mike Mitchell.

CC Number: 1105357

In 2012 the trust had assets of £24,000 and an income of £107,000, mostly from donations. Grants totalled £110,000, almost all of which was given in one £110,000 grant to the Good Shepherd Mission. The other beneficiaries were Teen Challenge London £200); and Release International (£15).

A further £6,500 was given in grants to individuals.

Applications

Ongoing support appears to be given to projects selected by the trustees.

Information gathered from:

Accounts; Charity Commission record.

The Queen Anne's Gate Foundation

Educational, medical and rehabilitative charities and those that work with underprivileged areas of society

£590,000 (2011/12)

Beneficial area

UK and Asia.

Correspondent: The Trustees, WillcoxLewis LLP, The Old Coach House, Bergh Apton, Norwich, Norfolk NR15 1DD (tel: 01508 480100)

Trustees: N. T. Allan; J. M. E. Boyer; Roger Wortley.

CC Number: 1108903

The foundation seeks to support projects and charities within the following broad criteria. It seeks to make a contribution that is meaningful in the context of the project/charity with which it is working. It tries to focus in particular on projects which might be said to make potentially unproductive lives productive. This tends to mean a bias towards educational, medical and rehabilitative charities and those that work with underprivileged areas of society. There is an attempt to focus a significant proportion of donations on Asia and the UK.

In 2011/12 the foundation had assets of £2.6 million and an income of £70,000. Grants totalled £590,000, broken down as follows:

Education	£322,000
Children's welfare	£101,000
General welfare	£81,000
Health and allied services	£55,000
Environment	£30,000

Beneficiaries included: Hong Kong Polytechnic University (£63,000); Friends of the Citizens Foundation (£50,000); Christian Friends of Korea (£31,000); Merlin and Families for Children (£30,000 each); CINI UK and The Marylebone Project (£25,000 each); English National Opera (£21,000); Indochina Starfish Foundation (£20,000); Support Street Children (£19,000); HH MH Singhji Charitable Foundation (£16,000); Hackney Music Development Trust and City of Exeter YMCA Community Projects (£10,000 each); and Mid-Wales Music Fund.

Applications

In writing to the correspondent. Trustees meet twice a year.

Information gathered from:

Accounts; Charity Commission record.

Quercus Trust

Arts, general

£1.3 million (2011/12)

Beneficial area

UK.

Correspondent: Helen Price, Trust Administrator, Gloucester House, 72 London Road, St Albans, Hertfordshire AL1 1NS (tel: 01727 869141)

Trustees: Lady Angela Bernstein; Kate E. Bernstein.

CC Number: 1039205

In February 1999 the trustees declared by deed that distributions would in future be directed principally (but not exclusively) to the arts and any other objects and purposes which seek to further public knowledge, understanding and appreciation of any matters of artistic, aesthetic, scientific or historical interest.

In 2011/12 the trust had assets of £3.9 million, an income of £145,000. Grants totalled £1.4 million including £52,000 to three individuals.

Beneficiaries included: Wayne McGregor Foundation (£1 million); Royal National Theatre (£100,000); Sadler's Wells Trust (£66,000); Royal Opera House Covent Garden Ltd (£50,000); Harley Street Osteopaths Ltd (£32,000); Dance UK (£26,000); Hofesh Shechter Company (£10,000); Rambert Trust Ltd (£7,500); Hunger Project Trust (£5,000); Starlight Children's Foundation (£2,000); and Tate Foundation (£850).

Exclusions

No grants to individuals.

Applications

The trust states in its grantmaking policy that: 'Proposals for distributions are generated internally.' No external applications for funding will be considered. The trust has informed us that they do not now consider, or even acknowledge unsolicited applications. Their available funds are fully absorbed by projects known to them.

Information gathered from:

Accounts; Charity Commission record.

R. J. M. Charitable Trust

Jewish

£120,000 (2011/12)

Beneficial area

UK and worldwide.

Correspondent: Joshua Rowe, Trustee, 84 Upper Park Road, Salford M7 4JA (tel: 01617 208787; email: joshua@broomwell.com)

Trustees: Joshua Rowe; Michelle Rowe.

CC Number: 288336

In 2011/12 the trust had assets of £117,000 and an income of £121,000, mostly from donations. Grants totalled £120,000.

The largest grant went to HR Crumpsall and Broughton (£101,000).

Other beneficiaries included: One to One (£10,000); Yeshun (£8,000); North Salford Synagogue (£7,400); South Manchester Synagogue (£5,000); Manchester Jewish Philanthropic (£3,000); Manchester Kellel (£2,000); Navas Chesed, OHR Elcharan and Sunderland Talmund (£1,000); British Friends Masat Moshe (£560); British Friends Israel War (£250); and Crisis (£20).

Applications

In writing to the correspondent.

Information gathered from:

Accounts; Charity Commission record.

R. S. Charitable Trust

Jewish, welfare

£267,000 (2011/12)

Beneficial area

UK.

Correspondent: Max Freudenberger, Trustee, 138 Stamford Hill, London N16 6QT

Trustees: Harvey Freudenberger; Michelle Freudenberger; Stuart Freudenberger; Max Freudenberger.

CC Number: 1053660

Established in 1996, this trust states that it supports Jewish organisations and other bodies working towards the relief of poverty.

In 2011/12 the trust had assets of £2.1 million and an income of £581,000. Grants totalled £267,000. A full list of beneficiaries was not included in the annual reports.

Previous beneficiaries have included British Friends of Tshernobil, Forty Ltd, NRST, Society of Friends of the Torah, Talmud Hochschule, Viznitz, Yeshiva Horomo and Yeshivas Luzern.

Applications

In writing to the correspondent.

Information gathered from:

Accounts; Charity Commission record.

The R. V. W. Trust

Music education and appreciation

£243,000 (2012)

Beneficial area

UK.

Correspondent: Ms Helen Faulkner, Administrator, 7–11 Britannia Street, London WC1X 9JS (tel: 020 7239 9139; email: helen@rvwtrust.org.uk; website: www.rvwtrust.org.uk)

Trustees: Hugh Cobbe; Michael Kennedy; Lord Armstrong; Andrew Hunter Johnston; Sir John Manduell; Jeremy Dale Roberts; Anthony Burton; Prof. Nicola Lefanu; Musicians Benevolent Fund.

CC Number: 1066977

The trust's current grantmaking policies are as follows:

1 To give assistance to British composers who have not yet

achieved a national or international reputation
2 To give assistance towards the performance and recording of music by neglected or currently unfashionable 20th century British composers, including performances by societies and at festivals which include works by such composers in their programmes
3 To assist UK organisations that promote public knowledge and appreciation of 20th and 21st century British music
4 To assist education projects in the field of music if the primary purpose is the performance of new or recent British music
5 To support postgraduate students of composition taking first masters degrees at British universities and conservatoires

In 2012 the trust had assets of £1.6 million and an income of £363,000. Grants totalled £265,000, including £20,000 to students studying masters in composition. Grants were broken down as follows:

Public performance	£152,000	57
Music festivals	£52,800	15
Public education	£44,000	24
Education grants	£27,000	8

Grant beneficiaries included: Vaughan Williams Memorial Library/English Folk Dance and Song Society (£25,000); Huddersfield Contemporary Music Festival (£12,000); Cheltenham Music Festival (£6,000); Northern Ireland Opera and National Youth Orchestra Composers' Course (£5,000); Royal Philharmonic Society Composition Prize (£4,500); British Youth Opera (£3,000); Little Missenden Festival (£2,500); and Stone Records and Onyx Brass (£2,000 each).

Exclusions

No grants for concerts, concert series or concert tours which do not include music by 20th and 21st century British composers; concerts for which income from box office receipts, together with support from other organisations, is forecast to amount to less than half of the estimated expenditure; commissions purely for youth or children's ensembles; grants for musicals, rock or pop music, ethnic music, jazz or dance music or multi-media and theatrical events in which music is not the primary art-form; 'workshops' with no planned public performance; grants to organisations directly administered by local or other public authorities; grants to managing agents and commercial promoters; vocal or instrumental tuition; the making, purchase or repair of musical instruments, computer or multi-media equipment; the construction or restoration of buildings. Grants cannot be made for the furtherance or performance of the founder's own work (Ralph Vaughan Williams).

Applications

In writing to the correspondent including the information detailed in the application guidelines which are available on the trust's website. For applicants for postgraduate funding there is a form available on the website. The trust will only fund up to 50% of the cost of any event. Trustees meet three times a year, in February, June and October to consider applications which should be received by 2 January, 1 May or 1 September respectively. Applications can be made either by email or post but a signed copy of the covering letter must be posted.

Percentage of awards given to new applicants: between 30% and 40%.

Common applicant mistakes

'Don't read the guidelines so apply for projects falling outside current policy.'

Information gathered from:

Accounts; Charity Commission record; further information provided by the funder; funder's website.

The Monica Rabagliati Charitable Trust

Children, humanitarian, medical, general

£60,000 (2011/12)

Beneficial area

UK.

Correspondent: Rachel Iles, S. G. Hambros Bank Ltd, Norfolk House, 31 St James's Square, London SW1Y 4JR (tel: 020 7597 3065; website: www.rabagliati.org.uk)

Trustees: S. G. Hambros Trust Company Ltd; R. L. McLean.

CC Number: 1086368

This trust was registered with the Charity Commission in April 2001. It makes grants in support of 'organisations that focus on the alleviation of child suffering and deprivation'. The trust also supports humanitarian and medical causes. 'The trustees have decided to prioritise small/medium sized organisations where possible.'

In 2011/12 the trust had assets of £1.8 million, an income of £37,000 and gave grants for £5,000 or less totalling £60,000.

Beneficiaries included: Nilyana Projects, The Special Yoga Centre and Travelling Light Theatre Company (£5,000 each); SignHealth (£4,700); Children's Safety Education Foundation (£3,800); Outward Bound Trust (£3,000); Getaway Girls (£2,500); Keynsham and District Mencap Society (£2,000); and Foundation UK and Youth at Risk (£1,000 each).

Applications

On a form available to download from the website. Grants are given twice yearly.

Information gathered from:

Accounts; Charity Commission record; funder's website.

The Racing Foundation

Horseracing industry, welfare and education, equine research

£357,000 (2013)

Beneficial area

UK.

Correspondent: Chris Mills, Executive Officer, 75 High Holborn, London WC1V 6LS (tel: 0300 321 1873; email: chris.mills@racingfoundation.co.uk; website: www.racingfoundation.co.uk)

Trustees: Michael Harris; Roger Weatherby; Kirsten Rausing; Sir Ian Good.

CC Number: 1145297

Background

The foundation was established in 2012 with funding derived from the UK government's sale of the Horserace Totalisator Board (Tote). It is expected to receive the proceeds from this sale over the seven year period from 2012–19, with the money being invested to provide a sustainable future income stream. The foundation has already received a £19 million endowment, to which it hopes to add a further £16 million by 2015, with the possibility of a further £50 million by 2021. Founding members include the British Horseracing Authority, The Horsemen's Group and the Racecourse Association. The foundation aims to use these funds to achieve a lasting legacy for the sport of horseracing. The foundation officially launched in October 2012.

The foundation website outlines their mission as follows:

> The foundation makes grants to charities associated with the UK horseracing and thoroughbred breeding industry, supporting work in social welfare, training and education, racehorse welfare, equine science research, heritage and culture.

Only one application may be submitted in any one year. The trust has forecast that it plans to distribute the following:

- 2014: £700,000
- 2015: £1 million

The first round of grants made in 2013 amounted to £228,000 with £129,000 scheduled for payment later in the year and £99,000 committed for future payment. Beneficiaries included: HEROS (Homing Ex-Racehorses Organisation Scheme); Moorcroft Racehorse Welfare Centre, National Horseracing Museum and New Astley Club – Newmarket.

Grants

The foundation is keen to attract applications that support the work of charities in the following areas (taken from the foundation's website):

Social Welfare

- The improvement in the health or the rehabilitation from injury of current or former members of the horseracing industry
- The prevention or relief of poverty among current or former members of the horseracing industry and their dependents
- Community development work in areas particularly connected with the horseracing industry (provided it is clear how such grant will benefit current or former members of the horseracing industry)

Education, Training & Participation

- The provision of education, training or retraining opportunities to disadvantaged individuals, currently or formerly employed within the horseracing industry
- The provision of work opportunities in the horseracing industry to unemployed people
- Enabling people, and especially young people, to participate in the sport of horseracing at an amateur level, including the training of amateur jockeys

Equine Science Research

- ?applied research in the field of equine science* insofar as the research has demonstrable practical benefits to thoroughbred horseracing (but only where the useful results of any such research will be published and publicised with open access)

* The use of the phrase equine science is intended to allow flexibility to applicants across a broad range of equine related disciplines, including veterinary, biological science, non-biological science and technical interests, with the focus on the application of relevant equine related scientific and technical knowledge to benefit thoroughbred horseracing.

Thoroughbred Horse Welfare

- The improvement of the welfare of current or former thoroughbred racehorses

Heritage and Culture

- The preservation or enhancement of the understanding of the history of the sport of horseracing, and its associated cultural impacts

What can be funded?

The foundation welcomes applications for project costs, core costs or capital projects, which may include funding for staff salaries and overheads. The foundation is happy to receive applications for multi-year grants, usually up to three years (although longer periods may be considered in exceptional circumstances). The foundation will also consider applications that are particularly innovative or risky if it can be shown that the work has the potential to achieve a substantial impact.

Who can be funded?

The foundation expects to make the majority of its grants to charities with objects that are directly associated with the horseracing and thoroughbred breeding industry. However, it may, on occasions, fund organisations that do not work exclusively within the horseracing and thoroughbred breeding industry when the work is of exceptional quality and can be shown to directly impact industry participants.

The foundation is only able to fund charities. This is defined as an institution established for exclusively charitable purposes. As well as charities registered with the Charity Commission, the Office of the Scottish Charity Regulator or the Charity Commission for Northern Ireland, this may include unregistered charities with an annual income of less than £5,000 and charities regulated by another body including higher education corporations, registered Industrial and Provident Societies and registered Friendly Societies.

The foundation has advised that the key criteria which they are looking for in an application include:

- Makes a difference
- Has a clearly identified need
- Addresses a significant gap in provision
- Monitoring and evaluates the impact of the work
- Working in a coordinated manner
- Provides value for money
- Proportion of the money from another source

The foundation has uploaded videos from their launch event detailing their priorities, the nature of their work as well providing guidance on the application process. These are viewable on its website.

Exclusions

Only one application, whether successful or not, may be submitted in any one year.

No grants can be given for the following:

- Work which does not deliver benefits associated with the UK horseracing and thoroughbreeding industry
- The promotion of religion
- Work that addresses gambling addiction (unless specifically focused on participants within the horseracing and thoroughbred breeding industry
- Retrospective funding
- Any work which is not legally charitable

The foundation will also not be able to provide match funding for projects funded by the British horseracing grants scheme. No general appeals or mailshots will be considered. The trustees will also not recognise any personal approaches in support of an application.

Applications

Equine Science grants:

Grants are managed and assessed in association with the Horserace Betting Levy Board. To make an application you must apply through the HBLB website (egs.hblb.org.uk) by registering with their equine grants system. To ensure your grant is considered by the Racing Foundation you must mark the relevant box on the application summary. Applications will be scrutinised by a number of external peer reviewers and HBLB's Veterinary Advisory Committee. The Racing Foundation trustees make the final decision.

The scheme tends to open in spring and close in summer with awards made in the winter. Exact closing dates are posted on the website.

All other grants:

First stage

In the first instance, charities must submit an online application. This will require charities to provide basic details about their organisation, upload a copy of the charity's most recent annual accounts and upload a short proposal.

The short proposal should be prepared as a Word document or PDF, and should address the following in no more than 600 words: what you would like the Racing Foundation to fund; how you know that there is a need for this work; what difference the work will make and who will benefit from it.

If you are successful in your first stage application, you will be invited to submit a second stage application form.

Second stage

At the second stage, charities will be asked to complete a more detailed application form.

Small charities submitting grant applications for less than £5,000 will be asked to complete a simple version of the second stage application form and will be offered assistance to do so.

During the application process, the Racing Foundation may ask to speak to you on the phone, or visit your charity, to obtain more information about your grant application. We will contact you if this is the case.

Applications are considered twice a year with a spring and autumn funding round. In the past the rounds have closed for first stage applications in December and June in, however, applicants are encourage to check the foundation's website for exact dates.

Information gathered from:

Accounts; Charity Commission record; funder's website.

The Radcliffe Trust

Music, crafts, conservation

£317,000 (2011/12)

Beneficial area

UK.

Correspondent: Belinda Hunt, Correspondent, 6 Trull Farm Buildings, Tetbury, Gloucestershire GL8 8SQ (tel: 01285 841900; email: radcliffe@thetrustpartnership.com; website: www.theradcliffetrust.org)

Trustees: Felix Warnock, Chair; Sir Henry Aubrey-Fletcher; Lord Balfour of Burleigh; Christopher Butcher; Mary Ann Sieghart; Timothy Wilson.

CC Number: 209212

The Radcliffe Trust was established in 1714 as a charitable trust under the will of Dr John Radcliffe, the most eminent physician of his day. The will provided for a permanent endowment, the income from which is used exclusively for charitable purposes.

By his will, Dr Radcliffe directed his Trustees to spend £40,000 on building a library, and today the Radcliffe Camera is one of Oxford's architectural glories. The trustees subsequently built two other important Oxford landmarks, the Radcliffe Observatory and the Radcliffe Infirmary, precursor of the modern John Radcliffe Hospital. In 1970 the agricultural holdings which Dr Radcliffe had bought in 1713 were acquired to become the new town of Milton Keynes, leaving the trustees with a substantial endowment and increased income.

Today the trust has a policy of making grants principally in two sectors: Music and Heritage and Crafts.

> *Music*
>
> The Radcliffe Trust supports classical music performance and training especially chamber music, composition and music education. Particular interests within music education are music for children and adults with special needs, youth orchestras and projects at secondary and higher levels, including academic research. The Trustees respond to applications and also initiate their own projects.
>
> *Craft*
>
> The Radcliffe Trust supports the development of the skills, knowledge and experience that underpin the UK's traditional cultural heritage and crafts sectors. This includes support for craft and conservation training, for practical projects and for strategic projects which demonstrate clear benefits to individuals and to the sector. However, the Trust remains committed to flexible, open and inclusive grant-giving and will consider other projects, should they fall broadly within its remit. The Radcliffe Trust wishes to promote standards of excellence through all its support.
>
> Applications are considered under two headings:
>
> - Heritage
> - Crafts.

In 2011/12 the trust had assets of £15 million, and an income of £408,000. Grants were made totalling £317,000, broken down as follows:

Music	48	£160,000
Heritage and Crafts	35	£140,000
Tercentenary	1	£15,000
Miscellaneous	2	£2,000

These figures do not include grants returned during the year.

Beneficiaries included: Church Buildings Council (£20,000); The Allegri String Quartet (£16,000); University of Buckingham Fund (£15,000); Guideposts Trust and Nordoff Robbins (£5,000 each); Abingdon Museum and Buxton Arts Festival (£4,000 each); Clod Ensemble and Quilters Guild (£2,000 each); Endellion Quartet (£1,000); and Orpheus Foundation (£600).

Exclusions

No grants to individual applicants. No retrospective grants are made, nor for deficit funding, core costs, general appeals or endowment funds. No new building appeals.

Applications

The trustees meet twice yearly to oversee the charity's activities and to make decisions on grants. The trust works with specialist advisers in each of its main sectors of activity: Sally Carter, Music Adviser and Carole Milner, Heritage and Crafts Adviser. There is also a Music Panel and a Heritage and Crafts Committee which each meet twice a year to consider applications. The day-to-day running of the trust's financial and administrative affairs and processing of grant applications is undertaken by the Trust Partnership.

How to Apply

Note that it is advisable to submit an application well in advance of the deadline.

- **Music Deadline:** 31 January for the June Trustee meeting; 31 August for the December Trustee meeting
- **Heritage and Crafts Deadline:** 28 February for the June Trustee meeting; 31 August for the December Trustee meeting

All applications must include:

- A cover letter, which should include official address, telephone number, email address and charity registration number. The letter should be headed with the project title and the applicant should make clear his/her position in the charity. Note that this letter should NOT include information on the project itself as this should be within the grant request
- No more than three pages outlining the proposal and the specific request to the Trust. This should be structured as follows:
  - The project title
  - A summary of the request in no more than 40 words
  - The timing of the project
  - The project background and description
  - A budget including a financial breakdown and total cost of the project as well as other income secured or requested and from what sources
  - The amount requested either as a one-off or recurrent grant
  - An indication of past grants from the Radcliffe Trust (year, amount and purpose)
- Other relevant supporting information, although applicants should be aware that this may not be circulated to Trustees

The cover letter and grant request should be emailed to the Administrator as Word or Excel documents and a hard copy also sent by post.

For full details of the trust's guidelines visit its website.

Information gathered from:

Accounts; Charity Commission record; funder's website.

The Bishop Radford Trust

Church of England

£495,000 (2011/12)

Beneficial area

UK.

Correspondent: Mr D. Marks, Correspondent, Devonshire House, 1 Devonshire Street, London W1W 5DR (tel: 020 7304 2000; email: thebishopradfordtrust@ntlworld.com)

Trustees: Janian Green; Suzannah O'Brien; Ruth Dare.

CC Number: 1113562

The trust was set up in 2006 to help 'promote the work of the Christian church in a manner consistent with the doctrines and principles of the Church of England', in particular:

- Church related projects promoting charitable purposes
- The education of priests, future priests and church workers
- Other support for the Church ministry

During 2011/12 the trust had assets of £6.9 million, an income of £2 million and gave grants totalling £495,000

Beneficiaries included: Anglican Investment Agency Trust (£125,000); Bible Society (£50,000); International Needs (£42,000); Bible Reading Fellowship (£41,000); Exeter College, Oxford (£27,000); Bristol Diocese (£25,000); Viva Network (£22,000); Wakefield Diocese (£20,000); Cuddesdon Ripon College (£15,000); Arthur Rank Centre (£13,000); Lambeth Partnership (£10,000); London Diocesan Board for Schools (£6,300); St Peter's Hereford (£1,000); and Queen Alexandra Hospital Home (£500).

Applications

In writing to the correspondent.

Information gathered from:

Accounts; Charity Commission record.

The Rainford Trust

Social welfare, general

£100,000 (2011/12)

Beneficial area

Worldwide, with a preference for areas in which Pilkington plc have works and offices, especially St Helens and Merseyside.

Correspondent: Mr William Simm, Executive Officer, c/o Pilkington plc, Prescot Road, St Helens, Merseyside WA10 3TT (tel: 01744 20574; email: rainfordtrust@btconnect.com)

Trustees: Dr F. Graham; Mrs A. J. Moseley; H. Pilkington; Lady Pilkington; D. C. Pilkington; S. D. Pilkington; Mrs L. F. Walker; Dr Clarissa Pilkington; John Pilkington.

CC Number: 266157

The trust's accounts stated that its objectives are to:

> Apply money for charitable purposes and to charitable institutions within the St Helens MBC area, and other places in the UK or overseas where Pilkington has employees. This does not prejudice the trustees' discretion to help charities that operate outside those areas.

Further to this the trust's charitable purposes are to support:

> - 'the relief of poverty, the aged, the sick, helpless and disabled, and the unemployed
> - The advancement of education including the arts, and other purposes with wide benefit for the community such as environmental and conservation projects'

In 2011/12 the trust had assets of £7.2 million, an income of £193,000 and gave grants totalling £100,000.

The trust offers the following explanation of its grantmaking in the 2011/12 annual report:

> In 2011 to 2012, charitable organisations within the St Helens MBC area received 49% of the total value of grants, in the categories of welfare, education and the humanities. Grants to charities for national and regional benefit in the UK amounted to almost 35% of the total, in the categories of medical, welfare, and education. 16% of grant value went to UK charities for overseas benefit, for medical, welfare, education and environmental causes.

Grants were broken down as follows:

Welfare	52,000
Education	21,000
Humanities	12,000
Medical	13,000
Environmental	500

Beneficiaries included: Clonter Opera (£13,000); The Citadel Arts Centre (£10,000); The Foundation for the Prevention of Blindness and Practical Action (£2,000 each); West Coast Crash Wheelchair Rugby (£1,500); Sue Ryder, Birchley Hall, National Benevolent Fund for the Aged, Health Poverty Action, Tibet Relief Fund and Rainford Carers Support Group (£1,000 each); Park Farm ACYP Centre (£850); Riders for Health (£800); and Galapogos Conservation Trust (£500).

Exclusions

Funding for the arts is restricted to St Helens only. Applications from individuals for grants for educational purposes will be considered only from applicants who are normally resident in St Helens.

Applications

On a form available from the correspondent. Applications should be accompanied by a copy of the latest accounts and cost data on projects for which funding is sought. Applicants may apply at any time. Trustees normally meet in November, March and July. A sub-appeals committee meets about ten times a year and they can either refuse, grant or pass on an application to the Trustees.

Percentage of awards given to new applicants: between 20% and 30%.

Common applicant mistakes

'Overloading of irrelevant information. Failure to send annual report and accounts without being requested. Sending reams of information, minus accounts when inquiring about eligibility. Mistaking a projected budget for actual accounts.'

Information gathered from:

Accounts; Charity Commission record; further information provided by the funder.

The Peggy Ramsay Foundation

Writers and writing for the stage

£22,000 to organisations (2012)

Beneficial area

British Isles.

Correspondent: Mr Laurence Harbottle, Trustee, Harbottle and Lewis Solicitors, Hanover House, 14 Hanover Square, London W1S 1HP (tel: 020 7667 5000; fax: 020 7667 5100; email: laurence.harbottle@harbottle.com; website: www.peggyramsayfoundation.org)

Trustees: G. Laurence Harbottle; Simon P. H. Callow; Michael Codron; Sir David Hare; John Tydeman; Harriet Walter; Tamara C. Harvey; Neil Adleman; Rupert J. Rhymes; Holly Kendrick.

CC Number: 1015427

This trust was established in 1992, in accordance with the will of the late Peggy Ramsay.

> Peggy Ramsay was one of the best-known play agents in the United Kingdom during the second half of the twentieth century. When she died in 1991 her estate was left for charitable purposes to help writers and writing for the stage.

The objects of the trust are:

- The advancement of education by the encouragement of the art of writing
- The relief of poverty among those practising the arts, together with their dependents and relatives, with special reference to writers
- Any charitable purpose which may, in the opinion of the trustees, achieve, assist in, or contribute to, the achievement of these objectives

Grants are made to:

- Writers who have some writing experience who need time to write and cannot otherwise afford to do so
- Companies which might not otherwise be able to find, develop or use new work
- Projects which may facilitate new writing for the stage

The main priority of the trust is to support semi-professional writers who fulfil the trust's application criteria. The trust also supports organisations and projects, which they review annually. Grants are normally for up to £5,000.

In 2012 the trust had assets of £5.2 million, an income of £255,000 and gave grants totalling £123,000. This included £101,000 given in 53 grants to individuals.

Organisational beneficiaries included: Pearson Management Services (£14,000); Alfred Fagon Prize Award (£6,500); and Society of Authors (£1,500).

Exclusions

No grants are made for productions or writing not for the theatre. Adaptations and plays intended primarily for younger audiences are accepted only in special circumstances which imply wider originality. Commissioning costs are often considered as part of production costs. Course fees are not considered. Aspiring writers without some production record are not usually considered.

Applications

Applications should be made in writing, including:

- A short letter explaining the need, the amount hoped for and the way in which any grant would be spent
- A full CV not limited to writing
- Separate sheet answers to these questions:
  1. when and where was the first professional production of a play of yours
  2. who produced the play which qualifies you for a grant
  3. when and where was your qualifying play produced, what was its run and approximate playing time and has it been revived
  4. for that production were the director and actors all professionals engaged with Equity contracts
  5. did the audience pay to attend

Trustees meet quarterly, but applications are considered between meetings. Allow six to eight weeks for a definitive answer. Urgent appeals can be considered at other times. All appeals are usually acknowledged.

Common applicant mistakes

'Failure to answer [our] website questions.'

Information gathered from:

Accounts; Charity Commission record; further information provided by the funder; funder's website.

The Joseph and Lena Randall Charitable Trust

General

£79,000 (2012/13)

Beneficial area

Worldwide.

Correspondent: Mr David Anthony Randall, Correspondent, Europa Residence, Place des Moulins, Monte-Carlo MC98 000 (tel: 0037793500382; email: rofrano.jlrct@hotmail.fr)

Trustee: Rofrano Trustee Services Ltd.

CC Number: 255035

It is the policy of this trust to provide regular support to a selection of charities providing medical, educational and cultural facilities.

In 2012/13 the trust had assets of £2.2 million, an income of £122,000 and gave grants totalling £79,000. A list of beneficiaries was not included in the accounts.

Previous beneficiaries have included: Cancer Research UK, Community Security Trust, Diabetes UK, Downe House 21st Century Appeal, Holocaust Educational Trust, Jewish Care, Jewish Deaf Association, LPO, LSE Foundation, Motor Neurone Disease Association, ROH Foundation and Transplant Trust.

Exclusions

No grants to individuals.

Applications

The trust stated in its 2012/13 annual report:

> The trustee received many appeals during the year, and a number of new charities have received the benefit of our philanthropy for the first time. All appeals are vetted but we desist from replying in the case of circular letters, or to letters inadequately franked, nor to appeals from individuals or from organisations lacking accreditation. We have always favoured appeals from established charities with proven track records that are successful and efficient in delivering services without being top heavy in terms of management and salaries.

Percentage of awards given to new applicants: between 20% and 30%.

Common applicant mistakes

'Inadequate core details of activities; too much spent on fundraising or salaries; inadequate postage or not personally signed.'

Information gathered from:

Accounts; Charity Commission record; further information provided by the funder.

Ranworth Trust

General

£190,000 (2011/12)

Beneficial area

UK and developing countries, with a preference for East Norfolk.

Correspondent: Jacquetta Cator, Trustee, The Old House, Ranworth, Norwich NR13 6HS (website: www.ranworthtrust.org.uk)

Trustees: Jacquetta Cator; Charles Cator; Mark Cator.

CC Number: 292633

This trust supports local registered charities in East Norfolk which are involved in care and education in the community and international charities with long-term commitment in providing technological initiative and support.

In 2011/12 the trust's assets stood at £4 million. It had an income of £168,000 and made grants to 21 organisations totalling £190,000.

Beneficiaries included: Practical Action and Water Aid (£20,000 each); Cancer Research UK and Médecins Sans Frontières (£15,000 each); Alzheimer's Research Trust and Sightsavers (£10,000 each); Hope and Homes for Children and Marie Curie Cancer Care (£5,000 each); Fairhaven C of E VA Primary School – South Walsham (£3,500); Coeliac Society (£2,000); and Canine Partners for Independence (£1,000).

In 2010 a grant of £350,000 was given to Norfolk Community Foundation to establish 'The Ranworth Grassroots Fund'. The aim of the fund is to support a wide range of charitable, voluntary and community activities across Norfolk.

Exclusions

No grants to non-registered charities.

Information gathered from:

Accounts; Charity Commission record; funder's website.

The Ratcliff Foundation

General

About £200,000 (2011/12)

Beneficial area

UK, with a preference for local charities in the Midlands, North Wales and Gloucestershire.

Correspondent: Christopher J. Gupwell, Secretary and Trustee, Woodlands, Earls Common road, Stock Green, Redditch B96 6TB (tel: 01386 792116; email: chris.gupwell@btinternet.com)

Trustees: David M. Ratcliff, Chair; Edward H. Ratcliff; Carolyn M. Ratcliff; Gillian Thorpe; Michael Fea; Christopher J. Gupwell.

CC Number: 222441

The foundation was established in 1961, by Martin Rawlinson Ratcliff. Grants are made to any organisation that has charitable status for tax purposes.

In 2011/12 the trust had an income of £214,000 and an expenditure of £217,000. Further financial information was not available.

Previous beneficiaries have included: Avoncroft Museum of Historic Buildings, Multiple Births Foundation, Harbury Village Hall, Cottage and Rural Enterprises Ltd, White Ladies Aston Parochial Church Council, Focus Birmingham, Full House Furniture, Recycling Service Ltd, Gloucestershire Wildlife Trust, and Colwyn Choral Society.

Exclusions

No grants to individuals.

Applications

In writing to the correspondent.

Information gathered from:

Accounts; Charity Commission record.

The Eleanor Rathbone Charitable Trust

Merseyside, women, deprivation, social exclusion and unpopular causes

£318,000 (2011/12)

Beneficial area

UK, with the major allocation for Merseyside; also international projects (Africa, the Indian Sub-Continent, plus exceptionally Iraq and Palestine).

Correspondent: Liese van Alwon, Administrator, 546 Warrington Road, Rainhill, Merseyside L35 4LZ (tel: 01514 307914; email: eleanorrathbonetrust@gmail.com; website: www.eleanorrathbonetrust.org.uk)

Trustees: William Rathbone; Jenny Rathbone; Andrew Rathbone; Angela Morgan; Mark Rathbone.

CC Number: 233241

Eleanor Rathbone was the first woman to be elected to Liverpool City Council, representing Granby from 1909 to 1934. In 1929 she was elected as an independent MP and campaigned for social reform, particularly on issues affecting women, human rights and refugees. This charitable trust was established in 1947 with money left by Eleanor following her death in 1946.

The trust concentrates on supporting charities which benefit women, girls, young people and families who are economically deprived or socially excluded and unpopular and neglected causes. In the future the trust wishes to 'continue to seek out innovative projects, with a particular focus on Merseyside, which tackle unpopular causes in an innovative way, celebrating the grassroots ability of people to help themselves or be supported to improve their lives'.

Most donations are one-off although requests for two or three year grants will be considered. Applications are considered from small to medium charities and are for £1,000 to £3,000, occasionally higher.

The current funding areas are:

- Merseyside: charities and projects which are based in or delivered in Merseyside (particularly the more deprived areas) and meet the funding priorities (grants in Merseyside accounted for 51% of total grants in 2011/12)
- Holiday Fund: Small grants for holidays and outings provided by charities helping disadvantaged children and adults from Merseyside
- National: Charities and projects which meet the priorities and have a nationwide reach
- International: Projects in Sub-Saharan Africa, the Indian Sub-Continent and exceptionally Iran, Palestine and Haiti. projects must be sponsored and monitored by a UK registered charity and do one or more of the following:
  - Benefit women or orphaned children
  - Demonstrate local involvement in scoping and delivery
  - Aim to repair the damage in countries recently ravaged by international or civil war
  - Deliver clean water and sanitation

In 2011/12 the trust had assets of £7.7 million and an income of £279,000. Grants totalled £318,000, broken down as follows:

Merseyside	75	£160,000
International	68	£78,000
National/Regional	36	£72,000
Holidays	8	£8,000

Beneficiaries included: Asylum Link; Buttle UK; DADA; Merseyside Congolese Association; Tomorrow's Women; The Basement; Art 4 Dementia; Counsel and Care; Islington Law Centre; Tonybee Hall; Working Families; Wirral Swallows and Amazons; Build it International; Burma Assist; Jeevika Trust; Women and Children First and ZOA-UK.

Exclusions

Grants are not made in support of: any activity which relieves a statutory authority of its obligations; individuals, unless (and only exceptionally) it is made through a charity and it also fulfils at least one of the other positive objects mentioned above; medical research; gap-year projects; lobbying or campaigning organisations or organisations whose primary purpose is the promotion of a religion, church or sect.

The trust does not generally favour grants for running costs, but prefers to support specific projects, services or to contribute to specific developments.

Applications

Using the online form including supporting documents which you can also print out and send by post. Receipt of applications and those that are unsuccessful are not acknowledged. Applications are accepted at any time and are considered at the Trustee meetings which occur three times a year.

Information gathered from:

Accounts; Charity Commission record; funder's website.

The E. L. Rathbone Charitable Trust

Social work charities

£67,000 (2011/12)

Beneficial area

UK, with a strong preference for Merseyside.

Correspondent: Liese Van Alwon, Rathbone Investment Management Ltd, Port of Liverpool Building, Pier Head, Liverpool L3 1NW (tel: 01512 366666)

Trustees: J. B. Rathbone; Mrs S. K. Rathbone; Caroline Rathbone; R. S. Rathbone.

CC Number: 233240

The trust has a special interest in social work charities. There is a strong preference for Merseyside with local beneficiaries receiving the major funding.

In 2011/12 the trust had assets of £1.9 million, an income of £74,000 and gave grants totalling £67,000.

Beneficiaries included: Liverpool Community and Voluntary Services (£5,000); Brathay Trust and Personal Service Society (£3,000 each); Prenton High School for Girls and Clatterbridge Centre for Oncology (£2,500 each); Catholic Children's Society, Honey Rose Foundation, Lifelites, Merseyside Youth Association, Options for Supported Living and Wood Street Mission (£2,000 each); Local Solutions (£1,500); Wirral Community Narrow Boat Trust (£1,400); Tomorrow's People, NSPCC, Fairbridge in Merseyside and Autistics (£1,000 each); and Clothing Solutions (£500).

Exclusions

No grants to individuals seeking support for second degrees.

Applications

In writing to the correspondent.

Information gathered from:

Accounts; Charity Commission record.

The Rayden Charitable Trust

Jewish

£45,000 (2011/12)

Beneficial area

UK.

Correspondent: The Trustees, c/o Beavis Morgan LLP, 82 St John Street, London EC1M 4JN (tel: 020 7417 0417)

Trustees: Shirley Rayden; Clive Rayden; Paul Rayden.

CC Number: 294446

In 2011/12 the trust had assets of £3,500 and an income of £44,000 from donations. Grants totalled £45,000.

A list of donations was not included in the accounts. Previous beneficiaries have included: NWJDS (£7,000); Or Chadash (£6,500); Yesodey Hatorah (£3,000); Holocaust Education and Jewish Care (£2,500); and Central London Mikveh and CTN Jewish Life (£1,000 each).

Applications

In writing to the correspondent.

Information gathered from:

Accounts; Charity Commission record.

The Roger Raymond Charitable Trust

Older people, education, medical

£147,000 (2011/12)

Beneficial area

UK (and very occasionally large, well-known overseas organisations).

Correspondent: Mr Russell Pullen, Suttondene, 17 South Border, Purley, Surrey CR8 3LL (tel: 020 8660 9133; email: russell@pullen.cix.co.uk)

Trustees: R. W. Pullen; M. G. Raymond; Alisdair Kruger Thomson.

CC Number: 262217

'The Roger Raymond Charitable Trust owns 100% of the issued share capital of Shaw White Estates Ltd whose principle business is that of property investment. Any profits attributable to the subsidiary undertaking are covenanted up to The Roger Raymond Charitable Trust.'

In 2011/12 the trust had assets of £12 million and an income of £483,000, Grants totalled £147,000.

The principal beneficiary during the year, as in previous years, was Bloxham School, which received a donation of £125,000.

The other beneficiary listed in the accounts was Macmillan Cancer Support (£2,000). Grants of less than £2,000 each totalled £20,000.

Exclusions

Grants are rarely given to individuals.

Applications

The trust stated that applications are considered throughout the year, although funds are not always available.

Information gathered from:

Accounts; Charity Commission record.

The Rayne Trust

Jewish organisations, older and young people and people disadvantaged by poverty or socially isolation, understanding between cultures

£118,000 (2011/12)

Beneficial area

Israel and UK.

Correspondent: Nurit Gordon, 100 George Street, London W1U 8NU (tel: 020 7487 9650; email: ngordon@raynetrust.org; website: www.raynefoundation.org.uk/RayneTrust.aspx)

Trustees: Jane Rayne; Robert A. Rayne; Damian Rayne.

CC Number: 207392

The Rayne Trust was established by Lord Rayne to support organisations in which its trustees (Lady Rayne and the Hon. Robert A Rayne) have a close personal interest.

The trust's mandate, as determined by the trustees, is to understand and engage with the needs of UK and Israeli society. The trust is involved in 'social bridge building', and looks for four main outcomes:

- Enlarging sympathies – increasing tolerance and understanding between communities and people of different backgrounds
- Reduced exclusion – helping to bring people in from the margins of society
- Reduced conflict in society – helping to heal divisions in society
- New productive relationships – bringing unconnected people and organisations together to benefit society

The criteria for assessing applications are:

- It is innovative
- It provides direct benefits to vulnerable or disadvantaged communities
- It brings in additional funding and encourages the involvement of other organisations

The trust will fund salaries, project costs and core costs, usually to a maximum of three years.

In 2011/12 the trust had assets of £19.8 million and an income of £284,000. Grants totalling £118,000 were made to 51 organisations, broken down into £87,000 in the UK and £32,000 in Israel.

Beneficiaries included: The Chicken Shed Theatre Trust (£25,000); Michael Sobell Sinai School (£15,000); and The Place2Be (£3,000).

Grants of less than £10,000 totalled £41,000.

Exclusions

No grants to:

- Organisations with free reserves that are higher than 75% of annual expenditure
- Individuals
- Retrospective applications
- Repayment of debts
- Organisations which have had a grant in the last year
- General appeals
- Endowments

Applications

Firstly fill out the Stage One application form, available to download from the website, and submit it to the correspondent. Applicants will be contacted within a month about whether or not they are invited to make a more detailed Stage Two application.

Information gathered from:

Accounts; Charity Commission record; funder's website.

The John Rayner Charitable Trust

General

£35,000 (2011/12)

Beneficial area

England, with a preference for Merseyside and Wiltshire.

Correspondent: Mrs J. Wilkinson, Trustee, Manor Farmhouse, Church Street, Great Bedwyn, Marlborough, Wiltshire SN8 3PE (tel: 01672 870362)

Trustees: Mrs J. Wilkinson; Dr J. M. H. Rayner; Louise McNeilage.

CC Number: 802363

This trust has general charitable purposes in the UK, with a preference for Merseyside. Support is given to smaller organisations for general charitable purposes including medical and disability, children and older people, community projects, carers, youth work, medical research and development and for the arts.

In 2011/12 the trust had assets of £768,000, an income of £25,000 and gave 14 grants totalling £35,000.

Grants were distributed in the following categories and amounts:

Medical	£12,000
General	£11,000
Children	£7,000
Arts	£3,000
Disabled	£2,000

Beneficiaries during the year were: Room to Read (£5,000); Alzheimer's Society, Live Music Now North West, Marie Curie Cancer Care, Prospect Hospice, Royal Marsden and Theodora Children's Trust (£3,000 each); Combat Stress; Home Start Wiltshire, Swindon Sea Cadet Unite, Wiltshire Bobby Van Trust and Ykids (£2,000 each); and The Royal Blind Society and Wirral Society for Blind and Partially Sighted (£1,000 each).

Exclusions

No grants to individuals or non-registered charities.

Applications

In writing to the correspondent by 31 January each year. Trustees meet to allocate donations in February/March. Only successful applicants will be contacted. There are no application forms or guidelines.

Percentage of awards given to new applicants: between 10% and 20%.

Common applicant mistakes

'Applying as individuals; applying by email.'

Information gathered from:

Accounts; Charity Commission record; further information provided by the funder.

Eva Reckitt Trust Fund

Welfare, relief-in-need, extension and development of education, victims of war

£37,000 (2012)

Beneficial area

UK and overseas.

Correspondent: David Birch, Trustee, 1 Somerford Road, Cirencester, Gloucestershire GL7 1TP (email: eva.reckitt.trust@gmail.com)

Trustees: Anna Bunney; Meg Whittaker; David Birch; Diana Holliday.

CC Number: 210563

Founded in 1940, in 2012 the trust had an income of £23,000 and a total expenditure of £43,000. 43 grants were made totalling £37,000.

The trust provides grants worldwide under the following headings:

- Education
- Relief of the poor and those suffering due to international or industrial unrest, injustice, tyranny, oppression or persecution
- Research on poverty
- Grants may also be given for the relief of poverty amongst persons who have been in the service of the family of the founder

Beneficiaries included: Navjyoti (£3,000); Rise and Shine School (£2,300); Workaid, Wythenshawe Law Centre, Islamic Relief, Peace Brigades International and Canon Collins Trust (£1,000 each); and Land Mines Museum Cambodia, Tourism Concern, Project Harar – Ethiopia, St Martin-in-the-Fields Christmas Appeal and The Pirate Castle (£500 each).

Exclusions

Grants are generally not given to individuals, although individual cases may be supported through other charities which are able to monitor the use of the funds.

Applications

Trustees are proactive in selecting organisations to support but unsolicited applications are also considered. Applications should be made in writing to the correspondent outlining the amount requested, a breakdown of its use and how the purpose of the grant fits with the objectives of the trust. Applications should be supported by material setting out the objective and recent activities of the charity and should also include a copy of the charity's most recent annual accounts. Trustees meet quarterly to discuss applications. They also like to meet with some of the organisations which they fund.

Information gathered from:

Accounts; Charity Commission record.

The Red Rose Charitable Trust

General with particular reference to educational expenses for students and ill health

£33,000 (2011/12)

Beneficial area

UK with a preference for Lancashire and Merseyside.

Correspondent: J. N. L. Packer, Trustee, c/o Rathbone Trust Company, Port of Liverpool Building, Pier Head, Liverpool L3 1NW (tel: 01512 366666)

Trustees: James Nigel L. Packer; Jane L. Fagan; Julian B. Rathbone.

CC Number: 1038358

This trust was established in 1994. It has a preference for supporting charities working with older people and people who have physical or mental disabilities and providing education expenses of students whose parents or guardians cannot afford the same. Grants are also made to individuals within these categories.

In 2011/12 the trust had assets of £915,000 and an income of £36,000. Grants were made totalling £33,000.

Beneficiaries included: Help the Aged, Mencap and Make-a-Wish Foundation (£2,000 each); Rethink, Mango Tree, Sense, The Leprosy Mission, Motor Neurone Disease Association and Hope House Children's Hospices (£1,000 each); and Local Solutions and The National Autistic Society (£500 each).

Applications

In writing to the correspondent.

Information gathered from:

Accounts; Charity Commission record.

The C. A. Redfern Charitable Foundation

General

£184,000 (2011/12)

Beneficial area

UK.

Correspondent: The Administrator, PricewaterhouseCoopers, 9 Greyfriars Road, Reading, Berkshire RG1 1JG (tel: 01189 597111)

Trustees: William Maclaren; David Redfern; Simon Ward; Julian Heslop.

CC Number: 299918

This foundation supports a wide range of organisations with some preference for those concerned with health and welfare.

In 2011/12 the trust had assets of £4.4 million and an income of £187,000 and gave grants totalling £184,000.

Beneficiaries included: Saints and Sinners and South Bucks Riding for the Disabled People (£30,000); White Ensign (£10,000); The Special Yoga Centre, Live Music Now and Help for Heroes, Canine Partners for Independence; Chicks Country Hospital for Inner City Kids and St Luke's Primary School (£5,000 each); Fund for Epilepsy (£3,000); Heads Up, The Para Dressage Training Trust and St Christopher's Hospice (£2,000 each); Vitalise, Institute of Hepatology, Fight for Sight and Hertfordshire Red Cross (£1,000); Bromley Churches Housing Action (£800); and The Royal Star and Garter Home (£500).

Exclusions

No grants for building works or individuals.

Applications

The trustees meet regularly to discuss the making of grants but do not invite unsolicited grant applications.

Information gathered from:

Accounts; Charity Commission record.

The Max Reinhardt Charitable Trust

Deafness, fine arts promotion

Around £30,000 (2011/12)

Beneficial area

UK.

Correspondent: The Secretary to the Trustees, Flat 2, 43 Onslow Square, London SW7 3LR

Trustees: Joan Reinhardt; Veronica Reinhardt; Magdalen Wade.

CC Number: 264741

The trust supports organisations benefiting people who are deaf and those which promote fine arts. In 2011/12 the trust had an income of £25,000 and an expenditure of £30,000. No further financial information was available.

Previous beneficiaries included: Paintings in Hospitals, The Art Room, Auditory Verbal UK and Modern Art Museum, Oxford, Deafblind UK, and Dogs Trust, Friends of the Earth, National Trust, Thrive, West London Homeless, Young and Free and Zane.

Exclusions

No grants to individuals.

Applications

In writing to the correspondent.

Information gathered from:

Accounts; Charity Commission record.

REMEDI

Medical research

£84,000 (2010/11)

Beneficial area

UK.

Correspondent: Rosie Wait, Director, Elysium House, 126–128 New Kings Road, London SW6 4LZ (tel: 020 7384 2929; email: info@remedi.org.uk; website: www.remedi.org.uk)

Trustees: Dr Anthony Clarke; Dr Adrian Heagerty; Michael Hines; Prof. Tony Ward; Prof. Nick Bosanquet; David Feld.

CC Number: 1063359

REMEDI seeks to provide funds that advance medical knowledge, education and research for medical purposes. The trust states in its annual report for 2010/11 'that it is dedicated to improving the journey from illness or disability back to a normal life'.

The trust's research strategy, which can be found on the trust's website states the following:

> With a broad remit, REMEDI supports research projects in any medical condition which causes impairment, activity limitation, restriction in participation and reduced quality of life for which rehabilitation is an appropriate response. We particularly support pilot or incubator projects which have the potential to lead to bigger projects. Also, each year we will fund a major research project in a specific condition which has been chosen by our trustees.

The medical research supported by the trust in rehabilitation and disability projects, often complete the 'incubator' or pilot study stage and this enables researchers to then seek funding from large organisations such as the Medical Research Council, who will then fund a much larger project to complete the studies which enable new advances in care for these diseases.

The 2011/12 accounts were over a year overdue for submission to the Charity Commission at the time of writing. In 2010/11 the trust's assets stood at just over £141,000. It had an income of £101,000 and made grants totalling £84,000.

Beneficiaries included: Dr Isabel White – King's College, London; Dr Lindsay Pennington – Newcastle University; and Dr Richard Wilkie et al – Leeds University.

Applications

Firstly, applicants should email a short summary of their project (two pages of A4), including a breakdown of costs, proposed start date and length of the research programme. If the project is considered of interest to the trustees they will request that a full application form be completed. Full applications are peer reviewed and, if successful, passed on to the trustees for a final decision at their biannual meetings (usually in June and December). On the completion of the research project a final report must be submitted before the final 10% of the award can be released.

For full guidelines visit the trust's website.

Information gathered from:

Accounts; Charity Commission record; funder's website.

The Rest Harrow Trust

Jewish, general

£52,000 (2012/13)

Beneficial area

UK.

Correspondent: Miss Judith S. Portrait, c/o Portrait Solicitors, 21 Whitefriars Street, London EC4Y 8JJ

Trustees: Mrs J. B. Bloch; Dominic B. Flynn; Judith Portrait.

CC Number: 238042

This trust was established in 1964, its main objectives are to distribute grants from its income for education, housing and to assist the deprived and the elderly.

In 2012/13 the trust had assets of £936,000, an income of £77,000 and gave 201 grants totalling £52,000. Most grants were for £500 or less.

Beneficiaries included: Pinhas Rutenberg Educational Trust (£15,000); Nightingale (£3,000); Weizmann UK (£2,000); Cheltenham Ladies' College (£1,000); World Jewish Relief (£1,000); Friends of Israel Educational Foundation and Age UK (£500 each); Action Medical Research, African Revival, Campaign to Protect Rural England, Combat Stress, Down's Syndrome Association and Project Harar Ethiopia (£200 each).

Exclusions

No grants to non-registered charities or to individuals.

Applications

In writing to the correspondent. Applications are considered quarterly. Only submissions from eligible bodies are acknowledged.

Information gathered from:

Accounts; Charity Commission record.

The Rhododendron Trust

Overseas aid and development, social welfare and culture

£49,000 (2011/12)

Beneficial area

UK and overseas.

Correspondent: The Administrator, 6 Bridge Street, Richmond, North Yorkshire DL10 4RW

Trustees: Sarah Ray; Sarah Oliver; Elizabeth Baldwin; Wendy Anderson.

CC Number: 267192

It is the current policy of the trustees to divide donations as follows: (i) 50% to charities whose work is primarily overseas; (ii) 40% for UK social welfare charities; and (iii) 10% for UK cultural activities.

In 2011/12 the trust had assets of £1.5 million, an income of £59,000 and gave grants totalling £49,000.

Beneficiaries included: Action for Blind People, Brandon Centre, De Paul UK, Street Child Africa and Find Your Feet (£1,000 each); and Womankind Worldwide, Tree Aid, Solace, Rethink, Phoenix Dance Theatre, Medical Aid for Palestinians, Ice and Fire Theatre Company, Anti-Slavery International, Contact the Elderly and Edinburgh Young Carers (£500 each).

Exclusions

The trust does not support medical research, individual projects, or local community projects in the UK.

Applications

In writing to the correspondent at any time. The majority of donations are made in March. Applications are not acknowledged.

Percentage of awards given to new applicants: between 10% and 20%.

Common applicant mistakes

'Letter too general, rabbits on about need instead of saying how specifically they will meet that need and how much each individual helped (in broad terms) will cost the charity (summary of accounts useful).'

Information gathered from:

Accounts; Charity Commission record; further information provided by the funder.

Daisie Rich Trust

General

£97,000 to organisations (2012/13)

Beneficial area

UK, with a preference for the Isle of Wight.

Correspondent: Mrs L. Mitchell, Administrator, The Hawthorns, Main Road, Arreton, Newport, Isle of Wight PO30 3AD (tel: 07866 449855; email: daisierich@yahoo.co.uk)

Trustees: Adrian H. Medley, Chair; Ann C. Medley; Maurice J. Flux; David J. Longford; James R. Woodward Attrill.

CC Number: 236706

The trust makes grants to former employees, or their spouses, of Upward and Rich Ltd. Further grants are made mainly to Isle of Wight institutions, charities and individuals.

In 2012/13 the trust had assets of £3.4 million, an income of £162,000 and gave grants to organisations totalling £97,000.

Beneficiaries included: Earl Mountbatten Hospice (£6,000); Hampshire and Isle of Wight Air Ambulance and Isle of Wight Scout Council (£5,000 each); SSAFA Forces Help – Isle of Wight branch (£4,000); CLIC Sargent, West Wight Sports Centre and Storeroom 2010 (£3,000 each); Shanklin Voluntary Youth and Community Centre, Quay Arts, Penny Brohn Cancer Care and Isle of Wight Citizens Advice (£2,000 each); Brading Roman Villa and Isle of Wight Foodbank (£1,000 each); Freshwater Independent Lifeboat (£650); and Greater Ryde Benevolent Trust, People's Dispensary for Sick Animals and St John's Church – Ryde (£500 each).

Grants to ex-employees of Upward and Rich Ltd, their dependents and other individuals totalled £30,000.

Applications

Contact the correspondent for an application form. The trustees hold regular meetings to decide on grant applications and are assisted by information gathered by the administrator.

Information gathered from:

Accounts; Charity Commission record.

The Clive Richards Charity

Churches, schools, arts, disability and poverty

£942,000 (2011/12)

Beneficial area

UK, with a preference for Herefordshire.

Correspondent: Mr Peter Henry, Trustee, Lower Hope, Ullingswick, Herefordshire HR1 3JF (tel: 01432 820557)

Trustees: Peter Henry; Clive Richards; Sylvia Richards.

CC Number: 327155

The trust gives predominantly to schools, churches and organisations which support disability and the arts. Help is also available to individuals, particularly those who suffer from disabilities.

In 2011/12 the trust had assets of £714,000 and an income of £1.3 million, which mostly came from donations. Grants were made to organisations totalling £942,000.

Beneficiaries included: Chance to Shine (£175,000); Archbishop McGrath School (£150,000); Balliol College (£100,000); The Hereford Castle Society (£85,000); Canine Partners (£70,000); Whitecross High School (£30,000); Mary Rose (£20,000); Belmont Abbey (£12,000); The St Kentigem Hospice (£10,000); Welsh National Opera (£5,0000); Seafarers UK (£2,500); Leominster Shopmobility (£2,000); and Bargoed Male Voice Choir (£1,000).

Applications

In writing to the correspondent. The trustees meet monthly to consider applications. Note, the trust has previously stated that due to its resources being almost fully committed it is extremely selective in accepting any requests for funding.

Percentage of awards given to new applicants: between 40% and 50%.

Common applicant mistakes

'Illegible applications; insufficient detail especially about other efforts being made to seek funding.'

Information gathered from:

Accounts; Charity Commission record; further information provided by the funder.

The Violet M. Richards Charity

Older people, ill health, medical research and education

£39,000 (2011/12)

Beneficial area

UK, with a preference for East Sussex, particularly Crowborough.

Correspondent: Mr Charles Hicks, Secretary, c/o Wedlake Bell, 52 Bedford Row, London WC1R 4LR (tel: 020 7395 3155; email: chicks@wedlakebell.com)

Trustees: Mrs E. H. Hill; G. R. Andersen; C. A. Hicks; Mrs M. Burt; Dr J. Clements.

CC Number: 273928

The trust's objects are the relief of age and ill health, through the advancement of medical research (particularly into geriatric problems), medical education, homes and other facilities for older people and those who are sick. Applications from East Sussex, particularly the Crowborough area are favoured by the trustees. Currently the trustees have changed their grantmaking policy so that rather than making a number of smaller donations they will focus on supporting three or four projects of medical research over a few years.

In 2011/12 the trust had assets of £1.9 million and an income of £60,000. The only beneficiary organisation in this financial year was: Stroke Association (£39,000).

Exclusions

No support for individuals.

Applications

In writing to the correspondent, however the trust states in its accounts that the trustees 'prefer to be proactive with charities of their own choice, rather than reactive to external applications.' The trustees generally meet to consider grants twice a year in the spring and the autumn. There is no set format for applying and only successful applications are acknowledged. Due to the change of grant policy to focus on a smaller number of projects, external applications are unlikely to be successful and are therefore discouraged.

Information gathered from:

Accounts; Charity Commission record.

The Ripple Effect Foundation

General, particularly disadvantaged young people, the environment and overseas development

£29,000 (2011/12)

Beneficial area

UK, with a preference for the South West of England, some overseas.

Correspondent: Ms Nicola Gannon, Trustee, Marlborough Investment Consultants Ltd, Wessex House, Oxford Road, Newbury, Berkshire RG14 1PA (tel: 01635 814470)

Trustees: Caroline D. Marks, Chair; I. R. Marks; I. S. Wesley.

CC Number: 802327

The accounts of this charity state: 'The objectives of the trustees are to support a range of charitable causes over a few years that meet their funding criteria. They proactively seek out projects that meet their criteria and do not respond to unsolicited applications.'

In 2011/12 the trust had assets of £1.3 million, an income of £30,000 and gave grants totalling £29,000.

The beneficiaries during the year were: COUL UK (£16,000); CHICKS (£6,000); Network for Social Change (£3,500); Devon Community Foundation (£1,800); and New Economics Foundation (£1,800).

Exclusions

No grants are made to individuals.

Applications

The trust states that it does not respond to unsolicited applications.

Information gathered from:

Accounts; Charity Commission record.

The Sir John Ritblat Family Foundation

Jewish, general

£130,000 (2011/12)

Beneficial area

UK.

Correspondent: The Clerk, c/o Baker Tilly, The Pinnacle, 170 Midsummer Boulevard, Milton Keynes, Buckinghamshire MK9 1BP (tel: 01908 687800)

Trustees: Sir John Ritblat; N. S. J. Ritblat; C. B. Wagman; J. W. J. Ritblat.

CC Number: 262463

The trust was established in 1971 and makes grants to organisations for general charitable purposes, with some preference for arts and Jewish organisations. The trust makes grants primarily to long-established organisations. Note, the trust was previously known as The John Ritblat Charitable Trust No. 1.

In 2011/12 the trust had assets of £526,000 and an income of £34,000. Grants totalling £103,000 were made to 26 organisations.

Beneficiaries included: Henry Jackson Society (£25,000); Jewish Care (£11,000); Hertford House Trust and The Outward Bound Trust (£10,000 each); The Wallace Collection (£5,500); Weizmann UK (£4,300); Mayor of London's Fund for Young Musicians (£4,000); Central Synagogue (£2,600); Weizmann Institute and Museum of London (£2,000); The Art Fund (£1,500); The Board of Deputies of British Jews and Open Europe (£1,000 each); Tate Foundation (£850); and Zoë's Place – Baby Hospice (£125).

Exclusions

No grants to individuals.

Applications

The trust has previously stated that its funds are fully committed.

Information gathered from:

Accounts; Charity Commission record.

The River Trust

Christian

£103,000 (2011/12)

Beneficial area

UK, with a preference for Sussex.

Correspondent: The Trustees, Kleinwort Benson Trustees Ltd, 14 St George Street, London W1S 1FE (tel: 020 3207 7008; email: elizabeth.fettes-neame@kleinworth.com)

Trustee: Kleinwort Benson Trustees Ltd.

CC Number: 275843

Gillian Warren formed the trust in 1977 with an endowment mainly of shares in the merchant bank Kleinwort Benson. It is one of the many Kleinwort trusts. The River Trust is one of the smaller of the family trusts. It supports Evangelical Christian causes.

In 2011/12 the trust had assets of £633,000, an income of £90,000 and gave grants totalling £103,000. Grants were divided into the following categories:

Advancement of the Christian faith	10	£37,000
Religious education	17	£35,000
Religious welfare work	10	£15,000
Church funds	1	£9,000
Missionary work	2	£6,000
Miscellaneous	1	£1,000

Grant recipients included: Youth With A Mission (£16,000); Youth With A Mission Scotland (£8,000); Care Trust (£6,800); St Stephen's Society (£4,000); Care for the Family (£3,700); Marriage Foundation, Release International and Stewardship Trust (£2,000 each); Society of Mary and Martha, Bible Society and Beauty from Ashes (£1,000 each).

Exclusions

Only appeals for Christian causes will be considered. No grants to individuals. The trust does not support 'repairs of the fabric of the church' nor does it give grants for capital expenditure.

Applications

In writing to the correspondent. It is unusual for unsolicited appeals to be successful. Only successful applicants are notified of the trustees' decision. Some charities are supported for more than one year, although no commitment is usually given to the recipients.

Information gathered from:

Accounts; Charity Commission record.

Rix-Thompson-Rothenberg Foundation

Learning disabilities

£114,000 to organisations (2012)

Beneficial area

UK.

Correspondent: The Administrator, RTR Administrative Office, White Top Research Unit, Springfield House, 15/16 Springfield, Dundee DD1 4JE (tel: 01382 385157; email: P-RTR@dundee.ac.uk)

Trustees: Lord Rix; David Rothenberg; Loretto Lambe; Fred Heddell; Barrie Davis; Jonathan Rix; Brian Baldock; Suzanne J. Marriott.

CC Number: 285368

The foundation is dedicated to supporting projects connected with the care, education, training, development and leisure activities of people with learning disabilities.

> Support is given through grants to voluntary organisations working with, or on behalf of, people with learning disabilities and their carers. A special emphasis is given to grants that will enhance opportunity and lifestyle.
>
> The foundation maintains a close relationship with the Baily Thomas Charitable Fund which gives it substantial donations towards the annual grant-making activity.

In 2012 the foundation had assets of £1.3 million, an income of £118,000 and gave grants totalling £129,000. Of this, £15,000 was given from the 'care fund' to individuals.

Grant beneficiaries include: Half Moon (£6,400); Self Unlimited (£5,800); Southend University Hospital Foundation Trust and No Handbags (£5,000); Create (£4,700); Soundabout (£4,400); Leeds Mencap and London Symphony Orchestra (£4,000); Tell me a Tale (£3,600); United Response (£2,700); and East Bristol Information and Advice Centres (£2,300).

Exclusions

Applications for specific learning difficulties are not supported.

Applications

In the first instance potential applicants should discuss the proposed work with the administrator by phone, email or letter at least four months before a board meeting, which are held in June and December. They may then be invited to complete an application form and submit it with a copy of their latest audited accounts. Applications received without going through this process will not be acknowledged or considered.

Information gathered from:

Accounts; Charity Commission record.

Thomas Roberts Trust

Medical, disability, relief in need

£42,000 (2011/12)

Beneficial area

UK.

Correspondent: Mr James Roberts, Trustee, Sheridan House, 40–43 Jewry Street, Winchester, Hampshire SO23 8RY (tel: 01962 843211; fax: 01962 843223; email: trtust@thomasroberts.co.uk)

Trustees: R. E. Gammage; J. Roberts; G. Hemmings.

CC Number: 1067235

Established in November 1997, this trust mainly makes grants to medical (particularly cancer support and research), disability and welfare organisations. Applications from employees and former employees of the Thomas Roberts Group of companies are also considered.

In 2011/12 the trust had an income of £22,000 and made grants totalling around £42,000.

Past beneficiaries have included: Cancer Research UK, Macmillan Cancer Relief, Marie Curie Cancer Care, Age Concern, Winchester Churches Nightshelter, Diabetes UK, Riding for the Disabled, Parkinson's Disease Society and Breast Cancer Campaign.

Applications

In writing to the correspondent. Applicants are required to provide a summary of their proposals to the trustees, explaining how the funds would be used and what would be achieved.

Percentage of awards given to new applicants: less than 10%.

Information gathered from:

Accounts; Charity Commission record; further information provided by the funder.

Edwin George Robinson Charitable Trust

Medical research

Around £40,000 (2011/12)

Beneficial area

UK.

Correspondent: Edwin Robinson, Trustee, 71 Manor Road South, Esher, Surrey KT10 0QB (tel: 020 8398 6845)

Trustees: Edwin Robinson; Susan Robinson.

CC Number: 1068763

The trust supports organisations which provide care for people with disabilities and older people, particularly in the area of medical research. Grants tend to be made for specific research projects and are not usually made to fund general operating costs.

In 2011/12 the trust had an income of £12,000 and an expenditure of £44,000. Grants probably totalled around £40,000. No further information was available.

Previous beneficiaries include: Marie Curie Cancer Care, Diabetes UK, Bath Institute of Medical Engineering, Deafness Research, Brainwave, Action for Medical Research, Ness Foundation, Cure Parkinson's, Holly Lodge Centre and Salvation Army.

Exclusions

No grants to individuals or for general running costs for small local organisations.

Applications

In writing to the correspondent.

Percentage of awards given to new applicants: between 10% and 20%.

Information gathered from:

Accounts; Charity Commission record; further information provided by the funder.

Robyn Charitable Trust

General charitable purposes, particularly the support of young people

Around £70,000 (2011/12)

Beneficial area

UK and overseas.

Correspondent: Malcolm Webber, Trustee, c/o Harris and Trotter, 64 New Cavendish Street, London W1G 8TB (tel: 020 7467 6300)

Trustees: Malcolm Webber; Mark Knopfler; Ronnie Harris.

CC Number: 327745

This trust was established in 1988 to advance education and relieve need amongst children in any part of the world.

In 2011/12 the trust had an income of £6,500 and a total expenditure of £70,000. No further information was available.

Previous beneficiaries have included: One to One Children's Fund, The Purcell School, Variety Club, The Honeypot Charity, Malawi Against Aids and Teenage Cancer Trust.

Exclusions

No grants to individuals.

Applications

In writing to the correspondent.

Information gathered from:

Accounts; Charity Commission record.

The Rock Foundation

Christian ministries and charities

£78,000 to organisations (2011/12)

Beneficial area

Worldwide.

Correspondent: Mr Richard Borgonon, Park Green Cottage, Barhatch Road, Cranleigh, Surrey GU6 7DJ (tel: 01483 274556)

Trustees: Richard Borgonon; Andrew Green; Kevin Locock; Jane Borgonon; Colin Spreckley; Peter Butler.

CC Number: 294775

Formed in 1986, this charity seeks to support charitable undertakings which are built upon a clear biblical basis and which, in most instances, receive little or no publicity. It is not the intention of the foundation to give widespread support, but rather to specifically research and invest time and money in the work of a few selected Christian ministries. As well as supporting such ministries, grants are also made to registered charities.

In 2011/12 the foundation had assets of £209,000 and an income of £176,000. Grants totalled £221,000 including £78,000 given in 40 grants to organisations and £142,000 given in 32 grants to individuals.

There were nine grants of over £5,000 listed in the accounts: Proclamation Trust (£23,000); Crosslinks and Lennox (£16,000 each); Carter (£14,000); Cranleigh Baptist Church (£13,000); Jackman (£12,000); Relite Africa Trust (£8,000), Baltic Reformed Theological Seminary (£6,500); and Lahore Evangelical Ministries (£6,000).

Applications

The trust has stated: 'the trust identifies its beneficiaries through its own networks, choosing to support organisations it has a working relationship with. This allows the trust to verify that the organisation is doing excellent work in a sensible manner in a way which cannot be conveyed from a written application. As such, all appeals from charities the foundation do not find through their own research are simply thrown in the bin. If an sae is included in an application, it will merely end up in the foundation's waste-paper bin rather than a post box.' They do not respond to unsolicited applications.

Information gathered from:

Accounts; Charity Commission record.

The Rock Solid Trust

Christian causes

About £20,000 (2011/12)

Beneficial area

Worldwide.

Correspondent: J. D. W. Pocock, Trustee, Beedings House, Nutbourne Lane, Nutbourne, Pulborough, West Sussex RH20 2HS

Trustees: J. D. W. Pocock; T. P. Wicks; T. G. Bretell.

CC Number: 1077669

This trust supports:

- Christian charitable institutions and the advancement of Christian religion
- The maintenance, restoration and repair of the fabric of any Christian church
- The education and training of individuals
- Relief in need

In 2011/12 the trust had an income of £13,000 and an expenditure of £29,000.

Previous beneficiaries have included: Clifton College Development Trust (£25,000); Crisis Centre Ministries (£20,000); Debate Mate (£5,000); Dolphin Society and Holy Trinity Cuckfield (£1,000 each); GL Enterprises (£500); and Paralympics GB and Naomi House/Jacksplace (£200 each).

Grants to individuals usually total around £10,000.

Applications

In writing to the correspondent. Support is given 'generally where the trustees can get personally involved. The trustees do not make donations to unknown persons or groups.'

Information gathered from:

Accounts; Charity Commission record.

The Rofeh Trust

General, religious activities

£56,000 (2011/12)

Beneficial area

UK.

Correspondent: Mr Martin Dunitz, 44 Southway, London NW11 6SA

Trustees: Martin Dunitz; Ruth Dunitz; Vivian Wineman; Henry Eder.

CC Number: 1077682

In 2011/12 the trust had assets of £929,000, an income of £53,000 and gave grants totalling £56,000. There was no further financial information given in the annual report filed with the Charity Commission.

Applications

In writing to the correspondent.

Information gathered from:

Accounts; Charity Commission record.

Rokach Family Charitable Trust

Jewish, general

£275,000 (2011/12)

Beneficial area

UK.

Correspondent: Mr Norman Rokach, Trustee, 20 Middleton Road, London NW11 7NS (tel: 020 8455 6359)

Trustees: N. Rokach; Mrs H. Rokach; Mrs E. Hoffman; Mrs M. Feingold; Mrs A. Gefilhaus; Mrs N. Brenig.

CC Number: 284007

This trust supports Jewish and general causes in the UK. Accounts for this trust are consistently very overdue when submitted to the Commission.

In 2011/12 the trust had assets of £2.4 million, an income of £573,000 and gave grants totalling £275,000. Investment management costs and governance totalled £129,000.

The beneficiaries were: Belz Heritage Foundation and Machzikei Hadass Ltd (£83,000 each); Cosmon Belz Ltd (£60,000); Before Trust and R.S.T. (£5,000); Beis Yaakov Primary School (£4,700); Belz Mercaz Torah Vechesed and Kehal Chasidei Wiznitz (£3,000 each); and Torah 5759 Ltd and WST Charity Ltd (£2,500 each).

Applications

In writing to the correspondent.

Information gathered from:

Accounts; Charity Commission record.

The Helen Roll Charitable Trust

General

£118,000 (2011/12)

Beneficial area

UK.

Correspondent: The Trustees, c/o Wenn Townsend Accountants, 30 St Giles, Oxford OX1 3LE (tel: 01865 559900; email: helen.roll@aol.co.uk)

Trustees: Christine Chapman; Christine Reid; Patrick J. R. Stopford; Paul Strang; Frank R. Williamson; Jennifer C. Williamson; Peter R. Williamson; Stephen G. Williamson.

CC Number: 299108

'One of the trustees' aims is to support work for which charities find it difficult or impossible to obtain funds from other sources. Some projects are supported on a start-up basis, others involve funding over a longer term'. The trust aims to distribute about £120,000 a year.

The charities supported are mainly those whose work is already known to the trustees and who report on both their needs and achievements. Each year a handful of new causes are supported. However the trust has previously stated that 'the chances of success for a new application are about 100–1'.

In 2011/12 the trust had assets of £1.6 million, an income of £47,000 and gave grants totalling £118,000.

Grants included those made to: Home Farm Trust (£12,000); Pembroke College Oxford and West Oxfordshire Citizens Advice (£10,000 each); Museum of Modern History and Wildlife Trust (£5,000 each); Oxford University Botanic Garden (£3,500); Sick Children's Trust (£3,000); Community of the Holy Fire (£2,500); Snowden Award Scheme (£2,000); Compassionate Friends (£1,500); and People's Dispensary for Sick Animals (£1,000).

Exclusions

No support for individuals or non-registered charities.

Applications

In writing to the correspondent during the first fortnight in February. Applications should be kept short, ideally on one sheet of A4. Further material will then be requested from those who are short-listed. The trustees normally make their distributions in March. Applications by email are welcomed.

Percentage of awards given to new applicants: less than 10%.

Common applicant mistakes

'Not applying within our application window – 75% apply outside this window.'

Information gathered from:

Accounts; Charity Commission record; further information provided by the funder.

The Sir James Roll Charitable Trust

General

£155,000 (2011/12)

Beneficial area

UK.

Correspondent: Mr Nicholas Wharton, Trustee, 5 New Road Avenue, Chatham, Kent ME4 6AR (tel: 01634 830111)

Trustees: N. T. Wharton; B. W. Elvy; J. M. Liddiard.

CC Number: 1064963

The trust's main objects are the:

- Promotion of mutual tolerance, commonality and cordiality in major world religions
- Promotion of improved access to computer technology in community based projects other than political parties or local government
- Funding of projects aimed at early identification of specific learning disorders
- Other charitable projects as the trustees see fit

In 2011/12 the trust had assets of £4.9 million, an income of £198,000 and gave grants totalling £155,000.

Beneficiaries included: St Clement's Parochial Church Council (£6,000); DEC East Africa Crisis Appeal (£5,000); REACT (£2,600); British Blind Sport, Challenging Behaviour Foundation, Independence at Home Ltd and Jubilee Sailing Trust Ltd (£1,300 each); Fair Trials International, Dystonia Society and OCD Action (£1,000 each); and International Refugee Trust (£500).

Applications

In writing to the correspondent. The trustees usually meet around four times a year to assess grant applications.

Information gathered from:

Accounts; Charity Commission record.

Rosa – the UK fund for women and girls

Women's organisations and projects supporting women

£3,800 (2011/12)

Beneficial area

UK.

Correspondent: Ms Jo Shaw, Executive Director, c/o Women's Resource Centre, United House, 4Th Floor, North Road, London N7 9DP (tel: 020 7697 3466; email: info@rosauk.org; website: www.rosauk.org)

Trustees: Marilyn List; Maggie Baxter; Gillian Egan; Lindsay Driscoll; Prof. Ruth Pearson.

CC Number: 1124856

Rosa is a charitable fund set up to support initiatives that benefit women and girls in the UK. Rosa's website gives the following information about what the organisation does:

> While many women and girls here do enjoy freedom of choice and the opportunity for success in their lives, that's simply not true for all. Our vision is of equality and justice for all women and girls in the UK.
>
> Women aren't short of ideas to help create positive change in their lives, but they are often short of the money needed to turn those ideas into reality. That's why Rosa was launched in 2008 – to help raise more money for women's projects and organisations.
>
> We do this in three key ways:
>
> We champion funding for women and girls – we can help inform, influence and advise other funders to promote greater investment in organisations working with women and girls.
>
> We raise funds and invest in change – Rosa raises money from individuals, companies, foundations and statutory donors so we can make grants to initiatives and groups that tackle specific issues around women's safety, economic justice, health and wellbeing, and representation in society.
>
> We act as a connector and advocate – by promoting awareness of women's organisations and the issues they tackle, showing how donations will help create lasting change, and bringing donors closer to the causes they support.
>
> *How we make a difference*
>
> Through Rosa you can support projects working with women and girls on these issues:
>
> - Economic justice
> - Health and well-being
> - Leadership
> - Safety

Our intention is to listen to and respect the voices of all women and girls in the work we do at Rosa. In particular we wish to work with those from groups who are heard less often for example due to their age, disability or migration status.

General Criteria

- Rosa will only fund organisations with charitable objectives that are also based in and working in the UK
- Rosa will fund projects run by women, based in women's organisations or based in mainstream organisations
- Rosa will consider funding capital and/ or revenue projects
- The grant can be used to fund project and/or core costs
- Organisations can only have one grant at a time and will normally be able to reapply after a break of three years after a grant has been awarded
- Rosa will not fund political parties or activity that promotes religion

In all its work Rosa seeks to support best practice on equality of opportunity and environmental sustainability.

In 2011/12 Rosa had assets of £109,000 and an income of £137,000. Although only one grants was listed in the accounts for the year (£3,800 to the Migrant and Refugee Communities Forum) the trust was working on projects that had been funded in the previous year. This included grants to: AnyBody, Platform 51, End Violence Against Women, Fawcett Society, Women's Budget Group, UK Feminista, Southall Black Sisters and collaborative work against Female Genital Mutilation.

Applications

The fund encourages organisations running projects or initiatives which match the current strategic priorities of the fund to contact them to discuss how the fund may be able to help. Potential applicants may contact the trust via email, phone or by visiting the office. The fund changes its priorities regularly so applicants are encouraged to visit the website regularly.

Information gathered from:

Accounts; Charity Commission record; funder's website.

The Cecil Rosen Foundation

Welfare, especially older people, infirm, people who are mentally or physically disabled

£283,000 (2011/12)

Beneficial area

UK.

Correspondent: Malcolm Ozin, Trustee, 22 Lisson Grove, London NW1 6TT (tel: 020 7258 2070)

Trustees: Malcolm Ozin; John Hart; Peter Silverman.

CC Number: 247425

Established in 1966, the charity's main object is the assistance and relief of the poor, especially older people, the infirm or people who have disabilities.

The correspondent has previously stated that almost all the trust's funds are (and will always continue to be) allocated between five projects. The surplus is then distributed in small donations between an unchanging list of around 200 organisations. 'Rarely are any organisations added to or taken off the list.'

In 2011/12 the foundation had assets of £5.7 million and an income of £446,000. Grants totalled £283,000, of which one grant was recorded. This was £135,000 given to the Jewish Blind and Physically Handicapped Society (of which two of the trustees are directors).

Exclusions

No grants to individuals.

Applications

The correspondent has previously stated that 'no new applications can be considered'. Unsuccessful applicants are not notified.

Information gathered from:

Accounts; Charity Commission record.

The Rothermere Foundation

Education, general

£569,000 (2011/12)

Beneficial area

UK.

Correspondent: Mr Vyvyan Harmsworth, Secretary, Beech Court, Canterbury Road, Challock, Ashford, Kent TN25 4DJ (tel: 01233 740641)

Trustees: Rt Hon. Viscount Rothermere; Viscountess Rothermere; V. P. W. Harmsworth; J. G. Hemingway.

CC Number: 314125

This trust was set up for the establishment and maintenance of 'Rothermere Scholarships' to be awarded to graduates of the Memorial University of Newfoundland to enable them to undertake further periods of study in the UK; and general charitable causes. The trustees have decided to designate £200,000 a year until further notice to make grants to Rothermere Fellows and support other such long-term projects.

In 2011/12 the foundation had assets of £25 million, an income of £851,000 and made grants totalling £569,000, broken down as follows:

Educational/children's charities	£321,000
Medical research	£30,000
The arts/sports	£6,200
Religious organisations	£5,600
Other charitable donations	£207,000

Three Rothermere scholarships were made totalling £57,000.

Other beneficiaries included: St Peter's College, Oxford (£130,000); Wycombe Abbey School (£80,000); Harmsworth Professorship (£77,000); London Library (£50,000); Shakespeare North (£25,000); National Osteoporosis Society (£10,000); St Christopher's Hospice, St Bride's Church, Salisbury International Arts and Coram's Field (£5,000 each); and Arts Logistics (£950).

Applications

In writing to the correspondent. Trustees meet twice a year to consider grant applications.

Information gathered from:

Accounts; Charity Commission record.

The Rowing Foundation

Water sports

About £26,000 (2011/12)

Beneficial area

UK.

Correspondent: Pauline Churcher, Secretary, 2 Roehampton Close, London SW15 5LU (tel: 020 8878 3723; fax: 020 8878 6298; email: applications@therowingfoundation.org.uk; website: www.therowingfoundation.org.uk)

Trustees: John Buchan; Simon Goodey; Philip Phillips; Dr Iain Reid; Roger Smith; John Chick; Francis Dale.

CC Number: 281688

The Rowing Foundation was set up in 1981 to generate and administer funds for the aid and support of young people (those under 18 or 23 if still in full-time education) and people who have disabilities, of all ages, through their participation in water sports, particularly rowing. Its income is mainly dependent on donations from the rowing fraternity.

The Foundation's preference is to make grants of between £500–£2000, up to 50% of the cost, usually to initiate projects when a club, school or other organisation can demonstrate their ability to complete the project. Grants are made to support rowing only.

The Rowing Foundation prefers to encourage participation in rowing by the young or disabled through the provision of equipment, such as boats, sculls, ergos, oars and essential safety equipment. Coaching, revenue or any commitment requiring long-term support are rarely approved.

To comply with their charity status, the Trustees must retain their absolute discretion when considering grant applications to ensure the objects are charitable, that is for public benefit. That requirement, and the conditions of the Rowing Foundation's charter, means that our support must be: non-elitist; for the benefit of young people; those in full time education; or disabled. However, the Trustees are always happy to discuss these how these criteria might be applied when the donor of a gift or legacy expresses a wish to help particular scheme.

In 2012 the foundation had an income of £13,000 and an expenditure of £26,000.

Beneficiaries included: Eastbourne RC, Eton Excelsior RC, Flushing and Mylor Pilot Gig Club, Portland Gig Club, City of Cambridge Rowing Club, The Great River Race Co., Hollowell Scullers and University of Northampton RC.

Exclusions

The foundation does not give grants to individuals, only to clubs and organisations, and for a specific purpose, not as a contribution to general funds. The foundation does not give grants to support sailing or swimming.

Applications

Applications should be made on a form, available to download from the foundation's website. Application deadlines are usually mid-May, August and November. Trustees have some preference for new applicants.

Percentage of awards given to new applicants: 50%.

Common applicant mistakes

'They simply do not read the form carefully.'

Information gathered from:

Accounts; Charity Commission record; further information provided by the funder; funder's website.

The Rowland Family Foundation

Relief-in-need, education, religion, community

£315,000 (2011/12)

Beneficial area

UK and overseas.

Correspondent: Lucy Gibson, Harcus Sinclair, 3 Lincoln's Inn Fields, London WC2A 3AA (tel: 020 7242 9700; email: lucy.gibson@harcus-sinclair.co.uk)

Trustees: Mrs A. M. Rowland; N. G. Rowland.

CC Number: 1111177

The foundation was registered with the Charity Commission in 2005. Its principal objectives are the relief of poverty, the advancement of education, the advancement of religion or other purposes beneficial for the community. The foundation is currently reducing its levels of grantmaking in order to protect assets in the long term.

In 2011/12 the foundation had assets of £4.8 million, an income of £106,000 and made three grants totalling £315,000.

Beneficiaries during the year were: Chailey Heritage School (£190,000); Child Welfare Scheme (£120,000); and Bevan Trust (£5,000).

Applications

In writing to the correspondent.

Information gathered from:

Accounts; Charity Commission record.

The Rowlands Trust

General, but mainly medical research, social welfare, music and the arts and the environment

£433,000 (2012)

Beneficial area

West and South Midlands including Hereford and Worcester, Gloucester, Shropshire and Birmingham.

Correspondent: Ms Gemma Wilkinson, Clerk to the Trustees, c/o Mills and Reeve, 78–84 Colmore Row, Birmingham B3 2AB (email: gemma.wilkinson@mills-reeve.com)

Trustees: A. C. S. Hordern; Mrs F. J. Burman; Mrs A. M. I. Harris; G. Barber; T. Jessop.

CC Number: 1062148

The trust primarily has an interest in supporting projects in the West Midlands, the South Midlands including Hereford and Worcester, Gloucester, Shropshire and Birmingham. Grants are given in the following areas:

- Research, education and training in the broadest sense with special regard to medical and scientific research
- The sick, poor, disabled and elderly
- Music and the Arts
- The environment

In 2012 the trust had assets of £4.9 million, an income of £217,000 and made grants totalling £433,000, broken down as follows:

Illness, poverty, older people and disability	39%
Research, education and training	32%
Church buildings	15%
Music and the arts	11%
The environment	3%

Beneficiaries included: Ruskin Mill Trust (£30,000); Shenley Academy and Baverstock Foundation School (£15,000 each); Hereford Cathedral (£12,000); Carpet Museum Trust (£10,000); Cure Leukaemia, Avoncroft Museum of Historic Buildings and West Midlands Central Accident Resuscitation and Emergency Team (£5,000 each); Focus, Birmingham (£3,000); Sight Concern Worcestershire, Castle Froma – Leamington Spa and Roses Theatre Trust Tewkesbury (£2,000 each); Cowley Parochial Church Council Gloucestershire and Royal Birmingham Society of Artists (£1,000 each); and Ledbury Poetry Festival (£800).

Exclusions

No support for individuals or to animal charities. No support is given for revenue funding.

Applications

Applications forms are available from the correspondent and are the preferred means by which to apply. Completed forms should be returned with a copy of the most recent accounts. The trustees meet to consider grants four times a year.

Information gathered from:

Accounts; Charity Commission record.

Royal Artillery Charitable Fund

Service charities

£217,000 to organisations (2012)

Beneficial area

UK and overseas.

Correspondent: Lt Col I. A. Vere Nicoll, Trustee, Artillery House, Royal Artillery House, Larkhill, Wiltshire SP4 8QT (tel: 01980 845698; email: AC-RHQRA-RACF-WelfareClk2@mod.uk; website: www.theraa.co.uk)

Trustees: Maj. Gen. J. Milne; Col. A. Jolley; Col. C. Fletcher-Wood; Maj. ATG. Richards; Maj. AJ. Dines; Brig. D. E. Radcliffe; Col. M. J. Thornhill; Brig. S. Humphrey; Maj. J. Leighton; Col. W. Prior; Col. R. Lee; Brig. K. Ford.

CC Number: 210202

The fund promotes the efficiency and welfare of all ranks of the Royal Artillery and gives relief and assistance to any past or present members, living or deceased, their dependents and families who are in need of such assistance by way of poverty, illness or disability.

In 2012 the trust had assets of £14 million and an income of £1.1 million. Grants to organisations totalled £217,000 and a further £799,000 was given in grants directly to individuals.

Grants to organisations included: Royal Artillery Sports (£65,000); Regiments and Batteries (£64,000); Army Benevolent Fund (£55,000); Gunner

Magazine (£18,000); RA Memorials (£8,100); King Edward VII Hospital (£2,800); Veterans Aid (£2,000); and Scottish Veterans Garden City Association (£500).

Applications

In writing to the correspondent.

Information gathered from:

Accounts; Charity Commission record; funder's website.

Royal Masonic Trust for Girls and Boys

Children, young people

£617,000 to non-Masonic charities (2012)

Beneficial area

UK.

Correspondent: Mr Leslie Hutchinson, Chief Executive, Freemasons' Hall, 60 Great Queen Street, London WC2B 5AZ (tel: 020 7405 2644; fax: 020 7831 4094; email: info@rmtgb.org; website: www.rmtgb.org)

Trustee: Council members appointed by a resolution of a General Court.

CC Number: 285836

This trust was established in 1982 and is largely focused on making grants to individual children of Freemasons who are in need. Grants are also made to UK non-Masonic organisations working with children and young people and to support bursaries at cathedrals and collegiate chapels.

Most grants are made to Masonic charities. According to the trust's website, it is currently running Stepping Stones: 'Through the scheme, we provide grants to charities and programmes working to alleviate poverty and improve educational outcomes among those children and young people who face financial hardship and are educationally disadvantaged.'

Potential applicants should check the charity's website for available schemes.

In 2012 the trust had assets of £123 million and an income of £6.9 million. Non-Masonic donations totalled £617,000, broken down as follows:

Lifelites programme	£211,000
Choral bursaries to individuals	£204,000
Other donations	£202,000

There was a further £6 million paid to individuals connected with Freemasonry and £382,000 through the TalentAid scheme, which aims to support children and young people who are exceptionally gifted in music, sport or the performing arts.

Stepping Stones grants have been awarded to: Aspire, British Exploring Society, Child Victims of Crime, Family Support Work, Home-Start Sutton, National Autistic Society, SkillForce, White Lodge Centre, Young Lives Foundation and Youth at Risk.

Applications

To apply to the Stepping Stones scheme: send a one page initial enquiry, comprising the charity's registration number, main area of work, the amount of funding requested and a description of the programme or project, including its location. If the enquiry fits the aims and requirements of the scheme, a full application form will be sent out.

Information gathered from:

Accounts; Charity Commission record; funder's website.

The RRAF Charitable Trust

General, medical research, children who are disadvantaged, religious organisations, aid for the developing world and support for the elderly

Around £26,000 (2011/12)

Beneficial area

UK and the developing world.

Correspondent: The Administrator, Rathbone Trust Company Ltd4th Floor1 Curzon StreetLondonW1J 5FB (tel: 020 7399 0807)

Trustees: Rathbone Trust Company Ltd; Claire Tufnell; Emilie Rathbone; Joanne McArthy; Rosemary McArthy; Elizabeth Astley-Arlington.

CC Number: 1103662

This trust was established in 2004. In 2011/12 it had an income of £25,000 and a total expenditure of £26,000. Accounts were received at the Charity Commission but due to the trust's low income were not published online.

Previous beneficiaries included: Refugee Support Network (£14,000); Dove Association and Kids Company (£7,000 each); Reaching Orphans for Care (£5,800); Hamlin Fistula (£5,000); Blues in Schools (£3,000); and Living Links (£1,500).

Applications

In writing to the correspondent. Only successful applicants are notified of the trustees' decision.

Information gathered from:

Accounts; Charity Commission record.

William Arthur Rudd Memorial Trust

General in the UK, and selected Spanish charities

£35,000 (2012)

Beneficial area

In practice UK and Spain.

Correspondent: Miss Alexandra Sarkis, Trustee, 12 South Square, Gray's Inn, London WC1R 5HH (tel: 020 7405 8932; email: mail@mmandm.co.uk)

Trustees: A. A. Sarkis; D. H. Smyth; R. G. Maples.

CC Number: 326495

In 2012 the trust had assets of £800,000, an income of £49,000 and gave grants totalling £35,000.

The trust's accounts state that donations were made to registered charities in the UK and to selected Spanish charities; however, no grants list was provided.

Applications

As the objects of the charity are not linked to any specific areas of charitable activity, the trustees receive a large number of applications for donations. They review the applications received and any wishes expressed by the settlor at their annual meeting and make their awards.

Percentage of awards given to new applicants: less than 10%.

Information gathered from:

Accounts; Charity Commission record; further information provided by the funder.

The Russell Trust

General charitable purposes

£268,000 (2011/12)

Beneficial area

UK, especially Scotland.

Correspondent: Iona Russell, Administrator and Trustee, Markinch, Glenrothes, Fife KY7 6PB (tel: 01592 753311; email: russelltrust@trg.co.uk)

Trustees: Fred Bowden; Cecilia Croal; Graeme Crombie; David Erdal; Don Munro; Iona Russell; Alan Scott; C. A. G. Parr.

SC Number: SC004424

This family trust was established in 1947 in memory of Capt. J P O Russell who was killed in Italy during the Second World War. The trustees prefer to make grants to pump-prime new projects, rather than giving on an ongoing basis. Grants of up to £10,000 can be distributed; however, generally the amounts given are for between £250 and £2,000. Three or four larger grants of up to £20,000 may be awarded annually.

In 2011/12 the trust had an income of £268,000. Grants were made totalling £201,000. No grants list was available, but donations are generally broken down into the following categories:

- Youth work
- Health and welfare
- Education
- Local
- Music and the Arts
- Church
- Preservation/conservation
- Archaeology
- St Andrew's University

Exclusions

Only registered charities or organisations with charitable status are supported.

Applications

On a form available from the correspondent. A statement of accounts must be supplied. Trustees meet quarterly, although decisions on the allocation of grants are made more regularly.

Information gathered from:

Accounts; OSCR record.

Ryklow Charitable Trust 1992

Education, health, environment and welfare

Around £223,000 (2011/12)

Beneficial area

UK and overseas, with a preference for the East Midlands.

Correspondent: Stephen Marshall, c/o Robinsons Solicitors, 10–11 St James Court, Friar Gate, Derby DE1 1BT (tel: 01332 291431; email: stephen.marshall@robinsons-solicitors.co.uk)

Trustees: Andrew Williamson; Ernest J. S. Cannings; Philip W. Hanson; Sheila Taylor.

CC Number: 1010122

The trust (also known as A B Williamson Charitable Trust) was established by Mr A B Williamson, a midlands industrialist, to provide financial assistance to small or individual charitable projects, students, and people in need, throughout the world.

Funding is given for the following activities:

- Projects in the developing world, especially those which are intended to be self-sustaining or concerned with education
- Help for vulnerable families, minorities and the prevention of abuse or exploitation of children and young persons
- Conservation of natural species, landscape and resources

The trust has now stopped accepting unsolicited applications.

In 2011/12 the trust had an income of £24,000 and an expenditure of £223,000. No further financial information was available.

Previous beneficiaries have included: Safe and Sound and Field Row Unitarian Chapel Belper.

Exclusions

Only organisations which are UK registered, have a UK sponsor, or are affiliated to a UK registered charity will be considered.

Applications

The trust is no longer accepting unsolicited applications. The trustees actively seek out charities which they invite to apply.

Percentage of awards given to new applicants: between 40% and 50%.

Information gathered from:

Accounts; Charity Commission record; further information provided by the funder.

The Jeremy and John Sacher Charitable Trust

General, including arts, culture and heritage, medical and disability, community and welfare, education, science and technology, children and youth, and religion

£72,000 (2011/12)

Beneficial area

UK and Israel.

Correspondent: The Trustees, H. W. Fisher and Company, Acre House, 11–15 William Road, London NW1 3ER (tel: 020 7388 7000)

Trustees: Simon Sacher; Jeremy Sacher; Hon. Rosalind Sacher; Elisabeth Sacher.

CC Number: 206321

This trust has general charitable purposes, with some interest in Jewish/ Israeli organisations. This trust is also known as the Michael Sacher Charitable Trust and should not be confused with the Michael Harry Sacher Trust (charity number 288973).

In 2012/13 the trust had assets of £5.3 million and an income of £161,000. Grants were made to 30 organisations totalling £72,000 and were broken down into the following categories:

Education, science and technology	53%	£38,000
Arts and culture	28%	£20,000
Medical and disability	10%	£7,000
Community and welfare	8%	£5,600
Children and youth	1%	£500
Environment		£350

A list of beneficiaries was not included in the accounts. Previous beneficiaries have included: Community Security Trust, Kings College London, The National Gallery, Royal Opera House Foundation, New Israel Fund, Beaminster Festival, Army Benevolent Fund and Dorset Children's Hospice.

Applications

In writing to the correspondent at any time.

Information gathered from:

Accounts; annual report; Charity Commission record.

The Michael Harry Sacher Trust

General, with a preference for arts, education, animal welfare, Jewish, health and social welfare

£72,000 (2011/12)

Beneficial area

UK and overseas.

Correspondent: The Trustees, c/o H. W. Fisher and Co., Acre House, 11–15 William Road, London NW1 3ER (tel: 020 7388 7000)

Trustees: Nicola Shelley Sacher; Michael Harry Sacher.

CC Number: 288973

The trust was established in 1984 and makes donations to registered charities which support a wide range of causes. Grants are only made to charities known personally to the trustees and generally range from £250 to £30,000.

In 2011/12 the trust had assets of £2.3 million and an income of £73,000. Grants were made to 24 organisations totalling £72,000 and were broken down into the following categories:

Children and youth	31%	£22,000
Arts and culture	19%	£14,000
Education	15%	£11,000
Community and welfare	10%	£7,500
Overseas aid	9%	£6,700
General	5%	£3,500
Health	5%	£3,300
Religion	5%	£3,200
Animal welfare	1%	£500

A list of beneficiaries was not included in the accounts. Previous beneficiaries have included: British Friends of the Art Museums of Israel, National Gallery Trust, Jewish Care, Nightingale House,

Jeremy and John Sacher Charitable Trust, Whale and Dolphin Conservation Society, The Mariinsky Theatre Trust and Venice in Peril.

Exclusions

No grants to individuals or organisations which are not registered charities.

Applications

In writing to the correspondent.

Information gathered from:

Accounts; Charity Commission record.

The Sackler Trust

Arts and culture, science, medical

£443,500 (2012)

Beneficial area

UK.

Correspondent: Mr Christopher Mitchell, Trustee, 9th Floor, New Zealand House, 80 Haymarket, London SW1Y 4TQ (tel: 020 7930 4944)

Trustees: Dame Theresa Sackler; Peter Stormonth Darling; C. B. Mitchell; R. M. Smith; Marissa Sackler; Sophia Dalrymple; Michael Sackler; Marianne Mitchell.

CC Number: 1132097

In 2012 the trust had assets of £51.7 million, due to substantial donations over recent years, and an income of £7.5 million. Grants were made totalling £443,500.

Beneficiaries included: Garden Museum (£100,000); The Prince's Foundation for Children and the Arts (£75,000); Watts Gallery (£60,000); Amnesty International (£50,000); The Charleston Trust Centenary Project (£35,000); and Houghton Hall and Commonwealth Youth Orchestra (£25,000 each).

Applications

In writing to the correspondent.

Information gathered from:

Accounts; Charity Commission record.

The Ruzin Sadagora Trust

Jewish causes

£454,000 (2011/12)

Beneficial area

UK and Israel.

Correspondent: Rabbi I. M. Friedman, Trustee, 269 Golders Green Road, London NW11 9JJ (tel: 020 8806 9514)

Trustees: Rabbi I. M. Friedman; Sara Friedman.

CC Number: 285475

The charity funds the cost, upkeep and activities of The Ruzin Sadagora Synagogue in London. The charity also funds and supports the parent and other associated and affiliated Sadagora institutions and other religious Jewish causes and charities.

In 2011/12 the trust had assets of £412,000, an income of £516,000 and made grants totalling £454,000. Support costs were £60,000. The trust's accounts were without a list of grants.

Previous grant beneficiaries include: Beth Israel Ruzin Sadagora (£196,000); Friends of Ruzin Sadagora (£180,000); Beth Kaknesset Ohr Yisroel (£91,600); Mosdos Sadigur (£40,000); Yeshivas Torah Temimah (£9,000); Chevras Moaz Lodol (£6,500); Pardes House (£2,000).

Applications

In writing to the correspondent.

Information gathered from:

Accounts; Charity Commission record.

The Jean Sainsbury Animal Welfare Trust

Animal welfare

£311,000 (2012)

Beneficial area

UK registered charities.

Correspondent: Mrs Madeleine Orchard, Administrator, PO Box 469, London W14 8PJ (tel: 020 7602 7948; email: orchardjswelfare@gmail.com; website: jeansainsburyanimalwelfare.org.uk)

Trustees: Colin Russell; Gillian Tarlington; James Keliher; Mark Spurdens; Adele Sparrow; Valerie Pike; Michelle Francine Allen.

CC Number: 326358

The trust was established in 1982 with the objective of benefiting and protecting animals from suffering. The policy of the trustees is to support smaller charities concerned with the following areas:

- Benefiting or protecting animals
- Relieving animals from suffering
- Conserving wild life
- Encouraging the understanding of animals

The Trust favours applications from smaller animal welfare charities registered in the UK and working in the UK or abroad:

- Which have at least one set of up-to-date annual accounts available for inspection
- Which demonstrate an active re-homing and rehabilitation policy for animals taken into their care
- Involved with conservation of wildlife, when the rescue, rehabilitation and (where possible) the release of animals is their main aim

Please note: the Trust expects all applicants to be charities registered with the Charity Commission unless their annual income is under £5,000.

The Trust aims to support UK registered charities by making donations toward the following:

- General running costs associated with the rescue, rehabilitation and re-homing of domestic, wild and exotic animals
- Feeding, capture, neutering and release of feral cats
- Assistance with vet's fees and neutering costs of animals owned by those on low incomes
- Donations towards capital purchases involving land, buildings, vehicles, equipment and educational material. The Trustees may pledge funds up to a maximum of £50k towards large capital building projects, which will only be released when all other funding is in place and the work is ready to commence.
- Donations toward the purchase or improvement of property or fixed buildings are only considered if:
  1. the property is clearly in the ownership of the charity, or
  2. at least 10 years is left to run on the charity's lease, or
  3. a letter from the landowner states that the charity will be reimbursed for the improvements on sale of the property or at the end of the lease. Otherwise, support for improvements can only be considered when they do not increase the saleable value of the property

There are two subsidiary funds:

- The Joyce Evelyn Shuman Bequest – animal rescue work overseas including rehoming and the neutering of feral cats and dogs; working equines and endangered species where the rehabilitation and release of the animals is the main aim
- The Colin Russell Award – given to one charity each year

In 2012 the trust had assets of £13 million, an income of £391,000 and made grants totalling £311,000. This total comprised of £281,000 given to charities working in the UK and £31,000 to UK charities working overseas

Beneficiaries included: All Creatures Great and Small (£30,000); North Clwyd Animal Rescue (£20,000); RVC Beaumont Sainsbury Animal Hospital (£15,000); Doris Banham Dog Rescue (£10,000); Southern Wildlife Animal Rescue (£7,000); Mayhew Animal Home, Caring for Cats – Yorkshire and Humber and Scratching Post (£5,000); South Yorkshire English Springer Spaniel Rescue (£4,000); Gambia Horse and Donkey Trust and Wildlife Vets International (£3,000 each); RSPCA Cardiff and District (£2,000); and Friends of the Tsunami Animal People Alliance (£500).

Exclusions

No grants are given to charities which:

- Are mainly engaged with the preservation of specific species of wild animals
- Have available reserves equal to more than one year's running costs (unless it can be demonstrated that reserves are being held for a designated project)
- Are offering sanctuary to animals, with no effort to re-home, foster or rehabilitate
- Do not have a realistic policy for animals that cannot be given a reasonable quality of life
- Are involved with assistance animals such as hearing dogs for the deaf, riding for the disabled
- Spend more than a reasonable proportion of their income on administration or cannot justify their costs per animal helped
- Are registered outside the UK

No support is given to veterinary schools (unless the money can be seen to be directly benefiting the type of animals the trust would want to support). No individuals are supported.

Applications

On a form available from the correspondent or to download from the trust's website. Applicants should complete and return nine copies of the form, their latest set of audited accounts and any other information which may be relevant to the application. Note: the trust requests that you do not send originals as these cannot be returned.

There are three trustees' meetings every year, usually in March, July and November and applications should be submitted by 15 January, 15 May and 15 September respectively. Further application information and policy guidelines are available by visiting the trust's website.

Information gathered from:

Accounts; Charity Commission record; funder's website.

Saint Luke's College Foundation

Research or studies in theology

£129,000 to organisations (2011/12)

Beneficial area

UK and overseas, with some preference for Exeter and Truro.

Correspondent: Dr David Benzie, Director, 15 St Maryhaye, Tavistock, Devon PL19 8LR (tel: 01822 613143; email: director@st-lukes-foundation.org.uk; website: www.st-lukes-foundation.org.uk)

Trustees: Prof. Mark Overton; The Bishop Of Exeter; Prof. Grace Davie; Dr Barbara Wintersgill; Dr Michael Wykes; David Cain; Alice Hutchings; Dick Powell; The Revd Dr David Rake; Very Revd Dr Jonathan Draper; Dr Karen Stockham; Phillip Mantell.

CC Number: 306606

This foundation encourages original work and imaginative new projects in theology. It supports St Luke's Chapel and funds the post of St Luke's Chaplain at Exeter University. It also supports the subject of Theology at Exeter and regional initiatives in ministerial formation.

Other awards are made in two main areas:

- *Corporate awards* are made to departments of theology and RE in universities, colleges and other agencies operating at university level, to enhance their capacity to provide theological and religious education. The awards are usually small and short-term and, consequently, priority is given to pump-priming initiatives and other such situations where, if the initiative proves itself, it may enable the grant-holder to demonstrate success to bodies which engage in longer-term funding. Occasionally the trustees make major awards.
- *Personal awards* are made to support individuals who are studying Theology or RE; or who are undertaking research leading to a Masters' degree or PhD in these fields. Around a third of the foundation's income is spent in this way.

In 2011/12 the foundation had assets of £3.8 million and an income of £184,000. Grants were made totalling £150,000, including £21,000 in personal awards.

Beneficiaries included: University of Exeter Dept of Theology (£28,000); Exeter Diocesan Board of Education (£15,000); University College Plymouth St Mark and St John (£13,000); National Association of Teachers of Religious Education (£2,800); and South West Youth Ministries (£720).

Exclusions

Funding is not available for building work or to provide bursaries for institutions to administer. Schools are not supported directly (although support is given to teachers who are taking eligible studies). Grants are not normally made for periods in excess of three years.

Applications

From 1 January each year, applicants can request an application pack from the correspondent. Applications are considered once a year and should be received by 1 May for grants starting in September.

Percentage of awards given to new applicants: between 20% and 30%.

Common applicant mistakes

'They don't look at the funding criteria!'

Information gathered from:

Accounts; Charity Commission record; further information provided by the funder; funder's website.

Saint Sarkis Charity Trust

Armenian churches and welfare, offenders

£148,000 (2011/12)

Beneficial area

UK and overseas.

Correspondent: Louisa Hooper, Secretary to the Trustees, 50 Hoxton Square, London N1 6PB (tel: 020 7012 1408; email: info@saintsarkis.org.uk; website: www.saintsarkis.org.uk)

Trustees: Martin Sarkis Essayan; Boghos Parsegh (Paul) Gulbenkian; Rita Vartoukian; Robert Brian Todd.

CC Number: 215352

The Saint Sarkis Charity Trust funds the following organisations:

- The Armenian Church of Saint Sarkis in London
- The Gulbenkian Library at the Armenian Patriarchate in Jerusalem
- Registered charities concerned with the Armenian community in the UK and/or overseas
- UK-registered charities developing innovative projects to support prisoners in the UK and so reduce the rates of re-offending; in particular, the trust is interested in helping people with short-term sentences to cope on their release from prison, women offenders and the families of offenders. The trust is no longer accepting unsolicited applications for this purpose

In 2011/12 the trust had assets of £7.9 million, an income of £245,000 and gave grants totalling £148,000.

The beneficiaries were: Armenian Church of St Sarkis (£35,000); Oxfam (£25,000); Lankelly Chase Foundation (£20,000); Centre for Armenian Information and Advice and Armenian Patriarchate (re Jerusalem Library) (£16,000 each); Tufenkian Foundation (£13,000); PRIME (£10,000); London Armenian Poor Relief (£8,500); Read Together (£5,200); and University of London (£300).

Exclusions

The trust does not give grants to:

- Individual applicants
- Organisations that are not registered charities
- Registered charities outside the UK, unless the project benefits the Armenian community in the UK and/or overseas

The trust does not fund:

- General appeals
- Core costs or salaries (as opposed to project costs)
- Projects concerning substance abuse
- Medical research

Applications

In writing to the correspondent. There is no standard application form so applicants should write a covering letter including the following:

- An explanation of the exact purpose of the grant
- How much is needed, with details of how the budget has been arrived at
- Details of any other sources of income (firm commitments and those still being explored)
- The charity registration number
- The latest annual report and audited accounts
- Any plans for monitoring and evaluating the work

Note: The trust is no longer accepting unsolicited applications for prisoner support projects.

Percentage of awards given to new applicants: between 10% and 20%.

Common applicant mistakes

'Not reading the guidelines on [our] website properly.'

Information gathered from:

Accounts; Charity Commission record; further information provided by the funder; funder's website.

The Saintbury Trust

General

£172,000 (2012)

Beneficial area

West Midlands and Warwickshire (which the trust considers to be postcode areas B, CV, DY, WS and WV), Worcestershire, Herefordshire and Gloucestershire (postcode areas WR, HR and GL).

Correspondent: Mrs J. P. Lewis, Trustee, P. O. Box 464, Abinger Hammer, Dorking, Surrey RH4 9AF (tel: 01306 730119; email: saintburytrust@btinternet.com)

Trustees: Victoria K. Houghton; Anne R. Thomas; Jane P. Lewis; Amanda E. Atkinson-Willes; Harry O. Forrester; C. E. Brogan.

CC Number: 326790

The trust gives grants for general charitable purposes, although the trust deed states that no grants can be given to animal charities. Grants are made to registered charities in Gloucestershire, West Midlands and Worcestershire. Areas of work include addiction, arts and leisure, care of the dying, childhood and youth, community work, disability, education, environment, health, heritage, homelessness, old age, other special needs and prisons.

In 2012 the trust had assets of £6.3 million, an income of £222,000 and gave 58 grants totalling £172,000.

Beneficiaries included: Enham (£25,000); Rehabilitation for Addicted Prisoners Trust and Alzheimer's Research Trust (£10,000 each); Birmingham Bach Choir (£6,000); Birmingham Boys' and Girls' Union and Emmaus (£5,000 each); Birmingham Settlement and Wildfowl and Wetlands Trust (£4,000 each); University Hospital Birmingham (£3,000); The Refugee and Migrant Centre and Hearing Dogs for Deaf People (£2,000 each); and The ASHA Centre, Sport 4 Life and Warley Woods Community Trust (£1,000 each).

Exclusions

No grants to animal charities, individuals (including individuals seeking sponsorship for challenges in support of charities), 'cold-calling' national charities or local branches of national charities. The trust only gives grants to charities outside of its beneficial area if the charity is personally known to one or more of the trustees.

Applications

In writing to the correspondent. Applications are considered in twice a year, usually in April and November.

Information gathered from:

Accounts; Charity Commission record.

The Saints and Sinners Trust

General but in practice mainly welfare and medical

£251,000 (2012)

Beneficial area

Mostly UK.

Correspondent: N. W. Benson, Trustee, Lewis Golden and Co., 40 Queen Anne Street, London W1G 9EL (tel: 020 7580 7313)

Trustees: N. W. Benson; Sir Donald Gosling; David Edwards; I. A. N. Irvine.

CC Number: 200536

This trust supports welfare and medical causes through the proceeds of its fundraising efforts. In 2012 the trust had assets of £80,000 and an income of £97,000, mainly from receipts from a golf tournament. Grants totalled £251,000.

Beneficiaries included: The Crimestoppers Trust (£128,000); The Gosling Foundation (£41,000); Marine Conservation Society and South Bucks Riding for the Disabled (£5,000 each); National Talking Newspapers and Magazines (£3,000); Police Rehabilitation Trust, Cowes Sea Cadets and The Stroke Association (£2,000 each); and International Childcare Trust, UCanDoIT and Sandy Gail's Afghanistan Appeal (£1,000 each).

Exclusions

No grants to individuals or non-registered charities.

Applications

Applications are not considered unless nominated by members of the club.

Information gathered from:

Accounts; Charity Commission record.

The Salamander Charitable Trust

Christian, general charitable purposes

£73,000 (2011/12)

Beneficial area

Worldwide.

Correspondent: Kate Douglas, The Old Rectory, 5 Stamford Road, South Luffenham, Oakham, Leicestershire LE15 8NT

Trustees: Sheila M. Douglas; Alison Hardwick; Phillip Douglas.

CC Number: 273657

Founded in 1977, the principal objects of the trust are the:

- The relief and assistance of poor and needy persons of all classes, irrespective of colour, race or creed
- The advancement of education and religion
- The relief of sickness and other exclusively charitable purposes beneficial to the community

In 2011/12 the trust had assets of almost £1.6 million and an income of £94,000. Grants were made to 100 organisations totalling £73,000, ranging from £250 to £2,500. A list of beneficiaries was not available.

Previous beneficiaries have included: SAT-7 Trust, All Nations Christian College, All Saints in Branksome Park, Birmingham Christian College, Christian Aid, Churches Commission on overseas students, FEBA Radio, International Christian College, London Bible College, Middle East Media, Moorland College,

St James Parochial Church Council in Poole, SAMS, Trinity College and Wycliffe Bible Translators.

Exclusions

No grants to individuals. Only registered charities are supported.

Applications

The trust's income is fully allocated each year, mainly to regular beneficiaries. The trustees do not wish to receive any further new requests.

Percentage of awards given to new applicants: less than 10%.

Information gathered from:

Accounts; Charity Commission record; further information provided by the funder.

Salters' Charitable Foundation

General, with project grants focused specifically on the environment, citizenship and community development and health

£192,000 (2011/12)

Beneficial area

Greater London and the UK.

Correspondent: Ms Vicky Chant, Charities Development Manager, The Salters' Company, Salters' Hall, 4 Fore Street, London EC2Y 5DE (tel: 020 7588 5216; email: charities@salters.co.uk; website: www.salters.co.uk)

Trustee: The Salters' Company.

CC Number: 328258

The foundation makes donations for a range of charitable purposes including, children and young people, health, homelessness, the developing world, the environment and members of the armed forces. Priority is given to funding small nationwide charities and organisations connected with the City of London, where the trust's contribution would make a 'real difference'. As a livery company, the trust pays particular attention to charities a liveryman is involved with. Many beneficiaries have received grants over a number of years.

The trust has two main grantmaking programmes:

- *Project grants* – three year grants of up to £20,000 are available. The foundation is currently prioritising the environment, citizenship and community development health and relief of need as areas of focus for its project grant support
- *General support* – a limited amount of small donations (up to £3,000) are available as general grants outside of the project grant programme. Applicants must have the support of a member of the Salters' Company to be eligible

In 2011/12 the trust had assets of £661,000, an income of £513,000 and made grants totalling £192,000, broken down as follows:

Project grants	8	£91,000
City of London	9	£23,000
Medical	5	£9,800
Armed Forces	5	£7,400
Masters' discretionary fund	7	£5,000
Children, schools and youth	1	£4,000
Environment/developing countries	2	£2,500
Homelessness	1	£2,000
Subscriptions	3	£900
Other donations	8	£16,000

Beneficiaries included: Mental Health Foundation (£18,000); Excellent Development Ltd (£17,000); Target Tuberculosis (£15,000); Drapers' Charitable Fund (£10,000); The Guildhall School Trust (£7,500); Arkwright Scholarships Trust (£4,000); The Passage (£2,000); The Royal Navy Benevolent Trust and Rehabilitation for Addicted Prisoners Trust (£1,500 each); and WWF UK (£500).

Exclusions

See the foundation's guidelines for information on restrictions.

Applications

Applicants must follow the relevant Guidelines ('Project Grant' or 'General Support') depending on the type of grant they are requesting:

- *Project grant* applicants need to fill in an application form, available from the foundation's website when the programme is open. The last deadline passed in January 2011
- *General support* applicants need to submit a covering letter, supporting document and annual report and accounts

Applications can be made via email or post. All supported organisations are regularly reviewed and visited by the Charities Development Manager, members of the Charity Committee and other interested parties within the Company.

Information gathered from:

Accounts; Charity Commission record; funder's website.

The Andrew Salvesen Charitable Trust

General

Around £1.3 million (2011/12)

Beneficial area

UK, with a preference for Scotland.

Correspondent: The Trustees, c/o Meston Reid and Co., 12 Carden Place, Aberdeen AB10 1UR (tel: 01224 625554; email: info@mestonreid.com)

Trustees: A. C. Salvesen; Ms K. Turner; V. Lall.

SC Number: SC008000

The trust gives grants for general charitable purposes; in particular it will support the arts, education/training, medical sciences and welfare of people who are young, elderly or ill.

In 2011/12 the trust had an income of £642,000 and an expenditure of £1.3 million.

Previous beneficiaries have included: Bield Housing Trust, William Higgins Marathon Account, Multiple Sclerosis Society in Scotland, Royal Zoological Society of Scotland, Sail Training Association, Scottish Down's Syndrome Association and Sick Kids Appeal.

Exclusions

No grants to individuals.

Applications

The trustees only support organisations known to them through their personal contacts. The trust has previously stated that all applications sent to them are 'thrown in the bin'.

Information gathered from:

OSCR record.

Basil Samuel Charitable Trust

General charitable purposes

£398,000 (2011/12)

Beneficial area

Worldwide, in practice, mainly UK.

Correspondent: Mrs Coral Samuel, Trustee, Smith and Williamson, 25 Moorgate, London EC2R 6AY (tel: 020 7131 4376)

Trustees: Coral Samuel; Richard M. Peskin.

CC Number: 206579

The trust was established in 1959 for such charitable purposes as the trustees decide, either in the UK or elsewhere. The trust describes its activities as making grants to medical, socially supportive, educational and cultural charities plus a number of donations to other charities.

In 2011/12 the trust had assets of £9.8 million, an income of £388,000 and gave 47 grants totalling £398,000. Grants were categorised as follows:

Medical/socially supportive	£206,000
Cultural	£140,000
Educational	£52,000

Beneficiaries included: Macmillan Cancer Support (£48,000); Historic Royal Palaces, National Hospital for Neurology and Neurosurgery and Westminster Abbey Foundation (£25,000 each); Jewish care (£10,000); Chair Lifeline Cancer Care, London's Air Ambulance and The Samaritans (£5,000 each); Medical Engineering Resource Unit, National Association of Deafened People and The Migraine Trust (£2,000 each); and Friends of the Elderly and The National Autistic Society (£1,000 each).

Exclusions

Grants are given to registered charities only.

Applications

In writing to the correspondent. The trustees meet on a formal basis annually and more frequently on an informal basis to discuss proposals for individual donations.

Information gathered from:

Accounts; Charity Commission record; further information provided by the funder.

The M. J. Samuel Charitable Trust

General, Jewish

£102,000 (2011/12)

Beneficial area

UK and overseas.

Correspondent: Mrs Lindsay Sutton, Secretary, Mells Park, Mells, Frome, Somerset BA11 3QB (tel: 020 7402 0602)

Trustees: Hon. Michael Samuel; Hon. Julia A. Samuel; Viscount Bearsted.

CC Number: 327013

The trust supports a wide range of causes, many of them Jewish, environmental or to do with mental health.

In 2011/12 the trust had assets of £3.5 million, an income of £101,000 and made grants totalling £102,000.

Beneficiaries of grants of £1,000 or more included: The Game and Wildlife Conservation Trust (£30,000); Oxfam (£25,000); Fact Check (£15,000); Spey Foundation (£10,000); Dress for Success London (£3,000); Osteoporosis Society (£2,000); Kindwood College Appeal (£1,500); and Mells Church of England School and The Anna Freud Centre (£1,000 each).

In addition 13 other donations were made to institutions of less than £1,000 each, totalling £4,000.

Exclusions

No grants to individuals.

Applications

In writing to the correspondent. The trustees have regular contact during the year to consider recommendations for, and make final decisions on, the awarding of grants.

Information gathered from:

Accounts; Charity Commission record.

The Peter Samuel Charitable Trust

Health, welfare, conservation, Jewish care

£92,000 (2011/12)

Beneficial area

UK, with some preference for local organisations in South Berkshire, Highlands of Scotland and East Somerset.

Correspondent: Miss Jenny Dance, Administrator, The Estate Office, Farley Hall, Castle Road, Farley Hill, Berkshire RG7 1UL (tel: 01189 730047; email: pa@farleyfarms.co.uk)

Trustees: Hon. Viscount Bearsted; Hon. Michael Samuel.

CC Number: 269065

The trust was established in 1975 and supports medical sciences, Jewish concerns, heritage, forestry/land restoration and the quality of life in local areas (south central Berkshire, east Somerset and the highlands of Scotland). The Hon Michael Samuel is also a trustee of: Col. Wilfred Horatio Micholls Deceased Charitable Trust Fund (Charity Commission no. 267472); The Hon. A. G. Samuel Charitable Trust (Charity Commission no. 1090481); The M. J. Samuel Charitable Trust (Charity Commission no. 327013); and The Peter Samuel Royal Free Fund (Charity Commission no. 200049).

In 2011/12 the trust had assets of £3.9 million, an income of £113,000 and gave grants totalling £92,000.

Beneficiaries included: The Game and Wildlife Conservation Trust and Marie Curie Cancer Care (£10,000 each); Anna Freud Centre (£7,000); Child Bereavement Trust (£6,000); Oxfam (£5,000); Community Security Trust and World Jewish Relief (£2,000 each); The Countryside Foundation for Education and Highland Hospice (£1,000 each); and Connexions Thames Valley and Anthony Nolan (£500 each).

Exclusions

No grants to purely local charities outside Berkshire or to individuals.

Applications

In writing to the correspondent. Trustees meet twice-yearly.

Information gathered from:

Accounts; Charity Commission record.

Coral Samuel Charitable Trust

General, with a preference for educational, cultural and socially supportive charities

£143,000 (2011/12)

Beneficial area

UK.

Correspondent: Mrs Coral Samuel, Trustee, c/o Smith and Williamson, 25 Moorgate, London EC2R 6AY (tel: 020 7131 4376)

Trustees: Coral Samuel; Peter Fineman.

CC Number: 239677

This trust was established in 1962 and makes grants to educational, cultural and socially supportive charities, plus a number of other charities.

In 2011/12 the trust had assets of £5.2 million and an income of £211,000. Grants were made to 30 organisations totalling £143,000, broken down as follows:

Cultural	£82,000
Medical/socially supportive	£41,000
Educational	£20,000

Beneficiaries included: Historic Royal Palaces (£25,000); The Foundation of the College of St George (£12,000); Glyndebourne Arts Trust (£10,000); Academy of St Martin-in-the-Fields, Jewish Music Institute and The Royal Horticultural Society (£5,000); Save Britain's Heritage (£2,000); Chicken Shed Theatre Co. and The Hertford House Trust (£1,000 each); and Museum of London (£500).

Exclusions

Grants are only made to registered charities.

Applications

In writing to the correspondent.

Information gathered from:

Accounts; Charity Commission record.

The Sandhu Charitable Foundation

General

£212,000 (2011/12)

Beneficial area

Worldwide.

Correspondent: The Trustees, First Floor, Santon House, 53–55 Uxbridge Road, Ealing, London W5 5SA (tel: 020 3478 3900; email: nsteele@thesantongroup.com)

Trustees: Bim Sandhu, Chair; Sean Carey.

CC Number: 1114236

The foundation was established in 2006 as a focus for the philanthropic activities of Bim and Pardeep Sandhu and their family.

In 2011/12 it had an income of £650,000 and assets stood at £4.5 million at year end. The trustees made 34 grants totalling £212,000.

Beneficiaries included: Variety, The Children's Charity (£32,500); Anne Frank Trust (£20,500); Magic Bus UK (£20,000); Latymer Foundation (£10,000); Choices Ealing, Coram, Enterprise Education Trust, Friendship Works Listening Books, Smile Train UK, Tree of Hope Children's Charity and The Ear Foundation (£5,000 each); Cystic Fibrosis and RNLI (£4,000 each); and EveryChild and Sightsavers (£3,000 each).

Applications

The charity supports individual charities or charitable causes, mainly on a single donation basis, which the trustees identify.

Information gathered from:

Accounts; Charity Commission record.

The Sants Charitable Trust

General

£57,000 (2011/12)

Beneficial area

UK.

Correspondent: The Trustees, 17 Bradmore Road, Oxford OX2 6QP (tel: 01865 310813)

Trustees: Alexander Sants; Caroline Sants; Hector W. H. Sants; John H. Ovens.

CC Number: 1078555

Registered with the Charity Commission in December 1999, the trust has general charitable purposes.

In 2011/12 the trust had assets of £1.1 million, an income of £99,000 and gave 19 grants totalling £57,000.

Beneficiaries included: Holy Trinity Brompton (£26,000); William Wilberforce Trust (£10,000); Children in Crisis, Family Links and Footsteps Foundation (£5,000 each); Wings (£3,000); Harry Mahon Cancer Research Trust and Tube Station (£1,000 each); trinity College (£300); and The Boxing Academy (£100).

Applications

In writing to the correspondent.

Information gathered from:

Accounts; Charity Commission record.

The Scarfe Charitable Trust

Churches, arts, music, environment

£110,000 (2011/12)

Beneficial area

UK, with an emphasis on Suffolk.

Correspondent: Eric Maule, Trustee, Salix House, Falkenham, Ipswich, Suffolk IP10 0QY (tel: 01394 448339; fax: 01394 448339; email: ericmaule@hotmail.com)

Trustees: Sean McTernan; Eric Maule; John McCarthy.

CC Number: 275535

The trust was established in 1978 by W S N Scarfe and supports mainly art and musical projects and the restoration of churches in Suffolk.

In 2011/12 the trust had assets of £1.2 million, an income of £57,000 and gave grants totalling £110,000.

Beneficiaries included: Aldeburgh Music (£8,000); Gainsborough's House and Woodbridge Tide Mill (£2,500); Aldeburgh Young Musicians (£1,800); East Anglia's Children's Hospices, John Peel Centre for Creative Arts and Suffolk Wildlife Trust (£1,000 each); Rosemary Hinton and Happy Days (£750 each); Canine Partners and Royal Northern College of Music (£500 each); Action on Hearing Loss, SCOPE and The Salvation Army (£375 each); St Peters Parochial Church Council (£200); and Friends of the Royal Academy (£90).

Applications

In writing to the correspondent by post or email. The trustees meet quarterly to consider applications. They will not respond to correspondence unless it relates to grants it has agreed to make.

Percentage of awards given to new applicants: between 10% and 20%.

Information gathered from:

Accounts; Charity Commission record; further information provided by the funder.

The Schapira Charitable Trust

Jewish, health, education

£639,000 (2011/12)

Beneficial area

UK.

Correspondent: Mr Isaac Yehuda Schapira, Trustee, 2 Dancastle Court, 14 Arcadia Avenue, Finchley, London N3 2JU (tel: 020 8371 0381; email: londonoffice@istrad.com)

Trustees: Isaac Y. Schapira; Michael Neuberger; Suzanne L. Schapira.

CC Number: 328435

This trust was established in 1989 and has a policy of supporting Jewish organisations and general health and education causes.

In 2011/12 the trust had assets of £6 million, an income of £215,000 and made grants totalling £639,000.

Beneficiaries included: British Friends of the Rabbi Meir Baal Hanes Charity (Kollel Shromrel Hachomos) (£136,000); The New Rachmistrivke Synagogue Trust (£91,000); Emuno Educational Centre Ltd (£84,000); Kahal Chassidim Boboy (£33,000); Friends of Mir (£22,000); Keren Association Ltd (£17,000); United Jewish Israel Appeal (£10,000); Rowanville Ltd (£8,400); Entindale Ltd (£5,500); Yeshivas Lev Simcha Ltd (£2,000); and Friends of Sanz Institutions (£1,000).

Applications

In writing to the correspondent.

Information gathered from:

Accounts; Charity Commission record.

The Annie Schiff Charitable Trust

Orthodox Jewish education

£115,000 (2011/12)

Beneficial area

UK, overseas.

Correspondent: Joseph Pearlman, Trustee, 8 Highfield Gardens, London NW11 9HB (tel: 020 8458 9266)

Trustees: Joseph Pearlman; Ruth Pearlman.

CC Number: 265401

The trust's objectives are:

- Relief of poverty, particularly amongst the Jewish community

- Advancement of education, particularly the study and instruction of Jewish religious literature
- Advancement of religion, particularly Judaism

In 2011/12 the trust had assets of £86,000 and an income of £63,000. Grants to 22 organisations totalled £115,000.

Grant recipients included: Friends of Beis Yisrael Trust and Menorah Grammar School Trust (£15,000 each); Elanore Ltd (£10,000); WST Charity Ltd (£8,000); Friends of Ohel Moshe (£6,000); Tifres High School, EMET and Yesamech Levav Trust (£5,000 each); North West Separdish Synagogue (£3,000); British Friends of Nadvorne (£1,500); Golders Charitable Trust (£1,100); Beth Jacob Grammar School for Girls Ltd (£1,000); and Ezra U'Marpeh (£500).

Exclusions

No support for individuals and non-recognised institutions.

Applications

In writing to the correspondent. Grants are generally made only to registered charities.

Information gathered from:

Accounts; Charity Commission record.

The Schmidt-Bodner Charitable Trust

Jewish, general

£241,000 (2011/12)

Beneficial area

UK and overseas.

Correspondent: Harvey Rosenblatt, Trustee, 5 Fitzhardinge Street, London W1H 6ED (tel: 020 7486 3111)

Trustees: Harvey Rosenblatt; Daniel Dover; Martin Paisner.

CC Number: 283014

This trust mainly supports Jewish organisations although it has also given a few small grants to medical and welfare charities.

In 2011/12 the trust had assets of £2.2 million and an income of £42,000. Grants were made to 14 organisations totalling £241,000.

The largest grants went to: Nightingale House (£60,000); and Menorah High School for Girls and Oak Family UK (£50,000 each).

Other beneficiaries included: World Jewish Relief (£15,500); Prostate Action (£10,000); and Chabad Lubavich UK, the Prince's Trust and United Jewish Israel Appeal (£5,000 each).

Applications

In writing to the correspondent. 'All applications received are considered by the trustees on their own merit for suitability of funding.'

Information gathered from:

Accounts; Charity Commission record.

The R. H. Scholes Charitable Trust

General, including children and young people who have disabilities or are disadvantaged, hospices, preservation and churches

Around £20,000

Beneficial area

England.

Correspondent: Roger Pattison, Trustee, Danehurst Corner, Danehurst Crescent, Horsham, West Sussex RH13 5HS (tel: 01403 263482; email: roger@rogpat.plus.com)

Trustees: Roger Pattison; Henrietta Sleeman.

CC Number: 267023

This trust currently only supports organisations in which the trustees have a special interest, knowledge of, or association with. Both recurrent and one-off grants are made depending upon the needs of the beneficiary. Core costs, project and research grants are made. Funding for more than three years will be considered.

In 2011/12 the trust had an income of £22,500 and a total expenditure of £24,500. Grants were estimated at around £20,000.

Previous beneficiaries included: Church of England Pensions Board, the Friends of Lancing Chapel and National Churches Trust.

Exclusions

Grants only to registered charities. No grants to individuals, animal charities, expeditions or scholarships. The trust tries not to make grants to more than one charity operating in a particular field, and does not make grants to charities outside England.

Applications

The trust has informed us that all of its funds are fully committed and they cannot accept unsolicited applications.

Information gathered from:

Accounts; Charity Commission record.

The Schreiber Charitable Trust

Jewish with a preference for education, social welfare and medical

£250,000 (2011/12)

Beneficial area

UK.

Correspondent: Graham S. Morris, Trustee, PO Box 35547, The Exchange, 4 Brent Cross Gardens, London NW4 3WH (tel: 020 8457 6500; email: graham@schreibers.com)

Trustees: Graham Morris; David A. Schreiber; Sara Schreiber.

CC Number: 264735

In 2011/12 the trust had an income of £311,000 and a total expenditure of £273,500. Grants were estimated at around £250,000.

Previous beneficiaries included: Friends of Rabbinical College Kol Tora, Jerusalem Foundation, SOFT, Gateshead Talmudical College, Dalaid Ltd and Aish Hatorah UK Ltd.

Applications

The trust states that the trustees 'regularly appraise new opportunities for direct charitable expenditure and actively seek suitable causes to reduce the unrestricted fund to the appropriate level'.

Information gathered from:

Accounts; Charity Commission record.

Schroder Charity Trust

General

£159,500 (2011/12)

Beneficial area

Worldwide, in practice mainly UK.

Correspondent: Sally Yates, Secretary, 81 Rivington Street, London EC2A 3AY

Trustees: Claire Fitzalan Howard; Charmaine Mallinckrodt; Bruno Schroder; T. B. Schroder; Leonie Fane; Frederick Schroder.

CC Number: 214050

The trust was established in 1944 by the Schroder banking family, and it continues to be governed by members of the family and associates. It supports a wide range of charitable causes in the areas of health and welfare, community, education, international relief and development, young people, arts, culture and heritage, the environment and rural issues. Preference is given to UK registered charities with a proven track record and those in which the trust has a special interest.

In 2011/12 the trust had assets of just under £7.5 million and an income of £201,000. Grants were made to 100 organisations totalling £159,500. All grants were for £5,000 or less.

Beneficiaries included: Army Benevolent Fund; Alzheimer's Research UK; Asperger's Syndrome Foundation; Civil Liberties Trust; Country Holidays for Inner City Kids; Foundation for Social Improvement; Game Conservancy Trust; Listening Books; National Youth Theatre; Raleigh International Trust; Samaritans; Toynbee Hall UK; and the Young Women's Christian Association (YWCA).

Exclusions

No grants to individuals.

Applications

In writing to the correspondent. Applicants should briefly state their case and enclose a copy of their latest accounts or annual review. Requests will be acknowledged in writing. The trust does not have the capacity to correspond with organisations on the progress of their application. Therefore, if you have not heard from the trust after six months, you can assume that the application has not been successful.

Information gathered from:

Accounts; Charity Commission record.

Scott (Eredine) Charitable Trust

Service and ex-service charities, medical, welfare

£250,000 (2012)

Beneficial area

UK.

Correspondent: Keith Bruce-Smith, Trustee, Harcus Sinclair, 3 Lincoln's Inn Fields, London WC2A 3AA (tel: 020 7242 9700)

Trustees: Lt Col. Michael Scott; Keith Bruce-Smith; Amanda Scott.

CC Number: 1002267

Set up in 1999, in 2012 the trust held assets of £232,000 and an income of £259,000. Grants were made to 61 organisations totalling £250,000.

Beneficiaries included: Scots Guards Charitable Trust (£52,000); Hampshire Youth Options (£10,000); Combat Stress and King Edward VII's Hospital for Officers (£5,500 each); Combined Services Disabled Ski Team (£5,000); Taste For Adventure Centre (£4,000); Tusk Trust (£3,000); RNLI (£2,000); and Malawi Trust Boat (£1,000).

Applications

In writing to the correspondent.

Information gathered from:

Accounts; Charity Commission record.

Sir Samuel Scott of Yews Trust

Medical research

£205,000 (2011/12)

Beneficial area

UK.

Correspondent: The Secretary, c/o Currey and Co., 21 Buckingham Gate, London SW1E 6LS (tel: 020 7802 2700)

Trustees: Lady Phoebe Scott; Hermione Stanford; Edward Perks.

CC Number: 220878

In 2011/12 the trust had assets of £5.8 million and an income of £107,000. Grants were made to 33 organisations totalling £205,000.

As in previous years, the largest grants was made to the Gray Institute at the University of Oxford (£106,500).

Other beneficiaries included: Cure Parkinson's Trust and Diabetes UK (£10,000 each); Alzheimer's Research UK and the Motor Neurone Disease Association (£5,000 each); British Lung Foundation (£4,000); Leukaemia and Lymphoma Research (£3,000); Blond McIndoe Research Foundation and the National Eye Research Centre (£2,000 each); and the British Council for Prevention of Blindness and the Inspire Foundation (£1,000 each).

Exclusions

No grants for: core funding; purely clinical work; individuals (although research by an individual may be funded if sponsored by a registered charity through which the application is made); research leading to higher degrees (unless the departmental head concerned certifies that the work is of real scientific importance); medical students' elective periods; or expeditions (unless involving an element of genuine medical research).

Applications

In writing to the correspondent. Trustees hold their half-yearly meetings in April and October. Applications have to be submitted two months before. There are no special forms, but applicants should give the following information: the nature and purpose of the research project or programme; the names, qualifications and present posts of the scientists involved; reference to any published results of their previous research; details of present funding; and if possible, the budget for the next 12 months or other convenient period.

All applications are acknowledged and both successful and unsuccessful applicants are notified after each meeting of the trustees. No telephone calls.

Information gathered from:

Accounts; Charity Commission record.

The Scouloudi Foundation

General charitable purposes

£188,500 (2012/13)

Beneficial area

UK charities working domestically or overseas.

Correspondent: The Trustees, c/o Haysmacintyre, 26 Red Lion Square, London WC1R 4AG (tel: 020 7969 5500; fax: 020 7969 5600)

Trustees: Sarah Baxter; David Marnham; James Sewell.

CC Number: 205685

The foundation has three types of grants:

- Historical grants are made each year to the Institute of Historical Research at University of London for fellowships, research and publications, to reflect the interests of the settlor, Irene Scouloudi, who was a historian
- Regular grants, generally of £1,300 each, are made to organisations on a five-year cycle
- Special grants are one-off grants in connection with capital projects

In 2012/13 the foundation had assets of £6.1 million and an income of £223,000. Grants were made totalling £188,500, broken down as follows:

Humanities	£81,000
Disability	£21,500
Medicine, health and hospices	£21,500
Children and young people	£15,000
Famine relief and overseas aid	£14,000
Social welfare	£12,500
Environment	£9,000
Armed forces and sailors	£9,000
Older people	£6,500

By far the largest donation was a historical grant made to the University of London – Institute of Historical Research (£72,000).

Other grants included those made to: Friends of the Elderly; British Institute for Brain Injured Children; Straight Talking Peer Education; Campaign to Protect Rural England; Campaign to Protect Rural England; Crossroads Caring for Carers; British Records Association; and Help the Hospices (£1,250 each).

Exclusions

Donations are not made to individuals, and are not normally made for welfare activities of a purely local nature. The rustees do not make loans or enter into leeds of covenant.

Applications

Only historical grants are open to application. Copies of the regulations and application forms for 'Historical Awards' can be obtained from: The Secretary, The Scouloudi Foundation Historical Awards Committee, c/o Institute of Historical Research, University of London, Senate House, Malet Street, London WC1E 7HU.

Information gathered from:

Accounts; Charity Commission record.

Seamen's Hospital Society

Seafarers and their dependents

£328,000 to organisations (2012)

Beneficial area

UK.

Correspondent: Peter Coulson, General Secretary, 29 King William Walk, Greenwich, London SE10 9HX (tel: 020 8858 3696; fax: 020 8293 9630; email: admin@seahospital.org.uk; website: www.seahospital.org.uk)

Trustees: Jeffery C. Jenkinson; Peter McEwan; Rupert Chichester; Alexander R. Nairne; Capt. Colin Stewart; Dr Charlotte Mendes da Costa; Capt. Duncan Glass; Mark Carden; Comm. Frank Leonard; Max Gladwyn; Graham Lane.

CC Number: 231724

The Seamen's Hospital Society was founded in 1821 by a group of philanthropists in response to the increasing number of homeless and impoverished seafarers living on the streets of London after the Napoleonic wars. By then the Mercantile Marine, as it was known, was clearly demarcated from the Royal Navy but had none of the Navy's medical services to support its men. The health of the sailors in the merchant service had been almost totally neglected.

It was in response to this neglect that, in 1817–18, a group of philanthropists established a charity for distressed seamen. Originally called the Society for Distressed (Destitute) Seamen, in 1821 it became the Seamen's Hospital Society.

The society makes grants to medical, care and welfare organisations working with seafarers and to individual seafarers and their dependents. The following information is taken from the funder's website:

Who can apply?

Any maritime organisation with charitable status may apply to the Seamen's Hospital Society for funding in support of activities that relate to the health and welfare needs of seafarers. Sometimes we fund projects run by non-charitable organisations, but only in exceptional circumstances.

Please contact us by phone, email or letter and ask for an application form.

When can we apply?

Grant application forms and instructions are circulated every summer to those who request them. They are considered during the autumn and grants are normally awarded in December. In exceptional circumstances grant applications may be considered at other times.

In 2012 the charity had assets of just over £7.8 million and an income of £462,000. Grants were made to nine organisations totalling £328,000. Grants directly benefiting individuals totalled £146,000.

As in previous years, the largest grant went to the Seafarers' Advice and Information Line (£230,000), which the society operates to help provide free confidential advice and information on welfare benefits, housing, consumer problems, legal matters, credit and debt, matrimonial and tax.

The other beneficiaries were: Nautilus Welfare Fund (£32,500); MCFG Development Programme (£30,000); Merchant Seamen's War Memorial Society (£17,500); Royal National Mission to Deep Sea Fishermen (£10,000); Scottish Nautical Welfare Society (£3,000); Apostleship of the Sea and Queen Victoria Seamen's Rest (£2,500 each); and Annual National Service for Seafarers (£150). The society mostly supports the same organisations each year, although this may reflect the application received from relevant organisations rather than a specific policy.

Applications

On a form available from the correspondent. Applicants are encouraged to contact the correspondent before making application.

Common applicant mistakes

'Incomplete information.'

Information gathered from:

Accounts; Charity Commission record; further information provided by the funder; funder's website.

The Searchlight Electric Charitable Trust

General

Around £65,000 (2011/12)

Beneficial area

UK, with a preference for Manchester.

Correspondent: H. E. Hamburger, Trustee, Searchlight Electric Ltd, 900 Oldham Road, Manchester M40 2BS (tel: 01612 033300; email: heh@slightdemon.co.uk)

Trustees: D. M. Hamburger; H. E. Hamburger; M. E. Hamburger.

CC Number: 801644

This trust has general charitable purposes, although most grants are given to Jewish organisations. A large number of grants are made in the Manchester area.

In 2011/12 the trust had an income of £19,000 and a total expenditure of £69,000. No further financial information was available but based upon previous years grants probably totalled around £65,000.

Previous beneficiaries include: UJIA; CST; Bnei a Kivah Sefer Torah; Guide Dogs for the Blind; Young Israel Synagogue; the Federation; Langdon College; Heathlands; Lubavitch Manchester; Manchester Eruv Committee; Reshet and the Purim Fund; Sense; Nightingales and Chabad Vilna.

Exclusions

No grants for individuals.

Applications

In writing to the correspondent, but note that in the past the trustees have stated that it is their policy to only support charities already on their existing list of beneficiaries or those already known to them.

Percentage of awards given to new applicants: less than 10%.

Information gathered from:

Accounts; Charity Commission record; further information provided by the funder.

The Searle Charitable Trust

Youth development with a nautical basis

£54,000 (2011/12)

Beneficial area

UK.

Correspondent: Sarah Sharkey, 30 Watling Street, St Albans, Hertfordshire AL1 2QB

Trustees: Andrew D. Searle; Victoria C. Searle.

CC Number: 288541

This trust was established in 1982 by Joan Wynne Searle. Following the death of the settlor in 1995 the trust was split into two. One half is administered by the son of the settlor (Searle Charitable Trust) and the other half by her daughter (Searle Memorial Trust).

The Searle Charitable Trust only supports projects/organisations for youth development within a nautical framework.

In 2011/12 the trust had assets of £3.8 million and an income of £88,000. One grant was awarded during the year, to the Rona Sailing Project, which received £54,000. This charity is the main regular beneficiary, although small grants are occasionally made to other charities.

Exclusions

No grants for individuals or for appeals not related to sailing.

Applications

In writing to the correspondent.

Information gathered from:

Accounts; Charity Commission record.

The Seedfield Trust

Christian, relief of poverty

£90,000 (2012)

Beneficial area

Worldwide.

Correspondent: Janet Buckler, Trustee, 3 Woodland Vale, Lakeside, Ulverston, Cumbria LA12 8DR (tel: 01539 530359)

Trustees: Paul Vipond; Keith Buckler; David Ryan; Janet Buckler; Valerie James; Eric Proudfoot.

CC Number: 283463

The trust's main objects are the furthering of Christian work and the relief of poverty. The trust rarely makes grants towards core funding or for activities that may require funding over a number of years, preferring to make one-off grants for projects which are also receiving support from other sources.

In 2012 the trust had assets of £2.5 million and an income of £111,000. Grants were made to 61 organisations totalling £90,000.

Beneficiaries included: Overseas Missionary Fellowship (£8,000); George Muller Charitable Trust (£5,000); Gideons International (£3,000); International Nepal Fellowship and Scripture Union (£2,000 each); Bible Study and Evangelism Fellowship, Church Urban Fund, Light for the Blind and Toy Box (£1,000 each).

Exclusions

No grants to individuals.

Applications

In writing to the correspondent, for consideration by the trustees who meet twice each year. Enclose an sae for acknowledgement.

Percentage of awards given to new applicants: between 10% and 20%.

Common applicant mistakes

'Requesting excessively large grants.'

Information gathered from:

Accounts; Charity Commission record; further information provided by the funder.

Leslie Sell Charitable Trust

Scout and guide groups

£87,500 (2011/12)

Beneficial area

UK, with some preference for the Bedfordshire, Hertfordshire and Buckinghamshire area.

Correspondent: Sharon Long, Secretary, Ashbrittle House, 2a Lower Dagnall Street, St Albans, Hertfordshire AL3 4PA (tel: 01727 843603; fax: 01727 843663; email: admin@iplLtd.co.uk; website: www.lesliesellct.org.uk)

Trustees: Mary Wiltshire; Adrian Sell; Nicola Coggins.

CC Number: 258699

Established in 1969 by the late Leslie Baden Sell, the trust mainly supports scout and guide groups. Most grants are made towards small projects such as building repair works, transport or equipment. Grants are also available to individuals and groups making trips in the UK and overseas.

In 2011 the trust set up the Peter Sell Annual Award, in memory of Peter Sell, a trustee and later chair of the Leslie Sell Charitable Trust who died in 2007. The award will give up to £5,000 to a project aimed at widening engagement and involvement in scouting and guiding.

In 2011/12 the trust had assets totalling £3.1 million and an income of £141,000. Grants were made totalling £87,500.

Applications

On an application form available from the trust's website. Applications should include clear details of the project or purpose for which funds are required, together with an estimate of total costs and details of any funds raised by the group or individual for the project. The trust states that: 'Applications are usually treated sympathetically provided they are connected to the Scouting or Guide movement'.

Applications to the Peter Sell Annual Award usually have to be submitted by the end of September. See the trust's website for full guidelines and future deadlines.

Percentage of awards given to new applicants: between 20% and 30%.

Common applicant mistakes

'They do not give sufficient detail of their project.'

Information gathered from:

Accounts; Charity Commission record; further information provided by the funder; funder's website.

Sellata Ltd

Jewish, welfare

£115,000 (2011/12)

Beneficial area

UK.

Correspondent: Eliezer Benedikt, Trustee, 29 Fountayne Road, London N16 7EA

Trustees: Eliezer Benedikt; Nechy Benedikt; Pinchas Benedikt; Joseph Stern.

CC Number: 285429

The charity supports the advancement of religion and the relief of poverty. In 2011/12 it had assets of £340,000 and an income of £246,000. Grants were made totalling £115,000. A list of beneficiaries was not available.

Applications

In writing to the correspondent.

Information gathered from:

Accounts; Charity Commission record.

SEM Charitable Trust

General, with a preference for educational special needs and Jewish organisations

£131,000 (2011/12)

Beneficial area

Mainly South Africa, Israel and UK.

Correspondent: David Ashman, The Trustees, Reeves and Co. LLP, 37 St Margaret's Street, Canterbury, Kent CT1 2TU (tel: 01227 768231; email: david.ashman@reeves.co)

Trustees: Sarah Radomir; Michael Radomir; David Wolmark.

CC Number: 265831

The trust operates in two main ways:

- Supporting and operating educational and training initiatives in South Africa
- Making ad hoc grants to organisations in the UK and Israel, particularly those supporting educational special needs

In 2011/12 the trust had assets of £960,000 and an income of £46,000. Grants were made totalling £131,000. A further £14,000 was spent on the trust's Diversity Camps.

By far the largest grant went to Natal Society for Arts (£65,000).

Other beneficiaries included: Africa Ignite (£7,400); Avon Riding Centre (£5,000); Disabled on Line Ltd and Magen David Adom UK (£3,000 each); Downs Syndrome Association, Dressability, Keren Laham, Manchester Jewish Community Care and Rutland House (£2,000 each); Friends of the Elderly, Garden Science and Lotem Limady Teva Meshulavium (£1,000 each); and The fifth Trust; Talking with Hands and Haifa LGBT Forum (£500 each).

Exclusions

No grants to individuals.

Applications

In writing to the correspondent.

Information gathered from:

Accounts; Charity Commission record.

The Seneca Trust

Social welfare, education, children and young people

£79,000 (2012)

Beneficial area

UK.

Correspondent: Natalie Wade, Trustee, c/o Aurum Fund Management, Ixworth House, 37 Ixworth Place, London SW3 3QH (tel: 020 7589 1130; fax: 020 7581 1780; email: ir@aurumfunds.com)

Trustees: Tatjana May; Adam Sweidan; Natalie Wade.

CC Number: 1137147

The trust was established in 2010 to support social welfare and education, with a particular emphasis on children and young people who are disadvantaged through disability, ill health or lack of education. The settlors of the trust are Kevin Gundle, co-founder of Aurum Funds Ltd and also a trustee of Absolute Return for Kids (ARK), and his wife Deborah, who amongst other things has been involved in publishing and film production – her most recent venture is NetBuddy (www.netbuddy.org.uk), an online resource offering tips, help and advice for parents and carers of children with learning disabilities.

In 2012 the trust had assets of £33,000 and an income of £106,000. Grants were made to ten organisations and two individuals totalling £79,000. A list of beneficiaries was not included in the accounts.

Applications

In writing to the correspondent.

Information gathered from:

Accounts; Charity Commission record.

The Ayrton Senna Foundation

Children's health and education

£0 (2012)

Beneficial area

Worldwide, with a preference for Brazil.

Correspondent: Christopher Bliss, Trustee, 8th Floor, 6 New Street Square, London EC4A 3AQ (tel: 020 7842 2000)

Trustees: Viviane Lalli; Milton Guerado Theodoro da Silva; Neyde Joanna Senna da Silva; Leonardo Senna da Silva; Christopher Bliss; Stephen Howard Ravenscroft.

CC Number: 1041759

The trust was established in 1994 by the father of the late Ayrton Senna, in memory of his son, the racing driver. The trust was given the whole issued share capital of Ayrton Senna Foundation Ltd, a company set up to license the continued use of the Senna trademark and copyrights. The trust supports the relief of poverty and the advancement of education, religion and health, particularly the provision of education, healthcare and medical support for children.

In 2012 the foundation had assets of £572,000, with an income of £108,500. Again, in this accounting year, the foundation did not make any charitable donations (£2.8 million in 2009). There is no indication in either the trustees' report or the accounts as to why no donations were made during the course of 2012.

Exclusions

No grants to individuals.

Applications

In writing to the correspondent.

Information gathered from:

Accounts; Charity Commission record.

The Seven Fifty Trust

Christian causes

£65,000 (2011/12)

Beneficial area

UK and worldwide.

Correspondent: Revd Andrew Cornes, Trustee, All Saints Vicarage, Church Road, Crowborough, East Sussex TN6 1ED (tel: 01892 667384)

Trustees: Revd Andrew Cornes; Katherine Cornes; Cannon Jonathan Clark; Mary Clark.

CC Number: 298886

This trust is for the advancement of the Christian religion in the UK and throughout the world.

In 2011/12 it had assets of £1.9 million and an income of £82,000. Grants were made totalling £65,000.

Beneficiaries included: All Saints Church (£21,000); St Matthew's Church (£6,000); Universities and Colleges Christian Fellowship (£4,500); Overseas Missionary Fellowship (£3,500); and Care for the Family (£2,500).

Exclusions

No support for unsolicited requests.

Applications

Unsolicited applications will not be considered.

Information gathered from:

Accounts; Charity Commission record.

The Cyril Shack Trust

Jewish, general

£124,000 (2011/12)

Beneficial area

UK.

Correspondent: The Clerk, c/o Lubbock Fine, Chartered Accountants, Russell Bedford House, City Forum, 250 City Road, London EC1V 2QQ (tel: 020 7490 7766)

Trustees: Jonathan Shack; Cyril Shack.

CC Number: 264270

In 2011/12 the trust had assets of £699,500 and an income of £118,000. Grants were made totalling £124,000.

A list of grants was not available. Previous beneficiaries have included Finchley Road Synagogue, Nightingale House and St John's Wood Synagogue.

Exclusions

No grants for expeditions, travel bursaries, scholarships or to individuals.

Applications

In writing to the correspondent.

Information gathered from:

Accounts; Charity Commission record.

The Jean Shanks Foundation

Medical research and education

£315,000 (2012/13)

Beneficial area

UK.

Correspondent: Paula Price-Davies, Administrator, Peppard Cottage, Peppard Common, Henley on Thames, Oxon RG9 5LB (email: administrator@jeanshanksfoundation.org; website: www.jeanshanksfoundation.org)

Trustees: Eric Rothbarth; Prof. Andrew Carr; Alistair Jones; Dr Julian Axe; Prof. Adrienne Flanagan; Prof. Sir James Underwood.

CC Number: 293108

Registered with the Charity Commission in November 1985, the foundation supports medical research and education, particularly in the area of pathology. Grants are made to fund medical students who wish to have an extra research year at medical school and also to other research projects the trustees consider worthwhile.

In 2012/13 the foundation had assets of £17.8 million and an income of £286,000. Grants were made to 27 institutions totalling £315,000.

Beneficiaries included: Royal College of Pathologists (£70,000); University of Oxford (£24,000); University of Cambridge (£21,000); University of Nottingham (£20,000); University of Birmingham, University of Manchester, University of Cardiff, University of Liverpool and Brighton and Sussex Medical School (£9,000 each); and University of Dundee (£5,500).

Exclusions

No grants for capital items. No grants for research which is already supported by another grant giving body or for projects of the type normally dealt with by bodies such as the MRC or Wellcome Trust.

Applications

In writing to the correspondent. Full grant guidelines are available on the foundation's website.

Information gathered from:

Accounts; Charity Commission record; funder's website.

The Shanley Charitable Trust

Relief of poverty

£155,000 (2011/12)

Beneficial area

Worldwide.

Correspondent: Steve Atkins, Trustee, Knowles Benning Solicitors, 32 High Street, Shefford, Bedfordshire SG17 5DG (tel: 01462 814824)

Trustees: C. A. Shanley; Roger Lander; Steve Atkins.

CC Number: 1103323

The trustees make grants to recognised international charities that operate for the relief of poverty.

In 2011/12 the trust had assets of £3 million and an income of £582,000, which included a donation of £500,000 from Bellcross Company Ltd, of which one of the trustees, C A Shanley, is a director. Grants were made to three organisations totalling £155,000.

The beneficiaries were: Water Aid (£100,000); Save the Children (£40,000); and Self Help Africa (£15,000).

Applications

In writing to the correspondent.

Information gathered from:

Accounts; Charity Commission record.

The Shanti Charitable Trust

General, Christian, international development

£37,000 (2011/12)

Beneficial area

UK, with preference for West Yorkshire, and developing countries (especially Nepal).

Correspondent: Barbara Gill, Trustee, Parkside, Littlemoor, Queensbury, Bradford, West Yorkshire BD13 1DB

Trustees: Barbara Gill; Andrew Gill; Ross Hyett.

CC Number: 1064813

This trust is a long-term supporter of the International Nepal Fellowship, although other funding is given. The trustees state that most of the beneficiaries are those which they already have links with.

In 2011/12 it had assets of £128,500 and an income of £34,000. Grants were made to seven organisations totalling £37,000.

Beneficiaries were: International Nepal Fellowship (£10,500); St John's Church (£9,000); Protac/Theotac, Nepal (£8,000); Development Associates International (£6,500); St John's Under 5's (£1,750); Marie Curie (£1,000); and Emmaus UK (£500).

Applications

In writing to the correspondent. Note, most beneficiaries are those the trustees already have contact with.

Information gathered from:

Accounts; Charity Commission record.

The Linley Shaw Foundation

Conservation

£60,000 (2011/12)

Beneficial area

UK.

Correspondent: The Trust Section, NatWest Trust Services, 5th Floor, Trinity Quay 2, Avon Street, Bristol BS2 0PT (tel: 0551 657 7371)

Trustee: National Westminster Trust Services.

CC Number: 1034051

The foundation supports charities working to conserve, preserve and restore the natural beauty of the UK countryside for the public benefit.

Generally the trustees prefer to support a specific project, rather than give money for general use. In his will, Linley Shaw placed particular emphasis on those charities which organise voluntary workers to achieve the objects of the foundation. This may be taken into account when considering applications. Grants can be given towards any aspect of a project. Previous examples include the cost of tools, management surveys and assistance with the cost of land purchase.

In 2011/12 the trust had an income of £247,000, mainly from assets sales. Grants were made to 17 organisations totalling £60,000 and ranging in value from £500 to £13,000.

Grant beneficiaries were: Protect Rural England, The National Trust, Cornwall Wildlife Trust, Nottinghamshire Wildlife Trust, Pond Conservation: The Water Habitats Trust, Moor Trees, John Muir

Trust, The Conservation Volunteers, Leicestershire and Rutland Wildlife Trust, Bardon Mill and Henshaw CVH Project Group, Campaign to Protect Rural England, Derbyshire Wildlife Trust.

Exclusions

No grants to non-charitable organisations, or to organisations whose aims or objects do not include conservation, preservation or restoration of the natural beauty of the UK countryside, even if the purpose of the grant would be eligible. No grants to individuals.

Applications

Applications must be in writing to the correspondent. All material will be photocopied by the trust so avoid sending 'bound' copies of reports and so on. Evidence of aims and objectives are needed, usually in the forms of accounts, annual reports or leaflets, which cannot be returned.

> Regular meeting are held by the Trustees where they discuss any applications received and consider which grants they wish to award.

Information gathered from:

Accounts; Charity Commission record.

The Shears Foundation

Health, education, children, arts, culture, recreation, heritage, conservation, environment

£610,500 (2011/12)

Beneficial area

Northumberland, Tyne and Wear, Durham and West Yorkshire.

Correspondent: Trevor Halliday Shears, Trustee, 35 Elmfield Road, Gosforth, Newcastle upon Tyne NE3 4BA

Trustees: Trevor Shears; Peter Shears; Lyn Shears; Patricia Shears; G. Lyall.

CC Number: 1049907

The foundation was established in 1994 by Trevor and Lyn Shears following the sale of their transport company. The foundation's annual report states that it 'aims to fund selected organisations and projects in the fields of community development, environmental issues, sustainable development, health and welfare and cultural development, all with an emphasis on education and raising awareness. There is also a proportion devoted to overseas projects in the same fields'.

In 2011/12 the foundation had assets of £11.2 million and an income of £494,000. There were 32 grants made totalling £610,500.

Beneficiaries included: Community Foundation for Tyne and Wear and Northumberland (£100,000 for the Linden Fund and £50,000 for the Local Environmental Action Fund); Alnwick Garden (£60,000); Whitley Fund for Nature (£50,000); and Samling Foundation and Bradford Grammar School (£30,000 each).

Exclusions

No grants for domestic animal welfare or religious organisations.

Applications

In writing to the correspondent.

Information gathered from:

Accounts; Charity Commission record.

The Sheldon Trust

General charitable purposes

£221,000 (2011/12)

Beneficial area

West Midlands.

Correspondent: The Trust Administrator, Pothecary Witham Weld Solicitors, 70 St George's Square, London SW1V 3RD (tel: 020 7821 8211; email: charities@pwwsolicitors.co.uk; website: www.pwwsolicitors.co.uk/funding-applications/8-the-sheldon-trust)

Trustees: A. Bidnell; Revd R. S. Bidnell; J. K. R. England; Mrs R. Beatton; Mrs R. Gibbins; Paul K. England.

CC Number: 242328

The trust's geographical area of giving is the West Midlands, with particular emphasis on the areas of Birmingham, Coventry, Dudley, Sandwell, Solihull, Wolverhampton and Warwickshire. The main aims continue to be the relief of poverty and distress in society. The trustees review their policy and criteria regularly. The trust merged with the Malcolm Chick Charity in 2013 and is keeping under review prospects for further mergers in order to reduce overheads costs.

The main purpose of the Sheldon Trust is to relieve poverty and distress in society, especially in deprived areas, by providing grants to registered charities working with disadvantaged people in the following four areas (taken from the trust's website):

> **Aims**
>
> 1. Community Projects*: primarily community-based organisations, run by local volunteers, perhaps with some paid staff. They would be addressing identified local needs of a community nature.
>
> 2. Special Needs Groups*: needs including age, health or learning issues which put them at a disadvantage within society.
>
> 3. Youth Development**: programmes which address the needs of 16–25 year olds, especially those not in education, employment or training. While individuals will not be supported directly, the trustees will encourage applications from programmes which encourage individual young people to expand their experiences and challenge their capacities.
>
> 4. Holidays for disadvantaged people***: Applications for this category are considered in the spring only and require a separate application form, which can be accessed on the trust's website and should be submitted by the end of April to be considered. The average value of these grants is £600.
>
> *West Midlands with particular emphasis on the following areas: Birmingham City, Coventry City, Dudley, Sandwell, Solihull, Wolverhampton and the County of Warwickshire. National charities wishing to apply under categories 1 and 2 may only do so where they have a branch in one or more of the defined areas which is responsible for its own financial management and fundraising and can provide separate accounts.
>
> **Nationally
>
> ***West Midlands or Greater London
>
> **Types of grants**
>
> The trustees fund projects, salaries, equipment, furnishings, refurbishments and running costs. The trustees do not consider appeals in respect of the cost of purchasing buildings or vehicles.
>
> Where appropriate, the trustees are prepared to consider multi-year grants, up to three years.
>
> The trustees may put aside a portion of their income for grants for special projects of which they have personal knowledge or an organisation which they have supported in the past.

In 2011/12 the trust had assets of £3.9 million and an income of £196,000. Grants were made to 47 organisations totalling £221,000. The average grant, excluding holiday funding, was £5,000.

Beneficiaries included: Action in the Community Trust (£31,000); Worth Unlimited and Rona Sailing School (£10,000 each); Cruise Bereavement Care – Coventry and Warwickshire (£9,000); The Spring Playgroup (£7,500); Yeldall Christian Centre (£5,000); Inclusion4U (£3,000); and Bag Books (£2,000).

Exclusions

No grants to charities with an income over £1 million and/or free unrestricted reserves to the value of more than six months of their annual expenditure.

Applications

Applications should be submitted online, via the trust's website. Trustees meet twice a year to consider applications, in March and September. Applications should usually be submitted two months prior to the meeting, although trustees may stop considering applications once sufficient numbers are received so sending applications early is advised. Precise deadlines are posted on the website.

Holiday applications differ from the other schemes. Application forms are made available online from the beginning of March and are usually accepted until late April/early May. Exact deadlines are posted on the website. Applications must include:

> A copy of the organisation's most recent signed accounts; a budget for the project for the current financial year; and, if the application envisages a salary, a job description. These documents can be uploaded at the end of the online application form. Applications will not be considered until all the relevant documentation has been received.
>
> The trust does not accept draft accounts. Please do not send any other information as it will be discarded.
>
> All applicants will be informed of the funding decision within 7 days of the Trustees meeting. Successful applicant will receive confirmation of the grant offer and any related conditions. Please do not contact the office before this time.
>
> Unsuccessful applicants can re-apply after two years. Successful applicants will not be considered for a period of two years following receipt of a grant (or final payment of repeat funding).

Information gathered from:

Accounts; Charity Commission record; funder's website.

The Patricia and Donald Shepherd Charitable Trust

General charitable purposes particularly those involving young people

£124,000 (2011/12)

Beneficial area

Worldwide, particularly the north of England and Scotland.

Correspondent: The Trustees, 5 Cherry Lane, Dringhouses, York YO24 1QH

Trustees: Patricia Shepherd; Iain Robertson; Jane Robertson; Michael Shepherd; Christine Shepherd; Patrick Shepherd; Joseph Shepherd; Rory Robertson; Annabel Robertson.

CC Number: 272948

The trust makes grants through charitable organisations to benefit people in need and society in general. There is a preference for supporting charities in the north of England and Scotland, or those connected with the trustees.

In 2011/12 the trust had assets of £512,000 and an income of £140,500. Grants were made to 168 organisations totalling £124,000.

Grants of £1,000 or more were made to: York Museum Trust (£12,500); Police Treatment Centres, Henshaws Society for the Blind, York Cemetery Trust and York Air Museum (£10,000 each); Special Boat Service Association (£5,000); Marrick Priory (£3,000); North Yorkshire Business and Education Partnership, ABF the Soldier's Charity and Involve Learning Centre (£2,000 each); and York Minster Fund (£1,000).

Applications

In writing to the correspondent.

Information gathered from:

Accounts; Charity Commission record.

The Archie Sherman Cardiff Foundation

Health, education, training, overseas aid, community and Jewish

£139,000 (2011/12)

Beneficial area

UK, Canada, Australia, New Zealand, Pakistan, Sri Lanka, South Africa, India, Israel, USA and other parts of the British Commonwealth.

Correspondent: The Trustees, Rothschild Trust Corp Ltd, New Court, St Swithins Lane, London EC4P 4DU (tel: 020 7280 5000)

Trustee: Rothschild Trust Corporation Ltd.

CC Number: 272225

Established in 1976, this foundation supports health and educational charities in the UK and overseas. The foundation is empowered to distribute its income as it sees fit but it tends to pay special regard to the following organisations: Society of Friends of the Jewish Refugees, UJIA, British Organisation for Rehabilitation and Training, JNF Charitable Trust, British Council of the Shaare Zedek Hospital, British Technion Society and Friends of the Hebrew University.

In 2011/12 the trust had assets of £2.2 million, an income of £69,000 and made grants totalling £139,000, broken down into:

Overseas aid	£115,000
Education and training	£24,000

Beneficiaries were: The Israel Children's Centres (£50,000); Jewish Child's Day (£35,000); JNF Charitable Trust (£30,000); The British Friends of the Bar-Ilan University (£19,000); and British Friends of the Hebrew University of Jerusalem (£5,000).

Exclusions

No grants to individuals.

Applications

In writing to the correspondent.

Information gathered from:

Accounts; Charity Commission record.

The Barnett and Sylvia Shine No. 2 Charitable Trust

General

£55,000 (2011/12)

Beneficial area

Worldwide.

Correspondent: Mr Martin Paisner, Trustee, Berwin Leiton Paisner, Adelaide House, London Bridge, London EC4R 9HA (tel: 020 7760 1000)

Trustees: Martin Paisner; Barbara J. Grahame; Rodney Grahame.

CC Number: 281821

In 1980, half the assets of the No. 1 Charitable Trust (see separate entry) were transferred to the No. 2 Charitable Trust. In 1981, the executors of the estate of the late Sylvia Shine transferred several paintings, jewellery and cash to the trusts. The No. 2 fund has some preference for organisations working with children and young adults, the elderly and people with disabilities.

In 2011/12 the trust had assets of £1.3 million, an income of £42,000 and made 16 grants to organisations totalling £55,000.

Beneficiaries included: The Samaritans, African Medical and Research Foundation, CAMFED International and Oxfam (£5,000 each); Médecins Sans Frontières and Macmillan Cancer Support (£3,000 each); and British Shalom-Salaam Trust, Children's Country Holidays Fund, NSPCC and UNICEF (£2,000 each).

Exclusions

No grants to individuals.

Applications

In writing to the correspondent. The trustees consider applications at formal and informal meetings.

Information gathered from:

Accounts; Charity Commission record.

The Bassil Shippam and Alsford Trust

Young and older people, health, education, learning disabilities, Christian

£75,500 to organisations (2011/12)

Beneficial area

UK, with a preference for West Sussex.

Correspondent: Iain MacLeod, Administrator, Thomas Eggar LLP, The Corn Exchange, Baffins Lane, Chichester, West Sussex PO19 1GE (tel: 01243 786111; fax: 01243 775640)

Trustees: John Shippam; Christopher Doman; Molly Hanwell; Simon MacFarlane; John Shippam; Richard Tayler; Susan Trayler; Stanley Young; Janet Bailey.

CC Number: 256996

This trust supports charities active in the fields of care for young and older people, health, education and religion. Many of the organisations supported are in West Sussex.

In 2011/12 the trust had assets of just under £3.8 million and an income of £145,000. Grants were made totalling £75,500, and were broken down as follows:

Furtherance of education	£41,000
Social welfare	£30,500
Performing arts	£2,500
Welfare of people in financial need	£1,000
Medical research	£750

Most grants were for less than £1,000. Beneficiaries of larger grants included: Chichester Boys' Club (£8,000); St Wilfrid's Hospice (£5,000); West Wittering Village Hall (£2,500); and the Tall Ships Trust (£1,000).

Grants were also made to individuals totalling £4,700.

Applications

In writing to the correspondent, including a copy of the latest set of reports, accounts and forecasts. The trustees meet three times a year to consider applications.

Information gathered from:

Accounts; Charity Commission record.

The Shipwrights' Company Charitable Fund

Maritime or waterborne connected charities

£86,000 (2011/12)

Beneficial area

UK, with a preference for the City of London.

Correspondent: The Clerk, Ironmongers' Hall, Shaftesbury Place, Barbican, London EC2Y 8AA (tel: 020 7606 2376; fax: 020 7600 8117; email: clerk@shipwrights.co.uk; website: www.shipwrights.co.uk)

Trustees: The Worshipful Company of Shipwrights; William Everard; Simon Sherrard; Sir Jock Slater; Simon Robinson; Graham Clarke; Archibald Smith.

CC Number: 262043

The Shipwrights' Company is a livery company of the City of London and draws its members from all the various aspects of marine commerce and industry in the UK. Its charitable interests therefore focus on the maritime, with an emphasis on young people, church work and the City.

Applications from individuals or, for example, schools to join sail training voyages are considered. A particular interest is support of sailing for people with disabilities.

In 2011/12 the trust had assets of £2.6 million and an income of £151,000. Grants were made to 25 organisations totalling £86,000. Most beneficiaries are supported on a regular basis.

Beneficiaries included: Tall Ships Youth Trust (£20,000 for bursaries); George Green's School (£14,500 in 3 grants); Marine Society and Sea Cadets (£13,000); Jubilee Sailing Trust (£5,000 for bursaries); British Maritime Federation (£2,000); and Thames Shipwright and the Ahoy Centre (£1,000 each).

Exclusions

Any application without a clear maritime connection.

Applications

In writing to the correspondent. Application forms and further guidelines are available from the trust's website. Applications are considered in February, June and November.

Percentage of awards given to new applicants: between 20% and 30%.

Information gathered from:

Accounts; Charity Commission record; further information provided by the funder; funder's website.

The Barbara A. Shuttleworth Memorial Trust

People with disabilities

£34,000 (2011/12)

Beneficial area

UK, with a preference for West Yorkshire.

Correspondent: John Baty, Chair, Baty Casson Long, 23 Moorhead Terrace, Shipley BD18 4LB (tel: 01274 584946; email: baty@btinternet.com)

Trustees: John Alistair Baty, Chair; Barbara Anne Shuttleworth; John Christopher Joseph Eaton; William Fenton.

CC Number: 1016117

The trust gives grants to organisations that aim to improve the circumstances of people who are disabled, and particularly those helping children. The trust prefers to make grants for what it calls 'hard' benefits such as equipment, premises or other permanent facilities but it will consider funding 'soft' benefits like holidays, training courses and visits.

In 2011/12 the trust held assets totalling £510,000 and had an income of £27,000. Grants totalled £34,000.

Beneficiaries included: The Being Bel Trust (£2,500); Whizz-Kidz (£1,900); Hollybank Special School (£1,400); Sunny Day's Children's Fund (£1,000); Making a Difference (£800); Disability Awareness UK, Seeing Ear, Alstrom Syndrome UK and Naomi House Children's Hospice (£500 each); and West Yorkshire ADHD Support Group and Autism Plus (£200 each).

Applications

In writing to the correspondent.

Information gathered from:

Accounts; Charity Commission record.

The Leslie Silver Charitable Trust

Jewish, general

£31,000 (2011/12)

Beneficial area

UK, but mostly West Yorkshire.

Correspondent: Ian J. Fraser, Trustee, R. S. M. Tenon Ltd, 2 Wellington Place, Leeds LS1 4AP (tel: 01132 445451)

Trustees: Leslie H. Silver; Hilary Brosh; Ian J. Fraser.

CC Number: 1007599

This trust principally supports Jewish-based charities and appeal funds launched in the West Yorkshire area.

In 2011/12 the trust had assets of £90,000 and an income of £33,000, mainly from donations. Grants totalled £31,000.

The beneficiaries were: Leeds Jewish Welfare (£10,000); The Zone and UJIA (£5,000 each); Coexistence Trust, Holocaust Centre, Variety Club Leeds and World Jewish Relief (£2,000 each); Donisthorpe Hall (£1,500); Ezer Mizion (£1,000); and Holocaust Education (£500).

Exclusions

No grants to individuals or students.

Applications

Organisation should submit a summary of their proposals 'in a specific format, together with outline appeals.'

Information gathered from:

Accounts; Charity Commission record.

The Simmons and Simmons Charitable Foundation

Social welfare, education

£62,000 (2011/12)

Beneficial area

London, with a preference for the City of London and Tower Hamlets.

Correspondent: The Trustees, Simmons and Simmons LLP, Citypoint, 1 Ropemaker Street, London EC2Y 9SS (tel: 020 7628 2020; fax: 020 7628 2070; email: diversity@simmons-simmons.com; website: www.simmons-simmons.com)

Trustees: Richard Dyton; Michele Anahory; Fiona Loughrey; Colin Passmore.

CC Number: 1129643

The foundation was established by the law firm Simmons and Simmons LLP. The following information is taken from the firm's website:

> The Simmons & Simmons Charitable Foundation was established in 2009 to further our goals in supporting access to justice and opportunities. The foundation is at the core of our pro bono, volunteering and community work, providing a vehicle for all our charitable giving and donations in alignment with the firm's corporate responsibility objectives.
>
> The foundation tends to favour smaller charities where the funding can be shown to make a sustainable impact.
>
> The foundation also prioritises charities in which the firm's staff can have an active involvement and address social inclusion i.e. by helping the less privileged to access financial and educational opportunities.
>
> Examples of charities we have helped are:
>
> ***Battersea Legal Advice Centre***
>
> Thirty volunteers from the firm attend a weekly surgery offering free legal advice to the local community. The volunteers have provided advice to several thousand people from all walks of life who otherwise would not be able to afford a lawyer. Our foundation gives an annual financial contribution towards the running of the centre.
>
> ***Simmons & Simmons Access 2 Law Scheme***
>
> Through our in-house 'Access 2 Law' scheme, Simmons & Simmons lawyers and trainees mentor A-level students at Tower Hamlets College and Crossways College in Lewisham, to encourage and support their aspirations in becoming lawyers. On completion of their A-levels the scheme continues to mentor students and provides further sponsorship throughout their degree and post-graduate qualification to assist them on their journey in qualifying as a solicitor.
>
> ***Pathways to Law***
>
> This is an innovative scheme aimed at widening access to the legal profession and to provide opportunities for students from state schools who are interested in a career in law. Established by the College of Law and the Sutton Trust, the programme targets students from under-represented backgrounds and provides support throughout years 12 and 13, and beyond into university.
>
> ***CSET – City Solicitors' Educational Trust***
>
> The foundation made a donation to CSET whose purpose is to identify and encourage university students from a diverse range of backgrounds to consider a career in the law and to provide financial assistance to university law faculties.

In 2011/12 the foundation had assets of £180,000 and an income of £198,000, which included a donation of £120,000 from Simmons and Simmons. Grants were made to 13 organisations totalling £62,000.

The beneficiaries were: The Mayor's Fund for London and Five Talents UK Ltd (£10,000 each); Bingham Appeal, Red Balloon, Opportunity International UK, Pennies Foundation, Big Issue Foundation and Twist (£5,000 each); Visionpath (£4,000); Stillbirth and Neonatal Death Charity (£2,500); Sunshine Action – Hong Kong (£2,200); Law Society riot helpline (£2,000); and YMCA (£1,000).

£8,000 was also given for the Tower Hamlets Mentoring Scheme.

Applications

On an application form available to download from the firm's website. Completed forms should then be emailed for consideration. The following information is given on the firm's website:

> The foundation meets quarterly and applications are reviewed in terms of how well they align with the criteria and the firm's objectives. Before submitting an application, please check the criteria below.
>
> - The charity/organisation for which the funds have been requested must have proper bookkeeping/accounts and a business case for how the funds will be used
> - The charity/project must be sustainable and any donation from the foundation must make a difference
> - The donation must be consistent with our policy by either:
>   - Creating opportunities for diverse or less privileged sections of society, particularly in regard to widening access to financial education and services
>   - Addressing social inclusion through opening opportunities to education and careers in law to those from less privileged backgrounds
>   - Supporting the rule of law and access to justice
>   - The charity should be local to a Simmons & Simmons office

In the UK donations would be restricted to charities in the City of London and Tower Hamlets areas.

Information gathered from:

Accounts; Charity Commission record; funder's website.

The Simpson Education and Conservation Trust

Environmental conservation

£31,500 (2011/12)

Beneficial area

UK and overseas, with a preference for the neotropics (South America).

Correspondent: Nigel Simpson, Trustee, Honeysuckle Cottage, Tidenham Chase, Chepstow, Gwent NP16 7JW (tel: 01291 689423; fax: 01291 689803)

Trustees: Dr Nigel Simpson, Chair; Prof. Donald Broom; Dr Michael Lock; Prof. Stanley Chang; Dr Katherine Simpson.

CC Number: 1069695

Established in 1998, the main objectives of this trust are:

- The advancement of education in the UK and overseas, including medical and scientific research
- The conservation and protection of the natural environment and endangered species of plants and animals with special emphasis on the

protection of forests and endangered avifauna in the neotropics (South America)

[T]he trust receives its income mainly [f]rom Gift Aid donations, which totalled [£]30,000 in 2011/12. Grants were made [t]otalling £31,500.

[I]ts priority for this year was again to [s]upport the Jocotoco Foundation in [E]cuador (£25,000). This charity is [d]edicated to the conservation of [e]ndangered special birds through the [a]cquisition of forest habitat. The chair of [t]his trust, Dr Nigel Simpson, an expert [i]n ornithology and conservation, is also [o]n the board of trustees for Jocotoco [C]onservation Foundation (JFC).

[O]ther grants were awarded to: RBG Kew [f]or Peru (£3,000); Linnean Society for [T]anzania, Dodwell Trust for Madagascar [a]nd Second Sight Trust for India (£1,000 [e]ach); and Lord Treloar School Trust (£500).

Exclusions

No grants to individuals.

Applications

In writing to the correspondent. The day-to-day activities of this trust are carried out by email, telephone and circulation of documents, since the trustees do not all live in the UK.

Information gathered from:

Accounts; Charity Commission record.

The Simpson Foundation

Roman Catholic purposes

£23,000 (2011/12)

Beneficial area

UK.

Correspondent: Patrick Herschan, Trustee, Pothecary Witham Weld, 70 St George's Square, London SW1V 3RD (tel: 020 7821 8211; fax: 020 7630 6484)

Trustees: Charles Bellord; Peter Hawthorne; Patrick Herschan.

CC Number: 231030

The trust supports charities favoured by the founder, Philip Witham Simpson, during his lifetime and other charities with similar objects, mainly Catholic charities. Only registered charities are supported.

In 2011/12 the trust had assets of £314,000 and an income of £37,500. Grants were made to 23 organisations totalling £23,000.

Beneficiaries included: Sisters of Providence and of the Immaculate Conception (£2,000); Apostleship of the Sea, The Passage and Friends of the Holy Trinity Monastery (£1,000 each); and Cardinal Hume Centre, Stonor Chapel and St Mungo's (£500 each).

Exclusions

No grants to non-registered charities or individuals.

Applications

In writing to the correspondent, at any time. No telephone applications will be considered.

Information gathered from:

Accounts; Charity Commission record.

The Huntly and Margery Sinclair Charitable Trust

General

£42,000 (2011/12)

Beneficial area

UK.

Correspondent: Wilfrid Vernor-Miles, Administrator, Hunters Solicitors, 9 New Square, Lincoln's Inn, London WC2A 3QN

Trustees: Noel Gibbs; Hugh Sherbrooke; Mrs J. Floyd.

CC Number: 235939

This trust has general charitable purposes at the discretion of the trustees. However, the trust states that nearly all grants are made to organisations already known to the trustees so unsolicited applications are rarely successful.

In 2011/12 the trust had assets of £1.3 million, an income of £47,000 and gave grants totalling £42,000.

Beneficiaries included: Injured Jockeys Fund (£5,000); Changing Faces (£4,000); Zetland Foundation (£3,000); Gloucester Cathedral and RNLI Special Appeal (£2,000); Army Benevolent Fund, Eton College, Action Water and Macmillan Cancer Support (£1,000 each); and National Parrot Sanctuary, Elkstone Church and Maggie's Cheltenham (£500 each).

Applications

Unsolicited applications are rarely successful and due to the high number such requests the trust is not able to respond to them or return any printed materials supplied.

Information gathered from:

Accounts; Charity Commission record.

Sino-British Fellowship Trust

Education

£255,500 to organisations (2012)

Beneficial area

UK and China.

Correspondent: Anne Ely, Trustee, Flat 23 Bede House, Manor Fields, London SW15 3LT (tel: 020 8788 6252)

Trustees: Prof. Sir Brian Heap; Ling Thompson; Prof. Hugh Baker; Anne Ely; Peter Ely; Dr Jeremy Langton; Lady Pamela Youde.

CC Number: 313669

The trust makes grants to institutions benefiting individual postgraduate students. It does this through: scholarships to Chinese citizens to enable them to pursue their studies in Britain; grants to British citizens in China to educate/train Chinese citizens in any art, science or profession.

In 2012 the trust had assets of £13.3 million and an income of £470,000. A total of £329,000 was made in grants, which included £255,500 to organisations in the UK and China, with the remainder awarded as individual scholarships.

Grants to institutions included: Royal Society (£51,500); British Library (£22,000); China Scholarship Council (£21,500); Great Britain China Educational Trust (£20,000); Hong Kong University (£15,000); Universities China Committee London (£13,000); Needham Research Institute (£8,000); and Universities China Committee London (£4,000).

Applications

On a form available by writing to the correspondence address.

Information gathered from:

Accounts; Charity Commission record.

The Charles Skey Charitable Trust

General

£88,000 (2011/12)

Beneficial area

UK.

Correspondent: John Leggett, Trustee, Flint House, Park Homer Road, Colehill, Wimborne, Dorset BH21 2SP

Trustees: Christopher Berkeley; John Leggett; Revd James Leggett; David Berkeley; Edward Berkeley; James Carleton.

CC Number: 277697

The trust's annual reports state:

> The trustees support causes on an annual basis, irregularly and on a one-off basis. For those charities receiving annual donations, the amount to be given is reviewed annually. For those receiving periodic donations, the trustees are the judge of when a further grant should be made. For one-off donations, the trustees examine the requests which have been received and have sole authority as to which to support. In general, the trust supports those causes where the grant made is meaningful to the recipient.

In 2011/12 the trust had assets of £3.9 million and an income of £285,000. Grants were made to 28 organisations totalling £88,000.

Beneficiaries included: Lloyds Patriotic Fund (£10,000); Trinity Hospice (£8,500); Roses Charitable Trust (£7,500); Battle of Britain Monument Fund (£5,000); Camphill Village Trust (£4,000); Dagenham Gospel Trust (£3,000); Water Aid (£2,500); Institute of Cancer Research (£1,500); and Rugbeian Society and King Edward VII Hospital for Officers (£1,000 each).

Applications

The trust has previously stated that no written or telephoned requests for support will be entertained.

Percentage of awards given to new applicants: less than 10%.

Information gathered from:

Accounts; Charity Commission record; further information provided by the funder.

The John Slater Foundation

Medical, animal welfare, general

£140,000 (2011/12)

Beneficial area

UK, with a strong preference for the north west of England especially West Lancashire.

Correspondent: Richard Thompson, Trust Manager, HSBC Trust Services, 10th Floor, Norwich House, Nelson Gate, Commercial Road, Southampton SO15 1GX (tel: 02380 722231; fax: 02380 722250; website: johnslaterfoundation.org.uk)

Trustees: D. J. Coke; B. A. Cook; H. Docherty; J. A. W. Doyle; N. G. Hinshelwood; D. J. Nibloe; V. Wales; D. L. Wells. (HSBC. Trust Co. (UK) Ltd.).

CC Number: 231145

The foundation gives grants for £1,000 to £5,000 to a range of organisations, particularly those working in the fields of medicine or animal welfare.

In 2011/12 it had assets of £4 million and an income of £292,500. There were 71 grants made to 38 organisations totalling £140,000.

Beneficiaries included: The Dogs Trust (£10,000); Trinity Hospital Bispham (£9,000); Adlington Community Centre (£8,000); Casterton School (£7,500); Verona Association Thornton Cleveleys and the North West Air Ambulance Trust (£6,000 each); Macmillan Cancer Relief (£5,000); Veterans Aid (£4,000); Cottingley Cornerstone Centre (£3,000); Wildlife Hospital Trust (£2,000); and Blackpool and Flyde Society for the Blind and the Marine Conservation Society (£1,000 each).

Exclusions

No grants to individuals.

Applications

The foundation's website states:

> The foundation is presently fully committed to its programme of giving and unfortunately is not able to receive any further new requests of any nature at this time.
>
> Should this situation change an appropriate announcement will be made on [the foundation's] website.

Information gathered from:

Accounts; Charity Commission record; funder's website.

Rita and David Slowe Charitable Trust

General

£83,000 (2011/12)

Beneficial area

UK and overseas.

Correspondent: The Trustees, 32 Hampstead High Street, London NW3 1JQ (tel: 020 7435 7800)

Trustees: Elizabeth Slowe; Graham Weinberg; Jonathan Slowe; Lilian Slowe; Robert Slowe.

CC Number: 1048209

The trust makes grants to a range of registered charities. In 2011/12 the trust held assets of £1.2 million and had an income of £264,000. Income is derived from holdings in the property and investment firm J Leon Group. Grants were made to eight organisations totalling £83,000.

Grants went to: Computer Aid International (£12,500); and Shelter, Books Abroad, Wells for India, Excellent Development, HERA, Big Issue Foundation and Crisis (£10,000 each). Most beneficiaries are supported on a recurrent basis.

Exclusions

No grants are made to individuals (including gap year students) or religious bodies.

Applications

In writing to the correspondent.

Information gathered from:

Accounts; Charity Commission record.

The SMB Charitable Trust

Christian, general charitable purposes

£238,000 (2011/12)

Beneficial area

UK and overseas.

Correspondent: Mrs Barbara O'Driscoll, Trustee, 15 Wilman Road, Tunbridge Wells, Kent TN4 9AJ (tel: 01892 537301; fax: 01892 618202; email: smbcharitabletrust@googlemail.com)

Trustees: Eric Anstead; Philip Stanford; Barbara O'Driscoll; Jeremy Anstead; Claire Swarbrick.

CC Number: 263814

The trust supports charities which meet one of the following criteria:

- Support of the Christian faith
- Provision of social care in the UK and abroad
- Provision of famine or emergency aid
- Protection of the environment and wildlife
- Support of education or medical research

Grants are generally of £1,000 each, although this can vary. The trustees make regular grants to a large number of 'core' charities, so while new applications are considered, only a small minority is likely to be successful. The founder's preferences are taken into account when deciding which of the applicants will be supported.

In 2011/12 the trust had assets of £8.6 million and an income of £349,000. Grants were made to 200 organisations totalling £238,000.

Beneficiaries included: London City Mission (£4,000); British Red Cross (£3,000); Baptist Missionary Society and Hospice of Hope (£2,500 each); Fegans Child and Family Care, In Golden Company and Leprosy Mission (£2,000 each); University and Colleges Christian Fellowship (£1,500); Torch Trust, World Wildlife Fund, Toybox in Nicaragua and Royal National College for the Blind (£1,000 each).

Exclusions

Grants to individuals are not normally considered, unless the application is made through a registered charity which can receive the cheque.

Applications

In writing to the correspondent, including the aims and principal activities of the applicant, the current financial position and details of any special projects for which funding is sought. Application forms are not used. Trustees normally meet in March, June, September and December and applications should be received before the beginning of the month in which meetings are held. Because of the volume of appeals received, unsuccessful applicants will only receive a reply if they enclose an sae. However, unsuccessful applicants are welcome to reapply.

Information gathered from:

Accounts; Charity Commission record.

The N. Smith Charitable Settlement

General including social work, medical research, education, environment/animals, arts and overseas aid

£143,500 (2011/12)

Beneficial area

Worldwide.

Correspondent: Anne Merricks, Linder Myers, Phoenix House, 45 Cross Street, Manchester M2 4JF (tel: 01618 326972; fax: 01618 340718)

Trustees: Anne Merricks; John Williams-Rigby; Graham Wardle; Janet Adam.

CC Number: 276660

This trust was established in 1978 by the late Miss Nora Smith.

In 2011/12 the trust had assets of £4.1 million and an income of £265,000. There were 152 grants made during the year totalling £143,500 to a wide range of organisations, all but one of which were for £2,000 or less.

Beneficiaries included: Disasters Emergency Committee (£5,000); Oxfam GB, Kidney Research UK and Genesis Appeal (£2,000 each); Epilepsy Research UK and Live Music Now (£1,500 each); and Anthony Nolan Bone Marrow Trust, Just Drop In, Fair Trials International and Pimlico Opera (£1,000 each). Numerous beneficiaries received grants for less than £1,000.

Exclusions

Grants are only made to registered charities and not to individuals.

Applications

In writing to the correspondent. The trustees meet three times a year.

Information gathered from:

Accounts; Charity Commission record.

The E. H. Smith Charitable Trust

General

£20,000 (2011/12)

Beneficial area

UK, some preference for the Midlands.

Correspondent: K. H. A. Smith, Trustee, Westhaven House, Arleston Way, Solihull, West Midlands B90 4LH (tel: 01217 137100)

Trustees: Kenneth Avery Smith; David Ensell.

CC Number: 328313

This trust has general charitable purposes and supports a range of local and national organisations.

In 2011/12 the trust had assets of £193,000, and income of £34,000 and made 60 grants to organisations totalling £20,000.

Beneficiaries included: Bible Learning Centre (£8,000); Hearing Dogs Charity Training Centre (£650); Perrywoods Football Club (£600); and Rubery Football Club (£500).

Other grants of £500 or less totalled £10,000.

Exclusions

No grants to political parties. Grants are not normally given to individuals.

Applications

In writing to the correspondent at any time.

Information gathered from:

Accounts; Charity Commission record.

The Smith Charitable Trust

General charitable purposes

£121,000 (2011/12)

Beneficial area

UK and overseas.

Correspondent: Paul Sheils, Trustee, c/o Moon Beever Solicitors, 24–25 Bloomsbury Square, London WC1A 2PL (tel: 020 7637 0661)

Trustees: A. G. F. Fuller; P. A. Sheils; R. I. Turner; R. J. Weetch.

CC Number: 288570

The trust supports registered charities, which are usually larger well-known UK organisations. Beneficiaries are chosen by the settlor and he has a set list of charities that are supported twice a year. Other charities are unlikely to receive a grant.

In 2011/12 the trust had assets of £6.8 million and an income of £126,000. Grants totalled £121,000.

Beneficiaries included: Sue Ryder Care (£11,000); British Red Cross, RNIB and Research Institute for the Care of the Elderly (£7,400 each); Action for Children and St Nicholas' Hospice (£5,600 each); and The Marine Society and Sea Cadets, The Salvation Army, Providence Row Charity, The Royal British Legion, SCOPE and MIND (£3,700 each).

Exclusions

No grants to animal charities or to individuals.

Applications

Unsolicited applications are not considered.

Information gathered from:

Accounts; Charity Commission record.

The Martin Smith Foundation

Art, music, sports and education

£57,000 (2011/12)

Beneficial area

UK.

Correspondent: Martin Smith, Trustee, PO Box 838, Oxford OX1 9LF

Trustees: Martin Smith, Chair; Elise Smith; Jeremy Smith; Katherine Wake; Elizabeth Buchanan; Bartholomew Peerless.

CC Number: 1072607

This trust mainly gives to projects and organisations connected to art, music, sports and education.

In 2011/12 the trust had assets of £69,000 and an income of £108,000, almost entirely from donations. Grants to 15 organisations totalled £57,000.

Beneficiaries included: Orchestra of St John's (£19,000); Bath Mozart fest, International Musicians Seminar Prussia Cove and Vocal Futures (£5,000 each); The Becket Collection (£4,000); Orchestra of the Age of Enlightenment and St Anne's College (£3,000 each); Tetbury Music Festival (£2,500); Wigmore Hall (£2,200); Insideworld Imagine (£2,000); Garsington (£1,500); and Kambia Appeal, Oxford Leider and Tetbury Parish Council/Long Newton Church (£1,000 each).

Applications

This trust does not consider unsolicited applications. 'The charity continues to look for new recipients and also, from time to time, review past and on-going projects for possible financial assistance they may require.'

Information gathered from:

Accounts; Charity Commission record.

The Leslie Smith Foundation

Children with illnesses, orphans and schools

£152,500 (2011/12)

Beneficial area

UK with a preference for London, Berkshire, Devon, Cornwall, Middlesex, Norfolk, Somerset and Wiltshire.

Correspondent: The Trustees, c/o Willcox and Lewis, The Old Coach House, Sunnyside, Bergh Apton, Norwich NR15 1DD (tel: 01508 480100; fax: 01508 480001; email: info@willcoxlewis.co.uk)

Trustees: Michael Willcox; Huw Young Jones.

CC Number: 250030

The foundation, which regularly reviews its grantmaking policy, is currently focusing on:

- Children with illnesses, both terminal and non-terminal, in the UK, excluding respite care and research
- Orphans
- Schools, specifically special needs schools based in the UK
- Recipients of previous grants

Furthermore, the foundation's annual report states:

> The trustees also seek to support charities either that do not receive funding from other grant-making bodies, or where the commitment by supporters of those charities is shown by the nature of their fundraising activities, and charities that have received grants in earlier years. The trustees' preference is for capital projects or specific appeals rather than ongoing funding. In addition, preference will be given to applications from London and the counties of Berkshire, Devon & Cornwall, Middlesex, Norfolk, Somerset and Wiltshire.

In 2011/12 the foundation had assets of £2.6 million and an income of £59,000. Grants were made to 22 organisations totalling £152,500, and were broken down as follows:

Health and allied service	£52,000
Children's welfare	£45,000
Ex-servicemen's welfare	£25,000
Counselling services	£10,000
Miscellaneous	£20,500

Beneficiaries included: Comic Relief and the Paul Strickland Scanner Centre Appeal (£15,000 each); Gaddum Centre and Whizz-Kidz (£10,000 each); Cystic Fibrosis Holiday Fund for Children, Prisoners Abroad and Water for All (£5,000 each); and Norfolk Accident Rescue Service (£2,000).

Exclusions

Grants are given to registered charities only. No grants for individuals.

Applications

In writing to the correspondent, including a summary of the project and a copy of the latest accounts. Only successful applications are acknowledged.

Information gathered from:

Accounts; Charity Commission record.

The Stanley Smith UK Horticultural Trust

Horticulture

£84,000 (2011/12)

Beneficial area

UK and overseas.

Correspondent: Dr James Cullen, Director, Cory Lodge, PO Box 365, Cambridge CB2 1HR (tel: 01223 336299; fax: 01223 336278)

Trustees: C. D. Brickell; Lady Renfrew; J. B. E. Simmons; A. De Brye; P. R. Sykes; Dr D. A. H. Rae; E. Reed.

CC Number: 261925

Established by deed in 1970, the trust's objects are the advancement of horticulture. In particular, the trustees have power to make grants for the following purposes:

- Horticultural research
- The creation, development, preservation and maintenance of public gardens
- The promotion of the cultivation and wide distribution of plants of horticultural value/other value to mankind
- The promotion of the cultivation of new plants
- Publishing books and work related to horticultural sciences

In 2011/12 the trust had assets of £3.3 million and an income of £137,000. Grants to 27 organisations and individuals totalled £54,000. A scholarship of £30,000 was also awarded to the Edinburgh Royal Botanic Garden. Historically, the majority of grants have been made to UK organisations with around 20% paid to overseas bodies.

Beneficiaries from the general fund included: Hackfalls Arboretum – New Zealand (£5,000); Alpine Garden Society Publications, Fauna and Flora International and PlantNetwork (£2,500 each); University of East London and Suffolk Punch Trust (£2,000); University of Lincoln (£1,500); Wentworth Castle Heritage Trust (£1,000); and Prenton High School (£500).

The director continues to provide advice to actual and potential applicants, and to established projects which have already received grants. Any grant provided by the trust bears the condition that the recipient should provide within six months, or some other agreed period, a report on the use of the grant.

Exclusions

Grants are not made for projects in commercial horticulture (crop production) or agriculture, nor are they made to support students taking academic or diploma courses of any kind, although educational institutions are supported.

Applications

In writing to the correspondent. Guidelines for Applicants are available from the trust. The director is willing to give advice on how applications should be presented. The factors which are taken into account when assessing an application include:

- Horticultural importance of the project
- Does the project involve a large element of horticulture
- Ability of applicant to carry out the project
- Quality of the application, including all necessary information
- If other funding may be more appropriate for the project

Grants are awarded twice a year, in spring and autumn. To be considered in the spring allocation, applications should reach the director before 15 February of each year; for the autumn allocation the equivalent date is 15 August. Potential recipients are advised to get their applications in early.

Information gathered from:

Accounts; Charity Commission record.

Philip Smith's Charitable Trust

Welfare, older people, children, environment, armed forces

£85,000 (2011/12)

Beneficial area

UK with a preference for Gloucestershire.

Correspondent: Helen D'Monte, Bircham Dyson Bell, 50 Broadway, London SW1H 0BL (tel: 020 7783 3685; fax: 020 7222 3480; email: helendmonte@bdb-law.co.uk)

Trustees: Hon. Philip R. Smith; Mary Smith.

CC Number: 1003751

The trust's grantmaking policy is outlined in its accounts: 'The trustees have adopted a policy of donating to those charities within the Gloucestershire area and also national charities supporting the environment, the elderly, the armed forces, children and the needy.'

In 2011/12 the trust had assets of £1 million and an income of £31,500. There were 43 grants made totalling £85,000.

Beneficiaries included: Save the Children (£10,000); League of Friends of Moreton-in-Marsh Hospital and the Gamekeepers Welfare Charitable Trust (£5,000 each); St James Parochial Church Council Chipping Campden (£4,000); The Salvation Army (£2,500); and the Army Benevolent Fund and Church Urban Fund (£1,000 each).

Applications

In writing to the correspondent. The trustees meet regularly to consider grants. A lack of response can be taken to indicate that the trust does not wish to contribute to an appeal.

Percentage of awards given to new applicants: between 10% and 20%.

Common applicant mistakes

'They do not look at the criteria applied by the trustees, shown on the Charity Commission.'

Information gathered from:

Accounts; Charity Commission record; further information provided by the funder.

Solev Co. Ltd

Jewish charities

£302,000 (2011/12)

Beneficial area

UK.

Correspondent: Romie Tager, Trustee, 1 Spaniards Park, Columbas Drive, London NW3 7JD (tel: 020 7420 9500)

Trustees: Romie Tager; Simon Tager; Joseph Tager; Chaim Frommer.

CC Number: 254623

In 2011/12 the charity had assets of £5.3 million and an income of £675,500. Grants were made totalling £302,000. No information on beneficiaries has been included in the accounts in recent years.

Further research shows that the trustees support numerous Jewish charities such as Norwood, London Jewish Cultural Centre, the Jewish Book Council and the Jewish Museum London.

Applications

In writing to the correspondent.

Percentage of awards given to new applicants: between 10% and 20%.

Information gathered from:

Accounts; Charity Commission record; further information provided by the funder.

The Solo Charitable Settlement

Jewish, general

£49,000 (2011/12)

Beneficial area

UK and Israel.

Correspondent: The Trustees, c/o Gallaghers Accountants, Titchfield House, 2nd Floor, 69–85 Tabernacle Street, London EC2A 4RR (tel: 020 7490 7774; fax: 020 7490 5354; email: partners@gallaghers.co.uk)

Trustees: Peter D. Goldstein; Edna A. Goldstein; Paul Goldstein; Dean Goldstein; Jamie Goldstein; Tammy Ward.

CC Number: 326444

Peter David Goldstein established the trust in 1983. The main object of the trust is to support Jewish charities, and where possible, to concentrate their efforts on the relief of suffering and poverty, and on education. The majority of grants were given to organisations that focused on Jewish related causes, medical research, the arts and palliative care.

In 2011/12 the trust had assets of £5.6 million and an income of £259,000. Grants were made to 29 organisations totalling £49,000, and were categorised as follows:

General charitable purposes	£24,500
Educational	£19,000
Medical/health	£2,300
Religious	£2,000
Services for the elderly	£1,200

Beneficiaries included: Norwood (£14,000); Jewish Leadership Council (£7,500); Mothers and Daughters Support Group (£2,200); and Israel Tennis Centres (£1,000).

Applications

In writing to the correspondent.

Information gathered from:

Accounts; Charity Commission record.

David Solomons Charitable Trust

Learning difficulties

£85,000 (2011/12)

Beneficial area

UK.

Correspondent: Graeme Crosby, Administrator, Jasmine Cottage, 11 Lower Road, Breachwood Green, Hitchin, Hertfordshire SG4 8NS (tel: 01438 833254; email: g.crosby@waitrose.com)

Trustees: Michael Chamberlayne; John Drewitt; Jeremy Rutter; Dr Richard Solomons; Dr Leila Cooke; Diana Huntingford.

CC Number: 297275

This trust supports research into, or the treatment and care of, people with learning difficulties, with a preference for smaller or localised charities. Most grants range from £1,000 to £2,000, although larger and smaller amounts are given. Administrative expenses and large building projects are not usually funded, although grants can be made towards furnishing or equipping rooms.

In 2011/12 the trust had assets of £2.3 million and an income of £104,000. There were 89 grants made during the year totalling £85,000.

As in previous years, the largest grant was made to Down's Syndrome Association (£8,000).

Other beneficiaries included: Columcille Centre (£3,000 in total); Acre Housing and Wessex Autistic Society (£2,000 each); Advocacy Trust Gloucester, Autism Sussex Ltd, Forest Forge Theatre Company, Papworth Trust and the Children's Adventure Farm Trust (£1,000 each); and Bedford Local Mencap, Ferring Country Centre and Outreach 3 Way (£500).

Exclusions

No grants to individuals.

Applications

The trustees conduct their own research into potential applicants.

Percentage of awards given to new applicants: between 40% and 50%.

Common applicant mistakes

'They apply in respect of mutual illness or physical problems instead of confining applications in respect of learning difficulties.'

Information gathered from:

Accounts; Charity Commission record; further information provided by the funder.

Songdale Ltd

Jewish, education

£214,000 (2011/12)

Beneficial area

UK and Israel.

Correspondent: Yechiel Grosskopf, Trustee, 6 Spring Hill, London E5 9BE (tel: 020 8806 5010)

Trustees: Yechiel Grosskopf; Myer Grosskopf; Malka Gitel Grosskopf.

CC Number: 286075

This trust was registered in 1983 for the advancement of the Orthodox Jewish Faith and the relief of poverty.

In 2011/12 the trust had assets of £2.5 million, an income of £233,000 and spent £214,000 on charitable activities.

A list of grant beneficiaries was not included in the accounts but previously grants have been given to: Cosmon Belz Ltd, Kollel Belz, BFOT, Ezras Yisroel, Forty Ltd, Darkei Ovois, Germach Veholachto, Keren Nedunnia Lchasanim, Belz Nursery and Bais Chinuch.

Applications

In writing to the correspondent.

Information gathered from:

Accounts; Charity Commission record.

The E. C. Sosnow Charitable Trust

Mainly education and arts

£53,000 (2011/12)

Beneficial area

UK and overseas.

Correspondent: The Trustees, PO Box 13398, London SW3 6ZL

Trustees: Mr E. R. Fattal; Mrs F. J. M. Fattal; Miss A. E. Fattal; Mr R. Fattal.

CC Number: 273578

The trust makes grants mainly to organisations working in education and the arts. Other areas of interest include disadvantage, healthcare, Judaism and emergency relief. In 2011/12 the trust had assets of £1.8 million and an income of £65,000. Grants were made to 19 organisations totalling £53,000.

Grants included those made to: Friends of Ascent and Weizman UK (£10,000 each); LSE (£5,000); Royal National Theatre and Youth Aliyah (£3,000 each); Holocaust Educational Trust (£2,500); British Technion Society and Society for Children with Diabetes (£1,000 each); and Parkinson's UK (£500).

Exclusions

No grants are made to individuals.

Applications

In writing to the correspondent.

Information gathered from:

Accounts; Charity Commission record.

The South Square Trust

General

£164,000 to organisations (2011/12)

Beneficial area

UK, with a preference for London and the Home Counties.

Correspondent: Nicola Chrimes, Clerk to the Trustees, PO Box 169, Lewes, East Sussex BN7 9FB (tel: 01825 872264; website: www.southsquaretrust.org.uk)

Trustees: Christopher Grimwade; Paul Harriman; Brand Inglis; Andrew Blessley; Stephen Baldock.

CC Number: 278960

The South Square Trust is governed by a trust deed dated 12 November 1979 and is established for general charitable purposes but in particular, education. The trustees, having due regard to the wishes of the original settlor, apply the income to such charities they choose and to such schools, colleges and other institutions selected by them which offer appropriate courses in the fine and applied arts. Grants are also made to individuals in connection with degree level educational courses in the fine and applied arts (especially goldsmithing and silversmithing), to include music, drama and dance.

The trustees have set up scholarship awards with a number of colleges, a full list of which can be obtained from the clerk to the trustees.

In 2011/12 the trust had assets of just over £3.6 million and an income of £192,000. Grants were made totalling £182,500, of which £164,000 went to 41 organisations and £18,500 to individuals.

Beneficiary organisations included: Fields in Trust and Woodlands Trust (£3,500 each); and World Child Cancer (£2,000).

Exclusions

No support for building projects, salaries or individuals wishing to start up a business. No grants given to individuals under 18 or those seeking funding for expeditions, travel, courses outside the UK, short courses or courses not connected with fine and applied arts.

Applications

In writing to the correspondent with details about your charity and the reason for requesting funding. Note, however, that the trust is not accepting applications until after July 2014 – check the trust's website for up-to-date information.

Information gathered from:

Accounts; Charity Commission record; funder's website.

The Stephen R. and Philippa H. Southall Charitable Trust

General

£28,500 (2011/12)

Beneficial area

UK, but mostly Herefordshire.

Correspondent: Philippa Southall, Trustee, Porking Barn, Clifford, Hereford HR3 5HE

Trustees: Philippa Southall; Anna Southall; Candia Compton.

CC Number: 223190

This trust has general charitable purposes, with a preference for promoting education and conservation of the natural environment and cultural heritage. A large number of grants are made in Herefordshire. The trust has previously stated that it uses its surplus income for world emergencies and the development of Hereford Waterworks Museum.

In 2011/12 the trust had assets of £3.2 million and an income of £76,500. Grants were made to 20 organisations totalling £28,500.

Beneficiaries included: Hereford Waterworks Museum Trust (£5,000); Bristol Museums Development Trust and Home-Start Herefordshire (£2,000 each); and Midlands Air Ambulance, Herefordshire Carers' Support and Britain Yearly Meeting Fund (£1,000 each).

Applications

The trust makes several repeat donations and has previously stated that: 'no applications can be considered or replied to'.

Information gathered from:

Accounts; Charity Commission record.

The W. F. Southall Trust

Quaker, general

£248,000 (2011/12)

Beneficial area

UK and overseas.

Correspondent: Margaret Rowntree, Secretary, c/o Rutters Solicitors, 2 Bimport, Shaftesbury, Dorset SP7 8AY (tel: 01747 852377; fax: 01747 851989; email: M.Rowntree@Rutterslaw.co.uk; website: wfsouthalltrust.org.uk)

Trustees: Donald Southall, Chair; Joanna Engelkamp; Claire Greaves; Mark Holtom; Daphne Maw; Annette Wallis; Richard Maw; Hannah Engelkamp.

CC Number: 218371

The trust was established in 1937 by Wilfred Francis Southall, a pharmacist and manufacturing chemist from Birmingham who was also a Quaker. The following information about the trust is given on its website:

> The Southall Trust is a trust which acts on Quaker principles and its policies reflect the values of the Religious Society of Friends. The trust is committed to supporting Quaker work, and initiatives which try to create a just and peaceful society. Emphasis is given to supporting relatively small grass roots innovative projects where the funding can make a real difference. The trust does not normally support mainstream education or healthcare establishments, and does not give gifts to individuals. It is not an official Quaker charity.

In 2011/12 the trust had assets of £7.8 million and an income of £273,500. Grants were made to 90 organisations totalling £248,000, and were categorised as follows:

Quaker and Society of Friends Charities	10	£89,500
Overseas development	37	£71,500
Community action	23	£44,000
Peace and reconciliation	12	£27,000
Alcohol, drug abuse and penal affairs	5	£10,000
Environmental action	3	£6,000

Beneficiaries included: Yearly Meeting – Society of Friends (£55,000); Woodbrooke Quaker Study Centre (£10,000); International Voluntary Services and Quaker Social Action (£5,000 each); Salt of the Earth (£4,000); and Campaign Against Arms Trade and World Orthopaedic Concern (£3,000 each).

Exclusions

No grants to individuals or large national charities.

Applications

On a form available from the trust's website. Further guidance on making an application is given as follows:

> When making an application, grant seekers should bear in mind the points below. We expect all applicants to complete the funding application form.
>
> Please ensure your application includes details regarding the following:
>
> - Your most recent annual report
> - Projected income and expenditure for the coming year
> - Your reserves
> - Particular features of your costs, e.g. high transport costs in rural areas
> - Details of other funding expected
> - Any significant achievements and/or problems or difficulties
> - Any 'matching funding' arrangements e.g. European Social Fund support
> - Timetable for when the proposed work is to start and finish
> - Applications should be accompanied by a stamped addressed envelope

Information gathered from:

Accounts; Charity Commission record; funder's website.

R. H. Southern Trust

Education, relief of poverty, disability, preservation and conservation

£174,000 to organisations (2011/12)

Beneficial area

England, Wales, Scotland, Republic of Ireland, Australia, Belgium, India.

Correspondent: Marion Wells, Trustee, 23 Sydenham Road, Cotham, Bristol BS6 5SJ (tel: 01179 425834; website: www.rhsoutherntrust.org.uk)

Trustees: Marion Wells; James Bruges.

CC Number: 1077509

This trust was registered with the Charity Commission in 1999. Grants tend to be made to a small number of organisations, mostly for long-term core funding and special projects. The trust's objects are:

- The advancement of education (including medical and scientific research)
- The relief of poverty
- Disability
- The preservation, conservation and protection of the environment (especially climate change)

The trust favours projects where the work is innovative, connected to other disciplines/bodies and has diverse application.

In 2011/12 the trust had assets of £2.9 million and an income of £100,500. Grants were made to 26 organisations totalling £174,000 and were broken down as follows:

Education	9	£68,000
Poverty	7	£42,000
Disabilities	3	£35,000
Environment	7	£29,000

Beneficiaries included: New Economics Foundation (£23,000); Equal Adventure (£20,000); Accord – Just Change, Salt of the Earth, World Development Movement and Oxford Research Group (£10,000 each); Action Village India (£7,500); Corporate Europe Observatory and Friends of the Earth (£5,000 each); EI Rural Links – Tamwed (£4,000); and CSIRO (£1,000).

Additionally, the trust made grants totalling £29,000 to individuals and businesses.

Applications

The trust's website states: 'The trust funds are fully committed for the foreseeable future. Please do not apply for funding and waste your time and resources and ours. Thank you.'

Information gathered from:

Accounts; Charity Commission record; funder's website.

Spar Charitable Fund

General, with a preference for children and young people

£114,000 (2012/13)

Beneficial area

UK.

Correspondent: Philip Marchant, Trustee, Mezzanine Floor, Hygeia Building, 66–68 College Road, Harrow, Middlesex HA1 1BE (tel: 020 8426 3700; email: philip.marchant@spar.co.uk)

Trustees: Kevin Hunt; Martin Agnew; Peter Dodding; Philip Marchant; Claire Bolton; Mark Gillett; Patrick Doody; Dominic Hall; Bryan Walters.

CC Number: 236252

This is the charitable trust of Spar UK Ltd. It tends to choose one main beneficiary, which receives most of its funds, with smaller grants being made to similar beneficiaries each year.

In 2012/13 it had assets of £879,500 and an income of £81,500. Grants were made totalling £114,000.

As in previous years, the main beneficiary was the NSPCC, which received £71,000. Other beneficiaries included: Spar Charitable Fund (£20,000); and Grocery Aid (£5,000).

Applications

In writing to the correspondent.

Information gathered from:

Accounts; Charity Commission record.

The Spear Charitable Trust

General, with some preference for animal welfare, the environment and health

£137,000 to organisations (2012)

Beneficial area

UK.

Correspondent: Hazel Spear, Secretary, Roughground House, Beggarmans Lane, Old Hall Green, Ware, Hertfordshire SG11 1HB (tel: 01920 823071; fax: 01920 823071)

Trustees: Philip Harris; Francis Spear; Hazel Spear; Nigel Gooch.

CC Number: 1041568

Established in 1994 with general charitable purposes, this trust has particular interest in helping employees and former employees of J W Spear and Sons plc and their families and dependents. Grants are given to UK organisations and occasionally those working overseas.

In 2012 the trust had assets of £4.9 million and an income of £169,000. Grants were made to 79 organisations totalling £137,000, whilst ex-employees received £4,500 in total.

Beneficiaries included: RSPCA – Enfield (£8,000); Camphill Village Trust and Tel Aviv University (£5,000 each); Centre for Alternative Technology and the Elm Farm Research Centre (£3,000 each); Bowel Disease Research Foundation and Lake Malawi Projects (UK) (£2,000 each); and ABF – The Soldiers' Charity, Canine Partners, Furniture Recycling Project and Wood Street Mission (£1,000 each).

Exclusions

Appeals from individuals are not considered.

Applications

In writing to the correspondent.

Information gathered from:

Accounts; Charity Commission record.

Spears-Stutz Charitable Trust

Relief of poverty, general

£117,000 (2011/12)

Beneficial area

Worldwide.

Correspondent: The Trustees, c/o Berkeley Law, 4th Floor, 19 Berkeley Street, London W1J 8ED (tel: 020 7399 0930)

Trustees: Glenn Hurstfield; Jonathan Spears.

CC Number: 225491

This trust was previously known as the Roama Spears Charitable Settlement. It states that it makes grants to organisations towards the relief of poverty worldwide. In practice it appears to support a range of organisations including a number of museums and arts organisations. It has some preference for Jewish causes.

In 2011/12 the trust had assets of £4.3 million and an income of £156,000. Grants totalled £117,000 and were made to various local and national charities, ranging from donations of £250 to £30,000. A list of grants was not provided in the accounts.

Previous beneficiaries include: Macmillan Cancer Fund, Royal Academy Trust, Royal Academy of Arts, Wellbeing, King Edward Hospital, Help the Aged and Westminster Synagogue.

Applications

In writing to the correspondent.

Information gathered from:

Accounts; Charity Commission record.

The Worshipful Company of Spectacle Makers' Charity

Visual impairment, general

£101,000 (2011/12)

Beneficial area

Worldwide, with a preference for the City of London.

Correspondent: John Salmon, Clerk, Apothecaries Hall, Blackfriars Lane, London EC4V 6EL (tel: 020 7236 2932; email: clerk@spectaclemakers.com; website: www.spectaclemakers.com)

Trustees: Christine Tomkins; Venerable John Morrison; Liz Shilling; Edward Middleton; James Osborne; Nigel Andrew; Michael Rudd.

CC Number: 1072172

Registered with the Charity Commission in October 1998, this livery company supports causes related to visual impairment and the City of London, however it has also supported a wide range of other projects worldwide. Grants tend to be made for specific projects, not general funds, and to national campaigns rather than local causes.

In 2011/12 the charity had assets of £670,000 and an income of £72,000. Grants were made to 27 organisations totalling £101,000.

The charity's accounts list a number of beneficiaries, without details of the value of individual grants. These included: Fight for Sight; Treloar Trust; British Council for the Prevention of Blindness; British Wireless for the Blind Fund; Skillforce; and Vision Aid Overseas.

Exclusions

No grants are made to individuals.

Applications

In writing to the correspondent including details of how the grant will be used and a copy of the latest audited accounts. Note: the trustees meet in early spring to decide on grants, meaning that applications received between June and March are unlikely to be addressed quickly.

Percentage of awards given to new applicants: less than 10%.

Common applicant mistakes

'Failure to appreciate that the trustees' prime concern is the fight against visual impairment; verbosity.'

Information gathered from:

Accounts; Charity Commission record; further information provided by the funder; funder's website.

The Jessie Spencer Trust

General

£91,000 (2012/13)

Beneficial area

UK, with some preference for Nottinghamshire.

Correspondent: John Thompson, Administrator, c/o 4 Walsingham Drive, Corby Glen, Grantham, Lincolnshire NG33 4TA (tel: 01476 552429; email: jessiespencer@btinternet.com)

Trustees: Victor Semmens; Mrs B. Mitchell; David Wild; Andrew Tiplady.

CC Number: 219289

The trust supports a range wide of causes, including welfare, religion and the environment amongst others. Whilst grants are made UK-wide, there is a preference for work in Nottinghamshire.

In 2012/13 the trust had assets of £4.1 million and an income of £141,500. Grants were made totalling £91,000.

Beneficiaries included: Nottinghamshire Historic Churches Trust (£10,000); Framework Housing Association and Bromley House Library (£5,000 each); Motability (£2,000); Independent Parental Special Education Advice, Alzheimer's Research UK and Dove Cottage Day Hospice (£1,000 each); and Clifton Methodist Church, Army Cadet

Force Association, Listening Books and Happy Days Children's Charity (£500 each).

Exclusions

Grants are rarely made for the repair of parish churches outside Nottinghamshire.

Applications

In writing to the correspondent, including the latest set of audited accounts, at least three weeks before the trustees' meetings in March, June, September and December. Unsuccessful applicants will not be notified.

Percentage of awards given to new applicants: less than 10%.

Common applicant mistakes

'They do not include a copy of their latest accounts.'

Information gathered from:

Accounts; Charity Commission record; further information provided by the funder.

Rosalyn and Nicholas Springer Charitable Trust

Welfare, Jewish, education, general

£142,000 (2011/12)

Beneficial area

UK and Israel.

Correspondent: Nicholas Springer, Trustee, 15 Park Village West, London NW1 4AE (tel: 020 7253 7272)

Trustees: Rosalyn Springer; Nicholas Springer; Judith Joseph.

CC Number: 1062239

This trust supports the relief and assistance of people in need, for the advancement of education, religion and other purposes beneficial to the community.

In 2011/12 the trust had assets of £31,000 and an income of £125,000. Grants were made to 58 organisations totalling £142,000, and were broken down as follows:

Medical health and sickness	21	£60,000
Education and training	18	£40,000
General charitable purposes	12	£26,000
Arts and culture	11	£9,000
Religious activities	4	£5,500
Relief of poverty	3	£2,000

Beneficiaries included: United Jewish Israel Appeal (£26,500); Magen David Adom UK (£13,000); British Council Of Shears Zedek (£11,000); Community Security Trust (£6,000); The Ear Foundation (£5,000); Chicken Shed Theatre Trust (£4,000); Proms at St Jude's (£2,500); Lifelites (£2,000); Regent's Park Open Air Theatre (£1,000); and Cancerkin, Train for Employment, Royal Ballet School and British Emunah (£500 each).

Applications

The trust has previously stated that it only supports organisations it is already in contact with. 99% of unsolicited applications are unsuccessful and because of the volume it receives, the trust is unable to reply to such letters. It would therefore not seem appropriate to apply to this trust.

Percentage of awards given to new applicants: less than 10%.

Information gathered from:

Accounts; Charity Commission record; further information provided by the funder.

The Spurrell Charitable Trust

General

£72,000 (2011/12)

Beneficial area

UK, with some preference for Norfolk.

Correspondent: Martyn Spurrell, Trustee, 78 Wendover Road, Aylesbury HP21 9NJ (tel: 01892 541565)

Trustees: Ingeburg Spurrell; Martyn Spurrell.

CC Number: 267287

The trust has previously stated that grants are only distributed to charities known personally to the trustees and that its funds are fully committed.

In 2011/12 the trust had assets of £2.3 million and an income of £64,500. Grants were made to 67 organisations totalling £72,000. Most grants were for less than £1,000.

Beneficiaries included: East Anglian Air Ambulance (£7,000); YMCA Norfolk (£3,500); Aylesbury High School (£3,000); Parkinson's UK (£2,500); and Alzheimer's Research UK, Brooke Hospital for Animals, Injured Jockeys Fund and Restore (£1,200 each).

Exclusions

No grants to individuals.

Applications

Income has fallen steadily over the last few years and is now insufficient to meet essential commitments. Therefore, new appeals are very unlikely to be considered.

Percentage of awards given to new applicants: 3%.

Common applicant mistakes

'They overlook: we do not give grants to individuals; we state [our] income is insufficient to meet existing requirements; we state we give only to charities known by the trustees.'

Information gathered from:

Accounts; Charity Commission record; further information provided by the funder.

St James's Trust Settlement

General

£317,500 (2011/12)

Beneficial area

UK and USA.

Correspondent: The Trustees, c/o Begbies Accountants, Epworth House, 25 City Road, London EC1Y 1AR (tel: 020 7628 5801; fax: 020 7628 0390; email: admin@begbiesaccountants.co.uk)

Trustees: Jane Wells; Cathy Ingram; Simon Taffler.

CC Number: 280455

The trust's main aims are to make grants to charitable organisations that respond to areas of concern which the trustees are involved or interested in. In the UK, the main concerns are health, education and social justice; in the USA the main areas are in education, especially to the children of very disadvantaged families, and in community arts projects. Grants are made by the trustees through their involvement with the project. Projects are also monitored and evaluated by the trustees.

In 2011/12 the trust had assets of £3.3 million and an income of £158,000. Grants were made during the year totalling £317,500, which included £37,000 to three organisations in the UK and £280,500 to 39 organisations in the USA.

The UK beneficiaries were: Homeopathy Action Trust (£15,000); CARIS (£12,000); and Highbury Vale Blackstock Trust (£10,000).

Exclusions

No grants to individuals.

Applications

The trust states that it 'does not seek unsolicited applications for grants and, without paid staff, are unable to respond to such applications'.

Information gathered from:

Accounts; Charity Commission record.

St Michael's and All Saints' Charities Relief Branch (The Church Houses Relief in Need Charity)

Health, welfare

£107,000 (2012)

Beneficial area

City of Oxford.

Correspondent: Rupert Sheppard, Administrator, 2 Churchill Place, Yarnton, Kidlington, Oxfordshire OX5 1GQ (tel: 01865 240940; email: rupert.sheppard@smng.org.uk)

Trustees: Patrick Beavis; Michael Lear; Lord Krebs; Ruth Loseby; Prudence Dailey; Robert Earl; Samia Shibli; The Very Revd Robert Wilkes; Simon Stubbings; Prof. Henry Woudhuysen; The Ven. Martin Gorick.

CC Number: 202750

Income of the charity is applied to relieve, either generally or individually, persons resident in the city of Oxford who are in conditions of need, hardship or distress. Grants may be made to institutions or organisations which provide services or facilities for such people.

In 2012 the trust had assets of £1.4 million and an income of £86,500. Grants were made to 20 organisations totalling £107,000.

Beneficiaries included: Leys Youth Programme (£11,000); Donnington Doorstep Family Centre (£10,000); Archway Foundation (£8,000); Oxford Sexual Abuse and Rape Crisis Centre (£6,000); Innovista International (£5,000); Abbeyfield Oxenford Society (£3,000); ACT (£2,000); and Blackbird Leys Neighbourhood Support Scheme (£1,000).

Exclusions

Individuals are very rarely supported.

Applications

In writing to the correspondent.

Information gathered from:

Accounts; Charity Commission record.

St Monica Trust (formerly known as St Monica Trust Community Fund)

Older people, disability

£584,000 to organisations (2012)

Beneficial area

Preference for the south west of England, particularly Bristol and the surrounding area.

Correspondent: Robert Whetton, Correspondent, Cote Lane, Bristol BS9 3UN (tel: 01179 494006; email: info@stmonicatrust.org.uk; website: www.stmonicatrust.org.uk)

Trustees: John Kane; Trevor Smallwood; Stuart Burnett; Richard Wynn-Jones; Jane Cork; John Laycock; Andrew Yates; Peter Rilett; Helen Moss; Dr Rebecca Slinn; Lady Paula Wills; Michael Lea; Charles Griffiths; Revd Canon Neil Heavisides.

CC Number: 202151

The St Monica Trust has provided accommodation, care and support for older and disabled people for over 85 years. The trust aims to provide sheltered accommodation; 'extra care' housing; care at home; care and support; and nursing care for elderly people, especially those living with Alzheimer's disease and other forms of dementia.

Another branch of its work, the community fund, offers financial help to individuals to help pay for essential items such as wheelchairs or adaptations to an individual's home; and monthly payments to an individual in the form of a short-term grant. The trust also provides LinkAge – an initiative that works locally with individuals, local groups and organisations to improve the well-being of older people.

As stated in 2012's accounts, the objects of the trust are:

> The relief of those individuals (and if appropriate their spouses) who are in need by reason of age, disability or ill-health by the provision of:
>
> - Accommodation and associated facilities
> - Other services or assistance

Grants of up to £15,000 are awarded to organisations which provide support to older people and adults with a physical disability or long-term illness.

In 2012 the trust had assets of £217 million and an income of nearly £24 million. The trust gave grants to organisations totalling £584,000. Information regarding grants was not provided.

Previous beneficiaries included: Citizens Advice (£9,800); St Peter's Hospice, Headway Bristol and Motor Neurone Disease Association (£7,500 each); IT Help@Home (£5,000); the New Place (£3,900); Bristol and Avon Chinese Women's Group (£2,000); Bath Institute of Medical Engineering (£1,500); and Western Active Stroke Group (£1,000).

The trust accepts applications from organisations that it has previously funded.

Exclusions

No grants to fund buildings, adaptations to buildings or minibus purchases.

Applications

On a form available from the correspondent, or to download from the fund's website. All applicants must submit a form together with additional information that is requested, for example, an annual report.

Applications are considered once a year; see the fund's website for deadline dates.

Information gathered from:

Accounts; Charity Commission record; funder's website.

The Late St Patrick White Charitable Trust

General

£31,500 (2012/13)

Beneficial area

UK.

Correspondent: R. Thompson, Trust Manager, HSBC Trust Co. UK Ltd, Norwich House, Nelson Gate, Commercial Road, Southampton SO15 1GX (tel: 02380 722240)

Trustee: HSBC. Trusts Co. (UK) Ltd.

CC Number: 1056520

The objects of the charity are to pay or to apply the income from the trust fund for the benefit of Barnardo's, Guide Dogs for the Blind, The Salvation Army, Age Concern and other charities benefiting people who are blind, cancer research, arthritis and rheumatism research.

In 2012/13 the trust had assets of £2.2 million and an income of £47,000. Grants were made to eight organisations totalling £31,500.

Each beneficiary received £4,500; they were: Age Concern; Age UK; Arthritis Care; Cancer Research UK; Barnardo's; Guide Dogs for the Blind; The Salvation Army; and Visability.

Applications

In writing to the correspondent. Applications are considered in February, May, August and November.

Information gathered from:
Accounts; Charity Commission record.

St Teilo's Trust

Evangelistic work in the Church in Wales

Around £40,000 (2011/12)

Beneficial area
Wales.

Correspondent: Patrick Mansel Lewis, Stradey Estate Office, 53 New Road, Llanelli SA15 3DP (tel: 01554 773059; email: info@saintteilostrust.org.uk; website: www.saintteilostrust.org.uk)

Trustees: Revd Canon Stuart Bell; Revd Peter Bement; Claire Mansel Lewis; Patrick Mansel Lewis; Revd Dr William Strange; Revd Bob Capper; John Settatree.

CC Number: 1032405

The trust supports evangelical work in the Church in Wales. It provides funding towards the cost of evangelical initiatives in parishes, Alpha courses, evangelical events and literature distribution for example. Grants are usually one-off and range from £50 to £1,000.

In 2011/12 the trust had an income of £3,500 and expenditure of £40,000. No grants list was available but examples of grant support are detailed on the trust's website.

Previous beneficiaries include: Christian Council for Schools for Wales, Gobaith i Gymru, St Michael's Aberystwyth, Complete Package Ministries, Red Cafe (a project of Linden Church Trust), St Michael's Aberystwyth, Trobwynt, and Youth For Christ.

Exclusions
No grants towards equipment or buildings.

Applications
In writing to the correspondent. Trustees meet in February, May and September. Applications should be sent by January, April and August. Guidelines are available from the trust.

Information gathered from:
Accounts; Charity Commission record; funder's website.

The Stafford Trust

Animal welfare, medical research, local community, relief in need

£250,500 (2012/13)

Beneficial area
UK, with a preference for Scotland.

Correspondent: Margaret Kane, Administrator, c/o Dickson Middleton CA, PO Box 14, 20 Barnton Street, Stirling FK8 1NE (tel: 01786 474718; fax: 01786 451392; email: staffordtrust@dicksonmiddleton.co.uk; website: www.staffordtrust.org.uk)

Trustees: A. Peter M. Walls; Hamish N. Buchan; Gordon M. Wyllie; Angus Morgan.

SC Number: SC018079

The Stafford Trust was set up in 1991 by the late Mrs Gay Stafford of Sauchie Estate near Stirling. During her lifetime, Mrs Stafford made substantial gifts to the trust and on her death in 2005, the residue of her estate was bequeathed to the trust. Over £10 million was received in the financial year 2006/07. The trust makes grants to charities from the income generated from the trust fund.

Grants vary, but most are for between £500 and £10,000. Occasionally the trustees make a recurring grant of up to three years.

Between 1991 and 2013, grants totalling £2.8 million were made in the following areas:

Adult welfare	23%
Medical research	19%
Child welfare	17%
Community projects	17%
Animal welfare	15%
Services personnel welfare	4%
Overseas appeals and support	3%
Sea Rescue	2%

In 2012/13 the trust had assets of £14.7 million and an income of £381,000. Grants were made to 55 organisations totalling £250,500.

Beneficiaries included: Animal Health Trust (£20,000); Quarriers (£15,000); CLIC Sargent (£10,000); Outfit Moray (£7,500); Toll Centre (£6,000); Aberlour Child Care Trust and SSPCA (£5,000 each); Brittle Bone Society, Music in Hospitals and the National Search and Rescue Dog Association (£4,000 each); Children with Cystic Fibrosis (£3,000); Scottish Seabird Centre (£2,000); and Borders Talking Newspapers (£1,500).

Exclusions
The trust does not support:

- Religious organisations
- Political organisations
- Retrospective grants
- Student travel or expeditions
- General appeals or mail shots

Applications
The trust has a short application form which can be downloaded from its website. Applicants are invited to complete the form using their own words without the restrictions of completing set questions. Also supply the following, where appropriate:

- A brief description of your charity
- A copy of your most recent annual report and accounts
- A description of the project/funding requirement – what do you want to achieve and how will it be managed. The trustees look for clear, realistic and attainable aims
- What is the expenditure budget for the project and the anticipated timescale
- What funds have already been raised and what other sources are being approached
- The need for funding must be clearly demonstrated
- What will be the benefits of the project and how do you propose to monitor and evaluate whether the project has been successful
- If applicable, what plans you have to fund the future running costs of the project

The trustees usually meet twice per annum to consider applications. Applicants may be contacted for more information or to arrange an assessment visit. Successful applicants must wait at least two years from the time of receiving a grant before reapplying. In the case of a two or three year recurring grant this applies from the time of receiving the last instalment.

Information gathered from:
Accounts; OSCR record; funder's website.

The Stanley Foundation Ltd

Medical care and research, education, social welfare, culture

£203,000 (2011/12)

Beneficial area
UK.

Correspondent: N. Stanley, Secretary, N. C. Morris and Co., 1 Montpelier Street, London SW7 1EX (email: nick@meristan.com)

Trustees: P. Hall; G. Stanley; N. Stanley; S. R. Stanley; E. Stanley; S. H. Hall; J. N. Raymond.

CC Number: 206866

The trust has traditionally supported medical care and research, education and social welfare charities. In 2011/12 it had assets of £3.1 million and an income of £100,000. Grants were made to 39 organisations totalling £203,000.

Beneficiaries included: Place 2 Be (£32,000); London Library (£22,000); Royal Opera House (£21,000); Holburne Museum (£15,000); National Theatre (£12,000); Tusk (£11,000); Cancer Research (£10,000); Camden Psychotherapy Unit (£7,000); Friends of Roy Kinnear House (£5,000); Multiple Sclerosis Society (£2,000); and Riding for the Disabled (£750).

Exclusions

No grants to individuals.

Applications

In writing to the correspondent.

Information gathered from:

Accounts; Charity Commission record.

The Star Charitable Trust

General

Around £35,000 (2011/12)

Beneficial area

UK.

Correspondent: The Trustees, PO Box 63302, London N2 2BU

Trustees: D. A. Rosen; David Taglight.

CC Number: 266695

Connected to the Star Diamond group of companies, this trust was established in March 1974.

In 2011/12 the trust had an income of £9,000 and a total expenditure of £37,500. Further information was not available.

Applications

In writing to the correspondent.

Information gathered from:

Accounts; Charity Commission record.

The Steinberg Family Charitable Trust

Jewish, health

£1.5 million (2011/12)

Beneficial area

UK, with a preference for Greater Manchester.

Correspondent: The Trustees, Lime Tree Cottage, 16 Bollingway, Hale, Altrincham WA15 0NZ (tel: 01619 038854; email: admin@steinberg-trust.co.uk)

Trustees: Beryl Steinberg; Jonathan Steinberg; Lynne Attias.

CC Number: 1045231

This trust is primarily concerned with the support of charities located in the North West region or active within the Jewish community (whether in the North West or Israel), particularly those involved with the provision of social or health services. There is a particular emphasis on the needs of children and young people within those areas.

During 2011/12 the trust had an income of £1 million, held assets of £22 million and made grants to 281 organisations totalling £1.5 million.

The most significant beneficiaries for this year were: Aish (£75,000); Fed, Hathaway Trust, UJIA and World Jewish Relief (£50,000); and Integrated Education Fund (£25,000).; SEED (£22,000); and Hale Adult Hebrew Education Trust (£20,000).

Beneficiaries of £15,000 or less included: Centre for Social Justice and Policy Exchange (£15,000); Ascent, Ezer Layeled, Imperial War Museum; MDA Israel, Menachim Begin Heritage Foundation and Yeshiva Bais Yisroel (£10,000 each); Chai Cancer Care and Holocaust Centre (£7,500 each); Hamayon and Hazon Yeshaya (£5,000 each); Henshaw's Society, Jewish Education in Manchester, NATA and Rainbow Trust (£2,500 each); and Prostate Cancer Charity (£1,000).

Exclusions

Registered charities only.

Applications

In writing to the correspondent on letter-headed paper, including evidence of charitable status, the purpose to which the funds are to be put, evidence of other action taken to fund the project concerned, and the outcome of that action.

Information gathered from:

Accounts; Charity Commission record.

The Sigmund Sternberg Charitable Foundation

Jewish, inter-faith causes, general

£267,000 (2011/12)

Beneficial area

Worldwide.

Correspondent: Jan Kariya, Star House, 104/108 Grafton Road, London NW5 4BA (tel: 020 7431 4200)

Trustees: Sir S. Sternberg; V. M. Sternberg; Lady Sternberg; Revd M. C. Rossi Braybrooke; M. A. M. Slowe; R. Tamir; M. D. Paisner.

CC Number: 257950

This trust supports the furtherance of the interfaith activities to promote racial and religious harmony, in particular between Christian, Jewish and Muslim faiths, and the education in, and understanding of, their fundamental tenets and beliefs. Most grants are made to Jewish and Israeli charities. The trust makes a small number of large grants, generally of £10,000 to £80,000 each, and a large number of smaller grants.

In 2011/12 the trust had assets of £4.3 million and an income of £442,000. Grants were made totalling £267,000, broken down as follows:

Promotion of interfaith understanding	39	£167,000
Religious activities	21	£71,000
Education	22	£14,800
Medical care and care of older people and people with disabilities	35	£7,200
Arts and culture	4	£5,400
Relief of poverty	17	£700
Bereavement care	1	£250

Grant beneficiaries included: Three Faiths Forum (£143,000); The Movement for Reform Judaism (£70,000); The Board of Deputies Charitable Foundation (£17,000); Leo Baeck College Centre for Jewish Education (£5,800); The Times/Sternbeck Active Life Award and UCL Development Fund (£5,000 each); World Congress of Faiths (£3,300); Oxford Centre for Hebrew and Jewish Studies (£2,000 each); Friends of the Hebrew University of Jerusalem (£1,600); and Age Exchange Theatre Trust (£1,000).

There were a further 87 grants of less than £1,000 totalling £11,000.

Exclusions

No grants to individuals.

Applications

In writing to the correspondent.

Information gathered from:

Accounts; Charity Commission record.

Stervon Ltd

Jewish

£200,000 (2011)

Beneficial area

UK.

Correspondent: A. Reich, Secretary, 109 St Ann's Road, Prestwich, Manchester M25 9GE (tel: 01617 375000)

Trustees: A. Reich; Gabriel Rothbart.

CC Number: 280958

'The principal objective of the company is the distribution of funds to Jewish, religious, educational and similar charities.'

In 2011 the trust had assets of £184,500 and an income of £203,000. Grants were made totalling £200,000. Unfortunately more recent information was not available at the time of writing as the charity consistently files its accounts late with the Charity Commission. Details on recent beneficiaries are also absent from the accounts.

Previous beneficiaries include: Eitz Chaim, Rehabilitation Trust, Chasdei Yoel, Beis Yoel, Friends of Horeinu, Beis Hamedrash Hachadash, Tashbar, Tov V' Chessed, Beth Sorah Schneirer and Asser Bishvil.

Applications

In writing to the correspondent.

Information gathered from:

Accounts; Charity Commission record.

Stevenson Family's Charitable Trust

Culture and arts, conservation and heritage, health, education, overseas aid and general charitable purposes

£501,000 (2012/13)

Beneficial area

Worldwide, in practice mainly UK.

Correspondent: Sir Hugh Stevenson, Trustee, Old Waterfield, Winkfield Road, Ascot SL5 7LJ

Trustees: Sir Hugh Stevenson; Lady Catherine Stevenson.

CC Number: 327148

This is the family trust of Hugh and Catherine Stevenson. A well-known City of London figure, Hugh Stevenson was formerly the chair of one of London's largest investment management companies. The trust operates with no premises or salaried staff of its own and is probably best seen simply as the vehicle for the personal donations of Mr and Mrs Stevenson, rather than as an institution with an independent existence.

The current policy of the trustees is in the main to support charitable causes in the fields of culture and the arts, conservation and heritage, and education, but they can exercise their discretion to make donations for other charitable purposes. In accordance with this policy the main donations made by the trustees during the year were in favour of places of culture and arts.

In 2012/13 the trust had assets of £2 million and an income of £228,000. Grants were made to 52 organisations totalling £501,000, and were categorised as follows:

Conservation and heritage	9	£182,500
General charitable purposes	14	£147,000
Culture and arts	14	£145,000
Education and training	5	£16,500
Health and medicine	7	£10,000
Overseas aid	3	£1,250

Beneficiaries included: Royal National Theatre and the Foundation and Friends of the Royal Botanic Gardens, Kew (£100,000 each); St Michael and All Angels, Sunninghill (£60,000); Berkshire Community Foundation (£40,000); the Abbotsford Trust and the Strawberry Hill Trust (£25,000 each); Royal Marines Charitable Trust Fund and the Watts Gallery Trust (£10,000 each); Berkshire County Blind Society and Prior's Court Foundation (£5,000 each); and Whitechapel Art Gallery and Charleston Trust (£1,000 each).

Exclusions

No grants to individuals.

Applications

'No unsolicited applications can be considered as the charity's funds are required to support purposes chosen by the trustees.'

Information gathered from:

Accounts; Charity Commission record.

The Stewards' Charitable Trust

Rowing

£250,000 (2011/12)

Beneficial area

Principally the UK.

Correspondent: Daniel Grist, Secretary, Regatta Headquarters, Henley Bridge, Henley-on-Thames, Oxfordshire RG9 2LY (tel: 01491 572153; fax: 01491 575509; website: www.hrr.co.uk)

Trustees: Michael Sweeney; Christopher Davidge; C. L. Baillieu; R. C. Lester; Sir Steve Redgrave.

CC Number: 299597

The Stewards' Charitable Trust was formally established by the governing body of the Henley Regatta in June 1988. The principal objective of the trust was to provide funds to encourage and support young people (still receiving education or undergoing training) to row or scull.

> The trust receives the bulk of its money from substantial annual donations made by Henley Royal Regatta and its trading arm, Henley Royal Regatta Ltd, but also benefits from the generosity of other donors, both corporate and individual, including several members of the Stewards' Enclosure.

The trust makes grants to organisations and clubs benefiting boys and girls involved in the sport of rowing. It supports rowing at all levels, from grassroots upwards; beneficiaries should be in full-time education or training. Support is also given to related medical and educational research projects. The trust works closely with British Rowing and the major current initiative is the long-term support of the Scholarship Coaching Scheme. Grants can be one-off or recurring and are especially made where matched funds are raised elsewhere.

In 2011/12 the trust had assets of £5.5 million and an income of £337,500. Grants were made totalling around £250,000.

Typical beneficiaries include: British Rowing Scholarships; London Youth Rowing; Rowing Foundation; Project Oarsome; Henley Rowing Club; Ball Cup Regatta; and Regatta for the Disabled.

Exclusions

No grants to individuals or for building or capital costs.

Applications

In writing to the correspondent. Applications are usually first vetted by Amateur Rowing Association.

Information gathered from:

Accounts; Charity Commission record; funder's website.

The Andy Stewart Charitable Foundation

General

£80,000 (2012)

Beneficial area

Worldwide.

Correspondent: The Trustees, Bridger, 14 Glategny Esplanade, St Peter Port, Guernsey GY1 1WP

Trustees: Andy Stewart; Mark Stewart; Paul Stewart.

CC Number: 1114802

The foundation was set up in 2006 by Andy Stewart, founder of Cenkos Securities and now chair of Ravenscroft Ltd, an investment and stockbroking firm.

In 2012 the foundation had an income of £19,000 and a total expenditure of £88,500. Due to a reduction in income in recent years the foundation's accounts were unavailable at the Charity Commission. Grant total is estimated at around £80,000.

Grants were made to organisations involved in spinal injuries care and research, other healthcare, animal welfare and assisting young people. Typical beneficiaries include: Spinal Research; Sir Peter O'Sullivan Charitable Trust; Spinal Injuries; Moorcroft Trust;

Brompton Foundation; and Racing Welfare.

Applications

In writing to the correspondent.

Information gathered from:

Accounts; Charity Commission record.

The Stoller Charitable Trust

Medical, children, general

£405,500 (2011/12)

Beneficial area

UK, with a preference for the Greater Manchester area.

Correspondent: Alison M. Ford, Secretary, Wrigley Partington Chartered Accountants, Sterling House, 501 Middleton Road, Chadderton, Oldham OL9 9LY (tel: 01616 220222; fax: 01616 275446; email: enquiries@stollercharitabletrust.co.uk)

Trustees: Norman K. Stoller; Roger Gould; Sheila M. Stoller; Andrew Dixon.

CC Number: 285415

The trust supports a wide variety of charitable causes, but with particular emphasis on those that are local (Greater Manchester), medically related or supportive of children. It also endeavours to maintain a balance between regular and occasional donations and between large and smaller grants. Grants can be considered for buildings, capital costs, projects, research costs, recurring costs and start-up costs. As well as one-off grants, funding may also be given for up to three years.

In 2011/12 the trust had assets of £5.4 million and an income of £203,000. Grants were made to organisations totalling £405,500.

Previous beneficiaries include: Bauern Helfen Bauern (Farmers Helping Farmers); Onside North West; Broughton House; Central Manchester Children's Hospitals; Live Music Now; Christie Hospital, Greater Manchester Appeal; Imperial War Museum North; National Memorial Arboretum; Cancer Research UK; Oldham Liaison of Ex-Services Associations; Church Housing Trust; Commandery of John of Gaunt; Mines Advisory Group; Salvation Army; and Windermere Air Show.

Exclusions

No grants to individuals.

Applications

In writing to the correspondent. Applications need to be received by February, May, August or November. The trustees usually meet in March, June, September and December.

Information gathered from:

Accounts; Charity Commission record.

The M. J C. Stone Charitable Trust

General

£390,000 (2012)

Beneficial area

UK.

Correspondent: Michael Stone, Trustee, Estate Office, Ozleworth Park, Wotton-under-Edge, Gloucestershire GL12 7QA (tel: 01453 845591)

Trustees: Michael Stone; Louisa Stone; Charles Stone; Andrew Stone; Nicola Farquhar.

CC Number: 283920

While the trust has general charitable objects, giving to a range of causes, it stated that its main area of interest is the advancement of education. Other areas include health, the environment and the relief of poverty.

In 2012 the trust had assets of £756,500 and an income of £310,000 (£1 million in 2011). Grants were made to 45 organisations totalling £390,000.

Beneficiaries included: Tennis for Free and the Diamond Jubilee Trust (£100,000 each); Bradfield Foundation (£50,000); Centre for Social Justice (£27,000); Game and Wildlife Trust (£18,000); Countryside Learning (£10,000); University of the Highlands and Islands, Evelina Children's Hospital, National Autistic Society, Wheelpower and the Outward Bound Trust (£5,000 each); Pestalozzi World Trust and Making the Change (£1,000 each).

Applications

In writing to the correspondent. 'The charitable trust makes grants to core charities on an annual basis. Grants to other charities are made on receipt of applications and after discussions between the trustees.'

Information gathered from:

Accounts; Charity Commission record.

The Samuel Storey Family Charitable Trust

General

£99,500 (2011/12)

Beneficial area

UK, with a preference for Yorkshire.

Correspondent: Hon. Sir Richard Storey, Trustee, 21 Buckingham Gate, London SW1E 6LS (tel: 020 7802 2700)

Trustees: Hon. Sir Richard Storey; Wren Hoskyns Abrahall; Kenelm Storey.

CC Number: 267684

This trust has general charitable purposes, supporting a wide range of causes, including the arts, children, gardens and churches. The grants list shows a large number of beneficiaries in Yorkshire.

In 2011/12 the trust had assets of £4.7 million and an income of £164,000. Grants were made to 131 organisations totalling £99,500. Most grants were for less than £1,000.

The largest grant again went to Hope and Homes for Children (£25,000). Other beneficiaries included: York University (£20,000); St John the Evangelist, Edinburgh (£6,000); Peter Buckley Learning Centre (£2,500); Archbishop of York Youth Trust (£2,000); and Justice First Ltd, Music at Paxton, Pebbles Project, Rainbow Trust and Smile Support and Care (£1,000 each).

Exclusions

No grants to individuals.

Applications

In writing to the correspondent. The trust informed us that, 'in order to give appropriately, we only really do so to personalised applications'.

Information gathered from:

Accounts; Charity Commission record.

Peter Stormonth Darling Charitable Trust

Heritage, medical research, sport

£131,000 (2012)

Beneficial area

UK.

Correspondent: Peter Stormonth Darling, Trustee, Soditic Ltd, 12 Charles II Street, London SW1Y 4QU

Trustees: John Rodwell; Peter Stormonth Darling; Elizabeth Cobb; Arabella Johannes; Christa Taylor.

CC Number: 1049946

The trust makes grants towards heritage, education, healthcare and sports facilities.

In 2012 it had assets of £3.6 million and an income of £192,500 (£1.1 million in 2011). Grants were made to 21 organisations totalling £131,000.

As in previous years, the largest grant was made to Winchester College Wykeham Campaign (£50,000). Other beneficiaries included: Friends of East Sussex Hospices and Westminster Abbey (£12,500 each); National Trust Scotland

(£5,000); Chailey Heritage and Fields in Trust (£2,500 each); Royal Commonwealth Ex-Services League (£1,500); and Arthritis Research UK (£1,000).

Exclusions

No grants to individuals.

Applications

This trust states that it does not respond to unsolicited applications.

Information gathered from:

Accounts; Charity Commission record.

Peter Storrs Trust

Education

£105,000 (2011/12)

Beneficial area

UK.

Correspondent: The Trustees, c/o Smithfield Accountants, 117 Charterhouse Street, London EC1M 6AA (tel: 020 7253 3757)

Trustees: Geoffrey Adams; Arthur Curtis; Julie Easton.

CC Number: 313804

The trust makes grants to registered charities working for the advancement of education in the UK. The trust informed us: 'We have around 30 regular recipients of grants, paid by annual standing order. Other [grants] are generally one-off payments.'

In 2011/12 the trust had assets of £2.5 million, an income of £118,000 and gave grants totalling £105,000. Of this grant total, £61,000 was given in recurring grants and £44,000 in one-off grants.

Beneficiaries included: Peter House (£5,400); Daylight Christian Prison Trust (£4,000); British Schools Exploring Society (£3,000), African Medical, British Bible Society, Hope and Homes for Children, Marie Curie Memorial, Radley College, SENSE, Voluntary Services Overseas, Excellent Development Ltd, The Archway Project and Wiltshire Guild of Spinners, Weavers and Dyers (£2,000 each); and SignAlong Group (£1,500).

Applications

In writing to the correspondent. Applications are considered every three to six months. Note the trust receives far more applications than it is able to support, many of which do not meet the criteria outlined above. This results in a heavy waste of time and expense for both applicants and the trust itself.

Percentage of awards given to new applicants: between 30% and 40%.

Information gathered from:

Accounts; Charity Commission record; further information provided by the funder.

The Strawberry Charitable Trust

Jewish, youth

Around £90,000 (2010/11)

Beneficial area

Not defined but with a preference for Manchester.

Correspondent: Anthony Leon, 4 Westfields, Hale, Altrincham WA15 0LL (tel: 01619 808484; email: anthonysula@hotmail.com)

Trustees: Emma Myers; Laura Avigdori; Anthony Leon.

CC Number: 1090173

Set up in January 2000, this trust supports the relief of poverty and hardship amongst Jewish persons and the advancement of the Jewish religion.

Unfortunately the trust's accounts for 2011/12 had not been filed with the Charity Commission at the time of writing. In 2010/11 the trust had an income of £3,500 and a total expenditure of £97,500. It is estimated that grants were made totalling around £90,000.

Previous beneficiaries included: United Jewish Israel Appeal; Community Security Trust; The Fed; Lubavitch South Manchester; King David School; World Jewish Relief; Belz and St John's Wood Synagogue; Action on Addiction; Mew Children's Hospital; and Tickets for Troops.

Applications

In writing to the correspondent.

Information gathered from:

Accounts; Charity Commission record.

The W. O. Street Charitable Foundation

Education, people with disabilities, young people, health, social welfare

£407,500 (2012)

Beneficial area

UK, with a preference for the North West of England, primarily Lancashire and Jersey.

Correspondent: The Trust Officer, Barclays Bank Trust Co. Ltd, Osborne Court, Gadbrook Park, Rudheath, Cheshire CW9 7UE (tel: 01606 313179)

Trustees: Barclays Bank Trust Co. Ltd; Clive Cutbill.

CC Number: 267127

In considering grants the trustees pay close regard to the wishes of the late Mr Street who had particular interests in education, support for people with financial difficulties (particularly the elderly, people who are blind or who have other disabilities), health and social welfare generally. Special support is given to the North West of England and Jersey.

In 2012 the trust had an income of £300,000 and assets of £15 million. Grants were made totalling £407,500.

Beneficiaries included: W O Street Jersey Charitable Trust (£40,000); Emmott Foundation (£30,000); The Fusilier Museum (£20,000); Ribblesdale High School and THOMAS Organisation (£5,000 each); Sahir House (£4,000); New Brighton Community Association (£3,000); Rochdale Connections Trust (£2,500); Norfolk Deaf Association (£2,000); and Fylde Community Link (£600).

Exclusions

No grants towards:

- Medical research
- Animal welfare
- Overseas projects or charities

Applications directly from individuals are not considered.

Applications

In writing to the correspondent. Applications are usually considered on a quarterly basis, at the end of January, April, July and October.

Information gathered from:

Accounts; Charity Commission record.

The A. B. Strom and R. Strom Charitable Trust

Jewish, general

Around £33,000 (2011/12)

Beneficial area

UK.

Correspondent: Regina Strom, Trustee, c/o 11 Gloucester Gardens, London NW11 9AB (tel: 020 8455 5949; email: m@michaelpasha.worldonline.co.uk)

Trustees: Regina Strom; Debbie Weissbraun.

CC Number: 268916

The objects of the charity are stated as follows:

- The advancement of education according to the tenets of the Orthodox Jewish faith
- The relief of poverty and sickness

However, according to the correspondent 'the trust only supports a set list of charities working with elderly people, schools/colleges, hospitals and Christian causes. It does not have any money available for any charities not already on the list.'

In 2011/12 the trust had an income of £5,000 and a total expenditure of £33,000. No further information was available.

Previously, grants in excess of £1,000 each were made to Yeshivas Hanegev (£10,000), JRRC (£10,000 in two grants); and Redcroft and Russian Immigrants (£5,000 each).

Information gathered from:

Accounts; Charity Commission record.

Sueberry Ltd

Jewish, welfare

£147,500 (2011/12)

Beneficial area

UK and overseas.

Correspondent: D. S. Davis, Trustee, 18 Clifton Gardens, London N15 6AP

Trustees: D. S. Davis, Chair; C. Davis; Mrs H. Davis; J. Davis; Mrs M. Davis; A. D. Davis; S. M. Davis; Y. Davis.

CC Number: 256566

The trust makes grants to Jewish organisations and to other UK welfare, educational and medical organisations benefiting children and young adults, at risk groups, people who are disadvantaged by poverty, or socially isolated people.

In 2011/12 the trust had assets of £100,000 and an income of £172,500. Grants were made totalling £147,500. A list of beneficiaries was not available. In previous years the trust has supported educational, religious and other charitable organisations.

Applications

In writing to the correspondent.

Information gathered from:

Accounts; Charity Commission record.

The Alan Sugar Foundation

Jewish charities, general

Around £220,000 (2011/12)

Beneficial area

UK.

Correspondent: Colin Sandy, Trustee, Amshold House, Goldings Hill, Loughton, Essex IG10 3RW (tel: 020 3225 5560; email: colin@amsprop.com)

Trustees: Lord Alan Sugar; Colin Sandy; Simon Sugar; Daniel Sugar; Louise Baron.

CC Number: 294880

This trust was established for general charitable purposes in 1986 by businessman and ex-chair of Tottenham Hotspur FC, Alan Sugar. It gives a small number of substantial grants each year to registered charities that are of current and ongoing interest to the trustees.

In 2011/12 the trust had an income of just £3,000 and a total expenditure of £232,000. Unfortunately the accounts were not available to view due to the low income, but it is estimated that grants were made totalling around £220,000.

Previous beneficiaries include: Jewish Care; Sport Relief; Macmillan Cancer; BBC Children in Need; Prostate Cancer Charitable Fund; Sightsavers; St Marylebone Church of England School; Cancer Research UK; and St Michael's Hospice.

Exclusions

No grants for individuals or to non-registered charities.

Applications

This trust states that it does not respond to unsolicited applications. All projects are initiated by the trustees.

Information gathered from:

Accounts; Charity Commission record.

The Adrienne and Leslie Sussman Charitable Trust

Jewish, general

£46,000 (2011/12)

Beneficial area

UK, in practice Greater London, particularly Barnet.

Correspondent: Adrienne Sussman, Trustee, 25 Tillingbourne Gardens, London N3 3JJ (tel: 020 8346 6775)

Trustees: Adrienne Sussman; Debra Sussman; Martin Paisner; Adam Sussman; Neal Sussman.

CC Number: 274955

The trust supports a variety of Jewish, medical and social welfare organisations, including many in the Greater London area.

In 2011/12 the trust had assets of £2 million and an income of £69,000. Grants were made totalling £46,000.

A list of beneficiaries was not available, however previous beneficiaries have included; BF Shvut Ami, Chai – Lifeline and B'nai B'rith Hillel Fund, Child Resettlement, Children and Youth Aliyah, Finchley Synagogue, Jewish Care, Nightingale House, Norwood Ravenswood and Sidney Sussex CLL.

Exclusions

No grants to branches of UK charities outside Barnet, non-registered charities and individuals.

Applications

In writing to the correspondent.

Information gathered from:

Accounts; Charity Commission record.

The Sutasoma Trust

Education, general

£98,500 (2011/12)

Beneficial area

UK and overseas.

Correspondent: Jane Lichtenstein, Trustee, PO Box 157, Haverhill, Suffolk CB9 1AH (tel: 07768 245384; email: sutasoma.trust@btinternet.com)

Trustees: Dr Angela Hobart; Marcel Burgauer; Jane Lichtenstein; Prof. Bruce Kapferer; Dr Sally Wolfe; Dr Piers Vitebsky.

CC Number: 803301

The trust's objects are 'to advance education and humanitarian activities by providing bursaries and support to institutions in the field of social sciences, humanities and humanitarian activities'. General grants may also be made. 'The trustees have indicated in the past that they prefer that annual donations should be made available to organisations on a recurring basis for the mid-to long-term.'

In 2011/12 the trust had assets of £2.6 million and an income of £103,500. Grants were made totalling £98,500. As in previous years, the largest grants went to Lucy Cavendish College Fellowship (£19,500); and University of Bergen (£12,000).

Other grants included those made to: Manipal Centre for Philosophy and Humanities (£9,000 in total); Livingstone Anglican Children's Project – Zambia (£7,000); HAU Journal of Ethnographic Theory (£4,000); Link Numeracy Project (£2,000); and the Medical Foundation Allotment Project and the Welfare Association (£1,000 each).

Applications

In writing to the correspondent.

Information gathered from:

Accounts; Charity Commission record.

The Suva Foundation Ltd

General

£245,000 (2011/12)

Beneficial area

Unrestricted with a preference for Henley-on-Thames.

Correspondent: Cristina Wade, Administrator, 61 Grosvenor Street, London W1K 3JE (tel: 020 3011 1100)

Trustees: Annabel Nicoll; Paddy Nicoll.

CC Number: 1077057

Set up in 1999, this is the foundation of Annabel Nicoll, who is the daughter of Sir Martyn Arbib, and her husband, Paddy Nicoll. The foundation has general charitable purposes, with a preference for education, health, medicine and culture. Along with the Arbib Foundation, the Suva Foundation is a supporter of the Langley Academy, where Annabel Nicoll is the vice chair of governors.

In 2011/12 the foundation had assets of £9.9 million and an income of £286,000. Grants were made totalling £245,000, which included £68,000 in support costs for the Langley Academy. A grant of £9,500 was also given to the academy.

Other beneficiaries included: Cancer Research UK (£101,000); Alfred Dunhill Links Foundation (£25,000); Rowing For Our Wounded (£20,000); Crazies Hill Educational Trust (£5,000); Henley Festival Trust (£2,500); and Lambrook School Trust Ltd (£1,000).

Applications

This trust does not accept unsolicited applications.

Information gathered from:

Accounts; Charity Commission record.

Swan Mountain Trust

Mental health, penal affairs

£42,500 (2012/13)

Beneficial area

UK.

Correspondent: Janet Hargreaves, Trustee, 7 Mount Vernon, London NW3 6QS (tel: 020 7794 2486; email: info@swanmountaintrust.org.uk; website: swanmountaintrust.org.uk)

Trustees: Dodie Carter; Janet Hargreaves; Peter Kilgarriff; Calton Younger.

CC Number: 275594

This trust supports organisations which are actively involved in the fields of mental health (not disability) and penal affairs. Provision is also made to help prisoners with educational needs. Grants are made to meet specific needs and rarely exceed £1,500.

The following information is given on the trust's website:

> We are a very small grant making trust and as such like to ensure that The Swan Mountain Trust's limited resources are used as effectively as possible. We do not consider contributing to large appeals but would rather consider a piece of equipment, or an activity for which we can consider meeting the cost in full – somewhere between £500 and £2000. Alternatively, the trust would consider meeting the final amount of a larger appeal after most of the costs have already been met.

In 2012/13 the trust had assets of £1.1 million and an income of £47,500. Grants were made to 27 organisations totalling £42,500.

Beneficiaries included: Prisoner's Education Trust (£5,000); Scottish Association for Mental Health (£3,000); Asha Women's Centre, Synergy Theatre and The Zahid Mubarek Trust (£2,000 each); Birmingham Centre for Arts Therapies (£1,500); Hope Housing, Training and Support Trust and Young Minds (£1,000 each); and Fair Shares (£500).

Exclusions

No grants for annual holidays, debt repayment, large appeals or for causes outside the trust's two main areas of work.

Applications

In writing to the correspondent, enclosing an up-to-date report on fundraising, and a copy of the most recent annual report and accounts (or any financial information available). The trustees meet in early February, June and October each year, but can occasionally reach decisions quickly in an emergency. Applications should be made at least four weeks before the trustees' next meeting. The trust tries to be as responsive as it can be to appropriate applicants.

Percentage of awards given to new applicants: between 40% and 50%.

Common applicant mistakes

'Outside our defined categories; individual applications (which we used to consider).'

Information gathered from:

Accounts; Charity Commission record; further information provided by the funder; funder's website.

The Swire Charitable Trust

General

£742,500 (2012)

Beneficial area

Worldwide.

Correspondent: The Trustees, Swire House, 59 Buckingham Gate, London SW1E 6AJ (tel: 020 7834 7717)

Trustees: Sir J. Swire; Sir Adrian Swire; B. N. Swire; J. S. Swire; M. Swire; J. W. J. Hughes-Hallett.

CC Number: 270726

This trust was established for general charitable purposes in 1975. In 2012 the trust had an income of £750,000 – almost entirely from donations received from John Swire and Sons Ltd. Assets stood at –£31,000 and grants to over 119 organisations totalled £742,500.

Beneficiaries included: Alzheimer's Research UK (£75,000); Marine Society and Sea Cadets (£50,000); Royal Ballet School (£30,000); Air League Trust (£26,000); Royal Academy of Arts and Textile Conservation Centre Foundation (£25,000 each); Walking with the Wounded (£15,000); British Red Cross, Combat Stress, Eden Project, Monte San Martino Trust St Mungo's and Voluntary Services Overseas (£10,000 each); Action for ME (£7,500); Ambitious about Autism, Children in Crisis and The Florence Institute (£5,000 each); Canine Partners, Dementia UK and Grey Coat Hospital (£2,500 each); and Survival International (£1,000).

Grants of less than £1,000 each totalled almost £1,500.

Applications

In writing to the correspondent. The trust states that: 'although the Trustees make some grants with no formal applications, they normally require organisations to submit a request explaining how the funds could be used and what would be achieved'. Applications are considered throughout the year.

Information gathered from:

Accounts; Charity Commission record.

The Adrian Swire Charitable Trust (formerly The Sammermar Trust)

General

£997,000 (2012)

Beneficial area

UK and overseas.

Correspondent: The Trustees, Swire House, 59 Buckingham Gate, London SW1E 6AJ (tel: 020 7834 7717)

Trustees: Lady Judith Swire; Timothy Cox; Richard Leonard; M. B. Swire; M. V. Allfrey.

CC Number: 800493

The trust, formerly known as the Adrian Swire Charitable Trust, was established in 1988 with general charitable purposes.

In 2012 the trust had assets of £18 million, an income of £970,000 and gave grants totalling £997,000.

Beneficiaries included: Eton College (£213,000); Collegiate Church of St Mary (£100,000); BSES (£75,000); The Inkerman Housing Association (£45,000); Brain Tumour Charity and Crisis Skylight Oxford (£20,000 each); British Lung Foundation (£11,000); Game and Wildlife Conservation Trust (£6,000); Independent Advice Centre (£5,000); Sparsholt Church (£3,000); 999 Club (£2,000); and Spitfire Society (£1,000).

Applications

In writing to the correspondent. The trust states that: 'although the trustees make some grants with no formal applications, they normally require organisations to submit a request saying how the funds could be used and what would be achieved'. The trustees usually meet monthly.

Information gathered from:

Accounts; Charity Commission record.

The Hugh and Ruby Sykes Charitable Trust

General, medical, education, employment

£77,000 (2012/13)

Beneficial area

Principally South Yorkshire, also Derbyshire.

Correspondent: Brian Evans, Administrator, The Coach House, Brookfield Manor, Hathersage, Hope Valley, Derbyshire S32 1BR (tel: 01433 651190; email: info@brookfieldmanor.com)

Trustees: Sir Hugh Sykes; Lady Ruby Sykes.

CC Number: 327648

This trust was set up in 1987 for general charitable purposes by Sir Hugh Sykes and his wife Lady Sykes. It supports local charities in South Yorkshire and Derbyshire, some major UK charities and a few medical charities.

In 2012/13 the trust had assets of £1.9 million and an income of £173,500. Grants were made totalling £77,000. A list of beneficiaries was not included in the accounts.

Exclusions

No grants are made to individuals. Most grants are made to organisations which have a connection to one of the trustees.

Applications

Applications can only be accepted from registered charities and should be in writing to the correspondent. In order to save administration costs, replies are not sent to unsuccessful applicants. If the trustees are able to consider a request for support, they aim to express interest within one month.

Information gathered from:

Accounts; Charity Commission record.

The Sylvanus Charitable Trust

Animal welfare, Roman Catholic

£31,000 (2012)

Beneficial area

Europe and North America.

Correspondent: Gloria Taviner, Trustee, Hunters Solicitors, 9 New Square, London WC2A 3QN (tel: 020 7412 0050; fax: 020 7412 0049; email: gt@hunters-solicitors.co.uk)

Trustees: John C. Vernor Miles; Alexander D. Gemmill; Wilfred E. Vernor Miles; Gloria Taviner.

CC Number: 259520

This trust was established in 1968 by the Countess of Kinnoull, who spent the last 40 years of her life in California, and supports animal welfare, the prevention of animal cruelty and the teachings and practices of the Roman Catholic Church pre Second Vatican Council. Organisations in North America and Europe are supported, with the trust splitting its finances into two sections, namely, the sterling section (Europe) and the dollar section (North America).

As the dollar section focuses solely on US giving only the sterling section is described here.

In 2012 it had assets of £2.3 million and an income of £84,000. Grants were made to 13 organisations totalling £31,000.

The beneficiaries included: Society of St Pius X (£5,000); Fauna and Flora International (£3,000); Durrell Wildlife Conservation Trust (£2,000); and Animal Health Trust and Help in Suffering (£1,000 each).

Exclusions

No grants for expeditions, scholarships or individuals.

Applications

The trustees usually make grants to charities known personally to them but occasionally make grants in response to unsolicited appeals. When considering applications for funding the trustees take into account how many years' reserves are held by an applicant and the proportionate costs of administration and fundraising. They also consider the degree to which the trustees have been informed of progress made since previous grants. The trustees do not give grants to individuals. Apply in writing to the correspondent. The trustees meet once a year.

Information gathered from:

Accounts; Charity Commission record.

T. and S. Trust Fund

Orthodox Jewish

£75,000 (2011/12)

Beneficial area

Greater London, Gateshead, Manchester City.

Correspondent: Aaron Sandler, Administrator, 96 Whitehall Road, Gateshead, Tyne And Wear NE8 4ET (tel: 01914 825050)

Trustees: Shoshana Sandler; Ezriel Salomon.

CC Number: 1095939

'The objects of the charity are the advancement of education according to the tenets of the Orthodox Jewish Faith, the advancement of the Orthodox Jewish Religion and the relief of poverty amongst the elderly or persons in need, hardship and distress in the Jewish Community.'

In 2011/12 the trust had assets of £142,500 and an income of £68,500. Grants were made totalling £75,000. Although submitted to the Charity Commission, the accounts which were available to view were incomplete and omitted the trust's beneficiaries.

Previous beneficiaries include: Orphan Children Fund; Centre for Advanced Rabbinics; New Hall Charitable Trust; Rozac Charitable Trust; Etz Chaim

School; Yeshaya Adler Memorial Fund; and Tashbar.

Applications

In writing to the correspondent.

Information gathered from:

Accounts; Charity Commission record.

The Tabeel Trust

Evangelical Christian

£67,000 (2011/12)

Beneficial area

Worldwide with a preference for Clacton (Essex).

Correspondent: Barbara Carter, Trustee, 3 Oak Park, West Byfleet, Surrey KT14 6AG (tel: 01932 343808)

Trustees: Douglas Brown; Barbara Carter; Dr Mary Clark; Jean Richardson; James Davey; Sarah Taylor; Nigel Davey.

CC Number: 266645

This trust primarily supports Evangelical Christian activities and projects which are either based in Clacton or are personally known to one or more of the trustees.

In 2011/12 the trust had assets of almost £1.1 million and an income of £29,000. Grants were made to 28 organisation totalling £67,000.

Beneficiaries included: Scargill House Building Project (£10,000); Spacious Places (£8,000); Sorted Magazine (£5,000); Barnabas Fund (£3,000); Galeed House and Retrak – Street Children Programme in Ethiopia and Uganda (£2,000 each); and Arise and Shine Children's Home – Kenya and Evangelical Alliance (£1,000 each).

Applications

Only charities with which a trustee already has contact should apply. Grants are considered at trustees' meetings in May and November and applications should be received by 31 March and 30 September respectively.

Percentage of awards given to new applicants: between 10% and 20%.

Common applicant mistakes

'[They are] unknown to us; too much waffle; no proper budget; no realistic target.'

Information gathered from:

Accounts; Charity Commission record; further information provided by the funder.

The Gay and Keith Talbot Trust

Overseas aid, health, famine relief

£116,000 (2012/13)

Beneficial area

Worldwide.

Correspondent: Keith Talbot, Chair, Fold Howe, Kentmere, Kendal, Cumbria LA8 9JW (tel: 01539 821504; email: rktalbot@yahoo.co.uk)

Trustees: Keith Talbot, Chair; Gay Talbot.

CC Number: 1102192

Established in 2004, this trust mainly supports charities working in developing countries.

In 2012/13 the trust had assets of £109,500 and an income of £120,000. Grants were made to eight organisations totalling £116,000

The beneficiaries were: CAFOD (£50,000, for water projects in Sudan); International Nepal Fellowship (£19,000, for a fistula repair camp); International Refugee Trust (£16,000, for aid in Sudan); Jesuit Missions (£10,000, to support torture victims in Zimbabwe); Medical Missionaries of Mary (£10,000 in total); Impact Foundation (£10,000 in total); Our Lady of Windermere and St Herbert (£500); and Amnesty International (£100).

Applications

In writing to the correspondent.

Information gathered from:

Accounts; Charity Commission record.

The Talbot Village Trust

General

£577,000 (2012)

Beneficial area

The boroughs of Bournemouth, Christchurch and Poole; the districts of east Dorset and Purbeck.

Correspondent: Gary S. Cox, Clerk, Dickinson Manser LLP, 5 Parkstone Road, Poole, Dorset BH15 2NL (tel: 01202 673071; email: garycox@dickinsonmanser.co.uk)

Trustees: Christopher Lees, Chair; James Fleming; Sir George Meyrick; Sir Thomas Salt; Russell Rowe; Earl of Shaftesbury.

CC Number: 249349

Support is given to 'other charitable bodies, churches, schools and the like for projects which support youth, the elderly and the disadvantaged in the boroughs of Bournemouth, Christchurch and Poole and the districts of East Dorset and Purbeck'. In addition, the trust also gives extensive support to charities in the form of loans. The charity owns and manages land and property at Talbot Village, Bournemouth, including almshouses which it maintains through an associated trust. There is a strong property focus in much of the trust's work.

As part of the trust's rolling five year plan it aims to make grants and loans averaging £800,000 per annum, in addition to its regular support of St Mark's Church, St Mark's School, the University Chaplaincy and others. The majority of grants are made for capital costs such as, equipment, refurbishment and building extensions.

In 2012 the trust had of assets of £37.8 million and an income of £1.8 million. Grants were made totalling £577,000, in line with the five year grant expenditure plan.

Grants authorised and paid during the year included those to: Strouden Park Community Association (£20,000); Richmond Hill St Andrew's United Reform Church (£15,000); Motability (£10,000); Dorset Blind Association (£7,000); Motor Neurone Disease Association East Dorset and New Forest (£4,500); and the Bus Stop Club (£1,000).

Exclusions

No grants for individuals.

Applications

In writing to the correspondent.

Percentage of awards given to new applicants: between 20% and 30%.

Common applicant mistakes

'[Applying] for funding in respect of projects which are outside of the trustees' criteria or area of benefit.'

Information gathered from:

Accounts; Charity Commission record; further information provided by the funder.

Talteg Ltd

Jewish, welfare

£203,000 (2012)

Beneficial area

UK, with a preference for Scotland.

Correspondent: Fred Berkley, Trustee, Gordon Chambers, 90 Mitchell Street, Glasgow G1 3NQ (tel: 01412 213353)

Trustees: Fred Berkley; Adam Berkley; Delia Lynn Berkley; Maxwell Berkley.

CC Number: 283253

In 2012 the trust had assets of £4.1 million and an income of £304,500. Grants were made during the year totalling £203,000. A list of grants was not included in the accounts.

Previous beneficiaries include: British Friends of Laniado Hospital, Centre for Jewish Studies, Society of Friends of the Torah, Glasgow Jewish Community Trust, National Trust for Scotland, Ayrshire Hospice, Earl Haig Fund – Scotland and RSSPCC.

Applications

In writing to the correspondent.

Information gathered from:

Accounts; Charity Commission record.

The Lady Tangye Charitable Trust

Catholic, overseas aid, general

£33,500 (2011/12)

Beneficial area

UK and worldwide, with some preference for the Midlands.

Correspondent: Colin Ferguson Smith, Trustee, 55 Warwick Crest, Arthur Road, Birmingham B15 2LH (tel: 01214 544698)

Trustees: Gitta Clarisse Gilzean Tangye; Colin Ferguson Smith; Michael Plaut.

CC Number: 1044220

This trust has general charitable purposes, with a preference for work in the Midlands and the developing world. Christian and environmental causes are also represented in grants awarded.

In 2011/12 it had assets of £946,000 and an income of £30,000. Grants were made totalling £33,500. The schedule to the accounts, detailing grant beneficiaries, was not published on the Commission's website.

Previous beneficiaries have included: West Midland Urban Wildlife Trust (£3,000); Spana, ChildLine – Midlands and Aid to the Church in Need (£2,000 each); Amnesty International, Priest Training Fund and Crew Trust (£1,500 each); St Saviour's Church, Walsall and District Samaritans, Life and European Children's Trust (£1,000 each); and Charity Ignite – Big Ideal (£500).

Applications

In writing to the correspondent.

Information gathered from:

Accounts; Charity Commission record.

The David Tannen Charitable Trust

Jewish causes

£222,000 (2011/12)

Beneficial area

UK and Israel.

Correspondent: Jonathan Miller, c/o Sutherland House, 70–78 West Hendon Broadway, London NW9 7BT (tel: 020 8202 1066)

Trustees: Jonathan Miller; Alan Rose; David Tannen.

CC Number: 280392

Established in 1974, the trust makes grants to Jewish causes.

> The objects of the charity are to relieve poverty, distress and suffering in any part of the world and to promote the Jewish religion through charitable means. The aims of the charity are to promote Jewish religion, education and social welfare by establishing, maintaining and supporting synagogues, schools, scholarships and charitable services by providing funds, either directly or by way of grants.

In 2011/12 it had assets of £22.5 million and an income of £1.2 million, all of which came from investments. The trust had a total expenditure of £964,000, which included 'investment management expenses' of £742,000 largely made up of interest payments on a bank loan. Grants were made totalling £222,000. A list of grant beneficiaries was not included in the trust's accounts.

Previous beneficiaries included: Cosmon Beiz Academy, Gevurath Ari Trust, Telz Academy Trust, Friends of Ohr Elchonon, Beis Ahron Trust, Wlodowa Charity, Chai Cancer Care, Kollel Skver Trust, Centre for Torah Trust, Gateshead Talmudical College, Jewish Women's Aid Trust, Torah 5759 Ltd and YTAF.

Applications

In writing to the correspondent.

Information gathered from:

Accounts; Charity Commission record.

The Tanner Trust

General

£397,000 (2011/12)

Beneficial area

UK, with a slight preference for the South of England, and overseas.

Correspondent: Celine Lecomte, Trust Administrator, Blake Lapthorn, Harbour Court, Compass Road, Portsmouth PO6 4ST (tel: 02392 221122 ext. 552)

Trustees: Alice P. Williams; Lucie Nottingham.

CC Number: 1021175

This trust has general charitable purposes, supporting organisations worldwide. There appears to be a preference for funding local organisations in the South of England with many other general purposes supported throughout the country and internationally including international development, health/medical, youth work, culture and conservation.

In 2011/12 the trust had assets of £5.4 million, an income of £462,000 and made 137 grants totalling £397,000.

Beneficiaries included: Homeopathic Action Trust (£12,000); Addington Fund (£10,000); National Trust (£7,000); Woodland Trust (£6,000); UNICEF and Phoenix Stroke Appeal (£5,000 each); Seeds for Africa and Sense (£4,000 each); Sheffield Industrial Museum Trust (£2,000); and Royal Hospital for Neuro-disability (£1,500).

Exclusions

No grants to individuals.

Applications

The trust states that unsolicited applications are, without exception, not considered. Support is only given to charities personally known to the trustees.

Information gathered from:

Accounts; Charity Commission record.

The Lili Tapper Charitable Foundation

Jewish

£79,000 (2011/12)

Beneficial area

UK.

Correspondent: Michael Webber, Trustee, Yew Tree Cottage, Artists Lane, Nether Alderley, Macclesfield SK10 4UA (tel: 01625 582320)

CC Number: 268523

The trust primarily supports organisations benefiting Jewish people.

In 2011/12 it had assets of £3.1 million, which generated an income of £39,000. Grants were made to 21 organisations totalling £79,000. No details of grant beneficiaries were available.

Previous beneficiaries include: UJIA, CST, Manchester Jewish Foundation, Teenage Cancer Trust, Keshet Eilon, Israel Educational Foundation, Chicken Shed Theatre Company and Jewish Representation Council.

Exclusions

No grants to individuals.

Applications

The trustees state that they do not respond to any unsolicited applications.

Information gathered from:

Accounts; Charity Commission record.

The Taurus Foundation

General

£106,000 (2011/12)

Beneficial area

UK.

Correspondent: Carole Cook, Trustee, Forsters LLP, 31 Hill Street, London W1J 5LS (tel: 020 7863 8333; email: carole.cook@forsters.co.uk)

Trustees: Denis Felsenstein; Michael Jacobs; Alan Fenton; Anthony Forwood; Priscilla Fenton; Wendy Pollecoff; Carole Cook.

CC Number: 1128441

The foundation was established in 2009 for general charitable purposes.

In 2011/12 the foundation had assets of £909,000 and an income of £144,000. Grants were made to nine organisations totalling £106,000.

The beneficiaries were: The Purcell School (£28,000); Concordia Foundation, Jewish Care, Just for Kids Law and Norwood Ravenswood (£10,000 each); Core Arts, Hillside Clubhouse and Magic Me (£5,000 each); and Royal Opera House (£2,500).

Applications

No grants to unsolicited applications.

Information gathered from:

Accounts; Charity Commission record.

The Tay Charitable Trust

General

Around £225,000 (2011/12)

Beneficial area

UK, with a preference for Scotland, particularly Dundee.

Correspondent: Mrs E. A. Mussen, Trustee, 6 Douglas Terrace, Broughty Ferry, Dundee DD5 1EA

SC Number: SC001004

This trust has general charitable purposes and supports a wide range of causes. Grants of up to £5,000 are made to charities with a first preference for Dundee based charities, then Scottish based charities although national charities have also been supported.

In 2011/12 the trust held assets of £5.5 million and had an income of £209,000. Grants to 233 organisations totalled £225,000.

Beneficiaries of grants of £1,000 or more included: V&A at Dundee (£10,000); University of Dundee and Ninewells Cancer Campaign (£5,000 each); Cerebral Palsy Africa (£3,000); Factory Skatepark, John Muir Trust and National Trust for Scotland (£2,000 each); St Giles' Cathedral, Trees for Life, Victim Support Dundee, Changing Faces and Dundee Science Centre (£1,000 each). 131 organisations received a grant of less than £1,000.

Exclusions

Grants are only given to registered charities. No grants to individuals.

Applications

No standard form; applications in writing to the correspondent, including a financial statement. 'The trustees regret to say they now do not notify applicants who have not succeeded due to the cost of postage.'

Percentage of awards given to new applicants: between 30% and 40%.

Common applicant mistakes

'Insufficient information and/or no figures.'

Information gathered from:

Accounts; OSCR record; further information provided by the funder.

C. B. and H. H. Taylor 1984 Trust

General charitable purposes, Quaker

£282,000 (2011/12)

Beneficial area

West Midlands, Ireland and overseas.

Correspondent: Clare Norton, Trustee, 266 Malvern Road, Worcester WR2 4PA (tel: 01905 412434; email: claregn@talktalk.net)

Trustees: Constance Penny; Elizabeth Birmingham; Clare Norton; John Taylor; Thomas Penny; Robert Birmingham; Simon Taylor.

CC Number: 291363

Registered in 1985, the trust's annual report provides the following information on its activities:

> The trust's geographical areas of benefit are:
>
> - Organisations serving Birmingham and the West Midlands
> - Organisations outside the West Midlands where the trust has well-established links
> - Organisations in Ireland
> - UK-based charities working overseas
>
> The general areas of benefit are:
>
> - The Religious Society of Friends (Quakers) and other religious denominations
> - Healthcare projects
> - Social welfare: community groups; children and young people; older people; disadvantaged people; people with disabilities; homeless people; housing initiatives; counselling and mediation agencies
> - Education: adult literacy schemes; employment training; youth work
> - Penal affairs: work with offenders and ex-offenders; police projects
> - The environment and conservation work
> - The arts: museums and art galleries; music and drama
> - Ireland: cross-community health and social welfare projects
> - UK charities working overseas on long-term development projects
>
> About 60% of grants are for the work and concerns of the Religious Society of Friends (Quakers). The trust favours specific applications. It does not usually award grants on an annual basis for revenue costs. Applications are encouraged from minority groups and women-led initiatives.

In 2011/12 the trust had assets of £9.9 million and an income of £341,000. Grants were made to 165 organisations totalling £282,000. Most grants were for £1,000 or less.

The largest grant went to Britain Yearly Meeting (£37,500). Other beneficiaries included: Oxfam East Africa (£8,000); Quaker Social Action (£7,500); Cape Town Quaker Peace Centre (£6,000); Ulster Quaker Service Committee (£7,000); Samaritans Birmingham (£4,000); Birmingham Association of Youth Clubs (£3,000); Freedom from Torture and Medical Aid for Palestinians (£2,000 each); and Construction Youth Trust, Birmingham Royal Ballet, Cerebral Palsy Birmingham and the International Childcare Trust (£1,000 each).

Exclusions

The trust does not fund: individuals (whether for research, expeditions, educational purposes and so on); local projects or groups outside the West Midlands; or projects concerned with travel or adventure.

Applications form UK registered charities only.

Applications

There is no formal application form. Applicants should write to the correspondent giving the charity's registration number, a brief description of the charity's activities, and details of the specific project for which the grant is being sought. Applicants should also include a budget of the proposed work, together with a copy of the charity's most recent accounts. Trustees will also wish to know what funds have already been raised for the project and how the shortfall will be met.

The trust states that it receives more applications than it can support. Therefore, even if work falls within its policy it may not be able to help, particularly if the project is outside the West Midlands.

Applications should be submitted at least six weeks in advance of the trustees' meeting. Trustees meet twice each year, in May and November. Applications will be acknowledged if an sae is provided.

Percentage of awards given to new applicants: between 20% and 30%.

Common applicant mistakes

'Appeals that are too long and wordy. Most these days, due to computer printing, are well laid out and illustrated. We favour less expensive glossy appeals since we think they are mostly well funded.'

Information gathered from:

Accounts; Charity Commission record; further information provided by the funder.

The Connie and Albert Taylor Charitable Trust

Medical research, hospices, education and recreation, preservation

£448,500 (2012)

Beneficial area

West Midlands.

Correspondent: Harry Grundy, Trustee, The Farmhouse, Darwin Park, Abnalls Lane, Lichfield, Staffordshire WS13 8BJ (email: applications@taylortrust.co.uk; website: www.taylortrust.co.uk)

Trustees: Alan Foster; Harry Grundy; Richard D. Long.

CC Number: 1074785

The trust was established by the will of Constance Iris Taylor in 1998 for the benefit of the West Midlands with the following objects:

- Research into the cure and causes of cancer, blindness and heart disease
- Provision and maintenance of nursing homes for older people or people who are unable to look after themselves
- Provision of maintenance of hospices for people with terminal illnesses
- Facilities for the education and recreation of children and young people
- The preservation, protection and improvements of any amenity or land of beauty, scientific or of horticultural interest and any building of historical, architectural or artistic or scientific interest

In 2012 the trust had assets of £4.7 million and an income of £141,000. Grants were made totalling £448,500, broken down as follows:

Care/hospice	£272,500
Education of children and young people	£121,000
Medical research	£40,000
Conservation	£15,000

Beneficiaries included: St Vincent's and St George's (£75,000); Donna Louise Children's Hospice (£40,000); Williams Syndrome Foundation (£30,000); Cure Leukaemia (£20,000); Norman Laud Association and the Black Country Museum (£15,000 each); Birmingham Royal Ballet (£10,000); and the Royal Wolverhampton Hospital (£2,000).

Applications

In writing to the correspondent, the trustees prefer to receive applications via email. The trust may visit applicants/ beneficiaries. The trust's annual report has the following information:

> The trustees normally meet quarterly to consider what grants they will make and to review any feedback they have received. Where possible they attempt to arrange these meetings to coincide with visits to organisations for which substantial donations are being considered.
>
> Nominations for grants are actively sought through the charity's website and from other sources. In all cases the trustees ask organisations to submit a formal application for specific projects. Decisions as to whether to make donations are made by all three trustees. Follow-up visits and feedback received are used to monitor the quality of grants made. No applications from individuals are considered.
>
> The trustees have been long-term supporters of certain projects. However, no ongoing pledge is for longer than three years, although a pledge may occasionally be extended.

Information gathered from:

Accounts; Charity Commission record; funder's website.

The Cyril Taylor Charitable Trust

Education

£200,000 (2011/12)

Beneficial area

Generally in Greater London.

Correspondent: Christopher Lintott, Trustee, Penningtons, Abacus House, 33 Gutter Lane, London EC2V 8AR (tel: 020 7457 3000; fax: 020 7457 3240; email: chris.lintott@penningtons.co.uk)

Trustees: Sir Cyril Taylor, Chair; Clifford D. Joseph; Robert W. Maas; Peter A. Tchereprine; Stephen Rasch; Christopher Lintott; Lady June Taylor; Michael Berry; William Gertz; Jack Burg; Thomas Kiechle.

CC Number: 1040179

This trust makes grants to organisations benefiting students in particular those studying at Richmond College and the American International University in London.

In 2011/12 the trust had assets of £391,000 and an income of £188,000. Grants were made to 11 organisations totalling £200,000.

Beneficiaries included: Richmond Foundation (£150,000); Focus Kensington and Chelsea (Chickenshed Theatre) (£10,000); the British Friends of Harvard Business School (£6,000); and Central African Mission, Educational Frontier Trust and Trinity Hall, Cambridge (£1,000 each).

Applications

In writing to the correspondent.

Information gathered from:

Accounts; Charity Commission record.

Rosanna Taylor's 1987 Charity Trust

General

Around £56,500 (2011/12)

Beneficial area

UK and overseas, with a preference for Oxfordshire and West Sussex.

Correspondent: Laura Gosling, Trust Administrator, c/o Millbank Financial Services, 4th Floor, Swan House, 17–19 Stratford Place, London W1C 1BQ (tel: 020 7907 2100; email: charity@mfs.co.uk)

Trustee: The Cowdray Trust Ltd.

CC Number: 297210

The trust has general charitable purposes, including support for medical, cancer, child development and environmental charities.

Accounts had been received at the Charity Commission but were unavailable to view. In 2011/12 the trust had an income of £11,000 and an expenditure of £56,500.

Previous beneficiaries include: Charities Aid Foundation (£24,000); Pearson Taylor Trust (£10,000); Disaster Emergencies Committee – Haiti Appeal (£5,000); and Resonance FM (£500).

Exclusions

No grants to individuals or non-registered charities.

Applications

In writing to the correspondent. Acknowledgements are not sent to unsuccessful applicants.

Information gathered from:

Accounts; Charity Commission record.

Tegham Ltd

Orthodox Jewish faith, welfare

£37,500 (2011/12)

Beneficial area

Barnet and Israel.

Correspondent: Nizza Fluss, Trustee, c/o Gerald Kreditor and Co., Hallswelle House, 1 Hallswelle Road, London NW11 0DH (email: admin@geraldkreditor.co.uk)

Trustees: Nizza Fluss; Daniel Fluss.

CC Number: 283066

This trust supports the promotion of the Jewish Orthodox faith and the relief of poverty.

In 2011/12 the trust had assets of £1.9 million and an income of £350,000. Grants were made totalling £37,500. No details of beneficiaries were included in the accounts.

Applications

The trust has stated that it has enough causes to support and does not welcome other applications.

Information gathered from:

Accounts; Charity Commission record.

Thackray Medical Research Trust

Research of medical procedures/products, medical supply trade

£161,500 (2012/13)

Beneficial area

Worldwide.

Correspondent: The Chair of the Trustees, c/o Thackray Museum, Beckett Street, Leeds LS9 7LN (email: johncampbell99@talktalk.net; website: www.tmrt.co.uk)

Trustees: William Kendall Mathie; Matthew Wrigley; Martin Schweiger; Christin Thackray; John Campbell; Steven Burt; Ian Mallinson.

CC Number: 702896

The following details on the trust's objects have been taken from its website:

> *Objects*
>
> The trust has three main purposes.
>
> - To support the Thackray Museum (Object 1)
> - To support charitable international medical supply organisations (Objects 2 and 3)
> - To support research into and publication of, the history of medical procedures and products. (Objects 4 to 7)
>
> ***Objects and Notes on the Objects***
>
> *Object 1*
>
> To support a museum in or near Leeds which has its objective bringing a greater awareness to the general public of advances in medical treatment, science, research and development with particular reference to the medical supply trade, with special regards to links with northern Great Britain and in particular Leeds and generally to educate the public in matters relating to the medical, technical and social aspects of medical products and procedures.
>
> Note: This object relates to the establishment of the museum and only the Thackray Museum may apply for funding under this heading.
>
> *Object 2*
>
> To support charitable international medical supply organisations, and in particular the Joint Missions Hospital Equipping Board (ECHO), for exceptional expenditure in the course of their charitable work in under-developed/Third World Countries.
>
> Note: Grants are provided for charitable organisations which specialise in supplying medical equipment to or within the third world. Support is unlikely to be for actual funding of equipment purchases but instead may be for 'pump-priming', start-up or organisational expenses where alternative funding is not available. Preference will be given where the charity is involved in value-for-money projects, e.g. the supply of used rather than new equipment.
>
> *Object 3*
>
> To relieve and prevent disease and sickness in under-developed or third-world countries by supporting for the public benefit appropriate research and manufacture of medical products calculated to achieve that aim.
>
> *Object 4*
>
> To promote research for the public benefit in the evaluation of medical procedures and products.
>
> *Object 5*
>
> To commission, fund and publish the results of research into the effect of health service investment decisions and product-related medical regulations on the supply of health services and the British health service in particular.
>
> *Object 6*
>
> To provide grants for research into, and publication of, the history of medical products and supplies.
>
> *Object 7*
>
> To provide grants for lectureships and prize money for essay competitions on the subjects of medical supplies, value-for-money evaluation of medical products and medical product history.

In 2012/13 the trust had assets of £6.5 million and an income of £238,000. Grants awarded totalled £161,500, of which £156,500 went to the Thackray Museum.

The only other beneficiary was Worldshare, which received £5,000 for the transportation of medicines to Senegal.

Applications

Application forms and guidance notes are available from the website. Applications are usually considered in October and April but may be considered at other times. The closing date for applications is the last day of July and January respectively.

Information gathered from:

Accounts; Charity Commission record; funder's website.

The Thames Wharf Charity

General charitable purposes

£20,500 (2011/12)

Beneficial area

UK.

Correspondent: Kenneth Hawkins, Administrator, HW Lee Associates, New Derwent House, 69/73 Theobalds Road, London WC1X 8TA (tel: 020 7025 4600; fax: 020 7025 4666)

Trustees: Avtar Lotay; Patrick Burgess; Graham Stirk; Audrey Gale.

CC Number: 1000796

Registered in 1990, the charity receives dividends from Rogers Stirk Harbour and Partners, the firm established by renowned architect Richard Rogers. In 2011/12 this produced an income of £443,000. During the year the charity's assets stood at £1.3 million. Grants were made to ten organisations totalling £20,500; however, during the previous year the charity awarded over 200 grants totalling £1.8 million.

The beneficiaries in 2011/12 were: World Wildlife Fund UK (£8,500); Milestone Academy (£5,000); Camden City, Islington and Westminster Bereavement Service (£4,200); Cycle to Cannes (£4,000); DEC – East Africa Crisis Appeal, Great Ormond Street Hospital and UNICEF UK (£1,500 each); Macmillan Cancer Support (£1,000); MIND (£500); and Antenatal Results and Choices (£550).

Exclusions

No grants for the purchase of property, motor vehicles or holidays.

Applications

In writing to the correspondent.

Information gathered from:
Accounts; Charity Commission record.

The Thistle Trust

Arts

£43,000 (2011/12)

Beneficial area
UK.

Correspondent: Elizabeth Fettes-Neame, Trust Officer, Kleinwort Benson Trustees Ltd, 14 St George Street, London W1S 1FE (tel: 020 3207 7337; email: elizabeth.fettes-neame@kleinwortbenson.com)

Trustees: Lady Madeleine Kleinwort; Catherine Trevelyan; Neil Morris; Donald McGilvray; Nicholas Kerr-Sheppard; Selina Kleinwort Dabbas.

CC Number: 1091327

This trust was established in 2002, and during the following year it received a £1 million endowment from the settlor. Its main objects are to promote study and research in the arts and to further public knowledge and education of art.

In 2011/12 the trust had assets of £1.1 million and an income of £37,000. Grants were made to 26 organisations totalling £43,000.

Beneficiaries included: Juventus Lyrica Associacion De Ope (£8,000); Awards for Young Musicians and the Bach Choir (£2,500 each); Bush Theatre and RADA (£2,000); and the Academy of St Martin-in-the-Fields, Handel House Museum, National Youth Orchestra of Scotland and Theatre Peckham (£1,000 each).

Exclusions
No grants to individuals.

Applications
In writing to the correspondent including most recent report and financial accounts. The trustees meet at least once a year with only successful applicants notified of the trustees' decision.

Information gathered from:
Accounts; Charity Commission record.

The Loke Wan Tho Memorial Foundation

Environment and conservation, general, medical causes, overseas aid

£70,000 (2011/12)

Beneficial area
Worldwide.

Correspondent: The Secretary to the Trustees, RBC Trust Company (International) Ltd, La Motte Chambers, St Helier, Jersey, Channel Islands JE1 1BJ (tel: 01534 602000)

Trustees: Tanis Tonkyn; Alan Tonkyn.

CC Number: 264273

The trust supports environment/ conservation organisations, medical causes and overseas aid organisations. In 2011/12 it had assets of £5.6 million and an income of £130,000. Grants totalled £70,000.

Only two organisations received grants during the year: North Hampshire Hospice Charity (£50,000); and Stichting Orchidee (£20,000).

Applications
In writing to the correspondent.

Information gathered from:
Accounts; Charity Commission record.

The Maurice and Vivien Thompson Charitable Trust

General

£37,000 (2011/12)

Beneficial area
UK.

Correspondent: Maurice Thompson, Trustee, 2 The Orchard, London W4 1JX (tel: 020 8995 1547)

Trustees: Maurice Thompson; Vivien Thomson; Paul Rhodes.

CC Number: 1085041

In 2011/12 the trust had assets of £1.1 million and an income of £31,000. Grants were made totalling £37,000.

Just one beneficiary was listed in the trust's accounts, Leicestershire First (£29,000), which has also been the main beneficiary in previous years and of which the three trustees of this trust are also on the board.

Applications
In writing to the correspondent.

Information gathered from:
Accounts; Charity Commission record.

The Sue Thomson Foundation

Christ's Hospital School, education

£122,000 (2011/12)

Beneficial area
UK, Sussex, London or Surrey.

Correspondent: Susannah Holliman, Administrator, Arcadia, 58a Woodland Way, Kingswood, Surrey KT20 6NW (email: stfsusannah@aol.com)

Trustees: Susan M. Mitchell, Chair; Timothy J. Binnington; Charles L. Corman; Kathleen Duncan.

CC Number: 298808

The foundation exists to support children in need in the UK, mainly by helping Christ's Hospital and the school in Horsham which caters specifically for children in need. Other areas of support include educational and self-help organisations and projects as well as organisations involved with the publishing industry. Grants have also been made to charities in recognition of pro-bono professional work done for the foundation by its trustees or others. The foundation's policies were reviewed in October 2012 and minor changes implemented. Grants are awarded for education and welfare in one of three categories: regular, Christ's Hospital student schemes and special (project) grants at the trustees' discretion. Grants from the latter category are usually in the range of £1,000 to £3,000 and made to small welfare or educational charities, likely to be working in London, Sussex or Surrey, and related to a particular need which cannot be readily alleviated by statutory bodies.

The foundation also explores, from time to time, new areas for possible future development that may lie outside its existing priority areas.

In 2011/12 the trust had assets of £2.7 million and an income of £214,000. Grants totalled £122,000, divided between education (£86,000) and welfare (£36,000). The total includes £7,000 paid to individual students.

The majority of the funds went to Christ's Hospital, which received £101,000. The foundation nominates one new entrant each year from a needy background to the school, subject to the child meeting Christ's Hospital's own admissions criteria academically, socially and in terms of need. The foundation commits to contributing to the child's costs at a level agreed with Christ's Hospital for as long as each of them remains in the school.

Other beneficiaries included: The Leonard Sainer Legal Education Foundation (£3,000); Book Trade Benevolent Society (£2,500); The Bridewell Foundation (£2,000); Hoskings House Trust, Broadfield Children's Project and Parent and Carers Support Association (£1,000 each); and The Stationers' Foundation (£500).

Exclusions
No grants to large, national charities (except Christ's Hospital) or individuals, except as part of a specific scheme. No research projects, charities concerned

with animals, birds, the environment, gardens or historic buildings.

Applications

In writing to the correspondent. Preliminary telephone or email enquiries are encouraged. Unsolicited applications are not acknowledged, unless accompanied by an sae or an email address. Grantmaking policies are published in the annual report and accounts, available from the Charity Commission website, and in relevant charity sector publications when the trustees are able to do so free of charge. This statement of policies is provided to anyone on request.

Percentage of awards given to new applicants: less than 10%.

Common applicant mistakes

'They have not bothered to make a preliminary phone call to establish eligibility and availability of funds. Far too much detail and sometimes expensive glossy literature.'

Information gathered from:

Accounts; Charity Commission record; further information provided by the funder.

The Thornton Foundation

General charitable purposes

£204,000 (2011/12)

Beneficial area

UK.

Correspondent: A. H. Isaacs, Jordans, Eashing, Surrey GU7 2QA

Trustees: R. C. Thornton, Chair; A. H. Isaacs; H. D. C. Thornton; S. J. Thornton.

CC Number: 326383

The object of the foundation is to make grants to charities selected by the trustees. The principal guideline of the trust is to use the funds to further charitable causes where their money will, as far as possible, act as 'high powered money', in other words be of significant use to the cause. Only causes that are known personally to the trustees and/or that they are able to investigate thoroughly are supported. The trust states it is proactive rather than reactive in seeking applicants.

In 2011/12 the trust had assets of almost £4.2 million and an income of £90,000. Grants totalling £204,000 were made to 26 organisations, some of which were supported in the previous year.

Beneficiaries included: Institute of Cancer Research (£111,000); Great Ormond Street Hospital (£25,000); The Cirdan Sailing Trust (£10,000); Helen House (£7,000); Action for Blind People, Help for Heroes, Keble College – Oxford and Prisoners of Conscience (£5,000 each); The Tait Memorial Trust (£2,000); Museum of London (£1,500); and Arrow Riding Centre and UCL HD Research (£1,000 each).

Applications

The trust strongly emphasises that it does not accept unsolicited applications and only organisations that are known to one of the trustees will be considered for support. Any unsolicited applications will not receive a reply.

Information gathered from:

Accounts; Charity Commission record.

The Thornton Trust

Evangelical Christianity, education, relief of sickness and poverty

£126,000 (2011/12)

Beneficial area

UK and overseas.

Correspondent: Douglas Thornton, Trustee, Hunters Cottage, Hunters Yard, Debden Road, Saffron Walden, Essex CB11 4AA (tel: 01799 526712)

Trustees: Douglas Thornton; Betty Thornton; James Thornton.

CC Number: 205357

This trust was created in 1962 for 'the promotion and furthering of education and the Evangelical Christian faith, and assisting in the relief of sickness, suffering and poverty'. The 2011/12 trustees' annual report states: 'Some organisations are involved in all of the activities referred to in the deed, but generally one third in supporting the Christian church, training and associated societies in the UK; a third in Christian missions and relief work overseas; and the balance in education, youth work, medical and other.'

In 2011/12 it had assets of £842,000 and an income of £70,000. Grants were made to 65 organisations totalling £126,000.

Beneficiaries included: Africa Inland Mission (£20,000); Saffron Walden Baptist Church (£10,000); Redcliffe Missionary College (£6,000); London Institute for Contemporary Christianity and London City Mission (£5,000 each); Hertford Community Church (£4,000); Bible Society and Young Life YHT (£3,000 each); Daughters Cambodia and Middle East Christian Outreach Ltd (£2,000 each); Abbeyfield Free Church (£1,000); and Alzheimer's Society and Guiding Herts (£100 each).

Applications

The trust states: 'Our funds are fully committed and we regret that we are unable to respond to the many unsolicited calls for assistance we are now receiving.'

Information gathered from:

Accounts; Charity Commission record.

The Thousandth Man- Richard Burns Charitable Trust (formerly known as The Hammonds Charitable Trust)

General charitable purposes directed towards the young, elderly and disabled

£39,500 (2011/12)

Beneficial area

Mainly Birmingham, London, Leeds, Bradford and Manchester.

Correspondent: Linda Sylvester, Correspondent, Squire Sanders (UK) LLP, Rutland House, 148 Edmund Street, Birmingham B3 2JR (tel: 01212 223318; email: linda.sylvester@squiresanders.com; website: www.squiresanders.com)

Trustees: John Forrest; Simon Miller; Susan Nickson; Robert Weekes; Robert Elvin.

CC Number: 1064028

The Thousandth Man- Richard Burns Charitable Trust (formerly known as The Hammonds Charitable Trust) usually makes donations to charitable organisations based locally to the trust. The trust's income was derived from the partners of Squire Sanders (UK) LLP.

In 2011/12 the trust 'supported a number of national charities in a wide variety of areas, but in particular the trustees were pleased to support smaller charities working within the areas in which its firm's offices are based – situated in Birmingham, London, Leeds and Manchester'.

During the year, the trust had assets of £141,000, an income of £118,000 and made grants to 99 organisations totalling £39,500.

Medical/health/sickness	30	£14,500
Educational/training	32	£12,300
General charitable purposes	27	£12,000
Disability	5	£1,200
Environment/conservation/heritage	1	£500
Arts/culture	1	£500
Animal welfare	1	£300
Religious activities	1	£250
Relief of poverty	1	£125

Beneficiaries included: Crohn's and Colitis in Childhood – 3C's (£5,000); Paddington Law Centre Ltd (£3,000); Help for Heroes (£2,300); Marie Curie Cancer Care (£1,200); the Prince's Trust and East Anglia's Children's Hospices (£1,000 each); Wooden Spoon Society (£700); Bowel Cancer and Research, Samaritan's Purse International Ltd and Action for Children (£500 each); Rett Syndrome Research Trust UK and Minge's Gift (£250 each); the Ickle Pickle Partnership Ltd and Royal Commonwealth Society for the Blind (£100 each); and the Candlelighters Trust (£50).

Exclusions

The charity generally supports smaller charities local to the firm's offices.

Applications

This trust does not accept unsolicited applications.

Information gathered from:

Accounts; Charity Commission record; funder's website.

The Three Oaks Trust

Welfare

£130,000 to organisations

(2011/12)

Beneficial area

UK and overseas, with a preference for West Sussex.

Correspondent: The Trustees, P. O. Box 893, Horsham, West Sussex RH12 9JD (email: contact@thethreeoakstrust.co.uk; website: www.thethreeoakstrust.co.uk)

Trustees: Dianne Margaret Ward; Polly Elizabeth Hobbs; Carol Vivian Foreman; Carol Johnson; Pam Wilkinson; Dr P. Kane; Sarah A. Kane; Giles Duncan Wilkinson; Three Oaks Family Trust Co. Ltd.

CC Number: 297079

Grants are made to organisations that promote the welfare of individuals and families. Grants are also made to individuals via statutory authorities or voluntary agencies. The trust regularly supports the same welfare organisations in the UK and overseas each year.

In 2011/12 the trust had assets of £6.3 million and a total income of £221,000. Donations made this year totalled £193,000. Of this, £83,000 was donated to charities and organisations that promote the welfare of individuals and families in the UK. As in previous years, a large number of small donations were made more directly for the benefit of individuals via statutory authorities and voluntary agencies. This year 353 such donations were made with a net value, taking account of refunds, of some £63,000.

Donations to charities and organisations whose focus of work is overseas, including donations in kind, were made to a value of £47,000.

Beneficiaries included: Raynauds and Scleroderma Association (£15,000); Crawley Open House (£10,000); Basildon Community Resource Centre, Wendy Gough Cancer Awareness Foundation and Springboard Project (£5,000 each); and MIND Brighton and Hove (£4,000).

Exclusions

No direct applications from individuals. Applications from students for gap year activities are not a priority and will not be funded.

Applications

The following guidelines are taken from the 2011/12 annual accounts: 'Grants are made to organisations that promote the welfare of individuals and families. In general, the trustees intend to continue supporting the organisations that they have supported in the past. Periodically and generally annually the trustees review the list of registered charities and institutions to which grants have been given and consider additions and deletions from the list. To save on administration, the trustees do not respond to requests unless they are considering making a donation. Requests from organisations for donations in excess of £2,000 are considered by the trustees on a quarterly basis in meetings usually held in January, April, July and September.'

For the full guidelines, visit the trust's website.

Information gathered from:

Accounts; Charity Commission record; funder's website.

The Thriplow Charitable Trust

Higher and further education and research

£87,000 (2011/12)

Beneficial area

Preference for British institutions.

Correspondent: The Trustees, PO Box 225, Royston SG8 1BG

Trustees: Sir Peter Swinnerton-Dyer, Chair; Dr Harriet Crawford; Prof. Christopher Bayly; Sir David Wallace; Dame Jean Thomas.

CC Number: 1025531

The charity was established by a trust deed in 1983. Its main aims are the furtherance of higher and further education and research, with preference given to British institutions.

Projects that have generally been supported in the past include contributions to research study funds, research fellowships, academic training schemes, computer facilities and building projects. Specific projects are preferred rather than contributions to general running costs. The trust prefers to support smaller projects where grants can 'make a difference'.

In 2011/12 it had assets of £4 million and an income of £458,000. Grants totalled £87,000.

Previous beneficiaries have included Cambridge University Library, Centre of South Asian Studies, Computer Aid International, Fight for Sight, Fitzwilliam Museum, Foundation for Prevention of Blindness, Foundation of Research Students, Hearing Research Trust, Inspire Foundation, Loughborough University, Marie Curie Cancer Care, Royal Botanic Gardens, Royal College of Music, Transplant Trust and University of Reading.

Applications

There is no application form. A letter of application should specify the purpose for which funds are sought and the costings of the project. It should be indicated whether other applications for funds are pending and, if the funds are to be channelled to an individual or a small group, what degree of supervision over the quality of the work would be exercised by the institution. Trustee meetings are held twice a year – in spring and in autumn.

Percentage of awards given to new applicants: between 20% and 30%.

Common applicant mistakes

'They are ineligible: many students apply for personal funding. Lack of costed specifics: trustees are not [able] to pay into general appeals but happy to buy specific items or services.'

Information gathered from:

Accounts; Charity Commission record; further information provided by the funder.

The Tinsley Foundation

Human rights, poverty and homelessness and health education in underdeveloped countries

£180,000 (2011/12)

Beneficial area

UK and overseas.

Correspondent: Henry Tinsley, Trustee, 14 St Mary's Street, Stamford,

Lincolnshire PE9 2DF (tel: 01780 762056; fax: 01780 767594; email: hctinsley@aol.com)

Trustees: Henry Tinsley; Rebecca Tinsley; Tim Jones.

CC Number: 1076537

The foundation was founded by Henry Tinsley in 1999 and will support:

- Charities which promote human rights and democratisation and/or which educate against racism, discrimination and oppression
- Charities which promote self-help in fighting poverty and homelessness
- Charities which provide reproductive health education in underdeveloped countries, but specifically excluding charities whose policy is against abortion or birth control

In 2011/12 the foundation had assets of £2.6 million, an income of £942,000 and made 17 grants totalling £180,000.

Beneficiaries included: SURF Survivors Fund (£50,000); Client Earth (£35,000); Network for Africa and Technoserve Europe (£25,000 each); Medact (£15,000); Article 1 Charitable Trust and Searchlight Education Trust (£10,000 each); and Computer Aid International, English National Opera, Fairtrade Foundation and Oxford Research Group (£1,000 each).

Applications

While the charity welcomes applications from eligible potential grantees, the trustees seek out organisations that will effectively fulfil the foundation's objectives.

Information gathered from:

Accounts; Charity Commission record.

The Tisbury Telegraph Trust

Christian, overseas aid, general

£186,000 (2011/12)

Beneficial area

UK and overseas.

Correspondent: Eleanor Orr, Trustee, 35 Kitto Road, Telegraph Hill, London SE14 5TW (email: tisburytelegraphtrust@gmail.com)

Trustees: Alison Davidson; John Davidson; Eleanor Orr; Roger Orr; Sonia Phippard; Michael Hartley.

CC Number: 328595

In 2011/12 this trust had assets of £327,000 and an income of £335,000. Grants were made to 63 organisations, including churches, totalling £186,000.

Beneficiaries included: Crisis and Tear Fund (£22,000 each); World Vision (£20,000); All Saints Church, Peckham (£15,500); Friends of Kiwoko Hospital (£15,000); Practical Action (£10,500); Helen and Douglas House (£10,000); Christian Aid and Wycliffe Bible Translators (£2,000 each); and Friends of the Earth, Habitat for Humanity, Pecan, Traidcraft and Salvation Army (£1,000 each).

Exclusions

No applications from individuals for expeditions or courses can be considered.

Applications

In writing to the correspondent. However, it is extremely rare that unsolicited applications are successful and the trust does not respond to applicants unless an sae is included. No telephone applications please.

Information gathered from:

Accounts; Charity Commission record.

Tomchei Torah Charitable Trust

Jewish

£60,000 (2011/12)

Beneficial area

UK and Israel.

Correspondent: Israel Kohn, 36 Cranbourne Gardens, London NW11 0HP (tel: 020 8458 5706)

Trustees: Israel Kohn; Sandra Kohn; Daniel Netzer.

CC Number: 802125

This trust supports Jewish educational institutions. Grants usually average about £5,000.

In 2011/12 the trust had assets of £71,000 and an income of £126,000 from donations. Grants were made totalling £60,000, and were broken down as follows:

Religion and community	£28,000
Education	£23,500
Relief of poverty	£9,000

A list of beneficiaries was not included in the accounts. Previous beneficiaries included: Friends of Mir; MST College; Friends of Sanz Institutions; United Talmudical Associates; Ezer North West; Menorah Grammar School; Friends of Torah Ohr; Ruzin Sadagora Trust; Achisomoch Aid Co. and Chesed Charity Trust.

Applications

In writing to the correspondent at any time.

Information gathered from:

Accounts; Charity Commission record.

The Torah Temimah Trust

Orthodox Jewish

£28,000 (2011/12)

Beneficial area

UK.

Correspondent: Mrs E. Bernath, Trustee, 16 Reizel Close, Stamford Hill, London N16 5GY (tel: 020 8800 3021)

Trustees: E. Bernath; M. Bernath; A. Grunfeld.

CC Number: 802390

This trust was set up in 1980 to advance/promote Orthodox Jewish religious education and religion. In 2011/12 it had assets of £127,000, an income of £38,000 and gave grants totalling £28,000.

Applications

In writing to the correspondent.

Information gathered from:

Accounts; Charity Commission record.

Toras Chesed (London) Trust

Jewish, education

£277,000 (2011/12)

Beneficial area

Worldwide.

Correspondent: Aaron Langberg, Trustee, 14 Lampard Grove, London N16 6UZ (tel: 020 8806 9589; email: ari@toraschesed.co.uk)

Trustees: Akiva Stern; Simon Stern; Aaron Langberg.

CC Number: 1110653

Set up in 2005, the objects of the charity are:

- The advancement of Orthodox Jewish religious education
- The relief of poverty and infirmity among persons of the Jewish faith
- To provide a safe and user friendly environment to share mutual problems and experiences
- To encourage active parental participation in their children's education
- The advancement of the Orthodox Jewish faith

The charity achieves its objectives by making grants to qualifying organisations and individuals.

In 2011/12 the charity had an income of £290,000 and gave grants totalling £277,000. There are no assets, income is received from donations.

Applications

'Applications for grants are considered by the trustees and reviewed in depth for final approval.'

Information gathered from:

Accounts; Charity Commission record.

The Tory Family Foundation

Education, Christian, medical

£82,000 (2011/12)

Beneficial area

Worldwide, but principally Folkestone.

Correspondent: Paul Tory, Trustee, The Estate Office, Etchinghill Golf Club, Canterbury Road, Etchinghill, Folkestone CT18 8FA (tel: 01303 862280)

Trustees: James Tory; Paul Tory; S. Tory; David Callister; Jill Perkins.

CC Number: 326584

The trustees' report for 2011/12 states:

> The charity was formed to provide financial assistance to a wide range of charitable needs. It is currently supporting a wide range of causes both from a national perspective and an international perspective. These causes include educational, religious, social and medical subjects and the donees themselves are often registered charities. The trustees continue to pursue the policy of donations and grants in line with the financial position of the charity.

The charity does not normally aim to fund the whole of any given project, and applicants are expected to demonstrate a degree of existing and regular support.

In 2011/12 the foundation had assets of almost £3.1 million, an income of £101,000 and made grants totalling over £82,000. These were broken down as follows:

Overseas	£27,500
Health	£17,500
Other	£17,000
Local	£8,500
Churches	£6,500
Education	£4,500
Elderly	£500

Previous beneficiaries have included: Ashford YMCA, Bletchley Park, Canterbury Cathedral, Concern Worldwide, Deal Festival, Disability Law Service, Folk Rainbow Club, Foresight, Friends of Birzett, Gurkha Welfare, Kent Cancer Trust, Royal British Legion, Uppingham Foundation and Youth Action Wiltshire.

Exclusions

Priority is given to applications from east Kent.

Applications

In writing to the correspondent. Applications are considered throughout the year. To keep costs down, unsuccessful applicants will not be notified.

Information gathered from:

Accounts; Charity Commission record.

The Toy Trust

Children

£340,500 (2012)

Beneficial area

UK.

Correspondent: Roland Earl, Administrator, c/o British Toy and Hobby Association, 80 Camberwell Road, London SE5 0EG (tel: 020 7701 7271; email: admin@btha.co.uk; website: www.btha.co.uk)

Trustees: The British Toy and Hobby Association Ltd; Clive Jones; Frank Martin; Kevin Jones; Philip Ratcliffe.

CC Number: 1001634

This trust was registered in 1991 to centralise the giving of the British Toy and Hobby Association. Prior to this, the association raised money from the toy industry, which it pledged to one charity on an annual basis. It was felt that the fundraising activities of the association were probably more than matched by its individual members, and that the charitable giving of the toy industry to children's charities was going unnoticed by the public. The trust still receives the majority of its income from fundraising activities, donating the proceeds to children's charities and charitable projects benefiting children.

In 2012 the trust had an income of £357,000, mostly in donations received. Grants were made to 92 organisations totalling £340,500.

The largest grant was made to Medic Malawi (£135,000). Other beneficiaries included: Toybox Charity (£10,000); Blaen Wern Farm Trust and Disability Challengers (£5,000 each); and Eden Coppice Trust (£4,000).

Applications

In writing to the correspondent.

Percentage of awards given to new applicants: between 40% and 50%.

Common applicant mistakes

'Don't include accounts; requesting money for salaries (we do not grant for salaries); not reading application criteria thoroughly.'

Information gathered from:

Accounts; Charity Commission record; further information provided by the funder; funder's website.

Annie Tranmer Charitable Trust

General charitable purposes, education

£216,500 to organisations (2012/13)

Beneficial area

UK, particularly Suffolk and adjacent counties.

Correspondent: M. Kirby, Correspondent, 51 Bennett Road, Ipswich IP1 5HX

Trustees: John Miller; Valerie Lewis; Nigel Bonham-Carter; Patrick Grieve.

CC Number: 1044231

The Annie Tranmer Charitable Trust was established in 1989. The objectives of the trust are to:

- Make grants in the county of Suffolk and adjacent counties
- Make grants to national charities according to the wishes of Mrs Tranmer during her lifetime
- Advance education and historical research relating to the national monument known at the Sutton Hoo burial site and Sutton Hoo estate
- To further the education of children and young people in Suffolk
- Make grants for general charitable purposes

In 2012/13 the trust had assets of £3.5 million and an income of £119,000. Grants were made totalling £229,000 of which £216,500 was donated to 74 organisations and £13,000 to 17 individuals.

Beneficiaries included: Royal National Lifeboat Institution (£128,500); Mid-Essex Hospital Services NHS Trust, Macmillan Cancer and Marie Curie Cancer (£5,000 each); St Elizabeth Hospice, Ovarian Cancer Action and the Salvation Army (£2,000 each); the National Strings Academy, Raynauds and Scleroderma Association and Wellbeing for Women (£1,000 each); and Wendy Gough Awareness Foundation and Missing People (£500 each).

Applications

This trust does not accept unsolicited applications.

Information gathered from:

Accounts; Charity Commission record.

The Treeside Trust

General

£75,000 (2011/12)

Beneficial area

UK, but mainly local in Oldham.

Correspondent: John Beresford Gould, 4 The Park, Grasscroft, Oldham OL4 4ES (tel: 01457 876422)

Trustees: Catherine Gould; Diana Ives; Richard Gould; Roger Gould; Richard Ives.

CC Number: 1061586

The trust supports mainly small local charities, and a few UK-wide charities which are supported on a regular basis. The majority of grants are made as a result of half-yearly reviews. In the main, the trustees' policy is to make a limited number of substantial grants each year, rather than a larger number of smaller ones, in order to make significant contributions to some of the causes supported.

In 2011/12 the trust had assets of £2 million and an income of £30,000. Grants totalling £75,000 were made during the year. The only, and largest, grant listed in the accounts was of £12,500 to Footprints Theatre Trust, of which John Beresford Gould is also a trustee.

Applications

The trust has stated that they 'do not welcome unsolicited applications'.

Percentage of awards given to new applicants: less than 10%.

Information gathered from:

Accounts; Charity Commission record; further information provided by the funder.

The Trefoil Trust (formerly known as Anona Winn Charitable Trust)

Health, young people, disability, the arts, armed forces

£90,000 (2012)

Beneficial area

UK.

Correspondent: Rupert Hughes, Correspondent, New Inn Cottage, Croft Lane, Winstone, Cirencester GL7 7LN (tel: 01285 821338)

Trustee: Trefoil Trustees Ltd.

CC Number: 1044101

Registered with the Charity Commission in February 1995, the trust will generally only support charities which are related to medicine, young people, people with disabilities, the arts and the armed forces.

In 2012 the trust had assets of £1.1 million and an income of £50,000. Grants to 26 organisations totalled £90,000.

Beneficiaries included: Charities Aid Foundation (£30,000); COPS (£5,000); Sussex Snowdrop Trust (£4,000); the Fire Fighters' Charity, Friends of Newmarket Day Centre and Gurkha Welfare Trust (£2,500 each); Sarah Greene Breakthrough Tribute Fund (£1,500); and ABF the Soldiers Charity, Alzheimer's Research and Crisis at Christmas (£1,000 each).

Exclusions

No applications are considered from individuals.

Applications

Applications will only be considered if received in writing and accompanied by the organisation's latest report and full accounts. The trustees usually meet in February and July to decide on distributions.

Percentage of awards given to new applicants: between 30% and 40%.

Information gathered from:

Accounts; Charity Commission record; further information provided by the funder.

The Tresillian Trust

Overseas aid, welfare

£40,000 to organisations (2011/12)

Beneficial area

Worldwide.

Correspondent: M. D. Willcox, Trustee, Old Coach House, Sunnyside, Bergh Apton, Norwich NR15 1DD (tel: 01508 480100; email: info@willcoxlewis.co.uk)

Trustees: G. E. S. Robinson; P. W. Bate; M. D. Willcox.

CC Number: 1105826

The trust is a general purpose charity and the trustees focus on particular areas of benefit from time to time. The strategy of the trustees for 2011/12 and the foreseeable future is to concentrate on donations to charities which fulfil one or more of the following criteria:

- In the UK, community based projects supporting the elderly and young people
- In Africa, Asia and South America, projects supporting the education and health of women and children
- Worldwide projects dealing with conflict and disaster areas and the environment

In 2011/12 this trust held assets of £2.7 million and had an income of £67,000 and made grants to 14 organisations totalling £40,000.

Beneficiaries included: Target TB (£6,000); St Andrew's Clinic for Children and Christian Friends of Korea (£5,000 each); Alive and Kicking UK and Blacksmith Institute (£2,000 each); and Homes for Zimbabwe (£1,000.).

Applications

In writing to the correspondent. 'The trust is very selective in the grant making process and applications are reviewed by the trustees personally.'

Information gathered from:

Accounts; Charity Commission record.

Truedene Co. Ltd

Jewish

£788,000 (2011/12)

Beneficial area

UK and overseas.

Correspondent: The Trustees, c/o Cohen Arnold and Co., 1075 Finchley Road, London NW11 0PU (tel: 020 8731 0777)

Trustees: Sarah Klein, Chair; Samuel Berger; Solomon Laufer; Sije Berger; Zelda Sternlicht.

CC Number: 248268

The charity's annual report of the trustees for 2011/12 states that this charity was established to support the activities of Jewish religious organisations, especially in the field of education and to provide philanthropic aid to the Jewish needy. It supports other charities both in respect of revenue and expenditure and capital projects.

In 2011/12 this trust had assets of over £4.1 million and an income of £445,000. Grants were made totalling £788,000. A list of beneficiaries was not included in the annual accounts.

Previous beneficiaries have included: Beis Ruchel D'Satmar Girls School Ltd, British Friends of Tshernobil, Congregation Paile Yoetz, Cosmon Belz Ltd, Friends of Mir, Kolel Shomrei Hachomoth, Mesifta Talmudical College, Mosdos Ramou, Orthodox Council of Jerusalem, Tevini Ltd, United Talmudical Associates Ltd, VMCT and Yeshivo Horomo Talmudical College.

Applications

In writing to the correspondent.

Information gathered from:

Accounts; Charity Commission record.

The Truemark Trust

General charitable purposes

£404,000 (2011/12)

Beneficial area

UK.

Correspondent: Clare Pegden, Correspondent, PO Box 2, Liss, Hampshire GU33 6YP (tel: 01730 894120)

Trustees: Sharon Knight; Wendy Collett; Judy Hayward; Stuart Neil; Sir Thomas Lucas.

CC Number: 265855

The trust's purpose is to make grants to other charitable bodies for the relief of all kinds of social distress and disadvantage. Donations mostly made to small local charities dealing with all kinds of disadvantage, with preferences to neighbourhood based community projects and for innovatory work with less popular groups.

Grants are usually one-off for a specific project or part of a project and range from £1,000 to £11,000. Core funding and/or salaries are rarely considered.

In 2011/12 the trust had assets of £12 million and an income of £550,000. There were 129 grants made in the year totalling £404,000.

Beneficiaries included: Iris Trust (£11,000); Music and Health in the Community and West Midlands Quaker Peace Education Project (£10,000 each); Unite and Wardens Centre for Disabled People (£5,000 each); Cape UK and Forces Support (£3,000 each); Hibiscus Caribbean Elderly Association (£2,500); Cranfold Job Seekers Club and Meridian Money Advice (£2,000 each); and Coventry Tamil Association, College of Psychic Studies, Playback Youth Theatre, Shetland Youth Information Service, South Copeland Disability Group and Young People Taking Action (£1,000 each).

Exclusions

Grants are made to registered charities only. Applications from individuals, including students, are ineligible. No grants are made in response to general appeals from large national charities. Grants are seldom available for churches or church buildings or for scientific or medical research projects.

Applications

In writing to the correspondent, including the most recent set of accounts, clear details of the need the project is designed to meet and an outline budget. Trustees meet four times a year. Only successful applicants receive a reply.

Information gathered from:

Accounts; Charity Commission record.

Truemart Ltd

General, Judaism, welfare

£175,000 (2011/12)

Beneficial area

UK-wide and overseas, with a preference for Greater London.

Correspondent: Mrs S. Heitner, Trustee, 34 The Ridgeway, London NW11 8QS (tel: 020 8455 4456)

Trustees: I. Heitner; Mrs S. Heitner.

CC Number: 1090586

The trust was set up to promote:

- The advancement of religion in accordance with the Orthodox Jewish faith
- The relief of poverty
- General charitable purposes

In 2011/12 the trust held assets of £83,000 and had an income from donations of £232,000. Grants totalled £175,000. A list of beneficiaries was not included with the accounts and no further information was available.

Applications

In writing to the correspondent.

Information gathered from:

Accounts; Charity Commission record.

Trumros Ltd

Jewish causes

£513,500 (2012)

Beneficial area

UK.

Correspondent: Ronald Hofbauer, Trustee, 282 Finchley Road, London NW3 7AD (tel: 020 7431 3282; email: r.hofbauer@btconnect.com)

Trustees: Ronald Hofbauer; Hannah Hofbauer.

CC Number: 285533

The aim of this charity is to advance religion in accordance with the Orthodox Jewish faith by the relief of poverty and supporting educational establishments.

The annual report for 2012 states:

> The charity delivers its charitable aims as follows:
>
> - Identification of suitable projects and causes through the existing Trustees' contacts and by building new relationships with a range of charitable organisations and intermediaries
> - The careful review of, with external advice where necessary, relevant applications taking account, inter alia, of the importance of the charitable work undertaken, the financial stability of the organisation and the competence of its management
> - The monitoring of the application of all grants made by the charity in the hands of the recipient to ensure that these have been used for the purpose for which they were made in an efficient and cost effective way
> - The monitoring of the investments of the charity and, when deemed necessary, managing the portfolio with a view to maintaining and, wherever possible, improving the market value and income of the underlying assets
>
> The current grant policy of the charity is to distribute a maximum of the annual income of the charity to beneficiaries unless a special project emerges which deserves additional support. The trustees welcome applications from any institution which meets the criteria set out above.
>
> Both of the trustees take an extremely active role in the management of the charity to ensure its aims are fulfilled. Regular contact is made with many beneficiaries in order to attempt to establish the needs of charities and the level of financial assistance that may be appropriate.

In 2012 the trust had assets of £9.1 million and a total income of £1.1 million. A total of £513,500 was given in 109 grants.

Beneficiaries included: Emuno Educational Centre (£51,000); Before Trust (£32,000); Ichud Mosdos Gur (£31,000); Chevras Mo'oz Ladol (£25,500); Am Ha Chessed (£20,000); Beis Yosef Zvi (£12,500); and Gesher Charitable Trust and Ozer Gemillas Chasodim (£10,000 each).

Applications

In writing to the correspondent.

Information gathered from:

Accounts; Charity Commission record.

Tudor Rose Ltd

Jewish

£252,000 (2011/12)

Beneficial area

UK.

Correspondent: Samuel Taub, Secretary, c/o Martin and Heller, 5 North End Road, London NW11 7RJ

Trustees: Miriam Lehrfield; Sylvie Taub.

CC Number: 800576

This trust works for the promotion of the Orthodox Jewish faith and the relief of poverty.

In 2011/12 the charity had assets of £3.2 million, an income of £418,000 and gave grants to organisations totalling £252,000.

Previous beneficiaries have included: Lolev Charitable Trust; Woodlands

Charity; KTV; Bell Synagogue; Hatzola; Lubavitch Centre; and TCT.

Applications

In writing to the correspondent.

Information gathered from:

Accounts; Charity Commission record.

The Tufton Charitable Trust

Christian causes

£293,000 (2012)

Beneficial area

UK.

Correspondent: The Trustees, Tufton Place, Ewhurst Place, Northiam, East Sussex TN31 6HL

Trustees: Lady Georgina Wates; Sir Christopher Wates; Joseph Lulham; Wates Charitable Trustees Ltd.

CC Number: 801479

This trust supports Christian organisations, by providing grants as well as allowing them to use premises leased by the trust for retreats.

In 2012 the trust had an income of £241,000 and grants totalled £293,000. Assets stood at £164,000.

Beneficiaries included: Stowe School Foundation (£60,000); St Michael's Hospice (£45,000); London Institute of Contemporary Christianity (£30,000); Soul Survivor (£25,000); Off the Fence, Mission Aviation Fellowship and Vincent's Appeal Trust (£15,000 each); Royal Opera House and Jesus College-Cambridge (£10,000 each); ReSource and Theos (£7,500 each); and the British Library and Spinnaker Trust (£5,000 each).

Exclusions

No grants for repair or maintenance of buildings.

Applications

In writing to the correspondent, including an sae. The trustees meet regularly to review applications.

Information gathered from:

Accounts; Charity Commission record.

The R. D. Turner Charitable Trust

General charitable purposes

£70,500 (for the nine months ending December 2012)

Beneficial area

UK, with a preference for the Worcestershire area.

Correspondent: Timothy Patrickson, Administrator, 3 Poplar Piece, Inkberrow, Worcester WR7 4JD (tel: 01386 792014; email: timpatrickson@hotmail.co.uk)

Trustees: John Del Mar; David Pearson; Stephen Preedy; Peter Millward; James Fea.

CC Number: 263556

This trust has general charitable purposes and the trustees have resolved that the following objectives be adopted:

- To support by means of grants and loans other registered charities, particularly in the Worcestershire area
- To maintain and enhance the amenities of the villages of Arley and Upper Arley
- Such other general charitable purposes in connection with the villages of Arley and Upper Arley as the trustees shall in their absolute discretion determine/decide

In the nine months to December 2012 the trust had assets of £29 million and an income of £566,000. The upkeep of the Ardley Estate was maintained and listed as a cost of £334,500. Grants to 25 organisations totalled £70,500 and were broken down as follows:

Hospices	2	£20,000
The arts	4	£10,500
The elderly	3	£9,500
People with disabilities/health	5	£9,500
Work in the community	4	£7,000
Social support	2	£5,000
Environment and heritage	1	£4,000
Medical research	1	£3,000
Children and young people	2	£2,000

There was no list of grant recipients with the accounts but previous beneficiaries have included: St Richard's Hospice (£15,000); Worcestershire and Dudley Historic Churches Trust (£12,000); British Red Cross Hereford and Worcester (£10,000); ARCOS, Cobalt Appeal Fund and Motor Neurone Disease Association (£5,000 each); County Air Ambulance Trust and Relate Worcestershire (£3,000); Sunfield Children's Homes (£2,000); Listening Books (£1,000); and Talking Newspapers of the UK (£500).

Exclusions

No grants to non-registered charities or to individuals.

Applications

The trust does not have a grant application form. Applicant Charities are requested to send a letter of no more than two pages describing their appeal, together with a copy of their latest accounts, to the Trust Administrator at the Grants Office. Phone calls and emails are welcome prior to submitting an application. Appeal guidelines are available on request.

Percentage of awards given to new applicants: between 20% and 30%.

Common applicant mistakes

'Too much information.'

Information gathered from:

Accounts; Charity Commission record; further information provided by the funder.

The Florence Turner Trust

General charitable purposes

£99,000 (2011/12)

Beneficial area

UK, but with a strong preference for Leicestershire.

Correspondent: Pamela Fowle, Correspondent, Shakespeares, Two Colton Square, Leicester LE1 1 QH (tel: 01162 576129; email: paula.fowle@Shakespeares.co.uk)

Trustees: Roger Bowder; Katherine Hall; Michael Jones.

CC Number: 502721

This trust has general charitable purposes, giving most of its support in Leicestershire. Grants are made to organisations and individuals. Smaller projects are favoured where donations will make a 'quantifiable difference to the recipients rather than favouring large national charities whose income is measured in millions rather than thousands.' Grants are made for the benefit of individuals through a referring agency such as social services, NHS trusts or similar responsible bodies.

In 2011/12 it had assets of £5.9 million and an income of £158,000. Grants totalled £99,000. Support costs were £17,000; auditor's remuneration £3,400 and 'trustees remuneration' was £6,000.

There was no list of beneficiaries included in the accounts. Previous beneficiaries included: Leicester Charity Link (£12,000); Leicester Grammar School – Bursary (£10,000); Age Concern Leicester, Leicester and Leicestershire Historic Churches Preservation Trust and VISTA (£2,400 each); LOROS (£2,000); New Parks Club for Young People (£1,500); and Four

Twelve Ministries and Help for Heroes (£1,000 each).

Exclusions

The trust does not support individuals for educational purposes.

Applications

In writing to the correspondent. Trustees meet every eight or nine weeks.

Information gathered from:

Accounts; Charity Commission record.

The Turtleton Charitable Trust

Arts, heritage, poverty, education

£75,000 (2012/13)

Beneficial area

Scotland.

Correspondent: Kenneth Pinkerton, Clerk to the Trustees, Turcan Connell, Princes Exchange, 1 Earl Grey Street, Edinburgh EH3 9EE (tel: 01312 288111; email: turtletontrust@turcanconnell.com; website: www.turcanconnell.com/turtleton)

SC Number: SC038018

Established in 2007, the trust makes grants in the fields of heritage and the arts, principally in Scotland. The following information is available from the administrator's website:

> The Turtleton Charitable Trust makes grant to charities which work in the following fields:
>
> - Advancement of the arts, culture and heritage – the trustees particularly favour heritage and the visual arts, but other aspects of the arts and culture will be considered. The vast majority of grants are made in this field
> - Support of the disadvantaged and the advancement of education – the trustees consider only a small number of grants in this field in any one year
>
> Please note that the trustees are unlikely to entertain applications which fall outside these two main areas.
>
> Grants typically range between £5,000 and £25,000. Larger grants and multi-year commitments may be available only in limited circumstances, at the trustees' discretion.

Grants are made totalling around £75,000.

Applications

The following information is given by the trust:

> Applications should be made in writing on no more than 3 sides of A4 by email to turtletontrust@turcanconnell.com. If your charity does not have access to email, a hard copy application may be sent.
>
> If this is the first time that you have applied to The Turtleton Charitable Trust, the most recent set of accounts for your charity should also be submitted, preferably by email, along with your application. Please do not send additional literature or materials such as DVDs, compact discs, etc, as additional materials will not be passed on to the trustees.
>
> The trustees meet once a year in Spring to decide on grants for the following 12 months.
>
> Applications should reach us by email or in hard copy not later than 31 January. The trustees normally pay grants prior to 30 June in each year.
>
> Please note that applications are not normally acknowledged on receipt. A note will be posted [on the administrator's website] once the trustees have met and successful applicants will be contacted after the trustees have held their annual meeting.

Information gathered from:

OSCR record; funder's website.

The TUUT Charitable Trust

General, particularly trade-union-favoured causes

£9,000 (2011/12)

Beneficial area

Worldwide.

Correspondent: Stephanie Ellis, TU Fund Managers Ltd, Congress House, Great Russell Street, London WC1B 3LQ (tel: 020 7637 7116; email: stephanie@tufm.co.uk; website: www.tufm.co.uk)

Trustees: Lord Christopher; M. Walsh; M. Bradley; B. Barber; Lord Brookman; E. Sweeney.

CC Number: 258665

'The TUUT Charitable Trust was set up by the trade union movement in 1969 for the sole purpose of owning TU Fund Managers Ltd. The intention was – and still is – that profits distributed by the company should go to good causes rather than individual shareholders.

> It is a requirement of the trust deed that all the trustees must be trades unionists, the intention being to ensure that causes benefiting should broadly be those that would be supported by the movement. Trade unions – and indeed individuals – are free to nominate favoured causes, all of which are reviewed by the trustees before any payment is made.

The trust considers requests from 'small to medium sized non-religious charitable organisations based in the UK'. The trustees stated in their 2011/12 annual report that they are:

> adopting a fresh approach which in the main and over perhaps a four year period, will provide support for one specific cause or project in the UK and one overseas.

In 2011/12 the trust had assets of £2.1 million and an income of £29,000. Grants totalled £9,000.

Beneficiaries during the year were: React (£1,700); Happy Days Children's' Charity (£1,200); Cares, Hope and Happy Homes for Children and Second Chance (£1,000); CICRA (£950); Derby Toc H Camp (£780); and RNLI and Royal British Legion (£500).

During the year the trust also awarded two fellowship awards to enable outstanding students to study for an MSc in Applied Animal Behaviour and Animal Welfare or similar courses, at University.

Exclusions

No grants to individuals or to charities based overseas.

Applications

'To apply for a grant, charitable organisations should apply for a Form of Request and submit this, duly completed. The Trustees meet three times a year to consider requests received.'

Information gathered from:

Accounts; Charity Commission record; funder's website.

TVML Foundation

General

£466,000 (2012)

Beneficial area

UK and overseas, with preference towards Brazil and Israel.

Correspondent: Tania Lima, Correspondent, 8 Sand Ridge, Ridgewood, Uckfield, East Sussex TN22 5ET

Trustees: Vivian Lederman; Marcos Lederman; Marcelo Steuer.

CC Number: 1135495

The TVML Foundation was established in 2010 for general charitable purposes. The settlor of the foundation is Marcos Lederman, founding partner of the hedge fund Spinnaker Capital Ltd.

In 2012 the foundation had an income of £103,000 and had assets of £4.6 million. Grants were made to organisations and individuals totalling £466,000.

There were no details of beneficiaries listed in the accounts, although the trust states that grants were to support educational and lifehood initiatives in Brazil and Israel.

Applications

In writing to the correspondent.

Information gathered from:

Accounts; Charity Commission record.

Ulting Overseas Trust

Theological training

£106,000 (2011/12)

Beneficial area

The developing world (mostly, but not exclusively, Asia, Africa and South and Central America).

Correspondent: Timothy Buckland, Correspondent, Pothecary, Witham Weld, 70 St George's Square, London SW1V 3RD (tel: 020 7821 8211)

Trustees: Tim Warren; Donald Ford; Mary Brinkley; Alan Bale; John Heyward; Dr Jean Kessler; Revd Joseph Kapolyo; Nicholas Durlacher; Roger Pearce; Dr Kang San Tan.

CC Number: 294397

According to the trustees' report for 2011/12, the objects of the trust are:

> To advance the Christian faith and to relieve poverty and disease in developing countries. This is done by making charitable grants to those training for Christian Ministry, teachers in theological education, theological institutions in developing countries and those seeking to assist in developing countries.
>
> The trust has made grants directly to training institutions but occasionally to individuals, so that they may further their Christian studies in order to return as faith leaders in their native countries.

The trust exists solely to provide bursaries, normally via grants to Christian theological training institutions or organisations with a training focus, for those in the developing world who wish to train for the Christian ministry, or for those who wish to improve their ministry skills. It gives priority to the training of students in their home countries or continents.

In 2011/12 it had assets of £3.4 million and an income of £104,000. There were 32 organisational grants and one individual grant made in the year totalling £106,000.

Beneficiaries included: International Fellowship of Evangelical Students (£15,000); Scripture Union International (£14,000); Langham Trust (£13,000); Interserve (£6,000); Asian Theological Seminary (£4,700); Evangelical Seminary Southern Africa, Discipleship Training Centre- Singapore and Langham Preaching (£2,000 each); University of Aberdeen and Alliance Development Fund (£1,000 each); and Bangladesh Bible Correspondence College (£750).

Exclusions

No grants are given for capital projects such as buildings or library stock, nor for training in subjects other than Biblical, theological and missionary studies. Grants are only made to institutions to pass on to their students; direct grants to individuals cannot be made.

Applications

In writing to the correspondent. Each application is examined against strict criteria.

Information gathered from:

Accounts; Charity Commission record.

The Ulverscroft Foundation

People who are blind or partially sighted, ophthalmic research

£642,000 (2011/12)

Beneficial area

Worldwide.

Correspondent: Joyce Sumner, Secretary, 1 The Green, Bradgate Road, Anstey, Leicester LE7 7FU (tel: 01162 361595; fax: 01162 361594; email: foundation@ulverscroft.co.uk; website: www.foundation.ulverscroft.com)

Trustees: John Bush; Peter Carr; Pat Beech; David Owen; Roger Crooks; John Sanford-Smith; Robert Gent.

CC Number: 264873

Ulverscroft Large Print Books Ltd, was formed in 1964. The company republished existing books in large type to sell to libraries and donate the profits to sight-related charitable causes. In 1972 The Ulverscroft Foundation was created.

The foundation supports projects which will have a positive effect on the quality of life of visually impaired people (blind and partially sighted). Funding is channelled via recognised organisations which help the visually impaired, for example, libraries, hospitals, clinics, schools and colleges, and social and welfare organisations.

In 2011/12 the foundation had assets of £18.3 million, an income of £11.7 million and a total expenditure of £11.2 million. Grants totalled £642,000.

Beneficiaries included: Ulverscroft Vision Research Group – Great Ormond Street Hospital (£446,000); University of Leicester (£130,000); Sightsavers and Force Foundation Netherlands (£10,000 each); Deafblind UK (£5,000); Cardiff Institute for the Blind (£3,000); Sight Support Derbyshire (£2,000); and Scarborough Blind and PS Society, Association Blind Asians Leeds and North Lanarkshire Libraries (£1,000 each).

Exclusions

Applications from individuals are not encouraged. Generally, assistance towards salaries and general running costs are not given.

Applications

In writing to the correspondent including the latest annual report and accounts, there is no application form. Proposals should be as detailed as possible, including: details of the current service provided to the visually impaired (if any) and how the proposed project will be integrated or enhanced; an estimate (if possible) of how many visually impaired people use/will use the service; the amount of funding obtained to date (if any); and the names of any other organisations to whom funding applications have been made.

Trustees meet quarterly to consider appeals in January, April, July and October each year; deadlines for appeals are the last day of the previous month.

Due to the large number of appeals received, the foundation will not consider fresh appeals until a period of 18 months to two years has elapsed since the last application. The success of any appeal is dependent on the level of funding available at the time of consideration.

Information gathered from:

Accounts; Charity Commission record; funder's website.

The Union of Orthodox Hebrew Congregation

Jewish causes

£438,000 to organisations (2012)

Beneficial area

UK.

Correspondent: The Administrator, Landau Morley, Lanmor House, 370–386 High Road, Wembley HA9 6AX (tel: 020 8903 5122)

Trustees: Benzion Se Freshwater; Chaim Konig; Rabbi A. Pinter.

CC Number: 249892

This charity works to protect and to further in every way the interests of traditional Judaism in the United Kingdom and to establish and support such institutions as will serve this object.

During 2012 the charity continued to support community projects and provide assistance to members. In this year it had assets of over £1.6 million and an income of £1.1 million. Grants to organisations totalled £468,000, which included £30,000 donated to individuals. Unfortunately there was no list of beneficiaries, however the annual report stated that the charity has donated significant sums for the renovation and building of Mikva'os in North and North West London.

Previous beneficiaries have included: Addas Yisoroel Mikva Foundation, Achieve Trust, Atereth Shau, Beis Malka, Beis Shmuel, Belz Nursery, Bnos Yerushaim, Chesed Charity Trust, London Board of Schechita, Mutual Trust, Maoz Ladol, North West London Mikvah, Needy Families and Poor Families Pesach, Society of Friends of the Torah, Talmud Centre Trust and VMCT.

Applications

In writing to the correspondent.

Information gathered from:

Accounts; Charity Commission record.

The David Uri Memorial Trust

General: Jewish, general

£0 (2011/12)

Beneficial area

Worldwide.

Correspondent: The Trustees, 244 Vauxhall Bridge Road, London SW1V 1AU

Trustees: Benjamin Blackman; Bianca Roden; Sandra Blackman.

CC Number: 327810

In 2011/12 the trust's assets totalled £3.2 million and it had an income of £285,000, mainly from property investment revenue. No grants were made during the year, however there were £63,000 worth of governance costs.

Previous beneficiaries have included: National Jewish Chaplaincy Board, Age Concern, Crisis at Christmas, Jefferies Research Wing Trust, NSPCC and Yakar Education Foundation.

Exclusions

No grants to individuals.

Applications

In writing to the correspondent.

Information gathered from:

Accounts; Charity Commission record.

Vale of Glamorgan – Welsh Church Fund

General

£29,000 (2011/12)

Beneficial area

Vale of Glamorgan and City of Cardiff council areas.

Correspondent: A. D. Williams, Director of Finance, ICT and Property, The Vale of Glamorgan Council, Civic Offices, Holton Rd, Barry CF63 4RU (tel: 01446 709250; email: adwilliams@valeofglamorgan.gov.uk; website: www.valeofglamorgan.gov.uk)

Trustee: Vale of Glamorgan County Borough Council.

CC Number: 506628

The fund makes grants in the following areas:

- Educational
- Relief in sickness
- Relief in need
- Libraries, museums, art galleries
- Social and recreational
- Protection of historical buildings
- Medical and social research and treatment
- Probation
- Older people
- Visual impairments
- Places of worship and burial grounds
- Emergencies or disasters
- Other charitable purposes

In practice grants are made to local churches. Grants are given on a one-off basis. Whilst no maximum/minimum grant levels are stipulated, awards are usually in the region of £1,500.

In 2011/12 there were assets of £3.7 million, an income of £42,000 and grants made totalling £29,000.

As in previous years grants were made solely to churches. These included: Ewenny Prior Church (£7,000); St Nicholas Parish Church (£5,000); All Saints Church, Barry (£3,000); Bethania Presbyterian Church (£2,300); All Saints Church, Llandaff North (£1,500); Tabernacle Baptist Church (£1,000); and Beacon Church Cardiff and Ararat Baptist Church, Whitchurch (£500 each).

Exclusions

No grants to individuals.

Applications

For organisations based in the Vale of Glamorgan, further information can be obtained from the correspondent. For organisations based in Cardiff, contact Robert Giddings at Cardiff County Council (029208537484/voluntarysectorgrants@cardiff.gov.uk). Applications are accepted throughout the year.

Information gathered from:

Accounts; Charity Commission record; funder's website.

The Albert Van Den Bergh Charitable Trust

Medical research, disability, community, general

£103,000 (2011/12)

Beneficial area

UK and overseas.

Correspondent: Jane Hartley, Trustee, Trevornick Farmhouse, Holywell Bay, Newquay, Cornwall TR8 5PW

Trustees: Jane Hartley; Nicola Glover; Bruce Hopkins.

CC Number: 296885

The trust was established in 1987. The majority of the organisations that receive donations are in the UK and concerned with health research and care for patients with cancer, multiple sclerosis, Parkinson's disease and other diseases and disabilities. Institutions which care for the elderly and children's charities are also supported.

In 2011/12 the trust had assets of £3.1 million and an income of £111,000. Grants to 100 organisations totalled £103,000 and were broken down as follows:

Medical research, care and support	£33,500
Help in the community	£20,000
Disability	£12,000
Overseas	£10,000
Hospices	£6,000
Service men and women	£4,000
Cultural	£3,500
Conservation	£3,000
Churches	£3,000
Homelessness	£2,000
Older people	£2,000
Other	£2,000
Disadvantaged	£1,000
Outward bound	£1,000

Previous beneficiaries have included: BLISS, Bishop of Guildford's Charity, British Heart Foundation, Counsel and Care for the Elderly, Leukaemia Research Trust, Multiple Sclerosis Society, Parentline Surrey, National Osteoporosis Society, RNID, Riding for the Disabled – Cranleigh Age Concern, SSAFA, St John Ambulance and United Charities Fund – Liberal Jewish Synagogue.

Applications

In writing to the correspondent, including accounts and budgets.

Information gathered from:

Accounts; Charity Commission record.

The Van Neste Foundation

Welfare, Christian, developing world

£205,000 (2011/12)

Beneficial area

UK (especially the Bristol area) and overseas.

Correspondent: Fergus Lyons, Secretary, 15 Alexandra Road, Clifton, Bristol BS8 2DD (tel: 01179 735167)

Trustees: M. T. M. Appleby; F. J. F. Lyons; G. J. Walker; J. F. Lyons; B. M. Appleby; Michael Lyons; Tom Appleby.

CC Number: 201951

The trustees currently give priority to the following:

- Developing world
- People who are disabled or elderly
- Advancement of religion and respect for the sanctity and dignity of life
- Community projects

These objectives are reviewed by the trustees from time to time but applications falling outside them are unlikely to be considered.

In 2011/12 the trust had assets of £6.9 million, an income of £261,000 and gave grants totalling £205,000.

Donations were broken down as follows:

Community and Christian family life	11	£75,000
Overseas	5	£64,000
Religious	2	£30,000
Disability and age	7	£26,00
Dignity and sanctity of life	1	£10,000

Beneficiaries included: CAFOD, DEKI and St James Priory (£25,000 each); CHAS Bristol (£21,000); Emmaus House Bristol (£10,000); African Promise, Bristol and District Tranquiliser Project and The Salvation Army (£5,000 each); For Ethiopia (£4,000); Mentoring Plus (£3,500); Cerebral Palsy Plus (£3,000); Avon Riding Centre (£1,000); and Have a Stick will Travel (£500).

Exclusions

No grants to individuals or to large, well-known charities. Applications are only considered from registered charities.

Applications

Applications should be in the form of a concise letter setting out the clear objectives to be obtained, which must be charitable. Information must be supplied concerning agreed funding from other sources together with a timetable for achieving the objectives of the appeal and a copy of the latest accounts. The foundation does not normally make grants on a continuing basis. To keep overheads to a minimum, only successful applications are acknowledged. Appeals are considered by the trustees at their meetings in January, June and October.

Information gathered from:

Accounts; Charity Commission record.

Mrs Maud Van Norden's Charitable Foundation

General

£41,000 (2012)

Beneficial area

UK.

Correspondent: The Trustees, BM Box 2367, London WC1N 3XX

Trustees: Ena Dukler; John Gordon; Elisabeth Humphryes; Neil Wingerath.

CC Number: 210844

Established in 1962, in 2012 the trust had assets of £1.1 million, an income of £40,000 and gave 23 grants totalling £41,000.

Most grants were for £1,500. Beneficiaries included: Salvation Army (£4,000); Women's Royal Voluntary Service (£3,000); Royal Hospital for Neuro-disability and Crisis UK (£2,500); and Action on Elder Abuse, Humane Slaughter Association, Gurkha Welfare Trust, Calibre Audio Library, The Cure Parkinson's Trust, Police Community Clubs of Great Britain and Princess Alice Hospice (£1,500 each).

Exclusions

No grants to individuals, expeditions or scholarships. The trustees make donations to registered UK charities only.

Applications

All appeals should be by letter containing the following:

- Aims and objectives of the charity
- Nature of the appeal
- Total target, if for a specific project
- Contributions received against target
- Registered charity number
- Any other factors

Letters should be accompanied by a copy of the applicant's latest reports and accounts.

Information gathered from:

Accounts; Charity Commission record.

The Vandervell Foundation

General

£351,000 (2012)

Beneficial area

UK.

Correspondent: Ms Valerie Kaye, Administrator, Hampstead Town Hall Centre, 213 Haverstock Hill, London NW3 4QP (tel: 020 7435 7546)

Trustee: Directors of the Vandervell Foundation Ltd.

CC Number: 255651

This trust has general charitable purposes, supporting both individuals and organisations. A wide range of causes has been supported, including schools, educational establishments, hospices and other health organisations, with the trust stating there are no real preferences or exclusions. Grants generally range from £1,000 to £20,000.

In 2012 the trust had assets of £6.7 million, an income of £301,000 and gave 98 grants to organisations totalling £351,000.

Social welfare	44	£133,000
Education	12	£105,000
Medical research	28	£68,000
Performing arts	6	£31,000
Environmental regeneration	8	£15,000

Beneficiaries included: The Big Issue Foundation (£30,000); Prisoners Education Trust (£20,000); PMS Foundation and Nottingham Trent University (£15,000 each); Kenwood Dairy Restoration Trust, The Outward Bound Trust and Weekend Arts College (£10,000 each); FareShare (£6,000); and London Air Ambulance, Royal National Theatre, Mayor of London and Salisbury Cathedral School (£5,000 each).

There was also one grant to an individual of £750.

Applications

In writing to the correspondent. Grants are reviewed by the board of the trustees which meets every two months.

Information gathered from:

Accounts; Charity Commission record.

Roger Vere Foundation

General

£262,000 (2011/12)

Beneficial area

UK and worldwide, with a special interest in High Wycombe.

Correspondent: Peter Allen, Trustee, 19 Berwick Road, Marlow, Buckinghamshire SL7 3AR (tel: 01628 471702)

Trustees: Rosemary Vere, Chair; Marion Lyon; Peter Allen.

CC Number: 1077559

This trust was established in September 1999 and it supports, worldwide:

- The relief of financial hardship in and around, but not restricted to, High Wycombe
- Advancement of education
- Advancement of religion
- Advancement of scientific and medical research
- Conservation and protection of the natural environment and endangered plants and animals
- Relief of natural and civil disasters
- General charitable purposes

In 2011/12 the trust had assets of £3.2 million, an income of £138,000 and made grants to organisations totalling £262,000.

A list of beneficiaries was not included in the accounts. Previous beneficiaries include: Cord Blood Charity, the Leprosy Mission, Claire House Children's Hospice, Angels International, SignAlong Group, Changing Faces, Women's Aid, St John Water Wing, UK Youth and Jubilee Plus.

Applications

In writing to the correspondent. The trustees meet regularly to consider requests.

Information gathered from:

Accounts; Charity Commission record.

The Nigel Vinson Charitable Trust

Economic/community development and employment, general

£282,000 (2011/12)

Beneficial area

UK, with a preference for north east England.

Correspondent: The Trustees, C. Hoare and Co, 37 Fleet Street, London EC4P 4DQ (tel: 020 7353 4522)

Trustees: Hon. Rowena A. Cowan; Rt Hon. Lord Vinson of Roddam Dene; Thomas O. C. Harris; Hon. Bettina C. Witheridge; Hon. Antonia C. Bennett; Miss E. Passey; C. Hoare and Co. Trustees.

CC Number: 265077

This trust was established in 1972. It supports economic/community development and employment as well as making grants to other causes.

In 2011/12 the trust received an exceptional gift of £5.5 million from the settlor which brought the income during the year to £5.6 million and the assets to £10 million. Grants totalled £282,000.

Beneficiaries included: The Injustice Foundation (£50,000); The Christian Institute (£37,000); Politics and Economics Research Trust (£30,000); Civitas (£15,000); Young Briton's Foundation and Chillingham Wild Cattle Association (£10,000 each); Northumberland and Newcastle Society, Christian Concern for our Nation, The Wing Appeal, Renewable Energy Research Foundation and Family Education Trust (£5,000 each); and European Foundation (£2,500).

Applications

In writing to the correspondent. The trustees meet periodically to consider applications for grants of £1,000 and above. All grants below £1,000 are decided by The Rt. Hon. Nigel Lord Vinson on behalf of the trustees.

Information gathered from:

Accounts; Charity Commission record.

Vision Charity

Children who are blind, partially sighted or dyslexic

£112,000 (2011/12)

Beneficial area

UK and overseas.

Correspondent: Peter Thompson, President, 59 Victoria Road, Surbiton, Surrey KT6 4NQ (tel: 01296 655227; email: info@visioncharity.co.uk; website: www.visioncharity.co.uk)

Trustee: William Vestey.

CC Number: 1075630

The objects of the charity are to combine the fundraising efforts of companies and individuals who use or benefit from, or work in, the visual communications industry for the benefit of children who are blind, partially sighted or dyslexic.

> The monies raised are used expressly to purchase equipment, goods or specialist services. The Vision Charity will make cash donations only in very exceptional circumstances, as approved by its board of trustees.
>
> Vision is keen to emphasise its increasing international focus, both in terms of its fundraising activities and in directing its donations.

In 2011/12 the charity had assets of £219,000 and an income of £252,000, most of which came from donations received and various fundraising events organised by the charity. Grants were made totalling £112,000.

There were nine grants of £1,000 or more listed in the accounts. The beneficiaries were: New College Worcester (£29,000); Priestley Smith School, Birmingham (£26,000 in two grants); VICTA (£20,000); Churchwood CP School (£12,000); Joseph Clarke School, London (£10,000); SENSE (£7,000); Autism Independent UK (£2,600); and The Bloomfield Learning Centre for Children (£1,600).

Applications

A brief summary of the request should be sent to the correspondent. If the request is of interest to the trustees, further details will be requested. If the request has not been acknowledged within three months of submission, the applicant should assume that it has not been successful. The charity is interested to receive such applications but regrets that it is not able to acknowledge every unsuccessful submission.

Percentage of awards given to new applicants: between 10% and 20%.

Common applicant mistakes

'Not defining application; too vague; too large!'

Information gathered from:

Accounts; Charity Commission record; further information provided by the funder; funder's website.

Vivdale Ltd

Jewish causes

£67,000 (2011/12)

Beneficial area

UK.

Correspondent: David Henry Marks, Trustee, 17 Cheyne Walk, London NW4 3QH (tel: 020 8202 9367)

Trustees: David Henry Marks; Francesca Zipporah Sinclair; Loretta Marks.

CC Number: 268505

In 2011/12 the trust's assets totalled £2.4 million, it had an income of £103,000 and made grants totalling £67,000.

Previous beneficiaries have included: Achisomach Aid Company Ltd, Beis Soroh Schneirer, Beis Yaakov Town, Beis Yisroel Tel Aviv, Comet Charities Ltd, Friends of Harim Bnei Brak, Jewish Teachers Training College Gateshead,

Mosdos Bnei Brak, Torah Vechesed Ashdod and Woodstock Sinclair Trust.

Applications

In writing to the correspondent.

Percentage of awards given to new applicants: between 10% and 20%.

Information gathered from:

Accounts; Charity Commission record; further information provided by the funder.

The Viznitz Foundation

Jewish

£120,000 (2011/12)

Beneficial area

UK and abroad.

Correspondent: Mr Heinrich Feldman, Trustee, 23 Overlea Road, London E5 9BG (tel: 020 8557 9557)

Trustees: Heinrich Feldman; Shulom Feldman.

CC Number: 326581

'The objects of the charity are to pay and apply and appropriate the whole of the trust fund to those purposes both in the UK and abroad recognised as charitable by English Law and in accordance with the trust deed and the wishes of the Grand Rabbi of Viznitz.'

In 2011/12 the foundation had assets of £2.2 million, an income of £204,000 and made 'donations' of £120,000. A list of beneficiaries was not included in the accounts.

Applications

In writing to the correspondent.

Information gathered from:

Accounts; Charity Commission record.

The Scurrah Wainwright Charity

Social reform

£112,000 (2011/12)

Beneficial area

Preference for Yorkshire, South Africa and Zimbabwe.

Correspondent: Kerry McQuade, Administrator, 16 Blenheim Street, Hebden Bridge, West Yorkshire HX7 8BU (email: admin@wainwrighttrusts.org.uk; website: www.wainwrighttrusts.org.uk)

Trustees: M. S. Wainwright, Chair; R. R. Bhaskar; H. P. I. Scott; H. A. Wainwright; P. Wainwright; T. M. Wainwright.

CC Number: 1002755

The Wainwright family runs two trusts, one charitable (The Scurrah Wainwright Charity), one non-charitable (The Andrew Wainwright Reform Trust Ltd), which prioritises grants for political and pressure group work that a registered charity could not support. The AWRT has a wide-ranging remit, striving for a just and democratic society, redressing political and social injustices.

> The trusts are based on the family's traditions of liberal values and support for the socially disempowered. The trustees are all family members, based in West Yorkshire.
>
> - The charity funds projects in England, primarily in Yorkshire and the North of England, as well as Zimbabwe and Southern Africa. It rarely funds work in any other part of the world
> - It looks for innovative work in the field of social reform, with a preference for 'root-cause' rather than palliative projects
> - It favours causes that are outside the mainstream, and unlikely to be funded by other charities
> - It will contribute to core costs

Typically, grants are between £1,000 and £5,000, but in cases of exceptional merit larger grants may be awarded. Organisations do not have to be charities to apply but it must have charitable objects. Large and national charities are only supported if they are specifically working in the Yorkshire region with clear evidence of local control and access to the grant.

In 2011/12 the charity had assets of £1.6 million, an income of £62,000 and gave grants to 37 organisations totalling £112,000.

Beneficiaries included: Heads Together Productions (£25,000); War on Want and Leeds Refuge Forum (£5,000 each); 32 Degrees East Ugandan Arts Trust (£4,500); HALE – Healthy Action Local Engagement (£4,000); Food Aware (£3,500); The Global Native (£3,000); Public Interest Investigations (£2,500); Helena Kennedy Foundation and Barnardo's Yorkshire (£2,000 each); Northern Indymedia – 1 in 12 Library Collective (£1,500); and Womankind Worldwide (£1,000).

Exclusions

No support is given to:

- Individuals
- Animal welfare
- Buildings
- Medical research or support for individual medical conditions
- Substitution for Government funding (e.g. in education and health)
- Charities that send unsolicited general appeal letters
- Activities that have already happened
- Applicants who do not have a UK bank into which a grant can be paid

Applications

Follow these preliminary steps:

- Check that the amount of money you need falls within the charity's limits
- Check deadlines: the trustees meet three times a year – in March, July and November – and applications must be submitted by 14 January, 14 May or 14 September respectively

Applications should include:

- An opening section that gives the name and postal address of your organisation, details of a named contact for the application and where you heard about the charity
- Background information about you and/or your organisation
- The nature of the project you wish to pursue and what it seeks to achieve
- Your plans for practical implementation of the work and a budget
- Your most recent accounts and details of any additional sources of funding already secured or to be sought
- Whether you will accept a contribution to the amount requested
- If the above information (excluding your accounts) takes up more than two sides of A4, include a summary of that information on no more than two sides of A4, using a font no smaller than 12-point

Applicants may contact the administrator, preferably by email, for any clarification.

If you have not heard from the administrator by the end of the month in which the trustees' meeting was held you must assume your application was not successful.

Percentage of awards given to new applicants: 90%.

Common applicant mistakes

'Applying as individuals; sending non-specific round-robin type applications; not including their most recent audited accounts.'

Information gathered from:

Accounts; Charity Commission record; further information provided by the funder; funder's website.

Wakeham Trust

Community development, education, community service by young people

Around £70,000 (2011/12)

Beneficial area

UK.

Correspondent: Miss Laura Gosling, Correspondent, Wakeham Lodge, Rogate, Petersfield, Hampshire GU31 5EJ (tel: 01730 821748; email:

wakehamtrust@mac.com; website: www.wakehamtrust.org)

Trustees: Harold Carter; Barnaby Newbolt; Tess Silkstone.

CC Number: 267495

> We provide grants to help people rebuild their communities. We are particularly interested in neighbourhood projects, community arts projects, projects involving community service by young people, or projects set up by those who are socially excluded.
>
> We also support innovative projects to promote excellence in teaching (at any level, from primary schools to universities), though we never support individuals.
>
> We aim to refresh the parts that other funding sources can't reach, especially new ideas and unpopular causes. Because we don't appeal to the public for funds, we can take risks.
>
> Because we are mostly run by volunteers, we can afford to make very small grants, without our funds being eaten up by administration costs.
>
> We favour small projects – often, but not always, start-ups. We try to break the vicious circle whereby you have to be established to get funding from major charities, but you have to get funding to get established. Grants are normally given where an initial £75 to £750 can make a real difference to getting the project up and running.

The trust is flexible and says that it sometimes 'breaks its own rules' but most projects share some of the following characteristics:

- It is something new for a particular area
- It is small
- It does not employ staff
- It is not well established
- It has the potential to become self-supporting
- It is outward looking and helps a lot of people
- It is a registered charity in the UK or can find one to accept funds on its behalf

In 2011/12 the trust had an income of £23,000 and a total expenditure of £83,000. Further financial information was not available but based on previous years there were about £70,000 worth of grants made.

Grants listed on the website include: A furniture reclamation and delivery enterprise (£500); a group of elderly and disabled volunteers for a children's cafe (£350); new youth club and The Kaiama Community Association (£250 each); community garden and toy boxes for DHSS offices (£200 each); Martin Youth Bikers (£150); and community football (£50).

Exclusions

No grants to individuals or large, well-established charities, or towards buildings and transport.

Applications

By letter or by filling in the online form on the trust's website, where full guidelines are also available. The trust prefers online applications.

Information gathered from:

Accounts; Charity Commission record; funder's website.

The Thomas Wall Trust

Education, welfare

£27,000 to organisations (2011/12)

Beneficial area

UK.

Correspondent: Louise Pooley, Skinners' Hall, 8 Dowgate Hill, London EC4R 2SP (tel: 020 7213 0564; email: information@thomaswalltrust.org.uk; website: www.thomaswalltrust.org.uk)

Trustees: Dr G. M. Copland; Mrs M. A. Barrie; P. Bellamy; C. R. Broomfield; Miss A. S. Kennedy; Mrs A. Mullins; Revd Dr R. Waller; Paola Morris.

CC Number: 206121

This trust makes grants to both individuals and charitable organisations. The applying organisation, movement or institution has to be a registered charity with objects in a broad sense educational and/or concerned with social service. Charities must have an annual income of less than £200,000 a year. Grants do not normally exceed £1,000 and are made for specific projects or activities, rather than general running costs.

Note on grants to individuals: 'The trustees consider applications from UK nationals only who are in financial need and who wish to undertake educational courses at any level and duration, especially courses which are vocational or are concerned with social service in a broad sense and which will lead to paid employment.'

In 2011/12 the trust had assets of £2.8 million and an income of £120,000. Grants to 28 organisations totalled £27,000 and to 41 individuals totalling £44,000.

Beneficiaries included: Crossroads Counselling (£1,100); Action Foundation; Barnet Lone Person Centre; Cued Speech Association; Foyle Down Syndrome Trust; Get Set Girls; Gospel Oak Action Link; Lincoln Toy Library; Westcliff Drop-In Centre (£1,000 each); Community Development Support (£900); Ulverston Inshore Rescue (£800); and Thomas Wall Nursery (£250).

Exclusions

Grants are not made: towards the erection, upkeep or renovation of buildings; to hospitals, almshouses or similar institutions; for objects which are purely medical; for projects outside of the UK; for charities that have received a grant from the trust in the last five years.

Applications

On a form available from the website which must be completed and returned via post or email along with a copy of the most recent audited accounts (if they are not available on the Charity Commission website). Charities will only be contacted if the application is successful.

The trustees meet twice a year, in July and November. Applications for the July meeting must be received by mid-May and for the November meeting by end of September.

Common applicant mistakes

'Applying when they fall outside the criteria. Not reading the guidance and not fully completing the form.'

Information gathered from:

Accounts; Charity Commission record; further information provided by the funder; funder's website.

Wallace and Gromit's Children's Foundation

Improving the quality of life for sick children

£100,000 (2011/12)

Beneficial area

UK.

Correspondent: Ms Anna Shepherd, Deputy Director, 24 Upper Maudlin Street, Bristol BS2 8DJ (tel: 01179 252744; email: info@wallaceandgromitcharity.org; website: www.wallaceandgromitfoundation.org)

Trustees: I. Hannah, Chair; S. Cooper; P. Lord; J. Moule; N. Park; D. Sproxton.

CC Number: 1096483

Wallace and Gromit's Children's Foundation is a national charity raising funds to improve the quality of life for children in hospitals and hospices throughout the UK.

'We are the only national charity raising funds for local children's hospitals and hospices to improve the quality of life for sick children across the UK.'

The foundation provides funding to support projects such as:

- Arts, music play and entertainment programmes to stimulate young minds and divert attention away from illness

- Providing welcoming and accessible environments and surroundings, designed specifically for children in a fun and engaging way
- Funding education and information programmes to educate young people and recognising the importance of self-help and health related issues
- Helping to fund the acquisition of medical facilities, which can help to improve diagnosis and treatment of a wide range of conditions and illnesses in children
- Sustaining family relationships helping to keep families together during emotionally difficult times
- Helping to meet the cost of care in a children's hospice where children and their families are cared for during good days, difficult days and last days
- Supporting children with physical and emotional difficulties empowering and increasing confidence

The charity raises its income through various fundraising activities such as the Wrong Trousers Day and Wallace and Gromit's BIG Bake.

In 2011/12 the charity had assets of £58,000 and an income of £221,000. Grants were made totalling £100,000.

Beneficiaries included: University Hospital Coventry and Warwickshire CW Charity, Coventry (£13,000); Alexander Devine Children's Hospice Service (£10,000); Wallace and Gromit's Grand Appeal (£9,000); Northern Ireland Children's Hospice (£7,700); The Sick Kids Friends Foundation, Alder Hey IMAGINE Appeal and Leeds Children's Hospital (£5,000 each); Little Havens Children's Hospice (£4,300); Chestnut Tree Children's Hospice (£3,500); and Chelsea Children's Hospital School (£1,000).

Exclusions

The foundation will not fund:

- Charities not supporting children's healthcare
- Organisations that do not have charitable status
- Animal, religious or international charities
- Retrospective funding
- Organisations that do not work within a hospital or hospice environment
- Organisations that provide excursions, holidays or away days
- No grants will be made to individuals
- Funding of Clown Doctors

The foundation does not give retrospective funding, grants to individuals or grants to replace statutory funding.

Applications

Grants are distributed on an annual basis. Application forms and guidelines are posted on the foundation's website from October and the closing date for applications is usually in December. All awards are made by the end of March.

Information gathered from:

Accounts; Charity Commission record; funder's website.

The F. J. Wallis Charitable Settlement

General

£4,500 (2011/12)

Beneficial area

UK, with some interest in Hampshire and Surrey.

Correspondent: Francis Hughes, Trustee, c/o Bridge House, 11 Creek Road, Hampton Court, East Molesey, Surrey KT8 9BE (tel: 020 8941 4455; email: francis@hughescollett.co.uk)

CC Number: 279273

The following information is taken from the 2011/12 trustees' annual report:

> In the past the trustees classified the causes that they sought to benefit and rotated the different classes of charities the benefited periodically. The Trustees found that the categorisation of the areas to benefit too restrictive, and so they have reverted to making discretionary donations to any global or local charitable purpose that either the trustees or the Wallis family particularly wish to support. This is subject to the proviso that any charity that has received a donation in the last 24 months will be unlikely to receive a further donation until 24 months has passed.
>
> The trustees canvass the Wallis family to see whether there are any charities that they particularly wish to favour and, in the absence of guidance, the trustees make decisions as to which charities to benefit at trustee meetings periodically. This used to normally take the form of making grants of £1,000, so that the maximum number of charities benefitted, although periodically it was decided to support a particular charity to a greater extent. The Trustees and the Wallis family found, in the last two years, great pleasure in supporting one single project, and so they have decided to follow this course of action in the future, and will only be looking to support charitable causes with a connection to the Wallis family, or to the Trustees.

In 2011/12 the settlement had assets of £1.2 million and an income of £49,000. Grants to organisations totalled £4,500.

Beneficiaries were: Our Lady's Nursery (£3,000); and RNLI (£1,000).

There was also a donation of £70,000 made to 4th New Forest North (Eling) Sea Scouts towards their new aquativity centre – this had been accrued for in the previous year's accounts.

Exclusions

No grants to individuals or to local charities except those in Surrey or in Hampshire. The same organisation is not supported twice within a 24-month period.

Applications

In writing to the correspondent. No telephone calls. Applications are not acknowledged and unsuccessful applicants will only be contacted if an sae is provided. Trustees meet in March and September and applications need to be received the month prior to the trustees' meeting.

Information gathered from:

Accounts; Charity Commission record.

The Ward Blenkinsop Trust

Medicine, social welfare, arts, education, general

£126,000 (2011/12)

Beneficial area

UK, with a special interest in Merseyside and surrounding counties.

Correspondent: Charlotte Blenkinsop, Trustee, PO Box 28840, London SW13 0WZ (tel: 020 8878 9975)

CC Number: 265449

The trust was established for general charitable purposes and currently supports charities in the Merseyside area and charities of a medical nature. We understand that all requests for funds are considered.

In 2011/12 the trust had assets of £1.8 million and an income of £137,000. Grants totalled £126,000.

The brief accounts did not contain a list of beneficiary organisations but previous beneficiaries have included Action on Addiction, BID, Chase Children's Hospice, Clatterbridge Cancer Research, Clod Ensemble, Comic Relief, Depaul Trust, Fairley House, Give Youth a Break, Halton Autistic Family Support Group, Hope HIV, Infertility Network, George Martin Music Foundation, Royal Academy of Dance, St Joseph's Family Centre, Strongbones Children's Charitable Trust, Walk the Walk, Winchester Visitors Group and Wirral Holistic Care Services.

Exclusions

No grants to individuals.

Applications

In writing to the correspondent.

Information gathered from:

Accounts; Charity Commission record.

The Barbara Ward Children's Foundation

Children

£516,000 (2012)

Beneficial area

England and Wales.

Correspondent: Christopher Banks, Trustee, 5 Great College Street, London SW1P 3SJ (tel: 020 7222 7040; fax: 020 7222 6208; email: info@bwcf.org.uk; website: www.bwcf.org.uk)

Trustees: Barbara Irene Ward, Chair; D. C. Bailey; J. C. Banks; A. M. Gardner; K. R. Parker; B. M. Walters.

CC Number: 1089783

This foundation makes grants to organisations working with children who are seriously or terminally ill, disadvantaged or otherwise. Grants made can range from one-off grants to project-related grants that run for two to five years. Grants are given to non-religious charities all over the world.

In 2012 the foundation had assets of £8.3 million, an income of £532,000 and gave grants to 69 organisations totalling £516,000.

Beneficiaries included: Friendship Works (£34,000) The Bubble Foundation (£27,000); Dame Vera Lynn Trust (£20,000); The Food Chain (£16,000); BIME – Bath Institute of Medical Engineering (£10,000); Wirral Swallows and Amazons (£6,500); Autism Bedfordshire, The Eyeless Trust and Stubbers Adventure Centre (£5,000 each); 4 Seasons Activity Group (£3,000); Friends of Mapledown School (£2,000); and Saffron Walden Opportunity Playgroup (£1,000).

Applications

In writing to the correspondent including latest set of audited financial statements. The trustees usually meet quarterly.

Percentage of awards given to new applicants: between 20% and 30%.

Information gathered from:

Accounts; Charity Commission record; further information provided by the funder; funder's website.

G. R. Waters Charitable Trust 2000

General

£101,000 (2011/12)

Beneficial area

UK, also North and Central America.

Correspondent: Michael Lewis, Finers Stephens Innocent, 179–185 Great Portland Street, London W1W 5LS (tel: 020 7323 4000)

Trustees: M. Fenwick; C. Organ.

CC Number: 1091525

This trust was registered with the Charity Commission in 2002, replacing Roger Waters 1989 Charitable Trust (Charity Commission no. 328574), which transferred its assets to the new trust (the 2000 in the title refers to when the declaration of trust was made.) Like the former trust, it receives a share of the Pink Floyd's royalties as part of its annual income. It has general charitable purposes throughout the UK, as well as North and Central America. The trust has provided funding for children with disabilities and serious illness, human rights campaigning, transport for people with illness or disabilities, older people and volunteer firemen in Chile.

In 2011/12 the trust had assets of £1.4 million, an income of £323,000 and gave grants totalling £101,000.

The beneficiaries were: Mandeville School (£50,000); Fundación Décimo Cuarta Compañía (£16,000); Wessex Children's Hospital rust, Freedom from Torture, Dream Holidays, Brecon and District disABLEd Club, React and Dream Connection (£5,000 each); and Lambourne Housing Trust (£100).

Applications

In writing to the correspondent.

Information gathered from:

Accounts; Charity Commission record.

Blyth Watson Charitable Trust

UK-based humanitarian organisations, hospices

£76,000 (2011/12)

Beneficial area

UK.

Correspondent: The Trustees, c/o Bircham Dyson Bell Solicitors, 50 Broadway, Westminster, London SW1H 0BL (tel: 020 7227 7000)

Trustees: Nicholas Brown; Ian McCulloch.

CC Number: 1071390

The trust dedicates its grant-giving policy in the area of humanitarian causes based in the UK. A number of hospices are supported each year. Loans have occasionally been given along with both one-off and recurring grants of £1,000 to £5,000.

In 2011/12 the trust had assets of £3.1 million, an income of £100,000 and gave grants totalling £76,000.

Beneficiaries included: St Martin-in-the-Fields Endowment Fund (£10,000 in two grants)); Trinity Hospice (£8,000 in two grants); St John's Hospice (£6,500 in two grants); Bread and Water for Africa (£5,000 in two grants); Royal Academy of Music (£3,000); Hospices of Hope (£2,500); Initiatives for Change (£1,500); and Comitato Fiori di Lavanda Onlus and Pace Centre (£1,000 each).

Applications

In writing to the correspondent. Trustees usually meet twice during the year in June and December.

Percentage of awards given to new applicants: between 20% and 30%.

Information gathered from:

Accounts; Charity Commission record; further information provided by the funder.

Weatherley Charitable Trust

General

About £180,000 (2012/13)

Beneficial area

Unrestricted.

Correspondent: Christine Weatherley, Trustee, Northampton Science Park Ltd, Newton House, Kings Park Road Moulton Park, Northampton NN3 6LG (tel: 01604 821841)

Trustees: Christine Weatherley; Richard Weatherley; Steven Chambers.

CC Number: 1079267

This trust was established in 1999 for general charitable purposes in particular research into mental and physical illness. In 2013 there had been no income for the past four years, suggesting the trust may be spending out. Expenditure totalled £197,000.

Applications

This trust does not accept unsolicited applications.

Information gathered from:

Accounts; Charity Commission record.

The Weavers' Company Benevolent Fund

Helping disadvantaged young people, offenders and ex-offenders

£264,000 (2012)

Beneficial area

UK.

Correspondent: Mrs Susie Williams, Charities Assistant, The Weavers Company, Saddlers' House, Gutter Lane, London EC2V 6BR (tel: 020 7606 1155; fax: 020 7606 1119; email: charity@weavers.org.uk; website: www.weavers.org.uk)

Trustee: The Worshipful Company of Weavers.

CC Number: 266189

This benevolent fund was set up in 1973 with funds provided by the Worshipful Company of Weavers, the oldest of the City of London Livery Companies. The fund states that its priorities are:

1. Helping disadvantaged young people

The object of the fund is to support projects working with disadvantaged young people to ensure that they are given every possible chance to meet their full potential and to participate fully in society. We normally define young people as being aged from 5 to 30 years.

2. Offenders and ex-offenders, particularly those under 30 years of age

Many offenders and ex-offenders suffer from a variety of difficult and complex problems and they are amongst the most vulnerable members of society. We will fund work that addresses the social and economic problems faced by this group and their families, and provide them with support, life skills training and a way back into education, training and/or employment, so that they may reintegrate and make a positive contribution to society.

We are especially interested in helping smaller organisations which offer direct services. They must be registered charities or in the process of applying for registration. Our grants are relatively modest, usually with an upper limit of £15,000 per annum, and to make sure grants of this size have an impact, we will not fund large organisations.

Applicants must show that they have investigated other sources of funding and made plans for the future, which should include replacement funding if appropriate.

What is funded?

Size of organisation – 'To be eligible for funding, local organisations such as those working in a village, estate or small town should normally have an income of less than about £100,000. Those working across the UK should normally have an income of not more than about £250,000.'

Funding limit – Grants are usually up to £15,000 per annum but smaller applications are also welcomed.

Duration – Grants may be awarded for up to three years.

Pump-priming – The trust particularly welcomes applications for pump-priming grants from small community-based organisations where a grant would form a major element of the funding. It prefers to support projects where its grant will be used for an identified purpose.

Core costs – Applications for core funding will be considered, such as general administration and training that enable an organisation to develop and maintain expertise.

Innovative or pioneering work – 'We like to encourage new ideas and to fund projects that could inspire similar work in other areas of the country.'

Continuation funding – The trust appreciates the importance of providing ongoing funding for successful projects, which have 'proved their worth'.

Salaries – Normally funded for up to three years but payment of the second and third year grants are subject to satisfactory progress reports.

Emergency or deficit funding – In exceptional circumstances, the trust may provide emergency or deficit funding for an established organisation. Applicants most likely to be granted emergency funding are charities which the company knows or has previously supported.

In 2012 the fund had assets of £8.4 million, an income of £383,000 and gave grants totalling £264,000.

Beneficiaries included: Weavers' Company Textile Education Fund (£90,000); Keep Out/Coldingly Crime Prevention Scheme (£13,000); The Helping Hands Trust (Gangsline) (£12,000); Trailblazers and Footprints (£10,000 each); Recycle Project (£8,500); Youth Empowerment (£7,800); The Ulysses Trust (£6,000); Grange Primary School and get Hooked on Fishing (£5,000 each); Prisoners' Penfriends (£4,700); Koestler Trust (£1,000); and Framlingham Area Youth Action Partnership (£500).

Exclusions

The fund provides the following information:

What will we not fund?

- General appeals – We will not support sponsorship, marketing or other fundraising activities
- Endowment funds – We will not support endowment funds, nor bursaries or long-term capital projects
- Grant-giving charities
- Retrospective funding – We will not make grants for work that has been completed or will be completed while the application is being considered
- Replacement funding – We will not provide grants for work that should be covered by statutory funding
- Building projects – We will not fund building work but may help with the cost of equipment or furnishings
- Disability Discrimination Act – We will not fund capital projects to provide access in compliance with the DDA
- Personal appeals – We will not make grants to individuals. Applicants must be registered charities, in the process of registering, or qualified as charitable
- Umbrella bodies or large, established organisations – We will not normally support projects in which the charity is collaborating or working in partnership with umbrella bodies or large, established organisations
- Overseas – We will not support organisations outside the UK, nor overseas expeditions or travel

Work that we cannot normally support includes:

- Work with children under five years of age
- Universities or colleges
- Medical charities or those involved in medical care
- Organisations of and for disabled people
- Environmental projects
- Work in promotion of religious or political causes

Applications

Detailed guidelines for applicants are available from the Weaver's Company website. Application forms can be downloaded from the fund's website, or by post or email. The grants committee meets in February, June and October of each year. Deadlines are available on the website; they are typically about three months prior to the meetings.

Percentage of awards given to new applicants: between 40% and 50%.

Common applicant mistakes

'Not reading the criteria.'

Information gathered from:

Accounts; Charity Commission record; further information provided by the funder; funder's website.

Webb Memorial Trust

Education, politics, social policy

£276,000 (2011/12)

Beneficial area

UK and Eastern Europe.

Correspondent: Mr Mike Parker, Secretary, Crane House, Unit 19 Apex Business Village, Annitsford, Newcastle NE23 7BF (email: webb@cranehouse.eu; website: www.webbmemorialtrust.org.uk)

Trustees: Richard Rawes, Chair; Mike Parker; Robert Lloyd-Davies; Dianne Hayter; Mike Gapes; Mike Gapes; Robert Lloyd-Davies; Katherine Green.

CC Number: 313760

The Webb Memorial Trust is a registered charity; it was established in 1947 as a memorial to the socialist pioneer Beatrice Webb.

The trust is set up with the aims of the advancement of education and learning with respect to the history and problem of government and social policy (including socialism, trade unionism and co-operation) in Great Britain and elsewhere by:

1 Research
2 Lectures, scholarships and educational grants
3 Such other educational means as the trustees may from time to time approve

In 2011 the trustees decided to spend down the remaining resources using at least 85% of the budget for a co-ordinated programme leaving a legacy worthy of Beatrice Webb. As such most of its funding resources are committed to a structured programme that will concentrate on the issues of poverty and inequality on the UK. Funding applications outside of these programmes may be considered if they reflect the original aims and ambitions of the Webbs.

In 2011/12 the trust had assets of £1.4 million, an income of £47,000 and gave grants totalling £276,000.

Beneficiaries included: Centris (£74,000); Smith Institute (£56,000); Children North East (£51,000); New Statesman (£20,000); Fabian Society, London School of Economics and Fair Pay Network (£15,000 each); Essays and Writings (£13,000); Campaign Transport (£8,500); and Northern Upstart (£5,700).

Exclusions

No grants in support of any political party. No grants for individuals including students.

Applications

Via the online form on the trust's website. Applications by post or email will not be accepted. Trustees meet three to four times a year.

Percentage of awards given to new applicants: between 10% and 20%.

Common applicant mistakes

'Not reading our website properly.'

Information gathered from:

Accounts; Charity Commission record; further information provided by the funder; funder's website.

The David Webster Charitable Trust

Ecological and broadly environmental projects

£214,000 (2011/12)

Beneficial area

UK.

Correspondent: Mrs Nikola Thompson, Trustee, Marshalls, Marshalls Lane, High Cross, Ware, Hertfordshire SG11 1AJ (tel: 01920 462001)

Trustees: Thomas Webster; Nikola Thompson.

CC Number: 1055111

Set up in 1995, in 2011/12 the trust had assets of £3.3 million, an income of £202,000 and gave grants totalling £214,000.

The beneficiaries during the year were: Bird Life International (£100,000); Natural History Museum and National Trust White Cliffs of Dover (£25,000 each); High Cross Church (£15,000); Isabel Hospice and Future Trees Trust (£10,000 each); National Churches Trust, Museum of the Broads, Berks, Beds and Oxford Wildlife Trust, National Trust and CPRE (£5,000 each); and Bat Conservation Trust and Norfolk Wherry Trust (£2,000 each).

Applications

In writing to the correspondent.

Information gathered from:

Accounts; Charity Commission record.

The Weinberg Foundation

General

Around £75,000 (2011/12)

Beneficial area

UK and overseas.

Correspondent: Nathan Steinberg, Correspondent, Munslows, 2nd Floor, Manfield House, 1 Southampton Street, London WC2R 0LR (tel: 020 7845 7500)

Trustees: Sir Mark Weinberg; Joy Whitehouse.

CC Number: 273308

Established in 1971 for general charitable purposes, this is the foundation of the financier Sir Mark Weinberg.

In 2011/12 the foundation had an income of £2,600 and a total expenditure of £75,000. Grants were made totalling around £85,000.

Previous beneficiaries included: Natan Foundation, Friends of EORTC, Amnesty International, Community Security Trust, Ability Net, Philharmonia Orchestra, Royal Shakespeare Theatre, St James's Palace Foundation, University of Cambridge, UJIA Campaign, South Bank Foundation, and the Elton John AIDS Foundation.

Information gathered from:

Accounts; Charity Commission record.

The Weinstein Foundation

Jewish, medical, welfare

£66,000 (2011/12)

Beneficial area

Worldwide.

Correspondent: Mr Michael Weinstein, Trustee, 32 Fairholme Gardens, Finchley, London N3 3EB (tel: 020 8346 1257)

Trustees: Stella Weinstein; Michael Weinstein; Philip Weinstein; Lea Anne Newman.

CC Number: 277779

This trust mostly supports Jewish organisations, although it does have general charitable purposes and supports a wide range of other causes, notably medical-related charities.

In 2011/12 the foundation had assets of £1.6 million, an income of £49,000 and gave grants totalling £66,000.

A list of beneficiaries was not included in the accounts; previous grants have been given to: Chevras Evas Nitzrochim Trust, Friends of Mir, SOFT UK, Chesed Charitable Trust, and Youth Aliyah.

Exclusions

No grants to individuals.

Applications

In writing to the correspondent.

Information gathered from:

Accounts; Charity Commission record.

The James Weir Foundation

General charitable purposes

£210,000 (2012)

Beneficial area

UK, with a preference for Ayrshire and Glasgow.

Correspondent: The Trustees, Mercer and Hole Trustees Ltd, Gloucester House, 72 London Road, St Albans, Herts AL1 1NS (tel: 01727 869141)

Trustees: Simon Bonham; Elizabeth Bonham; William Ducas.

CC Number: 251764

The James Weir Foundation was established in 1967. The foundation has general charitable purposes, giving priority to Scottish organisations, especially local charities in Ayrshire and Glasgow. The following six charities are listed in the trust deed as potential beneficiaries:

- The Royal Society
- The British Science Association
- The RAF Benevolent Fund
- The Royal College of Surgeons
- The Royal College of Physicians
- The University of Strathclyde

In 2012 the trust had an income of £225,000 and made 69 grants totalling £210,000. Assets stood at £6.9 million.

Beneficiaries included: Addaction, Age Scotland, Ayrshire Community Trust, Macmillan Cancer Support and Outward Bound Trust (£3,000 each); British Red Cross (£2,000); Kilbryde Hospice, Glasgow Women's Aid, Help for Heroes, Wiltshire Wildlife Trust and Scottish Refugee Council (£1,000 each); and St John Ambulance (£500).

Grants of £5,000 were given to five of the potential beneficiaries and £14,000 was given to the University of Strathclyde.

Exclusions

No grants to individuals.

Applications

The trustees' report for 2012 states:

> Applications should be received by letter with supporting evidence and a copy of the latest annual report. No applications can be received by email. The trustees meet twice a year in furtherance of the trust's objective of making grants to charitable bodies. Successful applicants are not able to submit a further application for two years.

Information gathered from:

Accounts; Charity Commission record.

The Barbara Welby Trust

General charitable purposes

£31,000 (2011/12)

Beneficial area

UK, with a preference for Lincolnshire.

Correspondent: The Trustees, Hunters, 9 New Square, Lincoln's Inn, London WC2A 3QN

Trustees: Nicolas Robertson; Charles Welby; Nevil Barker.

CC Number: 252973

The trust states that it considers supporting a range of charities, with particular emphasis on the Lincolnshire area.

In 2011/12 the trust had assets of £1 million and an income of £35,000. Grants were made to 38 organisations totalling almost £31,000.

Beneficiaries included: Lincolnshire Agricultural Society (£5,000); Community Action Northumberland (£2,500); Be Your Best Foundation, CAFOD and Stroxton Church (£1,000 each); and MS Therapy Centre, DEMAND, St Barnabas Hospice and Linkage Community Trust (£500 each).

Exclusions

The trust has stated that:

> Donations are generally made to established charitable organisations and not to individuals as the trustees have limited funds available to donate each year. In addition to providing regular support for a number of organisations, they consider all applications and, when possible, support exceptional appeals e.g. disaster funds.

Applications

In writing to the correspondent.

Information gathered from:

Accounts; Charity Commission record.

The Wessex Youth Trust

Youth, general

£122,000 (2011/12)

Beneficial area

Worldwide.

Correspondent: Jenny Cannon, Correspondent, Chelwood, Rectory Road, East Carleton, Norwich NR14 8HT (tel: 01508 571230; email: j.cannon@wessexyouthtrust.org.uk; website: www.wessexyouthtrust.org.uk)

Trustees: Robert Clinton; Mark Foster-Brown; Mary Poulton; Richard Parry; Kathryn Cavelle; Francesca Schwarzenbach.

CC Number: 1076003

The Wessex Youth Trust was established in 1999 at the wish of the Earl and Countess of Wessex.

According to the trustees' report for 2011/12:

> The primary aim of the Wessex Youth Trust is to provide financial assistance to other registered charities and charitable causes including those with which Their Royal Highnesses, the Earl and Countess of Wessex, have a personal connection or interest. The trust is particularly, although not exclusively, interested in supporting projects which provide opportunities to help, support and advance young people.

In 2011/12 the trust had an income of £106,000 mainly from donations. Assets stood at £436,000. Grants to 25 organisations totalled £122,000. Grants are generally made by means of single payments only.

The accounts state: 'the Charity Commission has been supplied with details of amounts given to each charity together with an explanation of the reason for the non-disclosure of individual amounts in the financial statements'.

Beneficiaries included: Freewheelers Theatre, New Horizon Youth Centre, Caring for Life, Adventure Unlimited, Ignito, Wessex Autistic Society, HopScotch Children's Charity, Carers Lewisham, and Carmarthen Women's Aid Ltd.

Non-disclosure of grants information should only be made where the information being made public may be potentially harmful to the trust or its recipients; failing to disclose information without providing an explanation in the public sphere may prompt unjustified speculation about the nature of grants made.

More information regarding grants can be found on the trust's website.

Exclusions

Grants are not made:

- To organisations or groups which are not registered as charities or charitable causes
- In response to applications by, or for the benefit of, individuals
- By means of sponsorship for individuals undertaking fundraising activities on behalf of any charity
- To organisations or groups whose main objects are to fund or support other charitable bodies
- Generally not to charities whose accounts disclose substantial financial resources and which have well

established and ample fundraising capabilities
- To charities with religious objectives, political, industrial or commercial appeal

Applications

Applicants must complete an application form which can be downloaded from the trust's website. Completed forms need to be submitted by 1 May or 1 November. Clarity of presentation and provision of financial details are among the qualities which impress the trustees. Successful applicants will receive a letter stating that acceptance of funding is conditional on an update report received within six months. Unsuccessful applicants will receive a letter of notification following the trustees' meeting. The trust cannot enter any further communication with applicants.

Information gathered from:

Accounts; Charity Commission record; funder's website.

West London Synagogue Charitable Fund

Jewish, general

£23,000 (2012)

Beneficial area

UK.

Correspondent: Simon Raperport, Trustee, 45 Arden Road, London N3 3AD (tel: 020 7723 4404)

Trustees: Michael Cutter; Simon Raperport; Vivien Feather; Jacqui Green; Jane Cutter; Jean Regen; Monica Jankel; Ruth Jacobs; Elizabeth Shrager; Hermy Jankel; Francine Epstein; Elaine Parry; Vivien Rose; Rabbi Debbie Young-Somers; Lucy Heath.

CC Number: 209778

The West London Synagogue Charitable Fund was established in 1959. According to the trustees' report for 2012, 'the objects of the fund are the collection of monies to be applied to charitable purposes. The aims and objectives of the fund for the year were the raising of money, to be achieved by the undertaking of various social activities.'

The trust has stated that it makes grants to both Jewish and non-Jewish organisations. It prefers to be involved with charities which synagogue members are involved with or helped by.

In 2012 the fund had assets of nearly £7,000, an income of £30,000 and made grants totalling just over £23,000. Grants were given to 24 organisations.

Beneficiaries included: Supporting Children with Diabetes (£5,000); Asylum Seekers Drop-In Centre (£4,000); Macmillan Nurses (£1,000); Fortune Riding Centre for the Disabled (£900); and Downs Syndrome Association, Helen House Hospice, OCD Action and Pets as Therapy (£500 each).

Exclusions

No grants to individuals.

Applications

In writing to the correspondent.

Information gathered from:

Accounts; Charity Commission record.

The Westcroft Trust

International understanding, overseas aid, Quaker, Shropshire

£92,000 (2011/12)

Beneficial area

Unrestricted, but with a special interest in Shropshire.

Correspondent: Martin Beardwell, Clerk, 32 Hampton Road, Oswestry, Shropshire SY11 1SJ

Trustees: Mary C. Cadbury; Richard G. Cadbury; James E. Cadbury; Erica R. Cadbury.

CC Number: 212931

Currently the trustees have five main areas of interest:

- International understanding, including conflict resolution and the material needs of the developing world
- Religious causes, particularly social outreach, usually of the Society of Friends (Quakers) but also for those originating in Shropshire
- Development of the voluntary sector in Shropshire
- Needs of people with disabilities, primarily in Shropshire

Medical aid, education and relief work in developing countries is mainly supported through UK-registered organisations. International disasters may be helped in response to public appeals.

The trust favours charities with low administrative overheads and that pursue clear policies of equal opportunity in meeting need. Grants may be one-off or recurrent; recurrent grants are rarely made for endowment or capital projects.

In 2011/12 the trust had assets of £2.2 million, which generated an income of £115,000. Grants were made totalling £92,000, broken down as follows:

Overseas Aid/Conflict Resolution	£33,000
Religious Society of Friends	£30,000
Social services/Health/Education	£29,000

Beneficiaries included: Northern Friends Peace Board (£3,600); British Epilepsy Association (£3,000); Community Council of Shropshire (£1,500); Institute of Orthopaedics (£1,300); Quaker Bolivia Link (£1,100); Disasters Emergency Committee (£1,000); Build It International and Bethesda Leprosy Hospital (£750 each); and Tolerance International and Derwen College (£500 each).

Exclusions

Grants are given to charities only. No grants to individuals or for medical electives, sport, the arts (unless specifically for people with disabilities in Shropshire) or armed forces charities. Requests for sponsorship are not supported. Annual grants are withheld if recent accounts are not available or do not satisfy the trustees as to continuing need.

Applications

In writing to the correspondent. There is no application form or set format but applications should be restricted to a maximum of three sheets of paper, stating purpose, overall financial needs and resources together with previous years' accounts if appropriate. Printed letters signed by 'the great and good' and glossy literature do not impress the trustees, who prefer lower-cost applications. Applications are dealt with about every two months. No acknowledgement will be given. Replies to relevant but unsuccessful applicants will be sent only if an sae is enclosed. As some annual grants are made by Bank Telepay, details of bank name, branch, sort code, and account name and number should be sent in order to save time and correspondence.

Percentage of awards given to new applicants: less than 10%.

Common applicant mistakes

'Little or no reference to the aims and objectives of the trust, as published.'

Information gathered from:

Accounts; Charity Commission record; further information provided by the funder.

The Barbara Whatmore Charitable Trust

Arts and music, relief of poverty

£50,000 (2011/12)

Beneficial area

UK.

Correspondent: Denise Gardiner, Correspondent, 3 Honeyhanger, Hindhead Road, Hindhead GU26 6BA (email: denise@bwct.org)

Trustees: David Eldridge; Denis Borrow; Gillian Lewis; Luke Gardiner; Patricia Cooke-Yarborough; Sally Carter; Stephen Bate.

CC Number: 283336

The Barbara Whatmore Charitable Trust was established in 1981. The objects of the charity, as stated in the trustees' report for 2011/12, are:

- To foster and promote the education of the general public in the appreciation of the arts and music
- The relief of poverty
- Such other purposes recognised by the law of England and Wales to be exclusively charitable

In 2011/12 it had assets of £1.45 million. It had an income of £58,000 and made 31 grants to organisations totalling £50,000.

Beneficiaries included: City and Guilds of London Art School (£4,500); Aldeburgh Music (£4,000); Campaign for Drawing (£3,500); National Youth Orchestra (£3,200); Edward Barnsley Educational Trust, the Garden Museum and Textile Conservation Centre (£2,000 each); Hereford Cathedral and Pro Corda (£1,500 each); English National Opera and the Old Operating Theatre (£1,000 each); Finchocks Musical Museum and Jericho House Productions (£500 each); and New Lanark Conservation (£250).

Applications

In writing to the correspondent.

Information gathered from:

Accounts; Charity Commission record.

The Whitaker Charitable Trust

Music, environment, countryside conservation

£375,000 (2011/12)

Beneficial area

UK, but mostly East Midlands and Scotland.

Correspondent: The Trustees, c/o Currey and Co., 21 Buckingham Gate, London SW1E 6LS (tel: 020 7802 2700)

Trustees: Edward Perks; David Price; Lady Elizabeth Whitaker.

CC Number: 234491

The trust has general charitable objects, although with stated preferences in the following fields:

- Local charities in Nottinghamshire and the east Midlands
- Music
- Agriculture and silviculture
- Countryside conservation
- Scottish charities

In 2011/12 the trust had assets of £7 million; it generated an income of £229,000. Grants to 41organisations totalled £375,000.

A substantial grant of £250,000 was made to The Jasmine Trust. Other beneficiaries included: Atlantic College (£42,000); Leith School of Art, Opera North Education and Royal Forestry Society (£10,000 each); Live Music Now (£5,000); Bassetlaw Hospice and Lincoln Cathedral Fabric Fund (£3,000 each); Bassetlaw Homestart and Prisoner Education Trust (£2,000 each); Babworth Church and Reality Adventure Works (£1,000 each); and Baronet's Trust (£500).

Exclusions

Support is given to registered charities only. No grants are given to individuals or for the repair or maintenance of individual churches.

Applications

In writing to the correspondent. Applications should include clear details of the need the intended project is designed to meet plus a copy of the latest accounts available and an outline budget. If an acknowledgement of the application, or notification in the event of the application not being accepted is required, an sae should be enclosed. Trustees meet on a regular basis.

Information gathered from:

Accounts; Charity Commission record.

The Colonel W. H. Whitbread Charitable Trust

Education, preservation of places of historic interest and natural beauty

£119,000 (2012)

Beneficial area

UK, with an interest in Gloucestershire.

Correspondent: Susan Smith, Correspondent, Fir Tree Cottage, World's End, Sinton Green (tel: 07812 454321; email: whwhitbread.trust@googlemail.com)

Trustees: H. F. Whitbread; Jeremy Barkes; Rupert Foley.

CC Number: 210496

The trustees have resolved to support charitable organisations and general areas of charitable activity which were, or in the opinion of the trustees would have been, of interest to the trust's founder, the late Colonel William Henry Whitbread, which comprise the following:

- The promotion of education and in particular: (a) the provision of financial assistance towards the maintenance and development of Aldenham School; and (b) the creation of Colonel W H Whitbread scholarships or bursaries or prizes to be awarded to pupils at Aldenham School
- Charitable organisations within Gloucestershire
- The preservation, protection and improvement for the public benefit of places of historic interest and natural beauty.

According to the trustees' report for 2012, 'the trustees will only in exceptional circumstances consider grant applications for purposes which fall outside those described above. Within the framework the trustees will generally distribute a minimum of £500 per distribution.'

In 2012 the trust had assets of £7.4 million and an income of £160,000. Grants made to organisations totalled £119,000.

Previous beneficiaries have included: 1st Queen's Dragon Guards Regimental Trust, Abbey School Tewkesbury, Army Benevolent Fund, CLIC Sargent, DEC Tsunami Earthquake Appeal, Friends of Alderman Knights School, Gloucestershire Historic Churches Trust, Great Ormond Street Hospital Children's Charity, Household Cavalry Museum Appeal, Hunt Servants' Fund, Queen Mary's Clothing Guild, Royal Hospital Chelsea and St Richard's Hospice.

Applications

A brief summary (no more than one side of A4) in writing (by email if possible) to the correspondent. It is not necessary to send any accompanying paperwork at this stage. Should the trustees wish to consider any application further, then an application form will be sent.

Information gathered from:

Accounts; Charity Commission record.

The Simon Whitbread Charitable Trust

General charitable purposes

Around £97,000 (2011/12)

Beneficial area

UK, with a preference for Bedfordshire.

Correspondent: Matthew Yates, Correspondent, Hunters, 9 New Square, Lincoln's Inn, London WC2A 3QN

Trustees: Sir Samuel Whitbread; Edward Martineau; Elizabeth Bennett.

CC Number: 200412

In 2011/12 the trust had assets of almost £3 million (2009/10: £63,000), an income of £129,000 and a total charitable expenditure of £97,000.

Beneficiaries included: Fun 4 Young People and St John Ambulance Bedfordshire (£10,000 each); Elizabeth Finn Care and Turn 2 Us and Stepping Stones Luton (£5,000 each); Bedfordshire Festival of Music, Speech and Drama, Age UK Milton Keynes and Onset Trust (£3,000 each); Young People of the Year and Victim Support Kempston (£2,000 each); Traffic of the Stage and Brainwave Centre Ltd (£1,000 each); and Goldington Family Centre (£500).

Exclusions

Generally no support for local projects outside Bedfordshire.

Applications

In writing to the correspondent. The trust has stated the following: 'when it is felt more appropriate, grantees are asked to report back. To minimise the costs, applicants are given no feedback or even acknowledgement unless they (a) are sent an application form or (b) specifically request feedback in which case it is given.'

Information gathered from:

Accounts; Charity Commission record.

The Melanie White Foundation Ltd

General

£131,000 (2011/12)

Beneficial area

Unrestricted.

Correspondent: Paula Doraisamy, 61 Grosvenor Street, London W1k 3JE (tel: 020 3011 1041; email: melaniewhitefoundation@gmail.com)

Trustees: Melanie White; Andrew White.

CC Number: 1077150

The charity's principal activity is its grantmaking programme which focuses on health, medicine and social welfare.

In 2011/12 the foundation had assets of £10.5 million, an income of £314,000 and gave grants totalling £131,000.

Beneficiaries included: Community Foundation for the CSRA (£50,000); CLIC Sargent (£30,000); Alfred Dunhill Foundation (£25,000); Dyslexia Association (£10,000); RNIB (£7,500); Right to Play (£1,000); Air Ambulance for Children (£500); and Centrepoint (£100).

Applications

This trust does not accept unsolicited applications.

Information gathered from:

Accounts; Charity Commission record.

The Whitecourt Charitable Trust

Christian, general

£52,000 (2011/12)

Beneficial area

UK and overseas, with a preference for South Yorkshire.

Correspondent: Gillian Lee, Trustee, 48 Canterbury Avenue, Fulwood, Sheffield S10 3RU (tel: 01142 305555)

Trustees: Peter Lee; Gillian Lee; Martin Lee.

CC Number: 1000012

Most of the grants given by the trust are recurrent and to Christian causes in the UK and overseas. Other grants are given to a few Christian and welfare causes in Sheffield.

In 2011/12 the trust had assets of £595,000 and an income of £40,000. There were 159 grants made totalling £52,000.

Beneficiaries included: Christ Church Fulwood (£7,000); Monkton Combe School Bursary Fund (£5,000); TEAR Fund (£2,500); Overseas Missionary Fellowship (£2,000); Church Pastoral Aid Society, Help for Heroes and Sudan Interior Mission (£1,000 each); The Cathedral Archer Project, Just 42, Riverside Church and VSO (£100 each); and The Prison Fellowship (£30).

Exclusions

No support for animal or conservation organisations or for campaigning on social issues.

Applications

In writing to the correspondent, at any time. However, the trust states very little money is available for unsolicited applications, due to advance commitments.

Percentage of awards given to new applicants: 55%.

Common applicant mistakes

'Nothing specifically Christian about their work to distinguish themselves from other similar projects.'

Information gathered from:

Accounts; Charity Commission record; further information provided by the funder.

A. H. and B. C. Whiteley Charitable Trust

General charitable purposes, particularly those causes based in Nottinghamshire

£36,000 (2012/13)

Beneficial area

England, Scotland and Wales, with a special interest in Nottinghamshire.

Correspondent: Ted Aspley, Trustee, Marchant and Co., Regent Chambers, 2A Regent Street, Mansfield NG18 1SW (tel: 01623 655111)

Trustees: Ted Aspley; Keith Clayton.

CC Number: 1002220

The trust was established in 1990 and derives most of its income from investments. The trust deed requires the trustees to make donations to registered charities in England, Scotland and Wales but with particular emphasis on charities based in Nottinghamshire.

In 2012/13 the trust had assets of almost £1.5 million and an income of £46,000. Grants were made to four organisations totalling almost £36,000.

Beneficiaries were: Lincolnshire and Nottinghamshire Air Ambulance and Macmillan Cancer Support (£10,000 each); Home Start Mansfield and Mansfield Choral Society (£5,000 each); Nottingham Churches Holding Fund (£3,000); and Southwell Minster (£2,500).

The trust's management and administration costs totalled £14,500.

Applications

The trust does not seek applications.

Information gathered from:

Accounts; Charity Commission record.

The Norman Whiteley Trust

Evangelical Christianity, welfare, education

£68,000 (2011/12)

Beneficial area

Worldwide, although in practice mainly Cumbria.

Correspondent: Mr D. Foster, Bovil Barn, Newbiggin on Lune, Kirkby Stephen, Cumbria CA17 4NT (email: normanwhiteleytrust@gmail.com)

Trustees: Miss P. Whiteley; P. Whiteley; D. Dickson; J. Ratcliff.

CC Number: 226445

This trust supports the furtherance of the Gospel, the relief of poverty and education. Grants can be made worldwide, but in practice are usually restricted to Cumbria and the surrounding areas as well as Austria.

In 2011/12 the trust had assets of £2.7 million and an income of £91,000. Grants over £500 were made to over 30 organisations totalling £68,000.

Beneficiaries included: Capernwray Miss Fellowship of Torchbearer and International Aid (£6,500 each); New Life Church (£5,000); Kinder Und Jugendwerk (£4,500); International Teams Austria (£2,700); Salvation Army and Christians Against Poverty (£1,000 each); and Baptisten Gemeinde (£800).

Applications

In writing to the correspondent along with an application form, available to download from the trust's DropBox account which can be accessed by sending an email to the trust. Applications should be made on headed paper or accompanied by a suitable reference. Applications are considered throughout the year.

Information gathered from:

Accounts; Charity Commission record.

The Whitley Animal Protection Trust

Animal welfare, conservation

£228,000 (2012)

Beneficial area

UK and overseas, with a preference for Scotland.

Correspondent: Michael Gwynne, Correspondent, Padmore House, Hall Court, Hall Park Way, Telford TF3 4LX (tel: 01952 641651)

Trustees: Edward Whitley; Edward Whitley; Jeremy Whitley; Penelope Whitley.

CC Number: 236746

The trustees' report for 2012 states that the trust supports charitable organisations that are 'concerned with the prevention of cruelty to animals or the promotion of the welfare of animals'. Grants are made throughout the UK and the rest of the world, with about 20% of funds given in Scotland.

In 2012 the trust had assets of £8.9 million and an income of £374,000. Grants to 18 organisations totalled £228,000. The total committed donation to Whitley Fund for Nature amounted to 46.19% of the total.

Beneficiaries included: Whitley Fund for Nature (£100,000); Shropshire Wildlife Trust (£25,000); WILDCRU Wildlife Conservation Research Unit (£20,000); Sustainable Inshore Fisheries Trust (£15,000); Songbird Survival (£10,000); Orangutan Foundation (£7,000); Tusk Trust and RSPC Scotland (£5,000 each); National Great Dane Rescue (£2,000); and Eden Rivers Trust and the Wye and Usk Foundation (£1,000 each).

Exclusions

No grants to non-registered charities.

Applications

The trust has previously stated that: 'the trust honours existing commitments and initiates new ones through its own contacts rather than responding to unsolicited applications.'

Percentage of awards given to new applicants: less than 10%.

Common applicant mistakes

'Not registered charities.'

Information gathered from:

Accounts; Charity Commission record; further information provided by the funder.

The Lionel Wigram Memorial Trust

General, particularly illness and disability

£65,000 (2011/12)

Beneficial area

UK, with a preference for Greater London.

Correspondent: Tracy Pernice, PA to A. F. Wigram, Highfield House, 4 Woodfall Street, London SW3 4DJ (tel: 020 7730 6820)

Trustees: Antony Wigram; Sally A. Wigram.

CC Number: 800533

The trustees 'have particular regard to projects which will commemorate the life of Major Lionel Wigram who was killed in action in Italy in 1944'. The trust makes grants to a wide range of organisations in the UK, especially those providing services or support for people who are disabled, particularly those who are blind or deaf. Preference is given to those with an income of less than £500,000 but occasionally larger charities are supported. Grants are generally for £400–£3,000.

In 2011/12 the trust had assets of £677,000 and an income of £69,000. There were 83 grants made totalling £65,000, broken down as follows:

Coping with illness and disability	55	£51,000
Community projects/helping the disadvantaged	20	£7,400
Performing arts and the arts	3	£4,000
Historical/restoration	3	£2,000
Conservation	2	£750

Beneficiaries included: U Can Do IT (£32,000 in four grants); The New English Ballet Theatre (£3,500); The Second World War Experience Centre (£1,500); The Cure Parkinson's Trust and Vision North Somerset (£750 each); Braille Chess Association; Finsbury Park Community Hub Ltd; The National Lobster Hatchery; The Trust Women's Project; Forest Sensory Services and The Anorexia and Bulimia Charitable Care Trust (£400 each).

Exclusions

No support for individuals, building projects or charities which do not have a three year record.

Applications

On a form available on the website. Applications are considered in December each year and successful applicants will receive a cheque at this time. Apart from this the trust does not communicate with applicants. Make sure your application is concise and try to limit it to a maximum of 400 words.

Percentage of awards given to new applicants: between 20% and 30%.

Common applicant mistakes

'Large charities making blanket appeals. Applications being too long and too detailed – our limit is 400 words.'

Information gathered from:

Accounts; Charity Commission record; further information provided by the funder.

The Felicity Wilde Charitable Trust

Children, medical research

£69,000 (2011/12)

Beneficial area

UK.

Correspondent: S. Wakefield, Trustee, Barclays Bank Trust Co. Ltd, Osborne Court, Gadbrook Park, Rudheath, Cheshire CW9 7UE (tel: 01606 313179)

Trustee: Barclays Bank Trust Co. Ltd.

CC Number: 264404

The trust supports children's charities and medical research, with particular emphasis on research into the causes or cures of asthma. In 2011/12 it held assets of £1.9 million and an income of £70,000. Grants were made to 38 organisations totalling £69,000.

Beneficiaries included: Kings College London – Respiratory Medicine and Allergy (£10,000); Hearing Dogs for Deaf People (£5,000); Action Medical Research and Cystic Fibrosis Trust (£3,000 each); The Roy Castle Lung Cancer Foundation and Prostrate Campaign (£2,000 each); The Sick Children's Trust (£1,500); and The Dream Team, The Stagecoach Charitable Trust, Autism Initiatives UK and Meningitis Trust (£1,000 each).

Exclusions

No grants to individuals or non-registered charities.

Applications

In writing to the correspondent at any time. Applications are usually considered quarterly.

Information gathered from:

Accounts; Charity Commission record.

The Wilkinson Charitable Foundation

Scientific research

£16,000 (2011/12)

Beneficial area

UK.

Correspondent: Barry Lock, Trustee, c/o Berkeley Law, 4th Floor, 19 Berkeley Street, London W1J 8ED (tel: 020 7399 0930)

Trustees: Glenn Hurstfield; Barry Lock; Anne Hardy.

CC Number: 276214

The trust was set up for the advancement of scientific knowledge and education at Imperial College – University of London. Grants are only given to academic institutions.

The trustees have continued their policy of supporting research and initiatives commenced in the founder's lifetime and encouraging work in similar fields to those he was interested in.

In 2011/12 the trust had assets of £1.4 million and an income of £40,000. Grants to 39 organisations totalled £16,000.

Beneficiaries included: Imperial College, London (£5,000); Lady Margaret Hall Development Fund (£2,500); University College, London (£1,000); Breast Cancer Campaign (£1,000) Blond McIndoe Research Foundation, Centre of the Cell, Forces Support and Wellbeing of Women (£500 each); and Elimination of Leukaemia Fund, Headstart, Murray Edwards College, The Smile Train UK and World Cancer Research Fund (£250 each).

In 2011/12 out of a total expenditure of £51,000 the trust spent £11,000 on portfolio management and £24,000 on governance.

Exclusions

No grants to individuals.

Applications

In writing to the correspondent.

Percentage of awards given to new applicants: between 10% and 20%.

Common applicant mistakes

'Not reading the fund's criteria.'

Information gathered from:

Accounts; Charity Commission record; further information provided by the funder.

The Williams Charitable Trust

£77,000 (2011/12)

Beneficial area

UK.

Correspondent: Stuart Williams, Trustee, Flat 85 Capital Wharf, 50 Wapping High Street, London E1W 1LY

Trustees: Stuart Williams; Hilary Williams; Andrew Williams; Matthew Williams; Keith Eyre-Varnier.

CC Number: 1086668

The trust stated in its 2011/12 annual report: 'The objects of the trust are to support education and training, the advancement of medicine and general charitable purposes.'

In 2011/12 the trust had assets of £2.3 million, an income of £83,000 and gave grants totalling £77,000.

Beneficiaries included: Donmar Warehouse (£24,000); Wilton's Music Hall Trust (£11,000); Royal Court Theatre and Children's Musical Theatre (£10,000); Fight for Peace (£6,000); The Shakespeare Globe Trust (£5,000); The Production Works – The Changeling (£2,500); The Soho Theatre (£2,000); and Mousetrap Theatre Project and British Film Institute (£1,000 each).

Five grants of less than £1,000 totalled £4,100.

Applications

In writing to the correspondent. 'The trustees adopt a proactive approach in seeking worthy causes requiring support.'

Information gathered from:

Accounts; Charity Commission record.

The Williams Family Charitable Trust

Jewish

£52,000 (2012)

Beneficial area

Worldwide.

Correspondent: Barry Landy, Trustee, 192 Gilbert Road, Cambridge CB4 3PB (tel: 01223 570417; email: bl10@cam.ac.uk)

Trustees: Barry Landy; Arnon Levy; Rabbi Shimon Bension.

CC Number: 255452

In 2012 this trust had an income of £48,000 and a total expenditure of £52,500. Grants totalled around £52,000. No further information regarding grant giving was available for this year.

Previous beneficiaries include: But Chabad, Friends of Mifalhtorah for Shiloh, Holon Association for Absorption of Immigrants, Ingun Yedidut, Israel Concern Society, Karen Denny Pincus, Mogdal Un, Yedidut Maabeh Eliahu and Yesodrey Hetorah Schools.

Applications

In writing to the correspondent.

Information gathered from:

Accounts; Charity Commission record.

Dame Violet Wills Charitable Trust

Evangelical Christianity

£57,000 (2012)

Beneficial area

UK and overseas.

Correspondent: Julian Marsh, Trustee, 3 Cedar Way, Portishead, Bristol BS20 6TT (tel: 1275848770)

Trustees: Julian Marsh; Revd Dr Ernest Lucas; Revd Alexander Cooper; Revd Ray Lockhart; Derek Cleave; John Dean; Rosalind Peskett; Janet Persson; Rachel Daws; Revd David Caporn; E. Street; Yme Potjewijd; Tim Kevan.

CC Number: 219485

Dame Violet Wills was interested in all forms of Christian work, especially those of an evangelical nature. The trust continues to operate within the original terms of reference, supporting evangelical Christian activities both within the UK and overseas. Grants are usually small and the trustees will not usually support long-term projects.

In 2012 the trust had assets of £1.75 million and an income of £71,000. Grants were made to 76 organisations totalling £57,000.

Beneficiaries included: WC and SWET Evangelists Fund (£12,000); Wycliffe Bibles Translators (£1,800); Bristol International Student Centre (£1,600); SWYM- the Rise Up Project, OMF and Sat-7 Trust (£1,500 each); Living Water Radio Ministry (£1,200); Open Air Campaigners (£800); True Freedom Trust, Open Doors and Eurovangelism (£500 each); France Mission Trust (£200); and Wales Evangelical School of Theology (£80).

Exclusions

No grants to individuals.

Applications

In writing to the correspondent. Trustees meet in March and in September.

Percentage of awards given to new applicants: between 20% and 30%.

Common applicant mistakes

'Asking for too much.'

Information gathered from:

Accounts; Charity Commission record; further information provided by the funder.

Sumner Wilson Charitable Trust

General

£70,000 (2011/12)

Beneficial area

UK.

Correspondent: N. Steinberg, Correspondent, Munslows, 2nd Floor, Manfield House, 1 Southampton Street, London WC2R 0LR (tel: 020 7845 7500; email: mail@munslows.co.uk)

Trustees: Michael Wilson; Amanda Christie; Anne-Marie Challen.

CC Number: 1018852

This trust has general charitable purposes, with no preferences or exclusions. In 2011/12 it had assets of £3.1 million, an income of £68,000 and made grants totalling £70,000.

There were 24 grants of £1,000 or more listed in the accounts. Beneficiaries included: St James's Place Foundation (£21,200); Lewisham Youth Theatre (£13,300); St Mungo's Community Housing Association (£3,000); Friends of Young Carers (£2,300); Mental Health Foundation, West London Centre for Counselling and Bramay Trust (£1,000 each); Land Aid (£900); Help for Heroes and SOS Children's Village (£800); and Tongole Foundation (£300).

Applications

In writing to the correspondent, or to the trustees.

Information gathered from:

Accounts; Charity Commission record.

The Benjamin Winegarten Charitable Trust

Jewish

£59,000 to organisations (2011/12)

Beneficial area

UK.

Correspondent: Benjamin Winegarten, Trustee, 25 St Andrew's Grove, Stoke Newington, London N16 5NF (tel: 020 8800 6669)

Trustees: Benjamin Winegarten; Esther Winegarten.

CC Number: 271442

This trust makes grants for the advancement of the Jewish religion and religious education. In 2011/12 it had assets of £942,000 and an income of £139,000, including £100,000 from donations and grants. Grants were made to 15 organisations totalling £59,000, with a further £13,000 going to seven individuals.

Previous beneficiaries have included Hechal Hatovah Institute, the Jewish Educational Trust, the Mechinah School, Merkaz Lechinuch Torani Zichron Ya'akov, Ohr Somayach Friends, Or Akiva Community Centre, Yeshivo Hovomo Talmudical College and ZSVT.

Applications

In writing to the correspondent.

Information gathered from:

Accounts; Charity Commission record.

The Francis Winham Foundation

Welfare of older people

£435,000 (2011/12)

Beneficial area

England.

Correspondent: Josephine Winham, Trustee, 41 Langton Street, London SW10 0JL (tel: 020 7795 1261; email: francinetrust@btopenworld.com)

Trustees: Francine Winham; Josephine Winham; Elsa Peters.

CC Number: 278092

This charity is established for the benefit of old people in England. Grants are given to both national organisations (including their local branches) and local charities. Many organisations are regular recipients, although not necessarily on an annual basis.

In 2011/12 the foundation had assets of £2.4 million, which generated an income of £341,000. There were 309 grants made totalling £435,000.

Beneficiaries included: Butterwick Hospice Care (£50,000); Age UK (£23,000 in eight donations); Help the Hospices and King Edward VII's Hospital (£20,000 each); U Can Do It (£10,000); and British Heart Foundation and Independence at Home (£5,000 each).

Applications

In writing to the correspondent. The trust regrets it cannot send replies to applications outside its specific field of help for older people. Applications should be made through registered charities or social services departments only.

Information gathered from:
Accounts; Charity Commission record.

The Witzenfeld Foundation

General charitable purposes, Jewish

£72,000 (2011/12)

Beneficial area
UK and Israel.

Correspondent: Alan Witzenfeld, Trustee, Porters House, Station Court, Radford Way, Billericay, Essex (tel: 01702 330032)

CC Number: 1115034

Set up in 2006, in 2011/12 the foundation had an income of £56,000 and made grants totalling £72,000. Assets totalled £5,500. The foundation made 22 donations in 2011/12. A list of beneficiaries was not available.

Applications
In writing to the correspondent.

Information gathered from:
Accounts; Charity Commission record.

The Michael and Anna Wix Charitable Trust

Jewish, general charitable purposes

£53,000 (2011/12)

Beneficial area
UK.

Correspondent: Sarah Hovil, Correspondent, c/o Portrait Solicitors, 21 Whitefriars Street, London EC4Y 8JJ (tel: 020 7092 6985)

CC Number: 207863

In 2011/12 the trust had assets of £1.7 million and an income of £67,000. 257 grants were made totalling £53,000.

Beneficiaries included: Weizmann UK (£3,000); British Friends of the Hebrew University and Jewish Care (£2,000 each) Pinhas Rutenberg Educational Trust and UJIA (£1,000 each). The remaining funds were distributed among over 200 beneficiaries in small grants of between £100–500. Beneficiaries included: YMCA, Ro-Ro Sailing Project, No Panic, Motability, Mencap, Meningitis Trust, Rehab UK, Independence at Home, Forces Support and Concern Worldwide.

Exclusions
Applications from individuals are not considered. Grants are to national bodies rather than local branches or local groups.

Applications
In writing to the trustees. Applications are considered half-yearly. Only applications from registered charities are acknowledged. Frequent applications by a single charity are not appreciated.

Information gathered from:
Accounts; Charity Commission record.

The Woodcock Charitable Trust

General, children

Around £30,000 (2012/13)

Beneficial area
UK.

Correspondent: Lucy Gibson, Correspondent, Harcus Sinclair, 3 Lincoln's Inn Fields, London WC2A 3AA (tel: 020 7242 9700)

CC Number: 1110896

Set up in 2005, in 2012/13 the trust had an income of just £31 and an expenditure of £33,000.

Previous beneficiaries have included: Egmont Trust, RNIB, George Adamson Wildlife Preservation Trust, Kids Company, Walden Spoon, Surrey Air Ambulance, Tusk Trust and Action on Addiction.

Applications
In writing to the correspondent.

Information gathered from:
Accounts; Charity Commission record.

Woodlands Green Ltd

Jewish causes

£202,000 (2010/11)

Beneficial area
Worldwide.

Correspondent: Daniel Ost, Trustee, 19 Green Walk, London NW4 2AL

CC Number: 277299

The charity's objectives are the advancement of the Orthodox Jewish faith and the relief of poverty. It mostly gives large grants to major educational projects being carried out by Orthodox Jewish charities.

The accounts for 2010/11 were the latest posted on the Commission's website at the time of writing. In that accounting year the trust had assets of £1.3 million and an income of £262,500. Grants made totalled £202,000. No further information was available.

Previous beneficiaries have included Achisomoch Aid Co., Beis Soro Schneirer, Friends of Beis Yisroel Trust, Friends of Mir, Friends of Seret Wiznitz, Friends of Toldos Avrohom Yitzchok, JET, Kahal Imrei Chaim, Oizer Dalim Trust, NWLCM, TYY Square and UTA.

Exclusions
No grants to individuals, or for expeditions or scholarships.

Applications
In writing to the correspondent.

Information gathered from:
Accounts; Charity Commission record.

Woodroffe Benton Foundation

General charitable purposes

£240,000 (2011/12)

Beneficial area
UK.

Correspondent: Alan King, Secretary, 44 Leasway, Wickford, Essex SS12 0HE (tel: 01268 562941; email: secretary@woodroffebenton.org.uk; website: www.woodroffebenton.org.uk)

CC Number: 1075272

This foundation was set up by trust deed in November 1988 by the late Alfred Woodroffe Benton. It later amalgamated with the S Wolfe Memorial Fund and is now governed by a scheme sealed by the Charity Commissioners for England and Wales on 6 April 1999.

The foundation clearly sets out its funding policy on its website as follows:

> The foundation provides grants to officially recognised charitable organisations within the UK only in respect of:
>
> - Relief of persons in need, hardship or distress by reason of disaster or as a consequence of social or economic circumstance
> - Provision/maintenance of care and accommodation for the sick and elderly
> - Promotion of education – in particular within the Derbyshire region
> - Environmental conservation/preservation/protection/improvement – in particular where this would encourage the provision of access by members of the general public

Any charitable organisation based in the UK is eligible to apply for a grant, as are any educational institutions (schools, universities, etc.) whether or not they have charitable status.

It is the trustees' present policy to assist smaller organisations with core costs.

Please note: applications may only be made to our small grants programme. These grants range from £250 – £2,000.

- The trustees' preference is to support smaller charities since modest donations are capable of providing potentially greater benefit in such cases
- They are happy to contribute to core operating costs rather than to a specific project where the funding will be legally 'restricted' – applications in this latter category are, however, not excluded
- They are unlikely to provide multiple grants to the same charity in a 12 month period
- The trustees have limited funds available and much regret that they are unable to help every eligible organisation that applies for a grant
- Meetings of the trustees are held quarterly, in the second or third week of January, April, July and October. The deadline for the receipt of applications is approximately 3 weeks prior to each meeting. Applications are not considered between meetings but any received after the deadline are automatically carried forward
- The foundation uses the application form available in the 'applications' section of [its] website. If you are unable to submit an application using this method but would like to be considered please submit your reasons via the 'Contact Us' form [on the foundation's website] and where reasonable, alternative methods of submission may be arranged
- Further correspondence is sent only to applicants for whom a grant is approved. If you have not received a cheque by the middle of the month following the meeting, you should assume that your application was not successful on that occasion. You should contact the secretary if you want confirmation of this outcome but note that the foundation does not comment on the reasons why an application proved unsuccessful

In 2011/12 the foundation had assets of almost £5.8 million and an income of £222,000. Grants were made to 223 organisations totalling £240,000. Beneficiaries of grants which receive ongoing support included: Queen Elizabeth's Grammar School (£18,000 in 4 grants); Community Links (£12,000); Action for Stammering Children, Friendship Works, Prisoners' Families and Friends Service and Young Peoples Trust for the Environment (£5,000 each); Beauchamp Lodge Settlement (£4,000); DEMAND (£3,000); and Theatre Peckham (£1,500).

Details of beneficiaries from unsolicited applications (the small grants programme) were not contained within the accounts.

Exclusions

The trustees do not usually make grants for:

- Organisations that operate primarily outside the UK or for the benefit of non-UK residents
- Places of worship seeking funds for restoration or upgrade of facilities
- Students requesting a grant for tertiary education or a gap year
- Educational organisations based outside the Derbyshire region – although the trustees may choose to do so
- Museums, historical or heritage organisations
- Medical research or palliative care
- Animal welfare organisations whose primary purpose is not conservation of the environment
- Bodies affiliated to or a local 'branch' of a national organisation, even when registered as a separate charity – if you are unsure whether you would fall within this category, submit a query via the foundation's website

Applications

Applications are made via an online form on the foundation's website – no supporting documentation is required. The funding policy on the website states:

> Meetings of the trustees are held quarterly, in the second or third week of January, April, July and October. The deadline for the receipt of applications is approximately 3 weeks prior to each meeting. Applications are not considered between meetings but any received after the deadline are automatically carried forward.

Information gathered from:

Accounts; Charity Commission record; funder's website.

The Woodward Charitable Trust

General

£243,000 (2011/12)

Beneficial area

Unrestricted.

Correspondent: Karin Hooper, Administrator, The Peak, 5 Wilton Road, London SW1V 1AP (tel: 020 7410 0330; fax: 020 7410 0332; email: contact@woodwardcharitabletrust.org.uk; website: www.woodwardcharitabletrust.org.uk)

Trustees: Camilla Woodward; Rt Hon. Shaun A. Woodward; Judith Portrait.

CC Number: 299963

This is one of the Sainsbury Family Charitable Trusts which share a joint administration but it operates quite differently to most others in this group in that it gives a large number of small grants in response to open application. It is the trust of Camilla Woodward (nee Sainsbury) and her husband Shaun Woodward MP for St Helens South and Whiston.

Guidelines

The trust's annual report states 'We favour charities which make good use of volunteers and encourage past and current users to participate. Our grant-making continues to be primarily reactive but with selected projects initiated by the trustees.' The trust's website offers the following guidance:

> The trustees favour small-scale, locally based initiatives. Funding is primarily for one-off projects, but the trustees are willing to consider funding running costs (including core costs and salaries).
>
> Please be clear when applying who the target users are and what your projected outcomes are. If this is a continuation of existing work what are your outcomes to date? If your project is on-going, how will it be sustainable? What are your plans for future/on-going funding? If your request is for a one-off project, what will be its legacy? How many people will benefit from the grant? Trustees are interested in helping smaller organisations which offer direct services. Any participation by past or current users of the service should be mentioned and is encouraged.
>
> The current areas of grant-making are set out below:
>
> *Funding Priorities*
>
> 1 Children and young people who are isolated, at risk of exclusion or involved in anti-social behaviour
> 2 Minority groups including refugees, gypsies and travellers. Projects that promote integration and community cohesion will be favoured
> 3 Prisoners and ex-offenders. Projects that help the rehabilitation and resettlement of prisoners and/or ex-offenders are supported as well as requests to help prisoners' families
> 4 Disability projects which can include rehabilitation and training for people who are either physically disabled or learning disabled, as well as help to improve employment prospects
> 5 Homelessness, especially affecting young people and women, and covering facilities such as women's refuges
> 6 Arts outreach work by local groups for the benefit of disadvantaged people
> 7 Environmental projects, especially with a strong educational element
>
> *Types of grants*
>
> Trustees review grant applications twice a year, usually in January and July. Please consult the diary page of the trust's website for up-to-date deadlines for receipt of applications.

Small grants
£100 – £5,000 (around 100 grants made per year)

Large grants
Over £5,000 (around 6 grants made per year). Large grants are mainly given to charities already known to the trustees. Applications for large grants will be rejected unless applications are discussed with the administrator prior to submission.

Children's summer play scheme grants
£500–£1,000 (usually about 35 grants made each year). Applications for these are made separately and considered in April each year. The charities annual income should be under £100,000.

Grantmaking in 2011/12

In 2011/12 the trust had assets of £10.1 million and an income of £206,000. Grants were paid during the year totalling £243,000, and were categorised as follows:

Category	No.	Amount
Community and social welfare	42	£94,000
Education	6	£52,000
Disability and Health	19	£37,000
Summer Schemes	31	£30,000
Arts	12	£24,000
Environment	4	£5,000

The following are examples of grants that were made during the year, including a description of the trust's interests in each category taken from the accounts.

Community and social welfare

Grants funded in this category relate to improving the wellbeing of vulnerable and homeless people; families living in deprivation; communities that encourage people to use their own skills and abilities as a resource for change and lead fuller roles in society.

Beneficiaries included: Noah's Ark Children's Venture and Jamie's Farm (£10,000 each); Outside Chance (£5,000); Westminster Befriend a Family, Soundmix and JAN Trust (£2,000 each); Lift People and Aylesbury Youth Action (£1,500); and Boys Clubhouse, Orchard Workshop and West London Churches Homeless Concern (£1,000 each).

Disability and health
Grants awarded in the disability and health category support people with disabilities to access vocational training; provide funding for support groups to cope with health issues; run workshops by disabled people to change social attitudes towards disability and difference and prevent isolation. Grants have enabled children and young people with additional needs access mainstream social activities.

Beneficiaries included: Deafness Research UK (£5,000); Proteus Theatre Company (£3,000); The Roby and Hearts and Minds (£2,000 each); Indigo Project (£1,500); Achieve Potentials (£1,200); Voluntary and Community Action East Cambridge and Kidz Aware (£1,000 each); and Horizons Children's Sailing Charity (£500).

Summer schemes
Every year the trustees make small grants for summer playschemes during the long summer holidays for children between the ages of 5 -16 who come from disadvantaged backgrounds. Only charities whose annual income is £100,000 or less can apply. The playschemes funded are inclusive and encourage integration both by accepting those of differing abilities as well as different social and racial backgrounds. Funds have also been made to train past users to come back as volunteers.

Beneficiaries included: West Euston Time Bank (£2,200); Lambeth Summer Projects Trust (£2,000); Heathside and Lethbridge Youth Project, Kids Together, and New Life Church – Oasis Community Gardens (£1,000 each); St Mark's Parish Church of Scotland – Stirling (£700); and African Caribbean Forum (£500).

Education
Support for the education category ranged from vocational training of young people to educational outreach for disadvantaged families.

Beneficiaries were: Trialogue Educational Trust (£30,000); Ideas Foundation (£10,000); Story Museum (£7,500); Furtherfield (£2,000); Pushkin Trust (£1,500); and The Sainsbury Archive (£1,300).

Arts
Trustees have supported a broad range of charities that run artistic programmes that help change the lives of those from disadvantaged communities, from the young to the old. Arts programmes that prevent isolation; improve mental health; encourage community cohesion and offer creative opportunities to help prevent destructive behaviour have been funded.

Beneficiaries included: Ark T Centre and Operahouse Music Projects (£2,500); Young Musicians Symphony Orchestra and Dance Action Zone Leeds (£2,000 each); Them Wifies (£1,500); and Art Against Knives (£1,000).

Environment
Family workshops and pupil-led programmes in schools were some of the grants funded in this category.

Beneficiaries were: British Trust for Conservation Volunteers (£2,000); and Dorset Scrapstore, Theatre Venture and Action for Sustainable Living (£1,000 each).

Exclusions

Trustees will not fund:

- Charities whose annual turnover exceeds £300,000
- Construction projects such as playgrounds, village halls, and disabled accesses
- General school appeals including out of hours provision
- Hospices
- Medical research
- Parish facilities
- Playgroups and pre-school groups
- Requests for vehicles
- Individuals in any capacity
- Educational fees

Applications

On simple application forms available from the trust, or via its website. Potential applicants whose project falls within the criteria are invited to telephone the administrator in advance to discuss the advisability of making an application. Do not skip sections on the application form and refer instead to supplementary material. Only send your accounts if they are not already available on the Charity Commission website.

Trustees advise that applicants address the following questions in their application:

> Please be clear when applying who your target users are, what your projected outcomes are and how many people will benefit from the grant. If this is a continuation of existing work what are your outcomes to date? If your request is for a one-off project, what will be its legacy? Trustees are interested in helping smaller organisations that offer direct services and those that encourage cross community participation. Any participation by past or current users of the service should be mentioned and is encouraged. It should be noted that a lack of this information may prejudice your application.

Main grants are allocated following trustees' meetings in January and July each year, with the exception of summer schemes, which are considered at the beginning of May each year. All application forms are assessed on arrival and if additional information is required you will be contacted.

The website has a useful diary of trustees' meetings and of the cut-off dates for applications. The trust advises that only around 15% of applicants are successful and the majority of grants are for less than £5,000.

Percentage of awards given to new applicants: 90%.

Common applicant mistakes

'Individuals apply when we say "no individuals". They apply if their income is over £300,000 when we say don't [consider them].'

Information gathered from:

Accounts; Charity Commission record; further information provided by the funder; funder's website.

The A. and R. Woolf Charitable Trust

General charitable purposes

£33,000 (2011/12)

Beneficial area

Worldwide; UK, mainly in Hertfordshire.

Correspondent: The Trustees, c/o Griffiths Preston Accountants, Aldbury House, Dower Mews, 108 High Street, Berkhamsted, Hertfordshire HP4 2BL (tel: 01442 870277)

Trustees: Andrew Rose; Dr Gillian Edmonds; Stephen Rose; Joyce Rose.

CC Number: 273079

The trust supports a range of causes, including animal welfare and conservation causes, Jewish organisations, children and health and welfare charities. Both UK and overseas charities (through a British-based office) receive support, together with local charities. Most of the grants are recurrent.

In 2011/12 the trust had assets of £2.6 million and an income of £44,000. Grants totalled £33,000. A detailed grants list was not provided but the trust did make the following comments on one of its major beneficiaries: 'Amongst the donations for the year was a donation of £5,250 to UNICEF. It is intended to continue our policy of making donations to UNICEF in subsequent years as the trustees are impressed with the work of that organisation in health and education provision internationally, particularly in Africa and Afghanistan for women and children.'

Previous beneficiaries include: Central British Fund for World Jewish Relief, the Peace Hospice, University of Hertfordshire Charitable Trust, Northwood Pinner Liberal Synagogue, RSPCA, WWF UK, the Multiple Sclerosis Society, Jewish Child's Day, Wellbeing for Women, National Schizophrenia Fellowship, International Primate Protection League UK, the Hertfordshire and Middlesex Wildlife Trust and Senahasa Trust.

Exclusions

No grants to individuals or non-registered charities unless schools, hospices and so on.

Applications

Support is only given to projects/organisations/causes personally known to the trustees. The trust does not respond to unsolicited applications.

Information gathered from:

Accounts; Charity Commission record.

The Diana Edgson Wright Charitable Trust

Animal conservation, social welfare, general

£67,500 (2012)

Beneficial area

UK with some preference for Kent.

Correspondent: Henry Moorhead, Trustee, c/o Henry Moorhead and Company Solicitors, 2 Stade Street, Hythe, Kent CT21 6BD (email: henmo4@talktalk.net)

Trustees: Robert Moorhead; Mrs G. Edgson Wright; Henry Moorhead.

CC Number: 327737

The trust has general charitable purposes; the policy is to support a small number of charities.

In 2012 the trust had assets of £1.3 million, an income of £63,000 and a total expenditure of £70,000. Grants were made to 52 organisations totalling £67,500.

Beneficiaries include: Shooting Star Children's Hospice and British Heart Foundation (£3,000 each); Friends of Canterbury Museum (£2,500); Gurkha Welfare Trust, The Donkey Sanctuary and Royal National Lifeboat Institution (£2,000 each); Campaign to Protect Rural England, Kent (£1,200); Friends of St Margaret's Church Bethersden and International Fund for Animal Welfare (£1,000 each); and The MFPA Trust for the Training of Handicapped Children in the Arts and War Memorial Trust (£500 each).

Applications

In writing to the correspondent.

Information gathered from:

Accounts; Charity Commission record.

The Matthews Wrightson Charity Trust

General, smaller charities

£50,000 to organisations and individuals (2012)

Beneficial area

UK and some overseas.

Correspondent: Jon Mills, Correspondent, The Old School House, Church Lane, Easton, Winchester SO21 1EH (tel: 0845 241 2574; email: matthewswrightson@gmail.com)

Trustees: Isabelle White; Guy Garmondsay Wrightson; Priscilla Wilmot Wrightson; Maria de Broe Ferguson; Robert Partridge.

CC Number: 262109

The trustees' report for 2012 states that 'grants are not normally made to large national charities and those with an income in excess of £250,000. The trustees would not normally support the maintenance of the fabric of churches and village halls, and do not make donations to animal charities.' The trust aims to support charities worldwide that work with young people, people with disabilities and those who are poverty-stricken.

In 2012 it had assets of £1.5 million and an income of £63,000. There were 96 grants made totalling £50,000, including grants to individuals. Grants were made to two individuals totalling £1,000. Donations were broken down as follows:

Disabled	26	£12,500
Students – Royal College of Art	15	£9,000
Youth	18	£9,000
Third world	5	£4,000
Rehabilitation	6	£3,000
Poor and homeless	5	£2,500
Miscellaneous	5	£2,500
Christian cause	5	£2,000
Arts	2	£1,500
Elderly	3	£1,500
Medical	5	£1,500
Individuals	2	£1,000

The trustees gave to a wide range of charities. Help Tibet, Karuna Home, Nishtha Rural Health Centre and Pimlico Opera each received £1,000. Most other donations, with a few exceptions, were for £500.

Awards totalling £9,000 were made to support students at the Royal College of Art who find their grants and other income inadequate (hardship grants).

The MWCT also gives to trainee doctors for medical elective expenses and to individuals undertaking voluntary work. Preference is given to overseas work.

Previous beneficiaries of larger grants included: Tools for Self Reliance (£2,400); and the Butler Trust, Childhood First, the Daneford Trust, DEMAND, Live Music Now! New Bridge and Practical Action (£1,200 each). Most other donations, with a few exceptions, were for £400 or £500 each.

Exclusions

Gap year projects; maintenance and repair of the fabric of church buildings; animal charities.

Applications

In writing to the correspondent including a set of accounts. Applications received are considered by the trustees on a monthly basis. Applicants who wish to be advised of the outcome of their application must include an sae. Successful applicants are advised of the trustees' decision at the earliest opportunity.

Percentage of awards given to new applicants: between 20% and 30%.

Common applicant mistakes

'Too much information; lack of clarity regarding their objectives and activities.'

Information gathered from:

Accounts; Charity Commission record; further information provided by the funder.

Wychdale Ltd

Jewish

£253,000 (2011/12)

Beneficial area

UK and abroad.

Correspondent: Sugarwhite Associates, 5 Windus Road, London N16 6UT

Trustees: C. D. Schlaff; J. Schlaff; Mrs Z. Schlaff.

CC Number: 267447

The objects of this charity are the advancement of the Orthodox Jewish religion and the relief of poverty in the UK and abroad. The charity stated in its 2011/12 accounts that it 'invites applications from religious and educational institutions as well as organisations providing services for the relief of poverty both in the UK and abroad'.

In 2011/12 the trust had assets of £1.4 million and an income of £277,000. Grants were made totalling £253,000 and were broken down into the following categories:

Advancement of religion	£126,000
Religious education	£97,000
General charitable purposes	£29,500
Medical	£1,000

Beneficiaries included: M. and R. Gross Charitable Trust (£50,000); Friends of the Yeshivat Shaar Hashamayim (£43,000); Friends of Beis Abraham (£21,000); and Chevras Machzikei Mesifta and Emuno Education (£20,000 each).

Exclusions

Non-Jewish organisations are not supported.

Applications

In writing to the correspondent.

Information gathered from:

Accounts; Charity Commission record.

Wychville Ltd

Jewish, education, general

About £1 million (2011/12)

Beneficial area

UK.

Correspondent: Mrs S. Englander, Trustee, 44 Leweston Place, London N16 6RH

Trustees: Mrs S. Englander; E. Englander; Mrs B. R. Englander.

CC Number: 267584

This trust supports educational, Jewish and other charitable organisations by way of grants.

In 2011/12 the trust had an income of £735,000, mostly from donations. Charitable activities were listed at £1 million exclusive of governance costs. There was no further information available regarding the grantmaking of the charity despite the high level of giving.

Applications

In writing to the correspondent.

Information gathered from:

Accounts; Charity Commission record.

The Wyseliot Charitable Trust

Medical, welfare, arts

£102,000 (2011/12)

Beneficial area

UK.

Correspondent: Jonathan Rose, Trustee, 17 Chelsea Square, London SW3 6LF

Trustees: Jonathan Rose; Emma Rose; Adam Raphael.

CC Number: 257219

This trust gives grants in the following areas: health, saving of lives, the arts and relief of those in need by reason of age and ill health.

In 2011/12 the trust had assets of £1.5 million, which generated an income of £87,000. Grants were made to 31 organisations totalling £102,000.

Beneficiaries, many of whom were supported in previous years, included: Avenues Youth Project and Time and Talents Association (£5,000 each); Royal Marsden Cancer Fund, Trinity Hospice and Macmillan (£4,000 each); Musicians Benevolent Fund (£3,000); and Brains Trust, Vitiligo Society and International Glaucoma Association (£2,000 each).

Exclusions

Local charities are not supported. No support for individuals; grants are only made to registered charities of national significance.

Applications

In writing to the correspondent; however, note that the trust states that the same charities are supported each year, with perhaps one or two changes. It is unlikely new charities sending circular appeals will be supported and large UK charities are generally not supported. Currently approximately one application is successful each year.

Percentage of awards given to new applicants: 1%.

Common applicant mistakes

'Don't meet our criteria.'

Information gathered from:

Accounts; Charity Commission record; further information provided by the funder.

Yankov Charitable Trust

Jewish

£81,000 (2011/12)

Beneficial area

Worldwide.

Correspondent: Jacob Schonberg, Trustee, 40 Wellington Avenue, London N15 6AS (tel: 020 3150 1227)

Trustees: Jacob Schonberg; Bertha Schonberg; Aryeh Schonberg.

CC Number: 1106703

The trust was established in 2004 for the advancement of the Jewish religion and culture among the Jewish community throughout the world.

In 2011/12 the trust had assets of £237,000 and an income of £129,500 including £80,000 from donations received. Grants totalled £81,000. No further grant information was available.

Previous grant beneficiaries include: European Yarchei Kalloh (£53,000); Keren Machzikei Torah (£23,000); Kollel Tiferes Chaim (£21,000); Agudas Israel Housing Association (£12,000); Ponovez Hachnosos Kalloh (£7,600); Freiman Appeal (£7,200); Beth Jacob Grammar School (£4,000); British Friends of Tiferes Chaim (£3,000); Yeshiva Tzemach Yisroel (£2,000); British Friends of Rinat Ahsron (£1,500); and Yeshivat Givat Shaul (£1,000).

Applications

In writing to the correspondent.

Information gathered from:

Accounts; Charity Commission record.

The Yapp Charitable Trust

Social welfare

£178,000 (2011/12)

Beneficial area

England and Wales.

Correspondent: Joanne Anderson, Administrator, 8 Leyburn Close, Ouston, Chester le Street DH2 1TD (tel: 01914 922118; email: info@yappcharitabletrust.org.uk; website: www.yappcharitabletrust.org.uk)

CC Number: 1076803

The Yapp Charitable Trust was formed in 1999 from the Yapp Welfare Trust (two-thirds share) and Yapp Education and Research Trust (one-third share). However, rather than combining the criteria for the two trusts, the trustees decided to focus on small charities, usually local rather than UK wide charities. The trust now accepts applications only from small charities with a total expenditure of less than £40,000 in the year of application. The objects are restricted to registered charities in England or Wales.

The trust's helpful website provides the following information:

Eligibility

We only offer grants to registered charities with a total annual expenditure of less than £40,000 who are undertaking work with our priority groups:

- Elderly people
- Children and young people aged 5 – 25
- People with physical impairments, learning difficulties or mental health challenges
- Social welfare – people trying to overcome life-limiting problems of a social, rather than medical, origin (such as addiction, relationship difficulties, abuse, offending)
- Education and learning (with a particular interest in people who are educationally disadvantaged, whether adults or children)

We will not fund work that does not focus on one of the above priority groups.

We only make grants for core funding. We define core funding as the costs associated with regular activities or services that have been ongoing for at least a year. We cannot fund new projects, extra services or additional delivery costs. This includes creating a paid post for work that is currently undertaken on a voluntary basis or rent for premises that are currently cost free.

We can only offer grants to registered charities that have been formally established for a minimum of three years. Newly registered charities may apply but the organisation must have appointed a management committee and adopted a governing document at least 3 years ago.

To ensure that our grants offer some realistic help we will not contribute towards organisational budgets with a shortfall in excess of £10,000 in the first year.

Grant making policy

We will fund running costs for up to three years. Grants are normally for a maximum of £3,000 per year. Most of our grants are for more than one year because we like to fund ongoing needs. We prefer to make a grant when other funding is coming to an end.

We prioritise:

- Work that is unattractive to the general public or unpopular with other funders
- Services that help to improve the lives of marginalised, disadvantaged or isolated people
- Applicants that can demonstrate an effective use of volunteers
- Charities that seek to be preventive and aim to change opinion and behaviour through raising awareness of issues, education and campaigning
- Applicants that can demonstrate (where feasible) an element of self-sustainability by charging subscriptions/fees to service users

Applications that don't address at least two of the above are unlikely to receive a grant.

How to apply

Please read our guidelines fully before pursuing an application. Potential applicants are strongly advised to review the eligibility questions below before completing an application form. We will only fund charities that can demonstrate they meet our eligibility criteria. If you answer 'No' to any of the questions then you will not be eligible to receive a grant from us and any application submitted will be rejected.

- Is your organisation registered as a charity in England or Wales with the Charity Commission?
- Is the charity's total annual expenditure budget for the next 12 months less than £40,000?
- Is the projected shortfall in that 12 month forecast less than £10,000?
- Has the charity been formally established for at least 3 years (i.e. was the governing document adopted at least 3 years ago)? NB – this will be verified with the Charity Commission's register of charities
- Does the work you are asking us to fund clearly fall within one of our priority areas (e.g. elderly, young people, disability) outlined in our guidelines?
- Is our grant required towards running costs for existing work that has been happening for at least one year?

If you prefer to discuss your eligibility then please contact Joanne Anderson, Trust Secretary on 01914 922118. If you can answer yes to all of the above questions then we may be able to consider you for a grant. The application form is available to download from the website.

In 2011/12 the trust had assets of £5.4 million and an income of £197,000. Grants were awarded to 49 charities and totalled £178,000. The largest number of grants was awarded in the London region (14 totalling £50,000) and most grants were to support work undertaken for people with disabilities.

Beneficiaries included: BCU Life Skills Centre (£7,500); Community Based Training Ltd, St George's Pop In and Sandwell Asian Development Association (£6,000 each); African Women's Health Group, Soundwaves Music Project and WHEAT Mentor Support Trust (£4,500 each); Llandrindod Wells YMCA (£3,000); and Eastern Enfield Good Neighbours, The Muslim Women's Organisation and Yeovil Shopmobility (£1,000 each).

Exclusions

The trust's website states that the trustees cannot fund:

- Charities with a total annual expenditure of more than £40,000
- Charities that are not registered with the Charity Commission in England and Wales. You must have your own charity number or be excepted from registration.
- Industrial Provident Societies and Community Interest Companies
- Work that is based in Scotland and Northern Ireland – the trust can only fund charities that are operating in England or Wales
- Charities with unrestricted reserves that equate to more than 12 months expenditure
- Branches of national charities. You must have your own charity number, not a shared national registration
- New organisations – you must have been operating as a fully constituted organisation for at least three years, even though you may have registered as a charity more recently
- New work that has not been occurring for at least a year
- New paid posts – even if the work is now being done by volunteers
- Additional activities, expansion or development plans
- Special events, trips or outings
- Capital expenditure – including equipment, buildings, renovations, furnishings, minibuses
- Work with under-5s
- Childcare
- Holidays and holiday centres
- Core funding of charities that benefit the wider community such as general advice services and community centres unless a significant element of their work focuses on one of the trust's priority groups
- Bereavement support

- Debt advice
- Community safety initiatives
- Charities raising money to give to another organisation, such as schools, hospitals or other voluntary groups
- Individuals – including charities raising funds to purchase equipment for or make grants to individuals

Applications

The trust states:

> We have a simple application form which we ask you to send in by post, together with a copy of your most recent annual report and accounts and any other information you wish to send.
>
> Applications are processed continuously. When we receive your application we will be in touch, usually within two weeks:
>
> - To ask for more information
> - Or to tell you the application will be going forward to the next stage of assessment and give an idea of when you can expect a decision
> - Or to let you know we can't help
>
> The time it takes to process an application and make a grant is usually between two months and six months. We always write to let you know the decision.
>
> *Previous Applicants*
>
> We will accept an application only once each year and you can have only one grant at a time from us. Current grant-holders may make a new application when their grant is coming to an end. If we refused your last application you must wait a year before applying again.
>
> The application form and guidelines can be downloaded in Word or pdf format from the trust's website. Alternatively they can be obtained from the trust's administrator.

Information gathered from:

Accounts; Charity Commission record; funder's website.

The Yardley Great Trust

General

£55,500 to organisations and individuals (2012)

Beneficial area

The ancient parish of Yardley now part of the County of West Midlands. This includes the wards of Yardley, Acocks Green, Fox Hollies, Billesley, Hall Green and parts of the wards of Hodge Hill, Shard End, Sheldon, Small Heath, Sparkhill, Moseley, Stechford, Sparkbrook and Brandwood. (A map is available on request.).

Correspondent: Mrs K. L. Grice, Clerk to the Trustees, Old Brookside, Yardley Fields Road, Stechford, Birmingham B33 8QL (tel: 01217 847889; fax: 01217 851386; email: enquiries@ygtrust.org.uk; website: www.yardley-great-trust.org.uk)

Trustees: Iris Aylin; Revd Andrew Bullock; Jean Hayes; Joy Holt; Cllr Barbara Jackson; Conrad James; Revd John Ray; Revd John Richards; Keith Rollins; Revd John Self; Revd Paul Leckey; Malcolm Cox; Revd William Sands; Andrew Veitch; Robert Jones.

CC Number: 216082

This charity is probably the earliest recorded Birmingham charity, originating when John de Yeardley made over all his lands to the poor in 1335. In 1531, other local charities were grouped together under the title the Yardley Great Trust. The trust still owns the freehold land, on which it has built five sheltered housing complexes and a care home and has a piece of land covering about eight acres in Sparkhill which is used for allotments.

The trust's priority is maintaining its own properties mentioned above. After this it makes grants to help the fight against poverty in South East Birmingham, supporting organisations as well as providing basic household essentials such as cookers and beds directly to individuals. In line with the trust's second broad aim of providing high quality care and housing for older people, the trust also owns a nursing home, which is operated by another charity.

In 2012 the trust had assets of £8.7 million and an income of £2.2 million. Grants to organisations totalled £28,000.

A further £27,500 was disbursed in grants of less than £500 to individuals and £3,000 was given to residents of Yardley Great Trust.

Beneficiaries include: The Springfield Project (£5,000); The Feast (£3,000); Fox Hollies Community Association (£2,500); St Richard's Lea Hall/Worth Unlimited (£2,000); St Thomas Church, Garrets Green (£1,300); Birmingham and Solihull Women's Aid (£1,000); St Richard's Church and Centre, Lea Hall (£700); and Hallmoor School, Yardley, Sport 4 Life UK and Yardley Church Forward Club (£500 each).

Applications

On a form available from the correspondent. Applications from individuals should be via a third party such as Neighbourhood Offices or Citizens Advice. Applications are considered on the second Thursday of each month.

Information gathered from:

Accounts; Charity Commission record; funder's website.

The Dennis Alan Yardy Charitable Trust

General charitable purposes

£16,000 (2011/12)

Beneficial area

Overseas and UK with a preference for the East Midlands.

Correspondent: The Secretary, PO Box 5039, Spratton, Northampton NN6 8YH

Trustees: Dennis Yardy; Christine Yardy; Jeffrey Creek; Joanne Stoney; Simon Bown.

CC Number: 1039719

This trust was established in 1993 and supports major UK and international charities and those within the East Midlands area. In 2011/12 the trust had assets of £557,000, an income of £25,500 and made grants totalling £16,000. Unfortunately, no further information was available.

Exclusions

No grants to individuals or non-registered charities.

Applications

In writing to the correspondent.

Information gathered from:

Accounts; Charity Commission record.

York Children's Trust

Young people under the age of 25

£49,000 (2012)

Beneficial area

Within 20 miles of York City.

Correspondent: Margaret Brien, Correspondent, 29 Whinney Lane, Harrogate HG2 9LS (tel: 1423504765; email: yorkchildren'strust@hotmail.co.uk)

Trustees: Colin Stroud; Mark Sessions; Lenore Hill; Keith Hayton; Peter Watson; William Miers; Alan Ward; Dr Anne Kelly; Rosalind Fitter; Julie Simpson; Dawn Moores; Kathy Pickard; Kitty Lamb; John Corden; Gail Tams; Vicky Mulvana.

CC Number: 222279

The trustees' report for 2012 states that the York Children's Trust's objects are 'the relief of needy children and needy young persons under 25 years of age, including advancement of the education of such children and young persons, living within a 20 mile radius of York.'

In 2012 the trust had assets of £2.8 million and an income of £93,000. Grants totalled £49,000, of which £32,000 was made to 40 organisations and £17,000 to 60 individuals. A total of 100 grants were made during the year, to schools, special schools, groups, local authorities, care trusts, charities and individuals. Grants were broken down as follows:

Youth, playgroups and organisations	£20,500
Social and medical	£14,500
Educational	£7,500
Travel and fostering talents	£6,500

Beneficiaries included: City of York Council (£5,200); Jack Raine Community Foundation (£3,300); Calverts Carpets and Osbaldwick and Murton Scouts (£2,500 each); York Sea Cadets Centre, Ocean Youth Trust and Home Start York (£2,200 each); LIPA (£1,600); and Osbaldwick Primary School and Hob Moor Community Primary School (£1,000 each).

Exclusions

The trust will not normally give grants for private education fees. Exceptions may be made where unforeseen circumstances, such as the death of a parent, would prevent a child from completing the last year of a critical stage of education such as A-levels.

Applications

In writing to the correspondent.

Information gathered from:

Accounts; Charity Commission record.

The John Young Charitable Settlement

General

About £35,000 (2011/12)

Beneficial area

UK and overseas.

Correspondent: Ken Hawkins, c/o H. W. Lee Associates LLP, New Derwent House, 69–73 Theobalds Road, London WC1X 8TA (tel: 020 7025 4600)

Trustees: John Young; Patrick Burgess.

CC Number: 283254

In 2011/12 the trust had an income of £8,000 and a total expenditure of £38,000. Grants totalled about £35,000.

Previous beneficiaries include: Caius House (£13,000); the Borlase Smart, Médecins du Monde, Pancreatic Cancer Research Fund, RSBP and St Barnabas Hospice Trust (£5,000 each); Chichester Harbour Trust (£2,000); and Action Aid (£250).

Applications

In writing to the correspondent.

Information gathered from:

Accounts; Charity Commission record.

The William Allen Young Charitable Trust

General, health, social welfare

£231,500 (2012/13)

Beneficial area

UK, with a preference for South London, occasionally overseas.

Correspondent: Torquil Sligo-Young, Trustee, Young and Co.'s Brewery plc, Riverside House, 26 Osiers Road, London SW18 1NH (tel: 020 8875 7000)

Trustees: Torquil Sligo-Young; James Young; Thomas Young.

CC Number: 283102

The trust supports humanitarian causes, with a large number of health organisations supported each year. Grants are made to local and national organisations throughout the UK, although there appears to be a preference for South London.

In 2012/13 the trust had assets of £24.5 million with an income of £466,000 and made 135 grants totalling £231,500.

Beneficiaries included: Anti-Slavery International (£20,000); St Mary's Wrestwood Children's Trust (£10,000); Somerset Otter Group (£7,000); Trinity Hospice (£4,000); 2boats (Halow Project) (£3,000); Back to Work, Canine Partners, Community Housing and Therapy, Dementia Concern, Fight for Sight, Jumbulance and Tall Ships Youth Trust (£2,000 each); and Age Concern Wandsworth, Battersea United Charities, Breast Cancer Care, Friends of the Elderly, Listening Books in South London, Stroke Association and Wisborough Green Cricket Club (£1,000 each).

Applications

The trust has stressed that all funds are committed and consequently unsolicited applications will not be supported.

Information gathered from:

Accounts; Charity Commission record.

Zephyr Charitable Trust

Community, environment, social welfare

£43,500 (2012/13)

Beneficial area

UK and worldwide.

Correspondent: The Trustees, Luminary Finance LLP, PO Box 135, Longfield, Kent DA3 8WF

Trustees: Elizabeth Breeze; Marigo Harries; David Baldock; Donald I. Watson.

CC Number: 1003234

The trust's grants are particularly targeted towards three areas:

- Enabling lower income communities to be self-sustaining
- The protection and improvement of the environment
- Providing relief and support for those in need, particularly from medical conditions or social or financial disadvantage

In 2012/13 the trust had assets of £1.6 million and an income of £63,000. There were 20 grants made totalling £43,500.

Beneficiaries during the year included: Friends of the Earth Trust; Medical Foundation for the Victims of Torture (£2,500 each); Organic Research Centre – Elm Farm; Hearing Research Trust (Deafness Research UK), UNICEF and Womankind (£2,000 each); and Margaret Pyke Trust and MERLIN (Medical Emergency Relief International) (£1,500 each).

Exclusions

No grants to individuals, expeditions or scholarships.

Applications

In writing to the correspondent. The trustees usually meet to consider grants in July each year. Unsolicited applications are unlikely to be successful, since the trust makes annual donations to a list of beneficiaries. However, the trust stated that unsolicited applications are considered on a quarterly basis by the trustees and very occasional support is given. Telephone applications are not accepted.

Information gathered from:

Accounts; Charity Commission record.

The Marjorie and Arnold Ziff Charitable Foundation

General, education, Jewish, arts, youth, older people, medicine

£256,000 (2011/12)

Beneficial area

UK, with a preference for Yorkshire, especially Leeds and Harrogate.

Correspondent: Sharon Hall, Secretary, Town Centre House, The Merrion Centre, Leeds LS2 8LY (tel: 01132 221234)

Trustees: Marjorie E. Ziff; Michael A. Ziff; Edward M. Ziff; Ann L. Manning.

CC Number: 249368

This trust likes to support causes that will provide good value for the money donated by benefiting a large number of people, as well as encouraging others to make contributions to the work. This includes a wide variety of schemes that involve the community at many levels, including education, public places, the arts and helping people who are disadvantaged. Capital costs and building work are particularly favoured by the trustees, as they feel projects such as these are not given the support they deserve from statutory sources.

In 2011/12 the trust had assets of £6.9 million and an income of £649,000. There were 71 grants made totalling £256,000 with further grants pledged over the next few years.

Beneficiaries included: United Jewish Israel Appeal (£53,000); Leeds Jewish Welfare Board (£34,000); The Haven (£30,000); Chief Rabbinate Trust (£10,000); Leeds University, Community Security Trust and Youth Aliyah – Child Rescue (£5,000 each); Association for Research into Stammering (£1,000); Little Sisters of the Poor (£400); and MS Society (£150).

Exclusions

No grants to individuals.

Applications

In writing to the correspondent. Replies will only be given to a request accompanied by an sae. Note that funds available from the trust are limited and requests not previously supported are unlikely to be successful. Initial telephone calls are welcome but note the forgoing comments.

Information gathered from:

Accounts; Charity Commission record.

Subject index

The following subject index begins with a list of categories used. The categories are very wide-ranging to keep the index as simple as possible. DSC's subscription website (www.trustfunding.org.uk)has a much more detailed search facility on the categories. There may be considerable overlap between the categories – for example, children and education, or older people and social welfare.

The list of categories is followed by the index itself. Before using the index, please note the following:

How the index was compiled

1) The index aims to reflect the most recent grant-making practice. It is therefore based on our interpretation of what each trust has actually given to, rather than what its policy statement says or its charitable objects allow it to do in principle. For example, where a trust states that it has general charitable purposes, but its grants list shows a strong preference for welfare, we index it under welfare.
2) We have tried to ensure that each trust has given significantly in the areas where it is indexed (usually at least £15,000). Thus small, apparently untypical grants have been ignored for index purposes.
3) The index has been complied from the latest information available to us.

Limitations

1) Policies may change; some more frequently than others.
2) Sometimes there will be a geographical restriction on a trust's grantgiving which is not shown in this index, or the trust may not give for the specific purposes you require under that heading. It is important to read each entry carefully.

   You will need to check:

   (a) The trust gives in your geographical area of operation.

   (b) The trust gives for the specific purposes you require.

   (c) There is no other reason to prevent you making an application to this trust.
3) It is worth noting that one or two of the categories list almost half the trusts included in this guide.

Under no circumstances should the index be used as a simple mailing list. Remember: each trust is different. Often the policies or interests of a particular trust do not fit easily into the given categories. Each entry must be read individually before you send off an application. Indiscriminate applications are usually unsuccessful. They waste time and money and greatly annoy trusts.

The categories are as follows:

Arts, culture, sport and recreation *page 350*

A very wide category including performing, written and visual arts, crafts, theatres, museums and galleries, heritage, architecture and archaeology, sports.

Children and young people *page 352*

Mainly for welfare and welfare-related activities.

Development, housing and employment *page 354*

This includes specific industries such as leather making or textiles.

Disability *page 354*

Disadvantaged people *page 355*

This includes people who are:

- Socially excluded
- socially and economically disadvantaged
- unemployed
- homeless
- offenders
- educationally disadvantaged
- victims of social/natural occurrences, including refugees and asylum seekers.

Education and training *page 356*

Environment and animals *page 359*

This includes:

- agriculture and fishing
- conservation
- animal care
- environment and education
- transport
- sustainable environment.

General charitable purposes *page 360*

This is a very broad category, and includes trusts that often have numerous specific strands to their programmes as a well as those that will consider any application (subject to other eligibility criteria).

Arts, culture, sport and recreation

Children and young people

Development, housing and employment

Disability

Disadvantaged people

Education and training

Environment and animals

General charitable purposes

Illness

Medicine and health

Older people

Philanthropy and the voluntary sector

Religion – Christianity

Religion – Inter-faith activities

Religion – Islam

Religion – Judaism

Religion – Religious understanding

Rights, law and conflict

Science and technology

Social sciences, policy and research

Social welfare

Geographical index

The following geographical index aims to highlight when a trust gives preference for, or has a special interest in, a particular area: county, region, city, town or London borough. Please note the following:

1) Before using this index please read the following information, as well as the introduction to the subject index on page 349. We must emphasise that this index:

   (a) should not be used as a simple mailing list, and

   (b) is not a substitute for detailed research.

   When you have used this index to identify relevant trusts, please read each entry carefully before making an application. Simply because a trust gives grants in your geographical area does not mean that it gives to your type of work.

2) Most trusts in this list are not restricted to one area; usually the geographical index indicates that the trust gives some priority for the area(s).

3) Trusts which give throughout England or the UK have been excluded from this index, unless they have a particular interest in one or more locality.

4) Each section is ordered alphabetically according to the name of the trust. The categories for the overseas and UK indices are as follows:

England

We have divided England into the following nine categories:

Some trusts may be found in more than one category due to them providing grants in more than one area e.g. those with a preference for northern England.

Overseas categories

This includes trusts which support missionary organisations when they are also interested in social and economic development.

The Middle East has been listed separately. Please note that most of the trusts listed are primarily for the benefit of Jewish people and the advancement of the Jewish religion.

England

North East

North West

Yorkshire and the Humber

East Midlands

West Midlands

Eastern England

South West

South East

Greater London

Channel Islands

Wales

Scotland

Northern Ireland

Republic of Ireland

Europe

Developing world

Africa

Americas and the West Indies

Asia

Middle East

Alphabetical index